The Handbook of
Discourse Analysis

Blackwell Handbooks in Linguistics

This outstanding multi-volume series covers all the major subdisciplines within linguistics today and, when complete, will offer a comprehensive survey of linguistics as a whole.

Published Works:

The Handbook of Child Language
Edited by PAUL FLETCHER and BRIAN MACWHINNEY

The Handbook of Phonological Theory
Edited by JOHN GOLDSMITH

The Handbook of Contemporary Semantic Theory
Edited by SHALOM LAPPIN

The Handbook of Sociolinguistics
Edited by FLORIAN COULMAS

The Handbook of Phonetic Sciences
Edited by WILLIAM HARDCASTLE and JOHN LAVER

The Handbook of Morphology
Edited by ANDREW SPENCER and ARNOLD ZWICKY

The Handbook of Japanese Linguistics
Edited by NATSUKO TSUJIMURA

The Handbook of Linguistics
Edited by MARK ARONOFF and JANIE REES-MILLER

The Handbook of Contemporary Syntactic Theory
Edited by MARK BALTIN and CHRIS COLLINS

The Handbook of Discourse Analysis
Edited by DEBORAH SCHIFFRIN, DEBORAH TANNEN, and HEIDI E. HAMILTON

The Handbook of Variation and Change
Edited by J. K. CHAMBERS, PETER TRUDGILL, and NATALIE SCHILLING-ESTES

The Handbook of Discourse Analysis

Edited by

Deborah Schiffrin, Deborah Tannen, and Heidi E. Hamilton

BLACKWELL
Publishers

Copyright © Blackwell Publishers Ltd 2001

First published 2001

2 4 6 8 10 9 7 5 3 1

Blackwell Publishers Inc.
350 Main Street
Malden, Massachusetts 02148
USA

Blackwell Publishers Ltd
108 Cowley Road
Oxford OX4 1JF
UK

Library of Congress Cataloging-in-Publication Data
The Handbook of discourse analysis / edited by Deborah Schiffrin, Deborah Tannen,
and Heidi Hamilton.
     p. cm. — (Blackwell handbooks in linguistics)
    Includes bibliographical references and index.
    ISBN 0–631–20595–0 (alk. paper)
    1. Discourse analysis—Handbooks, manuals, etc. I. Schiffrin, Deborah. II. Tannen,
Deborah. III. Hamilton, Heidi Ehernberger. IV. Series.

    P302 .H344 2001
    401'.41—dc21   2001018139

British Library Cataloguing in Publication Data
A CIP catalogue record for this book is available from the British Library.

Typeset in 9.5/12pt Palatino
by Graphicraft Limited, Hong Kong
Printed in Great Britain by T.J. International, Padstow, Cornwall

This book is printed on acid-free paper.

For our parents,

Marlye and Leonard Schiffrin
Dorothy and Eli Tannen
Claire and Gerald Ehernberger

Contents

Contributors

Carolyn Temple Adger is a Senior Researcher at the Center for Applied Linguistics in Washington, DC. Her research focuses on language in education, especially classroom discourse and teachers' professional talk. Recent co-authored and co-edited books include *Kids Talk: Strategic Language Use in Later Childhood* (Oxford University Press, 1998); *Dialects in Schools and Communities* (Lawrence Erlbaum, 1998); and *Making the Connection: Language and Academic Achievement among African American Students* (Delta Systems, 1999). carolyn@cal.org

Nancy Ainsworth-Vaughn is on leave from Michigan State University, where she is an Associate Professor in the Department of English. Her publications since the early 1990s have examined power, gender, and co-construction in the questions, stories, and topic transitions that constitute doctor–patient encounters. This work culminated in *Claiming Power in Doctor–Patient Talk* (Oxford University Press, 1998). ainswrth@pilot.msu.edu

Douglas Biber is Regents' Professor of English (Applied Linguistics) at Northern Arizona University. His research efforts have focused on corpus linguistics, English grammar, and register variation (in English and cross-linguistic; synchronic and diachronic). His publications include three books published by Cambridge University Press (*Variation Across Speech and Writing*, 1988; *Dimensions of Register Variation: A Cross-linguistic Comparison*, 1995; and *Corpus Linguistics: Investigating Language Structure and Use*, 1998, with Susan Conrad and Randi Reppen) and most recently the co-authored *Longman Grammar of Spoken and Written English* (1999). douglas.biber@nau.edu

Betty J. Birner is an Assistant Professor in the English Department at Northern Illinois University. Her research interests include the discourse functions of syntactic constructions, inferential relations in discourse, and reference. She is the author of *The Discourse Function of Inversion in English* (Garland, 1996) and co-author, with Gregory Ward, of *Information Status and Noncanonical Word Order in English* (Benjamins, 1998). bbirner@niu.edu

Diane Blakemore is Professor of Linguistics at the University of Salford. Her publications are mainly in the area of relevance theoretic pragmatics and investigate non-truth conditional meaning and the relationship between linguistic form and pragmatics interpretation. Her most recent articles include: "Indicators and procedures: 'nevertheless' and 'but' " (2000); "Restatement and exemplification: a relevance theoretic re-assessment of elaboration" (1997); and "Non-truth conditional meaning" (1998). d.blakemore@salford.ac.uk

Laurel J. Brinton is Professor of English Language at the University of British Columbia. Her main areas of interest include pragmatic markers, composite predicates, aspect, and grammaticalization in the history of English. Her most recent books include *Pragmatic Markers in English: Grammaticalization and Discourse Functions* (Mouton, 1996), the co-edited volume *Collocational and Idiomatic Aspects of Composite Predicates in the History of English* (Benjamins, 1999), and the text and CD-ROM workbook *The Structure of Modern English: A Linguistic Introduction* (Benjamins, 2000). brinton@interchange.ubc.ca

Marianne Celce-Murcia is Professor of Applied Linguistics at the University of California, Los Angeles. Her publications and research have dealt with English grammar and discourse, pedagogical grammar, and pronunciation instruction. Her most recent books include: *Teaching Pronunciation* (with Donna Brinton and Janet Goodwin; Cambridge University Press, 1996); *The Grammar Book: An ESL/EFL Teacher's Course* (with Diane Larsen-Freeman; Heinle and Heinle, 1999); and *Discourse and Context in Language Teaching* (with Elite Olshtain; Cambridge University Press, 2000). celce-m@humnet.ucla.edu

Wallace Chafe is Professor Emeritus of Linguistics at the University of California at Santa Barbara. His research has focused on languages of Native North America and on discourse and its relations to human thought. His most recent major publication is *Discourse, Consciousness, and Time* (University of Chicago Press, 1994), an exploration of how the flow and displacement of consciousness are reflected in speaking and writing. He is currently investigating ways in which prosody is used to express emotions and attitudes. chafe@humanitas.ucsb.edu

Herbert H. Clark is Professor of Psychology at Stanford University. He has published on a range of issues in linguistics and psycholinguistics. These include: spatial language, conventional and innovative word meaning, types of listeners, definite reference, the nature of common ground, interactive language in joint activities, quotations, gestures, and disfluencies. Much of this work is reviewed in two books, *Arenas of Language Use* (University of Chicago Press, 1992) and *Using Language* (Cambridge University Press, 1996). clark@psych.stanford.edu

Susan Conrad is an Assistant Professor in the Department of English and Program in Linguistics at Iowa State University. She is co-author of *Corpus Linguistics: Investigating Language Structure and Use* (Cambridge University Press, 1998) and the *Longman Grammar of Spoken and Written English* (Pearson, 1999), and co-editor of a collection of corpus-based studies of register and dialect variation, *Variation in English: Multi-dimensional Studies* (Pearson, 2001). Her work on register variation and corpus linguistics has appeared in *Applied Linguistics, Linguistics and Education, System,* and *TESOL Quarterly.*

Jenny Cook-Gumperz is a Professor of Education at the University of California, Santa Barbara. A sociologist and sociolinguist, she is well known for her work on literacy theory and the social context of children's language learning. She is the author of *Social Construction of Literacy, Social Control and Socialization*, and *Children's Worlds and Children's Language* (with William Corsaro and Jürgen Streeck), as well as numerous papers on literacy and language socialization. jenny@education.ucsb.edu

Colleen Cotter is an Assistant Professor at Georgetown University, dividing her time between the Linguistics Department and the Communication, Culture and Technology (CCT) master's program. Her former career as a daily newspaper reporter and editor (as well as journalism educator) has informed the ethnographic or community-situated approach she takes in studying media discourse. She is currently completing a book on news discourse and news language, examining news texts from the vantage point of journalistic practice and process and the perspectives of journalists themselves. It is provisionally entitled *News Values, News Practice: Shaping the Language and Culture of News*. She has also done research on the use of broadcast media to promote minority- or endangered-language development, focusing primarily on the case in Ireland. cotterc@georgetown.edu

Elizabeth Couper-Kuhlen is Professor of English Linguistics in the Department of Linguistics at the University of Konstanz, Germany. Her research interests include language use in interaction, prosody and conversation, and clause combining in spoken discourse. Among her major publications are *English Speech Rhythm: Form and Function in Everyday Verbal Interaction* (Benjamins, 1993); *Language in Time: The Rhythm and Tempo of Spoken Interaction* (co-authored with Peter Auer and Frank Müller; Oxford University Press, 1999); *Prosody in Conversation: Interactional Studies* (co-edited with Margret Selting; Cambridge University Press, 1996); *Cause, Condition, Concession, Contrast: Cognitive and Discourse Perspectives* (co-edited with Bernd Kortmann; Mouton, 2000); and *Studies in Interactional Linguistics* (co-edited with Margret Selting; Benjamins, in press). Elizabeth.Couper@uni-konstanz.de

Sylvie Dubois is Associate Professor at the Department of French at Louisiana State University. Her publications are mainly in the areas of discourse analysis, sociolinguistic methods and fieldworks, and vernacular varieties of French and English in North America, especially Cajun and Creole dialects spoken in Louisiana. She is the author of a book on discourse analysis, *L'analyse variationniste du discours en sociolinguistique* (American University Studies XIII, Peter Lang, 1997). Her most recent articles have been published in *Language Variation and Change, Language in Society*, and *Journal of Sociolinguistics*. sdubois@cmpsource.com

Jane A. Edwards is a Researcher at the Institute of Cognitive Studies, University of California at Berkeley. Her publications are mainly in the area of corpus linguistics, with special reference to spoken language description and robust use of electronic corpora in linguistic research. Her most recent publications include "Principles and alternative systems in the transcription, coding and mark-up of spoken discourse" (1995) and, as co-editor with Martin D. Lampert, *Talking Data: Transcription and Coding in Discourse Research* (Lawrence Erlbaum, 1993). edwards@icsi.berkeley.edu

Suzanne Fleischman was a Professor in the Department of French at the University of California at Berkeley for twenty-five years. Her research areas included Romance linguistics, historical linguistics, tense and aspect, grammaticalization, sociolinguistics, narrative analysis, linguistics and literature, medieval studies, and language and gender. Her publications covered all of these areas, and included *The Future in Thought and Language* (Cambridge University Press, 1982), *Tense and Narrativity* (University of Texas Press, 1990), *Discourse Pragmatics and the Verb* (co-edited with Linda Waugh; Routledge 1991), and *Modality in Grammar and Discourse* (co-edited with Joan Bybee; Benjamins, 1995). At the time of her death from myelodysplasia in 2000, Fleischman had been working on the cross-linguistic analysis of the grammaticalization of *like* and on a book integrating her own experience with illness with analyses of the relationship between language and medicine. A collection of her work is currently being prepared for publication by Eve Sweetser and Dan Slobin (both at University of California at Berkeley).

Allen Grimshaw is Emeritus Professor of Sociology at Indiana University; he served on the faculty from 1959 to 1994. During his last decades of teaching he specialized in courses on language in use in social contexts and on social conflict and violence, including war and genocide. He has written several books and numerous articles on these topics and continues research on them. His most recent writing includes encyclopedia and handbook articles on genocide, language topics, and racial violence. Among his publications are: *Conflict Talk: Sociolinguistic Investigations of Arguments in Conversations* (as editor; Cambridge University Press, 1990); *What's Going On Here? Complementary Studies of Professional Talk* (as co-editor; Ablex, 1994), "Genocide and democide" (1999); and "Control" (2000). grimsha@indiana.edu

John J. Gumperz is Professor Emeritus of Anthropology at the University of California at Berkeley. From his earlier work in the 1950s on dialect differences and social stratification in rural Michigan and as a member of an anthropological research team in a North Indian village community, he has consistently been dealing with the issue of language contact and linguistic diversity. Since the early 1970s he has turned to discourse and conversation analysis, concentrating on questions of bilingualism, bidialectalism, and intercultural communication. He is concerned with providing both the empirical evidence and the theoretical framework for investigating the varied but systematic ways in which talk both reflects and defines social and cultural boundaries. Among his best-known publications are *Directions in Sociolinguistics* (co-edited with Dell Hymes; Holt, Rinehart and Winston, 1972, reissued Blackwell, 1986, and to be republished in 2001); *Discourse Strategies* (Cambridge University Press, 1982); *Language and Social Identity* (Cambridge University Press, 1982), and *Rethinking Linguistic Relativity* (co-edited with Stephen Levinson; Cambridge University Press, 1996). Gumperz is currently at work on a follow-up volume to *Directions in Sociolinguistics* called *New Ethnographies of Communication*, to be co-edited with Marco Jaquemet, and on a set of theoretical essays. Gumperz@education.ucsb.edu

Heidi E. Hamilton is Associate Professor of Linguistics at Georgetown University. Her research focuses on language and Alzheimer's disease, language and aging, medical communication, and foreign language immersion programs. She is the author of *Conversations with an Alzheimer's Patient: An Interactional Sociolinguistic Study* (Cambridge

University Press, 1994) and *Discourse Analysis Across Disciplines* (Oxford University Press, forthcoming), and editor of *Language and Communication in Old Age: Multi-disciplinary Perspectives* (Garland, 1999). hamilthe@georgetown.edu

Rom Harré is Emeritus Fellow of Linacre College, Oxford, Professor of Psychology at Georgetown University, and Adjunct Professor of Philosophy at American University, Washington, D.C. His published work includes studies in the philosophy of the natural sciences such as *Varieties of Realism* (Blackwell, 1986) and *Great Scientific Experiments* (Oxford University Press, 1981). He has been among the pioneers of the "discursive" approach in the human sciences. In *Social Being* (Rowman and Littlefield, 1979), *Personal Being* (Harvard University Press, 1984), and *Physical Being* (Blackwell, 1991) he explored the role of rules and conventions in various aspects of human cognition, while in *Pronouns and People* (Blackwell, 1990), he and Peter Mühlhäusler developed the thesis that grammar and the sense of self are intimately related. harre@georgetown.edu

Monica Heller is Professor at the Ontario Institute for Studies in Education of the University of Toronto. Her publications and research are mainly in the areas of interactional sociolinguistics; code-switching; the political economy of multilingualism; and policy, ideology, and practice of French, English, and other languages in Canada. Her most recent books include *Linguistic Minorities and Modernity: A Sociolinguistic Ethnography* (Longman, 1999) and *Voices of Authority: Education and Linguistic Difference* (co-edited with Marilyn Martin-Jones; Greenwood, 2000). Recent articles have been published in such journals as the *Journal of Sociolinguistics*, *Estudios de Sociolinguistica*, *Discurso y Sociedad*, and *Grenzgaenge*. mheller@oise.utoronto.ca

Susan C. Herring is Associate Professor of Information Science and Linguistics at Indiana University, Bloomington. Her recent publications are mainly in the area of computer-mediated communication, where she applies linguistic methods of analysis to computer-mediated discourse. Her research investigates gender, politeness, interaction management, and changes over time in CMC. Her books include *Computer-mediated Communication: Linguistic, Social and Cross-Cultural Perspectives* (Benjamins, 1996) and *Computer-mediated Conversation* (forthcoming); she has also published numerous articles on CMC. herring@indiana.edu

Barbara Johnstone is Professor of Rhetoric and Linguistics at Carnegie Mellon University. In her book *Stories, Community, and Place* (Indiana University Press, 1990) she explored how shared story plots and shared conventions for storytelling help create community. She continues to explore connections between language, identity, and place. Johnstone is the author of several other books, including *Discourse Analysis: An Introduction* (Blackwell, 2001). bj4@andrew.cmu.edu

Christina Kakavá is Associate Professor of Linguistics at Mary Washington College. Her research interest is conflict management in intra- and interethnic communication. Her work has appeared in the *International Journal of the Sociology of Language*, *Georgetown Round Table on Languages and Linguistics*, and the *Journal of Modern Greek Studies*, and in other journals and books. ckakava@mwc.edu

Shari Kendall is Research Associate at Georgetown University. Her publications are mainly in the areas of gender and sexuality. Her research investigates the linguistic creation of gendered and other social identities in the workplace, the family, the courtroom, and the media. Her most recent articles include: "He's calling her Da Da!: A sociolinguistic analysis of the 'lesbianism as disease' metaphor in child custody cases" (with Keller Magenau; 1999); "Conversational patterns across gender, class and ethnicity: implications for classroom discourse" (with Deborah Tannen and Carolyn Temple Adger; 1997); and "Gender and language in the workplace" (with Deborah Tannen; 1997). kendalls@georgetown.edu

Amy Kyratzis is Assistant Professor of Early Childhood Education and Development at the Gevirtz Graduate School of Education, University of California, Santa Barbara. She has authored articles on children's early pragmatic development, communicative competence, and language socialization. She is co-editor of *Social Interaction, Social Context, and Language: Essays in Honor of Susan Ervin-Tripp* (with Dan Slobin, Julie Gerhardt, and Jiansheng Guo; Lawrence Erlbaum, 1996). kyratzis@education.ucsb.edu

Robin Tolmach Lakoff has been a Professor of Linguistics at the University of California at Berkeley since 1972. Her work is mostly in the areas of pragmatics and sociolinguistics, with particular emphasis on language and gender, politics of language, and discourse analysis. Earlier works include *Language and Woman's Place* (Harper & Row, 1975) and *Talking Power* (Basic Books, 1990). Her most recent book is *The Language War* (University of California Press, 2000). rlakoff@socrates.berkeley.edu

Charlotte Linde is a Senior Research Scientist at NASA Ames Research Center. Her publications focus on the social use of narrative, particularly in relation to individual and collective memory. Recent publications include "The Acquisition of a Speaker by a Story: How History Becomes Memory and Identity" (2000), "The Transformation of Narrative Syntax into Institutional Memory" (1999), and "Narrative: Experience, Memory, Folklore" (1997). Her book *Narrative and Institutional Memory* is to appear with Oxford University Press. clinde@mail.arc.nasa.gov

J. R. Martin is Professor in Linguistics (Personal Chair) at the University of Sydney. His research interests include systemic theory, functional grammar, discourse semantics, register, genre, multimodality and critical discourse analysis, focusing on English and Tagalog – with special reference to the transdisciplinary fields of educational linguistics and social semiotics. Publications include *English Text: System and Structure* (Benjamins, 1992); *Writing Science: Literacy and Discursive Power* (with M. A. K. Halliday; Falmer, 1993); *Working with Functional Grammar* (with C. Matthiessen and C. Painter; Arnold, 1997); *Genre and Institutions: Social Processes in the Workplace and School* (as co-editor with F. Christie; Cassell, 1997); and *Reading Science: Critical and Functional Perspectives on Discourses of Science* (as co-editor with R. Veel; Routledge, 1998). jmartin@mail.usyd.edu.au

Jacob L. Mey is Professor Emeritus of Linguistics at the University of Southern Denmark, Odense Main Campus. His publications are mainly in the areas of pragmatics and cognitive technology. His research investigates the use of pragmatic techniques in the production and consumption of literary texts, as well as the way the use of computers affects the way the mind organizes and uses knowledge and information. His most recent publications are *Concise Encyclopedia of Pragmatics* (as editor; Elsevier Science, 1999); *When Voices Clash: Studies in Literary Pragmatics* (Mouton de Gruyter, 2000); and *Pragmatics: An Introduction* (second, revised and enlarged edition; Blackwell, 2000). In addition, Mey publishes the *Journal of Pragmatics* and the new *Journal of Cognitive Technology* (with Barbara Gorayska and Jonathon Marsh). Jam@language.sdu.dk

John Myhill is Associate Professor in the Department of English at the University of Haifa. His publications are mainly in the field of discourse analysis, sociolinguistics, language typology, and semantics. His recent articles include "Towards a functional typology of agent defocusing" (1997); "A study of imperative usage in Biblical Hebrew and English" (1998); and "Quantitative methods of discourse analysis" (2001). john@research.haifa.ac.il

Neal R. Norrick holds the Chair of English Linguistics at Saarland University in Saarbrücken, Germany. His research specializations in linguistics include conversation, verbal humor, pragmatics, semantics, and poetics. In recent years, he has focused his research on spoken language, with particular interests in the role of repetition in discourse and verbal humor. His recent publications include: *Conversational Joking* (Indiana University Press, 1993); "Paradox and metaphor: a discourse approach" (1999); "Retelling again" (1998); "Retelling stories in spontaneous conversation" (1998); "Twice-told tales: collaborative narration of familiar stories" (1997); "Involvement and joking in conversation" (1994); "Repetition in canned jokes and spontaneous conversational joking" (1993); and *Conversational Narrative* (Benjamins, 2000). n.norrick@mx.uni-saarland.de

Elite Olshtain is Professor of Language Education at the School of Education, Hebrew University, Jerusalem, Israel. Her publications are mainly in the area of curriculum design and policy making, discourse analysis and teaching, and second language acquisition research. Her research investigates cross-cultural speech act behavior, language attrition and bilingualism, and language acquisition among immigrants. Her latest publications are *Discourse, Context and Language Teaching* (with Marianne Celce-Murcia; Cambridge University Press, to appear) and *Language Acquisition and Immigrant Patterns of Integration* (with G. Horenzyk; Magness Press, to appear). mselito@mscc.huji.ac.il

Livia Polanyi is Senior Research Scientist at FX Palo Alto Laboratories working in the area of computational discourse understanding. Before joining FXPAL, she taught at the University of Amsterdam and Rice University and was a Research Scientist at Bolt, Beranek, and Newman in Cambridge, MA. Polanyi has published widely. Her studies on formal, computational, linguistic, and cultural aspects of discourse understanding have appeared in journal and conference papers in many fields including theoretical linguistics, sociolinguistics, and computational linguistics, in addition to anthropology, literary theory, semiotics, and economics. Her book *Telling the American Story: Linguistic, Social and Cultural Constraints on the Meaning and Structure of Stories in Conversation* (Ablex, 1989) was reissued as a paperback by MIT Press. polanyi@pal.xerox.com

Martin Reisigl is a PhD candidate in Applied Linguistics at the University of Vienna and is a recipient of a research award from the Austrian Academy of Sciences. His publications are mainly in the areas of discourse analysis, (political) rhetoric, argumentation theory, and sociolinguistics. He is co-author of *The Discursive Construction of National Identity* (Edinburgh University Press, 1999) and *Discourse and Discrimination: The Rhetoric of Racism and Antisemitism* (Routledge, 2001), and co-editor of *The Semiotics of Racism* (Passagen, 2000). Mreisigl@hotmail.com

David Sankoff studied at McGill University and since 1969 has been at the Mathematics Research Centre of the University of Montreal, where he is also Professor of Mathematics and Statistics. He is a Fellow in the Evolutionary Biology Program of the Canadian Institute for Advanced Research. His research involves the formulation of mathematical models and the development of analytical methods in the sciences and humanities. This includes the design of algorithms for problems in computational biology, applied probability for phylogenetic analysis of evolution, and statistical methodology for studying grammatical variation and change in speech communities. His work since the early 1990s has focused on the evolution of genomes as the result of chromosomal rearrangement processes. sankoff@ere.umontreal.c

Emanuel A. Schegloff holds degrees from Harvard and the University of California at Berkeley, and has taught at Columbia and UCLA (since 1972). He has been a Fellow at the Netherlands Institute for Advanced Study in the Social Sciences and Humanities (1978–9) and at the Center for Advanced Studies in the Social Sciences at Stanford (1998–9), the latter while he held a Guggenheim Fellowship. He has lectured widely in the United States and Europe, and has published over seventy papers and chapters on a variety of topics concerning conversation and other forms of talk-in-interaction as the primordial site of human sociality. scheglof@soc.ucla.edu

Deborah Schiffrin is Professor of Linguistics at Georgetown University. Her research interests include narrative, life stories, oral histories of the Holocaust, discourse markers, referring terms, grammar and interaction, language and identity, and language and public memorial. Major publications include *Discourse Markers* (Cambridge University Press, 1987); *Approaches to Discourse* (Blackwell, 1994; second edition forthcoming); and *Language, Text and Interaction* (Cambridge University Press, forthcoming). schiffrd@georgetown.edu

Ron Scollon is Professor of Linguistics at Georgetown University. His publications are mainly in the areas of new literacy studies, mediated discourse analysis, and intercultural communication. His most recent books include *Professional Communication in International Settings* (with Yuling Pan and Suzanne Scollon) and *Mediated Discourse as Social Interaction*. scollonr@georgetown.edu

Suzanne Wong Scollon is Research Coordinator of Asian Sociocultural Research Projects and Adjunct Research Associate Professor in the Department of Linguistics at Georgetown University. Her publications are in the areas of critical semiotics, multimodal discourse analysis, and comparative rhetoric and professional presentation. Recent books include *Contrastive Discourse in Chinese and English: A Critical Appraisal* (with Ron Scollon and Andy Kirkpatrick) and *Intercultural Communication: A Discourse Approach* (with Ron Scollon; revised edition). suziescollon@earthlink.net

Roger W. Shuy is Distinguished Research Professor of Linguistics, Emeritus, Georgetown University. Over the years he has published his sociolinguistic and discourse analysis research on regional, social, education, ethnic, stylistic, and gender aspects of

English. Since the early 1970s, his major focus has been on forensic linguistics. His most recent books include *Language Crimes* (Blackwell, 1993); *The Language of Confession, Interrogation, and Deception* (Sage, 1998); and *Bureaucratic Language in Government and Business* (Georgetown University Press, 1998). shuyr@gusun.georgetown.edu

Michael Stubbs has been Professor of English Linguistics, University of Trier, Germany, since 1990. He was previously Professor of English, Institute of Education, University of London. His publications are mainly in educational linguistics, and in text and discourse analysis, including computer-assisted corpus linguistics. His publications include *Text and Corpus Analysis* (Blackwell, 1996) and *Words and Phrases: Studies in Corpus Semantics* (to appear). stubbs@uni-trier.de

Deborah Tannen is a University Professor and Professor of Linguistics at Georgetown University. She has published sixteen books and over eighty-five articles on such topics as spoken and written language, doctor–patient communication, cross-cultural communication, modern Greek discourse, the poetics of everyday conversation, the relationship between conversational and literary discourse, gender and language, workplace interaction, and agonism in public discourse. Among her books are *Talking Voices: Repetition, Dialogue and Imagery in Conversational Discourse* (Cambridge University Press, 1989); *Gender and Discourse* (Oxford University Press, 1994), and *Conversational Style: Analyzing Talk Among Friends* (Ablex, 1984). She has also written *I Only Say This Because I Love You* (Random House, 2001); *You Just Don't Understand: Women and Men in Conversation* (Ballantine, 1990); and *Talking from 9 to 5: Women and Men in the Workplace: Language, Sex, and Power* (Avon, 1995). Her book *The Argument Culture* (Random House, 1998) received the Common Ground Book Award. Tannen is co-recipient with Shari Kendall of a two-year grant from the Alfred P. Sloan Foundation, to examine the role of discourse in balancing work and family. tannend@georgetown.edu

Karen Tracy is Professor of Communication at the University of Colorado at Boulder and editor of the journal *Research on Language and Social Interaction*. She is a discourse analyst who studies face and identity troubles in institutional settings. Recent publications include *Colloquium: Dilemmas of Academic Discourse* (1997) and articles analyzing communicative trouble at emergency call centers, appearing in a variety of journals (*Human Communication Research, Journal of Applied Communication,* and *Discourse Studies*). She is beginning to write about deliberative difficulties in American school board meetings. karen.tracy@colorado.edu

Mija M. Van Der Wege is a Post-doctoral Research Assistant in the Psychology Department at Stanford University. She has published mainly in the area of language use and discourse processes. Her current research investigates issues of turn-taking, conventional and innovative word meanings, and reference processes. mija@psych.stanford.edu

Teun A. van Dijk is Professor of Discourse Studies at the University of Amsterdam, and Visiting Professor at the Universitat Pompeu Fabra in Barcelona. After earlier work on text grammar and the psychology of text processing, most of his work in the 1980s and 1990s dealt with the study of the discursive reproduction of racism. His new major project is on ideology and discourse. In each of these fields he has published several books. His latest are the two edited volumes *Discourse Studies* (Sage, 1997) and *Ideology* (Sage, 1998). He is founder and editor of the journals *Discourse and Society* and *Discourse Studies*. teun@hum.uva.nl

Gregory Ward is Professor and Chair of the Department of Linguistics at Northwestern University. His main research area is discourse, with specific interests in pragmatic theory, information structure, and reference/anaphora. Recent publications provide pragmatic analyses of various constructions, such as "do so" (with A. Kehler; Turner, 1999), Italian subject postposing (Kamio and Takami, 1998), and English "there"-sentences (with B. Birner; 1995). His recent book with Betty Birner, *Information Status and Noncanonical Word Order in English* (Benjamins, 1998), explores the discourse functions of a broad range of non-canonical syntactic constructions in English and other languages. With L. Horn, he is editor of the *Handbook of Pragmatics* (Blackwell, to appear). gw@northwestern.edu

Bonnie Lynn Webber is Professor of Intelligent Systems in the Division of Informatics, University of Edinburgh. She has published in both discourse semantics and natural language processing. Her most recent articles include "Inference through alternative-set semantics" (with Gann Bierner; 2000); "Discourse relations: a structural and presuppositional account using lexicalised TAG" (with Aravind Joshi, Alistair Knott, and Matthew Stone; 1999); and "Concession, implicature, and alternative sets (with Ivana Kruijff-Korbayová; 2001). bonnie@dai.ed.ac.uk

John Wilson is Professor of Communication and Dean of the Faculty of Social and Health Sciences and Education, University of Ulster. His research interests are in the areas of discourse, pragmatics, and sociolinguistics, in particular the applied use of theory in the understanding of everyday linguistic interaction. His early work concentrated on establishing a theory of conversation as a speech event. This is outlined in *On the Boundaries of Conversation* (Pergamon, 1987). He then moved on to consider the application of both pragmatic and discourse theory to an understanding of everyday language, most significantly political language (*Politically Speaking*: Blackwell, 1990; *Linguistic Forms of Political Life*: Mouton, forthcoming). His most recent publications indicate the breadth of his applied approach: *The Language of Peace and Conflict* (with J. Rose; 1997); *What Do You Have in Mind: Pragmatics and Language Impairment* (2000); and *Parameter Setting within a Socially Realistic Linguistics* (1998). jwilson@ulst.ac.uk

Ruth Wodak is Professor and Head of the Department of Applied Linguistics at the University of Vienna. Beside various other prizes, she was lately awarded with the Wittgenstein Prize for Elite Researchers (1996). She is Director of the Wittgenstein Research Centre Discourse, Politics, Identity (at the Austrian Academy of Sciences). Her publications are mainly in the areas of discourse and racism, discourse and discrimination, discourse analysis, gender studies, and organizational research. Her research also investigates studies in public and private discourse in Austria since 1945, with special focus on manifestations of antisemitism and racism towards foreigners. Most recently, she has focused on the deconstruction of a taboo on narratives of perpetrators in the Wehrmacht in World War II. Another main aim is the investigation of political language and political discourse: the study of media (printed and electronic) in 1988 in Austria and the impact of the "Waldheim Affair"; and the construction of Austrian and European identity in European Union policy making. Her recent books include *Methods of Critical Discourse Analysis* (with M. Meyer; Sage, forthcoming); *Racism at the Top* (with Teun A. van Dijk; Drava, 2000); *Discourse and Discrimination* (with Martin Reisigl; Routledge, in press); *The Semiotics of Racism* (with M. Reisigl; Passagen Verlag, in press); *Loss of Communication in the Information Age* (with R. de Cillia and H. J. Krumm; Austrian Academy of Sciences, forthcoming); and *Debating Europe: Globalisation Rhetoric and European Union Employment Policies* (with P. Muntigl and G. Weiss; Benjamins, forthcoming). ruth.wodak@univie.ac.at

Introduction

DEBORAH SCHIFFRIN, DEBORAH TANNEN, AND HEIDI E. HAMILTON

What Is Discourse Analysis?

Discourse analysis is a rapidly growing and evolving field. Current research in this field now flows from numerous academic disciplines that are very different from one another. Included, of course, are the disciplines in which models for understanding, and methods for analyzing, discourse first developed, such as linguistics, anthropology, and philosophy. But also included are disciplines that have applied – and thus often extended – such models and methods to problems within their own academic domains, such as communication, cognitive psychology, social psychology, and artificial intelligence.

Given this disciplinary diversity, it is no surprise that the terms "discourse" and "discourse analysis" have different meanings to scholars in different fields. For many, particularly linguists, "discourse" has generally been defined as anything "beyond the sentence." For others (for example Fasold 1990: 65), the study of discourse is the study of language use. These definitions have in common a focus on specific instances or spates of language. But critical theorists and those influenced by them can speak, for example, of "discourse of power" and "discourses of racism," where the term "discourses" not only becomes a count noun, but further refers to a broad conglomeration of linguistic and nonlinguistic social practices and ideological assumptions that together construct power or racism.

So abundant are definitions of discourse that many linguistics books on the subject now open with a survey of definitions. In their collection of classic papers in discourse analysis, for example, Jaworski and Coupland (1999: 1–3) include ten definitions from a wide range of sources. They all, however, fall into the three main categories noted above: (1) anything beyond the sentence, (2) language use, and (3) a broader range of social practice that includes nonlinguistic and nonspecific instances of language.

The definitional issues associated with discourse and discourse analysis are by no means unique. In his two-volume reference book on semantics, for example, Lyons (1997) illustrates ten different uses of the word *mean*, and thus an equal number of possible domains of the field of semantics. In his introductory chapter on pragmatics,

Levinson (1983) discusses twelve definitions of the field of pragmatics (including some which could easily cover either discourse analysis or sociolinguistics). Since semantics, pragmatics, and discourse all concern language, communication, meaning, and context it is perhaps not surprising that these three fields of linguistics are those whose definitions seem to be most variable.

The variety of papers in this *Handbook* reflects the full range of variation in definitions of – and approaches to – discourse analysis. The different understandings of discourse represented in this volume reflect the rising popularity of the field. Although it is not our intent to explain how or why discourse has gained so powerful an appeal for so wide a range of analytical imaginations (see Jaworski and Coupland 1999: 3–5; van Dijk 1997), our own intellectual/academic histories – all in linguistics – reveal some of the different paths that have led us to an interest in discourse. Since each of our paths is different, we here speak in our own voices – in the order in which we arrived at Georgetown University, where we all now teach.

Deborah Tannen

When I decided to pursue a PhD in linguistics, I held a BA and MA in English literature and had for several years been teaching remedial writing and freshman composition at Lehman College, the City University of New York. Restless to do something new, I attended the 1973 Linguistic Institute sponsored by the Linguistic Society of America at the University of Michigan. That summer I fell in love with linguistics, unaware that "language in context," the topic of that Institute, did not typify the field. Inspired by A. L. Becker's introductory course and by Robin Lakoff's course on politeness theory and communicative strategies, as well as by Emanuel Schegloff's public lecture on the closings of telephone conversations, I headed for the University of California, Berkeley, to pursue a PhD. There I discovered, along with Robin Lakoff, Charles Fillmore (then interested in frame semantics), Wallace Chafe (then interested in scripts theory and the comparison of speaking and writing), and John Gumperz (then developing his theory of conversational inference). Not for a moment did I think I was doing anything but linguistics. The word "discourse" was not a major category with which I identified. There were no journals with the word "discourse" in their titles. The only journal that specialized in language in context was *Language in Society*, which had a strongly anthropological orientation. I vividly recall the sense of excitement and possibility I felt when a fellow graduate student mentioned, as we stood in the halls outside the linguistics department, that another journal was about to be launched: *Discourse Processes*, edited by psychologist Roy Freedle at Educational Testing Service in Princeton.

When I joined the faculty of the sociolinguistics program at Georgetown University in 1979, I briefly redefined myself as a sociolinguist. That year I submitted an abstract to the annual LSA meeting and checked the box "sociolinguistics" to aid the committee in placing my paper on the program. But when I delivered the paper, I found myself odd man out as the lone presenter analyzing transcripts of conversation among a panel of Labovians displaying charts and graphs of phonological variation. I promptly redefined what I was doing as discourse analysis – the name I also gave to courses I developed in Georgetown. When invited to organize a Georgetown University Round Table on Languages and Linguistics in 1981, I titled the meeting (and the book that resulted) "Analyzing Discourse," and invited as speakers linguists, anthropologists, and psychologists, all of whom were examining language in context.

During these early years, a number of journals appeared that reflected and contributed to the development of the field: *Text*, the first of several journals founded and edited by Teun van Dijk in Amsterdam, and *Journal of Pragmatics*, co-edited by Jacob Mey and Hartmut Haberland in Denmark. As the years passed, many other journals were added – too many to name them all, but including *Pragmatics*, *Research on Language and Social Interaction*, *Discourse and Society*, *Multilingua*, *Journal of Linguistic Anthropology*, *Narrative Inquiry*, *Journal of Sociolinguistics*, and *Discourse Studies*. The proliferation of journals in itself testifies to the upsurge of interest in discourse analysis, and its many incarnations.

The changes I have seen in the two decades since I first began defining myself as a discourse analyst reflect the tremendous growth in this area. Work in discourse analysis is now so diverse that "discourse" is almost a synonym for "language" – coming full circle to where I saw such work at the start.

Deborah Schiffrin

I discovered linguistics and discourse analysis in a very roundabout way. In my senior year of college at Temple University, I read Erving Goffman's *Presentation of Self in Everyday Life* during a course in sociological theory (the last requirement of my major). I was so excited by his work that I went on to read everything else he had written and then decided to continue studying face-to-face interaction in a PhD program in sociology at Temple. There my studies included an eclectic blend of sociological and social theory, semiotics (which included initial forays into structural and transformational linguistics), statistics, and urban studies. While still at Temple, I wrote an article on the semiotics of the handshake, which I boldly sent to Goffman. What followed was an invitation to a personal meeting and then his permission to audit a course with him. (The course prerequisite was to read all his work before the first class!) When my advisor at Temple decided to leave for another position, I had already decided to try to work with Goffman. Ironically, it was Goffman himself who first turned my thoughts toward a PhD in linguistics: during our first meeting, he proclaimed his belief that linguistics could add rigor and respectability to the analysis of face-to-face interaction.

Once I was enrolled in the PhD Program in linguistics at the University of Pennsylvania, I quickly learned that although linguists knew that understanding social interaction was important, the *study* of social interaction itself had a somewhat peripheral role in the linguistics curriculum. What I found instead was Labov's sociolinguistics: an energizing mix of fieldwork, urban ethnography, variation analysis, and narrative analysis. I gladly immersed myself in the life and work of the faculty and students in the sociolinguistics community: we interviewed people, measured vowels, coded narratives, and wondered (and worried) about how to measure different "styles." Although many of my teachers published articles about discourse (Bill Labov on narrative and ritual insults, Ellen Prince on syntax, presupposition, and information status, Gillian Sankoff on grammaticalization in Tok Pisin), there was little sense of collective interest or of a community of discourse analysts.

As it became time for me to write my dissertation, I decided that I wanted to use what I had learned as a linguist to study social interaction. I remember my sense of confusion, though, when I tried to use what I had learned about the systematicity of language, as well as to follow the advice of both Labov and Goffman. Labov presented me with one mission: solve an old problem with a new method. But Goffman presented me with another: describe something that had not yet been described. After spending some time trying to apply these directives to the study of everyday arguments, I ended up focusing on discourse markers.

When I joined the faculty of Georgetown in 1982, I was immersed in the study of discourse, even though I was hired as a sociolinguist who could teach pragmatics and speech acts. Discourse analysis gradually filtered into those courses, as did face-to-face interaction, variation analysis, fieldwork, and even my old friend sociological theory. These various interests further jelled when I organized a Georgetown University Round Table on languages and linguistics in 1984, with the title "Meaning, Form and Use in Context: Linguistic Applications." Thanks to the interest in discourse created by Deborah Tannen, and the receptiveness of my sociolinguistics colleagues Roger Shuy and Ralph Fasold, I found – and continue to find – a community of faculty and students eager to pursue a collection of interests similar to my own under the rubric of "discourse analysis."

Heidi E. Hamilton

My motivation to study discourse came from my real-life experiences with what Gumperz has called "crosstalk." After receiving my bachelor's degree in German language/literature and cross-cultural studies, I worked in the field of international education for four years. Day after day I witnessed misunderstandings related to (what I would later learn were called) contextualization cues, framing, and complementary schismogenesis. I decided it was time to search for a graduate program to study the linguistic underpinnings of these misunderstandings. After culling through numerous graduate catalogues, I discovered that the courses that I had identified as the ones that seemed most intriguing and relevant led to a degree in linguistics at Georgetown University with a concentration on sociolinguistics. So off I went.

I was fortunate to begin my studies in 1981. The Georgetown University Round Table focusing on discourse had just been organized by Deborah Tannen. The entire department – students and faculty alike – was infused with a sense of excitement and open-ended possibility regarding the future of discourse studies. It was within this context that I worked as Deborah's research assistant and took her eye-opening courses on the analysis of conversation. In my second year of graduate study Deborah Schiffrin arrived at Georgetown as a new assistant professor, bringing with her a deep understanding of sociology and an approach to the analysis of discourse that was greatly influenced by Labov's work on variation. We graduate students were in the enviable position of working with two of the most innovative young discourse scholars at the time – a situation which became even more apparent to us a couple of years later.

In the summer of 1985, Georgetown University hosted 600 students and faculty who came from around the world to participate in the LSA Linguistic Institute organized by Deborah Tannen. Through the whirlwind of courses, lectures, and discussions, the interactional sociolinguistic approach to discourse analysis that we had been steeped in for several years was taking shape and gaining in prominence. Those of us educated at Georgetown kept hearing how very lucky we were to have the opportunity to study "this kind" of linguistics year-round. In retrospect, these comments seem to foreshadow the movement of the study of discourse from the fringes to a more mainstream position within linguistics.

Though my initial interest in crosstalk within international contexts never diminished (I came close to writing my dissertation on directness in German conversational style while living in Berlin for several years), I ended up shifting gears to another type of problematic talk – that of Alzheimer's disease. Little did I know that, with that choice of dissertation topic, I was jumping headfirst into a paradigmatic maelstrom. Being trained as an interactional discourse analyst, I was attempting to study a population that was firmly entrenched in the territory of neuro- and psycholinguistics. Time after time I found myself having to justify (to linguists and to gerontologists/neurologists alike) my attempt to marry the odd couple of interactional sociolinguistics and Alzheimer's disease. In the process, I learned quite a bit about how to talk across disciplinary boundaries, an enterprise that can be both frustrating and invigorating.

In 1990, when I joined the Georgetown Linguistics Department faculty, the program in discourse analysis was already very well established. Graduate students were entering our program better prepared than ever before and were ready to take their study of discourse to a new level. The field was mature enough to be expanded to include the study of "exceptional" discourse, which in turn can illuminate the often invisible workings of more ordinary, everyday discourse.

Purpose of the *Handbook*

Our own experiences in the field have led us to the conviction that the vastness and diversity of discourse analysis is a great strength rather than a weakness. Far from its being a liability to be lamented because of the lack of a single coherent theory, we find the theoretical and methodological diversity of discourse analysis to be an asset. We thus envision this volume as fostering the cooperative use – by linguists and others interested in empirically grounded studies of language – of the many theoretical and analytical resources currently proliferating in the study of discourse.

Our collection of forty-one articles suggests that the future cooperation which we hope will emerge will respect the many differences that distinguish the approaches reflected here. There are differences in the type of data drawn upon, ranging from political speeches to everyday conversation to literary texts. There are also differences in the types of context considered, including, for example, community, institutional, and ideological contexts. Finally, there is a varied range of theoretical paradigms, such as relevance theory and systemic-functional linguistics, and of methodology, including interpretive, statistical, and formal methods. As a result, the articles collected here suggest a foundational paradigm for "discourse analysis" that should be broad enough to support a wide range of assumptions, approaches, methods, analyses, and even definitions, of discourse.

What are the strengths and advantages of representing so wide a variety of discourse studies? Why have we collected so broad a set of articles and assumed so wide a scope for discourse analysis?

First, the scope of chapters reveals the range of problems that discourse analysis has addressed and can continue to address. These problems range from linguistic phenomena, such as preposing (Ward and Birner) and word meaning (Norrick, Schiffrin), to interdisciplinary phenomena, such as discourse flow (Chafe) and literary pragmatics (Mey), to social problems such as discrimination against minorities (Wodak and Reisigl) and patient compliance with doctors' instructions (Ainsworth-Vaughn). The problems addressed by the chapters also vary in focus, from historical discourse analysis (Brinton) to discourse and conflict (Kakavá); in analytical scope, from intonation (Couper-Kuhlen) to narrative (Johnstone); and in methodology, from case studies (Linde) to statistical surveys (Biber and Conrad).

Second, the inclusion of a range of chapters will immediately highlight analytical parallels among perspectives that are already substantively and methodologically aligned, such as the links among critical discourse analysis (van Dijk), the analysis of discourse and racism (Wodak and Reisigl), and political discourse (Wilson). However, we also hope that readers will discover parallels among areas whose similarities have been overlooked. Included here might be methodological parallels, such as the adoption of ethnographic methods across different institutional domains, as noted in Adger's on discourse in educational settings and Ainsworth-Vaughn's on the discourse of medical encounters. Readers may also find that they can apply empirical findings from one area to other areas: for example, insights into information structure (Ward and Birner) may be relevant to doctor–patient communication (Ainsworth-Vaughn) as well as discourse and conflict (Kakavá) or the discursive construction of the self (Harré). Similarly, the analysis of information flow (Chafe) may inform the formal demarcation of discourse units (Polanyi).

In a similar spirit, we hope that readers will find thematic parallels among chapters that approach similar domains of discourse in different ways. For example, "the computer" – so pervasive a force in linguistic and social dynamics – enters the *Handbook* in numerous sections and chapters. It is seen as a method in Edwards's chapter on transcription, and as both method and resource for data in Biber and Conrad's quantitative analyses of register variation and in Stubbs's discussion of corpus analysis. The computer provides a source of both data and genre in Herring's chapter on computer-mediated discourse, and as an algorithm in Webber's discussion of computational models of discourse.

It is with such patterns in mind, then, that we hope that the range of chapters – and perceived connections among them, many of which we have not described here or even foreseen – will enhance the ability of discourse analysts to deal with a variety of problems and phenomena in ways that are not only internally coherent, but also enriched by multiple connections with one another.

A third benefit to the wide scope of chapters is the reinforcement of the synergy between theory and data analysis that is reflected in the pervasive understanding of discourse analysis as the examination of actual (not hypothetical) text and/or talk. Although authors have pursued a range of formats within the general topic assigned to them, we have encouraged them – in keeping with the term "discourse analysis," as well as the strong empirical bent noted above – to illustrate and substantiate general points by drawing upon concrete analyses of real discourse data. This springs from our conviction that theory and data are inseparable and mutually enriching: theoretical insights are needed to move the analysis of discourse beyond instance-specific insights, at the same time as analysis must be grounded in actual instances of language in order to provide both realistic constraints and empirical bases for theory-building.

Fourth, though we have not asked contributors to address the need for – or even the desirability of – a single discourse theory, what contributors chose to include and emphasize, the themes and problems they address from the perspective of their specific areas, and the analyses and findings that they report all reveal the richness that needs to be respected and encompassed in discourse theories.

We hope that the breadth of articles collected here will provide a comprehensive view of the central issues in contemporary discourse analysis that is both accessible to students and informative to scholars. To this end, we have included articles by leading scholars in the field that provide an overview of their previous work, as well as chapters that survey the history of an area and summarize recent developments. In other articles, firmly established domains are assessed in order to link past approaches and findings with future challenges; in still others, authors develop relatively new fields of inquiry. Thus, we hope that the *Handbook* will serve not only as an authoritative guide to the major developments of discourse analysis, but also as a significant contribution to current research.

Organizational Structure

The organization of the *Handbook* reflects and builds upon the diversity of discourse analysis. Part I, "Discourse Analysis and Linguistics," locates the field in relation to the different aspects of, and perspectives on, language that typically constitute the field of linguistics. Of particular note is the growing interest in the influence of discourse from the traditional subfields of linguistics: phonology (Couper-Kuhlen), semantics (Martin, Norrick), syntax (Ward and Birner), and historical linguistics (Brinton). In all these chapters, we see scholars looking to naturally occurring discourse as the site within which to analyze sound, sense, and structure, as well as to understand diachronic processes such as language change. The chapters in this part thus demonstrate how examining utterances in discourse contributes to areas of linguistics traditionally limited to levels of analysis lower than that of discourse.

The part begins with sound (Couper-Kuhlen's discussion of intonation) and moves on to different views and levels of meaning (Martin, Schiffrin, Norrick), utterance interpretation (Blakemore), and sentence form (Ward and Birner). It concludes with an historical perspective on discourse (Brinton), as well as two comparative perspectives (Myhill on typology, Biber and Conrad on register variation). Not surprisingly, some of the chapters comfortably cross the borders not only between sentence and discourse, and between form and function, but also between traditionally conceived boundaries within linguistics itself: semantics and pragmatics (Norrick, Schiffrin), syntax and pragmatics (Ward and Birner), phonology and pragmatics (Couper-Kuhlen), and syntax, semantics, and pragmatics (Martin, Myhill, Brinton).

In general, then, chapters in part I provide an overview of specific linguistic issues that can be addressed through discourse analysis – how these issues (and their study) can not only reveal something about discourse, but also have an impact on the traditional subfields of linguistics. Such interest reflects not just a methodological shift to empirical data, but also a philosophical shift toward a humanistic linguistics in which language, theory, and practice inform and enrich one another.

The interdependence of theory and practice is the theme taken up in the next two parts, part II, "The Linking of Theory and Practice in Discourse Analysis," and part III, "Discourse: Language, Context, and Interaction." Our understanding of the term "practice" is slightly different in each of these two parts, roughly divided by whose practices are the focus of attention.

The focus in part II is upon analysts' practices, that is, the methodology of discourse analysis, and its relationship to theory. Collectively, the chapters address such questions as the following: how do the methodological practices through which we collect, represent, and analyze discourse reflect our theoretical assumptions and constructs? How might the kind of data we analyze not only reflect our theories, but also alter them? What tools should we use to analyze specific problems and issues? Just as it is possible to find interesting questions in any discourse that comes one's way (Chafe 1994: 12), it also behooves us to make use of any methods and theoretical insights that shed light on the discourse we have undertaken to analyze (cf. Chafe 1994: 18).

In this sense, the chapter by Lakoff sets the tone for the section, as she shows how a variety of theoretical and methodological constructs can be brought to bear on a single social/linguistic action, apologies. The part ends with Edwards's examination of an issue that must be addressed, tacitly or directly, by every discourse analyst: the development of a transcription system that is both theoretically motivated and methodologically justified. Included in the section are chapters that present retrospective overviews by two of the field's pioneers (Gumperz, Schegloff), a survey of varying methods and theoretical paradigms found in the analysis of discourse in interaction (Heller), and examples of approaches as varied as Polanyi's use of formal algorithms to represent discourse structures, Dubois and Sankoff's use of quantitative methods to analyze discourse, and Stubbs's examination of computer-based corpus analysis.

Although we do not use the term "practice" in the title of part III, "Language, Context, and Interaction," our focus here is on the interactive contexts in which (and through which) language is used. As a result, our attention shifts to examine the wide variety of ways that interlocutors draw upon the symbolic resources of language to accomplish the many different tasks of social life, including the presentation of self and other in a variety of institutional and interpersonal capacities.

This part is further divided into two sections. First comes "Political, Social, and Institutional Domains." Here we find a range of empirical studies and approaches showing how discourse is situated in different realms of social life and how these contextualized uses help to define interlocutors as members of specific discourse communities. The first set of chapters focuses on relatively public discourse: van Dijk on critical discourse analysis, Wodak and Reisigl on racism, Wilson on political discourse, and Cotter on the media. We then move to chapters summarizing research on discourse whose goals vary widely, from Shuy's focus on litigation, to chapters by Ainsworth-Vaughn and by Fleischman addressing the medical context, to Adger's chapter on education, and, finally, to Linde's discussion of the creation of institutional memory.

The second section continues to examine the nexus of discourse, context, and inter-action, but focuses on how discourse situated in "Culture, Community, and Genre" is reflected in, and enacted by, the language produced by groups of speakers in particular contexts. The section begins with Scollon and Scollon's account of the field of intercultural communication. We then move to chapters that survey research which addresses variation by groups of speakers identified by gender (Kendall and Tannen) and age (Hamilton on the aging, Cook-Gumperz and Kyratzis on children). The last three chapters in this section consider modes of communication by discourse type: Herring on computer-mediated discourse, Johnstone on narrative, and Kakavá on conflict.

Taken together, this part provides a wide range of empirical studies of discourse that will be useful not only to practitioners of discourse analysis, but also to those engaged in research on the specific domains of social life that are the focus of the analyses.

To this point, then, the *Handbook* begins with discourse analysis within linguistics (part I), continues by examining theoretical and methodological issues of discourse analysis (part II), and presents a wide range of empirical studies of discourse as social and linguistic practice (part III). Since many of the chapters are interdisciplinary in spirit and in application, we end the *Handbook* by considering how disciplines other than linguistics approach the analysis of discourse. Thus, part IV, "Discourse across Disciplines," provides an overview of how different disciplines have come to be interested in discourse. The chapters in this part reveal too not only ways that dis-course analysis can be expanded to incorporate insights from other disciplines, but also how questions asked by other disciplines (such as, "What is the 'self'?") can be fruitfully addressed through analyses of discourse.

The last part begins with Chafe's analysis of "discourse flow": an approach grounded firmly in the field of linguistics but which encompasses insights into cognition that can be revealed through analysis of discourse. Next, Harré explores the turn to analysis of discourse in social psychology, followed by Olshtain and Celce-Murcia's parallel account for language teaching, Tracy's for the discipline of communication, and Grimshaw's for sociology. Clark and Van Der Wege, coming from the field of psychology, introduce the notion of "imagination in discourse," while Mey introduces his analytic method for understanding the discourse of literary fiction. The part, and the *Handbook*, close with Webber's presentation of computational perspectives.

Conclusion

With these varied perspectives in mind, we return, in conclusion, to the question, "What is discourse?" Years ago, Charles Fillmore captured the essence of discourse by presenting the following two sentences, each of which appeared as a sign at a swimming pool. One sign said, *Please use the toilets, not the pool.* The other sign said, *Pool for members only.* Read separately, each sign is reasonable enough. But when the two sentences are read as if they were part of a single discourse, the second sentence forces a reinterpretation of the first that provokes laughter (or, if taken seriously, outrage). Fillmore's example captures what we might call the gift of discourse: new meanings are created through the relationship between sentences. But it also illustrates what we might call the curse of discourse: since more than one meaning can be created, how do we decide which meaning is intended, is justifiable, and/or makes the most sense?

We hope, through this *Handbook,* to offer a comprehensive sense of the scope and possibilities of discourse analysis, like the gift of multiple meanings. We know that some will see areas of meaning we have omitted, pathways we could have walked down but, due to the usual vagaries of human fallibility, we either did not pursue or were not able to realize. This is the curse of discourse: the directions in which its meanings may fan out are limitless. We have tried to provide a starting point from which the major highways emanate.

REFERENCES

Chafe, W. (1994). *Discourse, Consciousness, and Time.* Chicago: University of Chicago Press.

Fasold, R. (1990). *Sociolinguistics of Language.* Oxford: Blackwell.

Jaworski, A. and Coupland, N. (1999). *The Discourse Reader.* London and New York: Routledge.

Levinson, S. (1983). *Pragmatics.* Cambridge: Cambridge University Press.

Lyons, J. (1977). *Semantics.* Cambridge: Cambridge University Press.

van Dijk, T. (1997). *Discourse as Structure and Process.* London and Thousand Oaks CA: Sage.

I Discourse Analysis and Linguistics

1 Intonation and Discourse: Current Views from Within

ELIZABETH COUPER-KUHLEN

0 Introduction

In a millennium year we can expect increased stock-taking of the sort: where have we come from? Where are we now? Where do we go from here? The present contribution is an attempt to do this kind of stock-taking with respect to intonation and discourse. It consists of three millennialistic views organized temporally, starting with the view backwards, then the view of today, and finally a view of the future, near and far. Needless to say, all of these temporal viewings have their reference point at the moment of speaking, that is "now." Moreover, they are the author's views: they are anchored deictically to one researcher in the field.[1] Although it is difficult to avoid this natural bias, an adjunct like "from within" can at least recognize it as such.

1 Looking Back

What was the state of the art in the field of intonation and discourse a quarter of a century ago? Actually there was no such field. At that time most linguists felt that it was possible to have language without intonation and therefore to do linguistics without it. In fact, some even thought it imperative to think of intonation, like phonetics, as being outside of language. Not only do we have influential articles, like Bolinger's entitled "Around the edge of language" (1964), to remind us of this; it was (and still is) reflected institutionally in the fact that many renowned British universities had (and have) departments of "Linguistics and Phonetics", the latter subsuming the study of intonation.

Where did this idea come from? First, it was clearly promoted by the bias toward written language which has dominated much of twentieth-century linguistics. The fact that writing works perfectly well without intonation seems to bear out the proposition that we can do without it, and Occam's razor suggests we should. Moreover, the idea found nourishment in the competence–performance dichotomy of the generative paradigm in linguistics. Intonation was easy to relegate to the domain of performance because it only made itself apparent when language was used orally. Finally, *pace* Trager and Smith (1957), intonation did not fit very well into the structuralist mould of thinking anyway. Despite Halliday's (1967) efforts to adduce as much evidence as possible for its distinctive function, there were simply too many occasions when it appeared to be gradient rather than categorical. In fact, this was one of Bolinger's main reasons for saying that it was "around the edge of language," and it was Martinet's (1962) justification for excluding intonation from the functional system of language altogether.

So not only was intonation some thirty years ago a linguistic citizen with dubious credentials, if any at all.[2] Certainly no one had ever thought of combining the notion of intonation with that of discourse. Intonation was the difference between a sentence of written prose and that sentence read aloud. It was what you had when prose was spoken (see also Abercrombie 1965). This surely had nothing to do with discourse – or if it did, the connection was trivial, since discourse was merely a concatenation of sentences and each of these could be given an intonation on independent grounds.

The change has come slowly but surely. By the 1980s it was beginning to be apparent to some linguists that there might be a discourse function of intonation which would merit investigation (see inter alia Couper-Kuhlen 1986).[3] Brazil, Coulthard, and Johns's *Discourse Intonation and Language Teaching* (1980) was instrumental in bringing about this realization. Significantly the impulse to look at intonation in discourse came from language teachers (or rather, teachers of language teachers). In fact, this was the motivation for most of the early work done on English intonation: Armstrong and Ward's *Handbook of English Intonation* (1926), O'Connor and Arnold's *Intonation of Colloquial English* (1961), and even Halliday's *A Course in Spoken English: Intonation* (1970) are all didacticized texts intended to supplement the teaching of English pronunciation to foreign students. Small wonder then that it was language teachers who, with the turn to communicative skills in language teaching, were among the first to put intonation in this framework.

2   Looking at Now

What is the state of the art today? First, there has been a major paradigm shift with respect to the role of intonation in language. Few if any linguists today would wish to deny the fact that intonation impacts with language. It is hard to identify a single catalyst in this change of paradigm. Perhaps it is best seen as resulting from a slow accumulation of evidence which at some point reached a critical mass. But among those who waxed most persuasive the names of Bolinger, Halliday, Ladd, and Chafe should not be missing.

Three strands of research in the field of intonation in discourse, growing out of three different methodological approaches, may be identified today, in a state of more or less peaceful coexistence.[4] First there is the school of thought which sees intonation as a part of *grammar* broadly speaking.[5] This school actually has quite a tradition. Historically some of the earliest work on intonation tried to establish a correspondence between declarative, interrogative, and exclamatory sentence types and final falling or rising intonation (Couper-Kuhlen and Selting 1996). And there may even be some linguists who still think along these lines. But where speech act theory has been received, those who wish to see intonation as part of grammar will now usually assume that intonations are illocutionary-force-indicating devices and distinctive in the way they pair with different illocutions.

On the American scene, Pierrehumbert's model of intonation nominally belongs in this tradition;[6] it sets up a "grammar" of intonation, with an inventory of six tones or pitch accents, two phrasal tones, and two boundary tones and claims that all well-formed tunes can be generated from this inventory (Pierrehumbert 1980). Recently the intonation-as-grammar approach has addressed the "meaning of intonational contours in the interpretation of discourse" (Pierrehumbert and Hirschberg 1990). The tack taken is to see intonational contours as specifying a relationship between propositional content and the mutual beliefs of participants in the current discourse. One representative study, for instance, attempts to show a context-independent correspondence between a fall–rise pitch accent (L*+H L H%) and a propositional attitude of uncertainty (Ward and Hirschberg 1985; see also Hirschberg and Ward 1992). Here – as in general in the intonation-as-grammar approach – the term "discourse" is used on the grounds that test sentences are read out "in context," as follow-ups to prior sentences which are said to provide a "discourse context" for the interpretation in question.

In a second and no less lively tradition, intonation is thought of as related not to grammar but to *information flow*, the movement of ideas into and out of active, semi-active and inactive states of consciousness. In Chafe's work (1979, 1980, 1993), for instance, intonation is said to provide a window on consciousness via the establishment of two different types of unit: the intonation unit and the accent unit. The intonation unit encompasses the information that is in the speaker's focus of consciousness at a given moment (1993: 39); the accent units are the domains of activation for new, accessible and/or given information. Also within this tradition, Du Bois et al. (1992, 1993) have elaborated the notion of transitional continuity between one intonation unit and the next, marked by different sorts of terminal pitch contours. The term *transitional continuity* describes the extent to which "the discourse business at hand will be continued or has finished" (1993: 53). Thus, depending on whether some material is segmented into one or, say, two intonation units and on how these intonation units are linked transitionally to one another, claims can be made about its status in consciousness and about whether it is viewed as completed or not.

In contrast to the intonation-as-grammar approach, the intonation-and-information-flow approach has paid less attention to type of pitch accent and more attention to issues of unit segmentation and inter-unit continuity. Methodologically – also in marked contrast to the intonation-as-grammar school of thought – it has developed out of close observation of real discourse rather than from introspection and constructed examples. At times, the discourse under observation in the intonation-as-information-flow tradition has been prompted by an experimental set-up (for instance, the Pear Story film in Chafe 1979 or an instructional task e.g. in Swerts and Geluykens 1994). And it has tended to be primarily monologic as well as uniform in genre (e.g. oral narration, instructional monologue). In this sense the information-flow approach is different from the third school of thought, which takes a deliberately interactional approach.

The third approach might be called provisionally the intonation-as-contextualization approach, to make it comparable with its contemporaries. It is complementary, rather than contrastive, to the intonation-as-information-flow approach but stands in stark contrast to the intonation-as-grammar school of thought. The idea of contextualization goes back to seminal work by the anthropologist Bateson (1956, 1972). But it was first applied specifically to language and intonation in the second half of the 1970s (Cook-Gumperz and Gumperz 1976). Contextualization refers to the fact that linguistic signs need embedding in a context in order to be fully interpretable. In this sense *all* linguistic signs are indexical, not just a small subset of them. Contexts are not given but are said to be invoked, or made relevant, by participants through so-called contextualization cues. The cues may be verbal or nonverbal in nature: they include such stylistic uses of language as code-switching as well as gestural, proxemic, paralinguistic, and prosodic phenomena which accompany linguistic forms (see also Auer and di Luzio 1992). Contextualization cues function by indexing or evoking interpretive schemas or frames within which inferential understanding can be achieved (Gumperz 1982; Tannen 1993). Intonation – by its very nature nonreferential, gradient, and evocative – is seen as a prime contextualization cue in this approach.

Yet intonation – in the restricted sense of "pitch configuration" – rarely functions alone to cue an interpretive frame. The same frame may be cued by timing and volume as well. In fact, frames are cued best (most reliably) when their signals are multi-faceted and come in clusters (Auer 1992). Pitch, volume, and timing have in common that they are prosodic: syllable-based auditory effects produced by vocal-fold and air-flow manipulations orchestrated in time (Crystal 1969). This is why in the contextualization-cue approach there has been a subtle shift away from the study of "intonation" to the study of *prosody* and discourse. The third school of thought thus actually deserves to be called "prosody-as-contextualization cue."

In this approach contextualization cues, and consequently prosodic phenomena, are not seen as accidental or aleatory, nor as automatic reflexes of cognitive and affective states. They are thought to have their own systematicity, but a systematicity which can only be accessed in a context-sensitive fashion. This is why, methodologically, the contextualization-cue approach advocates situated empirical investigation of naturally occurring spoken data. To complement the intonation-as-information flow approach, it focuses less on monologue and more on interaction. In fact, prosodic contextualization research is *grounded* in verbal interaction. This has important consequences for the type of claim made and for the way in which the claims are warranted.

What do prosodic contextualization cues signal in discourse? Viewed from the perspective of interaction, prosodic phenomena can be thought of as furnishing a *format design* for turns at talk. This format design helps interactants meet two general sorts of requirement, which Goffman (1981) has dubbed "system requirements" and "ritual requirements." "System requirements" refer to "requirements that an interaction system must have, given that the participants have certain anatomical, physiological and information-processing capacities"; "ritual requirements" involve "rules that govern interaction, given that the participants are moral beings who are governed by reciprocally held norms of good or proper conduct" (Kendon 1988: 31f). In other words, prosodic contextualization cues help interactants make inferences about turn-taking and floor management, on the one hand, and about what actions or activities are being carried out, how they are being carried out, and how this might impinge upon participants' face, on the other.

How does one warrant claims about prosodically cued interactional meaning? Here the groundedness of the contextualization-cue approach affords a built-in methodology.

The local display which interactants provide to each other of how they have understood a prior turn and of what action is conditionally (or preferentially) relevant in a next turn can be exploited for warranting claims about prosodic signalling in interaction. That is, by viewing prosody as sequentially embedded in interaction, as occasioned by prior actions and occasioning subsequent actions, both embodied in turns with specific prosodic designs themselves, we can develop grounded hypotheses about what its function is from the interactional data and at the same time validate these hypotheses in the interactional data. This is the contextualization-cue paradigm for the study of prosody in discourse (see also Couper-Kuhlen and Selting 1996).

3   Looking Ahead

As work in this paradigm is just getting under way, it is only appropriate to place the following remarks under the heading of the future, albeit it should be thought of as the near future. What substantial gains in the study of prosodic contextualization can be anticipated over the next few years? The answer to this question will be influenced by the extent to which new territory can be explored. Some of this new territory lies beyond the intonation phrase, and some lies beyond intonation altogether. In the following, single-case analyses from these new territories will be used to show what kind of discovery can be expected with more systematic investigation.

3.1   *Beyond the intonation phrase*

As soon as one's perspective switches from the individual intonation phrase and events within it to sequences of intonation phrases – which is what should naturally happen in the study in discourse – then the question becomes: are all intonation units alike, merely juxtaposed in time, or are there differences between them? If there are differences, what is their effect? Do they create global intonational structure?

The groundwork for studying intonational structure beyond the intonation phrase has been laid by Chafe (1988), Schuetze-Coburn et al. (1991), and Du Bois et al. (1993). In particular, the notion of declination unit ('t Hart et al. 1990) – which, as Schuetze-Coburn et al. (1991) show, can be identified in naturally occurring discourse as well as in the laboratory – suggests one answer to the question of global intonational structure. Declination units create structures larger than the intonation unit. When there are several intonation units in a declination unit, they have slightly different shapes, depending on their relative position in the larger structure. The position of a single intonation unit within the larger unit is detectable in its final pitch, but also – importantly – in its initial pitch. It is the way intonation units *begin* which forms one of the new territiories for exploration beyond the intonation phrase.

3.1.1   *Onset level*

The notion of structure created by intonation phrase beginnings can be operationalized with the category of onset level (Brazil's "key"; see also Couper-Kuhlen 1986). The *onset* of an intonation phrase in English is defined as the first pitch accent in the phrase. If there is only one pitch accent, the onset is identical with the so-called nucleus, usually defined as the last pitch accent of the phrase. Brazil et al. (1980) suggest that at least three different onset levels can be identified in speech: High, Mid, and Low. These are to be thought of as pitch levels relative to that of a nucleus or onset in the prior intonation phrase. In the absence of a prior intonation phrase, they are presumably related to the speaker's default pitch range (which is itself related to that speaker's natural voice range: see below). Brazil has argued that the three different onset levels or keys have distinctive functions in discourse. Yet this statement is based more on introspection and carefully chosen constructed examples than on the analysis of large quantities of naturally occurring data. Whether indeed three levels are relevant in everyday conversational interaction is an empirical question which is still open at this time. Should conversationalists operate with only two, the following fragments suggest that an appropriate labeling might be High and Nonhigh.

In interaction there are two possible domains within which an intonational or a prosodic phenomenon may be relevant: (1) the turn or (2) a sequence of turns. In the first, a prosodic phenomenon makes itself apparent relative to surrounding prosody *within* a speaker's turn; in the second, a prosodic phenomenon is apparent relative to the prosody of a prior or subsequent turn, i.e. *across* speaker turns. Onset level is deployed in both domains by conversationalists, as the following extract demonstrates:

(1) **Kilimanjaro**
     (Ann and her boyfriend Chuck have returned for a visit to Minnesota and are having supper with Ann's high-school friend, Janet, and her husband Steve. Prior talk has centered on nature trips in the Upper Peninsula (U. P.) of Michigan. Ann is talking here about mountain treks in Scandinavia.)

```
     1    A:   there's some sort of rule though (there)
                when- when you're in a cabin,
                no (gh) in Sweden
                when you're in a cabin and someone comes?
     5           next day you have to leave.
                but other-
                if no one comes
                you can stay there as long as you want to.
                (.)
    10          so
                it's just (like)
                to get-
          J:   right
                to keep the process -
    15    S:   yeah
                (probably right)
          J:   going
                so someone doesn't have to ski for t(h)en days,
                heh heh heh
```

```
20  A:  oh ho [ho ho ho
    J:         [without sleep
            looking for the only open cabin,
    A:  No you end up with a lot of people going camping.
        but uh
25      (.)
    J:  °mhm°
        (.)
    J:  {acc} yeah that sounds nice.
→       There is a place like that in the U. P.;
30      uhm
        Porcupine Mountains.
        but they have cabins:
        up the mountain
        and you can hike
35      from one cabin
        and the next and
        (.)
    S:  [°yeah°
    J:  [perhaps this fall
40      we'll go do that
    S:  °yeah that'd be nice°
    J:  °yeah°
    A:  °in the fall°
        °mmm°
45  J:  shouldn't be very crowded then at all
        {1} it wasn't crowded when we were there
    A:  heh heh heh
    J:  no:
    A:  mmm
50  J:  nothing: in the U. P.;
        (.)
→   A:  Jane'll be hiking in the Kiliman↑jaro next week
    J:  {1}wo::w
        (.)
55  A:  mhm
        °poor Jane
        should've seen her when she went back°
        (.)
        °she had so: much stuff with he(h)r°
60  J:  yeah,
        (.)
        this is a friend from college
        that was teaching in Du:sseldorf
        for:: how long;
65      [four years?
```

Focusing on Janet's turn beginning in line 28, we notice that the first intonation phrase *yeah that sounds nice* has fast speech rate and begins relatively low in her pitch range. The low-pitched onset becomes particularly noticeable when it is contrasted with the next intonation phrase in line 29: *There is a place like that in the U. P.* Here the first pitch accent on *place* is noticeably higher than the first accent on *yeah* in the prior intonation phrase. (The high onset is indicated in transcription with a capital letter at the beginning of the line; a line which does not begin with a capital letter consequently lacks high onset.) Line 29 is thus a case of high onset being used within the domain of a turn. We identify the high start in relation to one or more other intonation phrases within that same speaker's turn. In the case at hand, since there is a transition relevance point (TRP) at the end of line 28, we might wish to say that lines 28 and 29 form separate turn-constructional units (TCUs). If so, we could then state that the intonational format of the second TCU lends it a different status compared to the first one.

What is the effect of high onset here? A line-by-line analysis of this fragment reveals that the TCUs in lines 28 and 29 are doing rather different things. Line 28 is responsive to the story Ann has just told about staying in mountain cabins in Sweden; its orientation is clearly backwards. Line 29, on the other hand, is more forward-looking. Despite its anaphoric reference with *that* to the place Ann was talking about, its primary business is to introduce a new topic, only tangentally related to the prior one. It puts this new topic *a place in the U. P.* on the floor and at the same time projects more talk about it. The intonational formatting of line 29 can thus be thought of as one of the ways this TCU is designed to do its work: it cues the introduction of a new topic.

Yet, looking somewhat further in the exchange, line 52 is worth considering. Here Ann appears to be introducing a new topic – there has been no mention of either Jane or Kilimanjaro in the forty minutes of talk preceding this fragment – and yet her onset is *not* noticeably higher than the onset of the surrounding intonation phrases.[7] Is this a counterexample to the postulation that new topics are cued with high onset, or is Ann strategically exploiting the contrast between high and nonhigh onset? The evidence suggests the latter. When examined more closely, Ann's new topic will be seen to be qualitatively rather different from Janet's. For one, it has a different sort of trajectory. Janet's TCU (line 29) introduces an entity into the discourse via a presentative construction with *There is* and an indefinite noun phrase *a place like that in the U. P.*, projecting more information on this entity in subsequent TCUs. Ann's TCU (line 52), on the other hand, treats *Jane* as a discourse entity already introduced and accessible, i.e. as common ground, and predicates something about this entity within the same unit. That is, Ann's TCU is constructed and executed as a complete turn of its own.

Second, notice that Janet's new topic receives uptake from all of the participants active in the conversation, whereas Ann's topic is acknowledged only by Janet. Moreover, the nature of Janet's response in line 53 reveals her to be a partially knowing recipient (Goodwin 1981). Were she unknowing, we would expect a response treating the components of Ann's turn – that Jane is or will be in Tanzania, that she will be hiking and that the hiking will be in the Kilimanjaro the following week – as news. Yet as it happens, Janet treats none of these pieces of information as particularly new or surprising. Instead her low-keyed, lengthened *wow* is heard as registering mild appreciation of something which was (at least partially) already known. That Janet knows that Jane has recently gone back to Tanzania is, moreover, implicit in the way

Ann's next turn is phrased: *should've seen her when she went back* (line 57) takes both the fact that she returned and where she returned as given.[8]

Third, Ann's follow-up talk on the new topic (lines 56–9) is delivered – in contrast to Janet's (lines 31–6) – sotto voce. And only one of the several participants responds (line 60). Ann's talk is thus insider talk: it is cued for, and receipted by, only a subset of those participating actively in the conversation. Janet's next move confirms this: she unilaterally begins to fill in the unknowing participants, explaining who Jane is and why she has gone to Tanzania (lines 60ff). The evidence thus conspires to suggest that "Jane" is not a full-fledged official topic for the general floor but an insider topic for a private floor. And the prosody of Ann's TCU introducing this topic – specifically its format *without* high onset – can be reconstructed as cueing its unofficial, insider status.

On a more general level, the above fragment demonstrates how participants use high onset and its absence as a strategic resource for cueing new topics. This does not mean that on other occasions high onset or its absence might not signal something different. The inferencing which the deployment of onset level cues must be expected to be sensitive to the sequential location and the verbal content of the TCU in question.

3.1.2 Register

In addition to onset level, there is another aspect of intonation beyond the intonation phrase which cues inferences in interactional discourse. This is *register*, defined as the relative position of an intonation phrase within a speaker's overall voice range (Cruttenden 1986: 129). The norm for register, according to Cruttenden, is for intonation phrases to be positioned roughly in the lower third of a speaker's voice range. Marked uses of register occur when the whole range of pitch configuration within an intonation phrase is moved to a higher, or within limits to a lower, position in the speaker's voice range.[9] Register is distinct from onset level because it affects all the pitches in a given intonation phrase rather than only that of the first accented syllable.

Just as with onset level, register and register shifts are deployed both within the speaking turn and across speaking turns in interaction. Well-known uses within speaking turns include the use of register shift to mark voicing in reported speech (see e.g. Klewitz and Couper-Kuhlen 1999), and the use of register shift to signal that a stretch of speech is parenthetic with respect to primary talk. But register, and more specifically register shift, may also be deployed across speakers' turns, as the next set of examples will demonstrate.

Let us begin by observing the unmarked case of two speakers using the same register in a sequence of turns. The use of the same (as opposed to a different) register by two different speakers is particularly noticeable if everything else in the two turns is held constant – that is, if one speaker is actually doing a repeat of what another speaker has said. For instance:

(2) **Brain Teaser: Fenella McNally**
     (*A Radio Picadilly phone-in program in Manchester, where listeners call in with answers to a riddle. M is the moderator, C the caller.*)

```
     1   M:   It is complete;
                though it seems it isn't.
                what do you reckon.
         C:   Well I think I've got this one;
     5          and I got it as you were reading it ou:t.
  →             Is the answer ho:le.
                (0.6)
  →      M:   Is the answer ho:le.
         C:   yes.
    10   M:   er: no.
         C:   ↑oh!
```

In auditory terms, judging register here involves (1) determining how high the caller's turn *Is the answer ho:le* is in relation to her voice range, (2) determining how high the moderator's repeat *Is the answer ho:le* is in relation to his voice range, and (3) comparing the two relatively. Register comparison across speakers is particularly difficult when the speakers have naturally different voice ranges, as here. However, the fact that the moderator comes off in line 8 as quoting what his caller has just said in line 6 suggests that his TCU is a good rendition of hers and consequently that the relative heights at which they are speaking are similar. Normalized measurements of fundamental frequency will back up this auditory judgment. Figure 1.1 shows a graph of fundamental frequency readings taken every one-tenth of a second for the two turns in question.

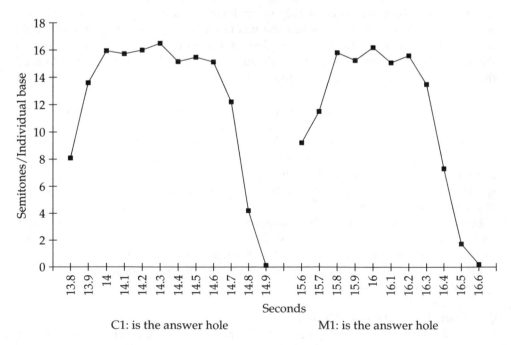

C1: is the answer hole   M1: is the answer hole

Figure 1.1

In order to normalize the readings and thus make different individual voices comparable, the Hertz values have been expressed here as semitones above the lowest pitch which each speaker is accustomed to use. Seen this way, it is quite obvious that the moderator is speaking at approximately the same height in his voice range as the caller is speaking in her voice range.

Compare now a similar interactional situation where there is a noticeable shift of register in the moderator's repetition of a caller's prior turn:

(3)   **Brain Teaser: Julie Salt**

```
      1   M:   h you can find reference,
                in any Latin dictionary -
                to a brigade.
           C:   .hh ↑troops!
      5        (0.5)
→          M:   {h}↑troops!
                erm
→               {h}↑troops!
                is wrong.
     10   C:   oh. hheh
```

Here the fact that the moderator has shifted to an exceptionally high register on *troops* is obvious from comparing it to the prior *you can find reference in any Latin dictionary to a brigade* (lines 1–3) or to the following *erm* (line 7) and *is wrong* (line 9). The normalized f_0 curves obtained from acoustic analysis of these turns are shown in figure 1.2.

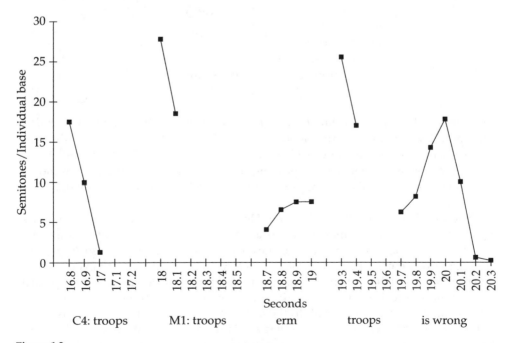

Figure 1.2

Figure 1.2 shows that the moderator is saying *troops* at a point much higher in his voice range than *erm* or *is wrong*. The latter expressions, however, are placed at approximately the same relative height in his voice range as is the caller's *troops* in hers.

What does the moderator cue with this register shift? As argued elsewhere, because he not only shifts his register higher but shifts it to exactly the same *absolute* pitch as his caller, the moderator is heard as mimicking his caller. In doing so, he seems to be subtly (or not so subtly) making a critical comment on the caller's guess – e.g. that it is a silly guess, or that it is delivered in an abnormally high voice (Couper-Kuhlen 1996). Due to the use of absolute pitch, this fragment is thus a special case of register shift. Yet it has in common with other cases of register shift that it cues special inferences about how talk is being produced and understood.

The exploitation of register across speaking turns is not restricted to guessing sequences nor to shifts to high. Here is a case on the same quiz show where a register shift to low is deployed by the moderator in quite a different context:

(4)   **Brain Teaser: Sexy Sharon**
```
      1   M:   then we go to Hardwick. (.)
                and there we get –
                (.) h sexy Sharon.
                ↓hi!
      5   C:   (0.4) °hello° –
 →        M:   {1} °hello° –
                how are you Sharon –
          C:   °all right [thanks°
          M:              [oh: ↑cheer up dear,
     10   C:   he hh
          M:   Cheer up;
                for goodness sake;
                don't- don't put me in a bad mood;
                at (.) one o'clock;
```

Focusing on the register of line 6, it will be observed that the moderator's *hello* is noticeably lower than his *sexy Sharon* in line 3. But it is at approximately the same relative height as Sharon's prior *hello* in line 5. This is a case of register shift to low which becomes noticeable across speaking turns by the same speaker. The moderator appears to be shifting to a register closer to that of his caller, as is evident from figure 1.3.

What does this register shift to low cue? Here too the moderator is heard as mimicking his caller and thereby making a critical comment on her turn. But in contrast to the prior example, where one of the messages was "Your voice is so high!," the message now seems to be "Your voice is so low!" This moderator has very definite expectations about his callers' register, especially his female callers. The upwards tendency in the register of his next TCU (*how are you Sharon*), visible in figure 1.3, may be another, more subtle hint to the caller to "raise her voice." If so, this would account nicely for why – when the strategy fails and Sharon continues with low pitch on *all right* (see figure 1.3) – he becomes more explicit in subsequent talk: *cheer up dear* (line 9) and *Cheer up for goodness sake* (lines 11–12).

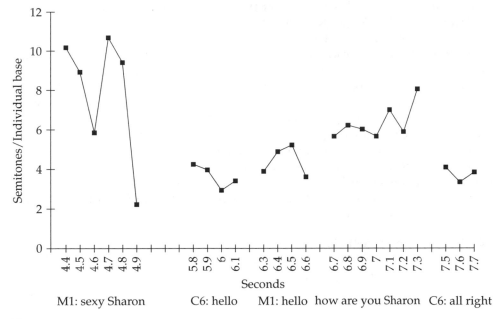

Figure 1.3

On a more general level, the above fragment provides a particularly clear demonstration of the fact that to make sense of what participants do in interaction, it is crucial to take the prosodic design of talk into consideration. Yet if we try to reconstruct why the moderator admonishes Sharon to cheer up, we will discover that there is more than just her pitch that is amiss: the volume and timing of her turn in line 5 are also off. This suggests that to fully understand the contextualization process the perspective must be broadened to include other prosodic phenomena.

3.2   *Beyond intonation*

A second type of new territory in the field of interactional prosody is that beyond pitch or intonation altogether. The focus here will be on *timing*. Needless to say, all spoken discourse unfolds in time. Moreover, our scientific tradition provides us with objective ways of dividing up time neatly and of measuring it precisely. Yet it is doubtful whether lay speakers *experience* time in interaction in terms of units measured objectively in minutes and seconds. To speak meaningfully about timing in interaction, the metric which is behind participants' subjective judgment of time must be identified. It is this metric which enables them to determine that "now" is the right time for some word or for a turn, and that someone has departed from this right time by pausing or by coming in too early or too late. Erickson and Shultz (1982) have proposed that subjective judgments of experienced time in interaction are made with reference to rhythmic cycles which organize the verbal and nonverbal behavior of participants. And, as Pike (1945), Halliday (1970), and others have pointed out, the basis for rhythm in English is the regular recurrence of accented syllables in time. Thus the hypothesis that *speech rhythm* provides a metric for timing in English interaction seems rather compelling (see also Couper-Kuhlen 1993).

Rhythm in the interactional sense refers to a regular beat which establishes itself in talk through the even placement of accented syllables in time (see Auer et al. 1999). The distance between two, typically adjacent accented syllables creates a temporal interval.[10] When two or more successive temporal intervals are perceived to be approximately equal in duration, the speaker (or speakers) can be said to be speaking rhythmically. Isochronously timed accents create the impression of a regular rhythmic beat in speech. Observation suggests that speakers use the rhythmic delivery of within-turn talk for a variety of structural and rhetorical purposes. And it appears to be the maintenance of a common rhythmic beat across turns at talk which counts as the well-timed option for turn transition in English conversation.

Consider the case of smooth interactional timing, i.e. where turn transition is wholly unremarkable. For instance:

(5) **Brain Teaser: Fenella McNally**
```
     1  M:  let's see how we do in Staleybridge,
             Fenella McNally;
             hi.
→        F:  hello!
→    5  M:  hello: Fenella,
→        F:  hello;
             we spoke last night.
             hehn
```

The first thing to notice about this opening is the fact that the moderator's accents on *see, Staleybridge, Fenella* and *hi* are timed regularly at the end of his first turn. The rhythmic beat which this timing establishes can be represented notationally as follows:[11]

(5′) Rhythmic analysis of **Fenella McNally** opening
```
     1  M:  let's /'see how we do in /
                  /'Staleybridge, Fe-/
                  /'nella McNally;    /
                  /'hi.
```

Fenella now picks up the moderator's rhythmic beat in the next turn by timing her accent on *hello* accordingly. Moreover, the moderator adjusts the timing of his next turn to synchronize with this beat:

(5″) Rhythmic analysis of **Fenella McNally** opening
```
     1  M:  let's /'see how we do in /
                  /'Staleybridge, Fe-/
                  /'nella McNally;    /
                  /'hi.
     5  F:                       hel-/
                  /'lo!
        M:                       hel-/
                  /'lo:
```

Moderator and caller collaborate here in the production of a common rhythm which they maintain across speaking turns by picking up in each new turn the beat established in the prior turn.

Now observe what happens in the continuation of line 5 in the orthographic transcript. The moderator shifts the rhythm slightly by placing an accent on *Fenella* which comes sooner than the next expected beat. This creates a number of rhythmic options for the timing of the next turn. (For instance, a next speaker could simply ignore the syncopation and continue according to prior timing. Or a next speaker could miss the next beat altogether, perhaps causing the rhythm to break down.) What this caller opts for, however, is to create a new, faster rhythmic pattern based on the timing of the moderator's accents on *hello* and *Fenella* by placing her next accents on *hello*, *spoke* and *night* accordingly. In rhythmic notation this can be shown as follows:

(5″) Rhythmic analysis of **Fenella McNally** opening

```
  1    M:   let's /'see how we do in /
                  /'Staleybridge, Fe-/
                  /'nella McNally;    /
                  /'hi.
  5    F:                          hel-/
                  /'lo!
       M:                          hel-/
                  /'lo: Fe-          /  (faster)
                  /'nella,
 10    F:                          hel-/
                  /'lo; we           /
                  /'spoke last/
                  /'night. hehn
```

The transitions in this exchange can thus be reconstructed as smooth due to the fact that each turn onset is rhythmically well-timed with respect to the prior turn.

Rhythmic coordination of this sort requires a fine sensing of timing on the part of participants. Unaccented syllables before the first accent of a new turn must be timed so that the first accent falls on the beat. Sometimes just a fraction of a second delay is necessary between turns in order to make the synchronization work. In fact, there are tiny micropauses at each of the transitions here, which suggests that speakers are timing their turn onsets rhythmically. In other words, they are not coming in at the earliest possible moment in time but at the earliest possible *rhythmic* moment in time. The micropauses are scarcely noticeable because they help maintain the regular rhythm rather than destroy it.

Now examine a case where transition timing is less successful:

(6) **Brain Teaser: Sexy Nora**

```
  1    M:   so I think we'll kick off;
            with er -
            sexy Nora;
            who lives in Heaton Chapel.
```

```
          5        hi!
    →      N:      (0.7) hi.
           M:      hi!
                   how are you Nora?
           N:      oh hello. heh
    10     M:      he- hello,
           N:      hello!
           M:      hello!
                   you're on the radio!
           N:      well that was a surprise.
    15     M:      surprise surprise.
```

In this opening the moderator also provides his caller with a clear rhythmic beat at the end of his first turn by regularly timing his accents on *sexy*, *lives*, and *hi*.[12] But she misses his cue. Her *hi* in line 6 is too late to coincide with the beat he has established:

(6')   Rhythmic analysis of **Sexy Nora** opening

```
    1   M:   so I 'think we'll kick off;
             with er -
             /'sexy Nora; who          /
             /'lives in 'Heaton 'Chapel./
    5        /'hi!
        N:   (0.7) 'hi.          (late)
```

As the subsequent development of talk here shows, the fact that Nora misses the moderator's cue creates a minor interactional "incident": the greeting sequence gets recycled twice, and accounts are offered on both sides for what has happened – *you're on the radio* (line 13) and *well that was a surprise* (line 14). Thus the hitch in turn transition in (6) can be reconstructed as rhythmic ill-timing: the caller's return of greeting is late with respect to the rhythm and timing established in prior talk.[13]

An appreciation of how crucial minor timing mishaps in turn transition can be for the order of interaction now casts a new light on what happened in fragment (4):

(4)   **Brain Teaser: Sexy Sharon**

```
    1   M:   then we go to Hardwick. (.)
             and there we get -
             (.) h sexy Sharon.
             ↓hi!
    5   C:   (0.4) °hello° -
    →   M:   {1} °hello° -
             how are you Sharon -
        C:   °all right [thanks°
        M:             [oh: ↑cheer up dear,
    10  C:   he hh
        M:   Cheer up;
             for goodness sake;
             don't- don't put me in a bad mood;
             at (.) one o'clock;
```

A rhythmic analysis of this opening reveals that Sharon too misses the timing cues in the moderator's first turn. He sets up a well-defined rhythm with accents on *sexy*, *Sharon*, and *hi*, but she comes in too late:

(4′) Rhythmic analysis of **Sexy Sharon** opening

```
      1  M:   and there we get -
               (.) h /'sexy     /
                    /'Sharon. /
                    /'↓hi!
      5  C:   (0.4) °hel'lo° - (late)
```

In sum, it is the fact that transition timing is off as much as the fact that Sharon's pitch is perceived as low which cues the moderator's inference that she is not cheerful. This fragment thus provides a concrete example of how prosodic contextualization cues cluster and jointly make interpretive frames relevant.

What provisional conclusions can be drawn about the way prosodic contextualization cues – here: onset, register, and rhythm – work in discourse? Onset and register have in common that they work to create a rudimentary sort of global structure: both are ways to format a TCU such that it will be heard as either prosodically matching or prosodically contrasting with surrounding TCUs. If matching, this may be interpretable structurally as, roughly speaking, continuing something that has already been started; if contrasting, it may be interpretable as doing something which is disconnected from what has gone before. Where the shift is to high, the structural inference may be that something new is beginning; where it is to low, that something is being subordinated. (On occasion, where sequential location and verbal content make a particular register or onset formatting expectable for a given TCU, the strategic avoidance of that format will cue the opposite interpretation.) Rhythm on the other hand is more of an equalizer: it pulls together units of different sizes and scope in an integrative fashion and sets them off from parts of surrounding talk which are rhythmically nonintegrated or which are patterned differently. What all three prosodic contextualization cues appear to have in common, however, is that they can have a structural (i.e. "system"-related) or an actional (i.e. "ritual"-related) interpretation, depending on the sequential context in which they occur and the syntactic-semantic content of the TCUs they are designed for.

4 Looking Far Ahead

To conclude, what are some of the directions prosodic research might take in the more distant future?

First, as the analysis of fragment (4) above suggests, *volume* needs to be looked at more closely. It will very likely turn out to be a prosodic contextualization cue like intonation and timing which is locally invoked and strategically deployed both within and across speaking turns. Just as with pitch, where the declination unit defines upper and lower gridlines within which pitch events are located, so a loudness declination unit will arguably need to be postulated within which loudness events are located (see also Pittenger et al. 1960 and Laver 1994). Whether loudness declination is coextensive with pitch declination is an open question. Moreover, how loudness declination is handled across turns requires investigation: Goldberg (1978) suggests that amplitude may shift or reset at structural points in discourse organization just as pitch has been shown to do.

Second and more significantly, paralinguistic voice-quality effects require investigation (see also Pike 1945; Trager 1958; Pittenger et al. 1960). This step of course goes not only beyond the intonation phrase and beyond intonation but beyond prosody altogether. Yet it is a logical step if one's goal is to reconstruct the vocal cues which contextualize language. Just as the same interpretive frame can be cued by pitch and timing at once, so it can also be cued by paralinguistic voice quality. *Voice quality* has often been thought of as resulting from the natural or habitual setting of laryngeal and supralaryngeal musculature in the vocal tract (Laver 1980). Yet speakers can and do assume different voice qualities at will. Some of those which appear to be deployed strategically in everyday English conversation are nasal voice, breathy voice, creaky voice, "smiley" voice, whisper, and falsetto. Others can and surely will be found on closer investigation. Here too the question must be: what resources do speakers have at their disposal? And how are these resources deployed in cueing interaction? The answers must be sensitive to possible sociolinguistic and sociocultural variation, but above all grounded in conversational interaction.

NOTES

1   I am grateful nonetheless to Wally Chafe, Jack Du Bois, and Sandy Thompson for listening to an early version of this chapter at the Linguistics Colloquium, University of California at Santa Barbara, and talking through the ideas with me. I bear full responsibility for not taking their advice when I should have.

2   Outside of linguistics, on the other hand, it was generally acknowledged as a prime metacommunicative device in face-to-face interaction. See e.g. Bateson et al. (n.d.) and Pittenger et al. (1960) for two early attempts to capture it on paper and describe its import.

3   Menn and Boyce (1982) was an early attempt to link quantified measurements of voice pitch with discourse structure.

4   Excluded from this survey are corpus-linguistic studies of discourse, many of which take intonation into consideration without making it the focus of investigation.

5   "Grammar" being understood loosely enough to include speech acts.

6   As does a fortiori Steedman (1991).

7   Nor is Ann's onset in line 52 as high as in line 23, where she *is* perceived as starting high.

8   Subsequent talk confirms that Janet knows not only that Jane has recently gone back to Tanzania but also why.

9   In addition, some analysts recognize the narrowing or widening of a speaker's register as significant departures from the norm (see Pittenger et al. 1960).

10   Occasionally nonadjacent accented syllables also mark off rhythmic

intervals; see (6) below for an example of this.

11 Left-hand slashes are placed before the accented syllables creating a rhythmic beat and are aligned underneath one another on the page to indicate regular timing. Right-hand slashes give a rough indication of tempo, or how close together/far apart the beats come in time.

12 Notice that the accents on *Heaton Chapel* are disregarded in the interest of a higher-level rhythmic pattern

created by the regular timing of accents on *sexy, lives,* and *hi.*

13 It is true that Fenella was probably on hold, waiting for her call to be put through, and that unpreparedness may account for why she misses the moderator's cue. Yet since presumably all callers to the show are put on hold, this fails to explain why the large majority of them have no trouble at all following the moderator's cue. In most calls a regular rhythm is established across speaking turns from the very beginning.

REFERENCES

Abercrombie, D. (1965). Conversation and spoken prose. In D. Abercrombie (ed.), *Studies in Phonetics and Linguistics* (pp. 1–9). Oxford: Oxford University Press.

Armstrong, L. E., and Ward, I. C. (1926). *A Handbook of English Intonation.* (Second edition, 1931). Cambridge: W. Heffer and Sons.

Auer, P. (1992). Introduction: J. Gumperz' approach to contextualization. In P. Auer and A. d. Luzio (eds), *The Contextualization of Language* (pp. 1–38). Amsterdam: Benjamins.

Auer, P., and Luzio, A. d. (eds), (1992). *The Contextualization of Language.* Amsterdam: Benjamins.

Auer, P., Couper-Kuhlen, E., and Mueller, F. (1999). *Language in Time: The Rhythm and Tempo of Spoken Interaction.* New York: Oxford University Press.

Bateson, G. (1956). The message "This is play". In B. Schaffner (ed.), *Group Processes* (pp. 145–242). New York: Josiah Macy Jr. Foundation.

Bateson, G. (1972). A theory of play and fantasy. In G. Bateson (ed.), *Steps to an Ecology of Mind* (pp. 177–93). New York: Ballatine.

Bateson, G., Birdwhistell, R., McKeown, N., Mead, M., Brasen, H. W., and Hockett, G. F. (n.d.). The Natural History of an Interview. Chicago: University of Chicago, unpublished.

Bolinger, D. (1964). Around the edge of language. *Harvard Educational Review,* 34, 282–96.

Brazil, D., Coulthard, M., and Johns, C. (1980). *Discourse Intonation and Language Teaching.* London: Longman.

Chafe, W. (1979). The flow of thought and the flow of language. In T. Givón (ed.), *Syntax and Semantics* (Vol. 12: *Discourse and Syntax,* pp. 159–81). New York: Academic Press.

Chafe, W. (1980). The deployment of consciousness in the production of a narrative. In W. Chafe (ed.), *The Pear Stories: Cognitive, Cultural and Linguistic Aspects of Narrative Production* (pp. 9–50). Norwood, NJ: Ablex.

Chafe, W. (1988). Linking intonation units in spoken English. In J. Haiman and S. A. Thompson (eds), *Clause Combining in Grammar and Discourse* (pp. 1–27). Amsterdam and Philadelphia: Benjamins.

Chafe, W. (1993). Prosodic and functional units of language. In J. A. Edwards and M. D. Lampert (eds), *Talking Data: Transcription and Coding Methods for Language Research*. Hillsdale, NJ: Lawrence Erlbaum.

Cook-Gumperz, J., and Gumperz, J. J. (1976). Context in children's speech. *Papers on Language and Context*, Working Paper No. 46, Language Behavior Research Laboratory, Berkeley.

Couper-Kuhlen, E. (1986). *An Introduction to English Prosody*. London and Tuebingen: Edward Arnold and Niemeyer.

Couper-Kuhlen, E. (1993). *English Speech Rhythm: Form and Function in Everyday Verbal Interaction*. Amsterdam: Benjamins.

Couper-Kuhlen, E. (1996). The prosody of repetition: on quoting and mimicry. In E. Couper-Kuhlen and M. Selting (eds), *Prosody in Conversation: Interactional Studies* (pp. 366–405). Cambridge: Cambridge University Press.

Couper-Kuhlen, E., and Selting, M. (1996). Towards an interactional perspective on prosody and a prosodic perspective on interaction. In E. Couper-Kuhlen and M. Selting (eds), *Prosody in Conversation* (pp. 11–56). Cambridge: Cambridge University Press.

Cruttenden, A. (1986). *Intonation*. Cambridge: Cambridge University Press.

Crystal, D. (1969). *Prosodic Systems and Intonation in English*. London: Cambridge University Press.

Du Bois, J. W., Schuetze-Coburn, S., Paolino, D., and Cumming, S. (1992). Discourse transcription. *Santa Barbara Papers in Linguistics*, 4, 1–225.

Du Bois, J. W., Schuetze-Coburn, S., Cumming, S., and Paolino, D. (1993). Outline of discourse transcription. In J. A. Edwards and M. D. Lampert (eds), *Talking Data: Transcription and Coding in Discourse Research* (pp. 45–89). Hillsdale, NJ: Lawrence Erlbaum.

Erickson, F., and Shultz, J. (1982). *The Counselor as Gate Keeper: Social Interaction in Interviews*. New York: Academic Press.

Goffman, E. (1981). *Forms of Talk*. Oxford: Blackwell.

Goldberg, J. A. (1978). Amplitude shift: a mechanism for the affiliation of utterances in conversational interaction. In J. Schenkein (ed.), *Studies in the Organization of Conversational Interaction* (pp. 199–218). New York: Academic Press.

Goodwin, C. (1981). *Conversational Organization: Interaction between Speakers and Hearers*. New York: Academic Press.

Gumperz, J. (1982). *Discourse Strategies*. Cambridge: University Press.

Halliday, M. A. K. (1967). *Intonation and Grammar in British English*. Mouton: The Hague.

Halliday, M. A. K. (1970). *A Course in Spoken English: Intonation*. London: Oxford University Press.

Hirschberg, J., and Ward, G. (1992). The influence of pitch range, duration, amplitude and spectral features on the interpretation of the rise–fall–rise intonation contour in English. *Journal of Phonetics*, 20, 241–51.

Kendon, A. (1988). Goffman's approach to face-to-face interaction. In P. Drew and W. Antony (eds), *Erving Goffman: Exploring the Interaction Order* (pp. 14–40). Oxford: Polity.

Klewitz, G., and Couper-Kuhlen, E. (1999). Quote-unquote: the role of prosody in the contextualization of reported speech sequences. *Pragmatics*, 9.4, 459–85.

Laver, J. (1980). *The Phonetic Description of Voice Quality*. Cambridge: Cambridge University Press.

Laver, J. (1994). *Principles of Phonetics.* Cambridge: Cambridge University Press.

Martinet, A. (1962). *A Functional View of Language, being the Waynflete Lectures.* Oxford: Clarendon.

Menn, L., and Boyce, S. (1982). Fundamental frequency and discourse structure. *Language and Speech,* 25.4, 341–83.

O'Connor, J. D., and Arnold, G. F. (1961). *Intonation of Colloquial English.* (Second edition, 1973). London: Longman.

Pierrehumbert, J. B. (1980). The Phonology and Phonetics of English Intonation. PhD thesis, MIT.

Pierrehumbert, J., and Hirschberg, J. (1990). The meaning of intonational contours in the interpretation of discourse. In P. R. Cohen, J. Morgan, and M. E. Pollack (eds), *Intentions in Communication* (pp. 271–311). Cambridge, MA: MIT Press.

Pike, K. L. (1945). *The Intonation of American English.* Ann Arbor, MI: University of Michigan Publications.

Pittenger, R. E., Hockett, C. F., and Danehy, J. J. (1960). *The First Five Minutes: A Sample of Microscopic Interview Analysis.* Ithaca, NY: Paul Martineau.

Schuetze-Coburn, S., Shapley, M., and Weber, E. G. (1991). Units of intonation in discourse: a comparison of acoustic and auditory analyses. *Language and Speech,* 34.3, 207–34.

Steedman, M. (1991). Structure and intonation. *Language,* 67, 260–96.

Swerts, M., and Geluykens, R. (1994). Prosody as a marker of information flow in spoken discourse. *Language and Speech,* 37.1, 21–43.

Tannen, D. (ed.), (1993). *Framing in Discourse.* New York and Oxford: Oxford University Press.

't Hart, J., Collier, R., and Collier, A. (1990). *A Perceptual Study of Intonation.* Cambridge: Cambridge University Press.

Trager, G. L. (1958). Paralanguage: a first approximation. *Studies in Linguistics,* 13.1, 1–12.

Trager, G. L., and Smith, H. L. J. (1957). An outline of English structure. *Studies in Linguistics: Occasional Papers,* 3, 40–52.

Ward, G., and Hirschberg, J. (1985). Implicating uncertainty: the pragmatics of fall–rise intonation. *Language,* 61, 747–76.

TRANSCRIPTION CONVENTIONS

One line	One intonation phrase
First word capitalized	High onset (= full declination reset)
[Line	
[Line	Overlapped utterances
Line=	
=Line	Latched utterances
Line.	Final pitch falling to low
Line!	Final pitch falling to low from high starting point
Line;	Final pitch falling slightly
Line -	Final level pitch
Line,	Final pitch rising slightly
Line?	Final pitch rising to high
{l}	Low register

{h}	High register
{*acc*}	Accelerando
{*dec*}	Decelerando
↑Word	Noticeable step-up in pitch
↓Word	Noticeable step-down in pitch
Wo::rd	Lengthened sound or syllable
Word-	Cut-off sound or syllable
WORD	Loud volume
°word°	Soft volume
'word	Accent or stress
/'word	/
/'word	/
/'word	Rhythmic patterning of accents
(h)	Breathiness
(gh)	Gutteralness
.hhh	Inbreath
hhh	Outbreath
(word)	Unsure transcription
(.)	Brief pause
(1.0)	Measured pause

2 Cohesion and Texture

J. R. MARTIN

0 Beyond the Clause

In this chapter I will outline a modular perspective on text organization, which places cohesion analysis within a broader framework for analyzing discourse. Cohesion is one part of the study of texture, which considers the interaction of cohesion with other aspects of text organization. Texture, in turn, is one aspect of the study of coherence, which takes the social context of texture into consideration. The goal of discourse analysis in this tradition is to build a model that places texts in their social contexts and looks comprehensively at the resources which both integrate and situate them.

Cohesion can be defined as the set of resources for constructing relations in discourse which transcend grammatical structure (Halliday 1994: 309). The term is generally associated with research inspired by Halliday (1964) and Hasan (1968) in systemic functional linguistics (hereafter SFL) and by Gleason (1968) in Hartford-based stratificational linguistics.[1] Halliday and Hasan (1976) is the canonical study in the former tradition, Gutwinski (1976) in the latter. Gutwinski draws on work by Halliday and by Hasan, and later SFL work by Martin (1992) was influenced by Gleason – so there has been a fruitful exchange of ideas across theories in this field. In section 1 below I will review the early work on cohesion analysis; then, in section 2, I will consider the next generation of research in this area, from the perspective of Australian SFL (for a complementary line of development see Winter 1982; Hoey 1983, 1991a; Jordan 1984).

Cohesion is one aspect of the study of **texture**, which can be defined as the process whereby meaning is channeled into a digestible current of discourse "instead of spilling out formlessly in every possible direction" (Halliday 1994: 311). Alongside cohesion, this process involves the text-forming resources of grammar and phonology[2] – for example, Theme and New in English (Davies 1989, 1992; Halliday 1994). Cohesion will be reconsidered in relation to texture in section 2.

Texture is one aspect of the study of **coherence**, which can be thought of as the process whereby a reading position is naturalized by texts for listener/readers. Alongside texture, this process involves understandings and expectations about the social context a text dynamically construes. In SFL, social context is modeled through register and genre theory (Halliday 1978; Halliday and Hasan 1985; Martin 1992; Christie and Martin 1997). Texture will be reconsidered in relation to social context in section 3.

All three variables – cohesion, texture, and coherence – will be illustrated from the children's story *Piggybook* by A. Brown. Section 1 looks at traditional approaches to cohesion as nonstructural resources for textual organization. Then in section 2, a more semantic perspective on cohesion in relation to texture is presented. Subsequently, in section 3, the social motivation of texture is considered.

1   Cohesion

Early work on cohesion was designed to move beyond the structural resources of grammar and consider discourse relations which transcend grammatical structure. Halliday (e.g. 1973: 141) modeled cohesion as involving nonstructural relations above the sentence, within what he refers to as the textual metafunction (as opposed to ideational and interpersonal meaning). In Halliday and Hasan (1976) the inventory of cohesive resources was organized as:

- reference
- ellipsis
- substitution
- conjunction
- lexical cohesion.

Gutwinski (1976: 57) develops a closely related framework, including these resources (and in addition grammatical parallelism).

Reference refers to resources for referring to a participant or circumstantial element whose identity is recoverable. In English the relevant resources include demonstratives, the definite article, pronouns, comparatives, and the phoric adverbs *here, there, now, then.* **Ellipsis** refers to resources for omitting a clause, or some part of a clause or group, in contexts where it can be assumed. In English conversation, rejoinders are often made dependent through omissions of this kind: *Did they win? – Yes, they did.* Some languages, including English, have in addition a set of place holders which can be used to signal the omission – e.g. *so* and *not* for clauses, *do* for verbal groups, and *one* for nominal groups. This resource of place holders is referred to as **substitution**.[3] Reference, ellipsis, and substitution involve small, closed classes of items or gaps, and have accordingly been referred to as grammatical cohesion (e.g. Hasan 1968; Gutwinski 1976).

Also included as grammatical cohesion is the typically much larger inventory of connectors which link clauses in discourse, referred to as **conjunction**. For Halliday and Hasan (1976) this resource comprises linkers which connect sentences to each other, but excludes paratactic and hypotactic (coordinating and subordinating) linkers within sentences, which are considered structural by Halliday. Gutwinski, however, includes all connectors, whether or not they link clauses within or between sentences. This difference reflects in part a territorial dispute over how much work the grammar is expected to do in discourse analysis (see also Schiffrin, this volume).

The complement of grammatical cohesion involves open system items, and so is referred to as **lexical cohesion**. Here the repetition of lexical items, synonymy or near-synonymy (including hyponymy), and collocation are included. Collocation was Firth's (1957) term for expectancy relations between lexical items (e.g. the mutual predictability of *strong* and *tea*, but not *powerful* and *tea*).

The relationship between a cohesive item and the item it presupposed in a text is referred to as a **cohesive tie**. Gutwinski (1976) contrasts the different kinds of cohesive tie that predominate in writing by Hemingway and James, with Hemingway depending more on lexical cohesion than does James. Halliday and Hasan (1976) provide a detailed coding scheme for analyzing cohesive ties, which takes into account the distance between a cohesive item and the item presupposed. This framework prompted a number of researchers to ask questions about the relationship between cohesive ties and evaluations of text as coherent or not (Rochester and Martin 1979; Fine et al. 1989), proficient or not (Hartnett 1986; Olson and Johnson 1989; Yang 1989), maturing or not (Martin 1983a; Chapman 1983; Nelson and Levy 1987; Pappas 1987), context dependent or not (Hawkins 1977), and so on. In general, the interpretation of patterns of cohesive ties depended in each study on the register, as had been predicted by Halliday and Hasan (1976: 23):

> The concept of cohesion can therefore be usefully supplemented by that of register, since the two together effectively define a text. A text is a passage of discourse which is coherent in these two regards: it is coherent with respect to the context of situation, and therefore consistent in register; and it is coherent with respect to itself, and therefore cohesive.

As reiterated by Halliday (1994: 339), for a text to be coherent "it must deploy the resources of cohesion in ways that are motivated by the register of which it is an instance."[4]

2   Discourse Semantics

As noted in section 1, from the perspective of grammar, cohesion was positioned as a set of nonstructural resources in the textual metafunction. Later work concentrated on the semantics of these cohesive resources and their relation to discourse structure. Martin (1992) worked on reformulating the notion of cohesive ties as discourse semantic structure, inspired by the text-oriented conception of semantics of the Hartford stratificationalists (Gleason 1968; Gutwinski 1976) with whom he studied in Toronto. In his stratified account, cohesion was reformulated as a set of discourse semantic systems at a more abstract level than lexicogrammar, with their own metafunctional organization. Halliday's nonstructural textual resources were thus reworked as semantic systems concerned with discourse structure, comprising:

- identification
- negotiation
- conjunction
- ideation.

Identification is concerned with resources for tracking participants in discourse. This system subsumes earlier work on referential cohesion in a framework which considers the ways in which participants are both introduced into a text and kept track of once introduced. In addition, the ways in which phoric items depend[5] on preceding or succeeding co-text, on assumed understandings, or on other relevant phenomena (images, activity, materiality, etc.) are considered. The questions addressed are similar to those pursued in Du Bois (1980) and Fox (1987).[6]

Negotiation is concerned with resources for exchange of information and of goods and services in dialog. This system subsumes some of the earlier work on ellipsis and substitution in a framework which considers the ways in which interlocutors initiate and respond in adjacency pairs. Drawing on earlier work at Birmingham (e.g. Sinclair and Coulthard 1975) and Nottingham (e.g. Berry 1981), a framework for exchanges consisting of up to five moves was developed, alongside provision for tracking and challenging side-sequences (Ventola 1987). This work is closely related to studies in conversation analysis (CA) but with a stronger grammatical orientation (such as that canvassed in Ochs et al. 1996). Eggins and Slade (1997) introduce ongoing SFL research in this area, in relation to wider questions of discourse structure and social context (Coulthard 1992 updates the Birmingham-based work).

Conjunction is concerned with resources for connecting messages, via addition, comparison, temporality, and causality. This system subsumes earlier work on linking between clauses in a framework which considers, in addition, the ways in which connections can be realized inside a clause through verbs, prepositions, and nouns (e.g. *result in, because of, reason*). Drawing on Gleason (1968) a framework for analysing internal[7] (pragmatic/rhetorical) and external (semantic/propositional) conjunctive relations was proposed, including the possibility of connections realized simply by the contiguity of messages (i.e. links unmarked by an explicit connector). This work is closely related to studies of relations between propositions in discourse by Longacre (e.g. 1976) and to rhetorical structure theory (RST) as developed by Mann, Matthiessen, and Thompson (e.g. 1992; Fox 1987).

Ideation is concerned with the semantics of lexical relations as they are deployed to construe[8] institutional activity. This system subsumes earlier work on lexical cohesion in a framework which considers the ways in which activity sequences and taxonomic relations (of classification and composition) organize the field of discourse (Benson and Greaves 1992). Drawing on Hasan (1985), a framework for a more detailed account of lexical relations was proposed – including repetition, synonymy, hyponymy, and meronymy; in addition, collocation was factored out into various kinds of "nuclear" relation, involving elaboration, extension, and enhancement (as developed by Halliday 1994 for the clause complex). This work is closely related to the detailed studies of lexical relations in discourse by Hoey (1991a), Francis (1985), and Winter (1977), and to work on the development of an ideational semantics by Halliday and Matthiessen (1999).

The result of these reformulations is a semantic stratum of text-oriented resources dedicated to the analysis of cohesive relations as discourse structure. Once stratified with respect to lexicogrammar, these resources can be aligned with metafunctions in the following proportions:

- identification   textual meaning
- negotiation   interpersonal meaning
- conjunction   logical[9] meaning
- ideation   experiential meaning.

In a stratified model of this kind the study of texture amounts to the study of patterns of interaction among discourse semantics, lexicogrammar, and phonology/graphology in realization.

As far as this interaction is concerned, research has concentrated on the discourse structure in relation to experiential grammar (cohesive harmony) and in relation to textual grammar (method of development). Some discussion of discourse in relation to information structure and intonation (point) and in relation to interpersonal grammar (modal responsibility) is presented in Martin (1992), but will not be developed here (Halliday and Martin 1993; Martin 1995).

Cohesive harmony and method of development will be briefly illustrated with respect to the Orientation stage of *Piggybook* (Brown 1989):

[1] Mr Piggott lived with his two sons, Simon and Patrick, in a nice house with a nice garden, and a nice car in the nice garage. Inside the house was his wife.

"Hurry up with the breakfast, dear," he called every morning, before he went off to his very important job.

"Hurry up with the breakfast, Mum," Simon and Patrick called every morning, before they went off to their very important school.

After they left the house, Mrs Piggott washed all the breakfast things . . . made all the beds . . . vacuumed all the carpets . . . and then she went to work.

"Hurry up with the meal, Mum," the boys called every evening, when they came home from their very important school.

"Hurry up with the meal, old girl," Mr Piggott called every evening, when he came home from his very important job.

As soon as they had eaten, Mrs Piggott washed the dishes . . . washed the clothes . . . did the ironing . . . and then she cooked some more.

[One evening when the boys got home from school there was no one to greet them . . .]

As far as identification is concerned this Orientation includes the following reference chains (in order of appearance):

Mr Piggott-his-his-he-he-his-they[10]-Mr Piggott-he-his-they . . .
a nice house-the house-the nice garage[11]-the beds-the carpets . . .
the breakfast-the breakfast-the breakfast things . . .
his two sons-Simon/Patrick-Simon/Patrick-they-their-they-the boys-they-
    their-they . . .
his wife-dear-Mum-Mrs Piggott-she-Mum-old girl-Mrs Piggott-she . . .
the meal-the meal-the dishes-the clothes-the ironing . . .

As far as ideation is concerned, the Orientation in addition includes the following lexical strings (based on repetition, synonymy, co/hyponymy, co/meronymy in this field of discourse):

> Mr-sons-wife-dear-Mum-Mrs-Mum-boys-girl-Mr-Mrs . . .
> nice-nice-nice-nice . . .
> house-garden-car-garage-house-house-beds-carpets . . .
> every-every-all-all-all-every-every . . .
> morning-morning-evening-evening . . .
> important-important-important-important . . .
> hurry up with-hurry up with-hurry up with-hurry up with-cooked . . .
> breakfast-breakfast-breakfast-meal-meal . . .
> dishes-clothes-ironing . . .
> called-called-called-called . . .
> went off-went off-left-went-came home-came home . . .
> job-school-work-school-job . . .
> washed-made-vacuumed . . .

In cohesive harmony analysis we are asking how strings and chains interact as far as experiential grammar is concerned (Hasan 1984, 1985). For example, at group rank the "nice" string and the "house" string are related through nominal group structure as Epithet to Thing: *nice house, nice garden, nice car, nice garage*. Similarly, at clause rank, the "calling" string is related to the "time of day" string as Process to Circumstance: *called every morning, called every morning, called every evening, called every evening*. Hasan defines interaction as taking place when two or more members of a string or chain relate in the same way to two or more members of another string or chain. Space does not permit an exhaustive analysis of cohesive harmony in text 1 here. However, since this is a feminist narrative, let us look briefly at cohesive harmony in relation to gender.

To simplify things, we will look simply at what the family does. Mrs Piggott's activity is outlined in table 2.1.[12] To make this analysis work effectively it is important to lexically render the text – that is, to make explicit all of the ellipsis and substitution so that points of interaction are not missed. From this display we can see that Mrs Piggott's identity chain interacts with two activity strings (cooking and cleaning), which in turn interact with domestic strings ("chores"). By definition, her identity chain does not *interact* with moving or work, since it relates to this activity (i.e. going to work) only once.

The boys on the other hand interact with verbal instructions every morning and evening; and with motion to and from work and school. The only thing they do not interact with at this stage of the story is eating (see table 2.2).

From this kind of analysis we can begin to access the construal of power relations in the story. At this stage only Mrs Piggott is agentive, and she affects only things inside the home. The boys on the other hand are not agentive; they do not transform or create anything inside the home but simply shout, come and go, and eat. The next phase of the narrative begins with Mrs Piggott leaving home, forcing the boys to try and act (unsuccessfully) on domestic goods; after a period of suffering she returns (I wonder why?), the boys become successfully agentive inside the home, and Mrs Piggott ends up outside mending the car.

Table 2.1 Mrs Piggott's activities (in sequence)

Agent (actor)	Process (range)	Medium (goal)	Circumstance
[Mrs Piggott][13]	hurry up with[14]	the breakfast	
[Mrs Piggott]	hurry up with	the breakfast	
Mrs Piggott	washed	all the breakfast things	
[Mrs Piggott]	made	all the beds	
[Mrs Piggott]	vacuumed	all the carpets	
she	went		to work
[Mrs Piggott]	hurry up with	the meal	
[Mrs Piggott]	hurry up with	the meal	
Mrs Piggott	washed	the dishes	
[Mrs Piggott]	washed	the clothes	
[Mrs Piggott]	did the ironing		
she	cooked		some more

Table 2.2 Mr Piggott and the boys' activities (regrouped)

Agent (actor)	Process (range)	Medium (goal)	Circumstance
he (Mr P)	called		every morning
Simon and Patrick	called		every morning
the boys	called		every evening
Mr Piggott	called		every evening
he (Mr P)	went off		to his . . . job
they (S and P)	went off		to their . . . school
they (Mr P/S/P)	left		the house
they (Mr P/S/P)	came (home)[15]		from . . . school
he (Mr P)	came (home)		from . . . job
they (Mr P/S/P)	had eaten		

For Hasan, the purpose of cohesive harmony analysis is to provide a measure of the coherence of a text. She defines peripheral tokens as meanings in the text which do not participate in identity chains or lexical strings, relevant tokens as meanings which do so participate, and central tokens as relevant tokens which interact (as illustrated above). She then suggests that:

- the lower the proportion of peripheral to relevant tokens, the more coherent a text is likely to be;
- the higher the proportion of central tokens to noncentral ones (i.e. of interacting to noninteracting relevant tokens), the more coherent a text is likely to be.

She also raises the issue of breaks in the overall pattern of interaction in a text, such as that which occurs in *Piggybook* when Mrs Piggott leaves home – obviously her identity chain does not interact much until she returns. Breaks of this kind may of course simply reflect the genre of a text as its moves from one stage to the next. As long as they are generically motivated, such breaks will not be felt as disruptive. However, it is likely that generically unmotivated breaks in string/chain inter-action will affect coherence. Hasan's technology for measuring coherence has been taken up by a number of scholars; see especially Pappas (1985) on children's stories, Parsons (1990, 1991) on scientific texts, and Yang (1989) (cf. Hoey 1991b and Martin 1992 on nuclear relations for closely related approaches to cohesion and coherence).[16] To the extent that scholars feel that readers' feeling about the coherence of a text is something that needs to be quantified, cohesive harmony is an effective, though labour-intensive, tool.

Note that cohesive harmony analysis is incomplete in various respects as an analysis of texture. For one thing it does not draw on conjunction analysis, so that temporal organization in text 1 is elided. But the point of the Orientation is to establish a habitual sequence of activity, through a series of messages that are either explicitly or implicitly related to each other with respect to temporal progression (explicit connections underlined, implicit connections in square brackets):

> "Hurry up with the breakfast, dear," he called every morning,
> before he went off to his very important job.
> [before/after/while?[17]]
> "Hurry up with the breakfast, Mum," Simon and Patrick called every morning,
> before they went off to their very important school.
> [later]
> After they left the house,
> Mrs Piggott washed all the breakfast things . . .
> [then] made all the beds . . .
> [then] vacuumed all the carpets . . .
> and then she went to work.
> [later]
> "Hurry up with the meal, Mum," the boys called every evening,
> when they came home from their very important school.
> [before/after/while?]
> "Hurry up with the meal, old girl," Mr Piggott called every evening,
> when he came home from his very important job.
> [later]
> As soon as they had eaten,
> Mrs Piggott washed the dishes . . .
> [then] washed the clothes . . .
> [then] did the ironing . . .
> and then she cooked some more.

Nor does cohesive harmony analysis consider negotiation,[18] which is relevant to the projected demands to hurry up in text 1 and the implied compliance by Mum. Nor is method of development, point, or modal responsibility considered. So while it has been proven a remarkably sensitive technique for measuring coherence, cohesive harmony analysis is not an adequate analysis of coherence, since in performing such analysis so many relevant parameters of texture can be aside.

Turning to the analysis of method of development, analysts are concerned with the interaction of identification and ideation with information flow in clause grammar, in particular Halliday's concept of Theme (which in English is realized via sequence, in clause-initial position). The canonical study is Fries (1981), who introduces the term (for a survey of recent work inspired by his seminal paper see Ghadessy 1995). Following Halliday (1994), *Piggybook* opens with an unmarked Theme, *Mr Piggott*; the next Theme is a marked one – a circumstantial item setting the story *inside the house*:

> Mr Piggott lived with his two sons, Simon and Patrick, in a nice house with a nice garden, and a nice car in the nice garage. Inside the house was his wife.

As far as participants are concerned this establishes the story's perspective on its field, which is overwhelmingly masculine. Mr Piggott is selected as Theme in 21 messages and his sons in 18; Mrs Piggott on the other hand is Theme in just 8 messages. This moral tale, in other words, is aimed at men.

Subsequently the Orientation unfolds in parallel waves (cf. Hymes 1995). The method of development iterates as follows:[19]

> "Hurry up with the breakfast, dear,"
> > he called every morning,
> > > before he went off to his very important job.
> "Hurry up with the breakfast, Mum,"
> > Simon and Patrick called every morning,
> > > before they went off to their very important school.
> After they left the house,
> > Mrs Piggott washed all the breakfast things . . .
> > [_] made all the beds . . .
> > [_] vacuumed all the carpets . . .
> > > and then she went to work.
>
> "Hurry up with the meal, Mum,"
> > the boys called every evening,
> > > when they came home from their very important school.
> "Hurry up with the meal, old girl,"
> > Mr Piggott called every evening,
> > > when he came home from his very important job.
> As soon as they had eaten,
> > Mrs Piggott washed the dishes . . .
> > [_] washed the clothes . . .
> > [_] did the ironing . . .
> > > and then she cooked some more.

Read globally, we have a cycle of morning activity followed by an evening one. Both cycles consist of three further cycles, two by the boys and one by Mum. Within the boys' cycles, Theme selection takes us from the quoted command (*Hurry up with*) to the commander (*he, Simon and Patrick, the boys, Mr Piggott*), temporally related to movers (*before he, before they, when they, when he*). For Mum's cycles, Theme selection takes us through a temporal transition (*after they, as soon as they*) to Mum working (*Mrs Piggott* – three times, twice ellipsed), extended temporally to Mum working some more (*and then she*). Overall then, the method of development in this part of the text takes us twice from the command to the boys, to Mum. The angle on the field this pattern constructs is that of domestic activity, verbally instigated by the boys and undertaken by Mum. Theme selections thus construe a method of development which foregrounds the division of labour in the home which the story works to deconstruct.

We will have to cut off our close reading of this text here. The main point we are focusing on at this stage is the sense in which cohesion is simply one aspect of texture, which has to be understood with respect to the interaction of identification, negotiation, conjunction, and ideation with each other and with the lexicogrammatical and phonological systems through which they are realized. Space also precludes a discussion of grammatical metaphor (Halliday and Martin 1993; Halliday 1994), which is a critical resource for catalyzing this interaction. Put simply, grammatical metaphor is a resource for grammatically reconstruing meanings as alternative wordings. Note for example the movement from a verbal to a more nominal construal of phenomena in the following series (Halliday and Martin 1993: 56):

> (the question of how) glass cracks, (the stress needed to) crack glass, (the mechanism by which) glass cracks, as a crack grows, the crack has advanced, will make slow cracks grow, speed up the rate at which cracks grow, the rate of crack growth, we can increase the crack growth rate 1,000 times . . .

What starts out as a process ends up as a participant, through an accumulating process of nominalization. Examples such as these underscore the power of grammar to construe and reconstrue participants in discourse (alongside realizing them) and shows the importance of adopting dynamic perspectives on texture which complement the synoptic accounts fossilized in tables, diagrams, counting, statistical analysis, and the like (Martin 1985).

Can we have texture without cohesion? Yes, providing our examples are short enough and carefully selected enough (cf. the two-sentence constructed example and excerpts presented as evidence in Brown and Yule 1983: 196). But in naturally occurring texts of more than a couple of clauses, some manifestation of cohesion is overwhelmingly the norm, even in discourse felt by listeners to be incoherent (cf. Rochester and Martin 1979 on thought-disordered schizophrenia).

3   Modeling Social Context: Register and Genre

To this point we have considered cohesive resources in relation to other aspects of text organization, and the contribution such texture makes to our sense that a text hangs together – its coherence. Can we have coherence without texture? Yes again, providing our examples are short and carefully excerpted – and providing we can access the social context of such examples. This brings us to the question of modeling

Table 2.3   Types of meaning in relation to social context

	"Reality construal"	*Contextual variable*
Interpersonal	Social reality	Tenor
Ideational (logical, experiential)	"Natural" reality	Field
Textual	Semiotic reality	Mode

social context in a functional theory which looks at what cohesion is realizing along-side the ways in which it is realized. In SFL social context is modeled through register and genre theory. Following Halliday (e.g. 1978), a natural relation is posited between the organization of language and the organization of social context, built up around the notion of kinds of meaning. Interpersonal meaning is related to the enactment of social relations (social reality) – tenor; ideational meaning is related to the con-struction of institutional activity ("naturalized reality") – field; and textual meaning is related to information flow across media (semiotic reality) – mode. A summary of these correlations is outlined in table 2.3.

Following Martin (1992), field is concerned with systems of activity, including descriptions of the participants, process, and circumstances these activities involve. For illustrative work see Rose et al. (1992), Halliday and Martin (1993), and Martin and Veel (1998). Tenor is concerned with social relations, as these are enacted through the dimensions of power and solidarity. For relevant work on tenor see Poynton (1985) and Iedema (1995). Mode is concerned with semiotic distance, as this is affected by the various channels of communication through which we undertake activity (field) and simultaneously enact social relations (tenor). For exemplary work on mode in print and electronic media see Iedema et al. (1994); for differences between speech and writing, see Halliday (1985).

In these terms, as far as *Piggybook* is concerned, the mode is written monologue, supported by images; the field, broadly speaking, is domestic activity; and the tenor involves adult-to-child narration about changing tenor relations in the Piggott family. The register motivates the patterns of cohesion in the text and their realization in turn through lexicogrammar. For example, its mode is reflected in the density of the lexical strings, which are denser than speaking but not so dense as more abstract writing; its tenor is reflected in direct imperative commands, implied compliance and patriarchal vocatives (*dear, Mum, old girl*); its field is reflected in the cohesive harmony and conjunctive sequencing analysis presented above.

Martin (1992) refers to the system of tenor, field, and mode collectively as register.[20] Technically, the relation of texture to register is termed "realization", which by defini-tion implies that interpersonal, ideational, and textual meaning construe, are con-strued by, and over time reconstrue and are reconstrued by tenor, field, and mode. Realization in other words is a dialectical process whereby language and social context coevolve.

Following Martin (1992), an additional level of context, above and beyond tenor, field, and mode, has been deployed – referred to as genre. This level is concerned with systems of social processes, where the principles for relating social processes

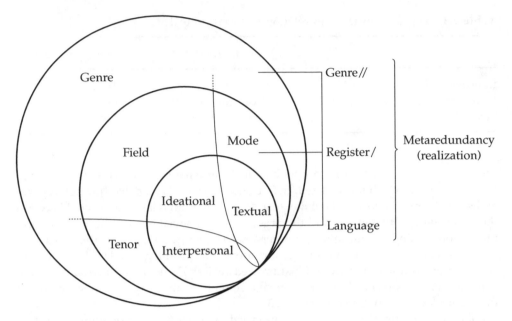

Figure 2.1   Metafunctions in relation to register and genre

to each other have to do with texture – the ways in which field, mode, and tenor variables are phased together in a text. In Australian educational linguistics, genres have been defined as staged, goal-oriented social processes (e.g. Martin et al. n.d.), a definition which flags the way in which most genres take more than a single phase to unfold, the sense of frustration or incompletion that is felt when phases do not unfold as expected or planned, and the fact that genres are addressed (i.e. formulated with readers and listeners in mind), whether or not the intended audience is immediately present to respond. In these terms, as a level of context, genre represents the system of staged, goal-oriented social processes through which social subjects in a given culture live their lives. An overview of this stratified model of context is presented in figure 2.1; this image includes Lemke's (e.g. 1995) notion of metaredundancy, whereby more abstract levels are interpreted as patterns of less abstract ones – thus register is a pattern of linguistic choices, and genre a pattern of register choices (i.e. a pattern of a pattern of texture). For further discussion see Christie and Martin (1997), Eggins and Martin (1977), Martin (1992, 1999), and Ventola (1987).

In terms of genre, *Piggybook* belongs to the narrative family of cultural practices (for relevant SFL research see Martin 1996b, 1997; Martin and Plum 1997; Rothery 1994). We analyzed the first phase of the narrative, its Orientation, above; this is followed by two phases in which equilibrium is disturbed. In the first, Mrs Piggott leaves home and the boys have to fend for themselves. In the second, their attempts to restore order create even more disequilibrium, to the point where they are rooting around as pigs for scraps on the floor; at which point Mrs Piggott arrives home (casting her shadow across the page in the relevant image). As predicted by Labov and Waletzky

(1967), the two crises of disruption are signaled by strongly evaluative language – first *You are pigs*, then *P-L-E-A-S-E come back.*

Beyond texture, then, we have the coherence deriving from the social context a text simultaneously realizes and construes. We read the text with respect to our expectations about the field of domestic activity, the evolving tenor of gender relations, and the nature of verbiage-to-image relations in children's books. And beyond this we read the text as a story, which in this case we recognize as a moral tale (related to fables, parables, exempla, and gossip; Eggins and Slade 1997). The genre phases field, tenor, and mode parameters together into a text with a message. It has been carefully designed to nudge along the redistribution of power across genders in western culture – to naturalize us into a reading position that interprets cohesion in relation to texture, and texture in relation to genre.

As readers, we may of course resist this positioning; or respond tactically, by refusing to read the text globally in a way that takes as many meanings as possible and their integration into account (e.g. simply snickering at the images and "piggy" lexis as the boys turn into swine: *pigsty–squealed–grunted–root around–snorted–snuffled*). But as discourse analysts we have a responsibility to build a model that accounts as fully as possible for the position that is naturalized, and this means building a model that places texts in their social contexts and looks comprehensively at the discourse semantics, lexicogrammar, and phonology (or graphology) that realize them.

4 Cohesion, Texture, and Coherence

In this chapter I have outlined a modular perspective on text, which places cohesion analysis within a broader framework[21] for analyzing discourse. Following Martin (1992), I described the ways in which cohesion can be recontextualized as discourse semantics (identification, negotiation, conjunction, ideation). Subsequently, the study of texture was briefly reviewed, drawing attention to work on patterns of interaction among discourse semantic, lexicogrammatical, and phonological systems (cohesive harmony, method of development, point, and modal responsibility). Finally, I approached coherence from the perspective of social context, suggesting that texture is motivated by tenor, field, and mode, and the way in which genre phases these register variables together into a trajectory of meanings that naturalizes a reading position for reader/listeners.

From an SFL perspective, I expect that in the future our understandings of cohesion, texture, and coherence will be enhanced by further work on cohesion in relation to other modules (both linguistic and social) – so that our sense of how the social motivates patterns of cohesion is improved. I expect some of these patterns to emerge, as recurrent units of discourse structure somewhere between what we currently understand as genre structure and clause structure. Early work on phase (e.g. Gregory 1995) and rhetorical units (Cloran 1995) has been encouraging in this respect. Heeding Firth (1957), however, it may be that a good deal of this kind of structure will turn out to be specific to particular registers, and not something we will choose to generalize across social contexts.

NOTES

1   For related European perspectives, see de Beaugrande and Dressler (1981).

2   For related work on cohesion and intonation see Gumperz et al. (1984).

3   Ellipsis and substitution are sometimes treated as a single resource (e.g. Halliday 1994). From the perspective of English, ellipsis is substitution by zero; more generally, looking across languages, it might be better to think of substitution as ellipsis (signaled) by something.

4   It is more than obvious from quotations such as these that Halliday and Hasan did not equate cohesion with coherence; cf. Brown and Yule (1983: 190–201).

5   For definitions of "phora" terms (e.g. anaphora, cataphora, endophora, exophora, homophora) see Martin (1992).

6   For work on cohesion in other languages other than English see Aziz (1988); Callow (1974); Martin (1983).

7   The terms "internal" and "external" are from Halliday and Hasan (1976), van Dijk (e.g. 1977) opposes pragmatic to semantic relations. The contrast is between *He came, because I just saw him* (internal = "why I'm saying he came") and *He came because I saw him and told him to* (external = "why he came").

8   I use the term "construe" to place emphasis on the role texts play in making meaning (knowledge if you will) and thus constructing social context (reality if you must); cf. Halliday and Matthiessen (1999).

9   In SFL the ideational metafunction includes two subcomponents, the experiential and the logical; experiential meaning is associated with orbital structure (mononuclear), and logical meaning with serial structure (multinuclear); Martin (1996).

10   The father-and-son chains join at times through *they*, included in each chain at this stage of the analysis.

11   An example of bridging (Clark and Haviland 1977; Martin 1992): the garage, the bed, and the carpets are bridged from the house (predictable contents), as the clothes and the ironing are later on from the dishes (predictable chores).

12   Experiential clause functions from Halliday (1994).

13   Ellipsed participants rendered in square brackets.

14   Treated as a phrasal verb.

15   Arguably *home* is a circumstance of location; but in the absence of either deixis or a preposition I have taken it as a specification of the process here.

16   Fries (1992) discusses the influence of cohesive harmony on the interpretation of words, demonstrating the dialectic between global and local features in the texturing of discourse.

17   Note that one of the advantages of implicit conjunction is that it is underspecified; we can read the connection here in various ways – as succeeding, preceding, or possibly simultaneous.

18   In the framework being developed here Brown and Yule's (1983: 196) *There's the doorbell. – I'm in the bath.* would be analyzed through conjunction as involving implicit internal concession ("although you're telling me to answer the door, I can't because I'm in the bath"), and through negotiation as involving an indirect command followed by a challenging rejoinder justifying noncompliance.

19   This text, and children's stories in general, foreground the cohesive

agency of grammatical parallelism (as suggested in Gutwinski 1976; Hasan 1985).

20   Halliday and Hasan (e.g. 1985) prefer the terms "context of culture" for these systems and "context of situation" for their instantiation, reserving the term "register" for the pattern of linguistic choices put at risk from one context of situation to another (for discussion see Matthiessen 1993).

21   The value of cohesion analysis is not something that can be separated from the general model of analysis in which it is positioned, something that seems often to have been lost on critics who take up an eclectic position as far as tools for discourse analysis are concerned – and who have been prepared to critique, say, Halliday and Hasan (1976) without taking into account its theoretical context, as provided by SFL.

REFERENCES

Aziz, Y. Y. 1988. Cohesion in spoken Arabic texts. In E. Steiner and R. Veltman (eds), *Pragmatics, Discourse and Text: Some Systemically-inspired Approaches*. London: Pinter (Open Linguistics Series). 148–57.

de Beaugrande, R. and W. Dressler. 1981. *Introduction to Textlinguistics*. London: Longman (Longman Linguistics Library 26).

Benson, J. D. and W. S. Greaves. 1992. Collocation and field of discourse. In W. A. Mann and S. A. Thompson (eds), *Diverse Analyses of a Fund Raising Text*. Amsterdam: Benjamins. 397–409.

Berry, M. 1981. Systemic linguistics and discourse analysis: a multi-layered approach to exchange structure. In M. Coulthard and M. Montgomery (eds), *Studies in Discourse Analysis*. London: Routledge and Kegan Paul. 120–45.

Brown, A. 1989. *Piggybook*. London: Little Mammoth.

Brown, G. and G. Yule. 1983. *Discourse Analysis*. Cambridge: Cambridge University Press (Cambridge Textbooks in Linguistics).

Callow, K. 1974. *Discourse Considerations in Translating the Word of God*. Grand Rapids, Mich.: Zondervan.

Chapman, J. 1983. *Reading Development and Cohesion*. London: Heinemann Educational.

Christie, F. and J. R. Martin. 1997. *Genre and Institutions: Social Processes in the Workplace and School*. London: Cassell (Open Linguistics Series).

Clark, H. H. and S. E. Haviland. 1977. Comprehension and the given–new contrast. In R. O. Freedle (ed.), *Discourse Production and Comprehension*. Norwood, N.J.: Ablex. 3–40.

Cloran, C. 1995. Defining and relating text segments: Subject and Theme in discourse. In R. Hasan and P. Fries (eds), *On Subject and Theme: A Discourse Functional Perspective*. Amsterdam: Benjamins (Amsterdam Studies in the Theory and History of Linguistic Science). 361–403.

Coulthard, M. (ed.). 1992. *Advances in Spoken Discourse Analysis*. London: Routledge.

Davies, M. 1989. Prosodic and non-prosodic cohesion in speech and writing. *Word* 40.1–2, 255–62.

Du Bois, J. W. 1980. Beyond definiteness: the trace of identity in discourse. In W. L. Chafe (ed.), *The Pear Stories: Cognitive, Cultural and Linguistic Aspects of Narrative Production*.

Norwood, N.J.: Ablex. 203–74.

Eggins, S. and J. R. Martin. 1977. Genres and registers of discourse. In T. A. van Dijk (ed.), *Discourse as Structure and Process*. London: Sage (*Discourse Studies: A Multidisciplinary Introduction*. Vol. 1). 230–56.

Eggins, S. and D. Slade. 1997. *Analysing Casual Conversation*. London: Cassell.

Fine, J., G. Bartolucci, and P. Szatmari. 1989. Textual systems: their use in creation and miscalculation of social reality. *Word* 40.1–2, 65–80.

Firth, J. R. 1957. A synopsis of linguistic theory, 1930–1955. *Studies in Linguistic Analysis* (special volume of the Philological Society). London: Blackwell. 1–31. [reprinted in F. R. Palmer (ed.). 1968. *Selected Papers of J. R. Firth, 1952–1959*. London: Longman. 168–205.]

Fox, B. A. 1987. *Discourse Structure and Anaphora: written and conversational English*. Cambridge: Cambridge University Press (Cambridge Studies in Linguistics 48).

Francis, G. 1985. *Anaphoric Nouns*. Discourse Analysis Monographs 11. English Language Research, University of Birmingham.

Fries, P. H. 1981. On the status of theme in English: arguments from discourse. *Forum Linguisticum* 6.1, 1–38. [republished in J. S. Petöfi and E. Sözer (eds). 1983. *Micro and Macro Connexity of Texts*. Hamburg: Helmut Buske Verlag (Papers in Textlinguistics 45). 116–52.]

Fries, P. F. 1992. Lexico-grammatical patterns and the interpretation of texts. *Discourse Processes* 15, 73–91.

Ghadessy, M. (ed.). 1995. *Thematic Development in English Texts*. London: Pinter (Open Linguistics Series).

Gleason, H. A. Jr. 1968. Contrastive analysis in discourse structure. *Monograph Series on Languages and Linguistics 21* (Georgetown University Institute of Languages and Linguistics). [reprinted in Makkai and Lockwood 1973: 258–76.]

Gregory, M. J. 1995. *Before and Towards Communication Linguistics: Essays by Michael Gregory and Associates*. Seoul: Department of English Language and Literature, Sookmyung Women's University.

Gumperz, J. J., H. Kaltman, and M. C. O'Connor. 1984. Cohesion in spoken and written discourse: ethnic style and the transition to literacy. In D. Tannen (ed.), *Coherence in Spoken and Written Discourse*. Norwood, N.J.: Ablex (Advances in Discourse Processes XII). 3–20.

Gutwinski, W. 1976. *Cohesion in Literary Texts: A Study of Some Grammatical and Lexical Features of English Discourse*. The Hague: Mouton (Janua Linguarum Series Minor 204).

Halliday, M. A. K. 1964. The linguistic study of literary texts. In H. G. Lunt (ed.), *Proceedings of the Ninth International Congress of Linguists*. The Hague: Mouton. 302–7. [reprinted in S. Chatman and S. R. Levin. 1967. *Essays on the Language of Literature*. Boston: Houghton Mifflin. 217–23.]

Halliday, M. A. K. 1973. *Explorations in the Functions of Language*. London: Edward Arnold.

Halliday, M. A. K. 1978. *Language as a Social Semiotic: The Social Interpretation of Language and Meaning*. London: Edward Arnold.

Halliday, M. A. K. 1985. *Spoken and Written Language*. Geelong, Vic.: Deakin University Press. [republished by Oxford University Press 1989.]

Halliday, M. A. K. 1994. *An Introduction to Functional Grammar*. (Second edition). London: Edward Arnold.

Halliday, M. A. K. and R. Hasan. 1976. *Cohesion in English*. London: Longman (English Language Series 9).

Halliday, M. A. K. and R. Hasan. 1985. *Language, Context, and Text: Aspects of Language in a Social-semiotic*

Perspective. Geelong, Vic.: Deakin University Press. [republished by Oxford University Press 1989.]

Halliday, M. A. K. and J. R. Martin. 1993. *Writing Science: Literacy and Discursive Power*. London: Falmer (Critical Perspectives on Literacy and Education).

Halliday, M. A. K. and C. M. I. M. Matthiessen. 1999. *Construing Experience Through Meaning: A Language Based Approach to Cognition*. London: Cassell.

Hartnett, C. 1986. Static and dynamic cohesion: signals of thinking in writing. In B. Couture (ed.), *Functional Approaches to Writing: Research Perspectives*. London: Pinter (Open Linguistics Series). 142–53.

Hasan, R. 1968. *Grammatical Cohesion in Spoken and Written English, Part One*. London: Longman (Programme in Linguistics and English Teaching, Paper No. 7).

Hasan, R. 1984. Coherence and cohesive harmony. In J. Flood (ed.), *Understanding Reading Comprehension: Cognition, Language and the Structure of Prose*. Newark, Del.: International Reading Association. 181–219.

Hasan, R. 1985. The texture of a text. In M. A. K. Halliday and R. Hasan, *Language, Context and Text*. Geelong, Vic.: Deakin University Press. 70–96. [republished by Oxford University Press 1989.]

Hawkins, P. 1977. *Social Class, the Nominal Group and Verbal Strategies*. London: Routledge and Kegan Paul (Primary Socialisation, Language and Education).

Hoey, M. 1983. *On the Surface of Discourse*. London: George Allen and Unwin.

Hoey, M. 1991a. *Patterns of Lexis in Text*. Oxford: Oxford University Press (Describing English Language).

Hoey, M. J. 1991b. Another perspective on coherence and cohesive harmony. In Ventola 1991: 385–414.

Hymes, D. 1995. Bernstein and poetics. In P. Atkinson, B. Davies and S. Delamont (eds), *Discourse and Reproduction: Essays in Honor of Basil Bernstein*. Cresskill, N.J.: Hampton Press. 1–24.

Iedema, R. 1995. *Literacy of Administration (Write it Right Literacy in Industry Research Project – Stage 3)*. Sydney: Metropolitan East Disadvantaged Schools Program.

Iedema, R., S. Feez, and P. White. 1994. *Media Literacy (Write it Right Literacy in Industry Research Project – Stage 2)*. Sydney: Metropolitan East Disadvantaged Schools Program.

Jordan, M. P. 1984. *Rhetoric of Everyday English Texts*. London: George Allen and Unwin.

Labov, W. and J. Waletzky. 1967. Narrative analysis. In J. Helm (ed.), *Essays on the Verbal and Visual Arts* (Proceedings of the 1966 Spring Meeting of the American Ethnological Society). Seattle: University of Washington Press. 12–44.

Longacre, R. E. 1976. *An Anatomy of Speech Notions*. Lisse: Peter de Ridder.

Makkai, A. and D. Lockwood. 1973. *Readings in Stratificational Linguistics*. Tuscaloosa, Al.: Alabama University Press.

Mann, W. C. and S. A. Thompson (eds). 1992. *Discourse Description: Diverse Linguistic Analyses of a Fund-raising Text*. Amsterdam: Benjamins (Pragmatics and Beyond, New Series).

Mann, W. C., C. M. I. M. Matthiessen, and S. A. Thompson. 1992. Rhetorical structure theory and text analysis. In Mann and Thompson 1992: 39–78.

Martin, J. R. 1983a. The development of register. In J. Fine and R. O. Freedle (eds), *Developmental Issues in Discourse*. Norwood, N.J.: Ablex (Advances in Discourse Processes 10). 1–39.

Martin, J. R. 1983b. Participant identification in English, Tagalog and

Kâte. *Australian Journal of Linguistics* 3.1, 45–74.

Martin, J. R. 1992. *English Text: System and Structure*. Amsterdam: Benjamins.

Martin, J. R. 1995. Interpersonal meaning, persuasion and public discourse: packing semiotic punch. *Australian Journal of Linguistics* 15.1, 33–67.

Martin, J. R. 1996. Types of structure: deconstructing notions of constituency in clause and text. In E. H. Hovy and D. R. Scott (ed.), *Computational and Conversational Discourse: Burning Issues – An Interdisciplinary Account*. Heidelberg: Springer (NATO Advanced Science Institute Series F – Computer and Systems Sciences, Vol. 151). 39–66.

Martin, J. R. 1997. Register and genre: modelling social context in functional linguistics – narrative genres. In E. Pedro (ed.), *Proceedings of the First Lisbon International Meeting on Discourse Analysis*. Lisbon: Colibri/ APL. 305–44.

Martin, J. R. and G. Plum. 1997. Construing experience: some story genres. *Journal of Narrative and Life History* 7.1–4 (special issue: *Oral Versions of Personal Experience: Three Decades of Narrative Analysis*; M. Bamberg, guest editor), 299–308.

Martin, J. R. and R. Veel. 1998. *Reading Science: Critical and Functional Perspectives on Discourses of Science*. London: Routledge.

Martin, J. R., F. Christie, and J. Rothery. n.d. Social processes in education: a reply to Sawyer and Watson (and others). In I. Reid (ed.), *The Place of Genre in Learning: Current Debates*. Geelong, Vic.: Centre for Studies in Literary Education (Typereader Publications 1). 46–57.

Matthiessen, C. M. I. M. 1993. Register in the round: diversity in a unified theory of register analysis. In M. Ghadessy (ed.), *Register Analysis:*

Theory and Practice. London: Pinter. 221–92.

Nelson, K. and E. Levy. 1987. Development of referential cohesion in children's monologues. In Steele and Threadgold 1987: 119–36.

Ochs, E., E. A. Schegloff, and S. A. Thompson (eds). 1996. *Interaction and Grammar*. Cambridge: Cambridge University Press (Studies in Interactional Sociolinguistics 13).

Olson, L. A. and R. Johnson. 1989. Towards a better measure of readability: explanation of empirical performance results. *Word* 40.1–2, 223–34.

Pappas, C. C. 1985. The cohesive harmony and cohesive density of children's oral and written stories. In J. D. Benson and W. S. Greaves (eds), *Systemic Perspectives on Discourse. Vol. 2: Selected Theoretical Papers from the 9th International Systemic Workshop*. Norwood, N.J.: Ablex. 169–86.

Pappas, C. C. 1987. Exploring the textual properties of "proto-reading." In Steele and Threadgold 1987: 137–62.

Parsons, G. 1990. *Cohesion and Coherence: Scientific Texts – A Comparative Study*. Department of English Studies, University of Nottingham (Monographs in Systemic Linguistics 1).

Parsons, G. 1991. Cohesion coherence: scientific texts. In Ventola 1991: 415–30.

Poynton, C. 1985. *Language and Gender: Making the Difference*. Geelong, Vic.: Deakin University Press. [republished London: Oxford University Press 1989.]

Rochester, S. and J. R. Martin. 1979. *Crazy Talk: A Study of the Discourse of Schizophrenic Speakers*. New York: Plenum.

Rose, D., D. McInnes, and H. Körner. 1992. *Scientific Literacy (Write it Right Literacy in Industry Research Project*

Stage 1). Sydney: Metropolitan East Disadvantaged Schools Program.

Rothery, J. 1994. *Exploring Literacy in School English (Write it Right Resources for Literacy and Learning)*. Sydney: Metropolitan East Disadvantaged Schools Program.

Sinclair, J. McH. and R. M. Coulthard. 1975. *Towards an Analysis of Discourse: The English Used by Teachers and Pupils*. London: Oxford University Press.

Steele, R. and T. Threadgold (eds). 1987. *Language Topics: Essays in Honor of Michael Halliday. Vol. 1*. Amsterdam: Benjamins.

van Dijk, T. A. 1977. *Text and Context: Explorations in the Semantics and Pragmatics of Discourse*. London: Longman.

Ventola, E. 1987. *The Structure of Social Interaction: A Systemic Approach to the Semiotics of Service Encounters*. London: Pinter.

Ventola, E. (ed.). 1991. *Functional and Systemic Linguistics: Approaches and Uses*. Berlin: Mouton de Gruyter (Trends in Linguistics, Studies and Monographs 55).

Winter, E. O. 1977. A clause relational approach to English texts: a study of some predictive lexical items in written discourse. *Instructional Science* 6.1, 1–92.

Winter, E. O. 1982. *Towards a Contextual Grammar of English*. London: George Allen and Unwin.

Yang, A. 1989. Cohesive chains and writing quality. *Word* 40.1–2, 235–54.

3 Discourse Markers: Language, Meaning, and Context

DEBORAH SCHIFFRIN

0 Introduction

The production of coherent discourse is an interactive process that requires speakers to draw upon several different types of communicative knowledge that complement more code-based grammatical knowledge of sound, form, and meaning per se. Two aspects of communicative knowledge closely related to one another are *expressive* and *social*: the ability to use language to display personal and social identities, to convey attitudes and perform actions, and to negotiate relationships between self and other. Others include a *cognitive* ability to represent concepts and ideas through language and a *textual* ability to organize forms, and convey meanings, within units of language longer than a single sentence.

Discourse markers – expressions like *well*, *but*, *oh* and *y'know* – are one set of linguistic items that function in cognitive, expressive, social, and textual domains.[1] Although there were scattered studies of discourse markers in the 1980s, their study since then has abounded in various branches of linguistics and allied fields, leading Fraser (1998: 301) to call discourse marker analysis "a growth market in linguistics." Markers have been studied in a variety of languages, including Chinese (Biq 1990; Kwong 1989; Or 1997), Danish (Davidsen-Nielsen 1993), Finnish (Hakulinen and Seppanen 1992; Hakulinen 1998), French (Cadiot et al. 1985; Hansen 1998; Vincent 1993), German (W. Abraham 1991), Hebrew (Ariel 1998; Maschler 1997, 1998; Ziv 1998), Hungarian (Vasko 2000), Indonesian (Wouk 2000), Italian (Bazzanella 1990; Bruti 1999), Japanese (Cook 1990, 1992; Fuji 2000; Matsumoto 1988; Onodera 1992, 1995), Korean (Park 1998), Latin (Kroon 1998), Mayan (Brody 1989; Zavala in press), Portuguese (Silva and de Macedo 1992), and Spanish (Koike 1996; Schwenter 1996; see also section 3 below). They have been examined in a variety of genres and interactive contexts, for example, narratives (Norrick forthcoming; Koike 1996; Segal et al. 1991), political interviews (Wilson 1993), health care consultations (Heritage and Sorjonen 1994), games (Greaseley 1994; Hoyle 1994), computer-generated tutorial sessions (Moser and Moore 1995), newspapers (Cotter 1996a), radio talk (Cotter 1996b), classrooms (de Fina 1997; Chaudron and Richards 1986; Tyler et al. 1988), and service encounters (Merritt 1984), as well as in a number of different language contact situations (Cotter

1996b; de Fina 2000; Gupta 1992; Heisler 1996; Maschler 1994; Sankoff et al. 1997). Synchronic studies have been supplemented by diachronic analyses of first (Andersen 1996; Andersen et al. 1995; Gallagher and Craig 1987; Jisa 1987; Kyratzis et al. 1990; Kryatzis and Ervin-Tripp 1999; Sprott 1992, 1994) and second language acquisition (Flowerdew and Tauroza 1995), as well as language change (Brinton 1996, ch. 7 this volume; Finell 1989; Fleischman 1999; Fludernik 1995; Jucker 1997; Stein 1985; Taavitsainen 1994; Traugott 1995).

The studies just mentioned have approached discourse markers from a number of different perspectives. After reviewing three influential perspectives (section 1) and presenting a sample analysis (section 2), I summarize a subset of recent studies that have provided a rich and varied empirical base that reveals a great deal about how discourse markers work and what they do (section 3). My conclusion revisits one of the central dilemmas still facing discourse marker research (section 4).

1   Discourse Markers: Three Perspectives

Perspectives on markers differ in terms of their basic starting points, their definition of discourse markers, and their method of analysis. Here I describe Halliday and Hasan's (1976) semantic perspective on cohesion (section 1.1); next is my own discourse perspective (Schiffrin 1987a (section 1.2)); third is Fraser's (1990, 1998) pragmatic approach (section 1.3). I have chosen these approaches not only because they have been influential, but because their differences (section 1.4) continue to resonate in current research.

1.1   *Markers and cohesion*

Halliday and Hasan's (1976) seminal work on cohesion in English provided an important framework for analyzing text by addressing a basic question stemming from the very inception of discourse analysis: what makes a text different from a random collection of unrelated sentences? Although Halliday and Hasan did not speak directly of discourse markers, their analysis of cohesion (based primarily on written texts) included words (e.g. *and, but, because, I mean, by the way, to sum up*) that have since been called markers and suggested functions for those words partially paralleling those of markers.

Halliday and Hasan propose that a set of cohesive devices (reference, repetition, substitution, ellipsis, and conjunction) help create a text by indicating semantic relations in an underlying structure of ideas (see Martin, this volume). A range of expressions (including, but not limited to, conjunctions) conveys conjunctive relations. Whereas most cohesive features establish cohesion through anaphoric or cataphoric ties to the text, conjunctive items "express certain meanings which presuppose the presence of other components in the discourse" (Halliday and Hasan 1976: 236).

The meanings conveyed by conjunctive items are relatively straightforward: additive, adversative, causal, and temporal. Within these general meanings, however, are specific subtypes: a causal relation, for example, includes general causal (with simple and emphatic subtypes), and specific causal (with reason, result, and purpose subtypes). Each (sub)type of cohesive meaning can be conveyed through a variety of words: a general causal simple conjunctive relation, for example, can be conveyed through *so, then, hence,* and *therefore*. Multiplicity is found not just in a FUNCTION (e.g. causal relation) → FORM (e.g. *so, hence*) direction, but also in a FORM → FUNCTION direction. Thus a single word [FORM] can convey more than one conjunctive relation [FUNCTION]: *then*, for example, can convey temporal, causal, and conditional relations, between clauses (cf. Biq 1990; Hansen 1997; Schiffrin 1992).

Whereas many analyses of conjunctions argue for either a simple semantic interpretation or a set of polysemous meanings (e.g. Posner 1980), Halliday and Hasan allow variation in the degree to which meaning results from the semantics of a word itself or from the propositions in a text. For example, although *and* is a texture-creating device that can contribute an additive meaning, its meaning can also reflect the semantic content of a text: thus, if *and* prefaces an upcoming proposition whose meaning contrasts with that of a prior proposition, *and* would then convey an adversative relation (comparable to *but* and *on the other hand*).

Just as contributions to meaning can vary in source – word meaning and/or propositions – so too, meanings can fluctuate between "external" and "internal" sources. External meaning is "inherent in the phenomena that language is used to talk about" (Halliday and Hasan 1976: 241); it is roughly analogous to referential meaning and the domain of semantics. Internal meaning is nonreferential pragmatic meaning: it is "inherent in the communicative process" (1976: 241), e.g. the speaker's choice of speech role, rhetorical channel, attitude (1976: 240). Rather than separate external and internal meanings, however, Halliday and Hasan posit a continuity. The additive meaning of *and*, for example, may be viewed "as an extension of the underlying patterns of conjunction into the communication situation itself, treating it, and thereby also the text . . . as having by analogy the same structure as 'reality'" (1976: 267).

Although *meaning* can be reshuffled – between word and propositions, between internal and external sources – the boundary between sentence and text is less permeable. The systemic-functional grammar in which Halliday and Hasan's analysis is located draws a sharp distinction between sentence and text: thus, the structural role of words like *and* (to coordinate clauses at a sentential level) is qualitatively different from its cohesive role (to mark interpretive dependencies between propositions, and thus create texture).

1.2   Markers and discourse

My analysis of discourse markers (Schiffrin 1987a) was motivated by several concerns. From a sociolinguistic perspective, I was interested in using methods for analyzing language that had been developed by variation theory to account for the use and distribution of forms in discourse. This interest, however, was embedded within my view of discourse not only as a unit of language, but as a process of social interaction (see Heller, Schegloff, both this volume). My analysis thus tried to reconcile both methodology (using both quantitative and qualitative methods) and underlying models (combining those inherited from both linguistics and sociology). Unifying the analysis was the desire to account for the distribution of markers (which markers occurred where? why?) in spoken discourse in a way that attended to both the importance of language (what was the form? its meaning?) and interaction (what was going on – at the moment of use – in the social interaction?).

My initial work (Schiffrin 1987a) defined discourse markers as sequentially dependent elements that bracket units of talk (1987a: 31), i.e. nonobligatory utterance-initial items that function in relation to ongoing talk and text. I proposed that discourse markers could be considered as a set of linguistic expressions comprised of members of word classes as varied as conjunctions (e.g. *and, but, or*), interjections (*oh*), adverbs (*now, then*), and lexicalized phrases (*y'know, I mean*). Also proposed was a discourse model with different planes: a participation framework, information state, ideational structure, action structure, exchange structure. My specific analyses showed that markers could work at different levels of discourse to connect utterances on either a single plane (1) or across different planes (2). In (1a) and (1b), for example, *because* connects actions and ideas respectively. In (1a), *because* connects a request (to complete a task) and the justification for the request:

(1) a.   Yeh, let's get back, because she'll never get home.

In (1b), *because* connects two idea units or representations of events:

(1) b.   And they holler Henry!!! Cause they really don't know!²

In (2), however, *but* connects an utterance defined on several different planes simultaneously, and hence relates the different planes to one another:

(2) *Jack*:   [The rabbis preach, ["Don't intermarry"
     Freda: [But I did-   [But I *did* say   those intermarriages
                that we have in this country are healthy.

Freda's *but* prefaces an idea unit ("intermarriages are healthy"), displays a participation framework (nonaligned with Jack), realizes an action (a rebuttal during an argument), and seeks to establish Freda as a current speaker in an exchange (open a turn at talk). *But* in (2) thus has four functions that locate an utterance at the intersection of four planes of talk.

Another aspect of my analysis showed that markers display relationships that are local (between adjacent utterances) and/or global (across wider spans and/or structures of discourse; cf. Lenk 1998). In (3), for example, *because* (in (d)) has both local and global functions (example from Schiffrin 1994b: 34, discussed also in Schiffrin 1997):

(3) *Debby*:   a.   Well some people before they go to the doctor, they talk to a friend,
                     or a neighbor.
                b.   Is there anybody that uh . . .
     Henry: c.   Sometimes it works!
                d.   Because there's this guy Louie Gelman.
                e.   he went to a big specialist,
                f.   and the guy . . . analyzed it wrong.
                     [narrative not included]
                o.   So doctors are – well they're not God either!

In (3), *because* has a local function: it opens a justification (that takes the form of a brief (three-clause) narrative about a friend's experience) through which Henry supports his claim to a general truth (going to someone other than a doctor *works*, i.e. can help a medical problem). But notice that Henry then follows this justification with a longer (eight-clause) narrative detailing his friend's experience. Thus, *because* also has a global function: *because* links *Sometimes it works* (defined retrospectively as an abstract) with a narrative (whose coda is initiated with the complementary discourse marker *so* also functioning at a global level).

Also considered in my analysis was the degree to which markers themselves add a meaning to discourse (i.e. as when *oh* displays information as "new" or "unexpected" to a recipient) or reflect a meaning that is already semantically accessible (e.g. as when *but* reflects a semantically transparent contrastive meaning). Markers can also occupy intermediate positions between these two extremes: *because* and *so*, for example, partially maintain their core meanings as cause/result conjunctions even when they establish metaphorical relationships on nonpropositional planes of discourse (cf. Schwenter 1996; Sweetser 1990).

Although I had initiated my analysis with what I called an "operational definition" of markers (quoted above), I concluded with more theoretical definitions of markers. First, I tried to specify the conditions that would allow a word to be used as a discourse marker: syntactically detachable, initial position, range of prosodic contours, operate at both local and global levels, operate on different planes of discourse (Schiffrin 1987a: 328). Second, I suggested that discourse markers were comparable to indexicals (Schiffrin 1987a: 322–5; cf. Levinson's 1983: ch. 2 notion of discourse deictics), or, in a broader sociolinguistic framework, contextualization cues (Schiffrin 1987b). Finally, I proposed that although markers have primary functions (e.g. the primary function of *and* is on an ideational plane, the primary function of *well* in the participation framework), their use is multifunctional. It is this multifunctionality on different planes of discourse that helps to integrate the many different simultaneous processes underlying the construction of discourse, and thus helps to create coherence.

1.3   Markers and pragmatics

Like the work reviewed thus far, Fraser's (1990, 1998) perspective on discourse markers is embedded within a larger framework that impacts upon the analysis of markers. In contrast to Halliday and Hasan – whose main interest was the cohesion of text – Fraser's theoretical framework concerns the meaning of sentences, specifically how one type of pragmatic marker in a sentence may relate the message conveyed by that sentence to the message of a prior sentence. And in contrast to my approach in Schiffrin (1987a) – whose starting point was to account for the use and distribution of markers in everyday discourse – Fraser's starting point is the classification of types of pragmatic meaning, and within that classification, the description of how some pragmatic commentary markers (discourse markers) dictate an interpretation of "the message conveyed by S2 [S = segment] vis-a-vis the interpretation of S1" (Fraser 1998: 302).

Fraser's framework depends upon a differentiation between content and pragmatic meaning. Content meaning is referential meaning: "a more or less explicit representation of some state of the world that the speaker intends to bring to the hearer's attention by means of the literal interpretation of the sentence" (1990: 385). Pragmatic meaning concerns the speaker's communicative intention, the direct (not implied) "message the speaker intends to convey in uttering the sentence" (1990: 386). It is conveyed by three different sets of pragmatic markers: basic pragmatic markers (signals of illocutionary force, e.g. *please*), commentary pragmatic markers (encoding of another message that comments on the basic message, e.g. *frankly*), and parallel pragmatic markers (encoding of another message separate from the basic and/or commentary message, e.g. *damn*, vocatives). Discourse markers are one type of commentary pragmatic marker: they are "a class of expressions, each of which signals how the speaker intends the basic message that follows to relate to the prior discourse" (1990: 387). Fraser's more recent work (1998) builds upon the sequential function of discourse markers, such that discourse markers necessarily specify (i.e. provide commentary on) a relationship between two segments of discourse: this specification is not conceptual, but procedural (it provides information on the interpretation of messages; see also Ariel 1998).

As suggested earlier, Fraser's framework presumes a strict separation between semantics (his content meaning) and pragmatics (his pragmatic meaning): speakers' use of commentary pragmatic markers – including, critically, discourse markers – has nothing to do with the content meaning of the words (cf. Halliday and Hasan 1976; Schiffrin 1987a; see also Norrick, this volume). Similarly, although discourse markers may be homophonous with, as well as historically related to, other forms, they do not function in sentential and textual roles simultaneously: "when an expression functions as a discourse marker, that is its exclusive function in the sentence" (1990: 189).

One consequence of these disjunctive relationships is that multiple functions of markers – including, critically, social interactional functions – are downplayed (if noted at all) and not open to linguistic explanation. What some scholars (e.g. Ariel 1998; Halliday and Hasan 1976; Schiffrin 1987a, 1992; Maschler 1998; Schwenter 1996) suggest is an interdependence (sometimes clear, sometimes subtle) between content and pragmatic meaning – explained by well-known processes such as semantic bleaching (Bolinger 1977) or metaphorical extensions from a "source domain" (Sweetser 1990) – becomes, instead, a matter of chance (e.g. homophony). Likewise, what scholars working on grammaticalization (Brinton, this volume; Traugott 1995) and particularly pragmaticization (e.g. Fleischman 1999; Onodera 1992, 1995) have found to be gradual changes in form/function relationships would have to be viewed, instead, as a series of categorical and functional leaps across mutually exclusive classes of form and meaning.

Fraser's classification of types of pragmatic meaning also has the important effect of redefining the set of expressions often considered as markers. Different markers are excluded for different reasons: whereas *oh*, for example, is considered akin to a separate sentence, *because* is viewed as a content formative or an interjection, and *y'know* is identified as a parallel pragmatic marker. These classifications create sets that end up containing tremendous internal variation. The large and varied group of interjections (Fraser 1990: 391), for example, includes not only *oh*, but also *ah, aha, ouch, yuk* (what Goffman 1978 has called response cries), *uh-huh, yeah* (what Yngve 1970 calls back channels and Schegloff 1981 calls turn-continuers), *hey* (a summons, see DuBois 1989), and *because* (which is an interjection when it stands alone as an answer (Fraser 1990: 392), and elsewhere a content formative (but see Schlepegrell 1991; Stenstrom 1998)).

1.4   Comparison of approaches

Along with the specific differences among approaches noted in interim comparisons above, we can also compare the approaches in relation to three recurrent themes. First, the source of discourse markers: although the three perspectives agree that markers have various sources, they differ on the contribution of word meaning and grammatical class to discourse marker meaning and function (Fraser positing the least contribution). Second, the relationship between discourse markers and contexts: although all agree that markers can gain their function through discourse, different conceptualizations of discourse produce different kinds of discourse functions. Fraser's focus is primarily how markers indicate relationships between messages (propositions); although Halliday and Hasan focus primarily on the propositional content of tests too, their overall theory also allows conjunctive relations to index facets of the communicative situation; Schiffrin explicitly includes various aspects of the communicative situation within her discourse model, such that indexing propositional relations is only one possible function of discourse markers. Third, the integration of discourse marker analysis into the study of language: whereas Halliday and Hasan embed the study of conjunctive relations in their study of cohesion, which in turn, is part of the larger theory of systemic-functional linguistics, Fraser's approach rests upon a pragmatic theory of meaning applied both within and across sentences, and Schiffrin's approach combines interactional and variationist approaches to discourse to analyze the role of markers in co-constructed discourse.

2   Theory, Method, Analysis: The Importance of the Data

Differences in the perspectives reviewed above stem from theoretical assumptions and goals, methodological practices, and choice of data (written texts, sociolinguistic interviews, hypothetical sentences). In this section, I present a brief (and partial) analysis of one marker (*and*) in one discourse (a list), primarily from my own approach (section 1.2). Although space prohibits explicit discussion of how every point of the analysis would be treated by different approaches, or how they would be relevant to the different themes discussed above (but see pp. 63, 65–6), I alert the reader to several key issues: what unit to consider (e.g. sentence, clause, intonation unit, turn), the relationship between sentence grammar and text, how to conceptualize and operationalize context, how to analyze multiple functions, and the difference between data-driven and theory-driven analyses.

The discourse in (4) is a list, i.e. a hierarchical description of members of a set (Schiffrin 1994a; see DuBois and Sankoff, this volume). All lists display a speaker's identification and organization of a set of items that are clearly the same in some ways (e.g. "my chores today," "members of my family") but different in others (e.g. "phone calls" vs. "post office," "siblings" vs. "cousins"). Thus, the central coherence relation (Knott and Sanders 1998) of lists is membership in a set; the central structure is coordination of subunits as equal level branches of a larger overarching unit (see Polanyi, this volume).

In (4), Kay is listing the race tracks near her house in response to a tag question from Anne (a sociolinguistic interviewer) about the popularity of racing. The list thus answers Anne's question by providing empirical justification for Anne's implicit claim that race tracks are locally popular (*big around here*). The Roman numerals and letters on the left of Kay's list indicate the organization of items in the list:[3]

(4) X LOCAL RACE TRACKS

		Anne:	a.	Racing's big around here, isn't it?
		Kay:	b.	Yeh.
		Anne:	c.	Yeh.
X1 RACE TRACKS IN NJ		Kay:	d.	Well, you got uh, Jersey.
X1a			e.	You got . . . Monmouth
X1b			f.	and you got Garden State.
X1c			g.	Y'got Atlantic City.
		Anne:	h.	Mhm.
X2/X2a RACE TRACKS IN PA		Kay:	i.	And then uh here you got Liberty Bell.
X2b			j.	And they're building a new one up in Neshaminy.
		Anne:	k.	That's right. [I've never seen that, =
X3/X3a RACE TRACK IN DE		Kay:	l.	[And uh . . . you got =
		Anne:		= [though.
		Kay:		= [Delaware.
X4 RACE TRACKS IN NY			m.	And of course, if you want to re- be- really go at it you can go up to New York.
		Anne:	n.	Mhm.
X4a		Kay:	o.	= You got Aqueduct
X4b			p.	and you got Saratoga
X4c			q.	and you have that Belmont, y'know.

And occurs frequently in the list: it prefaces seven list items; those not *and*-prefaced are X1a (e), X1c (g), X4a (o). Why does *and* occur with some list-items, but not with others?

Since lists represent set membership, one obvious suggestion is that *and* reflects the organization of set members being enumerated, and thus, the speaker's cognitive/conceptual organization (Knotts and Sanders 1998) of the set LOCAL RACE TRACKS. Notice, then, that *and* connects list-items at the *same* level: both lower level list-items (in (f), (j), (p), and (q)) and higher level list-items (linked in (i), (l), and (m)). But *and* does not connect list-items from different levels: *and* does not link X1 to X1a (e) or X4 to X4a (o).[4] This distribution suggests that the textual organization of the list-items parallels the grammatical role of *and* as a coordinating conjunction (Schiffrin 1986, 1987a: 182–90).

The ideational structure of the list is, of course, not the only discourse plane to consider. Since the list is presented as a relatively continuous turn at talk, we might be tempted to overlook any relationship between *and* and turn-taking. Notice in the data above, however, that Anne uses standard back-channel tokens ((h), (k), (n)) that not only show her attentiveness, but also function as turn-continuers (Schegloff 1981): *mhm* and *that's right* allow Kay to continue her turn despite a syntactically, intonationally and semantically marked (Ford and Thompson 1998) turn-transition space. In two of these exchanges ((g)–(i), (j)–(l)), Kay uses *and* to continue her turn after Anne's turn-continuers. Why does Kay not use *and* as a third turn-continuer (in (m)–(o))?

Recall our earlier observation that *and* connects equal level list-items on a list. The *and*-prefaced list-items within Kay's turn-continuation both have coordinate links ([X1] *and* [X2], [X2] *and* [X3]) at a global level. But the list item without *and* – *You got Aqueduct* (o) [X4a] – does not: because it is the first subcategory of [X4], there is not yet a coordinate level list-item with which it can be anaphorically linked. Thus, although the turn-taking environment of *You got Aqueduct* is consistent with the use of *and* (Schiffrin 1987a: 143–6), the ideational structure is not.

In this sample analysis, I have tried to explain both the presence and absence of *and* in a list by exploring two different aspects of context: ideational (conceptual) structure, exchange (turn-taking) structure. This has raised an important issue – the effect of multiple constraints on discourse options (Schiffrin 1985) – that is actually the flip side of the fact that markers are multifunctional.[5] We have already noted that discourse markers function in cognitive, expressive, social, and textual domains, i.e. simultaneously on different planes of discourse. If language served primarily one or another function at different times (and of course, it may, in certain registers; see Biber and Conrad, this volume), it would be relatively easy to decide on which plane to focus and to discover which aspect of discourse is indexed through a marker. But when language is multifunctional – as is certainly the case with discourse markers – it must be the data themselves that guide the selection of constraints to examine.

The approach to the multifunctionality of discourse markers illustrated here has clearly been data-driven. I asked why *and* occurred in some places, but not in others. I proposed explanations that I then explored in relation to the data: my goal throughout was to find the pattern of use for *and* and to explain that pattern. Although my brief analysis was certainly embedded within a general analytical interest in markers' functions and a set of theoretical principles about discourse (Schiffrin 1994b: 416), I did not take these as my starting points (cf. the theory-driven approaches of Andersen 1998; Rouchota 1998; Shloush 1998). Rather, it was the data themselves that suggested the constraints and the analytical frameworks that would be most pertinent to understanding the use of *and*.

3   Markers Across Contexts, Across Languages, and Over Time

Discourse marker research utilizes a variety of data sources that allow analysts to focus on markers across contexts, across languages, and/or over time. These three focal areas address many different specific issues that are part of several general themes of discourse marker research: what lexical items are used as discourse markers? Are words with comparable meanings used for comparable functions? What is the influence of syntactic structure, and semantic meaning, on the use of markers? How do cultural, social, situational, and textual norms have an effect on the distribution and function of markers? Since we have just discussed *and*, I begin with a review of some other studies of *and* that also provide a good entry point to several of these issues.

A conversation-analytic study of *and* (Heritage and Sorjonen 1994) studied its use as a preface to questions in clinical consultations. The primary use of *and* was to preface agenda-based questions either locally between adjacent turns, or globally across turns, and thus to orient participants to the main phases of the activity. An additional, more strategic, use of *and* was to normalize contingent questions or problematic issues (1994: 19–22). Whereas the former use of *and* was coordinating in both a metaphorical and structural sense (i.e. the questions were the "same" level in the question agenda), the latter use amplifies Halliday and Hasan's idea of external meaning: the additive meaning of *and* normalizes the problematic content and/or placement of a question.[6]

The coordinating function of *and* at both grammatical and discourse levels over a range of contexts has also been noted in studies of language development and child discourse (see also Meng and Sromqvist 1999; Kyratzis and Ervin-Tripp 1999; Cook-Gumperz and Kyratzis, this volume). Peterson and McCabe (1991) show that *and* has a textual use in childrens' (3 years 6 months to 9 years 6 months) narratives: *and* links similar units (i.e. narrative events) more frequently than information tangential to narrative plot (cf. Segal et al. 1991 for adults). Gallagher and Craig (1987) show how *and* connects speech acts during the dramatic role play of 4-year-olds. Sprott (1992) shows that the earliest appearance of *and* (as well as *but*, *because* and *well*) during children's (2 years 7 months to 3 years 6 months) disputes marks exchange structures; this function continues as action, and ideational (first local, then global) functions are added on at later ages.

Studies of bilingual discourse – those in which speakers either borrow or code-switch across two different languages (e.g. Heisler 1996) – also add to our understanding of the linguistic and contextual junctures at which markers work. A series of studies by Maschler (1994, 1997, 1998) on the use of Hebrew discourse markers in Hebrew/English conversations of bilingual women, for example, reveals a range of distributions across the two languages: some markers were roughly equivalent, others had no equivalents, still others were semantically, but not functionally, comparable. The last distribution has also been observed by Cotter (1996b: 140–216), who finds, despite a semantic equivalent in Irish, that English *well* is used during Irish radio call-in shows to fill in a perceived functional gap.

Other studies focus on the linguistic consequences of markers being borrowed across – and then coexisting within – different languages. Brody (1989) suggests that the general lexical meanings and structuring effects of Spanish conjunctions (including *bueno*; see below) reappear in Mayan use, but are sometimes used togther with native particles that have comparable uses. Zavala's (in press) analysis of the restructuring of the standard Spanish (causal or consecutive) conjunction *pues* by Quechua-Andean Spanish bilinguals shows that *pues* has lost its meaning at the sentence level and acquired meaning at the discourse level: *pues* is used to mark changes in information status, as well as commitment to the truth of information, in ways that reflect some of the functions of Quechua evidentials.[7]

Comparative studies of markers in monolingual speech situations also add to our understanding of the different junctures at which markers work. For example, studies of Spanish markers that are in some, but not all, contexts roughly comparable to English *well* suggest the importance of both context and lexical/semantic source. De Fina's (1997) analysis of *bien* (an adverb, glossed semantically as "well") in classroom talk shows that teachers use *bien* for both organizational functions (to redefine a situation, to move to another activity) and evaluative functions (as the feedback "move" in the three-part classroom exchange of question/answer/feedback). The organizational function of *bien* is most comparable to English *okay* (Beach 1993; Condon 1986; Merritt 1984). Like *okay*, the positive connotation (i.e. "I accept this") of *bien* has been semantically bleached (Bolinger 1977) in transitional (but not evaluative) environments. Travis's (1998) analysis of *bueno* (an adjective, glossed semantically as "good") in conversation in Colombian Spanish differentiates two functions. Although the first (mark acceptance) is comparable to the evaluative function of *bien* and English *okay*, the second (mark a partial response) is more comparable to uses of English *well*. Chodorowska-Pilch's (1999) research on Penisular Spanish suggests still another lexical source (*vamos*, literally "we go") for yet another function (mitigation) partially comparable to that of *well*. An analysis of *vamos* during service encounters in a travel agency suggests that *vamos* mitigates face-threatening speech acts by metaphorically moving the speaker away from the content of an utterance, and thus metonymically creating interpersonal distance.

The studies on *bien*, *bueno*, and *vamos* suggest that discourse functions can be divided very differently across languages. English *well*, for example, is used very generally with responses that are not fully consonant with prior expectations (Greaseley 1994; Lakoff 1973; Schiffrin 1987a: ch. 5; Svartvik 1980): hence its use in indirect and/or lengthy answers (as illustrated in line (d) of the list in (4)) and self-repairs. But in Spanish, it is only *bueno* that is used this way (Travis 1998): *bien* has the transitional function associated with *well* as a frame shift (Jucker 1993), and *vamos* the mitigating function associated with *well* in dispreferred responses (e.g. turning down a request). Thus, the functions of a marker in one language can be distributed among a variety of lexically based discourse markers in other languages.[8]

The importance of comparative studies for our understanding of grammaticalization is highlighted by Fleischman's (1999) analysis of markers comparable to English *like*. Fleischman finds that a variety of discourse/pragmatic functions associated with English *like* (e.g. focus, hedge) is replicated in languages as varied as Finnish, French, German, Hebrew, Italian, Japanese, Lahu, Portuguese, Russian, and Swedish. Although the words share neither etymologies nor a single lexical/semantic source, the processes that they undergo as they move toward their similar functions are strikingly similar.[9]

Studies of grammaticalization (both completed and in progress) within a single language also provide valuable insights into both the sources and developmental paths of markers (Onodera 1992, 1995; see also Brinton, this volume). Jucker (1997), for example, suggests that *well* underwent a process of continuous diversification, whereby new functions were added to old ones (cf. Finnell 1989). Warvik's (1995) analysis of two Middle English (ME) adverbial/conjunctions (glossed as "when" and "then") shows that when these words were supplanted by ME *then*, what was altered was not only a formal distinction (two forms shifted to one), but also a genre-based (narrative vs. non-narrative) distribution.

Research on a variety of words and expressions in contemporary English that have gained – or are gaining – pragmatic roles as discourse markers suggest a range of formal and functional relationships not just with their historical sources, but with their contemporary lexical sources. Whereas syntactic position, pronunciation, and meaning all differentiate the adverbial and discourse marker uses of *anyway* (Ferrera

1997), for example, it is pronunciation and meaning that differentiate the marker *cos* from its source *because* (Stenstrom 1998), and meaning and sequential distribution that differentiate the use of *yeh* as a "reaction" marker from its use as either agreement or turn-continuer (Jucker and Smith 1998; see also DuBois 1989 on *hey*, Sebba and Tate 1986 on *y'know what I mean*, and Tsui 1991 on *I don't know*). Finally, Swerts's (1998) analysis of filled pauses in Dutch monologues suggests that even vocalizations that are themselves semantically empty can provide an option within a set of paradigmatic choices that includes semantically meaningful markers (i.e. Dutch *nou* (cf. "now," "well") or *effe kijken* (cf. "let's see")). Thus, vocalizations that have no inherent meaning at all, and that occur elsewhere for very different reasons (see, e.g., Fromkin 1973 on the role of filled pauses, and other "speech errors" in language production), can also provide markers through which to structure discourse (for a parallel argument about gestures, see Kendon 1995).

In sum, research on discourse markers has spread into many areas of linguistic inquiry, drawing scholars from many different theoretical and empirical orientations.[10] Although this welcome diversity has led to an abundance of information about discourse markers, it has also led to knowledge that is not always either linear or cumulative. The result is that it is difficult to synthesize the results of past research into a set of coherent and consistent findings and, thus, to integrate scholarly findings into an empirically grounded theory. My conclusion in the next section thus returns to a very basic issue still confronting discourse marker analysis: what are discourse markers?

4   Conclusion: Markers and Discourse Analysis

Discourse markers are parts of language that scholars want to study, even if they do not always agree on what particular parts they are studying or what to call the object of their interest. Not only have discourse markers been called by various names (Fraser 1998: 301 lists 15 different names), but, like the definition of discourse itself (see Introduction, this volume), what often opens books (e.g. Brinton 1996; Jucker and Ziv 1998; Schiffrin 1987a: ch. 2) and articles (e.g. Holker 1991: 78–9; Sankoff et al. 1997: 195) about markers is a discussion of definitional issues. Rather than try to resolve these issues, I here take a more modest approach that addresses the definitional problem from the outside in: I suggest that the way we identify markers is an outgrowth of how we approach the study of discourse. I do so by considering the status of two words that are often, but not always, viewed as markers: *and*, *y'know*. Although the two markers present different definitional questions, resolving the status of both touches on broader discourse analytic issues of data, method, and theory.

Questions about the status of *and* revolve around the difference between sentences and texts, grammar and meaning. *And* has a grammatical role as a coordinating conjunction that seems to be (at least partially) paralleled in its discourse role. But can all tokens of *and* – even those that are intersentential and thus might seem to have a purely grammatical role – work as discourse markers?

In my sample analysis of *and* in a list (section 2), I began by including all occurrences of *and* regardless of linguistic environment: I included *and* between syntactically parallel clauses within one intonation unit (*You got . . . Monmouth and you got Garden State.*) and between syntactically different sentences in two intonation units (*And then uh here you got Liberty Bell. And they're building a new one up in Neshaminy.*).[11] My analysis suggested that all the tokens of *and* had both structural and additive roles. Because of their comparable function, I would argue that all the tokens of *and* in the list are all discourse markers.

My decision about the marker status of *and* was based not on an a priori theory, but on an analysis of the function of *and* in the data. Basing decisions about marker status on data analysis has an important consequence: there may very well be different decisions about the marker status of an expression depending upon the data. This should be neither surprising nor problematic. If discourse markers are, indeed, indices of the underlying cognitive, expressive, textual, and social organization of a discourse, then it is ultimately properties of the discourse itself (that stem, of course, from factors as various as the speaker's goals, the social situation, and so on) that provide the need for (and hence the slots in which) markers appear.

Of course data never exists in a vacuum. We all come to our data, and begin its analysis, with assumptions about what is important and principles that help us organize our thinking (theory), as well as sets of tools through which to first discover, and then explain, what we have perceived as a "problem" in the data (methodology). Although data and methodology both bear on the status of *y'know* as a marker, it is the role of underlying assumptions and principles about discourse that I want to stress in relation to decisions about *y'know*.

Disagreement about the status of *y'know* centers on the relationship between meaning and discourse. *Y'know* presents a set of distributional and functional puzzles: it is not always utterance-initial, it has variant degrees of semantic meaning. Despite general agreement that *y'know* is a marker of some kind, it is not always considered a *discourse* marker per se. Fraser (1990: 390), for example, excludes *y'know* from his discourse marker group because he claims that rather than signal a discourse relationship, it signals a speaker attitude of solidarity (cf. Holmes 1986).

To try to resolve disagreement about *y'know*, let us take a closer look, first, at where *y'know* occurs and, next, at the different views of discourse that underlie different analyses of markers. *Y'know* is often found in specific discourse environments: concluding an argument, introducing a story preface, evoking a new referent (Schiffrin 1987a: 267–95). These environments all mark transitions from one phase of discourse to another, and thus, they all relate (possibly large) discourse segments: the first connects a conclusion with prior evidence, the second connects a prior conversational topic with an upcoming story about that topic, and the third introduces a referent that will then be treated as familiar information. These connections certainly involve relationships between discourse segments. In fact, one might argue that it is precisely in transitional locations such as these – where interlocutors are jointly engaged in productive and interpretive tasks centered on establishing the relationship between somewhat abstract and complex discourse segments – that speakers may want to create, or reinforce, solidarity with their hearers.

What underlies decisions about expressions such as *y'know* are different conceptions of discourse itself. Sociolinguistic, interactional, and conversation-analytic analyses of markers begin with a view that language reflects (and realizes) rich and multifaceted contexts. This view leads such analysts to search for the varied functions of markers

– and thus to incorporate into their analyses and theories the multifunctionality that is one of the central defining features of discourse markers. But many current analysts who begin from semantic and pragmatic perspectives privilege the "message" level of discourse, thus restricting analysis of markers to the signaling of message-based relationships across sentences.[12] Also differently conceived is the notion of communicative meaning. Sociolinguistic approaches to discourse (Schiffrin 1994b: ch. 11) assume that communicative meaning is co-constructed by speaker/hearer interaction and emergent from jointly recognized sequential expectations and contingencies of talk-in-interaction. But many semantic and pragmatic analyses of markers are wed to a Gricean view of communicative meaning as speaker intention (and subsequent hearer recognition of intention). If the assignment of meaning is completely divorced from the study of the sequential and interactional contingencies of actual language use, however, then so are decisions about the functions of markers, and even more basically, decisions about the status of expressions as markers.

To conclude: I noted initially that the production of coherent discourse is an interactive process that requires speakers to draw upon several different types of communicative knowledge – cognitive, expressive, social, textual – that complement more code-based grammatical knowledge of sound, form, and meaning. Discourse markers tell us not only about the linguistic properties (e.g. semantic and pragmatic meanings, source, functions) of a set of frequently used expressions, and the organization of social interactions and situations in which they are used, but also about the cognitive, expressive, social, and textual competence of those who use them. Because the functions of markers are so broad, any and all analyses of markers – even those focusing on only a relatively narrow aspect of their meaning or a small portion of their uses – can teach us something about their role in discourse. If interest in discourse markers continues over the next 10 years, then, perhaps we will see an even broader empirical base from which to build an integrative theory. And perhaps this base will be built not only through analyses that continue to focus on specific markers, their uses, and/ or their contexts, but also through analyses of other topics in discourse analysis that can be illuminated by incorporating discourse markers into the set of basic tools through which we (as speaker/hearers *and* linguists) understand discourse.

NOTES

1   The names given to words such as *and, oh,* and *y'know* vary: for example, pragmatic particles (Ostman 1981), discourse particles (Schourup 1985), cue phrases (Moser and Moore 1995); some labels are used by other scholars to include words not typically considered as markers (e.g. Meyerhoff's (1994) use of "pragmatic particles" to refer to the tag *eh?*). More crucial than the range of labels, however, is the variety of definitions (see review in Jucker and Ziv 1998), for this has an impact on the items included within theories and analyses of discourse markers. I discuss this issue at the end of the chapter.

2   Compare Stenstrom (1998), who argues that *cos* (the phonologically reduced *because,* transcribed in (1b) as *cause*) is not used ideationally. For a range of research on *because,*

see E. Abraham (1991); Degand (1999); Ford (1994); Schlepegrell (1991).

3 Previous discussion of lists in general (Schiffrin 1994a) and this list in particular (Schiffrin 1994b: 294–6) points out the interdependence between the use of markers in lists and other list-making devices that reveal set membership and core vs. peripheral categories (e.g. intonation, repetition, presentational sentences, syntactic parallels, ellipsis). Note, also, that since it is the set membership of the list-item that underlies my assignment of levels in the list, I have assigned a dual status to the list-items in lines (i) and (l) because they are presented in one syntactic unit.

4 Explaining the lack of *and* in the coordinate level list-item [X1c] *Y'got Atlantic City* (g) requires using analytical tools beyond the space limitations of this chapter (but see Schiffrin forthcoming).

5 The term "constraints" itself is inherited more from variationist than from interactional approaches to discourse. Although it conveys more of a cause-and-effect relationship (i.e. aspects of context influence/constrain text) than is often assumed in most qualitative discourse analyses (i.e. that context is realized/constituted through text), it is useful to retain because it allows us to conceptualize and differentiate potentially discrete features of context that may either lead to (or be reflected through) features of text, such as markers.

6 See also Matsumoto (1999), whose linguistic analysis of questions in institutional discourse suggests that *and*-prefaced questions are also used when the questioner expects a positive answer, my discussion (Schiffrin 1998) of *well* and *okay*-prefaced questions during interviews, and various analyses of *and* in different texts and contexts

(Cotter 1996a; Schiffrin forthcoming; Skories 1998; Wilson 1993).

7 Compare studies on temporal, causal, and conditional connectives in English (Schiffrin 1992), Chinese (Biq 1990), and French (Hansen 1997).

8 These analyses also show that the use of markers is sensitive to social situation (e.g. classroom, service encounters) and to cultural norms of politeness. Compare, for example, the absence of a *well*-like marker in Hebrew among Israelis (Maschler 1994), speakers whose culture is said to value direct requests, direct statements of opinion, and open disagreement (Katriel 1986). See also studies on contrastive markers (noted in Fraser 1998; also Foolen 1991), as well as Takahara (1998) on Japanese markers comparable to *anyway*.

9 For comparisons of both forms and discourse functions across languages, see Park (1998); Takahara (1998).

10 Markers have been studied by scholars interested in relevance theory (see Andersen 1998; Blakemore 1988, this volume; Rouchota 1998; Shloush 1998; Watts 1986; Ziv 1998), computational linguistics (Hirschberg and Litman 1993; Elhadad and McKeown 1990; Miller 1998; Moser and Moore 1995), applied linguistics (Chaudron and Richards 1986; Schlepegrell 1996), variation analysis (Sankoff et al. 1997; Vincent 1993; Vincent and Sankoff 1993) formal linguistics (Unger 1996), language attitudes (Dailey-O'Cain 2000 on *like*; Watts 1989 on *well*), cognitive linguistics (Bell 1998), cognitive processing (Sanders 1997) and conversation analysis (Heritage 1984, 1998; Heritage and Sorjonen 1994).

11 The inclusion of all the tokens of *and* in the data differs from both conversation-analytic studies (Heritage and Sorjonen 1994; see also Matsumoto 1999) that considered

only turn-initial uses, and analyses of *and* as a formal connective (e.g. Unger 1996) that ignore not only turns at talk, but all interactionally emergent units.

12 Although discourse *is* often defined by linguists as "language beyond the sentence," the analysis of discourse as a set of connected sentences per se has evolved to become only a relatively small part of discourse analysis. Some scholars have argued that the sentence is not necessarily the unit to which speakers orient in constructing talk-in-interaction, suggesting, instead, a variety of alternatives (e.g. intonation/idea units, see Chafe 1994, this volume) and pointing out ways in which sentences are contingent outcomes of speaker/hearer interaction (Ochs et al. 1996). This is not to suggest, however, that analyses of different coherence relations, even within one particular semantic/pragmatic domain (e.g. Fraser's 1998 analysis of contrastive markers, and references within to comparative studies of contrast), cannot teach us a great deal about the complex network of meanings indexed (and perhaps realized) through markers.

REFERENCES

Abraham, E. 1991 Why *because*? *Text* 11(3), 323–9.

Abraham, W (ed.) 1991 *Discourse Particles: Descriptive and Theoretical Investigations on the Logical, Syntactic and Pragmatic Properties of Discourse Particles in German*. Amsterdam/Philadelphia: Benjamins.

Andersen, E. 1996 A cross-cultural study of children's register knowledge. In D. Slobin, J. Gerhardt, A. Kyratzis, and J. Guo (eds), *Social Interaction, Social Context, and Language: Essays in Honor of Susan Ervin-Tripp*. Hillsdale, NJ: Lawrence Erlbaum, pp. 125–42.

Andersen, E., M. Brizuela, B. DuPuy, and L. Gonnerman 1995 The acquisition of discourse markers as sociolinguistic variables: a cross-linguistic comparison. In E. Clark (ed.), *The Proceedings of the 27th Annual Child Language Research Forum*. Stanford University: CSLI Publications, pp. 61–9.

Andersen, G. 1998 The pragmatic marker *like* from a relevance-theoretic perspective. In A. Jucker and Y. Ziv (eds), *Discourse Markers: Description and Theory*. Amsterdam/Philadelphia: Benjamins, pp. 147–70.

Ariel, M. 1998 Discourse markers and form–function correlations. In A. Jucker and Y. Ziv (eds), *Discourse Markers: Description and Theory*. Amsterdam/Philadelphia: Benjamins, pp. 223–60.

Bazzanella, C. 1990 Phatic connectives as interactional cues in contemporary spoken Italian. *Journal of Pragmatics* 13, 629–47.

Beach, W. 1993 Transitional regularities for "casual" "okay" usages. *Journal of Pragmatics* 19, 325–52.

Bell, D. 1998 Cancellative discourse markers: a core/periphery approach. *Pragmatics* 8(4), 515–42.

Biq, Y. 1990 Conversation, continuation, and connectives. *Text* 10(3), 187–208.

Blakemore, D. 1988 *So* as a constraint on relevance. In R. Kempson (ed.), *Mental Representation: The Interface between Language and Reality*. Cambridge: Cambridge University Press, pp. 183–95.

Bolinger, D. 1977 *Meaning and Form.* London: Longman.

Brinton, L. 1996 *Pragmatic Markers in English: Grammaticalization and Discourse Functions.* The Hague: Mouton de Gruyter.

Brody, J. 1989 Discourse markers in Tojolabal Mayan. *Proceedings of the Chicago Linguistics Society 25,* 2.

Bruti, S. 1999 *In fact* and *infatti*: the same, similar or different. *Pragmatics* 9(4), 519–34.

Cadiot, A., O. Ducrot, B. Fraden, and T. Nguyen 1985 *Enfin,* marqueur métalinguistique. *Journal of Pragmatics* 2(3), 199–239.

Chafe, W. 1994 *Discourse, Consciousness, and Time.* Chicago: Chicago University Press.

Chaudron, C. and J. Richards 1986 The effect of discourse markers on the comprehension of lectures. *Applied Linguistics* 7(2), 113–27.

Chodorowska-Pilch, M. 1999 On the polite use of *vamos* in Penisular Spanish. *Pragmatics* 9(3), 343–55.

Condon, S. 1986 The discourse functions of okay. *Semiotica* 60, 73–101.

Cook, J. 1990 An indexical account of the Japanese sentence-final particle *ne. Discourse Processes* 13(4), 507–39.

Cook, J. 1992 Meanings of non-referential indexes: a case study of the Japanese sentence-final particle *ne. Text* 12(4), 507–39.

Cotter, C. 1996a Engaging the reader: the changing use of connectives in newspaper discourse. In J. Arnold, R. Blake, B. Davidson, S. Schwenter, and J. Solomon (eds), *Sociolinguistic Variation: Data, Theory and Analysis.* Stanford University: CSLI Publications, pp. 263–78.

Cotter, C. 1996b Irish on the Air: Media, Discourse, and Minority-language Development. University of California, Berkeley, PhD dissertation in linguistics.

Dailey-O'Cain, J. 2000 The sociolinguistic distribution of and attitudes toward focuser *like* and quotative *like. Journal of Sociolinguistics* 4(1), 60–80.

Davidsen-Nielsen, N. 1993 *Discourse Particles in Danish.* Pre-Publications of the English Department of Odense University, Denmark, No. 69, August.

de Fina, A. 1997 An analysis of Spanish *bien* as a marker of classroom management in teacher–student interaction. *Journal of Pragmatics* 28, 337–54.

de Fina, A. 2000 *Ma, pero, pero*: discourse markers in bilingual discourse. MS, Georgetown University, Department of Italian.

Degand, L. 1999 Causal connectives or casual prepositions? Discursive constraints. *Journal of Pragmatics* 32(6), 687–707.

DuBois, B. 1989 Pseudoquotation in current English communication: *"Hey, she didn't really say it!" Language in Society* 18(3), 343–60.

Elhadad, M. and K. McKeown 1990 Generating connectives. In *Proceedings of the 13th International Conference on Computational Linguistics.* Helsinki.

Ferrera, K. 1997 Form and function of the discourse marker *anyway*: implications for discourse analysis. *Linguistics* 35(2), 343–78.

Finell, A. 1989 *Well* now and then. *Journal of Pragmatics* 13, 653–6.

Fleischman, S. 1999 Pragmatic markers in comparative perspective. Paper presented at PRAGMA 99, Tel Aviv, Israel.

Flowerdew, J. and S. Tauroza 1995 The effect of discourse markers on second language lecture comprehension. *Studies in Second Language Acquisition* 17(4), 435–58.

Fludernik, M. 1995 Middle English *po* and other narrative discourse markers, In A. Jucker (ed.), *Historical Pragmatics.*

Amsterdam/Philadelphia: Benjamins, pp. 359–92.

Foolen, A. 1991 Polyfunctionality and the semantics of adversative conjunctions. *Multilingua* 10(1/2), 79–92.

Ford, C. 1994 Dialogic aspects of talk and writing: *because* on the interactive–edited continuum. *Text* 14(4), 531–54.

Ford, C. and S. Thompson 1998 Interactional units in conversation: syntactic, intonational, and pragmatic resources for the management of turns. In E. Ochs, E. Schegloff, and S. Thompson (eds), *Interaction and Grammar*. Cambridge: Cambridge University Press, pp. 134–84.

Fraser, B. 1990 An approach to discourse markers. *Journal of Pragmatics* 14, 383–95.

Fraser, B. 1998 Contrastive discourse markers in English. In A. Jucker and Y. Ziv (eds), *Discourse Markers: Description and Theory*. Amsterdam/Philadelphia: Benjamins, pp. 301–26.

Fromkin, V. (ed.) 1973 *Speech Errors as Linguistic Evidence*. The Hague: Mouton.

Fuji, S. 2000 Incipient decategorization of *mono* and grammaticalization of speaker attitude in Japanese discourse. In G. Andersen and T. Fretheim (eds), *Pragmatic Markers and Propositional Attitude*. Amsterdam/Philadelphia: Benjamins, pp. 85–118.

Gallagher, T. and H. Craig 1987 An investigation of pragmatic connectives within preschool peer interaction. *Journal of Pragmatics* 11(1), 27–37.

Goffman, E. 1978 Response cries. *Language* 54, 787–815.

Greaseley, P. 1994 An investigation in the use of the particle *well*: commentaries on a game of snooker. *Journal of Pragmatics* 22, 477–94.

Gupta, A. 1992 The pragmatic particles of Singapore Colloquial English. *Journal of Pragmatics* 18, 31–57.

Hakulinen, A. 1998 The use of Finnish *nyt* as a discourse particle. In A. Jucker and Y. Ziv (eds), *Discourse Markers: Description and Theory*. Amsterdam/Philadelphia: Benjamins, pp. 83–97.

Hakulinen, A. and E.-L. Seppanen 1992 Finnish *kato*: from verb to particle. *Journal of Pragmatics* 18, 527–50.

Halliday, M. and R. Hasan 1976 *Cohesion in English*. London: Longman.

Hansen, M. 1997 *Alors* and *donc* in spoken French: a reanalysis. *Journal of Pragmatics* 28(2), 153–88.

Hansen, M. 1998 *The Function of Discourse Particles: A Study with Special Reference to Spoken French*. Amsterdam/Philadelphia: Benjamins.

Heisler, T. 1996 *OK*, a dynamic discourse marker in Montreal French. In J. Arnold, R. Blake, B. Davidson, S. Schwenter, and J. Solomon (eds), *Sociolinguistic Variation: Data, Theory and Analysis*. Stanford University: CSLI Publications, pp. 293–312.

Heritage, J. 1984 A change-of-state token and aspects of its sequential placement. In J. Atkinson and J. Heritage, *Structures of Social Action*. Cambridge: Cambridge University Press, pp. 299–335.

Heritage, J. 1998 *Oh*-prefaced responses to inquiry. *Language in Society* 27(3), 291–334.

Heritage, J. and M. Sorjonen 1994 Constituting and maintaining activities across sequences: *and* prefacing. *Language in Society* 23(1), 1–29.

Hirschberg, J. and D. Litman 1993 Empirical studies on the disambiguation of cue phrases. *Computational Linguistics* 19(3), 501–30.

Holker, K. 1991 Französisch: Partikelforschung. In *Lexicon der Romantistischen Linguistik*, vol. V (1). Tubingen: Niemeyer, pp. 77–88.

Holmes, J. 1986 The functions of *you know* in women's and men's speech. *Language in Society* 15, 1–22.

Hoyle, S. 1994 Children's use of discourse markers in the creation of imaginary participation frameworks. *Discourse Processes* 17(3), 447–64.

Jisa, H. 1987 Connectors in children's monologue. *Journal of Pragmatics* 11(5), 607–22.

Jucker, A. 1993 The discourse marker *well*: a relevance-theoretical account. *Journal of Pragmatics* 19, 435–52.

Jucker, A. 1997 The discourse marker *well* in the history of English. *English Language and Linguistics* 1, 1–11.

Jucker, A. and S. Smith 1998 And people just you know like "wow": discourse markers as negotiating strategies. In A. Jucker and Y. Ziv (eds), *Discourse Markers: Description and Theory*. Amsterdam/Philadelphia: Benjamins, pp. 171–202.

Jucker, A. and Y. Ziv (eds) 1998 *Discourse Markers: Description and Theory*. Amsterdam/Philadelphia: Benjamins.

Katriel, T. 1986 *Talking Straight: "Dugri" Speech in Israeli "Sabra" Culture*. Cambridge: Cambridge University Press.

Kendon, A. 1995 Gestures as illocutionary and discourse structure markers in Southern Italian conversation. *Journal of Pragmatics* 23(3), 247–79.

Knott, A. and T. Sanders 1998 The classification of coherence relations and their linguistic markers: an exploration of two languages. *Journal of Pragmatics* 20, 135–75.

Koike, D. 1996 Functions of the adverbial *ya* in Spanish narrative discourse. *Journal of Pragmatics* 25(2), 267–80.

Kroon, C. 1998 A framework for the description of Latin discourse markers. *Journal of Pragmatics* 20(2), 205–24.

Kwong, L. 1989 The Cantonese utterance particle *la*. *Papers in Pragmatics* 3(1), 39–87.

Kyratzis, A. and S. Ervin-Tripp 1999 The development of discourse markers in peer interaction. In K. Meng and S. Sromqvist (eds), *Discourse Markers in Language Acquisition* (special issue). *Journal of Pragmatics* 31, 1321–38.

Kyratzis A., J. Guo, and S. Ervin-Tripp 1990 Pragmatic conventions influencing children's use of causal constructions in natural discourse. In K. Hall, J. Koenig, M. Meacham, S. Reinman, and L. Sutton (eds), *Proceedings of the 16th Annual Meeting of the Berkeley Linguistics Society*. University of California, Berkeley, pp. 205–15.

Lakoff, R. 1973 Questionable answers and answerable questions. In B. Kachru, R. B. Lees, Y. Malkiel, A. Pietrangeli, and S. Saporta (eds), *Issues in Linguistics: Papers in Honor of Henry and Renee Kahane*. Urbana: University of Illinois Press, pp. 453–67.

Lenk, U. 1998 Discourse markers and global coherence in conversation. *Journal of Pragmatics* 30(2), 245–57.

Levinson, S. 1983 *Pragmatics*. Cambridge: Cambridge University Press.

Maschler, Y. 1994 Metalanguaging and discourse markers in bilingual conversation. *Language in Society* 23, 325–66.

Maschler, Y. 1997 Discourse markers at frame shifts in Israeli Hebrew talk-in-interaction. *Pragmatics* 7(2), 183–211.

Maschler, Y. 1998 *Rotse lishmoa keta? Wanna hear something weird/funny?* Segmenting Israeli Hebrew talk-in-interaction. In A. Jucker and Y. Ziv (eds), *Discourse Markers: Description and Theory*. Amsterdam/Philadelphia: Benjamins, pp. 13–60.

Matsumoto, K. 1999 *And*-prefaced questions in institutional discourse. *Linguistics* 37(2), 251–74.

Matsumoto, Y. 1988 From bound grammatical markers to free discourse markers: history of some Japanese connectives. In S. Axmaker, A. Jaisser, and H. Singmaster (eds), *Proceedings of the 14th Annual Meeting of the*

Berkeley Linguistics Society. University of California, Berkeley, pp. 340–51.

Meng, K. and S. Sromqvist (eds) 1999 *Discourse Markers in Language Acquisition* (special issue). *Journal of Pragmatics* 31.

Merritt, M. 1984 On the use of *okay* in service encounters. In J. Baugh and J. Sherzer (eds), *Language in Use.* Englewood Cliffs, NJ: Prentice-Hall, pp. 139–47.

Meyerhoff, M. 1994 Sounds pretty ethnic, eh?: a pragmatic particle in New Zealand English. *Language in Society* 23(3), 367–88.

Miller, J. 1998 Intonation, vowel length and *well.* MS, Georgetown University, Department of Linguistics.

Moser, M. and J. Moore 1995 Investigating cue selection and placement in tutorial discourse. In *Proceedings of the 33rd Annual Meeting of the Association for Computational Linguistics*, pp. 130–5.

Norrick, N. (forthcoming) Discourse markers in oral narrative. *Journal of Pragmatics.*

Ochs, E., E. Schegloff, and S. Thompson 1996 *Interaction and Grammar.* Cambridge: Cambridge University Press.

Onodera, N. 1992 Pragmatic Change in Japanese: Conjunctions and Interjections as Discourse Markers. Georgetown University PhD dissertation in linguistics.

Onodera, N. 1995 Diachronic analysis of Japanese discourse markers. In A. Jucker (ed.), *Historical Pragmatics,* Amsterdam/Philadelphia: Benjamins, pp. 393–437.

Or, W. 1997 Chinese temporal adverbs of succession and overlap. Paper presented at the Annual Convention of the Midwest Modern Language Association, Chicago.

Ostman, J. 1981 *You Know: A Discourse Functional Approach.* Amsterdam/ Philadelphia: Benjamins.

Park, Y. 1998 The Korean connective *nuntey* in conversational discourse. *Journal of Pragmatics* 31(2), 191–218.

Peterson, C. and A. McCabe 1991 Linking children's connective use and narrative macrostructure. In A. McCabe and C. Peterson (eds), *Developing Narrrative Structure.* Hillsdale, NJ: Lawrence Erlbaum, pp. 29–54.

Posner, R. 1980 Semantics and pragmatics of sentence connectives in natural language. In F. Kiefer and J. Searle (eds), *Pragmatics and Speech Act Theory.* Dordrecht: D. Reidel, pp. 87–122.

Rouchota, V. 1998 Procedural meaning and parenthetical discourse markers. In A. Jucker and Y. Ziv (eds), *Discourse Markers: Description and Theory.* Amsterdam/Philadelphia: Benjamins, pp. 97–126.

Sanders, T. 1997 Semantic and pragmatic sources of coherence. *Discourse Processes* 24, 119–47.

Sankoff, G., P. Thibault, N. Nagy, H. Blondeau, M. Fonollosa, and L. Gagnon 1997 Variation in the use of discourse markers in a language contact situation. *Language Variation and Change* 9, 191–217.

Schegloff, E. 1981 Discourse as an interactional achievement: some uses of *uh huh* and other things that come between sentences. In D. Tannen (ed.), *Analyzing Discourse: Text and Talk.* Washington, DC: Georgetown University Press, pp. 71–93.

Schiffrin, D. 1985 Multiple constraints on discourse options: a quantitative analysis of causal sequences. *Discourse Processes* 8(3), 28–303.

Schiffrin, D. 1986 The functions of *and* in discourse. *Journal of Pragmatics.* 10(1), 41–66.

Schiffrin, D. 1987a *Discourse Markers.* Cambridge: Cambridge University Press.

Schiffrin, D. 1987b Discovering the context of an utterance. *Linguistics* 25(1), 11–32.

Schiffrin, D. 1992 Anaphoric *then*: aspectual, textual and epistemic meaning. *Linguistics* 30(4), 753–92.

Schiffrin, D. 1994a Making a list. *Discourse processes* 17(3), 377–405.

Schiffrin, D. 1994b *Approaches to Discourse.* Oxford: Blackwell.

Schiffrin, D. 1997 Theory and method in discourse analysis: what context for what unit? *Language and Communication* 17(2), 75–92.

Schiffrin, D. 1998 Stories in answer to questions in research interviews. *Journal of Narrative and Life History* 7(1–4), 129–37.

Schiffrin, D. (forthcoming) Conceptual, structural and interactional constraints on *and*. In D. Schiffrin, *Language, Text, and Interaction.* Cambridge: Cambridge University Press.

Schlepegrell, M. 1991 Paratactic *because*. *Journal of Pragmatics* 16, 323–37.

Schlepegrell, M. 1996 Conjunction in spoken English and ESL writing. *Applied Linguistics* 17(3), 272–85.

Schourup, L. 1985 *Common Discourse Particles in English Conversation: Like, Well, Y'know.* New York: Garland.

Schwenter, S. 1996 Some reflections on *o sea*: a discourse marker in Spanish. *Journal of Pragmatics* 25, 855–74.

Sebba, M. and S. Tate 1986 *Y'know what I mean?* Agreement marking in British Black English. *Journal of Pragmatics* 10(2), 163–72.

Segal, E., J. Duchan, and P. Scott 1991 The role of interclausal connectives in narrative structuring. *Discourse Processes* 14(1), 27–54.

Shloush, S. 1998 A unified account of Hebrew bekicur "in short": relevance theory and discourse structure considerations. In A. Jucker and Y. Ziv (eds), *Discourse Markers: Description and Theory.* Amsterdam/Philadelphia: Benjamins, pp. 61–83.

Silva, G. and A. de Macedo 1992 Discourse markers in the spoken Portuguese of Rio de Janeiro. *Language Variation and Change* 4, 235–49.

Skories, U. 1998 Features of a blame type using *and*. *Journal of Pragmatics* 30(1), 49–58.

Sprott, R. 1992 Children's use of discourse markers in disputes. *Discourse Processes* 15(4), 423–40.

Sprott, R. 1994 The Development of Discourse and the Acquisition of Connectives and Clause Combinations. University of California, Berkeley, PhD dissertation in psychology.

Stein, D. 1985 Discourse markers in early modern English. In R. Eaton, O. Fischer, and W. Koopman (eds), *Papers from the 4th International Conference on English Historical Linguistics.* Amsterdam/Philadelphia: Benjamins, pp. 283–302.

Stenstrom, A. 1998 From sentence to discourse: *cos* (*because*) in teenage talk. In A. Jucker and Y. Ziv (eds), *Discourse Markers: Description and Theory.* Amsterdam/Philadelphia: Benjamins, pp. 127–46.

Svartik, J. 1980 *Well* in conversation. In S. Greenbaum, G. Leech, and J. Svartvik (eds), *Studies in English Linguistics for Randolph Quirk.* London: Longman, pp. 167–77.

Sweetser, E. 1990 *From Etymology to Pragmatics.* Cambridge: Cambridge University Press.

Swerts, M. 1998 Filled pauses as markers of discourse structure. *Journal of Pragmatics* 30, 486–96.

Taavitsainen, I. 1994 Interjections in early modern English. In A. Jucker (ed.), *Historical Pragmatics.* Amsterdam/Philadelphia: Benjamins, pp. 439–65.

Takahara, P. 1998 Pragmatic functions of the English discourse marker *anyway* and its corresponding contrastive Japanese discourse markers. In A. Jucker and Y. Ziv (eds), *Discourse Markers: Descriptions and Theory*. Amsterdam/Philadelphia: Benjamins, pp. 327–51.

Traugott, E. 1995 The role of the development of discourse markers in a theory of grammaticalization. Paper presented at the 12th International Conference on Historical Linguistics, Manchester.

Travis, C. 1998 *Bueno*: a Spanish interactive discourse marker. In B. K. Bergen, M. C. Plauché, and A. C. Baily (eds), *Proceedings of the 24th Annual Meeting of the Berkeley, Linguistics Society, February 14–16*. University of California, Berkeley, pp. 268–79.

Tsui, A. 1991 The pragmatic functions of *I don't know*. *Text* 11(4), 607–22.

Tyler, A., A. Jefferies, and C. Davies 1988 The effect of discourse structuring devices on listener perceptions of coherence in nonnative university teachers' spoken discourse. *World Englishes* 7, 101–10.

Unger, C. 1996 The scope of discourse connectives: implications for discourse organization. *Journal of Linguistics* 32(2), 403–48.

Vasko, I. 2000 The interplay of Hungarian *de* (but) and *is* (too, either). In G. Andersen and T. Fretheim (eds), *Pragmatic Markers and Propositional Attitude*. Amsterdam/Philadelphia: Benjamins, pp. 255–64.

Vincent, D. 1993 *Les ponctuants de la langue et autres mots du discours*. Quebec: Nuit blanche.

Vincent, D. and D. Sankoff 1993 Punctors: a pragmatic variable. *Language Variation and Change* 4, 205–16.

Warvik, G. 1995. The ambiguous adverbial/conjunctions *Oa* and *oonne* in Middle English. In A. Jucker (ed.), *Historical Pragmatics*. Amsterdam/Philadelphia: Benjamins, pp. 345–57.

Watts, R. 1986 Relevance in conversational moves: a reappraisal of *well*. *Studia Anglica Posnaniensa* 19, 34–59.

Watts, R. 1989 Taking the pitcher to the "well": native speakers' perception of their use of discourse markers in conversation. *Journal of Pragmatics* 13, 203–37.

Wilson, J. 1993 Discourse marking and accounts of violence in Northern Ireland. *Text* 13(3), 455–75.

Wouk, F. 1998 Solidarity in Indonesian conversation: the discourse marker *kan*. *Multilingua* 17(4), 379–406.

Yngve, V. 1970 On getting a word in edgewise. In M. Campbell et al. (eds), *Papers from the Sixth Regional Meeting, Chicago Linguistic Society*. Chicago: Department of Linguistics, University of Chicago, pp. 567–78.

Zavala, V. (in press) Borrowing evidential functions from Quechua: the role of *pues* as a discourse marker in Andean Spanish. *Journal of Pragmatics*.

Ziv, Y. 1998 Hebrew *kaze* as discourse marker and lexical hedge: conceptual and procedural properties. In A. Jucker and Y. Ziv (eds), *Discourse Markers: Descriptions and Theory*. Amsterdam/Philadelphia: Benjamins, pp. 203–22.

4   Discourse and Semantics

NEAL R. NORRICK

0   Introduction

Semantics as a distinct field was first proposed by Bréal in 1883. He suggested the term "sémantique" for the study of "the laws which govern the transformation of sense, the choice of new expressions, the birth and death of locutions." The translation of Bréal's *Essai de sémantique* as *Semantics: Studies in the Science of Meaning* popularized the term in English. For the next fifty years, the field of semantics concerned itself with historical research on word meaning. Stern's (1931) *Meaning and the Change of Meaning* provides a worthy synthesis of this first phase of research in semantics.

Saussure inaugurated the study of word meaning as a linguistic sign process. Saussure's dyadic model of the sign postulated a psychological correspondence between the arbitrary but conventionalized form and meaning of the word. His *Cours de linguistique générale*, published posthumously in 1916, championed a new synchronic view of linguistic description alongside the traditional diachronic approach. Moreover, Saussure privileged study of the language system (langue) over study of language performance (parole), which relegated context and discourse to the status of outsiders in linguistic description.

Under the influence of Saussure's *Cours*, Trier produced in 1931 the first truly synchronic semantic investigation. His analysis of so-called semantic fields introduced an area of research still alive today. About the same time, Bloomfield (1933) popularized the behaviorist view of linguistic semantics. For Bloomfield, the definition of meaning explicitly included "the situation in which a speaker utters [an expression] and the response it calls forth in a hearer" (1933: 139). Though they eschew terms like "concept" and "feeling," behaviorists clearly see utterance function in context as central to meaning. Yet paradoxically the effect of behaviorism, particularly on American linguistics, was to narrow its focus to structural relations between lexical items, leaving the description of discourse meaning to neighboring disciplines such as rhetoric, stylistics, and poetics. Structural and generative treatments of language took the word and the sentence as the province of semantic theory. The meaning of the sentence was seen as the product of the meanings of its component lexical items and their structural relations, according to the so-called Principle of Compositionality. The role of the sentence in larger units received scant attention, as did figurative meaning and idiomaticity, which ran foul of this principle (but see Katz 1964; Chafe 1968).

In their influential monograph *The Meaning of Meaning* (1923), Ogden and Richards drew a fundamental distinction between symbolic and emotive meaning. Their symbolic meaning corresponds to what other authors call ideational, descriptive, propositional, or referential meaning, while their emotional meaning corresponds to interpersonal, expressive, nonpropositional, affective, and stylistic aspects of meaning. The assumption was that ideational meaning could be studied as a part of competence independent of context, while interpersonal meaning was a performance (or discourse) phenomenon unsuitable for systematic investigation.

In a very different vein, around this same time, Sapir (1921, 1929, 1949) and Whorf (1956) were raising questions about the relationship between language, meaning, culture, and personality which remain central concerns of semantic theory. The degree to which our language determines our perception, often discussed under the heading of the "Sapir–Whorf Hypothesis," has become an issue again especially in the cognitive semantics of G. Lakoff and his associates (G. Lakoff 1987; G. Lakoff and Johnson 1980; G. Lakoff and Turner 1989; Kövecses 1986). This research direction has revitalized the synchronic study of metaphor as well. Metaphor was already a staple concern of traditional diachronic semantics due to its concern with figurative meaning extensions as a factor in meaning change. The study of metaphor also received fresh input from semantic feature theory in the 1960s, a development to which we now turn.

With roots both in anthropological linguistics and in the phonological feature theory developed by Trubetzkoy (1939) and the Prague School, semantic feature theory (also called componential analysis, markerese, and lexical decomposition) was integrated into the so-called Standard Theory of generative transformational grammar by Katz and Fodor (1963) and Katz and Postal (1964). Katz (1966, 1972) continued to develop feature theory to describe such semantic notions as meaningfulness, anomaly, contradiction, tautology, synonymy, antonymy, paraphrase, and so on. The extension of componential analysis in the direction of logical notation, especially by McCawley (1968a, 1968b, 1968c, 1970) and G. Lakoff (1970, 1971), was a major tenet of the Generative Semantics movement. Proposals for the representation of sentence meanings in predicate logical notation, particularly in the intensional logic developed by Montague (1968, 1970, 1974), have continued to flourish as an area of semantic theory. Montague's position, deriving from formal logic, equates meaning with truth conditions in a model or a possible world. This research follows traditional practice in associating truth-functionality with ideational sentence meaning and competence, leaving interpersonal meaning as a nontruth-functional performance (read: discourse) phenomenon.

By contrast with most other work in semantics, the functional-systemic linguistics of Halliday (1967, 1977, 1978) recognizes not only ideational and interpersonal meaning, but also textual meaning. It associates various sorts of meaning with choices made all along the way in the production of a sentence in a text. This sort of analysis reflects the proposals Firth made about semantic analysis as early as 1935 (see Firth 1957). Thus, systemic linguistics has operated with the goal of describing discourse meaning all along.

In the following paragraphs, we will see how the notion of meaning has increasingly become bound to discourse contexts, since the early 1970s or so. Discourse context has been evoked ever more frequently to handle phenomena not describable in terms of truth-functional and structural semantics. Speaker intentions and audience responses found their way back into semantic theory via pragmatics and speech act theory. Research on talk in real contexts showed the necessity for considering the interactional goals and relationship of conversational participants in the description of meaning. The gradual inclusion of context began to erode the traditional dichotomy between competence and performance, and as it did, interpersonal elements of meaning returned to prominence in semantic analysis.

The rest of this chapter is organized as follows. First I will sketch some of the salient research which led to an incremental evolution in our view of semantics to include discourse phenomena. Then I will look in turn at indexicality and anaphora, presupposition, speech acts, entailment, and interpersonal, especially figurative, meaning, showing how they have developed in recent linguistic theory, and how our understanding of them has shifted toward discourse and away from structural and truth-functional semantics. This shift has two outcomes: first, a reanalysis and fuller understanding of these narrowly conceived topics; and second, an influx of new data and interesting topics, which has widened and deepened our understanding of linguistic semantics.

Certain topics arise only within a discourse study of meaning, for instance cohesion, coherence, register, framing (all of which have their own separate chapters in this *Handbook*), and the interpersonal meaning of such devices as repetition, parallelism, allusion, and formulaicity. I will review salient contributions to the understanding of these phenomena in real discourse from recent years, with the goal of developing a "poetics of talk" (Tannen 1989). Finally, I would like to show how a discourse-based analysis can shed new light on a traditional staple of semantics, namely figurative meaning. Figurative meaning was a concern of semantic theory from the beginning, since figurative extensions of word meaning were characteristic of historical language change. Research on metaphor, hyperbole, tautology, and paradox persisted in semantic theory, because they interfere with the truth-functional analysis of sentence meaning according to the Principle of Compositionality (Katz 1964; Weinreich 1966; Levin 1977). Most recent attention to figurative meaning grows out of work in the pragmatics of (Gricean) implicature or cognitive linguistics following G. Lakoff (1987) rather than focusing on real discourse. By contrast, I will attempt to show how analysis of figures in concrete discourse contexts can contribute to our understanding of figurative language. In particular, I focus on passages where participants themselves comment metalingually (Jakobson 1960) on the meaning of the figures.

1   The Shifting Paradigm

Various strands of research in philosophy and linguistics combined to extend the structural paradigm in semantics. In this old model, words had meaning due to their relations within the vocabulary of a language. Each word contributed its discrete meaning to a syntactic unit, the meaning of which was then computable from the component word meanings and their structural relations. This model gradually came to be considered a starting point for semantic analysis at best and a counterproductive fallacy at worst, as discourse increasingly came to serve as a site for the study not only of utterance meaning but even of word meaning. Austin's (1962) "performative analysis" showed that we use language to "do things with words" and not just to make true or false statements, which naturally entailed contextual correlates. Grice (1957, 1975) championed a theory of meaning grounded in speaker intentions, and he went on to show how context influences the meanings even of logical connectors. Moreover, Grice's notion of implicature gave linguists a way of developing inferential models of meaning, as witness for instance Gazdar (1979), Bach and Harnish (1979), Horn (1984), and Sperber and Wilson (1986).

Early on, G. Lakoff (1969) showed that deductions from contextual information and beliefs underlay judgments of grammaticality for many sentences (also Gordon and Lakoff 1975). Linguists began to feel the need for models of inference to determine grammaticality as well as meaning. Fillmore's interest in describing discoursal effects led him to propose frame theory as an approach to semantics (Fillmore 1976, 1985). Similarly, Labov's work on natural discourse, in particular oral narratives, led him to propose an analysis of affective meaning, which he termed "intensity" (Labov 1984). In response to truth-functional accounts of meaning, Harman (1977), Katz (1977), and others argued that linguistic meaning makes possible and explicates truth, not conversely. Finally, Reddy's (1969) recognition of the so-called "conduit metaphor" of communication exposed critical flaws in our traditional "message model" of linguistic interaction.

At the same time, Sacks (1992) and other sociologists were showing that everyday conversation was not only regular and describable, but contained mechanisms for clarifying and correcting factual content and linguistic form (in metalingual talk à la Jakobson 1960). This work reinforced the view of the audience as co-author (Duranti 1986; Goodwin 1986; Schegloff 1987) and meaning as subject to a process of negotiation in interaction. Meaning appeared to be negotiable even down to the level of the word (Lehrer 1983; Ochs 1984). Schegloff cited passages from natural conversation showing that the presumed lexical meaning of a word or the literal meaning of a sentence is often subordinate to – or even irrelevant compared with – the particular slot they occupy in interaction, the expectations participants have about the slot, and the response they elicit.

Halliday (1967, 1977, 1978) had long proposed – following Malinowski (1923, 1935) and Firth (1957) – that semantic theory recognizes interpersonal and textual aspects of meaning alongside ideational (or truth-functional) meaning. Further, Nunberg (1978) argued that polysemy and vagueness from any source require the same sort of inference-based processing, by which the recipient of an utterance seeks to reconstruct the speaker's goals, beliefs, and intentions. In this same vein, many linguists have sought to identify discourse strategies for determining contextual meaning rather than go on attempting to describe alleged discourse-independent meanings for sentence types, sentences, constructions, or even words. Moreover, as Stalnaker (1972, 1978), Cole (1978), and Green and Morgan (1981) argued, the presence of pragmatic principles in an integrated theory of linguistic descriptions clarifies the functions assigned to semantics and syntax. Hence, attempts to treat semantics and pragmatics in a single way, as Montague (1968) proposes, will necessarily miss important distinctions like that between referential and attributive uses of descriptions (Stalnaker 1972). After all, Grice (1975) proposed so-called implicatures as a way of keeping logical analysis clean and simple.

Some basic notions of semantic theory have been recognized to be discourse (or pragmatic) phenomena from their very introduction into considerations of linguistic meaning. Thus Bar-Hillel (1954) drew attention to indexicality (or deixis) and anaphora as aspects of meaning requiring inferences about speaker beliefs and intended referents, beyond truth-functional semantics proper. In fact, even traditional grammarians such as Christophersen (1939) and Jespersen (1924) had recognized the fundamental discourse orientation of pronouns. The notion of presupposition (versus assertion) entered into the discussion of linguistic semantics from philosophy (Frege 1892; Russell 1905; and especially Strawson 1950), as did the recognition of performative utterances with nontruth-functional meaning (Austin 1962; Searle 1969, 1979). Other notions like entailment are less clearly demarcated into semantic versus discourse areas. By contrast, lexical semantics (word meaning) has since Saussure (1916) been assigned to purely structural relations within the vocabulary as a more-or-less closed system. Semantic relations like synonymy, hyponymy, and antonymy were in principle described without recourse to discourse contexts. In every case, we can note a general trend toward discourse approaches in recent years. Increasingly, these topics have acquired discourse dimensions beyond whatever may be said of them from a structural or truth-functional point of view (Nunberg 1978; Lehrer 1983; Green 1996).

2   Indexicality and Anaphora

Indexicality or deixis is the only area of meaning universally acknowledged to belong in the area of discourse or pragmatics, since it pertains to the contextual determination of reference which necessarily precedes a decision as to the truth of falsity of an assertion. Bar-Hillel (1954) estimates that over 90 percent of our declarative sentences are indexical in requiring implicit reference to the speaker, the addressee, the time and place of utterance with pronouns like *I* and *you*, adverbs like *now* and *yesterday*, *here* and *there*, *right* and *left*, and demonstratives like *this* and *that*. The meanings of such lexical items are simply not describable without noting that their reference shifts each time the setting changes, each time a new speaker takes over or points in a different direction. This sort of meaning is irrevocably bound to context, and it represents a historical foothold for discourse analysis within semantic theory.

Of course, we must also find referents for third person pronouns like *she* and *them* within the local context or within the foregoing discourse, though they do not necessarily shift with a change of speaker as true indexicals do. Those pronouns used to point to people and things in the immediate context are being used indexically/ deictically, while those assigned to referents based on "coreference" with a noun phrase in the preceding discourse are called anaphoric. Often a single pronoun will have both indexical and anaphoric possibilities: thus in sentence (1) below, *she* and *him* can be interpreted as coreferential with *Sue* and *Al* respectively, or they may refer to other people indicated or otherwise prominent in the context of utterance:

(1)   Sue told Al she wished him luck.

Research on anaphora in generative linguistics offers a good example of the progressive inclusion of discourse considerations into an area of semantics. Transformational grammarians began with the question of coreference (e.g. Lees and Klima 1963; Langacker 1969); the interpretation of pronouns as bound variables was not discovered until later, and the question of how reference was established for deictic pronouns or for "referring expressions" generally was not considered. As research in the syntactic treatment of anaphora progressed, however, binding of anaphora through so-called c-command by a preceding or hierarchically dominating noun phrase took center stage (Langacker 1969; Chomsky 1973, 1981). In sentence (1) above *he* and *she* are c-commanded by the noun phrases *Sue* and *Al*, so they may be interpreted as bound by them.

Some scholars in the "interpretive semantics" camp among generative linguists, notably Jackendoff (1972), insisted that anaphora was a semantic phenomenon to be handled with devices such as coreference tables, identifying NPs and representing their relations. This same basic notion appears in Chastain's (1975) description of "anaphoric chains," which hold not just within sentences but between the sentences of a discourse; see also Donnellan (1978) in this regard. Really, the discourse basis of pronoun interpretation goes all the way back to traditional grammarians such as Christophersen (1939) and Jespersen (1924), who espoused what has been labeled the "familiarity theory of definiteness" (Hawkins 1978; Heim 1983), namely:

> A definite (description, name, pronoun) is used to refer to something that is already *familiar* at the current stage of conversation.
>   An indefinite (description) is used to introduce a *new* referent.

Karttunen (1976) sought to alleviate problems associated with this theory, by requiring that a definite must pick out an already familiar "discourse referent," while an indefinite introduces a new discourse referent. Heim (1983) expands on Karttunen's work and imbues the notion of "discourse referent" with substance in her "file change semantics." Kamp (1981) also looks to discourse for a unified treatment of deictic and anaphoric pronouns, proposing "discourse representation structures" similar to the "file cards" in Heim's approach: treating all anaphora as discourse anaphora solves problems associated with treating pronouns as bound variables in truth-functional semantic theories.

At the fringes of this shift in perspective, some linguists had been working on anaphora as a discourse problem all along. As early as 1967, Halliday was developing a treatment of anaphora in connected discourse built around his analysis of cohesion and text-semantic categories, namely *transitivity* (Actor, Process, Goal), *mood* (Subject, Predicate, Complement), and *theme* (Theme, Rheme). Chafe (1970, 1974, 1993) proposed a discourse-based interpretation of anaphora in terms of the given–new distinction as reflected in the presence of referents in consciousness. Givón (1973, 1982, 1985) argued for a pragmatic description of reference which would take discourse topicality and accessibility as well as cultural knowledge into account. Ariel (1988, 1990, 1991, 1994) works with a related notion of Accessibility in consciousness to account for anaphora in discourse. In order to develop pragmatic accounts of anaphora,

Prince (1981), Clark and his associates (Clark and Marshall 1981; Clark and Murphy 1982; Clark and Wilkes-Gibbes 1990), and Levinson (1987a, 1987b, 1991) all proposed hierarchies of referential expressions, where choice was determined by the Gricean Maxim of Quantity and related factors.

It slowly became clear that the determination of coreference was a discourse matter (Nunberg 1978; Reinhart 1983, 1986), and scholars of anaphora came to see syntactic binding within the sentence as *preventing* assignment of coreference within the discourse context (Lasnik 1976, 1981). Current theories of anaphora cover only bound variables within the (syntactic) binding theory; pronouns can act as bound variables only where they are syntactically bound (c-commanded), according to Reinhart (1983) and Reinhard and Reuland (1993). Otherwise, coreference is not established by syntactic binding; coreferencing is "just a subcase of the broader process of reference resolution" (Grodzinsky and Reinhart 1993: 77), which is a discourse-based process.

Tellingly, even the most "syntactic" of anaphoric relations, namely reflexivity, has been split into syntactic and discourse cases. As early as 1970 Ross noted that *myself* and *yourself* can occur without a sentential antecedent, thus requiring long-distance, that is discourse, interpretation; see also Kuno (1972, 1987) with examples from Japanese; Cantrall (1974) with examples from Ewe; and, for a summary, Zribi-Hertz (1989). Since then, long-distance reflexives, or *logophors*, have been described in several other languages, e.g. Icelandic (Mailing 1982), Italian (Giorgi 1983), and Norwegian (Hellan 1988). Accordingly, in sentence (2), the reflexive *herself* can be interpreted either as locally bound by and hence coreferential with *Sheila* or as logophorically coreferential with *Judy*:

(2)   Judy wishes she had been able to instill in Sheila respect for herself.

Zribi-Hertz (1989: 703, 724) argues that "a grammatical theory of English reflexive pronouns cannot be complete without a discourse component," and moreover that "structural constraints such as the binding conditions might actually draw their motivation from discourse." Reinhart and Reuland (1993) have demonstrated that discourse reflexives must be distinguished as either point-of-view logophors, following Clements (1975) and Sells (1987), like that in example (2) above, or emphatic logophors for focus, following Kuno (1987), Zribi-Hertz (1989), and others, like that in example (3):

(3)   The Joneses seem always to try and keep up with myself.

Thus the treatment of reflexivization in particular and of anaphora more generally illustrates the gradual shift from a syntactic to a discourse perspective on what was traditionally considered a semantic area of study.

3   Presupposition

Presupposition is also at heart a discourse or pragmatic notion, since the knowledge and beliefs of the speaker and the audience about things in the world are crucial in determining whether a sentence like the classic (4) makes sense:

(4)   The present king of France is bald.

For Russell (1905) and his followers (Sellars 1954; perhaps Donellan 1981) this sentence *entails* the existence of a particular individual, namely someone fitting the definite description "the present king of France." Hence the sentence counts as false in terms of truth-functional semantics – or perhaps simply false in any "possible world" in which there exists no king of France. By contrast, for Strawson and his (much more numerous) followers, existence does not count as a predicate at all. The existence of a present king of France amounts instead to a presupposition of sentence (4). In the absence of such a royal individual, the sentence simply fails to make any truth claim at all. For Strawson (1950) and his followers, the negation test for presuppositions is central: the presupposition that there is some current king of France adheres not only to sentence (4), but also to its negation (5):

(5)   The present king of France is not bald.

Strawson later (1964) expressed concerns about some apparent counterexamples to his presupposition theory, saying that our intuitions about the truth or falsity of sentences containing definite descriptions may depend on discourse matters such as the topic of conversation. Thus in a discussion about the potential audience for this text, if I said the present king of France would be among its readers, I think most real readers would be prepared to call my claim flat out false rather than to say it lacked a truth value; see Donnellan (1981). Still, the notion of presupposition received into linguistics was that of Strawson's original objection to Russell's theory of definite descriptions (Russell 1910).

Early linguistic treatments of presupposition saw it as a semantic property of sentences (Katz 1977) and even of particular lexical items (McCawley 1968a, 1975; Kiparsky and Kiparsky 1970; Fillmore 1971a, 1971b). Thus, the verbs *murder* and *kill* both assert that the object ends up dead, but *murder* presupposes the act was intentional on the part of the subject; similarly, *assassinate* presupposes over and above *murder* that its object held political office. Also the (a) sentences in (6) and (7) might be said to presuppose the (b) sentences by virtue of the presence of the so-called factive predicates *regret* and *know*, whereas no such presuppositions are found for the otherwise parallel (c) sentences:

(6)   a.   Judy regrets that she borrowed Roger's car.
      b.   Judy borrowed Roger's car.
      c.   Judy imagined that she borrowed Roger's car.

(7)   a.   Roger knows that Judy borrowed his car.
      b.   Judy borrowed Roger's car.
      c.   Roger believes that Judy borrowed his car.

Fillmore (1971b) makes presuppositions part of the lexical entries for predicates: a "verb of judging" like *blame* is characterized as presupposing that the activity for which culpability is assigned is "bad," and even as presupposing selection restrictions such as that the normal subject is human; see also McCawley (1975) on "verbs of bitching" and their presuppositions.

But the semantic notion of presupposition held by Katz and Langendoen (1976), Fodor (1979), and Martin (1979) came under increasing attack by such scholars as Karttunen (1973), Kempson (1975), and Wilson (1975). Gazdar (1979) argued that no coherent semantic definition of presupposition was possible, and that we must replace it with a pragmatic account along the lines of Keenan (1971), Stalnaker (1972, 1973, 1974), Karttunen (1973), and Karttunen and Peters (1979), who cast their definitions in terms of appropriateness, assumptions and dispositions of speakers, and reasonable inferences by their audiences. Notice in this regard particularly the reflexive assumptions in Stalnaker's (1974) definition of pragmatic presupposition:

> A proposition B is a **pragmatic presupposition** of a speaker **in** a given context just in case the speaker assumes or believes that B, assumes that his audience assumes or believes B, and assumes or believes that his audience recognizes that he is making these assumptions.

In this same spirit, most recent research tends to define presupposition in terms of reflective assumptions about knowledge shared by speakers and hearers (see e.g. Green 1989).

Many entailments or inferences first analyzed as presuppositions in the original philosophical semantic sense have come to be treated as implicata of various kinds (see Stalnaker 1973, 1978; Horn 1988), though Grice himself (1981) expresses doubts about analyzing the presuppositions of definite descriptions this way. But just how propositions end up as assumptions shared between speakers and their hearers – whether through presupposition or through implicature – is of less importance here than the fact that this whole area of meaning has come increasingly under the umbrella of discourse rather than truth-functional semantics.

4   Speech Acts

Since Austin (1962) described performative utterances as apparent declarative sentences with no truth-functional meaning as such, but instead with some illocutionary act potential, semantic theory has recognized for performatives a special discourse-based type of meaning. Searle's (1969, 1979) development of speech act theory enriched semantic theory in several parallel ways: he provided a functional classification of utterance types and interesting approaches to locutionary, illocutionary, and perlocutionary meaning. Speech act theory also offers a description of conditions for the successful performance of the different illocutionary acts, their so-called "felicity conditions." Finally, it proposes a model for deriving indirect meanings for utterances from their literal readings according to regular inferences, based on these felicity conditions.

Linguists reacted to speech act theory in several ways. Interest in the performative hypothesis by linguists led Ross (1970) and others (Cantrall 1974; Sadock 1974) to represent the pragmatic or discourse force of declarative sentences in (semantic) deep structure as a matrix sentence with the form *I tell you that* . . . , which spawned more work on contexts. Levinson (1983: 246–83) provides a history of the rise and fall of the performative hypothesis.

Generative semantics in effect tried to build discourse contexts into its deep syntactic analysis and trans-derivational constraints, for instance G. Lakoff (1970, 1971). Gordon and Lakoff (1975) argued that syntax requires a characterization of entailments in standardized contexts, and they proposed so-called "conversational postulates" to describe such entailments. Even though Green (1975), Morgan (1977), and others rejected conversational postulates on grounds that they were derivable from more general principles of inference, Gordon and Lakoff's proposal generated increased interest in contexts and ways to describe them.

In opposition to speech act theory, conversation analysis seeks to show that placement in the sequential organization of talk determines the force of an utterance. Even if one works from direct to indirect illocutionary force, placement will overrule both in concrete conversational contexts. Schegloff (1984, 1988) shows that apparent questions characteristically act as "pre-announcements." Thus, conversationalists tend to hear utterances like "Do you know who's going to that meeting?" as herolding an announcement. Only secondarily do they interpret such utterances as requests for an answer to the question of "Who's going." Moreover, the literal question about the hearer's knowledge seems to play no role at all. Speech act theory cannot develop a correct description of pre-sequences without taking sequentiality into account, and consequently does not offer a plausible model of conversational meaning, according to Schegloff. See Levinson (1983: 345–64) on the significance of pre-sequences generally.

Meanwhile, other semanticists were developing inferential approaches to meaning. Fodor (1975) argued for an inferential semantic theory versus the componential analysis of Katz (1972), while Bach and Harnish (1979) and Gazdar (1979) championed inferential models of meaning incorporating speech act theory and Gricean pragmatics. These attempts went along with an increasing awareness that the so-called "null context" posited by Katz and others in interpretive semantics was itself a special context or at least an invitation to image some context appropriate to the sentence in question.

5   Entailment

Areas of meaning like entailment divide less obviously into truth-functional semantic versus discourse areas. That *uncle* entails some feature like <male> and that *dead* entails <not alive> may be easily described within traditional structural semantics by means of so-called redundancy rules. Thus, sentence pairs like those in (8) and (9) can be recognized as logically sound within semantics alone:

(8)   a.   Sue's uncle arrived late.
      b.   Therefore, some male arrived late.

(9)   a.   Judy has been dead for years.
      b.   Judy is no longer alive.

Other entailments, however – say, that *rob* entails <commit crime> and <punishable by prison term> – become quite cumbersome in any structural semantics. Such entailments involve world knowledge over and above lexical information proper. Consequently, the characterization of the inferences from the (a) to the (b) sentences in the pairs below must be accomplished through some version of frame/script/ schema theory or the like:

(10)   a.   Harry robbed a bank.
      b.   Hence Harry committed a crime.

(11)   a.   Harry finally got out of prison last week.
      b.   That's because he robbed a bank in 1980.

6   Interpersonal Meaning

The interpersonal meanings of repetition, parallelism, allusion, and formulaicity must also count as discourse phenomena, because they can only manifest themselves within some concrete context. Historically such effects have been considered in part under the rubrics of *poetics* or even *prosody*. Jakobson (1960) placed the poetic focus of language – language directed at the message itself – on a par with the other five foci, namely the referential, the expressive, the conative (directive), the phatic, and the metalingual. Even the sociolinguist Sacks (1992) found repeated occasion to comment on the poetics of natural conversation, particularly the synonym, antonym, and punning relations between words close to each other in conversation. Tannen's (1989) *Talking Voices* concerns itself centrally with the poetics of everyday talk through the notion of *involvement*, which collects such features of talk as dialogue, detail, repetition, and formulaicity; and Tannen pioneered the study of conversational poetics in showing how such features as tempo, repetition, parallelism, and simultaneous speech go into determining "conversational style" (1984).

But phenomena associated with affect or stylistic meaning have also received attention under the umbrella of interpersonal meaning, especially in the British school following Firth (1957) and Halliday (1967, 1977, 1978). For Gumperz (1982a, 1982b) and Tannen (1984) this sort of meaning is also collected under the headings of interactional cues and involvement: it affects the alignment of conversational participants and their interpersonal relationships. R. Lakoff (1973, 1977) is responsible for drawing attention to the importance of politeness, power, and solidarity in everyday talk; and work by Brown and Levinson (1978) and Tannen (1986) has made politeness theory a major approach to inferencing in discourse.

In this general area of interpersonal meaning, we find linguists beginning to look at such phenomena as formulaicity (Tannen 1987a, 1989), for example the use of proverbs to wrap up stories (Norrick 1985; Sacks 1992) and the use of allusion and parody in jokes and joking (Norrick 1989b, 1993). Concern with the functions of repetition illustrates the growing concern with language in real discourse contexts: thus Tannen (1987b), Norrick (1987), and other contributions to the special number of *Text* Johnstone edited on the topic describe the role of repetition in the production and understanding of talk, in the coherence and interpersonal meaning of conversation.

7 Figurative Meaning

The figurative meaning of hyperbole, irony, and some metaphors has sometimes also been seen as context bound, though early attempts to describe metaphor often remained solidly within sentence semantics proper. Thus Katz (1964) described a procedure for developing interpretations for grammatically deviant and anomalous "semi-sentences." Semi-sentences, including many figurative examples, receive interpretations based on their relations to nonanomalous sentences sharing properties with them. Further, Katz and Postal (1964) proposed a device for assigning features from predicates to proforms and semantically depleted items. Since the verb *drip* usually requires subject noun phrases characterized by the feature <(liquid)>, *drip* can also transfer the feature <(liquid)> to *something* in (12) in order to effect semantic congruency. Weinreich (1966) extended this device so as to transfer features to any noun at all. He proposed that the verb *bark* can trigger the transfer of the feature <(canine)> to its subject *the sergeant* in (13). This transfer models the metaphorical process whereby we see the sergeant in terms of a dog:

(12)   Something dripped all over the new carpet.

(13)   The sergeant barked his orders to the new recruits.

Fillmore (1971a, 1971b) proposed that selectional restrictions as presuppositions could transfer this same way to account for metaphors. Van Dijk (1972) revises Weinreich's analysis as a case of feature *extension* rather than transfer; Levin (1977) and Norrick (1985) suggest further modifications of Weinreich's original proposal to account for a wide range of figurative possibilities. Still, early on (Reddy 1969; Schofer and Rice 1977; Nunberg 1978) there were arguments that figurative language required discourse/pragmatic treatment along the lines of contextual reference, or that metaphor represented a "performance phenomenon" outside the purview of semantics proper, for instance Cohen and Margalit (1972), Price (1974), and Abraham (1975). If sufficiently powerful interpretive strategies are independently required at the discourse level, they could eliminate the need for any narrowly conceived semantic rules for figures.

Nevertheless, many recent linguistic treatments of metaphor follow G. Lakoff's cognitive linguistic approach (G. Lakoff and Johnson 1980; G. Lakoff 1987; G. Lakoff and Turner 1989; Kövecses 1990; Sweetser 1990). Other approaches center on figurative meanings as implicatures from violations of Grice's maxims or similar principles (Grice 1978; Sperber and Wilson 1981, 1986). Still, neither of these approaches focuses on figures in concrete conversational contexts. By contrast, I would argue that the close analysis of figurative utterances in natural discourse contexts can provide evidence for real psychological strategies of interpretation.

We should note first that metaphors technically appear only at the discourse level; thus whereas a sentence like (14) will tend to provoke a nonliteral interpretation for the verb *dance* in most real-world contexts, it certainly does not force figurative interpretation, since it could apply literally to a scene from a cartoon, where anthropomorphized boats with legs indeed dance to appropriate background music:

(14)   The colorful fishing boats danced in the harbor.

All we know about (14) as a disembodied sentence is that it contains an incongruity between the subject *boats* and the verb *dance* which will presumably receive resolution in its discourse context. Other sentences like (15) are perfectly consistent within themselves:

(15)   The early bird catches the worm.

They trigger metaphorical interpretation only when they appear in contexts such as talk of the stock market, but not in talk about avian dietary habits – pace Matthews (1971), Katz (1964), and others who claim metaphor always involves selectional clashes. Similarly, hyperbole and irony are bound to discourse, since there is nothing intrinsic to sentences like (16) and (17) which marks them as necessarily involving overstatement or sarcasm:

(16)   I have about a thousand calls to answer by noon.

(17)   This is the kind of weather I like best.

It is the utterance of (16) to a colleague at 11.45 a.m. which makes it sound like an exaggeration, and the utterance of (17) during a downpour which makes it sound sarcastic.

8   Metalingual Perspectives on Figurative Meaning

Although we cannot directly observe the cognitive processing people go through when confronted with figures of speech, we do have access to several sorts of data which shed light on the process, namely the clarifications, corrections, and explicit metalingual comments in everyday talk. We can observe reactions of interlocutors to intentionally produced figures and to other incongruities which arise in conversation; and we can examine the verbal attempts conversationalists make to explain the apparent incongruities and outright contradictions in their own speech. When certain types of comments and attempts at clarification recur, they can claim a psychological reality as processing strategies which no proposed semantic rule shares. Moreover, they represent patterns which must be part of discourse competence in any case, so that it only makes good sense to see how far they go toward describing figurative meaning as well.

Since metaphor is not generally perceived as discourse incongruency the way contradiction is, we must glean what insight we can from "metalingual" comments about contradictions, then see what mileage we can derive from them for the analysis of metaphor. Talk counts as metalingual in the sense of Jakobson (1960) when it aims at questioning and clarifying linguistic forms and their meanings. Metalingual talk allows conversationalists to focus on the appropriateness of a word or turn of phrase – and hence, it helps them to negotiate the sort of meaning appropriate to their particular interaction. Jakobson's classic treatment of language functions leaves the impression that relatively few utterances exhibit primarily metalingual force. But thirty years of increasingly intense research on naturally occurring conversation have shown that quite a lot of everyday talk is directed at language forms themselves: we are at pains to agree on names and terminology; we work to clarify errors, contradictions, and misunderstandings; we negotiate grammar and meaning, turn-taking and topic choice; we take note of apt phrases, while we poke fun at inept phrasing and out-group (nonstandard) forms. See, for instance, Jefferson (1974), Schegloff (1987, 1988), and Schegloff et al. (1977) on misunderstanding and repair; M. H. Goodwin (1983), Ochs (1984), and Norrick (1991a) on correction and clarification; Tannen (1984, 1986) on reframing; Clark and Wilkes-Gibbs (1990) and Clark (1997) on negotiating reference. Certainly, the analysis of metalingual comments in everyday conversation can yield valuable input for any semantic theory.

The examination of metalingual talk to resolve incongruity in discourse reveals three patterns, which can be represented as operations on conflicting frames of reference of the sort Hrushovski (1984) proposes for the analysis of metaphor (see Norrick 1989a, 1991b). While metaphors oppose a literal and a figurative frame of reference, contradictions and paradoxes oppose two frames of reference on the same literal level. Yet the strategies themselves apply to metaphors in parallel ways. To see how the resolution of discourse contradiction illustrates the first of the three recurrent strategies identified, consider the following excerpt from Svartvik and Quirk (1980: 664). Here a contradiction arises through the conjunction of two adjacent utterances, the second of which is spoken rapidly as an attempt at correction, rather than with contrastive stress as the second part of a single utterance:

(18) B: but it was in the middle of this Dubrovniki Garden. which is a very over-
          grown kind of a garden. I mean it's not overgrown.
      A: Yeah?
      B: but things start off. with plenty of space between them. on the ground.
      A: Yes?
      B: but when they get up to the sort of foliage level.
      A: (laughs)
      B: they're all sort of interlinked.

In this passage, the speaker explains his contradictory statement at some length, apparently prodded by his hearer's repeated questioning. Speaker B resolves the contradiction he has produced by distinguishing two ways a garden can be overgrown. In doing so, he illustrates a common strategy of interpreting incongruity, which I call "separating frames of reference" (cf. Norrick 1985, 1989a). This strategy regularly applies to statements like *Sue's both right and wrong* to get a consistent interpretation such as, say "Sue is right theoretically and wrong practically"; Leech (1969) and Kiefer (1978) identify only this sort of interpretation for contradictory utterances.

In a second example from natural conversation (Craig and Tracy 1983: 320), speaker K shows with her *but, ah, so* that she realizes something has gone awry with her utterance:

(19)   K: they don't really get a lot of snow. Like – they got more than we did so far but, ah, so.
        B: This is an exceptional year I hear.
        K: Well they usually get – about as much as – we do.

In observing that the current year was exceptional, B already begins to relativize the clashing terms, then K goes on to find middle ground between them. She generalizes from this year to *usually*, and averages the two extremes of the contradiction with *about as much as*. We all employ this second strategy – call it "averaging opposites" – when we interpret a statement like *It's raining and it's not* to mean "it is just barely raining," and hence "it is drizzling." Here, clearly, we seek to coalesce entire frames of reference, rather than isolated lexical items.

The third major strategy speakers use to explain contradictory utterances takes one of the clashing terms as correct, and brings the other term into line with it. In responding to R's question in the example below (from Jefferson 1972: 337), K follows just this strategy of "modifying one term": he resolves the apparent contradiction R identifies by explaining what *can't dance* entails for him.

(20)   K: I can't dance, and – hell every time, every time the – the dance play – er every time there's a dance I'm always at it, an' I'm always dancin',
        R: An' yer al – yer dancing?
        K: Sure. I can't dance worth shit, I just move around hehh's all you gotta do.

We all employ this third strategy in finding consistent interpretations for statements like *Al is thirty-five going on twenty*, when we alter the second term to "acts like he's going on twenty."

Only the three foregoing strategies recur regularly in the cases of conversational incongruity I have identified in the literature on correction and clarification as well as in my own taped data. Furthermore, they seem to account for standard examples of intentionally crafted paradoxes, as I have shown in earlier work on proverbs (1985), proverbial phrases (1989c), and literary paradoxes (1989a). Hence these strategies should be included in complete semantics for discourse. Significantly, this sort of result seems obtainable only by direct reference to explaining and correcting behavior in real situated conversation.

Let us examine a final example of figurative meaning in natural conversation. Hearers do not usually remark explicitly on metaphors beyond an appreciative chuckle; the complimentary comment in the excerpt below comes only in response to an image of a rudderless boat, which summarizes the foregoing description in rather bold fashion. Mel, a professor of business, produces the figure during an interview about student writing assignments with Lou, a consultant on professional writing:

(21)   *Mel*:   None of these others maybe had a *stated* objective as to what they were trying to accomplish, but this is the only one that just seems to be kind of

adrift. The other ones- came to a con*clusion*. Even though you didn't know what they were trying to decide up *front*, at least there was a wrap-up saying, buy this, or sell that, or: invest in this, or this is a good project, or that's a bad project, or something ha ha ha ha hunh. This just doesn't seem to be going anywhere. It's kind of like a rudderless boat.

Lou: You're a good metaphor-maker.

Mel: (laughs)

Notice that the word *adrift* and the phrase *doesn't seem to be going anywhere* have already suggested a metaphor of aimless movement on the water, though their imagery is conventional and faded; the explicit image of the rudderless boat serves to focus this metaphor emerging in the preceding passage. Although Mel's phrase "like a rudderless boat" strictly counts as a simile rather than a metaphor in traditional parlance because of the explicit comparison with *like*, we know thanks to Ortony (1979a, 1979b) that similes themselves are metaphorical to greater or lesser degrees. With or without *like*, the image of the rudderless boat requires the same cognitive processing to relate it to the student writing assignment in question. An instinctive awareness of this non-literal meaning is marked by hedges such as *kind of* attached to the faded metaphor *adrift*. The hedges and Mel's rather embarrassed laughter show that he is somewhat reticent to have his metaphor noticed, while Lou's comment reveals a metalingual awareness of figurative language. The whole passage nicely illustrates how a speaker can use an explicit simile to bring out the metaphoric possibilities inherent in foregoing talk. Finally, the presence of *adrift* and *doesn't seem to be going anywhere* in the environment of the image of the rudderless boat point us in promising directions for its interpretation. By the strategy of modifying one term, we can generalize the rudderless boat to any undertaking without a fixed orientation toward its goal; and by the strategy of separating frames of reference, we can recognize that the comparison with a rudderless boat counts only for this abstract sense and not in any real frame of reference involving wooden vessels on water. This discussion illustrates the value of examining metaphors in their real-life conversational contexts for an understanding of their meaning potential, as well as to describe how speakers embed them in ongoing talk and how hearers react to them.

9   Conclusion

I hope the foregoing illustrates how linguistic analysis has become increasingly oriented toward discourse in recent years, and how this reorientation has detected new problems and discovered new solutions to old ones. The examination of discourse can reveal the working of interpretive strategies which obviate the need for narrowly semantic or syntactic explanations; including such independently motivated discourse strategies builds psychological reality into our linguistic descriptions and renders them more adequate to real linguistic behavior. Finally, investigation of utterances in their natural discourse contexts makes us appreciate the interrelations of the semantic phenomena we attempt to analyze into the separate species of referential, ideational, interpersonal, and affective meaning.

REFERENCES

Abraham, Werner (1975) *A Linguistic Approach to Metaphor*. Lisse: de Ridder.

Ariel, Mira (1988) Referring and accessibility. *Journal of Linguistics*, 24(1): 65–87.

Ariel, Mira (1990) *Accessing Noun-phrase Antecedents*. London: Routledge.

Ariel, Mira (1991) The function of accessibility in a theory of grammar. *Journal of Pragmatics*, 16: 443–63.

Ariel, Mira (1994) Interpreting anaphoric expressions: a cognitive versus a pragmatic approach. *Journal of Linguistics*, 30: 3–42.

Austin, John (1962) *How to Do Things with Words*. Cambridge, MA: Harvard University Press.

Bach, Kent and Harnish, Robert M. (1979) *Linguistic Communication and Speech Acts*. Cambridge, MA: MIT Press.

Bar-Hillel, Yehoshua (1954) Indexical expressions. *Mind*, 63: 359–79.

Bloomfield, Leonard (1933) *Language*. New York: Holt.

Bréal, Michel (1883) *Les lois intellectuelles du langage*. L'annuaire de l'association pour l'encouragement des études grecques en France.

Bréal, Michel (1897) *Essai de sémantique: Science des significations*. Paris: Librairie Hachette.

Bréal, Michel (1900) *Semantics: Studies in the Science of Meaning*. New York: Dover.

Brown, Penelope and Levinson, Stephen (1978) Universals in language usage: politeness phenomena. In E. N. Goody (ed.), *Questions and Politeness*, Cambridge: Cambridge University Press, 56–290. [Reissued as: *Politeness: Some Universals in Language Usage*. Cambridge: Cambridge University Press, 1987.]

Cantrall, William (1974) *View Point, Reflexives and the Nature of Noun Phrases*. The Hague: Mouton.

Chafe, Wallace (1968) Idiomaticity as an anomaly in the Chomskyan paradigm. *Foundations of Language*, 4: 109–27.

Chafe, Wallace (1970) *Meaning and the Structure of Language*. Chicago: University of Chicago Press.

Chafe, Wallace (1974) Language and consciousness. *Language*, 50: 111–33.

Chafe, Wallace (1993) *Discourse, Consciousness, and Time*. Chicago: University of Chicago Press.

Chastain, Charles (1975) Reference and context. In K. Gunderson (ed.), *Language, Mind, and Knowledge*. Minneapolis: University of Minnesota Press, 194–269.

Chomsky, Noam (1973) Conditions on transformations. In S. Anderson and P. Kiparsky (eds), *A Festschrift for Morris Halle*. New York: Holt, 232–86.

Chomsky, Noam (1981) *Lectures on Government and Binding*. Dordrecht: Foris.

Christophersen, Paul (1939) *The Articles: A Study of their Theory and Use in English*. Copenhagen: Einar Munksgaard.

Clark, Herbert H. (1997) Dogmas of understanding. *Discourse Processes*, 23: 567–98.

Clark, Herbert H. and Marshall, Catherine R. (1981) Definite reference and mutual knowledge. In A. K. Joshi, B. L. Webber, and I. A. Sag (eds), *Elements of Discourse Understanding*. Cambridge: Cambridge University Press, 10–63.

Clark, Herbert H. and Murphy, Gregory L. (1982) Audience design in meaning and reference. In J. F. Le Ny and W. Kintsch (eds), *Language and Comprehension*. Amsterdam: North-Holland, 287–99.

Clark, Herbert H. and Wilkes-Gibbs, W. (1990) Referring as a collaborative process. In P. R. Cohen, J. Morgan and M. E. Pollack (eds), *Intentions in Communication*. London: MIT Press, 463–93.

Clements, George N. (1975) The logophoric pronoun in Ewe: its role in discourse. *Journal of West African Languages*, 10: 141–77.

Cohen, L. Jonathan and Margalit, Avishai (1972) The role of inductive reasoning in the interpretation of metaphor. In D. Davidson and G. Harman (eds), *Semantics of Natural Language*. Dordrecht: Reidel, 722–40.

Cole, Peter (1978) On the origins of referential opacity. In P. Cole (ed.), *Syntax and Semantics, vol. 9: Pragmatics*. New York: Academic, 1–22.

Craig, Robert T. and Tracy, Karen (eds) (1983) *Conversational Coherence*. Beverly Hills: Sage.

Donnellan, Keith S. (1978) Speaker reference, descriptions and anaphora. In P. Cole (ed.), *Syntax and Semantics, vol. 9: Pragmatics*. New York: Academic, 47–68.

Donnellan, Keith S. (1981) Intuitions and presuppositions. In P. Cole (ed.), *Radical Pragmatics*. New York: Academic, 129–42.

Duranti, Alessandro (1986) The audience as co-author: an introduction. *Text*, 6: 239–47.

Fillmore, Charles J. (1971a) Verbs of judging. In C. J. Fillmore and D. T. Langendoen (eds), *Studies in Linguistic Semantics*. New York: Holt, 273–89.

Fillmore, Charles J. (1971b) Types of lexical information. In D. D. Steinberg and L. A. Jakobovits (eds), *Semantics: An Interdisciplinary Reader in Philosophy, Linguistics and Psychology*. New York: Holt, 370–92.

Fillmore, Charles J. (1976) The need for a frame semantics within linguistics. *Statistical Methods in Linguistics*: 5–29.

Fillmore, Charles J. (1985) Frames and the semantics of understanding. *Quaderni di Semantica: Rivista Internazionale di Semantica Teorica e Applicata*, 6: 222–54.

Firth, John R. (1957) *Papers in Linguistics, 1934–1951*. London: Oxford University Press.

Fodor, Jerry D. (1975) *Language of Thought*. New York: Crowell.

Fodor, Jerry D. (1979) In defense of the truth-value gap. In C. K. Oh and D. Dinneen (eds), *Syntax and Semantics, vol. 11: Presupposition*. New York: Academic, 199–224.

Frege, Gottlob (1892) Über Sinn und Bedeutung. *Zeitschrift für Philosophie und philosophische Kritik*, 100: 25–50. [Translated in: P. T. Geach and M. Black (eds) (1952) *Philosophical Writings*. Oxford: Blackwell, 17–38.]

Gazdar, Gerald (1979) A solution to the projection problem. In C. K. Oh and D. Dineen (eds), *Syntax and Semantics, vol. 11: Presupposition*. New York: Academic, 57–89.

Giorgi, Alexandra (1983) Toward a theory of long distance anaphors: A GB approach. *Linguistic Review*, 3: 307–61.

Givón, Talmy (1973) Opacity and reference in language: an inquiry into the role of modalities. In J. Kimball (ed.), *Syntax and Semantics, vol. 2*. New York: Academic Press, 95–122.

Givón, Talmy (1982) Logic vs. pragmatics, with human language as the referee: toward an empirically viable epistemology. *Journal of Pragmatics*, 6: 81–133.

Givón, Talmy (1985) The pragmatics of referentiality. In D. Schiffrin (ed.), *Meaning, Form and Use in Context (Georgetown University Roundtable on Languages and Linguistics 1984)*. Washington, DC: Georgetown University Press, 120–38.

Goodwin, Charles (1986) Audience diversity, participation and interpretation. *Text*, 6: 283–316.

Goodwin, Majorie H. (1983) Aggravated correction and disagreement in children's conversations. *Journal of Pragmatics*, 7: 657–77.

Gordon, David and Lakoff, George (1975) Conversational postulates. In P. Cole and J. Morgan (eds), *Syntax and Semantics, vol. 3: Speech Acts*. New York: Academic, 83–106.

Green, Georgia M. (1975) How to get people to do things with words: the whimperative question. In P. Cole and J. Morgan (eds), *Syntax and semantics, vol. 3: Speech Acts*. New York: Academic Press, 107–42.

Green, Georgia M. (1989) *Pragmatics and Natural Language Understanding*. Hillsdale, NJ: Erlbaum.

Green, Georgia M. (1996) Ambiguity resolution and discourse interpretation. In K. van Deemter and S. Peters (eds), *Semantic Ambiguity and Underspecification*. Stanford: CSLI, 1–26.

Green, Georgia M. and Morgan, Jerry L. (1981) Pragmatics, grammar, and discourse. In P. Cole (ed.), *Radical Pragmatics*. New York: Academic, 167–81.

Grice, H. Paul (1957) Meaning. *Philosophical Review*, 66: 377–88.

Grice, H. Paul (1975) Logic and conversation. In P. Cole and J. Morgan (eds), *Syntax and Semantics, vol. 3: Speech Acts*. New York: Academic, 41–58.

Grice, H. Paul (1978) Further notes on logic and conversation. In P. Cole (ed.), *Syntax and Semantics, vol. 9: Pragmatics*. New York: Academic, 113–27.

Grice, H. Paul (1981) Presupposition and conversational implicature. In P. Cole (ed.), *Radical Pragmatics*. New York: Academic Press, 183–98.

Grodzinsky, Yosef and Reinhart, Tanya (1993) The innateness of binding and coreference. *Linguistic Inquiry*, 24: 69–101.

Gumperz, John J. (1982a) *Discourse Strategies*. Cambridge: Cambridge University Press.

Gumperz, John J. (1982b) The linguistic bases of communicative competence. In D. Tannen (ed.), *Analyzing Discourse: Text and Talk (Georgetown University Roundtable on Languages and Linguistics 1981)*. Washington, DC: Georgetown University Press, 323–34.

Halliday, M. A. K. (1967) Notes an transitivity and theme in English: Part 2. *Journal of Linguistics*, 3: 199–244.

Halliday, M. A. K. (1977) Text as semantic choice in social contexts. In T. A. van Dijk and J. S. Petöfi (eds), *Grammars and Descriptions*. Berlin: de Gruyter, 176–225.

Halliday, M. A. K. (1978) *Language as Social Semiotic*. London: Arnold.

Hawkins, John A. (1978) *Definiteness and Indefiniteness: A Study in Reference and Grammaticality Prediction*. London: Croom Helm.

Harman, Gilbert (1977) Against universal semantic representation. In A. Rogers, B. Wall, and J. P. Murphy (eds), *Proceedings of the Texas Conference on Performatives, Presuppositions, and Implicatures*. Arlington: Center for Applied Linguistics, 1–11.

Heim, Irene (1983) File change semantics and the familiarity theory of definiteness. In R. Bäuerle, C. Schwarze, and A. von Stechow (eds), *Meaning, Use and Interpretation of Language*. Berlin: de Gruyter, 164–89.

Hellan, Lars (1988) *Anaphora in Norwegian and the Theory of Grammar*. Dordrecht: Foris.

Horn, Lawrence R. (1984) Toward a new taxonomy for pragmatic inference: Q-based and R-based implicature. In D. Schiffrin (ed.), *Meaning, Form and Use in Context (Georgetown University Roundtable on Languages and Linguistics*

1984). Washington, DC: Georgetown University Press, 11–42.

Horn, Lawrence R. (1988) Pragmatic theory. In F. J. Newmeyer (ed.), *Linguistics: The Cambridge Survey.* Cambridge: Cambridge University Press, 113–45.

Hrushovski, Benjamin (1984) Poetic metaphor and frames of reference. *Poetics Today,* 5: 5–43.

Jackendorff, Ray S. (1972) *Semantic Interpretation in Generative Grammar.* Cambridge, MA: MIT Press.

Jakobson, Roman (1960) Closing statement: linguistics and poetics. In T. A. Sebeok (ed.), *Style in Language.* Cambridge, MA: MIT Press, 350–77.

Jefferson, Gail (1972) Side sequences. In D. Sudnow (ed.), *Studies in Social Interaction.* New York: Free Press, 294–338.

Jefferson, Gail (1974) Error correction as an interactional resource. *Language in Society,* 3: 181–99.

Jesperson, Otto (1924) *The Philosophy of Grammar.* London: Allen and Unwin.

Kamp, Hans (1981) A theory of truth and semantic representation. In J. A. G. Groenendijk, T. Janssen, and M. Stokhof (eds), *Formal Methods in the Study of Language.* Amsterdam: Mathematisch Centrum, 277–322.

Karttunen, Lauri (1973) Presuppositions of compound sentences. *Linguistic Inquiry,* 4: 169–93.

Karttunen, Lauri (1976) What indirect questions conventionally implicate. In S. Mufwene, C. Walker, and S. Steever (eds), *Papers from the Twelfth Regional Meeting of the Chicago Linguistic Society:* 351–68.

Karttunen, Lauri and Peters, Stanley (1979) Conventional implicature. In C. K. Oh and D. Dinneen (eds), *Syntax and Semantics: Presupposition.* New York: Academic Press, 1–56.

Katz, Jerrold J. (1964) Semi-sentences. In J. Fodor and J. J. Katz (eds), *The Structure of Language: Readings in the Philosophy of Language.* Englewood Cliffs, NJ: Prentice-Hall, 400–416.

Katz, Jerrold J. (1966) *The Philosophy of Language.* New York: Harper and Row.

Katz, Jerrold J. (1972) *Semantic Theory.* New York: Harper and Row.

Katz, Jerrold J. (1977) *Propositional Structure and Illocutionary Force.* Hassocks: Harvester.

Katz, Jerrold J. and Fodor, Jerry A. (1963) The structure of a semantic theory. *Language,* 39: 170–210.

Katz, Jerrold J. and Langendoen, Terry D. (1976) Pragmatics and presupposition. *Language,* 52: 1–17.

Katz, Jerrold J. and Postal, Paul M. (1964) *An Integrated Theory of Linguistic Descriptions.* Cambridge, MA: MIT Press.

Keenan, Edward (1971) Two kinds of presupposition in natural language. In C. Fillmore and D. T. Langendoen (eds), *Studies in Linguistic Semantics.* New York: Holt, Rinehart and Winston, 45–52.

Kempson, Ruth M. (1975) *Presupposition and the Delimitation of Semantics.* Cambridge: Cambridge University Press.

Kiefer, Ferenc (1978) Zur Rolle der Pragmatik in der linguistischen Beschreibung. *Die Neueren Sprachen,* 77: 254–68.

Kiparsky, Carol and Kiparsky, Paul (1970) Fact. In M. Bierwisch and K. E. Heidolph (eds), *Progress in Linguistics.* The Hague: Mouton, 143–73.

Kövecses, Zoltán (1986) *Metaphors of Anger and Pride.* Philadelphia: John Benjamins.

Kövecses, Zoltán (1990) *Emotion Concepts.* New York: Springer.

Kuno, Susumu (1972) Pronominalization, reflexivization, and direct discourse. *Linguistic Inquiry,* 3: 269–320.

Kuno, Susumu (1987) *Functional Syntax: Anaphora, Discourse and Empathy.* Chicago: University of Chicago Press.

Labov, William (1984) Intensity. In D. Schiffrin (ed.), *Meaning, Form, and Use in Context (Georgetown University Roundtable on Languages and Linguistics 1984).* Washington, DC: Georgetown University Press, 43–70.

Lakoff, George (1969) Presupposition and relative grammaticality. *Journal of Philosophical Linguistics,* 1: 103–16.

Lakoff, George (1970) Global rules. *Language,* 46: 627–39.

Lakoff, George (1971) On generative semantics. In D. D. Steinberg and L. A. Jakobovits (eds), *Semantics: An Interdisciplinary Reader.* New York: Cambridge University Press, 232–96.

Lakoff, George (1987) *Women, Fire and Dangerous Things.* Chicago: University of Chicago Press.

Lakoff, George and Johnson, Mark (1980) *Metaphors We Live By.* Chicago: University of Chicago Press.

Lakoff, George and Turner, Mark (1989) *More than Cool Reason: A Field Guide to Poetic Metaphor.* Chicago: University of Chicago Press.

Lakoff, Robin (1973) The logic of politeness; or, minding your p's and q's. *Papers from the Ninth Regional Meeting of the Chicago Linguistic Society:* 292–305.

Lakoff, Robin (1977) What you can do with words: politeness, pragmatics, and performatives. In A. Rogers, B. Wall and J. P. Murphy (eds), *Proceedings of the Texas Conference on Performatives, Presuppositions and Implicatures.* Washington, DC: Center for Applied Linguistics, 79–105.

Langacker, Ronald W. (1969) On pronominalization and the chain of command. In D. A. Reibel and S. A. Schane (eds), *Modern Studies in English.* Englewood Cliffs, NJ: Prentice-Hall, 160–86.

Lasnik, Howard (1976) Remarks on coreference. *Linguistic Analysis,* 2: 1–22.

Lasnik, Howard (1981) On two recent treatments of disjoint reference. *Journal of Linguistic Research,* 1: 48–58.

Leech, Geoffrey N. (1969) *Towards a Semantic Description of English.* London: Longman.

Lees, Robert B. and Klima, Edward S. (1963) Rules for English pronominalization. *Language,* 48: 17–28.

Lehrer, Adrienne (1983) *Wine and Conversation.* Bloomington: Indiana University Press.

Levin, Samuel R. (1977) *The Semantics of Metaphor.* Baltimore: Johns Hopkins University Press.

Levinson, Stephen C. (1983) *Pragmatics.* Cambridge: Cambridge University Press.

Levinson, Stephen C. (1987a) Minimization and conversational interference. In J. Verschueren, and M. Bertuccelli-Papi (eds), *The Pragmatic Perspective: Proceedings of the International Pragmatics Conference. Viareggio, 1985.* Amsterdam: John Benjamins, 61–129.

Levinson, Stephen C. (1987b) Pragmatics and the grammar of anaphora: a partial pragmatic reduction of binding and control phenomena. *Journal of Linguistics,* 23: 379–434.

Levinson, Stephen C. (1991) Pragmatic reduction of the binding conditions revisited. *Journal of Linguistics,* 27: 107–61.

Mailing, Joan (1982) Non-clause-bounded reflexives in Icelandic. In T. Fretheim and L. Hellan (eds), *Papers from the Sixth Scandinavian Conference of Linguistics.* Trondheim: Tapir, 90–106.

Malinowski, Bronislaw (1923) The problem of meaning in primitive languages. In C. K. Ogden and I. A. Richards, *The Meaning of Meaning.* London: Routledge, 296–336.

Malinowski, Bronislaw (1935) *Coral Gardens and their Magic.* London: Allen and Unwin.

Martin, John N. (1979) Some misconceptions in the critique of semantic presuppositions. *Theoretical Linguistics*, 6: 235–82.

Matthews, Robert J. (1971) Concerning a "linguistic theory" of metaphor. *Foundations of Language*, 7: 413–25.

McCawley, James D. (1968a) The role of semantics in a grammar. In E. Bach and R. Harms (eds), *Universals in Linguistic Theory*. New York: Holt, 124–69.

McCawley, James D. (1968b) Lexical insertion in a transformational grammar without deep structure. *Papers from the Fourth Regional Meeting of the Chicago Linguistic Society*: 71–80.

McCawley, James D. (1968c) Concerning the base component of a transformational grammar. *Foundations of Language*, 4: 243–69.

McCawley, James D. (1970) Where do noun phrases come from? In R. A. Jacobs and P. S. Rosenbaum (eds), *Readings in English Transformational Grammar*. Boston: Ginn, 166–83.

McCawley, James D. (1975) Verbs of bitching. In D. Hockney (ed.), *Contemporary Research in Philosophical Logic and Linguistic Semantics*. Dordrecht: Reidel, 313–32.

Montague, Richard (1968) Pragmatics. In R. Klibansky (ed.), *Contemporary Philosophy*. Florence: La Nouva Italia Editrice, 102–21.

Montague, Richard (1970) Pragmatics and intensional logic. *Synthese*, 22: 68–94.

Montague, Richard (1974) *Formal Philosophy: Selected Papers of Richard Montague*. New Haven: Yale University Press.

Morgan, Jerry L. (1977) Conversational postulates revisited. *Language*, 53: 277–84.

Norrick, Neal R. (1985) *How Proverbs Mean*. Berlin: Mouton.

Norrick, Neal R. (1987) Functions of repetition in conversation. *Text*, 7: 245–64.

Norrick, Neal R. (1989a) How paradox means. *Poetics Today*, 10: 51–62.

Norrick, Neal R. (1989b) Intertextuality in humor. *Humor*, 2: 117–39.

Norrick, Neal R. (1989c) Proverbial paradox. *Proverbium*, 6: 67–73.

Norrick, Neal R. (1991a) On the organization of corrective exchanges in conversation. *Journal of Pragmatics*, 16: 58–83.

Norrick, Neal R. (1991b) Contradiction and paradox in discourse. In J. Verschueren (ed.), *Levels of Linguistic Adaptation*. Amsterdam: John Benjamins, 195–202.

Norrick, Neal R. (1993) *Conversational Joking: Humor in Everyday Talk*. Bloomington: Indiana University Press.

Nunberg, Geoffrey D. (1978) *The Pragmatics of Reference*. Bloomington: Indiana University Linguistics Club.

Ochs, Elinor (1984) Clarification in culture. In D. Schiffrin (ed.), *Meaning, Form, and Use in Context (Georgetown University Roundtable on Languages and Linguistics 1984)*. Washington, DC: Georgetown University Press, 325–41.

Ogden, C. K. and Richards, I. A. (1923) *The Meaning of Meaning*. London: Routledge.

Ortony, Andrew (1979a) Beyond literal simile. *Psychological Review*, 86: 161–80.

Ortony, Andrew (1979b) The role of similarity in similes and metaphors. In A. Ortony (ed.), *Metaphor and Thought*. Cambridge: Cambridge University Press, 186–201.

Price, J. T. (1974) Linguistic competence and metaphorical use. *Foundations of Language*, 11: 253–56.

Prince, Ellen (1981) Towards a taxonomy of given–new information. In P. Cole (ed.), *Radical Pragmatics*. New York: Academic Press, 223–56.

Reddy, Michael J. (1969) A semantic approach to metaphor. *Papers from the Fifth Regional Meeting of the Chicago Linguistic Society*: 240–51.

Reinhart, Tanya (1983) *Anaphora and Semantic Interpretation*. London: Croom Helm.

Reinhart, Tanya (1986) Center and periphery in the grammar of anaphora. In B. Lust (ed.), *Studies in the Acquisition of Anaphora*. Dordrecht: Reidel, 123–50.

Reinhart, Tanya and Reuland, Eric J. (1993) Reflexivity. *Linguistic Inquiry*, 24: 697–720.

Ross, John Robert (1970) On declarative sentences. In R. A. Jabobs and P. Rosenbaum (eds), *Readings in English Transformational Grammar*. Waltham: Ginn, 222–72.

Russell, Bertrand (1905) On denoting. *Mind*, 14: 479–93.

Russell, Bertrand (1910) *Principia Mathematica*. Cambridge: Cambridge University Press.

Sacks, Harvey (1992) *Lectures on Conversation*, 2 vols. Oxford: Blackwell.

Sadock, Jerrold M. (1974) *Toward a Linguistic Theory of Speech Acts*. New York: Academic.

Sapir, Edward (1921) *Language: An Introduction to the Study of Speech*. New York: Harcourt, Brace and World.

Sapir, Edward (1929) The status of linguistics as a science. *Language*, 5: 207–14. [Reprinted in Sapir 1949: 160–6.]

Sapir, Edward (1949) *Selected Writings of Edward Sapir in Language, Culture, and Personality*. Berkeley: University of California Press.

Saussure, Ferdinand de (1916) *Cours de linguistique générale*. Paris: Payot.

Schegloff, Emanuel A. (1984) On some questions and ambiguities in conversation. In J. M. Atkinson, and J. Hevitage (eds), *Structure of Social Action*. Cambridge: Cambridge University Press, 29–52.

Schegloff, Emanuel A. (1987) Some source of misunderstanding in talk-in-interaction. *Linguistics*, 25: 201–18.

Schegloff, Emanuel A. (1988) Presequences and indirection: applying speech act theory to ordinary conversation. *Journal of Pragmatics*, 12: 55–62.

Schegloff, Emanuel A., Jefferson, Gail, and Sacks, Harvey (1977) The preference for self-correction in the organization of repair in conversation. *Language*, 53: 361–82.

Schofer, Peter and Rice, Donald (1977) Metaphor, metonymy, and synechdoche revis(it)ed. *Semiotica*, 21: 121–49.

Searle, John R. (1969) *Speech Acts*. Cambridge: Cambridge University Press.

Searle, John R. (1979) *Expression and Meaning*. Cambridge: Cambridge University Press.

Sellars, Wilfried (1954) On presupposing. *Philosophical Review*, 63: 197–215.

Sells, Peter (1987) Aspects of logophoricity. *Linguistic Inquiry*, 18: 445–81.

Sperber, Dan and Wilson, Deidre (1981) Irony and the use–mention distinction. In P. Cole (ed.), *Radical Pragmatics*. New York: Academic, 295–318.

Sperber, Dan and Wilson, Deidre (1986) *Relevance: Communication and Cognition*. Cambridge: Harvard University Press.

Stalnaker, Robert C. (1972) Pragmatics. In D. Davidson and G. Harman (eds), *Semantics of Natural Language*. Dordrecht: Reidel, 380–97.

Stalnaker, Robert C. (1973) Presuppositions. *Journal of Philosophical Logic*, 2: 447–57.

Stalnaker, Robert C. (1974) Pragmatic presuppositions. In M. K. Munitz and P. K. Unger (eds), *Semantics and Philosophy*. New York: New York University Press, 197–214.

Stalnaker, Robert C. (1978) Assertion. In P. Cole (ed.), *Syntax and Semantics, vol. 9: Pragmatics*. New York: Academic, 315–32.

Stern, Gustaf (1931) *Meaning and the Change of Meaning*. Bloomington: Indiana University Press.

Strawson, Peter (1950) On referring. *Mind*, 59: 320–44.

Strawson, Peter (1964) Identifying reference and truth values. *Theoria*, 30: 96–118.

Svartvik, Jan and Quirk, Randolph (eds) (1980) *A Corpus of English Conversation*. Lund: Gleerup.

Sweetser, Eve (1990) *From Etymology to Pragmatics: Metaphorical and Cultural Aspects of Semantic Structure*. Cambridge: Cambridge University Press.

Tannen, Deborah (1984) *Conversational Style*. Norwood: Ablex.

Tannen, Deborah (1986) *That's Not What I Meant!* New York: Morrow.

Tannen, Deborah (1987a) Repetition in conversation: toward a poetics of talk. *Language*, 63: 574–605.

Tannen, Deborah (1987b) Repetition in conversation as spontaneous formulaicity. *Text*, 7: 215–44.

Tannen, Deborah (1989) *Talking Voices: Repetition, Dialogue, and Imagery in Conversational Discourse*. Cambridge: Cambridge University Press.

Trier, J. (1931) *Der deutsche Wortschatz im Sinnbezirk des Verstandes. Die Geschichte eines sprachlichen Feldes. I: Von den Anfängen bis zum Beginn des 13. Jh*. Heidelberg: Winter.

Trubetzkoy, Nikolaj S. (1939) *Grundzüge der Phonologie*. Prague: Cercle Linguistique de Prague.

van Dijk, Teun A. (1972) *Some Aspects of Text Grammars*. The Hague: Mouton.

Watzlawick, Paul, Beavin, Janet H., and Jackson, Don D. (1967) *Pragmatics of Human Communication*. New York: Norton.

Weinreich, Uriel (1966) Explorations in semantic theory. In T. A. Sebeok (ed.), *Current Trends in Linguistics, Vol. 3*. The Hague: Mouton, 395–477.

Whorf, Benjamin Lee (1956) *Language, Thought, and Reality: Selected Writings of Benjamin Lee Whorf*. New York: Wiley.

Wilson, D. (1975) *Presupposition and Non-truth-conditional Semantics*. London: Academic.

Zribi-Hertz, Anne (1989) Anaphor binding and narrative point of view. *Language*, 65: 695–727.

5 Discourse and Relevance Theory

DIANE BLAKEMORE

0 Introduction

It is generally agreed that the study of discourse takes us beyond the study of the sentence. However, as this book demonstrates, we are not always taken to the same place. In some cases, it seems, we are not taken that very far at all: thus according to the tradition set by Zellig Harris (1951), discourse is a structural unit which can be studied by analogy with the sentence. For example, Salkie (1995) suggests that while grammar is "basically about how words combine to form sentences, text and discourse analysis is about how sentences combine to form texts." And Hovy and Maier's (1994) work in artificial intelligence is based on the claim that "one of the first observations that one makes in analysing discourse is that it exhibits internal structure" (1994: 2).

In other cases, we are taken beyond and away from the notion of structure altogether to the notion of discourse as social behavior which must be studied in terms of its function. Thus Fasold (1990) defines the study of discourse as the study of any aspect of language use (1990: 65). And of course, one of the most influential books on linguistic aspects of discourse, Halliday and Hasan's (1976) *Cohesion in English*, is based on the view that a text is a "unit of language in use" (1976: 2) which must be studied in terms of its function in communication.

Notice that the analogy between discourse and language that is assumed by Zellig Harris is an analogy between discourse and what Chomsky has called externalized language (or E-language) (Chomsky 1986). This means that according to this view, a theory of discourse, like a grammar, is a collection of descriptive statements external to the human mind. Similarly, the functional view of discourse, in leading us from the study of the structural properties of discourse to the study of discourse as communicative behavior, has taken us to a phenomenon that is defined independently of the human mind.

If discourse is defined from either of these perspectives, then relevance theorists do not study discourse at all. For the object of study is not discourse, whether this be defined in terms of a structural phenomenon or a social phenomenon, but rather discourse understanding, or more particularly, the mental representations and computations underlying utterance understanding. In other words, the concern in relevance theory is with something internal to the human mind.

In drawing this analogy between relevance theoretic approaches to discourse and Chomskyan linguistics, I do not mean to suggest that there is an analogy between a theory of utterance understanding and grammar, or that a theory of discourse understanding is to be somehow accommodated within a theory of generative grammar. On the contrary, it is argued that Chomsky's modular view of the mind allows us to draw a principled distinction between a theory of grammar and a theory of utterance understanding. As we shall see in this chapter, while grammar plays a role in communication, this role is to deliver not representations of the thoughts that speakers communicate, but semantic representations which fall short of the complete interpretation intended. The contextual assumptions required for a complete interpretation of the speaker's intentions and the computations that are used in deriving this interpretation are *outside* the language module (grammar). As Deirdre Wilson (1995) has said, "there is no more reason to expect discourse to have the same structure as language than there is to expect it to have the same structure as vision." In particular, there is no reason to expect discourse to be analyzed in terms of a code or set of rules or conventions (see also Wilson and Sperber 1986).

1   Coherence and Discourse

The claim that a theory of discourse involves the search for the rules or conventions which govern it has dominated both structural and functional approaches to discourse. In structural approaches, the aim is to discover the rules which, if followed, result in an acceptable or well-formed text. In approaches which view discourse in terms of communicative behavior, the aim is to discover the social conventions which determine which utterances may occur and what they may be combined with. In other words, the main concern is with the *acceptability* of discourse.

According to one example of this approach, discourse is acceptable to the extent that it exhibits coherence relations between its segments. Thus for example Mann and Thompson (1987, 1988) argue that the reason why only the first of the sequences in (1) "works" is that our contextual assumptions about cars do not allow us to derive an interpretation of (1b) which is consistent with our assumption that the text is coherent:

(1)   a.   I love to collect classic automobiles. My favourite car is my 1899 Duryea.
      b.   I love to collect classic automobiles. My favourite car is my 1977 Toyota.
           (Mann and Thompson 1987: 57)

(1a) succeeds as a text because the contextual assumption that a 1899 Duryea is a member of the set of classic automobiles enables the hearer to establish that the two segments satisfy the relation of *elaboration*.[1]

This is not the only approach to coherence.[2] I focus on this approach here because some theorists who have taken it have also claimed that it provides the key to a theory of discourse *comprehension* in the sense that it is the search for coherence that leads to the successful comprehension of utterances. For example, Mann and Thompson (1987, 1988) have claimed that the search for coherence plays an essential role for the recovery of the implicatures recovered from an utterance. Hobbs (1979) has claimed that reference assignment is a consequence of the hearer's search for coherence. And Asher and Lascarides (1995) have argued that disambiguation can be seen as a consequence of the hearer's search for discourse coherence. My aim in this chapter is to outline the arguments which suggest that a theory of discourse comprehension should not be regarded as a by-product of a theory of discourse acceptability (or coherence), but is actually the key to the explanation of our intuitions about coherence. In other words, it is the notion of coherence that is derivative. More specifically, it can be seen as a consequence of the hearer's search for an interpretation that is consistent with Sperber and Wilson's (1986) Principle of Relevance.

Clearly, the success of a theory based on the assumption that the acceptability of discourse depends on coherence relations must be based on a complete taxonomy of coherence relations. However, this is the focus of considerable controversy. Mann and Thompson (1988) themselves propose a taxonomy based on 15 relations – rather fewer than the 70 relations proposed by Hovy and Maier (1994) but rather more than the four basic relations proposed by Sanders et al. (1993). Moreover, there are disagreements over how relations should be subclassified. For example, while Hovy and Maier (1994) suggest that both exemplification and restatement are subtypes of elaboration, Mann and Thompson (1988) include only exemplification as a subtype of elaboration and define restatement as a separate relation.

In fact, as we shall see, it is not clear that either restatement or elaboration provides an adequate theoretical basis for the analysis of reformulation sequences or for utterances intended as examples. More fundamentally, it is not clear that the assumptions underlying any taxonomy of coherence relations can be justified. Work by Blass (1990), Deirdre Wilson (1998), and myself (Blakemore 1988b, 1996, 1997) shows that coherence relations are necessary or sufficient for the acceptability of discourse or for its successful comprehension.

Coherence relations are structural relations which hold in virtue of formal properties of utterances. However, as Blass (1990) points out, intuitions about pragmatic acceptability are affected not only by the form of utterances, but also by their content. This means that it is possible to construct texts which are unacceptable even though they satsify formal coherence relations. Consider, for example, elaboration, which, for some writers, includes not only examples like (2), but also repetitions like (3):

(2)   Go down Washington Street. Just follow Washington Street three blocks to Adams Street. (from Hobbs 1979)

(3)   There's a mouse, a mouse.

As Blass's examples in (4) and (5) show, not every utterance recognizable as an elaboration or repetition is appropriate:

(4)   Go down Washington Street. Just pick up your left foot, place it down in front of your right foot, transfer your weight from right to left foot, lift your right foot . . .

(5)   [speaker goes into a shop] A box of cornflakes please. A box of cornflakes please. A box of cornflakes please . . .

In the same way, not every utterance satisfying a restatement relation would be appropriate. For example, a speaker who has just seen a mouse running across the bedroom floor is unlikely to produce the sequence in (6):

(6)   There's a mouse, a small grey furry rodent.

According to Mann and Thompson (1988), the intended effect of restatement is simply that the hearer recognize that a restatement is being made. However, it is difficult to see how this provides a means for distinguishing acceptable restatments from unacceptable ones or for distinguishing the effects of a restatment such as (7) from those derived from the sequence in (8):

(7)   a.   At the beginning of this piece there is an example of an anacrusis.
      b.   That is, it begins with an unaccented note which is not part of the first full bar. (Blakemore 1997a)

(8)   a.   A well-groomed car reflects its owner.
      b.   The car you drive says a lot about you. (Mann and Thompson 1988)

In the following section, we shall see how the interpretation of restatement sequences can be explained in terms of the notion of optimal relevance and the criterion of consistency with the principle of relevance.

It might be argued at this point that while the hearer's recognition of coherence relations is not enough to provide a full account of how these sequences are interpreted, the recognition of coherence relations is nevertheless necessary for comprehension. In other words, it could be claimed that in order to understand the utterance *U1* in the sequence *U1. U2* it is necessary to recover what Mann and Thompson (1987) call "relational proposition," which expresses a particular structural relation.

However, as Blass (1990) has pointed out, everyday discourse is full of acceptable utterances which cannot be understood in isolation from the context, but which cannot be said to be part of a coherent text. For example, travellers on the London Underground are able to recognize that the utterance displayed at the foot of escalators is not intended to be interpreted as a requirement that everyone using the escalator must carry a dog, but only that travellers who are travelling with dogs on the escalator must carry them:

(9)   Dogs must be carried.

It is not clear why the psychological processes involved in accessing and using contextual assumptions for the interpretation of isolated utterances like (9) and the principles governing those processes should be different from the ones involved in the interpretation of utterances which are part of a text.

As we have seen, repetitions are analyzed in a coherence approach in terms of a structural relation between adjacent segments. However, as Wilson (1995) points out, it is not clear how this approach would analyze repetitions which are not adjacent or repetitions in one-clause utterances like (10):

(10)   That was a really really stupid thing to do.

Wilson argues that since there is no obvious intonation break in (10), it could only be treated as a two-clause utterance because it is a repetition. Clearly, it would be more satisfactory to have an analysis which covers *all* cases of repetition whether or not they occur in adjacent segments.[3] However, as Blass (1990) has pointed out, an utterance may be part of an incoherent discourse, but still be understood by a hearer. For example, B's response in (11) has both a coherent interpretation in which it reports what she said, and an incoherent interpretation in which it describes what B has just seen:

(11)   A: What did she say?
         B: That man has a gun.

Some writers (for example, Tsui 1991) analyze interruptions as violations of a "coherence rule" which, unless they are justified, result in antisocial and impolite behavior. This raises the question of what justifies such violations. Giora (1996), who, unlike many coherence theorists, does not believe that coherence is analyzable in terms of a set of local coherence relations, regards the incoherent interpretation of B in (11) as unacceptable because it violates a "Relevance Requirement" (not to be confused with Sperber and Wilson's Principle of Relevance) which requires that all the propositions of a well-formed discourse be related to a discourse-topic proposition. However, she also suggests that violations from this requirement are acceptable provided that they are explicitly marked by an expression such as *by the way*, *incidentally*. However, as Wilson (1998) has shown, this would rule out B in (11) (which is not explicitly marked) but allow something like (12):

(12)   A: What's the time?
         B: By the way, Tutankhamen ate my dog. (example from Wilson 1998)

As we shall see in the following section, the interpretation of interruptions can be explained in terms of the notion of optimal relevance and the criterion of consistency with the principle of relevance. More generally, as Wilson (1998) points out, Giora's notion of topic relevance can be shown to be derivative in a relevance theoretic account. It is generally agreed that the function of the discourse topic is to provide access to contextual information required for comprehension. However, as Sperber and Wilson (1986) show, it is contextual information rather than the discourse topic that is essential for comprehension: on the one hand, a text may be comprehensible even where there is no explicitly stated topic, and, on the other hand, it may remain incomprehensible even where there is an explicitly stated topic.[4]

Although Giora (1996) does not analyze coherence in terms of local coherence relations between the segments of a text, she does recognize that we have intuitions about the way in which adjacent segments are related. And, indeed, there is no question that we are capable of recognizing coherence relations like restatement, elaboration, sequence. The question is whether these relations actually are computed in the course of utterance comprehension. In this section, we have seen that a coherence-based approach lacks the generality required for an account of comprehension which covers all utterances. In the following section I shall show that in a relevance theoretic framework the computation of coherence relations is not only unnecessary, since they can be derived as a consequence of the hearer's search for relevance, but may also be inconsistent with the Principle of Relevance.

2   Relevance and Coherence

The assumption that an utterance is consistent with the Principle of Relevance is based on the hearer's recognition that it is an act of ostensive communication – that is, an act of deliberate, overt communication in which the speaker not only intends to convey a particular message but is also actively helping the hearer recognize this. From the speaker's point of view, it is simply not worth engaging in such an act unless the audience pays attention to it. But equally, from the hearer's point of view it is not worth paying attention to an act of communication unless there is information worth processing – or in other words, unless it is relevant. This means that a speaker who requests the hearer's attention, for example by producing an utterance, communicates his or her assumption that his or her utterance is relevant.[5]

Relevance is defined in terms of *contextual effect* and *processing effort*. Contextual effects are simply the ways in which a new piece of information may interact with contextual assumptions to yield an improvement to the hearer's overall representation of the world. These are not confined to new assumptions derived from combining the new information with contextual assumptions, but may also include increased evidence for existing assumptions or even the elimination of existing assumptions. Processing effort is a function not only of the linguistic complexity of the utterance itself, but also of the cost of accessing and using contextual assumptions in the derivation of contextual effects.

Sperber and Wilson (1986) argue that the presumption of relevance carried by every act of ostensive communication has two aspects: first, it creates a presumption that the information it communicates interacts with the context for derivation of adequate *contextual effects*; and second, it creates a presumption that no gratuitous processing effort is required for the recovery of effects. Taken together, these presumptions define a level of *optimal relevance*. And the principle of relevance is simply the thesis that every act of ostensive communication communicates a presumption of its own optimal relevance.[6]

This is not to say that every act of ostensive communication is in fact optimally relevant. Suppose you grab my arm and point to the clock, which is now showing 3 o'clock. If I have seen the clock, then the presumption of optimal relevance communicated by your behavior is false. However, your behavior is still consistent with the principle of relevance inasmuch as it is not difficult for me to see how you *thought* it was optimally relevant.

Nor is it to say that the intended interpretation is always recovered. The Principle of Relevance does not guarantee that communication will succeed. Suppose, for example, the interpretation of A's utterance in (13) provides an immediately accessible context which, taken together with B's answer, yields adequate contextual effects. The resulting coherent interpretation, in which B's utterance is a report of what Jane said, will then be justified under the principle of relevance. However, it may not have been the one intended, and communication may fail:

(13)　A:　What did Jane say?
　　　　B:　It's 3 o'clock.

On the other hand, the coherent interpretation is not the only interpretation which might be justified under the principle of relevance. Obviously, the answer to A's question is relevant to him. Why otherwise would he have asked it? However, it is not difficult to imagine how B's utterance might trigger an immediately accessible context in which the information that it is 3 o'clock yields contextual effects. For example, A and B may have been planning to catch a train which leaves just after 3. They can always continue their discussion of Jane on the train. But the train will not wait.

In this case, B's utterance is processed for relevance in a context which is distinct from the one in which A's utterance is interpreted. There are no contextual assumptions used in the interpretation of B's utterance that are used in the interpretation of A's. Moreover, the contextual assumptions used in establishing the relevance of B's utterance do not include the content of A's utterance or any contextual effects derived from it. This, argues Blass, is the source of the incoherence. Putting this the other way round, if a discourse *is* coherent, then it is because there is continuity of context in the sense that assumptions made accessible by the interpretation of one segment are used in establishing the relevance of the next. Since the interpretation of information which has just been processed will provide a highly accessible context for the interpretation of an utterance, coherence can be regarded as a consequence of the hearer's search for optimal relevance.

If this is right, then it ought to be possible to show how particular coherence relations can be reanalyzed in terms of a consequence of the way relevance is established. This is the aim of the following section, where I shall outline a relevance theoretic reassessment of so-called sequential relations, and, then, some of the subtypes of elaboration. However, first, let us see how the claim that computation of coherence relations are necessary for comprehension would have to be justified in a framework which assumes that comprehension is constrained by the Principle of Relevance.

On the assumption that understanding an utterance is a matter of recovering its *explicatures* (or intended explicit content) and the *contextual effects* that the hearer is intended to derive from those explicatures, the claim that the computation of coherence relations is necessary for comprehension amounts to the claim that their identification is necessary for the recovery of an utterance's explicatures and intended contextual effects. If the identification of this relation is not necessary for the recovery of adequate contextual effects, then the effort required for its identification would be gratuitous, and would be ruled out by the second clause of the definition of optimal relevance (above). In other words, in a relevance theoretic framework a coherence relation should never be computed unless its identification contributes to adequate contextual effects.[7]

3   The Reassessment of Coherence Relations

3.1   *Sequence*

In a coherence-based framework the interpretation of sequences like the ones in (14) and (15) involve the identification of relations of temporal and causal sequence respectively:

(14)   a.   A number 16 bus finally arrived.
      b.   I asked the driver whether he was going to the university.

(15)   a.   The number 16 bus was half an hour late.
      b.   I missed most of the syntax lecture.

However, if Carston's (1993) analysis of these sequences is correct, these relations are a consequence of the way in which the hearer of these utterances uses contextual information to develop the linguistically determined semantic representation into a proposition which can achieve optimal relevance.[8] Her argument is that the linguistically determined semantic representation of these utterances underdetermines their propositional content in just the same way as the linguistic meaning underdetermines the explicit content of utterances like those in (16):

(16)   a.   It's too hot.
      b.   Too hot.

In order to recover a proposition which can achieve optimal relevance, the hearer must use contextual information to recover the reference of whatever is too hot, the intended sense of *hot* and the identity of what it is too hot for. Similarly, the search for optimal relevance will lead the hearer of (14) and (15) to use contextual assumptions in the recovery of the enriched propositional forms in (17) and (18) respectively:

(17)   a.   A number 16 bus finally arrived at time t_n.
      b.   At time t_{n+1} I asked the driver whether he was going to the university.

(18)   a.   [The number 16 bus was half an hour late]$_i$.
      b.   As a result of that$_i$ I missed most of the syntax lecture.

As Carston (1993) points out, this interpretation can be explained in terms of the fact that ready-made scripted knowledge makes the contextual assumptions that give rise to it highly accessible. However, she also points out that this cannot be the whole story, since there is a range of other cases in which sequential or causal enrichment cannot be a result of ready scripted knowledge – for example, (19) – and, moreover, a range of cases in which a sequential interpretation is not necessarily recovered at all – for example (20):

(19)   John broke his leg and skied over a precipice.

(20)   a.   John broke his leg.
     b.   He skied over a precipice. (examples from Smith 1990)[9]

Carston's suggestion that the causal interpretation of sequences like (19) can be seen as "the product of some quite general cognitive predisposition to forge certain connections and relations between states and events whenever it is reasonable to do so" (1993: 33) is not to be construed as a suggestion that hearers have a cognitive tendency to compute coherence relations in the course of comprehension, but rather that their information-processing capacities and their tendency to optimize relevance leads the hearer to enrich the linguistically determined semantic representation so that the proposition expressed has the sort of form given in (18). Once the hearer has recovered this proposition there is no justification (under the Principle of Relevance) for recovering a further proposition that a particular coherence relation holds (cf. Mann and Thompson 1987).

3.2   *Explanation*

However, as Carston (1993) recognizes, it still has to be explained why this causal interpretation is not necessarily recovered in nonconjoined utterances like (20). Carston's explanation of the difference between (19) and (20) hinges, first, on the claim that since we are "question-asking, explanation-seeking creatures" (1993: 38), our search for optimal relevance in a sequence in which the speaker has presented a fact involves asking "Why?," and, second, on the fact that a conjunction is a syntactic unit and hence a unit of relevance. If the first segment of (20) raises the question "Why?," then the second will achieve optimal relevance in virtue of answering that question. Once again, since the hearer has recognized that this is how the utterance achieves relevance, there is no justification for recovering the information that it stands in a particular coherence relation.

As Carston points out, this explanation is not restricted to the interpretation of utterances which follow an utterance that raises an implicit "Why?" question. In the following examples, which in a coherence framework would be analyzed in terms of elaboration, the (b) segments seem to answer implicit "Where?" and "Who?" questions:

(21)   a.   I ate at a good restaurant last week.
     b.   It was McDonald's.

(22)   a.   I met a great actress at the party.
     b.   It was Vanessa Redgrave. (examples due to Deirdre Wilson)

Questions and answers are by their very nature planned as separate utterances each carrying the presumption of relevance individually. However, as Carston argues, the fact that a conjoined utterance like (19) is a single syntactic unit means that it is a single processing unit which is interpreted for relevance as a whole. For Carston, this follows from syntactic considerations, in particular, the assumption that an utterance unit is in correspondence with a grammatical unit. However, I have argued (Blakemore 1987: 120) that this follows from relevance theoretic considerations: the processing effort that follows from the extra lexical and syntactic structure involved in conjoining can only be offset if the conjoined proposition carries the presumption of relevance. This suggests that both syntactic and pragmatic considerations could support an explanation of why the second conjunct of a conjoined utterance can never be interpreted as an answer to an implicit question raised by the first conjunct.

3.3 Exemplification

As Carston points out, these sorts of considerations also explain the interpretive difference between examples like the ones in (23a) and (b):

(23) a. The buses never arrive on time these days. Yesterday I waited 20 minutes for the number 16.

  b. The buses never arrive on time and yesterday I waited 20 minutes for the number 16.

On the assumption that "exemplification is a common way of providing evidence for a claim or, equivalently, giving a reason for believing something" (Carston 1992: 11), then it is not surprising that only the juxtaposed sequence in (23a) can be interpreted as a claim and exemplification. For to present a claim and then to present evidence for it is to present two utterances each of which carries the presumption of relevance individually. But why should exemplification be a means of providing evidence for a claim?

In Blakemore (1997) I argue that the answer to this question lies in the fact that once the state of affairs described by the speaker is recognized as an example, there is an expectation that it is typical in some respect and hence that there are other states of affairs which the speaker could have cited. For to say that there are a number of buses which are like the speaker's bus in virtue of their lateness is to provide support for the generalization that buses never arrive on time these days. It is possible for the speaker to strengthen her evidence by citing more examples. However, if these are recognized as examples, then no matter how many cases are cited, it will always be understood that there are others. In other words, it is the suggestion that there are other cases which could have been cited which makes exemplification such a good means of providing evidence for the claim exemplified.

This argument would seem to suggest that the hearer must recognize that an utterance is intended as an exemplification before he or she can understand it, for the assumption that the state of affairs is an example plays a central role in the recovery of its contextual effects. And indeed, it seems that a speaker who questions or denies the assumption that an utterance is an exemplification also questions or denies its intended contextual effects. For example, in the following, which is based on a radio interview (Radio 4, 12 August 1997), B is denying that the second segment of A's utterance provides support for the first by denying that it is an example.

(24) *A:* There seems to be something really wrong with the army. I assume you know about those soldiers who smashed up their hotel room in Uruguay?

  B: Yes, it was disgraceful, but it was just one isolated and very atypical incident.

However, it does not follow from this that the computation of coherence relations is essential for the comprehension of discourse. It only shows that the assumption that the utterance is intended as an exemplification is recovered because it contributes to the recovery of adequate contextual effects. Moreover, the crucial assumption in the inferential processes involved in establishing the relevance of the utterance is not so much the assumption that it is connected to the preceding text in a particular way as the assumption that the state of affairs it represents is typical in a particular respect. The role played by the interpretation of the preceding utterance is to give the hearer access to contextual assumptions which enable him or her to identify this respect.

3.4   Restatement

In my recent work on reformulations and reformulation markers (Blakemore 1993, 1994, 1997) I have argued that reformulations are on example of the way that utterances may be relevant as representations of utterances which they resemble. As Sperber and Wilson (1986) point out, all sorts of phenomena can be used as representations in this way; for example, pictorial representations and mimes. Of course, no two phenomena are exactly alike, and a communicator expects the hearer to identify the respects in which the resemblance holds. In the case of an utterance which is used to represent another, the resemblance may hold in virtue of resemblances in phonetic and phonological form, or resemblances in lexical and syntactic form, or resemblances in logical properties. For example, all the utterances in (27) could be produced as answers to (26) in a situation in which the director had produced the utterance in (25):

(25)   We will have to let her go.

(26)   What did the director say?

(27)   a.   We will have to let her go.
       b.   They'll have to let her go.
       c.   She's fired.

(27a) is a direct quotation and represents the director's utterance in virtue of resemblances in linguistic and semantic structure. (27b) has a different semantic structure (since it uses the third person pronoun instead of the original first person pronoun), but the two utterances share a common propositional form. (27c) has neither the same linguistic structure nor the same propositional form as the original. However, its propositional form may still be said to *resemble* the propositional form of the original in the sense that it is not difficult to imagine a context in which it gives rise to the same contextual implications. In such cases where the resemblance involves the sharing of logical and contextual implications, Sperber and Wilson say that the utterance can be said to be relevant as an *interpretation* of a propositional form or thought.

A speaker who produces an utterance which is relevant as a representation of another utterance cannot be taken to be creating expectations of truthfulness since she or he is not using that utterance *descriptively*. She or he can only be taken to be creating expectations of *faithfulness*. Faithfulness is a matter of degree, the degree of faithfulness being determined by the extent to which the two propositional forms share logical and contextual implications, and the degree of faithfulness attempted will vary from situation to situation. Thus in (7), repeated here as (28), the second segment achieves the same contextual effects as the first:

(28) a. At the beginning of this piece there is an example of an anacrusis.
      b. That is, it begins with a unaccented note which is not part of the first full bar. (Blakemore 1997)

Since the speaker is restating his own utterance, he is as committed to the factuality of the reformulation as he is to the original. However, the main point of utterance lies in the fact that it is a faithful interpretation of the preceding segment.

In an unplanned discourse, an utterance like (28b) would be justified under the Principle of Relevance if it followed the speaker's recognition that he had made a miscalculation of the hearer's contextual and processing resources, and that the original did not in fact achieve optimal relevance. However, sequences like (28) may also be part of a planned discourse. Why would a speaker aiming at consistency with the Principle of Relevance deliberately produce *both* the original and the reformulation if the second segment alone would have achieved the same contextual effects for less processing effort?

The use of a term with which the hearer is assumed to be unfamiliar and then its reformulation is characteristic of what might be called a pedagogical style, which itself can be justified in terms of the Principle of Relevance. For the speaker can be taken to communicate not just the information about the beginning of the piece of music, but also information about the term *anacrusis*. The assumption that it is relevant to teach the hearer what the term means by reformulating it is based on an assumption about the hearer's processing resources, and clearly a miscalculation here would result in a patronizing style.

A rather different effect is achieved in Mann and Thompson's example, repeated here as (29), which I assume is an advertisement for car polish:

(29) a. A WELL-GROOMED CAR REFLECTS ITS OWNER.
      b. The car you drive says a lot about you. (Mann and Thompson 1988)

The pun in the first segment captures the hearer's attention by presenting her with a sort of puzzle: the speaker could mean either that one's reflection shows on a well-groomed, shiny car or that owning a well-groomed car is evidence for being a well-groomed, smart kind of person. The second segment is an interpretation of only the second proposition and in this sense could be regarded as providing a solution to the puzzle posed by the pun, or, in other words, a means of constraining the hearer's interpretation of the first segment. However, the second segment alone would not have captured the hearer's attention in the way that the first segment does. Nor would it have yielded contextual effects about the shiny qualities of well-groomed cars. This means that although the interpretation of the first segment entails processing costs not entailed by the second segment, this effort is offset by, first, the way it captures the attention of the hearer and, second, contextual effects which would not have been achieved by the second segment alone.

These analyses have described (28b) and (29b) as reformulations. However, I have argued that this description must itself be analyzed in terms of the notion of interpretive representation. The question of whether an utterance is relevant as an interpretation (rather than a description) is not a question about how it is connected to the preceding text, but a question about the relationship between the proposition it expresses and the thought it represents. As Sperber and Wilson (1986, 1985/6) and Wilson and Sperber (1992) have shown, the notion of interpretive representation is involved in the analysis of a range of phenomena; for example, reported speech, free indirect speech, interrogatives, irony, and metaphor. In some cases, an utterance may be relevant as an interpretation of a thought that has been communicated by an utterance that is not part of a continuous text, and in other cases it may be relevant as an interpretation of a thought that has not been communicated at all. Indeed, according to relevance theory, the identification of an utterance as a reformulation follows from an aspect of interpretation which is fundamental to the way in which the relevance of all utterances is established, and will not itself contribute to the identification of contextual effects. This is not to say that a hearer, or, indeed, an analyst, will not describe the utterance as a reformulation. The point is that such a description is a consequence of the recognition that the utterance is an instance of interpretive rather than descriptive language use.

4   Implications for Discourse Understanding

In this chapter I have focused on an approach to discourse which assumes that discourse coherence provides the key to a theory of discourse comprehension, and have shown how in a relevance theoretic framework hearers' intuitions about coherence can be explained as a consequence of the hearer's search for an interpretation that is consistent with the Principle of Relevance. However, work in relevance theory is not just concerned with the reassessment of coherence relations. It has also shown how the notion of optimal relevance can be used to explain those aspects of comprehension which are claimed to be a consequence of the search for discourse coherence.

For example, recently Wilson and Matsui (1998) have compared the predictions made by Asher and Lascarides's (1995) coherence-based heuristics for disambiguation in discourse with those made by relevance theory. Whereas relevance theory claims that the same criterion of consistency with the Principle of Relevance explains disambiguation in both isolated utterances and extended texts, Asher and Lascarides's heuristics are designed to *supplement* the word-association heuristics given in the artificial intelligence literature for disambiguating isolated utterances. Wilson shows that neither the heuristics for isolated utterances nor the heuristics for discourse make the correct predictions and argues that disambiguation phenomena are more satisfactorily explained in terms of the notion of optimal relevance.

The criterion of consistency with the Principle of Relevance also provides a unitary explanation for the assignment of reference in isolated utterances and discourse sequences such as (30) (from Wilson 1992):

(30)   Sean Penn attacked a photographer. *The man* was quite badly hurt.

While it is often claimed that reference resolution is affected by the relative accessibility of the candidate referents, it is also agreed that an account based on accessibility alone would make the wrong predictions. For example, Herb Clark (1977) proposes that reference assignment in examples like (30) is affected by the number and plausibility of the assumptions needed to introduce the intended referent; but as Wilson (1992) and Matsui (1993, 1995) show, this proposal does not deal with all examples. Candidate referents must also be evaluated in terms of a pragmatic criterion that the overall interpretation is supposed to meet.

However, Wilson and Matsui (1998) have shown that neither the attempts to define such a criterion in terms of truth (cf. Lewis 1979; Sidner 1983) nor the attempts to develop a coherence-based criterion (cf. Hobbs 1979; Fox 1987) explain reference resolution in all cases. Moreover, a criterion which is powerful to choose among the various interpretations of an utterance on either of these grounds could do so only by considering them all. As Wilson (1995) says, this "would create a combinatorial explosion of gigantic proportions, and be quite unlike what hearers actually do." Her relevance theoretic analyses of examples that are problematic for both truth- and coherence-based accounts show that what hearers actually do is to accept the first interpretation that is consistent with the Principle of Relevance and that the speaker could have manifestly foreseen.

Within coherence-based approaches to discourse, expressions like utterance-initial *so, well, still, after all* are classified as *discourse markers*, a term which is intended to reflect the role that these expressions play in *marking, signaling,* or *indicating* how one unit of discourse is connected to another (cf. Levinson 1983: 87–8; Fraser 1990; Mann and Thompson 1987; Sanders et al. 1993; Knott and Dale 1994).[10] Since relevance-based approaches are concerned with processes of utterance understanding rather than the structure of discourse, and appeal to contextual effects rather than coherence relations, it is not surprising that relevance theoretic analyses of these expressions are significantly different from coherence-based ones.

For example, whereas Sanders et al. analyze *but* as an explicit guide to a range of coherence relations (namely, Contrast, Antithesis, Contrastive Cause–Consequence), my 1987 analysis treats *but* as an expression which constrains the interpretation process by narrowing down the search for the intended contextual effects. Thus while this analysis, like Sanders et al.'s, treats *but* as expressing either contrast or denial of expectation (cf. Lakoff 1971), it does this not by analyzing it in terms of a marker of coherence relations, but by analyzing it as an instruction for the recovery of contextual effects.[11]

The analysis of a discourse marker as an expression which links units of discourse would seem to imply that it cannot be used discourse initially. However, as the examples in (31–2) show, this is clearly not the case:

(31)   (speaker sees hearer come in laden with shopping) So you've spent all your
        money.

(32)   (speaker takes an enormous slice of cake) After all, it is my birthday.

If these expressions connect an utterance and a *context*, as my 1987 analysis suggests, this is not surprising. For while contextual assumptions may be derived from the preceding discourse, they may also be derived from the hearer's perception of the environment from memory. Not all discourse markers can be used discourse-initially, of course. However, as Blakemore (1998) shows, this can be explained in terms of the particular constraint that the expression imposes.

Within coherence-based approaches, discourse markers are said to have a *pragmatic meaning* on the grounds that they do not contribute to the truth conditions of the utterance that contains them. The relevance theoretic analysis I have described was an attempt to provide an explanation of the distinction between truth-conditional and nontruth-conditional meaning in terms of the cognitively motivated distinction between conceptual and procedural meaning. However, recent work within relevance theory has shown that the conceptual–procedural distinction is not coextensive with the truth-conditional–nontruth-conditional distinction, and that in particular there are discourse connectives which, although they do not contribute to truth conditions, nevertheless encode concepts (cf. Wilson and Sperber 1993; Blakemore 1996, 1997; Ifantidou-Trouki 1993). For example, in contrast with expressions like *but* and *well*, the so-called apposition marker *in other words* is both nontruth-conditional and conceptual.

Sperber and Wilson's (1995) speculation that the conceptual–procedural distinction will shed more light on linguistic semantics than the traditional distinction between truth-conditional and nontruth-conditional meaning provides an exciting agenda for future semantics research. Since expressions classified as discourse markers may encode either conceptual or procedural meaning, it seems that they will have an important part in this research.[12] At the same time, a relevance theoretic analysis of these expressions will play a significant role in showing how the approach I have outlined in this chapter can offer more insight into the psychological processes underlying discourse understanding than can an approach which analyses them as expressions which link units of discourse.

5   Conclusion

In this chapter, I have shown that according to relevance theory, discourse under-standing is not a by-product of discourse acceptability or coherence, and that our intuitions about the coherence of discourse are a consequence of our search for rel-evance. However, neither the relevance theoretic reassessment of coherence relations in section 3 nor the reanalysis of discourse phenomena in section 4 should be taken as an argument that we should simply replace talk of coherence relations by talk of "relevance relations." Coherence is a property of an object external to the human mind and is defined in terms of structural relations between subunits of that object. Relevance is a property of a mentally represented interpretation of the evidence a communicator provides for the thought(s) she or he intends to communicate, and is defined in terms of a function of the effects this interpretation has on the hearer's overall representation of the world and the effort that is needed for its derivation.

NOTES

1   For definitions of elaboration, see Hobbs (1979, 1983), Mann and Thompson (1987), and Hovy and Maier (1994).

2   For example, Samet and Schank (1984) propose that although local coherence must be defined in terms of coherence relations, global coherence must be analyzed in terms of stereotypic scripts and goals. Others, for example, Reinhart (1980), Giora (1996), and Sidner (1983), adopt a more functional approach and propose that coherence should be defined in terms of relevance to a discourse topic.

3   For a relevance theoretic analysis of repetitions, see Sperber and Wilson (1986). If the recognition of coherence relations is necessary for comprehension, then it would seem to follow that only coherent discourses are comprehensible.

4   For further discussion, see Sperber and Wilson (1987: 742).

5   Expository articles on Relevance Theory include Blakemore (1988b, 1995); Carston (1988, 1993); Smith and Wilson (1992); Wilson (1994); Wilson and Sperber (1986). For a précis of *Relevance*, see Sperber and Wilson (1987). For a book-length introduction, see Blakemore (1992).

6   This principle is what Sperber and Wilson (1995: 260–72) call *the communicative principle of relevance* and must be distinguished from *the cognitive principle of relevance*, which states that human cognition tends to be geared to the maximization of relevance. As Wilson (1998) points out, the confusion between these two principles has lead to misunderstandings about how relevance theory works (see for example, Giora 1996).

7   Unger (1986) makes a similar point.

8   See also Wilson and Sperber (1998).

9   Smith (1990) uses similar arguments against the view that a notion of narrative tense is necessary to account for the interpretation of narrative sequences.

10 Schiffrin's (1987) analysis of discourse markers is grounded in a more functional approach to discourse which assumes that language is designed for communication and attempts to show how their use is a consequence of structural, semantic, and pragmatic factors. In contrast with the approaches mentioned here, she argues that they play a role in establishing discourse coherence not just at a local level, but also from a global level. However, it should be noted that in contrast with relevance theoretic analyses, her analysis treats a marker like *so* as linking either ideas, premise, and conclusion in inference *or* acts of communication.

11 For other relevance theoretic analyses of discourse markers, see Blakemore (1988a); Blass (1990); Higashimori (1994); Itani (1993); Jucker (1993); Moeschler (1989, 1993); Rouchota (1998); Unger (1996). Ducrot (1984) has also developed a procedural approach to the analysis of discourse markers, but not from within a relevance theoretic framework.

12 For further discussion of this issue, see Blakemore (1997).

REFERENCES

Asher, N. and Lascarides, A. (1995) Lexical disambiguation in a discourse context. *Journal of Semantics*, 12. 69–108.

Blakemore, D. L. (1987) *Semantic Constraints on Relevance*. Oxford: Blackwell.

Blakemore, D. L. (1988a) *So* as a constraint on relevance. In R. Kempson (ed.) *Mental Representations: The Interface between Language and Reality*. Cambridge: Cambridge University Press. 183–96.

Blakemore, D. L. (1988b) The organization of discourse. In F. Newmeyer (ed.) *Linguistics: The Cambridge Survey* vol. 4. Cambridge: Cambridge University Press. 229–50.

Blakemore, D. L. (1992) *Understanding Utterances*. Oxford: Blackwell.

Blakemore, D. L. (1993) The relevance of reformulations. *Language and Literature*, 2(2). 101–20.

Blakemore, D. L. (1994) Relevance, poetic effects and social goals: a reply to Culpeper. *Language and Literature*, 3(1). 49–59.

Blakemore, D. L. (1995) Relevance theory. In J. Verschuerne, J-O. Ostman, and J. Blommaert (eds), *Handbook of Pragmatics*. Amsterdam: John Benjamins. 443–52.

Blakemore, D. L. (1996) Are apposition markers discourse markers? *Journal of Linguistics*, 32. 325–47.

Blakemore, D. L. (1997a) Restatement and exemplification: a relevance theoretic re-assessment of elaboration. *Pragmatics and Cognition*, 5(1). 1–19.

Blakemore, D. L. (1997b) Non-truth conditional meaning. *Linguistische Berichte*, 8. 92–102.

Blakemore, D. L. (1998) On the context for so-called "discourse markers." In K. Malmkjaer and J. Williams (eds) *Context in Language Learning*

Understanding. Cambridge: Cambridge University Press. 44–59.

Blass, R. (1990) *Relevance Relations in Discourse*. Cambridge: Cambridge University Press.

Carston, R. (1988) Language and cognition. In F. Newmeyer (ed.) *Linguistics: The Cambridge Survey* vol. III. Cambridge: Cambridge University Press. 38–68.

Carston, R. (1992) Conjunction, explanation and relevance. Unpublished ms. Revised (1993) version in *Lingua*, 90(1/2).

Carston, R. (1993) Conjunction, explanation and relevance. *Lingua* 90(1/2). 23–48.

Chomsky, N. (1986) *Knowledge of Language*. New York: Praeger.

Clark, H. (1977) Bridging. In P. Johnson-Laird and P. Wason (eds) *Thinking: Readings in Cognitive Science*. Cambridge: Cambridge University Press. 411–20.

Ducrot, O. (1984) *Le dire et le dit*. Paris: Minuit.

Fasold, R. (1990) *Sociolinguistics of Language*. Oxford: Blackwell.

Fox, B. (1987) *Discourse Structure and Anaphora*. Cambridge: Cambridge University Press.

Fraser, B. (1990). An approach to discourse markers. *Journal of Pragmatics*, 14. 383–95.

Giora, R. (1996) Discourse coherence and theory of relevance: stumbling blocks in search a unified theory. *Journal of Pragmatics*, 27. 17–34.

Halliday, M. A. K. and Hasan, R. (1976) *Cohesion in English*. London: Longman.

Harris, Z. (1951) *Methods in Structural Linguistics*. Chicago: University of Chicago Press.

Higashimori, I. (1994) A relevance theoretic analysis of *even, sae/sura/mo/*

temo/ddemo/datte/made. English Literature Review (Kyoto Women's University) 38. 51–80.

Hobbs, J. (1979) Coherence and coreference. *Cognitive Science*, 3. 67–90.

Hobbs, J. (1983) Why is discourse coherent? In F. Neubauer (ed.), *Coherence in Natural Language Texts*. Hamburg: Buske. 29–70.

Hovy, E. and Maier, E. (1994) Parsimonious or profligate: how many and which discourse structure relations? Unpublished.

Ifantidou-Trouki, E. (1993) Sentential adverbs and relevance. *Lingua*, 90(1/2). 65–90.

Itani, R. (1993) The Japanese sentence-final particle *ka*: a relevance theoretic approach. *Lingua*, 90(1/2). 129–47.

Jucker, A. (1993) The discourse marker *well*: a relevance theoretic account. *Journal of Pragmatics*, 19. 435–52.

Knott, A. and Dale, R. (1994) Using a set of linguistic phenomena to motivate a set of coherence relations. *Discourse Processes*, 18(1). 35–62.

Lakoff, R. (1971) Ifs ands and buts about conjunction. In C. J. Fillmore and D. T. Langendoen (eds) *Studies in Linguistic Semantics*. New York: Holt Rinehart and Winston. 115–50.

Levinson, S. (1983) *Pragmatics*. Cambridge: Cambridge University Press.

Lewis, D. (1979) Scorekeeping in a language game. In R. Bauerle et al. (eds) *Semantics from Different Points of View*. Berlin: Springer. 172–8.

Mann, W. C. and Thompson, S. (1987) Relational propositions in discourse. *Discourse Processes*, 9. 57–90.

Mann, W. C. and Thompson, S. (1988) Rhetorical structure theory: towards a functional theory of text organization. *Text*, 8(3). 243–81.

Matsui, T. (1993) Bridging reference and the notions of topic and focus. *Lingua*, 9(1/2). 49–68.

Matsui, T. (1995) Bridging and Reference. University of London, PhD thesis.

Moeschler, J. (1989) Pragmatic connectives, argumentative coherence and relevance. *Argumentation*, 3.3. 321–39.

Moeschler, J. (1993) Relevance and conversation. *Lingua* 90. 1/2. 149–71.

Reinhart, T. (1980) Conditions for text coherence. *Poetics Today*, 1(4). 161–80.

Rouchota, V. (1998). Procedural meaning and parenthetical discourse markers. In A. Jucker and Y. Ziv (eds) *Discourse Markers: Description and Theory*. Amsterdam: John Benjamins. 97–126.

Salkie, R. (1995) *Text and Discourse Analysis*. London: Routledge.

Samet, J. and Schank, R. (1984) Coherence and connectivity. *Linguistics and Philosophy*, 7(1). 57–82.

Sanders, T., Spooren, W., and Noordman, L. (1993) Towards a taxonomy of coherence relations. *Discourse Processes*, 15(1). 1–36.

Schiffrin, D. (1987). *Discourse Markers*. Cambridge: Cambridge University Press.

Sidner, C. (1983) Focusing and discourse. *Discourse Processes*, 6. 107–30.

Smith, N. (1990) Observations on the pragmatics of tense. *UCL Working Papers in Linguistics*, 2. 113–46.

Smith, N. and Wilson, D. (1992) Introduction to the special issue on relevance theory. *Lingua*, 87(1/2). 1–10.

Sperber, D. and Wilson, D. (1985/6) Loose talk. *Proceedings of the Aristotelian Society*, LXXXVI. 153–71.

Sperber, D. and Wilson, D. (1986) *Relevance: Communication and Cognition*. Oxford: Blackwell.

Sperber, D. and Wilson, D. (1987) Presumptions of relevance. *Behavioural and Brain Sciences*, 13(1). 736–54.

Sperber, D. and Wilson, D. (1995) *Relevance* (2nd edition). Oxford: Blackwell.

Tsui, A. (1991) Sequencing rules and coherence in discourse. *Journal of Pragmatics*, 15. 111–29.

Unger, C. (1996) The scope of discourse connectives: implications for discourse organization. *Journal of Linguistics*, 32(2). 403–38.

Wilson, D. (1992) Reference and relevance. *UCL Working Papers in Linguistics*, 4. 165–91.

Wilson, D. (1994) Relevance and understanding. In G. Brown, K. Malkmjaer, A. Pollit, and J. Williams (eds), *Language and Understanding*. Oxford: Oxford University Press. 35–58.

Wilson, D. (1995) Issues in pragmatics. Unpublished lectures.

Wilson, D. (1998) Discourse, coherence and relevance: a reply to Rachel Giora. *Journal of Pragmatics*, 29. 57–74.

Wilson, D. and Matsui, T. (1998) Recent approaches to bridging: truth coherence and relevance. *University of London Working Papers in Linguistics*, 10. 173–200.

Wilson, D. and Sperber, D. (1986) Pragmatics and modularity. Reprinted in S. Davis (ed.) 1991, *Pragmatics: A Reader*. Oxford: Oxford University Press. 377–93.

Wilson, D. and Sperber, D. (1992) On verbal irony. *Lingua*, 87(1/2). 53–76.

Wilson, D. and Sperber, D. (1993) Linguistic form and relevance. *Lingua*, 90. 5–25.

Wilson, D. and Sperber, D. (1998) Pragmatics and time. In R. Carston and S. Uchida (eds) *Relevance Theory:Implications and Applications*. Amsterdam: John Benjamins. 1–22.

6 Discourse and Information Structure

GREGORY WARD AND BETTY J. BIRNER

0 Introduction

In addition to deciding what to say, speakers must decide how to say it. The central premise of studies on the relationship between syntax and discourse function is that a speaker's use of a particular structural option is constrained by specific aspects of the context of utterance. Work in discourse has uncovered a variety of specific discourse functions served by individual syntactic constructions.[1] More recently, in Birner and Ward (1998) we examine generalizations that apply *across* constructions, identifying ways in which a given functional principle is variously realized in similar but distinct constructions.

1 Theoretical Framework

English, like many other languages, shows a tendency to order "given" information before "new" information in an utterance. Indeed, Prince (1981a: 247) posits a "conspiracy of syntactic constructions" designed to prevent NPs that represent relatively unfamiliar information from occupying subject position (see also Kuno 1971, inter alia). Chafe (1976) defines given information as "that knowledge which the speaker assumes to be in the consciousness of the addressee at the time of the utterance," while new information is defined as "what the speaker assumes he is introducing into the addressee's consciousness by what he says" (1976: 30). Other notions of given information have relied on such notions as predictability and shared knowledge, or assumed familiarity (see Prince 1981a). In reviewing the literature on givenness in discourse, Prince (1992) finds that three basic approaches may be distinguished, which she terms focus/presupposition, hearer-old/hearer-new, and discourse-old/discourse-new. Along similar lines, Lambrecht (1994) identifies three categories of "information structure" (Halliday 1967): presupposition and assertion (the structuring of propositional information into given and new); identifiability and activation (the information status of discourse referents); and topic and focus (the relative predictability of relations among propositions).

1.1 Focus/Presupposition

Although the term *focus* means different things to different people, we will use it here to refer to that portion of an utterance that represents new information, i.e. just that portion which augments or updates the hearer's view of the common ground (Vallduví 1992). A focused constituent is realized intonationally with some kind of prosodic prominence, generally unclear accent. **Presupposed** information is the complement of focus: it represents the information that the speaker assumes is already part of the common ground, i.e. either salient or inferable in context. A **presupposition** is a proposition that is presupposed in this way.

Because utterances are intended to be informative, the presupposition typically does not exhaust the information in the utterance; instead, the proposition being presupposed is "open" – that is, lacking certain information. Such a proposition is represented with a variable in place of one or more constituents. For example, the utterance in (1a) would give rise to the presupposed open proposition (OP) in (1b), in the sense that a person hearing (1a) would immediately thereafter be licenced to treat (1b) as part of the common ground:

(1) a. Pat brought those cookies to the BBQ.
     b. Pat brought X to the BBQ.

Although only a single word, or syllable, of the focus bears nuclear accent, the focus itself can be indefinitely large; consider (2):

(2) Pat brought a bag of those yummy cookies from Treasure Island to the BBQ.

In a context in which the speaker has been asked *What did Pat bring?*, the focus in (2) would be *a bag of those yummy cookies from Treasure Island*.

It is also possible for a clause to have more than one focus, as in the exchange in (3):

(3) A: Who brought what to the BBQ?
     B: Pat brought cookies.

The presupposition in this case is *X brought Y*, and *Pat* and *cookies* are foci. Notice that *Pat* need not represent entirely new information in order to count as new in this context. Even if Pat is salient in the discourse, *Pat* here is new as an instantiation of the variable in the presupposition. In effect, to say that *Pat* represents new information in this way is to say that the proposition *Pat brought cookies* is (believed to be) absent from the hearer's mental store of propositions, despite the presence of the proposition *X brought Y*.

Not all utterances involve presuppositions; for example, (2) may felicitously be uttered in a context in which it is not presupposed that anyone brought anything. In such a context, the entire utterance may be considered the focus (often called "broad focus").

1.2   *"New to the discourse" vs. "new to the hearer"*

Noting that a two-way division of information into given and new is inadequate, Prince (1992) offers a pair of cross-cutting dichotomies which classify information as, on the one hand, either "discourse-old" or "discourse-new" and, on the other hand, either "hearer-old" or "hearer-new." Discourse-old information is that which has been evoked in the prior discourse, while hearer-old information is that which the speaker believes to be present within the hearer's knowledge store.[2] This distinction captures the fact that what is new to the discourse need not be new to the hearer (cf. Firbas 1966; Chafe 1976; Lambrecht 1994); that is, an entity may be familiar to the hearer yet new to the discourse.

Thus, consider a simple discourse-initial utterance such as (4):

(4)   Last night the moon was so pretty that I called a friend on the phone and told him to go outside and look.

Here, *the moon* represents information that is discourse-new but hearer-old, denoting an entity that has not been evoked in the prior discourse but which can be assumed to be known to the hearer; *a friend* represents information that is both discourse-new and hearer-new, having not been previously evoked and also being (presumably) unknown to the hearer; and *him* represents information that is discourse-old and (therefore) hearer-old, having been explicitly evoked in the previous clause (as *a friend*). The status of what Prince calls "inferable" information (e.g. *the phone* in (4), since people are typically assumed to have telephones) is left unresolved in Prince (1992) and will be discussed below.

Constructions vary not only with respect to whether they are sensitive to discourse-familiarity or hearer-familiarity, but also with respect to whether they are sensitive to "absolute" or "relative" familiarity; the felicitous use of one construction may require that a certain constituent represent discourse-old information (an absolute constraint), while the felicitous use of another may require only that a certain constituent represent *less* familiar information within the discourse than does another constituent (a relative constraint). Thus, there exist three interacting pragmatic dimensions along which constructions can vary: old vs. new information, discourse- vs. hearer-familiarity, and relative vs. absolute familiarity. Moreover, in both preposing and inversion, the preposed constituent represents a discourse-old "link" (Reinhart 1981; Davison 1984; Fraurud 1990; Vallduví 1992; Birner and Ward 1998; inter alia) standing in a specific type of relation to information evoked in the prior context.[3] The range of relations that support this linking will be discussed next.

1.3   *Linking relations*

We will argue that the discourse-old link in a given utterance is related to previously evoked information via a partially ordered set, or **poset**, relationship.[4]

Two elements, A and B, that co-occur in a poset can be related to each other in one of three possible ways, in terms of their relative rank: A can represent a lower value than does B, A can represent a higher value than does B, or the two can be of equal rank, or "alternate values" sharing a common higher or lower value but not ordered with respect to each other:

(5)   a.   **Lower value**
G: Do you like this album?
M: Yeah, *this song I really like.* (M. Rendell to G. Ward in conversation)
b.   **Higher value**
C: Have you filled out the summary sheet?
T: Yeah. *Both the summary sheet and the recording sheet I've done.* (T. Culp to C. Wessell in conversation)
c.   **Alternate values**
G: Did you get any more [answers to the crossword puzzle]?
S: No. *The cryptogram I can do like that.* The crossword puzzle is hard. (S. Makais to G. Ward in conversation)

In (5a), the relation "is-a-part-of" orders the poset {album parts}, within which *this song* represents a lower value than does *this album*, since "this song" is a part of "this album." In (5b), *the summary sheet and the recording sheet* represents a higher value than does *the summary sheet* within the poset {forms}, ordered by "is-a-member-of" relation; that is, "the summary sheet and the recording sheet" is a superset of "the summary sheet."[5] Finally, in (5c), *the crossword puzzle* and *the cryptogram* represent alternate, equally ranked values within the poset {newspaper puzzles}, ordered by the relation "is-a-type-of."

An element in a poset may be associated with an entity, attribute, event, activity, time, or place, or with a set of such items (Ward and Hirschberg 1985; Ward 1988; Hirschberg 1991; Ward and Prince 1991). Examples of poset relations include not only scales defined by entailment (Horn 1972), but also a much broader range of relations, including the part/whole, entity/attribute, type/subtype, set/subset, and equality relations.

The **link** within an utterance is the linguistic material representing information which stands in a contextually licenced poset relation with information evoked in or inferable from the prior context, and serves as a point of connection between the information presented in the current utterance and the prior context. (See also Reinhart 1981; Davison 1984; Fraurud 1990; Vallduví 1992; and Birner and Ward 1998; inter alia.)

By a "contextually licenced" poset relation we mean a relation involving a poset that the speaker believes the hearer can construct or retrieve from his or her knowledge store based on the information evoked in the current discourse. This constraint is designed to restrict these posets to those that are salient or inferable in context, since in principle any random set of items could constitute a poset, yet most such combinations will not licence linking relations between utterances and their contexts:

(6)   a.   I walked into the kitchen. *On a/the counter was a large book.*
b.   I walked into the kitchen. #*On a/the jacket was a large book.*

In (6a), the inversion is licenced by the fact that the hearer may readily retrieve a culturally available poset containing both "kitchen" and "counter" – specifically, the poset {elements of a house}, ordered by the relation part-of, with "counter" representing a lower value than does "kitchen" (since a counter is part of a kitchen). In (6b), on the other hand, there exists no salient or inferable poset relating "kitchen" and "jacket"; hence, this poset is not contextually licenced.

We will refer to the poset relating the link and the prior context (in (6), {elements of a house}) as the **anchoring set**, or **anchor**. The relation between the link and the anchor, which we will refer to as the **linking relation** (cf. Strand 1996a), is always a poset relation. The relation between the anchor and the prior context, however, is not always a poset relation. Consider (7):

(7) a. I promised my father – *on Christmas Eve it was* – to kill a Frenchman at the first opportunity I had. (*The Young Lions*)
     b. She got married recently and *at the wedding was the mother, the stepmother and Debbie*. (E. B. in conversation)

In (7a), the link is *on Christmas Eve*. The prior context (*I promised my father*) renders inferable the notion that this promise was made at some time, which in turn licences the anchor {times}. This anchor stands in a poset relation with set member *Christmas Eve*. However, the anchoring poset {times} does not stand in a poset relation to the prior context; that is, *I promised my father* itself does not stand in a poset relation with the set {times}. Similarly, in (7b), mention of someone getting married renders inferable the anchor {the wedding}. Notice that here the linking relation that holds between the link and the anchor is one of identity, which is also a poset relation. That is, the link *the wedding* stands in the identity relation with the anchor {the wedding}.

We will call the linguistic or situational material that licences the inference to the anchor the **trigger** (Hawkins 1978).[6] As we have seen, this inference may be based on a poset relation (as in (6a)), but it need not be (as in (7)). The inference may be triggered by one or more items, one of which may be the link itself. Thus, in (6a), mention of *the kitchen* alone does not give rise to the poset {elements of a house}, since, if it did, every utterance of an NP would give rise to a cognitive explosion of instantaneously constructed part/whole relations in which the referent participates (Fraurud 1990). Rather, it is not until the speaker utters *on the counter* that mention of the kitchen and the counter combine to evoke the poset that relates the two.

Notice, finally, that it is entirely possible for the trigger, anchor, and link to all represent the same information, as in (8):

(8) On one of September's last blast-furnace days, Emil Peterson parked his car along a quiet street in the tiny Delaware County burg of Eddystone and pulled a yellow plastic bucket from the back seat. *In it he had expertly wedged an assortment of brushes and cans of cleanser, a hollyberry room deodorizer, knives, scissors, a couple of no-slip no-crease pants hangers and a box containing a boulder-sized zircon ring.* (*Philadelphia Inquirer*, October 2, 1983)

Here, the trigger *a yellow plastic bucket* evokes a singleton set containing the bucket as its only member. This set is the anchor, which in turn is related (trivially) to the link *it* via a linking relation of identity.[7] Thus, even cases where the machinery of posets and linking relations may not seem necessary are nonetheless consistent with this account, allowing the development of a unified theory.

With these theoretical primitives in hand, we can now proceed to see how they apply to some of the noncanonical constructions of English. Our analysis is based on a combined corpus consisting of several thousand naturally occurring tokens collected over a period of approximately ten years. The data can be described as more or less standard American English and were drawn from a wide range of sources. Whenever possible, the prior and subsequent context was noted for each token. Data were collected from both speech and writing; the written sources include newspapers, magazines, novels, nonfiction books, academic prose, and portions of the Brown Corpus (Kucera and Francis 1967). Spoken data were drawn from personal conversations, films, interviews from *Working* (Terkel 1974), transcripts of the 1986 Challenger Commission meetings,[8] and a variety of television and radio programs.

2   Preposing

As we use the term, a "preposing" is a sentence in which a lexically governed phrasal constitutent appears to the left of its canonical position, typically sentence-initially (Ward 1988).[9] Extending the theory of preposing presented in Ward (1988), we claim that felicitous preposing in English requires the referent or denotation of the preposed constituent to be anaphorically linked to the preceding discourse (see Prince 1981b, 1984; Reinhart 1981; Vallduví 1992). The information conveyed by the preposed constituent can be related to the preceding discourse in a number of ways, including such relations as type/subtype, entity/attribute, part/whole, identity, etc. These relations can all be defined as partial orderings, and in Ward (1988) it is argued that the range of relations that can support preposing are all poset relations:

(9) *Customer*:   Can I get a bagel?
     Waitress: No, sorry. We're out of bagels. *A bran muffin I can give you.* (service
                   encounter)

Here, the link (*a bran muffin*) and trigger (*bagels*) stand in a poset relation as alternate members of the inferred anchor set {breakfast baked goods}. The link could also have been explicitly mentioned in the prior discourse, as in (10):

(10) *A*:   Can I get a bagel?
      B: Sorry – all out.
      A: How about a bran muffin?
      B: *A bran muffin I can give you.*

Here, although the link *a bran muffin* is coreferential with the trigger explicitly evoked in A's second query, the salient linking relation is not identity. Rather, the link is related via a type/subtype relation to the anchoring set {breakfast baked goods}, of which both bagels and bran muffins are members. Some types of preposing also permit links to anchors with a single member:

(11)   Facts about the world thus come in twice on the road from meaning to truth: once to determine the interpretation, given the meaning, and then again to determine the truth value, given the interpretation. *This insight we owe to David Kaplan's important work on indexicals and demonstratives, and we believe it is absolutely crucial to semantics.* (Barwise and J. J. Perry 1983: 11. *Situations and Attitudes* (p. 11). Cambridge, MA: MIT Press).

Here, the link *this insight* stands in a relation of identity to the anchoring poset, consisting of a single member.

In addition, Ward (1988) shows that certain types of preposing constructions require a salient or inferable open proposition in the discourse (see also Prince 1981b, 1984). The variable in the OP is instantiated with the focus, which must be a member of a contextually licenced poset. Preposings can be classified into two major types based on their intonation and information structure: "focus preposing" and "topicalization." The preposed constituent of focus preposing contains the focus of the utterance, and bears nuclear accent; the rest of the clause is typically deaccented.[10] Topicalization, on the other hand, involves a preposed constituent *other than the focus* and bears multiple pitch accents: at least one on the preposed constituent and at least one on the (nonpreposed) focus.[11] Nonetheless, both types of preposing require a salient or inferable OP at the time of utterance for felicity.[12]

Consider first the focus preposing in (12), where the focus is contained within the preposed constituent:

(12)   *A*:   Where can I get the reading packet?
       B: In Steinberg. [Gives directions] *Six dollars it costs.* (two students in conversation)

The preposed constituent in this example, *six dollars*, contains the nuclear accent, which identifies it as the focus of the utterance:

(13)   OP = It costs X, where X is a member of the poset {prices}.
       "It costs some amount of money."
       Focus = six dollars

Here, *six dollars* serves as the link to the preceding discourse. Its referent is a member of the poset {prices}, which is part of the inferable OP in (13). The OP can be inferred on the basis of the prior context; from mention of a reading packet, one is licenced to infer that the packet costs some amount of money. While the anchoring poset {prices} is discourse-old, the preposed constituent itself represents information that has not been explicitly evoked in the prior discourse. In the case of focus preposing, then, since the anchoring poset must be discourse-old yet the link is the focus (and therefore new), it follows that the poset must contain at least one other member in addition to the link.

The focus in a topicalization, on the other hand, is not contained in the preposed constituent but occurs elsewhere in the utterance. Intonationally, preposings of this type contain multiple accented syllables: (at least) one occurs within the constituent that contains the focus and (at least) one occurs within the preposed constituent, which typically occurs in a separate "intonational phrase" (Pierrehumbert 1980). Consider (14):

(14)   G: Do you watch football?
       E: Yeah. *Baseball I like a lot better.* (G. McKenna to E. Perkins in conversation)

Here, the preposed constituent *baseball* is not the focus; *better* is. *Baseball* serves as the link to the inferred poset {sports}. This poset constitutes the anchor, and can be inferred on the basis of the link (*baseball*) and the trigger *football*. Note that *baseball* is accented in (14) not because it is the focus but because it occurs in a separate intonational phrase.

The OP is formed in much the same way as for focus preposing, except that the poset member represented by the preposed constituent is replaced in the OP by the anchoring poset, as in (15):[13]

(15)   OP = I like-to-X-degree {sports}, where X is a member of the poset {amounts}.
       I like sports to some degree.
       Focus = better

Here, the OP includes the variable corresponding to the focus, but note that the link *baseball* has been replaced by its anchoring set {sports}, i.e. the poset that includes both the trigger and the link. In other words, the OP that is salient in (14) is not that the speaker likes baseball per se, but rather that he likes sports to some degree, as indicated in (15).

3   Postposing

As used here, the term "postposing" denotes any construction in which a lexically governed phrasal constituent appears to the right of its canonical position, typically but not exclusively in sentence-final position, leaving its canonical position either empty or else occupied by an expletive (Birner and Ward 1996). The postposing constructions we will concentrate on are those in which the logical subject is postposed and the expletive *there* appears in the canonical subject position – i.e. what have traditionally been known as existential and presentational *there*-sentences, as in (16a) and (16b), respectively:

(16)   a.   *"There's a warm relationship, a great respect and trust"* between [United Air Lines]'s chairman, Stephen M. Wolf, and Sir Colin Marshall, British Air's chief executive officer, according to a person familiar with both sides. (*Wall Street Journal*, August 23, 1989)
       b.   *Not far from Avenue de Villiers there lived a foreign doctor, a specialist, I understood, in midwifery and gynecology.* He was a coarse and cynical fellow who had called me in consultation a couple of times, not so much to be enlightened by my superior knowledge as to shift some of his responsibility on my shoulders. (Munthe, A. 1929: 143. *The Story of San Michele*. London: John Murray)

Existential *there*-sentences, as in (16a), contain *be* as their main verb, whereas presentational *there*-sentences, as in (16b), contain some other main verb.[14]

We have shown that preposing requires that the marked constituent represent information that is "given" in the sense of being discourse-old; postposing, on the other hand, requires its marked constituent to represent information that is "new" in some sense, although the type of newness in question will be shown to vary by construction.

We will argue that, while each of these two sentence types requires the postverbal NP (PVNP) to represent information that is unfamiliar in some sense, they differ in the nature of this unfamiliarity – specifically, whether the information must be (believed to be) new to the discourse or new to the hearer.

3.1   English existential **there-*sentences***

As noted by Prince (1988, 1992) and Ward and Birner (1995), the postverbal NP of existential *there*-sentences is constrained to represent entities that the speaker believes are not familiar to the hearer:

(17)   What can happen is a hangup such as Rocky Smith ran into, as the independent hauler was traversing Chicago with a load of machinery that just had to get to a factory by morning. *"There was this truck in front of me carrying giant steel coils, and potholes all over the place,"* he remembers. (*Wall Street Journal*, August 30, 1989)

Here, the truck in question is hearer-new, being introduced to the reader for the first time.

On the other hand, hearer-old PVNPs produce infelicity:[15]

(18)   a.   I have some news you're going to find very interesting. #*There was on the panel your good friend Jim Alterman.*
       b.   President Clinton appeared at the podium accompanied by three senators and the Speaker of the House. #*There was behind him the vice president.*

The PVNPs in these examples represent entities that are new to the discourse, but presumably familiar to the hearer, and the existential *there*-sentences are unacceptable. Now consider *there*-sentences whose PVNPs are not only hearer-old but also discourse-old:

(19)   a.   A: Hey, have you heard from Jim Alterman lately? I haven't seen him for years.
            B: Yes, actually. #*There was on the panel today Jim Alterman.*
       b.   President Clinton appeared at the podium accompanied by three senators and the vice president. #*There was behind him the vice president.*

As predicted, such examples are infelicitous. Thus, whenever an NP represents a hearer-old entity, it is disallowed in the postverbal position of an existential *there*-sentence.

3.2   *English presentational* there-*sentences*

Unlike existential *there*-sentences, presentational *there*-sentences are sensitive to the discourse-status of the PVNP. In the vast majority of cases, the referent of the PVNP in a presentational *there*-sentence is both hearer-new and discourse-new, as in (20):

(20)   And so as voters tomorrow begin the process of replacing Mr. Wright, forced from the speaker's chair and the House by charges of ethical violations, *there remains a political vacuum in the stockyards, barrios, high-tech workshops and defense plants of Tarrant County.* (AP Newswire 1989)

In the news story from which this example is taken, the PVNP is the first reference to the political vacuum in question and can be assumed to represent a new entity to the readership.

However, the PVNP of presentational *there*-sentences may also represent a hearer-old referent:

(21)   a.   *There only lacked the moon*; but a growing pallor in the sky suggested the moon might soon be coming. (adapted from Erdmann 1976: 138)
        b.   *Suddenly there ran out of the woods the man we had seen at the picnic.* (= Aissen 1975: ex. 12)

In these examples, the referent of the PVNP is one that is familiar to the hearer, yet new to the discourse. Thus, while both types of *there*-sentences allow hearer-new, discourse-new PVNPs, they do so for different reasons: existential *there*-sentences require hearer-new PVNPs, while presentational *there*-sentences require discourse-new PVNPs.

As we would predict, presentational *there*-sentences – like existential *there*-sentences – disallow PVNPs representing discourse-old entities:

(22)   a.   *A:*   Hey, have you heard from Jim Alterman lately? I haven't seen him for years.
            B: Yes, actually. #*There appeared before the committee today Jim Alterman.*
        b.   President Clinton appeared at the podium accompanied by three senators and the vice president. #*There stood behind him the vice president.*

Note that both of the presentational *there*-sentences in (22) would be acceptable without prior mention of the PVNP's referent – i.e. with the PVNP representing an entity that is hearer-old but discourse-new.

4   Argument Reversal

While preposing involves the noncanonical leftward placement of a constituent, and postposing involves the noncanonical rightward placement of a constituent, argument reversal incorporates both. The English argument-reversing constructions we will consider are *by*-phrase passives and inversion. The data indicate that both constructions are subject to the same discourse constraint.

4.1 *Inversion*

In inversion, the logical subject appears in postverbal position while some other, canonically postverbal, constituent appears in preverbal position (Birner 1994), excluding cases where expletive *there* occupies syntactic subject position (which are both formally and functionally distinct). We will refer to the noncanonically positioned constituents as the "preposed" and "postposed" constituents for convenience, although again we wish to remain neutral with respect to the syntactic analysis of the construction.

As demonstrated in Birner (1994), felicitous inversion in English depends on the "discourse-familiarity" of the information represented by the preposed and postposed constituents, where discourse-familiarity is determined by prior evocation in the discourse, inferability based on the prior discourse, and recency of mention within the discourse. Information that has been evoked in the prior discourse or is inferable based on the prior discourse is discourse-old, while information that has not been evoked and is not inferable is discourse-new (Prince 1992). Among discourse-old information, that which has been mentioned more recently in general is treated as more familiar, in the sense of being more salient, than that which has been mentioned less recently.

In the study reported in Birner (1994), an examination of 1778 naturally occurring inversions showed that in 78 percent of the tokens, the preposed constituent represented discourse-old information while the postposed constituent represented discourse-new information:

(23) We have complimentary soft drinks, coffee, Sanka, tea, and milk. *Also complimentary is red and white wine.* We have cocktails available for $2.00. (Flight attendant on Midway Airlines)

Here, the preposed AdjP *also complimentary* represents information previously evoked in the discourse, while the postposed *red and white wine* is new to the discourse. There were no tokens in which the situation was reversed – i.e. in which a preposed discourse-new element combined with a postposed discourse-old element. Moreover, information that was merely inferable (Prince 1981a) behaved as discourse-old, occurring in the same range of contexts as explicitly evoked information.

It is not the case, however, that the preposed constituent need always be discourse-old, or that the postposed constituent need always be discourse-new. In 11 percent of the tokens in the corpus, for example, both the preposed and the postposed constituents represented discourse-old information. However, in these cases the preposed element was consistently the more recently mentioned of the two, as in (24):

(24) Each of the characters is the centerpiece of a book, doll and clothing collection. The story of each character is told in a series of six slim books, each $12.95

> hardcover and $5.95 in paperback, and in bookstores and libraries across the country. More than 1 million copies have been sold; and in late 1989 a series of activity kits was introduced for retail sale. *Complementing the relatively affordable books are the dolls, one for each fictional heroine and each with a comparably pricey historically accurate wardrobe and accessories.* (*Chicago Tribune*)

Here, although the dolls have been evoked in the prior discourse, they have been evoked less recently than the books. Switching the preposed and postposed constituents in the inversion results in infelicity:

(25)   Each of the characters is the centerpiece of a book, doll and clothing collection. The story of each character is told in a series of six slim books, each $12.95 hardcover and $5.95 in paperback, and in bookstores and libraries across the country. More than 1 million copies have been sold; and in late 1989 a series of activity kits was introduced for retail sale. #*Complementing the relatively affordable dolls are the books, one for each fictional heroine.*

Thus, even in cases where both constituents have been previously evoked, the postposed constituent nonetheless represents less familiar information, where familiarity is defined by prior evocation, inferability, and recency of mention. Therefore, what is relevant for the felicity of inversion in discourse is the relative discourse-familiarity of the information represented by these two constituents.

4.2   *Passivization*

Like inversion, English *by*-phrase passives reverse the canonical order of two constituents, and like inversion, they are also constrained pragmatically in that the syntactic subject must not represent newer information within the discourse than does the NP in the *by*-phrase (Birner 1996). We claim that passivization and inversion represent distinct syntactic means for performing the same discourse function in different syntactic environments.

By-phrase passives are passive sentences with a *by*-phrase containing the logical subject, as in (26):

(26)   The mayor's present term of office expires Jan. 1. *He will be succeeded by Ivan Allen Jr.* (Brown Corpus)

This restriction excludes such passives as that in (27):

(27)   A lamp was stolen yesterday.

We will refer to the preverbal NP in a *by*-phrase passive (e.g. *he* in (26)) as the syntactic subject, and to the postverbal NP (e.g. *Ivan Allen Jr.* in (26)) as the *by*-phrase NP.[16]

Based on an examination of the first 200 *by*-phrase passives appearing in the Brown Corpus, Birner (1996) shows that the syntactic subject of such passives consistently represents information that is at least as familiar within the discourse as that represented by the *by*-phrase NP. Moreover, when the information status of the relevant NPs is reversed, infelicity results. Consider again example (26), repeated here as (28a), as compared with (28b):

(28)   a.   The mayor's present term of office expires Jan. 1. *He will be succeeded by Ivan Allen Jr.* (= (26))
       b.   Ivan Allen Jr. will take office Jan. 1. *#The mayor will be succeeded by him.*

The subject *he* in (28a) represents discourse-old information, while the *by*-phrase NP, *Ivan Allen Jr.*, represents discourse-new information, and the token is felicitous. In (28b), on the other hand, the syntactic subject, *the mayor*, represents discourse-new information while the NP in the *by*-phrase, *him*, represents discourse-old information, and the passive is infelicitous. Thus, the subject NP in a *by*-phrase passive must not represent less familiar information within the discourse than does the NP within the *by*-phrase.

Given that passivization, like inversion, places relatively familiar information before relatively unfamiliar information, it too can be viewed as performing a linking function (see section 1.3). That is, in passivization as in inversion, the information represented by the preverbal constituent generally stands in a poset relationship with a previously evoked or inferable anchor.

5   Left-dislocation

Left-dislocation is superficially similar to preposing, but in left-dislocation a coreferential pronoun appears in the marked constituent's canonical position:

(29)   I bet she had a nervous breakdown. That's not a good thing. *Gallstones, you have them out and they're out.* But a nervous breakdown, it's very bad. (Roth, P. 1969: 162. *Portnoy's Complaint.* New York: Random House)

Here, the direct object pronoun *them* is coreferential with the sentence-initial constituent *gallstones*. Left-dislocation is also functionally distinct from preposing. As we have seen, preposing constructions constitute a functionally unified class in that the preposed constituent consistently represents information standing in a contextually licenced poset relationship with information evoked in or inferable from the prior context. No such requirement holds for left-dislocation, however.

Prince (1997) argues that there are three types of left-dislocation (LD), distinguishable on functional grounds. Type I LD is what Prince calls "simplifying LDs":

A "simplifying" Left-Dislocation serves to simplify the discourse processing of Discourse-new entities by removing them from a syntactic position disfavored for Discourse-new entities and creating a separate processing unit for them. Once that unit is processed and they have become Discourse-old, they may comfortably occur in their positions within the clause as pronouns. (1997: 124)

That is, LDs of this type involve entities that are new to the discourse and would otherwise be introduced in a nonfavored (i.e. subject) position. Consider the example in (30):

(30)   Two of my sisters were living together on 18th Street. They had gone to bed, and this man, their girlfriend's husband, came in. He started fussing with my sister and she started to scream. *The landlady, she went up and he laid her out.* (*Welcomat*, 12 February, 1981)

Here, the landlady is new to the discourse (and presumably to the hearer as well); however, the speaker is introducing her via an NP in subject position – a position disfavored for introducing new information. The dislocated NP creates a new information unit and thus, according to Prince, eases processing. The other two types of LD – triggering a poset inference and amnestying an island violation – typically do, according to Prince, involve discourse-old information.[17] This stands in stark contrast to true preposing constructions, in which the preposed constituent must represent a discourse-old link to the prior discourse.

6   Right-dislocation

Like existential and presentational *there*-insertion, right-dislocation involves the noncanonical placement of an argument of the verb in postverbal position. However, in contrast to both existential and presentational *there*-insertion, right-dislocation (RD) does not require the postverbal NP to represent new information. Consider the right-dislocations in (31):

(31)   a.   Below the waterfall (and this was the most astonishing sight of all), a whole mass of enormous glass pipes were dangling down into the river from somewhere high up in the ceiling! *They really were* ENORMOUS, *those pipes.* There must have been a dozen of them at least, and they were sucking up the brownish muddy water from the river and carrying it away to goodness knows where. (Dahl, R. 1964: 74–5 *Charlie and the Chocolate Factory*. New York: Knopf.)

   b.   Can't write much, as I've been away from here for a week and have to keep up appearances, but did Diana mention the desk drama? Dad took your old desk over to her house to have it sent out, but he didn't check to see what was in it, and forgot that I had been keeping all my vital documents in there – like my tax returns and paystubs and bank statements. Luckily Diana thought "that stuff looked important" so she took it out before giving the desk over to the movers. Phew! *She's a smart cookie, that Diana.* (personal letter)

In each of these examples, the sentence-final constituent represents information that has been evoked, either explicitly or implicitly, in the prior discourse. The functions that previous researchers have posited for RD, in fact, have generally assumed that the dislocated NP must represent information that is given or inferable within the discourse. For example, Davison (1984) argues that RD marks the referent of the dislocated NP as a topic, and thus also as having a "discourse antecedent" (1984: 802). Similarly, Ziv and Grosz (1994) argue that RD identifies a situationally or textually evoked entity as the most salient entity available for subsequent reference.[18] Indeed, our corpus-based study shows that, in every case, the dislocated NP represents information that is both hearer-old and discourse-old. Thus, right-dislocation cannot be viewed as marking information that is new in any sense, and in this way differs from existential and presentational *there*-insertion on functional grounds.

As we argued in previous work (Birner and Ward 1996), the difference in function can be attributed to the anaphoric pronoun of right-dislocation. Given that the marked NP in a right-dislocation is coreferential with the pronoun, and that the pronoun is anaphoric and therefore represents a discourse-old entity, it follows that the marked NP must also represent this same discourse-old entity. Thus, it is not accidental that right-dislocation does not require the marked NP to represent new information; the presence of the pronoun in fact precludes such a possibility.

7   Conclusion

We have suggested that a complete functional account of the noncanonical constructions of English requires reference to open propositions, discourse- and hearer-familiarity, and linking relations. By now it should be clear that these constraints are not randomly assigned to the various construction types, but rather that broad generalizations can be made regarding the correlation of syntax and discourse function. Specifically, we have argued that:

- preposing constructions require the preposed constituent to represent information that is old in some sense, while postposing constructions require the postposed constituent to represent information that is new in some sense;
- the constraints on preposing and postposing are absolute, while those placed on argument reversal are relative;
- the functional constraints observed for the classes of preposing and postposing constructions do not hold for superficially similar constructions in which the marked constituent's canonical position is filled by a referential pronoun (i.e. right- and left-dislocation).

Although we have found no necessary correspondence between particular constructions and specific functional constraints, discourse functions nonetheless correlate with syntactic constructions in a principled way. Our research indicates that the range of discourse functions a given construction may serve is constrained by the form of the construction; within that range, however, there is room for arbitrary variation. This approach reconciles both the strong correlations we have found among construction types and function types and the equally strong evidence of variation in the correlation between form and function.

NOTES

1   We use the term "construction" in the conventional sense, to refer to each of the various grammatical configurations of constituents within a particular language. See Fillmore (1988), Prince (1994), and Goldberg (1995), inter alia, for alternative views of what constitutes a linguistic construction.

2   What is relevant here is the presence of information within the hearer's knowledge store, not the hearer's beliefs regarding its truth (in the case of a proposition), existence (in the case of an entity), attributes, etc. That is, what matters for hearer-status is the hearer's knowledge *of*, rather than *about*, the information.

3   Strictly speaking it is the information itself that possesses some information status (and not the constituent representing that information), but where no confusion will result we will speak of constituents as being discourse-old, discourse-new, evoked, etc. for convenience.

4   Thus, the "discourse-old" link need not itself have been explicitly evoked within the prior discourse; as long as it stands in an appropriate relationship with previously evoked information, it is treated by speakers as discourse-old.

5   Higher-value preposings are actually quite rare, and are usually explicitly designated as such, as with the quantifier *both* in (5b).

6   The metaphorical use of the terms "anchor," "link," "linking relation," and "trigger" to describe the relationship between elements of the current sentence and the prior context is relatively widespread in the literature; see Reinhart (1981); Fraurud (1990); Garrod and Sanford (1994); and Strand (1996a, 1996b),

inter alia. Although the various studies utilizing these terms have by and large used them in very similar ways, these studies have failed to draw the (in our view) crucial distinctions among the linguistic items being related, the poset relation connecting the information represented by these items, and the poset itself.

7   In this example the preposition *in* does *not* constitute part of the link, unlike the preposition in (7a). The difference between the two types of links correlates with distinct preposing constructions; see Ward (1988) for discussion.

8   This corpus consists of over 1.3 million words of transcribed oral data drawn from the official transcripts of the Presidential Commission on the Space Shuttle Challenger Accident (1986). We are grateful to Julia Hirschberg for making an on-line version of these transcripts available to us.

9   For convenience, we will use terms like "preposing" and "postposing" to refer to the noncanonical placement of syntactic constituents, although we wish to remain neutral with respect to their actual syntactic analysis.

10   By "accent," we mean "intonational prominence" in the sense of Terken and Hirschberg (1994): "a conspicuous pitch change in or near the lexically stressed syllable of the word" (1994: 126); see also Pierrehumbert (1980).

11   Of course for both topicalization and focus preposing, other constituents may bear pitch accents. Intonationally speaking, the difference between focus preposing and topicalization is that only the former requires that the nuclear accent be on the preposed constituent.

12   As noted in Ward (1988), there is one preposing construction – "locative

preposing" – that does not require a salient OP but does require a locative element in preposed position.

13 While the link typically represents a subset of the anchoring poset, we shall for notational convenience use the set itself in the representation of the OP, e.g. "{sports}" as opposed to "y such that y stands in a poset relation to {sports}."

14 For terminological convenience and continuity, we will retain the terms "existential *there*" and "presentational *there*."

15 Although the PVNPs in (18) are formally definite, as well as hearer-old, we argue elsewhere (Ward and Birner 1995) that it is the information status of an NP – and not its morphosyntactic form – that determines whether or not an NP may appear in postverbal position of an existential *there*-sentence.

16 Breaking with traditional terminology (e.g. Siewierska 1984), we will not refer to the *by*-phrase NP as the agent, nor to these clauses as agentive passives, because in many cases the *by*-phrase NP does not act as a semantic agent (in the sense of Fillmore 1968). In (26), for example, *Ivan Allen Jr.* is not an agent.

17 Prince is not alone in claiming that at least some types of LD serve to introduce new entities into the discourse: Gundel (1974, 1985), Rodman (1974), and Halliday (1967) propose similar functions.

18 Those researchers that have not taken RD to mark the dislocated information as being given in some sense have taken it to be essentially a repair device for self-correcting potentially unclear references (Tomlin 1986; Geluykens 1987; inter alia). However, in cases like those in (31) above, it is not plausible to consider RD to be correcting for a possible reference failure. In (31a), for example, the identity of the referent of *they* in the right-dislocation is clear; not only do the pipes represent the only entity in the context realizable by a plural, but they also represent the most salient entity in the discourse at the time the pronoun is uttered. Similarly, in (31b), Diana is the only female mentioned in the prior discourse, and thus the only available referent for the pronoun *she*.

REFERENCES

Aissen, J. (1975). Presentational-*there* insertion: a cyclic root transformation. *Chicago Linguistic Society*, 11, 1–14.

Birner, B. J. (1994). Information status and word order: an analysis of English inversion. *Language*, 70, 233–59.

Birner, B. J. (1996). Form and function in English *by*-phrase passives. *Chicago Linguistic Society*, 32, 23–31.

Birner, B. J. and Ward, G. (1996). A crosslinguistic study of postposing in discourse. *Language and Speech: Special Issue on Discourse, Syntax, and Information*, 39, 111–40.

Birner, B. J. and Ward, G. (1998). *Information Status and Noncanonical Word Order in English*. Amsterdam and Philadelphia: Benjamins.

Chafe, W. (1976). Givenness, contrastiveness, definiteness, subjects, topics, and point of view. In C. Li (ed.), *Subject and Topic* (pp. 25–55). New York: Academic Press.

Davison, A. (1984). Syntactic markedness and the definition of sentence topic. *Language*, 60, 797–846.

Erdmann, P. (1976). *There Sentences in English*. Munich: Tuduv.

Fillmore, C. (1968). "The case for case." In E. Bach and R. Harms (eds), *Universals in Linguistic Theory* (pp. 1–90). New York: Holt.

Fillmore, C. (1988). The mechanisms of "construction grammar." *Berkeley Linguistics Society*, 14, 35–55.

Firbas, J. (1966). Non-thematic subjects in contemporary English. *Travaux Linguistiques de Prague*, 2, 239–56.

Fraurud, K. (1990). Definiteness and the processing of noun phrases in natural discourse. *Journal of Semantics*, 7, 395–433.

Garrod, S. C. and Sanford, A. J. (1994). Resolving sentences in a discourse context: how discourse representation affects language understanding. In M. A. Gernsbacher (ed.), *Handbook of Psycholinguistics* (pp. 675–98). New York: Academic Press.

Geluykens, R. (1987). Tails (right dislocations) as a repair mechanism in English conversations. In J. Nuyts and G. de Schutter (eds), *Getting One's Words into Line: On Word Order and Functional Grammar* (pp. 119–30). Dordrecht: Foris.

Goldberg, A. (1995). *Constructions: A Construction Grammar Approach to Argument Structure*. Chicago: University of Chicago Press.

Gundel, J. (1974). The role of topic and comment in linguistic theory. PhD dissertation, University of Texas.

Gundel, J. (1985). "Shared knowledge" and topicality. *Journal of Pragmatics*, 9, 83–107.

Halliday, M. A. K. (1967). Notes on transitivity and theme in English. Part 2. *Journal of Linguistics*, 3, 199–244.

Hawkins, J. A. (1978). *Definiteness and Indefiniteness*. Atlantic Highlands NJ: Humanities Press.

Hirschberg, J. (1991). *A Theory of Scalar Implicature*. New York: Garland.

Horn, L. R. (1972). On the semantic properties of logical operators in English. PhD dissertation, UCLA.

(reprinted 1976, Bloomington: Indiana University Linguistics Club.)

Kucera, H. and Francis, W. N. (1967). *Computational Analysis of Present-day American English*. Providence RI: Brown University Press.

Kuno, S. (1971). The position of locatives in existential sentences. *Linguistic Inquiry*, 2, 333–78.

Lambrecht, K. (1994). *Information Structure and Sentence Form*. Cambridge: Cambridge University Press.

Pierrehumbert, J. (1980). The phonology and phonetics of English intonation. PhD dissertation, MIT.

Prince, E. F. (1981a). Toward a taxonomy of given/new information. In P. Cole (ed.), *Radical Pragmatics* (pp. 223–54). New York: Academic Press.

Prince, E. F. (1981b). Topicalization, focus-movement, and Yiddish-movement: a pragmatic differentiation. *Berkeley Linguistics Society*, 7, 249–64.

Prince, E. F. (1984). Topicalization and left-dislocation: a functional analysis. In S. White and V. Teller (eds), *Discourses in Reading and Linguistics* (pp. 213–25). New York: Annals of the New York Academy of Sciences.

Prince, E. F. (1988). The discourse functions of Yiddish expletive *Es* + subject-postposing. *Papers in Pragmatics*, 2, 176–94.

Prince, E. F. (1992). The ZPG letter: subjects, definiteness, and information-status. In S. Thompson and W. Mann (eds), *Discourse Description: Diverse Analyses of a Fundraising Text* (pp. 295–325). Amsterdam and Philadelphia: Benjamins.

Prince, E. F. (1994). The notion "construction" and the syntax–discourse interface. Paper presented at the 25th Annual Meeting of the North East Linguistic Society, University of Pennsylvania.

Prince, E. F. (1997). On the functions of left-dislocation in English discourse.

In A. Kamio (ed.), *Directions in Functional Linguistics* (pp. 117–43). Amsterdam and Philadelphia: Benjamins.

Reinhart, T. (1981). Pragmatics and linguistics: an analysis of sentence topics. *Philosophica*, 27, 53–94.

Rodman, R. (1974). On left dislocation. *Papers in Linguistics*, 7, 437–66.

Siewierska, A. (1984). *The Passive: A Comparative Linguistic Analysis*. London: Croom Helm.

Strand, K. (1996a). Computing the implicatures carried by "the Φ." In *Computational Implicature: Computational Approaches to Interpreting and Generating Conversational Implicature. Working Notes* (pp. 103–9). American Association of Artificial Intelligence 1996 Spring Symposium Series.

Strand, K. (1996b). A taxonomy of linking relations. Paper presented at the Indiana Workshop on Indirect Anaphora, Lancaster, England.

Terkel, S. (1974). *Working*. New York: Avon.

Terken, J. and Hirschberg, J. (1994). Deaccentuation and words representing "given" information: effects of persistence of grammatical function and surface position. *Language and Speech*, 37.2, 125–45.

Tomlin, R. S. (1986). *Basic Word Order: Functional Principles*. London: Croom Helm.

Vallduví, E. (1992). *The Informational Component*. New York: Garland.

Ward, G. (1988). *The Semantics and Pragmatics of Preposing*. New York: Garland.

Ward, G. and Birner, B. J. (1995). Definiteness and the English existential. *Language*, 71, 722–42.

Ward, G. and Hirschberg, J. (1985). Implicating uncertainty: the pragmatics of fall–rise intonation. *Language*, 61, 747–76.

Ward, G. and Prince, E. F. (1991). On the topicalization of indefinite NPs. *Journal of Pragmatics*, 16, 167–77.

Ziv, Y. and Grosz, B. (1994). Right dislocation and attentional state. *Proceedings of the Ninth Annual Conference and of the Workshop on Discourse* (pp. 184–99). Israeli Association for Theoretical Linguistics.

7 Historical Discourse Analysis

LAUREL J. BRINTON

0 Introduction

Some dozen years ago, as evidenced by van Dijk's four-volume *Handbook of Discourse Analysis* (1985), the historical analysis of discourse was unrecognized.[1] However, the intervening period has seen a wealth of studies, which have been variously termed "New Philology" (Fleischman 1990), "post-/interdisciplinary philology" (Sell 1994), "historical discourse analysis" or "historical text linguistics" (Enkvist and Wårvik 1987: 222), "diachronic textlinguistics" (Fries 1983), or "historical pragmatics" (Stein 1985b; Jucker 1994). While providing an overview of some of these studies – which range from detailed accounts of particular discourse forms in individual languages to programmatic statements concerning the nature or usefulness of the undertaking – the following chapter will attempt to describe this new field of endeavor by locating discourse analysis in relation to historical linguistics and, alternatively, historical linguistics in relation to discourse analysis, and by exploring the mutual contributions of these disciplines as well as their possible synthesis.

0.1 Scope of discourse analysis

An initial difficulty which presents itself when one attempts to survey the field of historical discourse analysis is the determination of what is encompassed by discourse analysis itself. Standard treatments of discourse analysis (e.g. Stubbs 1983; Brown and Yule 1983; Schiffrin 1994) cover a wide range of topics, including cohesion and coherence, anaphora, information structuring (topic/comment, given/new, focus), turn-taking, boundary/peak marking, grounding, topic or participant tracking, discourse markers, and segmentation (paragraph or episode marking), on the one hand, and inference, implicature, presupposition, maxims of conversation, relevance, the Cooperative Principle, politeness, and speech acts, on the other hand.

Particularly problematic is the distinction between discourse analysis and pragmatics (see Ward and Birner, this volume), as suggested roughly by the division of topics above. A textbook account of pragmatics (e.g. Levinson 1983) covers many of the same issues as do accounts of discourse analysis; pragmatics is sometimes said to encompass discourse analysis – or the reverse. It has been suggested that discourse analysis is more text-centered, more static, more interested in product (in the well-formedness of texts), while pragmatics is more user-centered, more dynamic, more interested in the process of text production. Discourse analysis is frequently equated with conversational analysis, and pragmatics with speech act theory. It would seem difficult to distinguish the two with any conviction, however; for example, discourse markers, such as *well*, *so*, or *you know*, have both "textual" functions in organizing discourse (e.g. marking topic or participant change, narrative segmentation, discourse type, saliency, fore/background) – functions falling more under the rubric of discourse analysis – and "expressive functions," both subjective (e.g. expressing evaluation/ emphasis, focusing on the speaker) and interpersonal (e.g. evoking the hearer's attention, expressing common knowledge, denoting "negative" or "positive" politeness) – functions falling under the rubric of pragmatics proper (see Brinton 1996: 36–40).

While it is not possible in this chapter to define the range of topics included in the field of discourse analysis (these will be suggested by this *Handbook* in its entirety), it is useful to understand the field broadly as "the linguistic analysis of naturally occurring *connected* spoken or written discourse" (Stubbs 1983: 1), as being concerned with the level above that of the individual sentence: with intersentential connections, with global rather than local features, and with those forms that serve to bind sentences. No attempt will be made here to differentiate with any exactness between discourse analysis and pragmatics, though the emphasis will be on the more formal aspects of text structure, such as discourse markers or grounding, rather than on the more notional elements of text semantics, such as presupposition or conversational maxims, or on aspects of language use. For this reason, certain aspects of historical pragmatics, especially those relating to diachronic changes in the expression of conversational routines and politeness formulae or in the structuring of speech events, will not be treated here.

0.2 Scope of historical discourse analysis

As a cross-disciplinary field, historical discourse analysis may be approached from at least two different directions.

The first approach involves an application of discourse analysis to language history. It is the study of discourse forms, functions, or structures – that is, whatever is encompassed by discourse analysis (see above) – in earlier periods of a language. The attention of the discourse analyst is focused on historical stages of a language, yet the emphasis remains on discourse structure. This approach may be termed **historical discourse analysis** proper.[2] The advantage of such an approach is that it may more satisfactorily explain the functions of many features of older texts. Note, however, that this approach is essentially *synchronic*, since it involves an analysis, albeit a discourse-oriented one, of a language at a particular stage in its development. Within such an approach, there are two possible steps, one mapping form to function (the explication of the discourse functions of particular historical forms) and the other mapping function to form (the identification of historical forms which are exponents of particular discourse functions) (cf. Jacobs and Jucker 1995: 13ff). The former direction seems to be the more common in historical discourse analysis.[3]

The second approach involves an application of discourse analysis to historical linguistics. It is the study of "discourse-pragmatic factors" in language change or of the discourse motivations behind diachronic changes, whether phonological, morphological, syntactic, or semantic. The attention of the historical linguist is focused on discourse matters, yet the emphasis remains on language change. It should be noted that a consideration of discourse factors in certain kinds of diachronic change, such as word order change, is not recent, and an interest in discourse-driven or influenced change can now be seen as almost commonplace. Such an approach has the advantage of providing elucidation of certain changes and a fuller understanding of diachronic processes of change. It may be termed **discourse-oriented historical linguistics**.[4] An extension of this approach (dating back to Givón 1979a) involves the study of how an element functioning on the discourse level comes to function on the morphosyntactic or semantic level.

A third approach, though less well developed than the others, is more truly interdisciplinary, involving a synthesis of discourse and diachrony. It involves a study of the changes in discourse marking, functions, and structures over time. That is, discourse structure is treated on a par with phonological, morphological, syntactic, and semantic structure as something which changes and develops over time, so that one might legitimately talk of *discours(al) change* as well as, for example, *phonological change*. This approach may be termed **diachronic(ally oriented) discourse analysis**.

The remainder of the chapter will examine these three approaches.

1 Historical Discourse Analysis

Historical stages of a language often contain apparently meaningless words and particles, empty or repetitive phrases, inexplicable morphological forms or uses of inflectional forms, seemingly "primitive" stylistic features, and uncategorizable or odd text types. While traditionally many of these features have been viewed as grammatical pleonasms, metrical expedients, intensifiers or emphatics, colloquialisms, or defects of style, it has proved fruitful in recent years to re-examine these features using the tools of modern discourse analysis.

While a major stumbling block to such a re-examination would appear to be the lack of oral texts from earlier periods, since discourse analysis has typically been concerned with the oral medium, with naturally occurring conversations, and oral narratives, this is no longer considered a serious impediment to historical discourse analysis. First, it is generally agreed that earlier periods of most written languages, especially medieval texts in the Indo-European languages, are products of the transition from an oral to a literate culture and, though not oral texts, contain an "oral residue" (Ong 1984), the linguistic characteristics of an oral culture. For Fleischman, it is precisely because discourse analysis is concerned with oral texts that it will explain many of the features of medieval literature: "I am convinced that many of the disconcerting properties of medieval vernacular texts . . . can find more satisfying explanations if we first of all acknowledge the extent to which our texts structure information the way a spoken language does, and then proceed to the linguistic literature that explores the pragmatic underpinning of parallel phenomena in naturally occurring discourse" (1990: 23). Second, much can be deduced about the oral form of earlier languages from "speech-based" genres (Biber and Finegan 1992) such as court records, sermons, and dramatic dialogue as well as from more colloquial written genres such as personal letters. Finally, it has become increasingly common to apply the techniques of discourse analysis to written texts and to recognize separate principles of discourse structure in such texts: "written texts can be analyzed as communicative acts in their own right" (Jacobs and Jucker 1995: 10).

1.1 Discourse markers

In historical discourse analysis, perhaps the most attention has been paid to what Longacre terms "mystery particles," that is, to the "verbal and nominal affixes and sentential particles [which] continue to defy analysis even at a relatively advanced stage of research" (1976: 468); in contemporary discourse analysis, mystery particles are more typically termed *discourse markers* (Schiffrin 1987) or *pragmatic markers* (Brinton 1996: 29–30, 40) and include such forms as *well, now, so,* and *y'know* in Modern English.[5] Viewed traditionally, discourse markers are considered to be of indeterminate word class and uncertain meaning. But as Longacre observes, mystery particles almost inevitably "have a function which relates to a unit larger than the sentence, i.e. to the paragraph and the discourse" (1976: 468).

It has been convincingly argued that a number of particles can be understood as functioning as discourse markers with textual and interpersonal functions; here, space permits only a sampling of articles discussing particles in the history of the Germanic and Romance languages. For example, several works have treated Old English (OE) *þa* 'then'; it has been seen as a foregrounder, a foreground "dramatizer," a sequencer of events, a marker of colloquial speech, a peak marker, and a narrative segmenter (Enkvist 1972, 1986; Enkvist and Wårvik 1987; Wårvik 1990, 1995a, 1995b; see also Hopper 1979, 1992) or primarily as a shift marker (Kim 1992). Similar functions have been attributed to the cognate *thô* in Old Saxon and Old High German (Wilbur 1988; Betten 1992). OE adverbials such as *hēr* 'here' and *nū* 'now', as well as a variety of forms in the later periods (e.g. *before/afore/fore, above, the said, hereafter*), have a "text deictic" function in expressing the point where the speaker or writer is at the moment (Fries 1993, 1994). Comparing the OE adverbs *witodlice* 'certainly' and *soþlice* 'truly' with their most common Latin counterpart, *autem* (see Kroon 1995) and with the use of *þa*, Lenker (forthcoming) argues that they serve as highlighting devices and as markers of episode boundaries or shifts in the narrative (functionally equivalent to *þa gelamp hit þæt*; see below). It has also been suggested that *sona* and *þærrihte* 'immediately, at once' signal the "peak zone" of OE narratives (Wårvik 1995a). I have argued that OE *hwæt* 'what' serves as an attention-getter and as a marker of shared knowledge (Brinton 1996). Fludernik (1995, 1996: 101–20) has looked at the use of *so, but, and,* and *thenne* as episodic narrative markers in Middle English (ME). Fischer (forthcoming) exemplifies the use of *marry* (<*Mary*), beginning in ME and peaking in the sixteenth century, as a textual marker used to claim the floor at the beginning of a turn and as an interpersonal marker expressing a range of speaker attitude. In

Shakespeare, *why* may be used as a discourse marker to draw a logical conclusion from what has gone before, often giving a tone of superiority and potential disparagement, while *what* may be used to express surprise or incredulity, which often turns into contempt or scorn (Blake 1992). Interjections in Early Modern English (EModE), such as *ah, alas, fie, oh, tush,* and *welaway,* Taavitsainen argues (1995), are a subset of discourse markers; they "encode speaker attitudes and communicative intentions" (439), are "deliberate devices in manipulating reader involvement" (463), and may serve textual functions in some genres.

Similar arguments have been adduced for various mystery particles in the history of the Romance languages, such as Old French *mar* 'woe unto you', *si,* and the locative particles *ci, ça* 'here', *la, iluec* 'there' (see Fleischman 1990 for a summary of these articles). Fleischman (1992) argues that Old French *si* (untranslatable) functions as a main-clause marker of subject/topic continuity, while explicit subject pronouns mark switch-reference. Bolkestein and van de Grift (1994) show that the choice in Latin among the anaphoric particles *is, hic, ille, iste,* and Ø is pragmatically/functionally motivated. In a detailed study, Kroon (1995) argues that differences among the Latin adversative conjunctions *at, autem,* and *vero* and causal conjunctions *nam, enim, igitur,* and *ergo* cannot be explained adequately as a matter of relative strength, but that discourse type and communicative/expressive value must be considered: *nam* and *autem* occur primarily in monologic discourse and express textual connections in the strict sense; *enim* and *vero* occur primarily in dialogic discourse and function as "situating particles" indicating the involvement of the discourse participants, while *ergo* and *at* have an interactional function as well as a textual (connective) function. In another study of Latin particles, Risselada (1994) points out that a full understanding of directive markers (e.g. *dum, age, modo, quin, vero, sane, proinde*) depends on a knowledge not only of their basic meaning but also of the level of the utterance to which they pertain and the pragmatic and contextual properties of the utterance in which they are used.[6]

In sum, it has been possible to argue that erstwhile mystery particles in older stages of languages share many, if not all, of the features of discourse markers in modern languages. They are normally marginal in word class, heterogeneous in form, of high frequency, phonetically short, outside the syntactic structure of the clause, sentence-initial, lacking in propositional content, optional, difficult to translate, and stylistically stigmatized. Moreover, they exhibit all of the textual functions – grounding, saliency or peak marking, narrative segmentation – as well as the speaker- and hearer-oriented expressive functions, including those of internal and external evaluation, of modern discourse markers (see Brinton 1995).[7]

1.2   Inflectional forms

1.2.1   Verbal morphology

Tense-aspect morphology, because of its function in conceptualizing and placing events in time, plays a special role in discourse structuring and hence has been studied by historical discourse analysts.

For the student of medieval literature, the "historic(al) present" – the use of the present tense in a past-tense narrative, often with rapid and seemingly inexplicable alternations between past and present – offers the most obvious phenomenon where a discourse analysis might provide a more satisfactory explanation than has thus far been given. It has traditionally been explained either as a metrical expedient or as an intensifying, vivifying, or emphatic device. Numerous exceptions can be found, however, in which the appearance of the historical present cannot be accounted for by either theory. Extrapolating from work on the historic present in modern oral narratives, therefore, which has suggested its role in narrative segmentation, foregrounding, and internal evaluation, scholars have argued that the historical present in medieval texts from different traditions serves discourse roles: in Old French, it marks foregrounded events of "highest saliency," is a device for internal evaluation, and is characteristic of oral performed narrative (Fleischman 1985, 1986); in ME, it denotes main events, introduces central characters, and highlights key descriptive details (Richardson 1991); and in Old Norse, it frames and stages the narrative, marking transitions between episodes, distinguishing speakers, and providing internal evaluation (Richardson 1995). For both Fleischman and Richardson, vividness and excitement are a consequence of the text-organizing function of the historical present, not the primary function of the form. The overarching function of the present tense in Charlotte Brontë's nineteenth-century narrative seems to be that of evaluation, while the historical present is used for foregrounding and internal evaluation; "dramatization" and "vivid visualization" contribute to the form's evaluative function (Brinton 1992).

Discourse studies have also focused on the function of aspectual forms. Consonant with general principles of grounding, Hopper (1979: 219–26) concludes that in OE narrative the foreground is characterized by verbs in the perfective aspect denoting single dynamic, punctual, telic events, whereas the background is characterized by verbs in the imperfective aspect denoting states or durative/iterative/habitual atelic processes.[8] Looking at other aspectual forms in OE, Richardson argues that "nonperfective" forms, including motion, perception, and ingressive verbs, with accompanying infinitive, signal new episodes, accelerate actions for dramatic effect, and establish point of view; likewise, the perfect in ME serves to mark narrative boundaries (1994). I argue that ME inchoative *gan* 'began' serves a demarcating function and slows the narrative down, while perfective *anon* 'at once, immediately' marks salient action and speeds a narrative up (Brinton 1996). Finally, a number of studies have also suggested discourse functions for EModE *do* as a peak marker, information focuser, or event foregrounder (Stein 1985a; Wright 1989).[9]

Fleischman (1990: 36) concludes that tense-aspect forms serve a variety of important roles in discourse: they may have textual functions (e.g. grounding, creating cohesion, marking boundaries, or modulating pace), expressive functions (e.g. expressing evaluation or point of view), and metalinguistic functions (e.g. signaling text type).

1.2.2 Pronominal forms

Pronominal forms, because of their anaphoric and referential functions, play an important role in discourse structuring and hence have also received the attention of historical discourse analysts. For example, it has been suggested that the demonstrative pronoun *this* in ME (as in "this Pandarus") functions as a foregrounder (Fludernik 1995; Sell 1985). Work on EModE has attributed a discourse function to the variant personal pronominal forms *you/thou* (see references in Stein 1985b: 348): Calvo (1992) argues that in addition to negotiating social identities and expressing attitudinal features, these forms may denote a change in conversational topic and mark discourse boundaries; similarly, Hope (1994) sees these forms as having not only a "macro-pragmatic" function in encoding the differential status of the interlocutors, but a "micro-pragmatic" function in expressing emotional attitude. Wales (1995) also sees a discourse role for the generalizing *your* (i.e. "not your average person") in EModE; in addition to its generic or gnomic meaning, it has various kinds of expressivity: a deictic, focusing function, a second person discourse awareness, and a generally dismissive tone.

1.3   Fixed phrases and clauses

A number of the recognized discourse markers in Modern English consist of phrases (e.g. *after all, all right, and stuff like that*) or clauses, sometimes called "comment clauses" (e.g. *I mean, you see, that's right*). Thus, it is not surprising that fixed expressions in older language, in addition to their function as oral formulae, are coming to be recognized as discourse markers. For example, OE *þa gelamp hit þæt* and ME *then bifel it that* 'then it happened that' can best be understood as a metacommentary marking an episode boundary and expressing the "subsidiary foreground," the instigating event of an episode. OE *hwæt þa* 'what then' moves the narrative forward, expressing the fact that the event which follows can be inferred from the previous event. In contrast, ME *what (ho)* makes a claim on the attention of the interlocutor (Brinton 1996).

   Moreover, it is possible to find the origin of modern fixed expressions in earlier stages of a language. Modern English parentheticals such as *I think/suppose/guess* (subjective) or *it seems* (objective) arise in early ME as *I gesse/trowe/deme* or *it seemeth*; in addition to epistemic and evidential meaning, they serve purposes of intimacy and "positive" politeness (self-effacement and deference). Nonfirst person epistemic parentheticals (e.g. *God knows*) also arise in early ME as *God woot, trusteth me wel*, and serve as an attempt by the speaker to persuade the hearer of the truth of the utterance. Likewise, the very common Modern English discourse marker, *you know/y'know*, arises in ME as *ye knowen*, perhaps as a replacement for OE *hwæt* (see above) (Brinton 1996).

1.4   Word order

The relation of word order patterns to discourse factors such as topic/comment, thematization, and focus is well known. An account of such phenomena, which have been widely studied in the word order of older languages, is beyond the scope of this chapter. However, a somewhat broader view of discourse factors in the word order of an historical language is taken by Hopper (1979, 1992), who suggests that word order in OE can be accounted for by a theory of grounding. He argues that the foreground is characterized by (S)OV or VS (O) ("verb peripheral") word order, while the background is characterized by (S)VO word order. In respect to verb peripheral order, (S)OV is used internal to episodes with topical subjects and VS (O) is used at the beginning of minor episodes and with a change in subject or topic. (S)VO is used for the beginning of main episodes and for global backgrounding.

1.5   Text types

Finally, it has been suggested that typologies accounting for current texts and the enumeration of features characteristic of different text types may not be adequate for a classification of texts from the past, since conventions of genre are defined by a variety of factors, including forms of the language, topic, situation, and medium (see Görlach 1992: 736–44); Fries asserts, for example, that "it must not be taken for granted that text-linguistic rules for present-day English are also valid for the older periods of the language" (1983: 1013). Questions of differences of textual conventions fall under what Jacobs and Jucker (1995: 11) call "pragmaphilology," or "the contextual aspects of historical texts, including the addressers and addressees, their social and personal relationship, the physical and social setting of text production and text reception, and the goal(s) of the text." Within the field of historical discourse analysis, there have been studies of various genres at different periods, but no comprehensive accounts. For example, Fleischman (1990: 34–5) considers the discourse function of the *laisse* in the Old French epic genre, Görlach (1992) examines the conventions of English cookery books from the past, Hüllen (1995) uncovers the structures in Caxton's dialogues on language learning, and Virtanen (1995) looks at discourse strategies in EModE travelogues.

2   Discourse-oriented Historical Linguistics

The second approach to historical discourse analysis is one which seeks to find the origins and/or motivations of diachronic change in discourse. This approach has been ascendant in recent years. Since it would be impossible to give a complete picture of the results of this approach, this section can only hint at areas in which these types of studies have concentrated.

2.1   Discourse-driven change

It has become almost standard practice in linguistic research to consider discourse-pragmatic factors as possible causes, motivations, or essential aspects of historical change. Two areas of change in which discourse motivations seem most clearly at work are word order change and grammaticalization.

2.1.1   Word order change

It would seem obvious to conclude that just as there is an essential link synchronically between word order and discourse, there should be such a link between word order *change* and discourse. The work of Faarlund (1985, 1989) on "pragmatic syntax" is typical of this approach to word order change. Faarlund argues that "the goal [of pragmatic syntax] is to account for the choices speakers make between systematically related surface structures with equivalent cognitive content" in terms of factors such as theme, focus, and dominance; in other words, whenever two or more (synonymous) syntactic forms exist, there are pragmatic reasons for using one rather than the other. He believes that syntactic change can be explained in terms of pragmatic syntax, for if a new form appears and becomes pragmatically more useful, it may lead to syntactic restructuring, or what Faarlund calls the "grammaticalization of pragmatics" (1985: 366–8, 386). As an example of such change, he discusses the change from OV to VO word order in Germanic. The rightward movement of the object should not be explained as a rare and highly marked afterthought, but by a universal pragmatic principle of focusing. Similarly, Ramat (1990) argues that a discourse-functional explanation is needed for word order changes from Latin to Romance (loss of Wackernagel's Law, loss of verb-final order, cliticization of pronouns to the left of the verb).

2.1.2   Grammaticalization

More recently, it has come to be recognized that discourse factors play a role in the process of grammaticalization.[10] A widely accepted view of grammaticalization is that rather than involving semantic "bleaching" (loss of meaning) or metaphor, as has traditionally been assumed, it involves a change from conversational to conventional implicature; that is, a conversational implicature arising in certain local discourse contexts becomes "semanticized," or assimilated as part of the conventional meaning of the grammaticalized word. This type of change has been called "pragmatic strengthening" or "strengthening of informativeness" (Traugott and König 1991; Hopper and Traugott 1993: 63ff; Traugott 1995b).

Numerous examples of the role of conversational implicature in grammaticalization have been adduced by Traugott, primarily from the history of English. An instance of such a semantic shift is the change from temporal to causal meaning in the grammaticalization of OE *siþþan* 'since' from adverb to conjunction, from the meaning 'from the time that' to the meaning 'because', which results from semanticization of the meaning of 'cause' which arises in certain contexts. Working within the same framework, Carey (1994), considering the early grammaticalization of the perfect in OE, sees the shift from stative (adjectival) to perfect (verbal) meaning, that is, from present state of an object to past process performed on an object, as the conventionalization of an invited inference. Burridge (1995: 73–4) cites a number of examples from Pennsylvania German where increased pragmatic meaning is the outcome of grammaticalization: the change of *als* from an adverb > habitual aspectualizer > discourse particle; the development of futures with *geh* 'to go' and *zehle* 'to count'; the development of a progressive from the locative construction *sei* 'to be' + *am/draa* 'on, at'; and the change of *duh* 'to go' from habitual to present. Taking into account communicative intent, speaker attitude (prominence, (de)emphasis, viewpoint), grounding, and thematic continuity, Epstein (1994, 1995) has studied the grammaticalization of the Latin demonstrative *ille* as a definite article *le/Ø* in French; for example, the zero article in French expresses a low degree of individuation and hence has a backgrounding function; it serves a role in signaling the way a speaker manages the flow of information.[11]

2.2   From discourse to grammar/semantics

In 1979a, Givón argued for the following historical progression:

discourse > syntax > morphology > morphophonemics > zero[12]

He saw the first two steps as motivated primarily by communicative needs and the last two by phonological attrition. In discussions of this progression, interest has focused on the change from looser, conjoined, paratactic constructions to more tightly bound subordinated constructions, e.g. from finite clause to nonfinite complement, from topic clause to relative clause, and so on; other examples of this progression (with an emphasis on the initial discourse > syntax step) include the change from topic to subject marking or from old/new information marking to case functions.

The strong interpretation of Givón's now widely cited progression, which is probably not tenable, is that *all* syntax results from the fossilization of original discourse forms. A weaker interpretation – that what begins as a discourse strategy may sometimes be reanalyzed as syntax – has provided fruitful means of approaching some historical developments. For example, Burridge (1995) argues that in Pennsylvania German, the dative of possession, which begins as a rhetorical device for promoting personal involvement, develops into the regular syntactic marker of possession, displacing the original possessive genitive; furthermore, the semantic shift involves a conversational implicature from close relationship to possession. Faarlund (1985, 1989) sees the rise of an obligatory subject with specific syntactic properties from Old Norse to Modern Norwegian as the result of a topicalization rule moving the NP which is not most highly ranked semantically (but which is most highly ranked thematically) to the left; the moved NP then acquires the grammatical function of subject. Wiegand (1982, 1987) argues that the OE construction *for* + demonstrative pronoun (+ *þe*) begins as a pragmatic indicator of cohesion between two units of discourse, with the demonstrative indexing the cause. As case marking is lost in ME, the demonstrative is no longer analyzable as a deictic, and the construction is reanalyzed as a simple conjunction. König (1992) suggests that disjunctive (*whether*), quantificational (*what/where/ however*), and scalar (*even*) conditionals in English and German still show evidence of deriving from a juxtaposed or loosely connected clause.

3   Diachronically Oriented Discourse Analysis

The third type of historical discourse analysis is one which examines the evolution of discourse marking over time, whether focusing on the development of individual discourse markers or on changes in systems of discourse marking.[13]

3.1   The origin and development of discourse markers

A number of questions arise in the study of the development of discourse markers:

1   What is the source of discourse forms? What semantic and syntactic properties predispose them to express certain discourse notions?
2   What is the course of their semantic and syntactic development? Do they follow recognized principles of change?
3   How do they fare over time? What changes do they undergo and why? To what extent are they transient?

Most studies of the evolution of discourse markers have related their development to the unilinear course of grammaticalization proposed by Traugott (1982: 257), from propositional/ideational to (textual) to interpersonal/expressive meaning,[14] following three principles of semantic change (Traugott and König 1991: 208–9):

- tendency I: from meanings situated in the external described situation to meanings situated in the internal (evaluative/perceptual/cognitive) situation;
- tendency II: from meanings situated in the described external or internal situation to meanings situated in the textual/metalinguistic situation;
- tendency III: to meaning increasingly situated in the speaker's subjective belief-state/attitude toward the situation.

Tendencies I and II are metaphorically driven, while tendency III is metonymically driven, involving an increase in informativeness or a conventionalizing of conversational implicature (see above). Tendency III results in "subjectification," or "the development of a grammatically identifiable expression of speaker belief and speaker attitude toward what is said" (Traugott 1995b: 32).

Traugott gives the examples of the discourse markers *well*, *right*, and *why* moving from propositional to textual to interpersonal meaning (1982: 251, 252, 255), of *let's*, moving from a second person imperative to a first person hortative to a discourse marker meaning that the speaker is cognizant of the hearer, of *let alone* developing from an imperative to a discourse marker expressing the speaker's epistemic attitude, and of the subject of *I think* losing its referential properties and becoming the starting point of a perspective (1995b: 36–9). Schwenter and Traugott (1995; also Traugott forthcoming; Tabor and Traugott forthcoming) point to the acquisition of discourse functions for the "substitutive complex prepositions" *instead/in place/in lieu of*, which originate as purely locative expressions but come to encode an implicature of (counter)expectation. Citing the development of *indeed*, *in fact*, *besides*, and *anyway* in the history of English, Traugott (1995a, forthcoming; Tabor and Traugott forthcoming) argues for a cline: clause-internal adverbial > sentential adverb > discourse marker (denoting elaboration/clarification of discourse content). Rickford et al. (1995: 119–26) discuss the development of *as far as* from a marker of distance or extent to a topic restrictor beginning in the seventeenth century, again from a clause-internal adverb to a discourse marker (see also Traugott forthcoming).

Working within the same model,[15] Onodero (1995) sees the Japanese adversative conjunctions *demo* and *dakedo* changing from ideational > textual > expressive and interjections such as *ne* changing from expressive > textual/expressive, both moving from less to more personal. Kryk-Kastovsky (1997) looks at the shift in the adverbs *now* in English, *nun* in German, and *no/na* in Slavic (cf. OCS *nyně*) from propositional to textual/pragmatic meaning and their evolution as markers of speaker attitude.

Finell (1989, 1992) observes a similar course of development with *well* in English and with topic changers, including introducers (*now*), closers (*however*), and resumers (*anyhow*).[16]

In general, research has found that in their development, discourse markers undergo many of the morphosyntactic and semantic changes identified with the process of grammaticalization,[17] though never, of course, being fully "grammaticalized" in the sense of being incorporated into a recognized grammatical paradigm nor generally undergoing phonological reduction or morphological bonding.[18] They are subject to the following changes, all of which are thought to be typical of grammaticalization:

1 decategorialization: loss of the morphological and syntactic characteristics of their original word class);
2 change from open to closed class membership (Traugott forthcoming);
3 syntactic fixation: loss of syntactic variability and occupation of a fixed slot (but see Traugott 1995b);
4 "divergence" (Hopper 1991) or "split": retention of full lexical characteristics in some contexts alongside grammaticalization in other contexts; and
5 "layering" (Hopper 1991): continuation of older, more highly grammaticalized forms next to newer, less grammaticalized forms.

Semantically, discourse markers exhibit "semantic aptness," or appropriateness for the type of discourse marker that they become; more importantly, their semantic development provides evidence for unidirectionality, for referential (propositional) meaning being the source for pragmatic (textual and interpersonal) meanings (see Brinton 1995; Traugott 1995b, forthcoming). It might be argued that discourse markers do not undergo "condensation" (loss of syntactic scope), since in their discourse function they relate not to individual words or even clauses but to larger stretches of discourse; in fact, Tabor and Traugott (forthcoming) challenge the notion of scope reduction (from "loose" to "tight" syntax) in the process of grammaticalization generally.

I have argued (Brinton 1996) that in its evolution from interrogative to complementizer to discourse marker, OE *hwæt* becomes a particle of indeterminate status and assumes fixed, initial position, always occurring with first or second person pronoun. Its interrogative sense permits it to become a marker which questions common knowledge, expresses surprise, and focuses attention. ME *gan*, in its change from aspectual marker to turn-of-event marker to emphatic/intensive marker, develops from a full verb to a (quasi-)auxiliary, generally occurring with the bare infinitive, and becomes fixed in the third person preterite. Its inceptive semantics motivates its development as a textual marker which focuses on the ensuing action. ME *anon*, developing from locative/temporal meaning to the meaning of saliency/importance/sequence and then of willingness/readiness, loses the cardinal characteristerics of a predicate adverbial and follows Traugott's cline (see above). Its perfective semantics motivates its development as a textual marker which emphasizes the sequence of events. *Þa gelamp hit þæt* in OE and *then bifel it that* in ME become unitary and particle-like; their general meaning of 'happening' makes them suitable as episode boundary markers. In ME, parentheticals such as *I gesse* become fixed in the first person, present tense, and undergo a semantic change from act of cognition, to mode of knowing (evidentiality), to (un)certainty (epistemicity), and finally to intimacy/

politeness.[19] Using evidence such as its increasing fixedness in the first person, its occurrence sentence-initially without *that* or parenthetically, and even its orthography, Palander-Collin (1996, 1997) sees the grammaticalization of the impersonal verbal phrase *methinks* as a sentence adverbial indicating evidentiality, opinion, or subjective truth.[20] Akimoto (forthcoming) discusses the grammaticalization of *I pray you/thee > I pray > pray/prithee* as a "courtesy marker"; in taking on an interjectional use, occurring parenthetically in mid and final position, the verb *pray* undergoes decategorialization and syntactic subordination (or loss of scope) as well as semantic bleaching (see also Palander-Collin 1996: 148, 1997: 393). Finally, Lenker (forthcoming) observes the grammaticalization of OE *witodlice* and *soþlice* from truth-intensifying, speaker-oriented adverbs with sentential scope to discourse markers serving as highlighters and markers of discourse discontinuity.

3.2   *Changes in discourse marking*

In addition to the evolution of individual discourse studies, attention has also been paid to larger changes in patterns of discourse structuring, from one system of discourse marking to another system. For example, Wårvik (1990) sees a "typological" shift in the history of English from the explicit foreground-marking system of OE, centered on the use of *þa* "then", to the "fuzzy" backgrounding system of Modern English, which depends on the tense-aspect system (simple vs. expanded tenses) and the syntactic status of clauses; she relates this shift to a change from oral to literate techniques of grounding (cf. Aristar and Dry 1982). Fludernik (1995) sees the leveling of the foregrounding function of *þa* counteracted by various devices in ME, including *þis* NP, *so, thus*, and *anon* to denote foreground and present participles to denote background. ME *þenne/than* "then" becomes primarily a temporal marker of sequence (Wårvik 1995a; Fludernik 1995) or serves to mark the onset of a narrative episode, though with decreasing frequency (Fludernik 1996: 101).[21] A fundamental change in narrative organization which might also be attributed to the oral > literate shift is the replacement of foregrounded metacommentaries such as *þa gelamp hit þæt* denoting episode boundaries in OE with backgrounded, preposed *whan*-clauses in ME (Brinton 1996; also Fludernik 1995). Similarly, Finell (1992) notes that particles such as *now, however*, and *anyhow* tend to replace explicit phrases such as *and now let me tell you* as topic changers in EModE. In contrast, Taavitsainen (1995) sees interjections, as they become restricted to the oral context, as losing the textual functions (e.g. reader involvement, turning point in plot, vividness of narration, topic shift) that they had in EModE, while continuing the speaker- and addressee-focusing functions.

The loss of particular discourse markers has been accounted for by both grammatical changes and the shift from the literate to the oral mode. For instance, Fleischman (1992) attributes the loss of Old French *si* to a larger syntactic change, viz., the elimination of verb-second and the evolution of SVX order with obligatory subject pronouns, while Fujii (1991, 1992) argues that the development of explicit postpositional subject markers (*wa, ga*) in Japanese, where Old Japanese subjects were generally unmarked, results, internally, from the loss of implicit subject markers such as honorifics, as well as from external (language-contact) causes. The loss of discourse forms might also be attributable to a number of other causes (see Brinton 1996): to the form's co-optation as a metrical expedient and gradual loss of meaning (as in the case of ME *gan*), to its stylistic stigmatization, perhaps because of its affiliation with oral discourse (as in the case of ME *bifel*), or to its overextension of meaning (as in the case of *hwæt* > *what*, which in addition to its propositional uses as an interrogative pronoun, adverb, and adjective and its textual uses as an interrogative complementizer and marker of textual implication ('what then'), acquires expressive uses as a marker of shared knowledge, surprise (*what*, *why*), an exclamation (*what a*), and an attention-getter (*what ho*)).

Despite the changes in discourse forms over time or their loss, there would nonetheless seem to be a *continuity* of pragmatic functions over time, with the forms expressing discourse functions – forms which seem to be intrinsically ephemeral (see Stein 1985a) – continually being replaced; this process of "renewal" is characteristic of grammaticalization (Hopper 1991). For example, OE *hwæt* is replaced by *you know*, or in its attention-getting function by *y'know what*, OE *hwæt þa* by *so*, ME *anon* by *now*, and ME *gan* by the colloquial forms *up and*, *take and*, *go and*. In other cases, there seems to be a preservation of forms over a long period, as in the case of the ME epistemic parentheticals *I gesse*, the surprise sense of *what*, or the episode boundary marking *þa gelamp hit þæt* > *then it bifel that* > *it came to pass that* > *it happened that*, still a feature of modern, colloquial narrative (Brinton 1996).

3.3   Changes in text types

Although Stein (1985b: 351) suggests that the study of text types has always included an historical dimension, studies of changes in discourse or genre have focused almost exclusively on changes that result from the shift from the oral to the written medium.

Taking a global view of change in text type, Biber and Finegan (1989, 1992) have examined changes in a variety of written and speech-based genres in English in respect to a number of grammatical features. What they have found is a "drift" in all genres from features that can be described as more "literate" to ones that can be characterized as more "oral," that is, to features which they describe as more "involved" (e.g. private verbs, first and second person pronouns, contractions, *that*-deletion) rather than "informational" (e.g. nouns, prepositional phrases, "long" words); more "situation-dependent" (e.g. time and place adverbials) rather than "elaborated" (e.g. pied-piping, *wh*-relatives, nominalizations); and more concrete rather than abstract (e.g. passives, adverbial subordinators, past participles). However, Atkinson (1992), applying this type of analysis to medical research writing from 1735 to 1985 in English, has found a clear progression to more "informational," less narrative, more explicit reference, and less overt expression of persuasion, that is, the more literate norms of academic prose (apart from its abstractness). Confirmation of this trend is provided by Görlach (1992), who, in examining changes in the genre of cookery books from ME to the nineteenth century, finds evidence of a shift from oral to written traditions, of a gradual development of generic conventions, and of the introduction of social distinctions in the targeted audience in the linguistic, social, and technical aspects of the text type.

Given that the results of genre-specific study and cross-genre studies have shown opposite directions of change in respect to the oral/written continuum, it seems clear that this area needs much fuller study.[22] Moreover, the linguistic features defining "oral" and "written" texts need to be understood better than they currently are before a diachronic study of texts can come to any certain conclusions. One might also question whether the focus on oral and written features, given the uncertainties surrounding this topic, is the most useful one.

4   Conclusion

Some years ago, Clara Calvo issued the following challenge:

> For over twenty years the study of discourse has been almost exclusively concerned with synchronic analysis and . . . since we can no longer resort to the excuse that discourse studies are young and immature, we might find it necessary very soon to turn our minds to *diachronic* studies of discourse as well. (1992: 26)

Since the early 1980s, scholars have, in fact, been addressing this challenge in a variety of ways, and recently, historical discourse analysis has begun to take shape as a distinct discipline (see, e.g. Jucker 1995). However, it must be said that the field of historical discourse analysis, as it stands today, consists of somewhat disparate strands of study. One strand can be seen as philology tempered by discourse, the so-called "New Philology." That is, it focuses on many of the concerns of the philologist – on "mystery words," inflectional forms, collocations, textual structures – and seeks to understand them as exponents of discourse phenomena such as topic marking, participant tracking, given/new information, narrative segmentation, expressions of subjectivity, and internal or external evaluation, as we understand these phenomena in contemporary discourse. Perhaps the most rewarding of the new philological studies have been those reassessing "mystery particles" as "discourse markers." The second strand can be seen as historical linguistics tempered by discourse. That is, it involves the usual activities of diachronic linguistics combined with a consideration of discourse factors as sources, causes, or motivations of change. While discourse-pragmatic factors can affect many different kinds of diachronic processess, they have been seen as especially significant in grammaticalization and word order change. Certain grammatical structures have also been seen as developing from original discourse structures, and the reverse. The third and last strand of historical discourse analysis involves the study of the origin, diachronic development, and/or loss of discourse markers, of changes in discourse structures, and of alterations in text types over time. Unlike the first two strands, which are *cross*-disciplinary, this third strand is more truly *inter*disciplinary in uniting discourse analysis with diachronic linguistics; and perhaps represents the richest and most rewarding aspect of the new field of historical discourse analysis.

NOTES

1 The chapter "Historical discourse" in van Dijk (1985) is concerned primarily with a discourse analysis of historical writing.

2 Compare *historical (linguistic) pragmatics* (Jacobs and Jucker 1995: 5–6), which combines the first and third approaches discussed here, though it should be noted that the emphasis of the articles in the volume (Jucker 1995) is on the first approach.

3 In historical pragmatics, the latter direction, especially the historical study of the lexicalization of speech acts and changes in illocutionary acts, is common (see Stein 1985b: 350; Jacobs and Jucker 1995: 19–22).

4 Compare *pragmatic historical linguistics* (Jacobs and Jucker 1995: 5). This approach overlaps to some extent with "sociohistorical linguistics," or the study of how social factors (e.g. social class, ethnicity, regional origin, sex, occupation, education) influence linguistic change. In fact, Stein (1985b) defines sociohistorical linguistics as the "micro-approach" of historical pragmatics. In introducing a special volume on the topic, Romaine and Traugott (1985: 5) understand sociohistorical linguistics as encompassing such discourse topics as genre, topic, and oral vs. literate and see it as sharing some of the same concerns as traditional philology. One attempt to address a methodological problem of sociohistorical linguistics – the problem of extracting social information from written texts – is the Corpus of Early English Correspondence, where information concerning gender, social status, educational level, and so on is much more readily extractable (see Nevalainen and Raumolin-Brunberg 1996).

5 For a definition of discourse markers, see Brinton (1996: 29–40).

6 From other linguistic traditions, one might cite Onodero's (1995) study of the Japanese adversative conjunctions *demo* and *dakedo*, which acquired textual and expressive functions in the sixteenth and early twentieth centuries, respectively. In the classical, literary form of Malay used until the end of the nineteenth century, the particle *-lah* is a foregrounder, highlighting the event, giving it special prominence, and announcing it as one in a series of actions; use of the passive voice, marked by *-nya*, is a second means of foregrounding in Malay (Hopper 1979: 227–33).

7 "Propositional/ideational" denotes referential meaning or content, "interpersonal/expressive" is the expression of speaker attitude or judgment and aspects of the social exchange, and "textual" refers to devices for achieving intersentential connections and more global structuring of texts (see Brinton 1996: 38–9).

8 In contrast, Aristar and Dry (1982) argue that the grounding of aspectual forms in OE is ambiguous; the perfect and progressive forms are not restricted to the background, nor is the simple past restricted to the foreground (see also Wårvik 1990); grounding is accomplished through the use of aktionsart forms.

9 In a different vein, Stein (1985a, 1987), considering personal endings on verbs, argues that the variant third person endings *-th* and *-s* in EModE are originally distinguished stylistically (*-th* being used in the "higher" written register and elaborated prose style) and later come to have heterogeneous discourse

functions; *-s* is more common in the peak, and *-th* marks structural units, different narrative modes, characterization, or intensity.

10   For discussions of grammaticalization, see, for example, Lehmann (1985), Hopper (1991), Hopper and Traugott (1993), or Brinton (1996: 50–60).

11   Similarly, the grammaticalization of the demonstrative *se* as a definite article in spoken Finnish (see Laury 1995) also involves pragmatic factors. Since the demonstrative marks a discourse accessible referent, it is reanalyzed as a marker of identifiability in general; this change involves pragmatic strengthening (but not subjectification; see below).

12   Or as it has been reworded by Faarlund, echoing another of Givón's well-known phrases: "today's syntax may be the product of yesterday's discourse pragmatics" (1989: 70).

13   A further aspect of this approach – which will not be pursued here – is the reconstruction of discourse structures to protolanguages.

14   More recently, Traugott (1995b: 47–8) has come to question the unilinear course of development from propositional to textual to interpersonal, seeing grammaticalization operating along several "correlated diachronic continua," though she still considers the change from propositional function to discourse function – "the tendency to recruit lexical (propositional) material for purposes of creating text and indicating attitudes in discourse situations" – as central.

15   Working with a somewhat different framework, Fujii (1991, 1992) examines the development of the Japanese discourse-subject markers *wa* and *ga*: *wa* changes from a marker of contrast and local emphasis to a marker of theme/staging; *ga* changes from an associative marker to a nominative marker, while *no* becomes more fully associative. The markers *wo* and *ni* change from case markers to conjunctives.

16   In a more detailed examination of the history of *well*, Jucker (1997) argues, however, that the earliest form in OE (*wella, wel la*) is used interpersonally as an attention-getter; in ME, *well* begins to be used textually as a frame marker introducing direct reported speech, and in Early Modern and Modern English, it again develops interpersonal uses as a face-threat mitigator and qualifier.

17   Traugott (1995b, forthcoming) questions whether the development of discourse markers might be better understood as "lexicalization," "pragmaticalization," or "postgrammaticalization," but concludes that it most closely resembles the process of grammaticalization.

18   Some discourse markers may in fact undergo phonological reduction, such as *God woot > Goddot(h)* (Brinton 1996) or *indeed, in fact*/ndid, nfækt, fæk/ (see Traugott 1995a), morphological bonding, or other types of reduction, such as the ellipsis of {*is concerned, goes*} in the *as far as* construction (Traugott forthcoming).

19   It can be argued further that the semantic shifts undergone by all of these forms in the process of grammaticalization involve the conventionalization of contextual implicatures, as, for example, the meaning of salience/importance/ sequentiality of *anon* is an implicature of the word's sense of suddenness or urgency (see further Brinton 1996).

20   She considers *methinks* as a "sentence adverbial," though the functions and characteristics of the form that she identifies are comparable to those of discourse markers.

21 However, *then* preserves its foregrounding function in modern oral narratives.

22 For example, Taavistsainen (1994) shows that the development of medical writing is more complex than initially supposed, since even from the beginning of such writing in English, there exist different subtypes that vary in the expression of involvement (e.g. first/second person pronouns, imperatives) or objectivity (e.g. passive), audience, and textual form. A large-scale, corpus-based historical study of medical writing is currently being undertaken (see Taavistsainen and Pahta 1997).

REFERENCES

Akimoto, Minoji (forthcoming). The grammaticalization of the verb *pray*. In Stein and Fischer (forthcoming).

Andersen, Henning (ed.), (1995). *Historical Linguistics, 1993. Selected Papers from the 11th International Conference on Historical Linguistics, 16–20 August, 1993* (Current Issues in Linguistic Theory, 124). Amsterdam and Philadelphia: John Benjamins.

Andersen, Henning and Koerner, Konrad (eds), (1990). *Historical Linguistics, 1987: Papers from the 8th International Conference on Historical Linguistics (8. ICHL) (Lille, 31 August–4 September, 1987)* (Current Issues in Linguistic Theory, 66). Amsterdam and Philadelphia: John Benjamins.

Aristar, Anthony and Dry, Helen (1982). The origin of backgrounding tenses in English. In Kevin Tuite, Robinson Schneider, and Robert Chametzky (eds), *Papers from the Eighteenth Regional Meeting of the Chicago Linguistic Society* (pp. 1–13). Chicago: Chicago Linguistic Society.

Atkinson, Dwight (1992). The evolution of medical research writing from 1735–1985: the case of the *Edinburgh Medical Journal*. *Applied Linguistics*, 13, 337–74.

Betten, Anne (1992). Sentence connection as an expression of medieval principles of representation. In Gerritsen and Stein (1992), (pp. 157–74).

Biber, Douglas and Finegan, Edward (1989). Drift and the evolution of English style: a history of three genres, *Language*, 65, 487–517.

Biber, Douglas and Finegan, Edward (1992). The linguistic evolution of five written and speech-based English genres from the 17th to the 20th centuries. In Rissanen et al. (1992), (pp. 688–704).

Blake, Norman F. (1992). *Why* and *what* in Shakespeare. In Toshiyuki Takamiya and Richard Beadle (eds), *Chaucer to Shakespeare: Essays in Honour of Shinsuke Ando* (pp. 179–93). Cambrige: D. S. Brewer.

Bolkestein, A. Machtelt and van de Grift, Michel (1994). Participant tracking in Latin discourse. In Herman (1994), (pp. 283–302).

Brinton, Laurel J. (1992). The historical present in Charlotte Brontë's novels: some discourse functions. *Style*, 2, 221–44.

Brinton, Laurel J. (1995). Pragmatic markers in a diachronic perspective. In Jocelyn Ahlers, Leela Bilmes, Joshua S. Guenter, Barbara A Kaiser, and Ju Namkung (eds), *Proceedings of the Twenty-first Annual Meeting of the Berkeley Linguistics Society* (pp. 377–88). Berkeley: Berkeley Linguistics Society.

Brinton, Laurel J. (1996). *Pragmatic Markers in English: Grammaticalization and Discourse Functions* (Topics in English

Linguistics, 19). Berlin and New York: Mouton de Gruyter.

Brown, Gillian and Yule, George (1983). *Discourse Analysis* (Cambridge Textbooks in Linguistics). Cambridge: Cambridge University Press.

Burridge, Kate (1995). Evidence of grammaticalization in Pennsylvania German. In Andersen (1995), (pp. 59–75).

Calvo, Clara (1992). Pronouns of address and social negotiation in *As You Like It*. *Language and Literature: Journal of the Poetics and Linguistics Association*, 1, 5–27.

Carey, Kathleen (1994). The grammaticalization of the perfect in OE: an account based on pragmatics and metaphor. In Pagliuca (1994), (pp. 103–17).

Enkvist, Nils Erik (1972). Old English adverbial *þā* – an action marker? *Neuphilologische Mitteilungen*, 73, 90–6.

Enkvist, Nils Erik (1986). More about the textual functions of the Old English adverbial *þa*. In Dieter Kastovsky and Aleksander Szwedek (eds), *Linguistics across Historical and Geographical Boundaries: In Honour of Jacek Fisiak on the Occasion of his Fiftieth Birthday* (Trends in Linguistics, Studies and Monographs, 32), (Vol. 1, pp. 301–9). Berlin, New York, and Amsterdam: Mouton de Gruyter.

Enkvist, Nils Erik and Wårvik, Brita (1987). Old English *þa*, temporal chains, and narrative structure. In Anna Giacalone Ramat, Onofrio Carruba, and Giuliano Bernini (eds), *Papers from the 7th International Conference on Historical Linguistics* (Current Issues in Linguistic Theory, 48), (pp. 221–37). Amsterdam and Philadelphia: John Benjamins.

Epstein, Richard (1994). The development of the definite article in French. In Pagliuca (1994), (pp. 63–80).

Epstein, Richard (1995). The later stages in the development of the definite

article: evidence from French. In Andersen (1995), (pp. 159–75).

Faarlund, Jan Terje (1985). Pragmatics in diachronic syntax. *Studies in Language*, 9, 363–93.

Faarlund, Jan Terje (1989). Pragmatics and syntactic change. In Leiv Egil Breivik and Ernst Håkon Jahr (eds), *Language Change: Contributions to the Study of its Cause* (Trends in Linguistics, Studies and Monographs, 43), (pp. 71–114). Berlin and New York: Mouton de Gruyter.

Fernández, Francisco, Fuster, Miguel, and Calvo, Juan José (eds), (1994). *English Historical Linguistics: Papers from the 7th International Conference on English Historical Linguistics, Valencia, 22–26 September, 1992* (Current Issues in Linguistic Theory, 113). Amsterdam and Philadelphia: John Benjamins.

Finell, Anne (1989). *Well* now and then. *Journal of Pragmatics*, 13, 653–6.

Finell, Anne (1992). The repertoire of topic changers in personal, intimate letters: a diachronic study of Osborne and Woolf. In Rissanen et al. (1992), (pp. 720–35).

Fischer, Andreas (forthcoming). *Marry*: from religious invocation to discourse marker. In Raimund Borgmeier, Andreas Jucker, and Herbert Grabes (eds), *Anglistentag 1997*.

Fleischman, Suzanne (1985). Discourse functions of tense–aspect oppositions in narrative: toward a theory of grounding. *Linguistics*, 2, 851–82.

Fleischman, Suzanne (1986). Evaluation in narrative: the present tense in medieval "performed stories." *Yale French Studies*, 70, 199–251.

Fleischman, Suzanne (1990). Philology, linguistics, and the discourse of the medieval text. *Speculum*, 65, 19–37.

Fleischman, Suzanne (1992). Discourse and diachrony: the rise and fall of Old French *si*. In Gerritsen and Stein (1992), pp. 433–73.

Fludernik, Monica (1995). ME *þo* and other narrative discourse markers. In Jucker (1995), (pp. 359–92).

Fludernik, Monica (1996). *Towards a "Natural" Narratology*. London and New York: Routledge.

Fries, Udo (1983). Diachronic textlinguistics. In Shiro Hattori and Kazuko Inoue (eds), *Proceedings of the XIIIth International Congress of Linguists, August 29–September 4, 1982* (pp. 1013–15). Tokyo: Tokyo Press.

Fries, Udo (1993). Towards a description of text deixis in Old English. In Klaus R. Grinda and Claus-Dieter Wetzel (eds), *Anglo-Saxonica: Festschrift für Hans Schabram zum 65. Geburtstag* (pp. 527–40). Munich: Fink.

Fries, Udo (1994). Text deixis in Early Modern English. In Kastovsky (1994), (pp. 111–28).

Fujii, Noriko (1991). *Historical Discourse Analysis: Grammatical Subject in Japanese* (Discourse Perspectives on Grammar, 3). Berlin and New York: Mouton.

Fujii, Noriko (1992). Change in subject marking in Japanese. In Gerritsen and Stein (1992), (pp. 257–93).

Gerritsen, Marinel and Stein, Dieter (eds), (1992). *Internal and External Factors in Syntactic Change* (Trends in Linguistics, Studies and Monographs, 61). Berlin and New York: Mouton de Gruyter.

Givón, Talmy (1979a). From discourse to syntax: grammar as a processing strategy. In Givón (1979b), (pp. 81–112).

Givón, Talmy (ed.), (1979b). *Syntax and Semantics, Vol. 12: Discourse and Syntax*. New York: Academic Press.

Görlach, Manfred (1992). Text-types and language history: the cookery recipe. In Rissanen et al. (1992), (pp. 736–61).

Herman, Jósef (ed.), (1994). *Linguistic Studies in Latin: Selected Papers from the 6th International Colloquium on Latin Linguistics (Budapest, 23–27 March, 1991)* (Studies in Language Companion Series, 28). Amsterdam and Philadelphia: John Benjamins.

Hope, Jonathan (1994). The use of *thou* and *you* in Early Modern spoken English: evidence from depositions in the Durham ecclesiastical court records. In Kastovsky (1994), (pp. 141–51).

Hopper, Paul J. (1979). Aspect and foregrounding in discourse. In Givón (1979b), (pp. 213–41).

Hopper, Paul J. (1991). On some principles of grammaticization. In Traugott and Heine (1991), (pp. 17–35).

Hopper, Paul J. (1992). A discourse perspective on syntactic change: text-building strategies in Early Germanic. In Edgar C. Polomé and Werner Winter (eds), *Reconstructing Languages and Cultures* (Trends in Linguistics, Studies and Monographs, 58), (pp. 217–38). Berlin and New York: Mouton de Gruyter.

Hopper, Paul J. and Traugott, Elizabeth Closs (1993). *Grammaticalization* (Cambridge Textbooks in Linguistics). Cambridge: Cambridge University Press.

Hüllen, Werner (1995). A close reading of William Caxton's *Dialogues*: ". . . to lerne shortly frenssh and englyssh." In Jucker (1995), (pp. 99–124).

Jacobs, Andreas and Jucker, Andreas H. (1995). The historical perspective in pragmatics. In Jucker (1995), (pp. 3–33).

Jucker, Andreas H. (1994). The feasibility of historical pragmatics. *Journal of Pragmatics*, 22, 533–6.

Jucker, Andreas H. (ed.), 1995. *Historical Pragmatics: Pragmatic Developments in the History of English* (Pragmatics and Beyond, New Series, 35). Amsterdam and Philadelphia: John Benjamins.

Jucker, Andreas H. (1997). The discourse marker *well* in the history of English. *English Language and Linguistics*, 1, 91–110.

Kastovsky, Dieter (ed.), (1994). *Studies in Early Modern English* (Topics in English Linguistics, 13). Berlin and New York: Mouton de Gruyter.

Kim, Taijin (1992). *The Particle þa in the West-Saxon Gospels: A Discourse-level Analysis* (European University Studies, Series XIV, Anglo-Saxon Language and Literature, 249). Bern: Peter Lang.

König, Ekkehard (1992). From discourse to syntax: the case of concessive conditionals. In Rosemarie Tracy (ed.), *Who Climbs the Grammar-Tree* (pp. 423–33). Tübingen: Max Niemeyer.

Kroon, Caroline (1995). *Discourse Particles in Latin: A Study of nam, enim, autem, vero, and at* (Amsterdam Studies in Classical Philology, 4). Amsterdam: J.C. Gieben.

Kryk-Kastovsky, Barbara (1997). From temporal adverbs to discourse particles: an instance of cross-linguistic grammaticalization? In Terttu Nevalainen and Leena Kahlas-Tarkka (eds), *To Explain the Present: Studies in the Changing English Language in Honour of Matti Rissanen* (Mémoires de la Société Néophilologique de Helsinki, 52), (pp. 319–28). Helsinki: Société Néophilologique.

Laury, Ritva (1995). On the grammaticization of the definite article SE in spoken Finnish. In Andersen (1995), (pp. 239–50).

Lehmann, Christian (1985). Grammaticalization: synchronic variation and diachronic change. *Lingua e stile*, 2, 303–18.

Lenker, Ursula (forthcoming). *Soþlice and witodlice*: discourse markers in Old English. In Stein and Fischer (forthcoming).

Levinson, Stephen C. (1983). *Pragmatics* (Cambridge Textbooks in Linguistics). Cambridge: Cambridge University Press.

Longacre, Robert E. (1976). Mystery particles and affixes. In Salikoko S. Mufwene, Carol A. Walker, and Sanford B. Steever (eds), *Papers from the Twelfth Regional Meeting of the Chicago Linguistic Society* (pp. 468–75). Chicago: Chicago Linguistic Society.

Nevalainen, Terrtu and Raumolin-Brunberg, Helena (eds), (1996). *Sociolinguistics and Language History: Studies Based on the Corpus of Early English Correspondence*. Amsterdam: Rodopi.

Ong, Walter (1984). Orality, literacy, and medieval textualization. *New Literary History*, 16 (1), 1–12.

Onodero, Noriko Okada (1995). Diachronic analysis of Japanese discourse markers. In Jucker (1995), (pp. 393–437).

Pagliuca, William (ed.), (1994). *Perspectives on Grammaticalization* (Current Issues in Linguistic Theory, 109). Amsterdam and Philadelphia: John Benjamins.

Palander-Collin, Minna (1996). The rise and fall of METHINKS. In Nevalainen and Raumolin-Brunberg (1996), (pp. 131–49).

Palander-Collin, Minna (1997). A medieval case of grammaticalization, *methinks*. In Matti Rissanen, Merja Kyto, and Kirsi Heikkonen (eds), *Grammaticalization at Work: Studies of Long-term Developments in English* (Topics in English Linguistics, 24), (pp. 371–403). Berlin and New York: Mouton de Gruyter.

Ramat, Anna Giacalone (1990). Discourse functions and syntactic change. In Andersen and Koerner (1990), (pp. 175–90).

Richardson, Peter (1991). Tense, discourse, style: the historical present in "Sir Gawain and the Green Knight." *Neuphilologische Mitteilungen*, 92, 343–49.

Richardson, Peter (1994). Imperfective aspect and episode structure in

Beowulf. Journal of English and Germanic Philology, 93, 313–25.

Richardson, Peter (1995). Tense, structure, and reception in *Þorsteins þáttr stangarhǫlggs. Arkiv för nordisk filologi*, 110, 41–55.

Rickford, John R., Wasow, Thomas A., Mendoza-Denton, Norma, and Espinoza, Juli (1995). Syntactic variation and change in progress: loss of the verbal coda in topic-restricting *as far as* constructions. *Language*, 71, 102–31.

Rissanen, Matti, Ihalainen, Ossi, Nevalainen, Terttu, and Taavitsainen, Irma (eds), (1992). *History of Englishes: New Methods and Interpretations in Historical Linguistics* (Topics in English Linguistics, 10). Berlin and New York: Mouton de Gruyter.

Risselada, Rodie (1994). *Modo* and *sane*, or what to do with particles in Latin discourse. In Herman (1994), (pp. 319–43).

Romaine, Suzanne and Traugott, Elizabeth Closs (1985). Preface. In special volume of *Folia Linguistica Historica* (containing papers from the Workshop on Socio-historical Linguistics, Poznanń, Aug. 20, 1983), 6, 5–6.

Schiffrin, Deborah (1987). *Discourse Markers* (Studies in Interactional Sociolinguistics, 5). Cambridge: Cambridge University Press.

Schiffrin, Deborah (1994). *Approaches to Discourse*. Cambridge, MA: Blackwell.

Schwenter, Scott A. and Traugott, Elizabeth Closs (1995). The semantic and pragmatic development of substitutive complex prepositions in English. In Jucker (1995), (pp. 243–73).

Sell, Roger D. (1985). Politeness in Chaucer: suggestions towards a methodology for pragmatic stylistics, *Studia Neophilologica*, 57, 175–85.

Sell, Roger D. (1994). Postdisciplinary philology: culturally relativistic pragmatics. In Fernández et al. (1994), (pp. 29–36).

Stein, Dieter (1985a). Discourse markers in Early Modern English. In Roger Eaton, Olga Fischer, Willem Koopman, and Frederike van der Leek (eds), *Papers from the 4th International Conference on English Historical Linguistics* (Current Issues in Linguistic Theory, 41), (pp. 283–302). Amsterdam and Philadelphia: John Benjamins.

Stein, Dieter (1985b). Perspectives on historical pragmatics. *Folia Linguistica Historica*, 6, 347–55.

Stein, Dieter (1987). At the crossroads of philology, linguistics and semiotics: notes on the replacement of *th* by *s* in the third person singular in English. *English Studies*, 68, 406–31.

Stein, Dieter and Fischer, Olga (eds), (forthcoming). *Grammaticalization Processes in Older English*. Berlin and New York: Mouton de Gruyter.

Stubbs, Michael (1983). *Discourse Analysis: The Sociolinguistic Analysis of Natural Language* (Language in Society, 4). Chicago: University of Chicago Press.

Taavitsainen, Irma (1994). On the evolution of scientific writings from 1375 to 1675: repertoire of emotive features. In Fernández et al. (1994), (pp. 329–42).

Taavitsainen, Irma (1995). Interjections in Early Modern English: from imitation of spoken to conventions of written language. In Jucker (1995), (pp. 439–65).

Taavitsainen, Irma and Pahta, Päivi (1997). The Corpus of Early English Medical Writing. *ICAME Journal*, 21, 71–8.

Tabor, Whitney and Traugott, Elizabeth Closs (forthcoming). Structural scope expansion and grammaticalization. In Anna Giacalone Ramat and Paul J. Hopper (eds), *The Limits of Grammaticalization*. Amsterdam and Philadelphia: John Benjamins.

Traugott, Elizabeth Closs (1982). From propositional to textual and expressive meanings: some semantic-pragmatic aspects of grammaticalization. In Winfred P. Lehmann and Yakov Malkiel (eds), *Perspectives on Historical Linguistics* (pp. 245–71). Amsterdam and Philadelphia: John Benjamins.

Traugott, Elizabeth Closs (1995a). The role of the development of discourse markers in a theory of grammaticalization. Paper presented at the 12th International Conference on Historical Linguistics. Manchester, England.

Traugott, Elizabeth Closs (1995b). Subjectification in grammaticalization. In Dieter Stein and Susan Wright (eds), *Subjectivity and Subjectivisation: Linguistic Perspective* (pp. 31–54). Cambridge: Cambridge University Press.

Traugott, Elizabeth Closs (forthcoming). Constructions in grammaticalization. In Brian Joseph and Richard Janda (eds), *Handbook for Historical Linguistics*. Oxford: Oxford University Press.

Traugott, Elizabeth Closs and Heine, Bernd (eds), (1991). *Approaches to Grammaticalization, Vol. I: Focus on Theoretical and Methodological Issues* (Typological Studies in Language, 19). Amsterdam and Philadelphia: John Benjamins.

Traugott, Elizabeth Closs and König, Ekkehard (1991). The semantics-pragmatics of grammaticalization revisited In Traugott and Heine (1991), (pp. 189–218).

van Dijk, Teun A. (ed.), (1985). *Handbook of Discourse Analysis*. 4 vols. London: Academic Press.

Virtanen Tutja (1995). "Then I saw to antique heddes": discourse strategies in Early Modern English travelogues. In Jucker (1995), (pp. 499–513).

Wales, Katie (1995). Your average generalisations: a case study in historical pragmatics. In Jucker (1995), (pp. 309–28).

Wårvik, Brita (1990). On the history of grounding markers in English narrative: style or typology? In Andersen and Koerner (1990), (pp. 531–42).

Wårvik, Brita (1995a). The ambiguous adverbial/conjunctions *þa* and *þonne* in Middle English: a discourse-pragmatic study of *then* and *when* in early English saints' lives. In Jucker (1995), (pp. 345–57).

Wårvik, Brita (1995b). Peak marking in Old English narrative. In Brita Wårvik, Sanna-Kaisa Tanskanen, and Risto Hiltunen (eds), *Organization in Discourse. Proceedings from the Turku Conference* (Anglicana Turkuensia, 14), (pp. 549–58). Turku: University of Turku.

Wiegand, Nancy (1982). From discourse to syntax: *for* in early English causal clauses. In Anders Ahlqvist (ed.), *Papers from the 5th International Conference on Historical Linguistics* (Current Issues in Linguistic Theory, 21), (pp. 385–93). Amsterdam and Philadelphia: John Benjamins.

Wiegand, Nancy (1987). Causal Connectives in the Early History of English: a Study in Diachronic Syntax. Unpublished PhD dissertation, Stanford University.

Wilbur, Terence H. (1988). Sentence connectives in ancient Germanic texts. In Daniel G. Calder and T. Craig Christie (eds), *Germania: Comparative Studies in the Old Germanic Languages and Literatures* (pp. 85–95). Wolfeboro, NH: D. S. Brewer.

Wright, Susan (1989). Discourse, style and the rise of periphrastic DO in English. *Folia Linguistica Historica*, 10, 71–91.

8 Typology and Discourse Analysis

JOHN MYHILL

0 Introduction

The relationship between typology and discourse analysis has been characterized by, on the one hand, a general ideological compatibility and, on the other, inherent practical difficulties in combining the interests of the two subdisciplines. The general ideological compatibility is the result of the subdisciplines sharing the view that the study of language should be based upon analysis of empirical data rather than thought experiments. In syntax, semantics, and even pragmatics, intuitions have played a central role in gathering data, and interaction with discourse analysis has tended to be controversial from the outset because of the emphasis in discourse analysis upon the empirical analysis of linguistic data. A discourse analyst interested in the subdiscipline's relationship with, for example, syntax must immediately discuss performance data and phenomena that mainstream syntacticians simply reject as irrelevant; thus any syntax combined with discourse analysis can only be nonmainstream syntax. No such ideological problem arises in the case of typology: intuitions play essentially no role in the data analyzed by typologists, and typologists are only too happy, in principle, to consider the possible relevance of discourse phenomena to the problems they investigate.

In practice, however, it has been difficult to integrate work in these two disciplines, because of various empirical difficulties. There has, therefore, been relatively little research which can be said to have been the product of the interaction between these subdisciplines. Much of what I write here will therefore be programatic, although I will also discuss findings in this area to exemplify what can be done.

Before proceeding, it will be necessary to describe what I am taking to be "typology." The prototypical typological study has data from a wide variety of genetically unrelated languages, analyzed within a common descriptive paradigm which makes it possible to directly, systematically, and (relatively) simply compare data from these various languages and propose hypotheses regarding human language in general. This type of study was pioneered by Joseph Greenberg (1966a, 1966b), who categorized a large number of languages according to, e.g., most common order of subject, verb, and direct object, order of adposition and noun, etc., and, on the basis of this categorization, determined correlations which could be hypothesized as characteristic of human language in general (e.g. verb-object languages are very likely to have prepositions rather than postpositions). It is the use of a systematic common descriptive paradigm, allowing for direct comparison between a wide variety of languages, which distinguishes the methodology of typology from that of other approaches.

Within the field of discourse analysis, there have been many studies which have compared different languages but which would not, on this understanding, be considered to be specifically typological, because they are not focused upon developing a system for direct, systematic, and universal comparison of a wide variety of languages as Greenberg's studies were (e.g. Tannen 1981; Brown and Levinson 1987; Blum-Kulka 1991). Such works are discursive in nature, typically comparing English with one (or very rarely two) other language(s) and selecting examples which show how the languages differ in certain respects, or, alternatively, how they can fulfill similar discourse functions using constructions which may superficially appear to be different. Typically, there is no systematic, exhaustive, and quantitative analysis of a database, the examples are selected anecdotally depending upon which point the author wishes to make in a particular article without systematic demonstration that they represent a general pattern, comparison between actual usage in the languages is unsystematic, and it is not clear how additional languages would fit into the comparative framework of the study. Thus, although such studies are comparative, they are not really directed toward establishing a systematic universal framework for categorizing discourse phenomena in the way that Greenberg's studies established a systematic universal framework for categorizing syntactic phenomena. Because I am discussing the relationship of typology and discourse analysis, then, I will in the present chapter discuss those approaches which have been more similar to Greenberg's in this respect.

Section 1 of this chapter will describe general problems associated with methodology combining typology and discourse analysis. Sections 2 and 3 then discuss two approaches to these problems, the use of universal conceptual systems of classification and the use of translation data.

1   Problems of Typological Discourse Analysis

The study of discourse phenomena in a typological framework presents some inherent difficulties which are not found in other areas of typology. Traditional typological studies (Greenberg 1966a; Bybee 1985; Croft 1990) use as their main source of data reference grammars from a wide variety of languages, and the linguistic phenomena they consider are those which are likely to be found in a reference grammar, e.g. typical word order (of subject/object/verb, adposition/noun, etc.), structural characteristics of voice alternations, phonological inventory, etc. Unfortunately, this is not possible with the sort of phenomena typically of interest to discourse analysts. Existing reference grammars of less-known languages generally have very little in the way of discourse analysis, and what limited analyses they do have are not written in a way to allow for cross-linguistic comparison by someone who does not know the language very well. For example, if I were to attempt to do a typological study of the functions of contrastive connectives similar to English *but*, I could probably gather a list of words in a wide variety of languages with some type of generally similar function, but it would be impossible on the basis of the descriptions of these particles in reference grammars to understand and then compare the functions of these different words.

Another problem for typological discourse analysis as compared with more traditional discourse analysis is the degree of familiarity of the researcher with the languages to be analyzed; in a typological study the linguist is not going to know all the languages under investigation very well, while in a traditional discourse study the investigator is likely to be a native speaker of or very proficient in the language(s) under investigation. While there are recorded cases of individuals knowing a large number of languages, these are typically closely related or at least related languages; in typological studies, on the other hand, it is typical to have data from languages from 15–20 different language families. Although this problem can be alleviated to some extent through reliance on texts with interlinear glosses, this still does not entirely make up for the researcher's lack of in-depth knowledge of the language; additionally, the languages in which there are a large enough number of such texts of reasonable length which can be the basis for a discourse study are concentrated in just a few language families (Austronesian, Australian, and Semitic in particular), while the great majority of language families have no languages at all with a large number of texts with interlinear glosses.

Because such studies are not really feasible, linguists interested in discourse analysis and typology have instead focused upon using a narrower range of languages with which they themselves have some expertise. Even in this case there has to be much more dependence upon observations of textual patterns (so that longer texts must be used) and much less upon introspective judgments than would be the case for linguists working in their native languages. In such a situation, we cannot expect the relatively quick and impressive types of language-universal generalizations which individual typological studies of, e.g., word order patterns have been able to produce; in fact, it is unlikely that any single researcher will be able to conduct studies of a genetically diverse enough group of languages to allow for the degree of confidence in universality which typologists are accustomed to. Rather, in order to achieve an extensive genetic spread, it is necessary for a variety of discourse analysts, each working in a number of languages, to develop a uniform means of systematically comparing their results from these different languages.

1.1   Cross-linguistic comparison of discourse function and categories

Aside from the question of which data to analyze, it is also necessary for typological discourse analysts to consider the nature of the discourse categories to be used. It is very common for linguists describing discourse categories in different languages to use the same words to describe something in the language they are investigating, e.g. "topic," "focus," "contrast," etc., but this does not mean that they are referring to the same discourse phenomena. For example, although the term "topic" has been used to refer to a supposedly discourse-based category in a wide variety of languages, there is no cross-linguistic agreement about what a "topic" is. In each language, "topic" actually refers to whatever discourse properties result in a certain language-specific structure being used, so that the definition is a result of the language-specific pattern, and these structures in different languages actually serve clearly distinct functions. Thus in Japanese, anything marked with the postposition *wa* is called a "topic" (Kuno 1973), while in English, the term "topic" might be used for a clause-initial constituent whose syntactic role would call for some other position (e.g. **That book** *I don't like*), though usage differs (see Firbas 1966 and various articles in Li 1976 and Givón 1983a).[1]

Though linguists specializing in each of these languages may develop some sort of ostensibly discourse-based "definition" of a "topic" in this language (e.g. "What a sentence is about" or something which "sets a spatial, temporal, or individual framework within which the main predication holds" (Chafe 1976: 50)), these definitions are invariably quite vague. Thus, in practice, the only objective way to determine whether a constituent is actually a "topic" has been to apply some language-specific structural test (e.g. to see if it is marked with *wa* in Japanese). As a result, the "topics" in the different languages do not have the same discourse function at all, e.g. the translation of *I like Mary* into Japanese would have "I" as a "topic" (marked with *wa*), the translation of *I read the book* into Tagalog would have "the book" as a "focus" (marked with *ang*), etc. There is, then, no cross-linguistic idea of a "topic," and so such a category cannot serve as a basis for cross-linguistic comparison.

In order to deal with this problem of cross-linguistic comparison of function, linguists working in typological discourse analysis have focused upon developing a set of criteria which make it possible to give an objective, cross-linguistic definition of the discourse function of a particular form or construction. Using these criteria, a linguist can go through a text in a given language, note all the occurrences of a given form or construction in that language, determine numerical scores for that form or construction according to various parameters (e.g. for an NP, how recently its referent has been mentioned, whether it refers to a human being, etc.), and then compare these scores with those of other constructions in other languages. The question, of course, is exactly which scores should be used in which cases, and this is a matter of ongoing research. A second approach to the problem of comparison is to use translation data; we can get some idea of the functional similarity of and difference between constructions in different languages by seeing how often and in what circumstances they translate as each other. In section 2, I will discuss parameters used in classification of discourse function; in section 3, I will discuss the use of translation data.

2   Universal Systems of Classification of Discourse Function

I will describe here various text-count methods which have been developed to give an objective, cross-linguistically applicable description of the discourse function of a given construction. The use of such text counts does not suggest that speakers themselves go through any calculations similar to those of the linguist, nor does it imply that a given text-count score will predict with 100 percent accuracy which construction will be used on each occasion. Rather, such counts are purely descriptive tools to allow for cross-linguistic comparison.

2.1   Referential distance and topic persistence

The most widely used text-counts, associated particularly with Talmy Givón and students of his, are called Referential Distance (RD) and Topic Persistence (TP). For each NP in a text, RD counts the last time its referent was referred to (including zero anaphora) in the preceding text (e.g. RD = 2 if it was referred to two clauses before), while TP counts how many times it is referred to in the following text (e.g. TP = 1 if it is referred to again in the following clause but not in the clause after that). We can say that an NP is generally more topical if its RD is low and its TP is high, but of course we are really measuring two types of topicality here, anaphoric (RD) and cataphoric (TP).

RD and TP counts make it possible to give a functional profile of a given construction or NP type. For example, suppose that we are trying to give a general characterization of the function of the active–passive alternation in English, e.g. *Bill wrote that book* vs. *That book was written by Bill*. We go through a text, collecting all active transitive and passive constructions, and then count the average RDs for the Agents of actives (*Bill* in *Bill wrote that book*), the Agents of passives (*Bill* in *That book was written by Bill*), the Patients of actives (*that book* in *Bill wrote that book*), and the Patients of passives (*That book* in *That book was written by Bill*). We then calculate the mean and median RD and TP scores for active Agents, passive Agents, active Patients, and passive Patients, or list the populations in a table. By doing similar studies in a variety of languages, we can systematically compare the discourse functions of active and passive constructions in different languages. This approach has been useful in providing a typological perspective on functional alternations, clarifying the discourse motivations underlying these alternations, and also sharpening the descriptive tools for typological descriptions; it does not suggest that speakers make such calculations in deciding which construction to use (although RD can be interpreted as being generally correlated with cognitive accessibility). In the remainder of this section, I will discuss a number of studies which have been done using these measures.

2.1.1   RD and TP in analysis of voice systems

Voice alternations in different languages have been characterized in various descriptive grammars in a variety of ways, in particular *Active* vs. *Passive*, *Direct* vs. *Inverse*, *Ergative* vs. *Antipassive*, and (for Philippine languages) *Agent Focus* vs. *Goal Focus*. However, the basis for such characterizations has often been unclear. Consider, for example, the following constructions in Tagalog:

(1)   Bumasa ang lalaki ng diyaryo.
     read   man   newspaper
     "The man read a newspaper."

(2)   Binasa ng lalaki ang diyaryo.
       read   man   newspaper
       "The man read the newspaper."

Case functions in Tagalog are marked by prepositions, here *ang* and *ng*. It is clear that *ang* marks intransitive subjects (e.g. *matalino ang lalaki* "intelligent *ang* man" = "The man is intelligent"). The question here is what general function to ascribe to *ang* and *ng*. One possibility is to say that *ang* marks subjects (both intransitive and transitive) and *ng* marks direct objects and oblique NPs. Then (1) would be an active construction, with *lalaki* as the subject and *diyaryo* as the direct object, while (2) would be a passive construction, with *diyaryo* as the subject and *lalaki* as the oblique Agent. Alternatively, we might say that *ang* is an absolutive case marker (marking intransitive subjects and direct objects), while *ng* is an ergative (transitive subject) and oblique case marker. Then (1) would be an antipassive construction (grammatically intransitive), with *lalaki* as the intransitive subject marked with the absolutive preposition *ang*, and *diyaryo* (which is in this case an oblique rather than direct object) marked with the oblique preposition *ng*, and (2) would be an ergative construction, with *lalaki* as the transitive subject, marked with the ergative preposition *ng*, and *diyaryo* as the direct object, marked with the absolutive preposition *ang*. In fact, earlier studies of Philippine languages (e.g. Schachter and Otanes 1972) used yet another type of terminology, referring to *ang* as marking "focused" constituents (which causes confusion of another type in terms of cross-linguistic comparison, since the term "focus" is usually used with some sort of entirely different meaning) and *ng* as marking certain nonfocused constituents, so that (1) is an "Actor Focus" construction while (2) is a "Goal Focus" construction. Similar labeling problems arise in many other languages (see Givón 1994).

   The result of all of this has been that grammars of different languages have used a bewildering variety of labels for different constructions and it is unclear how to compare these. In response to this problem, linguists interested in functional factors such as discourse role began to develop discourse criteria for distinguishing these different types (see Givón 1994). The general criteria which have come out of these studies are:

1   The functionally unmarked type, which I will refer to by the general name **direct** (including constructions which have been called "Active" and "Ergative"), typically has an Agent (A) which is somewhat more topical (e.g. lower RD, higher TP) than its Patient (P).
2   If a construction is particularly used when the Patient is very high in topicality, this construction is referred to as an **inverse**. Such constructions can be used even when the Agent is relatively topical as well, in situations where the relatively high topicality of the Agent would prevent the use of a Passive.
3   If a construction is particularly used when the Agent is very low in topicality, this construction is referred to as a **passive**.
4   If a construction is particularly used when the Patient is very low in topicality, this construction is referred to as an **antipassive**.

Let us now see more specifically how text counts can be used as diagnostics for categorization of particular constructions in particular languages (table 8.1).

Table 8.1   Voice alternations in Koyukon and Dyirbal

		N	A RD	A TP	P RD	P TP
Koyukon	(a)	100	2.22	5.45	2.91	3.76
	(b)	110	4.99	3.90	1.51	6.83
	(c)	50	–	–	8.45	1.86
Dyirbal	(a)	225	3.42	2.00	5.19	1.16
	(b)	44	1.45	2.20	10.57	0.86

Data sources: Thompson (1994) (Koyukon); Cooreman (1988) (Dyirbal)

Each of the labels (a), (b), and (c) in table 8.1 refers to a particular construction in these languages, and the data in these tables can be used in combination with the characterizations of the different voice types given above to label these constructions in a cross-linguistically comparable and consistent manner. For both of these languages, the (a) construction is **direct/active**, having an Agent which is somewhat higher in topicality than its Patient (but the difference is not as great as would be characteristic of an antipassive construction). The Koyukon (b) construction has a P which is very high in topicality (the lowest RD and highest TP of any of the constructions here), and its A is not particularly high or low in topicality; this is therefore an **inverse** construction. The A in the Koyukon (c) construction, on the other hand, is very low in topicality (in fact obligatorily absent), and so this is a **passive** construction. The Dyirbal (b) construction is particularly characterized by having a very nontopical P (high RD, low TP), and so we can call this an **antipassive** construction (see Givón 1994 for similar discussion of a number of other languages).

2.1.2   RD and word order

Linguists have also applied RD to investigating word order variation. Studies from a variety of languages have found that preverbal arguments have on average a higher RD than postverbal arguments (there does not seem to be any corresponding clear pattern relating TP and word order). Table 8.2 shows data in this regard from a number of languages.

Table 8.2   RD and word order in four languages

	Ute (s)	Ute (o)	Biblical Hebrew	Spanish	Chamorro
Postverbal	1.81 (86)	4.21 (14)	6.52 (357)	3.54 (41)	7.45 (200)
Preverbal	5.49 (114)	7.78 (46)	10.64 (112)	8.55 (170)	10.90 (96)

Notes: Numbers are RD (N-size). All data are for subjects, except Ute (o), which is for direct objects.
Data sources: Givón (1983b) (Ute); Fox (1983) (Biblical Hebrew); Bentivoglio (1983) (Spanish); Cooreman (1983) (Chamorro).

These data have been taken from languages which are generally verb-initial (Biblical Hebrew and Chamorro), SVO (Spanish), and where the verb most often follows both the subject and the object (Ute) (see other studies in Givón 1983a showing a similar pattern); thus there is reason to suppose this may be a universal pattern. At first this appears surprising, because an often-repeated theme of functional linguistics is that "old information precedes new information" (e.g. Contreras 1978), whereas the data in table 8.2 suggest the reverse, that arguments are more likely to precede the verb if their RD is higher, so that they represent *newer* information. However, it is possible to suggest a resolution to this apparent contradiction (although this is speculative and should be checked against more data). Claims that old information generally precedes new information have been made on the basis of data from European languages which are generally SVO, using an existential-presentative construction like *On the roof stood a chimney*, where the preverbal *roof* is old information and the postverbal *chimney* is new information. It is possible that the distinctive use of VS order in this existential-presentative construction is specific to SVO languages, that such constructions constitute the only basis for the general claim that "old information precedes new information," and that if these constructions in these SVO languages are excluded, the reverse is generally true, and "new information precedes old information," as suggested by the data in table 8.2. Supporting this idea is the fact that in the data from the only SVO language here, Spanish, the researcher specifically excluded existential-presentative constructions from the counts (see Bentivoglio 1983); if these constructions are included, the picture changes, as the postverbal subjects have a *higher* RD (11.99, N = 141) than the preverbal ones (8.22, N = 180).[2]

2.2   *Temporal sequencing*

Another criterion for categorizing discourse function in different languages is **temporal sequencing** or **foregrounding**. Introduced in Labov (1972) (as the concept "narrative clause"), this was first extended to data in a variety of languages in Hopper (1979). According to this criterion, a clause is temporally sequenced if it has past time reference and refers to the next event in a story line (e.g. the second clause, but not the first, in *I was reading in the library and this guy came up to me . . .*). The sequencing function has been related to alternations in word order, voice, and verb form. For example, Schiffrin (1981) shows that the English historical present is associated with temporally sequenced clauses, while Hopper (1979) shows that temporal sequencing is associated with the use of the verbal forms with a *di*-prefix in Malay. Myhill (1992) argues that, in languages with a relatively high frequency of VS order, sequencing is particularly associated with VS word order, while SV order is associated with unsequenced clauses. On the other hand, in languages with a lower frequency of VS order, this correlation is not found. This is shown by the data in table 8.3 (see also data from Old English in Hopper 1979).

The Biblical Hebrew data here are particularly striking, in that they show that when the language changed to a lower frequency of VS order, the association between temporal sequencing and VS order disappeared. The concept of temporal sequencing therefore makes it possible to make a typological generalization regarding word order type.

Table 8.3   Word order and temporal sequencing

	Tzotzil	*EBH*	*Chorti*	*Spanish*	*LBH*	*Romanian*
All	80 (899)	65 (1099)	51 (184)	44 (2000)	40 (420)	31 (554)
Sequenced	92 (244)	80 (546)	72 (320)	58 (316)	20 (85)	22 (113)
Unsequenced	76 (655)	49 (553)	47 (152)	41 (1684)	46 (335)	33 (441)

Notes: Numbers are VS% (N-size). EBH = Early Biblical Hebrew, LBH = Late Biblical Hebrew.
Data sources: Givón (1977) (Hebrew); Myhill (1984) (others)

2.3   *Other types of text-counts*

Linguists have proposed other types of text-counts which can be useful in giving a profile of the discourse function of a construction. Myhill and Xing (1996) propose a definition of the term "contrast" which can be objectively applied to naturally occurring usages so as to categorize individual clauses as contrastive or not (and also to distinguish between different subtypes of contrast), so that one or another contrastive function can be shown to be statistically associated with the use of a certain word order, intonation pattern, or particle (e.g. Japanese *wa*, Korean *-(n)m*). In Forrest's (1994) study of voice alternations in Bella Coola, in addition to counts associated with NP information status such as RD and TP, she also uses a text-count distinguishing between NPs which refer to major characters in a story and those which do not, and shows that variation on this parameter correlates with the use of one or other voice construction. A related and more objective and universally applicable (though also more time-consuming) type of measure is Topicality Quotient, described in Thompson (1989). To determine this, one counts the number of clauses in which a referent is referred to in an entire text, divides this by the number of total clauses in the text, and then assigns this score to every mention of this referent. Other possible counts categorize referents according to their humanness, animacy, number, referentiality, function in previous clause, form (e.g. pronoun, unmodified noun, modified noun, common noun, proper noun, etc.), or, for that matter, anything else the linguist thinks is important which can be coded objectively.

3   Translation Data

Translation provides another means of comparing discourse functions in different languages. It is useful in that it gives some idea of the functional similarity or difference between constructions in different languages. For example, in Dryer's (1994) study of voice in Kutenai, he asked a bilingual Kutenai–English speaker to translate a Kutenai text into English. He found that, out of 70 clauses using a certain Kutenai construction clearly associated with highly topical Patients, only nine were translated into English as passives, the rest being translated as actives, suggesting that this Kutenai construction is functionally like an inverse rather than a passive.

Sometimes, translation data show that text-counts such as RD and TP do not give a true picture of the functional similarity or difference between different constructions in different languages. For example, Sun and Givón (1985) use data such as RD and TP to argue that object-fronting constructions in Chinese and Biblical Hebrew serve basically the same function. However, Myhill and Xing (1993) show that, if we look at translation data, we see that the object-fronting constructions in these languages are frequently not translated as each other; for example, of 82 OV constructions in a Biblical Hebrew database, 48 (59%) do *not* use an OV construction in the Chinese translation, while of 193 OV constructions in the Chinese translation, 159 (82%) do *not* use an OV construction in the Hebrew original. In other words, in the majority of cases, an OV construction in one language would not be used where an OV construction would be used in the other language. This shows that the Hebrew and Chinese OV constructions clearly differ significantly in discourse function, in spite of their RD and TP scores.

In such a situation, where established criteria for cross-linguistic comparison suggest functional similarity which is demonstrated to be incorrect by translation data, linguists interested in cross-linguistic comparison must develop other criteria which will capture these differences. In the case of the comparison of Biblical Hebrew and Chinese object-verb constructions, Myhill and Xing (1996) develop a text-count for contrast (see section 2.3 above), distinguishing between several subtypes of contrast, in order to describe exactly how these constructions are similar in function and how they are different; they find that certain types of contrastive functions result in OV order in both languages, but for other contrastive functions, only Biblical Hebrew fronts objects, while for still others, only Chinese does.

Another use of translation data can be to make it possible to distinguish between different functions which a particular construction can serve in a manner which is objective and uses parameters which languages themselves treat as significant; the studies described in section 2.1 make no such functional distinctions but simply lump all structurally similar constructions together. Myhill and Xing (1994) is a contrastive study of voice in Chinese, English, and Biblical Hebrew of this type, using Chinese and English translations of Genesis. Myhill and Xing divide up the database into one of a number of types of clauses, where all of the clauses in each type use a particular Hebrew construction translated as a particular Chinese construction and a particular English construction, and give a functional characterization of the type in general. Thus, for example, the combination of an English passive, a Chinese Patient–verb construction (suppressing the Agent), and a Hebrew niphal (an intransitive form often like a passive) occurs 12 times in the translation database, characteristically having an obscure Agent and an inanimate Patient (e.g. *The fountains of the deep and the floodgates of the sky were stopped up* (Genesis 8:2)), while the combination of an English passive, a Chinese active, and a Hebrew niphal occurs 19 times, characteristically with future time reference and a first or second person Agent (implied in the English and Hebrew, e.g. *By this you will be put to the test*, but Chinese *wo yao shiyishi nimen*, lit. "I will test you" (Genesis 42:15)), so that Chinese is the only one of the three languages which does not use an agent-suppressing construction to avoid mentioning first or second person Agents in such a potentially sensitive situation; similar patterns were found with other combinations of translations. Translation data of this type make it possible to divide up the functions of each of the constructions involved into subtypes and make the functional differences between the constructions in the different languages explicit.

Although translations are helpful in comparing functions across language, they have limitations. The most basic problem is the fact that, for many pairs of languages (e.g. Luganda and Zuni), it is hard to get direct translation data. One possibility is to use material from a third language which has been translated into both (the Bible is the most likely source here); another is for the linguist to get native speakers to make translations, although this will often be problematic as it will likely have to be done through a third language. Another problem with translations is that there is some tendency to translate according to certain conventions, with certain constructions translating as certain constructions and certain words translating as certain words even in cases where this might not result in the most idiomatic translations; for this reason, translation data are most significant when the translator does *not* follow the usual translating conventions, as this identifies cases where the functional differences between the constructions or words in question are great enough to overcome fixed translation practices.

A good source of cross-linguistic data is *The Pear Stories* (Chafe 1980a). A silent film was shown to people with a variety of first languages (more than 50 of English, at least 20 of Chinese, Japanese, Malay, Thai, Persian, Greek, German, Haitian Creole, and Sacapultec (Mayan)), and they were asked to retell the story in their own language. In this case there is no actual language-to-language translation, although the texts in the different languages are to some extent parallel. The linguistic studies which have been done of these stories, however, have thus far not been typological in nature, either focusing upon the question of how people report the plot of the movie in a single language (e.g. Chafe 1980b) or comparing English with a single other language without any attempt to integrate this into a general cross-linguistic framework for typological analysis (e.g. Tannen 1980).

4   Conclusion

Typology and discourse analysis are fields which have much to offer each other. Typological studies can provide a basis for discourse studies by offering a point of reference for discourse phenomena other than comparison with individual "other languages," which almost always turn out to be English. Discourse analysis offers typology a way of comparing different constructions in different languages and sorting through the enormous terminological confusion and inconsistency found in reference grammars which have plagued typological studies. There has thus far been relatively little work integrating these approaches, because of the inherent problems I have discussed, but some progress has been made in this regard. The most likely source of a breakthrough in this area is the development of a megacorpus of translation materials from a single text into a wide variety of genetically unrelated languages, with interlinear glosses, using perhaps the Bible, some other widely translated work, or *The Pear Stories*; a large enough corpus would to some extent mitigate the problems inherent in translation data. It will also be necessary to undertake further studies along the lines of Givón (1983a, 1994), where a number of researchers apply similar text-count methodology to study similar structural phenomena in texts from a variety of genetically diverse languages, but the methodology should be expanded to include not just RD and TP (useful though these have shown themselves to be) but other text-count methods as well. Another welcome move would be the development and application of similar text-count methods to the cross-linguistic analysis of other phenomena of concern to discourse analysts, e.g. politeness, definiteness, discourse particles, etc. Because typological discourse analysis has developed out of traditional typology, it has focused more upon issues such as word order and voice, which can be more directly related to syntax, but there is no reason why this has to continue to be the case in the future.

NOTES

1   A similar problem arises for "focus," which means a completely different thing when referring to Somali, Tagalog, Hungarian, or other languages.
2   Herring (1990) suggests a different type of universal account of word order patterns, one based upon categories which she refers to as "continuous topic," "shifted topic," "contrastive focus," and "presentative focus," and relating the position of these in a given language to the unmarked order of subject and verb in that language. Although Herring's proposals are interesting, she does not give quantitative data or an objective definition of exactly what she means by e.g. "continuous topic," nor does she attempt to integrate her findings with those of the papers in Givón (1983a); this should be addressed in future research.

   Payne (1992) has a number of papers discussing factors affecting word order in a variety of languages from a functional perspective. I am not focusing on the papers in that volume because of space limitations and because they are not intended to provide a systematic comparative typological framework as are the papers in, e.g., Givón (1983a, 1994).

REFERENCES

Bentivoglio, Paola. 1983. Topic continuity and discontinuity in discourse: a study of spoken Latin-American Spanish. In Givón 1983a, pp. 255–312.

Blum-Kulka, Shoshana. 1991. Interlanguage pragmatics: the case of requests. In R. Phillipson, ed., *Foreign/Second Language Pedagogy Research*, pp. 255–72. Clevedon: Multilingual Matters.

Brown, Penelope and Stephen C. Levinson. 1987. *Politeness: Some Universals in Language Usage*. Cambridge: Cambridge University Press.

Bybee, Joan L. 1985. *Morphology*. Amsterdam: John Benjamins.

Chafe, Wallace L. 1976. Givenness, contrastiveness, definiteness, subjects, topics, and point of view. In Li 1976, pp. 25–56.

Chafe, Wallace L., ed. 1980a. *The Pear Stories*. Norwood, NJ: Ablex.

Chafe, Wallace L. 1980b. The deployment of consciousness in the production of a narrative. In Chafe 1990a, pp. 9–50.

Contreras, Heles. 1978. *El orden de palabras en español*. Madrid: Catedra.

Cooreman, Ann. 1983. Topic continuity and the voicing system of an ergative language: Chamorro. In Givón 1983a, pp. 425–90.

Cooreman, Ann. 1988. Ergativity in Dyirbal discourse. *Linguistics* 26:717–46.

Croft, William. 1990. *Typology and Universals*. Cambridge: Cambridge University Press.

Dryer, Matthew. 1994. The discourse function of the Kutenai inverse. In Givón 1994, pp. 65–100.

Firbas, J. 1966. Non-thematic subjects in contemporary English. *Traveaux Linguistiques de Prague 2*.

Forrest, Linda B. 1994. The de-transitive clause in Bella Coola: passive vs. inverse. In Givón 1994, pp. 147–68.

Fox, Andrew. 1983. Topic continuity in Biblical Hebrew narrative. In Givón 1983a, pp. 215–54.

Givón, Talmy. 1977. The drift from VSO to SVO in Biblical Hebrew: the pragmatics of tense-aspect. In C. N. Li, ed., *Mechanisms of Syntactic Change*, pp. 181–254. Austin: University of Texas Press.

Givón, Talmy, ed. 1983a. Topic continuity in discourse. Amsterdam: John Benjamins.

Givón, Talmy. 1983b. Topic continuity and word-order pragmatics in Ute. In Givón 1983a, pp. 141–214.

Givón, Talmy, ed. 1994. *Voice and Inversion*. Amsterdam: John Benjamins.

Greenberg, Joseph. 1966a. Some universals of grammar with particular reference to the order of meaningful elements. In J. H. Greenberg, ed., *Universals of Grammar*, 2nd edn, pp. 73–113. Cambridge, Mass.: MIT Press.

Greenberg, Joseph. 1966b. Language universals, with special reference to

feature hierarchies. *Janua Linguarum, Series Minor, 59*. The Hague: Mouton de Gryter.

Herring, Susan C. 1990. Information structure as a consequence of word order type. *Berkeley Linguistics Society* 16:163–74.

Hopper, Paul J. 1979. Aspect and foregrounding in discourse. In T. Givón, ed., *Discourse and Syntax*, pp. 213–41. New York: Academic Press.

Kuno, Susumu. 1973. *The Structure of the Japanese Language*. Cambridge, Mass.: MIT Press.

Labov, William. 1972. The transformation of experience in narrative syntax. In W. Labov, *Language in the Inner City*, pp. 354–96. Philadelphia: University of Pennsylvania Press.

Li, Charles, ed. 1976. *Subject and Topic*. New York: Academic Press.

Myhill, John. 1984. A study of aspect, word order, and voice. University of Pennsylvania, PhD dissertation.

Myhill, John. 1992. Word order and temporal sequencing. In Payne 1992, pp. 265–78.

Myhill, John and Zhiqun Xing. 1993. The discourse functions of patient fronting: a comparative study of Biblical Hebrew and Chinese. *Linguistics* 31.1:25–57.

Myhill, John and Zhiqun Xing. 1994. A comparison of the function of voice in Biblical Hebrew, Chinese, and English. *Language Sciences* 16.2:253–83.

Myhill, John and Zhiqun Xing. 1996. Towards an operational definition of discourse contrast. *Studies in Language* 20.2:313–70.

Payne, Doris, ed. 1992. *The Pragmatics of Word Order Flexibility*. Amsterdam: John Benjamins.

Schachter, Paul and Fe T. Otanes. 1972. *Tagalog Reference Grammar*. Berkeley: University of California Press.

Schiffrin, Deborah. 1981. Tense variation in narrative. *Language* 57:45–62.

Sun, Chaofen and Talmy Givón. 1985. On the SOV word order in Mandarin Chinese. *Language* 61:2.

Tannen, Deborah. 1980. A comparative analysis of oral narrative strategies: Athenian Greek and American English. In Chafe 1980a, pp. 51–88.

Tannen, Deborah. 1981. Indirectness in discourse: ethnicity as conversational style. *Discourse Processes* 4:221–38.

Thompson, Chad. 1989. Voice and obviation in Navajo. In *Proceedings of the Fourth Annual Meeting of the Pacific Linguistics Conference*, pp. 466–88. Eugene: University of Oregon Department of Linguistics.

Thompson, Chad. 1994. Passive and inverse constructions. In Givón 1994, pp. 47–64.

9 Register Variation: A Corpus Approach

DOUGLAS BIBER AND SUSAN CONRAD

0 Introduction

Analyses of discourse context can be approached from two perspectives. First, they can focus on the textual environment, considering lexical, grammatical, and rhetorical features in the text. Alternatively, analyses can concentrate on the extratextual communicative situation. Furthermore, such extratextual analyses can differ in terms of their generality. For example, the communicative situation of a given interaction can be described in relation to the specific individuals involved, their precise relationship, their personal motivations for the interaction, etc. A different approach would be to focus on the general parameters defining the communicative situation of a text – for example, the mode, the level of interactiveness, the general purpose, etc.

Varieties defined in terms of general situational parameters are known as *registers*. We use the label *register* as a cover term for any variety associated with a particular configuration of situational characteristics and purposes. Thus, registers are defined in nonlinguistic terms. However, as illustrated in this chapter, there are usually important linguistic differences among registers as well.

There have been numerous studies that describe the situational parameters that are important for studies of discourse. As early as the 1930s, Firth identified crucial components of speech situations, applying principles from Malinowki's work. More recent and particularly well known is Hymes's (1974) framework for studying the ethnography of communication. In addition, a number of other anthropologists and sociolinguists have proposed frameworks or identified particularly important characteristics that can be applied to identifying registers (e.g. Basso 1974; Biber 1994; Brown and Fraser 1979; Crystal and Davy 1969; Duranti 1985). Throughout these discussions, the important characteristics that are identified include: the participants, their relationships, and their attitudes toward the communication; the setting, including factors such as the extent to which time and place are shared by the participants, and the level of formality; the channel of communication; the production and processing circumstances (e.g. amount of time available); the purpose of the communication; and the topic or subject matter. A register can be defined by its particular combination of values for each of these characteristics.

In many cases, registers are named varieties within a culture, such as novels, memos, book reviews, and lectures. However, registers can be defined at any level of generality, and more specialized registers may not have widely used names. For example, "academic prose" is a very general register, while "methodology sections in experimental psychology articles" is a much more highly specified one.

There are many studies that describe the situational and linguistic characteristics of a particular register. These studies cover diverse registers such as sports announcer talk (Ferguson 1983), note-taking (Janda 1985), personal ads (Bruthiaux 1994), classified advertising (Bruthiaux 1996), and coaching (Heath and Langman 1994). Analyses of register variation have also been conducted within a Hallidayan functional-systemic framework (see, e.g., the collection of papers in Ghadessy 1988, which include registers such as written sports commentary, press advertising, and business letters); several studies employing this approach are particularly concerned with describing school-based registers and their implications for education (e.g., Christie 1991; Martin 1993). Analysis of single registers has also been conducted for languages other than English, such as sports reporting in Tok Pisin (Romaine 1994). Atkinson and Biber (1994) provide an extensive survey of empirical register studies.

In addition to describing single registers, studies have also made comparisons across registers. These comparative studies have shown that there are systematic and important linguistic differences across registers, referred to as the patterns of *register variation*. This comparative register perspective is particularly important for two major arenas of research: (1) linguistic descriptions of lexical and grammatical features, and (2) descriptions of the registers themselves. With respect to traditional lexical and grammatical investigations, it turns out that functional descriptions based on texts without regard for register variation are inadequate and often misleading; we illustrate the importance of register for such analyses in section 1. For register descriptions, a comparative register perspective provides the baseline needed to understand the linguistic characteristics of any individual register. That is, by describing a target register relative to a full range of other registers, we are able to accurately identify the linguistic features that are in fact notably common in that register. We illustrate analyses of this type in section 2.1.

In recent years, studies of register variation have also been used to make cross-linguistic comparisons of registers. Such investigations are problematic because apparently similar linguistic features can have quite different functional roles across languages. However, from a comparative register perspective, researchers can first identify the configurations of linguistic features *within* each language that function to distinguish among registers; then, these parameters of variation can be used for cross-linguistic comparison. We briefly summarize an analysis of this type in section 2.2.

1   A Register Perspective on Traditional Linguistic Investigations

In general, any functional description of a linguistic feature will *not* be valid for the language as a whole. Rather, characteristics of the textual environment interact with register differences, so that strong patterns of use in one register often represent only weak patterns in other registers. We illustrate such patterns of use with analyses taken from the *Longman Grammar of Spoken and Written English* (Biber et al. 1999).

For lexical analysis, we illustrate these associations by considering the most common "downtoners" in English (section 1.1). These words are roughly synonymous in meaning, but they have quite different distributions across registers. Further, many of these words have distinctive collocational associations with following adjectives, but those typical collocations also vary in systematic ways across registers.

Similarly distinctive register patterns are typical with grammatical features. We illustrate those associations here by considering the textual factors that influence the omission versus retention of the complementizer *that* in *that*-clauses (section 1.2). It turns out that textual factors are most influential when they run counter to the register norm. For example, the complementizer *that* is usually omitted in conversation, so textual factors favoring the retention of *that* are particularly influential in that register. In contrast, the complementizer *that* is usually retained in news reportage, and as a result, the textual factors favoring the omission of *that* are particularly influential in that register.

Analyses of this type show that there is no single register that can be identified as "general English" for the purposes of linguistic description. Further, dictionaries and grammars based on our intuitions about "general" or "core" English are not likely to provide adequate exposure to the actual linguistic patterns found in the target registers that speakers and writers use on a regular basis.

1.1 Register variation in lexical descriptions

It is easy to demonstrate the importance of register variation for lexical analysis by contrasting the use of near-synonymous words. (See, for example, Biber et al. 1998: chs 2 and 4, on *big*, *large*, and *great*; *little* vs. *small*; and *begin* vs. *start*. See also Kennedy 1991 on *between* and *through*; and Biber et al. 1994 on *certain* and *sure*.)

We illustrate this association here by considering the use of *downtoners* (based on the analyses reported in Biber et al. 1999: ch. 7). Downtoners are adverbs that scale down the effect of a modified item, most often a following adjective. For example:

(1)   It did look *pretty* bad. (Conversation)

(2)   The mother came away *somewhat* bewildered. (News reportage)

(3)   Different laboratories have adopted *slightly* different formulations. (Academic prose)

Downtoners show that the modified item is not to be taken in its strongest sense. For example, in (1)–(3) above, *the way it looked*, *the mother*, and *formulations* do not have the full qualities of *bad*, *bewildered*, and *different*.

Many downtoners are roughly synonymous in meaning. For example, *pretty*, *somewhat*, and *slightly* could be interchanged in sentences (1)–(3) above with little change in meaning. However, it turns out that the most common downtoners have quite different distributions across registers. For the illustration here, we restrict our comparison

Table 9.1   Distribution of most common downtoners (immediately preceding adjectives) across two registers

	Conversation (AmE)	Academic prose
Pretty	********	.
Relatively	.	****
Rather	.	**
Fairly	.	**
Slightly	.	**
Almost	.	*
Somewhat	.	*
Nearly	.	.

Notes: Frequencies are based on analysis of texts from the Longman Spoken and Written English Corpus: *c*.2.5 million words from American English conversation and *c*.5 million words from academic prose. See Biber et al. (1999: ch. 1) for a complete description of the corpus.
Each * represents 50 occurrences per million words; . represents less than 20 occurrences per million words.
Source: Adapted from Biber et al. 1999: table 7.13

to two registers defined in relatively general terms: conversation (American English only) and academic prose. As displayed in table 9.1, in conversation, the downtoner *pretty* is very common, while all other downtoners are quite rare.[1] In contrast, academic prose uses a wider range of common downtoners, although none of them is extremely frequent.

Further analysis shows that downtoners are also used for different purposes in conversation and academic prose. For example, the downtoner *pretty* in conversation often occurs as a modifier of evaluative adjectives, as in *pretty good, pretty bad, pretty cool, pretty easy, pretty sure*. Typical examples include:

I'm *pretty good* at driving in the snow in my car.

That looks *pretty bad*.

That's a *pretty cool* last name, huh?

Is it a system that would be *pretty easy* to learn?

In contrast, downtoners in academic prose occur with a much wider range of descriptive adjectives. For example, the downtoner *fairly* occurs repeatedly with adjectives such as *resistant, consistent, constant, simple, obvious, common, recent*, and *direct*. Many of the downtoner + adjective collocations in academic prose have to do with marking the extent of comparison between two items (e.g. *slightly smaller, somewhat lower*). The downtoner *relatively* always has an implied comparison, as in *relatively simple, relatively stable, relatively unimportant*. In addition, several downtoners in academic prose commonly occur modifying the adjective *different*, specifying a comparison that gives the amount of difference (as in *rather different, slightly different, somewhat different,* etc.). Typical examples include:

> It does seem *fairly common* for children to produce project work consisting entirely of reiterations of knowledge they already have . . .

> . . . this regular periodicity of outbreaks suggests that the factors causing fluctuations in these populations are *relatively simple* and tractable . . .

> . . . the European study asked a *slightly different* question . . .

A complete description of downtoners obviously requires further analysis and interpretation, based on a fuller consideration of the individual items and a detailed analysis of particular downtoners in their discourse contexts. While it is not possible to undertake such an analysis here, the above discussion has illustrated the central importance of register differences in describing the meaning and use of related words.

1.2 Register variation in grammatical descriptions

Similar to lexical analysis, investigations of grammatical features require a register perspective to fully describe the actual patterns of use. Most grammatical features are distributed in very different ways across registers. For example, among the various types of dependent clause in English, relative clauses are many times more common in academic writing than in conversation, while *that*-complement clauses have the opposite distribution (i.e. much more common in conversation).

There are numerous book-length treatments of grammatical structures from a corpus-based register perspective; for example, Tottie (1991) on negation; Collins (1991) on clefts; Granger (1983) on passives; Mair (1990) on infinitival complement clauses; Meyer (1992) on apposition; and several books on nominal structures (e.g. de Haan 1989; Geisler 1995; Johansson 1995; Varantola 1984). The importance of a register perspective can be further highlighted by considering the distribution and use of roughly equivalent structures (such as *that*-clauses versus *to*-clauses; see Biber et al. 1998: chs 3 and 4).

In the present section, we consider differences in the use of *that*-clauses with the complementizer *that* retained versus omitted (based on analyses reported in Biber et al. 1999: ch. 9). In most *that*-clauses, the complementizer can be freely omitted with no substantial change in meaning. For example, compare:

> I hope *I'm not embarrassing you.* (Conversation)

with

> I hope ***that** Paul tells him off.* (Conversation)

However, there are several characteristics of the textual environment that influence the retention versus omission of *that,* and these textual factors interact in important

Table 9.2   Proportional retention versus omission of the complementizer *that*, by register

	% of that-*clauses* with that *retained*	% of that-*clauses* with that *omitted*
Conversation	***	******************
Fiction	********	************
News reportage	**************	******
Academic prose	*******************	*

Notes: Frequencies are based on analysis of texts from the Longman Spoken and Written English Corpus: *c*.4 million words from British English Conversation, and *c*.5 million words each from Fiction, British News Reportage, and Academic Prose. See Biber et al. (1999: ch. 1) for a complete description of the corpus.

Each * represents 5 percent of the occurrences of *that*-clauses in that register.

ways with register differences. In the following discussion we first review the register patterns for *that* retention versus omission; we then explain textual factors influencing the use of *that*; and we then proceed to describe the association between the register patterns and textual factors.

As table 9.2 shows, different registers have different overall norms for *that* retention versus omission: in conversation, *that*-omission is the typical case, with the complementizer being omitted in *c*.85 percent of all occurrences. At the other extreme, academic prose almost always retains the complementizer *that*.

These overall distributional patterns correspond to the differing production circumstances, purposes, and levels of formality found across registers. Conversations are spoken and produced on-line; they typically have involved, interpersonal purposes; and they are casual and informal in tone. These characteristics are associated with omission rather than retention of *that* as the norm. Academic prose has the opposite characteristics: careful production circumstances; an expository, informational purpose; and a formal tone. Correspondingly, *that* retention is the norm in academic prose.

Textual factors influencing the choice between omission and retention can be divided into two groups:

1   *Textual factors favoring the omission of* that:
    The omission of *that* is favored when the grammatical characteristics of the surrounding discourse conform to the most common uses of *that*-clauses. To the extent that a construction conforms to the characteristics typically used with *that*-clauses, listeners and readers can anticipate the presence of a *that*-clause without the explicit marking provided by the *that* complementizer.
    Two of the most important typical characteristics are:
    (a)   the use of *think* or *say* as the main clause verb (these are by far the two most common verbs taking a *that*-clause);
    (b)   the occurrence of coreferential subjects in the main clause and the *that*-clause (which is more common than noncoreferential subjects).

2 *Textual factors favoring the retention of* that:
   The retention of *that* is favored with grammatical characteristics that are not typical of *that*-clauses, making these structures difficult to process if the *that* were
   omitted. Three of the most important such factors are:
   (a)   the use of coordinated *that*-clauses;
   (b)   the use of a passive voice verb in the main clause;
   (c)   the presence of an intervening noun phrase between the main clause verb
         and the *that*-clause.

For the present discussion, the most interesting aspect of these discourse factors is
that they are mediated by register considerations. That is, textual factors are most
influential when they operate *counter* to the overall register norm. Table 9.3 describes
these patterns for conversation and news reportage.

For instance, because conversation has a strong register norm favoring the omission
of *that*, the factors favoring omission have little influence in that register. In contrast,
the factors favoring *that* retention are very powerful in conversation. For example:

- with coordinated *that*-clauses:

   Cos every time they use it, she reminds them *that it's her television* **and** *that
   she could have sold it.*

   I'm sure *they think I'm crazy* **and** *that I'm in love with him or something.*

- with a passive voice verb in the matrix clause:

   I **was told** *that Pete was pissed.*

   About two weeks after that it **was diagnosed** *that she had cancer of the ovary.*

- with an intervening noun phrase between the matrix clause verb and the
   that-clause:

   Then I told **him** *that I'm not doing it anymore.*

   I was busy trying to convince **him** *that he had to go to the doctor.*

   I promised **her** *that I wouldn't play it.*

News reportage shows the opposite tendencies: the overall register norm favors
that retention and thus the contextual factors favoring retention have comparatively
little influence. In contrast, the factors favoring *that* omission are relatively influential
in news. The following sentences from news reportage illustrate the most common
main verbs, together with coreferential subjects, co-occurring with *that*-omission:

   After a month she said (0) *she couldn't cope with it.*

   He thought (0) *he was being attacked.*

Table 9.3   Departure from the register norms for retention versus omission of the complementizer *that*, depending on textual factors

	← Greater proportion of that *retained* than the register norm	→ Greater proportion of that *omitted* than the register norm
Conversation:		
A Factors favoring omission:		
Main verb:		
think or *say* as matrix verb		>>
Other matrix verb	<<<	
Reference of subject:		
Coreferential		
Not coreferential	<	
B Factors favoring retention:		
Complex complement:		
Coordinated *that*-clauses	<<<<<<<<<<<<<<<<	
Simple *that*-clause		
Active/passive main verb:		
Passive	<<<<<<<<<<<	
Active		
Presence of indirect object:		
V + NP + *that*-clause	<<<<<<<<<<<<<<<<	
V + *that*-clause		
News reportage:		
A Factors favoring omission:		
Matrix verb:		
think or *say* as matrix verb		>>>>
Other matrix verb	<<	
Reference of subject:		
Coreferential		>>>>>>>>
Not coreferential	<<<	
B Factors favoring retention:		
Complex complement:		
Coordinated *that*-clauses	<<<<<	
Simple *that*-clause		
Active/passive main verb:		
Passive	<<<<<	
Active	<	
Presence of indirect object:		
V + NP + *that*-clause	<<<<	
V + *that*-clause	<	

Notes: Each < or > represents 5 percent departure from the register norm, for all occurrences of *that*-clauses in that register with the stated textual factor.

< marks proportionally greater use of *that* retention than the register norm.

> marks proportionally greater use of *that* omission than the register norm.

The present section has illustrated several ways in which a register perspective is important for grammatical analysis. First, grammatical features are used to differing extents in different registers, depending on the extent to which the typical functions of the feature fit the typical communicative characteristics of the register. However, there are also much more complex patterns of association, with textual factors interacting with register patterns in intricate ways. Although patterns such as those described here must be interpreted much more fully, the present section has illustrated the systematicity and importance of register patterns in describing the use of related grammatical features.

2   Register Comparisons

A major issue for discourse studies since the early 1970s concerns the relationship between spoken and written language. Early research on this question tended to make global generalizations about the linguistic differences between speech and writing. For example, researchers such as O'Donnell (1974) and Olson (1977) argued that written language generally differs from speech in being more structurally complex, elaborated, and/or explicit. In reaction to such studies, several researchers (including Tannen 1982, Beaman 1984, and Chafe and Danielewicz 1986) argued that it is misleading to generalize about overall differences between speech and writing, because communicative task is also an important predictor of linguistic variation; therefore equivalent communicative tasks should be compared to isolate the existence of mode differences.

Multidimensional (MD) analyses of register variation (e.g. Biber 1986, 1988) took this concern one step further by analyzing linguistic variation among the range of registers within each mode, in addition to comparing registers across the spoken and written modes. Further, these analyses included consideration of a wide range of linguistic characteristics, identifying the way that these features configured themselves into underlying "dimensions" of variation. These studies show that particular spoken and written registers are distinguished to differing extents along each dimension.

One potential biasing factor in most early studies of register variation is that they tended to focus on western cultures and languages (especially English). More recently, the MD approach has been used to investigate the patterns of register variation in nonwestern languages. Three such languages have been studied to date: Besnier's (1988) analysis of Nukulaelae Tuvaluan; Kim's (1990; Kim and Biber 1994) analysis of Korean; and Biber and Hared's (1992a, 1992b, 1994) analysis of Somali. Taken together, these studies provide the first comprehensive investigations of register variation in nonwestern languages. Biber (1995) synthesizes these studies, together with the earlier MD analyses of English, to explore cross-linguistic patterns of register variation, and to raise the possibility of cross-linguistic universals governing the patterns of discourse variation across registers.

In the following sections, we briefly describe and compare the patterns of register variation for three of these languages: English, Korean, and Somali.[2] These three languages represent quite different language types and social situations. Thus, they provide a good basis for exploring systematic cross-linguistic patterns of register variation. In section 2.1 we introduce the multidimensional approach to register variation with specific reference to the MD analysis of English. In 2.2 we then briefly summarize the major patterns of register variation across English, Korean, and Somali.

2.1   *Overview of the multidimensional (MD) approach to register variation*

The MD approach to register variation was developed to provide comprehensive descriptions of the patterns of register variation in a language. An MD analysis includes two major components: (1) identification of the underlying linguistic parameters, or *dimensions*, of variation; and (2) specification of the linguistic similarities and differences among registers with respect to those dimensions.

Methodologically, the MD approach has three major distinguishing characteristics: (1) the use of computer-based text corpora to provide a broad representation of the registers in a language; (2) the use of computational tools to identify linguistic features in texts; and (3) the use of multivariate statistical techniques to analyze the co-occurrence relations among linguistic features, thereby identifying underlying *dimensions* of variation in a language. MD studies have consistently shown that there are systematic patterns of variation among registers; that these patterns can be analyzed in terms of the underlying dimensions of variation; and that it is necessary to recognize the existence of a multidimensional space (rather than a single parameter) to adequately describe the relations among registers.

The first step in an MD analysis is to obtain a corpus of texts representing a wide range of spoken and written registers. If there are no pre-existing corpora, as in the case of the Korean and Somali analyses, then texts must be collected and entered into computer. The texts in these corpora are then automatically analysed (or "tagged") for linguistic features representing several major grammatical and functional characteristics, such as: tense and aspect markers, place and time adverbials, pronouns and nominal forms, prepositional phrases, adjectives, adverbs, lexical classes (e.g. hedges, emphatics, speech act verbs), modals, passives, dependent clauses, coordination, and questions. All texts are postedited interactively to correct mis-tags.

Next, the frequency of each linguistic feature in each text is counted. (All counts are normalized to their occurrence per 1000 words of text.) A statistical factor analysis is then computed to identify the co-occurrence patterns among linguistic features, that is, the dimensions. These dimensions are subsequently interpreted in terms of the communicative functions shared by the co-occurring features. Interpretive labels are posited for each dimension, such as "Involved versus Informational Production" and "Narrative versus Non-narrative Concerns." In addition, dimension scores for each text are computed by summing the major linguistic features grouped on each dimension; this score provides a cumulative characterization of a text with respect to the co-occurrence pattern underlying a dimension. Then, the mean dimension scores for each register are compared to analyze the salient linguistic similarities and differences among spoken and written registers.

To illustrate, consider English Dimension 1 in figure 9.1. This dimension is defined by two groups of co-occurring linguistic features, listed to the right of the figure. The top group (above the dashed line) consists of a large number of features, including

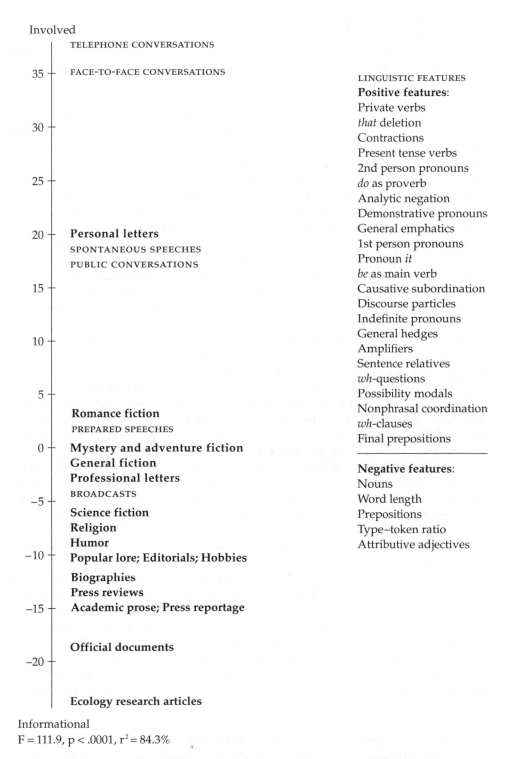

Figure 9.1   Mean scores of English Dimension 1 for twenty-three registers: "Involved versus Informational Production"

first and second person pronouns, questions, "private" verbs (such as *think* or *know*), and contractions. The bottom group has fewer features, including nouns, attributive adjectives, and prepositional phrases. The statistical analysis shows that these two groups have a complementary relationship and thus constitute a single dimension: when a text has frequent occurrences of the top group of features, it will tend to have few occurrences of the bottom group, and vice versa.

When dimension scores are computed for English Dimension 1, conversation texts are identified as the register that makes the most frequent use of the top group of features. Figure 9.1 plots the Dimension 1 score for several English registers, providing a graphic representation of the relations among registers with respect to this group of linguistic features. Conversation texts, with the largest positive Dimension 1 score, tend to have frequent occurrences of first and second person pronouns, questions, stance verbs, hedges, and the other features above the dashed line; at the same time, relative to the other registers, conversation texts have notably few occurrences of nouns, adjectives, prepositional phrases, and long words. At the other extreme, registers such as official documents and academic prose have the largest negative score, showing that they are marked for the opposite linguistic characteristics: very frequent occurrences of nouns, adjectives, prepositional phrases, and long words, combined with notably few occurrences of first and second person pronouns, questions, stance verbs, etc.

Considering both the defining linguistic features together with the distribution of registers, each dimension can be interpreted in functional terms. Thus, the top group of linguistic features on English Dimension 1, associated most notably with conversation, is interpreted as reflecting interactiveness, high involvement, and on-line production. For example, interactiveness and involvement are reflected in the frequent use of *you* and *I*, and the private verbs that convey the thoughts and feelings of the participants, as well as many other features. The reduced and vague forms – such as contractions, *that* deletions, and general emphatics and hedges – are typical of language produced under real-time constraints. The bottom group of linguistic features, associated most notably with informational exposition, is interpreted as reflecting careful production and an informational focus. That is, as exemplified below, nouns, prepositional phrases, and attributive adjectives all function to convey densely packed information, and the higher type–token ratio and longer words reflect a precise and often specialized choice of words. Such densely informational and precise text is nearly impossible to produce without time for planning and revision.

As noted earlier, one of the advantages of a comparative register perspective is to understand the linguistic characteristics of a particular register relative to a representative range of registers in the language. This advantage can be illustrated with respect to the specific register of research articles in biology (in the subdiscipline of ecology). Figure 9.1 shows that this register is extremely marked on Dimension 1, with a considerably larger negative score than academic prose generally.

Even a short extract from an article shows the high density of informational features from Dimension 1 (nouns are underlined, prepositions italicized, and attributive adjectives capitalized):

> There were MARKED <u>differences</u> *in* <u>root growth</u> *into* <u>regrowth cores</u> *among* the
> three <u>communities,</u> both *in* the <u>distribution</u> *of* <u>roots</u> *through* the <u>cores</u> and *in* the

response to ELEVATED CO^2. *In* the Scirpus community, root growth was evenly distributed *throughout* the 15-cm profile, *with* no SIGNIFICANT differences *in* root biomass *among* the 5-cm sampling intervals *within* a treatment.

All three of these features serve the purpose of densely packing the text with information about specific referents. Nouns refer to entities or concepts, and are then further specified by prepositional phrases, attributive adjectives, or other nouns which function as premodifiers (e.g. *root growth*). Clearly, the emphasis in this text is on transmitting information precisely and concisely, not on interactive or affective concerns.

Furthermore, by considering the scores of other registers on Dimension 1, we can see that such densely packed informational features are not typical in more colloquial registers of English. For this reason, it is not surprising that many novices experience difficulty when asked to read biology research articles or write up research reports like a professional (cf. Walvoord and McCarthy 1990; Wilkinson 1985). Even with this very brief examination of just one dimension in the MD model of English, we can see why, linguistically, these texts are challenging and why students are unlikely to have had practice with such densely informational prose.

2.2 Comparison of the major oral/literate dimensions in English, Korean, and Somali

The MD methodological approach outlined in the last section has been applied to the analysis of register variation in English, Korean, and Somali. Biber (1995) provides a full description of the corpora, computational and statistical techniques, linguistic features analyzed, and multidimensional patterns of register variation for each of these languages. That book synthesizes these studies to focus on typological comparisons across languages. Here we present only a summary of some of the more striking cross-linguistic comparisons.

Table 9.4 presents a summary of the major "oral/literate" dimensions in English, Korean, and Somali. Oral/literate dimensions distinguish between stereotypical speech – i.e. conversation – at one pole, versus stereotypical writing – i.e. informational exposition – at the other pole. However, as discussed below, each of these dimensions is composed of a different set of linguistic features, each has different functional associations, and each defines a different set of relations among the full range of spoken and written registers.

The first column in table 9.4 lists the co-occurring linguistic features that define each dimension. Most dimensions comprise two groups of features, separated by a dashed line on table 9.4. As discussed above for Dimension 1 in English, these two groups represent sets of features that occur in a complementary pattern. That is, when the features in one group occur together frequently in a text, the features in the other group are markedly less frequent in that text, and vice versa. To interpret the dimensions, it is important to consider likely reasons for the complementary distribution of these two groups of features as well as the reasons for the co-occurrence pattern within each group.

It should be emphasized that the co-occurrence patterns underlying dimensions are determined empirically (by a statistical factor analysis) and not on any a priori

Table 9.4 Overview of the major oral/literate dimensions in English, Korean, and Somali

Linguistic features	Characteristic registers	Functional associations
English: Dimension 1: 1st and 2nd person pronouns; questions; reductions; stance verbs; hedges; emphatics; adverbial subordination	Conversations (Personal letters) (Public conversations)	Interactive (Inter) personal focus Involved Personal stance On-line production
Nouns; adjectives; prepositional phrases; long words Dimension 3: Time and place adverbials	Informational exposition, e.g. official documents, academic prose Broadcasts (Conversations) (Fiction) (Personal letters)	Monologue Careful production Informational focus Faceless Situation-dependent reference On-line production
wh-relative clauses; pied-piping constructions; phrasal coordination Dimension 5: [No features]	Official documents Professional letters Exposition Conversations, fiction Personal letters Public speeches Public conversations Broadcasts	Situation-independent reference Careful production Nonabstract
Agentless passives; *by* passives; passive dependent clauses	Technical prose (Other academic prose) (Official documents)	Abstract style Technical, informational focus
Korean: Dimension 1: Questions; contractions; fragmentary sentences; discourse conjuncts; clause connectors; hedges	Private conversations TV drama (Public conversations) (Folktales)	Interactive On-line production Interpersonal focus
Postposition–noun ratio; relative clauses; attributive adjectives; long sentences; nonfinite and noun complement clauses	Literary criticism College textbooks Scripted speeches Written exposition (Broadcast news and TV documentary)	Monologue Informational focus Careful production
Dimension 2: Explanative conjuncts; explanative, conditional, coordinate, and discourse clause connectors;	Folktales (Conversations) (Speeches) (Public conversations)	Overt logical cohesion

Table 9.4 *(cont'd)*

Linguistic features	Characteristic registers	Functional associations
adverbial subordination Nouns; possessive markers; passive constructions	Written expository registers Broadcast news	Implicit logical cohesion Informational focus
Dimension 3: Verb and NP complements; emphatics; hedges; attitudinal expressions; private verbs; 1st person pronouns	TV drama (Private and public conversations) (Personal letters) (Personal essays)	Personal stance
Nouns	Newspaper reportage Official documents (Broadcast news)	Nonpersonal focus
Somali: **Dimension 1:** Main clause features; questions; imperatives; contractions; stance adjectives; downtoners; 1st and 2nd person pronouns	Conversations Family meetings Conversational narratives	Interactive (Inter) personal focus Involved Personal stance On-line production
Dependent clauses; relative clauses; clefts; verb complements; nouns; adjectives	Written expository registers	Monologue Informational focus Faceless Careful production
Dimension 2: [No features]	Sports broadcast (Other spoken registers)	On-line production Situation-dependent
Once-occurring words; high type–token ratio; nominalizations; compound verbs	Editorials Written political speeches and pamphlets Analytical press	Careful production Informational focus
Dimension 5: Optative clauses; 1st and 2nd person pronouns; directional particles; imperatives	Personal letters (Family meetings) (Quranic exposition)	Interactive Distanced and directive communication
[No features]	Press reportage and editorials Written expository registers	Noninteractive Nondirective

basis. Thus, the dimensions represent those groupings of linguistic characteristics that most commonly co-occur in the spoken and written texts of each corpus. Subsequent to the statistical identification of these co-occurrence patterns, each grouping is interpreted in functional terms, to assess the underlying communicative forces associated with each cluster of linguistic features. The functional associations for each dimension are summarized in the third column of table 9.4.

The dimensions can be used to compare spoken and written registers by computing a "dimension score" for each text (described in 2.1 above). The second column on table 9.4 lists those registers that have the most extreme dimension scores; that is, the registers that use the co-occurring linguistic features on a dimension to the greatest extent.

Table 9.4 summarizes only those dimensions that are closely associated with speech and writing. (Several additional dimensions in each of these languages have little or no association with physical mode.) Each of the dimensions listed in table 9.4 is defined by a different set of co-occurring linguistic features, and each identifies a different overall pattern of relations among registers. However, these dimensions are similar in that they all isolate written expository registers at one extreme (referred to below as the "literate" pole). These registers are formal, edited kinds of text written for informational, expository purposes: for example, official documents and academic prose in English; literary criticism and college textbooks in Korean; and editorials and analytical press articles in Somali.

The opposite extreme along these dimensions (referred to below as the "oral" pole) characterizes spoken registers, especially conversational registers. In addition, colloquial written registers, such as personal letters, are shown to have characteristics similar to spoken registers along several of these dimensions.

Table 9.4 shows that the two extremes of these dimensions are not equally associated with speech and writing: while the "literate" pole of each dimension is associated exclusively with written expository registers, the "oral" pole of many dimensions characterizes written registers, such as letters and fiction, as well as a range of spoken registers. Thus, written registers are characterized by both the "oral" and "literate" poles of English Dimensions 1, 3, and 5, Korean Dimension 3, and Somali Dimension 5.

These patterns indicate that the spoken and written modes provide strikingly different potentials. In particular, writers can produce dense expository texts as well as texts that are extremely colloquial, but speakers do not normally produce texts that are similar to written expository registers. This basic difference holds across all three languages considered here.

It should be emphasized that cross-linguistic similarities are found despite the fact that the statistical techniques used in MD analysis result in independent dimensions: each dimension is defined by a different set of co-occurring linguistic features, and each dimension defines a different set of overall relations among registers. Further, the MD analysis of each language is carried out independently, so there are no methodological factors favoring the identification of analogous dimensions across registers.

Despite this methodological independence, strong similarities emerge across these three languages. For example, three major patterns occur cross-linguistically with respect to the kinds of linguistic expression found exclusively in written expository registers:

1   frequent nouns, adjectives, and prepositional/postpositional phrases, reflecting an extremely dense integration of referential information;
2   high type–token ratio, frequent once-occurring words, and frequent long words, reflecting extreme lexical specificity and complex vocabulary;
3   greater use of nominal structural elaboration, including relative clauses and other nominal modifiers, reflecting elaboration of referential information.[3]

The existence of these linguistic characteristics particular to written exposition can be attributed to the cumulative influence of three major communicative factors (cf. Chafe 1982; Tannen 1982; Biber 1988): (1) communicative purpose, (2) physical relation between addressor and addressee, and (3) production circumstances:

1   *Communicative purpose:* Written expository registers have communicative purposes different from those found in most other registers: to convey information about non-immediate (often abstract) referents with little overt acknowledgement of the thoughts or feelings of the addressor or addressee. Spoken lectures are similar in purpose, but most other spoken registers (and many written registers) are more personal and immediately situated in purpose.
2   *Physical relation between addressor and addressee:* Spoken language is commonly produced in face-to-face situations that permit extensive interaction, opportunity for clarification, and reliance on paralinguistic channels to communicate meaning. Written language is typically produced by writers who are separated in space (and time) from their readers, resulting in a greater reliance on the linguistic channel by itself to communicate meaning.
3   *Production circumstances:* The written mode provides extensive opportunity for careful, deliberate production; written texts can be revised and edited repeatedly before they are considered complete. Spoken language is typically produced on-line, with speakers formulating words and expressions as they think of the ideas.

With respect to the last two of these factors, writing has a greater range of variability than speech. That is, while writing can be produced in circumstances similar to speech, it can also be produced in circumstances quite different from those possible in speech.

With regard to the relation between addressor and addressee, it is possible for readers and writers to be directly interactive (as in personal letters) and even to share the same place and time (e.g. passing notes in class). At the other extreme, though, writers of expository prose typically do not address their texts to individual readers; they rarely receive written responses to their messages; and they do not share physical and temporal space with their readers. In contrast, speaker and hearer must share the same place and time (apart from the use of telephones or tape recorders), and they typically interact with one another to some extent.

Written language is similarly adaptive with respect to production circumstances. At one extreme, written language can be produced in an on-line manner with little preplanning or revision (as in a hasty note or letter). At the other extreme, written texts can be carefully planned and allow for extreme levels of editing and revision. In contrast, while utterances in spoken language can be restated (as with false starts), it is not possible to edit and revise a spoken text.

The written mode thus provides the potential for kinds of language production not possible in typical speech.[4] Written language can be produced at any speed, with any amount of planning, and it can be revised and edited as much as desired. As a result, it is possible to package linguistic structures in writing in ways that cannot be sustained in spoken production.

The linguistic patterns of variation described in this section, taken from three widely different languages, show that the unique production potential of the written mode can be exploited to result in styles of linguistic expression not found in any spoken register. Specifically, expository registers seem to be the kind of writing that develops to maximally exploit the production potential of the written mode, apparently in response to the highly informational communicative purposes. In addition, these unique expository styles have similar linguistic correlates across languages: a dense packaging of nouns, adjectives, and prepositional/postpositional phrases; careful word choice and lexical elaboration; and extensive nominal modification. Further research is required to determine the extent to which these generalizations hold across a broader sample of languages.

2.3   *Register variation in more specialized domains*

The above discussion of register variation has focused on comparisons between broadly defined spoken and written registers across languages. In addition, MD analysis has also been applied to more specialized domains.

Conrad (1996a, 1996b) applies the MD model of variation in English to a study of disciplinary texts, comparing professional research articles, university-level textbooks, and university student papers in biology and history. The multiple perspectives provided by this analysis highlight similarities between all of these academic texts versus other nonacademic registers, as well as identifying systematic differences across the disciplines and types of texts. The study also highlights discipline-specific literacy demands and trends in writing development as students become more experienced in a discipline.

Reppen (1994, 1995; cf. Biber et al. 1998: ch. 7) uses MD analysis for a study of the spoken and written registers used by elementary school students in English. The study identifies and interprets the dimensions that characterize student registers, finding some dimensions with no counterparts in other MD analyses (such as one interpreted as "Projected scenario"). In addition, comparison of this student MD model and the adult English model discussed in the previous section provides a register perspective on the development of literacy skills.

The MD approach has also been used to study diachronic patterns of register variation in English and Somali. Biber and Finegan (1989, 1997; cf. Biber et al. 1998: ch. 8) trace the development of English written registers (e.g. letters, fiction, newspapers, science prose) and speech-based registers (e.g. drama, dialog in fiction) from 1650 to the present, along three different dimensions of variation. These studies describe a major difference in the historical evolution of popular registers (e.g. fiction, letters, drama) and specialized expository registers (e.g. science prose and medical prose): while popular registers have followed a steady progression toward more "oral" styles (greater involvement; less nominal elaboration; lesser use of passive constructions), the written expository registers have evolved in the opposite direction, developing styles of expression that were completely unattested in earlier historical periods (e.g. with extremely dense use of elaborated nominal structures and passive constructions). Biber and Finegan (1994b) use this same framework to compare the written styles of particular eighteenth-century authors (Swift, Defoe, Addison, and Johnson) across different registers.

In addition, two studies by Atkinson use the MD approach to trace the evolution of professional registers in English. Atkinson (1992) combines a multidimensional approach with a detailed analysis of rhetorical patterns to study the development of five subregisters of medical academic prose from 1735 to 1985, focusing on the *Edinburgh Medical Journal*. Atkinson (1996) employs a similar integration of multidimensional and rhetorical methodologies to analyze the evolution of scientific research writing, as represented in the *Philosophical Transactions of the Royal Society of London* from 1675 to 1975.

Biber and Hared (1992b, 1994) extend the MD analysis of Somali to study historical change following the introduction of native-language literacy in 1973. Finally, Biber (1995: ch. 8) integrates these diachronic analyses of English and Somali to discuss cross-linguistic similarities and differences in the patterns of historical register change.

3 Conclusion

In a chapter of this size, it is impossible to give complete accounts and interpretations of register analyses. Nevertheless, the chapter has illustrated the importance of register variation for diverse aspects of discourse study – whether more traditional descriptions of lexical and grammatical features, or more comprehensive characterizations of registers within a language or across multiple languages. The register perspective illustrated here has repeatedly shown that patterns of language use vary systematically with characteristics of the situational context. As a result, attempts to characterize a language as a whole are likely to misrepresent the actual language use patterns in any particular register.

Clearly, comparisons among registers will play an important role in any thorough description of a language. Furthermore, control of a range of registers is important for any competent speaker of a language. Thus, not only our understanding of discourse but also our understanding of language acquisition and issues within educational linguistics can also benefit from the analysis of register variation.

NOTES

1 The downtoner *pretty* is much less common in British English (BrE) conversation than in American English (AmE) conversation. In contrast, the adverb *quite* functioning as a modifier is very common in BrE conversation, where it often has a meaning similar to the other downtoners.

2 Nukulaelae Tuvaluan is spoken in a relatively isolated island community

and has a quite restricted range of register variation (only two written registers – personal letters and sermon notes – and five spoken registers). For these reasons, we have not included this study in our discussion here.

3   It is not the case that structural elaboration is generally more prevalent in written registers. In fact, each of these languages shows features of structural dependency distributed in complex ways. Certain types of structural complexity (e.g. adverbial clauses and complement clauses) can be found in conversational registers to a greater extent than written exposition,

while nominal modifiers are by far more common in written informational registers (cf. Biber 1992, 1995).

4   Oral literature, such as oral poetry in Somali, represents a spoken register that runs counter to many generalizations concerning speech. The original production of oral poetry depends on exceptional intellectual and verbal ability. While such texts can be extremely complex in their lexical and grammatical characteristics, they also conform to rigid restrictions on language form, including requirements for alliteration, rhythm, and number of syllables per line.

REFERENCES

Atkinson, D. (1992) The evolution of medical research writing from 1735 to 1985: the case of the *Edinburgh Medical Journal*. *Applied Linguistics*, 13, 337–74.

Atkinson, D. (1996) The *Philosophical Transactions of the Royal Society of London*, 1675–1975: a sociohistorical discourse analysis. *Language in Society*, 25, 333–71.

Atkinson, D., and Biber, D. (1994) Register: a review of empirical research. In Biber and Finegan (1994a), 351–85.

Basso, K. (1974) In R. Bauman and J. Sherzer (eds), *Explorations in the Ethnography of Speaking*. Cambridge: Cambridge University Press, 425–32.

Beaman, K. (1984) Coordination and subordination revisited: syntactic complexity in spoken and written narrative discourse. In D. Tannen (ed.), *Coherence in Spoken and Written Discourse*. Norwood, NJ: Albex, 45–80.

Besnier, N. (1988) The linguistic relationships of spoken and written Nukulaelae registers. *Language*, 64, 707–36.

Biber, D. (1986) Spoken and written textual dimensions in English: resolving the contradictory findings. *Language*, 62, 384–414.

Biber, D. (1988) *Variation across Speech and Writing*. Cambridge: Cambridge University Press.

Biber, D. (1992) On the complexity of discourse complexity: a multidimensional analysis. *Discourse Processes*, 15, 133–63.

Biber, D. (1994) An analytical framework for register studies. In Biber and Finegan (1994a), 31–56.

Biber, D. (1995) *Dimensions of Register Variation: A Cross-linguistic Comparison*. Cambridge: Cambridge University Press.

Biber, D., and Finegan, E. (1989) Drift and the evolution of English style: a history of three genres. *Language*, 65, 487–517.

Biber, D., and Finegan, E. (eds) (1994a) *Sociolinguistic Perspectives on Register Variation*. New York: Oxford University Press.

Biber, D., and Finegan, E. (1994b) Multidimensional analyses of authors' styles: some case studies from the eighteenth century. In D. Ross and D. Brink (eds), *Research in Humanities Computing 3*. Oxford: Oxford University Press, 3–17.

Biber, D., and Finegan, E. (1997) Diachronic relations among speech-based and written registers in English. In T. Nevalainen and L. Kahlas-Tarkka (eds), *To Explain the Present: Studies in the Changing English Language in Honour of Matti Rissanen*. Helsinki: Societe Neophilologique, 253–75.

Biber, D., and Hared, M. (1992a) Dimensions of register variation in Somali. *Language Variation and Change*, 4, 41–75.

Biber, D., and Hared, M. (1992b) Literacy in Somali: linguistic consequences. *Annual Review of Applied Linguistics*, 12, 260–82.

Biber, D., and Hared, M. (1994) Linguistic correlates of the transition to literacy in Somali: language adaptation in six press registers. In Biber and Finegan (1994a), 182–216.

Biber, D., Conrad, S., and Reppen, R. (1994) Corpus-based approaches to issues in applied linguistics. *Applied Linguistics*, 15, 169–89.

Biber, D., Conrad, S., and Reppen, R. (1998) *Corpus Linguistics: Investigating Language Structure and Use*. Cambridge: Cambridge University Press.

Biber, D., Johansson, S., Leech, G., Conrad, S., and Finegan, E. (1999) *The Longman Grammar of Spoken and Written English*. London: Longman.

Brown. P., and Fraser, C. (1979) Speech as a marker of situation. In K. Scherer and H. Giles (eds), *Social Markers in Speech*. Cambridge: Cambridge University Press, 33–62.

Bruthiaux, P. (1994) Me Tarzan, You Jane: linguistic simplification in "personal ads" register. In Biber and Finegan (1994a), 136–54.

Bruthiaux, P. (1996) *The Discourse of Classified Advertising*. New York: Oxford University Press.

Chafe, W. (1982) Integration and involvement in speaking, writing, and oral literature. In D. Tannen (ed.), *Spoken and Written Language: Exploring Orality and Literacy*. Norwood, NJ: Ablex, 35–54.

Chafe, W., and Danielewicz, J. (1986) Properties of spoken and written language. In R. Horowitz and S. Samuels (eds), *Comprehending Oral and Written Language*. New York: Academic Press, 82–113.

Christie, F. (1991) Pedagogical and content registers in a writing lesson. *Linguistics and Education*, 3, 203–24.

Collins, P. (1991) *Cleft and Pseudo-cleft Construction in English*. London: Routledge.

Conrad, S. (1996a) Academic discourse in two disciplines: professional writing and student development in biology and history. Unpublished PhD dissertation. Northern Arizona University.

Conrad, S. (1996b) Investigating academic texts with corpus-based techniques: an example from biology. *Linguistics and Education*, 8, 299–326.

Crystal, D. and Davy, D. (1969) *Investigating English Style*. London: Longman.

Duranti, A. (1985) Sociocultural dimensions of discourse. In T. van Dijk (ed.), *Handbook of Discourse Analysis, Vol. 1*. London: Academic Press, 193–230.

Ferguson, C. (1983) Sports announcer talk: syntactic aspects of register variation. *Language in Society*, 12, 153–72.

Firth, J. (1935) The technique of semantics. *Transactions of the Philological Society*, 36–72.

Geisler, C. (1995) *Relative Infinitives in English*. Uppsala: University of Uppsala.

Ghadessy, M. (ed.) (1988) *Registers of Written English: Situational Factors and Linguistic Features*. London: Pinter.

Granger, S. (1983) *The Be + Past Participal Construction in Spoken English with Special Emphasis on the Passive*. Amsterdam: Elsevier Science Publications.

de Haan, P. (1989) *Postmodifying Clauses in the English Noun Phrase: A Corpus-based Study*. Amsterdam: Rodopi.

Heath, S., and Langman, J. (1994) Shared thinking and the register of coaching. In Biber and Finegan (1994a), 82–105.

Hymes, D. (1974) *Foundations in Sociolinguistics*. Philadelphia: University of Philadelphia Press.

Janda, R. (1985) Note-taking English as a simplified register. *Discourse Processes*, 8, 437–54.

Johansson, C. (1995) *The Relativizers Whose and Of Which in Present-Day English: Description and Theory*. Uppsala: University of Uppsala.

Kennedy, G. (1991) *Between* and *through*: the company they keep and the functions they serve. In K. Aijmer and B. Altenberg (eds), *English Corpus Linguistics*. London: Longman, 95–127.

Kim, Y. (1990) Register variation in Korean: a corpus-based study. Unpublished PhD dissertation. University of Southern California.

Kim. Y., and Biber, D. (1994) A corpus-based analysis of register variation in Korean. In Biber and Finegan (1994a), 157–81.

Mair, C. (1990) *Infinitival Complement Clauses in English*. Cambridge: Cambridge University Press.

Martin, J. (1993) Genre and literacy – modeling context in educational linguistics. In *Annual Review of Applied Linguistics, Vol. 13*. New York: Cambridge University Press, 141–72.

Meyer, C. (1992) *Apposition in Contemporary English*. Cambridge: Cambridge University Press.

O'Donnell, R. (1974) Syntactic differences between speech and writing. *American Speech*, 49, 102–10.

Olson, D. (1977) From utterance to text: the bias of language in speech and writing. *Harvard Educational Review*, 47, 257–81.

Reppen, R. (1994) Variation in elementary student language: a multi-dimensional perspective. Unpublished PhD dissertation. Northern Arizona University.

Reppen, R. (1995) A multi-dimensional comparison of spoken and written registers produced by and for students. In B. Warvik, S. Tanskanen, and R. Hiltunen (eds), *Organization in Discourse* (Proceedings from the Turku Conference). Turku, Finland: University of Turku, 477–86.

Romaine, S. (1994) On the creation and expansion of registers: sports reporting in Tok Pisin. In Biber and Finegan (1994a), 59–81.

Tannen, D. (1982) Oral and literate strategies in spoken and written narratives. *Language*, 58, 1–21.

Tottie, G. (1991) *Negation in English Speech and Writing: A Study in Variation*. San Diego: Academic Press.

Varantola, K. (1984) *On Noun Phrase Structures in Engineering English*. Turku: University of Turku.

Walvoord, B., and McCarthy, L. (1990) *Thinking and Writing in College: A Naturalistic Study of Students in Four Disciplines*. Urbana, IL: National Council of Teachers of English.

Wilkinson, A. (1985) A freshman writing course in parallel with a science course. *College Composition and Communication*, 36, 160–5.

II The Linking of Theory and Practice in Discourse Analysis

10 Nine Ways of Looking at Apologies: The Necessity for Interdisciplinary Theory and Method in Discourse Analysis

ROBIN TOLMACH LAKOFF

0 Introduction: The Problems, Paradoxes, and Pleasures of Interdisciplinary Research

Of all the aspects of language, discourse analysis is singularly interdisciplinary – a word with a somewhat speckled past. At the moment, "interdisciplinary" is a good word. But it was not always so.

Originally all scholarship was implicitly multidisciplinary, in the sense that sharp distinctions were not explicitly recognized among disciplines. It was only in the mid-nineteenth century that disciplines were rigorously segmented into university departments, with all the budgetary and other turf rivalries that departmental structure brought in its train.[1] As knowledge in many fields, particularly in the social and physical sciences, increased exponentially and got more complex in the late twentieth century, departmental and disciplinary boundaries became at once more essential, to preserve order and identity, and more embarrassingly obstructionist to new ways of thought. The physical sciences seem to have solved the problem by creating new formal fields and new departmental structures to house and identify new ways of pursuing knowledge: molecular biology and biochemistry, for instance. But the social sciences – more unsure of both their legitimacy and their domains – seem to have had more of a problem in deciding what to do when ideas spill out of their original disciplinary receptacles.

Linguistics is a paradigmatic case. If our turf is, as we like to tell introductory classes, "the scientific study of language," what does "language" properly include? Some linguists interpret "language" as "language alone": they draw the line in the sand at the point where analysis involves interaction or persuasion, or anything we *do* with words.

Others incorporate these territories into linguistics, willingly or grudgingly, but still try to keep them separate. *Here*, in a central subdivision, we will discuss language-in-isolation; beyond this impregnable fence that guards the province of philosophy, speech acts and implicature; there, further than the eye can see, next to the kingdom of sociology, conversation; and far away, adjoining the duchies of rhetoric and mass communication, public discourse. Each area has developed its own language, as nations will, unintelligible to those within other areas of linguistics, and even those in adjoining principalities. These boundaries are guarded jealously and justified zealously.

There are certainly advantages to territoriality, not only political but genuinely intellectual. Within a field's strict confines one can achieve competence and control. No one, surely, can claim to know all of linguistics any more (as was perfectly possible a generation or two ago); but at least one can without undue strain claim mastery over an area like pragmatics or conversation analysis. But disadvantages, to the point of paradox, offset these advantages.[2] In this chapter I want to discuss the necessity of an inter-, cross-, and multidisciplinary approach for discourse analysis, an area that borrows from and contributes to many fields both within linguistics and outside of it. To illustrate my argument I will use as an example the speech act of apology, considering what we need to know about it in order to achieve a full and satisfying explanation of its properties and range of use.

0.1   Discourse analysis as interdisciplinary

Even if a case could be made for the autonomous treatment of some aspects of language (e.g. syntax, or phonetics), discourse cannot be satisfactorily analyzed in a vacuum, whether contextual or methodological. We might say of syntax that though it is located firmly within the boundaries of linguistics proper, sometimes reference to another subfield (suprasegmental phonology, or dialectology) or discipline (neurology) enhances the understanding of syntactic processes. But even in such cases the syntactician would be merely borrowing from outside, not obliterating the boundaries between syntax and the other field. But the assumption of autonomy works less well with discourse analysis. To do a thorough job of talking about "discourse," or "a discourse," the analyst must have recourse to the findings and methods of other (sub)disciplines; there is no "discourse analysis" otherwise. At the same time, our discovery procedures and methods of analysis, the questions we ask, and what we consider "answers" are uniquely our own, even as they represent the commingling of many diverse concepts. Our data may range from small units (sentences or turns) to much larger and more abstract entities (courtroom trials; novels; political events). And when we analyze those data, we must often consider them in terms of the smaller and more concrete units of which they are composed, using tools developed for the analysis of turns or sentences to understand the functions, meanings, and structurings of the larger and more abstract units we term "discourse." We may be concerned with any of several aspects of an extended utterance: its role in a longer document (a narrative); its interactive function (in creating small groups like couples or families); its role as a maker of institutional affiliation (academic language) and societal influence (journalism). Therefore our statements will reflect the belief systems of other fields: literary analysis; psychology; anthropology and sociology; political science, as well as areas closer to home (syntax, pragmatics, conversation analysis). This perspective is controversial both within linguistics (on the grounds that we are changing the rules or moving from the finite safety of autonomy to the chaos of interconnection) and from outside (on the basis that we are misusing the methods and languages of disciplines in which we are interlopers). But we must tolerate these critiques and learn to answer them if we are going to accomplish anything interesting, for it is precisely at the interstices of established disciplines and disciplinary thinking that the interesting work of discourse analysis will be done.

1   A Case in Point: Understanding Apology

Let me take as an example of the interdisciplinary nature of discourse analysis a case that at first may seem overly simple, hardly a part of "discourse analysis" at all, more typically considered as an exercise in pragmatics or conversation analysis: the apology. But we have to understand apologies as contributions to a larger discourse, viewing them from a variety of perspectives, formal and functional, cognitive and interactive, individual and group, intralanguage and societal; to examine the apology from the perspective of phonology, syntax, lexical semantics, speech act pragmatics, conversational analysis, narratology, and sociolinguistics. In some ways any speech act verb might illustrate the point. But apologies are particularly good examples, theoretically rich as well as practically important. They are hard to identify, define, or categorize, a difficulty that arises directly out of the functions they perform. Hence too, they occur in a range of forms from canonically explicit to ambiguously indirect; the functions served by those forms range from abject abasement for wrongdoing, to conventional greasing of the social wheels, to expressions of sympathy, advance mollification for intended bad behavior, and formal public displays of currently "appropriate" feeling. Thus, in terms of the relation between form and function, apologies are both one-to-many and many-to-one, a fact that only makes the analyst's task more daunting (and more exciting).

1.1   Form and function in apologies

Apology, more than most speech acts, places psychological burdens both on its maker and, less seriously, on its recipient. That is the reason for the plethora of indirect forms that, in appropriate contexts, we recognize as apologies. There does exist an unambiguous apology form, seen in:

> I apologize for eating your hamster.

But that form is rarely encountered in the most characteristic apologies, informal ones between intimates. In these cases we usually resort to any of a set of forms that involve one or another of the presuppositions or assertions of apologies (cf. section 2.2), either blurring it or explicitly stating it (allowing other aspects of the act of apology to be passed over in silence). For instance, the speaker's *responsibility* for the act can be downplayed in favor of an explicit statement conveying *regret*:

I'm sorry about your hamster,

or in extreme cases responsibility may be explicitly assigned elsewhere:

Well, *someone* left the hamster in the refrigerator!

or the utterance may deny that wrongdoing occurred at all:

Well, that's what hamsters are for, right?

The presence of *well* in extreme cases like this suggests an awareness that, as apologies, these utterances are not fully satisfactory, and that the addressee's goodwill is required to make them function appropriately (cf. Lakoff 1973; Schiffrin 1985). Note that *well* seems much less strongly mandated in the first case above, with *sorry*. Indeed, in the latter two cases the speech act may arguably have crossed over the line that separates apology from explanation (cf. section 2.2).

But some forms of apologies refer specifically to one of their functions, perhaps as a way to minimize the utterer's responsibility for the others:

I admit I ate the hamster. (Responsibility)

It was wrong of me to eat the hamster/I shouldn't have eaten the hamster. (Wrongdoing)

Can you find it in your heart to forgive me for eating the hamster? (Wish for forgiveness)

I'll never eat a hamster again as long as I live. (Abjuration of bad behavior)

These cases illustrate the many forms available for the performance of the single act of apology. The converse is also true (perhaps to a lesser degree): a single form, "I'm sorry," can function variously as an apology, an expression of non-responsible sympathy, and as a denial that an apology is, in fact, in order at all:

I'm sorry that I ate the hamster.

I'm sorry, Mr. Smith isn't available today.

Well, I'm sorry! but you don't know what you're talking about![3]

One advantage to having all these choices, for apologizers, is that they are thus enabled to calibrate the self-abasement to the perceived seriousness of the offense. It may seem that a full canonical apology would always be preferable to an offended party. But this is not necessarily true. Suppose you are at the movies. The show is in progress when someone moving past you steps on your foot. The occasion requires an expression of recognition of wrongdoing. But do you want the full canonical treatment? Both those around you, and you yourself, would be inconvenienced by it. A grunted "sorry" is all you desire; anything more is inappropriate and embarrassing.

On the other hand, some apologies, to be felicitous, require at least the *appearance* of contrition. In these cases the recipients must have the power and the right to enforce demands for "real remorse."

Another advantage of options is that an apologizer with power can, by making use of an ambiguous form, look virtuous while saving face. This is often seen in legally mandated "apologies." A particularly notorious case occurred at the University of California at Berkeley some years back, when a freshman woman accused several football players of acquaintance rape. She was persuaded to accept a plea bargain that involved an "apology" from the team members. Their apology stated that while they "apologized," they had not done what they were accused of doing. Some might argue that the second clause renders the first nonsensical or at least infelicitous (cf. section 2.4). Others might argue that this example perfectly illustrates the ability of institutional power to give meaning to otherwise bizarre utterances. If such vapid "apologies" have any meaning at all, it can only reside in the acknowledgment that the addressee has been hurt and has personhood or stature enough to require redress.

Similar cases occur in civil suits, in which corporate defendants refuse to publicly admit responsibility even though that might save them the expense and possible face-loss of a protracted trial. Their reasoning is that an apology is legally tantamount to a confession of wrongdoing via the presupposition of the speech act.

There are other problematic cases. One currently in vogue is the public-official apology, a statement made by someone in a position of power regretting bad behavior by previous holders of that office, in the name of the governed, against wronged ancestors of the aggrieved group. There are many such examples in recent years: e.g. President Clinton's apology to Africans for slavery, and Tony Blair's to the Irish for the potato famine. The willingness of many public officials to make such statements is striking compared with their reluctance to make apologies for their own, personal past misbehaviors. The reason is simple: the official cases are not true felicitous apologies, while the personal ones are. No one ever wants to make the latter kind, *especially* a powerful person, who stands to lose face, and therefore possibly power, by making one.

Most analyses of the apology speech act have focused on its felicity from the speaker's perspective, in particular the assessment of the speaker's state of mind (sincerity as manifested by signs of contrition). But this can create problems. For some speech acts (e.g. promises) felicity can be determined by the speaker's future actions alone. Others, though, like bets, require some sort of "uptake" from the addressee: "You're on!" or "It's a bet!" Apologies are normally considered members of the first class. But perhaps under some conditions – especially when the recipients have been outspoken in demanding apologies of a particular form – it may be appropriate to assign some responsibility to them for the felicity of the speech act. If, for instance, they make it clear that they have no intention of accepting any apology, no matter what, then surely no apology can be felicitous, and it is the demanders who make the entire performance infelicitous.

Even more confusing are forms that look like apologies but are not. Tannen (1994) has discussed the usage, especially common in women, of forms like "I'm sorry, Mr. Smith is out of town until Wednesday." As Tannen notes, these are not meant as apologies: the speaker does not mean to accept responsibility, nor is there any acknowledgment of misbehavior. At most in such cases, "I'm sorry" is a way for the speaker to head off the addressee's annoyance and prevent an unpleasant closure, by expressing sympathy and connectedness. Sometimes it is little more than a way of bringing a polite end to a less than satisfactory interchange. The "I'm sorry! but (you're an idiot)" type is similar in form, but quite different in function. It seems to be an example of a *but*-preface (Baker 1975). On a radio talk show recently about women raising children by themselves, the suggestion was made that this is often successful. A man called and, in the course of his comment, said, "I'm sorry! But [children need fathers]." This "I'm sorry!" is an apparent apology in advance for an utterance that is likely to be offensive. As such, it cannot be sincere, since if you know something you say will be offensive, and you care, you will not say it at all. Since these forms constitute challenges (= "I'm confronting you and you can't do anything about it!"), they are correctly felt to be rude, and so are seldom used by people with less power or something to lose by being offensive, while the former type are most often used by people in those positions.

2   The Function of Apologies

On both formal (forms like "I'm sorry," whether true apologies or not) and functional (the performance of apologies via many speech-act types) levels, apologies have a tendency to be ambiguous. That is in itself a good reason to study them, and a good reason why studying them well requires many disciplinary models and approaches. Some of us, especially in the earlier stages of our careers, have dismissed levels other than those we are comfortable working at as simplistic, subjective, or beyond the legitimate reach of linguistics. But each of the nine levels I will now discuss offers insights about what apologies are and, more generally, what discourse is; and to achieve a full analysis, we have to be aware that all these levels exist and contribute to the meaning and function of apologies.

2.1   *Phonological and nonverbal expressions in apology*

While there are in English no specific sounds associated with canonical or appropriate apology, there do exist suprasegmental and nonverbal levels that are important, especially for the addressee, in the determination of the acceptability of an apology. These levels are the basis for hearers' judgments about the apologizer's sincerity and sufficiency of "remorse," since we see them as beyond a speaker's control and therefore more likely to be truthful than the verbal utterance (cf. Ekman and Friesen 1969). So for instance an apology made too quickly, or in a monotone, will strike a hearer as scripted, nonspontaneous, and so not deeply felt. A breaking voice, on the other hand, bespeaks sincerity, as do certain nonverbal cues. An inability to make eye contact, generally judged negatively by Americans, has positive value (signifying appropriate shame) with apologies; the shuffling of feet and the use of self-adaptors (Ekman and Friesen 1968) like hand-wringing play a similar role. President Clinton is notorious on such occasions for biting his lip. While smiling is usually positively evaluated in American social interactions, its presence (often identified as a "smirk") usually detracts from the effectiveness of an apology.

A question for any analysis of this kind is the extent to which these assumptions are universal. It is popularly believed that nonverbal signifiers of emotion, like the emotions they signify, are universal: everyone feels, or should feel, remorse over the same events; the same amount of remorse; and therefore, should express it in the same way. But this is not necessarily true. What occasions embarrassment in one culture may not in another. The way genuine feelings are translated into surface representations (both how and how much), what Hochschild (1983) terms "emotion-work," may well differ across cultures, even cultures that are closely related and whose members speak the same (verbal) language.[4] Viewers of the 1997 "Cambridge Nanny" case on television, as well as jurors in that case, commented that the English nanny, Louise Woodward, accused of killing a baby in her care, did not show "enough remorse" on the stand.[5] Questioned about this later, she said that "we," that is, the English, did not "wear our hearts on our sleeves." Jurors basing their verdicts in part on witnesses' demeanor, as they are instructed to do, may make wrong decisions in cross-cultural situations like this.

2.2   The lexical semantics of apology: apology vs. explanation

The semantic problem of apology is this: what do we *mean* when we talk *about* "apologizing"? How does *apology* differ from *explanation* (the original sense of the word in Greek), *excuse*, and *justification*? The utterance "I apologize for X" involves several presuppositions (in that word's looser sense) and at least one assertion (Fillmore 1971):

- *Presuppositions:*
  X is bad for A(ddressee)
  Sp regrets X
  Sp undertakes not to do X again
  Sp (or someone under Sp's control) is responsible for X
  Sp could have done otherwise
- *Assertion:*
  Speech act puts Sp one-down vis-à-vis A

At least one of these conditions is missing in excuses, justifications, and explanations. In an excuse, the speaker denies either his or her own responsibility ("the cat made me do it") or ability to do otherwise ("I tried to, but your phone was busy"). In a justification, the speaker denies that the action was bad, if properly understood ("everybody else gets to do it"). In an explanation, the speaker takes responsibility for the action, but suggests that the addressee finds it bad because he or she does not understand it ("I did it for your own good"). So after apologies and excuses, the speaker ends up one-down; after justifications, both parties may be equal; and after an explanation, it is the recipient who ends up losing face as someone who does not get it. Explanations benefit their speakers, apologies their addressees.[6]

Semantic analyses like this can help us understand otherwise inexplicable choices in discourse. In 1983, Congress had passed a bill making the birthday of the Rev.

Dr. Martin Luther King a national holiday. Conservatives were unhappy about this, one of them arguing that King was "a man of immoral character whose frequent association with leading agents of communism is well-established." President Ronald Reagan, while privately indicating his agreement with that assessment, publicly waffled. Asked at a press conference whether he agreed with Senator Jesse Helms that King had had communist associations, the president said, "We'll know in about 35 years, won't we?"

With an election coming up, Reagan was urged by Democratic candidate Walter Mondale to apologize to King's widow. At first his spokesman said he would not, but eventually he phoned her. The call itself was not recorded, but asked later about its content, Coretta Scott King replied, "He apologized to me. He said it was a flippant response to what he considered a flippant question."

Prudence might dictate that the Reagan forces leave bad enough alone here. But shortly thereafter an assistant press secretary found it necessary to correct Mrs. King's statement: "It was an explanation," he said. "He didn't mean the remarks the way they sounded."

Now, suppose that the president had uttered precisely the words Mrs. King attributed to him (which would be appropriately described by the press secretary's statement). Why worry about whether "It was a flippant response to what I consider a flippant question" is an *apology* or an *explanation*? It might function as either: an apology for being "flippant" under inappropriate circumstances; or an explanation that "they" misunderstood a remark intended "merely" in jest.

The spokesman's insistence on defining the speech act differently from Mrs. King kept a divisive issue alive. There had to be a really good reason to do so. For presidents, and especially an imperial president like Reagan, it is crucial not to be one-down, because that constitutes a loss of power and influence. It was obviously considered more important to avoid this consequence than to remain on good terms with the constituency of the late Dr. King. But we can only understand what otherwise looks like pointless and even damaging intransigence in high places if we understand the lexical semantics of apologizing, and the importance of protecting the president of the United States from FTAs (face-threatening acts: Brown and Levinson 1987).

2.3   Syntax and the apology

Autonomous syntax does not have much to say about apologies. One might note the tendency of speakers to distance themselves from both the making of the apology itself, and the actions for which it offers redress, through indirect forms – either subjunctive equivalents like:

> I want to apologize

> I'd like to apologize

> I guess I owe you an apology

or the placement of the speaker/wrongdoer in other than subject position, or out of the sentence altogether:

It's too bad that X happened.

Sorry you got Xed.

or the sequestration of the apology in subordinate clauses, backgrounded and therefore less salient and accessible:

I feel I owe you an apology.

It looks to me like an apology might be in order.

While strictly speaking these are syntactic choices, only an autonomous syntactician would characterize them as principally artifacts of syntax. Rather, the embedded or subjunctive syntax is the handmaiden of other aspects of the utterance – pragmatics and semantics. We decide on the basis of semantics, pragmatics, and discourse considerations how noticeable a role we want ourselves to play in our reports, and the syntax obligingly provides us with the means to represent ourselves as we would like to be seen (or not seen). Syntactic form must be part of a discussion of apology, but it cannot be considered meaningful in isolation.

2.4 The pragmatics of apology: speech acts

Pragmatics occupies a realm intermediate between language-autonomous, decontextualized approaches and more complex theories entailing the consideration of the linguistic context and extralinguistic circumstances in which utterances occur. In his discussion of speech acts Austin (1962) referred to "utterances" rather than "propositions" or "sentences," because he was talking about language use, rather than mere form. His title indicates that we "do things with words." Since we alter reality by our utterances, it makes little sense to see language, or linguistics, as autonomous. In other ways, though, Austin's methods are akin to those of transformational syntax and its lineal descendants: the analysis of decontextualized structures constructed by the analyst.

Austinian analysis can help to explain both the numerousness and the specific forms of apologies, among them:

I'm sorry I Xed.

I guess I Xed.

I shouldn't have Xed.

You must be pretty mad that I Xed.

I was a real jerk to X.

... and I'll never X again.

Each of these forms comments on one of the conditions underlying the successful performance of an apology: a felicity condition in Austin's terminology, or preparatory or essential condition (according to Searle 1969). The first example expresses the speaker's regret; the second assumes (though it hedges on) the speaker's responsibility for the act; the third, that the act was wrong; the fourth, that the addressee was hurt; the fifth puts the speaker clearly one-down; and the sixth promises that such a thing will never happen again. This point was originally made by Gordon and Lakoff in their theory of conversational postulates (1971), though without an explanation for why conversational postulates are used.

In stating explicitly that one of the conditions for a felicitous apology is met, without explicitly acknowledging that an apology is being performed, a speaker necessarily places considerable responsibility for endowing the act with meaning on the addressee. The latter makes use of Gricean (1975) conversational maxims and implicatures to understand why the speaker is saying something the addressee has no demonstrated need to know – a flouting of the Gricean maxims of Quantity and Relevance. Ostensibly the addressee has no need to learn about the speaker's internal psychological state of regret – but if the first example above can be understood as implicating an apology, with all the interpersonal baggage that that entails, the utterance is clearly in obedience with the Cooperative Principle.

Although Austin framed his theory in terms of decontextualized utterances and assumed a strongly speaker-based perspective rather than seeing the discourse as created by all participants playing various roles, the interactive situations implied in his theory suggest a more contextualized, interactional model. For instance, Austin speaks of some speech acts as requiring certain forms of participation on the addressee's part to be felicitous. Thus, in a felicitous bet, an addressee has to say "it's a bet," or "you're on." Are apologies like bets in requiring some response, or some expectation, on the part of the addressee? If an addressee has no intention of accepting *anything* the speaker says, if no form at all will elicit forgiveness, Austin might say that no apology could be felicitous, but the fault would reside with the addressee rather than the speaker.

The apology battle between President Clinton and the Republican members of Congress in the fall of 1998 can be explained at least in part through this perspective.[7] Both sides contributed to the impasse. On the one hand, the President refused to apologize until the last possible moment, when the semen-stained dress made its public appearance. Even at that it took three or more attempts before, in the eyes of the public and the pundits, he got it right. In his first attempt, on August 17, he was angry and belligerent rather than contrite. He called his behavior "wrong" and the relationship with Monica Lewinsky "inappropriate," but did not say "I'm sorry."

He tried again on a trip to Europe in early September. The physical distance between Sp and A probably made it easier to utter the apology, but made it less effective. In Moscow on September 2, Clinton said, "I *have acknowledged* that I made a mistake, *said* that I regretted it, *asked* to be forgiven." The past tense reports of his earlier speech acts sound at first like apologies, but of course are not performative (as apologies must be), but merely reports of apologies, and therefore have no interactive value. On September 5, in Dublin, the President finally said that he was "very sorry about" the affair. But since he said it to people who were not the original addressees, not the people purportedly hurt by the behavior, again the utterance was not a felicitous apology.

On September 11, at a prayer breakfast, he tried again. "With tears in his eyes," the report in the *New York Times* begins, the President "admitted softly" that "I don't think that there is a fancy way to say that I have sinned." It should be noted that he has still not quite *said* "I have sinned," but merely said that these words could be said. Indeed, though all the correct language is there in the rest of the speech,

> It is important to me that everybody who has been hurt know that the sorrow I feel is genuine. . . . I have asked all for their forgiveness.

the expressions of contrition are all framed as indirect discourse, as presupposed rather than asserted, blunting their force and mitigating the speaker's responsibility. On the other hand, the nonverbal aspects are right in place, the tears and the soft voice. At this point the President's apology finally passed muster, suggesting that, as Ekman and Friesen point out, nonverbal signs mean more than verbal.

But even though the people, through the pollsters, voiced approval, the Republicans in Congress continued to withhold it. Asked what it would take to get their forgiveness, several asserted that nothing would serve. If that was their assumption from the start, could any apology by the President have been felicitous?

The assumptions of speech act theory shed light on why the President may have made the choices he made (we can only guess at his, or anyone's, intentions); and why Americans responded to the repeated attempts as they did. Lexical semantics shows why the President was reluctant to use the "s"-word, even running serious risks by his refusal to do so. Speech act theory helps explain why people were dissatisfied with his attempts, but also suggests that for one intended set of addressees at any rate, nothing the President said could be a felicitous apology.

2.5   The speech event

All participants in a discourse contribute to its meaning and perhaps even the form it takes (as Clinton's ultimate apology was shaped and reshaped by the "reviews" early versions got in the media). Utterances are situated in larger events, whether purely linguistic – an encompassing utterance, a conversation – or another human activity – a ritual, a job, a performance. Hence, no single canonical "apology" form will fit with equal appropriateness into any context. From the perspective of the situated discourse event, what is required in an apology is subsumed under several categories, among them:

- *register*. Even for equally heinous behaviors, an apology made in a close family context is different from one that is made publicly. Between intimates an apology may not be required ("love is never having to say you're sorry") for behavior for which one might be required in a more distant relationship. Different kinds of behavior may convey sincerity in intimate and in formal contexts (touching is often appropriate at home, less so in public).

- *genre*. In informal circumstances, a simple oral "OK" from the addressee may suffice to denote forgiveness. But in more formal settings (as in the settling of a lawsuit), a written statement exculpating the defendant may be required from the plaintiff to end the matter, with its wording carefully overseen by both sides.
- *key* (Hymes 1972). Under some conditions, an apology made ironically or otherwise humorously may be acceptable. My father once offended me and later sent me a copy of *The Portable Curmudgeon*, which I took to be an apology (= "I'm a curmudgeon all right, but I can't help it") and forgave him.

2.6   Conversation analysis: the apology adjacency pair

Conversation analysis (CA) as a research method has this analogy with autonomous syntactic analysis: because in both the analyst is prevented from dealing directly with meaning, intention, function, or understanding, the question "What constitutes an apology?" cannot be fully explored by either. Formal structures such as adjacency pairs can reveal what sort of second is preferred when the first member of a turn sequence is an apology.

For instance, the tools and methods of conversation analysis can clarify what constitutes a preferred second in response to an apology. If a concern of linguists is the determination of what can occur "grammatically" in the context of something else, then – if we are going to achieve a unified field and a cross-disciplinary perspective – conversation analysis has to be able to address the question: what form does a "preferred" utterance take, and why? Traditional CA cannot do this, or cannot do it very well, because it does not permit introspection or mentalistic analysis. But (as analysts like Gumperz (1982) and Tannen (1984) have pointed out) without the ability to address questions of intention and effect, the analysis of conversation bogs down much the way pretransformational syntactic analysis did. To shed light on apologies from a CA perspective, the analyst must note that, of the various possible seconds available in response to an apology, different ones are more apt to co-occur with differently formed apologies:

A: I apologize for my appalling conduct.
B: ?No prob, dude.
B':   ?Hey, we all make mistakes.
B":   ?Gosh, I never noticed.
B"':   I accept your apology/Accepted.
B"":   I forgive you/Forgiven.

But change A to A':

A':   Sorry 'bout that,

and the assignment of ?'s shifts abruptly.

Traditional CA, of course, would never utilize constructed examples or mentalistic judgments like these. Yet there must be some way of talking about what speakers believe, find plausible, and use.

2.7   *Narrative analysis: the story behind the apology*

Narrative analysis has become fashionable in many fields, from literature to law, psychology, anthropology, history, and political science. All these fields have come to the realization that humans make sense of their lives through the stories they construct. We develop psychological problems when our stories about our lives lack coherency (e.g. Schafer 1980; Spence 1982); in courtrooms, jurors determine whose "story" is more plausible, plaintiff or defendant, or whether the prosecutor's story has been successfully undermined by the defense attorney (cf. Delgado 1989). We can look at apologies as plot points in a story: what events led up to their making; how did the utterance of an apology move the story along? What happens when the internal stories of two people are in conflict – A sees B as someone who owes A an apology; B either does not believe she or he has done anything wrong, or believes that their social differences are such that no apology is necessary?

We might look at the tale told earlier of Ronald Reagan and Coretta Scott King as involving just such a set of conflicting narratives. King expected an apology, Reagan did not believe one was in order, for both of the reasons suggested above. Reagan (or his people) was (or were) ingenious enough to construct an utterance that could satisfy the plots of two different groups of storytellers, creating (possibly) successful conclusions to two very different stories. (This happy outcome works best, of course, if the duplicity does not come to light – as in this instance it did.)

When an apology is duly made and properly accepted, both parties come away satisfied. A good apology convinces both participants that their narratives are rational and permits both to have more or less happy endings. Even the humbled apologizer gets accepted back into the human fold, recognized as recognizing the need for an apology at this juncture, sharing with the addressee a common view of the narrative they have participated in creating. Even as apologizers are distanced momentarily from the fold of the virtuous, they are welcomed back as being, at any rate, competent.

2.8   *Sociolinguistic considerations*

Sociolinguistic analysis directly links the social group memberships of the pair involved in the apology and their options and expectations in the event. Larger cultural background plays a significant role in the understanding of the need for apologies and the determination of their appropriate form. For instance, in many societies "honor" is important, and may both keep an apology from being made where an American might readily make one, and make a formal explicit apology requisite where we might do without one. Apology is always face-threatening for the speaker; but not making a necessary apology may occasion more serious face loss in the long run. As Brown and Levinson (1987) would say, the weightiness of a contemplated apology as a face threat must be computed by giving consideration to the intimacy and power relationships of the parties involved, and the seriousness of the misdeed that occasioned it.

Other extralinguistic issues are equally relevant. If, for instance, as Tannen (1994) suggests, women tend to use "I'm sorry" as a smoother of difficult moments, but men are less likely to do so, the genders will misunderstand each other (and women, as people who traditionally are interpreted by others, will suffer more from the misunderstanding). Similarly, apologies raise the important question of when, how much, and in what way you divulge your "real self" or private persona to the world via language. As in the Cambridge Nanny case, when one culture believes it is shameful to let one's guard down at all in public, and another believes that the sincerity of a public apology is gauged by sobs, tears, and hand-wringing, it will be difficult for a member of one group to produce an apology that will at once gratify members of the other, and leave the apologizer herself or himself with any shred of self-esteem.

2.9   Text analysis: apology as a document

Finally, we can use much of the understanding gained at earlier levels to understand political and social events as reported in the media (both the choices of wording and the decisions as to what to discuss: the "text" and, perhaps, the "metatext(s)"). For instance, between the beginning of August and the end of September 1998 a large amount of space in the major American print media was dedicated to the analysis of and judgment upon the President's several apologies; polls of the American people, assessing their opinions about the satisfactoriness of each Presidential apology; reflections upon what apologies were and how they were appropriately made; and so on. We may deduce from this that apology had assumed a superhot, perhaps symbolic, importance at that moment (a search using Lexis-Nexus would tell the researcher that never before or since had the word "apology" received so much play in so many media over so long a time). At this level we can examine the subtext: why do "we," whoever "we" are, require a show of contrition at this time? And why are the demanders never satisfied? Answers to these questions require the examination of language at all the levels discussed above. In this way, through concentration on a particular speech act, located in a specific cultural and societal time and place, we can come to understand a great deal about who we are, what we want, and the rules and assumptions that bind us together as a society.

NOTES

I would like to thank Deborah Tannen for her perceptive comments and suggestions.

1   And there were many fewer areas of knowledge identified as "disciplines" or "departments." Within the humanities, for instance, modern

languages were recognized only in the late nineteenth century as valid subjects for university study. The first chair in English at Harvard was established in 1876; at Oxford, the English honors degree was created (with some sniping from traditionalists) in 1896 (Delbanco 1999). The social sciences are even newer, with anthropology and sociology dating from the first third of the twentieth century; departments of linguistics became commonplace only toward the end of the 1960s.

2 As an illustration, if the syntactician is permitted to offer analyses that take no cognizance of the fact that sentences are produced in the service of cognition and communication, then surely such analyses can function only as unintentional self-parodies, the ivory tower at its most aloof and irrelevant, social science turned antisocial (and not too scientific, since form divorced from function tends to offer very few useful or lasting generalizations).

3 Older readers may recall Steve Martin's line on *Saturday Night Live*, "Well, excu-u-use me!," to precisely this effect.

4 The relation between "real" feelings and "surface" ones proves as intriguing as it is vexing for several disciplines. It manifests itself in Ekman and Friesen's (1975) distinction between "automatic" expressions of emotion that represent universal human instincts (e.g. scowling to express anger) and those that people learn as part of their culture's communicative repertoire (e.g. Japanese giggling, vs. American joking, to cover embarrassment); in the various distinctions made within several versions of transformational generative grammar ("deep," "abstract," "underlying," or "logical" vs. "surface" structure); and in psychoanalytic discussion of the "latent" vs. "manifest" content of

dreams, symptoms, and errors. Here is another point at which disparate fields come together in a common quest, obscured by differences in vocabulary and methodology.

5 This was a notorious and controversial case shown on Court TV and tirelessly reported in network news and magazine shows nightly. Louise Woodward, a young British national employed in Cambridge MA as a nanny, was accused of shaking the baby in her charge to death. The evidence was ambiguous. Found guilty by the jury, she was placed on probation by the judge and allowed to go free, both decisions provoking controversy among the public and "experts" of various stripes.

6 However, the popularity in high places of the adage "Never apologize, never explain" argues that the two may be closer than the above analysis suggests.

7 For the historical record: in January of 1998, evidence came to light that President Clinton had engaged in sexual conduct with a White House intern, Monica Lewinsky. Shortly thereafter on a television interview he said, "I have never, at any time, had sexual relations with that woman, Miss Lewinsky." The question remained red-hot for several months, with continual denials on one side and insistences on the other. In August Lewinsky's "semen-stained dress" came to light, and subsequent DNA testing proved the semen to be the President's. Apologies were then demanded – for exactly what (the sexual behavior; the untruthfulness; the fact that the statement had been accompanied by wagging/shaking his finger at us/you/the American people) was never precisely clarified.

REFERENCES

Austin, J. L. 1962. *How to Do Things With Words*. Cambridge: Cambridge University Press.

Baker, Charlotte L. 1975. This is just a first approximation, but . . . In T. J. San, L. J. Vance, and R. E. Grossman (eds), *Papers from the Eleventh Regional Meeting of the Chicago Linguistic Society*, pp. 37–47.

Brown, Penelope and Stephen R. Levinson. 1987. *Politeness*. Cambridge: Cambridge University Press.

Delbanco, Andrew. 1999. The decline and fall of English literature. *New York Review of Books*, November 4, 1999:32–8.

Delgado, Richard. 1989. Storytelling for oppositionists and others: a plea for narrative. *Michigan Law Review*, 87, 2411.

Ekman, Paul and Wallace Friesen. 1968. The repertoire of nonverbal behavior: categories, origins, usage, and coding. *Semiotica* 1:49–97.

Ekman, Paul and Wallace Friesen. 1969. Nonverbal leakage and cues to deception. *Psychiatry* 32:88–105.

Ekman, Paul and Wallace Friesen. 1975. *Unmasking the Face: A Guide to Recognizing Emotions from Facial Cues*. Englewood Cliffs, NJ: Prentice-Hall.

Fillmore, Charles J. 1971. Verbs of judging. In C. J. Fillmore and D. T. Langendoen (eds), *Studies in Linguistic Semantics*. New York: Holt, Rinehart, and Winston, pp. 273–90.

Gordon, David and George Lakoff. 1971. Conversational postulates. In D. Adams, M. A. Campbell, V. Cohen, J. Lovins, E. Maxwell, C. Nygren, and J. Reighard (eds), *Papers from the Seventh Regional Meeting of the Chicago Linguistic Society*, pp. 63–84.

Grice, H. P. 1975. Logic and conversation. In P. Cole and J. L. Morgan (eds), *Syntax and Semantics 3: Speech Acts*. New York: Academic Press, pp. 41–58.

Gumperz, John J. 1982. *Discourse Strategies*. London: Cambridge University Press.

Hochschild, Arlie Russell. 1983. *The Managed Heart: Commercialization of Human Feeling*. Berkeley and Los Angeles: University of California Press.

Hymes, Dell. 1972. Models of the interaction between language and social life. In J. J. Gumperz and D. Hymes (eds), *Directions in Sociolinguistics*. London: Blackwell, pp. 35–71.

Lakoff, Robin T. 1973. Questionable answers and answerable questions. In B. Kachru et al. (eds), *Issues in Linguistics: Papers in Honor of Henry and Renée Kahane*. Urbana: University of Illinois Press, pp. 453–67.

Schafer, Roy. 1980. Narration in the psychoanalytic dialogue. *Critical Inquiry* Autumn 1980:29–53.

Schiffrin, Deborah. 1985. Conversational coherence: the role of well. *Language* 61.3:640–67.

Searle, John. 1969. *Speech Acts*. Cambridge: Cambridge University Press.

Spence, Donald. 1982. *Narrative Truth and Historical Truth*. New York: Norton.

Tannen, Deborah. 1984. *Conversational Style*. Norwood, NJ: Ablex.

Tannen, Deborah. 1994. *Talking from 9 to 5*. New York: William Morrow.

11 Interactional Sociolinguistics: A Personal Perspective

JOHN J. GUMPERZ

0 Introduction: Background

Interactional sociolinguistics (IS) is an approach to discourse analysis that has its origin in the search for replicable methods of qualitative analysis that account for our ability to interpret what participants intend to convey in everyday communicative practice. It is well known that conversationalists always rely on knowledge that goes beyond grammar and lexicon to make themselves heard. But how such knowledge affects understanding is still not sufficiently understood.

My perspective on verbal communication is grounded in earlier work on ethnography of communication (Hymes 1961); Hymes's key insight was that instead of seeking to explain talk as directly reflecting the beliefs and values of communities, structuralist abstractions that are notoriously difficult to operationalize, it should be more fruitful to concentrate on situations of speaking or, to use Roman Jakobson's term, speech events. Events are arguably more concretely available for ethnographic investigation (Gumperz and Hymes 1964, 1972). They constitute units of interaction subject to direct analysis by established empirical means. At the same time, what happens in such events frequently enters into public discussion, so that replicable information on relevant beliefs and values can readily be obtained through focused ethnographic inquiry.

The ethnography of communication debate stimulated a wide variety of empirical investigations. These early studies and particularly the findings, which tended to be presented in terms of grammar-like rules of speaking of the form "in situation A do or say X" (Bauman and Sherzer 1976), have been convincingly criticized on the grounds that they cannot capture everyday practice (Brown and Levinson 1979; Bourdieu 1977, 1994). Nevertheless it is clear that speech event analysis has played an important role in calling attention both to the importance of context in talk and to discourse as the principal site for language and culture studies. As a result, research on language and culture has increasingly come to concentrate on discourse as the basic research site. Ethnographic insight gained through long-term, first-hand immersion in strategically selected fieldwork situations is applied to the interpretation of what transpires in longer sequences and yields hypotheses on how native speakers think in everyday interaction. IS is one of several traditions concerned with these issues.[1]

To look at talk as it occurs in speech events is to look at communicative practices. Along with others I claim that such practices constitute an intermediate and in many ways analytically distinct level of organization. A sociological predecessor here is Erving Goffman, who proposed the concept of "Interaction Order" as a distinct level of discursive organization bridging the linguistic and the social. Goffman's work on this topic has greatly influenced the conversational analysts' argument that conversation is separate both from grammar and from macro social structures and must be analyzed in its own terms. In my early approach to interaction I took a position situated somewhere between those of Erving Goffman (1981) and Harold Garfinkel (1967). The former looked at encounters from an ethologist's perspective, while the latter was concerned with the often overlooked interpretive processes that make interaction work. I argue that all communication is intentional and grounded in inferences that depend upon the assumption of mutual good faith. Culturally specific presuppositions play a key role in inferring what is intended.

Suggestive evidence to indicate that sociocultural background knowledge does in fact enter into everyday decision making comes from Garfinkel's (1967) ethnomethodological experiments. Garfinkel sees interaction as constituted by goal-oriented moves, and his main concern is with the interpretive processes through which interactional outcomes are achieved. Based on a variety of illustrative examples taken from what he refers to as naturally organized situations, he argues that everyday talk can never be precise and detailed enough to convey what is really intended, so that interactants inevitably and necessarily rely on what he calls "practical reasoning" and unstated, taken-for-granted background knowledge to fill in for what is left unsaid. He goes on to point out that in so doing they display a built-in, deeply internalized, and for the most part unverbalized sense of social order. Yet apart from advocating that analysts resort to historical methods to trace how specific understandings come about so as to recover what types of knowledge are at work, Garfinkel gives no further specifics of how interpretive processes work in everyday talk.

It is the philosopher Paul Grice (1989) who lays the foundations for a truly social perspective on speaking, with his emphasis on conversational cooperation as a precondition for understanding. Arguing that communicating is by its very nature an intentional process, Grice goes on to develop a theory of meaning that brackets the traditional semanticists' concern with word-to-world relationships or denotation, to focus not on utterance interpretation as such, but on *implicature* – roughly, what a speaker intends to convey by means of a message. Grice coined the verb *implicate* to suggest that our interpretations, although often not closely related to context-free lexical meaning, are ultimately grounded in surface form. They are derived from what is perceptibly said through inference via processes of implicatures, processes that in turn rest on a finite set of general, essentially social *principles of conversational cooperation*. Grice cites a number of conversational examples, which show that situated implicatures often bear little denotational likeness to propositional or, loosely speaking, literal meaning. Exactly how Gricean principles of conversational implicature can be formulated more precisely is still a matter of dispute.

Garfinkel, by documenting the intrinsic incompleteness of everyday talk, and Grice, in claiming that listeners rely on assumptions about conversational cooperation to recast what is literally said, each in his own way argues for the importance of extracommunicative knowledge in human understanding. But in contrast to other interpretivist perspectives, which seek to explain a particular action in terms of general, community-wide or pan-human norms or values, their perspective on interpretation is basically a dialogic one. The fundamental problem is not deciding on what an expression means but determining what a speaker intends to convey by means of a specific message. This view, that inferences are rooted in discourse as well as in the local circumstances in which they were produced, is by now widely accepted in discourse studies.

Goffman has given us the outline of a communicative perspective on the social world. In his earlier work he sets aside traditional analytical categories such as role, status, identity, and the like to concentrate on the phenomenal bases of interactive processes. Among the questions that concern him are: how can we distinguish among various possible kinds of face-to-face gatherings? What are the observable interactive signs by which we can describe the types of involvement that mark them? What kind of speaking roles can we identify in interaction and how are these marked at the level of behavior? What are the dialogic processes through which interactants display shared perceptions of who they are, manage interpersonal relationships, and otherwise position themselves vis-à-vis others? In later work he provides vivid illustrations to argue how interactions are framed in such a way as to relate the ongoing interaction to broader classes of encounters and make what transpires intelligible in terms of prior experience. Among other things, he points out that "framing" can be viewed as something like a filtering process through which societal-level values and principles of conduct are transformed and refocused so as to apply to the situation at hand. It follows that we can no longer think of community-wide beliefs and ideologies as directly revealed in talk. Interaction, he goes on to claim, should be seen as a separate level of communicative organization: thus the interaction order, which bridges the verbal and the social, must be analyzed in terms of its own analytical units both at the level of language and in interaction. His arguments thus foreshadow current thinking on communicative practice. However, Goffman provides only illustrative information to flesh out his methodological arguments. He is not concerned with how grammar and lexicon function both to frame what is being said and to affect situated assessments of what is conveyed at any one point in an encounter.

Conversational analysis as it is currently practiced began as an attempt to apply something akin to Goffman and Garfinkel's program to the study of everyday talk. A major initial goal was to show how the essentially social orderliness of even the simplest, most casual exchanges is produced, by focusing on the verbal "methods" conversationalists themselves employ in managing verbal exchanges. For the purpose of analysis, talk is treated as constituted by sequentially organized strings of speaking turns, such that by means of these turns conversationalists indicate the meaning of their actions and their understanding of prior actions (Goffman 1989). Relationships among turns are examined to demonstrate empirically how conversational effects are achieved. The term "empirical" is important here, since many conversational analysts use it to justify the claim that only overtly lexicalized propositional content counts as data, so that the indirect inferences that play such an important role in other forms of discourse analysis are excluded.

From an IS perspective the question we must ask is: how do we know what aspects of background knowledge are relevant at any one time, and is extracommunicative background knowledge enough? We assume that information about contextual frames is communicated as part of the process of interacting, and therefore it becomes necessary to be clearer about the specifics of what happens in the interaction as such, to assess what is intended. Conversational analysts also set out to do this, and their work has brilliantly shown what can be learned through turn-by-turn sequential analyses. But I suggest that sequential analysis cannot by itself account for situated interpretation. It describes just one of the many indexical processes that affect inferencing. I argue that assessments of communicative intent at any one point in an exchange take the form of hypotheses that are either confirmed or rejected in the course of the exchange. That is, I adopt the conversational analysts' focus on members' procedures but apply it to inferencing. The analytical problem then becomes not just to determine what is meant, but to discover how interpretive assessments relate to the linguistic signaling processes through which they are negotiated.

1   Diversity as a Central IS Theme

A main IS theme is the inherent linguistic and cultural diversity of today's communicative environments. Research on the communicative import of diversity has been and continues to be plagued by deep theoretical divisions. On the one hand there are those who regard communicative practices as shaped by *habitus*: embodied dispositions to act and to perceive the world that directly reflect the macrosocietal conditions, political and economic forces, and relationships of power in which they were acquired (Bourdieu 1977, 1994). They argue that it is to such conditioning factors that we must look for insights into the nature of diversity. Others take a more constructivist approach, claiming that since our social worlds are ultimately shaped through interaction, it is necessary to begin by learning more about the way localized interactive processes work before we can turn to research on diversity. Since the two traditions differ in what they regard as relevant data and in the methods of analysis they employ, their findings are for the most part incommensurable.

IS seeks to bridge the gap between these two approaches by focusing on communicative practice as the everyday-world site where societal and interactive forces merge. Hanks (1996) defines communicative practice as largely resting on the discursive practices of actors acting in pursuit of their goals and aspirations. Therefore speaking, when seen in a practice perspective, is not just a matter of individuals' encoding and decoding messages. To interact is to engage in an ongoing process of negotiation, both to infer what others intend to convey and to monitor how one's own contributions are received. In other words, what is at issue is shared or nonshared interpretations rather than denotational meaning. And background knowledge of the kind I alluded to above, i.e. that goes beyond overt lexical information, always plays a key role in the interpretive process. IS analysis therefore concentrates on speech exchanges involving two or more actors as its main object of study. The aim is to show how individuals participating in such exchanges use talk to achieve their communicative goals in real-life situations, by concentrating on the meaning-making processes and the taken-for-granted, background assumptions that underlie the negotiation of interpretations.

As in-depth, discourse-level analyses of situated performances became available, it soon became evident that speech event categorizations cannot be treated as extralinguistically defined givens. More often than not, participants' definition of what the relevant event is and what it means in an encounter emerges in and through the performance itself (Bauman 1986; Bauman and Briggs 1990; Hymes 1981). As Hanks puts it in an article on genre and related questions of language use: "The idea of objectivist rules is replaced by schemes and strategies, leading one to view genre as a set of focal and prototypical elements which actors use variously and which never become fixed in a unitary structure" (1987: 681, quoted in Bauman and Briggs 1990). What holds for the literary theorists' *genre* is true also for events (Gumperz 1982a). In both cases we are dealing with schemata or frames, embodying presuppositions associated with ideologies and principles of communicative conduct that in a way bracket the talk, and that thereby affect the way in which we assess or interpret what transpires in the course of an encounter. Presuppositions that over time come to be associated with specific events may be metonymically evoked, in the course of communicative practice, to set the criteria or establish frames in terms of which constituent messages are interpreted, a point that will be taken up later in this chapter.

The analytical issue thus shifts from the search for grammar-like rules of language use as traditionally conceived, to questions such as (1) how and by what signaling devices language functions to evoke the contextual presuppositions that affect interpretation, and (2) what presuppositions are at work in particular talk exchanges. Thus the IS approach to diversity is essentially a semiotic one, which allows for a shifting balance between multiple inputs. Such an approach accounts for the fact that what count as different systems at the level of denotational structures can come to convey information at the level of communicative structure.

IS assumes that interpretive assessments always build on local or context-specific background knowledge that takes the form of presuppositions that shift in the course of an encounter. Analysis focuses on *conversational inference*, defined as the interpretive procedure by means of which interactants assess what is communicatively intended at any one point in an exchange, and on which they rely to plan and produce their responses. Sequential positioning of turns at speaking is clearly an important input to conversational inference, but many other, analytically prior factors are also involved. Furthermore, it is also true that individuals engaged in conversation do not just react to literal meaning – if there is such a thing – in the linguist's sense of the term. At issue is communicative intent; to assess what is intended, listeners must go beyond surface meaning to fill in what is left unsaid. For example, if Tom had just been talking to Fred and I asked what they had been doing, he might answer "I asked Fred if he was free this evening." From this I might infer that he might be planning to join Fred in some activity, although literally speaking this is clearly not what the utterance "means."

My interpretation is of course not the only possible one. I relied on background knowledge acquired through past communicative experience to infer what was intended. To the extent that background knowledge is not shared, interpretations may differ. What the presuppositions are that enter into conversational inference and how they are reflected in talk vary, among other things, with speakers' and listeners' communicative background. Sharing of inferential procedures cannot be taken for granted; it must be demonstrated through ethnographically informed, in-depth analysis of what transpires in an encounter. A main purpose of IS analysis is to show how diversity affects interpretation. Some of the best-known IS studies were conducted in urban workplace settings, where lay participants who are under great pressure to perform must deal with experts whose interpretive premises are quite different from theirs, and therefore operate with different background assumptions (Gumperz 1982a, 1982b; Gumperz and Roberts 1991).[2]

The following brief extracts will illustrate some of the above points. They are taken from a set of selection interviews recorded in the mid-1970s in the British Midlands. The applicants are applying for paid traineeships at a publicly funded institution, offering instruction in skills that are in short supply:

(1) Electrician:
    a. *Interviewer*: have you visited the skills center?
    b. *Applicant*: yes, I did.
    c. *Interviewer*: so you've had a look at the workshops?
    d. *Applicant*: yes.
    e. *Interviewer*: you know what the training allowance is? do you?
    f. *Applicant*: yeah.
    g. *Interviewer*: Do you know how much you've got to live on for the period of time.

(2) Bricklayer:
    a. *Interviewer*: have you visited the skills center?
    b. *Applicant*: yep. I've been there. yeah.
    c. *Interviewer*: so you've had a chance to look around?
        and did you look in at the brick shop?
    d. *Applicant*: ah yeah. we had a look around the brickshop.
        and uhm, it look o.k. I mean it's- . . .
    e. *Interviewer*: all right.
    f. *Applicant*: pretty good yeah.

Note that while the interviewer asks roughly the same questions in each case, the two applicants differ in the way they answer and the treatment they receive. In (2) the applicant (the bricklayer) elaborates his answers, enabling the interview to judge how he has interpreted the question. The two participants actively collaborate in constructing the exchange and we have the impression that they understand each other. In turn (d), for example, when the applicant hesitates as if he were searching for the right word ("I mean it's- . . ."), the interviewer helps him with "all right" and the exchange ends on a note of agreement. In (1), on the other hand, the applicant (the electrician) provides only minimal replies, volunteering no information on his own. We have the impression he is being rather passive, leaving the interviewer to do all the work. When the interviewer in turn (g) rephrases her question about the training allowance, it seems that she is not sure that the applicant understands what it is she wants.

The electrician, although he has been living in Britain for a number of years, is South Asian by background, and the bricklayer a native of the local region. We could argue therefore that ideology-based prejudice is at work. There is no question that ideology is an important factor, but experience with this and other similar workplace situations suggests that the treatment the two applicants receive is also due to the fact that, based on their communicative and cultural backgrounds, interviewers and applicants draw different inferences from what they see and hear. IS analyses of such inferential processes can provide evidence to show how such differences come about and how they affect the workplace climate. The latter part of this chapter will present a more detailed discussion of the electrician's interview, but first, more background on basic IS assumptions.

Initial insights into the role of language use in inferential processes came from studies of *code-switching* (Blom and Gumperz 1972), a term commonly used to refer to alternation among different speech varieties within the same event. Such alternations are employed throughout the world, particularly among participants in local networks of relationship. They are commonly described via rules of alternation similar in form to rules of language usage. For example, in the old Catholic church service Latin was said to be appropriate for prayer, while the native language was used for sermons. Yet if we examine switching as it enters into the discursive practices that constitute the event, it soon becomes apparent that it is not the objective situation that determines language use. The data show that the discursive juxtaposition of grammatically and lexically distinct ways of speaking in any one stretch of talk evokes a shift in contextual presuppositions which then in turn affects interpretation. As recent comparative empirical studies demonstrate (Auer 1998), code-switching constitutes a basic communicative resource that in many situations serves as a communicative strategy to achieve specific interpretive effects.

In IS analysis, speaking is treated as a reflexive process such that everything said can be seen as either directly reacting to preceding talk, reflecting a set of immediate circumstances, or responding to past events, whether directly experienced or indirectly transmitted. To engage in verbal communication therefore is not just to express one's thoughts. Speaking ties into a communicative ecology that significantly affects the course of an interaction. Conversational inference relies on two types of verbal signs: symbolic signs that convey information via the well-known lexical and grammatical rules and indexical signs that signal by direct association between sign and context. Terms like "here" and "there" or "this" and "that" are typical examples of indexicality, in that what is intended in any one instance can only be understood with reference to some physical or discursive environment. But context also can be and often is communicatively evoked through talk, and it is that evocation process that is at work in code-switching.

I use the term *contextualization cue* to refer to any verbal sign which, when processed in co-occurence with symbolic grammatical and lexical signs, serves to construct the contextual ground for situated interpretation and thereby affects how constituent messages are understood. Code-switching is one such contextualization cue. Others include pronunciation along with prosody (i.e. intonation and stress), rhythm, tempo, and other such suprasegmental signs. Contextualization cues, when processed in co-occurrence with other cues and grammatical and lexical signs, construct the contextual ground for situated interpretation and thereby affect how particular messages are understood (Gumperz 1982a). As metapragmatic signs (Lucy 1993), contextualization cues represent speakers' ways of signaling and providing information to interlocutors and audiences about how language is being used at any one point in the ongoing exchange. What sets them apart from communicatively similar lexicalized signs is that they are intrinsically oral forms. Since no utterance can be pronounced without such signs, contextualization cues are ever present in talk, and to the extent that they can be shown to affect interpretation, they provide direct evidence for the necessary role that indexicality plays in talk. Moreover, contextualization strategies signal meaning largely by cueing indirect inferences. In conversation, we could not possibly express all the information that interlocutors must have to plan their own contributions and attune their talk to that of their interlocutors, so it is easy to see the reason for this indirectness.

Finally, and perhaps most importantly, indirect (not overtly lexicalized) signaling mechanisms are for the most part culturally or subculturally specific. In fact prosody and "accent" (in the sense of phonetically marked features of pronunciation), for example, are among the principal means by which we identify where people are from and "who" they are, and assess their social identity, as happened in the above examples. The reason we can do this is that contextualization strategies are learned primarily through direct personal contacts of the kind characteristic of family, peer-group, and close friendship relations, where background knowledge is likely to be shared and speakers can be confident that others will understand their indirect allusions.

I will give some additional concrete examples to show how I view the process of understanding. Some time ago, while driving to the office, my radio was tuned to a classical radio station. At the end of the program, the announcer, a replacement for the regular host who was scheduled to return the next day, signed off with the following words: "I've enjoyed being with *you* these last two weeks." I had not been listening very carefully, but the extrastrong focal accent on *"you"* in a syntactic position where I would have expected an unaccented pronoun caught my attention. It sounded as if the announcer was talking to someone else. Yet there was no other person with him on the program. This led me to call on past communicative experience to construct an alternative, more plausible scenario which might suggest an interpretation. The speaker's words reminded me of a leave-taking exchange, where a first speaker might begin with "I've enjoyed being with you" and the second might respond with "It was fun being with *you*." I therefore inferred that the announcer, by accenting the personal pronoun as one would in the second part of the exchange, was actually implicating the first.

In the above examples, participants' as well as my own interpretations relied on background knowledge to construct possible scenarios or envisionments or to intertextually retrieve specific expressions in terms of which the speakers' words made sense. I use the term *activity type* or *activity* to refer to these evoked envisionments. My claim is that interpretation of communicative intent always – that is, not just in intercultural encounters – rests on such constructs. These imagined activities function like Goffman's frames, abstract representations of the actions of actors engaged in strategically planning and positioning their moves in order to accomplish communicative ends in real-life encounters.

I am not claiming that IS analysis can solve the problem of interpretive ambiguity. The aim is to find likely solutions, i.e. solutions that are plausible in that they show how constituent actions cohere in light of the event as a whole, and the assumptions in terms of which we assess the event's significance. This is of course quite different from determining the truth or falsity of specific interpretations. The method resembles the conversational analyst's procedures of reconstructing the strategies members employ in formulating specific actions. But IS differs from conversational analysis in that the concern is with situated interpretation of communicative intent, not with strategies as such, and that analysis is not confined to overtly lexicalized information. Instead of taking interpretive processes for granted, IS analysis suggests (1) what the most likely interpretations are, (2) what the assumptions and inferential processes are by which they are achieved, and (3) how they relate to what is literally said.

In studies of intercultural and interethnic communication, IS methods have been useful in isolating systematic differences in interpretive practices that affect individuals' ability to create and maintain conversational involvement, and consequently to get their views across. This is specially true for today's culturally diverse institutional and workplace settings, where goal-oriented interaction plays a key role. As pointed out above, the issue is not merely what someone means at any one time, but shared interpretation. And such sharing always presupposes the ability to negotiate repairs, agree on how parts of an argument cohere, and follow both thematic shifts and shifts in presupposition. Apart from focusing on interpretations as such, IS analysis attempts to illustrate how these tasks are accomplished. It is for this reason that the analysis places so much stress on contextualization processes.

2   IS Method

In empirical studies, IS analysts have worked out a set of procedures along the following lines. First there is an initial period of ethnographic research designed to (1) provide insight into the local communicative ecology; (2) discover recurrent encounter types most likely to yield communicative data relevant to the research problem at hand; and (3) find out through observation, interviewing key participants, and checking one's own interpretations with them how local actors handle the problems they encounter and what their expectations and presuppositions are. In the second stage, the ethnographic findings provide the basis for selecting events reflecting representative sets of interactions for recording. (4) The next phase of the analysis begins with scanning the recorded materials at two levels of organization: (a) content and (b) pronunciation and prosodic organization. The aim is to isolate sequentially bounded units, marked off from others in the recorded data by some degree of thematic coherence, and by beginnings and ends detectable through co-occurring shifts in content, prosody, or stylistic and other formal markers. Extending the ethnographer of communication's practice somewhat, I use the term *event* to refer to such temporally organized units. The aim is to discover strips of naturally organized interaction containing empirical evidence to confirm or disconfirm our analyst's interpretations, evidence against which to test assumptions about what is intended elsewhere in the sequence.

Once isolated, events are transcribed and *interactional texts* (that is, transcripts that account for all the communicatively significant, verbal and nonverbal signs perceived) (Silverstein 1992) are prepared by setting down on paper all those perceptual cues: verbal and nonverbal, segmental and nonsegmental, prosodic, paralinguistic, and others that, as past and ongoing research shows, speakers and listeners demonstrably rely on as part of the inferential process. This procedure enables us not only to gain insights into situated understandings, but also to isolate recurrent form–context relationships and show how they contribute to interpretation. These relationships can then be studied comparatively across events, to yield more general hypotheses about speakers' contextualization practices.

Now let us return to the electrician's interview, to show in more detail how the methodological principles outlined above work in analysis. This time a third person, the course instructor, joins in the questioning. In the first extract, the questioning is designed to test the applicant's knowledge of the course:

(3) a. *Interviewer*: and you've put here, that you want to apply for that course because there are more jobs in . . . the *trade*.
b. *Applicant*: yeah (low).
c. *Interviewer*: so perhaps you could explain to Mr. C. *apart* from *that* reason, *why* else you want to apply for *electrical* work.
d. *Applicant*: I think I like . . . this job in my- , as a profession.
e. *Instructor*: and *why* do you think you'll *like* it?
f. *Applicant*: why?
g. *Instructor*: could you explain to me why?
h. *Applicant*: why do I like it? I think it is more job *prospect*.

By using stress to foreground the word "trade" the interviewer is drawing the applicant's attention to the term the applicant used in the written questionnaire he filled out before the interview, relying on him to infer what she intended to convey by this strategy. That is, she is indirectly asking the applicant to elaborate his reply to questions about his interest in electrical work. But just as he did in the previous example, the applicant is treating her remarks literally, as if he had been asked a simple "yes or no" question. When the interviewer tries to elicit more information, by accenting key expressions to call attention to what needs explanation, the applicant simply paraphrases his earlier written response. At this point the course instructor takes over. Like his colleague, he also relies on indirect accenting strategies. Unable to infer what is intended and increasingly uncertain about what he is supposed to say, the applicant once again rephrases what he has just said. He does not seem to notice that the interviewers, by strategically positioning their accents, are attempting to direct his attention to significant points in the argument which they seem to think require more comment.

Research with British-resident South Asians in general, and other similar exchanges in the same set of interviews, indicate that such problems are not unique. By virtue of their communicative background, as native speakers of languages that employ other linguistic means to highlight information in discourse, South Asians often fail to recognize that accenting is used in English to convey key information, and thus do not recognize the significance of the interviewers' contextualization cues. Furthermore, we know from ethnographic data that the South Asian candidates have been socialized to expect interview practices that differ significantly from those the interviewers employ. They have learned to treat interviews as hierarchical encounters, where candidates are expected to show reluctance to dwell on personal likes or preferences and avoid giving the appearance of being too forward or assertive (Gumperz 1996).

The consequences of the miscommunication that results become clear in the following segment, when the instructor turns to the topic of the applicant's previous experience with electrical work:

(4) i. *Instructor*: what sorts of work have you done before in this particular field?
     j. *Applicant*: what do you mean please.
     k. *Instructor*: well, electrical installation and maintenance. some of it involves jobs done in your home. in your own *home* have you *done* work in your own home?
     l. *Applicant*: yes sir.
     m. *Instructor*: yeah, and what sorts of jobs have you done?
     n. *Applicant*: well I-, I wired up my own house.
     o. *Instructor*: you've wired your own house?
     p. *Applicant*: yeah.
     q. *Instructor*: yeah?
     r. *Applicant*: it is passed, by the authority, electricity board.
     s. *Instructor*: yeah?
     t. *Applicant*: first time.
     u. *Instructor*: so having wired your own house, could you tell me what the "consumer box" is?
     v. *Applicant*: yeah, where the fuses is.
     w. *Instructor*: where the fuses are. all right fine. have you done *anything* other than wiring your own house?

In turn (n) it seems that the applicant is finally about to provide the information the interviewers need. But he evidently did not expect the instructor's question. Coming as it does after the applicant's statement, a native speaker would interpret it as a request for elaboration. But the applicant treats it as a "yes or no" question. And when the instructor then questions his answer, the applicant changes topic. He does not understand that he is being asked to explain what the work he claims to have done involves. In turn (u) the instructor makes one more effort to test the applicant's knowledge. But the instructor gives only a lexical description of the term. From other interviews analyzed as part of this study, we know that when the interviewers change topic and ask about a specific technical term, they expect the applicant to use such questions as a point of departure for showing what they know about the work involved. We conclude therefore that the instructor is unimpressed with the information he has received and sees the applicant as a doubtful candidate. Although the applicant apparently has had quite a bit of experience doing electrical work, he has difficulty providing sufficient narrative detail to convince the interviewers that he has had relevant previous experience and is really interested in the course. In the end he does not gain admission.

Altogether, the evidence we have shows that many native speakers of South Asian languages respond similarly whenever interviewers rely on prosody, formulaic expressions, or other indirect means to contextualize their questions. Moreover, initial interpretive differences tend to be compounded rather than repaired in the course of the encounter (Gumperz 1982a, 1982b, 1996). We could say linguistic diversity is the cause of the difficulty such minority candidates encounter, but that is too simplistic an explanation.

The three principals in this example have lived in the region for over a decade and, apart from the Asian's accent and minor grammatical oddities, they all speak English well. Moreover, they agree on what a selection interview is about and understand what is being said at the level of literal or denotational meaning. Both interviewers and interviewee rely on inferencing to interpret what is intended. But their inferences rest on different context-bound presuppositions, and they are therefore unable to agree on what is intended. The communicative difficulties are interactively produced. The interpretive processes involved are automatic and not readily subject to conscious recall, so that those involved are likely to be unaware of the discursive reasons for the misunderstandings. The question is one of differences in principles of communicative etiquette and of conventions of interpersonal communication. Such conventions are typically learned through informal personal contact. Because of the political and economic conditions in which they live, minority group members' access to such learning opportunities is likely to be quite limited.

But interpersonal contact alone does not explain the inferential leap from differences in discursive practices to judgments of ability. How can we explain the fact that the interviewers regard the candidate's seeming unresponsiveness and his failure to be explicit in expanding on his answers as evidence for lack of professional knowledge? We need to go beyond the local encounter, and look at societal ideologies in terms of which the interaction is assessed, to find an explanation. While it is true that overt discrimination against minorities in western industrialized societies has significantly decreased over the last few years, the language ideologies that associate control of the officially accepted standard language with basic ability continue to prevail (Irvine and Gal 1999). In this sense, we can say that the interviewer's assessment was ideologically based and did not necessarily reflect the interviewee's technical abilities or his real interest in the course.

By revealing the underlying interpretive process at work in an encounter, which is otherwise bound to remain hidden, IS analysis of key situations in institutional life can provide insights into the interpretive and ideological bases of communicative assessments, while at the same time enabling participants to learn from some of the difficulties arising in their contacts with others.

3   Conclusion

The intercultural encounters I have discussed constitute an extreme case where participants represent historically and linguistically quite distinct traditions. All the participants had lived and worked in western industrial settings for much of their adult life, but they brought into that different linguistic and cultural background experiences which continue to resonate in these encounters. While such examples are useful in illustrating how inferential processes are grounded in both linguistic and other background knowledge, they also show that the social outcomes and interactional consequences of communicative misalignment are far greater than any single analysis can show. As some of the shorter examples cited above indicate, IS analysis is applicable to communicative situations of all kinds, monolingual or multilingual, as a means of monitoring the communication processes that are so important in institutional life.

NOTES

1 For other related approaches see, for example, Bauman (1986); Briggs (1996); Fairclough (1995); Guenthner (1993); Hill and Irvine (1993); Kallmeyer (1994); Sarangi and Roberts (1999); Sherzer (1983); Silverstein and Urban (1996); Tannen (1984, 1989); Young (1994).

2 For additional work on basic IS concepts, see Gumperz (1982b, 1992, 1996). For recent case study analyses see Gumperz (1998); Cook-Gumperz and Gumperz (1994, 1996).

REFERENCES

Auer, P. ed. 1998. *Code-Switching in Conversation*. London: Routledge.

Bauman, R. 1986. *Story Performance and Event: Contextual Studies of Oral Narrative*. Cambridge: Cambridge University Press.

Bauman, R. and Briggs, C. 1990. Poetics and performance as critical perspective on social life. *Annual Review of Anthropology*.

Blom, J. P. and Gumperz, J. J. 1972. Social knowledge in linguistic structures: code-switching in Norway. In J. J. Gumperz and D. Hymes, eds, *Directions in Sociolinguistics: The Ethnography of Communication*. New York: Holt, Rhinehart and Winston, pp. 407–34.

Briggs, C. ed. 1996. *Disorderly Discourse, Narrative Conflict and Inequality*. Oxford: Oxford University Press.

Bourdieu, P. 1977. *Outline of a Theory of Practice*. Cambridge: Cambridge University Press.

Bourdieu, P. 1994. *Language and Symbolic Power*. Cambridge: Polity.

Brown, P. and Levinson, S. C. 1979. Social structure, groups and interaction. In H. Giles and K. Scherer, eds, *Social Markers in Speech*. Cambridge: Cambridge University Press.

Cook-Gumperz, J. and Gumperz, J. 1994. The politics of a conversation: conversational inference in discussion. In A. Grimshaw et al., eds, *What's Going on Here? Complementary Studies of Professional Life*. Norwood, N.J.: Ablex, pp. 373–97.

Cook-Gumperz, J. and Gumperz, J. 1996. Treacherous words: gender and power in academic assessments. *Folia Linguistica*, XXX, 3–4.

Fairclough, N. 1995. *Critical Discourse Analysis*. London: Longman.

Garfinkel, H. 1967. *Studies in Ethnomethodology*. New York: Prentice-Hall.

Goffman, E. 1981. *Forms of Talk*. Philadelphia: University of Pennsylvania Press.

Goffman, E. 1989. The interaction order. *American Sociological Review*, 48, 1–17.

Grice, P. 1989. *Studies in the Ways of Words*. Cambridge, Mass.: Harvard University Press.

Guenthner, S. 1993. *Diskursstrategien in der Interkulturellen Kommunikation*. Tuebingen: Max Niemeyer Verlag.

Gumperz, J. J. 1982a. *Discourse Strategies*. Cambridge: Cambridge University Press.

Gumperz, J. J. ed. 1982b. *Language and Social Identity*. Cambridge: Cambridge University Press.

Gumperz, J. J. 1992. Contextualization and understanding. In A. Duranti and

C. Goodwin, eds, *Rethinking Context: Language as an Interactive Phenomenon.* Cambridge: Cambridge University Press, pp. 229–52.

Gumperz, J. J. 1996. The linguistic relativity of conversational inference. In J. Gumperz and S. C. Levinson, eds, *Rethinking Linguistic Relativity.* Cambridge: Cambridge University Press, pp. 359–406.

Gumperz, J. J. 1998. Culture in the cultural defense. In *Proceedings of the Sixth Annual Symposium about Language and Society, SALSA VI,* 91–121.

Gumperz, J. J. and Hymes, D., eds, 1964. The ethnography of speaking. Special issue, *American Anthropologist.*

Gumperz, J. J. and Hymes, D., eds, 1972. *Directions in Sociolinguistics.* New York: Holt, Rhinehart and Winston.

Gumperz, J. and Roberts, C. 1991. Understanding in intercultural encounters. In J. Blommaert and J. Verschueren, eds, *The Pragmatics of Inter-Cultural Communication.* Amsterdam: John Benjamins, pp. 51–90.

Hanks, W. F. 1987. Discourse genres in a theory of practice. *American Ethnologist,* 4(14), 668–96.

Hanks, W. F. 1996. *Language and Communicative Practice.* Boulder, Colo.: Westview Press.

Hill, J. H. and Irvine, J. T. 1993. *Responsibility and Evidence in Oral Discourse.* Cambridge: Cambridge University Press.

Hymes, D. H. 1961. The ethnography of speaking. In T. Gladwin and W. C. Sturtevant, eds, *Anthropology and Human Behavior.* Washington, D.C.: Anthropological Society of Washington, D.C. (Reprinted in J. A. Fishman, ed., 1968. *Readings in the Sociology of Language.* The Hague: Mouton, pp. 99–119.)

Hymes, D. H. 1981. *"In Vain I Tried to Tell You": Essays in Native American Ethnopoetics.* Philadelphia: University of Pennsylvania Press.

Irvine, J. T. and Gal, S. 1999. Language ideology and linguistic differentiation. In P. Kroskrity, ed., *Regimes of Language: Discursive Constructions of Authority, Identity and Power.* Santa Fe, N.M.: School of American Research, pp. 35–84.

Kallmeyer, W. 1994. *Kommunikation in der Stadt: Exemplarische Analysen des Sprachverhaltens in Mannheim.* Berlin: de Gruyter.

Knoblauch, H. 1995. *Kommunikationskultur: Die Kommunikative Konstruktion Kultureller Kontexte.* Berlin and New York: Mouton de Gruyter.

Lucy, J. A. 1993. *Reflexive Language: Reported Speech and Metapragmatics.* Cambridge: Cambridge University Press.

Sarangi, S. and Roberts, C., eds, 1999. *Talk Work and the Institutional Order.* Berlin, Mouton de Gruyter.

Sherzer, J. 1983. *Kuna Ways of Speaking.* Austin: University of Texas Press.

Silverstein, M. 1992. The indeterminacy of contextualization: when is enough enough? In P. Auer and A. Di Luzio, eds, *Contextualization of Language.* Philadelphia and New York: John Benjamins, pp. 33–58.

Silverstein, M. and Urban, G. eds, 1996. *Natural Histories of Discourse.* Chicago: University of Chicago Press.

Tannen, D. 1984. *Conversational Style.* Norwood, N.J.: Ablex.

Tannen, D. 1989. *Talking Voices: Repetition, Dialogue and Imagery in Conversational Discourse.* Cambridge: Cambridge University Press.

Young, L. W. L. 1994. *Crosstalk and Culture in Sino-American Communication.* Cambridge: Cambridge University Press.

12 Discourse as an Interactional Achievement III: The Omnirelevance of Action

EMANUEL A. SCHEGLOFF

0 Introduction

There are two themes on which I would like to focus attention, whose full incorporation into the analysis of discourse is, in my view, critical for its optimum further development. What needs to be incorporated is an orientation (1) to action and (2) to interaction. It will turn out that orientation to each of these themes confronts the student of discourse with a sort of challenge whose depth and consequentiality has not yet been fully registered or explored, but is likely to be substantial. What becomes inescapable in facing up to action and interaction is the challenge of contingency. What exactly I mean by "contingency" will only come into view over the course of the discussion of empirical materials; as it cannot be usefully elaborated here, I will return to the import of contingency at the end.

But before launching into this agenda, I need to make clear several premises of what I have to say – both as context for my central points and to make explicit my understanding of discourse's place in the world.

1 Points of Departure

The first point is that I take real-world, naturally occurring ordinary discourse as the basic target; it is as a student of *that* that I offer what follows. There may well be grounds for those with other interests to opt for a different point of reference or a different target of inquiry; but for me these involve departures from the natural and cultural bedrock.

Second, I take it that, in many respects, the fundamental or primordial scene of *social life* is that of direct interaction between members of a social species, typically ones who are physically copresent. For humans, *talking* in interaction appears to be a distinctive form of this primary constituent of social life, and ordinary conversation is very likely the basic form of organization for talk-in-interaction. Conversational inter-action may then be thought of as a form of social organization through which the work of the constitutive institutions of societies gets done – institutions such as the economy, the polity, the family, socialization, etc. It is, so to speak, *sociological* bed-rock. And it surely appears to be the basic and primordial environment for the devel-opment, the use, and the learning of natural language – both ontogenetically and phylogenetically.

Therefore, it should hardly surprise us if some of the most fundamental features of natural language are shaped in accordance with this home environment in copresent interaction – as adaptations *to* it, or as part of its very warp and weft (Schegloff 1989, 1996). For example, if the basic natural environment for *sentences* is in *turns at talk* in conversation, we should take seriously the possibility that aspects of their grammat-ical structure, for example, are to be understood as adaptations to that environment. In view of the thoroughly local and interactional character of the deployment of turns at talk in conversation (Sacks et al. 1974), grammatical structures – including within their scope discourse – should in the first instance be expected to be at least partially shaped by *interactional* considerations (Schegloff 1979a, 1996).

Third, in keeping with the foregoing, whereas for many linguists and other stu-dents of language, conversation is one type or genre of discourse, for me discourse is, in the first instance, one kind of product of conversation, or of talk-in-interaction more generally. How so? On the face of it, this claim is a puzzle.

Briefly: the term "discourse" at present has a variety of uses. In contemporary cultural criticism, for example, one can speak of the "discourse of modernity" or "the dis-courses of power" or "feminist discourse"; indeed, I was tempted to begin the present sentence by referring to "the discourse of contemporary cultural criticism." In a more technical usage current among linguists, "discourse" is (as one colleague has put it) "simply a broad term that includes interactional talk, but also includes written es-says, advertisements, sermons, folktales, etc. With this view of 'discourse,' your char-acterization is hard to interpret." My point is meant to contrast with this fundamentally taxonomic usage.

The taxonomic usage reflects academic interests in discriminating and conceptual-izing a variety of genres, and the relationship of these genres is derived from their relative positioning in this conceptual mapping, not in the naturally occurring pro-cesses which might conceivably have engendered them. It is this contrast that my earlier point is meant to invoke. That point turns on what is both a broader and a narrower sense of "discourse," one which underlies these other usages (and is a common characteristic of the usages discussed in the *Oxford English Dictionary*), and that is the usage which contrasts "discourse" with single sentences. If one examines the usage of a term like "discourse analysis," for example, one rarely finds it invoked to deal with single sentences. "Discourse" regularly refers to extended, multisentence "texts." And (unlike "text") it originally had reference to *speech* or *talk*. Hence my point, which is that discourse – extended or multi-unit talk production – be understood processually, that is, as one sort of (contingent) product of conversation, rather than conversation being understood taxonomically, as simply one subtype of discourse.

In this view, extended stretches of "text" by a single speaker have as their source environment turns-at-talk in conversation, in which an extended stretch of text by a single speaker is the concerted product of a company of participants in interaction, as, for example, in a spate of storytelling (a "concerted product," to mention just one aspect of the matter, in its dependence on others withholding talk to allow a single speaker to extend it). A kind of virtual natural history of interactional genres and speech exchange systems may then be conceived of, which would track the disengagement of such sustained, multi-unit talk production by a single speaker from the interactional environment of conversation into settings such as religious ceremony, political speech making, prophetic invocation, philosophical disquisition, etc., and the development of writing then enables an explosion of yet further genres.

Discourse can, then, be a *contingent* product of participants in *ordinary* conversation; or it can be the *designed* product of a form of talk-in-interaction (e.g. what is dubbed in Sacks et al. 1974 a "speech-exchange system") which is some systematic *variant* or *transformation* of ordinary conversation – like the interview or the lecture, of which an extended discourse is a "natural" outcome. But, as noted above, I take *conversation* to be the foundational domain, and the point of departure in the naturalistic study of the grounds of discourse is the production of a multi-unit stretch of talk by a single speaker in a turn at talk which initially provides for a speaker having rights to a *single* turn-constructional unit (Sacks et al. 1974: 703).

So much for premises. The two themes on which I want to focus your attention are endemic to the organization of talk-in-interaction, and follow from these points of departure. The first concerns the centrality of action.

Among the most robust traditional anchors for the analysis of language beyond the level of syntax are orientations to information and truth. This position needs to be reconsidered. It is critical that the analysis of discourse incorporate attention not only to the propositional content and information distribution of discourse units, but also to the *actions* they are doing.[1] Especially (but not exclusively) in conversation, talk is constructed and is attended by its recipients for the action or actions which it may be doing. Even if we consider only declarative-type utterances, because there is no limit to the utterables which can be informative and/or true, the informativeness or truth of an utterance is, by itself, no warrant or grounds for having uttered it – or for having uttered it at a particular juncture in an occasion. There is virtually always an issue (for the *participants*, and accordingly for professional analysts) of what is getting *done* by its production in some particular here-and-now.

In order to make vivid the consequentiality for conversational participants of the *action* which an utterance is doing, quite apart from the information which it is conveying, I offer a condensed and partial analysis of one conversational fragment. I hope thereby to show at least one way that action can matter, and to indicate an order of analysis which inquiry must incorporate if this view of the inescapability of action is correct.

2   The Decisive Consequences of Action for the Constitution of Discourse

In the conversation between Debbie and Nick (who is her boyfriend Mark's roommate) which is reproduced in its entirety in the appendix to this chapter, a peculiarly insistent exchange develops which can serve to exemplify my theme:[2]

(1)   Debbie and Nick, 34-59

```
34  Debbie:   hhh Um:: u- guess what I've-(u-)wuz lookin' in the
35            paper:.-have you got your waterbed yet?
36  Nick:     Uh huh, it's really nice °too, I set it up
37  Debbie:   Oh rea:lly? ^Already?
38  Nick:     Mm hmm
39            (0.5)
40  Debbie:   Are you kidding?
41  Nick:     No, well I ordered it last (week)/(spring)
42            (0.5)
43  Debbie:   Oh- no but you h- you've got it already?
44  Nick:     Yeah h! hh=                     ((laughing))
45  Debbie:   =hhh [hh hh]                    ((laughing))
46  Nick:          [I just]said that
47  Debbie:   O::hh: hu[h, I couldn't be[lieve you c-
48  Nick:             [Oh (°it's just) [It'll sink in 'n two
49            day[s fr'm now (then  )((laugh))]
50  Debbie:     [          ((l a u g h ))       ] Oh no cuz I just
51            got- I saw an ad in the paper for a real discount
52            waterbed s' I w'z gonna tell you 'bout it=
53  Nick:     =No this is really, you (haven't seen) mine, you'll
54            really like it.
55  Debbie:   Ya:h. It's on a frame and everythi[ng?
56  Nick:                                       [Yeah
57  Debbie:   hh Uh (is) a raised frame?
58  Nick:     °mm hmm
59  Debbie:   How: ni::ce,
```

At a point which I will characterize in a moment (l. 35), Debbie asks Nick whether he has gotten his waterbed yet. He tells her that he has, and this is met with three rounds of questioning, challenging, or disbelief – to settle for preanalytic characterizations initially. First, (at l. 37) "Oh really? Already?" When Nick confirms, she asks again (l. 40), "Are you kidding?" "No," he says, and notes that it has been a while since he ordered the waterbed. And still again she asks (l. 43) "Oh no but you h-you've got it already?" Finally, Nick complains (l. 46) that he has already said so. What *is* going on here?

Debbie has asked a seemingly simple, informational question, and Nick has answered it. Now questioning of the sort which Debbie engages in here can be undertaken in conversation (among other uses) as a kind of harbinger of disagreement – sometimes verging on challenge, and one response to such a usage is a backdown by its recipient. Sometimes this is a backdown in the substance of what was said,[3] sometimes in the epistemic strength with which it was put forward.[4] If a first questioning does not get such a backdown, sometimes a second one does. But what kind of backdown is possibly in order *here*? If Nick has in fact taken possession of his waterbed, is he now to deny it? Is he to retreat to a position of uncertainty or supposition about the matter? What could Debbie be after?

It is also true that, in keeping with the peculiar interactional "style" of teasing and laughing which some Americans in their late teens and early twenties practice, Nick has been indulging himself in unrelieved "kidding around" in the earlier part of this conversation, and it is not implausible that, if the first of Debbie's responses was audibly "surprise," the second could be checking out whether this is not just more teasing by Nick. But then what is the *third* about (at l. 43)? And why the persistence of her stance? Why should this information come in for such scrutiny and doubting?

We can get some analytic leverage on what is going on here if we attend to these utterances not only as a matter of information transfer involving issues of truth and confidence and stances toward that information, but as *actions* in a course of action, constituting an interactional sequence of a recurrent form.

Begin by noting (at l. 34) Debbie's "guess what." This is a usage virtually dedicated to a particular type of action referred to in past work as a "pre-announcement" (Terasaki 1976). Announcements, or other prospective "tellings," face the familiar constraint that they generally should not be done to recipients who already know "the news." Pre-announcements and their responses – pre-announcement *sequences*, that is – allow a prospective teller and recipient to sort out together whether the "news" is already known, so that the telling or announcement can be withheld or squelched, if need be. Of course, the very doing of a pre-announcement displays its speaker's supposition that there is indeed news to tell, and to tell *as* news to *this* recipient. Still, one thing prospective tellers can do (and regularly *do* do) before telling is to *check* whether the news is already known. And among the recurrent response forms to such pre-announcements, two central types are the "go-ahead" type of response (such as, in response to "guess what," "what"), which forwards the sequence to its key action – announcing or telling – and the blocking type of response (for example, a claim of knowledge, such as "I heard"), which aims to forestall such telling.[5]

Often the pre-announcement provides clues about the news to be told (e.g. "Y'wanna know who I got stoned with a few weeks ago?," or "You'll never guess what your dad is looking at," Terasaki 1976: 27–8), the better to allow the recipient to recognize it, if it is already known, and to provide a context for understanding it and an interpretive key, if it is not already known. And here Debbie *does* provide such clues; "I was looking in the paper" (at ll. 34–5) intimates that what she has to tell is something that one can find (and that she *has* found) in the newspaper. And then (at l. 35), "have you got your waterbed yet?" So the thing to be told (about) has something to do with waterbeds, and Nick's possibly being in the market for a waterbed in particular.

So there is another constraint on Debbie's telling here, one which is not generic to "telling" in the way in which "already known-ness" is. Debbie has information to offer – information which is relevant to Nick only contingently. Offers and offer sequences too can take what we call "presequences," just as announcements can and do. With *pre*-offers, prospective offerers can try to assess whether what they have to offer is relevant to their recipients and may be welcomed by them, so as to not make offers which will be rejected, for example. What Debbie has to offer is information on a cheap waterbed or an especially desirable one, but her pre-offer is designed to find out whether such information is relevant to Nick – whether what will be offered will be relevant. That is what "Have you got your waterbed yet?" appears designed to do – it is an analyzable pre-offer.[6] As such, it too (like pre-announcements) takes among its alternative response types a go-ahead response, which forwards the sequence to an offer, or a blocking response, which declines to do so.

So when Debbie asks, "Have you got your waterbed yet?" she is not just asking for information; she awaits a go-ahead to the pre-offer, on which her offer of the information which she has come across in the newspaper has been made contingent. And when Nick responds affirmatively, he is not only confirming the proposition at issue – that he already *has* his waterbed; he is *blocking her* from going on to tell the information which she has seen in the newspaper.

And *this* is the proximate sequential and interactional context for Debbie's repeated questionings. The backdown which is relevant here concerns not the facticity of the presence of a waterbed, and not Nick's confidence in asserting it; and perhaps not even whether he is teasing. What is at issue is a backdown from the blocking response to the presequences. One form it could take is, "why?" – as in (starting at ll. 37–8) "Oh really? Already?" "Mm hmm, why." Or (at ll. 40–1), "Are you kidding?," "No, why." Or (at ll. 43–4), "Oh- no but you h- you've got it already?" "Yeah! Why."

As it happens, it appears that Nick has not caught this, and so he responds only at the level of information transmission.[7] When for the third time Debbie asks, "You've got it already?" he says, "Yeah, I just said that . . . It'll sink in 'n two days from now." That is, he just says it again – and more pointedly; he makes her out to be not too quick on the uptake; she'll get it eventually.[8]

But it is *he* who has apparently not gotten it. And it will be *we* who do not get it if we do not systematically distinguish what an utterance is *about* or what is it *saying*, on the one hand, from what it is *doing* on the other. Backing down from the one is quite different from backing down from the other. Attention will virtually always need to be paid to the issue "what is someone *doing* with some utterance? What action or actions are involved?" Because overwhelmingly actions *are* involved, they *are* oriented to by the participants both in constructing and in understanding the talk, and the discourse cannot be appropriately understood without reference to them – precisely because they *are* key to the participants' conduct.

It follows, of course, that the actions to which analysis needs to attend are *not* classes of action defined by the conceptual commitments of *professional discourse analysts* (as, for example, in any of the varieties of academic speech act theory), but those units and understandings of action which are indigenous to the *actors'* – the interactional participants' – worlds. Hence, the appearance in my account of actions like "pre-offer" or "pre-announcement," which figure in no speech act theory with which I am familiar, but exemplars of which are laced through and through ordinary conversation.

That is the first theme I want to put before you: how an action done by a speaker – *taken as an action* – has decisive consequences in shaping the trajectory of the talk's development. The second theme concerns how the *absence of an action* can have such consequences. But the absent action here is not that of the *speaker* of the discourse but rather of its recipient, and this forces on us in another way the issue of the *interactivity* of discourse production – its "co-construction," as it were.

3 The Decisive Consequences of the Absence of Action for the Construction of Discourse

It is over twenty years now since Charles Goodwin (1979, 1981) gave a convincing demonstration of how the final form of a sentence in ordinary conversation had to be understood as an interactional product. He showed that the speaker, finding one after another prospective hearer not properly aligned as an actual recipient (that is, not looking at him), reconstructed the utterance in progress – the sentence – so as to design it for the new candidate hearer to whom he had shifted his gaze. He showed the effects on the utterance of both the candidate recipients' conduct and the speaker's orientation to the several possible recipients – a feature we call recipient design. Goodwin's account served at the time (and still serves) as a compelling call for the inclusion of the hearer in what were purported to be speaker's processes, and for the inclusion of the nonvocal in purportedly vocal conduct. In a paper published the following year, Marjorie Goodwin (1980) provided another such demonstration, showing how a hearer's displayed uptake and assessment of a speaker's in-process talk shaped the final form which the utterance took.[9]

The general point here is that units such as the clause, sentence, turn, utterance, discourse – *all* are in principle *interactional* units. For it is not only that turns figure in the construction of sequences (by which I mean *action* sequences implemented through talk and other conduct). Sequences – and their projected, contingent alternative trajectories – figure in the construction of turns, and of the extended turns which we sometimes call discourse(s). In examining the following conversation, I want to explicate how the *sequence* which is being incipiently constructed figures in the production of what appears to be an extended spate of talk by a single speaker – a discourse of sorts:[10]

```
(2)   Marcia and Donny, stalled
      01              1+ rings
      02  Marcia:     Hello?
      03  Donny:      'lo Marcia,=
      04  Marcia:     Yea[:h        ]
      05  Donny:         =[('t's) D]onny.
      06  Marcia:     Hi Donny.
      07  Donny:      Guess what.hh
      08  Marcia:     What.
      09  Donny:      hh My ca:r is sta::lled.
      10              (0.2)
      11  Donny:      ('n) I'm up here in the Glen?
      12  Marcia:     Oh::.
      13              {(0.4)}
      14  Donny:      {hhh}
      15  Donny:      A:nd.hh
      16              (0.2)
      17  Donny:      I don' know if it's po:ssible, but {hhh}/(0.2)} see
      18              I haveta open up the ba:nk.hh
      19              (0.3)
      20  Donny:      a:t uh: (·) in Brentwood?hh=
      21  Marcia:     =Yeah:- en I know you want- (·) en I whoa- (·) en I
      22              would, but- except I've gotta leave in aybout five
      23              min(h)utes.[((hheh)
      24  Donny:                 [Okay then I gotta call somebody
```

```
25              else.right away.
26              (·)
27 Donny:      Okay?=
28 Marcia:     =Okay [Don   ]
29 Donny:            [Thanks] a lot.=Bye-.
30 Marcia:     Bye:.
```

The "discourse of sorts" which eventually gets produced here (at ll. 9, 11, 15, 17–18, and 20) could be rendered as follows:

> My car is stalled (and I'm up here in the Glen?), and I don't know if it's possible, but, see, I have to open up the bank at uh, in Brentwood?

Put this way, each component (e.g. each clause or phrase) appears to follow the one before it, although I have tried to capture (with punctuation in my text, and with prosody in my articulation of it on delivery in conference settings) the possibly parenthetical character of the second component, with consequent revised understanding of the relative organization of the components surrounding it. Now aside from the "Oh" interpolated by Marcia (at l. 12) in response to this element, all that I appear to have left out in this rendering of the talk is . . . *nothing* – that is, silences, some of them filled by audible in- and out-breaths. But, of course, these silences are *not* nothing. The something that they are – the something that each is – is given by its sequential context, and it is *that* which requires us to attend to the *actions* being done here . . . and *not* being done here. Then we can see that – and *how* – this is not a unitary discourse produced by a single participant; and we can see that and how some of its components follow not the components of talk which preceded them, but the silence which *followed* the talk component that preceded them. Thereby we can come to see that it is not just a hearer's uptake and actions which can enter into the shaping of a speaker's talk; it can be the *absence* of them which does so.

To begin then, the utterance at l. 7 should now be readily recognizable for the action which it is doing: it is (doing) a pre-announcement. It may be useful to be explicit about what is involved in making and sustaining such a claim. Virtually always at least two aspects of a bit of conduct – such as a unit of talk – figure in how it does what it does: its position and its composition (Schegloff 1992c: 1304–20). A sketch will have to suffice.

We have already noted that this formulaic utterance "Guess what" is virtually dedicated to doing pre-announcements, as are various extensions and variants of it, such as "Guess what I did today," "Guess where I went," "Guess who I saw," etc.[11] I should say that this account of composition is only rarely available; there are precious few configurations of talk that are so dedicated, and even those that are are contingent on their position. "Hello," said by an actor upon tripping over a prone body in a British film, is *not* a greeting, however much that formulaic expression might appear dedicated to doing that action.

And what is the *position* of this utterance? How is it to be characterized? It comes just after the opening – the telephone ring's summons and the recipient's response (ll. 1–2), and the exchange of greetings intertwined with the explication of the identities of the two participants (ll. 3–6). I can only mention here something that would inform the parties' conduct of the ensuing interaction, namely the rushed, charged, almost breathless quality of Donny's participation, embodied here in his pre-emptive self-identification at l. 5, rather than waiting to be recognized (Schegloff 1979b). It is a way of doing "urgency," and it is a part of the positioning of "Guess what." Another part is the possible absence here of the start of an exchange of "Howaryous," a highly recurrent next sequence type in conversations between familiars under many (though not all) circumstances (Schegloff 1986). In moving directly to "first topic" and the "reason for the call," Donny pre-empts "Howaryous" as well, and this further informs the position in which "Guess what" is done. This position and the utterance in it, then, contingently foreshadow not only a telling of some news; they adumbrate the *character* of that news as well – that is, as urgent (or in some other respect "charged").

The pre-announcement projects further talk by its speaker, contingent on the response of the recipient, and we have already said a bit about the fairly constrained set of response types by the recipient which it makes relevant: a go-ahead response (the "preferred" one in the terminology of conversation analysis),[12] a blocking response, a pre-emptive response or a heckle-version of one. In the data before us, the response (at l. 8) is a go-ahead. Once again, it may prove worthwhile to make analytically explicit the practices by which this is achieved (which provide the warrant for the analysis being proposed), if only in a sketched version of the position and composition involved.

The *position* (at l. 8) is the turn after a pre-announcement which has made a response to it relevant next. The *composition* is a common one for responses to pre-announcements of the "guess + question word" form (as well as the "y'know + question clause" form): returning the question word from the pre-announcement ("Guess what." "What." "Y'know where I went?" "Where.", etc.).[13]

With this response, Marcia both shows that she understands Donny's prior turn to have been a pre-announcement (thereby further grounding *our* analysis of it along these lines in the just preceding text), and she provides an appropriate response to it. And note that that is how Donny hears Marcia's response; for otherwise, her "what" could invite treatment as displaying some trouble in hearing or understanding. It is *not*, of course, doing that, and it is not heard that way. "What" displays an understanding of "Guess what" as a pre-announcement; and Donny's ensuing turn displays *his* understanding of *it* as a go-ahead response to a pre-announcement. Of course Donny's ensuing turn – the one at l. 9 – is in the first instance otherwise engaged, and that is what we turn to next.

The pre-announcement sequence having been completed with a go-ahead, what is Donny's next utterance doing?

Well, in the first instance, it seems clearly enough designed to deliver the projected news. Note well: that it is *conveying information* is one formulation; that it does so by an utterance designed to be a recognizable action – "*announcing*" or "*telling*" – is another. For, of course, information can be conveyed by utterances designed to do something else in the first instance and on the face of it. But this one is clearly enough *designed* to do "telling."[14]

But what are the design features that make that "clear?" I can only tick off a series of observations whose development would be pertinent to such an analysis. First, the utterance is in an assertion or declarative format. Second, it refers to a speaker-specific event (what Labov and Fanshel 1977: 62 called an "A-event").[15] Third, it is presented as a recent, indeed as a *current*, event (Donny says "My car *is* stalled"). Fourth, as a current, A-event, it is not otherwise accessible to the recipient (by definition, else it would be an "A–B-event"). There is undoubtedly more; and surely none of this may appear to be itself news. Still, if we are to get clear on how the actions which people do with talk "are" transparently what they "are," we will have to make analytically explicit how they are *constructed* to be transparently that (or *equivocally* that, for that matter), and how they may therefore be *recognizable* as transparently that (or equivocally that) – both to their recipients and (derivatively) to us as analysts.

It is not enough that there was a pre-announcement sequence with a go-ahead response. What follows is not *necessarily* an announcement; it will have to be constructed by its speaker as a recognizable, analyzable announcement, though its position after a pre-announcement sequence will potentiate such recognition. Once again, then: position *and* composition matter. So if discourse analysis takes the actions being done in the discourse as key to understanding its organization, this will be part of the job.

Anyway, just as *pre*-announcements make sequentially relevant a response from some restricted set of next actions, so do announcements or tellings. Among them (and again, I must be brief) are some form of *information uptake* (such as registering the new information as new, for example through the use of the "oh" which Heritage (1984a) termed a "change-of-state token," or alternatively registering it as having already been known after all), or some form of *assessment* of what has been told – as good, awful, interesting, discouraging, etc. And indeed, these forms of action both regularly occur in the immediate sequential context of announcements. Not here, however.

It now becomes pertinent for us to note that what follows this bit of news – "My car is stalled" – is silence, at l. 10. Only two-tenths of a second of silence to be sure; still, it is a silence after the prior speaker has produced a possibly complete utterance, one which makes relevant a response from its recipient; indeed, as noted, one which makes relevant quite specific types of response. Although *everyone* is silent (which silence as a state requires), someone in particular is "relevantly not talking," and that is Marcia. For Donny has produced a possibly complete turn, one which implicates some responsive action next – by *Marcia*. Absence of talk is then, in the first instance, attributable to Marcia. So although the effect of her silence is that no action seems to get done, what she is specifically and relevantly "not doing" is registering some uptake of what has been told, and/or some assessment of it – for it is these which Donny's announcement has made conditionally relevant.

At least that is *some* of what she is not doing. For a bit of talk can do more than one action. And some sorts of actions regularly serve as the vehicle or instrument by which *other* actions are done – announcements or tellings prominent among them (as are "questions" and "assessments"). In this case, I suggest, "My car is stalled" is not only an announcement, it is as well a possible complaint.[16]

The features which provided for this utterance as a possible "announcement" do not, of course, analyze its status as a possible "complaint." Here again I must be brief. In a variety of contexts it appears that formulating a state of affairs or an event as an absence, as a failure, as a *non*occurrence is a way of constructing a recognizable complaint. And although the utterance under examination here is not as distinct an embodiment of such a usage in its "surface" realization as many others (for example, "You didn't get an ice cream sandwich," analyzed in Schegloff 1988c: 118–31), "stalled" *is* used to mean "engine will not start or run," i.e. it does formulate a failure.

Again, a complaint or report of trouble makes *different* types of response relevant next than does an announcement. Among such sequentially implicated next turns to complaints can be (depending on the character and target of the complaint or reported trouble) such ones as a sympathy expression, apology, excuse or account, agreement and co-complaint or disagreement and rejection, and – perhaps most relevant here – a remedy or help, or the offer of a remedy or help.[17] So the silence at l. 10 is to be understood not only for its withholding of news uptake and assessment, but for its withholding – by Marcia – of an offer to help. Though the silence by definition has no talk, *it is as fully fledged an event in the conversation as any utterance, and as consequential for the ensuing talk.* The talk which follows is properly understood as following *not* the utterance "My car is stalled," *not* the information which that utterance conveys, and *not* the announcement which that utterance embodies or the complaint which that announcement implements; rather, it follows the *silence* following that announcement/complaint, in which its "preferred" response (in the technical conversation analytic sense of that term)[18] is audibly and analyzably withheld.

Note well: not every silence in conversation can be accorded an analysis along these lines. Silences get their interactional import from their sequential context (their "position"). A silence developing where an utterance has not been brought to possible completion is generally heard *not* as the interlocutor's, but as a pause in the continuing turn of the one who was talking (Sacks et al. 1974: 715). And not all silences following a turn's possible completion are equivalent either: the silence following a question has a different import and consequence than one following an answer, or one following receipt of an answer. *That* something is missing, and *what* something is missing, should not simply be asserted; both need to be analytically grounded, based on structural analyses of relevant empirical materials. (This is so not only when silence develops, but at any apparent juncture in the talk where the analyst is drawn to introduce claims about what is "missing.")

Were sufficient space available, it would repay the effort to continue tracking in detail the development of this interaction, the whole of which lasts barely 18 seconds. A selective set of observations will have to suffice, focusing on the recurrent re-entries of Donny in the aftermath of "My car is stalled":

```
(3)  Marcia and Donny, stalled (partial)
     09  Donny:    hh My ca:r is sta::lled.
     10            (0.2)
     11  Donny:    ('n) I'm up here in the Glen?
     12  Marcia:   Oh::.
     13            {(0.4)}
     14  Donny:    {hhh}
     15  Donny:    A:nd.hh
     16            (0.2)
     17  Donny:    I don' know if it's po:ssible, but {hhh}/(0.2)} see
     18            I haveta open up the ba:nk.hh
     19            (0.3)
     20  Donny:    a:t uh: (·) in Brentwood?hh=
     21  Marcia:   =Yeah:- en I know you want- (·) en I whou- (·) en I
     22            would, but- except I've gotta leave in aybout five
     23            min(h)utes.[(hheh)
```

Note to begin with that each of these re-entries (at ll. 11, 15, 17, and 20) is constructed by Donny as an increment to the earlier talk, with the series of "turns-so-far" laced with silences, at many of which intervention from Marcia with an offer of help might be relevant. This incrementally constructed discourse is a multiply renewed effort (or series of efforts) to elicit help from Marcia, without ever requesting it (as we say in the vernacular) explicitly.

First, although we lack independent ethnographic knowledge, "'n I'm up here in the Glen" appears designed to reassure Marcia of Donny's proximity, and thereby to mitigate the costs or difficulty of helping for Marcia. Note further that it is delivered as a sort of parenthetical insert,[19] projecting a further continuation. In making itself out to be a continuation of what preceded (note that it begins – at l. 11 – with a compressed conjunction), it treats what preceded as having not been complete, and the silence which it breaks as having been not a postcompletion withholding of response, but a pause in the continuing production on an ongoing turn. That something might have been missing is thereby suppressed or camouflaged.[20]

The projection of continuation carried by the parenthetical informing is echoed and renewed (after Marcia's receipt of the informing, once again with no response to the complaint) by a substantial, audible (pretalk) in-breath (l. 14), and an isolated continuation marker "A:nd" (l. 15), after which another silence is allowed to materialize (l. 16), with provision already made that further talk by Donny (should it be necessary) will be a further continuation of the utterance-in-progress. It turns out to be necessary.

With "I don't know if it's possible, but" Donny adumbrates the conventional grounds of rejection of requests (cf. n. 16 above), and thereby comes to the very verge of doing an outright request himself, for this usage virtually serves as a form of marking an utterance or an incipient utterance as a request. It serves, then, as a form of *pre*request, a form cognate with the earlier-mentioned pre-announcement and pre-offer. But unlike those forms, the preferred response to a prerequest does not promote the sequence to doing the request; it pre-empts the request with an offer (Schegloff 1979b: 49, 1990: 61). So here again, as in the initial installment of this now-extended turn, Donny is providing for help to be offered without requesting it explicitly, but by now the utterance has become not a complaint, but a prerequest. That is, as the turn is extended, the action which it is analyzably doing can be – and here is – transformed.

At just the point at which the request itself would be specified, and thereby brought to realization, Donny self-interrupts (with "See" at l. 17), and suppresses the clearly projected request. In its place, "I haveta open up the bank" underscores both the urgency and the potential costs of failure. Here again, for the first time since "My car is stalled," the utterance is brought to possible completion both grammatically and prosodically (cf. Ford and Thompson 1996), and once again there is no uptake or response from Marcia. Once again Donny breaks the silence (as he did at l. 11), again with talk built as an increment to the prior – otherwise apparently completed – talk, again with a place reference delivered with upward intonation, in the manner of a try-marked recognitional reference (Sacks and Schegloff 1979) for a place, inviting its recipient's claim of recognition, and whatever other response might be forthcoming to this by now elaborately constructed, multiply laminated utterance.

Each of these increments comes after, and is analyzably directed to, the *absence of any response to the complaint or (later) to the prerequest* which Donny had presented as the reason for his call. When she eventually responds, Marcia declines to offer help, without ever saying "no." But her response does display (l. 21) her understanding that a solicitation of help was being made relevant ("en I know you want-") and that she would ordinarily comply ("en I would,"), but for a disabling circumstance.

Donny's "discourse of sorts," with the presentation of which this discussion began, has now been analyzed into the components from which it was assembled through a series of sequential and interactional contingencies, and its elaborate pursuit of help anatomized as the proposed underlying action. Here is one use of such analytic and terminological tools as the "parts" of an "adjacency pair," which are sometimes bemoaned as merely jargon. It is the analysis of "My car is stalled" as a possible announcement (a first pair part which makes one of a set of potential second pair parts relevant next), and consultation of other empirical announcement sequences (to establish what kinds of utterances serve as second pair parts which satisfy these sequence-organizational constraints), which grounds claims about what is missing in the following silence. It is analysis of that utterance as also a possible complaint (another type of first pair part), and examination of complaint sequences, that provides for the possible relevance next of the variety of responsive turn types proposed above, and characterizations of them as preferred or dispreferred, and underwrites further claims about what might be audibly missing. Without some such analytic resource (as well as analytic resources bearing on turn organization such as "possible completion" and further talk as either new "turn-constructional unit" or "increment" to the prior unit), it is easy for a *post hoc* observer (unlike an *in situ* participant) to overlook that an action is missing – precisely because the prior speaker (here Donny) may talk in such a manner as covers over and obscures that missingness, and makes it appear a mere pause in an ongoing utterance in progress. That action by the speaker, together with our vernacular inclination to normalize and naturalize the events in the interactional stream, can give the air of inevitability to what ends up having transpired. Stopping to say of "My car is stalled" that it is a possibly complete turn that is a first pair part, and what type or types of first pair part, prompts thinking explicitly about the possibly relevant second pair parts, prompts looking for them, and finding them "missing" if they are not there. The relevant "missing" is, of course, "missing for the participants," and one must then go back to the data to find evidence of an orientation to something being awry for the participants.

The point of this analysis, however, has been that not only is action a relevant facet and upshot of the talk, but that *actions by other than the speaker are relevant to understanding a speaker's construction of discourse*; and, relatedly, that the absence of actions by recipient – *the absence of actions made relevant by the speaker's prior talk, the speaker's turn-so-far* – may be crucial to understanding the speaker's further construction of the discourse.

This, then, is my second theme: discourse involves not just action, but action in *inter*action, and the consequential eventfulness of its absence. Once again, then, "co-construction" may be most critical to our analysis of discourse when one of the participants is *not* producing talk – or doing anything else visible or hearable. For the very *production* of a discourse may be one contingent response by a prior speaker to the absence of a response by a co-participant to an apparently completed, action-implementing turn constructional unit.

This logic – an interactional or sociologic, if you will – is at work throughout talk-in-interaction. To get at it, information will not suffice. It is the *action* import of utterances and not just what they are about or what they impart – the action import or *non*action import – which regularly drives the interactional construction of extended spates of talk, or discourses.

APPENDIX: DEBBIE AND NICK

```
01                    ((ring ring))
02                    ((click/pick-up))
03    Nick:           H'llo
04    Debbie:         hh- 'z <Who's this,
05                    (0.2)
06    Debbie:         This'z Debbie
07                    (0.3)
08    Nick:           Who's this.
09    Debbie:         This'z Debbie
10    Nick:           This is >the Los Angeles Poli[ce<
11    Debbie:                                      [Nno:=
11a                   =[(((Laugh))
12    Nick:           =[ ha ha [ha
13    Debbie:                  [Hi Nicky how are ya.
14    Nick:           O:kay
15    Debbie:         hh u- Did Mark go to Ohio?
16    Nick:           Ohio?
17    Debbie:         Uh huh¿
18    Nick:           I dunno did he?
19    Debbie:         hh I: dunn[o::]
20    Nick:                     [ ha]ha
21    Debbie:         Ny-
22    Nick:           Yeah I think he's (com-)/(still (  )-
23                    when's Mark come back, Sunday¿ ((off phone))
24                    (0.8)
25    Nick:           Yeah I think he's comin back Sunday=
26    Debbie:         =Tomorrow¿ Is Rich gonna go get 'im?
27                    (0.2)
28    Nick:           I guess
29    Debbie:         Or is he gonna ca:ll¿
30                    (0.8)
31    Nick:           h! (h)I du(h)nno he didn't tell me=
32    Debbie:         =Oh:: you have nothin' t'do with it
33    Nick:           (n)ha ha
34    Debbie:         hhh Um:: u- guess what I've-(u-)wuz lookin' in the
35                    paper:.-have you got your waterbed yet?
36    Nick:           Uh huh, it's really nice °too, I set it up
37    Debbie:         Oh rea:lly? ^Already?
38    Nick:           Mm hmm
39                    (0.5)
40    Debbie:         Are you kidding?
```

```
41   Nick:     No, well I ordered it last (week)/(spring)
42             (0.5)
43   Debbie:   Oh- no but you h- you've got it already?
44   Nick:     Yeah h! hh=                    ((laughing))
45   Debbie:   =hhh [hh  hh]                  ((laughing))
46   Nick:          [I just] said that
47   Debbie:   O::hh: hu[h, I couldn't be[lieve you c-
48   Nick:              [Oh (°it's just)[It'll sink in 'n two
49             day[s fr'm now (then  ) ((laugh))]
50   Debbie:      [          (( l a u g h ))     ] Oh no cuz I just
51             got- I saw an ad in the paper for a real discount
52             waterbed s' I w'z gonna tell you 'bout it=
53   Nick:     =No this is really, you (haven't seen) mine, you'll
54             really like it.
55   Debbie:   Ya:h. It's on a frame and everythi[ng?
56   Nick:                                       [Yeah
57   Debbie:   hh Uh (is) a raised frame?
58   Nick:     °mm hmm
59   Debbie:   How: ni::ce, Whadja do with Mark's cou:ch,
60             (0.5)
61   Nick:     P(h)ut it out in the cottage,
62             (0.2)
63   Nick:     goddam thing weighed about two th(h)ousand
64             pound[s
65   Debbie:        [mn:Yea::h
66             I'll be[:t
67   Nick:            [ah
68             (0.2)
69   Debbie:   Rea:lly
70             (0.3)
71   Debbie:   hh O:kay,
72             (·)
73   Debbie:   Well (0.8) mmtch! I guess I'll talk tuh Mark later
74             then.hh
75   Nick:     Yeah I guess yo[u will. [eh heh huh huh huh [huh
76   Debbie:                  [ hhh    [ W e : l l : -       [eh heh
77             hh that that: (·) could be debatable too I dunno
78             (0.2)
79   Debbie:   Bu:t hh so um: hh=
80   Nick:     =So (h!) um [uh [let's see my name's Debbie=
81   Debbie:               [hh [um
82   Nick:     =[I don't ((laugh))
83   Debbie:   =[ ((laugh))
84   Debbie:   hhh! Okay I'll see you later Nick=
85   Nick:     =Okay
86   Debbie:   Buh bye
87   Nick:     Bye bye
88             ((phone hung up))
89             ((click))
```

NOTES

This chapter is a slightly revised version of a paper first published in the journal *Research on Language and Social Interaction*, 28.3: 185–211, 1995. That publication was an adaptation of part of a larger paper ("Issues of relevance for discourse analysis: contingency in action, interaction and co-participant context") first prepared for a conference, "Burning Issues in Discourse Analysis," organized by Donia Scott and Eduard Hovy, sponsored by NATO, convened in Maratea, Italy, April 1993, and published in E. H. Hovy and D. Scott (eds), *Computational and Conversational Discourse: Burning Issues – An Interdisciplinary Account* (Heidelberg: Springer Verlag, 1996), pp. 3–38. In the larger paper there is other material of interest to discourse analysts, including a methodological appendix contrasting conversation-analytic and experimental/computational approaches to discourse – material which could not be accommodated within the space constraint of the present volume, but which may be of interest to its readers. My title alludes to two earlier papers on the theme "Discourse as an interactional achievement" (Schegloff 1982, 1987, 1988b). My thanks to John Heritage, Sally Jacoby, and Sandra Thompson for helpful comments on earlier drafts of the present effort.

1   As will become clear below, I do not mean here to be invoking speech act theory, whose ability to deal with real ordinary discourse is subject to question, but that is another story (cf. Schegloff, 1988a, 1992a, 1992b: xxiv–xxvii).

2   Readers are invited to access the audio of the data extracts in this paper in a format suitable for most platforms on my home page, which can be addressed at: <http://www.sscnet.ucla.edu/soc/faculty/schegloff/action/>. Should this web

page cease to be available, readers should contact me directly or search the California Digital Library at: <http://www.cdlib.org>.

3   For example:

```
A:  Is Al here?
B:  Yeah
    (0.?)
C:  He is?
B:  Well he was.  ←
```

4   For example, in the following fragment from a conversation in a used furniture store (US, 27:28–28:01), Mike is angling to buy (or be given) Vic's aquarium when Rich intervenes with a challenge to Vic's ownership of it (at line a). Note the backdowns in epistemic strength at lines (c) and (e) in response to Vic's questionings at lines (b) and (d) respectively – first from assertion to assertion plus tag question, and then to fully interrogative construction. (Note finally that in the end Vic does disagree with Rich's claim, and rejects his challenge.)

```
  MIK:  Wanna get some-
        wannuh buy some fish?
  RIC:  Ihhh ts-t
  VIC:  Fi:sh,
  MIK:  You have a tank I
        like tuh tuh- I-I
        [like-
  VIC:  [Yeh I gotta fa:wty::
        I hadda fawtuy? a
        fifty, enna twu[nny::
        en two ten::s,
  MIK:              [Wut-
        Wuddiyuh doing wit
        [dem. Wuh-
a RIC:              [But
        those were uh:::
a       [Alex's tanks.
  VIC:  [enna fi:ve.
```

```
   b  VIC:  Hah?
   c  RIC:  Those'r Alex's tanks
             weren't they?
   d  VIC:  Pondn' me?
   e  RIC:  Weren't- didn' they
             belong tuh Al[ex?
      VIC:              [No:
             Alex ha(s) no tanks
             Alex is tryintuh buy
             my tank.
```

5 For a more general treatment, cf.
   Terasaki (1976); Schegloff (1990).
   For an instance with both – indeed,
   simultaneous – go-ahead and
   blocking responses, see Schegloff
   (1995).

6 Among the design features which
   make it so analyzable is the negative
   polarity item "yet," which displays
   its speaker's orientation to a "no"
   answer, and builds in a preference
   for that sort of response (note that
   "yet" is replaced by "already" after
   Nick's affirmative response). The
   placement of the pre-offer after the
   pre-announcement is a way of
   showing the former to be in the
   further service of the latter, and part
   of the same "project." For a formally
   similar series of sequences, see the
   data excerpt in n. 14 below, where
   positioning "Didjer mom tell you
   I called the other day?" after
   "Wouldju do me a favor?" puts
   it under the jurisdiction of the
   projected request sequence, and
   in pursuit of that project.

7 It is possible, of course, that he *has*
   caught it, but prefers not to hear of
   the better buy he could have had,
   having just taken possession of, and
   pride in, his new acquisition.

8 Let me just mention without
   elaboration that Debbie does find a
   way of conveying what she saw in
   the newspaper in spite of it all,
   namely, in the questions she
   eventually asks about Nick's

waterbed – specific questions (about
the bed being on a frame, on a raised
frame, etc.: cf. ll. 55–7), almost
certainly prompted by what she saw
in the paper.

9 Others have contributed to this theme
   as well. I leave with a mere mention
   Lerner's work (1987, 1991, 1996),
   pursuing several observations by
   Sacks (1992: I, 144–7 *et passim*; 1992: II,
   57–60 *et passim*), on "collaboratives,"
   in which two or more speakers
   collaborate in producing a turn, in the
   sense that each actually articulates
   part of it. See also Schegloff (1982,
   1987); Mandelbaum (1987, 1989); and
   in a somewhat different style of work,
   Erickson (1992) and the papers in
   Duranti and Brenneis (1986).

10 The following discussion documents
   another point as well. A number of
   papers (e.g. Jefferson and Schenkein
   1978; Schegloff 1980, 1988c, 1990)
   describe various ways in which
   sequences get expanded as the vehicle
   for interactionally working out some
   course of action between parties to
   talk-in-interaction. Sequence
   expansion is embodied in the number
   of turns composing the trajectory of
   the sequence from start to closure.
   But the amount of talk in a sequence
   can increase in ways other than
   expansion in its sequence structure.
   Among these is expansion of the
   component turns that make up the
   sequence. (Cf. Zimmerman 1984:
   219–20 and the discussion in
   Schegloff 1991: 62–3 concerning
   different formats of citizen complaint
   calls to the police.) Most commonly it
   is the second part of an adjacency-
   pair-based sequence which gets this
   sort of elaboration, as when a
   question gets a story or other
   elaborated response as its answer.
   There may then still be a "simple,"
   unexpanded (or minimally expanded)
   sequence structure of question/

answer, or question/ answer/receipt, with the second of these parts being quite a lengthy "discourse unit." "Turn expansion" may then stand as a contrast or alternative to sequence expansion, rather than in a subsuming or subsumed relationship to it (compare Schegloff 1982: 71–2). In the data examined in the next portion of the text, the discourse or turn expansion occupies not the second part position in the sequence, but the first.

11 Cf. Terasaki (1976). Note that such utterances are neither designed nor heard as commands or invitations to guess, i.e. to venture a try at what their speaker means to tell, though hecklers may heckle by so guessing (though I must say that I have seen very few empirical instances of this). On the other hand, some recipients of pre-announcements who know – or think they know – what the pre-announcer has in mind to tell may not simply block the telling by asserting that they know; they may *show* that they know by pre-empting the telling themselves.

12 Cf. for example Heritage (1984b: 265–92); Levinson (1983: 332–56); Pomerantz (1984); Sacks (1987[1973]); Schegloff (1988d: 442–57).

13 Again, cf. Teraski (1976) for a range of exemplars; Schegloff (1988a).

14 See, for example, Schegloff (1990: 63, n. 6) for a discussion of the same bit of information first being conveyed in an utterance designed to do something else, and immediately thereafter done as a "telling" at arrows (a) and (b) respectively in the following exchange:

```
B:   But- (1.0) Wouldju do me
     a favor? heheh
J:   e(hh) depends on the
     favor::, go ahead,
```

```
B:   Didjer mom tell you I
     called the other day? ← a
J:   No she didn't.
     (0.5)
B:   Well I called. (·) [hhh] ←
J:                      [Uhuh]
```

15 By this they refer to "representations of some state of affairs . . . drawn from the biography of the speaker: these are A-events, that is, known to A and not necessarily to B" (Labov and Fanshel 1977: 62).

16 Alternatively, it could be characterized as a possible troubles telling (cf. Jefferson 1988; Jefferson and Lee 1981) or a prerequest (see below), though I cannot here take up the differences between these formulations, which in any case are not material to the issues I am presently concerned with.

17 Drew (1984: 137–9 *et passim*) describes the use of reportings which leave it to the recipient to extract the upshot and the consequent appropriate response. He addresses himself specifically to the declining of invitations by reporting incapacitating circumstances. His materials share with the present data the feature that a "dispreferred" action is circumlocuted by the use of a simple reporting of "the facts" – there declining invitations, here requesting a service.

18 Cf. n. 12.

19 For recent treatments of parenthetical prosody from a variety of approaches see the papers by Local (1992) and Uhmann (1992).

20 On the use of additional increments to otherwise possibly completed turns after developing silences portend incipient disagreement or rejection, see Ford (1993).

REFERENCES

Drew, P. (1984). Speakers' reportings in invitation sequences. In J. M. Atkinson and J. C. Heritage (eds), *Structures of Social Action* (pp. 152–64). Cambridge: Cambridge University Press.

Duranti, A. and Brenneis, D. (eds) (1986). Special issue on "The audience as co-author." *Text*, 6(3).

Erickson, F. (1992). They know all the lines: rhythmic organization and contextualization in a conversational listing routine. In P. Auer and A. diLuzio (eds), *The Contextualization of Language* (pp. 365–97). Amsterdam: John Benjamins.

Ford, C. (1993). *Grammar in Interaction: Adverbial Clauses in American English.* Cambridge: Cambridge University Press.

Ford, C. and Thompson, S. A. (1996). Interactional units in conversation: syntactic, intonational and pragmatic resources for the management of turns. In E. Ochs, E. A. Schegloff, and S. A. Thompson (eds), *Interaction and Grammar* (pp. 138–84). Cambridge: Cambridge University Press.

Goodwin, C. (1979). The interactive construction of a sentence in natural conversation. In G. Psathas (ed.), *Everyday Language: Studies in Ethnomethodology* (pp. 97–121). New York: Irvington.

Goodwin, C. (1981). *Conversational Organization.* New York: Academic Press.

Goodwin, M. H. (1980). Processes of mutual monitoring implicated in the production of description sequences. *Sociological Inquiry*, 50, 303–17.

Heritage, J. C. (1984a). A change-of-state token and aspects of its sequential placement. In J. M. Atkinson and J. C. Heritage (eds), *Structures of Social Action* (pp. 299–345). Cambridge: Cambridge University Press.

Heritage, J. C. (1984b). *Garfinkel and Ethnomethodology.* Oxford: Polity.

Jefferson, G. (1988). On the sequential organization of troubles-talk in ordinary conversation. *Social Problems*, 35(4), 418–41.

Jefferson, G. and Lee, J. R. L. (1981). The rejection of advice: managing the problematic convergence of a "troubles-telling" and a "service encounter." *Journal of Pragmatics*, 5, 399–422.

Jefferson, G. and Schenkein, J. (1978). Some sequential negotiations in conversation: unexpanded and expanded versions of projected action sequences. In J. Schenkein (ed.), *Studies in the Organization of Conversational Interaction* (pp. 155–72). New York: Academic Press.

Labov, W. and Fanshel, D. (1977). *Therapeutic Discourse.* New York: Academic Press.

Lerner, G. H. (1987). Collaborative turn sequences: sentence construction and social action. Unpublished PhD dissertation, University of California, Irvine.

Lerner, G. H. (1991). On the syntax of sentences-in-progress. *Language in Society*, 20, 441–58.

Lerner, G. H. (1996). On the "semi-permeable" character of grammatical units in conversation: conditional entry into the turn space of another speaker. In E. Ochs, E. A. Schegloff, and S. A. Thompson (eds), *Interaction and Grammar* (pp. 238–76). Cambridge: Cambridge University Press.

Levinson, S. (1983). *Pragmatics.* Cambridge: Cambridge University Press.

Local, J. (1992). Continuing and restarting. In P. Auer and A. diLuzio (eds), *The Contextualization of Language* (pp. 273–96). Amsterdam: John Benjamins.

Mandelbaum, J. (1987). Couples sharing stories. *Communication Quarterly*, 35(2), 144–70.

Mandelbaum, J. (1989). Interpersonal activities in conversational storytelling. *Western Journal of Speech Communication*, 53(2), 114–26.

Pomerantz, A. (1984). Agreeing and disagreeing with assessments: some features of preferred/dispreferred turn shapes. In J. M. Atkinson and J. C. Heritage (eds), *Structures of Social Action: Studies in Conversation Analysis* (pp. 57–101). Cambridge: Cambridge University Press.

Sacks, H. (1987[1973]). On the preferences for agreement and contiguity in sequences in conversation. In G. Button and J. R. E. Lee (eds), *Talk and Social Organization* (pp. 54–69). Clevedon: Multilingual Matters.

Sacks, H. (1992). *Lectures on Conversation*. Vols 1 and 2. Ed. G. Jefferson, intro. E. A. Schegloff. Oxford: Blackwell.

Sacks, H. and Schegloff, E. A. (1979). Two preferences in the organization of reference to persons in conversation and their interaction. In G. Psathas (ed.), *Everyday Language: Studies in Ethnomethodology* (pp. 15–21). New York: Irvington.

Sacks, H., Schegloff, E. A., and Jefferson, G. (1974). A simplest systematics for the organization of turn-taking for conversation. *Language*, 50, 696–735.

Schegloff, E. A. (1979a). The relevance of repair for syntax-for-conversation. In T. Givón (ed.), *Syntax and Semantics 12: Discourse and Syntax* (pp. 261–88). New York: Academic Press.

Schegloff, E. A. (1979b). Identification and recognition in telephone openings. In G. Psathas (ed.), *Everyday Language: Studies in Ethnomethodology* (pp. 23–78). New York: Irvington.

Schegloff, E. A. (1980). Preliminaries to preliminaries: "Can I ask you a question?" *Sociological Inquiry*, 50, 104–52.

Schegloff, E. A. (1982). Discourse as an interactional achievement: some uses of "uh huh" and other things that come between sentences. In D. Tannen (ed.), *Georgetown University Roundtable on Languages and Linguistics* (pp. 71–93). Washington, D.C.: Georgetown University Press.

Schegloff, E. A. (1986). The routine as achievement. *Human Studies*, 9, 111–51.

Schegloff, E. A. (1987). Analyzing single episodes of interaction: an exercise in conversation analysis. *Social Psychology Quarterly*, 50(2), 101–14.

Schegloff, E. A. (1988a). Presequences and indirection: applying speech act theory to ordinary conversation. *Journal of Pragmatics*, 12, 55–62.

Schegloff, E. A. (1988b). Discourse as an interactional achievement II: an exercise in conversation analysis. In D. Tannen (ed.), *Linguistics in Context: Connecting Observation and Understanding* (pp. 135–58). Norwood, N.J.: Ablex.

Schegloff, E. A. (1988c). Goffman and the analysis of conversation. In P. Drew and A. Wootton (eds), *Erving Goffman: Exploring the Interaction Order* (pp. 89–135). Cambridge: Polity.

Schegloff, E. A. (1988d). On an actual virtual servo-mechanism for guessing bad news: a single case conjecture. *Social Problems*, 35(4), 442–57.

Schegloff, E. A. (1989). Reflections on language, development, and the interactional character of talk-in-interaction. In M. Bornstein and J. S. Bruner (eds), *Interaction in Human Development* (pp. 139–53). Hillsdale, N.J.: Lawrence Erlbaum.

Schegloff, E. A. (1990). On the organization of sequences as a source of "coherence" in talk-in-interaction. In B. Dorval (ed.), *Conversational Organization and its Development* (pp. 51–77). Norwood, N.J.: Ablex.

Schegloff, E. A. (1991). Reflections on talk and social structure. In D. Boden and D. H. Zimmerman (eds), *Talk and Social Structure* (pp. 44–70). Cambridge: Cambridge University Press.

Schegloff, E. A. (1992a). To Searle on conversation: a note in return. In J. R. Searle et al., *(On) Searle on Conversation* (pp. 113–28). Amsterdam and Philadelphia: John Benjamins.

Schegloff, E. A. (1992b). Introduction. In G. Jefferson (ed.), *Harvey Sacks: Lectures on Conversation*, vol. 1 (pp. ix–lxii). (Oxford: Blackwell).

Schegloff, E. A. (1992c). Repair after next turn: the last structurally provided defense of intersubjectivity in conversation. *American Journal of Sociology*, 97(5), 1295–345.

Schegloff, E. A. (1995). Parties and talking together: two ways in which numbers are significant for talk-in-interaction. In P. ten Have and G. Psathas (eds), *Situated Order: Studies in Social Organization and Embodied Activities* (pp. 31–42). Washington, D.C.: University Press of America.

Schegloff, E. A. (1996). Turn organization: one intersection of grammar and interaction. In E. Ochs, E. A. Schegloff, and S. Thompson (eds), *Interaction and Grammar* (pp. 52–133). Cambridge: Cambridge University Press.

Shannon, C. and Weaver, W. (1949). *The Mathematical Theory of Communication*. Urbana: University of Illinois Press.

Terasaki, A. (1976). Pre-announcement sequences in conversation. *Social Science Working Paper 99*, School of Social Sciences, Irvine, California.

Uhmann, S. (1992). Contextualizing relevance: on some forms and functions of speech rate changes in everyday conversation. In P. Auer and A. diLuzio (eds), *The Contextualization of Language* (pp. 297–336). Amsterdam: John Benjamins.

Zimmerman, D. H. (1984). Talk and its occasion: the case of calling the police. In D. Schiffrin (ed.), *Georgetown University Round Table on Languages and Linguistics 1984* (pp. 210–28). Washington, D.C.: Georgetown University Press.

13 Discourse and Interaction

MONICA HELLER

0 Introduction

When the editors of this volume first asked me for a contribution, they proposed the title "The interactional analysis of discourse". However, it seemed to me that that title revealed but one perspective on a historical, intellectual relationship among approaches to the study of language practices which is in fact multifaceted. Historically, I think it is fair to say that a variety of disciplines (notably social psychology and sociology, later linguistic anthropology and sociolinguistics) undertook the study of social inter-action in order to understand how people construct the world around them. In this perspective, it has not necessarily been the case that the object of analysis has been understood or constructed as "discourse". However, the notion of "discourse" has become increasingly important to this endeavor, as it has become clear that the specifics of linguistic practices are linked to more broadly shared, and ideologically framed, ways of using language. At the same time, the study of discourse has increasingly come to include the study of the conditions of production of discourse (whatever its form), and hence to draw on analyses of interactions. It is just as useful to talk about the discourse analysis of interactions as it is to talk about the interactional analysis of discourse. As a result, what I will focus on in this chapter is a variety of facets of the relationship between the two (and I have changed the title in order to reflect this attempt to place the one in relation to the other, although I could just as easily have called it "Interaction and discourse"). The common thread nonetheless remains the same: what we can learn by understanding what goes on in interactions as the production of discourse.

What we have thought we can learn has the following major threads: (1) the nature of the interactional, discursive mechanics of the social construction of reality, and, in particular, what dimensions of these mechanics are universal and what are culturally, socially, or historically contingent or even specific; (2) the nature of the relationship between those mechanics and the conditions of their existence. Put differently, our goals have been to explore the nature of discourse in interaction itself as a way of understanding how we construct social reality, and to explain what we understand to be the nature of discourse in terms of the (local or elsewhere, or, to use Mehan's

(1987) terms, proximal or distal) social, political, and economic conditions of discursive production. At the same time, once the question of that relationship between discourse and conditions of discursive production is posed, it is no longer clear what it is that affects what, and our focus shifts to approaching discourse itself as a form of social action.

I will treat each one of these threads in turn, beginning with the issue of examining discourse in interaction as a way of discovering how social reality is constructed. Here it is important to situate this concern (how is social reality constructed?), which had long been expressed in a variety of ways within the disciplines of philosophy, social psychology (principally through the work of symbolic interactionists), sociology, and anthropology, in the context of new interests in focusing on the structure and function of talk. These new interests can be in part explained through reactions against universalist nonempirical tendencies in linguistic and social theory, in part perhaps simply through the availability of the tape recorder as a data collection device for fieldwork. In any case, what is central here is a combination of concerns rooted in the emerging disciplines (or subdisciplines, depending on your point of view) of ethnomethodology/ conversation analysis, pragmatics, linguistic anthropology, and sociolinguistics (with echoes and influences in cognitive science and philosophy of language). These concerns focus on discovering the patterns of discourse as they emerge in interaction, and on understanding them as primary acts of meaning-making.

For some, a strict focus on discourse in interaction was, however, unsatisfying, since such a focus could not provide the kind of data needed to explain where any observable patterns might have come from, or what kinds of consequences they might have. The second thread consists, then, of work intended to link discourse patterns to the conditions of their production, that is, to situate them socially and historically. From this line of inquiry has emerged a slightly different way of posing the original question, in the form of work which sees discourse not as a product of conditions of interaction, but rather as dialectically embedded in them. In this (for the purposes of argument, third) perspective, discourse in interaction becomes a privileged site for analyzing social action and social structure (and the relationship between the two).

In the final section, I will discuss some theoretical issues which remain unresolved in this line of inquiry. One of the most significant among them is the problem of the extent to which language can be treated as an autonomous system, put into play in discourse, or whether, more radically, language cannot be understood at all outside of its use. Equally important is the counterpart of the first question, namely where discourse in interaction fits in the spectrum of forms of social action, and the extent to which such discourse deserves the privileged status it has enjoyed in recent decades among those who study the nature and functioning of social action. Both of these are important questions for linguists and for (other kinds of?) social scientists.

1   The Social Construction of Reality

The question of the nature of reality has a long and noble history. Stances with respect to that question have constituted some of the most important fault lines in intellectual debates. The perspective that concerns us here is that which characterizes

reality as a social construct, and which locates the process of construction in the interaction between an individual and his or her world, most importantly as mediated by
interaction with other people. For some, notably within the tradition of psychology
and cognitive science, this has meant an empirical focus on the individual's experience
of that interaction, and on the consequences of interactional processes for individual
development (see Case 1996 for an overview). For others, it has meant a focus on
interactional processes themselves, as revealing the social dimensions of the construction of reality. Here, I will concern myself with work in the second vein.

Approaches to the question of the nature of interactional processes can be loosely
grouped into two categories: *ethnomethodological* and *interpretivist* (or *interactionist*).
There are many ways in which the two are related, and in particular in which the
first has influenced the second, but for the purposes of exposition it is useful to
divide them. The major distinction which I want to make between them has to do
with their stance with respect to data. Ethnomethodologists have a strong preference
for restricting analysis to what is actually observable. Interpretivists or interactionists
are prepared to bring other sources of data to bear on the analysis of interactional
data. Needless to say, the distinction in specific cases may be largely heuristic, even
inaccurate, but nonetheless it describes at least the difference between extreme outliers
of each group, and captures something of the orientation of practitioners situated
somewhere on the fuzzy boundary between the two groups.

An ethnomethodological approach to analysis of discourse in interaction has perhaps the strongest tendency to treat interactional data as text. The object of analysis
is the text of the transcription of the interaction, whether the text is a literal, verbal
one, based on audiotapes, or whether it combines verbal and nonverbal material,
as has become possible with the availability of videorecording. (Indeed, as we will
see below, one branch of ethnomethodology now prefers simply to think of itself as
conversation analysis, reflecting this focus on observable interaction.) The reason for
this is that social action is held to be ongoing and reflexive; one can only see how
participants make sense out of the world by observing their actions in it, or more
specifically, their reflexive interactions (Heritage 1984).

These interactions can be shown to be nonrandom; Garfinkel, the founder of
ethnomethodology, showed that it was possible to uncover the normative order
indexed by interactional routines by breaching those routines and watching all hell
break loose. As Heritage points out, the patterns observed in interactional data are
held to point to an "underlying pattern" (Garfinkel 1967, cited in Heritage 1984: 84).
This "underlying pattern" is some form of social order. While it is not clear exactly
what form of social order is involved here (this problem will be taken up in the
following section), the ethnomethodological insight is that it is possible to see it by
discovering its manifestations in the normative order of interaction, and especially
helpfully where that normative order is breached. Other sociologists, notably Goffman,
also were concerned to discover social order through the patterns of everyday life,
arguing that much of what happens interactionally is the constant construction and
reconstruction of forms of normative social order (cf. Goffman 1959, 1974, 1981).

While ethnomethodology did not begin by focusing on discourse in interaction,
it is not surprising that it would turn to such data, given the primacy accorded
to observable action. Heritage (1984: 235) cites Harvey Sacks' explanation for why
he turned to tape-recorded data: "So the question was, could there be some way

that sociology could hope to deal with the details of actual events, formally and informatively? . . . I wanted to locate some set of materials that would permit a test." Together with Emanuel Schegloff and Gail Jefferson, Sacks laid the groundwork for *conversation analysis*, ethnomethodology's major contribution to the analysis of discourse in interaction.

Conversation analysis focuses on the discovery of the patterns whereby people orient themselves (and each other) to specific dimensions of some underlying normative order. Frequently, these have concerned the normative order of talk itself, that is, how talk is supposed to be organized. Most important here have been studies concerned with: (1) how participants construct an orientation to talk, that is, how they make themselves available to each other for the purposes of interaction (for example, through the use of greeting routines; cf. Schegloff 1972) and otherwise organize their orientation to each other and to the activity at hand; (2) the distribution of talk among participants; and (3) how participants construct an orientation to a topic of conversation. In addition to a focus on observable routines, ethnomethodologists look at the structure of conversation, notably at such phenomena as turn-taking (beginning with the influential Sacks et al. 1974); sequencing and adjacency; and, of course, repair, which highlights the normative order by analyzing its breakdown and reconstruction.

There are a number of reasons why the normative order of talk might be interesting. For some, the underlying pattern it relates to is cognitive and potentially universal: what the normative order of talk reveals is the way in which we, as sentient organisms, organize our experience and understand it. For others, the interest lies in the direction of the social order, which requires relating the normative order of talk to other dimensions of social relations, that is, to the normative regulation of relations among people who, by virtue of their position with respect to (normatively salient) social categories, bear some set of (normatively salient) relations to each other as well as to others who can be said to be interactionally "present" (whether they are physically present or not), but who do not themselves speak (or write) in the interaction at issue. Here the underlying pattern might be universal, but is more likely historically contingent.

For those interested in problems of social order, ethnomethodological methods provide a way to do three things. One is to discover how interaction (as seen in actors' ways of knowing and being) contributes to the construction of a social order which extends far beyond any given analyzable interaction; conversely, another is to examine how the relationship between social action and social structure constrains how individuals can come to know and act in their world. The third is to identify the interactional manifestations of social problems (in which interactions are seen as potential sources of problems, as potential sites for discovering sources which are interactionally indexed, and as potential sites for intervention). As we shall see, however, pursuing these questions has provoked something of an ideological split. Some researchers continue to hold to the ethnomethodological principle of confining analysis to what is observable, and analyze interactions in and of (and for) themselves. Others have been posing questions about interactions and what goes on in them which lead them to consider phenomena beyond the bounds of the analysis of specific interactions. Some of these questions, as we shall see below, have to do with explaining why things happen the way they do, and others have to do with consequences of interactional patterns.

Indeed, while such work shares concerns and methods originating in ethno-methodology, one can also note parallel developments in sociology itself as well as in anthropology and linguistics, and a certain degree of convergence among some trends within sociolinguistics and linguistic anthropology (the difference between these two subdisciplines is in fact becoming less and less evident). Within sociology, the work of Goffman (see above) has been highly influential. While Goffman shares with ethnomethodologists a concern for understanding interactional processes as funda-mental to the construction of the social order, his work pointed to the importance of situating specific interactions not in the context of some abstract underlying pattern, but rather in the living tissue of everyday life, itself understood as part of a dynamic pattern of socially constituted frames (which he understood as the basis of social institutions).

In anthropology, the emergence of the ethnography of communication (Gumperz and Hymes 1972; Bauman and Sherzer 1974) opened the way toward yet another approach to interaction, one which borrowed ethnomethodology's respect for the routines and patterns of language use in interaction, but which went beyond that to consider those patterns as embedded in complex cultural processes. While one impetus for this work has been to contest the Chomskyan insistence on taking an abstract structural idea of language as the proper object of linguistic inquiry (and as the right way to think about what language is), many of the questions which have informed this work have been more oriented to issues traditionally treated within sociology and anthropology, namely questions about the social order, about the nature of culture, and about social problems (notably the consequences of social difference and social inequality; cf. Gumperz 1982a, 1982b). One of the major ideas behind the ethnography of communication was that long-standing questions in social and cultural anthropology could be addressed by problematizing language as social process, rather than taking it as a neutral and transparent reflection of the social order. Language had to be seen as a privileged site for the study of society and culture. Here it joined sociological concerns for capturing the nature of the construc-tion of social reality.

Similar concerns surfaced in linguistics, in particular with respect to accounting for meaning within inquiries regarding linguistic structure. Here, work in semantics (influenced also by the philosophy of language, notably work by Austin, Grice, and Searle; cf. Austin 1965; Grice 1975; Searle 1969, 1971) turned into the field of prag-matics, with a focus on local practices of meaning construction as manifested in the communicative exploitation of linguistic form (see Blommaert et al. 1995; Verschueren 1999; Levinson 1993). In France, another take on this problem produced an approach called *la praxématique*, which takes meaning construction to be a form of praxis, and its object of inquiry the forms of linguistic praxis which can be shown to be central to the construction of meaning (see notably the journal *Cahiers de praxématique*; and, for example, Bres 1989).

In this line of inquiry, work has tended to focus on interactions in institutional settings, for a variety of reasons. One is that the problem of the relationship between interaction, culture, and social order can be seen as a problem of a relationship between interaction and social institutions, which themselves can be taken as social categories (such as gender) or as organized realms of activity (such as regulation of behavior, management of health, or socialization). In the English-speaking world, there have been studies focused on the "doing" of social categories, for reasons having to do with movements for equity and justice in socially heterogeneous communities. As a result, we have work on "doing" gender, and on the construction of the other, that is, on the ways in which we do the work of setting up and maintaining social differences based largely on nationality, race, and ethnicity (see, for example, work on gender in Hall and Bucholtz 1995; Tannen 1993a; Ochs 1992; West and Zimmerman 1987; and on nationality, race, and ethnicity in Rampton 1995; Blommaert and Verschueren 1991). Work on the construction of the other overlaps with work on multilingualism, since multilingualism so often involves the interplay of identities (e.g. Oesch-Serra and Py 1996; Lüdi and Py 1995; Heller 1994, 1999). There are, of course, countless other social categories which could be investigated in the same way, such as Watts's (1991) study of family relations or Dannequin (1976) on class; the ones we choose are the ones which pose particular problems for us.

Despite its social significance, work on the construction of specific social categories has not been quite as prominent as work in institutions taken as organized, normatively regulated realms of activity. This may have to do with the more ready accessibility and identifiability of data in such settings (where you find the activity of construction of gender categories may not be as immediately obvious as where you might find the construction of knowledge about the body or about what counts as illegal), and with the kinds of packages in which data seems to come in such settings. In schools, hospitals, and courts of law, interactions are often highly routinized and temporally circumscribed; one can easily identify the beginning and end of an interaction, and interactions are not so long as to be analytically unwieldy. It may also have to do with the salience of the social problems visible in institutions such as schools, hospitals, workplaces, and courts of law, where unequal treatment, for example, is often highly visible, and has profound consequences for society at large.

One can look at this body of work, then, as motivated in two ways. The first motivation consists of attempts to understand how interaction in institutional settings produces knowledge about what is important in the world and how to act in it (socialization at home, in the community and at school; cf. e.g. Ochs and Schieffelin 1979; Schieffelin and Ochs 1986; Mehan 1979); how it produces knowledge about the physical world, notably the body (as in intake and diagnostic procedures in medical settings; cf. e.g. Cicourel 1987; Heller and Freeman 1987; Freeman and Heller 1987; Fisher and Todd 1983; Mishler 1984); and how it produces and reproduces the moral order, notably through the legal and political systems (cf. e.g. O'Barr 1982; Conley and O'Barr 1990; Brenneis and Myers 1984; Mertz 1998; Philips 1998). This work involves relating what happens in interactions in these settings to institutional processes themselves, that is, it involves understanding the nature of social categories and forms of social organization that can be seen to be important both in terms of how they constrain interaction and in terms of how interaction affects them. This would include things like understanding what it means to be, say, a "patient" or a "doctor," a "student" or a "teacher," and so on, as well as what it means to do "diagnosis," "legal defense," or "learning" (or "marking homework" or "filing" or "pulling a chart," and so on), and then understanding how they relate to each other.

The second kind of motivation concerns applying conversation analytic tools to the understanding of the kind of work institutions do, that is, what it is that they actually produce. Here, an interest in institutional activity frequently relates to addressing some social problem, especially since so many institutional settings are sites of social selection and for the regulation of production and distribution of valued resources (that is, sites where people are evaluated in ways that make a difference to their lives, and where someone decides whether or not they get access to things that are important to them). Thus, for example, a look at educational settings allows us to understand how they contribute to the production and reproduction of social categories, and to the construction and distribution of what counts as knowledge. In this area, examples can be found, for instance, of work on the interactional bases of language learning and teaching (cf. e.g. Oesch-Serra and Py 1996; Lüdi and Py 1995) and on the social construction of literacy (Cook-Gumperz 1986; Heath 1983), as well as of knowledge in other subject areas, like mathematics or science (O'Connor and Michaels 1993). A critical take on these processes produces questions like these: why do schools privilege some forms of knowledge over others? Why is the knowledge brought to school by some categories of students treated as valuable and legitimate while that brought by others is devalued and marginalized? Why are some groups of students more academically successful than others?

In the area of education, a great deal of work has been devoted to precisely this question of the interactional dynamics of social and cultural reproduction in school. Class, race, ethnicity, and gender have all been examined (see, for example, Gumperz 1982b; Heath 1983; Erickson and Shultz 1982; Collins 1988, 1991; Swann 1992; Heller 1995a, 1999; Martin-Jones and Heller 1996, in press). Such analyses of interaction in school settings (usually, but not only, in classrooms) show that discourse in interaction is involved in the process of social and cultural production and reproduction (that is, the maintenance or transformation of relations of power and of social boundaries and categories) in a number of ways. First, the value attached to linguistic varieties shows up in the judgments made about the intellectual competence of their users (individually and collectively), judgments which are based on the use of elements of these varieties in all kinds of interactional performances. Second, the social organization of discourse itself (who gets to talk when, for example), allows certain actors to exercise such judgments over others, to control access to educational interactions where knowledge is constructed, and to control what gets to count as knowledge. Third, the structure of discourse generally indexes frames of reference which must be shared in order for an activity (like, say, learning) to be considered to be taking place; the ability of participants to build such shared frames on the basis of normatively conventionalized discourse structures affects their ability to do the work of doing "learning" together, to display their activity to each other, and to make appropriate judgments on the basis of the behavior displayed.

Similar kinds of questions have arisen with respect to other institutions, such as the workplace, medicine, and law, where other kinds of crucial judgments can be made about people, and where a great deal rides on the linguistic resources people can muster interactionally, and on the uses they put them to there (cf. Sarangi and Roberts 1999; Roberts et al. 1992; Goldstein 1997; Mertz 1998; Philips 1998). In particular, researchers in medical settings have been concerned to understand the differences between lay and practitioner understanding of health and illness, and their discursive construction in the process of formulating diagnoses and decisions regarding treatment (this kind of research can have immediate applications in areas like the development of computer-based screening procedures, which are designed to save on health care costs). In areas concerning the law, researchers have also been interested in the discursive construction of legal arguments, on the extent to which they are received as being persuasive or not, and with what consequences for judges' and juries' decision-making. In the workplace, research has focused on the nature of knowledge required for the accomplishment of interactions between workers and clients, as well as among coworkers or between employers and employees. While the lay versus practitioner, or worker versus employee, distinction is clearly central to these inquiries (social position is connected to access to resources, including knowledge, and to the power to influence the production and distribution of knowledge and of other resources), it is also clear that that categorical distinction overlaps with others (not all lay people and practitioners, not all workers and employees, are the same). What is more, the salient dimensions of difference may shift over the course of an interaction.

While work in what might be called a strictly ethnomethodological vein certainly continues, in many other instances the initial insights of ethnomethodology have been taken over, incorporated and modified in the course of using ethnomethodological tools to answer a wide variety of what still remain fundamentally sociological and anthropological questions. In so doing, researchers have found that it is difficult to explain where observable interactional differences come from and what their consequences are (for the structure of the social order, for the content of belief systems, for the life chances of specific groups, and so on) if they stay focused on the observable routines of specific interactions. In the following section, I will describe further some of the problems that interaction analysis has tried to deal with, and some ways it has tried to preserve the central insights and descriptive and explanatory power of an interactional approach, while resolving some of the problems caused by its limitations.

2   Situating Interactions

Lines of questioning in work on the interactional construction of social categories and of social relations have led to a number of issues unresolvable by interaction analysis alone. For example, a central issue in the study of the construction of social categories has been the source and nature of the differences involved. Both studies of gender and of intercultural communication have pointed out that members of different social categories use different conversational routines (or discourse strategies, to use Gumperz's 1982a term), which in turn index different frames of reference (different sets of assumptions about the world and how to act in it). (The nature and functioning of indexicality and framing in discourse have, not surprisingly, become the object of much research as a result; cf. Goffman 1974; Tannen 1993b; Silverstein 1998.) The question is to what extent these palpable cultural differences are the result of distinct socialization experiences, and to what extent they are the result of different social positions with respect to the distribution of power (Cameron 1992; Kandiah 1991). The answer to that question has implications for understanding the ways in which such differences may enter into the construction of relations which are perceived (at least by somebody) as being problematic, normally because they lead to misunderstanding (and hence an inability to accomplish goals, to gain access to valued resources), to conflict, or to some form of unequal treatment (as manifested for example in high dropout, alcoholism and unemployment rates among members of the Native North American population; coincidence of racial and educational stratification; gender bias in occupational specialization; and gender-based income stratification, to mention just a few). Of course, while these are central to understanding processes of production and reproduction of social categories and of social relations, they are not readily amenable to a conversation analytic approach. In addition, the linkage of the problem of social categorization and social relations through the concept of social problems becomes itself an important theoretical and empirical question.

Attempts to resolve these issues have led researchers to rethink the old problem of interaction and the social order. In particular, the question of how to situate interactions with respect to other forms of social life became a central analytical problem, one which came to be posed as a problem of understanding the nature of context.

Earlier work had established that one of the powerful means by which interaction functions to produce and reproduce the social order is by indexing the frames of reference with respect to which local action is interpretable. Clearly, those frames of reference were an important locus for understanding social order, but the only means to address their nature would be through understanding the process of indexing, or of *contextualization* itself, that is, the process by which frames of reference are called into play, defined and modified in interaction. Auer (1992: 4) defines it as follows: "(C)ontextualization . . . comprises all activities by participants which make relevant, maintain, revise, cancel . . . any aspect of context which, in turn, is responsible for the interpretation of an utterance in its particular locus of occurrence." Gumperz (1982a) was highly influential in calling attention to the importance of this process, and his work inspired that of others, who examined the wide variety of communicative means called upon in order to accomplish it (see notably Auer and di Luzio 1992).

While work on contextualization as an interactional process has clearly helped understand the nature of the linkages between local interactional processes and phenomena and the contexts or frames they index, it has not addressed the question of the nature of the relationship between interaction and context. In sociology, this relationship has long been thought of as one between so-called macrosocial processes and structures and so-called microlevel ones. This distinction connotes a separation of realms, which therefore should be empirically distinct. However, one of the results of the turn toward studying interaction as a locus of construction of social order has been to call that distinction into question. Empirically it does not seem possible to identify phenomena anywhere other than at the so-called microlevel (this is, of course, why people started examining interactional data in the first place). If the macrolevel is not empirically observable, what use is there in maintaining the concept? On the other hand, as we have seen, it is impossible to explain everything that goes in at the microlevel by focusing on particular interactions, no matter how carefully chosen.

Many authors have proposed ways of rethinking the macro–micro distinction (see, for example, Cicourel 1980; Collins 1981; Mehan 1987; Giddens 1984; Marcus 1986). All of them share the view that methodologically and theoretically it is necessary to begin with what is empirically observable, namely interactions and their traces. At the same time, it is clear that social order cannot be simply read off from any particular interaction. The solution that all propose, in their different ways, is to explore the linkages among interactions.

There are two main ways in which people have tried to do this. One is through examining the traces within interactions of their linkages with others. The study of contextualization processes certainly forms part of this endeavor, but it has also taken other forms. Mehan (1987) and Cicourel (1987), for example, have examined interactions which have an observable outcome, usually in the form of a decision of some kind. Some of these are what Erickson and Shultz (1982) call "gate-keeping" encounters, because the decisions taken there affect petitioners' access to resources; examples of such encounters are job interviews, medical intake interviews, and educational placement committee meetings. In this way, interactional processes can be tied to outcomes, and it is possible to separate out the effects of local interactional processes (which Mehan calls "proximal" effects) and those of interactions which are removed in time and space from the one at hand (and which are, for Mehan, "distal"). In this approach, texts too play a particularly important role as institutional traces of other interactions (and other decisions), which turn up and are incorporated (interpreted and reinterpreted, applied in a variety of ways to new interpretive problems) into new interactions; these texts might be texts of laws or other regulations which constrain what it is institutionally possible to do, or texts like minutes of previous meetings, or diagnostic charts, which situate an interaction in a chain of temporally and institutionally interconnected encounters.

Another approach to this problem is to practice what Marcus (1986) calls "multi-locale ethnography," that is, to focus on more than one interaction in order to discover the spatial, temporal, and most importantly social linkages among them. Here Marcus joins the anthropological dimensions of sociolinguistic work carried out within the tradition of the ethnography of communication, since that tradition too privileged using ethnographic knowledge to choose sites where interactions would be particularly revealing of whatever issues were of immediate concern. It also developed concepts which can be understood in a similar way, in particular the notion of *communicative repertoire*, as well as the concept of *speech situation* or *speech event*. All these concepts, central to the ethnography of communication, are based on the assumption that people use language in ways which vary systematically in co-occurrence with other dimensions of their social relations. At the community level, there therefore exist communicative repertoires, that is, sets of linguistic resources, from which people can draw for the purposes of any given interaction. From this perspective, it is clear that only by making linkages among interactions in a variety of situations is it possible to arrive at some broader understanding both of the significance of any specific interaction and of the social system of which it is a part. In addition, individuals possess sets of linguistic resources which vary according to their access to the communicative situations in their community.

The major problem confronted by the ethnography of communication approach has been that it turns out to be empirically next to impossible (outside of highly routinized and institutionalized encounters) to draw boundaries around interactions, or repertoires, or communities. The concept of co-occurrence, which drew attention to the fact that behaviors and conditions of their production tend to cluster, permitted the development of a recognition of the social variability of linguistic practice, but was unable to account for the socially creative force of those practices, since it emphasized conventional, repetitive associations, rather than change. Instead, the descriptive and explanatory potential of the ethnographic grounding of interactions had to be wedded to the ethnomethodological and sociological recognition of linguistic practice as social process, to the anthropological concern for understanding behavior in everyday life as the basis of cultural production and reproduction, and to a linguistic approach to the multiplexity and multivocality of language.

Hence a Marcus-type multilocal ethnography, applied to the concerns outlined here, entails using ethnographic methods to understand where any particular interaction comes from, and where it might be going, that is, what consequences it might have and for whom (whether they were actually present during the interactions examined or not). There is a certain amount of debate as to what the appropriate ethnographic methods might be, however, and this debate revolves around the ontological status of various forms of data, based on insights derived precisely from the study of interactions.

The specific concern has to do with the extent to which ethnographic methods should be confined to examining what is observable, or whether participant reports can provide useful information. Participant reports are of course interactional constructs (whether someone calling themselves a sociolinguist or a linguistic anthropologist or whatever is there or not), and so their narratives, elicited in interviews or captured in the course of a spontaneous exchange with a neighbor, have to be understood in the same way as we understand any interaction, namely as social process (Briggs 1986; Cicourel 1988; Lafont 1977). It is, however, generally accepted that this is merely one variant of an old problem in the social sciences, namely that of how the interpretation of data has to take into account the subjectivity of all involved. Bearing this in mind, it has nonetheless been possible to address some of these problems in a number of ways. One has been to triangulate data, that is, to collect data from a variety of sources to see to what extent they confirm or contradict each other. More important, perhaps, has been the use of interaction and discourse analysis techniques to understand the nature of the construction of data, and hence what kinds of claims can be made on the basis of it.

The question still remains, however, of the kind of ethnographic knowledge most appropriate to the selection of sites. Here the issue is profoundly theoretical. Some researchers have adopted principles based on political economic notions of explanation (Gal 1989; Heller 1995b, 1999), that is, on the idea that the symbolic order is closely tied to the material world, and that language practices can often be explained in terms of the interests people have with respect to valued resources (including language itself). This requires locating sites where valued resources are produced and distributed, and understanding what goes on there not only in terms of a site's relationship to other sites of resource production and distribution, but also in terms of the social position participants occupy (or would like to occupy) with respect to them. The study of interaction then becomes one of examining the workings of human agency with respect to the obstacles and opportunities presented by social conditions produced elsewhere. The workings of human agency are understood as discourse in the sense that they are a take on the world, an endeavor to construct meaning and to situate oneself and others with respect to it, but in ways that are also profoundly interested and situated in the material, as well as the social, world.

3 Conclusion

The interactional analysis of discourse is, then, at the intersection of our analyses of human understandings of the world, of the conditions which produce those understandings, and of their role in the construction of the social order. Debate remains as to what can be learned by examining interactions as it were from the "inside," in isolation from the conditions of their existence, as opposed to what can be learned by situating interactions as part of broader, long-term processes, only parts of which we can ever hope to apprehend.

The question of what affects what also remains open; while it seems clear that behavior is patterned at a number of levels, from linguistic structure through conversational and discourse structure to the social organization of interactions, the nature of the sources of those patterns and of the relations among them remains obscure, as does the extent to which they actually function autonomously (as opposed to being able to be described that way). It is not yet clear what kinds of methods might allow us to pursue those questions, although obviously methods derived from several disciplines (cognitive science, sociology, anthropology, linguistics, history) seem relevant.

Nonetheless, the interactional analysis of discourse opens up not just these questions, but also those related to the nature of the interests at stake in any given interaction. Social actors creatively exploit linguistic, discursive resources to accomplish local as well as long-term goals, whether consciously or not. In addition, what goes on among people has palpable, observable effects on the conditions of their own lives and on the conditions of the lives of others; our understanding of how things happen to people is thus enriched by seeing how they make it happen (or have it happen to them).

The interactional analysis of discourse is both a means for advancing theories of human cognition, of language, and of the social order, and a means for addressing social problems affecting numbers of lives. The integration of the two provides for a socially grounded and reflexive means for building theory, as well as a conceptually informed basis for social action.

REFERENCES

Auer, P. 1992. Introduction: John Gumperz' approach to contextualization. In: P. Auer and A. di Luzio (eds), *The Contextualization of Language*. Amsterdam: John Benjamins, pp. 1–37.

Auer, P. and A. di Luzio (eds). 1992. *The Contextualization of Language*. Amsterdam: John Benjamins.

Austin, J. 1965. *How To Do Things With Words*. New York: Oxford University Press.

Bauman, R. and J. Sherzer (eds). 1974. *Explorations in the Ethnography of Speaking*. Cambridge: Cambridge University Press.

Blommaert, J. and J. Verschueren (eds). 1991. *The Pragmatics of International and Intercultural Communication*. Amsterdam: John Benjamins.

Blommaert, J., J.-O. Östman, and J. Verschueren (eds). 1995. *Handbook of Pragmatics*. Amsterdam: John Benjamins.

Brenneis, D. and F. Myers (eds). 1984. *Dangerous Words: Language and Politics in the Pacific*. New York: New York University Press.

Bres, J. 1989. Praxis, production de sens/identité, récit. *Langages* 93: 23–44.

Briggs, C. 1986. *Learning How to Ask: A Sociolinguistic Reappraisal of the Social Science Interview*. Cambridge: Cambridge University Press.

Cameron, D. 1992. *Feminism and Linguistic Theory*. London: Macmillan.

Case, R. 1996. Changing views of knowledge and their impact on educational research and practice. In: D. Olson and N. Torrance (eds), *The Handbook of Education and Human Development: New Models of Learning, Teaching and Schooling*. Cambridge, MA: Blackwell, pp. 75–99.

Cicourel, A. 1980. Three models of discourse analysis: the role of social structure. *Discourse Processes* 3: 101–32.

Cicourel, A. 1987. Cognitive and organizational aspects of medical diagnostic reasoning. In: M. Heller and S. Freeman (eds), "Discourse as Organizational Process", special issue of *Discourse Processes* 10(4): 347–68.

Cicourel, A. 1988. Elicitation as a problem of discourse. In: U. Ammon, N. Dittmar, and K. Mattheier (eds), *Sociolinguistics: An International Handbook of the Science of Language and Society*. Berlin: Walter de Gruyter, pp. 903–10.

Collins, J. 1988. Language and class in minority education. *Anthropology and Education Quarterly* 19(4): 299–326.

Collins, J. 1991. Hegemonic practice: literacy and standard language in public education. In: C. Mitchell and K. Weiler (eds), *Rewriting Literacy: Culture and the Discourse of the Other*. New York: Bergin and Garvey, pp. 228–54.

Collins, R. 1981. On the micro-foundations of macro-sociology. *American Journal of Sociology* 86(5): 985–1014.

Conley, J. and W. O'Barr. 1990. *Rules versus Relationship: The Ethnography of Legal Discourse*. Chicago: University of Chicago Press.

Cook-Gumperz, J. (ed.) 1986. *The Social Construction of Literacy*. Cambridge: Cambridge University Press.

Dannequin, C. 1976. *Les enfants baillonnés*. Paris: CEDIL.

Erickson, F. and J. Shultz. 1982. *The Counsellor as Gatekeeper: Social Interaction in Interviews*. New York: Academic Press.

Fisher, S. and A. Todd (eds). 1983. *The Social Organization of Doctor–Patient Communication*. Washington, DC: Center for Applied Linguistics.

Freeman, S. and M. Heller (eds). 1987. "Medical discourse". Special issue of *Text* 7(1): 1–87.

Gal, S. 1989. Language and political economy. *Annual Review of Anthropology* 18: 345–67.

Garfinkel, H. 1967. *Studies in Ethnomethodology*. Englewood Cliffs, NJ: Prentice-Hall.

Giddens, A. 1984. *The Constitution of Society*. Berkeley and Los Angeles: University of California Press.

Goffman, E. 1959. *The Presentation of Self in Everyday Life*. Garden City, NY: Anchor Books.

Goffman, E. 1974. *Frame Analysis: An Essay on the Organization of Experience*. Cambridge, MA: Harvard University Press.

Goffman, E. 1981. *Forms of Talk*. Philadelphia: University of Pennsylvania Press.

Goldstein, T. 1997. *Two Languages at Work: Bilingual Life on the Production Floor*. Berlin and New York: Mouton de Gruyter.

Grice, P. 1975. Logic and conversation. In: P. Cole and J. Morgan (eds), *Syntax and Semantics, Vol. 3*. New York: Academic Press, pp. 41–58.

Gumperz, J. 1982a. *Discourse Strategies*. Cambridge: Cambridge University Press.

Gumperz, J. (ed.) 1982b. *Language and Social Identity*. Cambridge: Cambridge University Press.

Gumperz, J. and D. Hymes (eds). 1972. *Directions in Sociolinguistics: The Ethnography of Communication*. New York: Holt, Rhinehart and Winston.

Hall, K. and M. Bucholtz (eds). 1995. *Gender Articulated: Language and the Socially Constructed Self*. London: Routledge.

Heath, S. B. 1983. *Ways With Words*. Cambridge: Cambridge University Press.

Heller, M. 1994. *Crosswords: Language, Education and Ethnicity in French Ontario*. Berlin: Mouton de Gruyter.

Heller, M. 1995a. Language choice, symbolic domination and social institutions. *Language in Society* 25(3): 373–404.

Heller, M. 1995b. Code-switching and the politics of language. In: L. Milroy and P. Muysken (eds), *One Speaker, Two Languages: Cross-disciplinary Perspectives on Code-switching*. Cambridge: Cambridge University Press, pp. 158–74.

Heller, M. 1999. *Linguistic Minorities and Modernity: A Sociolinguistic Ethnography*. London: Longman.

Heller, M. and S. Freeman. 1987. First encounters: the role of communication in the medical intake process. In: M. Heller and S. Freeman (eds), "Discourse as Organizational Process", special issue of *Discourse Processes* 10(4): 369–84.

Heritage, J. 1984. *Garfinkel and Ethnomethodology*. Cambridge: Polity.

Kandiah, T. 1991. Extenuatory sociolinguistics: diverting attention from issues to symptoms in cross-cultural communication studies. *Multilingua* 10(4): 345–80.

Lafont, R. 1977. À propos de l'enquête sur la diglossie: l'intercesseur de la norme. *Lengas* 1: 31–9.

Levinson, S. 1993. *Pragmatics*. Cambridge: Cambridge University Press.

Lüdi, G. and B. Py. 1995. *Changement de langage, langage du changement*. Lausanne: L'Âge d'Homme.

Marcus, G. 1986. Contemporary problems of ethnography in the modern world system. In: J. Clifford and G. Marcus (eds), *Writing Culture*. Berkeley and Los Angeles: University of California Press, pp. 165–93.

Martin-Jones, M. and M. Heller (eds). 1996. "Education in Multilingual Settings: Discourse Identities and Power", special issues of *Linguistics and Education* 8(1, 2): 1–228.

Martin-Jones, M. and M. Heller (eds). In press. *Voices of Authority: Education and Linguistic Difference*. Oxford: Elsevier.

Mehan, H. 1979. *Learning Lessons*. Cambridge, MA: Harvard University Press.

Mehan, H. 1987. Language and power in organizational process. In: M. Heller and S. Freeman (eds), "Discourse as Organizational Process", special issue of *Discourse Processes* 10(4): 291–302.

Mertz, E. 1998. Linguistic ideology and praxis in U.S. law school classrooms. In: B. Schieffelin, K. Woolard, and P. Kroskrity (eds), *Language Ideologies: Practice and Theory*. Oxford: Oxford University Press, pp. 149–62.

Mishler, E. 1984. *The Discourse of Medicine*. New York: Academic Press.

O'Barr, W. 1982. *Linguistic Evidence: Language, Power and Strategy in the Courtroom*. New York: Academic Press.

Ochs, E. 1992. Indexing gender. In: A. Duranti and C. Goodwin (eds), *Rethinking Context: Language as Interactive Phenomenon*. Cambridge: Cambridge University Press, pp. 335–8.

Ochs, E. and B. Schieffelin (eds). 1979. *Developmental Pragmatics*. New York: Academic Press.

O'Connor, M. C. and S. Michaels. 1993. Aligning academic task and participation status through revoicing: analysis of a classroom discourse strategy. *Anthropology and Education Quarterly* 24(4): 308–35.

Oesch-Serra, C. and B. Py (eds). 1996. Le bilinguisme. *Acquisition et interaction en langue étrangère (AILE)* 7: 3–183.

Philips, S. 1998. *Ideology in the Language of Judges: How Judges Practice Law, Politics and Courtroom Control*. New York and Oxford: Oxford University Press.

Rampton, B. 1995. *Crossing: Language and Ethnicity Among Adolescents*. London: Longman.

Roberts, C., E. Davies, and T. Jupp. 1992. *Language and Discrimination: A Study of Communication in Multiethnic Workplaces*. London: Longman.

Sacks, H., E. Schegloff, and G. Jefferson, 1974. A simplest systematics for the organization of turn-taking for conversation. *Language* 50: 696–735.

Sarangi, S. and C. Roberts (eds). 1999. *Talk, Work and Institutional Order: Discourse in Medical, Mediation and Management Settings*. Berlin and New York: Mouton de Gruyter.

Schegloff, E. 1972. Sequencing in conversational openings. In: J. Gumperz and D. Hymes (eds), *Directions in Sociolinguistics: The Ethnography of Communication*. New York: Holt, Rhinehart and Winston, pp. 346–80.

Schieffelin, B. and E. Ochs (eds). 1986. *Language Socialization Across Cultures*. Cambridge: Cambridge University Press.

Searle, J. 1969. *Speech Acts*. Cambridge: Cambridge University Press.

Searle, J. (ed.) 1971. *Philosophy of Language*. Oxford: Oxford University Press.

Silverstein. M. 1998. The uses and utility of ideology: a commentary. In: B. Schieffelin, K. Woolard, and P. Kroskrity (eds), *Language Ideologies: Practice and Theory*. Oxford: Oxford University Press, pp. 123–48.

Swann, J. 1992. *Girls, Boys and Language*. Oxford: Blackwell.

Tannen, D. (ed.) 1993a. *Gender and Conversational Interaction*. Oxford: Oxford University Press.

Tannen, D. 1993b. *Framing in Discourse*. New York: Oxford University Press.

Verschueren, J. 1999. *Understanding Pragmatics*. Amsterdam: Benjamins.

Watts, R. 1991. *Power in Family Discourse*. Berlin: Mouton de Gruyter.

West, C. and D. Zimmerman. 1987. Doing gender. *Gender and Society* 1(2): 125–51.

14 The Linguistic Structure of Discourse

LIVIA POLANYI

0 Introduction

We take as the goal of our formal work in discourse analysis explaining how speakers almost without error interpret personal, temporal, and spatial deixis, recover the objects of anaphoric mention, and produce responses which demonstrate that they know what is going on in the talk despite disturbances to orderly discourse development (Polanyi 1978, 1987, 1996; Polanyi and van den Berg 1996; Polanyi and Scha 1984; Scha and Polanyi 1988). With the informal description of the Linguistic Discourse Model (LDM) in this chapter, we take a first step toward this goal by proposing answers to three basic questions: what are the atomic units of discourse? What kinds of structures can be built from the elementary units? How are the resulting structures interpreted semantically? After sketching machinery to account for discourse segmentation, parsing, and interpretation, we will conclude by addressing the concerns readers of the present volume may have about the utility of a formal theory of discourse. What sort of work could such a theory do? To argue for our approach, we will examine the data and discussion presented in Prince's (1988) account of Yiddish expletive, ES + Subject Postposing. We will use the Yiddish data to show how the LDM analysis allows us to give a much more principled account than has been possible before of what it means for an entity to be "new in the discourse." In the concluding section of the chapter, we will broaden the discussion to argue for the benefits to sociolinguists and other discourse researchers of the formal methods we have proposed.

1 Discourse Segmentation

In the LDM framework, two types of basic discourse units are recognized: the propositional content carrying the elementary discourse constituent unit (E-DCU) and the extrapropositional discourse operator. These two units reflect the traditional linguistic distinction between **content** and **function**. We claim that discourse can be segmented exhaustively into these basic units which are then combined into more complex units by the rules of complex discourse unit formation discussed in section 2 below.

1.1   *The e-discourse constituent unit (E-DCU)*

We define the **e-discourse constituent unit** (E-DCU) as a contextually indexed representation of information conveyed by a semiotic gesture, asserting a single state of affairs or partial state of affairs in a **discourse context** (DC). We can informally think of a DC as some sort of conceptual world modeled by the discourse construction process. Each DCU, whether linguistically or paralinguistically encoded,[1] expresses an event or in general a state of affairs in some spatiotemporal location, involving some set of (defined or as of yet undefined) participants (Davidson 1967). The event will be either positive or negative, generic or specific.

Under the LDM, higher-level discourse structures such as genre-defined constituents and **speech events** (Hymes 1972) play an important role in discourse interpretation. Genre units such as stories, negotiations, or arguments have a characteristic constituent structure in which expected types of information are deployed in a conventionally agreed-upon manner. Similarly, in speech events such as doctor–patient interactions, formal lectures, business meetings, church services or blind dates, etc., the participants know when they are in one phase of the activity or in another and behave accordingly. The proper interpretation of a DCU depends critically on its participation in a specific structured discourse text as well as its relationship to the speech event in which it was uttered. Similar prosodically related strings of words will express very different information if used to build the semantic representation of one story embedded in one interactional context rather than another. Therefore, discourse genre unit and speech event information, along with the spatio/temporally located participant structure we call **interaction**, contextually index the semiotic DCUs and operators that make up any spoken, written, gestural, or multimodal discourse event.

In summary, E-DCUs which give information about events in the same discourse context will necessarily present information from the same points of view, empathy status, and modality, and relate to the identical genre-defined and socially constructed interactional frames.

1.2   *Discourse operators*

In addition to semantic structures which express states of affairs about a DC, utterances may also involve nonpropositional elements which make explicit the nature of links among pieces of information, thereby facilitating proper semantic interpretation. These **discourse operators** modify discourse constituents and may have scope over long stretches of discourse (Schiffrin 1987, this volume; references in Di Eugenio et al. 1997).

Although some metacommunicative propositional utterances such as *As we were saying before we were interrupted* may function as operators as well as expressing propositional content and must be interpreted as a complex structure, most linguistic structures functioning as operators, such as English *yes, uh, ok, but, because, well, so, if, then, therefore, hello, goodbye, now, or, what, why, and, anyway, on the other hand, by the way,* and any proper name used as a vocative, do not assert information about states of affairs in a context but give information about the state of the discourse and the relation of discourse entities and discourse representations to one another. Discourse operators, while themselves lacking in propositional content, often make explicit the shift in the indices of the content-bearing DCUs. Sometimes that shift is not linguistically encoded at all; body position, eye gaze, and tone of voice may all signal a shift in footing – a shift in interpretive context.

1.3   Segmentation and discourse surface structure

Under the LDM, discourse is segmented maximally. Initiation of a new elementary unit is signaled whenever phonological (i.e. pausal or prosodic) criteria indicate a break, whenever sentential syntactic criteria indicate a clause break (except for a lexically limited set of matrix verbs governing infinitival clauses), and whenever sentential semantics requires a change in any of the contexts (spatial, temporal, modal, etc.) that index the discourse contexts where the events (and in general, states of affairs) are interpreted.[2]

Discourse segmentation is determined by semantic criteria and guided by syntax and intonation. For example, the sentence *I went downtown but Mary stayed home* (discussed in Longacre 1976: 261) is analyzed under the LDM as a three-unit structure consisting of two DCUs (*I went downtown* and *Mary stayed home*) and a discourse operator *but,* a logical connective which asserts the relationship that obtains between two states of affairs, while the utterance *Actually, I slept* expresses a single state of affairs, "speaker slept," which obtains in one context and an attitudinal evaluation of that state of affairs uttered from the point of view of the speaker situated in another. This utterance thus maps into two discourse-level units, the discourse operator *actually* and the E-DCU *I slept.*

2   Complex Discourse Units and Discourse Parsing

In this section, we discuss the rules specifying the syntax and semantics of well-formed discourse structures recursively built from elementary DCUs and develop a typology of higher-level constituents. Discourse operators are peripheral to this undertaking: the central data structure, the **discourse parse tree** (DPT), has propositional DCUs at the leaves.[3] Under the LDM, the DPT is constructed on a DCU-by-DCU basis built up sequentially through a process of discourse parsing. After examining the rules for complex DCU formation, we will briefly consider the DPT construction process.

2.1   Complex discourse units

We distinguish three basic types of higher structures: **coordination**, **subordination**, and **binary** constructions. Nonterminal nodes of the DPT are always one of these, and will be labeled by *C, S,* or *B* accordingly.

2.1.1 Coordination structures

Adding a next item to a list, giving a next episode of a story, beginning a new topic in a conversation when discussion of a previous topic has been concluded, or going on to a next expected activity in a speech event such as a church service can all be analyzed as continuing the development of an ongoing discourse activity. In the DPT such continuing activities are depicted as a sequence of coordinated constituents, i.e. as a nonterminal C node immediately dominating arbitrarily many constituents that share a single type. **Lists**, **topic chains**, and **narratives** are common sequential structures.

Consider the simple discourse fragment given in (1):

(1) *I like to read sci-fi. I like to ski and I like to sleep late.*

The structure of (1) can be characterized by the tree given in (2):

(2)

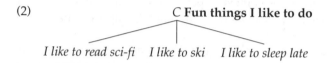

In (2), the first DCU, *I like to read sci-fi*, could be an item on lists of many types such as "What I like to do," "What I do on Tuesdays," "What I like to read," "What people in my family like to do," and so on. When the second DCU is encountered, and the information in the proposition "speaker likes to ski" is compared with the information in the proposition "speaker likes to read sci-fi," a competent language understander using world knowledge would infer that what is being communicated is a list of items of what we could gloss as "fun things the speaker likes to do." This higher-level, more general information, referred to as the **common ground**, is used in the DPT as further specification of the C node label.[4] When the third DCU, *I like to sleep late*, is encountered, it is compared in form and meaning to *I like to ski*, a computation of the common ground between DCU 2 and DCU 3 nets the same higher-level common ground "fun things the speaker likes to do" as was computed to obtain between the first two DCUs. This means that all three DCUs are specific instances of the same general list and can be accommodated under the same higher-level node.

2.1.2 Subordination structures

Discourse activities which interrupt the completion of other ongoing activities are treated in a structurally uniform manner. **Elaborations** on a point just made, **digressions** to discuss something else, **asides**, **appositives**, sections of **direct discourse**, or true **interruptions** are all treated as subordinated to activities which continue the development of an ongoing unit, be it a story, a proposal for a course of action, a lecture, or a move in speech event. We also recognize **sentential subordination** which obtains between a matrix clause and its subordinated clause[5] or appositive or parenthetical element[6] as discourse subordinations.

In the general case, the subordinated constituent will be encoded as the right daughter Y in an elementary tree such as (3):

(3)
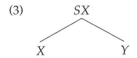

Notice that the superordinate constituent X does not dominate Y – the fact that the relation between the two is one of subordination is expressed by the label of the mother node. Unlike the coordination case, where the interpretation of the mother node is computed by conjoining the interpretations of the daughters, the interpretation of structures such as (4) is as in (5). The mother node inherits all the information of its left daughter; the right daughter has no impact whatsoever:

(4) a. *I like to do fun things on vacation*
     b. *I like to read sci-fi.*

(5)

Should the discourse continue, *I like to ski*, this new DCU would be coordinated to Y *I like to read sci-fi* under a newly created C node interpreted as "Fun things I like to do" as in (6):

(6)
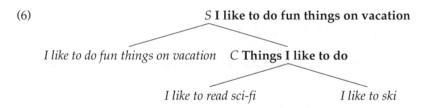

The identical DPT process operates in the case of interruptions. Since no semantic relationship obtains between the sister DCUs, and the newly incoming interrupting sister is breaking off an ongoing discourse activity, the fact that the content of the right sister does not influence the interpretation of the unit it is interrupting is very reasonable. The only relationship between an interrupting and an interrupted constituent is the structural relationship of contiguity.

We will pay special attention to one type of elaboration, which plays an important role in the analysis of the Yiddish anecdote we will be discussing below. **Reported speech and thought** are common in stories, arguments, and other forms of discourse. What is spoken or thought by the character is interpreted relative to an interaction in a story discourse world among characters in that discourse world. The narrator, in asserting a reporting event such as *I said* or *Suzie thought*, which typically is an event on the mainline of the narrative, communicates directly to the story recipients in a context that includes narrator and recipient as participants but which excludes the characters in the story. Because the reporting DCUs are events on the story mainline and the reported speech or thought interrupts the development of the narrated world by interposing an interaction among other participants, we subordinate reported speech and thought to the DCU of the reporting narrative as shown in (7):

(7)

reporting DCU   *reported* DCU

2.1.3   Binary structures

Binary structures construct a DCU out of two DCUs commonly joined by an explicit or implicit relation. Semantically, binary relations are very complex. Binary relations hold between two constituents related logically (e.g. *if/then, then/if, or, therefore*), rhetorically, (e.g. *sum up*), or interactionally (e.g. *question/answer, warrant/response, error/repair*).[7] The discourse parsing of (8):

(8)   a.   *If John goes to the store*
      b.   *he'll buy tomatoes*
      c.   *Otherwise, we'll just have lettuce in the salad.*

begins with setting up an intrasentential binary node dominating both DCUs in the first sentence:

(9)

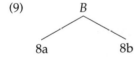

When (8c) becomes available, it is subordinated to the *B* node, since at this point it is a digression as shown in (10):

(10)

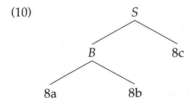

At this time it is not known how many types of binary relations (and thus how many binary node types) need to be distinguished, though there is no reason to believe that the number of binary discourse structures commonly found in a language, and which should be stipulated in a grammar, would greatly exceed the number of complement types that sentential syntax requires us to differentiate. It is to be expected that different languages may have quite different binary relations (Longacre 1976).

One binary structure deserving special mention is **repair**, which differs from other discourse relations because, instead of an instruction to semantics to create a new representation or update an existing one, the repair node calls for the removal of information previously added to a representation. Because of repairs, discourse which is syntactically monotonic is semantically nonmonotonic.

2.2 The discourse parse tree

From the preceding discussion of the major construction types it is clear that at a high level of abstraction all DPTs can be described by a simple context-free grammar. Elementary DPTs will have either a *C* mother node and two or more daughters, or an *S* or *B* mother node and exactly two daughters.[8] But this is no more than the syntactic skeleton of the grammar. As soon as we annotate the nodes by the semantic interpretation of the constituents, matters become much more complex. The main difference between DPTs and the trees familiar from sentential syntax is that in DPTs we allow attachment only at the right edge: discourse POPS which resume an interrupted constituent will always close off the interrupting (elaborating or otherwise subordinated) constituents and make it impossible to attach (coordinate or subordinate) any subsequent DCUs to them. It is this property of the DPT that we refer to as being **right open**.

It should be emphasized that, together with other computational discourse analysts, by stipulating restrictions on DCU attachment we are making a very strong claim about the structure of discourse. The openness of the right edge makes the DPT in this respect equivalent to the **intention stack** mechanisms proposed by Grosz and Sidner (1986) and the **right frontier** of Webber (1988), as opposed to Reichman's (1985) **context spaces** and Johnson-Laird's (1986) **mental models**, which always remain open and available for incrementation. This restriction permits predictions to be made about the encoding forms of incoming propositions. Any attempt to add propositions to a closed unit will be accompanied by an intonational repair or initiation signal and will receive a syntactic and phonological encoding as a new rather than a resumed unit (see Grosz and Sidner 1986; Polanyi 1988; Hirschberg and Pierrehumbert 1986; Hirschberg and Litman 1987; Webber 1988). The open right edge offers a simple formal mechanism for the analyst to keep track of what is happening at any given moment in a discourse. Ongoing activities that have been interrupted and are expected by the participants to be resumed are all encoded by nodes on the right edge.

2.3 Discourse parsing

Suppose a DPT has already been built over the first k DCUs $d_1, \ldots, d_k$. When the sentential component provides a new DCU d_{k+1}, we first determine the relationship of this incoming unit to the immediately preceding DCU d_k. If this is an elaboration relationship, then we attach d_{k+1} as the right sister to d_k at a newly created *S* node, and label this node with the structural and semantic characteristics of d_k. Otherwise, we continue up the open right edge of the DPT, looking for semantic or syntactic matches. When a match is made, we adjoin the newly parsed DCU as a terminal under a higher-level existing or newly created nonterminal node. If no match is made, we adjoin d_{k+1} as the right sister of a newly created *S* node at the bottom of the DPT, assuming that the new DCU is interrupting all ongoing discourse activities.

A DCU which initiates an entirely new discourse activity will be added to the DPT as a daughter of a high-level mother, which may be created especially to close off the old discourse activities and begin the new. In this case, the new node is inserted above the highest existing node in the tree and the new daughter becomes the new right sister of the previous discourse, rendering the entire previously existing tree inaccessible. Less dramatically, a DCU which initiates a discourse activity is often the first utterance of a new constituent, such as a new **move** or **episode** in an ongoing higher level unit such as a **speech event** or **story**. Both stories and speech events (linguistically realized socially meaningful activities; see Hymes 1972) are internally organized, and while the full details of this organization are complex, the highest level of organization is essentially sequential. For example, in a doctor–patient interaction first there is a greeting, followed by a statement of complaint, an examination, discussion of the findings, suggestions for follow-up, and finally, leave-taking. If a DCU (such as the doctor's summary of the findings) begins a new move, the previous moves become structurally inaccessible. Interruptions and other real-world exigencies do not cause the analysis to fail, since they are embedded into the matrix speech event at the moment of occurrence, and the speech event is resumed after the digression is ended. Needless to say, there can be attachment ambiguities, but the problem of finding higher-level discourse units does not appear to be any more complex than in the sentential case, and since our grammar is context-free, the same techniques of ambiguity resolution are applicable.

3   Discourse Interpretation

So far we have addressed two important issues for our theory: (1) what the atomic units of discourse are and (2) what kinds of structures can be built from these elementary units. These are issues for discourse syntax. Now we will turn to discourse semantics and ask how the resulting structures can be interpreted semantically.

3.1   Discourse contexts

Contemporary semantic theory has a great deal to say about isolated propositions, and we believe that a model-theoretic component along the lines of Montague (1973) or Groenendijk and Stokhof (1991) is indispensable for elucidating the meaning of natural language utterances. Yet we find it necessary to use a richer notion of semantic representation both for individual DCUs and for larger structures than is available in standard formal semantic models. In addition to the propositional **content** of a DCU we will also talk of its **context** and use the formal mechanism of **indexation** to express the fundamental dependency of propositional content on context.

To some extent, the importance of context has already been recognized in sentential semantics, especially for lexical items such as indexicals, where interpretation clearly depends on the identity and location of the speaker (Kaplan 1989). There was an attempt in situation semantics (Barwise and Perry 1983) to incorporate spatiotemporal and polarity indices, and a growing recognition in the formal semantics community that modality plays a very similar role (Roberts 1987; Farkas 1997). Under the LDM the range of contextual categories is considerably broader than generally assumed, and presents a hierarchy (partial ordering) of contexts:

interaction > speech event > genre unit > modality > polarity > point of view.

The LDM semantics is a version of dynamic semantics (Discourse Representation Theory (DRT): Kamp 1981; File Change Semantics (FCS): Heim 1982; Dynamic Logic: Groenendijk and Stokhof 1991), and the graphical similarity between our DC representations and those used in DRT/FCS is intentional. But the top half of the representation, which in these theories is used for keeping track of discourse referents, will in our notation be used to keep track of contextual indices. The change in notation reflects a shift in emphasis. While the central concern of DRT is pronominal reference and the equations between variables that implement coreferentiality, the central concern of the LDM is the setting and resetting of contexts.

In the simplest case, we depict a DC in (11):

(11)

$$
\begin{array}{|c|}
\hline
\textit{interaction} \\
\textit{speech event} \\
\textit{genre unit} \\
\textit{modality} \\
\textit{polarity} \\
\textit{point of view} \\
\hline
e_1 \text{ at } t_1 \\
e_2 \text{ at } t_2 \\
\cdots \\
e_k \text{ at } t_k \\
\hline
\end{array}
$$

We treat discourse contexts as purely technical devices of semantics, no more mentally real than variables or generalized quantifiers. For our purposes, discourse contexts are simply intermediate representations between natural language expressions and model structures, much as in DRT. Rather, we talk about the embedding of one discourse world in another, as in the case of reported speech depicted in (12) below:

(12)

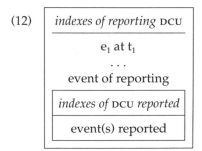

In general, discourse contexts can be recursively embedded in one another. They may also be related to one another by logical and other relations. We indicate these relations by arrows running between the related structures.[9]

4   The Explanatory Power of the LDM

In earlier sections of this chapter, we have presented a very brief and superficial overview of the LDM. Now we turn our attention to arguing for the usefulness of the machinery we have proposed. Specifically, in this section we will argue that the LDM allows us to construct a general, independently motivated theory of what *evoked in the discourse* entails. We will build our account on Prince's (1988) exemplary analysis of 1804 clauses from a corpus of Yiddish anecdotes, *Royte pomenantsen* (Olsvanger 1947: 208), "in which the subject is Postposed with a concomitant use of expletive ES."

We use Prince's examples given in (13)–(15) below to illustrate the phenomenon:

(13)   *es* is geshtorbn *a raykher goy.*
      it is died   a rich   gentile
      A rich gentile died.

(14)   *es* veln oyfahteyn *groyse khakhomin fun   daytshland* . . .
      it will upstand big   sages   from Germany.
      Great sages from Germany will stand up.

(15)   *es* geyt epes   in vald   *a yid*
      it goes something in wood a Jew
      Some Jew seems to be walking in the woods.

Prince argues that "Postposed subjects of ES-sentences indicate that they do not represent entities which have already been evoked in the discourse" (1988: 184). Her conclusion is well supported by the data given: out of 1804 examples of ES+Subject postposing, there are only two putative counterexamples to this generalization, which both occur in the same story. These counterexamples bring into question the apparently unremarkable idea of what it means *to be evoked in the discourse*.

4.1   *Nondiscourse initial Postposed subjects of* ES *sentences*

In the article we are considering, Prince explains that the full NP *the horse and wagon* occurs six times in the text of a single anecdote, *What my father did*.[10] In two cases, the postposed subject in an ES sentence is not "discourse initial in the story" (Prince p. 184):
Prince explains these apparent anomalies as follows:

> The second occurrence[11] [of the phrase in the text] is Postposed [and] is in an interior monologue of the hero – and since, as far as we know, *he* has not spoken about the horse and wagon *recently* it is discourse-initial in his private discussion with *himself*.
>
>   The fourth occurrence[12] [of the phrase in the text] is [also] Postposed, but this time it is in his public announcement back in the inn, addressed to the guests, and in that speech-event it is discourse-initial.

Thus it seems that the generalization is maintained that Postposed subjects of ES-sentences may not represent entities already evoked in the discourse, with the unsurprising caveat that discourses have internal structure and may themselves include sub-discourses in each of which some discourse entity may be new.[13]

Prince's analysis of how these cases differ from the norm is compelling. However, as stated, the explanation of the key data is ad hoc and unrelated to any more systematic linguistic theory. No explanation of what it means for a discourse to have internal structure is given. Let us now turn to a discussion of how the LDM can account for Prince's data within a comprehensive theory of discourse structure.

4.2 Reanalysis of Prince (1988, 1993)

In order to see how Prince's data are treated under the LDM, let us consider a shortened version of the Yiddish anecdote she provides. For readability, we have removed the glosses. We have already segmented the text according to LDM criteria:

What my father did
(a) A guy once went by an inn. (b) He left his horse and wagon outside (c) and went alone into the inn. (d) Inside the inn, (e) he ordered a couple of eggs (f) or some chicken (g) and ate it. (h) Then he got up (i) to travel further. (j) He goes outside the inn. (k) He looks around. (l) There's no horse and no wagon. (m) He thought, (n) there was probably a thief among the people in the inn (o) that had stolen the horse and wagon. (p) He goes back into the inn (q) and shouts (r) "The horse and wagon should be returned." (s) The thief got scared. (t) He quickly went out (u) and brought back the horse and wagon.

This discourse consists of constituents of various types, including: the List, Elaboration, Sum Up, Subordinate Clause, Operator/Sentence, Interruption, Direct Discourse, Reported Thought, If/Then, Because, Antecedent/Consequent, Yiddish Anecdote, and Written Yiddish Anecdote.

The Written Yiddish Anecdote is a coordinate structure consisting of several co-ordinated constituents (as a first analysis and based on this one example):

Yiddish anecdote → (Opening), Orientation, Action, Question, Answer

A Written anecdote involves an Interaction between a Reader and a Modeled Writer in which an Interaction between a Modeled Narrator and Modeled Story Recipient takes place. The rule for Written Yiddish Anecdote consists of the constituents of Yiddish Anecdote plus an initial Title constituent:

Written Yiddish Anecdote → Title, Yiddish Anecdote.

4.3 DPT of What my father did

Following the rules of discourse segmentation and discourse syntax given above, results in the discourse parse tree for *What my father did* are given in figure 14.1.[14]

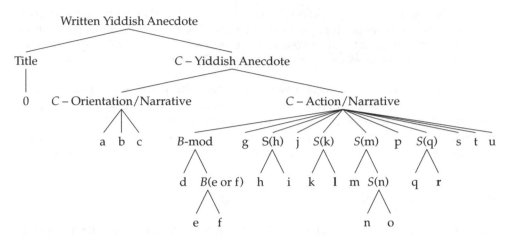

Figure 14.1   DPT for *What my father did*

An examination of the DPT for *What my father did* reveals its hierarchical structure. The events of the narrative mainline are represented as daughters of one coordinate ACTION node, while reported speech, thought and perception are shown as embedded constituents under *S* nodes.

From this purely structural representation, however, it is not clear why the subjects in (l) and (r) are not postposed. For an explanation of this phenomenon we must look further to the semantic representation.

4.4   *Evoked in which discourse?*

As you will recall, LDM analysis of discourse requires that each DCU be tagged for a number of context variables. If we now examine the semantic representation for this text constructed following the LDM, it is clear that *the horse and wagon* is evoked within the scope of three separate interactional contexts: Interaction 1, involving a Modeled Narrator and a Modeled Story Recipient; Interaction 2, in which the participant set is the Guy who acts as both enunciator of perception and receiver of the enunciation; and Interaction 3, in which the Guy interacts with the crowd at the inn. These three DCUs correspond to DCUs marked (b), (l), and (r). These are the first mention of *horse and wagon* in the Yiddish anecdote we have been examining, and the two putative counterexamples to Prince's generalization.

Since the LDM requires tagging of each DCU for Interactional Context as well as for a host of other context types, our analysis provides the machinery to rephrase Prince's theory of Yiddish expletive ES + Subject Postposing without extending the model at all. The analysis of this under the LDM specifies that any entity mentioned initially in any Interaction Context will be marked in Yiddish as a first mention.

In figure 14.2, we have prepared an informal representation of the semantics of this text.[15]

Interaction 1: Participants: Modeled Narrator and Story Recipient
Speech Event 1: Storytelling   Discourse Unit 1: Anecdote
modality: indicative   point of view: omniscient narrator

---

guy goes by an inn
GUY leaves his horse and wagon outside
GUY goes alone into the inn

GUY orders FOOD   ←

Participants: Modeled Narrator and Story Recipient Speech Event 1: Storytelling modality: indicative point of view: omniscient narrator
GUY orders a couple of eggs *or* GUY orders some chichen

GUY eats FOOD

GUY gets up   ←

Participants: Modeled Narrator and Story Recipient Speech Event 1: Storytelling modality: irrealis   point of view: omniscient narrator
GUY travels further

GUY goes outside the inn
GUY looks around

Interaction 2: Participants: GUY modality: Direct Perception   point of view: GUY polarity: negative
Horse and wagon exists

Interaction 2: Participants: GUY and GUY Speech Event 3: introspection modality: epistemic factivity: "PROBABLE" point of view: GUY	Interaction 2: Participants: GUY and GUY Speech Event 3: introspection modality: epistemic factivity: "PROBABLE" point of view: GUY temporal location: "FLASHBACK"
thief is among the people	THIEF steals horse and wagon

←

GUY goes back into the inn

Interaction 3: Participants: GUY and INN-CROWD Speech Event 3: making-a-fuss modality: "MUST"   point of view: GUY
Horse and wagon are returned

thief gets scared
THIEF goes out
THIEF brings back horse and wagon

Figure 14.2   Informal semantic representation of *What my father did*

5   Summary and Conclusions

In describing the LDM, we have dealt with discourse as an autonomous linguistic module while, almost paradoxically, insisting that the physical and social identity of the speaker are of crucial importance in discourse interpretation. Where, one might wonder, is the speaker in this theory of discourse? Although accounting for the social concerns, motivations and actions of the speaker, along with the cognitive processing apparatus brought into play during discourse production and reception, lay well beyond the scope of the present discussion, the model of discourse presented here is potentially of use to the working sociolinguist concerned with the analysis and manipulation of complex interactive data, and the psycholinguist interested in understanding the nature of linguistic competence and performance.

For the sociolinguist, we offer analytic machinery which can handle incomplete utterances, hesitations, repairs, interruptions, and changes in social roles and identities (for a survey of work in the interactive and cultural dimensions of language use, see Duranti and Goodwin 1992). The indexing and segmentation requirements allow the sociolinguist to track what is going on in the discourse in a more consistent manner than has been possible previously. In addition, the definition of the DCU permits the form of encoding of propositional (or operator) material to be nonlinguistic. Deictic points, grimaces, or the actions of a machine may all be integrated into the discourse history. The structures of specific instances of a socially recognized speech event can be compared with one another, and far more robust descriptions of the sequences of expected actions can be produced.

To the psycholinguist we offer the opportunity to formulate testable hypotheses about discourse processing and to investigate the relationship between discourse structure, sentence form, and memory limitations in terms of an integrated framework. Although we make no specific cognitive claims and pointedly avoid using psychologically appealing terms such as "mental model," "salience," or "attention," we nonetheless provide a semantic representation in terms of which one can inquire into the mental model any given speaker might build, the differential salience accorded by a speaker to the entities and events in that model, and the degree of attention entities command (see Levelt 1993 for an overview of much relevant work in this area).

In conclusion, we would maintain that the LDM provides a significant set of tools for systematic investigation of discourse-level linguistic phenomena. We have made explicit the nature of our atomic units, the rules for combining them into more complex structures, and the framework in which both simple and constructed units may be interpreted. Linguists, especially the more formally minded, are often held back from the study of discourse by the belief, strongly felt though seldom clearly articulated, that discourse itself is simply an unstructured soup of sentences. Our goal has been to demonstrate that this belief is false: a theoretically well-founded characterization of the domain of rule applicability and the distribution of linguistic structures in discourse is both possible and necessary.

NOTES

1 Paralinguistic signaling includes the use of deictic hand gestures, ad hoc head nods, eye movements, facial expressions, etc. Gestural languages such as American Sign Language and other signed languages encode DCUs in linguistic signs realized nonverbally.

2 This segmentation methodology can operate even if discourse operators are entirely absent from the text. Semantic criteria, alone, will force breaks among the E-DCUs. Similarly, segmentation does not depend on any notion of "coherence" and operates even if the discourse is fragmentary or incoherent.

3 Operators, if present in the text, are treated as clitics attached to propositional hosts.

4 For details of how the computation is done on the lower-level DCUs to create the specification on the higher-level DCU see Polanyi (1985); Caenepeel and Moens (1994); Prüst et al. (1994).

5 Matthiessen and Thompson (1988) build on Halliday's notions of rankshifting (Halliday 1967) and treat subordinated clauses as discourse-embedded.

6 The general constraint in discourse subordination requiring the subordinated element to be to the right of its matrix in the linear ordering of the text (and thus in the discourse parse structure, which is strictly bound to text order) is relaxed in sentential subordination, where the normal order of embedding can be reversed.

7 Longacre (1976) refers to logical and rhetorical structures as "binary paragraphs."

8 If we use different types of parentheses to encode the type of the mother node, () for coordination, [] for subordination, and {} for binary relations, we can describe the language of well-formed DPTs with a single rule $N \rightarrow (NN^+) \mid [NN] \mid \{NN\} \mid t$, where N is the only nonterminal (the start symbol) and t is the terminal denoting an elementary DCU.

9 How logical inferences are drawn on the basis of such relations is a matter too complex and digressive to discuss here (for recent work in this direction see Lascarides and Asher 1991, 1993; Asher 1993; Farkas 1997.)

10 The translated shortened form of the anecdote is in section 4.2 below.

11 **es iz nito**   *der vogn*   **un nit**
It is not here the wagon and not
dos ferdl
the horse
There's no **horse and no wagon**.

12 **es zol teykef**   **Vern**
It shall immediately become
der vogn mith ferdl
the wagon with the horse
The horse and wagon must come back immediately.

13 Emphasis added.

14 For the sake of simplicity the terminal nodes are labeled only with the letter corresponding to the terminal DCU in the segmented text; nonterminals are labeled only with C, S, or B and the simplest indication of semantic extension. Full node labels are much more extensive and allow for the computation on the nonterminal nodes necessary to express recursive DCU formation.

15 In order to make the diagram a bit more easily understood, only particularly relevant contexts are identified. After the first DCU, the contexts which hold for the entire are not repeated.

REFERENCES

Asher, N. 1993. *Reference to Abstract Objects in Discourse*. Dordrecht: Kluwer.

Barwise, J. P. 1983. *Situations and Attitudes*. Cambridge, MA: MIT Press.

Caenepeel, M. and M. Moens. 1994. Temporal structure and discourse structure. In *Tense and Aspect in Discourse*, eds C. Vet and C. Vetter, 5–20. Berlin: de Gruyter.

Davidson, D. 1967. The logical form of action sentences. In *The Logic of Decision and Action*, ed. N. Rescher. Pittsburgh: University of Pittsburgh Press.

Di Eugenio, B., J. D. Moore, and M. Paolucci. 1997. Learning features that predict cue usage. *Proceedings of the 35th Annual Meeting of the Association for Computational Linguistics, Association of Computational Linguistics 97*, Madrid, Spain.

Duranti, A. and C. Goodwin. 1992. *Rethinking Context: Language as an Interactive Phenomenon*. New York: Cambridge University Press.

Farkas, D. 1997. Evaluation indices and scope. In *Ways of Scope Taking*, ed. A. Szabolcsi, 183–215. Dordrecht: Kluwer.

Groenendijk, J. and M. Stokhof. 1991. Dynamic predicate logic. *Linguistics and Philosophy*, 14(1).39–100.

Grosz, B. and C. Sidner. 1986. Attention, intention and the structure of discourse. *Computational Linguistics*, 12(3).175–204.

Halliday, M. A. K. 1967. Notes on transitivity and theme, part 2. *Journal of Linguistics* 3.199–244.

Heim, I. 1982. The semantics of definite and indefinite noun phrases. Cambridge, MA, MIT dissertation. Department of Linguistics.

Hirschberg, J. and D. Litman. 1987. Now let's talk about now: identifying cue phrases intonationally. *Proceedings of the 25th Annual Meeting of the Association for Computational Linguistics*, 163–71.

Hirschberg, J. and J. Pierrehumbert. 1986. The intonational structuring of discourse. *Proceedings of the 24th Annual Meeting of the Association of Computational Linguistics*, 136–44.

Hymes, D. S. 1972. Models of the interaction of language and social setting. *Journal of Social Issues*, 23(3).

Johnson-Laird, P. 1986. *Mental Models*. Cambridge MA: Harvard University Press.

Kamp, H. A. 1981. A theory of truth and semantic representation. In *Formal Methods in the Study of Language, Part 1*, eds J. Groenendijk, T. Janssen, and M. Stokhof. Amsterdam: Mathematisch Centrum.

Kaplan, D. 1989. Demonstratives in demonstratives. In *Themes from Kaplan*, eds J. Almog, J. Perry, and H. Wettstein, 481–563. Oxford: Oxford University Press.

Lascarides, A. and N. Asher. 1991. *Discourse Relations and Common Sense Entailment*. Edinburgh: HCRC/RP-6 Edinburgh Human Communication Centre.

Lascarides, A. and N. Asher. 1993. Temporal interpretation, discourse relations, and common sense entailment. *Linguistics and Philosophy*, 16(5).437–93.

Levelt, W. J. M. 1993. *Speaking: From Intention to Articulation*. Cambridge, MA: MIT Press.

Longacre, R. 1976. *An Anatomy of Speech Notions*. Lisse: Peter de Ridder Press.

Matthiessen, C. and S. Thompson. 1988. The structure of discourse and "subordination." In *Clause Combining in Grammar and Discourse*, eds J. Haiman and S. Thompson, 275–330. Amsterdam: John Benjamins.

Montague, R. 1973. The proper treatment of quantification in ordinary English. In *Approaches to Natural Language: Proceedings of the 1970 Stanford Workshop on Grammar and Semantics*, eds J. Hintikka, J. Moravcsik, and P. Suppes, 247–70. Dordrecht: D. Reidel.

Olsvanger, I. ed. 1947. *Royte pomerantsen*. New York: Schocken Books.

Polanyi, L. 1978. False starts can be true. *Proceedings of Berkeley Linguistics Society*, 4. 628–38.

Polanyi, L. 1985. A theory of discourse structure and discourse coherence. *Proceedings of the 21st Annual Meeting of the Chicago Linguistics Society*. Chicago: University of Chicago, Department of Linguistics.

Polanyi, L. 1987. Keeping it all straight: interpreting narrative time in real discourse. *West Coast Conference on Formal Linguistics*, 6.229–245.

Polanyi, L. 1988. A formal model of discourse structure. *Journal of Pragmatics*, 12.601–38.

Polanyi, L. 1996. *The Linguistic Structure of Discourse*. Stanford, CA: CSLI Technical Report.

Polanyi, L. and R. Scha. 1984. A syntactic approach to discourse semantics. *Proceedings of the 6th International Conference on Computational Linguistics*, 413–19. Stanford, CA.

Polanyi, L. and M. H. van den Berg. 1996. Discourse structure and discourse interpretation. *Proceedings of the 10th Amsterdam Colloquium*, 113–31. Amsterdam: ILLC, Department of Philosophy, University of Amsterdam.

Prince, E. 1988. The discourse functions of Yiddish expletive ES+subject-postposing. *Papers in Pragmatics*, 2(1/2).176–94.

Prince, E. 1993. On the discourse functions of syntactic form in Yiddish: expletive ES and subject-postposing. In *The Field of Yiddish*, 5th collection, eds D. Goldberg, M. Herzog, B. Kirshenblatt-Gimblett, and D. Miron, 59–86. Northwestern University Press/YIVO.

Prust, H., R. Scha, and M. v. d. Berg. 1994. Discourse structure and verb phrase anaphora. *Linguistics and Philosophy*, 17.261–327.

Reichman, R. 1985. *Getting Computers to Talk Like Me and You*. Cambridge, MA: MIT Press.

Roberts, C. 1990. *Modal Subordination*. New York: Garland.

Scha, R. and L. Polanyi. 1988. An augmented context-free grammar for discourse. *Proceedings of the 12th International Conference on Computational Linguistics*, 573–7. Budapest, August.

Schiffrin, D. 1987. *Discourse Markers*. Cambridge: Cambridge University Press.

Webber, B. L. 1988. *Discourse Deixis and Discourse Processing*. Technical Report MS–CIS–86–74. Linc Lab 42. Pennsylvania: Department of Computer and Information Science. University of Pennsylvania.

15 The Variationist Approach toward Discourse Structural Effects and Socio-interactional Dynamics

SYLVIE DUBOIS AND DAVID SANKOFF

0 Introduction

Sociolinguists tend to focus on spontaneous speech used in ordinary conversational situations. The variationist approach to sociolinguistics involves open-ended procedures to obtain representative and comparable data, which contrasts with principles of control and predictability in other experimental-evaluative approaches (see Sankoff 1989 for more details). The variationist method relies on quantitative analysis to validate interpretations of the data. The purpose of the quantitative method is to highlight the sociocultural meaning of linguistic variation and the nature of the relationships among the linguistic aspects in probabilistic terms. The use of quantitative analysis is not a minor methodological detail. It provides a more accurate understanding of the usage and the frequency of the forms within the community as well as a way of detecting linguistic change. The frequency of forms and speakers' preferences give a more realistic overview of the usage of linguistic structures. More importantly, statistical tools allow us to pinpoint the social and linguistic conditioning as well as the tendencies and regularities within the linguistic system. Being a more objective and accurate basis of analysis than intuitions and judgments of value, the quantitative method is a powerful and efficient tool.

Sociolinguists view discourse as the product of a specific verbal interaction resulting from a set of choices vis-à-vis the set of all the potential choices within a language. Discursive competence implies the knowledge of linguistic forms, the context within which they might be used, and the sociolinguistic circumstances which permit them to be realized; these circumstances include the conceptual universe of the speakers, their sociocultural characteristics, and the interactional strategies between speakers. Several analysts (Labov 1978; Lavandera 1978; Dines 1980; Romaine 1981; Thibault 1982; Weiner and Labov 1983; Vincent 1983, 1986; Horvath 1985; Dubois 1992) have identified five characteristics of variation analysis within discourse. First, discourse variables involve a finite number of discrete variants, independent and autonomous, which do not form part of a continuum of surface realizations, but are related to each other only by their identical function. Second, it is not feasible to contrast the presence of a discourse form to its absence as is done in phonological studies. The linguistic context where the form will appear cannot be anticipated even though it is possible to characterize some linguistic contexts that favor its usage. Third, substitutions among the different manifestations of most discourse processes have consequences at several linguistic levels (pragmatic, interactional, etc.). Fourth, we cannot delimit and define in advance the set of different discourse functions. In addition, discourse forms are structurally diverse and can occur at distinct levels of analysis; they can be complex processes (narration, description, argument), large units (repetition, rhetorical questions, reported speech), or more circumscribed forms (markers and particles). Fifth, the discourse variable has in general a large number of variants (different forms) and, in consequence, requires a more complex quantitative treatment than the usual variable rule method elaborated for binomial variants (Dubois and Sankoff 1997).

Sociolinguists argue that the only way to access the multidimensional scoop of discourse structure is: (1) to adopt a quantitative procedure which respects the principle of accountability; (2) to recognize the various levels of analysis and to integrate them into the observation and analysis of the distribution of a discourse form; (3) to focus the analysis on the conditioning that holds among the multiple linguistic levels (structural, referential, pragmatic, interactional, social, etc.) that form the canvas of discourse process; and (4) to highlight the polyvalent associations (the co-occurrences) between the components of a discourse structure at its various linguistic levels.

0.1 The holistic understanding of the discourse system

The goal of the variationist approach is to highlight the "potential of signification of discourse" (term used by Halliday 1978), that is, the different levels of meaning which are intertwined to create discourse. Four general principles are representative of this framework:

1 *The specific conditions of oral speech:* The segmentation of oral speech based on the concept of the sentence as it is formulated for written speech is inappropriate (Blanche-Benveniste and Jeanjean 1987: 89). The identification of a discourse process must take into account the specific conditions of formation of oral speech.

2 *The type of corpus:* Factors taken into account in the study of a discourse structure within a specific corpus might not be applicable or relevant to or significant in another type of corpus. Consequently, the selection and the nature of the factors or linguistic levels, which may influence the occurence of a discourse structure, are constrained and valid to a single corpus.

3 *The identification of the significant levels conditioning a discourse process:* There are many levels on which discourse is organized. The important point is that the number and the type of levels are not fixed: they vary according to the object of study, the corpus, the type of linguistic data (political speech, interaction among friends, reporter-type interview) and the observed material (written or oral discourse).

The division into two or more is a conceptual distinction,[1] which presupposes that all the levels participate in the creation of a discourse process, and are dependent on each other.

4   *The dynamic nature of discourse:* In examining the discourse system, sociolinguists aim at understanding the dynamic interaction between the different levels of signification constituting the discourse system. All levels are intertwined and interact with each other, but they all can be theoretically classified into categories. The conceptual division aims at identifying where, when, and how each level participates in the organization of a discourse form.

The variationist approach is not without difficulties. The definition and the delimitation of a discourse object – that is, the distinction of what is inherent in this object (the definition) and what constitutes the strategies of support or the variable environment of this object (the groups of factors) – itself represents a difficult task. The analyst must deal with numerous and extremely varied groups of factors. Their study requires different scientific competences; spotting all of them is not evident and is a tedious task. More importantly, their study requires linguistic intuition and good comprehension of discourse organization. Moreover, the systematic analysis of all the relations between groups of factors and the verification of the associations detected oblige the researcher to manipulate a lot of data and evaluate the significance of many statistical quantities, which requires care, energy, and critical judgment.

Nevertheless, the solid scientific basis of the empirical procedure as well as the quantitative method transcend these difficulties. The representation of a given discourse process in its multidimensional aspects, rather than as an inventory of its forms, allows us to unveil the network of associations between different factors which influence the construction of such a process.

The rest of this chapter is divided into two parts. In the following section, we set out the formal criteria and discourse roles that characterize the enumerative process in the spoken language. These provide the operational basis for the collection of data on several thousand tokens of enumeration. We present a variety of structural factors – the number of components; their syntactic nature; the use of coordinating markers and of the processes of repetition, reduction and expansion – which are among the most salient aspects of variation within the structure of enumeration. We intend to show that these processes do not, however, vary completely independently, but in a patterned way, and this patterning should reveal much about functional constraints on the construction of enumerative expressions by speakers.

The second part of the chapter deals with the stylistic dimension that accounts for the considerable variation among speakers in the overall use of enumeration. Stylistic factors are not as regularly employed as sociodemographic factors in quantitative studies, partly because stylistic distinctions are not directly accessible to objective approaches, and because variation along the stylistic dimension generally seems to parallel that along some social parameter. However, there has recently been much debate over the direction and extent of variation due to stylistic or interactional parameters in general versus the analogous effects of age, sex, and class.[2] Rickford and McNair-Knox (1994) emphasize the importance of empirical testing of hypotheses and the predictions of certain models of stylistic variation, such as the audience design model of Bell (1984) and the communication accommodation model of Coupland and Giles (1988). Rickford and McNair-Knox also note that the quantitative study of style in sociolinguistics adds an important perspective. Combined with social aspects (age, sex, race, etc.) and with internal linguistic conditioning, the quantitative study of stylistic variation gives rise to a range of intriguing problems in sociolinguistics. It helps distinguish between the effects of internal constraints (linguistic factors) and external constraints (social and stylistic dimensions), and to assess the independence of the latter. In order to determine whether enumeration in spontaneous discourse exemplifies the kind of stylistic observations found to be recurrent in sociolinguistics by Finegan and Biber (1994), we compare and contrast social and stylistic conditioning on the use of enumeration.

1   Enumeration as a Discourse Strategy

Studies of figures of speech have been limited in traditional rhetoric, as well as in stylistics and in modern literary fields, because analysts have confined their role to exceptional, ornamental uses. Because they generally pick only one or a few striking examples to illustrate their points, they have tended to underestimate the regular, routine use of these figures; this is true even in literary studies. While enumeration as a figure of speech has engrossed rhetoricians since classical times, as well as modern text analysts, little attention has been paid to it in spoken discourse. Enumeration is a frequently used discourse strategy – in compiling shopping lists, in presenting evidence in an argument, in counting one's blessings, in comparing costs and benefits – and its use in oral interaction differs considerably from its role in the written language (Gilbert 1989). Because it is made up of, or overlaps with, numerous other linguistic processes, enumeration has not usually been studied for its own sake, but rather in terms of related topics: repetition, structural parallelism, semantic progression. As an example, Schiffrin (1987) and Jefferson (1990) discuss lists, a distinct type of construction, though overlapping to a considerable extent with enumeration.

Enumeration is a complex process, combining a variable number of different structural components of the same type to evoke a single, more general, referent. It is a rhetorical device in French as well as in other languages which have received less attention. With some effort it can be operationally identified and isolated in a text (see Dubois 1995 for more detail). *Enumeration represents a cumulative discursive procedure made up of at least two different components that belong to the same or equivalent morphological and functional categories. This procedure evokes a homogeneous referential ensemble to which the enumerated constituents refer.* The surprising variety, not only of types of enumeration but also of syntactic and discursive procedures used in their elaboration, is of particular interest in the enumerative procedure. Examples (a) and (b) correspond well to the intuitive notion of enumeration as the sequential naming of the elements of some set. In assembling our data set, however, it became clear that referential and syntactically more complex constructions like examples (c), (d), and (e) should also be included:

(1)   **Examples of enumeration encountered in the corpus**[3]

a.   1.   Okay then: your family,
your children do they live
near here?
2.   No, my children . . .
my daughter lives in
Snowdon (yes)
one of my sons lives in
Repentigny
the other lives in . . . well,
since this morning, in
Boucherville (ah ah)
and the third is in La-Cité
(uh-huh)

1.   OK puis: c'est ça: Votre famille
vos enfants est-ce-qu'ils habitent
pas loin d'ici?
2.   Non mes enfants:
ma fille habite à Snowdon <oui>
un autre de mes fils habite à
Repentigny
l'autre habite à: bien depuis ce
matin à Boucherville <ah ah>
et le troisième est à La-Cité
<humhum> (79:3)

b.   She's got a title, she might make
. . . I don't know, twenty-five
cents more than the other, but
she's got all the responsibilities.
Open the shop
close the shop (uh-huh)
cash-receiving all of that
taking stock shipments then . . .
Because I have a friend like that
(uh-huh)

Il lui donne un titre, elle a peut-être:
je sais pas moi vingt-cinq cents de
plus' que l'autre mais elle a toutes les
responsabilités.
Ouvrir la porte
fermer la porte <humhum>
le cash receiving tout' ça là
recevoir le stock puis:
Parce-que j'ai une amie comme ça
<humhum> (7:56)

c.   So the principles of life haven't
changed. There has been no
evolution in that. <humhum>
The idiots
we've had some
we will have some
and then we'll have some more
and there will always be some

Fait-que donc les principes de vie
ont pas changé. Il y a eu aucune
évolution là-dedans. <humhum>
Des idiots
tu en as eus,
tu vas en avoir
puis tu vas en avoir encore
puis il y en aura tout le temps
(2-84:18)

d.   Everybody in the hall. "I salute
the flag." And the principal reads
the prize-winners, and this and
that <y yes yes> Finally it's time
to salute the flag,
the brigadiers in front
the white belt
the flag carrier
the first in the class

Tout le monde dans la salle. "Je te
salue ô drapeau." Puis le principal
lit des mentions puis ci, puis ça.
<oui oui oui> Là un moment
donné c'est le salut au drapeau,
les brigadiers en avant
la ceinture blanche
le porte-drapeau
le premier de classe

the second	le deuxième
and the third in the class	puis le troisième de classe
the Quebec one	celui du Québec
the American one. Fantastic.	celui des Etats-Unis. Fantastique.
The Canadian one in the middle.	Celui du Canada dans le milieu.
You get the picture?	Tu vois la scène? <oui (rire)> Bon,
<yes (laughs)> Good, perfect.	parfait.
The girls on one side,	Les filles sur un bord,
the guys on the other.	les gars sur l'autre. (2-84:51)

e. I mean [language] it's probably
not important
when you go to work in a factory,
I don't think it's very important.
<humhum>
When you're a doctor really I am
not even sure it's important.
But when you're a lawyer, then
it surely is. <humhum>
When you're a journalist, then
it surely is.
When you're a university
professor, then it is.
<yes yes yes> Yes yes.

Je veux dire [la langue] c'est
probablement pas important
quand tu t'en vas travailler dans
une usine, je pense pas que ça
soit bien important. <humhum>
Quand tu es médecin à la rigueur je
suis même pas sûr c'est important.
Mais quand tu es-t-avocat ce l'est
sûrement. <humhum>
Quand tu es journaliste ce l'est
sûrement.
Quand tu es professeur d'université
ce l'est.
<oui oui oui> Oui oui. (117-84:43)

We used the following operational criteria to identify enumerations:

1 There must be at least two components. Traditionally three have been required, but we also accepted just two when they are followed by an "extension particle" (Dubois 1992). Look at the second sequence in example (c), where we find *puis*, etc. There were more than 400 enumerations with two components, 2000 with three components, and 900 with four or more, to a maximum of 17.

2 Each component must constitute an autonomous prosodic and syntactic unit, and they cannot simply be repeated items with the same referent.

3 The components are linked in a coordinate structure, either explicitly (by a conjunction) or implicitly.

4 The components have identical functional roles. They are subjects of the same verb, adjectives qualifying the same noun, subordinate clauses attached to the same noun or the same verb, a series of independent sentences, etc.

5 They have morphological equivalence. Though the components are not constrained to be in exactly the same word class, they must be paradigmatically substitutable from the syntactic viewpoint.

6 The components of the enumeration together evoke some larger set of which they are part and which is larger than any one of them.

7 They have prosodic coherence. The same rhythmic value is assigned to each component that distinguishes the enumerative sequence from its general context.

2   Data and Methodology

The 1984 Montréal corpus serves as database for our study of enumeration. Composed of 72 semiclosed interviews, this corpus is a continuation of the Sankoff–Cedergren corpus completed in 1971. It contains 60 interviews with speakers in 1971 and 12 interviews with speakers aged 15–20 (to represent a new cohort of young speakers). On average, each interview included 1.5 hours of conversation, usually recorded in the informant's home. The interviewers were directed to create a climate conducive to informal conversation and to elicit the most discourse possible from the informant (Thibault and Vincent 1990: 46).

In total, we collected 3464 enumerations in the corpus. All speakers use the enumerative procedure, but to varying degrees; we find 12–156 enumerations per interview. No social factor influences the overall rate of use of enumeration. General use of enumerations neither rises nor falls with the age of the speaker. Women and men use it in similar ways and the socioprofessional code assigned to speakers does not affect the overall use of enumeration. To measure the association between aspects of the interactional context of enumeration and its properties at the structural, referential, and discourse levels, we used a systematic protocol for generating and evaluating large numbers of cross-tabulations of two or three variables. To analyze the social effects on these same properties, we used GoldVarb, a logistic regression package.

The interview is divided into two parts, each corresponding to a specific interactional dynamic. Open questions dealing with such themes as residence, occupation, education, and language constitute the first part, henceforth called the interview. The goal was largely to stimulate as much natural, uninterrupted discourse as possible. A closed (more or less) questionnaire on tastes and consumer habits represents the second part, which was designed to probe a more specific set of attitudes, customs, and experiences. In the corpus, there are not (properly speaking) two separate communication events: it is the same interview, and the interviewer and the roles (interviewer and informant) do not change. However, the use of two questionnaires modifies the dynamic of the interviews. The distinction between the general interview and the questionnaire is one of style, or more precisely of discourse elicitation, although this stylistic differentiation is weaker than that provoked by two very different communication events (e.g. at home, in public).

The distribution of the enumerations within the interviews is not affected by the subject matter. On the other hand, the use of enumeration is very sensitive to the two interactional dynamics set in place by the interviewer: one in the general interview and the other in a questionnaire. It was the latter that provoked the greater production of enumeration. The nature of some of the questions in the questionnaire partially explains this high frequency of occurence. Specific questions, such as "Do you read the newspaper?," "Which one?," "Do you play games or sports?," "Which ones?," "Do you go see shows?," "What kind?," implicitly assume more than one newspaper, more than one game, and more than one kind of show.

The two interactional dynamics also lead to enumerations that tend to have somewhat different properties at all levels of analysis. Distinctions between them on the interactional level are summarized in table 15.1.

Table 15.1 Summary of relations on the interactional level

Enumerations in general interview	*Enumerations in questionnaire*
+ monologic section	+ dialogic section (+ back-channel)
+ indirect orientation	+ direct orientation

The enumerations produced in the interview tend not to be directly elicited by the interviewer, and to be in more monologic discourse. Enumerations collected in the questionnaire tend to occur in more dialogic discourse, as part of an immediate answer to the interviewer, who accompanies their production with back-channel signals.

In this chapter, we will discuss only the most salient linguistic aspects of the construction of multiple forms of enumeration.

In first place is the length of the enumeration:

1 The number of enumerated constituents (elements), which varies from two to seventeen in speech.
2 Enumeration composed of complete sentences (SVO) is distinguished from that composed of sentence fragments (for example an enumeration of adjectivals).
3 Third is the specific experience of the informant, including autobiographical observations and the experience of his or her friends and relations, and the general experience of the world.
4 Following this is the particular functional organization of the enumeration (schemas: that of synonymous or antonymous value versus that of sets), particularly the inventory or the list of heterogeneous elements, in which several distinct elements are concatenated to evoke the entirety of the set.
5 Enumerations are sometimes anchored in the discourse by an opening theme (produced by the interviewer or the speaker) which does not participate in the specific structure of the enumeration but which is instead an optional part of its general structure.
6 The enumeration may have an informative function, or it may play a persuasive role such as justification, illustration, counterargument, etc.

3 Structural Effects on Enumeration

Enumerations are used to evoke some set larger than any of the components and generally larger than all of them put together. The expressive potential of this device is thus very great, but its use entails a number of potential problems of processing for the speaker and of interpretation for the hearer. The concatenation of several syntactically homologous components in a slot that ordinarily contains just one item may disrupt the expected sequence of categories for the hearer. An enumeration entails a longer delay than usual between the part of the sentence or utterance preceding it and that following it, possibly creating problems for both the speaker and hearer. For the speaker, the condition of equivalent categories may be too constraining and too time-consuming, but for the hearer it may be essential for decoding. Summarizing, the cross-cutting pressures on enumerations that may account for their variability, then, are of three different types, which we operationalize as follows:

1   *Expressivity:* The more components there are, the more there is in each component, and the more different the content of each component, the more the expressive potential of the enumeration.
2   *Processing:* The more components there are, the more there is in each component, and the more different the content of each component, the greater the processing difficulty. Conversely, the shorter the enumeration, the shorter the components, and the more parallel the components are, the easier the enumeration is to process.
3   *Length:* The shorter the enumeration, the shorter the components are, the more efficient is the use of enumeration in carrying out its function. Parallelism of components is redundant and represents a decrease of efficiency.

Of course, we have greatly oversimplified these considerations (see Slobin's 1977 charges to performance). They may not apply in particular instances, but simply represent hypotheses about statistical tendencies.

The linguistic structure of the enumerative expression and of its individual components referring to a set of elements is quite variable, as can be seen in the examples. The first of the structural factor groups to be examined is simply the number of components in the enumerative sequence. Example (b) has four components, example (d) has eleven. According to our operational criteria, it is clear that increasing the number of components in an enumeration allows for greater expressivity but is costly in terms both of communicative efficiency and of processing.

The second factor, that of component complexity, contrasts enumeration via independent propositions with the situation where the components constitute a part of a sentence. We also distinguish a category of dislocated, independent, or detached units that are associated with a sentence but do not form part of the basic sentence matrix. Increasing complexity should allow for increased expressivity but cause increased processing costs and decreased efficiency, much as increasing the number of components does.

When the third, fourth, etc. component shows an ellipsis of an element that "should have" appeared by analogy with the first two components, the enumeration was coded as "reduced." Example (d) shows several degrees of reduction. Inversely, when lexical elements are added to the purely paradigmatic content of the second or later component, this was coded as "expanded." The sixth component in example (d) is expanded.

Both reduction and expansion decrease the homology among components and hence could increase the difficulty for the hearer of recognizing that the enumerative procedure has been used. With respect to efficiency, the two processes should have opposite effects, reduction increasing it and expansion impeding it. In addition, expansion definitely should allow for increased expressivity.

For the fifth factor group, enumerations where some elements are repeated in at least two components were coded as such (e.g. example c). This was a widespread feature in the data. Repetition results in increased parallelism among components and hence should decrease processing difficulties while also decreasing efficiency.

The sixth aspect of enumeration that we coded was the use of explicit markers to indicate the coordination of components and their integration into the linear sequence. Thus, markers decrease processing difficulties while decreasing efficiency by adding additional material to the utterance. In the written language, by far the most common pattern is the presence of a conjunction between the penultimate and the final components of an enumeration. In the spoken language, in stark contrast, almost half of the enumerations simply concatenate the components without any explicit marker.

Table 15.2 summarizes the hypothesized effect of each of the parameters on processing difficulties, expressivity, and efficiency.

Table 15.2 Hypothesized effects of parameters on use of enumeration

Parameters	Processing ease	Expressivity	Efficiency
Number of components	–	+	–
Complexity	–	+	–
Reduction	–		+
Expansion	–	+	–
Repetition	+		–
Markers	+		–

The empirical relationships among the six factor groups as found by the detailed statistical analysis described in Dubois (1995) are summarized in figure 15.1. The strength of the relationship between number of components and complexity is somewhat surprising; from table 15.2 it might have been expected that as the number of components increased, the complexity of each one would *decrease* to compensate, from both processing and efficiency viewpoints. That this is not the case casts doubts on our initial hypotheses about the processing difficulties associated with these two parameters, or else the increase in expressivity outweighs the processing and efficiency costs.

	Complexity	Reduction	Expansion	Repetition	Markers
Number	+	+	–	(+)	(+)
Complexity				+	
Reduction				+	+
Expansion				–	+
Repetition					(–)

Figure 15.1 Correlation among six factor groups

The connections between number of components and reduction and expansion are both compatible with the criterion of efficiency, but only the decrease in expansion conforms to expectations according to processing difficulties. The divergent behavior of expansion and reduction reflects the requirements for efficiency and not processing.

Expansion and repetition both reduce efficiency, while reduction and repetition compensate. Finally, the use of markers in the presence of reduction and expansion compensates for the processing difficulties due to the loss of parallelism between components. This is not necessary in the case of repetition since the latter actually increases this parallelism.

The associations summarized in figure 15.1 lead us to conclude that marking and repetition do indeed play a role in reducing potential processing difficulties, especially those due to lack of parallelism within components introduced by reduction and expansion. On the other hand, the increase in processing difficulties we hypothesized due to the number of components in an enumeration and the complexity of these components are either nonexistent or completely outweighed by the increased expressivity obtained.

4   Interactional and Social Effects on Enumeration

The interactional situation (general interview versus questionnaire) conditions properties of enumeration on the referential, discourse, and structural levels,[4] producing two sets of enumeration which show clearly divergent tendencies, as summarized in table 15.3.

Although no social factor influences the overall rate of enumerations in the interviews within the corpus, several linguistic aspects are tied to age (table 15.4).

The youngest in the corpus (15–33) exhibit a greater number of their enumerations in the questionnaire. Conversely, older speakers (34+) more often elaborate their enumerations within the general interview.[5] Why do the younger speakers produce enumerations: (1) in a context in which the interviewer intervenes strongly (questionnaire, dialogic discourse, direct orientation, or expressly as an interviewer); (2) putting their personal experience into play in the form of a list (biography/others, specific

Table 15.3   Properties of two sets of enumerations

General interview	Questionnaire
Referential:	*Referential:*
++ things/objects, general experience	++ biographical
++ synonymy (antonymy), gradation	++ inventories
Discourse:	*Discourse:*
++ argumentative function	++ informative function
++ Ø OT or + OT from informant	++ OT from interviewer
Structural:	*Structural:*
+ or − partial sentences	++ full sentences

Notes: ++ indicates strong associations (binary factors co-occurring less than 40 percent or more than 60 percent of the time.)
+ represents weaker relations (factors co-occurring between 40 percent and 60 percent of the time).
OT = opening theme of an enumeration, e.g. "Do you eat any particular fruits?"

Table 15.4   Effects of social factors on properties of enumerations

Older speakers (34+):	*Younger speakers (33–):*
++ interview	++ questionnaire
+ ref. things/objects, general experience	++ biographical
of the world	+ inventory
+ synonymy (antonymy)	++ informative function
+ argumentative function	++ OT from interviewer
Middle class:	*Working class:*
+ parts of sentences	+ full sentences

Notes: All indicated relations are significant with p < 0.001.
See notes to table 15.3 for key to symbols.

framework, inventory); (3) as an informative function of which the thematic ensemble is put into perspective by an announced theme? We do not pretend to have a simple response, as several social phenomena contribute. Nevertheless, certain facts can explain the observed tendencies.

First, more or less experience in diverse formal situations (the sociolinguistic interview being a more formal situation than a family discussion) partially explains the behavioral differences between younger and older speakers. In the questionnaire, the interviewer is more visible. She or he poses a series of questions designed to promote the formation of enumeration, as we pointed out previously. Younger speakers, more than older, use enumeration to replace the interactive task requested by the interviewer. Also, younger speakers are particularly sensitive to the interactional behavior of the interviewer. Among other things, they let the interviewer decide the themes of their enumerations. The interactional behavior of the interviewer has repercussions on the referential and discursive organization of enumerations of young speakers: they hold more strongly to their personal experience and generalize it less, contenting themselves with informing the interviewer on their own lives. They assign greater importance to enumeration in a dialogic discourse of an informative nature.

In the interview, an interactional dynamic in which the interviewer grants more freedom to the speaker and poses more general questions, younger speakers use enumeration less but older speakers use it more. We can explain the particular behavior of older speakers by the fact that they possibly associate use of enumeration with a more formal or educational task less than do younger speakers. They enumerate little when the interviewer's questions lend themselves to it and distance themselves from the linguistic behavior of the interviewer. However, this does not explain why they enumerate more in the interview. There is certainly an interactional process underlying the behavior of older speakers, but it is more implicit and diffuse than that within the questionnaire.

The age of the interviewers may also play a role, even though one group of informants (15–20 years old) was younger than the interviewers. Although the authors of the corpus attempted to minimize the role of the interviewer, clear behavioral differences between younger and older speakers remain. Still, all younger speakers do not let themselves be continuously guided by the interviewer. For example, one young speaker takes control of the interview for granted. At this point, it is the relations of authority or solidarity which are established between the speaker and the interviewer, rather than the repercussions of the role of the interviewer, that explain the different behaviors.

5   Four Recurrent Observations and the Case of Enumeration

In examining the results in tables 15.3 and 15.4, we may discuss the validity, for enumeration, of the four observations considered to be recurrent in sociolinguistics according to Finegan and Biber (1994):

1   Social and stylistic factors influence the usage of linguistic processes.
2   The type of linguistic variation influenced by stylistic factors is parallel to that of social factors.
3   Certain interactional situations (generally more formal) present a more frequent usage of elaborated forms, while other situations (generally more informal) contain a greater utilization of reduced forms.
4   Speakers of higher social class show a proportionally more important usage of elaborated forms, while speakers of lower social class tend to use a greater number of reduced forms.

Both social factors and the interactional dynamic influence the formation of enumeration, which constitutes another instance of observation (1), leaving aside for the moment the nature of the link between the two extralinguistic aspects.

The interaction situation does not influence exactly the same linguistic factors as do age or social class, though some parallelism can be seen between social and interactional effects on enumeration; an observation of type (2). For example, although the situation has no effects on complexity, this property is clearly linked to the social dimension. The use of the inventory schema, while influenced somewhat by the interaction situation, is subject to the effects of age, but not class. Although the associations are weak, we do find one property, complexity, that is conditioned by SP class and not by age (an effect verified by other statistical analyses). In our opinion, this fact is explained in terms of priorities by the absence of ties between interaction and the structure of the enumerations. As we have seen, while the effect of age is mediated by interactional factors, that of class is not. Structural variation in enumeration results from a real sociological effect and, contrary to discursive and referential variation, it is relatively free from what happens on the interactional level. In other words, it is not the informants' reaction to the type of interaction which determines the structure of the enumeration, but the SP class as an individual characteristic.

Contrary to observation (2) (the parallelism pattern), we have thus documented three types of extralinguistic effects on the properties of enumeration:

1   Some properties are influenced by interactional and social effects together.
2   Some factors are exclusively influenced by the social dimension (only SP class has an incidence upon structure properties).
3   Some factors are linked solely or largely to the interactional dynamic. For example, the total number of enumerations is directly influenced only by the interview situation, and the effects of the interview situation on the choice of schema (inventory versus synonymy or gradation) and the type of referent (evaluation, things, etc.) of the enumeration clearly dominate those of age.

These last effects run counter also to the prediction of Bell's (1984) model. He contends that certain linguistic processes are subject to social and stylistic effects, others only to social effects, but none is influenced solely by stylistic effects. Moreover, he adds, the degree of stylistic variation does not exceed the degree of social variation (Bell 1984: 152). How can we explain the origin and dominance of stylistic effects on certain aspects of enumeration?

Interactional factors capable of influencing the production of a process are numerous, quite different (some govern interactional organization, while others participate in its implementation), and linked to thematic and pragmatic aspects. Some of the relations between interactional factors and properties of discourse are predetermined by the nature of the interview situation itself (such as subjects broached or the choice of interviewer), being the interactional organization within which the participants agree to act. This is inescapable; each speaker has to respond to questions either from the general interview or from the questionnaire. Language phenomena influenced by personal and social characteristics of the participants may or may not occur within the questionnaire or the interview, but the contrasting interaction situations are both imposed, so whatever influence they have must always occur in each interview. On the other hand, the variable number and the formulation of questions (other than those determined by inquiry methodology), the emission of back-channel signals, and the mode of discourse (monologic or dialogic) of the speaker represent aspects of the implementation of the interaction. Social factors such as age, sex, ethnicity, etc. of the speaker or of the interviewer can constrain linguistic variation and dominate stylistic effects (Dubois and Horvath 1992, 1993).[6]

Bell's hypothesis about the dominance of social factors holds up better when the properties being influenced are involved in the implementation of the interaction, while stylistic effects can surpass social effects when the former govern the organization of interaction. Since stylistic factors have a different impact on linguistic variation at various levels (e.g. structural, referential, discourse organization), then their relation to social effect can also differ: stylistic effects can be exclusive, dominant, or parallel to social effects. Bell's model does not take into account the dominance or exclusivity of stylistic effects, since he considers the way factors act only on one level, namely structural.

In Finegan and Biber's observation (3), determining what is reduced or elaborated poses a problem in discourse, since the use of a discourse strategy is not opposed to its "nonuse." Nevertheless, from the specific point of view of structure, it may be considered that an enumeration of complete sentences is more elaborate than an enumeration of words, and that an enumeration of three constituents is reduced in comparison to another of five constituents. As an instance of observation (3),

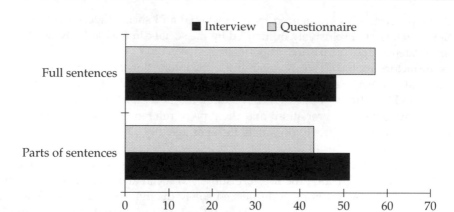

Figure 15.2   Percentage of enumerations composed of full sentences and parts of sentences within the general interview and the questionnaire

elaborated enumerations – namely more constituents and more full sentences – are frequently produced in the (formal) questionnaire, while more reduced ones are more frequent in the general interview (figure 15.2).

However, the type of interactional behavior imposed by the interviewer determines a greater or lesser elaboration of the enumeration than does the type of formality (in terms of theme) in the interview. Given that use of a questionnaire generally favours a dialogic discourse, use of back-channel signals and theme questions ("What are your favorite restaurants?") favorable to enumeration, it is not surprising that construction of these enumerations differs from those found in the general interview. Nonetheless, how is it that the greater presence of the interviewer prods the speaker to pad out his or her enumeration with a larger number of constituents?

The presence of a specific theme question of the interviewer, which often becomes the OT (opening theme) of an enumeration, can be interpreted as a mark of authorization. The OT of the interviewer (like the use of back-channel signals) explicitly legitimizes the construction of the enumeration which the speaker will produce, which in turn authorizes a more complex elaboration. Since the interviewer has predefined the thematic set to be evoked by the enumeration of some of its elements, the speaker must assure cohesion of enumerated elements as well as cohesion of all elements in accordance with the interviewer's request (while this is not obligatory for self-initiated enumerations). This is carried out by using a larger number of enumerated elements and elements of more complex structure.

Were an observation of Finegan and Biber's fourth type pertinent to enumeration, we would find more elaborated enumerations from speakers of higher SP class and more reduced enumerations in the discourse of speakers of lower SP class. However, it is the converse that is clearly supported by analysis. Speakers of higher social class show a proportionally greater use of reduced enumerations, while speakers of lower social class tend to use a greater number of elaborated enumerations (figure 15.3).

The link between complexity of enumerations and social class is better explained from the point of view of "discourse strategy" than, as contended by Finegan and Biber (1994), by greater or lesser access to a specific style by a social group. When speakers of disadvantaged SP utilize enumeration in a sociolinguistic interview, they

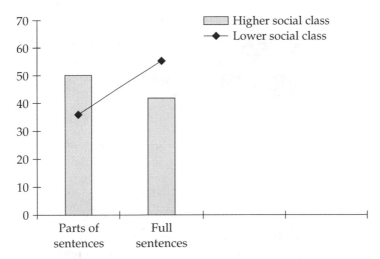

Figure 15.3   Percentage of enumerations composed of full or part sentences, by social class

make its use stand out more clearly, in structural terms, than do speakers of other SP classes. The fact that this social group favors the use of linguistic aspects causing a greater structural breadth (an enumeration that is longer and constituted of more structurally elaborated elements) does not signify that it prefers more complex enumerations in and of themselves, or that it is more able than another group to make use of this process.

There is no necessary link between the linguistic factors involved in the structural variation of a discourse process and the intrinsic complexity of that process, for two major reasons:

1   The structure of a discourse process is much more complex than the scope of observation (3), since that structure is linked to other aspects at different levels (referential, discourse, etc.).
2   Because of interactional laws (goals or maxims) that assure good transmission of the message and that govern all discourse (for example, it is impossible to enumerate indefinitely without incurring certain consequences), a balance exists among the processes that participate on the structural level. Thus, the use of a process which augments the structural complexity of a form (the length of an enumeration) counterbalances another one which reduces it (surface reduction of enumerated elements).

The greater the structural complexity of an enumeration (complete sentences), the more a part of the sentence is repeated in each sentence (and repetition diminishes complexity). Or, the smaller the complexity (enumeration of parts of sentences), the more certain enumerated elements benefit from a structural expansion (more complex) (figure 15.4). To sum up, a long enumeration of sentences of which a part is repeated has a degree of complexity equal to a short enumeration of words, interspersed with paraphrases designed to orient the listener, or to a long enumeration of subordinate clauses of which some undergo a surface reduction.

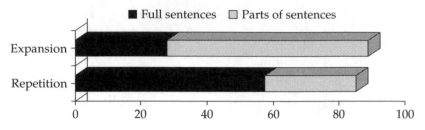

Figure 15.4   Percentage of expansion and repetition by structural complexity

Few analysts take into account the interrelation of structural and other factors in the construction of a form and of the balance of functions within discourse. We often see an oversimplified view of the frequently demonstrated association between social class and linguistic structure. It is difficult to contend that the link between these two aspects is summarized in the form of the following: higher class = elaborated structure, lower class = reduced structure. Observation (4), which in our context would see more elaborate discourse forms employed by speakers of higher SP than by speakers of lower SP, cannot be made for the phenomenon of enumeration.

6   Conclusion

We have demonstrated that there are three types of extralinguistic effects on the properties of enumeration: (1) some properties are influenced by interactional and social effects together; (2) some factors are exclusively influenced by the social dimension; and (3) some factors are linked solely or largely to the interactional dynamic.

Finegan and Biber (1994), unlike Bell (1984), hold that stylistic variation can prevail over social variation. They contend that the sociolinguistic methodology through which Bell examines the conditioning of linguistic variation prevents the discovery of the weight of stylistic effects. Contrary to what these authors hold, our results indicate that traditional sociolinguistic methodology can reveal the stylistic effects on variation in the same way as an analysis of different situations, although it is true that the number of stylistic factors taken into account in the corpus is lower than that of social factors. In other respects, according to Finegan and Biber (1994: 343), a stylistic analysis such as that of enumeration has no external validity and no empirical status, as it is not built on diverse situations or different interviewers. It is evident that stylistic variation that speakers show within a corpus constitutes only a part of their stylistic repertoire. Still, nothing assures us that interactional or social factors insignificant to enumeration will become significant in other situations.

For example, interactional level has little influence on the structure of enumerations (the interview situation has a weak effect on the complexity of enumerated elements but no effect on all the other structural factors that we analyzed, such as number of elements, repetition, markers, etc.). If we analyze the same procedure in diverse situations, it is possible that the structure will remain indifferent to all stylistic variation. We might also multiply the situations without interactional factors becoming influential. The results of our study are empirically valid in the sociolinguistic inquiry, but they may also be so for the ensemble of the stylistic repertoire of the speakers. The important point is to examine the effect of social and stylistic levels separately on factors that are implied in the production of a discursive procedure, and to take into account this vast network of linguistic and extralinguistic associations. Thus the analysis may determine whether one level (social or stylistic) explains the other's effects, and reveal the process of complex elaboration of the discourses.

Discourse analysis has traditionally focused on the study of individual examples to illuminate rather general and abstract principles about texts and interactions viewed holistically. In contrast, variationism depends on hundreds or thousands of tokens to prove rather circumscribed points about specific phonological or syntactic structures. While the scope of discourse analysis is broad, methodologically it does not search for reproducibility, objectivity, or even necessarily scholarly consensus. The opposite is true about variationism, where even proponents of opposite viewpoints can agree on the nature of the data and the validity of analytical procedures, but the investigation is confined to one issue within a single level of linguistic structure. Can we (and should we) hope to harness the methodological power of quantitative methodology in probing the richness of discourse, with its multiple facets spanning both structural and interactional relationships? We propose our study of enumeration as a prototype of an approach which succeeds in operationalizing discourse concepts on many levels, so that an exhaustive study of a large corpus can reveal and characterize with some precision the deep connections among the various processes implied in the motivation, construction, use, and interpretation of this figure. The keys to this approach include:

1 avoidance of one-dimensional, highly modular, or other oversimplified models of performance. What is needed is an eclectic and inclusive vision of what may be in play during a particular production, and an open-mindedness about what surface indications and what analytical interpretations are appropriate for coding the various aspects of a token.
2 taking seriously the principle of accountability. This involves willingness to undertake the tedious job of extracting and analyzing all the eligible examples in a corpus, and understanding that although every occurrence is different, they are comparable at many levels.
3 avoidance of highly parameterized and other restrictive statistical models for analyzing the data. What is needed is straightforward but systematic two-way and three-way assessments of association, at least as a first step.
4 a great deal of reflection in order to integrate the welter of results likely to emerge from such a study. A series of isolated correlations without any emergent framework is what gives quantitative studies a bad name. No analysis is complete without an understanding as coherent and elegant as the discourse phenomena themselves.

NOTES

1 For example, several researchers
(Labov 1972, 1978; Linde and Labov
1974; Labov and Fanshel 1977; Labov
and Waletsky 1967; Sacks et al. 1974;
Tannen 1984, 1989; Bell 1984; Schiffrin
1994; Horvath 1997; Horvath and
Eggins 1987; Dubois 1994, 1995, 1997;
Dubois and Horvath 1992; Vincent and
Dubois 1996, 1997; Dubois et al. 1995;
Dubois and Sankoff 1994, 1997) have
paid attention to the description of
a number of high-level discourse
structures (argumentative, informative,
and narrative structures as well as
reported speech, interruption, overlap,
repetition, etc.) and their particularities.
Others have concentrated on signals
or local small units (markers and
particles) which mark prospectively or
retrospectively the linguistic or the
interactional structure of discourse
(Schiffrin 1987; Dines 1980; Laforest
1992, 1996; Vincent 1983; Vincent and
Rains 1988; Vincent and Sankoff 1992;
Vicher and Sankoff 1989; Dubois 1992;
Dubois et al. 1995).

2 Atkinson and Biber (1994) give a
systematic and detailed summary
of empirical studies dealing with
language style.

3 All constituents of the enumerations
cited as examples are boldfaced and
placed one after another so that each
appears on a different line. Such a
configuration lends more perspective
to the constituents (or to internal
movements of enumeration) and
marks the enumeration of that which
precedes or follows in the discursive
context. I have respected the diacritical
marks and the punctuation used in the
transcriptions of the interviews.

4 We mentioned earlier that the situation
or style influenced the choice of
dialogic or monologic mode as well as
the orientation of the enumerations.
Mode and orientation also share all the
associations between the interactional
situation and the other parameters that
it conditions. To avoid redundancy of
results, only those of the interactional
situation will be given, with the
understanding that these associations
are valid for the two other parameters
as well.

5 If we take the interactional situation,
in each SP class, younger speakers
produce more enumerations in the
questionnaire than do their elders.
No matter what the age, informants of
disadvantaged SP class will always
have more enumerations in the
questionnaire than other SP classes.

6 Dubois and Horvath (1992) measured
the influence of interviewers in varying
the ethnicity of the interviewees.
Request strategies of Australian
interviewers (number and formulation
of questions that are unforeseen in the
original questionnaire) are significantly
different according to the addressee
(Greek, Italian, or Australian).

REFERENCES

Atkinson, Dan and Douglas Biber.
1994. Register: a review of
empirical research. In D. Biber and
E. Finegan (eds), *Sociolinguistic
Perspectives on Register*. Oxford,
Oxford University Press,
351–85.

Bell, Allen. 1984. Language style as
audience design. *Language in
Society* 13. 145–204.

Blanche-Benveniste, Claire and Claude Jeanjean. 1987. *Le français parlé: transcription et édition.* Paris, Didier-érudition.

Coupland, Nicholas and Giles Howard (eds). 1988. Communicative accommodation: recent developments. *Language and Communication* 8(3/4). 175–327.

Dines, Elizabeth. 1980. Variation in discourse "and stuff like that." *Language in Society* 9. 13–33.

Dubois, Sylvie. 1992. Extension particles, etc. *Language Variation and Change* 4(2). 179–203.

Dubois, Sylvie. 1994. Social effects and interactional dynamics: Their relative importance for a discourse procedure. *Sociolinguistic Variation: Data, Theory, and Analysis.* Stanford University, Center for the Study of Language and Information. 279–92.

Dubois, Sylvie. 1995. Structural processes in enumeration. *Language Variation and Change* 7(1). 113–37.

Dubois, Sylvie. 1997. *L'analyse variationniste du discours en sociolinguistique: l'approche modulaire pour décrire l'usage et la formation des procédés discursifs.* American University Studies XIII. New York, Peter Lang.

Dubois, Sylvie and Barbara Horvath. 1992. Interactional influences on descriptive style. *Actes du XV congrès international des linguistes*, vol. 3. Québec, Presses de L'Université Laval. 331–4.

Dubois, Sylvie and Barbara Horvath. 1993. Interviewer's linguistic production and its effect on speaker descriptive style. *Language Variation and Change* 4(2). 125–35.

Dubois, Sylvie and David Sankoff. 1994. The organization of relations among variables: background, methods, and software. Paper presented at NWAV-XXIII, Stanford University, California.

Dubois, Sylvie and David Sankoff. 1997. Discourse enumerators and Schegloff's denominator. In G. Guy, J. Baugh, D. Schiffrin, and C. Feagin (eds), *Towards a Social Science of Language: Papers in Honor of William Labov*, Amsterdam, Benjamins. 153–82.

Dubois, Sylvie, Martine Boutin, and David Sankoff. 1995. The quantitative analysis of turn-taking in multiparticipant conversations. *Proceedings of NWAV-XXIV*, University of Pennsylvania, Philadelphia. 257–65.

Finegan, Edward and Douglas Biber. 1994: Register and social dialect variation: An integrated approach. In D. Biber and E. Finegan (eds), *Sociolinguistic Perspectives on Register*, Oxford, Oxford University Press. 315–50.

Gilbert, Beatrice. 1989. La série énumérative. Étude linguistique et stylistique s'appuyant sur dix romans français publiés entre 1945 et 75. Geneva and Paris, Librairie Droz.

Halliday, Michael K. 1978. *Language as Social Semiotic.* Baltimore, University Park Press.

Horvath, Barbara. 1985. *Variation in Australian English: The Sociolects of Sydney.* Cambridge, Cambridge University Press.

Horvath, Barbara. 1987. Text in conversation: variability in story-telling texts. In Keith M. Denning et al. (eds), *Variation in Language NWAV-XV.* Department of Linguistics, Stanford University.

Horvath, Barbara. 1997. Horse-racing calls. In G. Guy, J. Baugh, D. Schiffrin, and C. Feagin (eds), *Towards a Social Science of Language. Papers in Honor of William Labov*, Amsterdam, Benjamins. 103–20.

Horvath, Barbara and Susan Eggins. 1987. Opinion texts in conversation. In P. H. Fries and M. J. Gregory (eds),

Discourse in Society: Functional Perspectives, Norwood, NJ, Ablex. 29–45.

Jefferson, Gil. 1990. List construction as a task and interactional resource. In G. Psathas (ed.), *Interaction Competence*, Washington, DC, University Press of America. 63–92.

Labov, William. 1972. The transformation of experience in narrative syntax. In W. Labov (ed.), *Language in the Inner City*, Philadelphia, University of Philadelphia Press. 354–96.

Labov, William. 1978. Where does the linguistic variable stop? A response to Beatriz Lavandera. *Sociolinguistic Working Paper 44*. Austin, TX, Southwest Educational Development Laboratory.

Labov, William and David Fanshel. 1977. *Therapeutic Discourse*. New York, Academic Press.

Labov, William and J. Waletsky, 1967. Narrative analysis. In J. Helm (ed.), *Essays on Verbal and Visual Arts: Proceedings of the 1966 Annual Spring Meeting of the American Ethnological Society*, Seattle, University of Washington Press. 12–44.

Laforest, Marty. 1992. *Le back-channel en situation d'entrevue sociolinguistique*. Quebec, Université Laval, CIRAL.

Laforest, Marty (ed.). 1996. Autour de la narration. Québec, Nuit blanche éditeur.

Lavandera, Beatriz. 1978. Where does the sociolinguistic variable stop? *Language in Society* 7. 171–83.

Linde, C. and Willam Labov. 1974. Spatial networks as a site for the study of language and thought. *Language* 51. 924–39.

Rickford, John R. and Fair McNair-Knox. 1994. Addressee and topic-influenced style shift: a quantitative sociolinguistic study. In D. Biber and E. Finegan (eds), *Sociolinguistic Perspectives on Register*, Oxford, Oxford University Press. 235–76.

Romaine, Susan. 1981. On the problem of syntactic variation: a reply to Beatriz Lavandera and William Labov. *Sociolinguistic Working Papers 82*. Austin, TX, Southwest Educational Development Laboratory.

Sacks, Harvey, Emmanuel Schegloff, and Gail Jefferson, 1974. A simplest systematics for the organisation of turn-taking for conversations. *Language, Journal of the Linguistic Society of America* 50(4). 696–735.

Sankoff, David. 1989. Sociolinguistics and syntactic variation. In F. Newmeyer (ed.), *Linguistics: The Cambridge Survey 4, Language: The Socio-cultural Context*, Cambridge, Cambridge University Press. 140–61.

Schiffrin, Deborah. 1987. *Discourse Markers*. Cambridge, Cambridge University Press.

Schiffrin, Deborah. 1994. Making a list. *Discourse Processes* 17. 377–406.

Slobin, Dan. 1977. Language change in childhood and in history. In J. MacNamara (ed.), *Language Learning and Thought*. New York, Academic. 185–214.

Tannen, Deborah. 1984. *Conversational style: Analyzing Talk Among Friends*. Norwood, NJ, Ablex.

Tannen, Deborah. 1989. *Talking Voices. Repetition, Dialogue, and Imagery in Conversational Discourse*. Cambridge, Cambridge University Press.

Thibault, Pierrette. 1982. Style, sens, fonction. In N. Dittmar and B. Schlieben-Lange (eds), *La sociolinguistique dans les pays de langue romane*, Tübingen, Gunter Narr Verlag. 73–81.

Thibault, Pierrette and Diane Vincent. 1990. *Un corpus de français parlé: Recherches Sociolinguistiques 1*. Quebec, Centre International de Recherches en Aménagement Linguistique.

Vicher, Anne and David Sankoff. 1989. The emergent syntax of pre-sentential turn-opening. *Pragmatics* 13. 81–97.

Vincent, Diane. 1983. Les ponctuants de la langue. Unpublished PhD dissertation. Montreal, Université de Montréal.

Vincent, Diane. 1986. Que fait la sociolinguistique avec l'analyse du discours et vice-versa. *Langage et Société* 38. 7–17.

Vincent, Diane and Sylvie Dubois, 1996. A study on the use of reported speech in spoken language. In J. Arnold et al. (eds), *Sociolinguistic Variation. Data, Theory and Analysis*, Stanford, CSLI Publications. 361–74.

Vincent, Diane and Sylvie Dubois, 1997. *Le discours direct: collection langue et pratiques discursives*. Quebec, Centre International de recherche en aménagement linguistique.

Vincent, Diane and Charlene Rains. 1988. Discourse particles in narratives. In K. J. Denning (ed.), *Variation in Language. Proceedings of NWAV-XV*, Stanford, Stanford University. 424–31.

Vincent, Diane and David Sankoff. 1992. Punctors: a pragmatic variable. *Language Variation and Change*, 4. 206–16.

Weiner, E. and William Labov. 1983. Constraints on the agentless passive. *Journal of Linguistics* 19. 29–58.

16 Computer-assisted Text and Corpus Analysis: Lexical Cohesion and Communicative Competence

MICHAEL STUBBS

0 Introduction

When we read or hear a piece of connected text, we may find the language used familiar or not, and correspondingly easy or difficult to follow. Difficulties in understanding a written or spoken text – such as a set of instructions, a textbook, a lecture, or a story in a conversation – can have many causes. However, by and large, we find a text easy to understand if it consists of familiar topics being talked about in familiar ways. If everything is totally familiar, of course, the text will strike us as boring or full of clichés. But there are limits to the rate at which we can take in new information, and we can understand connected text only if we are able to predict, at least partly, what is going to be said. Conversely, we find a text difficult to understand if it is lexically and semantically dense: that is, if there is too little repetition of vocabulary, if frequent topic changes mean that too much new vocabulary is being introduced too rapidly, and if too many of the words are unfamiliar or being used in unusual combinations.

These expectations of what is likely to be said – our knowledge of what is probable and conventional – can only come from other texts which we have read or heard in the past. This means that individual texts are interpreted against an intertextual background of norms of language use. These norms, which are expressed largely in recurring collocations of words, can be revealed by the computer-assisted analysis of large corpora. That is, we can compare what occurs in individual texts with what frequently occurs in large numbers of texts of different kinds.

In this chapter I will discuss methods for making such comparisons, under the following main topics:

- the contribution of words and phrases to text cohesion;
- the intertextual relations between texts;
- the extent to which our linguistic competence includes knowledge of norms of language use.

1   Data and Terminology

My main aim is to illustrate some computer-assisted methods of analyzing the use of words and phrases in texts and corpora, and for this, I require some simple terminology as follows.

A **text** is any stretch of naturally occurring language in use, spoken or written, which has been produced, independently of the analyst, for some real communicative purpose. A **corpus** is a large collection of computer-readable texts, of different text-types, which represent spoken and/or written usage. No corpus can be a fully representative sample of the whole language, but such collections can at least be designed to represent major dimensions of language variation, such as spoken and written, casual and formal, fiction and nonfiction, British and American, intended for different age groups, for experts and lay persons, and so on. **Large** means at least millions, and possibly hundreds of millions, of running words (tokens).

All examples of text fragments and phrases in this article are attested in such corpora. The frequency data are mainly from the Bank of English corpus created by COBUILD at the University of Birmingham in the UK. (COBUILD stands for Collins Birmingham University International Language Database.) This corpus has been used in the design of major dictionaries and grammars (including Cobuild 1995a; Francis et al. 1996, 1998). By the late 1990s, the corpus totalled some 330 million words, including fiction and nonfiction books, newspapers, and samples of spoken English. The corpus is available in different forms: I have here mainly used a 56-million word subcorpus which is available over the internet as CobuildDirect.[1] I have also used a database on CD-ROM (Cobuild 1995b), which was constructed from a 200-million word subcorpus. Sinclair (1991: 13–26) describes the early corpus development.

Other individual examples are from the LOB (Lancaster–Oslo–Bergen) and Lund corpora, and from the Longman–Lancaster corpus. For descriptions of these corpora, see Biber (1988: 66ff) and Summers (1993).[2]

Since I am going to compare the use of words and phrases in texts and corpora, I also need to make some terminological distinctions here. A **lemma** is a lexeme or dictionary headword, which is realized by a **word form**: e.g. the lemma TAKE (upper case) can be realized by the word forms *take, takes, took, taking,* and *taken* (lower-case italicized). Corpus work has shown that different forms of a lemma often have quite different collocational behaviour.

A **node** (the word form, lemma, or other pattern under investigation) co-occurs with *collocates* (word forms or lemmas) within a given *span* of word forms, for example 4:4 (four words to left and right). Position in the span can be given if relevant: e.g. $N-1$ = one word to the left of the node, $N+3$ = three words to the right. A **collocation** is a purely lexical and nondirectional relation: it is a node–collocate pair which occurs at least once in a corpus. Usually it is frequent co-occurrences which are of interest, and **typical collocates** of a node are given in diamond brackets, for word forms or lemmas, or for a set of semantically related words:

(1)   untold <$N+1$: damage, misery, . . . ; millions, riches, . . . >

(2)   CAUSE

These examples are discussed in more detail below. Such sets are usually open-ended, and the relations probabilistic, but measures of typicality can filter out idiosyncratic collocates, and reveal the typical cases. (Statistical methods are discussed by Clear 1993; Stubbs 1995a; Barnbrook 1996.)

A **prosody** is a feature which extends over more than one unit in a linear string. Here I will refer to **discourse prosodies** which extend over a span of words, and which indicate the speaker's attitude to the topic. Unpleasant prosodies are more frequent, but pleasant prosodies do occur:

(3)   BREAK out <"unpleasant things", such as: disagreements, riots, sweat, violence, war>

(4)   PROVIDE <"valuable things", such as: aid, care, employment, facilities, food, housing, jobs, money, opportunities, security, services, support, training; an answer, data, information>

The concept of prosody in this sense was first proposed by Sinclair (1991: 74–5, 112). Louw (1993) provides the first detailed discussion, and Stubbs (1996) and Bublitz (1996) give other examples.

Finally, it has become fairly standard to distinguish between **cohesion** and **coherence** (Widdowson 1979: 146; Brown and Yule 1983: 24–5, 194–9). Cohesion refers to linguistic features (such as lexical repetition and anaphora) which are explicitly realized in the surface structure of the text: Halliday and Hasan (1976) provide a thorough account. Coherence refers to textual relations which are inferred, but which are not explicitly expressed. Examples include relations between speech acts (such as offer–acceptance or complaint–excuse), which may have to be inferred from context, or other sequences which are inferred from background nonlinguistic knowledge.

2   Lexical Cohesion: An Introductory Example

Here then is an initial example of the intertextual relations between a text fragment and typical language use, as documented in large corpora. It shows how a cohesive text is built up through the use of variations on typical collocations. As Sinclair (1991: 108) puts it: "By far the majority of text is made of the occurrence of common words in common patterns, or in slight variations of those common patterns." The text fragment is from a book on the environment published in 1990 in the UK:[3]

(5)   Here the Green Party has launched its Euro-election campaign. Its manifesto, "Don't Let Your World Turn Grey", argues that the emergence of the Single European Market from 1992 will cause untold environmental damage. It derides the vision of Europe as "310 million shoppers in a supermarket". The Greens want a much greater degree of self-reliance, with "local goods for local needs". They say they would abandon the Chunnel, nuclear power stations, the Common Agricultural Policy and agrochemicals. The imagination boggles at the scale of the task they are setting themselves.

For many readers, the cohesion of this text fragment will be due both to repeated words and to familiar phrasings. It is sometimes thought that lexical cohesion is mainly due to chains of repeated and related words, such as:

(6)   Green, Grey, Greens; Euro-, European, Europe; Party, election, campaign, manifesto; Market, shoppers, supermarket, goods

In an influential critique of attempts at text analysis, Morgan and Sellner (1980: 179–80) objected that such lexical chains are of no linguistic interest, but merely "an epiphenomenon of coherence of content." However, I will argue that lexical cohesion is not only a reflex of content, but that it is also due to the stringing together and overlapping of phrasal units.

In the text fragment, some of these units are simply fixed multiword phrases:

(7)   the Green Party; the Single European Market; the Common Agricultural Policy; nuclear power stations

Other chunks are more complex to identify: they are variants on frequent combinations, such that certain words greatly increase the expectation that other words will occur. However, this assumes that we know the norms of co-occurrence in the language, and it is these norms that can be investigated only via the frequency of co-occurrences in large corpora. I will take a series of phrases, in the order in which they occur in the text, and show to what extent they are typical usages:

(8)   **from (5):** has launched its Euro-election campaign

For example, the word form *launched* co-occurs with restricted sets of semantically related words. Native speakers might think initially of phrases such as *launched a satellite*, *lifeboats were launched*. However, the corpus data show that a much more frequent usage (about 50 times as frequent) is with abstract nouns, involving a plan, which may be military:

(9)   launched <appeal, bid, campaign, programme, project, strategy; attack, offensive, invasion>

Most occurrences collocate with a time reference, especially a reference to a first, new, or recent launch, and/or (as here) a *has*-form which indicates present relevance of a recent event.

(10)   **from (5):** cause untold environmental damage

Here, the corpus data show that the most frequent collocates of CAUSE (as a verb) are overwhelmingly unpleasant. I studied the collocates of CAUSE (verb and noun) in a 425,000-word corpus of texts about environmental issues (discussed by Gerbig 1996). Frequent collocates were:

(11)   CAUSE <blindness, damage, danger, depletion, harm, loss, ozone, problems, radiation, warming>

If different corpora gave different results, then these unpleasant associations might be an artifact of the data, not a collocational property of the word. However, I also studied the 38,000 occurrences of CAUSE in a much larger corpus of 120 million words of general English (Stubbs 1995a). Amongst the 50 most frequent collocates within a span of 3:3, there were only words (most frequently abstract nouns) with unpleasant connotations. The most frequent were:

(12)   CAUSE <problem(s) 1806, damage 1519, death(s) 1109, disease 591, concern 598, cancer 572, pain 514, trouble 471>

In addition, CAUSE often occurs in the syntactic structure verb + adjective + noun, such as:

(13)   cause considerable damage; cause great problems; cause major disruption; cause severe pain; cause untold damage

The last example is the one in the text. In turn, *untold* is usually followed by an abstract noun denoting something bad and unpleasant, or a large number and/or a large amount of money:

(14)   untold <damage, misery, problems, suffering; billions, riches>

A few cases are positive (*brought untold joy*): but in this context CAUSE is not used.

(15)   **from (5):** a much greater degree of self-reliance

Other patterns are more variable again, but still detectable. In the corpus data, there were hundreds of examples of the pattern: *a* + quantity adjective + *degree of* + abstract noun. The most frequent adjectives were *greater* and *high*, as in *a far greater degree of clarity, a high degree of support*. After *greater*, almost all the nouns expressed positive ideas: e.g. *cooperation, democracy, success*.

(16)   **from (5):** the imagination boggles at

Some words have very restricted uses: only *mind* and the semantically related *imagination* frequently co-occur with *boggles*:

(17)   **from (5):** the scale of the task

The combination *the scale of the* is followed by abstract nouns (such as *challenge, operation, problem*) which refer back to a general discourse topic. Logically, the *scale* could be large or small, but *the scale of the* is almost always used of something very large, and usually something bad. Typical phrases are *underestimated the scale of the destruction* and *cannot cope with the scale of the fraud*.

(18)   **from (5):** the task they are setting themselves

The task has no single anaphoric referent. *Task* is often used as a metalinguistic label to encapsulate a preceding stretch of text (see below on such vocabulary). Things one commonly sets oneself are goals which are challenging or demanding. Typical collocates are abstract nouns, such as *aim, challenge, goal, objective, standards, target,* or *task*.

(19)   **from (17) and (18):** the scale of the task – the task they are setting themselves

Where chunks overlap with each other in this way, Hunston and Francis (1998: 68) talk of pattern flow.

   We now have examples of the expectations generated by some of the individual words and phrases. A mechanism of text cohesion becomes clearer if we now look at these phrases from the text together, because we see that several have to do with the meaning "large size." There are explicit references to size in the text fragment (*310 million, greater*), but also implicit references. If a campaign is *launched*, the implication is that it is a major event. *Untold, boggles,* and *the scale of the* all usually co-occur with large numbers or large amounts. These patterns are not explicit in the text, but implicit in the intertextual references to norms of language use. Each individual pattern is probabilistic, but cumulatively the intertextual expectations convey "large size" as a discourse prosody distributed across the text.

3 Collocations and Cohesion

What follows? Collocational facts are linguistic, and cannot be explained away on grounds of content or logic. Such combinations are idiomatic, but not "idioms," because although they frequently occur, they are not entirely fixed, and/or they are semantically transparent. More accurately, such idiomatic combinations pose no problem for decoding, but they do pose a problem for encoding: speakers just have to know that expected combinations are *brought untold joy*, but *caused untold damage*. (Makkai 1972 and Fillmore et al. 1988: 504–5 draw this distinction.)

   Much recent linguistics emphasizes creative aspects of language at the expense of predictable combinations, which nevertheless constitute a large percentage of normal language use. The pervasiveness of such conventionalized language use, the correspondingly large role played by memory, and the implications for fluent and idiomatic native speaker competence have, however, been emphasized by Bolinger (1976), Allerton (1984), Pawley and Syder (1983), Sinclair (1991), and Miller (1993).

   Such observations concern probabilistic features of English. It is possible to have the "pleasant" combination *cause for celebration*, but vastly more frequent are combinations such as *cause for concern*. With the verb, there is nothing illogical (and nothing ungrammatical?) about the collocation *?cause an improvement*, yet it seems not to occur. (What does occur is *make an improvement*, or *achieve, bring about, lead to, produce, result in,* and *secure an improvement*.) Such syntagmatic patterning is much more detailed than is generally shown in grammars: it stretches well beyond words and short phrases, and provides a relatively unexplored mechanism of text cohesion. However, as I have illustrated, such analysis cannot be restricted to isolated texts, since it requires an analysis of intertextual relations, and therefore comparison of the actual choices in a given text, typical occurrences in other texts from the same text-type, and norms of usage in the language in general.

The literature on cohesion tends to neglect the role of collocations. For example, Halliday and Hasan (1976), in the standard reference on cohesion in English, have only four pages on collocations and regard them as "the most problematical part of lexical cohesion" (1976: 284). However, the role of collocations in text cohesion is discussed by Kjellmer (1991) and Bublitz (1996, 1998). Moon (1994, 1998: 259) argues that semi-fixed phrases provide a way of presenting stereotyped ideas, which avoids explicit evaluation, but encodes shared schemas which are institutionalized in the culture. Sinclair (1996) provides further detailed examples of the kind of lexical, grammatical, and semantic relations which make such extended lexical units cohesive.

Conversely, the large literature on collocations and phrase-like units almost always regards them in their own right as linguistic units, and neglects their contribution to text cohesion. Early work on "word clustering" was done by Mandelbrot (who is nowadays more often associated with chaos theory), and as early as the 1970s he used a 1.6-million-word corpus to identify the strength of clustering between co-occurring words (Damerau and Mandelbrot 1973). More recent work (e.g. Choueka et al. 1983; Yang 1986; Smadja 1993; Justeson and Katz 1995) has used computer methods to identify recurrent phrasal units in natural text. Cowie (1994, 1999) provides useful reviews and discussions of principles.

These characteristics of language use – frequency, probability, and norms – can be studied only with quantitative methods and large corpora. However, cohesion (which is explicitly marked in the text) must be distinguished from coherence (which relies on background assumptions). Therefore, we also have to distinguish between frequency in a corpus and probability in a text. In the language as a whole, *launched an attack* is much more frequent than *launched a boat*. But if the text is about a rescue at sea, then we might expect *launched the lifeboat* (though *launched a plan* is not impossible). The probability of coming across a given word combination will be stable across the language: this is probability across a sequence of events. But this is not the same as the probability of a single event in a specific text: especially given that linguistic events are not independent of each other (unlike successive flips of a coin). Our linguistic competence tells us that one of these general semantic patterns (*launched* "a plan" or *launched* "a boat") is highly likely: but given what we know about the topic under discussion, we know which pattern is more likely in a given text.

4   Grammatical, Feasible, Appropriate, Performed

The significance of extended lexicosemantic units for a theory of idiomatic language use is discussed by Pawley and Syder (1983). They argue that native speakers know hundreds of thousands of such units, whose lexical content is wholly or partly fixed: familiar collocations with variants, which are conventional labels for culturally recognized concepts. Speakers have a strong preference for certain familiar combinations of lexis and syntax, which explains why nonnative speakers can speak perfectly grammatically but still sound nonnative.

A reference to Hymes's (1972) influential article on communicative competence can put this observation in a wider context. Hymes proposes a way of avoiding the oversimplified polarization made by Chomsky (1965) between competence and performance. Hymes not only discusses whether (1) a sentence is formally possible (= grammatical), but distinguishes further whether an utterance is (2) psycholinguistically feasible or (3) sociolinguistically appropriate. In addition, not all possibilities are actually realized, and Hymes proposes a further distinction between the possible and the actual: (4) what, in reality, with high probability, is said or written. In an update of the theory, Hymes (1992: 52) notes the contribution of routinized extended lexical units to the stability of text.

Whereas much (Chomskyan) linguistics has been concerned with what speakers *can* say, corpus linguistics is *also* concerned with what speakers *do* say. But note the *also*. It is misleading to see only frequency of actual occurrence. Frequency data become interesting when they can be interpreted as evidence for typicality, and speakers' communicative competence certainly includes tacit knowledge of behavioral norms.

5 Collocations and Background Assumptions

An important approach to discourse coherence has used the concept of semantic frames and schemas. For example, Brown and Yule (1983) discuss the background assumptions we make about the normality of the world: "a mass of below-conscious expectations" (1983: 62), which contribute to our understanding of coherent discourse. They argue that "we assume that" doors open, hair grows on heads, dogs bark, the sun shines. These assumptions depend in turn on expected collocations: in English, hair is blond, trees are felled, eggs are rotten (but milk is sour, and butter is rancid), we kick with our feet (but punch with our fists, and bite with our teeth), and so on. Many such examples go back to an early study of syntagmatic relations in German by Porzig (1934). Examples are often restricted to the small set of such items available to intuition, and their very banality contributes to our sense of a predictable and stable world. In an influential sociological discussion, Berger and Luckmann (1966) point to the importance of frequent "institutional formulae" in the construction of a taken-for-granted everyday reality.

However, it is important to distinguish between those collocations which are accessible to introspection and those which actually occur in running text. Both have to be studied, precisely because they reveal differences between intuition and behavior. For example, the very fact that KICK implies FOOT means that the words tend *not* to collocate in real text, since they have no need to. I checked over 3 million running words, and found almost 200 occurrences of KICK. But in a span of 10:10 (ten words to left and right), there were only half-a-dozen occurrences each of *foot* and *feet*, in cases where more precision was given:

(20) with his left *foot* he gave a wild *kick* against the seat

(21) she swam [. . .] with *kicks* of her thick webbed hind*feet*

Words often make general predictions about the content of surrounding text. Loftus and Palmer (1974) showed that words for "hit" trigger different assumptions, and affect perception and memory, when witnesses to a traffic accident are questioned in different ways about what they have seen, as in: *How fast were the cars travelling when they bumped* (versus *smashed*) *into each other?* Such assumptions do not arise from nowhere, but are created by recurrent collocations. In the 56-million-word corpus, I studied verbs in the semantic field of "hit." Collocates of HIT itself show its wide range of uses, often metaphorical and/or in fixed phrases (*hit for six, hit rock bottom*). In contrast, BUMP has connotations of clumsiness, and collocates such as *accidentally, lurched, stumbled*. COLLIDE is used predominantly with large vehicles, and has collocates such as *aircraft, lorry, ship, train*. SMASH has connotations of crime and violence, and has collocates such as *bottles, bullet, looted, police, windscreen*.

6   Collocations and Cultural Connotations

Such collocations contribute to textual coherence via the assumptions which they trigger. In a detailed study of such connotations, Baker and Freebody (1989) investigated the distribution of collocations in children's elementary reading books. They found that the adjective *little* was very frequent, and that 50 percent of the occurrences of *girl*, but only 30 percent of the occurrences of *boy*, collocated with *little* (p < 0.01). They argue (1989: 140, 147) that such frequent associations make some features of the world conceptually salient, but the associations are implicit, and appear to be a constant, shared, and natural feature of the world (cf. above on Berger and Luckmann 1966). Thus, *little* connotes cuteness, and its frequent collocation with *girl* conveys a sexist imbalance in such books. Such ideas ("girls are smaller and cuter than boys") are acquired implicitly along with the recurrent collocation.

Again, collocations can have such connotations only because patterns in a given text reflect intertextual patterns in the language. I studied 300,000 occurrences of the adjectives *little, small, big*, and *large*, and found that they occur in largely complementary distribution, with quite different uses and collocates (Stubbs 1995b). In particular, *little* has strong cultural connotations. The following facts are very simple, but not explicitly presented in any dictionary I have found. In the database constructed from a 200-million-word corpus (Cobuild 1995b), the most frequent noun to co-occur with *little* is GIRL, and the most frequent adjective to co-occur with *girl* is *little*. The phrase *little girl(s)* is nearly 20 times as frequent as *small girl(s)*, whereas *little boy(s)* is only twice as frequent as *small boy(s)*. *Little* typically occurs in phrases such as *charming little girl* (or *funny little man*), and *small* typically occurs in rather formal phrases such as *relatively small amount*.

What follows from such data? First, even on its own, one of the most frequent words in the language can convey cultural stereotypes, and this provides an intertextual explanation of why *little* has the connotations it does in phrases such as *Little Red Riding Hood*. In combination with other words, however, *little* conveys even stronger expectations. The combination *little old* is cute and folksy, or critical and patronizing; it can also be used purely pragmatically, with an atypical adjective–pronoun construction:

(22)   this frail little old woman; the dear little old church; a ramshackle little old van; any weedy little old man

(23)   little old New York; little old me

Of over 70 instances, selected at random from the corpus data, of *little old* before a noun, over half were in phrases such as *little old lady/ies* and *little old grandma*. The combination *little man* has two distinct uses. Both convey speaker attitude, one pejorative, and one approving:

(24)   a ridiculous little man; an evil, nasty, frightful and revolting little man

(25)   the little man against the system; little man versus Big Business; a victory for the little man

Second, paradigmatic oppositions (e.g. *little–big*, *old–young*) might appear to be permanently available in the language system. But coselection severely limits such choices in syntagmatic strings. There are stereotyped phrases such as *little old lady*, but combinations such as **little young lady* or *?small old lady* are impossible or highly unlikely. Indeed it is frequent for paradigmatically contrasting items to co-occur (syntagmatically) within a text. Justeson and Katz (1991) discuss quantitative aspects of several adjective pairs including *large* and *small*, such as the tendency (highly statistically significant) of lexically antonymous adjectives to co-occur within a span of a few words, as in:

(26)   from the *large* departmental store to the *small* shoe-mender

(27)   a *large* area of the *small* kitchen

In summary: in terms of cohesion, the word *little*, especially in frequent collocations, allows a hearer/reader to make predictions about the surrounding text. In terms of communicative competence, all words, even the most frequent in the language, contract such collocational relations, and fluent language use means internalizing such phrases. In terms of cultural competence, culture is encoded not just in words which are obviously ideologically loaded, but also in combinations of very frequent words. (Cf. Fillmore 1992 on *home*.) One textual function of recurrent combinations is to imply that meanings are taken for granted and shared (Moon 1994).

7   Lexis and Text Structure

In this section, I will review some further aspects of lexical cohesion which I have not yet mentioned.

Some words function primarily to organize text: see Halliday and Hasan (1976) on general nouns which can refer to whole topics (such as *affair, business, matter*); Winter (1977) on cohesive lexical items (such as *conclude, fact, reason, subsequent*); Widdowson

(1983) on "procedural vocabulary"; and Tadros (1994) on "prospective vocabulary." These studies do not use computational techniques, though their lists can be used in such work. Yang (1986) identifies technical and subtechnical vocabulary by its distribution: technical words are frequent only in a restricted range of texts on a specialized topic, but not evenly distributed across academic texts in general; whereas subtechnical words (e.g. *accuracy, basis, decrease, effect, factor, result*) are both frequent and evenly distributed in academic texts, independent of their specialized topic. And Francis (1994) uses corpora to identify noun phrases typically used to encapsulate and evaluate topics in written argumentative texts (e.g. *this far-sighted recommendation, this thoughtless and stupid attitude*); such discourse labels often occur in frequent collocations, which may be recognizable as newspaper language (e.g. *reverse this trend, the move follows, denied the allegations*).

Words from given lexical fields will co-occur and recur in particular texts. For example, here are the ten most frequent content words (i.e. excluding very high-frequency grammatical words), in descending frequency, from two books:

(28)   people, man, world, technology, economic, modern, development, life, human, countries

(29)   women, women's, discrimination, rights, equal, pay, work, men, Act, government

Such lists fall intuitively into a few identifiable lexical fields, tell us roughly what the books are "about," and could be used as a crude type of content analysis. Work on the structural organization of vocabulary usually considers paradigmatic relations, but words in lexical fields can also be discovered by simple syntagmatic analysis. The classic work on lexical fields was done on German between the 1920s and 1940s by Trier (1931) and Weisgerber (1950): it is summarized by Ullmann (1957) and Lyons (1977).

Morris and Hirst (1991) identify topical units in texts via chains of word relations (such as synonymy, antonymy, part–whole) taken from a thesaurus. They implement, by hand, a procedure which can "delineate portions of text that have a strong unity of meaning," but claim that the procedure is computable (1991: 23, 29). Topic and content are signaled by vocabulary, which must provide at least some formal signals of text structure, since lexis is not distributed evenly across corpora or across individual texts. As Church and Mercer (1994: 10–11) put it, content words tend to appear in bunches, "like buses in New York City." If we divide a large corpus into 10,000-word segments, the occurrence of a given word, say *Kennedy*, will be distributed quite unevenly across the segments: perhaps several occurrences in two or three segments, but none at all elsewhere, and this uneven distribution is itself one mechanism of cohesion. Phillips (1985, 1989) therefore uses entirely automatic methods to study the distribution of lexis in the syntagmatic, linear stream of science textbooks. When we remember what a text is "about," we do not remember the syntactic structure: there are forms of organization to which grammatical classification is irrelevant. Phillips finds syntagmatic lexical sets, but, by carrying out the kind of objective, knowledge-free distributional analysis originally proposed by Harris (1952), he also finds that sets of words intercollocate. This shows distinct lexical networks within different chapters, and thus reveals semantic units not directly observable in the original text.

Even finer lexical clustering can be studied as follows. For the first few words of a text, all words occur for the first time. But very soon, words start to recur: that is, the number of word types (new words) rises more slowly than the number of word tokens (running words). Exceptions will occur only with texts of restricted kinds, such as a shopping list in which each word probably occurs just once. Such features of texts can be studied via their type–token ratio. On its own, this ratio provides only an overall characterization of a text. However, as new topics are introduced into a text, there will be bursts of new words, which will in turn start to recur after a short span. Youmans (1991, 1994) uses this observation to study the "vocabulary flow" within a text. He shows that if the type–token ratio is sampled in successive segments of texts (e.g. across a continuously moving span of 35 words), then the peaks and troughs in the ratio across these samples correspond to structural breaks in the text, which are identifiable on independent grounds. Therefore a markedly higher type–token ratio means a burst of new vocabulary, a new topic, and a structural boundary in the text. (Tuldava 1995: 131–48 also discusses how the "dynamics of vocabulary growth" correspond to different stages of a text.)

8 Observational Methods

This chapter has been mainly about empirical methods of studying lexis in texts and corpora. So I will end with some more general remarks on computer-assisted observational methods.

There are many aspects to the Saussurian paradox (Labov 1972: 185ff). In much recent linguistics, langue or competence is seen as systematic and as the only true object of study: but, since it is abstract ("a social fact" or an aspect of individual psychology), it is unobservable. Parole or performance is seen as unsystematic and idiosyncratic, and therefore, at best, of only peripheral interest: but, although concrete, it is observable only in passing fragments, and, as a whole, also unobservable. Mainstream linguistics – from Saussure to Chomsky – has defined itself with reference to dualisms, whose two poles are equally unobservable.

Observational problems arise also in connection with the traditional dichotomy between syntagmatic and paradigmatic. For Saussure (1916/1968: 171), the syntagmatic relation holds between items *in praesentia*, which co-occur in a linear string. A text is a fragment of parole, where instances of syntagmatic relations can be observed. However, we are interested in more than what happens to occur in such a fragment. A paradigmatic ("associative") relation is a potential relation between items *in absentia*, which have a psychological reality ("des termes *in absentia* dans une série mnémonique virtuelle", 1916/1968: 171). However, since paradigmatic relations are a virtual mental phenomenon, they are unobservable.

In an individual text, neither repeated syntagmatic relations, nor any paradigmatic relations at all, are observable. However, a concordance makes visible repeated events: frequent syntagmatic co-occurrences, and constraints on the paradigmatic choices. The co-occurrences are visible on the horizontal (syntagmatic) axis of the individual concordance lines. And the paradigmatic possibilities – what frequently recurs – are equally visible on the vertical axis: especially if the concordance lines are merely reordered alphabetically to left or right (Tognini-Bonelli 1996).

As a very brief illustration, here are examples of one of the patterns discussed above, in (15):

(30)   a certain degree of humility
       an enormous degree of intuition
          a greater degree of social pleasure
          a high degree of accuracy
          a high degree of confidence
          a large degree of personal charm
          a mild degree of unsuitability
       a reasonable degree of economic security
       a reasonable degree of privacy
       a substantial degree of association

This tiny fragment of data, extracted from a concordance, is not claimed in any way as representative: these are only ten examples from many hundreds. They simply illustrate that concordance lines make it easy to see that *degree of* is often preceded by a quantity adjective (the full concordance shows that by far the most frequent is *high*), and is often followed by an abstract noun (the majority of which express positive ideas). Concordances provide a powerful method of identifying the typical lexicogrammatical frames in which words occur.

The classic objection to performance data (Chomsky 1965: 3) is that they are affected by "memory limitations, distractions, shifts of attention and interest, and errors." However, it is inconceivable that typical collocations and repeated coselection of lexis and syntax could be the result of performance errors. Quantitative work with large corpora automatically excludes idiosyncratic instances, in favor of what is central and typical.

It is often said that a corpus is (mere) performance data, but this shorthand formulation disguises important points. A corpus is a sample of actual utterances. However, a corpus, designed to sample different text-types, is a sample not of one individual's performance, but of the language use of many speakers. In addition, a corpus is not itself the behavior, but a record of this behavior, and this distinction is crucial. Consider a meteorologist's record of changes in temperature. The temperatures are a sequence of physical states in the world, which cannot be directly studied for the patterns they display. But the record has been designed by human beings, so that it can be studied. The intentional design of the record can convert the physical states in the world into a form of public knowledge. (This example is from Popper 1994: 7.) And, developing Halliday's (1991, 1992) analogy, such temperature records can be used to study not only local variations in the weather (which are directly observable in a rough and ready way), but also longer-term variations in the climate, which are certainly not directly observable.

Chomskyan linguistics has emphasized creativity at the expense of routine, which is seen as habit and as the unacceptable face of behaviorism. Other linguists (such as Firth 1957 and Halliday 1992) and sociologists (such as Bourdieu 1991 and Giddens 1984) have emphasized the importance of routine in everyday life. Corpus linguistics provides new ways of studying linguistic routines: what is typical and expected in the utterance-by-utterance flow of spoken and written language in use.

Large corpora provide a way out of the Saussurian paradox, since millions of running words can be searched for patterns which cannot be observed by the naked eye (compare devices such as telescopes, microscopes, and X rays). We can now study patterns which are not visible directly to a human observer, but which are nevertheless stable across the language performance of many speakers. An elegant defense and detailed study of such patterns is provided by Burrows (1987: 2–3), who talks of:

> evidence to which the unassisted human mind could never gain consistent, conscious access. Computer-based concordances, supported by statistical analysis, now make it possible to enter hitherto inaccessible regions of the language [which] defy the most accurate memory and the finest powers of discrimination.

In this chapter, I have illustrated methods which can identify the intertextual patterns which contribute to the cohesion of individual texts. As Hymes (1972) argued thirty years ago, tacit knowledge of the probabilities of such patterns is a significant component of linguistic competence.

NOTES

For access to the Bank of English corpus, I am very grateful to colleagues at Cobuild in Birmingham. For permission to use other corpus materials, I am grateful to the Norwegian Computing Centre for the Humanities and Longmans Group UK Ltd. For comments on earlier drafts, I am grateful to Wolfram Bublitz, Andrea Gerbig, Gabi Keck, and Henry Widdowson. For corpus preparation and programming, I am grateful to Oliver Mason and Oliver Hardt.

1   CobuildDirect is available on-line, with access software, at http:// titania.cobuild.collins.co.uk/form.html.
2   LOB consists of one million words of written British English; Lund consists of half a million words of spoken British English. These are very small corpora by modern standards, but carefully constructed, and still useful as reference corpora. The Longman–Lancaster corpus consists of 30 million words of written English, fiction and nonfiction. A useful further source is the 100-million-word British National Corpus, available on-line at http:// thetis.bl.uk/lookup.html.
3   The book is *A Year in the Greenhouse* by John Elkington (London: Gollancz). A large part of the book is contained in the Longman–Lancaster corpus, reference LL 40433.

REFERENCES

Aijmer, K. and Altenberg, B. eds. (1991). *English Corpus Linguistics*. London: Longman.

Allerton, D. J. (1984). Three (or four) levels of word co-occurrence restriction. *Lingua*, 63: 17–40.

Armstrong, S. ed. (1994). *Using Large Corpora*. Cambridge, Mass.: MIT Press.

Baker, C. and Freebody, P. (1989). *Children's First School Books*. Oxford: Blackwell.

Baker, M., Francis, G., and Tognini-Bonelli, E. eds. (1993). *Text and Technology*. Amsterdam: Benjamins.

Barnbrook, G. (1996). *Language and Computers*. Edinburgh: Edinburgh University Press.

Berger, P. and Luckmann, T. (1966). *The Social Construction of Reality*. London: Allen Lane.

Biber, D. (1988). *Variation across Speech and Writing*. Cambridge: Cambridge University Press.

Bolinger, D. (1976). Meaning and memory. *Forum Linguisticum*, 1, 1: 1–14.

Bourdieu, P. (1991). *Language and Symbolic Power*. Oxford: Polity.

Brown, G. and Yule, G. (1983). *Discourse Analysis*. Cambridge: Cambridge University Press.

Bublitz, W. (1996). Semantic prosody and cohesive company: "somewhat predictable." *Leuvense Bijdragen: Tijdschrift voor Germaanse Filologie*, 85, 1/2: 1–32.

Bublitz, W. (1998). "I entirely dot dot dot": copying semantic features in collocations with up-scaling intensifiers. In R. Schulze, ed., *Making Meaningful Choices in English*. Tuebingen: Narr. 11–32.

Burrows, J. F. (1987). *Computation into Criticism*. Oxford: Clarendon.

Chomsky, N. (1965). *Aspects of the Theory of Syntax*. Cambridge, Mass.: MIT Press.

Choueka, Y., Klein, S. T., and Neuwitz, E. (1983). Automatic retrieval of frequent idiomatic and collocational expressions in a large corpus. *ALLC Journal*, 4, 1: 34–8.

Church, K. and Mercer, R. L. (1994). Introduction to the special issue on computational linguistics using large corpora. In Armstrong 1994: 1–24.

Clear, J. (1993). From Firth principles: computational tools for the study of collocation. In Baker et al. 1993: 271–92.

Cobuild. (1995a). *Collins Cobuild English Dictionary*. London: HarperCollins.

Cobuild. (1995b). *Collins Cobuild Collocations on CD-ROM*. London: HarperCollins.

Coulthard, R. M. ed. (1994). *Advances in Written Text Analysis*. London: Routledge.

Cowie, A. P. (1994). Phraseology. In R. E. Asher, ed., *The Encyclopedia of Language and Linguistics*. Oxford: Pergamon. 3168–71.

Cowie, A. P. (1999). Phraseology and corpora. *International Journal of Lexicography*, 12, 4: 307–23.

Damerau, F. J. and Mandelbrot, B. B. (1973). Tests of the degree of word clustering in samples of written English. *Linguistics*, 102: 58–75.

Fillmore, C. J. (1992). Corpus linguistics or computer-aided armchair linguistics. In Svartvik 1992: 35–60.

Fillmore, C. J., Kay, P., and O'Connor, M. C. (1988). Regularity and idiomaticity in grammatical constructions: the case of let alone. *Language*, 64, 3: 501–38.

Firth, J. R. (1957). A synopsis of linguistic theory, 1930–55. In *Studies in Linguistic Analysis*. Special Volume, Philological Society. Oxford: Blackwell. 1–32.

Francis, G. (1993). A corpus-driven approach to grammar: principles, methods and examples. In Baker et al. 1993: 137–56.

Francis, G. (1994). Labelling discourse: an aspect of nominal-group lexical cohesion. In Coulthard 1994: 83–101.

Francis, G., Hunston, S., and Manning, E. (1996). *Grammar Patterns 1: Verbs*. London: HarperCollins.

Francis, G., Hunston, S., and Manning, E. (1998). *Grammar Patterns 2: Nouns and Adjectives*. London: HarperCollins.

Gerbig, A. (1996). *Lexical and Grammatical Variation in a Corpus*. Frankfurt: Peter Lang.

Giddens, A. (1984). *The Constitution of Society*. Cambridge: Polity.

Halliday, M. A. K. (1991). Corpus studies and probabilistic grammar. In Aijmer and Altenberg 1991: 30–43.

Halliday, M. A. K. (1992). Language as system and language as instance: the corpus as a theoretical construct. In Svartvik 1992: 61–77.

Halliday, M. A. K. and Hasan, R. (1976). *Cohesion in English*. London: Longman.

Harris, Z. (1952). Discourse analysis. *Language*, 28: 18–23.

Hoey, M. ed. (1993). *Data, Description, Discourse*. London: HarperCollins.

Hunston, S. and Francis, G. (1998). Verbs observed: a corpus-driven pedagogic grammar. *Applied Linguistics*, 19, 1: 45–72.

Hymes, D. (1972). On communicative competence. In J. Pride and J. Holmes, eds, *Sociolinguistics*. Harmondsworth: Penguin. 269–93.

Hymes, D. (1992). The concept of communicative competence revisited. In M. Pütz, ed., *Thirty Years of Linguistic Evolution*. Amsterdam: Benjamins. 31–58.

Justeson, J. S. and S. M. Katz (1991). Redefining antonymy: the textual structure of a semantic relation. In *Using Corpora*. Proceedings of 7th Annual Conference of the UW Centre for the New OED and Text Research. Oxford. 138–53.

Justeson, J. S. and Katz, S. M. (1995). Technical terminology. *Natural Language Engineering*, 1, 1: 9–27.

Kjellmer, G. (1991). A mint of phrases. In Aijmer and Altenberg 1991: 111–27.

Labov, W. (1972). The study of language in its social context. In *Sociolinguistic Patterns*. Philadelphia: University of Pennsylvania Press. 183–259.

Loftus, E. F. and Palmer, J. C. (1974). Reconstruction of automobile destruction: an example of the interaction between language and memory. *Journal of Verbal Learning and Verbal Behavior*, 13: 585–9.

Louw, B. (1993). Irony in the text or insincerity in the writer? The diagnostic potential of semantic prosodies. In Baker et al. 1993: 157–76.

Lyons, J. (1977). *Semantics*. Cambridge: Cambridge University Press.

Makkai, A. (1972). *Idiom Structure in English*. The Hague: Mouton.

Miller, J. (1993). Spoken and written language. In R. J. Scholes, ed., *Literacy and Language Analysis*. Hillsdale, NJ: Erlbaum. 99–141.

Moon, R. (1994). The analysis of fixed expressions in text. In Coulthard 1994: 117–35.

Moon, R. (1998). *Fixed Expressions and Idioms in English*. Oxford: Clarendon.

Morgan, J. L. and Sellner, M. B. (1980). Discourse and linguistic theory. In R. J. Spiro, B. C. Bruce, and W. F. Brewer, eds, *Theoretical Issues in Reading Comprehension*. Hillsdale, NJ: Erlbaum. 165–200.

Morris, J. and Hirst, G. (1991). Lexical cohesion computed by thesaural relations as an indicator of the structure of text. *Computational Linguistics*, 17, 1: 21–48.

Pawley, A. and Syder, F. H. (1983). Two puzzles for linguistic theory. In J. C. Richards and R. W. Schmidt, eds, *Language and Communication*. London: Longman. 191–226.

Phillips, M. K. (1985). *Aspects of Text Structure*. Amsterdam: North-Holland.

Phillips, M. K. (1989). Lexical structure of text. *Discourse Analysis Monograph 12*. Birmingham: English Language Research.

Popper, K. R. (1994). *Knowledge and the Body–Mind Problem*. London: Routledge.

Porzig, W. (1934). Wesenhafte Bedeutungsbeziehungen. *Beiträge zur Geschichte der deutschen Sprache und Literatur*, 58: 70–97.

Saussure, F. de (1916/1968). *Cours de Linguistique Générale*. Paris: Payot.

Sinclair, J. McH. (1991). *Corpus, Concordance, Collocation*. Oxford: Oxford University Press.

Sinclair, J. McH. (1996). The search for units of meaning. *Textus*, IX: 75–106.

Smadja, F. (1993). Retrieving collocations from text. Xtract. *Computational Linguistics*, 19, 1: 143–77.

Stubbs, M. (1995a). Collocations and semantic profiles. *Functions of Language*, 2, 1: 1–33.

Stubbs, M. (1995b). Collocations and cultural collocations of common words. *Linguistics and Education*, 7, 4: 379–90.

Stubbs, M. (1996). *Text and Corpus Analysis*. Oxford: Blackwell.

Summers, D. (1993). Longman/Lancaster English language corpus: criteria and design. *International Journal of Lexicography*, 6, 3: 181–95.

Svartvik, J. ed. (1992). *Directions in Corpus Linguistics*. Berlin: Mouton.

Tadros, A. (1994). Predictive categories in expository text. In Coulthard 1994: 69–82.

Tognini-Bonelli, E. (1996). Corpus Theory and Practice. Unpublished PhD dissertation. University of Birmingham, UK.

Trier, J. (1931). *Der deutsche Wortschatz im Sinnbezirk des Verstandes*. Heidelberg: Winter.

Tuldava, J. (1995). *Methods in Quantitative Linguistics*. Trier: WVT (Wissenschaftlicher Verlag Trier).

Ullmann, S. (1957). *The Principles of Semantics*. Oxford: Blackwell.

Weisgerber, L. (1950). *Vom Weltbild der deutschen Sprache*. Dusseldorf: Schwann.

Widdowson, H. G. (1979). *Explorations in Applied Linguistics*. Oxford: Oxford University Press.

Widdowson, H. G. (1983). *Learning Purpose and Language Use*. Oxford: Oxford University Press.

Winter, E. (1977). A clause-relational approach to English texts: a study of some predictive lexical items in written discourse. *Structional Science*, 6: 1–92.

Yang, H. (1986). A new technique for identifying scientific/technical terms and describing science texts. *Literary and Linguistic Computing*, 1, 2: 93–103.

Youmans, G. (1991). A new tool for discourse analysis: the vocabulary management profile. *Language*, 67, 4: 763–89.

Youmans, G. (1994). The vocabulary management profile: two stories by William Faulkner. *Empirical Studies of the Arts*, 12, 2: 113–30.

17 The Transcription of Discourse

JANE A. EDWARDS

0 Introduction

Recordings are essential tools in discourse research, but are not sufficient by themselves for the systematic examination of interaction. It is simply impossible to hold in mind the transient, highly multidimensional, and often overlapping events of an interaction as they unfold in real time.

For this reason, transcripts are invaluable. They provide a distillation of the fleeting events of an interaction, frozen in time, freed from extraneous detail, and expressed in categories of interest to the researcher.

As useful as they are, transcripts are not unbiased representations of the data. Far from being exhaustive and objective, they are inherently selective and interpretive. The researcher chooses what types of information to preserve, which descriptive categories to use, and how to display the information in the written and spatial medium of a transcript. Each of these choices can affect the researcher's perceptions of the structure of the interaction (Ochs 1979), making some types of regularities easier to detect in the data and others more difficult.

For example, arranging utterances by different speakers in separate columns (**column-based format**) gives the impression of asymmetry between the speakers, with the leftmost speaker appearing to be the most dominant. In contrast, arranging them one above the other in a single column (**vertical format**) gives the impression of interdependence and equal dominance. Vertical format is useful for conversations between adults of equal status, but would be misleading for interactions between adults and very young children, which tend to be child-centered and therefore child-dominated. For those interactions, Ochs (1979) recommended using column-based format, with the child's column leftmost.

The best choice of conventions in a given instance depends on the nature of the interaction, the theoretical framework, and the research question. In fact, Mishler (1991) presents several examples from published literature in which the same interaction was transcribed differently for contrasting purposes – in some cases, even by the same researcher at different times.

Transcription is an open-ended process. A transcript changes as the researcher's insights become progressively refined (Ehlich 1993; Ehlich and Switalla 1976; Gumperz and Berenz 1993). To ensure that significant but subtle factors are not left out, it is important to listen to recordings repeatedly throughout the course of a study and to update the transcript to reflect developing insights.

This chapter focuses on the interplay of theory and methods. It begins with general principles of design which are relevant regardless of research question. Next it surveys alternative conventions and their underlying assumptions. Then discussion turns to practical issues of applying transcription conventions to actual data in a consistent and efficient manner. Finally, it reviews some historical precursors to transcription, and summarizes developing standards and future trends.

1   General Principles

1.1   Encoding processes

Transcripts contain basically three types of encoding, termed here **transcription**, **coding**, and **markup**.

Transcription is the process of capturing the flow of discourse events in a written and spatial medium. This includes primarily: *who* said *what, to whom, in what manner,* and *under what circumstances*. It involves the kinds of information found in the script of a play, only with more systematic and detailed specification.

Many categories found useful in discourse research are interpretive in nature, rather than being tied strictly to objective physical measurements. Interpretive categories are necessary because the goal of discourse research is to capture aspects of interaction as they are perceived by human participants, and these are not yet specifiable by means of physical parameters. For example, perceived pause length depends not only on physically measurable time, but also on speech rate, location of the pause (e.g. within a clause, between clauses, between speaker turns), and other factors. There are many distinctions of interest to discourse researchers which have less obvious relationships to physically measurable properties. This is not a problem, so long as they can be applied reliably by human observers, on the basis of clearly specified criteria.

At a certain level of abstraction and complexity, transcribing shades into coding (also called "annotation" or "tagging"), which is even more interpretive and more closely tied to particular theoretical frameworks. Some examples of coding include: syntactic categories (such as nouns, verbs, adjectives, etc.), semantic distinctions (e.g. motion verbs, manner verbs), or pragmatic acts (e.g. directive, prohibition, claim). Coding establishes equivalence classes which expedite analysis and computer search by enabling otherwise dissimilar items to be efficiently brought together for closer examination.

Mark-up concerns format-relevant specifications rather than content. It is intended to be interpreted by a typesetter or computer software for such purposes as proper segmentation of the text and cataloging of its parts, in the service of formatting, retrieval, tabulation, or related processes. It also plays a central role in data exchange and emergent encoding standards, discussed in the closing section of this chapter.

1.2   Other representations

An important technological advance in recent years has been the ability to link transcripts to recordings. Bloom (1993) linked transcripts to videotaped recordings by means of SMTPE time codes, for purposes of navigating through the recordings more easily.

Some projects link transcripts to digitized audiorecordings (e.g. the MARSEC project, described in Knowles 1995; the HCRC project, described in Thompson et al. 1995, and the ToBI project, described in Roach and Arnfield 1995; the "Transcriber" interface, described in Barras et al. 1998). The listener can relisten to any utterance (or turn), with a simple click of a mouse.   .

Some projects link transcripts to digitized videorecordings (e.g. the SignStream project, described in Neidle and MacLaughlin 1998), enabling systematic encoding and analysis of visual language data (e.g. sign language and data). Duranti (1997) mentions the value of photographs, maps, and diagrams for providing supplementary information about an interaction. These other representations do not usually affect the form or content of transcripts, but are simply alternative perspectives on the same data.

The focus of this chapter is the representation of spoken language in a written/ spatial medium. There are three general design principles which are pertinent regardless of research question. These are principles of category design, computational tractability, and readability.

1.3   Principles of category design

Transcription and coding systems are divided into subdomains (e.g. pause length, intonation contour, syntactic category). The categories used in describing a particular subdomain (e.g. "short" or "long" pause) function as alternatives to one another. That is, they constitute a "contrast set." To be descriptively useful, the categories within each contrast set must satisfy three general principles:

1   They must be *systematically discriminable*. That is, for each portion of the interaction it must be clear whether or not a given category applies. Category membership can be based on either defining characteristics or similarity to prototypical exemplars.
2   They must be *exhaustive*. That is, for each relevant aspect or event in the data, there must be a category which fits (even if, in hopefully rare cases, it is only "miscellaneous").
3   They must be *usefully contrastive*. That is, they must be focused on distinctions of importance to the research question. For example, a "short" pause in information flow in monologues might be 0.2 seconds, whereas a "short" pause in research on turn-taking might be 0.5 seconds.

The categories within a contrast set usually cannot be interpreted without knowledge of the number and type of other categories in that set. Firth (1957: 227) expressed this property as follows: "The 'meaning' of the grammatical category noun in a grammatical system of, say, three word classes, *noun*, *verb*, and *particle*, is different from the meaning of the category *noun* in a system of five classes in which *adjective* and *pronoun* are formally distinguished from the *noun, verb*, and *particle*."

This is true also when interpreting symbols in a transcript. Punctuation marks are convenient and hence ubiquitous in transcripts, but may not serve the same purposes in all projects. They may be used to delimit different types of units (e.g. intonational, syntactic, pragmatic) or to signify different categories of a particular type. For example, a comma might denote a "level" utterance-final contour in one system and "nonrising" utterance-final contour in another. The only guarantee of comparability is a check of how the conventions were specified by the original sources. (For instances of noncomparability in archive data, see Edwards 1989, 1992b.)

1.4 *Principles of computational tractability*

For purposes of computer manipulation (e.g. search, data exchange, or flexible reformatting), the single most important design principle is that *similar instances be encoded in predictably similar ways.*

Systematic encoding is important for uniform computer retrieval. Whereas a person can easily recognize that *cuz* and *'cause* are variant encodings of the same word, the computer will treat them as totally different words, unless special provisions are made establishing their equivalence. If a researcher searches the data for only one variant, the results might be unrepresentative and misleading. There are several ways of minimizing this risk: equivalence tables external to the transcript, normalizing tags inserted in the text, or generating exhaustive lists of word forms in the corpus, checking for variants, and including them explicitly in search commands. (Principles involved in computerized archives are discussed in greater detail in Edwards 1992a, 1993a, 1995.)

Systematic encoding is also important for enabling the same data to be flexibly reformatted for different research purposes. This is an increasingly important capability as data become more widely shared across research groups with different goals. (This is discussed in the final section, with reference to emerging standards for encoding and data exchange.)

1.5 *Principles of visual display*

For many researchers, it is essential to be able to read easily through transcripts a line at a time to get a feel for the data, and to generate intuitive hypotheses for closer testing. Line-by-line reading is often also needed for adding annotations of various types. These activities require readers to hold a multitude of detail in mind while acting on it in some way – processes which can be greatly helped by having the lines be easily readable by humans. Even if the data are to be processed by computer, readability is helpful for minimizing error in data entry and for error checking.

In approaching a transcript, readers necessarily bring with them strategies developed in the course of extensive experience with other types of written materials (e.g. books, newspapers, train schedules, advertisements, and personal letters). It makes sense for transcript designers to draw upon what readers already know and expect from written media, both because readers are good at extracting information in these ways, and because strategies based on reading habits and perceptual predispositions may be difficult to suspend even if it is desired to do so.

Written materials often make systematic use of two cues in particular: space and visual prominence. For example, chapter titles are expected to be printed in a large font, possibly centered or ruled off, and placed above the body of the text at some vertical distance, rather than, say, being embedded in the body of a text and in the same font size and type.

In looking across transcripts of various types, one notices some recurring strategies using these two cues for highlighting information and indicating relationships of interest. Six of them are summarized here. Some of these overlap with properties discussed by Du Bois (1991) and Johansson (1991). These are discussed with examples in Edwards (1992b, 1993b).

1 *Proximity of related events:* Events or types of information which are more closely related to each other are placed spatially nearer to each other than those which are less closely related. For example, prosodic information, such as prominent syllable stress, is often indicated by a mark (e.g. an apostrophe or an asterisk) placed immediately before the relevant syllable (cf. Svartvik and Quirk 1980; Gumperz and Berenz 1993).

2 *Visual separability of unlike events:* Events or types of information which are qualitatively different from each other (e.g. spoken words and researcher comments, codes, and categories) tend to be encoded in distinctly different ways. For example, codes may be enclosed in parentheses, or expressed as nonalphabetic characters (rather than alphabetic) or upper case letters (in contrast to lower case). This enables the reader to know what kind of information is about to be read before actually reading it, and thereby speeds reading and minimizes false attributions (e.g. perceiving a word as having been part of the speech stream, when it was really part of a metacomment or code).

3 *Time-space iconicity:* Temporally prior events are encountered earlier on the page (top to bottom or left to right) than temporally later events. This can include utterances, gestures, door slams, laughs, coughs, and so forth.

4 *Logical priority:* Logically prerequisite information for interpreting utterances tends to be encountered earlier on the page than the utterance(s) for which it is relevant. Information concerning the circumstances of data gathering and the relationships among the speakers tends to be given at the top of the transcript, whereas changes in circumstances or activities during the course of the interaction tend to precede the utterances they contextualize or potentially influence.

5 *Mnemonic marking:* Coded categories are encoded either in directly interpretable abbreviations or in symbolically iconic ways in order to expedite recovery of their meaning during rapid reading. An example of this is the use of a slash (/) for rising intonation and a backslash (\) for falling tone, rather than vice versa or instead of an arbitrary numerical code (e.g. "7"), as in the following example:

(1) **London–Lund Corpus, text 1.3 (Svartvik and Quirk 1980):**
    1 3   7212280 1 1 A   11   and at ^h\/ome#.   /
    1 3   7212290 1 1 A   11   she's not a ^b\it the way she is at c/ollege# /

Direct readability is also helped by using conventions already known from other written contexts. Du Bois (1991) notes that a number of transcription conventions derive from literary conventions found in novels and plays. Some examples are the use of three dots (. . .) for pauses, or a dash (–) for interrupted thoughts or utterances.

6   *Efficiency and compactness:* Coded distinctions should be marked with as few symbols as possible (e.g. nonredundantly, using short abbreviations), so long as meaning is easily recoverable (i.e. encoded mnemonically). This serves to minimize nonessential and distracting clutter in the transcript. For example, the use of a slash (/) for rising tone is more compact and efficiently read than would be the use of the full word, "rising." The encoding of spoken words and prosodic information on the same line instead of on separate lines is also a type of compactness.

All transcripts contain at least some of these devices. They vary in the specific types of information they foreground, background, and interrelate.

We turn now to a brief survey of some of their differences and how they relate to underlying theories of interaction.

2   Contrasting Methods and Assumptions

There are primarily two types of decisions which affect researcher perceptions in transcripts: format-based decisions and content-based decisions.

2.1   *Format-based decisions*

Format-based decisions are those involving layout and symbol choice. If the data have been systematically encoded, it is possible to convert between these choices by means of computer programs.

2.1.1   *Layout*

The main layout considerations are: arrangement of speaker turns (i.e. vertical, column-based, and partiture formats) and placement of codes and researcher comments relative to the discourse events they clarify (multilinear, column-based, and interspersed formats).

2.1.1.1   *Arrangement of speaker turns*
The three main choices are vertical format, column-based format, and "partiture" or musical score notation.

As mentioned in the opening section, **vertical** format implies symmetry and equal dominance of speakers, whereas **column-based** format gives the impression (due to left-to-right reading bias) that the speaker whose utterances are leftmost is more dominant in the interaction. Vertical and column-based format are similar in highlighting the incremental aspect of interaction – that is, the fact that discourse is built up gradually out of smaller units, contributed one at a time. For both vertical and column-based formats, time is preserved vertically from the top to the bottom of the transcript, and to a more limited degree from left to right. In both of these formats, overlapping stretches of speech are signaled by marks placed before and after the parts which overlap. In vertical format, indentation and brackets may also be used:

(2) **From Du Bois et al. (1993: 49):**
    Jeff: That's all it does.
           It doesn't [even] reach a conclusion.
    Sarah: [mhm]

Similar conventions are found in Jefferson (1984) and Psathas (1990).

In **partiture** notation (e.g. Ehlich 1993; Erickson and Shultz 1982), turns by different speakers are put on different lines in a manner similar to instruments on a musical score. This format highlights the collaborative aspects of interaction – that is, that discourse is a unified "accomplishment" achieved jointly by multiple participants. Partiture preserves both time and simultaneity in a directly interpretable manner (which is why it is useful for musical notation), and eases the study of temporal coordination, overlaps, and conjoined action. Its disadvantage is that it may require specialized software (such as HIAT2 – Ehlich 1993) to ensure the alignment is preserved whenever changes are made. Also, the boundaries of turns are less prominent than in vertical format.

2.1.1.2 Placement of codes and comments

The three main possibilities are multitier, column-based, and interspersed formats.

Multitier (or interlinear or multilayer) format: The most widespread format involves placing codes or annotations on separate lines beneath the datum they clarify. It was used in the Berkeley Crosslinguistic Language Acquisition project (Slobin 1967), which was one of the earliest coded computer corpora:

(3) 2;0a 002A ALL CLOSE UP Q. {notes back of bus is open}.
    2;0a 002B = -NO -V PC -YN QT
    2;0a 002C == CPSP {close-up} PERF {all}
    2;0a 002D (Q+POT PERF (C (P SP))) #

In this example, the top tier contains the child's utterance and contextual comments, and subsequent tiers contain syntactic and semantic analyses of the utterance. In the ChiLDES archive of child language data (MacWhinney 1995), the top tier contains the child utterance and subsequent tiers contain phonetic, prosodic, gestural-proxemic, or other types of information. In multilingual studies, the top line is used for the utterance, the second line for an interlinear morpheme by morpheme gloss, and the third line for a free translation (discussed in Duranti 1997: 158; see also Du Bois et al. 1993). In the ToBI (Tones and Break Indices) project, concerning prosody, the orthographic rendering of the utterance is followed by three tiers: a tone tier (for specifying the tonal properties of the fundamental frequency contour), a break index tier (for specifying the degree of disjuncture between adjacent words), and a miscellaneous tier (for additional notations). Multitier format is also used in the MATE

(Multilevel Annotation Tools Engineering) project, a large European project concerned with establishing standards for encoding for speech and language technologies using corpus data.

Multitier format enables users to access each type of information independently from the others in an efficient manner. However, this format also has some drawbacks. Unless there is a strict, sequential, one-to-one correspondence between main-tier elements and elements on the other tiers, additional provisions are needed (such as numerical indices) to indicate the word(s) to which each code or comment pertains (that is, its "scope"). Otherwise it is not possible to convert data automatically from this format into other formats, and the data are less efficient to use where it is necessary to correlate individual codes from different tiers (see Edwards 1993b for further discussion).

Also, it is generally less useful in discourse research than other methods because it requires the reader to combine information from multiple tiers while reading through the transcript, and because it spreads the information out to an extent which can make it difficult to get a sense of the overall flow of the interaction.

Column-based format: Rather than arranging the clarifying information vertically in separate lines beneath the discourse event, codes may be placed in separate columns, as in the following example from Knowles (1995: 210) (another example is the Control Exchange Code described in Lampert and Ervin-Tripp 1993):

(4)

phon_id	orthog	dpron	cpron	prosody
525400	the	Di	D@	the
525410	gratitude	'gr&tItjud	'gr&tItjud	,gratitude
525420	that	D&t	D@t~p	that
525430	millions	'mIll@@nz	'mill@nz	~millions
525440	feel	fil	'fil	*feel
525450	towards	t@'wOdz	t@'wOdz	to'wards
525460	him	hIm	Im	him

If the codes are mostly short, column-based format can be scanned more easily than multitier format because it is spatially more compact.

Column-based coding is also preferable when annotating interactions which require a vertical arrangement of speaker turns, such as interactions with very young children. For this reason, Bloom's (1993) transcript contained columns for child utterances, coding of child utterances, adult utterances, coding of adult utterances, and coding of child play and child affect. The columns in her transcript are of a comfortable width for reading, and it is relatively easy to ignore the coding columns to gain a sense of the flow of events, or to focus on the coding directly.

Interspersed format: Where codes are short and easily distinguished from words, they may be placed next to the item they refer to, on the same line (i.e. "interspersed"), as in this example from the London–Oslo–Bergen corpus:

(5)   A10 95 ^ the_ATI king's_NN$ counsellors_NNS couched_VBD their_PP$
      A10 95 communiqué_NN in_IN vague_JJ terms_NNS ._.

Brackets may be used to indicate scope for codes if they refer to more than one word. Gumperz and Berenz (1993) indicate such things as increasing or decreasing tempo or loudness across multiple words in a turn in this manner.

Information is encoded in both the horizontal and vertical planes in the following example, from the Penn Treebank, in which the vertical dimension indicates larger syntactic units:

(6) **(from Marcus et al. 1993):**

```
((S
    (NP Battle-tested industrial managers
        here)
    always
    (VP buck
        up
        (NP nervous newcomers)
        (PP with
            (NP the tale
                (PP of
                    (NP (NP the
                            (ADJP first
                                (PP of
                                    (NP their countrymen)))
                        (S (NP *)
                            to
                            (VP visit
                                (NP Mexico))))
                        ,
                        (NP (NP a boatload
                            (PP of
                                (NP (NP warriors)
                                    (VP-1 blown
                                        ashore
                                        (ADVP (NP 375 years)
                                            ago)))))
                        (VP-1 *pseudo-attach*))))))))
.)
```

2.1.2 Symbol choice

The choice of symbols is mainly dictated by the principles of readability already discussed above. Examples (5) and (6) are readable despite their dense amount of information. This is due to the visual separability of upper and lower case letters, and to a consistent ordering of codes relative to the words they describe. That is, in (5), the codes follow the words; in (6) they precede the words.

With systematic encoding and appropriate software, it is possible for short codes, such as those in example (5), to serve as references for entire data structures, as is possible using the methods of the Text Encoding Initiative (TEI) (described more fully in McEnery and Wilson 1997: 28). Alternatively, tags can be left out of the text entirely, by numbering the words in a text sequentially and linking data structures to their identification numbers (as in Du Bois and Schuetze-Coburn 1993).

2.1.3   Converting between formats

With consistent encoding and appropriate software, it is possible to translate easily between alternative formats, and to protect the user from clutter by displaying only those parts of the information which are needed for specific research purposes.

This kind of flexibility of representation was the main motivation behind the TEI, a large international project designed to establish guidelines for text exchange among the various fields using textual data, discussed in greater detail in the final section of this chapter.

2.2   Content-based decisions

Unlike "format-based" biases, "content-based" biases cannot be adjusted by computer program. To change these, it is often necessary to change both the number and type of categories used to encode the interaction. It is the content-based aspects which most distinguish different systems and which are primarily of interest with respect to the issue of the impact of theory on methods.

Content-based decisions are of mainly two types: the sorts of information which are encoded, and the descriptive categories used.

Though transcripts differ across many dimensions, some of the domains in which transcripts differ most often (and which are often the most theory-relevant) are the following:

* words
* units of analysis
* pauses
* prosody
* rhythm and coordination
* turn-taking
* nonverbal aspects and events.

2.2.1   Words

In encoding words, there are mainly two types of decision to be made. The first is whether standard orthography is sufficient, or whether to preserve nuances of pronunciation (e.g. regional accents or idiolects). If details of pronunciation are to be preserved, the second choice is whether to use phonemic or phonetic transcription (which is rigorous but requires some special training) or modified orthography (which requires less training but is also less precise).

Because English spelling has many inconsistencies, modified orthography is often ambiguous. It is also likely to be less accessible for nonnative speakers of English than for native speakers. In addition, it suggests departure from the educated standard

(Duranti 1997) and may cause participants to appear less educated or intelligent (Gumperz and Berenz 1993; Preston 1985). Where modified orthography is used for words which are pronounced in the standard way (e.g. "wuz" in place of "was"), it serves to imply a manner of speaking without actually adding precision regarding pronunciation. Duranti (1997) observes that modified orthography may serve in some cases to remind researchers of specific aspects of a recording which they know intimately, rather than encoding events in a manner precisely interpretable by those who have not heard the recording. (For further discussion, see Duranti 1997; Edwards 1992c.)

2.2.2   Units of analysis

Next the researcher must decide how to subdivide the text into units for purposes of analysis. Should the unit of analysis be an idea unit, a unit containing a predicate, a speaker turn, a unit bounded by pauses or uttered under a completed intonational contour, or some combination of these? Should text be subdivided into paragraphs or episodes? These are just a few of the possibilities.

This choice will determine which dimensions of structure are highlighted for purposes of analysis (e.g. prosody, syntax, information packaging), as well as the relevant scope of descriptive codes. (For further discussion, see Edwards 1993b; Lampert and Ervin-Tripp 1993.)

This choice affects the location of line breaks. In some transcription systems, line breaks occur before each intonation or ideational unit (as in Du Bois et al. 1993). Where analysis is focused on turn-taking, line breaks may be less common, perhaps occurring only between turns, or for long utterances (to keep them on the screen or page).

The unit of analysis also has implications for the temporal organization of the transcript. In the ChiLDES archive, utterances are the primary units of analysis. Gestures are treated as clarifying information, tied to specific utterances. They are placed on subordinate tiers beneath the utterances they are believed to clarify. If the gesture occurs before the utterance, this is indicated by adding the tag "<bef>" to the gestural-proxemic tier. Time is preserved spatially only for utterances in that format. Where a gesture or event is deemed relevant to more than one utterance, it is duplicated for each utterance (without notation distinguishing this case from the case in which the gesture itself is repeated in the interaction). This introduces ambiguity, and hinders automatic conversion from this format to others.

An alternative approach is to place verbal and nonverbal communication events in the transcript in order of occurrence. This approach is more theory-neutral because researchers are not required to guess the scope of relevance of nonverbal events (as is required in the former approach). In addition, having utterances and nonverbal acts in chronological order provides a more immediate sense of the flow of an interaction. This second approach is the more common in discourse research (e.g. Bloom 1973; Ehlich 1993; Jefferson 1984; Psathas 1990; Gumperz and Berenz 1993).

2.2.3   Pauses

Some researchers measure pauses to the nearest tenth of a second (Jefferson 1984). However, a pause may seem longer if embedded in rapid speech than if embedded in slower speech. For this reason, some researchers quantify pauses as the number of beats of silence, based on the speaker's preceding speech rate. If all participants have the same speech rate, these approaches will be equivalent.

The perceived length of a given pause is also affected by its location in the discourse. It may seem longer if it is within an utterance than between turns by different speakers. Pauses which are longer or shorter than expected for a given location may be highly significant to interactants, indicating communicative strain or high rapport depending on communicative norms of that social group (as discussed by Erickson and Shultz 1982; Tannen 1984). For this reason, some researchers include normative judgments in their estimates of pause length. (To avoid circularity, communicative significance is established independently of the pause.)

Some systems explicitly mark all detectable pauses (e.g. Chafe 1993; Du Bois et al. 1993), while others mark only pauses that depart strongly from expectation (e.g. Ehlich 1993; Gumperz and Berenz 1993).

Even if the pause is measured in tenths of a second, its classification as "short" or "medium" depends on the research purpose. Researchers concerned with turn-taking smoothness may consider a "short" pause to be 0.5 seconds, while those interested in information packaging may consider it to be 0.2 seconds.

Another issue is the positioning of the pause relative to units of analysis. For monologs, it is sufficient to adopt a consistent convention, such as putting the pause at the beginning of each intonation unit (e.g. Chafe 1987, 1993). For dialogs, decisions are needed regarding who is responsible for an interturn pause. If a pause is perceived as "shared" by interactants, it makes sense to place it midway between the two turns (e.g. on a separate line in vertical format). If the first speaker asks a question and the second speaker says nothing, the pause may signal reticence. In that case, there is some logic to viewing it as belonging to the second speaker and transcribing it as if it is an empty turn (Tannen 1981).

All of these categories are potentially useful in some contexts. It is important simply to be aware of their interpretive nature (Tannen 1981) and to make allowances for their biases in the results.

2.2.4   Prosody

Prosodic features are properties that "generally extend over stretches of utterances longer than just one sound" (Cruttenden 1997: 1). These include such things as perceived duration, prominence, and intonation. These are perceptual/linguistic rather than acoustic phenomena. Although they are related to objectively measurable properties, the correspondence is far from perfect.

Listeners make many adjustments which acoustic measuring machines do not. There are far more frequency variations in the speech signal than are noticed by the listener (see, for example, Couper-Kuhlen 1986: 7). An utterance may be sprinkled with sudden high frequencies at high vowels (e.g. /i/) and silent spots at devoiced stop consonants (e.g. /p/) (Cruttenden 1997), but somehow the listener looks past these perturbations and perceives what seem to be reasonably smooth frequency contours.

Seemingly simple categories such as "rising intonation" actually cover a wide variety of acoustic contours. Contours may stretch over utterances of different lengths, or have differing numbers of pitch peaks or different speeds of pitch change, and still be judged as belonging to the same contour category. These adjustments rely on norms:

> As Crystal (1975) has pointed out, we apparently do use norms or standards in auditory perception. For one, we can form a notion of "natural speaking level" and are able to determine (regardless of individual voice range) whether someone is speaking near the top or the bottom of his/her voice. (Couper-Kuhlen 1986: 9)

Since discourse researchers wish to describe interactions in categories which are as similar as possible to perceptions by participants, it is necessary to use interpretive categories. A variety of interpretive categories has been found useful. We examine them with reference to three aspects of prosodic encoding: prominence, duration, and intonation.

Prominence: A common feature of English is that some syllables are perceived as more prominent than others. The location of a prominence is determined in part lexically. In *ELephants* the first syllable is the most prominent; in *esCAPED*, the last. When these words occur in the same utterance, one of them will typically receive more prominence than the other, depending on such things as information focus or surprisingness of content (cf. Bolinger 1986; Tench 1996). For example, in response to "What happened today?" the reply might be "The *elephants* escaped," with the greater prominence on *elephants*, whereas in response to "Did you feed the elephants today?" the response might be "The elephants *escaped*."

All transcription systems mark unusual prominence (e.g. contrastive stress and "boosters"). Some systems mark many other prominences as well, such as primary stress (') and secondary stress (^) in the following example:

(7) **From Du Bois, et al. 1993: 58:**
>   G: ... (2.2) 'a=nd of course,
>   a 'lot of herb ^tea,
>   when I'd 'rather be drinking ^whiskey.

These prominences are also marked in the London–Lund Corpus (Svartvik and Quirk 1980).

Perceived prominence presents considerable challenges to automatic detection by computer. It may arise from a marked change in pitch, or increased intensity, lengthening, or a combination of these and other factors. The same speaker may use different combinations of these cues in different types of discourse, or even within a single stretch of discourse (Brown et al. 1980).

Duration (lengthening and shortening): The length of syllables is determined to some degree lexically, as a function of which syllable is stressed in the word. For example, the second syllable is longer in *subJECT* than in *SUBject*. In addition, speech rate tends to speed up at the beginnings of phrases (**anacrusis**) and to slow down at the ends (**phrase-final lengthening**). Those discourse researchers who mark syllable lengthening or shortening tend to mark it only where it deviates from norms or is interactively significant for other reasons.

Intonation: There is no definitive "phoneme" in prosodic research, that is, no units which correlate with meaning in such a way that the principle of distinctive contrast

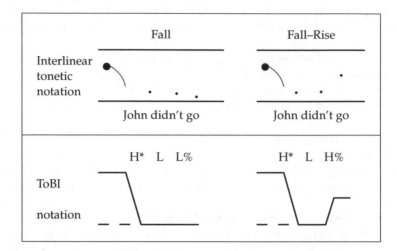

Figure 17.1   Interlinear tonetic and ToBI notations

can apply. However, we know that intonation is used systematically for communication – quite apart from the contributions of words and syntax. The analyst's task is to determine, as Crystal (1969) expressed it, what nonsegmental contrasts are meaningful, within a set of postulated systems.

Researchers differ in the size of unit they believe to be meaningful. Some have attributed meanings to entire contours (e.g. Bolinger 1986). Others have subdivided the contours and sought meaningful generalizations regarding those subparts (e.g. that a falling unit-final contour suggests conviction or closure). Tench (1996) compares a number of those proposals. Some researchers attribute meaning to the degree of rise (or fall) relative to the speaker's comfortable range (cf. "boosters", described in Altenberg 1990).

Systems also differ in their treatment of "declination," that is, the tendency for fundamental frequency to drift downward from the beginning to the end of an intonation unit. Acoustically oriented researchers may represent intonation contours as being superimposed upon a declining baseline (e.g. 't Hart et al. 1990). Others draw the contours as being superimposed on a level baseline – an approach which is less acoustic and more interpretive.

A widespread and intuitively accessible notation is that known as "interlinear tonetic notation," which is illustrated in the top pane of figure 17.1. In that format, "the top and bottom lines represent the top and bottom of the speaker's pitch range and each dot corresponds to a syllable, the larger dots indicating stressed and/or accented syllables" (Cruttenden 1997: xv).

An especially important difference between researchers is that between "levels" and "movements." Some researchers encode the relative height of individual syllables – e.g. Pike (1945); Ladd (1996); and the ToBI (Tones and Break Indices) prosodic conventions (Beckman and Ayers 1997). Others focus on pitch movements, or "nuclear tones" – e.g. the "British School" (Cruttenden 1997; Crystal 1980; Svartvik and Quirk 1980).

Notational systems of "movements" have included: (1) "nuclear tones," which extend from the main prominence in a stretch of speech to the end of that unit (e.g.

high-rising, low-falling, fall–rise); (2) pitch change on the final syllable of the unit (e.g. rising, falling, continuing); (3) larger patterns such as the rise–fall–rise pattern observed in the so-called "contradiction contour" (see Cruttenden 1997).

The focus on levels versus movements inspired considerable differences in their notation conventions. Figure 17.1 compares their notations with reference to two very common contours in American and British English. Within the British school, represented by Cruttenden (1997: 61), they are called "falling" and "fall–rise" nuclear tones, and are expressed in "interlinear tonetic notation." In ToBI notation, represented here by Pierrehumbert and Hirschberg (1990: 281), these receive less immediately transparent labels: H* L L% and H* L H%.

There is a variety of other differences between British school and ToBI notations (see Cruttenden 1997). For tables of partial correspondences between the two systems, see Ladd (1996: 83) and Roach (1994). Additional methods of prosodic transcription are surveyed by Ehlich and Switalla (1976), Gibbon (1976), and Leech et al. (1998).

An important branch of prosody research involves comparing observed acoustic properties (i.e. measured aspects of waveforms) with the auditory perceptions of listeners (i.e. psychological and linguistic categories). This work serves to clarify the acoustic substrates of listener perceptions of prosody (e.g. 't Hart et al. 1990). Text-to-speech conversion (e.g. Dutoit 1997; Svartvik 1990) is another area which promises to advance our knowledge of prosody. These approaches seek the most reliable correspondences between acoustic and auditory descriptions, often making explicit also contributions of other factors (i.e. syntax, semantic, pragmatic, and other information) in order to generate acceptably natural prosodic contours.

Because the prosodic distinctions are difficult to convey in writing alone, documentation should include recordings in addition to manuals. This was appreciated by Armstrong and Ward (1942), who made their examples available for purchase on three grammophone records (1942: vii). Audiorecordings are available for the following recent systems: Cruttenden (1997) (via audiocassette, Cambridge University Press ISBN: 0 521 62902 0), Du Bois et al. (1993) (via tutorial on computer diskette, available from the Linguistics Department, University of California at Santa Barbara), and Beckman and Ayers (1997) (via audiocassette and ftp-transferable digital records, available from Mary Beckman).

2.2.5 Rhythm and coordination

One key property not discussed so far is that of rhythm and coordination. Regardless of the degree to which nonverbal actions and utterances contribute independently to the content of an interaction, they are often unfolding jointly in time. Some researchers have attempted to systematize these observations and look into their temporal organization and coordination with one another. Erickson and Shultz (1982) and Ehlich (1993) did this by incorporating nonverbal actions as well as utterances into their "partiture" (or musical score) format, and by looking for synchrony within and across speakers as a reflection of communicative smoothness or difficulty in interview situations.

Scollon (1982) suggests that people contribute to an interaction in keeping with its rhythm at the time. This is an exciting area, not yet routinely indicated in transcripts. This may be due in part to a premature dismissal of stress timing (though see

Couper-Kuhlen 1993 and Dutoit 1997 for reasons why this was unjustified). It may also be due to a lack of tools facilitating this type of encoding (such as exist now for prosodic encoding). A practical and systematic approach to encoding it is found in Couper-Kuhlen (1993).

2.2.6   Turn-taking

Categories concerned with turn transition include unusually short pauses between one speaker and the next (**latching**), interruption by the second speaker, and simultaneous talk (**overlap**). These conventions are among those devised by Gail Jefferson for **conversation analysis** (Jefferson 1984; Psathas 1990) and used widely in any area of discourse research concerned with coordination of turns across speakers (e.g. Gumperz and Berenz 1993).

Transcription systems differ as to whether they mark only the beginnings of overlapping sections or also the ends (see Leech et al. 1998). They differ too in whether they mark overlap only by adjacent marks or also by indentation.

2.2.7   Nonverbal aspects and events

Nonverbal actions constitute a communicative resource which is partially independent of spoken language. As such, it raises many of the issues already discussed with reference to spoken language, such as how detailed the descriptive system can be without overburdening a viewer, and what is the best format for displaying the information.

Partiture format is the one most often used for capturing nonverbal events (e.g. Ehlich 1993; Neidle and MacLaughlin 1998). One approach (by Farnell 1995, cited in Duranti 1997: 149) involves the use of Laban notation, borrowed from choreography. The SignStream Project (discussed in the next section) provides a computer interface for handling complex data of this type as well as linking the transcript to the videorecording.

For capturing gaze patterns during conversations, Jefferson (1984) proposed inserting a line above or below an utterance to indicate the stretch of words during which mutual gaze occurred. A couple of additional conventions are used to indicate transition into and out of mutual gaze, to identify who is involved, and other details. This system has been found useful in several studies (e.g. Goodwin and Goodwin 1992).

3   Practicalities

Transcription is a notoriously time-consuming process. The exact amount of time required depends on the type of speech involved (e.g. amount of interruption, self-repair, or overlapping speech) and the amount of detail (e.g. word flow, prosodics, turn-taking). Estimates for word-level transcription with minimal added information are in the range of 10 or 11 minutes of transcribing for every 1 minute of speech (e.g. Crowdy 1995; Gibbon et al. 1997: 171). To produce a transcript containing the types of information encoded in most discourse transcripts (e.g. overlaps, pauses, stress or prominence, notable changes in rate or loudness, etc.), the time estimates increase to 20:1 (Ervin-Tripp 2000). Coding can take considerably longer, depending on the number and complexity of the categories involved.

A great saving in time would be possible if off-the-shelf speech recognition software (such as that produced by Dragon Systems, Lernhout and Hauspie, or IBM) could be used to produce word-level discourse transcripts. When attempted, this has so far yielded only modest results (e.g. Coniam 1998). Current off-the-shelf speech recognizers need a training phase, are designed to recognize only one person's speech per session, and are hindered by noisy conditions. Perhaps it may be possible someday. Automatic speech recognition is progressing not only in word recognition (for an overview, see Bourlard and Morgan 1994), but also in automatic detection of speaker shift, topic shift, utterance boundaries, and stressed syllables. In the meantime, specialized software interfaces can greatly facilitate human efforts on both transcription and coding.

Transcriber (Barras et al. 1998) is a highly developed software tool, which gives the human transcriber virtually unlimited control over the playback of a digital recording, and provides a convenient computer interface for data entry. Transcriber is distributed as free software under GNU General Public License, at www.etca.fr/CTA/gip/Projects/Transcriber/. Its basic format is what was above called vertical format, that is, speaker turns are arranged in a single column down the page. It does not yet allow fine-grained encoding of overlapping speech, but it is in others ways surprisingly flexible, and seems likely to continue to develop.

For partiture or multitiered format including nonverbal information, relevant software includes HIAT-DOS (Ehlich 1993; http://www.daf.uni-muenchen. de/HIAT/HIAT.HTM) and SignStream (Neidle and MacLaughlin 1998; www.bu.edu/asllrp/SignStream/), the latter linking the transcript to a digitized videorecording.

Software supporting coding or annotation includes: the Corpus/Annotation Toolbox (Garside and Rayson 1997; McEnery and Rayson 1997), which is associated with Lancaster University's UCREL research center (www.comp.lancs.ac.uk/ucrel/); the SAM (Speech Assessment Method) software tools (Gibbon et al. 1997: appendix E), which is part of the EAGLES project (Expert Advisory Group on Language Engineering); and the MATE Coding Workbench, which is part of the Multilevel Annotation Tools Engineering project (described at mate.nis.sdu.dk/). Additional software is listed on the resources web page of the Linguistic Data Consortium (morph.ldc.upenn.edu/annotation/).

Apart from the practicalities of adding distinctions to a transcript, several guidelines may help ensure that the resulting encoding (transcription or coding) is as accurate and consistent as possible.

Lampert and Ervin-Tripp (1993) note that learning to use a coding system is similar to learning a second language: in both cases, the learner must learn how to extend what is already known in useful ways. To expedite learning, they recommend that coders be trained in groups using clear and concrete documentation, and that intercoder agreement be evaluated regularly, to guard against differential uses and "category drift." Intercoder agreement can be assessed with Cohen's Kappa. It is preferable to percent agreement because it corrects for chance agreement. If Kappa is low for a particular section of a code, it may indicate the need for additional coder training or better documentation, or it may signal the need for revising the categories themselves.

Additional suggestions for transcription are the following:

- Do not encode more than what is known to be needed in a project. Additional distinctions can always be added later, as needed.
- Limit the load on working memory by restricting the number of decisions made on any one pass through the data.
- Carefully document all distinctions in the form of a transcription manual or coding manual. Where possible the manual should contain not only a conceptual definition, but also both good examples of a category and boundary cases (Lampert and Ervin-Tripp 1993). For prosodic distinctions, audiorecordings are useful in documenting distinctions, and are being made available increasingly by their authors. Manuals serve not only in encoding but also when using data encoded by others.
- Documentation should also include information regarding the participants and their relationships, the social context and setting, the task (if any), and other factors. For discussion of typologies of discourse types, see Leech et al. (1998).

4   Transcription: Past and Future

Much as phoneticians believed, prior to Abercrombie, that phonetics began in 1830 (Fromkin and Ladefoged 1981), one sometimes finds claims in discourse literature such as the following: "transcription – the entextualization of speech – has only recently been taken seriously. [E]arlier research practices assumed . . . that what was said could be represented adequately in the form of paraphrases or summaries" (Mischler 1991). In fact, attempts to transcribe discourse can be traced to antiquity.

4.1   Ancient origins

The earliest attempts to capture spoken language in writing date back at least 22 centuries, to the golden age of oratory in ancient Greece. According to Parkes (1993), during the fourth century BCE, when the ideal of eloquence was central, writing was viewed as a record of the *spoken language*:

> Texts were mostly read aloud. A reader on his own might murmur the sounds of the words to himself, but the ideal was a kind of expressive declamation with well modulated pronunciation, in which the text was carefully phrased (*distincta*) by means of appropriate pauses. (Parkes 1993: 9)

Punctuation marks came to be added to early texts by teachers and educated readers in order to clarify structure and facilitate oral performance. There are parallels in the types of properties which were marked even if the specific distinctions were not the same. Some texts from the first and second centuries CE show a tripartite division of pauses: "minor medial pause" (a low dot), "major medial pause" (a dot at medium height), and "final pause" (a high dot). By the sixth century CE, punctuation marks had been employed to signal various aspects of interest in modern transcripts:

unit boundaries, pauses, rising and falling intonation on syllables, and some aspects of rhythm (Parkes 1993; Steele 1779). Some modern work even uses ancient distinctions (e.g. *ictus* and *remiss*, in Abercrombie's and in Halliday's work on rhythm, cited in Butler 1985: 139).

There are parallels in the typographical devices as well, dictated no doubt by perceptual and cognitive factors such as what is most easily noticed amidst words on a page, and most consistently produced with the methods and materials at hand. These fall into four categories.

Punctuation: The ad hoc marks devised by ancient readers (as today) tended to be simple geometric forms (wedges, curls, dots, dashes, hooks, etc.), placed on the line or elevated above it (similar to our distinction between comma and apostrophe), alone or in combination (similar to our semicolon and colon). In Parkes (1993), one encounters discussions concerning what, whether, and how much to punctuate. For example, Cicero argued that the reader should be guided by the constraint of rhythm, "not by the need for breath nor by copyists' marks," and used only few marks in his texts. In 1220, Bene of Florence "ridiculed the notion that punctuation should attempt to represent intonation or delivery: 'for if we wish to vary the written marks according to our manner of delivery it would look like an antiphonary'" (Parkes 1993: 45).

Metacomments: Prior to the development of quotation marks and question marks, scribes indicated these by means of linguistic markers, such as "dicit" for indirect speech, or "scriptum est" for quotations (Parkes 1993: 11). This is similar to the modern-day use of abbreviations such as "ac" meaning "accelerando," in Gumperz and Berenz's (1993) conventions, to indicate some property of a stretch of speech.

Visual prominence: In inscriptions from as early as 133 BCE the practice is already seen of placing the first letters of a new paragraph to the left of the line, enlarging it (*litterae notabiliores*) (Parkes 1993: 10). This is not unlike contemporary practices of printing stressed words in captial letters (e.g. Tedlock 1983; Bolinger 1986) or boldface (e.g. Goodwin and Goodwin 1992).

Spatial arrangement: Scribes in the second century BCE were already leaving blank space between major sections of a text (e.g. chapters or paragraphs (*per capitula*) (Parkes 1993: 10). In the fourth century CE, St. Jerome introduced a spatial innovation into the formatting of Bibles, for the purpose of clarifying the structure of ideas and avoiding misunderstandings of religious doctrine. This format, *per cola et commata*, involves starting each sense unit on a new line. "Where the unit of sense is too long to be accommodated in a single line, the remainder is inset on the next line and the insetting is continued until the end of the unit" (Parkes 1993: 16). In his prologue to his translation of Ezekiel, Jerome writes: "that which is written *per cola et commata* conveys more obvious sense to the readers" (Parkes 1993: 15). St. Jerome applied it only to Isaiah and Ezekiel; scribes later extended it to all the other books of the Bible. The Codex Amiatinus (from 716 CE), which was one of the earliest complete Bibles to survive, used these spacing conventions (from Parkes 1993: 179):

(8)   SED IN LEGE DOMINI UOLUNTAS EIUS
        ET IN LEGE EIUS MEDITABITUR
            DIE AC NOCTE

The English translation is:

(9)   But his will is in the law of the Lord
      and in His law shall he meditate
            day and night

   Many centuries later, this format is found in virtually any transcript which is organized in terms of idea units, such as the following (from Schegloff 1982: 82):

(10)   B: Uh now I could've walked, the three or
            four blocks,
            to that cab stand,

or Chafe's (1987) work on information flow, or Tedlock's (1983) work on Native American narratives. This use of space is especially pronounced in the Penn Treebank, where there are several more levels of indentation to signal additional subordination (see example 6).
   After the sixth century CE, it became fashionable to read silently (Parkes 1993), and written conventions diverged progressively from spoken ones, took on properties of their own, and became less relevant to transcription.

4.2   The novel

During the eighteenth century, the novel arose as a new literary form, which attempted to capture conversations in a realistic way. Some conventions which arose in this medium and became adopted in some transcription conventions are the use of three dots (. . .) for pauses, or a dash (–) for interrupted thoughts or utterances (Du Bois 1991), interpretive metacomments (e.g. "he said cheerfully"), and modified spelling to capture variant phonology or dialects.

4.3   Scientific notations

As early as the 1500s, scholars attempted to encode spoken language for scientific study. Some of their practices have parallels in modern transcripts.
   In 1775, Joshua Steele proposed a notation intended to capture the melody and rhythm of English "in writing" (1775: 15), in a manner similar to musical notation. With no access to modern devices for recording or measuring speech, Steele repeated a sentence over and over, while finding its notes on his bass viol, and expressed rhythms with reference to human gait or the beats of a pendulum.
   The use of quasi-musical notation is found in modern approaches, though stylized in various ways. In interlinear tonetic transcription (e.g. Cruttenden 1997), a two-line staff is used to represent the top and bottom of the speaker's natural pitch range; Brown et al. (1980: 64) use a three-line staff. In Bolinger's work (e.g. Bolinger 1986), the words themselves flow up and down with no staffs and no lines.

Phoneticians had been devising shorthand systems for capturing speech sounds since the sixteenth century (MacMahon 1981), and Fromkin and Ladefoged (1981) speak of "the seventeenth-century search for a universal phonetic alphabet that could be distinguished from the separate alphabets required for particular languages" (1981: 3). In the 1800s, many different shorthand systems were being developed in England and continental Europe. Among the developers were Alexander Melville Bell (1867) and Henry Sweet (1892), whose work contributed to the development of the International Phonetic Alphabet (IPA).

In the mid-1800s one finds sporadic mention of markings for stress, voice quality including ingressive versus egressive whisper, and voice (Bell 1867: 48). Stress markings are found in all intonation-oriented transcripts; ingressive/egressive is part of Gail Jefferson's conventions (Jefferson 1984), which is the standard used in conversation analysis. Bell (1867) distinguished fall–rise and several other intonation types, which are widespread in contemporary approaches.

Despite these parallels with modern work, researchers attempting to systematically study any of these factors before the twentieth century faced serious technological limitations. In the 1930s, Boas relied on native speakers' ability to speak slowly and clearly as he wrote down their narratives (Duranti 1997: 122). This method worked less well for conversations, where his informants were less careful in their speech. Henry Sweet's shorthand methods reportedly enabled a recording rate of 150 words per minute (MacMahon 1981: 268), but here too there were no double checks on accuracy. Joshua Steele's methods, though resourceful, enabled at best a very crude approximation of melody and rhythm compared to what is possible with modern signal processing technology. Even as late as the 1920s, prosodic analyses were still often impressionistic, and conflicting claims were difficult to assess (Crystal 1969).

4.4 Technological advances

In the 1950s, recording technology became available for research use, making it possible to replay an interaction indefinitely many times, and to analyze timing and pronunciation to virtually unlimited degrees of refinement. Signal processing technology has made it possible to measure the physical properties of the speech signal, reflecting such things as fundamental frequency, energy, or other parameters. And computer interfaces make it possible to enter data effortlessly, to search quickly through even the largest databases, and to view transcripts and acoustic wave forms simultaneously, enabling an increasing interpenetration of visual and verbal information.

Technology does not provide answers on its own, however. For example, the measured aspects of a speech signal (such as wave frequency and amplitude) do not correspond perfectly with the perceived aspects (such as fundamental frequency and loudness). The ability to connect transcripts to acoustic measurements is an important step toward understanding those relationships, but it does not arise automatically with the technology of linking the two. The technology itself must be harnessed in various ways to be of benefit to research. The transcript draws attention to distinctions which people find meaningful and can make consistently. By providing categories which are relevant to human interactants, the transcript helps bridge the gap between technology and discourse understanding.

4.5   Convergence of interests

There is now an increasing convergence of interests between discourse research and computer science approaches regarding natural language corpora. This promises to benefit all concerned.

Language researchers are expanding their methods increasingly to benefit from computer technology. Computer scientists engaged in speech recognition, natural language understanding, and text-to-speech synthesis are increasingly applying statistical methods to large corpora of natural language. Both groups need corpora and transcripts in their work. Given how expensive it is to gather good-quality corpora and to prepare good-quality transcripts, it would make sense for them to share resources to the degree that their divergent purposes allow it.

Traditionally, there have been important differences in what gets encoded in transcripts prepared for computational research. For example, computational corpora have tended not to contain sentence stress or pause estimates, let alone speech act annotations. This is partly because of the practicalities of huge corpora being necessary, and stress coding not being possible by computer algorithm. If discourse researchers start to share the same corpora, however, these additional types of information may gradually be added, which in turn may facilitate computational goals, to the benefit of both approaches.

One indication of the increasing alliance between these groups is an actual pooling of corpora. The CSAE (Corpus of Spoken American English), produced by linguists at UC Santa Barbara (Chafe et al. 1991), was recently made available by the LDC (Linguistics Data Consortium), an organization previously distributing corpora guided by computational goals (e.g. people reading digits, or sentences designed to contain all phonemes and be semantically unpredictable).

4.6   Encoding standards

Another indication of the increasing alliance is the existence of several recent projects concerned with encoding standards relevant to discourse research, with collaboration from both language researchers and computational linguists: the TEI, the EAGLES, MATE, and the LDC. While time prevents elaborate discussion of these proposals, it is notable that all of them appear to have the same general goal, which is to provide coverage of needed areas of encoding without specifying too strongly what should be encoded. They all respect the theory-relevance of transcription.

McEnery and Wilson (1997: 27) write: "Current moves are aiming towards more formalized international standards for the encoding of any type of information that one would conceivably want to encode in machine-readable texts. The flagship of this current trend towards standards is the Text Encoding Initiative (TEI)." Begun in 1989 with funding from the three main organizations for humanities computing, the TEI was charged with establishing guidelines for encoding texts of various types, to facilitate data exchange. The markup language it used was SGML (Standard

Generalized Markup Language) – a language which was already widely used for text exchange in the publishing industry. Like HTML (the markup language of the worldwide web), SGML and XML (the eXtensible Markup Language) use paired start and end tags (e.g. <s> and </s>) to indicate the boundaries of format-relevant segments of text, which are then interpreted by an appropriate interface (or browser) so that the desired visual display is accomplished without the user needing to see the tags themselves. SGML and XML derive their power in addition from other structural aspects, which are discussed in detail elsewhere (Burnard 1995; Johansson 1995; Mylonas and Allen 1999).

The subcommittee on Spoken Language Encoding for the TEI (Johansson et al. 1992) began its work with a large-scale survey of transcription methods, in order to identify as comprehensively as possible all major dimensions encoded in transcripts. Then the subcommittee proposed how each dimension should be encoded in TEI-compliant format. Rather than dictating what users should encode in a transcript, the TEI approach was to catalog distinctions used by others and to establish TEI-compliant ways of encoding them if the researcher wishes to include them in a transcript. TEI standards were designed to facilitate data exchange across projects, to enable the same transcript to be flexibly formatted in different ways for different research purposes, and to support technological upgrading from text-only to text aligned with digital records.

TEI conventions have been adopted in the 100,000,000-word British National Corpus (Crowdy 1995), and in the 1,000,000-word International Corpus of English (McEnery and Wilson 1997: 29). The TEI is now a consortium, and is shifting from SGML to XML. For more information see Burnard (1995), Johansson (1995), Mylonas and Allen (1999), and the website, http://www.tei-c.org/.

Within the EAGLES project, three developments are relevant here. The first is the impressive survey of LE (language engineering) transcription and annotation methods prepared by Leech et al. (1998). The second is the *Handbook of Standards and Resources for Spoken Language Systems* (Gibbon et al. 1997), which offers precise, extensive, and useful technical guidelines on such things as recording equipment and computer-compatible IPA, based on European projects. The third is the XCES (XML Corpus Encoding Standard) developed for EAGLES by Nancy Ide and Patrice Bonhomme at Vassar College (www.cs.vassar.edu/XCES).

Leech et al.'s (1998) survey concerns encoding conventions which can be of use in large corpora for applied purposes involving training and the use of computer algorithms. Leech et al. feel it is premature to favor a particular standard at this point and instead favor the general approach taken in the TEI: "For future projects, we recommend that as much use as possible should be made of standardized encoding schemes such as those of the TEI, extending them or departing from them only where necessary for specific purposes" (1998: 14).

In a domain which is as theory-relevant as transcription, TEI (or something like it) is really the only workable basis for standardization. A standard of this type seeks to provide a mechanism (via markup conventions) for systematic encoding of data, such that the data can be flexibly reformatted later in various ways as dictated by the purpose at hand, but leaves it to the discretion of individual researchers to decide what exactly to encode and what categories to use.

5   General Discussion and Conclusion

The present chapter has provided an overview of factors which are relevant whenever transcripts are used. The transcript is an invaluable asset in discourse analyses, but it is never theory-neutral. Awareness of alternatives and their biases is an important part of their use. It is hoped that this chapter contributes to effective use of transcripts and to the continued development of discourse methodology more generally.

REFERENCES

Altenberg, B. 1990. Some functions of the booster. In *The London–Lund Corpus of Spoken English: Description and Research*, ed. Jan Svartvik. 193–209. Lund: Lund University Press.

Armstrong, Lilias E., and Ward, Ida C. 1942. *Handbook of English Intonation*. Cambridge: W. Heffer and Sons.

Barras, Claude, Geoffrois, Edouard, Wu, Zhibiao, and Liberman, Mark. 1998. Transcriber: a free tool for segmenting, labeling and transcribing speech. *Proceedings of the First International Conference on Language Resources and Evaluation (LREC)*, 1373–6. May 1998. (Available at www.etca.fr/CTA/gip/publis.html.)

Beckman, Mary E., and Ayers, Gayle Elam. 1997. *Guidelines for ToBI Labelling, Version 3*. Columbus, OH: Ohio State University Research Foundation.

Bell, Alexander Melville. 1867. *Visible Speech: The Science of Universal Alphabetics, or Self-interpreting Physiological Letters, for the Writing of All Languages in one Alphabet*. London: Simpkin, Marshall.

Bloom, Lois. 1973. *One Word at a Time: The Use of Single Word Utterances Before Syntax*. The Hague, Mouton.

Bloom, Lois. 1993. Transcription and coding for child language research: the parts are more than the whole. In *Talking Data: Transcription and Coding in Discourse Research*, eds Jane A. Edwards and Martin D. Lampert. 149–66. Hillsdale, NJ: Lawrence Erlbaum.

Bolinger, Dwight. 1986. *Intonation and its Parts: Melody in Spoken English*. Stanford: Stanford University Press.

Bourlard, Herve, and Morgan, Nelson. 1994. *Connectionist Speech Recognition: A Hybrid Approach*. Boston: Kluwer Academic.

Brown, Gillian, Currie, Karen L., and Kenworthy, Joanne. 1980. *Questions of Intonation*. London: Croom Helm.

Burnard, Lou. 1995. The Text Encoding Initiative: an overview. In *Spoken English on Computer: Transcript, Mark-up and Application*, eds Geoffrey Leech, Greg Myers, and Jenny Thomas. 69–81. New York: Longman.

Butler, Christopher. 1985. *Systemic Linguistics: Theory and Applications*. London: Batsford Academic and Educational.

Chafe, Wallace L. 1987. Cognitive constraints on information flow. In *Coherence and Grounding in Discourse*, ed. Russell S. Tomlin. 21–51. Philadelphia: John Benjamins.

Chafe, Wallace L. 1993. Prosodic and functional units of language. In *Talking Data: Transcription and Coding in Discourse Research*, eds Jane A. Edwards and Martin D. Lampert. 33–43. Hillsdale, NJ: Lawrence Erlbaum.

Chafe, Wallace L., Du Bois, John W., and Thompson, Sandra A. 1991. Towards a new corpus of spoken American English. In *English Corpus Linguistics*, eds Karin Aijmer and Bengt Altenberg. 64–82. New York: Longman.

Coniam, David. 1998. Speech recognition: accuracy in the speech-to-text process. *TEXT Technology*, 8.1–13.

Couper-Kuhlen, Elizabeth. 1986. *An Introduction to English Prosody*. London: Edward Arnold.

Couper-Kuhlen, Elizabeth. 1993. *English Speech Rhythm: Form and Function in Everyday Verbal Interaction*. Philadelphia: John Benjamins.

Crowdy, Steve. 1995. The BNC Corpus. In *Spoken English on Computer: Transcript, Mark-up and Application*, eds Geoffrey Leech, Greg Myers, and Jenny Thomas. 224–34. New York: Longman.

Cruttenden, Alan. 1997. *Intonation*. 2nd edn. Cambridge: Cambridge University Press.

Crystal, D. 1969. *Prosodic Systems and Intonation in English*. New York: Cambridge University Press.

Crystal, D. 1975. *The English Tone of Voice: Essays in Intonation, Prosody and Paralanguage*. London: Edward Arnold.

Crystal, D. 1980. The analysis of nuclear tones. In *The Melody of Language*, eds Linda R. Waugh and C. H. van Schooneveld. 55–70. Baltimore: University Park Press.

Du Bois, John W. 1991. Transcription design principles for spoken language research. *Pragmatics*, 1.71–106.

Du Bois, John W., and Schuetze-Coburn, Stephan. 1993. Representing hierarchy: constitute hierarchy for discourse databases. In *Talking Data: Transcription and Coding in Discourse Research*, eds Jane A. Edwards and Martin D. Lampert. 221–60. Hillsdale, NJ: Lawrence Erlbaum.

Du Bois, John W., Schuetze-Coburn, Stephan, Cumming, Susanna, and Paolino, Danae. 1993. Outline of discourse transcription. In *Talking Data: Transcription and Coding in Discourse Research*, eds Jane A. Edwards and Martin D. Lampert. 45–89. Hillsdale, NJ: Lawrence Erlbaum.

Duranti, Alessandro. 1997. *Linguistic Anthropology*. New York: Cambridge University Press.

Dutoit, Thierry. 1997. *An Introduction to Text-to-speech Synthesis*. Boston: Kluwer Academic.

Edwards, Jane A. 1989. *Transcription and the New Functionalism: A Counterproposal to CHILDES' CHAT Conventions*. Technical Report, No. 60. Berkeley: UC Berkeley, Cognitive Science Program.

Edwards, Jane A. 1992a. Computer methods in child language research: Four principles for the use of archived data. *Journal of Child Language*, 19.435–58.

Edwards, Jane A. 1992b. Design principles for the transcription of spoken discourse. In *Directions in Corpus Linguistics: Proceedings of the Nobel Symposium 82, Stockholm, August 4–8, 1991*, ed. Jan Svartvik. 129–47. New York: Mouton de Gruyter.

Edwards, Jane A. 1992c. Transcription in discourse. In *Oxford International Encyclopedia of Linguistics, vol. 1*, ed. William Bright. 367–71. Oxford: Oxford University Press.

Edwards, Jane A. 1993a. Perfecting research techniques in an imperfect world. *Journal of Child Language*, 20.209–16.

Edwards, Jane A. 1993b. Principles and contrasting systems of discourse transcription. In *Talking Data: Transcription and Coding in Discourse Research*, eds Jane A. Edwards and Martin D. Lampert. 3–31. Hillsdale, NJ: Lawrence Erlbaum.

Edwards, Jane A. 1995. Principles and alternative systems in the transcription, coding and markup of spoken discourse. In *Spoken English on Computer: Transcript, Mark-up and Application*, eds Geoffrey Leech, Greg Myers, and Jenny Thomas. 19–34. New York: Longman.

Ehlich, Konrad. 1993. HIAT: a transcription system for discourse data. In *Talking Data: Transcription and Coding in Discourse Research*, eds Jane A. Edwards and Martin D. Lampert. 123–48. Hillsdale, NJ: Lawrence Erlbaum.

Ehlich, Konrad, and Switalla, B. 1976. Transkriptionssysteme – Eine exemplarische Uebersicht. *Studium Linguistik*, 2.78–105.

Erickson, Frederick, and Shultz, Jeffrey. 1982. *The Counselor as Gatekeeper: Social Interaction in Interviews*. New York: Academic Press.

Ervin-Tripp, Susan. 2000. Methods for studying language production. In *Studying Conversation: How to Get Natural Peer Interaction*, eds Lise Menn and Nan Bernstein Ratner. 271–90. Mahwah: Lawrence Erlbaum.

Farnell, Brenda. 1995. *Do You See What I Mean?: Plains Indian Sign Talk and the Embodiment of Action*. Austin: University of Texas Press.

Firth, J. R. 1957. *Papers in Linguistics 1934–1951*. Oxford: Oxford University Press.

Fromkin, Victoria A., and Ladefoged, P. 1981. Early views of distinctive features. In *Towards a History of Phonetics*, eds R. E. Asher and Eugenie J. A. Henderson. 3–8. Edinburgh: Edinburgh University Press.

Garside, Roger, and Rayson, P. 1997. Higher-level annotation tools. In *Corpus Annotation: Linguistic Information from Computer Text Corpora*, eds Roger Garside, Geoffrey Leech, and A. M. McEnery. 179–93. London: Longman.

Gibbon, Dafydd. 1976. *Perspectives of Intonation Analysis*. Bern: Herbert Lang.

Gibbon, Dafydd, Moore, Roger, and Winski, Richard. 1997. *Handbook of Standards and Resources for Spoken Language Systems*. New York: Mouton de Gruyter.

Goodwin, C., and Goodwin, M. H. 1992. Assessments and the construction of context. In *Rethinking Context: Language as an Interactive Phenomenon*, eds Allessandro Duranti and Charles Goodwin. 147–89. Cambridge: Cambridge University Press.

Gumperz, John J., and Berenz, Norine B. 1993. Transcribing conversational exchanges. In *Talking Data: Transcription and Coding in Discourse Research*, eds Jane A. Edwards and Martin D. Lampert. 91–121. Hillsdale, NJ: Lawrence Erlbaum.

't Hart, Johan, Collier, Rene, and Cohen, Antonie. 1990. *A Perceptual Study of Intonation: An Experimental–Phonetic Approach to Speech Melody*. Cambridge: Cambridge University Press.

Jefferson, Gail. 1984. Transcript notation. In *Structures of Social Action: Studies in Conversation Analysis*, eds J. Maxwell Atkinson and John Heritage. ix–xvi. Cambridge: Cambridge University Press.

Johansson, Stig. 1991. *Some Thoughts on the Encoding of Spoken Texts in Machine-readable Form*. Oslo: University of Oslo, Department of English.

Johansson, Stig. 1995. The approach of the Text Encoding Initiative to the encoding of spoken discourse. In *Spoken English on Computer: Transcript, Mark-up and Application*, eds Geoffrey Leech, Greg Myers, and Jenny Thomas. 82–98. New York: Longman.

Johansson, Stig, Burnard, Lou, Edwards, Jane, and Rosta, Andrew. 1992. *Chapter P2.34: Text Encoding Initiative.*

Spoken Text Working Group, Final Report. TEI, Department of English, University of Oslo.

Knowles, Gerry. 1995. Converting a corpus into a relational database: SEC becomes MARSEC. In *Spoken English on Computer: Transcript, Mark-up and Application*, eds Geoffrey Leech, Greg Myers, and Jenny Thomas. 208–19. New York: Longman.

Ladd, D. Robert. 1996. *Intonational Phonology*. Cambridge: Cambridge University Press.

Lampert, Martin D., and Ervin-Tripp, Susan M. 1993. Structured coding for the study of language and interaction. In *Talking Data: Transcription and Coding in Discourse Research*, eds Jane A. Edwards and Martin D. Lampert. 169–206. Hillsdale, NJ: Lawrence Erlbaum.

Leech, Geoffrey, Weisser, Martin, Wilson, Andrew, and Grice, Martine. 1998. Survey and guidelines for the representation and annotation of dialogue. LE-EAGLES-WP4-4. Working paper for the EAGLES Project (http://www.ling.lancs.ac.uk/eagles/).

MacMahon, W. K. C. 1981. Henry Sweet's system of shorthand. In *Towards a History of Phonetics*, eds R. E. Asher and Eugenie J. A. Henderson. 265–81. Edinburgh: Edinburgh University Press.

Marcus, Mitchell P., Santorini, Beatrice, and Marcinkiewicz, Mary Ann. 1993. Building a large annotated corpus of English: the Penn Treebank. *Computational Linguistics*, 19.313–30.

MacWhinney, Brian. 1995. *The CHILDES project: Tools for Analyzing Talk*. 2nd edn. Hillsdale, NJ: Lawrence Erlbaum.

McEnery, A. M., and Rayson, P. 1997. A Corpus/annotation toolbox. In *Corpus Annotation: Linguistic Information from Computer Text Corpora*, eds Roger Garside, Geoffrey Leech, and A. M. McEnery. 194–208. London: Longman.

McEnery, A. M., and Wilson, Andrew. 1997. *Corpus Linguistics*. Edinburgh: Edinburgh University Press.

Mishler, Elliot G. 1991. Representing discourse: the rhetoric of transcription. *Journal of Narrative and Life History*, 1.255–80.

Mylonas, Elli, and Renear, Allen (eds). 1999. The Text Encoding Initiative at 10: not just an interchange format anymore – but a new research community. *Computers and the Humanities*, 33, Issues 1 and 2.

Neidle, Carol, and MacLaughlin, D. 1998. SignStream[tm]: a tool for linguistic research on signed languages. *Sign Language and Linguistics*, 1.111–14.

Ochs, Elinor. 1979. Transcription as theory. In *Developmental Pragmatics*, eds Elinor Ochs and Bambi B. Schieffelin. 43–72. New York: Academic Press.

Parkes, M. B. 1993. *Pause and Effect: An Introduction to the History of Punctuation in the West*. Berkeley: University of California Press.

Pierrehumbert, Janet, and Hirschberg, Julia. 1990. The meaning of intonational contours in the interpretation of discourse. In *Intention in Communication*, eds Philip R. Cohen, Jerry Morgan, and Martha E. Pollack. 271–311. Cambridge, MA: MIT Press.

Pike, Kenneth L. 1945. *The Intonation of American English*. Ann Arbor: University of Michigan Press.

Preston, Dennis R. 1985. The Li'l Abner syndrome: written representations of speech. *American Speech*, 60.328–36.

Psathas, George. 1990. Appendix: transcription symbols. In *Interaction Competence*, ed. George Psathas. 297–307. Washington, DC: University Press of America.

Roach, Peter. 1994. Conversion between prosodic transcription systems – Standard British and ToBI. *Speech Communication*, 15.91–9.

Roach, Peter, and Arnfield, Simon. 1995. Linking prosodic transcription to the time dimension. In *Spoken English on Computer: Transcript, Mark-up and Application*, eds Geoffrey Leech, Greg Myers, and Jenny Thomas. 149–60. New York: Longman.

Schegloff, Emanuel A. 1982. Discourse as an interactional achievement: some uses of "uh huh" and other things that come between sentences. In *Analyzing Discourse: Text and Talk*, ed. Deborah Tannen. 71–93. Washington, DC: Georgetown University Press.

Scollon, Ron. 1982. The rhythmic integrity of ordinary talk. In *Analyzing Discourse: Text and Talk*, ed. Deborah Tannen. 335–49. Washington, DC: Georgetown University Press.

Slobin, Dan I. 1967. *A Field Manual for Cross-cultural Study of the Acquisition of Communicative Competence*. Berkeley: University of California, Department of Psychology.

Steele, Joshua. 1775. *An Essay Towards Establishing the Melody and Measure of Speech to be Expressed and Perpetuated by Peculiar Symbols*. London: J. Almon.

Steele, Joshua. 1779. *Prosodia Rationalis: or, An Essay Towards Establishing the Melody and Measure of Speech, to be Expressed and Perpetuated by Peculiar Symbols*. London: J. Nichols.

Svartvik, J. (ed.). 1990. *The London–Lund Corpus of Spoken English: Description and Research*. Lund: Lund University Press.

Svartvik, J., and Quirk, Randolph (eds). 1980. *A Corpus of English Conversation*. Lund: C. W. K. Gleerup.

Sweet, Henry. 1892. *A Manual of Current Shorthand, Orthographic, and Phonetic*. Oxford: Clarendon Press.

Tannen, Deborah. 1981. [Review of W. Labov and D. Fanshel, *Therapeutic Discourse: Psychotherapy as Conversation*]. *Language*, 57.481–6.

Tannen, Deborah. 1984. *Conversational Style*. Norwood, NJ: Ablex.

Tedlock, Dennis. 1983. *The Spoken Word and the Work of Interpretation*. Philadelphia: University of Pennsylvania Press.

Tench, Paul. 1996. *The Intonation Systems of English*. New York: Cassell.

Thompson, Henry S., Anderson, Anne H., and Bader, Miles. 1995. Publishing a spoken and written corpus on CD-ROM: the HCRC Map Task experience. *Spoken English on Computer: Transcript, Mark-up and Application*, eds Geoffrey Leech, Greg Myers, and Jenny Thomas. 168–80. New York: Longman.

III   Discourse: Language, Context, and Interaction

A Political, Social, and Institutional Domains

18 Critical Discourse Analysis

TEUN A. VAN DIJK

0 Introduction: What Is Critical Discourse Analysis?

Critical discourse analysis (CDA) is a type of discourse analytical research that primarily studies the way social power abuse, dominance, and inequality are enacted, reproduced, and resisted by text and talk in the social and political context. With such dissident research, critical discourse analysts take explicit position, and thus want to understand, expose, and ultimately resist social inequality.

Some of the tenets of CDA can already be found in the critical theory of the Frankfurt School before the Second World War (Agger 1992b; Rasmussen 1996). Its current focus on language and discourse was initiated with the "critical linguistics" that emerged (mostly in the UK and Australia) at the end of the 1970s (Fowler et al. 1979; see also Mey 1985). CDA has also counterparts in "critical" developments in sociolinguistics, psychology, and the social sciences, some already dating back to the early 1970s (Birnbaum 1971; Calhoun 1995; Fay 1987; Fox and Prilleltensky 1997; Hymes 1972; Ibáñez and Iñiguez 1997; Singh 1996; Thomas 1993; Turkel 1996; Wodak 1996). As is the case in these neighboring disciplines, CDA may be seen as a reaction against the dominant formal (often "asocial" or "uncritical") paradigms of the 1960s and 1970s.

CDA is not so much a direction, school, or specialization next to the many other "approaches" in discourse studies. Rather, it aims to offer a different "mode" or "perspective" of theorizing, analysis, and application throughout the whole field. We may find a more or less critical perspective in such diverse areas as pragmatics, conversation analysis, narrative analysis, rhetoric, stylistics, sociolinguistics, ethnography, or media analysis, among others.

Crucial for critical discourse analysts is the explicit awareness of their role in society. Continuing a tradition that rejects the possibility of a "value-free" science, they argue that science, and especially scholarly discourse, are inherently part of and influenced by social structure, and produced in social interaction. Instead of denying or ignoring such a relation between scholarship and society, they plead that such relations be studied and accounted for in their own right, and that scholarly practices be based on such insights. Theory formation, description, and explanation, also in discourse analysis, are sociopolitically "situated," whether we like it or not. Reflection on the role of scholars in society and the polity thus becomes an inherent part of the discourse analytical enterprise. This may mean, among other things, that discourse analysts conduct research in solidarity and cooperation with dominated groups.

Critical research on discourse needs to satisfy a number of requirements in order to effectively realize its aims:

- As is often the case for more marginal research traditions, CDA research has to be "better" than other research in order to be accepted.
- It focuses primarily on *social problems* and political issues, rather than on current paradigms and fashions.
- Empirically adequate critical analysis of social problems is usually *multidisciplinary*.
- Rather than merely *describe* discourse structures, it tries to *explain* them in terms of properties of social interaction and especially social structure.
- More specifically, CDA focuses on the ways discourse structures enact, confirm, legitimate, reproduce, or challenge relations of *power* and *dominance* in society.

Fairclough and Wodak (1997: 271–80) summarize the main tenets of CDA as follows:

1. CDA addresses social problems
2. Power relations are discursive
3. Discourse constitutes society and culture
4. Discourse does ideological work
5. Discourse is historical
6. The link between text and society is mediated
7. Discourse analysis is interpretative and explanatory
8. Discourse is a form of social action.

Whereas some of these tenets have also been discussed above, others need a more systematic theoretical analysis, of which we shall present some fragments here as a more or less general basis for the main principles of CDA (for details about these aims of critical discourse and language studies, see, e.g., Caldas-Coulthard and Coulthard 1996; Fairclough 1992a, 1995a; Fairclough and Wodak 1997; Fowler et al. 1979; van Dijk 1993b).

1 Conceptual and Theoretical Frameworks

Since CDA is not a specific direction of research, it does not have a unitary theoretical framework. Within the aims mentioned above, there are many types of CDA, and these may be theoretically and analytically quite diverse. Critical analysis of conversation is very different from an analysis of news reports in the press or of lessons and teaching at school. Yet, given the common perspective and the general aims of CDA, we may also find overall conceptual and theoretical frameworks that are closely related. As suggested, most kinds of CDA will ask questions about the way specific discourse structures are deployed in the reproduction of social dominance, whether they are part of a conversation or a news report or other genres and contexts. Thus, the typical vocabulary of many scholars in CDA will feature such notions as "power," "dominance," "hegemony," "ideology," "class," "gender," "race," "discrimination," "interests," "reproduction," "institutions," "social structure," and "social order," besides the more familiar discourse analytical notions.[1]

In this section, I focus on a number of basic concepts themselves, and thus devise a theoretical framework that critically relates discourse, cognition, and society.

1.1   Macro vs. micro

Language use, discourse, verbal interaction, and communication belong to the micro-level of the social order. Power, dominance, and inequality between social groups are typically terms that belong to a macrolevel of analysis. This means that CDA has to theoretically bridge the well-known "gap" between micro and macro approaches, which is of course a distinction that is a sociological construct in its own right (Alexander et al. 1987; Knorr-Cetina and Cicourel 1981). In everyday interaction and experience the macro- and microlevel (and intermediary "mesolevels") form one unified whole. For instance, a racist speech in parliament is a discourse at the microlevel of social interaction in the specific situation of a debate, but at the same time may enact or be a constituent part of legislation or the reproduction of racism at the macrolevel.

There are several ways to analyze and bridge these levels, and thus to arrive at a unified critical analysis:

1   *Members–groups:* Language users engage in discourse *as* members of (several) social groups, organizations, or institutions; and conversely, groups thus may act "by" their members.
2   *Actions–process:* Social acts of individual actors are thus constituent parts of group actions and social processes, such as legislation, newsmaking, or the reproduction of racism.
3   *Context–social structure:* Situations of discursive interaction are similarly part or constitutive of social structure; for example, a press conference may be a typical practice of organizations and media institutions. That is, "local" and more "global" contexts are closely related, and both exercise constraints on discourse.
4   *Personal and social cognition:* Language users as social actors have both personal and social cognition: personal memories, knowledge and opinions, as well as those shared with members of the group or culture as a whole. Both types of cognition influence interaction and discourse of individual members, whereas shared "social representations" govern the collective actions of a group.

1.2   Power as control

A central notion in most critical work on discourse is that of power, and more specifically the *social power* of groups or institutions. Summarizing a complex philosophical and social analysis, we will define social power in terms of *control*. Thus, groups have (more or less) power if they are able to (more or less) control the acts and minds of (members of) other groups. This ability presupposes a *power base* of privileged access to scarce social resources, such as force, money, status, fame, knowledge, information, "culture," or indeed various forms of public discourse and communication (of the vast literature on power, see, e.g., Lukes 1986; Wrong 1979).

Different *types of power* may be distinguished according to the various resources employed to exercise such power: the coercive power of the military and of violent men will rather be based on force, the rich will have power because of their money, whereas the more or less persuasive power of parents, professors, or journalists may be based on knowledge, information, or authority. Note also that power is seldom absolute. Groups may more or less control other groups, or only control them in specific situations or social domains. Moreover, dominated groups may more or less resist, accept, condone, comply with, or legitimate such power, and even find it "natural."

The power of dominant groups may be integrated in laws, rules, norms, habits, and even a quite general consensus, and thus take the form of what Gramsci called "hegemony" (Gramsci 1971). Class domination, sexism, and racism are characteristic examples of such hegemony. Note also that power is not always exercised in obviously abusive acts of dominant group members, but may be enacted in the myriad of taken-for-granted actions of everyday life, as is typically the case in the many forms of everyday sexism or racism (Essed 1991). Similarly, not all members of a powerful group are always more powerful than all members of dominated groups: power is only defined here for groups as a whole.

For our analysis of the relations between discourse and power, thus, we first find that access to specific forms of discourse, e.g. those of politics, the media, or science, is itself a power resource. Secondly, as suggested earlier, action is controlled by our minds. So, if we are able to influence people's minds, e.g. their knowledge or opinions, we indirectly may control (some of) their actions, as we know from persuasion and manipulation.

Closing the discourse–power circle, finally, this means that those groups who control most influential discourse also have more chances to control the minds and actions of others.

Simplifying these very intricate relationships even further for this chapter, we can split up the issue of discursive power into two basic questions for CDA research:

1   How do (more) powerful groups control public discourse?
2   How does such discourse control mind and action of (less) powerful groups, and what are the social consequences of such control, such as social inequality?

I address each question below.[2]

1.2.1   Control of public discourse

We have seen that among many other resources that define the power base of a group or institution, *access to* or *control over* public discourse and communication is an important "symbolic" resource, as is the case for knowledge and information (van Dijk 1996). Most people have active control only over everyday talk with family members, friends, or colleagues, and passive control over, e.g. media usage. In many situations, ordinary people are more or less passive targets of text or talk, e.g. of their bosses or teachers, or of the authorities, such as police officers, judges, welfare bur-eaucrats, or tax inspectors, who may simply tell them what (not) to believe or what to do.

On the other hand, members of more powerful social groups and institutions, and especially their leaders (the elites), have more or less exclusive access to, and control over, one or more types of public discourse. Thus, professors control scholarly dis-course, teachers educational discourse, journalists media discourse, lawyers legal discourse, and politicians policy and other public political discourse. Those who have more control over more – and more influential – discourse (and more discourse properties) are by that definition also more powerful. In other words, we here pro-pose a discursive definition (as well as a practical diagnostic) of one of the crucial constituents of social power.

These notions of discourse access and control are very general, and it is one of the tasks of CDA to spell out these forms of power. Thus, if discourse is defined in terms of complex communicative events, access and control may be defined both for the *context* and for the *structures of text and talk themselves*.

Context is defined as the mentally represented structure of those properties of the social situation that are relevant for the production or comprehension of discourse (Duranti and Goodwin 1992; van Dijk 1998b). It consists of such categories as the overall definition of the situation, setting (time, place), ongoing actions (including discourses and discourse genres), participants in various communicative, social, or institutional roles, as well as their mental representations: goals, knowledge, opin-ions, attitudes, and ideologies. Controlling context involves control over one or more of these categories, e.g. determining the definition of the communicative situation, deciding on time and place of the communicative event, or on which particip-ants may or must be present, and in which roles, or what knowledge or opinions they should (not) have, and which social actions may or must be accomplished by discourse.

Also crucial in the enactment or exercise of group power is control not only over content, but over the structures of text and talk. Relating text and context, thus, we already saw that (members of) powerful groups may decide on the (possible) dis-course *genre(s)* or *speech acts* of an occasion. A teacher or judge may require a direct answer from a student or suspect, respectively, and not a personal story or an argu-ment (Wodak 1984a, 1986). More critically, we may examine how powerful speakers may abuse their power in such situations, e.g. when police officers use force to get a confession from a suspect (Linell and Jonsson 1991), or when male editors exclude women from writing economic news (van Zoonen 1994).

Similarly, genres typically have conventional *schemas* consisting of various *categor-ies*. Access to some of these may be prohibited or obligatory, e.g. some greetings in a conversation may only be used by speakers of a specific social group, rank, age, or gender (Irvine 1974).

Also vital for all discourse and communication is who controls the *topics* (semantic macrostructures) and topic change, as when editors decide what news topics will be covered (Gans 1979; van Dijk 1988a, 1988b), professors decide what topics will be dealt with in class, or men control topics and topic change in conversations with women (Palmer 1989; Fishman 1983; Leet-Pellegrini 1980; Lindegren-Lerman 1983).

Although most discourse control is contextual or global, even local details of *meaning, form*, or *style* may be controlled, e.g. the details of an answer in class or court, or choice of lexical items or jargon in courtrooms, classrooms or newsrooms (Martín Rojo 1994). In many situations, volume may be controlled and speakers ordered to "keep their voice down" or to "keep quiet," women may be "silenced" in many ways (Houston and Kramarae 1991), and in some cultures one needs to "mumble" as a form of respect (Albert 1972). The public use of specific words may be banned as subversive in a dictatorship, and discursive challenges to culturally dominant groups (e.g. white, western males) by their multicultural opponents may be ridiculed in the media as "politically correct" (Williams 1995). And finally, action and interaction dimensions of discourse may be controlled by prescribing or proscribing specific speech acts, and by selectively distributing or interrupting turns (see also Diamond 1996).

In sum, virtually all levels and structures of context, text, and talk can in principle be more or less controlled by powerful speakers, and such power may be abused at the expense of other participants. It should, however, be stressed that talk and text do not always and directly enact or embody the overall power relations between groups: it is always the context that may interfere with, reinforce, or otherwise transform such relationships.

1.2.2 Mind control

If controlling discourse is a first major form of power, controlling people's minds is the other fundamental way to reproduce dominance and hegemony.[3] Within a CDA framework, "mind control" involves even more than just acquiring beliefs about the world through discourse and communication. Suggested below are ways that power and dominance are involved in mind control.

First, recipients tend to accept beliefs, knowledge, and opinions (unless they are inconsistent with their personal beliefs and experiences) through discourse from what they see as authoritative, trustworthy, or credible sources, such as scholars, experts, professionals, or reliable media (Nesler et al. 1993). Second, in some situations participants are obliged to be recipients of discourse, e.g. in education and in many job situations. Lessons, learning materials, job instructions, and other discourse types in such cases may need to be attended to, interpreted, and learned as intended by institutional or organizational authors (Giroux 1981). Third, in many situations there are no pubic discourses or media that may provide information from which alternative beliefs may be derived (Downing 1984). Fourth, and closely related to the previous points, recipients may not have the knowledge and beliefs needed to challenge the discourses or information they are exposed to (Wodak 1987).

Whereas these conditions of mind control are largely *contextual* (they say something about the participants of a communicative event), other conditions are *discursive*, that is, a function of the structures and strategies of text or talk itself. In other words, given a specific context, certain meanings and forms of discourse have more influence on people's minds than others, as the very notion of "persuasion" and a tradition of 2000 years of rhetoric may show.[4]

Once we have elementary insight into some of the structures of the mind, and what it means to control it, the crucial question is how discourse and its structures are able to exercise such control. As suggested above, such discursive influence may be due to *context* as well as to the *structures of text and talk themselves.*

Contextually based control derives from the fact that people understand and represent not only text and talk, but also the whole communicative situation. Thus, CDA typically studies how context features (such as the properties of language users of powerful groups) influence the ways members of dominated groups define the communicative situation in "preferred context models" (Martín Rojo and van Dijk 1997).

CDA also focuses on how *discourse structures* influence mental representations. At the *global level* of discourse, *topics* may influence what people see as the most important information of text or talk, and thus correspond to the top levels of their mental models. For example, expressing such a topic in a headline in news may powerfully influence how an event is defined in terms of a "preferred" mental model (e.g. when crime committed by minorities is typically topicalized and headlined in the press: Duin et al. 1988; van Dijk 1991). Similarly, argumentation may be persuasive because of the social opinions that are "hidden" in its implicit premises and thus taken for granted by the recipients, e.g. immigration may thus be restricted if it is presupposed in a parliamentary debate that all refugees are "illegal" (see the contributions in Wodak and van Dijk 2000) Likewise, at the *local level*, in order to understand discourse meaning and coherence, people may need models featuring beliefs that remain implicit (presupposed) in discourse. Thus, a typical feature of manipulation is to communicate beliefs implicitly, that is, without actually asserting them, and with less chance that they will be challenged.

These few examples show how various types of discourse structure may influence the formation and change of mental models and social representations. If dominant groups, and especially their elites, largely control public discourse and its structures, they thus also have more control over the minds of the public at large. However, such control has its limits. The complexity of comprehension, and the formation and change of beliefs, are such that one cannot always predict which features of a specific text or talk will have which effects on the minds of specific recipients.

These brief remarks have provided us with a very general picture of how discourse is involved in dominance (power abuse) and in the production and reproduction of social inequality. It is the aim of CDA to examine these relationships in more detail. In the next section, we review several areas of CDA research in which these relationships are investigated.[5]

2   Research in Critical Discourse Analysis

Although most discourse studies dealing with any aspect of power, domination, and social inequality have not been explicitly conducted under the label of CDA, we shall nevertheless refer to some of these studies below.

2.1   Gender inequality

One vast field of critical research on discourse and language that thus far has not been carried out within a CDA perspective is that of gender. In many ways, feminist work has become paradigmatic for much discourse analysis, especially since much of this work explicitly deals with social inequality and domination. We will not review it here; see Kendall and Tannen, this volume; also the books authored and edited by, e.g., Cameron (1990, 1992); Kotthoff and Wodak (1997); Seidel (1988); Thorne et al. (1983); Wodak (1997); for discussion and comparison with an approach that emphasizes cultural differences rather than power differences and inequality, see, e.g., Tannen (1994a); see also Tannen (1994) for an analysis of gender differences at work, in which many of the properties of discursive dominance are dealt with.

2.2 Media discourse

The undeniable power of the media has inspired many critical studies in many disciplines: linguistics, semiotics, pragmatics, and discourse studies. Traditional, often content analytical approaches in critical media studies have revealed biased, stereotypical, sexist or racist images in texts, illustrations, and photos. Early studies of media language similarly focused on easily observable surface structures, such as the biased or partisan use of words in the description of Us and Them (and Our/Their actions and characteristics), especially along sociopolitical lines in the representation of communists. The critical tone was set by a series of "Bad News" studies by the Glasgow University Media Group (1976, 1980, 1982, 1985, 1993) on features of TV reporting, such as in the coverage of various issues (e.g. industrial disputes (strikes), the Falklands (Malvinas) war, the media coverage of AIDS.)

Perhaps best known outside of discourse studies is the media research carried out by Stuart Hall and his associates within the framework of the cultural studies paradigm. (See, e.g., Hall et al. 1980; for introduction to the critical work of cultural studies, see Agger 1992a; see also Collins et al. 1986; for earlier critical approaches to the analysis of media images, see also Davis and Walton 1983; and for a later CDA approach to media studies that is related to the critical approach of cultural studies, see Fairclough 1995b. See also Cotter, this volume.)

An early collection of work of Roger Fowler and his associates (Fowler et al. 1979) also focused on the media. As with many other English and Australian studies in this paradigm, the theoretical framework of Halliday's functional-systemic grammar is used in a study of the "transitivity" of syntactic patterns of sentences (see Martin, this volume). The point of such research is that events and actions may be described with syntactic variations that are a function of the underlying involvement of actors (e.g. their agency, responsibility, and perspective). Thus, in an analysis of the media accounts of the "riots" during a minority festival, the responsibility of the authorities and especially of the police in such violence may be systematically de-emphasized by defocusing, e.g. by passive constructions and nominalizations; that is, by leaving agency and responsibility implicit. Fowler's later critical studies of the media continue this tradition, but also pay tribute to the British cultural studies paradigm that defines news not as a reflection of reality, but as a product shaped by political, economic, and cultural forces (Fowler 1991). More than in much other critical work on the media, he also focuses on the linguistic "tools" for such a critical study, such as the analysis of transitivity in syntax, lexical structure, modality, and speech acts. Similarly van Dijk (1988b) applies a theory of news discourse (van Dijk 1988a) in critical studies of international news, racism in the press, and the coverage of squatters in Amsterdam.

2.3   Political discourse

Given the role of political discourse in the enactment, reproduction, and legitimization of power and domination, we may also expect many critical discourse studies of political text and talk (see Wilson, this volume). So far most of this work has been carried out by linguists and discourse analysts, because political science is among the few social disciplines in which discourse analysis has remained virtually unknown, although there is some influence of "postmodern" approaches to discourse (Derian and Shapiro 1989; Fox and Miller 1995), and many studies of political communication and rhetoric overlap with a discourse analytical approach (Nimmo and Sanders 1981). Still closer to discourse analysis is the current approach to "frames" (conceptual structures or sets of beliefs that organize political thought, policies, and discourse) in the analysis of political text and talk (Gamson 1992).

In linguistics, pragmatics, and discourse studies, political discourse has received attention outside the more theoretical mainstream. Seminal work comes from Paul Chilton; see, e.g., his collection on the language of the nuclear arms debate (Chilton 1985), as well as later work on contemporary nukespeak (Chilton 1988) and metaphor (Chilton 1996; Chilton and Lakoff 1995).

Although studies of political discourse in English are internationally best known because of the hegemony of English, much work has been done (often earlier, and often more systematic and explicit) in German, Spanish, and French. This work is too extensive to even begin to review here beyond naming a few influential studies.

Germany has a long tradition of political discourse analysis, both (then) in the West (e.g. about Bonn's politicians by Zimmermann 1969), as well as in the former East (e.g. the semiotic-materialist theory of Klaus 1971) (see also the introduction by Bachem 1979). This tradition in Germany witnessed a study of the language of war and peace (Pasierbsky 1983) and of speech acts in political discourse (Holly 1990). There is also a strong tradition of studying fascist language and discourse (e.g. the lexicon, propaganda, media, and language politics; Ehlich 1989).

In France, the study of political language has a respectable tradition in linguistics and discourse analysis, also because the barrier between (mostly structuralist) linguistic theory and text analysis was never very pronounced. Discourse studies are often corpus-based and there has been a strong tendency toward formal, quantitative, and automatic (content) analysis of such big datasets, often combined with critical ideological analysis (Pêcheux 1969, 1982; Guespin 1976). The emphasis on automated analysis usually implies a focus on (easily quantifiable) lexical analyses (see Stubbs, this volume).

Critical political discourse studies in Spain and especially also in Latin America has been very productive. Famous is the early critical semiotic (anticolonialist) study of Donald Duck by Dorfman and Mattelart (1972) in Chile. Lavandera et al. (1986, 1987) in Argentina take an influential sociolinguistic approach to political discourse, e.g. its typology of authoritarian discourse. Work of this group has been continued and organized in a more explicit CDA framework especially by Pardo (see, e.g., her work on legal discourse; Pardo 1996). In Mexico, a detailed ethnographic discourse analysis of local authority and decision-making was carried out by Sierra (1992). Among the many other critical studies in Latin America, we should mention the extensive work of Teresa Carbó on parliamentary discourse in Mexico, focusing especially on the way delegates speak about native Americans (Carbó 1995), with a study in English on interruptions in these debates (Carbó 1992).

2.4   *Ethnocentrism, antisemitism, nationalism, and racism*

The study of the role of discourse in the enactment and reproduction of ethnic and "racial" inequality has slowly emerged in CDA. Traditionally, such work focused on ethnocentric and racist representations in the mass media, literature, and film (Dines and Humez 1995; UNESCO 1977; Wilson and Gutiérrez 1985; Hartmann and Husband 1974; van Dijk 1991). Such representations continue centuries-old dominant images of the Other in the discourses of European travelers, explorers, merchants, soldiers, philosophers, and historians, among other forms of elite discourse (Barker 1978; Lauren 1988). Fluctuating between the emphasis on exotic difference, on the one hand, and supremacist derogation stressing the Other's intellectual, moral, and biological inferiority, on the other hand, such discourses also influenced public opinion and led to broadly shared social representations. It is the continuity of this sociocultural tradition of negative images about the Other that also partly explains the persistence of dominant patterns of representation in contemporary discourse, media, and film (Shohat and Stam 1994).

Later discourse studies have gone beyond the more traditional, content analytical analysis of "images" of the Others, and probed more deeply into the linguistic, semiotic, and other discursive properties of text and talk to and about minorities, immigrants, and Other peoples (for detailed review, see Wodak and Reisigl, this volume). Besides the mass media, advertising, film, and textbooks, which were (and still are) the genres most commonly studied, this newer work also focuses on political discourse, scholarly discourse, everyday conversations, service encounters, talk shows, and a host of other genres.

Many studies on ethnic and racial inequality reveal a remarkable similarity among the stereotypes, prejudices, and other forms of verbal derogation across discourse types, media, and national boundaries. For example, in a vast research program carried out at the University of Amsterdam since the early 1980s, we examined how Surinamese, Turks, and Moroccans, and ethnic relations generally, are represented in conversation, everyday stories, news reports, textbooks, parliamentary debates, corporate discourse, and scholarly text and talk (van Dijk 1984, 1987a, 1987b, 1991, 1993). Besides stereotypical topics of difference, deviation, and threat, story structures, conversational features (such as hesitations and repairs in mentioning Others), semantic moves such as disclaimers ("We have nothing against blacks, but . . .", etc.), lexical description of Others, and a host of other discourse features also were studied. The aim of these projects was to show how discourse expresses and reproduces underlying social representations of Others in the social and political context. Ter Wal (1997) applies this framework in a detailed study of the ways Italian political and media discourse gradually changed, from an antiracist commitment and benign representation of the *"extracommunitari"* (non-Europeans) to a more stereotypical and negative portrayal of immigrants in terms of crime, deviance, and threat.

The major point of our work is that racism (including antisemitism, xenophobia, and related forms of resentment against "racially" or ethnically defined Others) is a complex system of social and political inequality that is also reproduced by discourse in general, and by elite discourses in particular (see further references in Wodak and Reisigl, this volume).

Instead of further elaborating the complex details of the theoretical relationships between discourse and racism, we shall refer to a book that may be taken as a prototype of conservative elite discourse on "race" today, namely, *The End of Racism* by Dinesh D'Souza (1995). This text embodies many of the dominant ideologies in the USA, especially on the right, and it specifically targets one minority group in the USA: African Americans. Space prohibits detailed analysis of this 700-page book (but see van Dijk 1998a). Here we can merely summarize how the CDA of D'Souza's *The End of Racism* shows what kind of discursive structures, strategies, and moves are deployed in exercising the power of the dominant (white, western, male) group, and how readers are manipulated to form or confirm the social representations that are consistent with a conservative, supremacist ideology.

The overall strategy of D'Souza's *The End of Racism* is the combined implementation, at all levels of the text, of the positive presentation of the in-group and the negative presentation of the out-group. In D'Souza's book, the principal rhetorical means are those of hyperbole and metaphor, viz., the exaggerated representation of social problems in terms of illness ("pathologies," "virus"), and the emphasis of the contrast between the Civilized and the Barbarians. Semantically and lexically, the Others are thus associated not simply with difference, but rather with deviance ("illegitimacy") and threat (violence, attacks). Argumentative assertions of the depravity of black culture are combined with denials of white deficiencies (racism), with rhetorical mitigation and euphemization of its crimes (colonialism, slavery), and with semantic reversals of blame (blaming the victim). Social conflict is thus cognitively represented and enhanced by polarization, and discursively sustained and reproduced by derogating, demonizing, and excluding the Others from the community of Us, the Civilized.

2.5   From group domination to professional and institutional power

We have reviewed in this section critical studies of the role of discourse in the (re)production inequality. Such studies characteristically exemplify the CDA perspective on power abuse and dominance by specific social groups.[6] Many other studies, whether under the CDA banner or not, also critically examine various genres of institutional and professional discourse, e.g. text and talk in the courtroom (see Shuy, this volume; Danet 1984; O'Barr et al. 1978; Bradac et al. 1981; Ng and Bradac 1993; Lakoff 1990; Wodak 1984a; Pardo 1996; Shuy 1992), bureaucratic discourse (Burton and Carlen 1979; Radtke 1981), medical discourse (see Ainsworth-Vaughn and Fleischman, this volume; Davis 1988; Fisher 1995; Fisher and Todd 1986; Mishler 1984; West 1984; Wodak 1996), educational and scholarly discourse (Aronowitz 1988;

Apple 1979; Bourdieu 1984, 1989; Bernstein 1975, 1990; Bourdieu et al. 1994; Giroux 1981; Willis 1977; Atkinson et al. 1995; Coulthard 1994; Duszak 1997; Fisher and Todd 1986; Mercer 1995; Wodak 1996; Bergvall and Remlinger 1996; Ferree and Hall 1996; Jaworski 1983; Leimdorfer 1992; Osler 1994; Said 1979; Smith 1991; van Dijk 1987, 1993), and corporate discourse (see Linde, this volume; Mumby 1988; Boden 1994; Drew and Heritage 1992; Ehlich 1995; Mumby 1993; Mumby and Clair 1997), among many other sets of *genres*. In all these cases, power and dominance are associated with specific social domains (politics, media, law, education, science, etc.), their professional elites and institutions, and the rules and routines that form the background of the everyday discursive reproduction of power in such domains and institutions. The victims or targets of such power are usually the public or citizens at large, the "masses," clients, subjects, the audience, students, and other groups that are dependent on institutional and organizational power.

3 Conclusion

We have seen in this chapter that critical discourse analyses deal with the relationship between discourse and power. We have also sketched the complex theoretical framework needed to analyze discourse and power, and provided a glimpse of the many ways in which power and domination are reproduced by text and talk.

Yet several methodological and theoretical gaps remain. First, the cognitive interface between discourse structures and those of the local and global social context is seldom made explicit, and appears usually only in terms of the notions of knowledge and ideology (van Dijk 1998). Thus, despite a large number of empirical studies on discourse and power, the details of the multidisciplinary *theory* of CDA that should relate discourse and action with cognition and society are still on the agenda. Second, there is still a gap between more linguistically oriented studies of text and talk and the various approaches in the social. The first often ignore concepts and theories in sociology and political science on power abuse and inequality, whereas the second seldom engage in detailed discourse analysis. Integration of various approaches is therefore very important to arrive at a satisfactory form of multidisciplinary CDA.

NOTES

I am indebted to Ruth Wodak for her comments on an earlier version of this chapter, and to Laura Pardo for further information about CDA research in Latin America.

1   It comes as no surprise, then, that CDA research will often refer to the leading social philosophers and social scientists of our time when theorizing these and other fundamental notions. Thus, reference to the leading scholars of the Frankfurter School and to contemporary work by Habermas (for instance, on legitimation and his last "discourse" approach to norms and democracy) is of course common in critical analysis. Similarly, many critical studies will refer to Foucault

when dealing with notions such as power, domination, and discipline or the more philosophical notion of "orders of discourse." More recently, the many studies on language, culture, and society by Bourdieu have become increasingly influential; for instance, his notion of "habitus." From another sociological perspective, Giddens's structuration theory is now occasionally mentioned. It should be borne in mind that although several of these social philosophers and sociologists make extensive use of the notions of language and discourse, they seldom engage in explicit, systematic discourse analysis. Indeed, the last thing critical discourse scholars should do is to uncritically adopt philosophical or sociological ideas about language and discourse that are obviously uninformed by advances in contemporary linguistics and discourse analysis. Rather, the work referred to here is mainly relevant for the use of fundamental concepts about the social order and hence for the metatheory of CDA.

2   Space limitations prevent discussion of a third issue: how dominated groups discursively challenge or resist the control of powerful groups.

3   Note that "mind control" is merely a handy phrase to summarize a very complex process. Cognitive psychology and mass communication research have shown that influencing the mind is not as straightforward a process as simplistic ideas about mind control might suggest (Britton and Graesser 1996; Glasser and Salmon 1995; Klapper 1960; van Dijk and Kintsch 1983). Recipients may vary in their interpretation and uses of text and talk, also as a function of class, gender, or culture (Liebes and Katz 1990). Likewise, recipients seldom passively accept the intended opinions of specific discourses. However, we should not forget that most of our beliefs about

the world are acquired through discourse.

4   In order to analyze the complex processes involved in how discourse may control people's minds, we would need to spell out the detailed mental representations and cognitive operations studied in cognitive science. Since even an adequate summary is beyond the scope of this chapter, we will only briefly introduce a few notions that are necessary to understand the processes of discursive mind control (for details, see, e.g., Graesser and Bower 1990; van Dijk and Kintsch 1983; van Oostendorp and Zwaan 1994; Weaver et al. 1995).

5   Note that the picture just sketched is very schematic and general. The relations between the social power of groups and institutions, on the one hand, and discourse on the other, as well as between discourse and cognition, and cognition and society, are vastly more complex. There are many contradictions. There is not always a clear picture of one dominant group (or class or institution) oppressing another one, controlling all public discourse, and such discourse directly controlling the mind of the dominated. There are many forms of collusion, consensus, legitimation, and even "joint production" of forms of inequality. Members of dominant groups may become dissidents and side with dominated groups, and vice versa. Opponent discourses may be adopted by dominant groups, whether strategically to neutralize them, or simply because dominant power and ideologies may change, as is for instance quite obvious in ecological discourse and ideology.

6   Unfortunately, the study of the discursive reproduction of class has been rather neglected in this perspective; for a related approach, though, see Willis (1977).

REFERENCES

Agger, B. (1992a). *Cultural Studies as Critical Theory*. London: Falmer Press.

Agger, B. (1992b). *The Discourse of Domination. From The Frankfurt School to Postmodernism*. Evanston, IL: Northwestern University Press.

Albert, E. M. (1972). Culture patterning of speech behavior in Burundi. In J. J. Gumperz and D. Hymes (eds), *Directions in Sociolinguistics: The Ethnography of Communication* (pp. 72–105). New York: Holt, Rhinehart, and Winston.

Alexander, J. C., Giesen, B., Münch, R., and Smelser, N. J. (eds). (1987). *The Micro–Macro Link*. Berkeley, CA: University of California Press.

Apple, M. W. (1979). *Ideology and Curriculum*. London: Routledge and Kegan Paul.

Aronowitz, S. (1988). *Science as Power: Discourse and Ideology in Modern Society*. Minneapolis: University of Minnesota Press.

Atkinson, P., Davies, B., and Delamont, S. (eds). (1995). *Discourse and Reproduction. Essays in Honor of Basil Bernstein*. Cresskill, NJ: Hampton Press.

Bachem, R. (1979). *Einführung in die Analyse politischer Texte. (Introduction to the Analysis of Political Discourse)*. Munich: Oldenbourg Verlag.

Barker, A. J. (1978). *The African Link: British Attitudes to the Negro in the Era of the Atlantic Slave Trade, 1550–1807*. London: Frank Cass.

Bergvall, V. L. and Remlinger, K. A. (1996). Reproduction, resistance and gender in educational discourse: the role of critical discourse analysis. *Discourse and Society* 7(4), 453–79.

Bernstein, B. (1975). *Class, Codes and Control. Volume 3, Towards a Theory of Educational Transmissions*. London: Routledge and Kegan Paul.

Bernstein, B. (1990). *The Structuring of Pedagogic Discourse*. London: Routledge and Kegan Paul.

Birnbaum, N. (1971). *Toward a Critical Sociology*. New York: Oxford University Press.

Boden, D. (1994). *The Business of Talk. Organizations in Action*. Cambridge: Polity.

Bourdieu, P. (1984). *Homo Academicus*. Paris: Minuit.

Bourdieu, P. (1989). *La noblesse d'état. Grandes écoles et esprit de corps*. Paris: Minuit.

Bourdieu, P., Passeron, J. C. and Saint-Martin, M. (1994). *Academic Discourse. Linguistic Misunderstanding and Professorial Power*. Cambridge: Polity Press.

Bradac, J. J., Hemphill, M. R., and Tardy, C. H. (1981). Language style on trial: effects of "powerful" and "powerless" speech upon judgments of victims and villains. *Western Journal of Speech Communication*, 45(4), 327–41.

Britton, B. K. and Graesser, A. C. (eds). (1996). *Models of Understanding Text*. Mahwah, NJ: Erlbaum.

Burton, F. and Carlen, P. (1979). *Official Discourse. On Discourse Analysis, Government Publications, Ideology and the State*. London: Routledge and Kegan Paul.

Caldas-Coulthard, C. R. and Coulthard, M. (eds). (1996). *Texts and Practices: Readings in Critical Discourse Analysis*. London: Routledge and Kegan Paul.

Calhoun, C. (1995). *Critical Social Theory*. Oxford: Blackwell.

Cameron, D. (ed.) (1990). *The Feminist Critique of Language. A Reader*. London: Routledge and Kegan Paul.

Cameron, D. (1992). *Feminism and Linguistic Theory*. Second edition. London: Macmillan.

Carbó, T. (1992). Towards an interpretation of interruptions in Mexican parliamentary discourse. *Discourse and Society*, 3(1), 25–45.

Carbó, T. (1995). *El discurso parlamentario mexicano entre 1920 y 1950. Un estudio de caso en metodología de análisis de discurso. (Mexican Parliamentary Discourse between 1920 and 1950. A Case Study in the Methodology of Discourse Analysis)*. 2 volumes. Mexico: CIESAS and Colegio de México.

Chilton, P. (ed.) (1985). *Language and the Nuclear Arms Debate: Nukespeak Today*. London and Dover, NH: Frances Printer.

Chilton, P. (1988). *Orwellian Language and the Media*. London: Pluto Press.

Chilton, P. (1996). *Security Metaphors. Cold War Discourse from Containment to Common House*. Bern: Lang.

Chilton, P. and Lakoff, G. (1995). Foreign policy by metaphor. In C. Schäffner and A. L. Wenden (eds), *Language and Peace*, (pp. 37–59). Aldershot: Dartmouth.

Collins, R., Curran, J., Garnham, N., Scannell, Schlesinger, P., and Sparks, C. (eds). (1986). *Media, Culture, and Society*. London: Sage.

Coulthard, R. M. (ed.) (1994). *Advances in Written Text Analysis*. London: Routledge and Kegan Paul.

Danet, B. (ed.) (1984). Legal discourse. *Text*, 4, 1/3, special issue.

Davis, H. and Walton, P. (eds). (1983). *Language, Image, Media*. Oxford: Blackwell.

Davis, K. (1988). *Power Under the Microscope. Toward a Grounded Theory of Gender Relations in Medical Encounters*. Dordrecht: Foris.

Derian, J. D. and Shapiro, M. J. (1989). *International/Intertextual Relations*. Lexington, MA: D. C. Heath.

Diamond, J. (1996). *Status and Power in Verbal Interaction. A Study of Discourse in a Close–knit Social Network*. Amsterdam: Benjamins.

Dines, G. and Humez, J. M. M. (eds). (1995). *Gender, Race, and Class in Media. A Text–reader*. London, CA: Sage.

Dorfman, A. and Mattelart, A. (1972). *Para leer el Pato Donald. Comunicación de Masa y Colonialismo. (How to Read Donald Duck. Mass Communication and Colonialism)*. Mexico: Siglo XXI.

Downing, J. (1984). *Radical Media: The Political Experience of Alternative Communication*. Boston: South End Press.

Drew, P. and Heritage, J. (eds). (1992). *Talk at Work. Interaction in Institutional Settings*. Cambridge: Cambridge University Press.

D'Souza, D. (1995). *The End of Racism: Principles for Multiracial Society*. New York: Free Press.

Duin, A. H., Roen, D. H., and Graves, M. F. (1988). Excellence or malpractice: the effects of headlines on readers' recall and biases. National Reading Conference (1987, St Petersburg, Florida). *National Reading Conference Yearbook*, 37, 245–50.

Duranti, A. and Goodwin, C. (eds). (1992). *Rethinking Context: Language as an Interactive Phenomenon*. Cambridge: Cambridge University Press.

Duszak, A. (ed.) (1997). *Culture and Styles of Academic Discourse*. Berlin: Mouton de Gruyter.

Ehlich, K. (ed.) (1989). *Sprache im Faschismus. (Language under Fascism)*. Frankfurt: Suhrkamp.

Ehlich, K. (ed.) (1995). *The Discourse of Business Negotiation*. Berlin: Mouton de Gruyter.

Essed, P. J. M. (1991). *Understanding Everyday Racism: An Interdisciplinary Theory*. Newbury Park, CA: Sage.

Fairclough, N. L. (1992a). *Discourse and Social Change*. Cambridge: Polity Press.

Fairclough, N. L. (ed.) (1992b). *Critical Language Awareness*. London: Longman.

Fairclough, N. L. (1995a). *Critical Discourse Analysis: The Critical Study of Language.* Harlow, UK: Longman.

Fairclough, N. L. (1995b). *Media Discourse.* London: Edward Arnold.

Fairclough, N. L. and Wodak, R. (1997). Critical discourse analysis. In T. A. van Dijk (ed.), *Discourse Studies. A Multidisciplinary Introduction, Vol. 2. Discourse as Social Interaction* (pp. 258–84). London: Sage.

Fay, B. (1987). *Critical Social Science.* Cambridge: Polity.

Ferree, M. M. and Hall, E. J. (1996). Rethinking stratification from a feminist perspective: gender, race, and class in mainstream textbooks. *American Sociological Review*, 61(6), 929–50.

Fisher, S. (1995). *Nursing Wounds. Nurse Practitioners, Doctors, Women Patients, and the Negotiation of Meaning.* New Brunswick, NJ: Rutgers University Press.

Fisher, S. and Todd, A. D. (eds). (1986). *Discourse and Institutional Authority. Medicine, Education, and Law.* Norwood, NJ: Ablex.

Fishman, P. (1983). Interaction: the work women do. In B. Thorne, C. Kramarae, and N. Henley (eds), *Language, Gender, and Society* (pp. 89–101). New York: Pergamon Press.

Fowler, R. (1991). *Language in the News. Discourse and Ideology in the Press.* London: Routledge and Kegan Paul.

Fowler, R., Hodge, B., Kress, G., and Trew, T. (1979). *Language and Control.* London: Routledge and Kegan Paul.

Fox, C. J. and Miller, H. T. (1995). *Postmodern Public Administration. Toward Discourse.* London, CA: Sage.

Fox, D. R. and Prilleltensky, I. (1997). *Critical Psychology. An Introduction.* London: Sage.

Gamson, W. A. (1992). *Talking Politics.* Cambridge: Cambridge University Press.

Gans, H. (1979). *Deciding What's News.* New York: Pantheon Books.

Giroux, H. (1981). *Ideology, Culture, and the Process of Schooling.* London: Falmer Press.

Glasgow University Media Group. (1976). *Bad News.* London: Routledge and Kegan Paul.

Glasgow University Media Group. (1980). *More Bad News.* London: Routledge and Kegan Paul.

Glasgow University Media Group. (1982). *Really Bad News.* London: Writers and Readers.

Glasgow University Media Group. (1985). *War and Peace News.* Milton Keynes and Philadelphia: Open University Press.

Glasgow University Media Group. (1993). Getting the message. In J. Eldridge (ed.), *News, Truth and Power.* London: Routledge and Kegan Paul.

Glasser, T. L. and Salmon, C. T. (eds). (1995). *Public Opinion and the Communication of Consent.* New York: Guilford Press.

Graesser, A. C. and Bower, G. H. (eds). (1990). *Inferences and Text Comprehension. The Psychology of Learning and Motivation*, vol. 25. New York: Academic Press.

Gramsci, A. (1971). *Prison Notebooks.* New York: International Publishers.

Guespin, L. (ed.) (1976). Typologie du discours politique (Typology of political discourse). *Languages*, 41.

Hall, S., Hobson, D., Lowe, A., and Willis, P. (eds). (1980). *Culture, Media, Language.* London: Hutchinson.

Hartmann, P. and Husband, C. (1974). *Racism and the Mass Media.* London: Davis–Poynter.

Holly, W. (1990). *Politikersprache. Inszenierungen und Rollenkonflikte im informellen Sprachhandeln eines Bundestagsabgeordneten. (Politician's Language. Dramatization and Role Conflicts in the Informal Speech Acts of a Bundestag Delegate).* Berlin: Mouton de Gruyter.

Houston, M. and Kramarae, C. (eds). (1991). Women speaking from silence. *Discourse and Society*, 2(4), special issue.

Hymes, D. (ed.) (1972). *Reinventing Anthropology*. New York: Vintage Books.

Ibáñez, T. and Iñiguez, L. (eds). (1997). *Critical social psychology*. London: Sage.

Irvine, J. T. (1974). Strategies of status manipulation in the Wolof greeting. In R. Bauman and J. Sherzer (eds), *Explorations in the Ethnography of Speaking* (pp. 167–91). Cambridge: Cambridge University Press.

Jaworski, A. (1983). Sexism in textbooks. *British Journal of Language Teaching*, 21(2), 109–13.

Klapper, J. T. (1960). *The Effects of Mass Communication*. New York: Free Press.

Klaus, G. (1971). *Sprache der Politik (Language of Politics)*. Berlin: VEB Deutscher Verlag der Wissenschaften.

Knorr–Cetina, K. and Cicourel, A. V. (eds). (1981). *Advances in Social Theory and Methodology. Towards an Integration of Micro- and Macrosociologies*. London: Routledge and Kegan Paul.

Kotthoff, H. and Wodak, R. (eds). (1997). *Communicating Gender in Context*. Amsterdam: Benjamins.

Lakoff, R. T. (1990). *Talking Power. The Politics of Language*. New York: Basic Books.

Lauren, P. G. (1988). *Power and Prejudice. The Politics and Diplomacy of Racial Discrimination*. Boulder, CO: Westview Press.

Lavandera, B. R., García Negroni, M. M., López Ocón, M., Luis, C. R., Menéndez, S. M., Pardo, M. L., Raiter, A. G., and Zoppi–Fontana, M. (1986). Análisis sociolingüístico del discurso político. *Cuadernos del Instituto de Lingüística*, 1(1). Buenos Aires: Instituto de Lingüística, Universidad de Buenos Aires.

Lavandera, B. R., García Negroni, M. M., López Ocón, M., Luis, C. R., Menéndez, S. M., Pardo, M. L., Raiter, A. G., and Zoppi–Fontana, M. (1987). Análisis sociolingüístico del discurso político (II). *Cuadernos del Instituto de Lingüística*. Buenos Aires: Instituto de Lingüística, Universidad de Buenos Aires.

Leet-Pellegrini, H. (1980). Conversational dominance as a function of gender and expertise. In H. Giles, W. P. Robinson, and P. Smith (eds), *Language: Social Psychological Perspectives* (pp. 97–104). Oxford: Pergamon Press.

Leimdorfer, F. (1992). *Discours académique et colonisation. Thèmes de recherche sur l'Algérie pendant la période coloniale. (Academic Discourse and Colonization: Research on Algeria during the Colonial Period)*. Paris: Publisud.

Liebes, T. and Katz, E. (1990). *The Export of Meaning: Cross–cultural Readings of "Dallas."* New York: Oxford University Press.

Lindegren–Lerman, C. (1983). Dominant discourse: the institutional voice and the control of topic. In H. Davis and P. Walton (eds), *Language, Image, Media* (pp. 75–103). Oxford: Blackwell.

Linell, P. and Jonsson, L. (1991). Suspect stories: perspective-setting in an asymmetrical situation. In I. Markova and K. Foppa (eds), *Asymmetries in Dialogue. The Dynamics of Dialogue* (pp. 75–100). n.d. Barnes and Noble Books/Bowman and Littlefield Publishers: Harvester Wheatsheaf.

Lukes, S. (ed.) (1986). *Power*. Oxford: Blackwell.

Martín Rojo, L. (1994). Jargon of delinquents and the study of conversational dynamics. *Journal of Pragmatics*, 21(3), 243–89.

Martín Rojo, L. and van Dijk, T. A. (1997). "There was a problem, and it was solved!" Legitimating the expulsion of "illegal" immigrants in Spanish parliamentary discourse. *Discourse and Society*, 8(4), 523–67.

Mercer, N. (1995). *The Guided Construction of Knowledge. Talk Amongst Teachers and Learners*. Clevedon: Multilingual Matters.

Mey, J. L. (1985). *Whose Language. A Study in Linguistic Pragmatics*. Amsterdam: Benjamins.

Mishler, E. G. (1984). *The Discourse of Medicine. Dialectics in Medical Interviews*. Norwood, NJ: Ablex.

Mumby, D. K. (1988). *Communication and Power in Organizations: Discourse, Ideology, and Domination*. Norwood, NJ: Ablex.

Mumby, D. K. (ed.) (1993). *Narrative and Social Control: Critical Perspectives*. Newbury Park, CA: Sage.

Mumby, D. K. and Clair, R. P. (1997). Organizational discourse. In T. A. van Dijk (ed.), *Discourse as Social Interaction. Discourse Studies. A Multidisciplinary Introduction*, vol. 1 (pp. 181–205). London: Sage.

Nesler, M. S., Aguinis, H., Quigley, B. M., and Tedeschi, J. T. (1993). The effect of credibility on perceived power. *Journal of Applied Social Psychology*, 23(17), 1407–25.

Ng, S. H. and Bradac, J. J. (1993). *Power in Language*. Newbury Park: Sage.

Nimmo, D. D. and Sanders, K. R. (eds). (1981). *Handbook of Political Communication*. Beverly Hills, CA: Sage.

O'Barr, W. M., Conley, J. M., and Lind, A. (1978). The power of language: presentational style in the courtroom. *Duke Law Journal*, 14, 266–79.

Osler, A. (1994). Still hidden from history: the representation of women in recently published history textbooks. *Oxford Review of Education*, 20(2), 219–35.

Palmer, M. T. (1989). Controlling conversations: turns, topics, and interpersonal control. *Communication Monographs*, 56(1), 1–18.

Pardo, M. L. (1996). *Derecho y lingüística: Cómo se juzga con palabras* (*Law and Linguistics: How to Judge with Words*). Buenos Aires: Nueva Visión.

Pasierbsky, F. (1983). *Krieg und Frieden in der Sprache.* (*War and Peace in Language*). Frankfurt: Fischer.

Pêcheux, M. (1969). *Analyse Automatique du Discours*. Paris: Dunod.

Pêcheux, M. (1982). *Language, Semantics and Ideology*. New York: St Martin's Press.

Radtke, I. (ed.) (1981). *Die Sprache des Rechts und der Verwaltung. Vol. 2. Deutsche Akademie für Sprache und Dichtung, Die öffentliche Sprachgebrauch.* (*The Language of the Law and the Administration. Vol. 2. German Academy of Language and Literature, Official Language Use*). Stuttgart: Klett–Cotta.

Rasmussen, D. M. (ed.) (1996). *The Handbook of Critical Theory*. Oxford: Blackwell.

Said, E. W. (1979). *Orientalism*. New York: Random House (Vintage).

Seidel, G. (ed.) (1988). *The Nature of the Right. A Feminist Analysis of Order Patterns*. Amsterdam: Benjamins.

Shohat, E. and Stam, R. (1994). *Unthinking Eurocentrism. Multiculturalism and the Media*. London: Routledge and Kegan Paul.

Shuy, R. W. (1992). *Language crimes. The Use and Abuse of Language Evidence in the Court Room*. Oxford: Blackwell.

Sierra, M. T. (1992). *Discurso, cultura y poder. El ejercio de la autoridad en los pueblos hñähñús del Valle del Mezquital.* (*Discourse, Culture and Power. The Exercise of Authority in the Hñähñú (Otomí) Villages of the Mezquital Valley*). Gobierno del Estado de Hidalgo: Centro de Investigaciones y Estudios Superiores en Antropología Social.

Singh, R. (ed.) (1996). *Towards a Critical Sociolinguistics*. Amsterdam: Benjamins.

Smith, D. E. (1991). Writing women's experience into social science. *Feminism and Psychology*, 1(1), 155–69.

Tannen, D. (1994a). *Gender and Discourse*. New York: Oxford University Press.

Tannen, D. (1994b). *Talking from 9 to 5. How Women's and Men's Conversational Styles Affect Who Gets Heard, Who Gets Credit, and What Gets Done at Work*. New York: Morrow.

Ter Wal, J. (1997). The reproduction of ethnic prejudice and racism through policy and news discourse. The Italian case (1988–92). Florence: PhD, European Institute.

Thomas, J. (1993). *Doing Critical Ethnography*. Newbury Park: Sage.

Thorne, B., Kramarae, C., and Henley, N. (eds). (1983). *Language, Gender and Society*. Rowley, MA: Newbury House.

Turkel, G. (1996). *Law and Society. Critical Approaches*. Boston, MA: Allyn and Bacon.

UNESCO. (1977). *Ethnicity and the Media*. Paris: UNESCO.

van Dijk, T. A. (1984). *Prejudice in Discourse*. Amsterdam: Benjamins.

van Dijk, T. A. (1987). *Communicating Racism: Ethnic Prejudice in Thought and Talk*. Newbury Park, CA: Sage.

van Dijk, T. A. (1987). *Schoolvoorbeelden van Racisme. De Reproduktie van Racisme in Maatschappijleerboeken (Textbook Examples of Racism. The Reproduction of Racism in Social Science Textbooks)*. Amsterdam: Socialistische Uitgeverij Amsterdam.

van Dijk, T. A. (1988a). *News as Discourse*. Hillsdale, NJ: Erlbaum.

van Dijk, T. A. (1988b). *News Analysis. Case Studies of International and National News in the Press*. Hillsdale, NJ: Erlbaum.

van Dijk, T. A. (1991). *Racism and the Press*. London: Routledge and Kegan Paul.

van Dijk, T. A. (1993a). *Elite Discourse and Racism*. Newbury Park, CA: Sage.

van Dijk, T. A. (1993b). Principles of critical discourse analysis. *Discourse and Society* 4(2), 249–83.

van Dijk, T. A. (1996). Discourse, power and access. In R. C. Caldas–Coulthard and M. Coulthard (eds), *Texts and Practices: Readings in Critical Discourse Analysis* (pp. 84–104). London: Routledge and Kegan Paul.

van Dijk, T. A. (1998a). *Ideology. A Multidisciplinary Study*. London: Sage.

van Dijk, T. A. (1998b). Towards a theory of context and experience models in discourse processing. In H. van Oostendorp and S. Goldman, (eds), *The Construction of Mental Models During Reading*. Hillsdale, NJ: Erlbaum.

van Dijk, T. A. and Kintsch, W. (1983). *Strategies of Discourse Comprehension*. New York: Academic Press.

Van Oostendorp, H. and Zwaan, R. A. (eds). (1994). *Naturalistic Text Comprehension*. Norwood, NJ: Ablex.

Van Zoonen, L. (1994). *Feminist Media Studies*. London: Sage.

Weaver, C. A., Mannes, S. and Fletcher, C. R. (eds). (1995). *Discourse Comprehension. Essays in Honor of Walter Kintsch*. Hillsdale, NJ: Erlbaum.

West, C. (1984). *Routine Complications: Troubles with Talk between Doctors and Patients*. Bloomington: Indiana University Press.

Williams, J. (ed.) (1995). *PC Wars. Politics and Theory in the Academy*. New York: Routledge and Kegan Paul.

Willis, P. (1977). *Learning to Labour: How Working Class Kids Get Working Class Jobs*. London: Saxon House.

Wilson, C. C. and Gutiérrez, F. (1985). *Minorities and the Media*. Beverly Hills, CA, and London: Sage.

Wodak, R. (1984). Determination of guilt: discourses in the courtroom. In C. Kramarae, M. Schulz, and W. M. O'Barr (eds), *Language and Power* (pp. 89–100). Beverly Hills, CA: Sage.

Wodak, R. (1985). The interaction between judge and defendant. In T. A. van Dijk (ed.), *Handbook of Discourse Analysis. Vol. 4. Discourse Analysis in Society* (pp. 181–91). London: Academic Press.

Wodak, R. (1987). "And where is the Lebanon?" A socio–psycholinguistic investigation of comprehension and intelligibility of news. *Text*, 7(4), 377–410.

Wodak, R. (1996). *Disorders of Discourse*. London: Longman.

Wodak, R. (1997). *Gender and Discourse*. London: Sage.

Wodak, R. and van Dijk, T. A. (eds) (2000). *Racism at the Top*. Klagenfurt: Drava Verlag.

Wrong, D. H. (1979). *Power: Its Forms, Bases and Uses*. Oxford: Blackwell.

Zimmermann, H. D. (1969). *Die politische Rede. Der Sprachgebrauch Bonner Politiker. (Political Speech. Language use of Bonn's Politicians)*. Stuttgart: Kohlhammer.

19   Discourse and Racism

RUTH WODAK AND MARTIN REISIGL

0   Introduction

"Racism" is a stigmatizing headword and political "fighting word" that seems to be on almost everyone's lips today. Perhaps this is because the meaning of "racism" has become extraordinarily expanded and evasive. There is talk of a "genetic," "biological," "cultural," "ethnopluralist," "institutional," and "everyday racism," of a "racism at the top," of an "elite racism," of a "racism in the midst," of and "old" and a "new" or "neo-racism," of a "positive racism," and of an "inegalitarian" and a "differentialist racism." (For an explanation of most of the terms just mentioned see Reisigl and Wodak 2001: ch. 1, section 1.2.)

The starting point of a discourse analytical approach to the complex phenomenon of racism is to realize that racism, as both social practice and ideology, manifests itself discursively. On the one hand, racist opinions and beliefs are produced and reproduced by means of discourse; discriminatory exclusionary practices are prepared, promulgated, and legitimated through discourse. On the other hand, discourse serves to criticize, delegitimate, and argue against racist opinions and practices, that is, to pursue antiracist strategies. Because we are bound by constraints of space, we have to do without detailed and extensive analyses of concrete discursive examples that help to show and reconstruct the discursive production and reproduction of racism and the accompanying discursive counteractions. However, after briefly reviewing concepts of "race" (section 1) and explanations of racism (section 2), we present five discourse analytic approaches to racism (section 3), including an illustration of how our own discourse-historical approach works through an analysis of a short excerpt from an interview with an Austrian politician. Our conclusion poses several questions that are still unanswered (section 4).

1 The Concept of "Race": A Historical-political Etymological Overview

It is currently an undeniable fact for geneticists and biologists that the concept of "race," in reference to human beings, has nothing to do with biological reality (e.g. Jacquard 1996: 20). From a social functional point of view, "race" is a social construction. On the one hand, it has been used as a legitimating ideological tool to oppress and exploit specific social groups and to deny them access to material, cultural, and political resources, to work, welfare services, housing, and political rights. On the other hand, these affected groups have adopted the idea of "race." They have turned the concept around and used it to construct an alternative, positive self-identity; they have also used it as a basis for political resistance (see Miles 1993: 28) and to fight for more political autonomy, independence, and participation.

From a linguistic point of view, the term "race" has a relatively recent, although not precisely clear, etymological history. The Italian "razza," the Spanish "raza," the Portuguese "raça," and the French "race" had been documented rarely from the thirteenth century onwards and with more frequent occurrences beginning in the sixteenth century, when the term also appeared in English. It has, at different times, entered different semantic fields, for example (1) the field of ordinal and classificational notions that include such words as "genus," "species," and "varietas"; (2) the field that includes social and political group denominations such as "nation" and "Volk" (in German), and, more rarely, "dynasty," "ruling house," "generation," "class," and "family"; and (3) the field that includes notions referring to language groups and language families[1] such as "Germanen" (Teutons) and "Slavs" (see Conze and Sommer 1984: 135). The prescientific (up to the eighteenth century) meaning of "race" in regard to human beings[2] was mainly associated with aristocratic descent and membership, to a specific dynasty or ruling house. The term primarily denoted "nobility" and "quality," and had no reference to somatic criteria yet. However, in the eighteenth and nineteenth centuries pseudobiological and anthropological systematizations soon conformed its meaning to overgeneralized, phenotypic features designated to categorize people from all continents and countries. The idea of "race" became closely incorporated into political-historical literature and was conceptually transferred to the terminology of human history. In the second half of the nineteenth century, the concept, now with historical and national attributes, was linked to social Darwinism – which can be traced to Darwin's theory of evolution only in part – and became an "in-word" outside the natural sciences. "Race theorists" interpreted history as a "racial struggle" within which only the fittest "races" would have the right to survive. They employed the political catchword with its vague semantic contours almost synonymously with the words "nation" and "Volk" for the purposes of their biopolitical programs of "racial cleansing," eugenics, and birth control.

The extremely radicalized "race" theory of the German antisemites and National Socialists in the tradition of Arthur de Gobineau, Houston Stewart Chamberlain, and Georg Ritter von Schönerer tied together syncretistically religious, nationalist, economist, culturalist, and biologistic antisemitism,[3] which then served as the ideology to legitimize systematic, industrialized genocide. It was this use of "race theory" "that stimulated a more thorough critical appraisal of the idea of 'race' in Europe and

North America and the creation of the concept of racism in the 1930s" (Miles 1993: 29).[4] Since 1945, use of the term "race" in the German-language countries of Germany and Austria has been strictly tabooed for politicians, for academicians, and even for the people in general. In France, the expression "relations de race" would also be regarded as racist (Wieviorka 1994: 173). On the other hand, the term "race relations" is still commonly used in the United Kingdom and in the United States. Research about racism must take into account these differences in language use. Misinterpretations can lead to difficulties in translation and even to mistakes in shaping different analytical categories used when dealing with the issue of racism (see Wieviorka 1994: 173).

2   How to Explain "Racism"

Many approaches from different disciplines reflect on the material, economical, social, political, social psychological, cognitive, and other causes and motives for racism. The explanations offered by each have an important impact on the choice of specific antiracist strategies. Let us mention some of the most prominent approaches (for an overview of theoretical accounts see, for example, Poliakov et al. 1992: 145–96 and Zerger 1997: 99–164; for a more detailed overview see also Reisigl and Wodak 2001: ch. 1, section 2).

Social cognitive accounts focus on social categorization and stereotyping, relying on the cognitive concepts of "prototypes," "schemas," "stereotypes," and "object classification." Some social cognition researchers, for example Hamilton and Trolier (1986), "argue that the way our minds work, the way we process information, may in itself be sufficient to generate a negative image of a group. They point to several strands of evidence but most notably to the illusory correlation studies" (Wetherell and Potter 1992: 38). Their concepts of society and social environment are quite static, and they assume that prejudicial apperceptions and categorizations (inherent in all persons) are inevitable and cognitively "useful." In presuming this, they risk playing down and even – at least implicitly – justifying racism as a "survival strategy." In addition, they cannot explain why some people are more susceptible to racist ideology than others.

Social identity theory (e.g. Hogg and Abrahams 1988; Tajfel 1981; Tajfel and Turner 1985; Turner 1981, 1985; Turner and Giles 1981; Turner et al. 1987) places the concept of social identity in the center of its social psychological theory of intergroup relations. In contrast to the above-mentioned approach, it recognizes the importance of socialization and group experiences in the development and acquisition of social categories. From the perspective of social identity theory, the social structures individual perception, identity, and action. Categorizations are assumed to be necessary for reducing the complexity of the social world. Individual perception is formed by patterns aligned with group memberships and nonmemberships. These learned patterns of perception tend to favor the in-group and to derogate the out-groups. The image of the in-group is more differentiated than the images of the out-groups, which, all in all, are much more characterized by "internal attributions" than the in-group. Racism and ethnocentrism are, in large part, seen as the interpersonal result of group membership and as the psychological effects of identifying with a specific group in economic and social competition with other groups. Some of the causal assumptions of this theory are rather too simple and reductionist. Apart from the simplistic frustration–aggression hypothesis, and the hasty analogical generalization of the results of small-group experiments, the relationship between experiences, thinking, and practices is simply assumed without any closer differentiation. Like the social cognition approach, social identity theory suffers from "a tendency to universalize the conditions for racism and a lingering perceptualism" (Wetherell and Potter 1992: 47). The implications for antiracism are therefore very pessimistic ones.

Several nativist *psychoanalytical theories* (for psychoanalytical accounts, see also Poliakov et al. 1992: 175–82 and Ottomeyer 1997, 111–31; for psychological accounts, see Mecheril and Thomas 1997) hold this universalistic viewpoint in common with the two approaches already noted above. Allport (1993: 10) is right to criticize psychoanalytical theories for tending to ascribe to all persons the same dependency on unconscious aggressions and fixations which undoubtedly characterize the inner life of neurotic and psychotic persons. In positing the "thanatos," that is to say, innate death instincts, many varieties of psychoanalysis naturalize aggressions against "the other" as an anthropological invariant and thus relinquish their political potential to be critical of society (see Masson 1984 and especially Jacoby 1983 for his critique of the politically self-disarming and self-immunizing medicalization and professionalization of conformist psychoanalysis).

In contrast to these approaches, which are inclined to legitimate the social status quo, *critical theory* (e.g. Adorno 1973, 1993; Adorno et al. 1950; Fromm 1988; Horkheimer 1992; Horkheimer and Flowerman 1949f; Horkheimer et al. 1987; Fenichel 1993; Simmel 1993; Reich 1986; and more recently Outlaw 1990), combine neo-Marxism, politically committed psychoanalysis, and sociopsychology. In this way, they connect economic, political and cultural structures, as well as social dynamics, with the character structure of a person that has been fundamentally formed through childhood socialization. Thus, critical theory does not merely describe racist, and especially antisemitic, prejudice, but primarily tries to explain it in order to illuminate the conditions for the emergence and social maintenance of Nazi fascism and antisemitism and in order to help to eradicate authoritarianism and racist prejudice. Adorno (1973: 8) regards insight into the character structure as the best protection from the tendency to ascribe constant traits to individuals as "innate" or "racially determined." As a specific character structure – the authoritarian personality – makes an individual susceptible to antidemocratic propaganda, the social and economic conditions under which the potential turns into active manifestation have to be uncovered.

Outlaw (1990: 72ff) develops early critical theory to propagate a critical theory of "race" which challenges the commonsense assumption that "race" is a self-evident, organizing, explanatory concept. Stressing the sociohistorical constructivist dimensions of "race," Outlaw points to the danger, particularly widespread in the United States, of taking an essentializing and objectivizing concept of "race" as the focal point of contention, thereby supplying a shorthand explanation for the source of contentious differences.[5] Outlaw pleads for emancipatory projects informed by traditions of critical thought which might help to move beyond racism, without reductionism, to pluralistic socialist democracy.

The *colonial paradigm* or *race relations approach* (Cox 1970; Szymanski 1985; Wallerstein 1979; Fox-Genovese 1992; Genovese 1995) – the notion was coined by Miles – views racism within the classical Marxist tradition as the consequence of colonialism and imperialism in the context of capitalism. It analyzes racism in the light of the development of a capitalist world economic system. One of the first to analyze "race relations" within this framework is Cox (1970) (see Miles 1993: 30ff). Cox characterizes "race relations" as "behavior which develops among people who are aware of each other's actual or imputed physical differences" (1970: 320). Although Cox claims that "races" are social constructions, he reifies them as distinctive, permanent, immutable collectivities distinguished by skin color. As Miles (1991, 1994) criticizes, the "colonial paradigm," assuming that racism was created to legitimate colonial exploitation, externalizes the problem of racism one-sidedly, one consequence being its inability to explain antisemitism and the negative racialization of other "interior" minorities (e.g. "gypsies") in Europe before and after the Second World War.

The *political economy of migration paradigm* (Castles and Kosack 1972, 1973; Nikolinakos 1975; Lawrence 1982; Sivanandan 1982, 1990; Miles 1993) analyzes the processes of "racialization" in the capitalist centers in connection with migration, capital accumulation, and class formation. Rejecting the sociological paradigm of "race relations," Castles and Kosack (1972, 1973) focus on worldwide migration after 1945 as a consequence of uneven capitalist development on a world scale. They identify immigrant workers "as having a specific socio-economic function found in all capitalist societies, namely to fill undesirable jobs vacated by the indigenous working class in the course of the periodic reorganization of production. This stratum of immigration workers thereby came to constitute a 'lower stratum' of the working class which was thereby fragmented" (Miles 1993: 36). In common with the proponents of the "race relations approach" Castles and Kosack do not reject the idea of "race" as an analytical concept. "Rather, they subordinate it to a political economy of labor migration and class relations: that is, they retained the category of 'race' in order to deny its explanatory significance" (Miles 1993: 36). The analyses by Sivanandan (1982, 1990) suffer from the absence of any critical evaluation of "race" and "race relations" as analytical concepts as well. They suggest at least indirectly that the human population is composed of a number of biological "races." Beyond that, they ascribe to "race" more or less the same status of reality as to "social class" and reduce racism primarily to economical factors.

The *postmodern approaches* and *the cultural studies perspective* – which except for its neo-Marxist orientation partly relies on postmodernism – (CCCS/Center for Contemporary Cultural Studies 1982; Hall 1978, 1980, 1989, 1994; Gilroy 1987; Rattansi and Westwood 1994; Rattansi 1994; Westwood 1994; Bhabha 1990; Said 1978, 1993; Fanon 1986; Bauman 1989, 1991) primarily try to analyze the cultural, ideological, and political construction of racism. They emphasize "that ethnicities, nationalisms, racism and other forms of collective identities[6] are products of a process to be conceptualized as a cultural politics of representation, one in which narratives, images, musical forms and popular culture more generally have a significant role" (Rattansi 1994: 74). Rejecting Western "metanarratives" constructed around particular "collective subjects" like "nations," "races," "ethnic groups," and "classes," Rattansi and Westwood (1994: 2) point out that the conceptual vocabulary of "nationalism," "racism," "ethnicism," and "class struggle" can no longer provide the basis for a viable taxonomy of violent social antagonisms and clashes.[7] In their view, these concepts no longer enable the creation of convincing, all-encompassing explanatory frameworks, since subjectivities and identifications are multiple and shifting under the "postmodern condition" (Lyotard 1984) of chronic disembedding, decentering, de-essentialization, and reinvention of traditions and "collective" identities.

Cultural studies and postmodern approaches regard the western genocide of aboriginal people, slavery, imperialist and colonial domination and exploitation, and the Holocaust, in all of which western doctrines of "racial" and cultural superiority have played a constitutive role, as the other side of western modernity.[8] Relying on poststructuralist psychoanalysis (Lacan, Kristeva), they link racism to sexuality, considering racism to be one response of the generically fragile, split, fragmented ego (see Frosh 1987, 1989, 1991) and of the repressed homosexual desire leading into ambivalence and projection of unwanted feelings about the body toward others, whether Jews, "black" people, or Asians (Fanon 1986: 163–78).

Miles proposes the *racism after race relations* paradigm (see Miles and Phizacklea 1979; Guillaumin 1991, 1992; Goldberg 1993; Taguieff 1987) as an alternative neo-Marxist theorization of racism. It is not his intention to revive the classical argumentation that racism is "only" a utilitarian invention of the bourgeoisie to divide the working class and to legitimate colonialism (Miles 1994: 204). Rather, he locates the explanation for racism in the "disorganization of capitalism," strictly speaking in a field of several contradictions "between, on the one hand, universalism and humanism, and, on the other, the reproduction of social inequality and exploitation" (Miles 1994: 207). Miles sees the first contradiction in the conflict between the universalizing and equalizing tendencies embodied in the "commodification of everything" (Wallerstein 1988) and the capitalist necessity to reproduce social inequality. Here, racism mediates ideologically by attributing specified essential, naturalizing traits to social collectivities, thereby justifying social inequality and uneven development. The second contradiction Miles (1994: 205) identifies is that "between the capitalist universalizing tendencies and the reality of extensive cultural diversity rooted in the disaggregation of social formations, within which material reproduction was socially organized prior to the development of the capitalist mode of production, and which have been reproduced parallel with that development while those social formations have not been fully incorporated into the capitalist world economy." Here, racism makes it possible to racialize social groups resisting capitalist "progress" as primitive and inferior. The third contradiction Miles makes out is that between the economic globalization tendencies and the nationalization of social formations, that is to say, the partial confinement of capitalist relations of production within the political form of nation-states wherein political subjects are nationalized and racialized.

Like Miles (1994: 207), we recognize the multiple determination of racism and do not seek to propose a holistic explanation for the expression of contemporary racism in Europe. We believe that no monocausal and monodimensional approach is adequate to grasp the complexity of racism. Racialization is criss-crossed by ethnic, national, gender, class, and other social constructions and divisions, thus rendering a separating view on "race" or "racialization" as an isolated determinant of social relations short-sighted. Multidimensional analysis is required in order to obtain adequate historical reconstructions, actual diagnoses, and anticipatory prognoses, all of which are necessary to develop promising antiracist strategies. Among many other things, a multidimensional analysis of racism requires taking into account adjacent and overlapping phenomena like antisemitism, nationalism, ethnicism, and sexism.

3   Five Discourse Analytical Approaches to Racism

Now that we have reviewed the meanings of the word "race" and a variety of explanations for racism, it is time to turn to the approaches through which the discursive manifestations of racism have been analyzed.

3.1   *Prejudices and stereotypes*

One of the first discourse analysts to attempt to study and categorize prejudiced discourse was Uta Quasthoff (1973, 1978, 1980, 1987, 1989, 1998). Quasthoff distinguishes between "attitudes," "convictions," and "prejudices." She defines *attitudes* as the affective position taken towards a person one relates to and to whom one can express dislike or sympathy. *Convictions* ascribe qualities to others and often provide rationalizations for negative attitudes (e.g. that "blacks smell bad"). *Prejudices* are mental states defined (normally) as negative attitudes (the affective element) toward social groups with matching stereotypic convictions or beliefs.

For the purposes of linguistic access, Quasthoff defines the term *stereotype* as the verbal expression of a certain conviction or belief directed toward a social group or an individual as a member of that social group. The stereotype is typically an element of common knowledge, shared to a high degree in a particular culture (see Quasthoff 1987: 786, 1978). It takes the logical form of a judgment that attributes or denies, in an oversimplified and generalizing manner and with an emotionally slanted tendency, particular qualities or behavioral patterns to a certain class of persons (Quasthoff 1973: 28).

Quasthoff's investigations cover all kinds of social prejudices and stereotypes, not only racist and nationalist ones.[9] According to Quasthoff (1973), sentences are the linguistic unit most amenable to her type of analysis. However, Quasthoff (1987: 786; 1989: 183) herself points out that "the definitional quality that the grammatical unit of the linguistic description of stereotypes is the sentence does not mean that stereotypes empirically have to appear in the form of complete sentences. It solely implies that the semantic unit of a stereotype is a proposition, i.e. reference and predication, as opposed to a certain form of reference as such."

Since 1973, Quasthoff herself has done considerable analysis of stereotypes on the empirical basis of their use in very different kinds of discourse; among others, in everyday argumentation (Quasthoff 1978, 1998) and narratives (Quasthoff 1980), thus broadening her linguistic horizons to social prejudice and transcending the single-sentence perspective. When, for example, she applied Toulmin's schematism (1969) to the microstructural level of argumentation, Quasthoff came to the conclusion that stereotypes do not exclusively, or even primarily, appear as warrants. If they are used to support a claim, they appear usually as a backing (Quasthoff 1978: 27). Moreover, stereotypes can themselves be either data or claims, supported, in their turn, by other kinds of propositions.

3.2   The sociocognitive approach

The model of prejudice use by Teun van Dijk is partially based on sociopsychological considerations similar to those of Quasthoff. According to van Dijk, prejudice:

> is not merely a characteristic of individual beliefs or emotions about social groups, but a shared form of social representation in group members, acquired during processes of socialization and transformed and enacted in social communication and interaction. Such ethnic attitudes have social functions, e.g. to protect the interests of the ingroup. Their cognitive structures and the strategies of their use reflect these social functions. (van Dijk 1984: 13)[10]

While Quasthoff most generally stresses the marking of distance toward out-groups and the establishment of in-group solidarity (and phatic communion) as social functions of prejudice, van Dijk focuses on the "rationalization and justification of discriminatory acts against minority groups" in more detail (van Dijk 1984: 13). He designates the categories used to rationalize prejudice against minority groups as "the 7 Ds of Discrimination". They are dominance, differentiation, distance, diffusion, diversion, depersonalization or destruction, and daily discrimination. These strategies serve in various ways to legitimize and enact the distinction of "the other"; for example, by dominating the minority groups, by excluding them from social activities, and even by destroying and murdering them (see van Dijk 1984: 40).

For the elaboration of a discourse analytical theory about racist discourse, one of the most valuable contributions of van Dijk's model is the heuristic assistance it provides in linking the generation of prejudice to discursive units larger than the sentence. Van Dijk's initial assumption is that those parts of long-term memory directly relevant to the production and retention of ethnic prejudices (recognition, categorization, and storage of experience) can be divided into three memory structures: semantic memory, episodic memory, and control system.

According to van Dijk, *semantic memory* is social memory: it is here that the collectively shared beliefs of a society are stored. These beliefs are organized as attitudes, which are of a generalized and abstract nature and are determined by their organization in socially relevant categories of the group that is being evaluated (e.g. national origin and/or appearance, socioeconomic status, and sociocultural norms and values, including religion and language). *Episodic memory* retains personal or narrated experiences and events as well as patterns abstracted from these experiences. The listener constructs a textual representation of a story in episodic memory. General situational models are the link between narrated events or personally retained experiences and the structures of the semantic memory.

In his new context model (van Dijk 1998a), van Dijk distinguishes between specific *event models* and *context models*. He views both types of models as being personal and not shared by a group. Accordingly, van Dijk conceptualizes the third structure of long-term memory, the *control system*, as a personal model of the social situation. The control system's task is to link communicative aims and interests (e.g. persuasion) with the situational and individual social conditions (e.g. level of education, gender, and relationship to the person one is addressing). Van Dijk calls the processes involved in the perception, interpretation, storage, use, or retrieval of ethnic information about minority groups and their actions "strategies." The control system coordinates these various strategies and at the same time monitors the flow of information from long-term memory to short-term memory, as well as the storage or activation of situation models in episodic memory.

One of the main strategies of the control system is to link a positive self-presentation – i.e. one acceptable to society and signaling tolerance – with an existing negative attitude to foreigners. Positive self-presentations are expressed in phrases such as "Personally, I have nothing against Jews, but the neighbors say . . ." The interaction of these three memory systems thus both directly and indirectly influences the decoding and encoding – which take place in the short-term memory – of the received and/or self-produced remarks about minorities. Van Dijk's model can thus explain the cognitive processes of the text recipients: isolated experiences, statements, and symbols are assigned to general schemas and confirm existing prejudices.

More recently, van Dijk (1991, 1993, 1998a, 1998b) has turned to the analysis of "elite racism" and to the integration of the concept of "ideology" into his sociocognitive model. He mainly focuses on the investigation of newspaper editorials, school books, academic discourse, interviews with managers, political speeches, and parliamentary debates, with the basic assumption that "the elite" produces and reproduces the racism that is then implemented and enacted in other social fields. We certainly believe that "the elite" plays a significant role in the production and reproduction of racism, but we prefer to assume a more reciprocal and less monocausal and unidirectional top-down relationship of influence between "the elite" and other social groups and strata within a specific society.

3.3   Discourse strands and collective symbols

Siegfried Jäger and the Duisburg group are probably the most prominent researchers in Germany dealing with issues of racism and discourse (see S. Jäger 1992, 1993; M. Jäger 1996a; S. Jäger and Jäger 1992; S. Jäger and Januschek 1992; S. Jäger and Link 1993; Kalpaka and Räthzel 1986; Link 1990, 1992).[11] The research was triggered largely by the violent racism that started shortly after 1992, when new and stricter immigration laws were implemented in Germany. Simultaneously, the unification of West Germany and the former communist East Germany erupted in racist violence against many foreigners, who were physically attacked and whose asylum homes were set afire. Among others, this violence was and continues to be connected to the fact that the unification poses tremendous cultural and economic problems for the Germans and that foreigners provide a comfortable scapegoat for these problems (e.g. that millions of people lost their jobs postunification). The Duisburg group has been very active not only in its research and documentation of racism, but also in proposing strategies against it (e.g. see M. Jäger et al. 1998: 167–236).

In several respects, the Duisburg group follows and extends the research of van Dijk. Among others, they interview different groups of people to elicit their attitudes toward foreigners and Jews. In contrast to standard methods for conducting interviews, their method leads people to tell their personal stories in depth. Besides studying everyday racism, the Duisburg group also does media analysis, in particular of the German tabloid *Bildzeitung*, which launches large campaigns against foreigners, but also of the conservative quality daily *Frankfurter Allgemeine Zeitung*, the regional daily newspapers *Frankfurter Rundschau, Westdeutsche Allgemeine Zeitung*, and *Rheinische Post*, and the social liberal weekly *Der Spiegel*. A primary interest in the analysis of all these newspapers is the press coverage about criminal acts. A recent analysis (see M. Jäger et al. 1998) shows that most of the papers tend toward singularization and individualization of (alleged) German perpetrators and toward collectivization of "foreigners" who have (allegedly) committed a criminal offence. Moreover, "foreign perpetrators" are marked by reference to their national or ethnic origin in half of the press articles of all newspapers except *Der Spiegel*.

The main focus in many of the Duisburg studies is discourse semantics, and especially the uncovering of "collective symbols" that are tied together in "discourse strands," best explained as thematically interrelated sequences of homogeneous "discourse fragments" (S. Jäger 1993: 181),[12] which appear on different "discourse levels" (i.e. science, politics, media, education, everyday life, business life, and administration). "Collective symbols" are designated as "cultural stereotypes" in the form of metaphorical and synecdochic symbols that are immediately understood by the members of the same speech community (see Link 1982, 1988, 1990, 1992). "Water," natural disasters like "avalanches" and "flood disasters," military activities like "invasions," all persuasively representing "immigration" or "migrants" as something that has to be "dammed," are examples of collective symbols, just as are the "ship" metaphor, symbolizing the effects of immigration as on an "overcrowded boat," and the "house" and "door" metaphor that metaphorizes the in-groups' (e.g. "national") territory as "house" or "building" and the stopping of immigration as "bolting the door" (see also Jung et al. 1997). The Duisburg group also analyzes the construction of "the Other" with a focus on the pronominal system, on the connotations of specific nouns, verbs, and adjectives, on stylistic features, on tense, mood, and modality, on specific syntactic means and structures, and on argumentation strategies, which are all employed in self-presentation and other-presentation through discourse (S. Jäger 1993).

3.4   The Loughborough group

The sociopsychologists Margaret Wetherell and Jonathan Potter (1992) criticize the approaches of Robert Miles and of critical theory (see above) for Marxist "determinism" (Wetherell and Potter 1992: 18ff) and for a traditional Marxist concept that refers to "ideology" as "false consciousness" (Wetherell and Potter 1992). They also oppose sociocognitive approaches that give absolute priority to the cognitive dimension in the analysis of racism and tend to universalize the conditions for racism (see also Potter and Wetherell 1987) and reject the concept of an immutable identity (see also Wodak et al. 1998 for a dynamic conceptualization of "identity"), as well as social identity theory and the social cognition approach (see above) for their "lingering perceptualism" (Wetherell and Potter 1992: 69) – a critique that, in our view, is at best partly valid.

Wetherell and Potter (1992: 70) argue, instead, that attitudes and stereotypes are not simply mediated via cognition, but discourse is actively constitutive of both social and psychological processes, and thus also of racist prejudices. In the manner of Billig (1978, 1985, 1988) and Billig et al. (1988), Wetherell and Potter (1992: 59) posit that racism must be viewed as a series of ideological effects with flexible, fluid, and varying contents. Racist discourses should therefore be viewed not as static and homogeneous, but as dynamic and contradictory. Even the same person can voice contradictory opinions and ideological fragments in the same discursive event.

Wetherell and Potter (1992: 70) also sympathize with, and adopt, the concepts of the "politics of representation" and the "definitional slipperiness" of postmodern theoreticians (see e.g. Hall 1989, 1994). In part, they have been influenced theoretically by some of Foucault's theses and remarks on discourse, power, and truth, as well as by the neo-Marxist theoreticians.

Finally, like the Duisburg group and in our own discourse-historical theorization (section 3.5), the Loughborough group stresses the context dependence of racist discourse. They define their task as "mapping the language of racism" in New Zealand, and draw up a "racist topography" by charting themes and ideologies through exploration of the heterogeneous and layered texture of racist practices and representations that make up a part of the hegemonic taken-for-granted in this particular society. They bring out the ideological dilemmas and the manifest and latent argumentation patterns (Wetherell and Potter 1992: 178ff, 208ff).

Similarities between the Loughborough and Duisburg approaches go beyond emphasis on context dependence and poststructuralist alignment. Somewhat similar to the Duisburg concept of "interdiscourse" (in which the shared culture and traditions of a society at a certain time are sedimented and conceptualized as systems of collective symbols) is the Loughborough concept of "interpretative repertoire":

> broadly discernible clusters of terms, descriptions and figures of speech often assembled around metaphors or vivid images . . . systems of signification and . . . the building blocks used for manufacturing versions of actions, self and social structures in talk . . . some of the resources for making evaluations, constructing factual versions and performing particular actions. (Wetherell and Potter 1992: 90)

However, in its concrete analyses, the Loughborough group mainly focuses on narratives and argumentation and does not pay as much attention to metaphors or symbols as do Jürgen Link, Siegfried Jäger, and their associates.

3.5   The discourse-historical approach

The four discourse analytical approaches presented thus far have all influenced – either through more or less favorable reception or critical discussion – the theoretical and methodological approach we introduce in this section. We agree with many of Quasthoff's general sociopsychological assumptions of the social function of prejudices as a sociocohesive means for obtaining in-group solidarity and "phatic communion," but transcend the single-sentence perspective prevailing in her early work and also try to take into consideration the more latent and allusive meanings of discourses. We adopt several of van Dijk's concepts and categories (e.g. the notions of "positive self-presentation" and "negative other-presentation"), but put no stress on his sociocognitivism, the latter being incompatible with the hermeneutic basis of our model. Moreover, we do not want to overemphasize a top-down causality of opinion making and manipulation (i.e. a manipulative impact from the allegedly homogeneous "elite" on the allegedly homogeneous masses of ordinary people). We share the Duisburg group's transtextual, interdiscursive, sociopolitical, and historical perspective as well as their interest in the analysis of collective symbols and metaphors, but we do not align ourselves with their affiliation with Foucaultian and postmodernist theories of discourse and power, which reify or personify language and discourse as autonomous, collusive actors. We partially share the constructivist approach of Wetherell and Potter as well as their critique of universalizing the conditions for racist discrimination, though without adopting their rather relativist (postmodernist) viewpoint.

One of the most salient distinguishing features of the discourse-historical approach in comparison to the four approaches already mentioned is its endeavor to work interdisciplinarily, multimethodologically, and on the basis of a variety of different empirical data as well as background information. Depending on the object of investigation, it attempts to transcend the pure linguistic dimension and to include more or less systematically the historical, political, sociological, and/or psychological dimension in the analysis and interpretation of a specific discursive occasion (see, for example, Wodak 1986, 1991a, 1991b; Wodak et al. 1990, 1994, 1998, 1999; Mitten and Wodak 1993; Matouschek et al. 1995; Reisigl and Wodak 2001).

In accordance with other approaches devoted to critical discourse analysis (see van Dijk, this volume), the discourse-historical approach perceives both written and spoken language as a form of social practice (Fairclough 1992; 1995; Fairclough and Wodak 1997; Wodak 1996). We assume a dialectical relationship between particular discursive practices and the specific fields of action (including situations, institutional frames, and social structures) in which they are embedded: we consider discourses to be linguistic social practices that constitute nondiscursive and discursive social practices and, at the same time, are being constituted by them.

"Discourse" can be understood as a complex bundle of simultaneous and sequential interrelated linguistic acts which manifest themselves within and across the social fields of action as thematically interrelated semiotic (oral or written) tokens that belong to specific semiotic types (genres). "Fields of action" (Girnth 1996) may be understood as segments of the respective societal "reality" which contribute to constituting and shaping the "frame" of discourse. The spatiometaphorical distinction among different fields of action can be understood as a distinction among different functions or socially institutionalized aims of discursive practices. Thus in the area of political action we distinguish among the functions of legislation, self-presentation, manufacturing of public opinion, developing party-internal consent, advertising and vote-getting, governing as well as executing, and controlling as well as expressing (oppositional) dissent (see figure 19.1). A "discourse" about a specific topic can find its starting point within one field of action and proceed through another one. Discourses and discourse topics "spread" to different fields and discourses. They cross between fields, overlap, refer to each other, or are in some other way sociofunctionally linked with each other (some of these relationships are often described under such labels as "textual chains," "intertextuality," "interdiscursivity," "orders of discourse," and "hybridity"; see Fairclough 1992: 101–36; Fairclough 1995: 133). We can illustrate the connection between fields of action, genres, and discourse topics with the example of the area of political action in figure 19.1.

Field of action: lawmaking procedure	Field of action: formation of public opinion and self-presentation	Field of action: party-internal development of an informed opinion	Field of action: political advertising/propaganda	Field of action: political executive/administration	Field of action: political control
Genres: laws, bills, amendments, speeches and contributions of MPs, regulations, recommendations, prescriptions, guidelines, etc.	*Genres:* press releases, press conferences, interviews (press, TV), talk shows, "round tables," lectures/contributions to conferences, articles/books, commemorative speeches, inaugural speeches, speeches of MPs, speeches of the head, speeches of ministers	*Genres:* party programs, declarations/ statements/speeches of principle, speeches on party conventions, etc.	*Genres:* election programs, slogans, speeches in election campaigns, election announcements, posters, election brochures, direct mail advertising, fliers, etc.	*Genres:* decisions (approval/rejection: asylum, stay, work) inaugural speeches, coalition papers, speeches of ministers/heads, governmental answers to parliamentary questions	*Genres:* declarations of opposition parties, parliamentary questions, speeches of MPs, petitions for a referendum, press releases of opposition parties, etc.

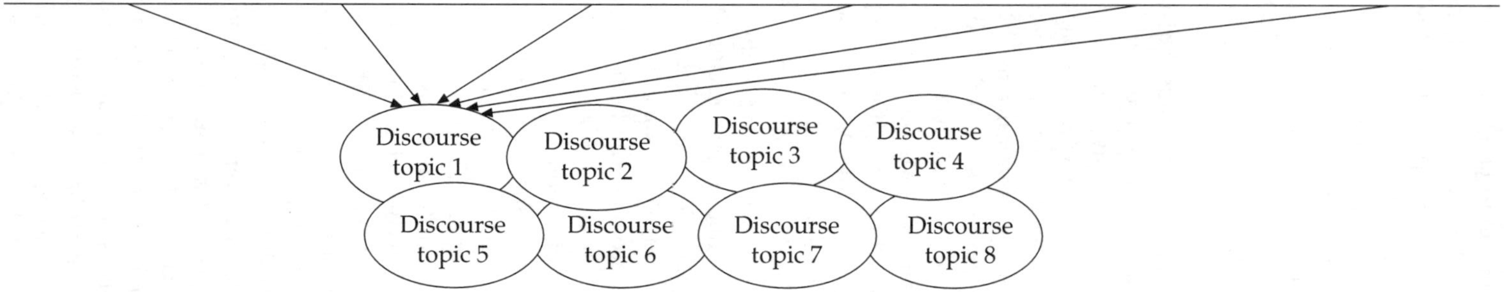

Figure 19.1

Discursive practices are socially constitutive in a number of ways: first, they play a decisive role in the genesis and production of certain social conditions. This means that discourses may serve to construct collective subjects like "races," nations, ethnicities, etc. Second, they might perpetuate, reproduce, or justify a certain social status quo (and "racialized," "nationalized," and "ethnicized" identities related to it). Third, they are instrumental in transforming the status quo (and "racializing concepts," nationalities, ethnicities related to it). Fourth, discursive practices may have an effect on the dismantling or even destruction of the status quo (and of racist, nationalist, ethnicist concepts related to it). According to these general aims one can distinguish between constructive, perpetuating, transformational, and destructive social macrofunctions of discourses.

Our triangulatory approach is based on a concept of "context" which takes into account (1) the immediate, language, or text-internal cotext, i.e. the "synsemantic environment" (see Bühler 1934) of a single utterance (lexical solidarities, collocational particularities and connotations, implications, and presuppositions as well as thematic and syntactic coherence) and the local interactive processes of negotiation and conflict management (including turn-taking, the exchange of speech acts or speech functions, mitigation, hesitation, perspectivation, etc.); (2) the intertextual and interdiscursive relationship between utterances, texts, genres, and discourses (discourse representation, allusions/evocations, etc.); (3) the language-external social/sociological variables and institutional frames of a specific "context of situation" (the formality of situation, the place, the time, the occasion of the communicative event, the group/s of recipients, the interactive/political roles of the participants, their political and ideological orientation, their sex, age, profession, and level of education as well as their ethnic, regional, national, and religious affiliation or membership, etc.); and (4) the broader sociopolitical and historical context that the discursive practices are embedded in and related to, that is to say, the fields of action and the history of the discursive event as well as the history to which the discursive topics are related.

The specific discourse analytical approach applied in the different studies carried out in Vienna during the last two decades (for the history of the discourse-historical approach see Reisigl and Wodak 2000: ch. 2, section 1.2) was three-dimensional: after (1) having found out the specific *contents* or *topics* of a specific discourse with racist, antisemitic, nationalist, or ethnicist ingredients, (2) the *discursive strategies* (including argumentation strategies) were investigated. Then (3), the *linguistic means* (as types) and the specific, context-dependent *linguistic realizations* (as tokens) of the discriminatory stereotypes were investigated.

There are several discursive elements and strategies which, in our discourse analytical view, deserve to get special attention. Picking five out of the many different linguistic or rhetorical means by which people are discriminated in ethnicist and racist terms, we orient ourselves to five simple, but not at all randomly selected, questions: (1) How are persons named and referred to linguistically? (2) Which traits, characteristics, qualities, and features are attributed to them? (3) By means of which arguments and argumentation schemes do specific persons or social groups try to justify and legitimate the exclusion, discrimination, suppression, and exploitation of others? (4) From which perspective or point of view are these nominations, attributions, and arguments expressed? (5) Are the respective discriminating utterances articulated overtly, are they even intensified, or are they mitigated?

According to these questions, we are especially interested in five types of discursive strategies which are all involved in the positive self- and negative other-presentation. By "strategy" we generally mean a more or less accurate and more or less intentional plan of practices (including discursive practices) adopted to achieve a certain social, political, psychological, or linguistic aim. As far as the discursive strategies are concerned, that is to say, systematic ways of using language, we locate them at different levels of linguistic organization and complexity.

First, there are *referential strategies* or *nomination strategies* by which one constructs and represents social actors; for example, in-groups and out-groups. Among others, this is done via membership categorization devices, including reference by tropes like biological, naturalizing, and depersonalizing metaphors and metonymies as well as by synecdoches (see Zimmerman 1990).

Second, once constructed or identified, the social actors as individuals, group members, or groups are linguistically provided with predications. *Predicational strategies* may, for example, be realized as stereotypical, evaluative attributions of negative and positive traits in the linguistic form of implicit or explicit predicates. These strategies aim at labeling social actors either positively or negatively, deprecatorily or appreciatively. Some of the referential strategies can be considered to be specific forms of predicational strategies, because the pure referential identification very often already involves a denotatively or connotatively depreciatory or appreciative labeling of the social actors.

Third, there are *argumentation strategies* and funds of *topoi*, through which positive and negative attributions are justified, through which, for example, the social and political inclusion or exclusion, and the discrimination or preferential treatment, of the respective persons or groups of persons are suggested to be warranted.

Fourth, discourse analysts may focus on the *perspectivation, framing*, or *discourse representation* by which speakers express their involvement in discourse and position their point of view in the report, description, narration, or quotation of discriminatory events.

Fifth, there are *intensifying strategies* on the one hand, and *mitigation strategies* on the other. Both of them help to qualify and modify the epistemic status of a proposition by intensifying or mitigating the illocutionary force of racist, antisemitic, nationalist, or ethnicist utterances. These strategies can be an important aspect of the presentation, inasmuch as they operate upon it by sharpening it or toning it down.

We now briefly illustrate the discourse-historical approach with an example of political discourse, taken from an interview with Jörg Haider, the leader of the Austrian Freedom Party (FPÖ). The interview was printed in the Austrian weekly *profil* on February 24, 1997, on page 19. The topic was a directive (*Weisung*) issued on November 26, 1996, by the FPÖ politician Karl-Heinz Grasser, at that time deputy head of the government of the province of Carinthia in Austria and also the highest official (*Landesrat*) in the building and tourist industries in Carinthia. In his directive, Grasser instructed his consultant (*Referenten*) for roadwork to include a regulation in the tender invitations for public building projects that such projects were exclusively to be carried out by indigenous (*heimisch*) workers or by workers from states of the European Union. As a consequence, an intense public discussion arose, and there was strong protest against Grasser's proposal to institutionalize such an exclusionary practice. Finally, Grasser revoked the directive. During the discussion, Jörg Haider was interviewed about the "Grasser affair." The journalist from *profil*, Klaus Dutzler, asked Haider what he, as leader of the FPÖ, was going to recommend to Grasser, his fellow party member and protégé at that time:

> *profil*: You will not recommend Karl-Heinz Grasser to give in?
> *Haider*: We never thought differently and will continue to do so. The indignation, of course, only comes from the side of those like the Carinthian guild master for construction, a socialist, who makes money out of cheap labor from Slovenia and Croatia. And if, today, one goes by one of Hans Peter Haselsteiner's "Illbau" building sites, and there, the foreigners, up to black Africans, cut and carry bricks, then the Austrian construction worker really thinks something. Then one must understand, if there are emotions.[13]

Haider's answer is remarkable with respect to the employed referential strategies, the negative other-presentation by the attributions and predications directed against the different groups of "them," and the enthymemic argumentation serving the justification of "emotions" against "the foreigners up to black Africans."

The social actors mentioned by the journalist are "Jörg Haider," social-deictically addressed as "Sie" (the German formal term of address), and "Karl-Heinz Grasser." The social actors mentioned by Haider are – in chronological order of their sequential appearance – "we," "the socialist Carinthian guild master for construction," "the cheap labor from Slovenia and Croatia," "the building contractor (and politician of the Austrian party Liberales Forum) Hans Peter Haselsteiner," "the foreigners," "black Africans," and "the Austrian construction worker."

There are at least three strategic moves in this short transcript from the interview. The first is the political self-presentation of the FPÖ as a party with firm positions that acts publicly in unison. Thus, Haider woos the voters' favor. According to the question asked by the journalist, one would expect an answer with a transitivity structure in which Haider (as a sayer) would recommend (a verbal or/and mental process in Halliday's 1994 terms) to Grasser (the receiver or target) that he do something (a proposal). Haider does not meet this expectation. He refuses to show himself explicitly as a leader advising his fellow party member in public (and thereby threatening Grasser's and the party's reputation) and instead finds refuge in a referentially ambiguous "we" (rather than using the expected "I"), which helps to evade the exclusive referential focus both on Grasser and on himself. The ambivalent "we" allows for different, although not mutually exclusive, interpretations. On the one hand, it can be understood as a "party-we" which is designated to demonstrate a closed, unanimous, fixed position of the whole party on the issue in question. The temporal deixis by past and future tense backs this conjecture. If one knows the history of the FPÖ and the fact that Haider has been an authoritarian party leader since he came into power in 1986, on the other hand, one is led to interpret the "we" as a sort of *pluralis maiestatis* that is employed to regulatively prescribe how the party members of the FPÖ are required to think at that moment and in future.

However, after having introduced this ambiguous "we," which, in addition to having the two functions just mentioned, invites the potential voters of the FPÖ to acclaim or join Haider's position, Haider then sets out to present the critics of the directive negatively. This is the second strategic move. Haider deliberately chooses two prominent critics (who are also political adversaries) as *partes pro toto* in the groups of critics. He debases the socialist Carinthian guild master (whom he does not identify by proper name) by depicting him as an unsocial, capitalist socialist who exploits "the cheap labor (*Arbeitskräfte*) from Slovenia and Croatia" (here, one may take note of Haider's impersonal and abstract reference to human beings as a cheap labor force). This image of the unsocial capitalist who egoistically wants to profit from wage dumping is also inferentially passed on to the second political opponent mentioned by Haider. (We can assume that the reader knows from the Austrian political context that the building contractor, Hans Peter Haselsteiner, is a politician.) Viewed from an argumentation analytical perspective, Haider argues here at one and the same time *secundum quid*, i.e. taking a part (as = two critics) for the whole (as = for all critics of Grasser's directive), and *ad hominem*, i.e. he employs a fallacy of relevance (see Lanham 1991: 779), and he disparages the character of the critics in order to call into question the credibility of all critics – instead of attacking their arguments.

The third strategic move by Haider is partly embedded in the negative presentation of Hans Peter Haselsteiner. It is realized as an imaginary scenario (with the character of an argumentative *exemplum*) and aims to justify the "emotions" of hostility toward foreigners. This move relies on a shift of responsibility, in rhetorical terms, on a *traiectio in alium* that places the blames on Haselsteiner and the socialist Carinthian guild master, instead of on those who have racist "emotions" and instead of on Haider himself (for instigating polulism).

Haider's third move contains a blatant racist utterance. Here, the party leader discursively constructs a discriminatory hierarchy of "foreigners" around the phenotypic feature of skin color – strictly speaking, around the visible "deviation" (the color black) of a specific group of "foreigners" (i.e. black Africans) from the "average white Austrian." Most probably it is no accident that Haider refers to "black Africans," that is to say, that he explicitly uses the word "black." In the context given, the attribute "black" has an intensifying function. It helps Haider (who, though he explicitly denies it later on in the interview, wants to emotionalize) to carry his black-and-white portrayal to extremes in a literal sense as well. Haider seems to intend to construct the greatest possible visual difference between Austrians and "foreigners." His utterance can thus be seen as an example of "differentialist racism" in its literal sense. The out-groups of "the foreigners, up to black Africans" (the definite article is characteristic for stereotypical discourse) employed as construction workers are opposed to the in-group of construction workers. Haider apostrophizes the latter synecdochically as "the Austrian construction worker". As their self-appointed spokesman, he asks for understanding for the Austrian workers' "emotions" in the face of the "foreigners, up to black Africans."[14]

At this point, Haider does not argue why "one" should understand the "emotions." He simply relies on the discriminatory prejudice (functioning as an inferable "warrant" in this enthymemic argumentation) that "foreigners" take away working places from "in-group members." Furthermore, he relies on the unspoken postulate that "Austrians," in comparison with "foreigners," should be privileged with respect to employment.

However, it is not just Haider's argumentation that is shortened, incomplete, and vague. In particular, the naming of the prejudicial (mental, attitudinal), verbal, and actional hostilities to "foreigners" is extremely evasive and euphemistic in Haider's utterance. In this regard, Haider exclusively identifies and names mental and emotional processes: with respect to "foreigners" (including black Africans), "the Austrian construction worker" is clearly thinking of something (the German particle *schon* ("really") serves here as an inference-triggering device that suggests comprehensibility). And in his last sentence, Haider deposits a very euphemistic concluding overall claim with an instigatory potential: "one" is obligated ("must") to be understanding if there are emotions. In other words, the "emotions," and whatever the reader of Haider's interview connects with this nonspecific cover-term that opens the way to a vast variety of associations, are totally justifiable.

4   Conclusion

In this chapter, we have provided an overview of definitions of "race" and explanations of "racism," as well as a synopsis of five discourse analytical approaches to the problem of racism, and an illustration of the discourse-historical approach. Our discussion has shown that racism remains a multifaceted and theoretically complex issue that leaves us without comprehensive answers to many questions: what exactly are we supposed to take "racist" and "racism" to mean? Which specific forms of "genetic," "culturalist," and "institutional racism" do we nowadays face and what causes them? How do these different forms of racism manifest themselves in discourse? Is it possible to delimit racism from adjacent or possibly overlapping discriminatory phenomena like antisemitism, nationalism, ethnicism, and sexism? Which analytical – including discourse analytical – criteria, if any, can be used to set at least somewhat clear boundaries between these different "-isms"? Despite the vast amount of specialist literature in the areas of social science, history, philosophy, and even discourse analysis, these are only a small number of the many questions that still await satisfactory answers. We hope to have suggested some of the paths that can be taken toward such answers.

NOTES

1   The contribution of philology and linguistics to the construction and taxonomization of "races" and to the legitimation of racism was an extraordinarily inglorious one. Apart from the synecdochical usurpation and generalization and the mythicalization of the "Aryan" (see Poliakov 1993; Römer 1985; Conze and Sommer 1984: 159), philology and linguistics are responsible for at least three serious faults, viz. (1) for the confusion of language relationship and speaker relationship, (2) for the discriminatory hierarchy of languages and language types, and (3) for the metaphorical, naturalizing description of languages as organisms which provided the basis for the connection and approximation of race and language classifications (see Römer 1985).

2   We omit discussion of language-specific usage of the term "race" in

reference to animals, plants, and even extrabiological groupings of things, such as "type" or "sort" (see Il Nuovo Dizionario di Garzanti 1984: 725; Duden 1989: 1214f).

3 The terms "antisemitism" and "antisemitic", which *post festum* cover the whole range of religious, economist, nationalist, socialist, Marxist, culturalist, and racist prejudicial aversion and aggression against Jews, were most probably coined in 1879 in the agitational, antisemitic circle of the German writer Wilhelm Marr (see Nipperdey and Rürup 1972). At that time the word "antisemitic" was employed as a self-descriptive, political "fighting word." In 1935, the National Socialist ministry of propaganda (*"Reichspropagandaministerium"*) issued a language regulation in which it prescribed that the term should be avoided in the press and replaced with the term "anti-Jewish" ("antijüdisch"), "for the German policy only aims at the Jews, not at the Semites as a whole" (quoted from Nipperdey and Rürup 1972: 151). Undoubtedly, the term "antisemitic" has been used in postwar Germany and in postwar Austria more often than during the National Socialist reign of terror. This is because the term has become a politically "stigmatic word" for describing others and its meaning has been expanded in the analysis of anti-Jewish aggression throughout history.

4 The term "racism," with its suffix "-ism," which denotes a theory, doctrine, or school of thought as well as the related behavior (Fleischer/ Barz 1992: 190), was probably first used in a title for an unpublished German book by Magnus Hirschfeld in 1933/4. In this book, which was translated and published in English in 1938, Hirschfeld argued against the pseudoscientifically backed contention that there exists a hierarchy of biologically distinct "races" (see Miles 1993: 29). The actual linguistic "career" of the term started in the postwar period (Sondermann 1995: 47).

5 For a similar critique see Claussen (1994: 2), who complains that in the public world (*"Weltöffentlichkeit"*) almost all violent social tension in the United States, for example the street fights in Los Angeles in 1992, are reported as "race riots" – "a headword that seems to make superfluous every analysis."

6 For a critique of the notion of "collective identity" see Berger and Luckman (1980: 185) and Wodak et al. (1998: 58); for a critique of the terminological confusion see below.

7 Postmodernists are not completely consistent in their refusal of "metanarratives" and large-sized "collective subjects." Rattansi (1994), for example, makes use of the abstract notion of "Western identities" as completely unquestioned reified entities.

8 Wieviorka (1991, 1994) relates racism to modernity as well. He holds the view that the current spread of racism has to do with the actual destructuration of industrial societies, with increasing difficulties of state and public institutions, and with the ongoing transformations of national identities (for a critique of Wieviorka's postindustrial framework see Miles 1994).

9 For the concepts of "social" and "linguistic prejudice" see also Heinemann (1998).

10 Van Dijk does not neatly distinguish between ethnicism, racism and adjacent forms of discrimination (for a recent discussion of these concepts see also van Dijk et al. 1997), as he believes that they are fuzzy and overlapping concepts.

11 Margret Jäger adopts the same theoretical framework as Siegfried Jäger. One of her main interests is the relationship between gender and racism. In her analysis of interviews, she proves that sexism and racism are interconnected in multiple ways, especially in discourse about Turkish men and women (see M. Jäger 1996). We are limited by considerations of space and so omit discussion of this issue to concentrate on the theoretical and methodical innovations proposed by the Duisburg group.

12 A "discourse fragment" is a text or a part of a text that deals with a specific topic; for example, with the topic of "foreigners" and "foreigner issues" (in the widest sense) (S. Jäger 1993: 181).

13 The excerpt in the original German is as follows:

> *profil*: Sie werden Karl-Heinz Grasser nicht empfehlen nachzugeben?
> *Haider*: Wir haben zu keiner Zeit anders gedacht und

werden das weiter tun. Die Empörung kommt ohnehin nur aus der Richtung jener wie dem Kärntner Bau-Innungsmeister, einem Sozialisten, der sein Geschäft mit Billigarbeitskräften aus Slowenien und Kroatien macht. Und wenn man heute in Kärnten an einer Illbau-Baustelle von Hans Peter Haselsteiner vorbeigeht und dort die Ausländer bis hin zu Schwarzafrikanern Ziegel schneiden und tragen, dann denkt sich der österreichische Bauarbeiter schon etwas. Da muß man verstehen, wenn es Emotionen gibt.

14 The racist intensification "up to black Africans" implies that in Austria, black African workers, because of their most visible "otherness," are "an even worse evil" than other "foreigners," and therefore functions as argumentative backing.

REFERENCES

Adorno, T. W. (1973). *Studien zum autoritären Charakter*. Frankfurt: Suhrkamp.

Adorno, T. W. (1993). Antisemitismus und faschistische Propaganda. In E. Simmel (ed.), *Antisemitismus* (pp. 148–61). Frankfurt: Fischer.

Adorno, T. W., Fränkel-Brunswik, E., Levinson, D. J., and Stanford, P. N. (1950). *The Authoritarian Personality*. New York: American Jewish Committee.

Allport, G. W. (1993). Vorwort. In E. Simmel (ed.), *Antisemitismus* (pp. 9–11). Frankfurt: Fischer.

Bauman, Z. (1989). *Modernity and the Holocaust*. Cambridge: Polity.

Bauman, Z. (1991). *Modernity and Ambivalence*. Cambridge: Polity.

Berger, P. and Luckman, T. (1980). *Die gesellschaftliche Konstruktion der Wirklichkeit. Eine Theorie der Wissenssoziologie*. Frankfurt: Fischer.

Bhabha, H. K. (ed.) (1990). *Nation and Narration*. London and New York: Routledge and Kegan Paul.

Billig, M. (1978). *Facists. A Social Psychological Analysis of the National Front*. London: Academic Press.

Billig, M. (1985). Prejudice, categorisation and particularisation. From a perceptual to a rhetorical approach. *European Journal of Social Psychology*, 15, 79–103.

Billig, M. (1988). The notion of "prejudice." Some rhetorical and ideological aspects. *Text*, 8, 91–111.

Billig, M., Condor, S., Edwards, D., Gane, M., Middleton, D., and Radley, A. (1988). *Ideological Dilemmas. A Social Psychology of Everyday Thinking.* London: Sage.

Bühler, K. (1934). *Sprachtheorie. Die Darstellungsfunktion der Sprache.* Stuttgart and New York: Gustav Fischer.

Castles, S. and Kosack, G. (1972). The function of labour immigration in Western European capitalism. *New Left Review*, 73, 3–21.

Castles, S. and Kosack, G. (1973). *Immigrant Workers and Class Structure in Western Europe.* London: Oxford University Press.

CCCS/Centre for Contemporary Cultural Studies (ed.) (1982). *The Empire Strikes Back. Race and Racism in 70s Britain.* London: Hutchinson/Centre for Contemporary Cultural Studies.

Claussen, D. (1994). *Was heißt Rassismus?* Darmstadt: Wissenschaftliche Buchgesellschaft.

Conze, W. and Sommer, A. (1984). Rasse. In O. Brunner, W. Conze, and R. Koselleck (eds), *Geschichtliche Grundbegriffe: historisches Lexikon zur politisch-sozialen Sprache in Deutschland. Volume 5: Pro-Soz* (pp. 135–77). Stuttgart: Klett-Cotta.

Cox, O. C. (1970). *Caste, Class and Race.* New York: Monthly Review Press.

Duden. (1989). *Deutsches Universalwörterbuch A–Z* (2nd edn). Mannheim, Vienna, and Zurich: Duden.

Fairclough, N. (1992). *Discourse and Social Change.* Oxford and Cambridge, MA: Polity and Blackwell.

Fairclough, N. (1995). *Critical Discourse Analysis: The Critical Study of Language.* London and New York: Longman.

Fairclough, N. and Wodak, R. (1997). Critical discourse analysis. In T. A. van Dijk (ed.), *Discourse as Social Interaction. Discourse Studies: A Multidisciplinary Introduction, Volume 2* (pp. 258–84). London, New Delhi, and Thousand Oaks: Sage.

Fanon, F. (1986). *Black Skin, White Masks.* London: Pluto Press.

Fenichel, O. (1993). Elemente einer psychoanalytischen Theorie des Antisemitismus. In E. Simmel (ed.), *Antisemitismus* (pp. 35–57). Frankfurt: Fischer.

Fleischer, W. and Barz, I. (1992). *Wortbildung der deutschen Gegenwartssprache.* Tübingen: Niemeyer.

Fox-Genovese, E. (1992). *Within the Plantation Household. Black and White Women of the Old South.* Chapel Hill, NC: University of North Carolina Press.

Fromm, E. (1988). *Die Furcht vor der Freiheit (Escape from Freedom).* Frankfurt: Ullstein.

Frosh, S. (1987). *The Politics of Psychoanalysis.* London: Macmillan.

Frosh, S. (1989). Psychoanalysis and racism. In B. Richards (ed.), *Crisis of the Self.* London: Free Association Books.

Frosh, S. (1991). *Identity Crisis. Modernity, Psychoanalysis and the Self.* London: Macmillan.

Genovese, E. D. (1995). *The Southern Front. History and Politics in the Cultural War.* Columbia, MO: University of Missouri Press.

Gilroy, P. (1987). *"There Ain't No Black in the Union Jack." The Cultural Politics of Race and Nation.* London: Hutchinson.

Girnth, H. (1996). Texte im politischen Diskurs. Ein Vorschlag zur diskursorientierten Beschreibung von Textsorten. *Muttersprache*, 106/1/96, 66–80.

Goldberg, D. T. (1993). *Racist Culture. Philosophy and the Politics of Meaning.* Oxford: Blackwell.

Guillaumin, C. (1991). RASSE. Das Wort und die Vorstellung. In U. Bielefeld (ed.), *Das Eigene und das Fremde.* *Neuer Rassismus in der Alten Welt* (pp. 159–73). Hamburg: Junius.

Guillaumin, C. (1992). Zur Bedeutung des Begriffs "Rasse". In Institut für Migration und Rassismusforschung e.V. (ed.), *Rassismus und Migration in Europa.* Beiträge des Kongresses "Migration und Rassismus in Europa" Hamburg, 26 bis 30 September 1990 (pp. 77–87). Hamburg, Berlin: Argument.

Hall, S. (1978). Racism and reaction. In Commission for Racial Equality (ed.), *Five Views of Multi-Racial Britain* (pp. 22–35). London: Commission for Racial Equality.

Hall, S. (1980). Race, articulation, and societies structured in dominance. In UNESCO (ed.), *Sociological Theories. Race and Colonialism* (pp. 305–45). Paris: UNESCO.

Hall, S. (1989). Rassismus als ideologischer Diskurs. *Das Argument*, 178, 913–21.

Hall, S. (1994). *Rassismus und kulturelle Identität. Selected Writings 2.* Hamburg, Berlin: Argument.

Halliday, M. A. K. (1994). *An Introduction to Function Grammar* (2nd edn). London: Edward Arnold.

Hamilton, D. and Trolier, T. (1986). Stereotypes and stereotyping. An overview of the cognitive approach. In J. F. Dovidio and S. L. Gaertner (eds), *Prejudice, Discrimination, and Racism.* Orlando, FL: Academic Press.

Heinemann, M. (ed.) (1998). *Sprachliche und soziale Stereotype.* Frankfurt: Lang.

Hirschfeld, M. (1938). *Racism.* London: Gollancz, Ryerson Press.

Hogg, M. A. and Abrahams, D. (1988). *Social Identifications.* London: Routledge and Kegan Paul.

Horkheimer, M. (1992). *Traditionelle und Kritische Theorie. Fünf Aufsätze.* Frankfurt: Suhrkamp.

Horkheimer, M. and Flowerman, S. H. (eds) (1949). *Studies in Prejudice.* New York: American Jewish Committee.

Horkheimer, M., Fromm, E., Marcuse, H., Mayer, H., Wittfogel, K. A., and Honigsheim, P. (1987). *Studien über Autorität und Familie. Forschungsberichte aus dem Institut für Sozialforschung* (2nd edn). Klampen.

Il Nuovo Dizionario di Garzanti. (1984). Milan: Garzanti.

Jacoby, R. (1983). *Die Verdrängung der Psychoanalyse oder Der Triumph des Konformismus.* Frankfurt: Fischer.

Jacquard, A. (1996). Ein unwissenschaftlicher Begriff. *Unesco-Kurier*, 3, 18–21.

Jäger, M. (1996). *Fatale Effekte. Die Kritik am Patriarchat im Einwanderungsdiskurs.* Duisburg: DISS.

Jäger, M., Cleve, G., Ruth, I., and Jäger S. (1998). *Von deutschen Einzeltätern und ausländischen Banden. Medien und Straftaten. Mit Vorschlägen zur Vermeidung diskriminierender Berichterstattung.* Duisburg: DISS.

Jäger, S. (1992). *BrandSätze. Rassismus im Alltag.* Duisburg: DISS.

Jäger, S. (1993). *Kritische Diskursanalyse. Eine Einführung.* Duisburg: DISS.

Jäger, S. and Jäger, M. (eds) (1992). *Aus der Mitte der Gesellschaft (I–IV). Zu den Ursachen von Rechtsextremismus und Rassismus in Europa.* Duisburg: DISS.

Jäger, S. and Januschek, F. (eds) (1992). *Der Diskurs des Rassismus. Ergebnisse des DISS-Kolloquiums November 1991.* Osnabrück: Redaktion Obst (OBST 46).

Jäger, S. and Link, J. (eds) (1993). *Die vierte Gewalt. Rassismus in den Medien.* Duisburg: DISS.

Jung, M., Wengeler, M., and Böke, K. (eds) (1997). *Die Sprache des Migrationsdiskurses. Das Reden über "Ausländer" in Medien, Politik und Alltag.* Opladen: Westdeutscher Verlag.

Kalpaka, A. and Räthzel, N. (eds) (1986). *Die Schwierigkeit, nicht rassistisch zu sein.* Berlin: Express Edition.

Lanham, R. A. (1991). *A Handlist of Rhetorical Terms* (2nd edn). Berkeley: University of California Press.

Lawrence, E. (1982). Just plain common sense. The "roots" of racism. In CCCS (eds), *The Empire Strikes Back. Race and Racism in 70s Britain* (pp. 47–94). London: Hutchinson/CCCS.

Link, J. (1982). Kollektivsymbolik und Mediendiskurse. *kultuRRevolution*, 1, 6–21.

Link, J. (1988). Über Kollektivsymbolik im politischen Diskurs und ihren Anteil an totalitären Tedenzen. *kultuRRevolution*, 17/18, 47–53.

Link, J. (1990). *Schönhuber in der Nationalelf. Halbrechts, rechtsaußen oder im Abseits? Die politische Kollektivsymbolik der Bundesrepublik und der Durchbruch der neorassistischen Schönhuberpartei.* Duisburg: DISS.

Link, J. (1992). Die Analyse der symbolischen Komponenten realer Ereignisse. Ein Beitrag der Diskurstheorie zur Analyse neorassistischer Äußerungen. In S. Jäger and F. Januschek, (eds), *Der Diskurs des Rassismus. Ergebnisse des DISS-Kolloquiums November 1991* (pp. 37–52). Osnabrück: Redaktion Obst (OBST 46).

Lyotard, J.-F. (1984). *The Postmodern Condition. A Report of Knowledge.* Manchester: Manchester University Press.

Masson, J. M. (1984). *The Assault on Truth. Freud's Suppression of the Seduction Theory.* New York: Farrar, Strauss and Giroux.

Matouschek, B., Wodak, R., and Januschek, F. (1995). *Notwendige Massnahmen gegen Fremde? Genese und Formen von rassistischen Diskursen der Differenz.* Vienna: Passagen Verlag.

Mecheril, P. and Thomas T. (eds) (1997). *Psychologie und Rassismus.* Reinbeck bei Hamburg: Rowohl.

Miles, R. (1991). Die Idee der "Rasse" und Theorien über Rassismus:

Überlegungen zur britischen Diskussion. In U. Bielefeld (ed.), *Das Eigene und das Fremde. Neuer Rassismus in der alten Welt* (pp. 189–218). Hamburg: Junius.

Miles, R. (1993). *Racism after "Race Relations."* London: Routledge and Kegan Paul.

Miles, R. (1994). Explaining racism in contemporary Europe. In A. Rattansi and S. Westwood (eds), *Racism, Modernity and Identity. On the Western Front* (pp. 189–221). Cambridge: Polity.

Miles, R. and Phizacklea, A. (eds) (1979). *Racism and Political Action in Britain.* London: Routledge and Kegan Paul.

Mitten, R. and Wodak, R. (1993). On the discourse of racism and prejudice. In *Folia Linguistica. Acta Societatis Linguisticae Europaeae*, XXVII/3–4, special issue: *Discourse Analysis and Racist Talk* (pp. 191–215). Berlin and New York: de Gruyter.

Nikolinakos, M. (1975). Notes towards a general theory of migration in late capitalism. *Capital and Class*, 17/1, 5–18.

Nipperdey, T. and Rürup, R. (1972). Antisemitismus. In O. Brunner, W. Conze, and R. Koselleck (eds), (1984), *Geschichtliche Grundbegriffe: historisches Lexikon zur politisch-sozialen Sprache in Deutschland. Volume 1: A–D.* (pp. 129–53). Stuttgart: Klett-Cotta.

Ottomeyer, K. (1997). Psychoanalytische Erklärungsansätze zum Rassismus. Möglichkeiten und Grenzen. In P. Mecheril and T. Thomas (eds), *Psychologie und Rassismus* (pp. 111–31). Reinbeck bei Hamburg: Rowohl.

Outlaw, L. (1990). Toward a critical theory of "race." In: T. D. Goldberg (ed.), *Anatomy of Racism* (pp. 58–82). Minneapolis and London: University of Minnesota Press.

Poliakov, L. (1993). *Der arische Mythos. Zu den Quellen von Rassismus und Nationalismus.* Hamburg: Junius.

Poliakov, L., Delacampagne, C., and Girard, P. (1992). *Rassismus. Über Fremdenfeindlichkeit und Rassenwahn.* Hamburg and Zurich: Luchterhand.

Potter, J. and Wetherell, M. (1987). *Discourse and Social Psychology. Beyond Attitudes and Behaviour.* London: Sage.

Quasthoff, U. (1973). *Soziales Vorurteil und Kommunikation. Eine sprachwissenschaftliche Analyse des Stereotyps.* Frankfurt: Athenäum.

Quasthoff, U. (1978). The uses of stereotype in everyday argument. *Journal of Pragmatics,* 2/1, 1–48.

Quasthoff, U. (1980). *Erzählen in Gesprächen. Linguistische Untersuchungen zu Strukturen und Funktionen am Beispiel einer Kommunikationsform des Alltags.* Tübingen: Narr.

Quasthoff, U. (1987). Linguistic prejudice/stereotypes. In U. Ammon, N. Dittmar, and K. Mattheier (eds), *Sociolinguistics/Soziolinguistik. An International Handbook of the Science of Language and Society/Ein internationales Handbuch zur Wissenschaft von Sprache und Gesellschaft.* Vol. 1/Erster Halbband (pp. 785–99). Berlin and New York: de Gruyter.

Quasthoff, U. (1989). Social prejudice as a resource of power: towards the functional ambivalence of stereotypes. In R. Wodak (ed.), *Language, Power, and Ideology* (pp. 137–63). Amsterdam: Benjamins.

Quasthoff, U. (1998). Stereotype in Alltagsargumentationen. Ein Beitrag zur Dynamisierung der Stereotypenforschung. In M. Heinemann (ed.), *Sprachliche und soziale Stereotype* (pp. 47–72). Frankfurt: Lang.

Rattansi, A. (1994). "Western" racism, ethnicities, and identities in a "postmodern" frame. In A. Rattansi and S. Westwood (eds), *Racism, Modernity and Identity. On the Western Front* (pp. 15–86). Cambridge: Polity.

Rattansi, A. and Westwood, S. (eds) (1994). *Racism, Modernity and Identity. On the Western Front.* Cambridge: Polity.

Reich, W. (1986). *Die Massenpsychologie des Faschismus.* Cologne: Kiepenheuer und Witsch.

Reisigl, M. and Wodak, R. (2001). *Discourse and Discrimination. Rhetorics of Racism and Antisemitism.* London and New York: Routledge and Kegan Paul.

Römer, R. (1989). *Sprachwissenschaft und Rassenideologie in Deutschland* (2nd edn). Munich: Fink.

Said, E. W. (1978). *Orientalism.* Harmondsworth: Penguin.

Said, E. W. (1993). *Culture and Imperialism.* New York: Knopf.

Simmel, E. (ed.) (1993). *Antisemitismus.* Frankfurt: Fischer.

Sivanandan, A. (1982). *A Different Hunger. Writings on Black Resistance.* London: Pluto Press.

Sivanandan, A. (1990). *Communities of Resistance. Writings on Black Struggles for Socialism.* London: Verso.

Sondermann, K. (1995). *O Deutschland! Oi Suomi! Vielgeliebtes Österreich! Zur politischen und gesellschaftlichen Karriere vorgestellter Wesen.* University of Tampere: Forschungsinstitut für Sozialwissenschaften.

Szymanski, A. (1985). *The structure of race. Review of Radical Political Economics,* 17/4, 106–20.

Taguieff, P.-A. (1987). *La Force du Préjugé Essai sur le racisme et ses doubles.* Paris: Editions La Découverte.

Tajfel, H. (1981). *Human Groups and Social Categories. Studies in Social Psychology.* Cambridge: Cambridge University Press.

Tajfel, H. and Turner, J. C. (1985). The social identity theory of intergroup behaviour. In S. Worchel and W. G. Austin (eds), *Psychology of Intergroup Relations* (pp. 7–24). Chicago, Ill.: Nelson-Hall.

Toulmin, S. (1969). *The Uses of Argument.* Cambridge: Cambridge University Press.

Turner, J. C. (1981). The experimental social psychology of intergroup behaviour. In J. C. Turner and H. Giles (eds), *Intergroup Behaviour* (pp. 66–101). Oxford: Blackwell.

Turner, J. C. (1985). Social categorisation and the self-concept: a social cognitive theory of group behaviour. In J. Lawler (ed.), *Advances in Group Processes, Vol. 2* (pp. 77–102). Greenwich: JAI Press.

Turner, J. C. and Giles, H. (eds), (1981). *Intergroup Behaviour.* Oxford: Blackwell.

Turner, J. C., Hogg, M. A., Oakes, P., Reicher, S., and Wetherell, M. (1987). *Rediscovering the Social Group. A Self-Categorisation Theory.* Oxford: Blackwell.

van Dijk, T. (1984). *Prejudice in Discourse.* Amsterdam: Benjamins.

van Dijk, T. (1991). *Racism and the Press. Critical Studies in Racism and Migration.* London: Routledge and Kegan Paul.

van Dijk, T. (1993). *Elite Discourse and Racism.* Newbury Park, CA: Sage.

van Dijk, T. (1998a). Context models in discourse processing. In H. Oostendorp and S. Goldman (eds), *The Construction of Mental Models during Reading* (pp. 123–48). Mahwah, NJ: Erlbaum.

van Dijk, T. (1998b). *Ideology. A Multidisciplinary Study.* London: Sage.

van Dijk, T., Ting-Toomey, S., Smitterman, G., and Troutman, D. (1997). Discourse, ethnicity, culture and racism. In T. A. van Dijk (ed.), *Discourse as Social Interaction. Vol. 2* (pp. 144–80). London: Sage.

Wallerstein, I. (1979). *The Capitalist World-Economy.* Cambridge: Cambridge University Press.

Wallerstein, I. (1988). Universalisme, racisme, sexisme. Les tensions ideologiques du capitalisme. In E. Balibar and I. Wallerstein (1988), *Race, Nation, Classe. Les Identités Ambigues.* Paris: Editions La Découverte.

Westwood, S. (1994). Racism, mental illness and the politics of identity. In A. Rattansi and S. Westwood. (eds), *Racism, Modernity and Identity. On the Western Front* (pp. 247–65). Cambridge: Polity.

Wetherell, M. and Potter, J. (1992). *Mapping the Language of Racism. Discourse and the Legitimation of Exploitation.* New York: Harvester Wheatsheaf.

Wieviorka, M. (1991). *The Arena of Racism.* London: Sage.

Wieviorka, M. (1994). Racism in Europe: unity and diversity. In A. Rattansi and S. Westwood (eds), *Racism, Modernity and Identity. On the Western Front* (pp. 173–88). Cambridge: Polity.

Wodak, R. (1986). *Language Behavior in Therapy Groups.* Los Angeles: University of California Press.

Wodak, R. (1991a). Turning the tables. Antisemitic discourse in post-war Austria. *Discourse and Society,* 2/1, 65–84.

Wodak, R. (1991b). The Waldheim affair and antisemitic prejudice in Austrian public discourse. *Patterns of Prejudice,* 24/2–4, 18–33.

Wodak, R. (1996). *Disorders of Discourse.* London: Longman.

Wodak, R., De Cillia, R., Reisigl, M., and Liebhart, K. (1999). *The Discursive Construction of National Identity.* Edinburgh: Edinburgh University Press.

Wodak, R., Menz, F., Mitten, R., and Stern, F. (1994). *Die Sprachen der Vergangenheiten.* Frankfurt: Suhrkamp.

Wodak, R., De Cillia, R., Reisigl, M., Liebhart, K., Hofstätter, K., and Kargl, M. (1998). *Zur Konstruktion nationaler Identität.* Frankfurt: Suhrkamp.

Wodak, R., Nowak P., Pelikan, J., Gruber, H., De Cillia, R. and Mitten, R. (1990). *"Wir sind alle unschuldige Täter."* *Diskurshistorische Studien zum Nachkriegsantisemitismus*. Frankfurt: Suhrkamp.

Zerger, J. (1997). *Was ist Rassismus? Eine Einführung*. Göttingen: Lamuv.

Zimmerman, E. N. (1990). Identity and difference: the logic of synecdochic reasoning. *Texte. Revue de critique et de Théorie Litteraire 1988*, 8/9, 25–62.

20 Political Discourse

JOHN WILSON

0 Introduction

The study of political discourse, like that of other areas of discourse analysis, covers a broad range of subject matter, and draws on a wide range of analytic methods. Perhaps more than with other areas of discourse, however, one needs at the outset to consider the reflexive and potentially ambiguous nature of the term *political discourse*. The term is suggestive of at least two possibilities: first, a discourse which is itself political; and second, an analysis of political discourse as simply an example discourse type, without explicit reference to political content or political context. But things may be even more confusing. Given that on some definitions almost all discourse may be considered political (Shapiro 1981), then all *analyses* of discourse are potentially political, and, therefore, on one level, *all* discourse analysis is political discourse.

This potentially confusing situation arises, in the main, from definitions of the political in terms of general issues such as *power, conflict, control*, or *domination* (see Fairclough 1992a, 1995; Giddens 1991; Bourdieu 1991; van Dijk 1993; Chilton and Schaffer 1997), since any of these concepts may be employed in almost any form of discourse. Recently, for example, in a study of a psychotherapeutic training institution, Diamond (1995) refers to her study of the discourse of staff meetings as "political," simply because issues of power and control are being worked out. They are being worked out at different levels, however: at interpersonal, personal, institutional, and educational levels for example, and in different strategic ways (Chilton 1997). By treating all discourse as *political*, in its most general sense, we may be in danger of significantly overgeneralizing the concept of *political discourse*.

Perhaps we might avoid these difficulties if we simply delimited our subject matter as being concerned with formal/informal political contexts and political actors (Graber 1981); with, that is, *inter alia*, politicians, political institutions, governments, political media, and political supporters operating in political environments to achieve political goals. This first approximation makes clearer the kinds of limits we might place on thinking about political discourse, but it may also allow for development. For example, analysts who themselves wish to present a political case become, in one sense, political actors, and their own discourse becomes, therefore, political. In this sense much of what is referred to as *critical linguistics* (Fairclough 1992b) or *critical discourse analysis* (van Dijk 1993; Wodak 1995) relates directly to work on political discourse, not only because the material for analysis is often formally political but also, perhaps, because the analysts have explicitly made themselves political actors (see van Dijk, this volume).

But such a delimitation, like all delimitations, is not without its problems. For example, how do we deal with the work of Liebes and Ribak (1991) on family discussions of political events? Is this political discourse, or family discourse of the political? In one sense it is both – but the issue of which may simply be a matter of emphasis (see, for example, Ochs and Taylor 1992). While delimitations of the political are difficult to maintain in exact terms, they are nevertheless useful starting points. Equally, while one can accept that it is difficult to imagine a fully objective and nonpolitical account of political discourse, analysts can, at best, and indeed should, make clear their own motivations and perspectives. This may range from setting some form of "democratic" ideal for discourse against which other forms of political discourse are then assessed (Gastil 1993) to explicitly stating one's political goals in targeting political discourse for analysis (as in the case of a number of critical linguists: Fairclough 1995; Wodak 1995; van Dijk 1993). It also allows for more descriptive perspectives (Wilson 1990, 1996; Geis 1987), where the main goal is to consider political language first as discourse, and only secondly as politics. The general approach advocated above would respond to the criticism of Geis (1987), who argues that many studies of political language reveal their own political bias. Most of us who write about political discourse may do this at some level, but as long as this is either made clear, or explicitly accepted as a possibility, then this seems acceptable.

1   Studying Political Discourse

The study of political discourse has been around for as long as politics itself. The emphasis the Greeks placed on rhetoric is a case in point. From Cicero (1971) to Aristotle (1991) the concern was basically with particular methods of social and political competence in achieving specific objectives. While Aristotle gave a more formal twist to these overall aims, the general principle of articulating information on policies and actions for the public good remained constant. This general approach is continued today.

Modern rhetorical studies are more self-conscious, however, and interface with aspects of communication science, historical construction, social theory, and political science (for an overview see Gill and Whedbee 1997). While there has been a long tradition of interest in political discourse, if one strictly defines political discourse analysis in broadly linguistic terms (as perhaps all forms of discourse analysis should be defined: see Fairclough and Wodak 1997), it is only since the early 1980s or 1990s that work in this area has come to the fore. Indeed, Geis (1987) argues that his is the first text with a truly linguistic focus on political language/discourse. There is some merit in this argument, but without opening up issues about what is and what is not linguistics, many of the earlier studies in *social semiotics* and *critical linguistics* should also be included in a general linguistic view of political discourse (Fowler et al. 1979; Chilton 1990, 1985; Steiner 1985). While language is always clearly central to political discourse, what shifts is the balance between linguistic analysis and political comment. Distinguishing the direction of this balance, however, is not always straightforward.

2   Political Discourse: Representation and Transformation

In more modern times it was perhaps Orwell who first drew our attention to the political potential of language. This is seen in his classic article "Politics and the English Language," where he considers the way in which language may be used to manipulate thought and suggests, for example, that "political speech and writing are largely the defence of the indefensible" (1969: 225). His examples are types of inverted logic (reflected in literary detail in his book *Nineteen Eighty Four*) and they echo through much of the present work on political discourse. Instances include the use of "pacification" to refer to the bombing of defenseless villages, or the use of "rectification of frontiers" to refer to the relocation or simply removal of thousands of peasants from their homes.

Orwell was concerned with a general decline in the use of English, and politicians had a central responsibility for this decline. They have a general reputation for the construction of what Americans call "fog" or the British "political gobbledygook" (see Neaman and Silver 1990: 320). For example, the American navy have described high waves as "climatic disturbances at the air–sea interface," while in the 1970s, President Nixon's press secretary coined the phrase "biosphere overload" for overpopulation (also called "demographic strain" by some government officials) (see Neaman and Silver 1990: 317–21). The British are not exempt from such excesses of lexical production, however; an antivandalism committee of the Wolverhampton District Council was given the title, "The Urban Conservation and Environmental Awareness Work Party" (Neaman and Silver 1990: 321).

However, it is not simply manipulation that is at issue in the case of political language; it is the goal of such manipulation which is seen as problematic. Politicians seem to want to hide the negative within particular formulations such that the population may not see the truth or the horror before them. This is the general thrust of Orwell's comments, and it emerges again and again throughout work on political discourse, but with perhaps different levels of emphasis and analysis. The influential work of the political scientist Murray Edleman (1971, 1977, 1988) mirrors Orwell's concerns and looks at the symbolic manipulation of reality for the achievement of political goals. In a more directed political sense Pêcheux (1982, 1978), following Althusser's claim that ideology is not just an abstract system of thought but becomes actualized in a variety of material forms, set about studying discourse as one type of material form. Pêcheux argued that the meanings of words became transformed in terms of who used them, or, in Foucault's (1972) terms, in relation to particular "discourse formations." Here words (and their interaction) in one formation were differently interpreted within another. Conservative or right-wing views of terms like "social benefit" and "defense spending" may differ radically from interpretations available within a socialist or left-wing discourse (see below).

The general principle here is one of transformation. Similar words and phrases may come to be reinterpreted within different ideological frameworks. Linked directly to this process is the concept of "representation." Representation refers to the issue of how language is employed in different ways to represent what we can know, believe, and perhaps think. There are basically two views of representation: the universalist and the relativist (Montgomery 1992). The universalist view assumes that we understand our world in relation to a set of universal conceptual primes. Language, in this view, simply reflects these universal possibilities. Language is the vehicle for expressing our system of thought, with this system being independent of the language itself. The relativist position sees language and thought as inextricably intertwined. Our understanding of the world within a relativist perspective is affected by available linguistic resources. The consequences here, within a political context, seem obvious enough. To have others believe you, do what you want them to do, and generally view the world in the way most favorable for your goals, you need to manipulate, or, at the very least, pay attention to the linguistic limits of forms of representation.

While many analysts accept the relativist nature of representation in language, i.e. that experience of the world is not given to us directly but mediated by language, there is a tendency to assume that politically driven presentation is in general negative. In Fairclough's (1989) view of critical linguistics/discourse, for example, political discourse is criticized as a "form of social practice with a malign social purpose" (Torode 1991: 122). The alternative goal is "a discourse which has no underlying instrumental goals for any participant, but is genuinely undertaken in a co-operative spirit in order to arrive at understanding and common ground."

Examples of this malign social purpose are highlighted in work on the political discourse of what has been referred to as "nukespeak." As is clear, the very title "nukespeak" is formed on analogy with Orwell's famous "newspeak," where the assumption was that if one could manipulate or limit what was possible in language then one could manipulate or limit what was possible in thought. Chilton (1985) and others argue, using a range of analytic techniques, that in the political discourse of nuclear weapons efforts are made to linguistically subvert negative associations. An example from Montgomery (1992: 179) highlights this general issue (see also Moss 1985):

> *Strategic nuclear weapon* – large nuclear bomb of immense destructive power
> *Tactical nuclear weapon* – small nuclear weapon of immense destructive power
> *Enhanced radiation weapon* – neutron bomb (destroys people not property)
> *Demographic targeting* – killing the civilian population

In this example Montgomery is performing a type of translation in which he explicitly attempts to show how the language on the left of the dash is manipulating reality as represented by the translation on the right. For Montgomery, the language of nuclear weapons is clearly "obscurantist and euphemistic."

3   Syntax, Translation, and Truth

A similar and related point to that noted in Montogmery's work has been made specifically in the case of syntax (Montgomery 1992; Simpson 1988, 1993; Chilton 1997). The system of "transitivity," for example (Halliday 1985), provides a set of choices for describing "what is going on in the world." One such choice is referred to as a "material process," where what is going on may be described as an *action*, *transaction*, or *event*. An example from Goodman (1996: 56) clearly illustrates these options:

Actions
a. The solider   fired
    (Actor)   (material process: action)

Transactions
b. The soldier   killed   innocent villagers
    (Actor)   (material process: transaction) (goal)

Event
c. Innocent villagers   died
    (goal: material process)   (material process: event)

Goodman (1996: 57) comments on the possible reasons behind such selections, suggesting:

> Writers with a technical interest in weaponry (in a specialist magazine) might have an interest in obscuring the pain and destruction that weapons cause. Writers who are on the same side as the soldiers might also have an interest in obscuring their army's responsibility for the death of innocent civilians.

Although Goodman is writing in 1996, we can note the similarity with Orwell's comments some 50 years previously (see also Chilton 1997; Stubbs 1996). While many of Goodman's claims may be true, Fairclough (1995) notes that such claims are often built around single, isolated utterances, taking no account of the textual or historical context of production. One might, for example, decide to present the sentences highlighted by Goodman by sequencing the events for the listener in very specific ways:

Announcement

> Innocent villagers died last night. It was the soldiers who fired on them. It was the soldiers who killed them!

In the first sentence here it is the villagers who are highlighted, not the soldiers. One might argue, as does Goodman, that such a form obscures those responsible. However, not only are those responsible highlighted in the next two sentences, but the very contrast that is indicated by their exclusion from the first and not the following sentences might lead readers back to the first sentence to confirm their originally hidden responsibility. By inviting readers/listeners to revisit the first sentence, this small text may emphasize not only the responsibility of the soldiers, but that they have tried to avoid that responsibility.

Issues of representation, however, need not only revolve around specific syntactic transformations: without any seemingly manipulative intent one can achieve personal and political goals by relatively uncontroversial structural selections. Consider the general area of evidentiality. Evidentiality refers to the way in which forms of evidence become grammaticalized in different languages and to the attitude one takes or adopts toward this evidence (see papers in Chafe and Nichols 1986), since not all evidence is of a similar type. There is a complex interaction here between such things as beliefs, assumptions, inferences, and physical experiences (sight, hearing, smell, touch, etc.): *I saw John yesterday; I believe I saw John yesterday; I was told John was seen yesterday; it is possible that John was seen yesterday.*

In a study of political discourse just prior to American entry into the 1990 Gulf War, Dunmire (1995) argues that newspaper articles in both the *New York Times* and the *Washington Post*, and statements made by representatives of the American government, actively assisted the USA in positioning itself for intervention. They did this by shifting their concerns from Iraq's invasion of Kuwait to a series of claims regarding a potential attack on Saudi Arabia. Dunmire argues that, through an increased use of nominal clauses to represent the threat of Iraq's attack on Saudi Arabia, what was speculation came to be accepted as fact.

Equally, it may be that in some cases it is not simply the syntactic form which is chosen, but rather the relative distribution of particular syntactic selections which carries the political implications. Work by Stubbs (1996) on the distribution of *ergative* forms within two school geography textbooks may be used to illustrate this point. As Stubbs (1996: 133) explains, ergatives are verbs which:

> can be transitive or intransitive, and which allow the same nominal group and the same object group in transitive clauses and as subject in intransitive clauses:
> several firms *have closed their factories*
> factories *have been closed*
> factories *have closed*

The important point is that ergatives have agentive and nonagentive uses. This allows ergatives, like transitivity in active and passive sentences, to be used differentially depending on the ideological goals of the text.

Using a computer analysis of two different types of school text, one which looked at human geography from a fact-based perspective (text G), and one which adopted an environmentalist position (text E), Stubbs discovered significant distributional differences between the two:

> Relative to text length texts G and E have almost the same number of ergative verbs: slightly fewer than one per 100 words of running text. However, the distribution of transitive, passive, and intransitive choices is significantly different (p < 0.001). Text E has many more transitive forms with correspondingly fewer passives and intransitives. Consistent with explicit orientation to the responsibility for environmental damage, Text E expresses causation and agency more frequently. (Stubbs 1996: 137)

Clearly, text E's author has adopted an explicit political role within the text and this is revealed through both a grammatical and a distributional analysis of specific verb forms.

The idea that similar grammatical categories may be operationalized in different ways is taken up by Kress and Hodge (1979), who have argued that several different types of strategy might be subsumed under a general heading of *negation*. They explore the use of a variety of options available to politicians which allow them to articulate some contrastive alternatives to what they are saying: I agree with you *but* . . . ; that is a fair point, *nevertheless* . . . ; I see your point *yet*. . . . However, such stylistic assumptions seem to overlap with other levels of structure such as discourse, for example, and indeed forms such as *but, nevertheless, well*, etc. are now normally referred to as discourse markers (Schiffrin 1987; Gastil 1993; see Schiffrin, this volume). Wilson (1993) explicitly treats such forms as discourse markers and suggests that they may function differentially in the marking of ideological contrasts. In an analysis of students' debates on specific political subjects, it is noted that "and" may be used for either planned coordination (as in X, Y, and Z) or unplanned coordination (as in X and Y and Z). The choice one adopts relates to the way one wishes to present the elements coordinated by "and." In political terms, unplanned coordination is used where one wishes the elements to be treated independently (Scotland and England and Wales and Northern Ireland), whereas planned coordination treats the elements as naturally linked (Scotland, England, Wales, and Northern Ireland).

4   Politics, Representation, and Textual Production

Linguistic options for representing the world are clearly, then, central issues in political discourse, but so are issues of action and textual production. Utterances within the context of political output are rarely isolated grammatical cases; they operate within historical frameworks and are frequently associated with other related utterances or texts (Bakhtin 1981). In 1993, for example, the prime minister of Britain responded to a question in the House of Commons in the following way:

> PM John Major: "If the implication of his remarks is that we should sit down and *talk* with Mr. Adams and the Provisional IRA, I can say only that would *turn my stomach* and those of most hon. Members; we *will not do it*. If and when there is a total ending of violence, and if and when that ending of violence is established for a significant time, we shall *talk* to all the constitutional parties that have people elected in their names. I will *not talk* to people who murder indiscriminately". (Hansard Official Report, November 1, 1993: 35)

Despite this statement, however, on November 15, 1993, Gerry Adams, the leader of Sinn Fein, claimed that the British government was, in fact, involved in protracted dialogue with Sinn Fein. The claim was rejected by the British government, but Adams went on to claim that Major had broken off the contact "at the behest of his Unionist allies" (*Belfast Telegraph*, December 15, 1993). The next day Sir Patrick Mayhew, the secretary of state for Northern Ireland, when asked on BBC Television if there had been contact with Sinn Fein or the IRA by people who could be regarded as emissaries or representatives of the British government, said "No there hasn't." The controversy over government contacts with the IRA resurfaced when, on November 22, Mayhew announced that "Nobody has been authorised to *talk* to or to negotiate on behalf of the British Government with Sinn Fein or any other terrorist organisation" (*Belfast Telegraph*, December 15, 1993). However, reports in the *Observer* newspaper later that week forced the government to admit having been in contact with the IRA in response to an IRA peace overture in February of that year.

Both journalists and Unionist politicians were by now beginning to argue that at best the government had misled them, and at worst lied to them (see Ian Paisley's comments in Hansard, November 29, 1993: 786). The government insisted that any contact had been at arm's length. On November 28 Sir Patrick admitted that the meetings had been going on for three years. The following day in the Commons he was forced to account for the seeming discrepancy between government statements and government actions.

The general claims made by Mayhew in the House of Commons were summarized and paraphrased in Wilson (1993: 470) as follows:

(1a)   We did not *talk* to the IRA, we had channels of communication/contacts.

(1b)   We did not *authorise* anyone to talk with the IRA.

In the first case a semantic contrast between *talk* and *communication* is presented, the claim seemingly being that the British government did not have articulate verbal contact, but did communicate with the IRA using selected channels of communication. In (1b) negation is employed in the context of a particular type of presuppositional verb (authorize) which creates two possible interpretations, both of which are equally acceptable:

We did not authorize anyone to talk to the IRA, so no one did.

We did not authorize anyone to talk to the IRA, although someone did (unauthorized).

Which statement was intended was never made clear in the debates that took place. However, as a number of politicians indicated at the time, the issue was not whether the government had communication channels with the IRA, but that John Major (and the secretary of state in other statements) implied by their comments ("[to] *talk* with Mr. Adams and the Provisional IRA ... would *turn my stomach*") that the British government would not have *any* contact with the IRA until they gave up violence. For some of the politicians who listened to John Major's original claims, any contact at whatever level, authorized or unauthorized, was in breach of such claims.

This particular incident involves a complex of textual and historical issues as well as examples of particular forms of representation. It illustrates the need for arguments about political manipulation to draw on larger-scale linguistic structures, as well as general grammar and single words or phrases.

This is not to deny the significance of single words or phrases in the discussion of political discourse; the aim is merely to highlight other relevant aspects in delimiting political discourse. But even at the level of words and phrases themselves, as Stubbs has shown, it may not merely be the single occurrence of a term that is important but sets of collocational relationships, which in their turn produce and draw upon ideological schemas in confirming or reconfirming particular views of the world. For example, Stubbs (1990: cited in Stubbs 1996: 95) analyzed a newspaper text of riots in South Africa and showed how blacks and whites were frequently described by different sets of words (see Wodak and Reisigl, this volume):

> Blacks act in *mobs, crowds, factions, groups*. They constitute *millions*, who live in *townships* and *tribal homelands*. They *mass* in *thousands* and are followers of *nationalist leaders*. But Whites (who are also reported as committing violence) are *individuals* or *extremists*. By implication different from other (normal) Whites.

On a related level there is a further potential problem with some of the examples of political representation noted above, and this is that relativism affects everyone, including the analyst. The descriptive and, indeed, manipulative element in analyses concerned with the way in which representation may become systemically structured for specific effect is not in doubt. The derived implications may sometimes, however, be more political than analytical. At one level there is a suggestion that heroic terms for weapons, such as *tomahawk, peacekeeper, Hawkeye*, etc. (Moss 1985: 56), or the reordering of events (active vs. passive), reconstitute the world for hearers such that the truth or reality of an event is subverted. I have no doubt of the general truth in this, but along with Horkheimer (1972) and Garfinkel (1967), I do not view participants to communication as potential "interactional" dopes but rather, as Giddens (1991) suggests, social actors capable of making choices, no matter how constrained the conditions. As Giddens notes, an agent who has no choice is no longer an agent.

Equally, since the transitive system of English syntax is available to all English speakers, alternative ways of representing the world may not be interpreted by hearers in exactly the ways that producers intend. As suggested above, the transformation of a passive sentence in production into an active sentence in interpretation is perfectly feasible. Indeed, research into political information processing clearly indicates that interpretation in affected by cognitive bias (St Evans 1989). Once information is encoded into memory in terms of one set of concepts, it is unlikely to be retrieved and interpreted in terms of other, alternative sets presented at a particular point in time. For example, people who have conceptualized their view of blacks in a particular negative way are unlikely to adjust that view on reading or hearing a text which has manipulated any presentation of this group in a more positive manner. This does not suggest there are no possibilities for change, however. Views can be reformulated given forms of counterevidence presented over time and brought forward in particular ways, and part of this reformulation will, of course, be through different linguistic presentations. The fact is, however, that specific biases may override structural presentation.

This may be seen clearly in attempts to model ideological reasoning in a computational form. One of the best known systems is POLITICS (see Carbonell 1978; see also

Hart 1985), which is a program designed to interpret political events in relation to differing ideological frames. For example, if the input is (2), then the output for a conservative interpretation of the event would be (3) and that for a liberal interpretation of the same event would be (4):

(2)   The United States Congress voted to fund the Trident Submarine project.

Conservative interpretation:
(3)   a.   The United States Congress wants the United States armed forces to be stronger.
      b.   The United States Congress should be strong to stop communist expansion.

Liberal interpretation:
(4)   a.   The United States Congress fears falling behind in the arms race.
      b.   The United States should negotiate to stop the arms race. (adapted from Carbonell 1978: 30)

The reference to an arms race or communist threat dates the POLITICS system. The important point nevertheless is that such systems generally work on the basis of key propositions within the input. These are then linked to particular scripts or frames (Schank and Ableson 1977); for instance, what the USA should do in the case of nuclear threat. These scripts provide a mechanism for grouping inferences and defining the context in which interpretation takes place. Such contexts are modified relative to certain ideological formations (conservative or liberal). While it would be possible to build in specific parsing constraints which may be sensitive to structural dimensions of syntax, the important features for the system are elements such as "Congress" and "fund," not necessarily their syntactic embedding.

5   A Word about Politics

As suggested above, syntactic selection undoubtedly affects interpretation, but this must be seen in relation to other contextual factors, and indeed in relation to the impact of lexical choices themselves. Wilson and Rose (1997) argue, for example, that the problems of interpretation which accompanied one piece of controversial legislation, the 1985 Anglo-Irish Agreement, seemed to revolve around single lexical items. Making use of Sperber and Wilson's (1996) theory of relevance, Wilson and Rose describe how a single lexical item, in this case *consultation*, drives differing interpretations of the agreement. This controversial legislation brought together the Irish and British governments in an intergovernmental forum. The British government described the relationship as one of "consultation," and modified this as "merely consultation," revealing their view that they were only talking to the Irish government as opposed to being influenced by them. The Irish government, in contrast, viewed "consultation" as a process of influence. One does not normally consult someone unless one is willing to take the person's advice. In this case, consultation meant more than discussion; it was *discussion plus impact*. This was also the interpretation given by the

Unionist parties within Northern Ireland, who were vehemently opposed to the agreement. On the other hand Sinn Fein accepted the British interpretation, and for this very opposite reason (i.e. the British would do nothing more than talk to the Irish government) they also opposed the agreement. The point is, however, that in the myriad debates which took place at the time, the syntax of presentation seemed to have little impact on ideologically contrived lexical interpretations.

Such conflicts over lexical interpretation are not new, of course. Everyday words, organized and structured in particular ways, may become politically implicated in directing thinking about particular issues, and with real and devastating effects. Even the process of uttering someone's name may become a political act, as it did in the infamous McCarthy trials of the 1950s (see also Wilson 1990: ch. 3).

McCarthy's witch-hunt for communists created a context where "naming names" became a central issue (see Navasky 1982). The McCarthy trials raised questions about the very act of naming and what it means to name someone in certain kinds of social context. If one agreed to name names, was one an "informer" or an "informant," for example? Ultimately, this depended on which side of the semantic fence you stood on. J. Edgar Hoover, the head of the Federal Bureau of Investigation, was quite clear on his position:

> They stigmatize patriotic Americans with the obnoxious term "informer," when such citizens fulfil their obligations of citizenship by reporting known facts of the evil conspiracy to properly constituted authorities. It would require very little time for these critics to pick up a dictionary; Webster's unabridged volume specifically states that an "informant" is one who gives information of whatever sort; an informer is one who informs against another by way of accusation or complaint. Informer is often, informant almost never, a term of opprobrium. (cited in Navasky 1982: xviii)

Whatever one's reasons for providing names to McCarthy's committee – and Navasky notes that justification ranged from the protection of the country (where one Manning Johnson admitted he would lie in a court of law in the course of protecting his country) to liberal outrage (James Wechsler argued that only by cooperating with the committee could he gain access to a transcript of the trials, which he could then use to attack the committee itself) – in those cases where names were provided a number of analysts took a simpler and alternative view to Hoover's: Navaksy (1982) states quite straightforwardly that anyone who gave names "was an informer."

The interesting issue in all this is in relation to what one believes a word means, and what effect, beyond a word's core or semantic meaning, the use of the word has. Hoover objected to the use of the word "informer" not because it cannot be, in one sense, correctly applied to anyone who gives names, but because it carries negative connotations, and he believed that the actions of naming within the context of the search for communists and communist sympathizers ought to be seen as positive. Navasky takes an opposing view; despite Hoover's suggested semantic arguments, he points out that most of those who gave evidence thought of themselves as informers, and, says Navasky, "that's what I will call them" (1982: xviii).

Or consider another context where ordinary, everyday words are organized differently within the discourse of speechmaking. The following extracts are taken from a speech given by Neil Kinnock, at the time the Labour Opposition leader in Britain, on Tuesday June 2, 1987, at a Labour Party rally in Darlington, England:

> unemployment is a contagious disease . . . it infects the whole of the economic body . . .
>   If limbs are severely damaged the whole body is disabled. If the regions are left to rot, the whole country is weakened . . .
>   . . . just as the spread of unemployment, closure, redundancy, rundown . . . affects the economic life in that region so the same ailments in a country gradually stain the whole country.
>   . . . if the battered parts and people of Britain don't get noisy they will just get neglected. Silent pain evokes no response.

What is clear from these extracts, and many others within the same speech, is that the semantic fields of *illness* and *health* are being evoked in an attempt to produce relevant political images. Some of the vocabulary employed in this effort is highlighted below:

> fracture, illness, decay, deprivation, contagious, (contagious) disease, body, strength, (shrivel), cuts, limbs, damage (severe), disabled (body), weakened, spread (disease), rundown, ailments, battered (parts), pain, dose (decline), deaden, waste, accident, healing, caring, disabled, short-sighted, welfare, chronically ill, affliction, handicapped, medicine, infects

It is also clear that many of these terms are negatively marked. Examples are *weak* as opposed to *strong*; *dead* as opposed to *alive*; *decline* as opposed to *revival*; and *ill* as opposed to *well*. It would, of course, be possible for Kinnock to use these terms to actually refer to the health issues of real groups of people, and within the speech the use of *handicapped* would fall into this category. Nevertheless, the majority of words taken from the area of health (see below) are employed out of context, that is, in this case, metaphorically.

This is a further reflection of Fairclough's (1995) general point about not looking at isolated sentences, or in this case isolated words. While much has been made of single words in political discourse (Wodak 1989; Hodge and Fowler 1979; Geis 1987; Bolinger 1982), the reality is that in most cases it is the context, or reflected form (Leech 1995), of the words which carries the political message. This is particularly true of the kinds of metaphorical uses made by Kinnock. As Lakoff and Johnson (1980) have shown, metaphorical uses may describe the world for us in particular ways such that we come to understand the world in that way (representation again: see Chilton and Ilyin 1993). And this is what Kinnock is trying to do. What he wants is for us to understand the world in such a way that all aspects of Conservative government control lead to disease and decay.

The issue here, as with both the POLITIC system interpretation and the human interpretation of the Anglo-Irish Agreement, is that some humans, like some systems, may be biased in their mode of interpretation from the start. For such individuals, manipulations of transitivity, or other aspects of structure, may have little effect on interpretation, which is not to say that such structural forms may not have an impact elsewhere. The point is that there are many dimensions of language involved in political output, and all of these have the potential in their own way for political impact. Even individual sounds may become political, and a much-neglected area of political language is what we might call "political phonology."

6   Sounds Political

It may be initially difficult to grasp how specific sounds come to be interpreted as political, although where one sees politics as tied directly to forms of ideology, the issue becomes a central plank of variationist sociolinguistics, and beyond (see Cameron 1995; Lippi-Green 1997). Research on accent clearly indicates that selected phonological variables can carry political loading. By their very nature, phonological variables have been tied to issues such as class, gender, and ethnicity, and, in turn, to the social and political implications of the use of such variables (at both macro- and microlevels; Wilson and O Brian 1998).

Despite this natural link between phonological work in variationist sociolinguistics and political and social facts, there have been few studies of the potential of phonology in the *direct* construction of political discourse. There is no reason to presuppose, however, that this level of linguistic structure may not also be available for political orientation. There is general evidence, for example, that Margaret Thatcher modified her speech in very particular ways in order to make herself more attractive to voters. And in the work of Gunn (1989; Wilson and Gunn 1983) it is claimed that leading politicians and political supporters may make adjustments within their phonological systems for political effect. For example, Gerry Adams is said to have adopted phonological forms as representative of southern Irish dialect alternatives, and placed these within his own Belfast phonological system. Similarly, selected members of the Democratic Unionist Party, at the opposite end of the political spectrum from Adams's Sinn Fein, were shown to modify some of their phonology in the direction of a perceived and geographically (North Antrim) located Ulster Scots dialect. What this means is that politicians can choose to *sound* ideological/political, and indeed that such modifications are perceptually salient to the public. Matched guise studies (see Lambert et al. 1960), manipulating the kinds of phonological variables noted by Gunn (Wilson and Gunn 1983), revealed that certain variables were associated with political factors such as Unionism and Republicanism and general social factors such as Protestantism, Catholicism, Britishness, and Irishness. By adopting particular alternative phonological forms, one could be perceived as either more Catholic/Irish/Republican or more Protestant/British/Unionist.

7   Conclusions and Summary

One of the core goals of political discourse analysis is to seek out the ways in which language choice is manipulated for specific political effect. In our discussions we have clearly seen that almost all levels of linguistics are involved; i.e. most samples of political discourse may be mapped onto the various levels of linguistics from lexis to pragmatics. At the level of lexical choice there are studies of such things as loaded words, technical words, and euphemisms (Graber 1981; Geis 1987; Bolinger 1982). In grammar, as we have seen, there are studies of selected functional systems and their organization within different ideological frames (Fowler and Marshall 1985). There are also studies of pronouns and their distribution relative to political and other forms of responsibility (Maitland and Wilson 1987; Wilson 1990; Pateman 1981; Lwaitama 1988) and studies of more pragmatically oriented objects such as implicatures, metaphors, and speech acts (van Dijk 1989; Wilson 1990; Holly 1989; Chilton and Ilyin 1993).

As we have discussed above, defining political discourse is not a straightforward matter. Some analysts define the political so broadly that almost any discourse may be considered political. At the same time, a formal constraint on any definition such that we only deal with politicians and core political events excludes the everyday discourse of politics which is part of people's lives. The balance is a difficult one, and perhaps all we can expect from analysts is that they make clear in which way they are viewing political discourse, because they too, like politicians, are limited and manipulated in and by their own discourse. As we have seen, in a number of cases (Stubbs and van Dijk, for example) the text which is being analyzed has already been delimited as a specific political type. Stubbs refers to his chosen text as an "environmentalist one," and van Dijk refers to specific speeches as "racist." In both cases, social and political judgments have been made before analysis commences. In other studies (Gunn and Wilson, for example) the data generate their own stories, and the initial constraint is usually only linguistic, the political being drafted in later to explain why patterns may have emerged as they have. I am not suggesting that these are mutually exclusive alternatives, or that one or the other has any specific problems. The point is made to illustrate the way in which some analyses may become as much political as linguistic; and I think political discourse is made up of, and must allow for, both.

Since the early 1980s, there has been a growing interest in the area of political discourse (with studies emerging from across the globe: see Chilton 1997). While many studies have adopted (explicitly or implicitly) a critical perspective (see van Dijk, this volume), there has also been a variety of other approaches available, ranging from the descriptive to the psychological. The essential issue in political discourse is, as we have noted, the balance between linguistic analysis and political analysis, and we have perhaps emphasized the former in this chapter as opposed to the latter, since, in general, this is what distinguishes political discourse analysis from political research as found, say, in political science.

It is also now a growing trend in political discourse to combine social theory with linguistic theory (see Fairclough 1992a; Wodak 1995). The trick, however, is not to lose linguistic rigor for the sake of sociopolitical claims, but equally not to simply continue producing language-based analyses which do not fully consider why, in social and political terms, specific linguistic choices have been made. There is also an emerging argument for a more integrated semiotic view of public and political communications which combines analyses of a range of sign-based systems (Kress and van Leeuwen 1990, 1996). But certain core features will, and must, remain constant in the field of political discourse, and central to this is the role of language and language structure, and its manipulation for political message construction and political effect.

REFERENCES

Aristotle. (1991) *On Rhetoric: A Theory of Civil Discourse*, trans. G. Kennedy. Oxford: Oxford University Press.

Bakhtin, M. (1981) *The Dialogical Imagination*, ed. M. Holquist, trans. C. Emerson and M. Holquist. Austin: University of Texas Press.

Bolinger, D. (1982) *Language: The Loaded Weapon*. London: Longman.

Bourdieu, P. (1991) *Language and Symbolic Power*. Cambridge: Polity.

Cameron, D. (1995) *Verbal Hygiene*. London: Routledge and Kegan Paul.

Carbonell, J. G. (1978) POLITICS: automated ideological reasoning. *Cognitive Science* 2, 27–51.

Chafe, W. and Nichols, J. (1986) *Evidentiality: The Linguistic Coding of Epistemology*. Norwood, NJ: Ablex.

Chilton, P. (1985) Words, discourse and metaphors: the meanings of *deter*, *deterrent* and *deterrence*. In P. Chilton (ed.), *Language and the Nuclear Arms Debate*. London: Pinter, 103–27.

Chilton, P. (1987) Discourse and politics. In T. van Dijk (ed.), *Discourse as Social Interaction*. London: Sage, 206–30.

Chilton, P. (1990) Politeness and politics. *Discourse and Society* 1(2), 201–24.

Chilton, P. and Ilyin, M. (1993) Metaphor in political discourse. The case of the common European house. *Discourse and Society* 4(7), 7–31.

Chilton, P. and Schaffer, C. (1997) Discourse and politics. In T. van Dijk (ed.), *Discourse as Social Interaction*. Vol. 2. London: Sage, 206–31.

Cicero. (1971) *Selected Works*, trans. M. Grant. Harmondsworth: Penguin.

Diamond, P. (1995) *Status and Power in Verbal Interaction: A Study of Discourse in a Close-knit Social Network*. Amsterdam: Benjamins.

Dunmire, P. L. (1995) Realising the hypothetical: a critical linguistic analysis of a projected event. Paper presented to the conference on Political Linguistics, University of Antwerp.

Edleman, M. (1971) *Politics as Symbolic Action*. New York: Academic Press.

Edleman, M. (1977) *Political Language*. New York: Academic Press.

Edleman, M. (1988) *Constructing the Political Spectacle*. Chicago: University of Chicago Press.

Edwards, D. and Potter, J. (1992a) *Discursive Psychology*. London: Sage.

Fairclough, N. (1989) *Language and Power*. London: Longman.

Fairclough, N. (1992a) *Discourse and Social Change*. Oxford: Blackwell.

Fairclough, N. (1992b) *Critical Language Awareness*. London: Longman.

Fairclough, N. (1995) *Critical Linguistics*. London: Longman.

Fairclough, N. and Wodak, R. (1997) Critical discourse analysis. In T. van Dijk (ed.), *Discourse as Social Interaction*. Vol. 2. London: Sage, 258–85.

Foucault, M. (1972) *The Archaeology of Knowledge*. London: Tavistock Publications.

Fowler, R. and Marshall, J. (1985) Power. In T. van Dijk (ed.), *Handbook of Discourse Analysis*. London: Academic Press, 47–63.

Fowler, R., Hodge, B., Kress, G., and Trew, T. (eds) (1979) *Language and Control*. London: Routledge and Kegan Paul.

Garfinkel, H. (1967) *Studies in Ethnomethodology*. Englewood Cliffs, NJ: Prentice-Hall.

Gastil, J. (1993) Undemocratic discourse: a review of theory and research on political discourse. *Discourse and Society* 3(4), 469–500.

Geis, M. (1987) *The Language of Politics*. New York: Springer Verlag.

Giddens, A. (1991) *Modernity and Self Identity*. Cambridge: Polity.

Gill, A. M. and Whedbee, K. (1997) Rhetoric. In T. van Dijk (ed.), *Discourse as Structure and Social Process*. London: Sage, 157–85.

Goodman, S. (1996) Visual English. In S. Goodman and D. Graddol (eds), *Redesigning English: New Texts, New Identities*. London: Routledge, 38–72.

Graber, D. A. (1981) Political languages. In D. Nimmo and K. Sanders (eds), *Handbook of Political Communication*. Beverly Hills: Sage, 195–224.

Gunn, B. (1989) The Politic Word. Unpublished PhD thesis, University of Ulster at Jordanstown.

Halliday, M. A. K. (1985) *An Introduction to Functional Grammar*. London: Arnold.

Hansard Offical Report, November 1st, 1993.

Hansard Official Report, November 29th, 1993.

Hart, R. P. (1985) Systematic analysis of political discourse: the development of DICTION. In K. R. Sanders, L. L. Kaid, and D. Nimmo (eds), *Political Communication Yearbook 1984*. Carbondale: Southern Illinois University Press, 92–137.

Hodge, B. and Fowler, R. (1979) Orwellian linguistics. In Fowler et al. (1979).

Holly, W. (1989) *Credibility and Political Language*. In R. Wodak (ed.), *Language Power and Ideology*. Amsterdam: John Benjamins, 115–35.

Horkheimer, M. and Adorno, T. W. (1972) *The Dialectic of Enlightenment*. New York: Herder and Herder.

Kress, G. (1988) *Linguistic Processes in Sociocultural Practice*. Oxford: Oxford University Press.

Kress, G. and Hodge, G. (1979) *Language as Ideology*. London: Routledge.

Kress, G. and van Leeuwen, T. (1990) *Reading Images*. Deakin, Vic.: Deakin University.

Kress, G. and van Leeuwen, T. (1996) *Reading Images: The Grammar of Visual Design*. London: Routledge and Kegan Paul.

Lakoff, G. and Johnson, M. (1980) *Metaphors We Live By*. Chicago: University of Chicago Press.

Lambert, W., Hodgson, R., Gardner, and Fillenbaum, S. (1960) Evaluative reactions to spoken language. *Journal of Abnormal and Social Psychology* 60, 44–51.

Leech, G. (1995) *Semantics*. Harmondsworth: Penguin.

Liebes, T. and Ribak, R. (1991) A mother's battle against TV news: a case study of political socialisation. *Discourse and Society* 2(2), 202–22.

Lippi-Green, R. (1997) *English With An Accent*. London: Routledge and Kegan Paul.

Lwaitama, A. F. (1988) Variations in the use of personal pronouns in the political oratory of J. K. Nyerere and A. H. Mwinyi. *Belfast Working Papers in Language and Linguistics* 1, 1–23.

Maitland, K. and Wilson, J. (1987) Ideological conflict and pronominal resolution. *Journal of Pragmatics* 11, 495–512.

Montgomery, M. (1992) *An Introduction to Language and Society*. London: Routledge.

Moss, P. (1985) The rhetoric of defence in the United States: language myth and ideology. In P. Chilton (ed.), *Language and the Nuclear Arms Debate*. London: Pinter, 45–62.

Navasky, V. (1982) *Naming Names*. Boston: John Calder.

Neaman, J. S. and Sliver, C. G. (1990) *Kind Words*. New York: Facts on File.

Ochs, E. and Taylor, C. (1992) Family narratives as political activity. *Discourse and Society* 3(3), 301–40.

Orwell, G. (1969) Politics and the English language. In W. F. Bolton and D. Crystal (eds), *The English Language*

Vol. 2: Essays by Linguists and Men of Letters, 1858–1964. Cambridge: Cambridge University Press, 217–19.

Pateman, T. (1981) Linguistics as a branch of critical theory. *UEA Papers in Linguistics* 14–15, 1–29.

Pêcheux, M. (1982) *Language Semantics and Ideology.* London: Macmillan.

Pêcheux, M. (1978) Discourse-structure or event. In C. Nelson and L. Grossberg (eds), *Marxism and the Interpretation of Culture.* London: Macmillan, 251–66.

Richardson, K. (1985) Pragmatics of speeches against the peace movement in Britain: a case study. In P. Chilton (ed.), *Language and the Nuclear Arms Debate.* London: Pinter, 23–40.

Richardson, K. (1991) The debate about nukespeak. *Belfast Working Papers in Language and Linguistics* 11, 15–48.

Rose, J. (1989) The Relevance of Ulster Politics. Unpublished PhD thesis, Department of Communication, University of Ulster at Jordanstown.

Schank, R. and Ableson, R. P. (1977) *Scripts, Plans, Goals, and Understanding.* Hillsdale, NJ: Lawrence Erlbaum.

Schiffrin, D. (1987) *Discourse Markers.* Cambridge: Cambridge University Press.

Shapiro, M. J. (1981) *Language and Political Understanding.* New Haven, CT: Yale University Press.

Simpson, P. (1988) Language and ideology. *Critical Studies in Mass Communication* 7, 166–88.

Simpson, P. (1993) *Language Ideology and Point of View.* London: Routledge and Kegan Paul.

Sperber, B. and Wilson, D. (1996) *Relevance.* Oxford: Blackwell.

St Evans, J. B. (1989) *Bias in Human Reasoning.* Hove: Lawrence Erlbaum.

Steiner, E. (1985) The concept of context and the theory of action. In P. Chilton (ed.), *Language and the*

Nuclear Arms Debate. London: Pinter, 213–27.

Stubbs, M. (1990) Knowledge about language: grammar, ignorance and society. Special professorial lecture. Institute of Education, University of London.

Stubbs, M. (1996) *Text and Corpus Analysis.* Oxford: Blackwell.

Torode, B. (1991) Review of Fairclough, N., *Language and Power* (1989). *Discourse and Society* 2(1), 121–2.

van Dijk, T. (1989) Structures of discourse and structures of power. In J. A. Anderson (ed.), *Communication Yearbook 12.* Newbury Park, CA: Sage, 163–83.

van Dijk, T. (1991) *Racism and the Press.* London: Routledge and Kegan Paul.

van Dijk, T. (1993) The principles of critical discourse analysis. *Discourse and Society* 4(2), 249–83.

Wiesner, M. J. (1991) Mario M. Cuomo decides to run: the construction of the political self. *Discourse and Society* 2(1), 85–104.

Wilson, J. (1990) *Politically Speaking.* Oxford: Blackwell.

Wilson, J. (1993) Discourse marking and accounts of violence in Northern Ireland. *Text* 13(3), 455–75.

Wilson, J. (1997) Metalinguistic negation and textual aspects of political discourse. In J. Blommaert and C. Bulcaen (eds), *Political Linguistics.* Amsterdam: John Benjamins, 69–89.

Wilson, J. (forthcoming) *Linguistic Forms of Political Life.*

Wilson, J. and Gunn, B. (1983) Political affiliation. Paper presented to Sociolinguistics Symposium, University of Liverpool.

Wilson, J. and O Brian, K. (1998) Language gender and employability. Mimeo, School of Behavioural and Communication Sciences, University of Ulster.

Wilson, J. and Rose, J. (1997) The language of peace and conflict: Relevance

Theory and the Anglo-Irish agreement. *Journal of Conflict Studies* XVII(2), 51–73.

Wodak, R. (1989) 1968: The power of political jargon – a "Club 2"

discussion. In R. Wodak (ed.), *Language Power and Ideology.* Amsterdam: John Benjamins, 137–63.

Wodak, R. (1995) *Disorders of Discourse.* London: Longman.

21 Discourse and Media

COLLEEN COTTER

0 Introduction and Approaches

The average weekday *New York Times* contains more than 10,000 column inches of text and is seen worldwide by an estimated 3.37 million readers.[1] The news that the *Times* sees fit to print often finds its way into discussions by policy-makers and politicians, meaning that it effectively sets (or follows) the national agenda for public discussion, as well as functions as a "paper of record" for society. On the other side of the United States, the average *Corning (California) Observer* publishes some 1000 column inches of copy three times a week and is read by a community of barely 10,000. Each word is an open invitation to comment and criticism by citizens of varying enthusiasms who watch closely whether the paper strays too far as a player on the civic team. Meanwhile, television offers an array of up to dozens of channels for 24-hour consumption. By one estimate, by the time a child is 18, she or he will have ingested 10,000 hours of talk on the tube. The flexible medium of radio shows no signs of abating, and the Internet has given us up-to-the-last-possible-minute news from all over the world.

As the scope of the media is so far-reaching, in the US and throughout the world, and so globally situated and influential, it is not surprising that it is the subject of a great deal of intellectual scrutiny. Within academic areas such as cultural studies, media studies, critical theory, semiotics, rhetoric, film studies, and the like, the impacts, roles, and cultural reproductions of what is broadly termed "media" are dissected and deconstructed. The discourse and language of the media are also addressed by academics, and increasingly by linguists.

The discourse of the news media encapsulates two key components: the news story, or spoken or written text; and the process involved in producing the texts. The first dimension, that of the text, has been the primary focus of most media researchers to date, particularly as the text encodes values and ideologies that impact on and reflect the larger world. The second dimension, that of the process – including the norms and routines of the community of news practitioners – has been on the research agenda for the past several years, but to date no significant work has been completed.

It is thus a ripe area for further research, especially as factors in the process significantly influence – and define – news discourse.

The relative paucity of attention to process, however, does not mean that the text has been examined as only a static artifact. Most linguists consider the news text from one of two vantage points: that of discourse structure or linguistic function, or according to its impact as ideology-bearing discourse. Either view assumes an emergent, dynamic mechanism that results in the unique display of media discourse over time, culture, and context. In the first view, Bakhtin's notions of voicing ([1953]1986), Goffman's concept of framing (1981), Bell's work on narrative structure and style (1991, 1994, 1998), and Tannen's positioning of the media as agonists and instigators of polarized public debate (1998) have led to valuable insights into discourse structure, function, and effect – and have characterized the very significant role the media play in the shaping of public, as well as media, discourse. In the latter view, the interdisciplinary framework of critical discourse analysis (CDA) – including Fairclough's deployment of social theory and intertextuality in the illumination of discourse practice (1992, 1995a, 1995b), Fowler's critical scan of social practice and language in the news (1991), and van Dijk's work on the relation of societal structures and discourse structures, particularly as this relation implicates racism (1991) – has been seminal, and indeed, with Bell (1991, etc.) has created the foundations of the field of media discourse studies thus far (for an extended discussion of CDA, see Fairclough 1995b; van Dijk, this volume).

In this chapter, I will discuss the major developments in media discourse research, and suggest areas for further work, particularly research that seeks to explain media discourse in terms of the community that produces it. To refer to the content or output of journalists, in qualifying "discourse," I will use "media" and "news" interchangeably, in part because what is considered news comprises a great portion of what is transmitted through the media. One could divide media content into two main parts: news and advertising (cf. Schudson 1981; Bell 1991), or also add a third category, entertainment (cf. Fairclough 1995a). The references to news or media discourse will concern the broad range of stories, features, and genres that makes up "news" – in the modalities of print, broadcast, and web – as opposed to advertising or entertainment. I also use "media" interchangeably with "practitioner" or "journalist," referring to the people who produce or write the news vs. the news itself.

The chapter addresses the following: (0) introduction and summary of approaches and methods; (1) the inception of media discourse research; (2) audience considerations; (3) data; (4) insights for discourse, which highlights two areas of current analysis: narrative structure and style; and (5) directions for future research. But first, a brief summary of the field in terms of its primary *approaches, methods,* and *topics* of investigation is in order, as most discussion of language and discourse factors relates to them and even integrates them.

The three main approaches to the study of media discourse can be characterized as (1) discourse analytic, (2) sociolinguistic, and (3) "nonlinguistic." While the discourse analytic approach is the primary focus of the chapter, it is well to note the other approaches as media discourse researchers tend to blend aspects of all three approaches in a single work. Indeed, even the discourse analytic approaches that underlie a great deal of the research on media can be characterized as hybrids of existing frameworks – pragmatics (e.g. Verschueren 1985; Wortham and Locher 1996), conversation analysis (e.g. Greatbatch 1998), variation (led by Bell 1991), Labovian narrative analysis (incorporated by Bell 1991, 1998; van Dijk 1988) and interactional sociolinguistics (Goffman 1981; Cotter 1999a) – optionally interlaced with sociological content analysis. Or, for example, the approach can be "critical" in the sense of looking at social impact or inequality (cf. Santa Ana 1999); or concern political economy in the sense of the social value of language (cf. Jaffe 1999), without necessarily aligning with a major tradition, such as critical discourse analysis or media studies.

At this juncture, I have reserved the term "sociolinguistic" for work that involves variation and style in the media or a similar close analysis of language. In doing so, I make a key differentiation with the "discourse analytic" paradigm, which addresses discourse-level matters related to larger stretches of talk and text beyond the word or sentence level, including questions of participant, topic, function, and discourse structure, as well as a range of topics that includes news interviews, quotation and reported speech, register issues, politeness, positioning and framing, and so forth. (As discourse structure has been an important area of focus, work in this area will be highlighted in subsection 4.1.)

Researchers often rely on sociolinguistic insights, either to characterize some dimension of media language, such as variation and style, or to inform related discourse-level work, such as genre and register. (As style and register considerations have been well studied they will be discussed in greater detail in subsection 4.2.) The "nonlinguistic" research involves work in political science, media studies, or communication studies paradigms and, to some degree, in cultural studies. While the nonlinguistic research is beyond the scope of this chapter, it is important to note that work in the nonlinguistic domains is referred to by media discourse researchers perhaps more than in any other topical area of discourse analysis (e.g. Jamieson 1990, 1996; Campbell and Jamieson 1990; Schudson 1981, 1986; Tuchman 1980; Haraway 1991).

Likewise, the methods used by media language researchers often are managed in a cross-disciplinary manner, roughly falling out along the lines of the three dominant approaches noted above. Nonetheless, research methods tend to cluster in one of several areas irrespective of the approach or field: *critical* (discourse approach), *narrative/pragmatic* (discourse/sociolinguistic approaches), *comparative/intercultural* (discourse/sociolinguistic approaches), and *media studies* (nonlinguistic approach). Less systematically explored to date, but increasingly important, are the *practice-based or ethnographic* (discourse/sociolinguistic approaches) and *cognitive or conceptual* methods (discourse/nonlinguistic approaches).

To further elaborate, the primary methods of analysis at this juncture are:

1 **Critical:** This method is "critical" in the sense of revealing societal power operations and invoking a call to social responsibility. It is informed by social theory, the systemic-functional approach to linguistics developed by Halliday (1985), and the earlier critical linguistics work of Fowler et al. (1979), as well as notions of mediated action (Fairclough 1989, 1995a, 1995b; Fowler 1991; Scollon 1998; van Dijk 1988, 1991, 1993).

2 **Narrative/pragmatic/stylistic:** A great deal of research focuses on discourse-level elements and explanations, often in tandem with pragmatic analyses, discussions of presentation and perspective, style and register, and issues of audience response to texts (Bell 1991; R. Lakoff 1990; Meinhof 1994; Richardson 1998; Verschueren 1985; Tannen 1989; Weizman 1984; Wortham and Locher 1996; etc.).

The structure of news discourse has probably received the greatest attention to date (the researchers just cited dealing in some way with structural issues), often in relation to other linguistic elements (e.g. Leitner's 1998 sociolinguistic examination of discourse parameters underscores the heterogeneity of media forms).

3   **Comparative/cross-cultural:** Researchers in this area reveal important understandings of the role of culture and politics in the production of news discourse and delineate the variable aspects of news practice not apparent in solely western media-focused treatments (Leitner 1980; Love and Morrison 1989; Pan 1999; Satoh 1999; Scollon 1997; Scollon and Scollon 1997; Waugh 1995; etc.).

4   **Media/communication studies:** Researchers in this heterogeneous area either employ traditional positivistic research protocols and content analyses or work from the insights of cultural studies, semiotics, social theory, and social history; aspects of language or discourse may not be addressed as such (Glasgow Media Group 1976, 1980; Hall 1994; Hardt 1992; Cappella and Jamieson 1997; Schudson 1981; etc.).[2]

5   **Practice-focused:** Currently advanced by "journo-linguists" (linguists with newsroom experience or professional training which informs their analyses) who look to aspects of the situated practices of news reporters and editors, the practice-focused method, often informed by ethnographic procedures, aims for a holistic reading of media discourse (Bell 1991, 1998; Cotter 1993, 1996a, 1996b, 1999a–c, in press, in preparation; Knight and Nakano 1999; Peterson 1991, 1999).[3]

6   **Cognitive:** Cognitive methods, relative either to comprehension or to other aspects of mental structure, seek to reveal the relations between cognitive processes, conceptual metaphor, social meaning, and discourse (G. Lakoff 1996; Santa Ana 1999; van Dijk 1988, 1998; van Dijk and Kintsch 1983).

The different approaches and methods cover some of the same analytical territory, often focusing on the following primary topics:

- the narrative or sociolinguistic elements that construct or underlie news discourse (see subsections 4.1 and 4.2);
- the implications of quotation and reported speech;
- the exercise of power, bias, and ideology in the press;
- the effects of the media in perpetuating social imbalance, notably racism and immigration (the focus of European researchers) and minority representation (the focus of US researchers);
- key genres, including broadcast interviews;
- the role of the audience (see section 3) in terms of sociolinguistic news "design" (Bell 1984, 1991), reception (Richardson 1998), discourse comprehension (van Dijk 1987), and position within the media process (Cotter 1996a, 1996b, 1999a);
- issues of production and process of newsgathering and writing.

1   The Inception of Media Discourse Analysis

Now that the main approaches and methods have been outlined, I turn to the development of the subfield of media discourse analysis, discussing early work and applications.

The United Kingdom has been the leader in most of the dominant approaches to media language research. The work of the Glasgow University Media Group, collected in the books *Bad News* (1976), *More Bad News* (1980), and their successors, have been influential in setting the stage for research on media discourse, particularly in Britain, Europe, and Australia.[4] The *Bad News* books are well known as canonical examples of the study of media language, despite well-reported flaws that subsequent researchers in the British media studies tradition acknowledge. The researchers in these early ideological analyses of the British press investigated the content of industrial reporting in the British broadcast media. Lexical choices, the positioning of information, and the use of quotations are evaluated through content analysis and offered as evidence of bias in the press.

The other major contribution by British scholars over the past decade or so has been in the development of media studies – led by many researchers and building on the established cultural studies work undertaken at the University of Birmingham – which borrows from semiotics and critical theory-oriented traditions. As an example, Graddol and Boyd-Barrett's (1994) volume is an early survey of the range of approaches to investigating media texts by scholars working in the British tradition, and details how multifaceted and multidisciplinary the media studies approach can be. For one, Australian functional linguist M. A. K. Halliday – whose systemic-functional analytic framework is the basis of much current work – contributes research on oral and written texts. In the same volume, cultural studies scholar Stuart Hall discusses audience familiarity with the "negotiated code" of the dominant culture (Hall 1994: 210), and applied linguist Ulrike Meinhof discusses the heteroglossic verbal and visual messages on TV, a situated semiotics that makes the medium's effects difficult to predict.

To date, the work of British scholars, as well as that of researchers from Germany, Holland, Australia, and New Zealand (mentioned previously), has formed the basis of media discourse work that has established the subfield. As researchers, they have been laboring primarily to articulate larger theories of news language using national or international stories as data. Their work stands in contrast, particularly as language and discourse are addressed, to that of their American counterparts. The American contributions to media research have largely been outside of linguistics, either continuing along the lines of traditional, quantitative communications research or based on political science. Within linguistics, there is little work by American scholars (but see Scollon 1998), as well as very little discussion by linguistically oriented researchers of American newsgathering traditions (noted by Cotter 1996a, 1999a).

Thus far, a primary objective of most media discourse analysis (from the linguistic to the sociological) is often the registering of the presence of bias or ideology in language, or the problematizing of power relations in society. As such, social theory has often been more a basis for analysis than linguistic theory. This is especially the case in the early work of the Glasgow University Media Group (1976, 1980), Davis and Walton (1983), and Kress and Hodge (1979). The literature as a body tends to focus variously on the ideological implications of language in the media, and thus critiques of the approaches are organized around the validity of findings of bias, whether instigated through linguistic or sociological means.[5] The fundamental concerns are: to what extent is language evidence used to support the ideological frame or bias a researcher believes is there? To what extent does focus on ideology as a research goal obscure the potential contribution that a linguistic examination could bring to bear?

Early critiques of media discourse analysis came notably from Verschueren (1985), whose work is grounded in pragmatics and "metapragmatics," and Bell (1991), whose initial sociolinguistic research on language style and variation in media language has expanded to include issues of narrative and discourse. Verschueren, for instance, noted that either the linguistic work was not sufficiently contextualized, ignorant of the "structural and functional properties of the news gathering and reporting process in a free press tradition" (1985: vii), or the ideology work drew obvious conclusions, "simply predictable on the basis of those structural and functional properties" (1985: vii; see also Cotter 1999a). Bell, for his part, critiques the earlier content-analytic approaches to media language analysis, which in his view suffer from a "lack of sound basic linguistic analysis" (1991: 215). Approaches that are too simplistic do not advance the field, erroneously presuming "a clearly definable relation between any given linguistic choice and a specific ideology" and assigning to "newsworkers a far more deliberate ideological intervention in news than is supported by the research on news production" (Bell 1991: 214).

Currently, as more work is being done in both social theory and linguistics-situated frameworks, and the interdisciplinarity of media research is more firmly established, the issues under consideration tend to focus less on methodological or theoretical limitations than on what the different approaches – taken together – can usefully reveal.

2   Audience Considerations

Attention to audience is the first step away from text-focused analyses of media, and many researchers are aware that a theoretical position of media discourse that includes the audience is desirable.

Different linguists or theorists offer different conceptualizations of the audience and its role in the construction of media realities. In the approaches I address here, the audience is conceived of as part of the discourse mechanism. This is in contrast with more conventional assumptions about mass communication which rely on the active sender–passive receiver "conduit" model, which is now contested. The position of the audience may be one of the more salient differentiating features of the various research paradigms. A great deal of the research (from within discourse analysis and sociolinguistics and outside of it) either casts the audience as individuals who do not have much choice in resisting media power, or credits the audience's role with more equality in the relationship: as being *both* active and acted upon.

There are different ways to explore the concept of audience agency or interaction in media discourse. Goffman's frame analysis of radio talk (1981) was one of the first to articulate and apply the insight that the relationships among the different interlocutors determine the nature of the speech event and the talk that is appropriate to it. Similarly, in Bell's view (1991), which builds on Goffman's categories of participant roles, the media audience takes on multiple roles: that of speaker, addressee, auditor, overhearer, and eavesdropper. As media-savvy participants in the larger culture, we recognize audience roles and embedded points of view and are conscious when an interviewee – or an interviewer – departs from a prescribed position. (Bell 1991 cites former US President Jimmy Carter's oft-quoted post-*Playboy* interview remarks, in which he admits to lusting "in his heart": Carter's words were appropriate for the immediate addressee, but not for the ultimate listening audience, especially coming from a candidate for president.) In a related, but less Goffmanian way, Cappella and Jamieson (1997) employ the concept of frame to account for the influence of media language on public opinion. Their work on political campaign coverage determined that audiences who read stories about strategy became more cynical about politicians and politics than those who read stories that focused on, and were thus framed in terms of, issues.

Meinhof's work on the visual and textual double messages in television news, which she argues have cross-cultural implications, is consciously predicated on a focus away from "text-internal readings, where readers are theorized as decoders of fixed meanings, to more dynamic models, where meanings are negotiated by actively participating readers" (Meinhof 1994: 212). Her own three-part taxonomy of communication, which circumvents the sender–receiver model and is briefer than Goffman's and Bell's characterizations, includes *actors, activities or events*, and *the affected, the effect, or outcome*.

The audience is considered from cognitive perspectives, as well. Van Dijk and Kintsch (1983) led the early work on the cognitive factors in the processing of information that influence comprehension of texts by readers. They establish that hierarchical relations exist among discourse strategies; that information comes from many sources within text and context; and that "forward" and "backward" interpretation strategies operate on the local level to specify the meaning and constrain interpretation – insights that background many current assumptions about audience interplay with text.

In comprehension research such as this, the audience and its range of innate psycholinguistic abilities are assumed and essentially backgrounded in the discussion of other issues. This stands in contrast to the work by investigators who incorporate the tenets of reception analysis in their investigation of media discourse, a blend of methodologies that has received little attention by linguists (Richardson 1998). In Richardson's work, the audience is foregrounded as a key element in the production of discourse meaning both through the researchers' emphasis on audience comprehension of texts, and by the audience's response to texts in the data-eliciting process itself.

Bell (1984, 1991) has worked to articulate a framework for considering the role of the audience on the sociolinguistic level, using phonological, lexical, syntactic, and pragmatic evidence to construct a theory of "audience design." Major insights of the framework involve the role of style, which in different ways can either be responsive to the linguistic norms of an audience, or refer in some way to a "third party, reference group or model" outside of the speech community (Bell 1991: 127). Style strategies, thus, can be seen as playing an essential role in redefining and renegotiating the media's relationship to the audience.

Finally, Cotter (1993, 1999a) attempts to characterize the nature of the relationship between the news community and the "community of coverage" it serves. This work focuses on the interactive properties of the "pseudo-dyadic" relationship that exists between the two communities, as well as on the dynamic of "reciprocal transmission"

– "the interplay of texts, creators, and audience" which allows the media to engage on the social or phatic level, at the same time providing content that "captures facts about our social worlds" (Cotter 1999a: 168).

3   The Nature of Data

The ubiquity of media language and its easy accessibility make it a natural data source for linguists interested in the components of language and discourse and for other researchers interested in assessing the effects of language on culture. Given that the media is such a widespread purveyor of talk about our world and our position in it, it is a bit surprising that not more linguists attempt to work with it. However, those who have explored media discourse tend to select and utilize data that will allow answers to fundamental questions about language, about the nature of the news and the media, and about more abstract issues of language, action, thought, and society.

Newspapers are convenient repositories of large bodies of data, and this fact has allowed the development of research backed up by quantity of example. As illustration, Suter (1993), aiming to expand the development of the study of text-types, goes to the newspapers to find a "prototype text." The "wedding report" is the case study with which he develops his working model of text analysis. He uses data on the wedding report – an account of a wedding which includes time–place–date details as well as other wedding-related information – from a variety of British newspapers to analyze text structure, incorporating the frameworks of Biber (1988), Bell (1991), Halliday (1985), and van Dijk (1988). Suter aims to determine the constitutive features of the four areas that delineate a text type: *situational context*, *function*, *content*, and *form*. His work is a good example of a multidisciplinary approach informed by a broad reading of media as situated social and textual practice.[6]

Other sociolinguists studying media language outside of discourse analysis per se have also made noteworthy use of the extensive database that a single newspaper, or a single media entity, can produce, bolstering with quantity of example a number of claims about media language and its indexing of social stereotype and attitude. For example, Santa Ana (1999) uses a corpus of thousands of stories to analyze metaphors of racism in the *Los Angeles Times'* coverage of anti-immigrant ballot initiatives; and Lippi-Green (1997) uses a film archive of the entire Disney animated oeuvre to correlate accent and stereotyped renderings of nonwhite, mainstream characters in Disney films. Meanwhile, Fasold et al. (1990) look at issues of gender representation in the *Washington Post* before and after gender-inclusion policies were instated. Fasold et al. used a substantial corpus of data and rigorous statistical method as well as a qualitatively informed reading of newsroom style guides.

4   Insights for Discourse

Media data enrich the examination of more traditional discourse parameters, often offering the "third alternative" to standard dichotomies such as the continuum of spoken and written discourse, or public and private language. Media research offers a challenge to some of our *a priori* assumptions about how discourse might operate in varied, active contexts. For example, Zeliger (1995) observes that quotes present an "interface" between written and oral modes of communication, as they blend aspects of talk and text, an outcome that is present whether or not the channel of delivery is broadcast or print. Similarly, Cotter (1993) notes how the routinized intonation of radio news, which can be viewed as a way to cue listener expectations in a particular discourse environment, is in part a result of the communicative requirements of producing radio news. What are understood as requirements of the job by broadcast professionals cause the broadcast news register to combine features of discourse modes which are traditionally viewable as distinct: written vs. spoken, conversational vs. more public forms, and formal vs. casual style.

Unique distributions of discourse features occur in other media discourse, demonstrating more fully the range of social and textual meanings implicit on the discourse level. Sentence-initial connectives in news stories show a communicative function overriding a prescriptive one (the "don't start a sentence with a connective" rule). The pragmatic and ideational meanings in sentence-initial connectives such as *and* or *but* in news stories (Cotter 1996b) allow the discourse to invoke both conversational immediacy and an authoritative distance – seemingly contradictory goals that are resolved through the multifunctionality of discourse.

The use of quotation or reported speech[7] – by newsmakers, from a range of texts, by direct or indirect means – is another example of a journalistic practice that has been addressed by discourse analysts from many perspectives, in the process illuminating a range of discursive behaviors across contexts. For example, Leitner (1998) examines the use of reported speech in TV news, looking at the distribution of more than a dozen grammatical and textual elements, noting how their presence was instantiated by journalistic assumptions about what is normative in news presentations. Scollon and Scollon (1997) compare quotation, among other features involving point-of-view and citation, in 14 Chinese and English versions of a single story. They note that a complement of discourse features (including author acknowledgement through bylines) works together to project a story with a traceable lineage to its official publishing source. Caldas-Coulthard (1997), on the other hand, notes how some features, particularly the representation of nonlinguistic elements as in face-to-face interaction, are lost as a story undergoes its process of transformation.

Other discourse-level insights exist that could be applied to the study of media discourse, particularly if one is concerned with issues of involvement and detachment (Beaman 1984; Chafe 1982), code elaboration in the written and spoken channels (Tannen 1982), the differences in speech and writing as outcomes of different processes of production (Chafe 1982; Nunberg 1990), the shift from a literacy-based model of communication standard to an oral-based one (R. Lakoff 1982), and the intersection of meaning, intonation boundaries, and grammatical junctures in talk (Ford and Thompson 1992).

Discourse-level analysis also works to pinpoint the key features and behaviors of the language of news. The media context produces unique manifestations of language and discourse, the study of which enriches our understanding of the media as well as of discourse behaviors. In this vein, many researchers have examined the narrative structure of news discourse, the role of quotation and voicing, variation in register and style, and the relation of conventionalized or standardized language to news routines, among other topics. The approaches adopted and the methods used to examine these components, taken as a whole, draw from the entire range of discourse analysis frameworks familiar to most sociolinguists and linguistic anthropologists, encompassing the critical, narrative/pragmatic/stylistic, and comparative/crosscultural methods outlined in section 0. Increasingly, too, work that compares news discourse across culture and community has lent substance and sophistication to discussion of discourse issues (e.g. Leitner 1980; Pan 1999; Scollon 1997; Scollon and Scollon 1997; Weizman 1984; see Scollon and Scollon, this volume, on intercultural communication).

As previously mentioned, *narrative structure* and *style and register* are two productive areas of analysis and produce unique results when media data are considered, and so they will be discussed in greater detail.

4.1   Narrative structure

Journalists write stories, and consequently, research into story structure or narrative becomes relevant to account for their motivations. Frameworks that have been successfully applied to other domains of talk, such as Labov's (1972) narrative framework (see Johnstone, this volume), have also been applied to news discourse. For example, Bell (1991) uses Labov's framework to examine the global narrative structure of news across local and national news boundaries, while van Dijk (1988) outlines a "theory of discourse schemata," which includes the traditional Labovian narrative schema as well as a more elaborated "news schema" – a "series of hierarchically ordered categories" that helps define the discourse (van Dijk 1988: 49).

Bell (1991, 1994, 1998) has long compared the structure of news stories to personal narratives, noting their similarities and divergences, and using the Labovian framework as a point of departure. A key result is the insight that the narrative "evaluation" component, which cues our reading of a news story's salience, is focused in the lead (that is, the very important first paragraph in a news story). The discursive elaboration and alteration of time elements in the news narrative are another feature distinctive to media discourse. Linear chronology is not important in a news story to the extent one would think: "Perceived news value overturns temporal sequence and imposes an order completely at odds with the linear narrative point" (Bell 1991: 153; see also 1995, 1996). In their manipulation of temporal elements, reporters are not stenographers or transcribers; they are storytellers and interpreters (Cotter in press).

This point about a reordered "news chronology," constrained by the norms of text and content that underlie news discourse, comes up again in the work of media researchers Manoff and Schudson (1986). Their collection of nonlinguistic essays looks at the various elements that comprise the news and the process of journalism, namely, "The Five Ws and How": who, what, when, where, why, and how. These are the basic questions reporters answer, and the authors use these components as a way of organizing their discussion of news practice. Bell (1998) uses the Five Ws as an organizing principle in his recent discussion of news parameters. Similarly, Cotter (1999a) talks about the Five Ws in relation to news values and story organization.

Ultimately, the researchers are trying to determine what the placement of these profession-circumscribed informational elements means in the context of news structure and discourse organization.

The surface simplicity of the writing rules (which are standard across newswriting textbooks) and the complexity of their outputs (which varies across presentation domains) have only begun to get the attention they deserve. Bell (1991), for instance, notes the common practice in news-story construction of embedding one speech event into another. For example, a quotation from an interview is surrounded by information from a press release, but on the surface it is realized as a seamless, coherent "story." Likewise, Cotter (1999a, in press), in discussing the progress of a story through time, and Knight and Nakano (1999), in delineating the "press release reality" that informed reporting of the historic 1997 Hong Kong handover, elaborate on the role of multiple texts and multiple authors in the production of news. This multiparty/multi-element infrastructure has been remarked on by other researchers (such as van Dijk 1988; Verschueren 1985; Bell 1991; 1994; Cotter 1999a), who draw a range of conclusions, depending on their research focus.

4.2   Style and register

Linguistic style becomes an operative concept in media discourse, as a means both of characterizing the register and the unique features of news language, and also of considering the dynamic role of many speech communities in the production of discourse.

The many social tasks a journalistic text intentionally or unconsciously accomplishes are reflected in the different dimensions of register that many researchers have noted as constitutive of media discourse. For example, Chimombo and Roseberry (1998) see news register as a result of the informing role of news producers and its attendant linguistic correlates. Weizman (1994) notes preliminarily how quotation marks convey a reporter's stance toward the material he or she has included in the news story and in the process help constitute the news register. And Scollon and Scollon (1999) notes that the journalistic register is marked in part by the reporter's standardized practice of avoiding brand names and copyrighted material, an activity that integrates a "hidden dialogicality" with intellectual property priorities.

Style issues have also been addressed in the context of the media of bilingual societies, including Gonzalez's (1991) study of stylistic shifts in the English of the Philippine print media and Cotter's (1996a) research on English discourse-marker insertion in Irish-language radio interviews.[8] Gonzalez notes that a stylistic formality and consistency in Philippine English print media can be attributed to an underlying insecurity toward the colonizing language as well as to the site of English acquisition, i.e. the school. Cotter discusses the presence of discourse markers as a strategy for discourse coherence in a domain in which fluency is expected but not necessarily available, and for the negotiation of identity in a bilingual frame. (See Schiffrin, this volume.) In both cases, the discourse requirements of a well-formed news story or interview condition the use of language.

The constraints on style also derive from the larger culture in which the media discourse is being produced. Leitner (1980) was one of the first to conclude that language on the radio is marked in culturally constrained ways by stylistic variation and reflects social contradictions (Naro and Scherre's 1996 work on Brazilian Portuguese similarly points to the impact of a media presence on linguistic variation). Employing a comparative approach to investigate the characteristics of language on the radio, Leitner's work on understanding the differences between German and British radio emphasizes the importance of sociopolitical contexts in characterizing media language.

Bell's audience design framework bears mention again, as reference group affiliation would also explain the circumstances in which the media influences or reflects variation in the larger community. Bell (1991) cites several studies of status determinants in both print and broadcast discourse, e.g. in French radio in Montreal and with Hebrew dialects on Israeli radio, a point that is also relevant in minority-language radio broadcasts in places as diverse as Zambia (Spitulnik 1992), Corsica (Jaffe 1999), and Ireland (Cotter 1996a). Social class is also a factor in the work by Roeh and Feldman (1984), who looked at two Hebrew dailies and observed how numbers, particularly in headlines, index social class. They found that numbers were used for rhetorical value more often in the popular daily than in the elite daily.

Journalists' own perceptions of their roles in the public sphere and their changing job duties also influence style and speak to the dynamic construction of media identities. For example, Quirk (1982) notes how speaking style on the radio has changed over time. He compares British broadcast texts from the first half and the latter half of the twentieth century. Initially, news readers were just that: readers, agents for conveying information, reading from a prepared text. Rhetorical devices, such as ad libbing or joking (in what has been called "happy talk") to lessen the distance between broadcaster and listener, were not present as they are in abundance now. Quirk points out that the changing roles of the broadcaster – in particular in relation to audience and in relation to medium – influence style.

Finally, changes in technology itself influence media discourse at the same time as they offer the researcher an opportunity to consider the stability (or intractability) of cultural categories. For example, McKay's (1988) work on voice amplification and gender observes how discourse styles had to alter to fit changing production modes in the early days of technology-assisted communication, from the megaphone to radio. Her focus on the role of gender in questions of authoritative voice indicates that culturally projected views of women's "appropriate" place did not stop at the door of the recording studio. Her observations speak to the perseverance of cultural attitudes over technological boundaries. (See also Moses 1994; Cotter 1999c.)

5 Directions for Continued Research

In the beginning of this chapter, I referred to the discourse of news media as encapsulating two key components: the dimension of text or story, and the dimension of the process involved in the production of texts. The text dimension has been considered productively and work is now well established and organized around a range of research questions, methodologies, and topics that are continuing to bear fruit.

However, as I pointed out earlier, aspects of the production of news texts and the processes involved in newsgathering, reporting, and editing have not been addressed in any degree of depth. It is this latter dimension that I will now consider, elaborating on points I have made elsewhere (see Cotter 1996a, 1996b, 1999a–c, in preparation) that can be considered as researchers change focus from text to process. In particular, it is important to look at *the role of the audience in relation to the practitioner*, and the sites of news production and dissemination from *the larger context of community*. Additionally, a focus on process, production, and practice likely will require an expansion of method – and in that light I propose developing more ethnographic, community-situated research.

5.1   *From text to practice*

In the research to date, news texts have not been viewed particularly as an *outcome of a discourse process* that comprises key communicative routines and habits of practice that work to constitute the journalistic community; a journalist reports, writes, edits, and produces in the context of his or her discourse community. Nor does the typical researcher think of process and production at first mention of media discourse (but see Bell 1991, 1998; Cotter 1999a, etc.; Knight and Nakano 1999, whose professional experience as journalists has informed their continuing research). And thus, the way is clear for even more work in a newly burgeoning field of academic endeavor that, taken as a whole, incorporates research orientations from a wide variety of disciplines.

Indeed, the multidisciplinary ethos that undergirds existing research can be extended to even more holistic scholarly endeavors. Ideally, developing an ethnographic component is a logical next step, one which would work to explain communicative behaviors from the perspective of the community in which the discourse is situated (for an elaboration on this point, see Cotter 1999a, 1999b, and in preparation). This approach means looking at the "community of coverage" – the audience, readers, listeners, consumers, users – as well as the community of practice (cf. Cotter 1999a, in press, in preparation). A process- or practice-oriented approach would allow new insights into the integrated examination of news practice, news values, and audience role – the key elements that comprise the professional ideology of journalists (Cotter 1993, 1996a, 1996b, in preparation).

A key aspect in the production of media discourse is the role of the *audience in relation to* the media practitioner (Cotter 1993, 1996b, 1999a). Key questions I propose asking are: what is the role or position of the audience in the practitioner's mind? How does this influence creation of the news text? How does it affect discourse structure, style choice, syntax, or phonology? Whom is the practitioner writing for? I argue that a deeper knowledge of the practitioner's focus on his or her readership or audience would allow a more nuanced discussion of media practice and its relation to audience or the communities that are covered (Cotter 2000). While mass communication models position the audience in a nearly invisible role, and some media discourse researchers have made the strong claim that journalists are only interested in reporting for their peers, I make the strong counterclaim that these assumptions can be challenged, and then better characterized, by ethnographic evidence, and by a consideration of the intentions (if not outcomes) of journalists in relation to their audience (see Cotter 1993, 1996a, 1996b, 1999a–c).

5.2   Community-based research

Researchers would do well to consider the range and scope of journalistic practice that exists worldwide. Since most researchers take their data from major newspapers or broadcast outlets, one area for further research pertains to community journalism. With some exceptions (e.g. Bell 1991; Cotter 1999b; Dorian 1991; Jaffe 1999; Spitulnik 1992) extensive study of community journalism (as opposed to metro or international reporting) is fairly minimal in the literature – this despite the fact that community journalists, like their bigger counterparts, apply the profession's standard, which then mediates with local norms (Cotter 1999a), contributing to linguistic heterogeneity as much as larger news outlets do (cf. Leitner 1980; and see the comparative/ cultural work cited earlier in this chapter).

I have noted elsewhere that research is rarely focused on the smaller, local paper, or the smaller national paper, despite their pervasive function as main news sources for countless communities worldwide (Cotter 1996a).[9] Additionally, to meaningfully interpret locally produced stories in the speech community in which they are situated, the researcher would conceivably need to possess a fair amount of ethnographic and contextual information – which suggests a range of methodological issues that must be identified and addressed. It is well to remember that a local paper effects results similar to the big metropolitan or national daily on the discourse or sociolinguistic level, using largely the same linguistic currency and intending similar discourse goals but within a different sphere (Cotter 1999a). Roughly the same conditions for language use in the media appear to apply across the board, whether urban or rural, big or small – even transnationally to some extent. I have noted that while the conditions for the formulation of media language are similar, since practitioners are bound by the strictures of their discourse community of media-makers, the results are realized differently in different local contexts (Cotter 1993, 1996a, 1996b, 1999a, in preparation).

Community-based research has implications for other domains, including that of lesser-used or endangered languages. Much of minority-language media is modeled on community journalism practices, primarily because the population that is served by such media is often small and community boundaries are well defined.[10] For example, in Ireland, the community status of the Dublin-based, Irish-language radio station Raidió na Life not only is a legal designation (upon which a broadcast license is issued), and a practical one (the broadcast range is limited to the immediate environs), but also allows for a wider participation of its community of listeners in creating what actually goes on the air than a commercial or state station would have or allow. Not only do community members influence what goes on the air, they can go on the air themselves. The discourse community of journalists then intermixes with the speech community it serves. In the case of community journalism, the community of practitioners has a chance to interact more directly with the audience it serves

(Cotter 1996a, 1999b). This proximity affords us another vantage point from which to scrutinize media discourse processes, practices, and impacts.

6   Summary and Coda

This chapter has outlined a range of work that considers media discourse from several vantage points, examining many aspects of discourse structure, representation, and involvement with audience and society. What has been emphasized has been the importance of media-language work – to articulate a better understanding of the news media, the unique handling of language and text, and the impact on thought and culture – and the challenges it can provide researchers using the tools of linguistics and discourse analysis.

As I have summarized it, the primary approaches to media language analysis are discourse analytic and sociolinguistic, often blended in some way. Analyses of media texts and impacts have been additionally informed by the insights of work in fields other than linguistics: cultural studies, critical theory, and semiotics comprise one area of research that has attracted the attention of many discourse analysts; political science, sociology, history, and a broad range of scholarly activities that make up communication and media studies comprise the other.

I have noted that the methods of investigating media discourse, while uniquely cross-disciplinary in many respects, can be organized into four primary areas and two secondary but rising ones, characterized differently by method of investigation and theoretical focus. These are primarily: critical, narrative/pragmatic/stylistic, comparative/cultural, and "nonlinguistic" media/communication; and secondarily: cognitive/conceptual and practice-based or ethnographic.

In proposing extensions of current research, I pointed out that the news media can be studied in terms of its texts or stories, and also in terms of the process involved in the production of texts and stories. Text-level analyses, including those incorporating aspects of audience involvement or interaction, have been the province of most research to date. Process and production issues have yet to be considered more fully. In that realm, a methodology that includes ethnographic or community-situated research may well be the next area for discourse analysts and linguists to develop, with the prospect of new and exciting insights into media discourse and its linguistic and cultural dimensions.

We play the radio when we drive to work, and hear it at the office. We check on-line news sites for everything from stock quotes to movie listings to the latest breaking news. We get the world in a glance from rows of news racks or over the shoulder of someone reading a paper. The television's steady stream of talk is often a counterpoint to social visits, household activities, and dinnertime conversation, not to mention its other position as social focal point. The media's words intersect with our own. And we discuss the movements of recent and not-so-recent media icons that have received worldwide attention as if they were curious members of our extended community. The media sets a standard for language use, be it to enhance social position or to bond with others. "BBC English" in Britain, "network English" in the US, and "news English" in the Philippines are considered targets for prestigious usage, while advertisements, sitcoms, music videos, rap songs, and movies give us verbal riffs or catch-phrases that can be shared by like-minded members of our social circle. The technology available to millions of people in the global village ensures that this "franchised" media language, like McDonald's, is accessible, understood, and consumed across a wide geographical and ethnographic swathe. To study media discourse, then, is to work to make sense of a great deal of what makes up our world.

NOTES

1   Figures for 1995 from Paul Beissel, *Times* marketing researcher.

2   Note that discussions of the media by journalists themselves are not included in this listing as their work often does not cross over into academic treatments of media language.

3   Altheide (1996) adapts an ethnographic methodology to the traditional quantitative-oriented content analysis, showing another way that research can be practice-focused.

4   Broad American correlates might be Herman and Chomsky's *Manufacturing Consent* (1988), or Lee and Solomon's *Unreliable Sources* (1991), but these books have not had the same academic impact – or language focus – as the Glasgow University Media Group work.

5   Ideology is defined and investigated differently by different researchers.

6   Reading data from a contextualized position, such as the researchers mentioned in this chapter adopt, can be contrasted to work, often nondiscourse-analytic, that uses newspaper databases or corpora to make claims about usage or linguistic form. Since these claims are often divorced from awareness of text, context, or process, they are thus less defensible – and often erroneous – when extrapolated to language behaviors outside of the media realm.

7   Tannen (1989) refers to quotation practice such as this as "constructed dialogue."

8   On-line news and entertainment sites on the worldwide web afford an accessible source of multilingual, comparative data. For example, in spring 2000, the *Miami Herald* offered 11 different web publications through its portal site to appeal to different audiences, according to Janine Warner, former Director of Site Operations for the Miami office of KnightRidder.com. Especially interesting is the contrast between the English-language news site, the Spanish-language news site (*El Nuevo Herald*), and the youth news site, which cover similar topics framed according to the interests of their different constituencies.

9   The number of papers overall in the US is significant: 1538 dailies and 7176 weeklies in the mid-1990s, according to information supplied by the Newspaper Association of America (dailies) and National Newspaper Association (weeklies).

10   Community journalism is also known as "participatory journalism" in Europe, particularly in Eastern Europe, where a correlation with communism is avoided (Ronán Ó Dubhthaigh, 1995 interview).

REFERENCES

Altheide, David. 1996. Ethnographic content analysis. In *Qualitative Media Analysis*, 13–23. Thousand Oaks, CA: Sage.

Bakhtin, Mikhail. [1953] 1986. The problem of speech genres. In *Speech Genres and Other Late Essays*, Caryl Emerson and Michael Holquist, eds, 60–102. Austin: University of Texas Press.

Beaman, Karen. 1984. Coordination and subordination revisited: syntactic complexity in spoken and written narrative discourse. In *Coherence in Spoken and Written Discourse*, Deborah Tannen, ed., 45–80. Norwood, NJ: Ablex.

Bell, Allan. 1984. Language style as audience design. *Language and Society* 13(2): 145–204.

Bell, Allan. 1991. *The Language of News Media*. Oxford and Cambridge, MA: Blackwell.

Bell, Allan. 1994. Telling stories. In *Media Texts, Authors and Readers: A Reader*, David Graddol and Oliver Boyd-Barrett, eds, 100–18. Clevedon: Multilingual Matters.

Bell, Allan. 1995. News time. *Time and Society* 4: 305–28.

Bell, Allan. 1996. Text, time and technology in news English. In *Redesigning English: New Texts, New Identities*, Sharon Goodman and David Graddol, eds, 3–26. London: Routledge. Milton Keynes: Open University.

Bell, Allan. 1998. The discourse structure of news stories. In Bell and Garrett 1998: 64–104.

Bell, Allan and Peter Garrett, eds. 1998. *Approaches to Media Discourse*. Oxford and Malden, MA: Blackwell.

Biber, Douglas. 1988. *Variation across Speech and Writing*. Cambridge: Cambridge University Press.

Caldas-Coulthard, Carmen Rosa. 1997. News as social practice. In *A Study in Critical Discourse Analysis*, 59–86. Forianopolis: Pos-Graduagco em Ingles/UFSC.

Campbell, Karlyn Kohrs and Kathleen Hall Jamieson. 1990. *Deeds Done in Words: Presidential Rhetoric and the Genres of Governance*. Chicago: University of Chicago Press.

Cappella, Joseph N. and Kathleen Hall Jamieson. 1997. *Spiral of Cynicism: The Press and the Public Good*. New York: Oxford University Press.

Chafe, Wallace. 1982. Integration and involvement in speaking, writing, and oral literature. In *Spoken and Written Language: Exploring Orality and Literacy*, Deborah Tannen, ed., 35–53. Norwood, NJ: Ablex.

Chimombo, Moira and Robert L. Roseberry. 1998. The discourse of news media. In *The Power of Discourse: An Introduction to Discourse Analysis*, 307–36. Hillsdale, NJ: Lawrence Erlbaum Associates.

Cotter, Colleen. 1993. Prosodic aspects of broadcast news register. In *Proceedings of the 19th Annual Meeting of the Berkeley Linguistics Society* 19: 90–100. Berkeley: Berkeley Linguistics Society.

Cotter, Colleen. 1996a. Irish on the air: media, discourse, and minority language development. Unpublished PhD dissertation. University of California, Berkeley.

Cotter, Colleen. 1996b. Engaging the reader: the changing use of connectives in newspaper discourse. In *Sociolinguistic Variation: Data, Theory, and Analysis*, Jennifer Arnold, Renée Blake, Brad Davidson, Scott Schwenter, and Julie Solomon, eds, 263–78. Stanford: CSLI Publications.

Cotter, Colleen. 1999a. Language and media: five facts about the Fourth

Estate. In *The Workings of Language: Prescriptions to Perspective*, Rebecca S. Wheeler, ed., 165–79. Westport, CT: Praeger Publishing.

Cotter, Colleen. 1999b. Raidió na Life: innovations in the use of media for language revitalization. *International Journal of the Sociology of Language* 140: 135–47.

Cotter, Colleen. 1999c. From folklore to "News at 6": managing language and reframing identity through the media. In *Reinventing Identities: From Category to Practice in Language and Gender Research*, Mary Bucholtz, A. C. Liang, and Laurel Sutton, eds, 369–87. Oxford: Oxford University Press.

Cotter, Colleen. 2000. "Story meetings": the negotiation of news values in the journalistic discourse community. Paper presented at Georgetown University Round Table on Language and Linguistics, Washington, DC, May.

Cotter, Colleen. In press. The pragmatic implications of "boilerplate" in news coverage of California's immigration and race discrimination initiatives. *Proceedings of GURT 1999*. Georgetown University, Washington, DC.

Cotter, Colleen. In preparation. *News Values, News Practice: Shaping the Language of News*.

Davis, Howard and Paul Walton. 1983. *Language, Image and Media*. Oxford: Blackwell.

Dorian, Nancy. 1991. Surviving the broadcast media in small language communities. *Educational Media International* 28: 134–7.

Fairclough, Norman. 1989. *Language and Power*. London: Longman.

Fairclough, Norman. 1992. Intertextuality. In *Discourse and Social Change*, 101–36. Cambridge: Polity.

Fairclough, Norman. 1995a. *Media Discourse*. London: Edward Arnold.

Fairclough, Norman. 1995b. *Critical Discourse Analysis*. London: Longman.

Fasold, Ralph et al. 1990. The language-planning effect of newspaper editorial policy: gender differences in the Washington Post. *Language in Society* 19.4: 521–40.

Ford, Cecilia E. and Sandra Thompson. 1992. On projectability in conversation: grammar, intonation and semantics. MS. University of Wisconsin, Madison.

Fowler, Roger. 1991. *Language in the News: Discourse and Ideology in the Press*. London: Routledge.

Fowler, Roger and Bob Hodge, Gunther Kress, and Tony Trew. 1979. *Language and Control*. London: Routledge.

Glasgow University Media Group. 1976. *Bad News*. London: Routledge.

Glasgow University Media Group. 1980. *More Bad News*. London: Routledge.

Goffman, Erving. 1981. *Forms of Talk*. Philadelphia: University of Philadelphia Press.

Gonzalez, Andrew. 1991. Stylistic shifts in the English of the Philippine print media. In *English Around the World: Sociolinguistic Perspectives*, Jenny Chesire, ed., 333–63. Cambridge: Cambridge University Press.

Graddol, David and Oliver Boyd-Barrett, eds. 1994. *Media Texts: Authors and Readers*. Clevedon: Multilingual Matters.

Greatbatch, David. 1998. Conversation analysis: neutralism in British news interviews. In Bell and Garrett 1998: 163–85.

Hall, Stuart. 1994. Encoding/decoding. In Graddol and Barrett 1994: 200–11.

Halliday, M. A. K. 1985. *Introduction to Functional Grammar*. London: Edward Arnold.

Halliday, M. A. K. 1994. Spoken and written modes of meaning. In Graddol and Barrett 1994: 51–73.

Haraway, Donna J. 1991. *Simians, Cyborgs, and Women: The Reinvention of Nature*. London: Routledge.

Hardt, Hanno. 1992. *Communication, History and Theory in America*. London and New York: Routledge.

Herman, Edward S. and Noam Chomsky. 1988. *Manufacturing Consent: The Political Economy of the Mass Media*. New York: Pantheon Books.

Jaffe, Alexandra 1999. *Language Politics on Corsica*. Berlin: de Gruyter.

Jamieson, Kathleen Hall. 1990. *Eloquence in an Electronic Age: The Transformation of Political Speechmaking*. Oxford: Oxford University Press.

Jamieson, Kathleen Hall. 1996 (3rd edn). *Packaging the Presidency: A History and Criticism of Presidential Campaign Advertising*. Oxford: Oxford University Press.

Knight, Alan and Yoshiko Nakano, eds. 1999. *Reporting Hong Kong: Foreign Media and the Handover*. Richmond: Curzon.

Kress, Gunther and Robert Hodge. 1979. *Language as Ideology*. London: Routledge.

Labov, William. 1972. The transformation of experience in narrative syntax. In *Language in the Inner City*, William Labov, 354–96. Philadelphia: University of Pennsylvania Press.

Lakoff, George. 1996. *Moral Politics: What the Conservatives Know that Liberals Don't*. Chicago and London: University of Chicago Press.

Lakoff, Robin. 1982. Some of my favorite writers are literate: the mingling of oral and literate strategies in written communications. In *Spoken and Written Language: Exploring Orality and Literacy*, Deborah Tannen, ed., 239–60. Norwood, NJ: Ablex.

Lakoff, Robin. 1990. *Talking Power: The Politics of Language and Our Lives*. New York: Basic Books.

Lee, Martin A. and Norman Solomon. 1991. *Unreliable Sources: A Guide to Detecting Bias in the News Media*. New York: Lyle Stuart.

Leitner, Gerhard. 1980. BBC English and Deutsche Rundfunksprache: a comparative and historical analysis of the language on the radio. *International Journal of the Sociology of Language* 26: 75–100.

Leitner, Gerhard. 1998. The sociolinguistics of communication media. In *The Handbook of Sociolinguistics*, Florian Coulmas, ed., 187–204. Oxford and Cambridge, MA: Blackwell.

Lippi-Green, Rosina. 1997. *English with an Accent. Language, Ideology, and Discrimination in the United States*. London and New York: Routledge.

Love, Alison and Andrew Morrison. 1989. Readers' obligations: an examination of some features of Zimbabwean newspaper editorials. *ELR Journal* 3: 137–72.

Manoff, Robert Karl and Michael Schudson, eds. 1986. *Reading the News*. New York: Pantheon Books.

McKay, Anne. 1988. Speaking up: voice amplification and women's struggle for public expression. In *Technology and Women's Voices: Keeping in Touch*, Cheris Kramarae, ed., 187–206. London: Routledge.

Meinhof, Ulrike. 1994. Double talk in news broadcasts. In Graddol and Boyd-Barrett 1994: 212–23.

Moses, Rae. 1994. Gendered dying: the obituaries of women and men. In *Cultural Performances: Proceedings of the Third Berkeley Women and Language Conference*, 542–50. Berkeley: Berkeley Women and Language Group.

Naro, Anthony J. and Maria Marta Pareira Scherre. 1996. Contact with media and linguistic variation. In *Sociolinguistic Variation: Data, Theory, and Analysis*, Jennifer Arnold et al., eds, 223–8. Stanford: CSLI Publications.

Nunberg, Geoffrey. 1990. *The Linguistics of Punctuation*. Cambridge: Cambridge University Press.

Pan, Yuling. 1999. MS. Beyond face strategies: linguistic politeness in Chinese newspapers.

Peterson, Mark Allen. 1991. Aliens, ape-men and whacky savages: anthropologists in the tabloids. *Anthroplogy Today* 7.5: 4–7.

Peterson, Mark Allen. 1999. Getting to the story: off-the-record discourse as interpretive practice. Paper presented at the American Anthropological Association conference, Chicago.

Quirk, Randolph. 1982. Speaking into the air. In *The Future of Broadcasting, Essays on Authority, Style and Choice*, Richard Hoggart and Janet Morgan, eds, 81–99. London: Macmillan Press.

Richardson, Kay. 1998. Signs and wonders: interpreting the economy through television. In Bell and Garrett 1998: 220–50.

Roeh, Itzhak and Saul Feldman. 1984. The rhetoric of numbers in front-page journalism: how numbers contribute to the melodramatic in the popular press. *Text* 4.4: 347–68.

Satoh, Akira. 1999. Constructing identities and social relations: speech representation in journalistic narrative and conversational discourse. Unpublished PhD dissertation. Georgetown University.

Santa Ana, Otto. 1999. "Like an animal I was treated": anti-immigrant metaphor in US public discourse. *Discourse and Society* 10.2: 191–224.

Schudson, Michael. 1981. *Discovering the News: A Social History of American Papers*. New York: Basic Books.

Schudson, Michael. 1986. *Advertising, the Uneasy Persuasion: Its Dubious Impact on American Society*. New York: Basic Books.

Scollon, Ron. 1997. Attribution and power in Hong Kong news discourse. *World Englishes* 16.3: 383–93.

Scollon, Ron. 1998. *Mediated Discourse as Social Interaction: A Study of News Discourse*. London: Longman.

Scollon, Ron and Suzanne Wong Scollon. 1997. Point of view and citation: fourteen Chinese and English versions of the "same" news story. *Text* 17.1: 83–125.

Scollon, Ron and Suzanne Wong Scollon. 1999. Hidden dialogicality: when infelicity becomes fear of infringement. Talk given at 7th International Congress of the International Association for Dialogue Analysis. Birmingham.

Spitulnik, Debra. 1992. Radio time sharing and the negotiation of linguistic pluralism in Zambia. *Pragmatics* 2.3: 335–54.

Suter, Hans-Jürg. 1993. *The Wedding Report: A Prototypical Approach to the Study of Traditional Text Types*. Amsterdam: John Benjamins.

Tannen, Deborah. 1982. The oral/literate continuum in discourse. In *Spoken and Written Language: Exploring Orality and Literacy*, Deborah Tannen, ed., 1–16. Norwood, NJ: Ablex.

Tannen, Deborah. 1989. *Talking Voices: Repetition, Dialogue, and Imagery in Conversational Discourse (Studies in Interactional Sociolinguistics 6)*. Cambridge: Cambridge University Press.

Tannen, Deborah. 1998. *The Argument Culture: Moving from Debate to Dialogue*. New York: Random House.

Tuchman, Gaye. 1980. *Making News: A Study in the Construction of Reality*. New York: Free Press.

van Dijk, Teun A. 1985. *Discourse and Communication: New Approaches to the Analysis of Mass Media Discourse and Communication*. Berlin and New York: Walter de Gruyter.

van Dijk, Teun A. 1987. Episodic models in discourse processing. In *Comprehending Oral and Written Language*, Rosalind Horowitz and S. Jay Samuels, eds, 161–96. San Diego, CA: Academic Press.

van Dijk, Teun A. 1988. *News Analysis. Case Studies of International and National News in the Press*. Hillsdale, NJ: Erlbaum.

van Dijk, Teun A. 1991. *Racism and the Press*. London: Routledge.

van Dijk, Teun A. 1993. *Elite Discourse and Racism*. Newsbury Park, CA: Sage.

van Dijk, Teun A. 1995. Discourse semantics and ideology. *Discourse and Society* 6: 243–89.

van Dijk, Teun A. 1998. Opinions and ideologies in the press. In Bell and Garrett 1998: 21–63.

van Dijk, Teun A. and Walter Kintsch. 1983. *Strategies of Discourse Comprehension*. New York: Academic Press.

Verschueren, Jef. 1985. *International News Reporting: Metapragmatic Metaphors and the U-2 (Pragmatics and Beyond 6/5)*. Amsterdam and Philadelphia: John Benjamins.

Waugh, Linda. 1995. Reported speech in journalistic discourse: the relation of function and text. *Text* 15.1: 129–73.

Weizman, Elda. 1994. Some register characteristics of journalistic language: are they universals? *Applied Linguistics* 5.1: 39–50.

Wortham, Stanton and Michael Locher. 1996. Voicing on the news: an analytic technique for studying media bias. *Text* 16: 557–85.

Zeliger, Barbie. 1995. Text, talk and journalistic quoting practice. *Communication Review* 1(1): 33–51.

22   Discourse Analysis in the Legal Context

ROGER W. SHUY

0   Introduction

One of the defining characteristics of discourse analysis is that it is capable of application in a wide variety of settings and contexts. Wherever there is continuous text, written or spoken, there is a potential analysis of such text. The area of law provides an open opportunity for discourse analysis, especially since law is such a highly verbal field. It is generally regarded as a field containing written discourse, for care is taken to record in print all oral interactions that occur in court. Cases are preserved in written form to serve as the basis for later decisions and to record the cases for later review. Law libraries, therefore, house immense collections of written text, such as motions, counterclaims, and judges' opinions, but they also contain spoken words, transcribed in writing, such as trial testimony, questioning, and argument. Law, therefore, is a fertile field for discourse analysts.

1   A Brief History of Discourse Analysis and Law

Forensic linguistics is a somewhat newly recognized subfield of study, having spawned its own academic organizations and journal only recently. In the 1990s, forensic linguistics, in the broader sense, seems to have flowered, with important general collections of articles on language and law (Gibbons 1994; Levi and Walker 1990; Rieber and Stewart 1990), and books on the language of the courtroom (Solan 1993; Stygall 1994), bilingualism in the courtroom (Berk-Seligson 1990), and aircraft communication breakdown (Cushing 1994). Discourse analysis plays a role in these studies, but it is not the centerpiece of these works.

There were, of course, instances of the application of linguistics to law much earlier than this. Individual linguists have been called upon to assist attorneys for many years, but, as far as I can tell, without much documentation. For example, I know from personal correspondence that the late Raven I. McDavid, Jr., was used by Chicago area lawyers to help with the identification of dialects of defendants in law cases. There were probably other linguists used in the same way throughout the years. During the 1960s, linguists were called upon to assist both the government and local and state school systems in interpreting and evaluating issues related to new laws on bilingual education and desegregation. Again, official documentation of such consultation is either nonexistent or spotty.

Before the 1980s, it is clear that linguists who engaged in such work did so as a side-issue application of their primary work as dialectologists, phonologists, syntacticians, or, in some cases, applied linguists in the most general sense. There were several phonologists doing forensic work in voice identification (Tosi 1979), but there is no record of any linguists referring to themselves as forensic linguists, those specializing in the relationship of linguistics, in its broadest sense, and law.

It appears that the advent of surreptitious tape recordings of conversations had an important effect on expanding and organizing forensic linguistics to what it is today, largely because of two developments. By the 1970s, thanks to vast improvements in electronics and the passage of new laws related to electronic surveillance, the government had begun to increase its use of taped evidence in matters of white-collar and organized crime. It is perhaps serendipitous that during this same period, linguistics was expanding its domain to include the systematic analysis of language beyond the level of the sentence and its study of meaning beyond the level of words. "Discourse analysis," "pragmatics," "speech acts," "intentionality," "inferencing," and other such terms began to find their way into common academic use. The advent of these two developments made it possible to merge them in the use of discourse analysis to analyze the tape recorded conversations gathered by law enforcement agencies as evidence against suspects.

Nor is discourse analysis limited to criminal law cases with tape recorded evidence. Its uses were also immediately apparent and available as a further tool to be used in the stylistic identification of authors of written documents, in the patterned language use of voice identification, in the discovery of systematic language patterns that serve as profiles of suspects, and in the identification of crucial passages in civil cases such as disputes over contracts, product warning labels, and defamation.

2   Using Analysis to Analyze Criminal Cases

2.1   Using familiar tools to analyze criminal cases

2.1.1   Topic and response analyses

One of the early uses of discourse analysis in criminal cases involving tape recorded evidence appears to be *Texas* v. *Davis* in 1979 (Shuy 1982). T. Cullen Davis was a Fort Worth oil millionaire who was accused of soliciting the murder of his wife. The government used undercover tape recordings of conversations between Davis and an employee to attempt to show that Davis indeed solicited murder. But the tapes had some very odd qualities. For one thing, topic analysis showed that Davis never brought up the subject of killing, casting doubt on this as Davis's agenda in those conversations. Response analysis showed that when the topic of murder was introduced by the undercover employee, Davis responded with no agreement and, in fact, no recognizable interest in the matter. His response strategies were to change the subject, say nothing at all, or offer only feedback marker "uh-huh" responses. One battle in court concerned the meaning of these "uh-huhs," the prosecution arguing that they signaled agreement with the employee's offer and the defense arguing that they indicated only that Davis was listening, but not agreeing, to what the other man was saying.

The context of the event also shed some light on Davis's verbal behavior. Davis had just been acquitted in a trial in which he had been accused of breaking into his own home, wearing a ski mask, and killing his wife's boyfriend. After his acquittal, Davis, perhaps understandably, brought divorce proceedings against his wife. During these proceedings, Davis heard, correctly or not, that his wife was running around with the judge in the divorce trial. To obtain evidence of this, Davis asked that employee to spy on his wife and catch her with the judge. The employee went to the police and told them that Davis had asked him to find someone to kill the wife and the judge. The police then wired the employee with a tape recorder and sent him to get the verbal evidence on Davis. This produced two brief meetings, both requested by the employee, in which the two men sat in a car and talked. The employee carried a gun (not uncommon in Texas) and had a black belt in karate. Davis, a slight man, appeared nervous throughout.

The "smoking gun" evidence held by the prosecution was a passage on one of the tapes in which the employee reports to Davis, "I got the judge dead for you." To this, Davis is alleged to respond, "Good," followed by the employee saying, "And I'll get the rest of them dead for you too." These words do indeed appear on the tape but not *in response* to the employee's statement, as the government's own evidence would show. As it turns out, the police not only had the employee wear a mike but also made a videotape of the meeting, taken from a van parked across the parking lot. Correlation of the voice tracks of the audio- and videotapes indicated that Davis was getting out of the car as they were discussing the employee's boss, a man named Art. As he got out of the car, Davis continued to talk about Art while the employee, anxious to get incriminating evidence on tape, talked about getting the judge and others dead.

At trial, I testified that two separate conversations went on at the same time here. I had the jury read everything that Davis said, beginning with the preceding conversation about Art and continuing as he moved around the side of the car. It read as a continuous topic, with the "smoking gun" word, "Good," an integral and grammatical part of his own sentence. Davis's "good" was not in response to the employee's topic at all. Likewise, I had the jury read the employee's discourse continuously, also beginning with the mutual topic or Art, and showed how the moment Davis was out of clear hearing distance, the employee lowered his head to his chest, presumably where the mike was hidden, and peppered the tape with words that Davis would not be likely to hear. It was only by sheer coincidence that Davis uttered "Good" at a point where listeners who did not attend to body position changes could have heard this as a response to the bad stuff on the tape. In the courtroom, even if language evidence is tape recorded, attention is given almost entirely to the written transcript. In this case, the prosecution followed this pattern, to its ultimate disadvantage.

This case opened the door for discourse analysis in many other criminal cases over the years. The Davis case showed that topic and response analyses are salient units of analysis for any conversation, but are especially vital in criminal cases involving tape recorded evidence. Likewise, the significance of identifying dialogic discourse as needing a participatory addressee in order to have interactional meaning was emphasized in this case. Tape recordings have only minimal ways to demonstrate that interactants are different distances from each other when they utter their words. Relative degrees of loudness help, but the on- or off-topic relevance of their answers also contributes to understanding of such distance.

I have had several cases since Davis in which participants' off-topic responses indicate that they either had a hearing problem or were simply out of hearing range. Another possibility, of course, is that they were either so uninterested in the topic that they did not bother to reply to it or so afraid of the topic that they avoided it. All of these analyses, however, usually work to the benefit of the suspect and cast serious doubt on the accusation of the prosecution.

2.1.2   Speech act and pragmatic analysis

Speech acts, such as promising, offering, denying, agreeing, threatening, warning, and apologizing, have been well documented as central to conversation used as evidence in criminal cases (Shuy 1993) as well as to the intent and understanding of contracts, warning labels, and other written documents in civil cases (Dumas 1990; Shuy 1990).

One example of how speech act analysis was used in civil litigation took place in Fort Worth, Texas. In an effort to price a used car, a congenitally deaf man charged the dealership with the infliction of false imprisonment, fraud, emotional distress, and violating the state's deceptive trade practices act as well as the human resources code's protection of the handicapped. Handwritten exchanges between the customer and the salesperson constituted the evidence for the charges. During the four hours of this event, he made it clear that he would not buy that day, but his only promise was to think about it and come back when he was ready. Nevertheless, the salesperson took the keys to the customer's current car and refused to return them. The salesperson also solicited, and got, a returnable check from the customer which was allegedly to be used to convince the supervisor that the customer was interested, supposedly to produce a better deal in the long run. After less than an hour of this, the customer requested that his check and keys be returned. By the second hour, he was demanding. By the fourth hour, he took matters into his own hands, scooped up all the written exchanges, rifled the salesperson's desk until he found his check, and headed for the door, only to be blocked by the salesperson, who smiled and dangled the keys tauntingly. The customer snatched the keys out of the salesperson's hand and headed straight for an attorney.

Speech act analysis of all of the hundred or so written exchanges made it clear that the customer gave no indication that he would buy that day. He reported facts about his financial status seven times, requested information about the vehicle six times, promised to return at a later date three times, disagreed with the salesman's offers 14 times, requested his check back 12 times, and clearly said "no" to the salesperson's offer 11 times. Despite this evidence, the dealership claimed that the customer was, indeed, interested in buying that day and, even worse, that he had agreed to purchase the vehicle, which is why they justified keeping him there so long.

This rather simple use of speech act analysis complemented other linguistic analyses in this case and contributed to the ultimate jury finding for the customer (Shuy 1994).

Speech act analysis has been especially helpful in cases involving alleged bribery. A classic example, again in Texas, involved the charge that a state politician had agreed to accept money in exchange for switching the state employee insurance program to a new carrier. But was the speech act of offering the deal what the prosecution said it was? First of all, it was couched in the perfectly legal context of an offer to save the state money by getting a better insurance contract. Then suddenly the agents made a second offer, for a campaign contribution of $100,000 (perfectly legal at that time in that place), to which the politician replied, "Let's get *this* done first, then let's think about *that*." The agents then upped the ante, saying, "There's $600,000 every year . . . for whatever you want to do with it to get the business." To this, the politician replied, "Our only position is that we don't want to do anything that's illegal or anything to get anybody in trouble and you all don't either. This [the insurance plan] is as legitimate as it can be because anytime somebody can show me how we can save the state some money I'm going to be for it." As for the campaign contribution, the politician accepted it as a legal campaign contribution and clearly said that he would report it. The agent urged him not to do so. He reported it anyway. Although the state did not switch insurance policies, the politician was indicted for bribery. Speech act analysis was used to show that there were two separate offers here and that the politician clearly denied the connection between the two, both by his own words and by his act of reporting it to the state campaign finance committee. The politician was acquitted.

2.2 Newer areas for discourse analysis

Although discourse analysis has been used in many cases such as those described above, it is not limited to cases of solicitation to murder or bribery. Other areas of law, such as voice identification and defamation, are equally promising for future work.

2.2.1 Voice identification

Throughout recorded history, people have been identified, or misidentified, by their voices. An early record of such practice is found in Genesis 27, where Jacob, stole the inheritance of his older brother Esau. In the modern American context, one of the earliest known cases involving voice identification is *U.S.* vs. *Hauptmann* in 1935, in which the famous aviator Charles Lindberg claimed at trial that he recognized Hauptmann's voice in a telephone call demanding ransom money for Lindberg's kidnapped child. Controversy over the validity of voice identification led to the modern era of scientific voice analysis (Tosi 1979). Today, those interested in the field that has come to be called forensic phonetics can benefit from starting their reading with Baldwin and French's *Forensic Phonetics* (1990), Hollien's *The Acoustics of Crime* (1990), and a special issue of the journal *Forensic Linguistics* (vol. 3, number 1, 1996). As might be expected, these works deal primarily with the sounds of language used in voice identification and not with the discourse patterns of those whose voices come under analysis.

What can discourse analysis add to the issue of identifying the voices of otherwise unidentified speakers? The need to identify voices on a tape recording is not always limited to the types of cases normally examined by forensic phoneticians. For example, in a typical criminal case in which tape recorded conversations serve as evidence, not only must the words of each speaker be identified and transcribed, but also the speakers must be identified accurately. In most cases, this is not too difficult, especially if there are only two speakers on a tape and those two speakers have distinctively different voices. But when there are multiple speakers, things get complicated. And when some of the multiple speakers have, for example, equally deep voices, the same southern dialect, or other speaker attribution similarities, attention must be given to other voice identification features. Complicating matters even further for the use of forensic phoneticians, accurate voice identification usually requires a tape recording which is of good enough quality to be submitted to sophisticated spectographic instrumentation. This rules out many, if not most, surreptitious tape recordings made in criminal investigations, since such recordings are done under less than optimal laboratory conditions.

Earlier I briefly noted how the interruption patterns of a given speaker helped identify him as the speaker of certain passages in a tape recorded business meeting. There were discourse speaker identification features as well. One of the three speakers with the same first name, for example, dominated certain sections of the conversation, bringing up the most topics and responding first to the topics introduced by others. This pattern of dominance helped identify him as the speaker on several occasions.

A similar voice identification procedure was made in the case of *U.S.* vs. *Harrison A. Williams*, in his noted Abscam case in the early 1980s. Both Senator Williams and Camden Mayor Angelo Errichetti had deep, bass voices. Both were recorded together on several of the undercover tapes. Even when videotapes were made, the visual quality was so fuzzy and the angles and lighting were so poor that it was not always possible to determine who was speaking. On several critical occasions, the government transcript showed Senator Williams as the speaker where my analysis showed it to be Errichetti doing the talking. Since their voices were otherwise similar and the poor quality of the tape ruled out spectographic analysis, the major diagnostic clues to speech identification were found in their distinctive discourse patterns. Among other things, Errichetti interrupted other speakers frequently; Williams did not. Errichetti repeated himself regularly; Williams tended not to. Williams used frequent discourse markers (Schiffrin 1987), such as "Well," "And" (lengthened and slowed down), "So" (also lengthened), and "You know," usually as sentence starters; Errichetti did not. Attending to such discourse features, to which the courts are unaccustomed, led me to the proper speaker identification where the government had erred.

If the potential of discourse analysis for voice identification has been underrealized to date, it is probably because the opportunities to use discourse features have been few. In much of the research on discourse analysis, the significance of such features may be considerably less apparent and significant than in a law case involving the potential loss of property or individual freedom. In that even today there is a relatively small number of linguists active in the field of forensic linguistics, the frequency of using discourse analysis for voice identification has not been great.

2.2.2 Defamation

In recent years linguists have begun to be called as witnesses in cases involving charges of libel or slander. Defamation laws specify that if something is published (in writing or orally) that contains information that is not true and is put forth as fact rather than as opinion, the author of such material is subject to prosecution for defamation of character. The issue of the truth of the statement is arguable by both parties but the way in which the statement is put forth is the proper subject of linguistics. There are structural ways that a statement can be identified as either fact or opinion.

An opinion is defined as a view, judgment, or appraisal formed in the mind about a particular matter. The structure of opinion statements, however, calls on linguistic expertise. There are what might be called performatively stated opinions, usually accompanied by words such as "I think that . . . ," "I believe that . . . ," "It appears to me . . . ," or, best of all, "In my opinion, ..." Opinions are often accompanied by conditional modals, such as "I would think . . . ," "One could believe . . . ," or "It would appear that . . . ."

A fact is defined as a thing done, the quality of being actual, information having objective reality, something that has actual existence. Facts are represented grammatically in the past or present tense, but not in the future. Information conveyed as fact is capable of independent verification while information conveyed as opinion is not.

Defamation law and dictionaries are in agreement with the definitions of both "opinion" and "fact," but both law and lexicography are predictably silent about their linguistic structure. Yet it is the discourse structure of the language used as evidence of defamation that is often most crucial to the resolution of the case.

Defamation is an extremely sensitive area in which to cite actual cases. Therefore, the following examples will protect participants by maintaining anonymity with pseudonyms.

A defamation case was brought by Roy Harris against a television station which, he claimed, went beyond calling him a suspect to accusing him of committing the crime in news segments of two different programs. In most of the two programs, Harris was consistently referred to as "the only suspect" or "the one and only suspect." Being the only suspect does not defame him, however, since this is a verifiable fact. Nor does it mean that he actually committed the crime, for that is a different conclusion. In fact, the use of these words might even have been defended by the station as evidence of police incompetence. However, in one of the broadcasts, the police investigator said, "The suspect went directly into the house, into the kitchen, and shot the victim in the head." Elsewhere in the programs, Harris was said to be the only suspect. Now we are told that the suspect shot the victim. Put these together and one can easily understand the program to be stating as a fact, not opinion, that Roy Harris killed the victim. This referential definition was overlooked by both the plaintiff and the defense, until the linguist called it to their attention.

Referential definition is not the only discourse analysis procedure found useful in defamation cases. Discourse framing, for example, also played a role in the Harris case. Television news programs characteristically frame their stories with introductions and conclusions that relevantly focus on the specific news item. In this case, the introductory frame went a bit beyond this, as follows:

(1)   *Female announcer*: During the past few weeks, you've probably heard about the latest in the murder of a suburban Kenmore housewife.
      Male announcer: A husband and his one-time girl friend have been indicted for murder in that case. Well, tonight's special examines another case where the victim's husband is coming under close scrutiny.

Here the murder story frame makes use of an analogy. An analogy is defined as an inference that if two or more things agree with one another in some respects, they will probably agree in others as well. Thus by using the analogy of the husband's indictment in the prior Kenmore murder with the current Harris case, the discourse frame encourages the inference that these two separate and unrelated cases are alike even though Harris was never indicted. The use of the discourse marker, "Well," uttered with a lengthened vowel, signals that what follows has semantic cohesion with the Kenmore murder. The male announcer's use of "another" strengthens this connection. The use of analogical discourse framing encourages listeners to infer that Harris, like the Kenmore husband, is more than just a suspect.

As with other areas of the legal context, discourse analysis has been underutilized in defamation cases so far.

3   Using Criminal Cases to Address Linguistic Problems

To this point we have noted how discourse analysis can be used to address legal issues in certain criminal and civil cases. Such a process is one definition of applied linguistics. There are those, however, who believe that the relationship of linguistics to real world problems is more iterative. They aver that through the process of addressing real-world problems, new insights emerge in the development of linguistics. Such may well be the case with discourse analysis.

3.1   Discourse analysis and intentionality

Topic and response analysis has the advantage of opening the door a bit to the perplexing problem of intentionality. Nobody, linguist, psychologist, or anybody else, can get into the mind of a speaker and figure out exactly what that person's intentions are. But tape recordings make it possible for us to freeze the lightning-fast pace of everyday conversation, to examine it over and over again, and to determine *clues* to such intentions that reside in the speakers' topics and response strategies, much like the way pieces of pottery give clues to past civilizations in archeological studies. This difference between actual intentions and clues to such intentions is very important. When I introduce such ideas, attorneys often accuse me of mind-reading. When they do so, however, they fail to listen carefully to the distinction I am making.

One way to determine the intention of people is to simply ask them about their intentions. But the possibility of getting an accurate and truthful answer in a court case is diminished by the fact that participants naturally want to protect their own best interests. In everyday life, people may not even be aware of their own intentions or, more likely, they are unable to articulate them clearly. In any case, self-report data are not highly regarded in the social sciences. Short of inventing a machine that gets into the mind and captures actual intentions, the topics one introduces in a conversation come closer to indicating agendas or intentions than anything else. One should be very careful not to claim that these clues to intention are actually the real intentions. But real intentions can certainly be inferred justifiably from them.

Likewise, the responses people make to the topics of others can also provide *clues* to their intentions. We have a number of response strategies available to us. We can agree or disagree with the other person's topic. We can elaborate on that topic in ways that indicate that we accept/reject it or even agree/disagree with it. In either case, the intentions are reasonably clear, even performative. Alternatively, we can change the subject, an act which offers several possible interpretations, including lack of interest in it, inability or unwillingness to hear it, mental wandering from it, rudeness, or fear of getting involved in that topic. But in any of these alternatives, it is very difficult to claim that the responder had the intention of either agreeing or disagreeing with the topic. In a court of law it is very difficult, if not impossible, to prove that such responses indicate agreement to participate in a crime.

3.2   Discourse analysis and ambiguity

Ambiguity in the use of language is often thought to be the sole province of semantics. Discourse ambiguity, however, is equally present in both written and spoken language. The sequencing of discourse can create an ambiguity that is not always immediately apparent in the individual words or sentences.

For example, the criminal case of *U.S.* v. *John DeLorean* hinged on whether or not DeLorean, the auto manufacturer whose new car plant in Ireland was built with money from the British government but had run into financial difficulties when the government changed, had agreed to purchase and then sell drugs in order to salvage his company from impending bankruptcy (Shuy 1993). The prosecution thought that it had DeLorean when, on tape, he agreed that "investment" was a good thing. Undercover agents had tried for several months to entice DeLorean to invest in their fake drug business but DeLorean had never bitten. In fact, he had previously rejected such a plan outright.

Closer examination of the context that led up to DeLorean's agreement makes it clear, however, that the discourse sequence puts a quite different spin on his agreement that investment would be a good thing. As it turns out, the undercover agents, though admitting that they were in the drug business, had actually made two separate propositions to DeLorean. One was to make him a kind of partner in their drug business, which he rejected, and the second was to continue to try to help him find legitimate investors in his car business. Thus, when they met on the occasion of DeLorean's alleged agreement that investment was a good thing, two different contextual meanings of "investment" were operational. The government chose to believe that DeLorean meant that he would invest in their drug business, get a quick resale turnaround, and gain enough money to keep his company afloat. DeLorean's position, argued by the defense and supported by my analysis, was that he agreed that it would be best for these people to find investors in his company. The word "investment" was used by both the agent and DeLorean without benefit of any sentence context definition. Such definition had to be discovered by carefully examining the discourse context and sequence.

Many criminal law cases center on the words used by the participants. Elsewhere I have referred to such as language crimes (Shuy 1993). That is, there is no physical damage done to victims, such as robbery, murder, or assault. Such crimes are based solely on the language used in cases involving bribing, buying or selling illegal property or substances, illegal soliciting of various sorts, extorting, and conspiring to do something illegal.

Often in such cases, the participants are not crystal clear in their interactions with each other. Sometimes they speak in vague generalities. Sometimes they even use code. This makes it difficult for suspects to understand what agents are getting at and for law enforcement to pinpoint the intentions of the suspects. Nevertheless, ambiguity of interaction will not produce convictions at trial.

The reasons for ambiguous statements vary greatly. Speakers may intend to be ambiguous, they may be on totally different wave lengths and be unintentionally ambiguous, or they simply may be verbally sloppy. In criminal cases, both the government and the defense tend to hear what they want to hear and interpret ambiguous utterances in a way that best serves their own goals. The prosecution often puts the worst spin on it, interpreting the suspect's ambiguity as an intentional ploy to disguise obvious guilt. The defense often interprets the same passage as evidence that the suspect was thinking of something entirely different, something nonincriminating.

Different types and interpretations of discourse ambiguity can be illustrated in a 1997 criminal conspiracy case brought against the president of a Texas manufacturer of helicopters (*U.S. vs. David Smith*, 18 U.S.C. 371). Smith's company, a subsidiary of a French manufacturer, held a contract to produce a number of military-style helicopters for the nation of Israel. Israel, as an ally of the US, comes under the provisions of the Foreign Military Financing (FMF) Program, which was set up to assist allies in the purchase of hardware and equipment manufactured in the US, using US government funds while also promoting the interests of domestic American business. In short, as long as the helicopters were made in America, FMF funds could support a large amount of Israel's costs. If only part of the helicopters were manufactured in the US, only a proportional amount of the purchase would receive FMF support.

For reasons that are unclear, the government suspected Smith's company of falsely documenting the amount of FMF moneys to which Israel was entitled. They first went after Smith's employee in charge of the contract with Israel, Ron Tolfa. Having convinced him that there was, indeed, something illegal going on, they gained his cooperation in tape recording Smith and others in their meetings and discussions of this matter. The evidence against Smith consisted of these tapes alone. Thus, the indictment rested only on tape recorded conversation evidence.

It is possible that the French parent company may well have had some knowledge of or involvement in misconduct in this matter but the case against Smith was whether or not he and his company had such knowledge or, as the indictment put it, "should have known" about it. Tolfa's assignment was to elicit Smith's knowledge on tape. Four conversations between Smith and Tolfa were recorded, none of which produced clear evidence that Smith had any knowledge of this matter. Nevertheless, the government cited some passages of these conversations that they believed suggested Smith's complicity or knowledge of the parent company's complicity, and indicted him. Needless to say, these passages were, at best, ambiguous.

At the center of the government's case was the issue of whether or not the Israeli broker, Ori Edelsburg, was being paid a commission out of FMF funds. If so, and if Smith knew that this was the case or if he should have known this, it would prove that Smith was involved in the alleged conspiracy. On the other hand, if Edelsburg were receiving a commission from the French parent company on some other aspect of the transaction that did not involve FMF funding, there could be no case against Smith.

As it turns out, this transaction was very complicated. Edelsburg had created a deal that involved not only the sale of new helicopters to Israel but also, combined in his brokering, the sale of old equipment from Israel to Chile. The latter was a deal between Edelsburg and the Israeli government alone, for which a commission was entirely proper. Naturally, confusion about Edelsburg's alleged commission was at the center of the trial.

Tolfa tried his best to elicit Smith's knowledge of any commission that Edelsburg might get, but did not disambiguate what the commission was for. The best he could get out of Smith, however, were feedback marker "uh-huhs," expressions of surprise, and eventual outright denials that the broker received any commission growing out the FMF moneys. Aided by my analysis of Smith's responses to Tolfa's suggestions of illegality, Smith's Dallas attorney, Mark Werbner, led Smith to an acquittal of all charges.

In his earlier conversations with Smith, Tolfa provided many opportunities for Smith to self-generate his own guilt. In this, Tolfa's effort was totally unsuccessful. Tolfa then began to gingerly suggest that the broker, Ori Edelsburg, was getting a commission out of FMF funding, as follows:

(2) **(Feedback marker)   April 11, 1995 meeting**
  Tolfa: Ori's calling me every day . . . he's worried, I guess, about his payment, his commission.
  Smith: Uh-huh.

The government obviously believed that Smith's feedback marker response, "uh-huh," was enough to send Tolfa back for another try, even though Smith offered absolutely no self-generated statements that could be used against him.

Over a month later, Tolfa tried again, this time with the obvious FBI instructions to focus on tying Ori's commission to the milestone payments Smith's company was receiving from Israel, as follows:

(3) **(Surprise about procedure)   May 19, 1995 meeting**
  Tolfa: Ori's been . . . beatin' me over the head about this payment . . . He wants his commission.
  Smith: So he gets paid when we get paid huh? Is that how it works?

Again, the tapes provided little for the government's case. The best that Tolfa could get out of Smith was his surprise that Ori's commission was timed with the milestone payments Israel made to the company. The possible reason for such a tie was not suggested or discussed. In fact, it is not even clear that Ori was making such calls to Tolfa. Tolfa's ambiguity could well have worked for the government, if Smith had self-generated any type of complicity in the matter. But he did not.

So five months later, Tolfa tried again.

(4) **(Denial of involvement)   October 2, 1996 meeting**

> *Tolfa*:   ECF [the French parent company] has, you know, Ori's contract.
> *Smith*:   Uh-hmm.
> *Tolfa*:   If they get their hands on that, then we have a problem with the certification.
> *Smith*:   We didn't want the same signature on the cert as on the main (contract). That was check and balance.
> *Tolfa*:   If they can get ECF's documentation and find out that Ori's getting a commission –
> *Smith*:   AEC [Smith's company] did not have one on this contract. ECF will tie Ori to the Chilean transaction.

This time, Tolfa became a bit more specific, stating that the French parent company, ECF, indeed has Ori under contract and suggesting that Smith's company has a problem with their certification to the government about the extent of FMF funding to which Israel was entitled. That Smith did not really catch Tolfa's ambiguous drift here is evidenced by his response. Smith realized that he, as president, signed the main contract but that he had some other company official sign the certification about FMF entitlements to Israel. He interprets Tolfa's "we have a problem with the certification" in this benign way. Tolfa, recognizing that he would have to be even less ambiguous, finally comes out with a nonambiguous statement, attempting to connect the French parent company's files with Ori's commission. Now that Tolfa's drift is out in the open, Smith categorically denies, saying that his company has no contract with the broker, Ori Edelsburg, and that any contract Ori Edelsburg might have with the French parent company is connected with the part of the transaction that involved the Israeli's sale of equipment to the Chilean military.

As an elicitation strategy, ambiguity can be a very effective tool for uncovering language crime, at least in the initial stages of an investigation. The less explicit one is, the more opportunity there is for respondents to clarify the ambiguity and implicate themselves. If such clarification leads to incrimination, the government has done its work effectively. On the other hand, when suspects do not even seek clarification, we may suspect (1) that they understand the drift of the ambiguity and may be, indeed, guilty, (2) that their minds are on something else, (3) that they are so fearful of talking about the issue that they retreat into silence, perhaps even suspecting that they are being taped, or (4) that they are so innocent that they do not even catch the drift of the hinted ambiguity or innuendo. The first three of these interpretations may suggest to the government that it is worth another try at tape recording conversations with the suspect. Elicitation of responses in the fourth interpretation suggest that future taping may well yield nothing again.

Table 22.1

Tolfa suggests	Smith responds
1. Ori gets a commission	Feedback marker "uh-huh"
2. Ori's commission repeated	New information to Smith: "Is that how that works?"
3. Parent company has contract with Ori that we must hide from the investigators	Misunderstands thrust and explains something else
4. Specific request for what Ori's involvement is	Explanation that any pay to Ori is paid by parent company for legal sale of equipment to Chile, not from FMF money

The government obviously wanted to try once more, even though they still had nothing solid to show that Smith knew or should have known that Edelsburg was getting a broker's commission illegally out of FMF funds. Now Tolfa, probably with instructions from the FBI case agent, abandons ambiguity and goes for the homerun, as follows:

(5)   **(Denial of involvement)   July 26, 1996**
    Tolfa: How does Ori get involved in this?
    Smith: Ori's gonna have to be paid through ECF you know, the outbound loop.

Obviously, the ploy fails completely, for Smith, finally understanding what Tolfa had only hitherto hinted at, explicitly points out that any pay Ori gets will have to be from the parent company concerning the "outbound loop." It was not contested that "outbound loop" refers to Israel's sale of used military equipment to Chile.

Table 22.1 summarizes the agent's use of ambiguity in this case.

One cannot fault the government's elicitation strategy of starting with ambiguity and gradually moving toward explicitness. It is not unlike the strategy of salesmanship, in which the seller speaks benignly about what features the buyer might like in a product before trying to make the sale (Shuy 1994). What was lacking in the government's pursuit of this case was an effective intelligence analysis that would have revealed the hopelessness of their case before time, money, and the suspect's emotional state of mind were unnecessarily expended. Using ambiguity may have been an effective strategy but when that ambiguity was finally resolved, the case against Smith evaporated.

Law enforcement agencies, such as the FBI, often have guidelines for undercover agents to follow. One of the specified FBI guidelines that agents are required to follow is that "of making clear and unambiguous to all concerned the illegal nature of any opportunity used as a decoy" (United States Congress 1984: 36). In the Smith case above, that representation of illegality was finally made clear and the suspect clearly distanced himself from it. But often the ambiguity is far from resolved. In such instances suspects may well agree to do something that is quite different from that which the undercover agent means. When this happens, it is not uncommon for the prosecution to extract from the discourse context words, phrases, or sentences that seem to indicate guilt but which, when seen holistically in context, easily can be understood to mean something else. We have seen this in each of the cases described thus far.

3.3   *Discourse analysis and stylistics*

Stylistic analysis is the examination of the characteristic use of language features by a given writer or writers. The analyst reviews the material presented, written or spoken, and compares the text of unknown origin with that of the known. Such comparison focuses on language features of which speakers or writers have little or no conscious knowledge or control as they speak or write. For example, writers have rather high levels of consciousness and control over vocabulary choices but considerably less consciousness and control over their grammar, spelling, or punctuation patterns. Discourse style is another language feature of which most speakers and writers have little or no conscious awareness or control.

This is not to say that such features as patterns of vocabulary and punctuation are not central to the identification of authorship. Indeed, Vassar professor Donald Foster concluded (correctly, as it turns out) that the anonymous author of the novel *Primary Colors* was *Newsweek*'s Joe Klein by comparing his use of adverbs derived from adjectives ending in -y, such as "scarily" and "huffily," the common use of the nouns, "mode" and "style," and the tendency to use the colon excessively (Garreau and Weeks 1996).

Perhaps the most celebrated investigators of authorship in recent years are Walter Stewart and Ned Feder, the NIH scientists who created what came to be called "The Plagiarism Machine," a program that searched for and compared duplicated phrases and sentences, using modern scanning and computerized approaches. But finding plagiarism is not the same thing as finding style and it was soon discovered that their "machine," geared as it was to scientific writing alone, could not pinpoint the writer of *Primary Colors*.

The contribution of stylistics to the broad field of forensic linguistics is well documented by Gerald McMenamin's comprehensive text *Forensic Stylistics* (1993), a book which is an excellent resource for this field. The major thrust of forensic stylistics, however, has been the study of linguistic forms, such as vocabulary, grammatical categories, syntax, punctuation, and length of expressions or text, rather than discourse style. The latter has been dealt with ably in nonforensic contexts (Tannen 1982, 1984; Brown and Yule 1983), especially with written text, but the application to forensic discourse is only recently beginning.

What then can discourse analysis add to the mix of current forensic stylistics? Although features of discourse style have not been focused commonly on characteristics of author or speaker identification, there is no reason why they cannot be. The use of discourse markers (Schiffrin 1987), for example, has served as an identifier of an individual's style in at least one known legal dispute (Katherine Thomas, pers. comm.). The analyst was able to determine that the speaker in question was not the one suspected by comparing that person's use of discourse markers in known speech samples with the sample in question.

Patterns of interruption can characterize not only the social relationship of speakers (Tannen 1984) but also their group or individual styles. In a business meeting involving the sale of an insurance company, for example, a dispute arose over whether or not the company's real assets and liabilities were accurately revealed to the buyer, leading to a civil suit. A rather poor-quality tape recording was made openly at that meeting by the selling party. I was called on to prepare a transcript of the meeting, which involved a dozen participants. No help was to be given me in identifying the speakers. All were male and, to make speaker identification even more difficult, three had the same first name and two others had the same last name. One characteristic language feature which I found helpful in identifying one of the speakers was his style of interrupting other speakers. Not only was this far more frequent than that of any other person but also there were predictable points in the discourse at which these interruptions took place, and predictable persons whom he interrupted.

Other indicators of discourse style are available for similar analysis and comparison, such as organizational style, patterns and types of register shifting or mixing, patterns of sequencing given versus new information (Brown and Yule 1983), the use of cohesion (Halliday and Hassan 1976; Scinto 1986), and many others.

4 Directions and Future Connections

The legal context appears ot be just beginning to take advantage of discourse analysis to help unravel the complexities of litigation. Whether the language evidence is written or spoken, whether the case is criminal or civil, and whether the analysis is done for the defense, prosecution, or plaintiff, discourse analysis has a bright future in legal disputes. Issues of intentionality, ambiguity, stylistics, voice identification, defamation, bribery, solicitation, and many others provide a vast arena for linguists to explore the uses of these, and other, aspects of discourse analysis. The field of law seems to be more and more open to such assistance (Wallace 1986). It is up to linguists to respond.

REFERENCES

Baldwin, John and Peter French. 1996. *Forensic Phonetics*. London: Pinter.

Berk-Seligson, Susan. 1990. *The Bilingual Courtroom*. Chicago: University of Chicago Press.

Brown, G. and Yule, G. 1983. *Discourse Analysis*. New York: Cambridge University Press.

Cushing, Steven. 1994. *Fatal Words*. Chicago: University of Chicago Press.

Dumas, Bethany K. 1990. An analysis of the adequacy of federally mandated cigarette package warnings. In Judith Levi and Anne Walker (eds), *Language in the Judicial Process*. New York: Plenum, 309–52.

Forensic Linguistics. 1996. Vol. 3, no. 1.

Garreau, Joel and Linton Weeks. 1996. Anonymous sleuths get a byte. *Washington Post*, February 16, F1, F6.

Gibbons, John. 1994. *Language and the Law*. London: Longman.

Halliday, M. A. K. and Ruqaiya Hasan. 1976. *Cohesion in English*. London: Longman.

Halliday, Michael and Raquia Hassan. 1986. *Cohesion in English*. London: Longman.

Hollien, Harry. 1990. *The Acoustics of Crime*. New York: Plenum.

Levi, Judith and Anne Walker (eds). 1990. *Language in the Judicial Process*. New York: Plenum.

McMenamin, Gerald. 1993. *Forensic Stylistics*. Amsterdam: Elsevier.

Rieber, Robert and William Stewart (eds). 1990. *The Language Scientist as Expert in the Legal Setting*. New York: New York Academy of Sciences, 606, no. 6, 85–105.

Schiffrin, Deborah. 1987. *Discourse Markers*. Cambridge: Cambridge University Press.

Scinto, Leonard. 1986. *Written Language and Psychological Development*. Sydney: Academic Press.

Shuy, Roger. 1982. Topic as the unit of analysis in a criminal law case. In Deborah Tannen (ed.), *Analyzing Discourse: Text and Talk*. Washington DC: Georgetown University Press, 113–26.

Shuy, Roger. 1990. Warning labels: language, law and comprehensibility. *American Speech*, 65.4: 291–303.

Shuy, Roger. 1993. *Language Crimes*. Oxford: Blackwell.

Shuy, Roger. 1994. Deceit, distress, and false imprisonment. *Forensic Linguistics*, 1.2: 133–49.

Solan, Lawrence. 1993. *The Language of Judges*. Chicago: University of Chicago Press.

Stygall, Gail. 1994. *Trial Language*. Philadelphia: John Benjamins.

Tannen, Deborah (ed.). 1982. *Analyzing Discourse: Text and Talk*. Washington DC: Georgetown University Press.

Tannen, Deborah. 1984. *Conversational Style*. Norwood NJ: Ablex.

Tannen, Deborah (ed.). 1988. *Linguistics in Context*. Norwood NJ: Ablex.

Tosi, Oscar. 1979. *Voice Identification*. Baltimore: University Park Press.

United States Congress. 1984. FBI Undercover Operations. Washington: US Government Printing Office.

Wallace, William. 1986. The admissibility of expert testimony on the discourse analysis of recorded conversations. *University of Florida Law Review*, 38.1: 69–115.

23 The Discourse of Medical Encounters

NANCY AINSWORTH-VAUGHN

0 Introduction

There is a huge cross-disciplinary literature on medical encounters. Lipkin et al. estimate 7000 titles (1995: ix) overall, and one computerized bibliography contains 3000 articles (Putnam and Sherman 1995). However, as Fleischman (this volume) points out, there are significant differences among the interests, theories, and methodologies brought to bear on talk in medical encounters. In this huge literature, most studies of medical encounters are atheoretical about language. Since most of the linguistically atheoretical studies are oriented toward medical praxis, I will refer to this group as the "praxis literature."

In the praxis literature, talk-as-data usually disappears in the first steps of the research. These first steps involve assigning a single functional meaning (e.g. information-giving, affective display) to each utterance and then coding utterances into functional categories, so that they can be quantified. Language is assumed to be the transparent vehicle of meaning. For these reasons, the praxis literature does not provide discourse data, although it does provide data on speakers' intuitions and it can have tangential bearing upon discourse issues.

The "discourse literature," by contrast, consists of analyses of talk itself. The analyses grow out of contemporary theories about sequential, situated discourse (e.g. conversation analysis, interactional sociolinguistics, the ethnography of communication). The discourse literature is a relatively new one. Although articles date from the 1970s (e.g. Shuy 1976), the major books devoted entirely to the discourse of medical encounters have all been published since 1984 (Mishler 1984; West 1984b; Fisher 1986; Silverman 1987; Davis 1988; Todd 1989; von Raffler-Engel 1990; Fisher and Todd 1993; Weijts 1993; Ferrara 1994; Ainsworth-Vaughn 1998a).

In the praxis literature, and to a large extent in the discourse literature, research has had an explicit or implicit orientation toward the balance of power between patient and physician. An overt or underlying research question is: what is the relationship between the power balance and what participants say?

In order to address this question, we need first to analyze power (see Ainsworth-Vaughn 1995, 1998a, for a complete discussion of power and discourse). Power is usually defined as implementing one's agenda. Doctor and patient may each have an agenda regarding who will speak, about what, and when; and doctor and patient may each have an agenda regarding treatment. So there are two kinds of power at issue: control over the emerging discourse, and control over future action.

The praxis literature includes discussion of the second type of power, control over future action: what are the outcomes of talk? Do patients follow physicians' recommendations? One striking theme in this discussion is that of improved physical health following upon certain types of talk within the encounter (Kaplan et al. 1989).

The discourse literature, however, is concerned with the first type of power: control over emerging discourse.

In both literatures, researchers have tended to focus upon three dimensions of the discourse organization of the medical encounter: sequential phases of the encounter; its discourse genre (usually, interview vs. conversation); and its major constitutive speech activities. Following is a selective, issue-oriented review organized by these three categories.

1   Sequential Phases

It is in this dimension that the two literatures diverge the most. Much of the discourse literature contains no mention of phases in the overall encounter, focusing instead upon one or a few sequential speech activities. By contrast, in the praxis literature, phases are accepted as fundamental, a given (e.g. Byrne and Long 1976, discussed below). Helman's (1984) description of encounters as "ritualized" refers in part to their organization into phases.

In the study of medical discourse, it is helpful to return to assessment of ritual in both institutional and noninstitutional talk. Though we seldom notice ritual in every-day life, it interpenetrates conversational talk – for example, simply getting through a grocery store checkout line can involve as many as five ritualized routines of greeting, thanking, and farewell. These are ritualized in three ways: the type of speech activity is culturally predetermined, its place of occurrence in sequential talk is prescribed, and its phrasing is routinized. All this operates at such a low level of awareness that we do not normally consider such encounters to have ritualized dimensions.

In the medical encounter, all three of these dimensions show ritualization, but – for physicians and medical educators, at least – there is a conscious attempt to design these ritual aspects of talk. As is the case with religious rituals, the approved speech activities, their phrasing, and their sequence are taught explicitly by the ordained to the neophyte (in medical school). Another similarity to religious rituals is the fact that the design of the discourse is subject to overt debate and change (e.g. Smith and Hoppe 1991, discussed below).

However, conversational discourse co-occurs with ritualized discourse in medical encounters. Medical discourse is unpredictable, and in being so, it is like conversation. Also, many of the constitutive speech activities of medical encounters are shared with conversation – though these speech activities may be modified or restricted differently in the two genres. Relationships between conversation and talk in medical encounters are discussed in section 2.

The model of ritualized phases has been adopted into the discourse literature from the praxis literature. For instance, Heath (1992) cites a phase model drawn from the praxis literature (Byrne and Long 1976). Byrne and Long suggest six phases: "[Phase] I, relating to the patient; II, discovering the reason for attendance; III, conducting a verbal or physical examination or both; IV, consideration of the patient's condition; V, detailing treatment or further investigation; and VI, terminating" (Heath 1992: 237). Note that Byrne and Long name each phase after the physician's activity rather than joint activity. This focus upon the physician and neglect of patients' role in co-constructing the discourse is a significant limitation of both literatures.

Conscious design of the discourse of medical encounters is illustrated by a variation on the phase model in the praxis literature (Smith and Hoppe 1991). This model also illustrates the relationship between this speech event and the larger society. Smith and Hoppe explicitly construe the encounter as sequential phases, but propose that initial phases should change away from the traditional physician-centered history-taking. Instead, they call upon physicians to make the first two phases of the encounter "patient-centered." In the first phase, the physician would not talk beyond an opening remark and occasional back-channels or brief repetitions of the patient's words. In the second phase, the physician would ask questions directed at eliciting the patient's feelings. In this second phase, "When patients redirect conversation away from the personal dimension and begin to give data related to organic disease, the interviewer should try to refocus the patient on the already-developed . . . emotion, as in the following example: 'Before going into your hospitalization, tell me more about what that was like for you to be scared'" (Smith and Hoppe 1991: 474).

Smith and Hoppe's model is a kind of discourse planning that is ongoing in medical education. It illustrates the pitfalls in overt attempts to design the discourse of encounters without understanding the ways power is claimed through discourse. The model is an attempt to respond to the recent well-documented rejection, in American society, of traditional authoritarian roles for physicians (Starr 1982). Ironically, in Smith and Hoppe's model the physician is enjoined to make highly consequential unilateral decisions about topic transitions (cf. West and Garcia 1988). A physician who did this would enact the very authoritarian role the model seeks to subvert, since he or she would be unilaterally choosing topics and enforcing predetermined phases.

If the praxis literature is overinfluenced by the notion of phases, the discourse literature shows a paucity of attention to the notion. One sophisticated analysis which does assert the relevance of a phase model is that of ten Have (1989).

Ten Have's model brings together the phase, genre, and speech activities dimensions of medical encounters. He regards "the consultation as a genre" (the title of his article). For ten Have, this genre is marked by orientation to phases. At the same time, it is realized through locally negotiated speech activities.

Ten Have speaks of medical encounters as organized into an "ideal sequence" of six phases: opening, complaint, examination or test, diagnosis, treatment or advice, and closing. "The sequence is called 'ideal' because one observes many deviations from it that seem to be quite acceptable to the participants" (ten Have 1989: 118).

Shuy's (1983) analysis also bears upon the nature and existence of planned phases for medical encounters. Like ten Have, Shuy (1983) found a great deal of variation in the sequential organization of encounters. Physicians in Shuy's data apparently were filling out a written questionnaire during the encounter. Shuy expected that the topics of the encounters' discourse would be clearly related to the questionnaire. He reports:

> One startling conclusion faced me at the end of my examination of some 100 interviews: It would be very difficult to reconstruct the written questionnaire on the basis of the tape-recorded interviews. . . . not all interviews cover the same topics and by no means are all questions covered consistently across all interviews. The range of variability was, in fact, gross. (1983: 22).

In other words, in Shuy's data, patients' and doctors' local negotiation changed the encounter away from the doctors' previously established design for the discourse.

Shuy's subsequent discussion casts his results in terms of the possibility that medical encounters can be conversational to a degree. Shuy suggests that patients are more comfortable with encounters that are more conversational. This raises the issue of genre: are encounters fundamentally interviews which can be modified toward conversation, or fundamentally conversations that have been modified to create interviews?

2   Genre

The question whether medical encounters are fundamentally conversational or interview-like appears in several major analyses. Frankel points to early studies in which researchers suggested that the encounter "is essentially conversational in nature" (1979: 232). Frankel remarks that the "case [has not] been made convincingly" (1979: 233).[1] Instead, he suggests, the restricted turn-taking system of the medical encounter is in contrast with that of conversational discourse, especially in regard to questions.

Ten Have's (1989) discussion of genre in medical encounters suggests that there is "simultaneous relevance of several different interactional formats" (1989: 115). Ten Have examines one such format, troubles-telling, a conversational activity. Confusions occur when patients think they are being invited to do troubles-telling. So ten Have sees that conversation can be one of the interactional formats that participants in encounters orient themselves toward, but that this can be "problematic," as physicians resist the format.

Heritage appears to agree with Frankel that institutional discourse is defined by restrictions on speech activities: "Institutional interaction seems to involve specific and significant narrowing and respecifications of the range of options that are operative in conversational interaction" (1989: 34). But, in contrast to Frankel, Heritage's formulation might suggest that he sees medical discourse as essentially conversational in nature.

Both Maynard (1991) and Ainsworth-Vaughn (1998b) identify speech activities which are found in conversation and in the medical encounters the researchers studied. Maynard shows that "doctor–patient interaction involves sequences of talk that have their home in ordinary conversation" (1991: 449). This sequence is neither problematic, as in ten Have's data, nor peripheral, as in Shuy's. The sequence Maynard finds in both medical encounters and ordinary conversations is a "perspective display series." For instance, a clinician and his team have developed a diagnosis of developmental delay in a child, and the clinician must now convey that diagnosis to the parents. The clinician asks the parents, "What do you see? – as his difficulty" (Maynard 1991: 468). The clinician then uses the parents' perspectives, as displayed in their answers, in co-constructing a formulation of the difficulty. Because the parents helped construct the formulation, they are more easily persuaded of its validity. Maynard suggests that this persuasive power can be abused by clinicians.

Maynard points to the theoretical significance of finding overlap between conversation and medical encounters: "If, at the level of conversational sequencing, we find deep connections between everyday life and the medical encounter, implications [for theories of] clinical and other institutional discourses are vast" (1991: 449). One such implication is that the structures of institutional discourse should be studied in conjunction with those of ordinary conversation, rather than in isolation, as is often the case now.

Ainsworth-Vaughn (1998b) also found a conversational structure fundamental to medical encounters. She studied narratives and stories used by doctors and patients in speculating upon and ruling out possible diagnoses. Three types of narratives appeared in this process: Labovian (Labov 1972), habitual (Riessman 1991), and hypothetical (Riessman 1991). Doctors and patients used these types of narrative to tell what happened (Labovian), what typically happens (habitual), or what might happen (hypothetical), in a story-world embodying a diagnosis. Labovian narratives about what did not happen were used to rule out possible story-worlds that had been offered. Often these Labovian, habitual, and hypothetical narratives were evaluated, becoming stories. These data are particularly significant for the "conversation as fundamental" approach, because narration and stories are often cited as archetypal conversational speech activities.

Psychotherapy sessions are an outgrowth of medical encounters. Ferrara's (1994) list of contrasts between conversation and talk in psychotherapy sessions is relevant to discussion of genre.

Ferrara labels seven differences between conversation and psychotherapy sessions: parity, reciprocality, routine recurrence, bounded time, restricted topic, remuneration, and regulatory responsibility. Three of the seven – routine recurrence, bounded time, and remuneration – are contextual features. These unarguably constitute the event, but they do not directly control or define the speech activities in the event. These three contextual features are found in both psychotherapeutic and medical encounters, but not in ordinary conversation.

The other four features have to do with discourse structure. They often are prominent in medical encounters, but have varying salience. Restricted topic, for instance, is a feature of encounters; but that statement must be qualified, for both topic sequence and topic itself. Shuy's (1983) above-mentioned data show the unpredictability of topic sequences in encounters. In my data on topic in oncology encounters (aspects of which are discussed in Ainsworth-Vaughn 1992), the restriction operated to require discussion of the relevant medical topic, but not necessarily to exclude discussion – even extensive discussion – of other, nonmedical topics.

In reviewing my data on medical encounters (Ainsworth-Vaughn 1998d), I find two more of Ferrara's contrasts to be borne out: lack of reciprocality (e.g. patient and doctor have unequal rights to ask questions) and regulatory responsibility (the physician has an asymmetrical right to initiate and terminate the encounter).

This leaves parity. Parity, or lack of it, in Ferrara's data refers to a client's agreement that the therapist is a helper and that the client needs help, through the discourse itself. Here therapeutic talk can differ from that of medical encounters. Since the discourse itself is treatment, the therapist has rights that may or may not be ceded to physicians in medical encounters.

In psychotherapeutic encounters, patients are presenting themselves for on-the-spot treatment through discourse, including discussion of intimate topics as the therapist deems therapeutic. So parity is relinquished, at least in selection of topics. This is not necessarily the case with medical encounters. This is why the model proposed by Smith and Hoppe, discussed above, is not appropriate for every medical encounter.

In medical encounters, parity is negotiated among participants, apart from the genre (conversational or ritualized talk). When the physician puts forth a diagnosis and treatment plan, this act is sometimes accepted as desired help and is ratified as a plan of action. The sequence of offering and accepting then constitutes lack of parity.

But the same act may be taken as constituting an opinion, and the patient may hold in abeyance any plans for action. In my data, an oncologist suggested that a young man with testicular cancer should have an exploratory operation to see whether cancer was in the nearby lymph nodes. Because the couple had no children, and the operation could lead to impotence, the man's wife suggested a different plan, and her plan was eventually adopted. She had negotiated parity; her plan was on a par with that of the physician.

In sum, we cannot characterize all medical encounters as having a matrix of conversational features, or as having a matrix of interview-like restrictions. We can suggest that encounters exist on a continuum between interrogation, as described in Mishler (1984), and friendly conversation with a small amount of time devoted to satisfying medical goals, as I found in studying unproblematic oncology checkups.

At the interrogation end, the sequence of speech activities is heavily ritualized (primarily questions and answers) and reciprocality is not present. At the conversation end, only a brief part of the sequence of speech activities is ritualized, and reciprocality may be present in varying degrees. Regulatory responsibility (the right of the physician to begin and end the event) is present throughout the continuum. Parity is negotiated locally, apart from discourse genre.

All analogies are deficient, by nature. A continuum metaphor provides for construing two possible directions for the discourse – toward the two ends of the continuum – rather than depicting the possible shifts that actually take place among multiple interactional frames (cf. Tannen and Wallat 1987). Perhaps the emblematic designs in medieval woodcuts would serve better; these web-like designs show connections among a variety of symbols. In an emblem, movement would be possible back and forth in a variety of directions. But the continuum metaphor does allow a representation, however limited, of variation in discourse genre – variation that has not yet received adequate attention in either the medical or the discourse literature on the medical encounter.

3 Constitutive Speech Activities

Framing moves and questions are the constitutive speech activities that have been of most interest to analysis of medical talk. Framing moves are related to the constitution of self in the medical encounter. Questions are the speech activity usually seen as embodying asymmetry in the encounter.

3.1 Frames

Framing is a critical act, because a frame is the definition of the speech activity underway (Tannen 1993). Frames are related to schemas, which are mental constructs, organized chunks of information (Tannen and Wallat 1987). We have schemas about all aspects of our lives, including our and others' social identities, the normal conduct of types of talk, and relationships between the two. I suggest that speakers make attempts to instantiate their schemas for the conduct of speech activities. In my terminology, such an attempt is a framing act, and an instantiated schema for a speech activity is a frame. Frames are constituted by participants' interactive behavior and by the way this behavior indexes the sociocognitive schemas associated with speech activities.

Goffman speaks of "the building up of an information state known to be common to the participants," which is "dependent on the question of the [interactional] unit as a whole" (1981: 131). Theories of frame and schema suggest that by proffering a frame, a speaker attempts to constitute the self. When the doctor–patient encounter is framed as part of the medical institution, participants are constituted as doctors, patients, nurses. But when a friendship frame is invoked, participants are constituted as peers. As frames are offered and ratified, a recursive process takes place. In this process, favorable or unfavorable attributes are added to the cognitive schemas participants can refer to during future constitution of their own and other's social identities.

A great deal of framing takes place at the beginning of an encounter. Introductory talk cannot be dismissed as just a prefatory segment preceding, and walled off from, the real work of the medical encounter. Talk at the first and last of the encounter is rich in meaning; as Ferrara says, "Information about differences is stacked at the edges of events" (1994: 42).

Coupland et al. found framing in physicians' small talk at the first of medical encounters in a small hospital in England. There were greetings and welcomings, apologies, compliments, teases, and other talk that "constitute[s] a predominantly social frame for consultation openings" (1994: 102); "doctors' willingness to pursue non-medical topics [was] strikingly at odds with the findings of most previous studies" (1994: 104). Coupland et al. see these framing gestures in a positive light. However, Cheepen (1988), referring to data on a job interview, suggests that when this early small talk is initiated by the institutional member of the group, it may be patronizing.

Although framing moves are typically proffered at the first of the encounter, they can occur anywhere within it. Tannen and Wallat (1987) studied a pediatrician who was videotaped for the purpose of teaching medical students how to conduct a medical encounter. The physician joked with the child, addressed her audience of medical students, and spoke to the mother, moving back and forth among frames. Tannen and Wallat locate their study within an extensive, detailed theoretical apparatus, showing that medical discourse (indeed, any discourse) may involve the coexistence of multiple frames.

Ten Have (1989) most likely had framing in mind when he remarked upon "different interactional formats" that can occur during medical consultations (1989: 115). Unlike Tannen and Wallat, who found multiple frames in peaceful coexistence, ten Have was interested in difficulties – "activity contamination" – that might arise from the salience of multiple frames.

Storytelling has been linked with framing in medical discourse. Stories are rich in both referential and social meaning (Schiffrin 1984), and therefore they play an interesting role in constituting frames and selfhood.

3.2   Stories

Sandelowski (1991) provides a masterly review of narrative studies relevant to medicine and medical discourse. In the praxis literature, narration has been linked primarily to patients' histories. "The patient's story," whether told by patient or by physician, usually is a term that conflates localized storytelling with an overview of the illness or of the patient's life history in relation to illness (Brody 1987; Kleinman 1988; Charon 1989; Hunter 1991; Frank 1995). For example, Waitzkin suggests that "doctors should let patients tell their stories, with fewer interruptions, cut-offs, and returns to the technical" (1991: 273). "Story" here refers both to localized talk and to the development of an overarching, abstract narrative.

Analysts of sequential discourse, however, are interested primarily in localized stories. A localized story is talk about a sequence of events. In the cross-disciplinary literature on stories, it is generally agreed that stories function to display core values and thus characterize the storyteller (e.g. Bauman 1986; Josselson and Lieblich 1993; Riessman 1993). Localized storytelling establishes both interactive frames and cognitive schemas important to the encounter.

Localized stories in the medical encounter have been associated with patients and thought of as patient's actions in a fundamentally conflictual relationship with the physician. Davis (1988) and Young (1989) looked at stories being used by patients. The stories they studied had two purposes:

- to define the interaction so that the social distance between patient and physician was reduced;
- to assert a self which had been suppressed in the institutional discourse.

Young (1989) describes encounters in which stories have little overt relation to the patient's presenting illness. Young analyzes both "links and splits" between stories and their surrounding medical context, but her emphasis is on the splits. For Young, stories are "enclaves of the self." The self is "sealed inside a story" (1989: 153).

Ainsworth-Vaughn (1998c) describes storytelling with multiple functions, in the introductory small talk in two oncology encounters. Rather than being the production of only one speaker, as in Young's study, in these encounters stories – even stories with no direct relation to cancer – were co-constructed, as doctor and patient worked to constitute a valued social self for the patient.

But this willingness to co-construct story and self may be unusual in medical encounters. Like Young, others who write about patient–physician talk have found patients having little success with their attempts to secure respect for their life worlds (Mishler 1984; Henzl 1990). Davis (1988) analyzed storytelling in Dutch medical encounters. In her data, "Myriad instances were available of the patient's 'lifeworld' being 'absorbed' into medical frameworks" (1988: 357). Davis makes it clear that she does not mean this in a positive way – as an enriching integration of the two – but rather as the disappearance of the life world.

The functions of storytelling as described by Davis (1988) and Ainsworth-Vaughn (1998b) are quite complex. Davis chose four encounters which show that patients' storytelling can range from being continuous throughout the encounter (creating and being created by a friendship frame) to being stymied at every attempt (creating and being created by a medical/professional dominance frame). And Ainsworth-Vaughn (1998c) suggested that stories functioned not only to frame but also to mitigate discussion of cancer, introduce a candidate diagnosis, and validate the patient's experience.

Also, as described in the preceding section, Ainsworth-Vaughn (1998b) found encounters in which joint storytelling became a way of constituting a diagnosis. Doctor and patient used narratives and stories to propose, argue against, augment, or accept – i.e. to construct – an overarching diagnostic hypothesis and its associated treatment plan.

Because it can determine diagnosis and treatment, and because it embodies our selves, storytelling claims power. Its presence in medical encounters is rich in significance for discourse theory and also for medical praxis.

3.3 Questions

The study of questions in medical encounters illustrates two fundamental problems with the extant research. One is the difficulty of defining a speech activity, and the other is the difficulty of generalizing on the basis of situated talk, without fully assessing the influence of varying contextual features, such as setting, gender, or diagnosis.

3.3.1 Questions and power

The term *question* sometimes is used to refer only to linguistic form, e.g. inversion of subject and auxiliary verb, or rising intonation at the end of a sentence. However, I follow Stenström (1984), West (1984a), and Frankel (1979) in using "question" to mean "request for information." Stenström shows that linguistic markings alone cannot identify questions (e.g. rhetorical questions are linguistically marked but function otherwise), but that linguistic markings and situational features have some conventionalized relationships which speakers understand as suggesting and confirming question function.

The number of questions doctors and patients ask has been a central issue in research on medical discourse because to ask a question is to claim power over emerging talk. Studies in various cultures (e.g. West 1984b (United States); Hein and Wodak 1987 (Austria); Weijts 1993 (Netherlands)) have shown beyond doubt that medical encounters often consist primarily of doctors asking questions and patients answering. The usual conclusion is that medical encounters are an "interview" genre – highly asymmetrical, with only one person having the right to question.

The relationship between questions and power is important to specify. Questions are directives. By using directives, a speaker proposes to exert control over other conversational participants (Goodwin 1990), i.e. to direct their actions in the discourse. There are several ways in which questions claim power:

- A question addressed to another participant chooses that participant as the next speaker – an obvious exercise of control.
- A question, even an "open-ended" question, always in some way restricts the topic of the response – the referential content of the conversation. This second point is especially important in the medical encounter, because time for the encounter is limited and choice of topic determines which of the patient's problems will be addressed and which will not.
- Some questions entail the expectation that the floor will be returned to the questioner (Frankel 1979: 234), and control of the floor is usually thought to embody the "up" position in conversational asymmetry (Edelsky 1993; James and Drakich 1993).

In institutional dyads (attorney–witness, teacher–student, physician–patient), typically, the speaker who has the power to reward (attorney, teacher, physician) has asked the most questions, and the imbalance in numbers has been dramatic (Dillon 1982, 1986, 1990). In conversational settings, however, questions need not be solely claims to power over the emerging discourse. Sometimes questions also propose to share or give up that power. Notably, a question can hand over the floor to other participants and demonstrate the questioner's interest in the answer (Goody 1978; Fishman 1983).

Questions in medical encounters demonstrate both power-claiming and power-sharing. However, it is power-claiming that has occupied researchers' attention. Comparative numbers and percentages of questions asked have been assumed to be rough indices to the balance of power between doctor and patient (Frankel 1979; West 1984a; Ainsworth-Vaughn 1994; see Ainsworth-Vaughn 1995 for a critique of this assumption). But these quantitative studies often rest upon differing definitions.

3.3.2   Defining and counting questions

Discourse acts depend upon both culturally agreed signals and interpretations made in real time by the participants. Interpretations are made by assessing talk within its local context. So speakers are assessing widely varying combinations of syntactic, referential, discourse, and other features. These combinations cannot be reduced to brief definitions. Referential meaning is particularly difficult to delimit with a definition (Ainsworth-Vaughn 1992).

The problem of definition is central in research on questions in medical encounters, in both the medical and the discourse literature. In the praxis literature, studies often have no articulated definition for questions (Bain 1976; Davis 1971; Korsch and Negrete 1972) or an idiosyncratic definition (Roter 1977, 1984).

In the discourse literature, the best-known article on questions is Frankel (1979). Frankel's definition acknowledges the role of referential content but rests upon the status of the question as the first part of an adjacency pair, itself a controversial concept (Stenström 1984: 24; Tsui 1989).

Frankel studied a very narrow subset of questions, which he called "patient-initiated." In audiotapes of ten ambulatory care visits, Frankel found that fewer than 1 percent of the total number of questions asked by physicians and patients were "patient-initiated." In order to be "initiated" by the patient, the question had to be the first utterance in the turn and also had to introduce new information. In addition, Frankel excluded "'normal' troubles such as requests for clarification, information, etc." (1979: 239).

Frankel's count of "patient-initiated" questions, based upon a well-articulated definition, is an example of quantitative and qualitative methods supporting one another in a productive way. It meets the qualitative demand for a discourse-based definition and the quantitative goal of providing an overview of the occurrence of the activity.

Unfortunately, there has been a widespread tendency to generalize Frankel's 1 per cent finding to all questions, when in fact it only applies to narrowly defined "patient-initiated" ones.[2] This inappropriately generalized finding is probably the best-known result of all research done on medical encounters and has contributed materially to a prevalent stereotype of patients as passive and powerless.

West (1984a, 1984b) also used an adjacency pair definition of questions; however, she placed few restrictions upon it, excluding only requests for repetition, because one person did not hear the other, and markers of surprise ("Oh, really?"). West studied questions in 21 encounters in a clinic whose population was primarily drawn from lower socioeconomic strata. She found 773 questions, of which 91 percent (705) were asked by physicians. Only 9 percent of the questions were asked by patients. West's data may suggest that medical encounters between residents and poor patients in a clinic do in fact belong to the "interview" genre, with doctors asking questions and the patients' role being largely limited to answering. But there is little contextual information on these 21 encounters. West does not say what the diagnoses were or whether the patients and doctors had met before.

She does say that there were 18 physicians, all of whom were white. Fourteen of the physicians were men and four were women. There were nine male patients (five white, four black) and 11 female patients (six white, five black). So both gender and ethnicity are complicating factors in evaluating West's results.

In my quantitative study of questions, I also used an adjacency pair definition, comparable to that used by West. I studied 40 encounters, evenly divided as to gender of both physician and patient. The setting was oncology in 28 of the 40 encounters, but the other 12 encounters were spread over a variety of medical specialties and diagnoses.

Compared with West's (9 percent) numbers, patients in this study asked a high percentage – 38.7 percent – of the 838 questions physicians and patients asked one another. This percentage is not out of line with other research. Roter et al. (1988)

summarize the results of nine quantitative studies of medical encounters in which some form of questioning was studied; by my count of their reported figures, patients asked 25 percent of the questions. In Roter's own 1984 study, patients asked 43 percent of the questions.

Diagnosis, gender, and initial versus repeat visit all appeared to make a difference in the numbers of questions patients asked, in the Ainsworth-Vaughn study. Gender was a particularly interesting issue. When the physician was a woman, male patients asked 10.9 questions per encounter and female patients asked 10.8. When the physician was a man and the patient a woman, the patient asked 8 questions per visit. Finally, the man–man dyad produced only 3.7 patient questions per visit. The percentages of physicians' questions in these same encounters are equally interesting. Overall, when the physician was a woman, she asked 49.9 percent (216) of the 433 questions. When the physician was a man, he asked 73.3 percent (297) of the 405 questions.

Gender has not been well studied in medical discourse. The studies that focus upon gender (West 1984c, 1990; Pizzini 1991; Davis 1988; Ainsworth-Vaughn 1992) have involved small numbers of female physicians (e.g. Davis looks only at the male physician–female patient combination). With these qualifications, it can be said that the studies of gender in medical discourse tend to support the possibility that women are more likely to be cooperative in discourse, while men are more likely to be competitive.

These quantitative/qualitative studies bear directly upon the problem of describing a genre – in this case, the medical encounter. They show that for some patients, the medical encounter was an interview in which physicians asked, and patients answered, questions; but for others, it was not. They suggest that subgenres exist, related to such factors as diagnosis and setting. They call attention to the need for further study of gender. In short, quantitative studies with a strong base in qualitative methods can provide important data on the control of emerging discourse.

4   Conclusion

In sum, research on medical discourse has provided data of great interest for theoreticians and practitioners. The medical encounter is an ideal locus for studies of institutional discourse because of the disparities between doctor and patient and the consequentiality of the talk. Practical problems of recording institutional discourse are minimal in medical encounters because of the temporal and spatial boundaries of the talk – usually 10–15 minutes, in a private room – and the small number of participants.

On the other hand, it is difficult to establish the trust that allows physicians and patients to consent to being recorded. Most studies have been based upon recordings made as part of residents' training, in free or low-cost clinics. In these settings, it is debatable whether patients can freely give consent. Perhaps because of the difficulty of obtaining consent for data other than that on free or low-cost clinics, the discourse literature is fragmentary.

There are several problems with the extant literature: first, we lack broadly tested discourse models of medical encounters. Therefore we cannot assume that phases are the most salient discourse organization in this speech event. Secondly, the event's constitutive speech activities have often gone undefined – or defined in idiosyncratic ways – and this casts doubt upon many quantitative studies of such critical activities as questions. Other important features of the event also need closer attention; so far we have an inadequate base of data on important discourse features such as contrasting medical settings, characteristics of the illness and patient, and gender. And finally, theories about power – its use and abuse – in relation to institutional discourse have not yet been well articulated, in spite of the centrality of power issues to debates in the literature.

We need research upon talk in a wider variety of medical settings, with balanced numbers of men and women as participants, and with ethnographic observation and attention to the way talk is situated – setting, diagnosis, interactional history, prospective length of the relationship. Research should exploit the creative tension that can exist between qualitative and quantitative methodologies, so that data on both sequence and frequency are represented in the analysis.

Research on medical encounters is used by medical educators, who attempt to design this consequential discourse event. New data on the event and on the attempt will continue to hold an unusual degree of interest for discourse analysts because of its theoretical, practical, and human implications.

NOTES

1 The publication date for this study is variously given as 1979 and 1984. As I read the publication data in Psathas's book, 1979 is the correct date.
2 For example, the phrasing in Beckman and Frankel (1984) allows overgeneralization: "In two studies (Frankel 1979, West 1984) physicians were found to control 91% and 99% of the questions asked in routine office visits to internists and family practitioners" (Beckman and Frankel 1984: 694).

REFERENCES

Ainsworth-Vaughn, Nancy. 1992. Topic transitions in physician–patient interviews: power, gender, and discourse change. *Language in Society* 21:409–26.

Ainsworth-Vaughn, Nancy. 1994. Negotiating genre and power: questions in medical discourse. In *Text and Talk in Professional Contexts*, eds Britt-Louise Gunnarsson, Per Linell, and Bengt Nordstrom, 149–66.

Uppsala: Association Suedoise de Linguistique Appliquée.

Ainsworth-Vaughn, Nancy. 1995. Claiming power in the medical encounter: the "Whirlpool" discourse. *Qualitative Health Research* 5(3):270–91.

Ainsworth-Vaughn, Nancy. 1998a. *Claiming Power in Doctor–Patient Talk*. New York: Oxford University Press.

Ainsworth-Vaughn, Nancy. 1998b. Diagnosis as storytelling. In *Claiming*

Power in Doctor–Patient Talk, Nancy Ainsworth-Vaughn, 147–71. New York: Oxford University Press.

Ainsworth-Vaughn, Nancy. 1998c. "Geez where'd you find THAT?": Co-constructing story and self in oncology encounters. In *Claiming Power in Doctor–Patient Talk*, Nancy Ainsworth-Vaughn, 125–46. New York: Oxford University Press.

Ainsworth-Vaughn, Nancy. 1998d. A sense of the moment: theory, methodology, data. In *Claiming Power in Doctor–Patient Talk*, Nancy Ainsworth-Vaughn, 15–32. New York: Oxford University Press.

Bain, J. G. 1976. Doctor–patient communication in general practice consultations. *Medical Education* 10:125–31.

Bauman, Richard. 1986. *Story, Performance, and Event: Contextual Studies of Oral Narrative*. Cambridge Studies in Oral and Literate Culture. Cambridge: Cambridge University Press.

Beckman, Howard B., and Richard M. Frankel. 1984. The effect of physician behavior on the collection of data. *Annals of Internal Medicine* 101:692–96.

Brody, Howard. 1987. *Stories of Sickness*. New Haven, CT: Yale University Press.

Byrne, P. S., and B. E. L. Long. 1976. *Doctors Talking to Patients*. London: HMSO.

Charon, Rita. 1989. Doctor–patient/reader–writer: learning to find the text. *Soundings* 72:137–52.

Cheepen, Christine. 1988. *The Predictability of Informal Conversation*. London: Pinter.

Coupland, Justine, Jeffrey D. Robinson, and Nikolas Coupland. 1994. Frame negotiation in doctor–elderly patient consultations. *Discourse and Society* 5(1):89–124.

Davis, Kathy. 1988. *Power Under the Microscope*. Dordrecht: Foris.

Davis, Milton S. 1971. Variation in patients' compliance with doctors' orders: medical practice and doctor–patient interaction. *Psychiatry in Medicine* 2:31–54.

Dillon, James T. 1982. The multidisciplinary study of questioning. *Journal of Educational Psychology* 74(2):147–65.

Dillon, James T. 1986. Questioning. In *A Handbook of Communication Skills*, ed. Owen Hargie, 95–127. New York: New York University Press.

Dillon, James T. 1990. *The Practice of Questioning*. New York: Routledge.

Edelsky, Carole. 1993. Who's got the floor? In *Gender in Conversational Interaction*, ed. Deborah Tannen, 189–230. New York: Oxford University Press.

Ferrara, Kathleen Warden. 1994. *Therapeutic Ways with Words*. Oxford Studies in Sociolinguistics. New York: Oxford University Press.

Fisher, Sue. 1986. *In the Patient's Best Interest: Women and the Politics of Medical Decisions*. New Brunswick, NJ: Rutgers University Press.

Fisher, Sue and Alexandra Todd, eds. 1993. *The Social Organization of Doctor–Patient Communication*. Second edition. Norwood, NJ: Ablex.

Fishman, Pamela M. 1983. Interaction: the work women do. In *Language, Gender, and Society*, eds Barrie Thorne, Cheris Kramarae, and Nancy Henley, 89–102. Cambridge, MA: Newbury House.

Frank, Arthur W. 1995. *The Wounded Storyteller: Body, Illness, and Ethics*. Chicago: University of Chicago Press.

Frankel, Richard. 1979. Talking in interviews: a dispreference for patient-initiated questions in physician–patient encounters. In *Everyday Language: Studies in Ethnomethodology*, ed. George Psathas, 231–62. New York: Irvington.

Goodwin, Marjorie Harness. 1990. *He-Said-She-Said: Talk as Social Organization among Black Children*. Bloomington, IN: Indiana University Press.

Goody, Esther N. 1978. Towards a theory of questions. In *Questions and Politeness*, ed. Esther N. Goody, 17–43. New York: Cambridge University Press.

Have, Paul ten. 1989. The consultation as genre. In *Text and Talk as Social Practice*, ed. Brian Torode, 115–35. Dordrecht: Foris.

Heath, Christian. 1992. Diagnosis in the general-practice consultation. In *Talk at Work*, eds Paul Drew and John Heritage, 235–67. Cambridge: Cambridge University Press.

Hein, Norbert, and Ruth Wodak. 1987. Medical interviews in interbal medicine: some results of an empirical investigation. *Text* 7(I):37–65.

Helman, Cecil G. 1984. The role of context in primary care. *Journal of the Royal College of General Practitioners* 34:547–50.

Henzl, Vera M. 1990. Linguistic means of social distancing in physician–patient communication. In *Doctor–Patient Interaction*, ed. Walburga von Raffler-Engel, 77–91. Amsterdam: John Benjamins.

Heritage, J. 1989. Current developments in conversation analysis. In *Conversation*, eds D. Roger and P. Bull, 21–47. Philadelphia: Multilingual Matters.

Hunter, Kathryn M. 1991. *Doctors' Stories: The Narrative Structure of Medical Knowledge*. Princeton, NJ: Princeton University Press.

James, Deborah, and Janice Drakich. 1993. Understanding gender differences in amount of talk: a critical review of research. In *Gender and Conversational Interaction*, ed. Deborah Tannen, 281–312. New York: Oxford University Press.

Josselson, Ruthellen, and Amia Lieblich. 1993. *The Narrative Study of Lives*. Newbury Park, CA: Sage.

Kaplan, S. H., S. S. Greenfield, and J. E. Ware. 1989. Assessing effects of physician–patient interaction on outcomes of chronic disease. *Medical Care* 27(3):110–27.

Kleinman, Arthur. 1988. *The Illness Narratives: Suffering, Healing and the Human Condition*. New York: Basic Books.

Korsch, Barbara M., and Vida F. Negrete. 1972. Doctor–patient communication. *Scientific American* 227(2):66–74.

Labov, William. 1972. The transformation of experience in narrative syntax. In *Language in the Inner City*, William Labov, 354–96. Philadelphia: University of Pennsylvania Press.

Lipkin, Mack, Jr., Samuel M. Putnam, and Aaron Lazare, eds. 1995. *The Medical Interview: Clinical Care, Education, and Research*. New York: Springer-Verlag.

Maynard, Douglas W. 1991. Interaction and asymmetry in clinical discourse. *American Journal of Sociology* 97:448–95.

Mishler, Elliot. 1984. *The Discourse of Medicine*. Norwood, NJ: Ablex.

Pizzini, Franca. 1991. Communication hierarchies in humor: gender differences in the obstetrical gynaecological setting. *Discourse and Society* 2(4):477–88.

Putnam, Sam, and Scott Sherman. 1995. Bibliography of the medical interview. Computerized. 6728 Old McLean Village Drive, McLean, Virginia 22101–3906: American Academy on Physician and Patient.

Riessman, Catherine Kohler. 1991. Beyond reductionism: narrative genres in divorce accounts. *Journal of Narrative and Life History* 1(1):41–68.

Riessman, Catherine Kohler. 1993. *Narrative Analysis*. Qualitative Research Methods series. Newbury Park, CA: Sage.

Roter, D. L. 1977. Patient participation in the patient–provider interaction: the effects of patient question asking on the quality of interaction, satisfaction, and compliance. *Health Education Monographs* 5:281–315.

Roter, D. L. 1984. Patient question asking in physician–patient interaction. *Health Psychology* 3:395–409.

Roter, Debra L., Judith A. Hall, and Nancy R. Katz. 1988. Patient–physician communication: a descriptive summary of the literature. *Patient Education and Counseling* 12(2):99–119.

Sandelowski, Margarete. 1991. Telling stories: narrative approaches in qualitative research. *Image: Journal of Nursing Scholarship* 23 (Fall):161–6.

Schiffrin, Deborah. 1984. How a story says what it means and does. *Text* 4(4):313–46.

Shuy, Roger W. 1976. The medical interview: problems in communication. *Primary Care* 3(3):365–86.

Shuy, Roger W. 1983. Three types of interference to an effective exchange of information in the medical interview. In *Social Organization of Doctor–Patient Communication*, eds Sue Fisher and Alexandra D. Todd, 189–202. Washington, DC: Center for Applied Linguistics.

Shuy, Roger W. 1987. Conversational power in FBI covert tape recordings. In *Power through Discourse*, ed. Leah Kedar, 43–56. Norwood, NJ: Ablex.

Silverman, David. 1987. *Communication and Medical Practice*. London: Sage.

Smith, R. C., and R. Hoppe. 1991. The patient's story: integrating a patient-centered approach to interviewing. *Annals of Internal Medicine* 115:470–7.

Starr, Paul. 1982. *The Social Transformation of American Medicine*. New York: Basic Books.

Stenstrom, Anna-Brita. 1984. *Questions and Responses in English Conversation*. Lund studies in English. Malmo, Sweden: Liber Forlag.

Tannen, Deborah. 1993. *Framing in Discourse*. New York: Oxford University Press.

Tannen, Deborah, and Cynthia Wallat. 1987. Interactive frames and knowledge schemas in interaction: examples from a medical examination interview. *Social Psychology Quarterly* 50(2):205–16.

Todd, Alexandra Dundas. 1989. *Intimate Adversaries: Cultural Conflict between Doctors and Women Patients*. Philadelphia: University of Pennsylvania Press.

Tsui, Amy B. M. 1989. Beyond the adjacency pair. *Language in Society* 18:545–64.

von Raffler-Engel, Walburga, ed. 1990. *Doctor–Patient Interaction*. Pragmatics and Beyond: new series. Amsterdam: John Benjamins.

Waitzkin, Howard. 1991. *The Politics of Medical Encounters: How Patients and Doctors deal with Social Problems*. New Haven, CT: Yale University Press.

Weijts, Wies. 1993. Seeking information. In *Patient Participation in Gynaecological Consultations: Studying Interactional Patterns*, Wies Weijts, 39–64. Maastricht: Uniprint Universitaire Drukkerij.

Weijts, Wies, Guy Widdershoven, Gerko Kok, and Pauline Tomlow. 1992. Patients' information-seeking actions and physicians' responses in gynecological consultations. Mimeo, University of Limburg.

West, Candace. 1984a. Questions and answers between doctors and patients. In *Routine Complications: Troubles with Talk Between Doctors and Patients*, Candace West, 71–96. Bloomington, IN: Indiana University Press.

West, Candace. 1984b. *Routine Complications: Troubles with Talk Between Doctors and Patients*. Bloomington: Indiana University Press.

West, Candace. 1984c. Turn-taking in doctor–patient dialogues. In *Routine Complications: Troubles with Talk Between Doctors and Patients*, Candace West, 51–70. Bloomington, IN: Indiana University Press.

West, Candace. 1990. Not just doctor's orders: directive–response sequences in patients' visits to women and men physicians. *Discourse and Society* 1(1):85–112.

West, Candace, and Angela Garcia. 1988. Conversational shift work: a study of topical transitions between women and men. *Social Problems* 35 (December):551–73.

Young, Katharine. 1989. Narrative embodiments: enclaves of the self in the realm of medicine. In *Texts of Identity*, eds John Shotter and Kenneth Gergen, 152–65. Newbury Park, CA: Sage.

24 Language and Medicine

SUZANNE FLEISCHMAN

Medicine . . . forfeited pretension to be deemed a Science, because *her Professors and Doctors . . . refuse to consider, in express terms, the relations between Things, Thoughts and Words involved in their communication to others.*

F. G. Crookshank, M. D., 1923

0 Introduction

A lot has been written on language and medicine. More than one might imagine, judging by the extent to which the research in this hybrid field – which staked its place on the Great Map of Knowledge essentially in the 1980s[1] – has had a demonstrable impact in three areas we might take to be "diagnostic": medical language itself, communication between patients and physicians, and our everyday discourse about illness and disease.[2] The second of these areas alone has spawned an extensive body of literature, which percolates down slowly into medical education and medical practice.

For practical reasons, this chapter will concentrate on western biomedicine (vs. other models of medicine studied, e.g., by medical anthropologists and semioticians) and on research in and about English. The choice of topics for inclusion, and their relative foregrounding and backgrounding, reflects to a degree my own biases and interests within the field. It could not be otherwise.

This chapter is organized into five sections. Section 1 touches briefly on doctor–patient communication (surveyed in depth in Ainsworth-Vaughn, this volume), focusing on differences in thinking, orientation, and research methodology between studies coming out of biomedicine and studies from humanities and social science fields. Section 2 deals with medical language as an "occupational register" and its constituent written genres. Section 3 looks at the literature–medicine interface, notably at theoretical notions and approaches to the reading/interpretation of texts that medical discourse analysts have borrowed from the field of literature, in particular the study of narrative. Section 4 deals with metaphors, in and of medicine. Section 5 probes the relationship of medical language to the "real world" of sickness and health.

We regret that this line of inquiry can no longer be pursued by Fleischman herself due to her untimely death from myelodysplastic anemia.

1   Doctor–Patient Communication

By far the lion's share of literature on language and medicine is about doctor–patient communication. As this is the topic of a separate chapter (Ainsworth-Vaughn, this volume), I limit my remarks here to noting interesting differences between the approaches and methodologies of researchers from biomedicine and those of discourse analysts, coming mainly from linguistics, English for science and technology (EST), and social science fields.

Discourse analysts (DA) tend to look at lexicogrammatical features (lexical choices, tense–mood variables, hedging devices, pronouns and passive voice, transitivity relationships), discourse structures and organization ("moves," schemas and frames, thematic progression, topic–focus relations, foregrounding and backgrounding), features of conversation analysis (turn-taking, structures of adjacency), and particularly at the functions these phenomena fulfill in the discourse forms in question. By contrast, the interactional analysis systems (ISAs) developed within medicine – "observational instruments" (the term itself is revealing) designed to analyze the medical encounter – typically involve the methodic identification, categorization, and notably quantification of salient features of doctor–patient communication. Ong et al. (1995) compare twelve such systems with regard to what they measure, their clinical relevance, observation strategies used, "inter-rater reliability validity," and "channels" of communicative behavior (i.e. applicability of the model to verbal and/or nonverbal behavior). Their study is based on 112 publications on doctor–patient communication from medical journals on hospital practice, medical education, social aspects of medicine, and in several medical specialties (notably oncology).[3] This research is highly quantitative (findings are based on survey/questionnaire data) and minimally linguistic, in the sense that the variables investigated involve general phenomena of communicative behavior (posing questions, interrupting, using technical language, giving "bad news"), physician and patient attitudes (about death, bad diseases, how much information to give patients), patient expectations, and measures of patient satisfaction (the influence of certain communicative behaviors on "patient outcomes"). For the most part, this literature does not look at texts (spoken or written), hence there is virtually no analysis, distributional or functional, of lexicogrammatical features, discourse organization, or rhetorical conventions. There is some attention to semantics (Bourhis et al. 1989; Hadlow and Pitts 1991), since the meaning of isolated words is easier to study using the methodologies these studies employ.

In order to produce the kinds of data ISAs are designed to manipulate, communicative behaviors must be identified (e.g. as "privacy behaviors" or "high physician-control" vs. "low physician-control" behaviors; Stewart and Roter 1989), categorized (e.g. as "instrumental" (task-focused, cure-oriented) vs. "affective" (socioemotional, care-oriented)), and quantified. On the basis of two studies in their survey, for example, Ong et al. report that only 7 percent of "affective" behavior is conveyed verbally, 22 percent is transferred by voice tone, but 55 percent is conveyed by visual cues such as eye contact, body positioning, etc. (1995: 908). One wonders how these statistics are produced.

The research generated within the two "camps" shows a fundamental difference in approach and orientation. Whereas the discourse analytical literature tends to be concerned with the interpretation of data, the goal of the biomedical literature is taxonomy/quantification. Case in point: a considerable literature has been generated in both camps on the subject of interruption. One study on the effect of physicians' communicative behavior in medical interviews (Beckman and Frankel 1984) has determined that 18 seconds is the mean length of time that elapses before a doctor interrupts a patient's first response to a physician-initiated question. This finding is unreflectively categorized as exemplifying "high physician-control behavior." Yet the sociolinguistic/discourse analytical literature on interruption has demonstrated that this speech behavior cannot automatically be interpreted as a dominance-associated violation of the speaking rights of others. Interruption serves various functions in conversation; in order to assess its function in a particular situation it is necessary to know, e.g. something about the roles and identities of the participants (for a review of this literature and a summary of the functions of interruption, see James and Clarke 1993: esp. 238–47).

Some of the results obtained from these biomedical studies might seem trivially obvious, e.g. that "the frequency with which patients ask questions seems to be strongly related to the prevalence of doctors' information-giving behaviors" (Ong et al. 1995: 908), or that "review of the literature suggests that patients often do not recall or understand what the doctor has told them" (Ong et al. 1995: 911). Most of the studies surveyed by Ong et al. (I cannot give an exact percentage) rely on statistically evaluable questionnaires and surveys, a staple of science and much social science methodology. Apparently, even the intuitively obvious is more authoritative when set on a foundation of statistical evidence.

Discourse analytical approaches, on the other hand, while not necessarily eschewing quantitative methodologies (intrinsic, e.g. to variation analysis), might ask questions like: what kinds of speech acts do the various questions instantiate (questions do not have a single, universal function)? How do they relate to/shed light on the identities/roles of the participants or the situation context in which they occur? (cf. Schiffrin's analysis (1994) of questions in interview situations, as presented in §3 of her chapter on the ethnography of communication). Does "speaker meaning" differ from "semantic meaning" and if so how? Since physicians are not trained to look at language from these perspectives or, therefore, to ask these kinds of questions, one can only hope that some of the findings of the DA literature surveyed in Ainsworth-Vaughn, this volume, might eventually come to their attention. Which brings us to the question of audience.

A significant factor accounting for the differences between the two bodies of literature involves their audiences and objectives. The overall objective of the medically generated research is to improve the physician–patient relationship as part of a broader agenda of improving health-care delivery. It is directed to physicians, with the ultimate goal of producing more satisfied patients. While this is undoubtedly an agenda of the discourse literature as well, it seems in most cases not to be the primary agenda, which is rather to extend the methodologies of DA into another field of application. The "proof of the pudding" is that this literature is rarely cited by medical researchers,[4] from which one might infer that they do not read it.

2 Medical Language and Discourse Genres

French writer Julien Green once observed that while thought flies, words walk. Jammal (1988) comments similarly that science flies and its terminology walks – typically at a pace that lags far behind scientific advances.

There is less literature than one might expect on medical language, the occupational register of a tribe of white-coated speakers that gets passed from one generation of physicians to the next through the highly ritualized institutions of medical education. It is widely recognized as what sociolinguistics would call an "in-group dialect," i.e. largely opaque outside the medical "confraternity."

2.1 Spoken and written genres

The literature on medical language tends to concentrate in two areas: doctor–patient communication (section 1 above and Ainsworth-Vaughn, this volume), where the focus is on *spoken* discourse, and the language of particular genres of medical discourse. The latter are primarily *written*, save for case presentations, formal oral performances made by physicians in training to their peers and superiors, typically in the context of hospital "grand rounds" or other types of case conferences. The case presentation is a highly conventionalized linguistic ritual[5] involving stylized vocabulary, syntax, and discourse structures which, when examined under a linguistic microscope, reveal tacit and subtle assumptions, beliefs, and values concerning patients, medical knowledge, and medical practice to which physicians in training are covertly socialized (see Anspach 1988).

With regard to spoken language, attention has also been paid to the in-group dialect physicians use in speaking to one another, notably about patients (cf. Klass 1984; Donnelly 1986; and Anspach 1988: 358–9 for additional references). The (largely ethnographic) literature on this topic uses medical language, particularly teaching-hospital slang, as a key to understanding the subculture that develops among physicians-in-training partly as a response to stresses generated by their work environment. Ethnographers of medical socialization, Anspach notes, have been particularly intrigued by the "black humor" and pejorative expressions for referring to hospital patients (*gomers, turkeys, crocks, brainstem preparations*)[6] or their clinical status (a terminally ill patient is *CTD*, "circling the drain," a patient who has died is said to have *boxed*), since these language phenomena fly in the face of the ostensible aim of medical training: to impart humanitarian values or a service orientation.

2.2 The lexicon and semantics of medicine

From a statistical study of 100,000 words from medical English texts, Salager (1983) distills "the core lexis of medicine" across specialties, while Jammal (1988) looks at how and why (mainly how) the technical vocabularies of medical specialties come to be constituted. Based on his experience compiling a dictionary of epidemiology, he offers a practical guide to the creation of terminology for fields of specialization.

Since the dictionary he worked on was bilingual (French–English), he pays particular attention to problems of translation from English, the international language of medicine (see Maher 1986). A question Jammal raises is: who ultimately decides which name/word should be chosen, among competing alternatives, to refer to a concept or disease entity? I doubt that the arbiter in these matters is, as he suggests, the lexicographer ("because it is his/her job to think about such questions," 1988: 536); more likely, a consensus ultimately emerges from discussions among specialists. For a fascinating window onto a terminological controversy of this sort, see the debate over the naming of "preleukemic states" (INSERM 1975, discussed in Fleischman 1999).

2.2.1   *Vocabulary of family medicine*

Dixon (1983) looks at the vocabulary of family medicine and finds it sadly wanting, offering up "a restricted and very biomedical view of the world." In the *International Classification of Health Problems in Family Care*, which serves as a dictionary for research in family practice, he notes a sizable vocabulary for classifying and describing respiratory infections, but only one word for poverty. Similarly, infectious diseases are categorized and subcategorized, while marital and family problems are presented in amorphous chunks (1983: 360). Occupying a kind of half-way house between the everyday language patients use to talk about the "lifeworld"[7] and the technical language of the biomedical world, the language of family practice in particular, Dixon argues, needs to be modified so as to make more of a place for human values in a professional framework that is largely committed to a reductionist, biomedical view of health. (One finds this theme reiterated throughout the literature in humanistic medicine.)

2.2.2   *Euphemism*

Johnson and Murray (1985) explore the role of euphemism in medical language. Nineteenth-century disease names, like popular disease names since earliest times, were often euphemistic – consumption, St. Vitus' dance, shingles, "tourista" – testifying to the hope, mystification, and resignation of patient and physician alike. Our elaborate system of euphemistic signifiers apparently evolved for the purpose of allowing medical teaching to take place with the patient present. While this language is still used in many cultures, particularly when the diagnosis is "bad,"[8] American doctors, Johnson and Murray report, claim to avoid euphemisms with their patients.[9] Johnson and Murray offer several possible explanations for this change in communicative practice. On the one hand, there is a sense in which "the real, solemn, Latin [or Greek!] name of something (put there by doctors) confers upon a disease, or on its sufferer, an importance which may be a kind of comfort" (1985: 151). This is the name, at any rate, that the sufferer will repeat to friends, telling them that she or he has *pityriasis rosea* (a harmless rash), *lymphadenopathy* (swollen glands), or *pernicious anemia* (a low red blood count, easily treated). Another rationale for scientific names is obviously pragmatic. Johnson and Murray (1985: 156–7) report that US physicians prefer "a clear and carefully worded scientific explanation of a patient's condition" as a precaution against lawsuits (cf. Gordon 1996). But in patients' experience "scientific explanations" are frequently anything but "clear" (cf. West 1984; Hirschberg 1985;

Bourhis et al. 1989; Hadlow and Pitts 1991; Platt 1992). Scientific nomenclature has thus, paradoxically, come to carry out the original function of euphemism.

2.2.3 *Technical language and ordinary language*

Some attention has been paid to the linguistic "gray area" in which the occupational register of medicine overlaps with ordinary language (Hadlow and Pitts 1991; Fleischman 1999; sporadically in the literature on doctor–patient communication). Occupational registers provide an efficient code for the transfer of information among specialists. Within knowledge communities, they provide a practical and convenient shorthand for talking about complex matters specific to a field. They are largely opaque outside the esoteric circle. A particularly slippery situation arises when technical language passes for ordinary language, i.e. when words have meanings – different meanings – in both dialects. Looking at psychological disorders the names of which have entered common parlance (e.g. depression, hysteria, eating disorder, obsession, "psychomatic" disorders generally), Hadlow and Pitts (1991) and Kirkmayer (1988) find that patients and medical professionals have different understandings of these terms. And in my own initial forays into medical literature, as a naive patient, I was unaware, for example, that the euphemism "supportive care" was a technical term (an umbrella term for a variety of actual therapies); it did not mean, as I had imagined, that patients were to be treated with empathy and respect. Nor did I realize that an "indolent" clinical course was a desirable thing to have. This latter expression, like a nurse's reference to Oliver Sacks's "lazy muscle" that prompted a mini-diatribe on descriptors (Sacks 1984: 46), illustrates medical language's potential for "guilt by association" (metonymic contamination), subtle slippages through which characteristics of a disease or affected body part transfer to the sufferer as an individual (see also Donnelly 1986 and section 4.3 below). One of the most striking examples of the ambiguous gray area in which the esoteric dialect confronts the exoteric dialect is the term "morbidity" – coin of the realm in medical discourse, the affective charge of which is clearly more noxious in ordinary language.

2.2.4 *"Illness language" and "disease language"*

Medical language, as various observers have pointed out (McCullough 1989; Mintz 1992), is an abstract discourse about disease and organs; it is not about patients and their experience of illness. In principle, McCullough argues, only patients can employ illness language; physicians *qua* physicians have no other language at their disposal than the abstract (because it is not *about* patients) language of disease (1989: 124). Those who urge changes in physicians' communicative practices, however, are less inclined to accept that physicians' "hands are tied" by the traditional orientation of medical language (see Donnelly 1986, forthcoming, and section 2.3.2 below on case histories). One wonders too whether physicians' language changes when they "cross over" and become patients? The "polyphonic" passages of Oliver Sacks's (1984) narrative of his experience of a severe leg injury shed interesting light on this question (see also Hahn 1985).

Mintz (1992) emphasizes the *distancing* function of medical language, an artifact of its commitment to objectivity. The distance, he argues, develops not only out of poor communication between physician and patient but also, and more importantly, *as the language physicians use comes to modulate their experience of patients* (1992: 223).[10] Shades of Sapir–Whorf.[11] (What Mintz describes using the word "distance" is perhaps better characterized as language's imperfect representation of the extralinguistic world – a paradoxical view for a Whorfian!) In particular, he dislikes the spatial metaphors and reification of diseases intrinsic to western discourse on medicine (the latter an artifact of our tendency to lexicalize diseases as nouns; see section 5 below). This discourse also tends to cast the sufferer in the role of a passive substrate, or medium, on which the more interesting player in the game, the disease, operates. Translating this into functional linguistic terms, we might say that the sufferer is assigned the "dative/ experiencer" role and the disease the "agent" role (see Fleischman 1999);[12] or, in terms of "grounding" relationships, that the disease is foregrounded, the sufferer backgrounded. My own reading of a fairly large body of medical literature – research papers, even case reports – confirms this distribution of roles. In the highly competitive "scientific" world of medical research, illness sufferers risk being eclipsed in biomedicine's crusade against disease – a state of affairs that is both reflected in and furthered by its language. Intrinsic to the "medicine as war" metaphor (section 4.2), for example, is biomedicine's emphasis on *fighting disease* rather than caring for sick patients. Which, in turn, licenses a rhetoric of blame that casts the patient as the agent responsible when things do not work out as hoped or expected: "she failed chemo" rather than "chemotherapy failed in/with her" (cf. Kirkmayer 1988).

2.3   *The genres of medical writing*

Among the genres of medical writing that have attracted discourse analysts' attention are the research article (Pettinari 1983; Salager-Meyer et al. 1989; Nwogu 1990), its abstract (Salager-Meyer 1990a, 1991; Nwogu 1990), popularizations of medical research in the news media or popular science magazines (Dubois 1986; Salager-Meyer et al. 1989; Nwogu 1990), textbooks of medicine and home medical books (Kahn 1983), and – by the lion's share of the literature – hospital patients' medical records or case histories (I use these terms synonymously; references in section 2.3.2 below), including those of bioethics cases (Brock and Ratzan 1988; Chambers 1996a, 1996b).

2.3.1   *Comparative genre analysis*

Several studies have undertaken to compare the discourse of different medical genres from the standpoint of rhetoric or surface-structure variables. Yanoff (1989) analyzes the "rhetorical features" (syntax, semantics, pragmatics, discourse function and organization, logic of argumentation, style) of "the six major genres" of medical discourse (as determined by a survey of medical schools),[13] with attention to cultural and situational contexts. Nwogu (1990) compares research articles, abstracts, and popularizations (parallel texts dealing with the same subject matter) in terms of three aspects of discourse organization: schematic units or "moves" (segments of a text identified by a distinctive rhetoric and/or function within the text as a whole), types of thematic progression, and textual cohesion. The studies by Salager(-Meyer) and colleagues likewise compare (through quantitative analysis) the constituent "moves" of the research paper, abstract, case report, and editorial, with attention to the communicative functions of particular variables (tense, active vs. passive voice, exponents of modality, hedging devices, connectives, negatives, interrogatives) within each one. A secondary agenda of the research by this group is pedagogical/ESL-oriented, i.e. to help nonnative medical students to recognize the discursive conventions of genres of medical English and to write well-structured texts. Also ESL-oriented are Van Naerssen's study on the lexicon, syntax, and discourse organization of the medical record (1985) and Pettinari (1983) on the use in surgical reports of distinct constructions for introducing "thematic" and "non-thematic" information (defined in terms of relevance, from the surgeon's perspective, to the goal of the surgical event).

2.3.2   Case histories

Among written genres of medical discourse, the case history has garnered the most attention, by far, and elicited the loudest call for reform – of its language as well the approach to medical practice that it reflects.[14]

The case history follows a ritualized format involving the frequent use of certain words, phrases, and syntactic forms, and a characteristic discourse organization. It includes information on how the patient's condition was noticed and diagnosed, how the condition has been treated, and how the patient responded to treatment. Psychosocial aspects of the case are presented (if at all) only after the medical problems have been discussed. The "problem-oriented medical record" favored by most teaching hospitals today (Weed 1970) organizes this information into four macro-categories, hygienically abbreviated SOAP: Subjective (the patient's statement of his or her condition), Objective (the physician's observations of the patient's condition), Assessment, and Plan.

Significant in this model is the fact that patients' accounts are set apart and relegated to the domain of the "subjective" – a negatively valued category in the world of science (see below) – and their observations are typically introduced using nonfactive predicators. Patients "state," "report," "claim," "complain of," "admit," or "deny" (see the excerpt below);[15] physicians "note," "observe," or "find" (Anspach 1988: 368) – factive predicators that put a stamp of truth/objectivity on the information that follows. Writers of case histories tend to present information obtained from physicians (themselves or others) as factual, while treating information from patients as "an account" (Anspach 1988: 369; cf. n. 31 below). This is presumably done unconsciously; the "evidential"[16] skewing is an artifact of the linguistic conventions of the genre. The example below is the history portion of the hospital admission summary (written by a resident) of a patient admitted for obstetrical care (from Anspach 1988: 373–4, my emphasis):

E. HISTORY (OB)   DATE OF ADMISSION:
                                                  11/07/84

The patient is a 21 year old Gravida III, Para I, Ab I black female at 32 weeks gestation, *by her dates*. *She states* that she has been having uterine contractions every thirty minutes, beginning two days prior to admission. *The patient* has a history of vaginal bleeding on 10/23, at which time *she reports* she was seen in the _____ Emergency Room and sent home. Additionally, *she does state* that there is fetal movement. *She denies* any rupture of membranes. *She states* that she has a known history of sickle-cell trait.

PAST MEDICAL HISTORY: Positive only for spontaneous abortion in 1980, at 12 weeks gestation. *She* has had no other surgeries. *She denies* any trauma. *She denies* any allergies.
REVIEW OF SYSTEMS: *Remarkable only for* headaches in the morning. *She denies* any dysuria, frequency, or urgency. *She denies* any vaginal discharge or significant breast tenderness. HABITS: *She denies* tobacco, alcohol, coffee, or tea. MEDICATIONS: *She* takes pre-natal vitamins daily.
FAMILY HISTORY: *Positive for* a mother with sickle-cell anemia. It is unknown whether she is still living. *The patient* also has a male child with sickle-cell trait. Family history is otherwise non-contributory.

Medical records are, conventionally, highly condensed summaries of large amounts of information. The example above is more fleshed out, less elliptical, than many. Hunter (1991: 91) sees the minimalism as "a goal of medical storytelling and an emblem of the efficiency that is an ideal of scientific medicine."

Most analysts of this genre focus on (1) how case histories are written – and how they might be improved – and (2) the "translation process" through which patients' *stories of illness* find their way into the medical record, transformed into *instances of disease* by the terse, objectifying, formulaic code that is the norm for this genre (cf. Mishler 1984; Kleinman 1988; Anspach 1988; Donnelly 1988, 1997; Hunter 1991: ch. 5; Charon 1992; Poirier et al. 1992; Smith 1996). Case in point: an individual tells the interviewing physician in training about his puzzled shock and dismay after noting passage of a black or "tarry" stool. This gets translated in the student's written account as "melena." Donnelly comments: "In one stroke, substituting 'melena' strips the event of the patient's wonder, shock, and dismay and consigns it to a universe of anonymous stools blackened by the presence of digested blood. Not only has the patient's subjective experience been objectified, but its particularity has been transcended by an abstraction" (1988: 824).

Among "questionable language practices" of the conventional case history, Donnelly (1997) includes:

> Categorizing what the patient says as "subjective" and what the physician learns from physical examination and laboratory studies as "objective." It is true that these terms . . . *can* be used *ontologically*, as I believe Weed intended when he made the[m] . . . part of the problem-oriented medical record . . . (*subjective* mental states and processes versus *objective* physical and biological phenomena). Unfortunately, the distinction is more commonly understood, especially in a science-using activity, *epistemically*, marking "different degrees of independence of claims from the vagaries of special values, personal prejudices, points of view, and emotions" [Searle 1992: 19]. Inevitably, then, categorizing what the patient says as "subjective" stigmatizes the patient's testimony as untrustworthy. On the other hand, calling physical findings and laboratory studies "objective data" gives an air of infallibility to the quite fallible *observations* of doctor and laboratory.

This statement expresses one facet of a broader *cri de guerre* against the widely perceived "loss of humaneness or humanity in medicine" (Fein 1982: 863). It is representative of an increasing body of literature, produced largely within the enclave known as humanistic medicine, calling for reforms in medical education, with a specific focus on language. The broader goal of these reforms is to restore to medicine the "personhood" of patients, who have been banished from a discursive stage on which organ systems essentially play out their dramas. (On the absent voice of the patient from medical case histories, see Poirier et al. 1992; for a nuanced analysis of how the *language* of case histories objectifies patients and devalues their subjective experience, see Anspach 1988). In an unorthodox attempt to remedy this situation, Charon (1986, 1989) asks second-year medical students to write stories about illness and disability *from the patient's point of view* in addition to conventional histories of present illness.[17]

Discourse analysis of the medical case history ranges from highly quantitative (Van Naerssen 1985) to highly interpretive (Anspach 1988). From the various studies on this genre (see n. 14 above), two will be singled out for discussion: Anspach (1988) and Francis and Kramer-Dahl (1992).

Anspach looks at the rhetorical features through which claims to knowledge are made and conveyed and at the epistemological assumptions underlying them. She focuses on four aspects of case histories:

1   *Depersonalization*, i.e. the separation of biological processes from the individual. See the opening sentence of the excerpt above; throughout this excerpt the woman is referred to as "the patient" or "she," no name, and ellipted altogether from statements of the physician's observations ("positive for . . . ," "remarkable (only) for . . .").

2   *Omission of agents*, e.g. through existential "there was . . ." constructions and agentless passives. These have the effect of emphasizing *what* was done rather than *who* did it let alone *why* a decision was made to engage in a given course of action.[18]

3   *Treating medical technology as the agent* ("The CT scan revealed . . . ," "Angiography showed . . ."). These formulations carry the process of objectification a step further than the passive voice: not only do the writers fail to mention the person(s) who performed the diagnostic procedures, but they also omit mention of the often complex processes by which angiograms and CT scans are interpreted. In treating medical technology as if it were the agent, such formulations support a view of knowledge in which instruments rather than people create the "data."

4   *The use of non-factive predicators* such as "states," "reports," and "denies" (Anspach calls these "account markers"), which emphasize the subjectivity of the patient's accounts.

What distinguishes this study from many others is not only its lucid and insightful analysis of the style of this genre of medical discourse, but also the author's attempt to ferret out the (unconscious) epistemological assumptions informing this style (1988: 369–72). Language, as Dr. Freud reminds us, is never innocent.

Another illuminating study of the medical case history is Francis and Kramer-Dahl's comparison (1992) of the title essay of Oliver Sacks's collection *The Man Who Mistook His Wife for a Hat* (Sacks 1985) with a "standard" case report of a patient with the same neuropsychological disorder. Through a nuanced analysis of lexicogrammatical patterns (using Halliday's transitivity model), the authors show how Sacks's linguistic choices reflect his beliefs about neurologically afflicted human beings, their conditions, and their relationships with their physicians, beliefs that tend to be erased by the language and text-structure of conventional case reports. The authors also emphasize the intertextual dialogue Sacks's "clinical tale" (his term, cf. Sacks 1986) engages in with "standard" case histories, questioning the ideology they encode. Sacks's view of professional case reports is that "their rigor and exactness may be useful in the construction of hypotheses about neurological conditions, but they can never convey the 'experience of the person, as he faces, and struggles to survive, his disease'" (Francis and Kramer-Dahl 1992: 81). As we have seen, this is a "chief complaint" of humanistic medicine, which often looks to language for remedies. Sacks's clinical tales spin out a heteroglossic discourse in which two "languages" illuminate one another: on the one hand, the scientific community's rigorous mode of observation and discovery, and on the other, the traditional storytelling mode.[19]

3   What Does Literature Have To Do with Medicine?

In recent years a number of medical discourse analysts (notably those trained in English departments) have turned to the field of literature for methodologies, models, and concepts for text analysis/interpretation.[20] Among the more productive analogies, to my mind, is the notion that doctors can learn to "read" patients using the interpretive strategies readers apply to literary texts (Charon 1986, 1989; King and Stanford 1992). Certain of the phenomena on which attention has been focused, however, are not specific to literature: repetition and parallelism, formulaicity, narrative "voice," point of view, description of participants ("character development" in fiction), "reading for the plot." But perhaps because they have been studied initially or primarily with respect to literary discourse, or because of the analysts' literary background, they are thought of as "literary" devices. In particular, research into narrative's role in medicine is often informed by an (unstated) assumption that literary narrative is the unmarked form of narrative (e.g. Poirier and Ayres 1997), an assumption many nonliterary narratologists might dispute.

This section will focus on three topics relevant to the literature–medicine interface: the role of narrative in medical discourse and medical thinking (section 3.1), narrative "voice" and point of view (section 3.2), and "pathographies," personal narratives about an experience of illness (section 3.3).

3.1   Narrative in medicine

Narratologists who have studied (nonfictional) narrative are keenly aware that what storytellers provide is not a verbal icon of a pre-existing structure of real-world experience. Rather, they cull from, and configure, the experiential database from which the story is constructed, notably in ways that support "the point" they wish to make in telling the story (see, e.g. Labov 1972; Fleischman 1990: section 4.1). This commonplace of narratology comes as "news" to at least some researchers who have undertaken to analyze medical case histories from a narrative point of view.

Observing that bioethicists have generally paid little attention to the rhetorical features of case presentations (but see Brock and Ratzan 1988), Chambers (1996a) compares four presentations of one of the best-known bioethics cases in the history of the field, the story of burn victim Donald "Dax" Cowart, who was not allowed to die. By comparing the different redactions of Cowart's story, with particular attention to features such as character development, narrative voice, and point of view, Chambers demonstrates how case writers suppress elements of the case that would challenge the premises of their theories. His broader agenda is to demonstrate the "constructed" nature of ethics cases and the extent to which the constructions are driven by particular ethical theories (see also Chambers 1996b). As stated above, this conclusion comes as no surprise to investigators of narrative in other settings (conversation, ritual performance, the courtroom, etc.). But apparently in the field of medicine (including medical ethics), which joins with "scientific" disciplines[21] in its ideological investment in objectivity, the case must still be made that narrative accounts are subjective, "constructed," and shaped by the point the teller wishes to make.

The terms "narrative" and "story" (here used synonymously) have different meanings in different disciplines. In the literature on the medical encounter and the documents it generates, notably the patient's chart and case history, the phrases "doctors' stories" and "patients' stories" come up frequently. The latter is fairly straightforward, inasmuch as patients typically "tell a story" that explains their presence in the physician's office, and that story is a constituent element of the medical interview "frame." The phrase "doctors' stories," however, seems to have a greater range of meanings. In some studies it seems to be synonymous simply with "explanation" or "prognosis" (Boyd 1996), whereas in others it refers to more prototypical narratives.

The phrase "doctors' stories" provides the title for Kathryn Hunter's book (1991), the main agenda of which is to call attention – particularly within the medical community – to the crucial importance of narrative to the institution and practice of medicine. Narrative, Hunter argues, is integral to the medical encounter, to communications by and about the patient, and to the structure and transmission of medical knowledge (cf. also Hunter 1996; Epstein 1995). The patient's story is told to and interpreted by the physician, who then tells another story about the patient, in case format, to other physicians, and records that story in a formulaic chart entry. Hunter observes that most of the rituals and traditions of medicine and medical training are narrative in structure – the "medicine is a detective story" metaphor rests on the notion that "diagnostic reasoning [i]s a fundamentally narrative enterprise" (Epstein 1995: 43) – and explains why narratives such as cautionary tales, anecdotes, case reports, and clinical-pathological conferences must be seen as central, not peripheral, to medicine. This thesis is further developed as a "take-home message" to physicians: that if they will recognize the narrative structure of medicine, they will attend better to their patients, in part by acknowledging the details and importance of their patients' life stories.

Hunter is not alone in advocating that physicians accord greater importance to patients' stories than has traditionally been the case in biomedicine. There is a strong impetus in this direction, particularly among advocates of the "biopsychosocial model" of health and illness (Engel 1977; cf. Charon 1986, 1989; Donnelly 1988, 1997; Poirier et al. 1992; Smith 1996; and references provided in Ainsworth-Vaughn, this volume).

Chapter 7 of Hunter's book is devoted to the "narrative incommensurability" of doctors' and patients' stories. Doctors differ from patients in the ways in which they use language and the purposes to which they put words. Doctors use words to contain, to control, to enclose (Charon 1992 and Epstein 1995 express a similar view). One of the central assertions of Epstein's book is that medical narratives are produced, in part, to "contain human beings, . . . to hold their anarchic potential in check" or "to rein in the threatening aberrational potential of the human body" (1995: 4, 20).[22] Patients, on the other hand, use language to express the sensations of things being amiss. Rather than categorizing and reducing, patients enlarge and embroider. Doctors simplify, patients complicate (Charon 1992: 116).

3.2 Narrative "voice" and point of view

Literary narratology insists on a distinction between "narrative voice" (who is speaking?) and "point of view" (whose perception orients the report of information?).[23] Since narrators commonly undertake to tell what other individuals have seen or experienced (this is standard in the medical chart or case history, where the patient's words and experiences are entered into the record using the physician's language), it is necessary to keep these two notions distinct at the theoretical level. In the literature on medical discourse the two notions are often conflated and the terms used interchangeably. Poirier et al.'s discussion of "the absent voice of the patient" (1992: 7–9) is really about the absence from the chart of the patient's *point of view* (they mention, in fact, that the Subjective entry in SOAP notes (see section 2.3.2) typically begins with a direct quote from the patient). This use of the term "patient's voice" is also encountered in regard to pathographies (section 3.3). King and Stanford (1992) implicitly address the issue of point of view in arguing for a "dialogic" (patient and physician) rather than the traditional "monologic" (physician only) storying of patients. In the studies surveyed in this connection, the collapsing of the theoretical distinction between voice and point of view is not problematic, though it could be, a fortiori since in "medically plotted" stories, the observing, narrating speaker is conventionally effaced and the story written as if "the medical facts" speak for themselves.

Bioethics cases in particular can be "evidentially" problematic as a result of the case writer's failure to properly identify participants' distinct points of view, all reported through the narrator's voice. Chambers (1996b) discusses a case that revolves around what to do about a psychiatric patient who refuses to complete a course of electroshock therapy but has become violent and suicidal. What Chambers finds problematic about the ethicists' write-up of this case in their textbook, which claims to present "accurate accounts of actual cases," is that although there are three points of view in this story – the physician's, the patient's, and the ethicists' – the story told reflects only the point of view of the physician (as determined by identifying linguistic features).

3.3 Pathography

Narratives about an experience of illness have proliferated in America over the past several decades, notably in the form of biographies and autobiographies often referred to as "pathographies." Hawkins (1984, 1993) surveys this burgeoning body of literature, tracing the metaphors and patterns of myth-making at work, and examining the ways in which writers of pathographies borrow from the metaphorical archetypes – the journey, war/battle, death and rebirth, the body/soul analogy – to describe and come to terms with the experience of serious illness. Whereas Hunter (1991) sees pathography as a genre of protest literature against the medical reification of patients (see n. 10 on the "metonymic imperialism" through which "patients" are transformed into "cases"), Hawkins views it as complementary to the medical case report. Using a striking visual metaphor, she observes: "Case reports and pathography function as mirrors set at an oblique angle to experience: each one distorts, each one tells the truth" (1993: 13).

A comparison of two reviews of Hawkins 1993 (= H.), from the journals *Theoretical Medicine* (*TM*) and *Literature and Medicine* (*LM*), sheds illuminating light on the ideological divide alluded to above (section 1) between a traditional biomedical approach and a humanistic approach to illness. The reviewer for *TM*, a psychiatrist, fails to engage H.'s study on its own terms, opting instead to elaborate his "dislike [of] the genre to which Hawkins gives the name of *pathography*" (the term is in fact from Freud). Too often, he opines, "pathographies represent an attempt to impose the patient's subjective interpretation as an objective fact, . . . a kind of power trip." H. makes clear that she reads pathography *not for reportorial accuracy* but to understand the prevalent metaphors used by illness sufferers to "formulate" their experiences.[24] In her view pathography "restores the person ignored or cancelled out in the medical enterprise, . . . [and] gives that person a voice" (1993: 12). Is it a bias of psychiatry (or of the particular reviewer) or is it endemic to biomedicine that "effective therapy may depend on convincing the patient that his voice is wrong, or at least unhelpful" (*TM*)? By contrast, the reviewer for *LM* credits H. with giving these narratives of illness experiences "the status they deserve as a major resource for clinical teaching and reflection." As an occasional reader of pathographies, I share the *TM* reviewer's dismay at the tabloid quality of many of these accounts, those in the *New Yorker* and Sacks's *A Leg to Stand on* (1984) being notable exceptions.[25] However, I recognize their value as cultural documents, of particular interest for their use of metaphors. Which brings us to the topic of the next section.

4 Metaphors in Medicine

Since the publication in 1980 of Lakoff and Johnson's *Metaphors We Live By*, which argues for the pervasiveness of metaphor in everyday life and thought, researchers have undertaken to explore the metaphorical substrate of a wide range of domains of experience and fields of inquiry. Medicine is no exception. The topics one might discuss under the rubric of "metaphors in medicine" are many and the studies too numerous to survey in depth. I will of necessity be selective. After a brief introduction (section 4.1), I will look primarily at the use of metaphors within medicine – western medicine's predominant conceptual metaphors (section 4.2) and the metaphors generated by body parts and their afflictions (section 4.3) – and secondarily at metaphors medicine has "exported" (section 4.4). I conclude this section with a "balance sheet" assessing the advantages and disadvantages of metaphorical language/thinking in medicine (section 4.5).

4.1   Introduction

In 1989 the interdisciplinary journal *Soundings* devoted a special section to "Metaphors, Language, and Medicine" (Carter and McCullough 1989), offering a spectrum of essays on topics that include the metaphoric language of pain (Landon 1989); metaphors in doctor–patient communication (McCullough 1989; Donnelly (repr. of Donnelly 1988); Carter 1989); the familiar metaphors of "Medicine is war" (Ross 1989; Diekema 1989) and "The body is a machine" (Osherson and AmaraSingham 1981; Kirkmayer 1988; Diekema 1989), and metaphors of destruction and purgation (Maher 1989); as well as the moral and cultural implications of medicine's metaphors (Kirkmayer 1988; Diekema 1989). The other major study of metaphor in medicine, van Rijn-van Tongeren (1997), looks at metaphors in medical texts (specifically in cancer research, but with broader implications). Following Lakoff and Johnson, van Rijn-van Tongeren (= V.) starts from the position that metaphors should be seen as surface representations of an underlying conceptual system, then proceeds to identify (1) the kinds of metaphors used to structure medical concepts and (2) the functions of metaphorical expressions in medical texts. Analysis of how the "recipient," or target, field of a metaphor is structured by the "donor,"[26] or source, field is used to reveal which aspects of a phenomenon are "highlighted" and which are "obscured" (see section 4.5) by the metaphor applied to it.

V. sees metaphorical expressions in medical texts as serving three functions: catachretic, didactic, and theory-constitutive. The first two are applied to objects or phenomena that are already known: *catachretic* metaphors fill gaps in a vocabulary, e.g. the initial "blood vessels as rivers" metaphors, instantiating the conceptual metaphor "Anatomy is a landscape", while *didactic* metaphors explain new concepts by means of familiar concepts, e.g. the *transcription machinery* of m[essenger]RNA (itself a metaphor), instantiating both "The body is a machine" (specifically "Cells contain machinery") and "A genome is a text." *Theory-constitutive* metaphors, on the other hand, are applied to phenomena that are not yet known in order to structure them and discover what they are "like"; they cannot, therefore, be replaced by "literal" terms. V. emphasizes that the function of a metaphor *is context dependent and may change* in the course of investigation. Especially theory-constitutive metaphors may change their function and acquire a didactic function, when discoveries are made on the basis of the theory metaphor.

Though conceived with regard to texts in medical research, V.'s typology of metaphors has applications elsewhere in medicine. Didactic metaphors in particular are "coin of the realm" in doctor–patient communication, as physicians are called upon to explain complex pathophysiological phenomena to their patients (cf. Carter 1989; Fleischman 1999). Some of the most profound aspects of the physician–patient relationship are not easily talked about – cf. Dixon's (1983) article on the language of family practice, aptly subtitled "at a loss for words" – and thus lend themselves to catachretic metaphors. These metaphors can reveal dimensions of an ailing individual not accessible through medical models (Marston 1986), and thereby tap into healing resources within the patient (Carter 1989). The challenge, of course, is to discover which metaphors best serve the individual patient's healing (Fleischman 1999).

4.2   Biomedicine's conceptual metaphors

As Diekema (1989: 19) points out, there is a dialectic between the metaphors of a culture and the medicine that evolves within that culture. In American culture and among American physicians there is a prevailing view that disease is an *outrage*, a violation of the true nature of life rather than a natural part of it (cf. section 5.1). Viewing disease as an outrage, Ross (1989: 40) argues, lays the groundwork for what is undoubtedly the dominant conceptual metaphor of biomedicine: "Medicine is war."

"Medicine is war" has long informed the thinking/discourse about infectious disease (Sontag 1978; Burnside 1983), and more recently about cancer, AIDS, and other epidemic diseases (Sontag 1978, 1989;[27] Brandt 1988; Ross 1988, 1989; Norton et al. 1990 van Rijn-van Tongeren 1997; among many). It constitutes a major piece of the ideological underlay of the biomedical model (cf. Hawkins 1984; Hodgkin 1985; Diekema 1989; Mintz 1992). It is this metaphor, for example, that underwrites biomedicine's emphasis on *fighting disease* rather than caring for sick patients.

The rising expectations for cure on the part of illness sufferers in western industrialized societies are due in no small part to the prominence in these cultures of the "Medicine as war" metaphor, which government and the media have seized upon – how better to unite a fractured society than through opposition to a universally acknowledged "enemy"? – but which certain cultural critics (Sontag, Ross) find inappropriate, if not covertly insidious. Ironically, as Sontag points out in her "deconstruction" of this metaphor that informs the discourse around cancer and a fortiori around AIDS, the patient emerges as both victim and responsible agent (1978: 57; cf. also Kirkmayer 1988).

Like all metaphors, "Medicine is war" has advantages and drawbacks (see section 4.5). While the imagery of fighting provides many patients with motivation, optimism, and comradery, whence its prominence in pathographies, it can also contribute to despondency if the disease becomes terminal (Stibbe 1997) or to a sense of personal failure. And Hodgkin (1985) points out that certain entailments of this metaphor – action is a virtue, doctors are fighters, technologies are weapons, disease is the enemy – only further the view that patients are not the "real" focus of medicine but merely the clinical stage on which the main protagonists of the drama do battle. Finally, to the extent that war is still a largely male enterprise, this metaphor subtly reinforces medicine's traditional gender bias.

As noted above, the language of medicine assigns physicians an active role and patients, by default, a passive role (cf. Burton 1982). This "transitivity" relationship is supported by both the war metaphor and the other major conceptual metaphor of biomedicine: "The body is a machine" (see Hodgkin 1985; Diekema 1989; Mintz 1992; van Rijn-van Tongeren 1997). This metaphor has a long tradition, from Descartes through nineteenth-century positivism. According to this view, the individual is seen as the sum of the body's parts, many of which have their own individual mechanical analogues: "The heart is a pump," "The digestive system is plumbing," "The brain is a computer,"[28] "A cell is a machine," and "Cells contain machinery."

The conceptual macrometaphor suggests that we place our bodies in a custodial relationship to the medical establishment analogous to the relationship of our vehicles, for example, to the confraternity of auto mechanics to whom we turn for repairs or replacement parts (on the "fix-it" metaphor, see Kirkmayer 1988; Carter 1989). Doctors and patients alike may find objectionable, because dehumanizing, the image of physicians who work as mechanics or technicians and of illness sufferers metonymically reduced to a malfunctioning body part (see section 4.3). Warner (1976) goes so far as to suggest that the power of this metaphor might contribute to an overuse of surgical procedures.

Another prominent set of metaphors in medicine are those of "marketplace economics." These metaphors inform our language about diseases (TB, cancer, and now AIDS), and with the current emphasis in America on "managed care," health care itself. Sontag (1978) points out that the fantasies about TB that arose in the nineteenth century (and continued into the twentieth) echo the attitudes of early capitalist accumulation: one has a limited amount of energy, which must be properly spent. Energy, like savings, can be depleted, run out, or be used up through reckless expenditure. The body will start "consuming" itself, the patient will "waste away" (1990: 62; see also Rothman 1994). *Mutatis mutandis*, this network of metaphors has migrated into the thinking/discourse about AIDS. And if TB was conceptualized via images that sum the negative economic behavior of nineteenth-century *Homo economicus* – consumption, wasting, squandering of vitality – then cancer is conceptualized through images that sum up the negative behavior of twentieth-century *Homo economicus* – unregulated, abnormal growth, repression of energy (refusal to consume or spend) (Sontag 1990: 63).

Health care in America today is more than ever before a matter of economics. Discussions of treatment, procedures, drugs, and hospitalization are suffused with marketplace concepts and vocabulary, which have clearly influenced our thinking about the treatment of illness. Particularly since the rise of the carefully controlled biomedical economy referred to as "managed care," commodification has become a reality and not simply a way of thinking and speaking. "Health care is a commodity": treatments are "sold" by physicians and hospitals and "bought" by patients (the euphemism "health-care consumers" proliferates in policy statements and media discourse), and physicians are employees of medical "businesses." Optimal "delivery" of health care is "calculated" according to a balance sheet, notably by the "bottom line" (cf. Fein 1982; Diekema 1989). Medical education, too, is increasingly subject to the "law of supply and demand," notably as regards the training of physicians in subspecialties.

Other conceptual metaphors of medicine have been or will be dealt with in other sections of this chapter: "the patient as text" (section 3), "disease as an object" and its corollary "the patient as container" (section 5.1), and spatial metaphors, notably "causation (etiology) as a line" (section 4.5). A leitmotif running throughout Hunter's *Doctors' Stories* (1991) is the metaphor of "medicine as a detective story" (cf. also Hodgkin 1985).

4.3   *The body and its metaphors*

As linguists, anthropologists, and cultural investigators of the body have long recognized, in virtually every language and every culture *body parts serve as metaphors.*

They come to stand for perceived physical or mental states, and as such, take on "a new life" in language. One need only think of expressions such as *eat your heart out!*, *he hasn't a leg to stand on*, *it makes my blood boil*, *she gets under my skin*, *a gut reaction*, *get off my back!*, or *in your face* – all based on associative meanings that attach to the respective body parts in English. Some of these associations extend across languages and across cultures.

The symbolic and metaphorical meanings that attach to body parts naturally carry over to illnesses affecting those body parts, and may have as profound an impact on the sufferer, consciously or unconsciously, as the bodily distress occasioned by the symptoms of the pathology. A disease of the *heart*, for example, calls up a potent symbolic universe in virtually every culture of the world (see Good 1997; Matisoff 1978), confronting us directly and unavoidably with our mortality. (The recent redefinition of death in terms of the *brain* and not the *heart* is bound to yield some interesting metaphorical shifts.) The metaphoric potential of a disease of the *eyes* is likewise far-reaching, given the primacy of vision among our perceptual senses and its quasi-universal link to cognition ("I see" means "I understand"). Since *blood* is universally viewed as the transmitter of lineage, the taint of a blood disorder may extend symbolically (if not also in actuality) down through the entire vertical line of the sufferer's "blood relations." And especially in recent times, blood has also become the organ of contagion par excellence. And a disease that affects the *bone marrow* is symbolically one that touches the deepest cellular recesses, the core of one's being (Fleischman 1999).

When a person suffers from an illness, the affected organ or body part is never *just* a body part. Illnesses typically evoke the symbolic meanings that body parts acquire in the context of a culture, which are frequently metaphorical (on the ways in which signs of health and illness serve as metaphors and metonyms generally, see Staiano 1986). Staiano also observes a tendency to express diffuse, ill-defined, unstated, or unstable social or personal concerns (fears, anxieties) in concrete, physiological terms. In this metaphoric process of somaticizing the social and personal, reference is often made to body parts ("my blood is stagnating," "there must be something wrong with my liver," "I have heart distress," "my guts are in a knot," etc.).

Health-care professionals too commonly engage in linguistic (and conceptual) troping. The trope most frequently commented on involves reducing patients to an afflicted body part. Just as a waiter in a restaurant might say, metonymically, "the ham sandwich wants his check" (Lakoff and Johnson 1980), the physician or nurse may come to regard body parts as synechdoches standing in place of the patient as a whole: "the gall bladder in 312 needs his IV changed." On consequence of such troping, which apparently occurs not only in biomedicine but also in traditional forms of medical therapy (Staiano 1986: 27), is the exclusion of the patient from the ensuing treatment, which becomes directed toward the synecdochic sign.

But if from the healer's perspective the sufferer becomes the affected body part, from the sufferer's perspective the synechdochic process may work in the other direction: the ailing body part becomes you. Oliver Sacks articulates this feeling of the body part's takeover of the self when he writes: "What seemed, at first, to be no more than a local, peripheral breakage and breakdown now showed itself in a different, and quite terrible, light – as a breakdown of memory, of thinking, of will – *not just a lesion in my muscle, but a lesion in me*" (1984: 46).

4.4   Medicine's metaphorical "exports"

In any culture the body provides a powerful set of metaphors for talking about society and the "body politic" (Benthall and Polhemus 1975; Staiano 1986), about social institutions, and about the character of individuals (on the influence of the medieval doctrine of the humors/temperaments on our contemporary vocabulary, see Geeraerts and Grondelaers 1995). It follows, then, that the body's ills will become metaphors for "the ills of society" (see n. 29). The illness/disease metaphors that medicine has "exported" are too numerous to list. Some that come readily to mind are being *blind* to reality, *deaf* to all entreaties; having a *lame* excuse, an *anemic* economy, or your style *cramped*. Public transit systems become *paralyzed*, traffic *arteries blocked*, college majors *impacted*. The terms *pathology/pathological* have extended their domain of reference from "the branch of medicine that studies diseased tissues" to groups, individuals, or behavior "deviating from a sound or proper condition" (the relationships in that family are *pathological*, standard languages are *pathological* in their lack of diversity).

As various investigators have pointed out, Sontag in particular, epidemic diseases offer wide possibilities for metaphorization to the social body or body politic (the term *epidemic* itself has become a metaphor, as in an *epidemic* of house selling). The discourse of social complaint is rife with allusions to *poxes on, plagues to,* and *cancers of* society, often expressed using *inflammatory* rhetoric. Sontag notes (1990: 14–15) that the earliest figurative uses of cancer are as a metaphor for "idleness" and "sloth." But as cancer biology became better understood, these were replaced by uses privileging the notions of "abnormal proliferation" and "unregulated spread or growth." Albeit one of the most thoughtful commentators on medicine's metaphorical legacy, Sontag is strongly of the opinion that "illness is *not* a metaphor, and that the most truthful way of regarding illness – and the healthiest way of being ill – is one most purified of, most resistant to, metaphoric thinking" (1990: 3).

4.5   Highlighting and obscuring

Like others who have looked at metaphor, van Rijn-van Tongeren (1997) emphasizes that metaphors can limit as well as advance our thinking. Because they always structure partially, metaphors foreground certain aspects of a phenomenon, while others remain backgrounded, or obscured altogether (Lakoff and Johnson's 1980 "highlighting and hiding"). For example, what is highlighted when a "body as machine" metaphor is used is that the process is controllable by humans. Machine metaphors suggest that the "mechanism" of a phenomenon is understood (by some at least), since machines are made by people. Applied to natural phenomena, these metaphors hide the fact that many of the "secrets" and "laws" of nature – including many aspects of bodily functioning – are still poorly understood. Likewise, the metaphor "(Tumor) cells are human beings acting independently and autonomously," used in descriptions of cancer at the cellular level, may obscure other factors, both external (chemicals, radiation, dietary fat) and internal to the body (hormones, the enzyme "telomerase," thought to be responsible for cellular *immortality*), that have been implicated in carcinogenesis.

Similarly, the pervasiveness of certain metaphors may exclude other equally valid ways of viewing health and illness. Warner (1976) suggests that European languages' extensive use of spatial metaphors to express abstract concepts (e.g. "Causation is a line") may encourage a rigid categorization of disease and inhibit our ability to conceive of diseases as having more than one cause. Van Rijn-van Tongeren (1997: 93) makes a similar claim for "agent" metaphors.[29]

Moreover, therapies are linked with theories, as van Rijn-van Tongeren points out (1997: 96), and metaphors constituting medical theories thus determine the therapeutic possibilities. When therapies are deemed inadequate, alternative theory-constitutive metaphors have to be found. The issue of "highlighting and hiding" is important in connection with medical theories, since valuable therapeutic possibilities may be obscured by the metaphors constituting those theories. For example, the development of new cancer therapies based on regulating "apoptosis" (a mechanism for cellular *suicide*, or *programmed cell death*) or inhibiting the expression of telomerase in malignant cells (see above) supports but also challenges the metaphor "(Tumor) cells are human beings acting independently and autonomously." Research in these areas is consistent with the view of tumor cells as human beings; it challenges the view that cells act independently. As van Rijn-van Tongeren suggests (1997: 96), analysis of the way in which the target field of a metaphor is structured by the source field may reveal which aspects of a phenomenon are highlighted and which hidden, and thus contribute to finding alternative metaphors to establish new theories.

As possibilities for alternative metaphors that medicine might draw on, Hodgkin (1985) suggests: "Medicine is collaborative exploration," "The body is an enduring pattern," "The body is a biochemical dance," commenting on the kinds of thinking each implies. While these all point toward a "kinder, gentler" model of medicine, desirable from just about everyone's point of view, they seem excessively complex and sophisticated for basic conceptual metaphors and, thus, unlikely to capture the ordinary metaphorical imagination.

5   Language in Relation to the "Real" World of Sickness and Health

Warner (1976) offers a brief but penetrating cross-cultural exploration, Whorfian in inspiration, of language's role in shaping our conceptions of health and illness. Changes in biomedical practice and orientation since the mid 1970s render certain of his observations now inaccurate (though nonetheless insightful). Still, the study stands as one of the few in the linguistic literature to address the issue of how the lexicogrammatical resources of a language influence speakers' conceptions of illness and disease (this issue looms larger for medical anthropologists and semioticians than for linguists).

5.1   The nominalization of disease

Warner's most interesting remarks concern lexical categorization and grammar. The use of nouns instead of verbs to express the idea of illness (he *has cancer/hypertension* vs., e.g. *he is cancering/hypertenses*) has interesting implications. It may, he argues, lead to a view of diseases as static entities rather than dynamic processes; and if there is anything disease is *not*, it is not static (cf. also Hodgkin 1985; on what gets expressed as a noun and what as a verb across languages, see Hopper and Thompson 1984, 1985). In addition, the nominalization of diseases serves to segregate illnesses as distinct entities rather than defining them as aspects of bodily functioning. Warner quotes Lambo (1964) as stating that "the concepts of health and disease in African culture can be regarded as constituting a continuum with almost imperceptible gradations" – this in contrast to our notion of "the sick" and "the well" constituting discrete communities (Sontag 1990).

An entailment of the "Diseases are objects" metaphor – and consistent with the biomedical view of health – is that "Illness sufferers are containers" for those objects: he's *full of* cancer, let's *get in there* and control the bleeding (Hodgkin 1985). This conceptualization is useful in that one can physically put pills, injections, IVs into patients and take gall bladders and appendixes out of them. Yet to the extent that patients are thought of as mere vessels of disease, their importance in the arena of medical care diminishes.

Various investigators have commented on the lexicalization of diseases as *things* (Crookshank 1923; Cassell 1976; Fleischman 1999). Fleischman introduces this topic as part of a broader argument that disease entities are ultimately *constructs* – of medical diagnostics in the first instance and ultimately of language. The examples involve blood disorders that commonly evolve into one another – supporting the notion of disease as dynamic process – but are thought of as discrete entities (especially in the exoteric circle) *because of* the different names given to them. The other side of this coin is where a single diagnostic label, e.g. *schizophrenia* (Warner 1976) or the less familiar *myelodysplastic syndrome(s)* (Fleischman 1999), is applied to a heterogeneity of pathology. Such situations can have significant repercussions for recipients of these diagnoses, in that potentially important differences regarding treatment and prognosis may be obscured by the common signifier.[30] Both situations come into play in the fascinating history Crookshank details (1923: 347–55) of medicine's attempts to disentangle the "diseases" named influenza, poliomyelitis, polioencephalitis, and encephalitis lethargica. Generalizing, he states:

> disease concepts, or, more simply, *diseases*, . . . are symbolized by *Names* which are, of course, the *Names of Diseases*. But, as time goes on, and the range and complexity of our experience (or *referents* [afflicted individuals]) extend, we find it necessary to revise our *references* [disease-concepts] and rearrange our groups of *referents*. Our symbolization is then necessarily involved and we have sometimes to devise a new symbol [name] for a revised reference, while sometimes we retain an old symbol for what is really a new reference.
>
> **These processes are usually described as the discovery of a new disease, or the elucidation of the true nature of an old one.** . . . But when, as so often happens, a *name* is illegitimately transferred from the *reference* it symbolizes to particular *referents*, confusion in thought and perhaps in practice is unavoidable. (Crookshank 1923: 341, bolding mine)

5.2 Naming across languages

Kay (1979) studies the lexicon of illness terms used by bilingual Mexican-American women. This is a paradigm study on issues raised by bilingualism and "medical biculturalism" (the coexistence of different health systems), with implications for medical anthropology (e.g. though the vocabulary of disease terms reflects linguistic and cultural interference, the different names do not represent compartmentalized participation in different health systems; cognitions of illness seem to be situated within a single unified theory) as well as for linguistics (new disease names emerge, and changes are observed in the meanings of established disease names). Among linguistic changes, Kay shows that in some instances an English term is simply borrowed (*virúses* "viruses" and *microbios* "microbes" replacing *animalitos* "little animals"), in others a cognate is coined from an English disease name (*fiebre de heno*, literally "hay fever"); terms no longer useful may be dropped (*mal ojo* "evil eye" and metonymic *daño* "witchcraft," lit. "harm" caused by witchcraft), while some Spanish disease names lacking equivalents in English, or in modern biomedicine generally, may be retained, but with a shift in the meaning (*bilis* "bile" is now the term for "gallbladder disease"; *mollera caída*, lit. "fallen soft spot," is coming to mean "dehydration"). The direction of these shifts, not surprisingly, is toward semantic correspondence with the concepts of biomedicine.

The model of lexical change and semantic shift that Kay demonstrates for Mexican-American Spanish can be applied to monolingual disease nomenclature too. The English category "arthritis," she notes (1979: 90), has undergone changes: *gout* has narrowed in meaning from subsuming all arthritis to one specific type; *lumbago* as a type of arthritis is now known only to elderly people; and *rheumatism* has gone from being a technical to a lay term.

5.3 The grammar of illness and disease

Staiano (1986) draws an illuminating contrast between the construction "I am," e.g. a diabetic, and "I have" or "I suffer from" diabetes. Elaborating on this distinction, I point out (Fleischman 1999) that the existential statement ("I am") posits an identification with the pathology, an incorporation of it as part of the self, while the genitive construction ("I have") casts the pathology as an external object in one's possession (Warner 1976 characterizes it as "a separate entity, *illness*, [that] is added to, or inflicted upon, the individual"), and the dative construction ("I suffer from") construes the affected individual as the experiencer of a particular state of ill health. Both the genitive and the dative constructions reflect the western "ontological" view of diseases as *objects* (section 5.1). As medical anthropologists have shown, cultures differ in how they construe the relationship between disease states and affected individuals. In certain cultures disease is never incorporated into the self; in the languages of such cultures we do not find the "I am" construction. In cultures where disease is construed as simply as change in the individual's processes, we expect different grammar, as Warner (1976) and Cassell (1976) suggest.

Even within "disease-incorporating" cultures, some diseases lend themselves to construal as part of the self while others do not, remaining linguistically outside the individual. In English, for example, it seems normal to say: *He's a diabetic/manic-depressive/hemophiliac*, but most speakers would not say (in ordinary parlance, at least – these examples might occur in speech between clinicians): **She's a pneumoniac/lymphomic/sickle-celler*. Warner links acceptability of the existential construction to conditions that are *chronic*, hence intimately entwined with the patient's way of life, in contrast to *acute* conditions, which are often transitory. But as the above examples show, not all chronic conditions accept the existential construction. One can, however, go even further than the genitive and dative constructions in putting distance between the patient and the pathology.

For a time following diagnosis with a serious but little-known illness, I would respond to the question "What do you have?" by saying: *I've been diagnosed with _____*. This construction combines the passive voice with a verb that licenses the interpretation that I may not in fact *have* the disease in question, I have just been *diagnosed with it*. It took some time before I found myself moving toward "I have."

Distancing is also achieved by use of a definite article or neuter pronoun "it" with diseases and afflicted body parts (*the leg doesn't feel* right (see n. 25); *make* it [a tumor in the patient's breast] *go away!*) rather than the personal "my" or "I." Cassell (1976) notes, however, that some diseases (hypertension, diabetes) seem not to be objectified and are not referred to impersonally; the more frequent usage is "my diabetes" or "my irritable bowel syndrome." Here again, a chronic vs. acute condition may be the distinctive feature, with the personal pronoun signaling acceptance of a chronic condition.

I conclude this section, and this chapter, with a citation from Warner that sums up the relationship between the resources of a language and how we think about sickness and health:

> Standard Average European language binds us to a Standard Average European conception of illness. Although we know a disease to consist of multifactorial changes in biological processes, we continue to think of it as a rigidly defined, unchanging, unicausal object, inflicted upon an individual and distinct from him. In other words, a *thing*. Our conception of disease is only a little less concrete than that of the Eskimos who brush and blow disease away. (1976: 66)

Lest his statement be interpreted too strongly, he clarifies that:

> [he] does not wish to give the impression that our language is the direct *cause* of our objectification of illness: it is at least as likely that our disease concepts have shaped some of the linguistic forms we use to describe them. It does appear, however, that our language holds us back from a view of disease process which matches our current knowledge of how illness happens.

Given the advances biomedicine has made in understanding the pathogenesis of many diseases in the years since Warner's article was written, and the changes that have occurred in medical models and in our thinking about the mind–body relationship (cf. Osherson and AmaraSingham 1981; Kirkmayer 1988),[31] his statement is a fortiori apt. The pathology of language – as distinct from the language of pathology – is when it inhibits changes in concepts and interferes with new ways of understanding disease and treating illness.

NOTES

1 This is not to deny the existence of literature on this topic prior to 1980. Studies on the medical interview and guides for teaching the conventions of certain medical genres began to appear in the 1960s. And among studies on the relationship of language to the "real world" of medicine, two of the most illuminating date from the 1970s (Warner 1976; Cassell 1976). The epigraph for this chapter, it will be noted, is drawn from an essay dated 1923; its thesis remains valid three-quarters of a century later.

2 In this chapter I follow the distinction, introduced by Eisenberg (1977) and elaborated by Kleinman (1988), between illness and disease. "Illness" incorporates our *human perception and experience* of states of bodily or mental dysfunction, while in "disease" the patient is abstracted out of the pathology. In the western biomedical tradition, doctors are trained to treat disease. They do not necessarily treat illness.

3 The task is rendered easier than a comparable survey of the DA/EST literature by virtue of the fact that medical articles are always accompanied by an abstract that "tells all." One need not read the article to extract the "bottom line." The abstracts from language-oriented fields, on the other hand, are often crafted so as to draw the reader into the article through a seductive advertisement of topics to be addressed and broader implications of the study (this is an impression based on extensive reading of the literature; a quantitative comparison has not been carried out.) Also, books and monographs (which do not have abstracts) are rare from the medical camp, save for practical guides to medical interviewing (Cassell 1985: vol. 2; Platt 1992, 1995; Smith 1996).

4 Medical professionals who enter the debate about medicine's language all tend to cite the same three "language authorities": Susan Sontag, Lakoff and Johnson, and Benjamin Lee Whorf (Sapir is occasionally thrown in for good measure – or through guilt by association; see n. 11).

5 The *performative* dimension of case presentations and their formulaic language prompt Ratzan's (1992) comparison of this genre to orally composed song-poetry of the type analyzed by Parry and Lord (see Lord 1960). While the process through which medical students learn the formulae of medicine's tribal language (see Klass 1984) may bear similarities to oral poets' apprenticeship in the art of formulaic composition, the comparison falters on the level of the *functions* of the respective texts – poetic entertainment vs. imparting clinically relevant information about hospital patients – which necessarily influence their construction. Ethnographic approaches to discourse, in particular, emphasize the crucial role of *situation*

context in interpreting language behavior, while speech act theory stresses the importance of illocutionary acts. Moreover, in drawing the comparison Ratzan seems to underestimate the extent to which *all* discourse is formulaic (i.e. displays genre- or frame-specific conventions).

6   *Gomers* (an acronym for "get out of my emergency room"), like the earlier term *crocks* (of uncertain origin), refers to the decrepit patients who do not get better but do not die (Donnelly 1986: 82). A *brainstem preparation*, as used in neurological research, is an animal whose higher brain functions have been destroyed so that only the most primitive reflexes remain (Klass 1984).

7   Mishler (1984) distinguishes two "voices" in medical discourse: the (dominant) voice of medicine and the voice of the "lifeworld" that serves to communicate the beliefs and attitudes of people in everyday life. He sees these voices as discrete (nonoverlapping) and asymmetrical in terms of the power and authority they carry.

8   Holland et al. (1987) conducted a cross-cultural study on the communication of cancer diagnoses. They found that use of the word "cancer" – unparalleled among disease names for its metaphoric power (cf. Sontag 1978) – was often avoided in discussions with patients in favor of substitutes implying a swelling ("tumor," "growth," "lump"), inflammation, or pathophysiologic change ("blood disease," "precancerous" or "unclean" tissue), or, alternatively, of technical terms unlikely to be understood by the patient ("neoplasm," "mitotic figure").

9   Studies coming out of biomedicine (which are based largely on survey data) seem inclined to accept without question physicians' assessments of their own language behavior; linguists, from experience, prefer to listen for themselves.

10   Donnelly (1986: 84) states that "decades of absent-minded substitution of 'case' for 'patient' have resulted in dictionary recognition of usage that blurs this distinction between the patient and his disease." Undiagnosed metonymies proliferate in the discourse of medicine.

11   A scattering of writers from within biomedicine (Warner 1976; Fein 1982; Dixon 1983; Donnelly 1986) invoke the Sapir–Whorf hypothesis (explicitly or unknowingly) in acknowledging that the vocabulary and grammatical/discourse structures of the medical dialect play a role in shaping physicians' attitudes about, and behavior toward, patients. Citing Sapir (1949), Donnelly observes that "the world . . . of trainees in teaching hospitals, like all 'real worlds', is to a great extent unconsciously built upon the language habits of the group" (1986: 93).

12   Alternatively, the physician assumes the agent role, the disease the object or "patient" role, with the real-world patient assuming third place in the line-up.

13   Her "top six" include (the conventional author of each is given in parentheses): the case write-up (medical student), discharge summary (house officer), consultation letter and case report (private practitioner), research article and grant proposal (academic physician). This roster – like most of the literature on medical genres – shows a bias toward academic medicine as well as an EST agenda (teaching medical writing).

14   Cf. Van Naerssen (1985); Anspach (1988); Poirier and Brauner (1988); Poirier et al. (1992); Donnelly (1988, 1997); Hunter (1991: ch. 5, 1992);

Charon (1986, 1989, 1992); Ratzan (1992); Francis and Kramer-Dahl (1992); Trautmann and Hawkins (1992); Epstein (1995); and "Case stories," a regular feature of the journal *Second Opinion*. For a historiography of the medical case history, see Hunter (1992: 165–8).

15 Case histories show a curious usage of "admit" and "deny," both of which impose a negative judgment on the proposition of the complement clause and/or imply an accusation. Often, however, these verbs are used simply to report a patient's "yes" or "no" response, respectively, to a physician's question. "Do you smoke, or drink alcohol, coffee, or tea? No" gets translated into the medical record as "Patient denies tobacco, alcohol, ..." Is having an allergy something one must "admit to" or "deny" (see the excerpt that follows in the chapter)? "Deny," in particular, casts doubt on the truthfulness of the patient's account and his or her credibility as an historian (see below).

16 Jakobson (1957) introduced the term "evidential" as a tentative label for a verbal category that indicates the source of the information on which a speaker's statement is based. As currently understood, evidentiality covers a range of distinctions involved in the identification of the *source of a speaker's knowledge* or the *speaker's willingness to vouch for the propositional content of an utterance*. In English, evidentiality is generally expressed lexically (*allegedly, he claims that . . . , reports confirm that . . .*); other languages have "dedicated" evidential morphology.

17 A parallel to Charon's exercise for medical students is Burton's analysis (1982) of a passage from Sylvia Plath's *The Bell Jar* in which the protagonist undergoes electroshock therapy. Using Halliday's transitivity

model (Halliday 1973, 1978), Burton asks her English composition students to rewrite the passage from the patient's point of view, with the comparison intended to reveal the extent to which language is ideological.

18 As Anspach points out (1988: 367), to delete mention of the person who made an observation ("The baby was noted to have congestive heart failure") suggests that the observer is irrelevant to what is being observed or "noted," or that anyone would have "noted" the same "thing." In other words, in this type of discourse the agentless passive takes on an evidential function (see n. 16) of imbuing what is being observed with an unequivocal, authoritative factual status.

19 Notwithstanding their enthusiasm for Sack's particular brand of case histories, Francis and Kramer-Dahl caution about the limits of comparing his clinical tales to hard-core case reports, notably in view of the different ways the two text-types function within the knowledge community of biomedicine. The case history, as Charon (1992) observes, is meant to be read only within the esoteric circle, i.e. by professional readers with competence in the medical tradition. It is a purely utilitarian document that does not aspire to the "display" function that is always a metafunction of the well-told tale. Moreover, Sacks – like Freud and the Russian neuropsychologist A. R. Luria (cf. Hawkins 1986) – writes in a medical specialty that still relies for diagnosis almost entirely on the subjectively reported details of the patient's experience. For neurologists and psychiatrists and their patients, disease and personal identity are often inextricably linked.

Consequently, their case histories may be qualitatively and discursively different from those in clinical fields "in which phenomenological studies have less warrant, where both patient and narrator are ghostly presences in the case" (Hunter 1992: 173).

20 The founding of the journal *Literature and Medicine* (1982–) testifies to this new hybridization. See in particular the special issues guest edited by Trautmann and Pollard (1982) and Trautmann Banks (1986).

21 Though most physicians today accept the idea that medicine is not a science but a "science-using activity," the rhetorical power of language (together with wishful thinking) so sways the intellect that the phrase "medical science" strongly colors popular thinking about medicine.

22 Apropos, Hodgkin (1985) comments on the "Emotions are fluids" metaphor (to be *swamped with* feeling, *boiling over* with rage, to *channel* one's grief into productive activities) that supplies "a network of . . . subconscious plumbing" for the containment effort expected of medical and especially surgical professionals.

23 The latter concept is alternatively referred to as "angle of vision," "focalization," "reflector (character)," or "filter."

24 "Formulation," as H. uses this concept from Robert J. Lifton (1967), "involves the discovery of patterns in experience, the imposition of order, [and] the creating of meaning – all with the purpose of mastering a traumatic experience and thereby re-establishing a sense of connectedness with objective reality and with other people" (Hawkins 1993: 24).

25 A salient linguistic feature of Sacks's account is his alienation of the injured body part, which appears more often accompanied by a definite article (*the* leg, *the* knee, *the* quadriceps) or "distal" demonstrative (*that* leg of mine) than by a personal pronoun (*my* good leg).

26 The "donor–recipient" pair is conceivably a metaphor drawn from medicine, specifically from the field of (organ/bone-marrow) transplantation.

27 Sontag's essays (1978, 1989, repr. together in Sontag 1990) stimulate a careful re-evaluation of the place of metaphor in our thinking about illness. While she touches on metaphors intrinsic to medicine, and acknowledges that thinking about illness without recourse to metaphor is probably neither desirable nor possible, her main agenda – and focus of her discontent – is the use of *illness as metaphor* (see section 4.4).

28 Computer "viruses" and other metaphors of cyber-contamination offer an interesting reversal of this conceptual metaphor. Once we have mentally constructed a basic conceptual metaphor, it lends itself to proliferation. In fact, the basic conceptual metaphor (here "Computers are bodies") is rarely used as such; we must mentally reconstruct it on the basis of actually occurring metaphorical expressions (computers get *viruses*) before creating further extensions of it ("Sharing software is unsafe sex").

29 Presenting the other side of the coin, Sontag (1978: 61) argues that *multiple causation* is considered only in cases of diseases whose causation is *not* understood. And it is these "mysterious" diseases, she notes, "that have the widest possibilities as metaphors for what is felt to be

socially or morally wrong." For an
opposing view, see Brandt (1988).

30   Crookshank (1923: 343), in his quaint
idiom, states: "In modern Medicine
this tyranny of names is no less
pernicious than is the modern form
of scholastic realism [the view that
diseases are "morbid entities" of
the phenomenal world]. Diagnosis,
which, as Mr Bernard Shaw has
somewhere declared, should mean
the finding out of all there is wrong
with a particular patient and why,
too often means in practice that
formal and unctuous pronunciation
of a Name that is deemed appropriate
and absolves from the necessity of
further investigation."

31   For a history of this epistemological
dualism that subordinates subjective
awareness (the patient's) to direct
observation (the physician's), see
Sullivan (1986).

REFERENCES

Anspach, R. R. (1988). Notes on the
sociology of medical discourse: the
language of case presentation. *Journal
of Health and Social Behavior*, 29,
357–75.

Beckman, H. B. and Frankel, R. M. (1984).
The effect of physician behavior on
the collection of data. *Annals of
Internal Medicine*, 101, 692–6.

Benthall, J. and Polhemus, T. (eds). (1975).
The Body as a Medium of Expression.
London: Allen Lane.

Bourhis, R., Roth, S., and MacQueen, G.
(1989). Communication in the hospital
setting: a survey of medical and
everyday language use amongst
patients, nurses, and doctors.
Social Science and Medicine, 28(4),
339–47.

Boyd, J. W. (1996). Narrative aspects of a
doctor–patient encounter. *Journal of
Medical Humanities*, 17(1), 5–15.

Brandt, A. (1988). AIDS and metaphor:
toward the social meaning of
epidemic disease. *Social Research*, 55,
413–32.

Brock, H. and Ratzan, R. (eds). (1988).
Literature and Medicine, 7: special issue
on "Literature and Bioethics."

Burnside, J. (1983). Medicine and war:
a metaphor. *Journal of the American
Medical Association*, 249, 2091.

Burton, D. (1982). Through glass darkly:
through dark glasses. In R. Carter
(ed.), *Language and Literature. An
Introductory Reader in Stylistics*
(pp. 195–212). London: Allen and
Unwin.

Carter, A. H. (1989). Metaphors in the
physician–patient relationship.
Soundings, 72(1), 153–64.

Carter, A. H. and McCullough, L. W.
(eds). (1989). *Soundings*, 72(1), 7–164:
Special section on "Metaphors,
language, and medicine."

Cassell, E. (1976). Disease as an "it":
concepts of disease revealed by
patients' presentation of symptoms.
Social Science and Medicine, 10,
143–6.

Cassell, E. J. (1985). *Talking with Patients.
Vol. 1: The Theory of Doctor–Patient
Communication; Vol. 2: Clinical
Technique.* Cambridge, MA and
London: MIT Press.

Chambers, T. (1996a). Dax redacted:
the economics of truth in bioethics.
Journal of Medicine and Philosophy, 23,
287–302.

Chambers, T. (1996b). From the ethicist's
point of view: the literary nature
of ethical inquiry. *Hastings Center
Report*, January–February,
pp. 25–33.

Charon, R. (1986). To render the lives of patients. *Literature and Medicine*, 5, 58–74.

Charon, R. (1989). Doctor–patient/reader–writer: learning to find the text. *Soundings*, 72(1), 137–52.

Charon, R. (1992). To build a case: medical histories as traditions in conflict. *Literature and Medicine*, 11(1), 115–32.

Crookshank, F. G., MD (1923). The importance of a theory of signs and a critique of language in the theory of medicine. In C. Ogden and I. Richards (eds), *The Meaning of Meaning*, 5th edn 1938 (pp. 337–55). London: Kegan Paul, Trench, Trubner; New York: Harcourt Brace.

Diekema, D. S. (1989). Metaphors, medicine, and morals. *Soundings*, 72(1), 17–26.

Dixon, A. (1983). Family medicine – at a loss for words? *Journal of the Royal College of General Practitioners*, 33, 358–63.

Donnelly, W. J. (1986). Medical language as symptom: doctor talk in teaching hospitals. *Perspectives in Biology and Medicine*, 30, 81–94.

Donnelly, W. J. (1988). Righting the medical record: transforming chronicle into story. *Journal of the American Medical Association*, 12 August, 823–35.

Donnelly, W. J. (1997). The language of medical case histories. *Annals of Internal Medicine*, 127, 1045–8.

Dubois, B. L. (1986). From *New England Journal of Medicine* and *Journal of the American Medical Association* through the *Associated Press* to local newspaper: scientific translations for the laity. In T. Bungarten (ed.), *Wissenschaftsprache und Gessellschaft*. Hamburg: Edition Akademion.

Eisenberg, L. (1977). Disease and illness: distinctions between professional and popular ideas of sickness. *Culture, Medicine and Psychiatry*, 1, 9–24.

Engel, G. L. (1977). The need for a new medical model: a challenge for biomedicine. *Science*, 8 April, 129–36.

Epstein, J. (1995). *Altered Conditions: Disease, Medicine, and Storytelling*. New York: Routledge.

Fein, R. (1982). What is wrong with the language of medicine? *New England Journal of Medicine*, 306, 863–4.

Fleischman, S. (1990). *Tense and Narrativity: From Medieval Performance to Modern Fiction*. Austin: University of Texas Press; London: Routledge.

Fleischman, S. (1999). I am . . . , I have . . . , I suffer from . . . : a linguist reflects on the language of illness and disease. *Journal of Medical Humanities and Cultural Studies*, 20(1).

Francis, G. and Kramer–Dahl, A. (1992). Grammaticalizing the medical case history. In M. Toolan (ed.), *Language, Text, and Context. Essays in Stylistics* (pp. 56–90). London: Routledge.

Geeraerts, D. and Grondelaers, S. (1995). Looking back at anger: cultural traditions and metaphorical patterns. In J. R. Taylor and R. E. MacLaury (eds), *Language and the Cognitive Construal of the World* (pp. 153–79). Berlin, New York: Mouton de Gruyter.

Good, B. J. (1977). The heart of what's the matter: the semantics of illness in Iran. *Culture, Medicine and Psychiatry*, 1(1), 25–58.

Gordon, D. (1996). MDs' failure to use plain language can lead to courtroom. *Canadian Medical Association Journal*, 15 October, 1152–4.

Hadlow, J. and Pitts, M. (1991). The understanding of common health terms by doctors, nurses, and patients. *Social Science and Medicine*, 32(2), 193–7.

Hahn, R. (1985). Between two worlds: physicians and patients. *Medical Anthropology Quarterly*, 16, 87–98.

Halliday, M. (1973). *Explorations in the Function of Language*. London: Edward Arnold.

Halliday, M. (1978). *Language as Social Semiotic*. London: Edward Arnold.

Hawkins, A. H. (1984). Two pathographies: a study in illness and literature. *Journal of Medicine and Philosophy*, 9, 231–52.

Hawkins, A. H. (1986). A. R. Luria and the art of clinical biography. *Literature and Medicine*, 5, 1–15.

Hawkins, A. H. (1993). *Reconstructing Illness: Studies in Pathography*. West Lafayette: Purdue University Press (reviewed in *Theoretical Medicine*, 16 (1995), 389–402, and *Literature and Medicine* 12 (1993), 248–52).

Hirschberg, S. E. (1985). Diagnosis: chronic progressive abstrusity. *Verbatim*, Winter, 3–4.

Hodgkin, P. (1985). Medicine is war. *British Medical Journal (Clinical Research Edition)*, 291, 1820–1.

Holland, J. C., Geary, N., Marchini, A., and Tross, S. (1987). An international survey of physician attitudes and practice in regard to revealing the diagnosis of cancer. *Cancer Investigation*, 5(2), 151–4.

Hopper, P. J. and Thompson, S. (1984). The discourse basis for lexical categories in universal grammar. *Language*, 60, 703–52.

Hopper, P. J. and Thompson, S. (1985). The iconicity of the universal categories "noun" and "verb." In J. Haiman (ed.), *Iconicity in Syntax* (pp. 151–83). Amsterdam: Benjamins.

Hunter, K. M. (1991). *Doctors' Stories: The Narrative Structure of Medical Knowledge*. Princeton: Princeton University Press.

Hunter, K. M. (1992). Remaking the case. *Literature and Medicine*, 11(1), 163–79.

Hunter, K. M. (1996). Narrative, literature, and the clinical exercise of practical reason. *Journal of Medicine and Philosophy*, 21, 303–20.

INSERM Symposium 1975. (1976). Is preleukemic states an adequate designation? *Blood Cells*, 2, 347–51.

Jakobson, R. (1957). Shifters, verbal categories and the Russian verb. In *Selected Writings* (II, pp. 130–47). The Hague: Mouton, 1971.

James, D. and Clarke, S. (1993). Women, men, and interruptions: a critical review. In D. Tannen (ed.), *Gender and Conversational Interaction* (pp. 231–80). New York and Oxford: Oxford University Press.

Jammal, A. (1988). Les vocabulaires des spécialités médicales: pourquoi et comment les fabrique-t-on? (The vocabularies of medical specialties: why and how are they created?) *Meta*, 33(4), 535–41.

Johnson, D. and Murray, J. F. (1985). Do doctors mean what they say? In D. Enright (ed.), *Fair of Speech: The Uses of Euphemism* (pp. 151–8). Oxford: Oxford University Press.

Kahn, J. (1983). *Modes of Medical Instruction*. Berlin: Mouton.

Kay, M. (1979). Lexemic change and semantic shift in disease names. *Culture, Medicine and Psychiatry*, 3, 73–94.

King, N. M. and Stanford, A. F. (1992). Patient stories, doctor stories, and true stories: a cautionary reading. *Literature and Medicine*, 11(2), 185–99.

Kirkmayer, L. (1988). Mind and body as metaphors: hidden values in biomedicine. In M. Lock and D. Gordon (eds), *Biomedicine Examined* (pp. 57–93). Lancaster: Kluwer.

Klass, P. (1984). "Hers" column. *New York Times*, 4 October, p. C2.

Kleinman, A. (1988). *The Illness Narratives: Suffering, Healing, and the Human Condition*. New York: Basic Books.

Labov, W. (1972). The transformation of experience in narrative syntax. In *Language in the Inner City* (pp. 354–96). Philadelphia: University of Pennsylvania Press.

Lakoff, G. and Johnson, M. (1980). *Metaphors We Live By*. Chicago: University of Chicago Press.

Lambo, T. (1964). Patterns of psychiatric care in developing African countries. In A. Kiev (ed.), *Magic, Faith, and Healing*. New York: Free Press.

Landon, L. H. (1989). Suffering over time: six varieties of pain. *Soundings*, 72(1), 75–82.

Lifton, R. J. (1967). *Death in Life: Survivors of Hiroshima*. New York: Simon and Schuster.

Lord, A. B. (1960). *The Singer of Tales*. Cambridge, MA: Harvard University Press.

Maher, E. L. (1989). Burnout: metaphors of destruction and purgation. *Soundings*, 72(1), 27–37.

Maher, J. (1986). The development of English as an international language of medicine. *Applied Linguistics*, 7(2), 206–18.

Marston, J. (1986). Metaphorical language and terminal illness: reflections upon images of death. *Literature and Medicine*, 5, 109–21.

Matisoff, J. A. (1978). *Variational Semantics in Tibeto-Burman: The "Organic" Approach to Linguistic Comparison*. Philadelphia: Institute for the Study of Human Issues.

McCullough, L. B. (1989). The abstract character and transforming power of medical language. *Soundings*, 72(1), 111–25.

Mintz, D. (1992). What's in a word? The distancing function of language in medicine. *Journal of Medical Humanities*, 13, 223–33.

Mishler, E. G. (1984). *The Discourse of Medicine: Dialectics of Medical Interviews*. Norwood, NJ: Ablex.

Norton, R., Schwartzbaum, J. and Wheat, J. (1990). Language discrimination of general physicians: AIDS metaphors used in the AIDS crisis. *Communication Research*, 17(6), 809–26.

Nwogu, K. N. (1990). *Discourse Variation in Medical Texts: Schema, Theme and Cohesion in Professional and Journalistic Accounts*. Nottingham: Department of English Studies, University of Nottingham.

Ong, L., de Haes, C., Hoos, A., and Lammes, F. (1995). Doctor–patient communication: a review of the literature. *Social Science and Medicine*, 40(7), 903–18.

Osherson, S. and Amara Singham, L. (1981). The machine metaphor in medicine. In E. Mishler, L. AmaraSingham, S. Osherson, S. Hauser, N. Wexler, and R. Liem, *Social Contexts of Health, Illness and Patient Care* (pp. 218–49). New York: Cambridge University Press.

Pettinari, C. (1983). The function of grammatical alternation in fourteen surgical reports. *Applied Linguistics*, 55–76.

Platt, F. W. (1992). *Conversation Failure: Case Studies in Doctor–Patient Communication*. Tacoma, WA: Life Sciences Press.

Platt, F. W. (1995). Foreword. In J. Gregory Carroll, *Conversation Repair: Case Studies in Doctor–Patient Communication*. Boston: Little, Brown.

Poirier, S. and Ayres, L. (1997). Endings, secrets, and silences: overreading in narrative inquiry. *Research in Nursing and Health*, 20, 551–7.

Poirier, S. and Brauner, D. J. (1988). Ethics and the daily language of medical discourse. *Hastings Center Report*, August–September, 5–9.

Poirier, S., Rosemblum, L., Ayres, L., Brauner, D. J., Sharf, B. F., and Stanford, A. F. (1992). Charting the chart – an exercise in interpretation(s). *Literature and Medicine*, 11(1), 1–22.

Ratzan, R. (1992). Winged words and chief complaints: medical case histories and the Parry-Lord oral-formulaic tradition. *Literature and Medicine*, 11(1), 94–114.

Ross, J. W. (1988). Ethics and the language of AIDS. In C. Pierce and D. Van DeVeer (eds), *AIDS: Ethics and Public*

Policy (pp. 39–48). New York: Wadsworth Press.

Ross, J. W. (1989). The militarization of disease: do we really want a war on AIDS? *Soundings*, 72(1), 39–58.

Rothman, S. (1994). *Living in the Shadow of Death*. New York: Basic Books.

Sacks, O. (1984). *A Leg to Stand on*. New York: Summit Books (reissued 1993 by HarperPerennial.).

Sacks, O. (1985). *The Man Who Mistook His Wife for a Hat*. London: Picador.

Sacks, O. (1986) Clinical tales. *Literature and Medicine*, 5, 16–23.

Salager, F. (1983). The lexis of fundamental medical English: classificatory framework and rhetorical function (a statistical approach). *Reading in a Foreign Language*, 1(1), 54–64.

Salager-Meyer, F. (1990a). Discoursal movements in medical English abstracts and their linguistic exponents: a genre study analysis. *Interface: Journal of Applied Linguistics* (Tijdschrift-voor-Toegepaste-Linguistiek, Brussels), 4(2), 107–24.

Salager-Meyer, F. (1990b). Metaphors in medical English prose: a comparative study with French and Spanish. *English for Specific Purposes*, 9(2), 145–59.

Salager-Meyer, F. (1991). Medical English abstracts: how well are they structured? *Journal of the American Society for Information Science*, 2(7), 528–31.

Salager-Meyer, F., Defives, G., Jensen, C., and de Filipis, M. (1989). Function and grammatical variations in medical English scholarly papers: a genre analysis study. In C. Lauren and M. Nordman (eds), *Special Language: From Humans Thinking to Thinking Machines* (pp. 151–60). Clevedon: Multilingual Matters.

Schiffrin, D. (1994). *Approaches to Discourse*. Oxford: Blackwell.

Searle, J. R. (1992). *The Rediscovery of the Mind*. Cambridge, MA: MIT Press.

Smith, R. C. (1996). *The Patient's Story: Integrated Patient–Doctor Interviewing*. Boston: Little, Brown.

Sontag, S. (1978). *Illness as Metaphor*. New York: Farrar, Strauss and Giroux. Also in *Illness as Metaphor and AIDS and its Metaphors*. New York: Anchor Doubleday. (1990).

Sontag, S. (1989). *AIDS and its Metaphors*. New York: Farrar, Strauss and Giroux. Also in *Illness as Metaphor and AIDS and its Metaphors*. New York: Anchor Doubleday. (1990).

Sontag, S. (1990). *Illness as Metaphor and AIDS and its Metaphors*. New York: Anchor Doubleday.

Staiano, K. V. (1986). *Interpreting Signs of Illness: A Case Study in Medical Semiotics*. Berlin: Mouton de Gruyter.

Stewart, M. and Roter, D. (1989). Introduction. In M. Stewart and D. Roter (eds), *Communicating with Medical Patients*. Newbury Park: Sage.

Stibbe, A. (1997). Fighting, warfare and the discourse of cancer. *South African Journal of Linguistics*, 15(2), 65–70.

Sullivan, M. (1986). In what sense is contemporary medicine dualistic? *Culture, Medicine and Psychiatry*, 10, 331–50.

Trautmann, J. and Hawkins, A. H. (eds). (1992). The art of the case history. *Literature and Medicine*, 11(1): special issue.

Trautmann, J. and Pollard, C. (1982). *Literature and Medicine: An Annotated Bibliography* (rev. ed.). Pittsburgh: University of Pittsburgh Press.

Trautmann Banks, J. (ed.). (1986). Use and abuse of literary concepts in medicine. *Literature and Medicine*, 5(1): special issue.

Van Naerssen, M. M. (1985). Medical records: one variation of physicians' language. *International Journal of the Sociology of Language*, 51, 43–73.

van Rijn-van Tongeren, G. W. (1997). *Metaphors in Medical Texts*.

Amsterdam and Atlanta, GA:
Rodopi.

Warner, R. (1976). The relationship
between language and disease
concepts. *International Journal of
Psychiatry in Medicine, 7,* 57–68.

Weed, L. L. (1970). *Medical Records, Medical
Education and Patient Care.* Cleveland:
Case Western Reserve University.

West, C. (1984). Medical misfires:
mishearings, misgivings, and
misunderstandings in the physician–
patient dialogues. *Discourse Processes,
7,* 107–34.

Yanoff, K. L. (1989). The rhetoric of
medical discourse: an analysis of the
major genres. (Dissertation). DAI,
49(10), 3011A.

25 Discourse in Educational Settings

CAROLYN TEMPLE ADGER

0 Introduction

In an early study of language use in schools, Shuy and Griffin (1981) noted that whatever else goes on there, what they do in schools on any day is talk. To a great extent, the fabric of schooling is woven of linguistic interaction. One of the central concerns of discourse analysis in educational settings has been to uncover the ways in which talk at school is unique and thus what children must be able to do linguistically in order to succeed there. Attention focuses on the socialization functions that schools serve, especially but not exclusively those connected to teaching and learning. Another analytic perspective cross-cuts that one: discourse analysis is helping to explicate the actions in which the primary goal of schools – learning – is realized. This chapter offers a selective overview of some of the chief analytic constructs that have been employed in describing classroom interaction and some of the topics of discourse study in educational settings. It closes by considering how insights from discourse analysis in schools can help to make them better.

1 Focus on Linguistic Practices in Schools

Since the early 1970s, research on language in schools has moved from a focus on discrete chunks of language to a concern with "communication as a whole, both to understand what is being conveyed and to understand the specific place of language within the process" (Hymes 1972: xxviii). Highly inferential coding of classroom linguistic activity receded (though it persists still) as scholars with disciplinary roots in anthropology, social psychology, sociology, and sociolinguistics began to focus on structural cues by which interactants understand what is going on (e.g. Gumperz and Herasimchuk 1975; McDermott et al. 1978; Mehan 1979). An early sociolinguistic study of instructional interaction in primary classrooms (Griffin and Shuy 1978) combining ethnographic, ethnomethodological, and pragmatic perspectives and research methods contributed significantly to developing analytic techniques for classroom talk. Analysis of one important structure – sequences in which teachers elicited knowledge from students – found that elicitation turns could not be explained in terms of formal linguistic characteristics alone, as Sinclair and Coulthard (1975) had proposed. Griffin and Shuy adopted the notion of topically relevant sets of talk as outlined in Mehan et al. (1976), linking talk to an element that might lie outside the discourse. A lesson's instructional goals motivate certain tasks and topics that constrain interpretation. Thus a teacher utterance that consists solely of a student's name, one of the phenomena occurring more frequently in instructional discourse than elsewhere, can function as elicitations because they recycle a question previously asked:

(1) *The teacher has just completed instructions for a math activity to a first grade class:*[1]
   1 *Teacher*: Who can tell Carter what group one does, when they're done with their number book.
   2 *Hai*: I know.
   3 *Teacher*: Hai?
   4 *Hai*: Um . . after you finish your workbook, you get something quiet to do. (Adger 1984: 250)

This early work on elicitation sequences providing the apparatus for a functional analysis of classroom talk allowed principled description of talk as social interaction. The elicitation sequence composed of teacher initiation, student response, and teacher evaluation (IRE), proposed as a basic unit of instructional interaction, was tested against empirical evidence. For example, Mehan et al. (1976) had argued that the evaluation turn was optional, but Griffin and Shuy (1978) found it to be obligatory: when it does not occur, some reason for its absence can be located in the discourse by reference to interactional rules:

(2) *The teacher is checking student understanding of her directions for a math worksheet to first graders:*
   1 *Teacher*: What will you color in this row?
   2 *Students*: Blue
   3 *Teacher*: How many blue squares?
   4 *Students*: Three
   5 *Teacher*: Same on twenty-five, and twenty-six the same thing. (Adger 1984: 249)

L. 1 is an initiation; l. 2, a response. No overt evaluation occurs, but it is inferable: the teacher's initiation of a second sequence in l. 3 in place of evaluation implicitly conveys positive evaluation. (It is also possible to withhold a negative evaluation and initiate a new sequence, but eventually the faulty response may need to be evaluated to advance the lesson and preserve the evaluator's authority.)

Illuminating the IRE and principled means of linking talk and task laid the groundwork for investigating other aspects of context. Shultz et al. (1982) and Green and Wallat (1981), for instance, examined social interaction in classrooms and homes in terms of participation structures. These account for who is participating, what turn-taking patterns are in effect, who has rights to the conversational floor, proxemics, all aspects of talk (such as directness, register, paralinguistic cues), and gaze. O'Connor and Michaels (1996) use Goffman's (1974, 1981) notion of participant framework in explicating the ways that expert teachers socialize children into academic discussion, particularly through revoicing children's lesson contributions. This participant framework "encompasses (a) the ways that speech event participants are aligned with or against each other and (b) the ways they are positioned relative to topics and even specific utterances" (O'Connor and Michaels 1996: 69). Talk and the participant frameworks it entails compose speech activities (Gumperz 1982).

The IRE continues to be featured in discourse analytic accounts of academic talk. But communication in classrooms frequently proceeds in ways that do not follow the sequential, reciprocal model of interaction between teacher and students that the IRE captures so well. Erickson (1996) shows that classroom interaction frequently demonstrates a complex ecology of social and cognitive relations.[2] The flow of interaction in dyadic (Erickson and Shultz 1982) and multiparty talk alike is governed by timing and contextualization cues: "any aspect of the surface form of utterances which, when mapped onto message content, can be shown to be functional in signaling of interpretive frames" (Gumperz 1977: 199), such as gaze, proxemics, intonational contours, and volume. Cues cluster to establish a cadence that facilitates the social organization of attention and action in conversation. Using evidence from a combination kindergarten–first grade classroom, Erickson shows that successful participation in a whole-group lesson requires responding with a correct answer in the appropriate interactive moment. Weak turns fall prey to the "turn sharks" hovering in the interactional waters to snatch them up.

The following excerpt from a first grade class demonstrates that the ecology of social and cognitive relations obtains in other instructional settings. Here the teacher responds to four students who have been given the same math task but who contextualize it differently. Each is engaged in an individual vector of activity involving the teacher (Merritt 1998), but their joint interaction coheres around social relations and the shared instructional task:

(3) *The students, who are seated in four clusters, are working on math worksheets requiring them to demonstrate number sets. The teacher moves among them, checking students' work and assisting them:*

  1 *Teacher*: You don't have what?
  2 *Coong*: I don't have scissors.
  3 *Teacher*: Scissors. What do you need scissors for.
  4 *Coong*: Um: cut.=
  5 *Blair*: =Lots of things.
  6 *Teacher*: Why do you need scissors.
  7 ____: //
  8 *Hai*: I can't make no <u>nother</u> one, Miss.
  9 *Teacher*: (to Coong) In Mrs. K . . Mrs. K's room?
10 ____: //
11 *Teacher*: Okay, go and get it.
12 /*Coong*/: //
13 *Teacher*:   [Okay, get it tomorrow.

14	*Katie*:	(approaching from another table) [Mrs. D, what happened to [my number line.
15	*Teacher*:	(to Coong) [Oh you mean for tomorrow in your class?
16	*Coong*:	Um hum.
17	*Teacher*:	I'll let you borrow one tomorrow.
18	*Katie*:	Mrs. D, what happened to my. um . [number line?
19	*Teacher*:	(to Coong, loud) [Tomorrow. I will get you one. <u>Now</u> you go and work on your m<u>ath</u>:.
20	*Katie*:	Mrs. D, what happened to my li. number line.
21	*Teacher*:	(soft) Well it was coming off your desk.
22	*Katie*:	Huh <u>uh</u>:.
23	*Teacher*:	//
24	*Katie*:	Who took mine.
25	*Teacher*:	<u>I</u> did. // cleaning off the <u>desks</u>. (looking at Blair's math worksheet) Why did you erase the other one. The other one was fine. And this is=
26	*Coong*:	[/See/
27	*Teacher*:	=[the same.
28	*Hai*:	[Mine's the only one that=
29	*Blair*:	Oh.
30	*Hai*:	=stays [down.
31	*Teacher*:	[You. you can make four sentences with these numbers. // a little harder. (Adger 1984: 331–2)

The teacher and students construct three intersecting discourse tasks that are relevant to the math lesson in progress but individually negotiated (Bloome and Theodorou 1988). In the teacher/Coong discourse task (ll. 1–19), the teacher works to challenge Coong's scissors issue as irrelevant to the math task that she has assigned, then to defer it, and then to direct him to the task. In the overlapping teacher/Katie inter-action (ll. 14–25), Katie manages to initiate an interaction about her missing number line. Despite the relevance of Katie's topic to the lesson task, the teacher treats Katie's talk as socially inappropriate, both in terms of timing and in terms of politeness. The teacher's nonresponse to Katie's first two turns (ll. 14, 18) suggests that she views them as attempts to interrupt the scissors talk with Coong. She treats Katie's question about the missing number line as an unwarranted complaint in light of the teacher's right to maintain a neat classroom, even when it means removing a lesson-relevant resource. The overlapping teacher/Blair interaction (ll. 25–31), in which the teacher points out an error and urges him on, requires the least negotiation. He shows evid-ence of having attended to the task and thus there are no task or social structure issues to be aired. The teacher critiques his work, he acknowledges her, and she moves on.

   Hai does not succeed in engaging the teacher, apparently because of trouble with timing. He makes an unsuccessful bid for the teacher's attention at what seems to be a transition relevant point in her interaction with Coong, complaining in l. 8 that he cannot draw another of the items required to demonstrate his grasp of math sets. In l. 28, his comment that his number line is still firmly attached to his desk is relevant to the topic of the discourse task at hand, which is itself relevant to the math lesson, but ill-timed in terms of topic development and turn exchange.

This bit of classroom life instantiates Erickson's observation that classroom conversation is often more than a dialog, more than reciprocal or sequential interactive turns. In (3), lesson talk inheres in a discourse ecosystem in which students assemble their individual versions of the math lesson in concert with others, balancing academic and social interactional concerns. The teacher participates in advancing the math lesson with Coong, Katie, and Blair, but as a responder more than an initiator or an evaluator, the roles that the IRE attributes to the teacher. Her goal seems to be to urge them to adopt her interpretation of the math task. She negotiates, directs, explains, and corrects. She also nonresponds, protecting the interaction with Coong against interruptions from Blair in l. 5, from Hai in l. 8, and from Katie in l. 14. In the discourse task that is most directly related to the math lesson, the one involving Blair, she initiates the talk, but as critique rather than as request for information. These interwoven tasks reflect the teacher's responsibility to see that her version of the math lesson gets done and that interactional order is preserved, but they also show students as agents in both of those school agendas.

2 Topics of Discourse Analysis in School Settings

The rise in discourse analytic study of educational settings is part of a broader embracing of qualitative study in a domain long dominated by behavioral theory and quantitative research methods. Reasons for this shift are complex, but a prime influence came from the imperative – moral, legal, and economic – to educate a diverse population of students. The entrenched middle-class traditions dominating schooling have not succeeded in producing equitable student achievement, and resulting concern with socioeducational processes has opened the door to descriptive methods. Discourse analysis scrutinizing classroom interaction has found evidence of poorly matched cultural and social norms that contribute to inequity. In addition, a number of studies have focused on the processes of literacy development and second language learning. More recently there has been significant use of discourse analysis to discover the nature of cognitive development in social space. Many studies have combined more than one of these foci.

2.1 Classroom interaction as cultural practice

Discourse analysis has been instrumental in locating the educational failure of children from certain groups within classroom practices, particularly where the cultural background of the teacher and the pervasive culture of the school is different from that of the students. Microanalysis of classroom interaction shows mismatched frames (Tannen 1993) and participation style in classroom routines, with the result that over time students accumulate individual profiles of failure that mirror the statistics for their groups derived from standardized tests.

Ethnographic studies have illuminated the community basis of some interactive behavior that schools find anomalous. Philips's (1993) study conducted on the Warm Springs Indian Reservation in the early 1970s explained some aspects of Native

American students' classroom participation style. What teachers saw as failure – students' demurring from individual engagement with the teacher in whole-group lesson talk – reflected community values that favor collective talk. The discontinuity between the community and the school norms for interaction also led to schools' disciplining Native American students who had misinterpreted the school norms for physical activity. (For related study of contrasting norms between Native American communities and Anglo schools, see also Erickson and Mohatt 1982; Scollon and Scollon 1981.)

Another strand of ethnographic research on classroom discourse developed microethnographic research methods that contributed new understanding of the role of nonverbal communication and timing, in particular the ways in which cultural differences between home and school may systematically constrain the chances of success for some groups of students (e.g. McDermott 1976; Mehan 1979; Erickson and Shultz 1982). For example, Florio and Shultz (1979) undertook a complex analysis of participation structures during mealtime at home and lessons at school, events that exhibited some structural similarities. Comparison showed differences between home and school in the alignment between a participation structure and the phase of an event. Thus when dinner was being prepared in the Italian American homes that were studied, conversation had a single focus and one person talked at a time. But in the preparation phase of a lesson, several conversations could co-occur and children could chime in. Italian American children had trouble meeting the expectations for classroom participation structure in various lesson phases.

Studies of cross-cultural mismatch illuminate the culturally based discourse practices that schools have taken for granted – patterns based on the middle-class European-American traditions that have predominated in US institutions. A few studies shed light on classroom discourse patterns that are based on other traditions. Foster's (1995) description of interaction in a community college class taught by an African American professor showed strategic use of stylistic features associated with African American culture. The professor's lecture style included the call and response typical of gospel meetings, repetition, vowel elongation, alliteration, marked variation in pitch and tempo, and features of African American Vernacular English – discourse strategies that invited her mostly African American students to chime in. Foster suggests that where cultural norms are shared, this interactive style may serve a special instructional function. Students reported to Foster that the professor repeated information that they needed to know, but the data did not bear that out. Foster surmises that the students' sense that some information had been stressed may have derived from the teacher's discourse style rather than from actual repetition of information.

The following excerpt shows an African American teacher using such an interactional style in an upper elementary school classroom. The effect here is to engage more than one student in a discourse task that is part of preparation for a high-stakes standardized test:

(4)   *The teacher is introducing a worksheet on frequently misspelled words:*
       1   *Teacher*:   It's a word called a spelling demon. These letters sometimes are silent letters. What is a word that means to eat little by little. Which letter would . be missing.

2	*Eric:*	Ooh.
3	*Teacher:*	Now here's the word.
4	*Robert:*	Oh, I-I think [I know.
5	*Teacher:*	[All right.
6	*Eric:*	Gnaw.
7	*Teacher:*	What does this say.
8	*Several:*	Gnaw. Gnaw.
9	*Teacher:*	What is it?
10	*Several:*	Gnaw. [Gnaw.
11	*Teacher:*	[Gnaw. (softly) All right. Now that's really saying the word=
12	*Damien:*	I know.
13	*Teacher:*	=To eat little by little is <u>gnaw</u>. But it is a letter missing=
14	*Damien:*	k
15	*Harold:*	A k.
16	*Teacher:*	=And that letter is . a . si: :=
17	*James:*	Si=
18	*Thad:*	Ooh.
19	*Teacher:*	=lent=
20	*James:*	=lent=
21	*Teacher:*	=letter.
22	*James:*	=letter.
23	*Teacher:*	Now. How do you spell <u>gnaw</u>.
24	*Damien:*	K n=
25	*David:*	K n a=
26	*Damien:*	=a w
27	*Several:*	K n a w.
28	*David:*	=w.
29	*Teacher:*	Wrong.
30	*Robert:*	It's g.
31	*Teacher:*	What is it Robert?
32	*Sonny:*	Yes, g.
33	*Robert:*	G, g.
34	*Pierre:*	K.
35	*Teacher:*	(loud) It's G::=
36	*Robert:*	G.
37	*Teacher:*	=n:a:=
38	*Sam:*	We all look//
39	*Teacher:*	=w. It's G::=
40	*Quentin:*	I got it.
41	*Teacher:*	=n:a:w. Which is why this paper is called sixty demons. (Adger and Detwyler 1993: 10–12)

Clearly, eliciting the correct answer is not the sole point of this lesson. The teacher's question in the first turn, "What is a word that means to eat little by little," is repeated in ll. 7 and 9, even after the answer, *gnaw*, is supplied in l. 6. Through repetition (e.g. *letter* in ll. 13, 16, and 21), vowel elongation (e.g. the first vowel in *silent*, l. 16), and volume shifting ll. 11 and 35), the teacher establishes a cadence that engages many more students than those who supply the information needed to advance the lesson. She transforms a technical exercise into a drama by emphasizing the unknown, spotlighting the speaker of the delayed correct answer (Robert, l. 31), and then supplying the coda in l. 41.

Another study of classroom discourse in which the teacher and all of the students are African American showed shared dialect norms that do not match idealized norms for academic talk (Adger 1998). In an upper elementary classroom (not the one from which (4) was taken), the teacher consistently used Standard English for instructional functions, but the students shifted along a dialect continuum as they changed registers within a literacy event. For a literary analysis task in which they spoke with authority about a text, students selected Standard English features, but elsewhere within the literacy event they used African American Vernacular English. Students appeared to be using dialect resources in ways that mirror the linguistic norms of their community.

2.2   Classroom discourse and literacy development

Sociocultural studies have been concerned especially with the ways in which students develop literacy, broadly defined to include the acquisition and increasingly skilled use of written language, the interweaving of talk and text, and the genres or discourses associated with school. Often literacy studies also consider cultural norms, with a focus on explicating contrasts between school and community that constrain literacy success (e.g. Gee 1989; Heath 1983; Scollon and Scollon 1981).

Michaels's work on "sharing time," the class meeting that has typified elementary classrooms, identified two patterns of thematic progression in children's narratives: a topic-centered pattern and a topic-associating pattern (Michaels 1981). In the topic-centered pattern used by European American children, a narrow topic is mentioned and fixed in time to start the story, with subsequent utterances adhering to it. In the topic-associating pattern more usual with African American children, a general topic is put forth and other topics are raised in relation to it. The styles differ both in what can constitute the topic and in how topics are developed. From the perspective of the European American teacher whose classroom Michaels studied, the topic-associating style was illogical and deficient.

Subsequent work on narrative style at a graduate school of education further illuminated the role that teachers' culturally based expectations for literacy-related discourse routines can play in student achievement. To test whether teacher reactions to children's stories were ethnically based, researchers recorded topic-associating (episodic) and topic-centered stories, both told in Standard English. As anticipated, white graduate students (teachers or teacher interns) preferred the topic-centered stories. They attributed the episodic stories to low-achieving students with language problems or even family or emotional problems. Black graduate students, on the other hand, approved of both styles, commenting that the episodic stories showed interesting detail and description. They imagined that the story that had suggested serious language problems to the white graduate students had come from a highly verbal, bright child (Cazden 1988).

Anthropological study of storytelling in Hawaiian communities described a collaborative narrative style that European American teachers had noticed in schools because it conflicts with narrative practices expected there. The speech event referred to in the community as "talk story" is characterized by co-narration among multiple speakers (Watson-Gegeo and Boggs 1977). By contrast, the idealized classroom discourse pattern involves one student speaking at a time, at the teacher's bidding. Although this pattern is very often superseded, teachers expect students to comply when the one-at-a-time rule is invoked. In the Hawaiian schools, an experimental instructional program was created, based on the community co-narration event. It involved teachers participating in co-narration with the students, rather than leading IRE-based discussion (Au and Jordan 1981).

2.3 Discourse study of second language development

Discourse analysis has become an increasingly attractive analytic method for researchers in second language development because of what it can show about that process and what it can suggest about second language pedagogy. I mention only one example, since other chapters in this volume treat second language discourse at length (see Olshtain and Celce-Murcia, this volume). In a study of the development of biliteracy, Moll and Dworin (1996) examine the written work in two languages of two young bilingual speakers (Spanish and English). They conclude that there are many paths to biliteracy, made up of students' own histories and the social contexts for their learning, and that the ways in which bilingualism is typically characterized in schools are simplistic. In these two students' classrooms, the freedom to use both English and Spanish meant that children developed literate skills in both languages – not just the means of writing two languages but the ability for "literate thinking" where writing in English involves reflecting on Spanish language experience.

2.4 Classroom discourse as learning

In recent years, discourse analysis has played an important role in testing and extending the theories of Vygotsky (1978) and other contributors to the sociocognitive tradition (e.g. Wertsch 1991; Rogoff 1991). While Vygotsky's thinking has been interpreted in very different ways (Cazden 1996), some of his insights have been highly influential in research on teaching and learning: that individuals learn in their own zones of proximal development lying just beyond the domains of their current expertise, and that they learn through interacting in that zone with a more knowledgeable individual and internalizing the resulting socially assembled knowledge. Thus learning is inherently both social and personal (Bakhtin 1981). A central question for scholars working in this tradition concerns the ways in which discourse between learner and expert mediates cognitive development. But research addressing this question has often given short shrift to the social dimension, viewing the discourse as an accomplishment – the product of learning – and leaving underexamined the flow of interactional, interpretive acts through which it is accomplished (Erickson 1996). Hicks (1996) observes that while sociocognitive theories have contributed significantly to educational theory, methods for testing them are not well developed (but see Wells 1993). Hicks lays out a complex methodology that combines the study of interaction and the study of the group's texts, oral and written. This methodology is welded to sociocognitive theory: it examines the process of social meaning construction in light of the group's history, as well as the process of the individual's internalization or appropriation of social meaning.[3]

2.5   School as a venue for talk

Most studies of discourse at school concern the language of teaching and learning, examining classroom interaction as social practice or cognitive work – or both. But school is also a site in which children's repertoires for strategic language use expand (Hoyle and Adger 1998). Classrooms and other school settings present social tasks that differ from those of home and neighborhood and thus inspire innovation in register repertoires, framing capacities, and assumptions about appropriateness (Merritt 1998). Instructional settings in which students work without direct teacher participation, such as cooperative learning groups, allow them to construct knowledge and social structures through talk (Rosebery et al. 1992; Schlegel 1998; Tuyay et al. 1995) – though this may happen in ways that do not match teachers' intentions (Gumperz and Field 1995).

School is also a site of social interaction that is not academic. Eder's (1993, 1998) work on lunchtime interaction in a middle school shows that collaborative retelling of familiar stories functions to forge individual and group identities that partition young people from adults. Here school structures and participants – teachers and students – are recast as background for other socialization work that young people do together through discourse.

3   Application of Discourse Studies to Education

Most work on classroom discourse can be characterized as applied research: by illuminating educational processes, the research is relevant to critiquing what is going on in classrooms and to answering questions about how and where teaching and learning succeed or fail. Much of it has been conducted by scholars who work in or with schools of education and who address the most troubling questions about schools and schooling, especially in areas of differential educational success. But relating the detailed findings to educational practice is far from straightforward. Teacher education programs often require their interns to read studies of children's language use in context (Heath 1983 has been especially influential), but making explicit recommendations for educational practice based on discourse study is difficult.

One program linking research and educational practice that has grown out of the work on literacy instruction reported by Au and Jordan (1981) is exceptional in terms of longevity, coherence, and influence. Beginning in the late 1960s, teaching methods that approximated the community narrative style, talk story, were developed and tested by a team of teachers, psychologists, anthropologists, and linguists at the Kamehameha Early Education Program (KEEP), a research and development center in Honolulu. The approach had positive effects on students' reading achievement there and later on test scores in other Hawaiian schools (Vogt et al. 1987). Findings from that project subsequently informed the development of sociocognitive theory in which the discourse of learning was highlighted (e.g. Rogoff 1991; Tharp and Gallimore 1988). Currently, some of the researchers who began the Kamehameha work, along with others, continue researching and developing educational approaches that promote school success, especially for language-minority students and others placed at risk for school failure. Their work is based on five principles for educational practice derived from their research and review of the literature on the influence of culture and gender on schooling:

1. Facilitate learning through joint productive activity among teachers and students
2. Develop competence in the language and literacy of instruction through all instruction activities
3. Contextualize teaching and curriculum in the experiences and skills of home and community
4. Challenge students toward cognitive complexity
5. Engage students through dialog, especially the instructional conversation. (Tharp 1997: 6–8)

These principles stress interaction that involves teachers as assistants to children rather than as drivers of dialog and deliverers of information (Tharp 1997). Instructional conversations involve a teacher and a group of students in constructing meaning by linking texts and student knowledge as they talk (Goldenberg and Patthey-Chavez 1995). The challenge for the teacher, accustomed to taking every other turn in IRE-dominated classrooms, is to avoid responding to each student's response so that students can talk in each other's zones of proximal development.

4   Conclusion

This chapter touches on some methodological advances and topical interests within the corpus of discourse analysis in education settings. This corpus is by now encyclopedic (Cazden 1988; Corson 1997; Bloome and Greene 1992), and that is both the good and the bad news. The good news is that many of the educational processes that are the very stuff of school are being scrutinized. We now have methods and researchers skilled in their use for asking and answering questions about why we see the educational outcomes that fuel funding and policy decisions. The bad news is that discourse analysis and other qualitative methods are not widely accepted even within the educational establishment. One way of bringing this scholarship into the mainstream of educational research is through research and development programs that make the applications of discourse analysis very concrete. There is a need for more interdisciplinary collaboration in research design, data collection, and analyses requiring close attention to talk. The challenge is to avoid an atheoretical, merely commonsense approach to the study of talk and text and to knit together and build on the rather disparate work so far amassed.

NOTES

1 Transcription conventions are as follows (based on Tannen 1984):

.	sentence-final falling intonation
?	sentence-final rising intonation
,	continuing intonation
..	noticeable pause, less than half-second
...	half-second pause; each extra dot represents additional half-second pause
underline	emphatic stress
CAPITALS	extra emphatic stress
italics	graphemes
//	slash marks indicate uncertain transcription or speaker overlap
=	speaker's talk continues or second speaker's talk is latched onto first speaker's without a noticeable pause
:	lengthened sound (extra colons represent extra lengthening)
( )	information in parentheses applies to the talk that follows; continues until punctuation

2 Labov and Fanshel (1977: 29) made a similar claim about dyadic interaction: "Conversation is not a chain of utterances, but rather a matrix of utterances and actions bound together by a web of understandings and reactions."

3 Although this is not the point that Hicks wants to make, the methodology for which she argues is able to make evident the dimensions of a discursive event that Fairclough identifies: "language use, analyzed as text, discourse practice and social practice" (Fairclough 1993: 138).

REFERENCES

Adger, C. T. (1984). Communicative competence in the culturally diverse classroom: negotiating norms for linguistic interaction. Unpublished doctoral dissertation, Georgetown University.

Adger, C. T. (1998). Register shifting with dialect resources in instructional discourse. In S. Hoyle and C. T. Adger (eds), *Kids Talk: Strategic Language Use in Later Childhood* (pp. 151–69). New York: Oxford.

Adger, C. T., and Detwyler, J. (1993). Empowering talk: African American teachers and classroom discourse. Paper presented at the annual meeting of the American Education Research Association, Atlanta, April.

Au, K., and Jordan, C. (1981). Teaching reading to Hawaiian children: finding a culturally appropriate solution. In H. Trueba, G. Guthrie, and K. Au (eds), *Culture and the Bilingual Classroom: Studies in Classroom Ethnography* (pp. 139–52). Rowley, MA: Newbury House.

Bakhtin, M. (1981). *The Dialogic Imagination: Four Essays by M. M. Bakhtin.* Ed. M. Holquist trans. C. Emerson and M. Holquist. Austin: University of Texas Press.

Bloome, D., and Greene, J. (1992). Educational contexts of literacy. In W. Grabe, (ed.), *Annual Review of Applied Linguistics*, 13, 49–70.

Bloome, D., and Theodorou, E. (1988). Analyzing teacher–student and student–student discourse. In J. Green and J. Harker (eds), *Multiple Perspective Analyses of Classroom Discourse* (pp. 217–48). Norwood, NJ: Ablex.

Cazden, C. (1988). *Classroom Discourse: The Language of Teaching and Learning*. Portsmouth, NH: Heinemann.

Cazden, C. (1996). Selective traditions: readings of Vygotsky in writing pedagogy. In D. Hicks (ed.), *Discourse, Learning, and Schooling* (pp. 165–88). New York: Cambridge University Press.

Corson, D. (ed.) (1997). *Encyclopedia of Language and Education*, 8 vols. Dordrecht: Kluwer.

Eder, D. (1993). "Go get ya a French!": romantic and sexual teasing among adolescent girls. In D. Tannen (ed.), *Gender and Conversational Interaction* (pp. 17–31). New York: Oxford University Press.

Eder, C. (1998). Developing adolescent peer culture through collaborative narration. In S. Hoyle and C. T. Adger (eds), *Kids Talk: Strategic Language Use in Later Childhood* (pp. 82–94). New York: Oxford University Press.

Erickson, F. (1996). Going for the zone: the social and cognitive ecology of teacher–student interaction in classroom conversations. In D. Hicks (ed.), *Discourse, Learning, and Schooling* (pp. 29–63). New York: Cambridge University Press.

Erickson, F., and Mohatt, G. (1982). Cultural organization of participation structures in two classrooms of Indian students. In G. D. Spindler (ed.), *Doing the Ethnography of Schooling* (pp. 132–75). New York: Holt, Rhinehart, and Winston.

Erickson, F., and Shultz, J. (1982). *The Counselor as Gatekeeper: Social Interaction in Interviews*. New York: Academic Press.

Fairclough, N. (1993). Critical discourse analysis and the marketization of public discourse: the universities. *Discourse and Society*, 4, 133–68.

Florio, S., and Schultz, J. (1979). Social competence at home and at school. *Theory into Practice*, 18, 234–43.

Foster, M. (1995). Talking that talk: the language of control, curriculum, and critique. *Linguistics and Education*, 7, 129–50.

Gee, J. P. (1989). Two styles of narrative construction and their linguistic and educational implications. *Discourse Processes*, 12, 287–307.

Goffman, E. (1974). *Frame Analysis*. Cambridge, MA: Harvard University Press.

Goffman, E. (1981). *Forms of Talk*. Philadelphia: University of Pennsylvania Press.

Goldenberg, C., and Patthey-Chavez, G. (1995). Discourse processes in instructional conversations: interactions between teacher and transition readers. *Discourse Processes*, 19, 57–73.

Green, J., and Wallat, C. (1981). Mapping instructional conversations – a sociolinguistic ethnography. In J. Green and C. Wallat (eds), *Ethnography and Language in Education Settings* (pp. 161–205). Norwood, NJ: Ablex.

Griffin, P., and Shuy, R. (1978). *Children's Functional Language and Education in the Early Years*. Arlington, VA: Center for Applied Linguistics.

Gumperz, J. (1977). Sociocultural knowledge in conversational inference. In M. Saville-Troike (ed.), *Linguistics and Anthropology* (pp. 191–211). 28th Annual Round Table Monograph Series in Languages and Linguistics. Washington, DC: Georgetown University Press.

Gumperz, J. (1982). *Discourse Strategies*. Cambridge: Cambridge University Press.

Gumperz, J., and Field, M. (1995). Children's discourse and inferential practices in cooperative learning. *Discourse Processes*, 19, 133–47.

Gumperz, J., and Herasimchuk, E. (1975). The conversational analysis of social meaning: a study of classroom interaction. In M. Sanches and B. Blount (eds), *Sociocultural Dimensions of Language Use* (pp. 81–115). New York: Academic Press.

Heath, S. B. (1983). *Ways with Words: Language, Life, and Work in Communities and Classrooms*. New York: Cambridge University Press.

Hicks, D. (1996). Contextual inquiries: a discourse-oriented study of classroom learning. In D. Hicks (ed.), *Discourse, Learning, and Schooling* (pp. 104–44). New York: Cambridge University Press.

Hoyle, S., and Adger, C. T. (1998). Introduction. In S. Hoyle and C. T. Adger (eds), *Kids Talk: Strategic Language Use in Later Childhood* (pp. 3–22). New York: Oxford University Press.

Hymes, D. (1972). Introduction. In C. Cazden, V. Johns, and D. Hymes (eds), *Functions of Language in the Classroom* (pp. xi–lvii). New York: Teachers College Press.

Labov, W., and Fanshel, D. (1977). *Therapeutic Discourse: Psychotherapy as Conversation*. New York: Academic Press.

McDermott, R. (1976). Kids make sense: an ethnographic account of the interactional management of success and failure in one first grade classroom. Unpublished dissertation, University of Stanford.

McDermott, R. P., Gospodinoff, K., and Aron, J. (1978). Criteria for an ethnographically adequate description of concerted activities and their contexts. *Semiotica*, 24, 245–75.

Mehan, H. (1979). *Learning Lessons: Social Organization in the Classroom*. Cambridge, MA: Harvard University Press.

Mehan, H., Cazden, C., Coles, L., Fisher, S., and Mauroles, N. (1976). *The Social Organization of Classroom Lessons*. San Diego: University of California, Center for Human Information Processing.

Merritt, M. (1998). Of ritual matters to master: structure and improvisation in language development at primary school. In S. B. Hoyle and C. T. Adger (eds), *Kids Talk: Strategic Language Use in Later Childhood* (pp. 134–50). New York: Oxford University Press.

Michaels, S. (1981). "Sharing time": children's narrative styles and differential access to literacy. *Language in Society*, 10, 423–42.

Moll, L., and Dworin, J. (1996). Biliteracy development in classrooms: social dynamics and cultural possibilities. In D. Hicks (ed.), *Discourse, Learning, and Schooling* (pp. 221–46). New York: Cambridge University Press.

O'Connor, M. C., and Michaels, S. (1996). Shifting participant frameworks: orchestrating thinking practices in group discussion. In D. Hicks (ed.), *Discourse, Learning, and Schooling* (pp. 63–104). New York: Cambridge University Press.

Philips, S. (1993). *The Invisible Culture: Communication in Classroom and Community on the Warm Springs Indian Reservation*. 2nd edition. Prospect Heights, IL: Waveland Press.

Rogoff, B. (1991). Social interaction as apprenticeship in thinking: guidance and participation in spatial planning. In L. B. Resnick, J. M. Levine, and S. Teasley (eds), *Perspectives on Socially Shared Cognition* (pp. 349–64). Washington, DC: APA Press.

Rosebery, A., Warren, B., and Conant, F. (1992) Appropriating scientific discourse: findings from language minority classrooms. *Journal of the Learning Sciences*, 2, 61–94.

Schlegel, J. (1998). Finding words, finding means: collaborative learning and distributed cognition. In S. B. Hoyle and C. T. Adger (eds), *Kids Talk: Strategic Language Use in Later Childhood* (pp. 187–204). New York: Oxford University Press.

Scollon, R., and Scollon, S. (1981). *Narrative, Literacy and Face in Interethnic Communication*. Norwood, NJ: Ablex.

Shultz, J., Florio, S., and Erickson, F. (1982). "Where's the floor?": aspects of social relationships in communication at home and at school. In P. Gilmore and A. Glatthorn (eds), *Children In and Out of School: Ethnography and Education* (pp. 88–123). Washington, DC: Center for Applied Linguistics.

Shuy, R. W., and Griffin, P. (1981). What do they do any day: studying functional language. In W. P. Dickson (ed.), *Children's Oral Communication Skills* (pp. 271–86). New York: Academic Press.

Sinclair, J., and Coulthard, R. M. (1975). *Towards an Analysis of Discourse*. London: Oxford University Press.

Tannen, D. (1984). *Conversational Style: Analyzing Talk Among Friends*. Norwood, NJ: Ablex.

Tannen, D. (1993). What's in a frame? Surface evidence for underlying expectations. In D. Tannen (ed.), *Framing in Discourse* (pp. 14–56). New York: Oxford University Press.

Tharp. R. G. (1997). *From At-risk to Excellence: Research, Theory, and Principles for Practices*. University of California, Santa Cruz: Center for Research on Education, Diversity and Excellence.

Tharp, R., and Gallimore, R. (1988). *Rousing Minds to Life: Teaching, Learning, and Schooling in Social Context*. Cambridge: Cambridge University Press.

Tuyay, S., Jennings, L., and Dixon, C. (1995). Classroom discourse and opportunities to learn: an ethnographic study of knowledge construction in a bilingual third-grade classroom. *Discourse Processes*, 19, 75–110.

Vogt, L., Jordan, C., and Tharp, R. (1987). Explaining school failure, producing school success: two cases. *Anthropology and Education Quarterly*, 19, 276–86.

Vygotsky, L. S. (1978). *Mind in Society*. Cambridge, MA: Harvard University Press.

Watson-Gegeo, K., and Boggs, S. (1977). From verbal play to talk story: the role of routines in speech events among Hawaiian children. In S. Ervin–Tripp and C. Mitchell–Kernan (eds), *Child Discourse* (pp. 67–90). New York: Academic Press.

Wells, G. (1993). Reevaluating the IRF sequence: a proposal for the articulation of theories of activity and discourse for the analysis of teaching and learning in the classroom. *Linguistics and Education*, 5:1, 1–38.

Wertsch. J. (1991). *Voices of the Mind*. Cambridge, MA: Harvard University Press.

26 Narrative in Institutions

CHARLOTTE LINDE

0 Introduction

Within discourse analysis, narrative has been one of the major areas of research. Researchers have explored various levels of questions ranging from the formal structure of narrative, the relation of discourse structure to morphological and syntactic structure, and the use of narrative in the presentation of self to the work of narrative in small group interactions. This chapter provides review of research on narratives in institutions, considering both the effect on the forms of narratives of their location within institutions, and the work that narratives do within and for those institutions. This question is important for linguistics, and for discourse analysis in particular, since institutional constraints have a strong shaping effect on the narratives told within them, and reciprocally, narratives have a strong part in the creation and reproduction of institutions.

In this chapter, I propose that there are two basic approaches to the study of narrative in institutions. The first approach is the study of the way narrative is used to carry out the daily work of the institution. This can include both the use of narrative by members of the institution to do its daily work and the attempts of nonmembers to use narrative in professional settings, such as legal or medical situations, where professionals require the use of specialized, privileged forms of discourse. The second approach is the study of the work that narrative performs in institutions to reproduce the institution, reproduce or challenge its power structures, induct new members, create the identity of the institution and its members, adapt to change, and deal with contested or contradictory versions of the past. We may understand this as the way an institution uses narrative to create and reproduce its identity by the creation and maintenance of an institutional memory.

I use the term "institution" rather than organization, although both terms are used in different fields, for the phenomena examined here. The first reason for the choice is that "institution," in common use, is a broader term than "organization," and this chapter surveys work on formal organizations, such as an insurance company, as well as studies of what are normally called institutions such as the practice of education, law, and medicine. I therefore use the term "institution" to represent any social group which has a continued existence over time, whatever its degree of reification or formal status may be. Thus, an institution may be a nation, a corporation, the practice of medicine, a family, a gang, a regular Tuesday night poker game, or the class of '75.

1 Narratives and Institutional Work

As we have all experienced, a great deal of storytelling goes on in every institution. While some of this narrative is recreational or personal, a surprising amount of it functions to get the work of the institution done. This section reviews studies of narrative's role in getting work done within and across the boundaries of institutions.

1.1 Narratives help institutions do their daily work

Recently, there have been a number of linguistic and ethnographic studies of work in institutional contexts, which contribute indirectly to our understanding of narratives in these settings. In most cases, the contribution is indirect, since the focus is on other forms of institutional discourse, with narrative described only in passing. For example, Wasson (1996) provides a linguistic analysis of decision-making processes in managerial meetings of a large technology company, and the use of the discourse of these meetings to create identity, agency, and reputation for the participants and the corporation. Similarly, Bargiela-Chiappini and Harris (1997) provides a comparison of the discourse of British and Italian quality assurance team meetings. They focus on meetings as a genre, with detailed attention to linguistic issues of cohesion: theme, pronominalization, metaphor, and the role of the chair. Wodak (1996) provides detailed linguistic descriptions of the work of discourse in a medical clinic, school governance committees, and group therapy sessions, but touches on narrative only in passing. Kunda (1992) presents an influential ethnography of a technical firm, focusing on the rituals and narratives which construct the self as a member, but does not give the narratives themselves, since the data was gathered by note-taking, not recording.

The most important description of narrative in work settings is Orr's analysis of the use of narrative in the work of copier repair technicians (1990, 1996). He shows that narrative forms a major part of their work practice, and that these technicians could not properly do their jobs without participating in a community which tells endless stories about copiers, clients, and repair technicians, as part of the work of maintaining an ongoing community memory of difficult problems, unexpected and undocumented solutions, and heroic diagnoses.

1.2 Narratives at the boundaries of the institution

Within linguistics proper, one of the most-studied aspects of institutional discourse has been what I call discourse at the boundaries of the institution. The issue for these studies is what happens to the structure of narrative (and to the narrators) when one of the interlocutors is in an institutional position to require other interlocutors to provide narratives or other discourse forms in an institutionally specified form. Narrative is a vernacular form, and narratives (and narrators) can get mangled at the boundaries of powerful institutions.

Agar (1985), indeed, proposes this as the central characteristic of institutional discourse, which he defines as discourse produced when "one person – a citizen of a modern nation/state – comes into contact with another – a representative of one of its institutions" (1985: 147). Looking particularly at medical and legal discourse, he proposes a three-part framework for institutional discourse, which typically consists of an interaction – usually a series of question–answer pairs – to diagnose the client, directives given by an institutional representative either to the client or to the institution, and a report made by the institutional representative of the diagnosis and directives.

While Agar does not deal directly with the question of narratives at institutional boundaries, his account suggests why the production of narratives at these boundaries is often contested. An important part of the work of the institutional representative is to use his or her control to fit the client into the organizational ways of thinking about the problem. As we shall see in the discussion of narrative at institutional boundaries, the framing of the problem is most frequently the disputed issue across the boundary. We find these issues in studies of medicine, law, and education.

Frankel (1983) and Todd (1981) demonstrate the conflict between the narrative form in which patients prefer to offer information about their condition, and the question–answer form which physicians prefer, since it matches the record which the physician must construct and the diagnosis tree which they use to determine a condition. Frankel also finds that production pressure affects medical discourse: physicians fear that allowing patients to tell their stories will produce an unfocused discourse which will not provide the needed information within the allotted time. Yet he also finds a conflict between the physician's notion of "presenting problem" which is the focus of diagnosis, and the fact that patients do not always mention the health issue of greatest concern first in their presentation.

Similarly, there have been a number of studies of legal language which show tensions between narrative structure and a question–answer format required by institutional settings. For example, when people on the witness stand try to tell stories, which by their structure require personal judgment in the evaluation sections, they are confined by the questions and directions of lawyers and judges to just telling the facts (Conley and O'Barr 1990; O'Barr and Conley 1996). Similarly, Whelan (1995), in a study of the work of public safety dispatchers (9-1-1 operators), shows how an operator taking a call is tightly constrained by the demands of filling out a form on the computer, while the caller attempts to tell a story about two guys who were shooting.

Both of these cases represent narratives told across the boundary of institutional membership: the two interlocutors do not share knowledge and agreement of what is relevant, what is permitted, and what should be next for a narrative in that context. Witnesses do not normally know the legal rules governing admissible testimony. The person calling 9-1-1 does not know what form the operator must fill out, nor does he or she know that the computer requires him or her to proceed through its fields in order, rather than being able to sieve out the information needed as it comes up in his or her narrative.

There have been a number of studies of discourse in school settings which argue that schools require students to produce particular forms of spoken discourse shaped by the conventions of expository written texts. These conventions require decontextualization of information, address to a generalized audience rather than those particular persons present, focus on a single topic, and explicit lexicalization of topic shifts. This discourse is quite different from the vernacular forms that students normally use for narration. A number of works argue that while white middle-class children are trained in such decontextualization skills even before entering kindergarten, children of other ethnic groups may not understand these discourse norms, and hence may produce narratives which are not acceptable in a classroom context (Michaels 1981; Scollon and Scollon 1981).

2 Narrative and Institutional Reproduction

We now turn from the use of narrative in the work of institutions to the use of narrative in the work of institution-making: the reproduction and maintenance of institutions, as well as contestations and changes in the institutions' self-representation.

My primary data-source for these questions is a major American insurance company, here called MidWest Insurance, founded in the 1920s. My colleagues and I performed a three-year ethnographic study, including observations and recording of the training and work of insurance sales agents, as well as observations of ongoing training programs, sales conventions, regional meetings, task forces, and management meetings. This work was originally commissioned by MidWest to answer questions about agents' sales practices, customers' understanding of insurance purchases, and the success of the company's new agent training program. This study gave us detailed access to the company's culture during a period of great cultural change.

3 Nonparticipant Narratives in Institutions

Within the boundaries of an institution, many stories are told daily. Social life is created by, and reproduced by, narrative, and life within institutions is no exception. Of these uncountable stories, it is the class of repeated narratives which is the most useful in understanding the work of stories in institutions. Linde (1993: 194) shows that the individual life story is a discontinuous discourse unit, composed of those narratives with long-term repeatability.

In studying narrative in institutions, it is equally important to find the long-term narratives. There are many ephemeral institutional narratives: the stories in the lunchroom about today's computer crash, the terrible traffic, or a manager's momentary fit of generosity or bad temper, stories told during the course of the day or perhaps the week, but which will not survive the weekend. Such narratives also show something about the ways in which membership and identity are created through discourse. However, this study concentrates on those institutional narratives that are repeatable through time and across tellers. I define this class as nonparticipant narrative (NPN): the narrative told by a speaker who was not a participant or witness to the events narrated, but heard them from someone else. Thus, NPNs have an extended life in the institution, since their very form assures us that they have been retold at least once. (See Linde 1996 for a discussion of the use of evidentials in NPNs to mark group membership.)

NPNs have a special status within institutions because, as we shall show, they form a particular part of the way that institutions remember their past and use that remembering to create current identities for both the institution and its members. At MidWest, the one NPN that everyone knows is the company's history, told as the story of the founder. All versions include the following evaluative points:

- a charismatic founder with a strong vision: the idea that farmers of good moral character should be charged lower rates for auto insurance, since they ran lower risks than city drivers, and an exclusive relation between the company and its sales agents;
- the American rural and small-town origins of the founder and of the company, which still shape its values;
- the development of the company from selling auto insurance to a full service company offering fire, life, and health insurance as well, presented as an ever-growing commercial and ethical success;
- the idea that the company is a family, and represents family values.

Note that this story of the institution's origin gives a coherent account of the company's identity and values. For a member to know this story means to know what the institution is, and what that member must do to be a part of it.

3.1   In what media are narratives represented?

I now turn to the range of media used to convey the institutional narratives.

3.1.1   Authorized biography and history

Although MidWest was founded early in the 1920s, its founder is still vividly present. He is referred to by name, Mr. McBee, and is often quoted by management. His biography, which is also a history of the company, was written in the mid-1950s, and is still in print. Copies are to be seen prominently displayed in executives' offices, with the front cover turned outward. Our fieldwork team was told that we must read it to really understand MidWest.

I initially had some questions about whether this book functioned more like a ritual object, whose function is to be displayed, or as a text which is assumed always to be relevant to the present, and quoted and interpreted continuously (see Smith 1993). In fact, the biography is read and quoted, particularly by managers. For example, one manager explained that she mines it for materials for speeches since "I don't come by it by blood." She explained that this meant that she was relatively new to MidWest, having previously worked at another insurance company, and so does not yet claim full storytelling rights at MidWest. (It is also possible that the remark is to be understood literally, since over half of the members of this company have kin currently or formerly employed by MidWest, while this manager did not.)

Taking the story of the founder as exemplary means that his virtues are to be emulated by all members of the company. And yet, an important part of knowing how to use an exemplary narrative is to learn what parts of the model are unique to the founder, and are *not* to be emulated. For example, in religious exemplary narratives, Christians may expect to have to take up their cross, but they understand that this will not include literally being crucified and rising from death after the third day. (Linde (2000) gives a fuller discussion of the use of exemplary narratives.) Similarly, part of being a member of MidWest means not only generally knowing Mr. McBee's book, but also knowing which parts of it should directly guide one's actions. So agents, who are independent contractors, not employees of MidWest, describe themselves as determined, highly principled entrepreneurs, just like Mr. McBee. But while they are business owners like him, they are not business founders. A dramatic turning point in Mr. McBee's life came when he complained about the insurance company he worked for, and was told "Well, T.D., if you don't like the way we run things, go start your own company." This is repeatedly told as an indication of his determined character. This story is told not to inspire agents to found their own companies, but rather to make them proud of having founded their own agency offices, thus showing the same entrepreneurial spirit as the founder.

3.1.2 Newsletter articles

Another source of institutional narratives at MidWest Insurance is a monthly magazine sent to all agents, which frequently retells the history of the company at various levels. It makes continuous reference to stories of Mr. McBee. It often profiles older agents, using their stories to spotlight changes in the business, and to mark the continuity of underlying values. Several years ago, it ran a year-long series of the history of MidWest by decade, highlighting the key events of each.

3.1.3 Speeches and training

Official speeches are frequent at MidWest, at national and regional sales conventions, at special task force meetings, and at events organized by local management. At all of these, we have observed managers retelling stories of MidWest's past. Very frequently, these stories of the company's past are told as a guide to the present and inspiration for the future. The message is: "We have faced difficult times before and won, we have changed before without sacrificing our essential character, and we can do so again. We can rely on our history to guide us in how to change."

As the initial data for the study were being collected, the insurance company was in the process of introducing a new contract for agents. Acceptance of this was voluntary for agents already working under the old one. During a contract rollout meeting, a number of executives used references to known stories about the company's history to make the point that the company has changed before. They cited such changes as "moving our offices out of our back bedrooms, bringing on trained staff, incorporating microfiche and then computers." One speaker noted that this was his third contract introduction: "In both the previous cases, the people who did not sign the new contract were sorry. Those who failed to change failed to advance."

All new employees hear the history of the company as part of their training. This is particularly relevant for newly promoted managers, who will be authorized speakers for the company, permitted and required to retell these stories. This type of training is often extremely lively and humorous. One training program I observed devoted five hours of the first day of a three-month training to the history and values of MidWest. A video was shown, which included movies of the early headquarters of the company and the typical Model T Fords they insured, still photographs of the presidents, interviews with retired employees, early radio and television commercials for MidWest, etc. During the video, the trainer stopped the tape to add comments or stories of her own. At the end of the video, she then asked the students what they remembered from it, throwing a small roll of candy with MidWest's logo to each person who answered. She then passed out sheets of company milestones by decade, and discussed them, interspersed with stories of her own involvement with MidWest.

Similarly, I have observed a training event for new managers in which someone who describes himself as the "unofficial historian" of the company covered MidWest's history. The audience undoubtedly already knew most of the facts and had read the book. But the speaker was lively and humorous, framing parts of the speech as a sermon or a revival meeting. For example, he ended a story about the founder's ambitious sales goals by saying: "Now brothers and sisters, that's *sales leadership*. If you want to say amen, go ahead. (*applause*)" He also added details not in the official history: an alternative version of a well-known slogan, the origins of the names of local buildings. It was striking how engaging the speaker was, and how engaged the audience was.

3.1.4   Individual retellings or citations

In addition to official retellings of the founding stories, I have collected examples of individuals telling or citing these stories to members of the ethnographic team, to potential business partners, and, infrequently, to clients.

In one example, an agent explained that MidWest was better than his previous company because it had been founded by a farmer, and retained the strong ethical values of farmers. What I find extraordinary about this agreement with the founding story is that the speaker had lived his entire life in either a major city or a densely populated suburb. (This location of virtue and probity on the farm is, of course, not exclusive to MidWest. It has formed a central theme in American discourse about virtue and vice for at least 150 years.)

In addition to the telling of stories, insiders often index them: that is, they refer to stories their interlocutors already know. For example, a favorite story in MidWest's history is that when the growth in auto policies caused logistical problems in processing applications, the company hired a number of young women who roller-skated applications around the enormous processing building. Pictures of these skating workers are among the most frequently reproduced in the company. On one occasion, as a number of agents were moving through a long buffet line, I heard one agent remark to another: "We could use roller-skates to get through this line." This reference indexes a known story; it serves as an inside joke, which supports the status of both interlocutors.

3.1.5 *Narratives of personal experience and paradigmatic narratives*

We now turn to the question of the relation between the narratives of personal experience told within the institution and the official institutional narrative. In particular, we may focus on the repeated narratives that form a part of the teller's life story. For the sales agents, these narratives almost always include socially defined milestones of their careers: how the agent was recruited, relationship to the first manager, the first years of developing a business, moves from one office location to another, addition of staff, winning of specific awards, etc. Each agent has many of these narratives, which are frequently told, not only to the inquiring ethnographer, but also to other agents and managers. While these narratives frame the stages of individual careers, they are told against the background of what we call the *paradigmatic narrative*, which gives an account of the trajectory of an ideal sales agent career. We may distinguish the paradigmatic narrative from a myth or folktale, because the full paradigmatic narrative is never told on any given occasion; rather, pieces of it are told as possibilities. Thus, a manager recruiting a possible new agent might cite the beginning part of the story: "You'll work hard for the first seven years or so, and then you can start to reap the rewards." Further, the paradigmatic narrative gives salience to the telling of stories of individual agents' careers. Thus when an agent tells a success story, or a manager tells a new recruit a story about old Bob down the street, the story has particular relevance if it approximates to the ideal agent career. As Goffman has pointed out (1981), it is the task of a narrator to justify taking up airtime by making the story that of Everyman – what any reasonable person would do in similar circumstances. The paradigmatic narrative represents the work of an entire institution to create such relevance for particular narratives.

4 When and How Are Narratives Told?

Having surveyed the media available for narration, we now turn specifically to the question of how and when narratives are told. When we consider the range of institutions, it appears that there are large differences between how many narratives they maintain, and more generally, how intensely they work their pasts. Thus, it is not enough to ask what narratives about an institution exist; we must also ask what form of existence they have. Narratives may be collected by a company archivist, or an external historian, but if they exist only in a rarely consulted archive, they have no real life. Rather, the key question is: what are the occasions that allow for the telling and retelling of this stock of stories? An important way institutions differ is in the kinds of occasions for narration they maintain, and the ways these occasions are used. This section offers a taxonomy of types of occasions for the telling of narratives. The first axis of this taxonomy is modality: time, both regular and irregular; space;

Table 26.1   Occasions for narrative remembering

	Designed for remembering	*Used for remembering*
Time: Regular occurrences	Anniversaries, regular audits, regular temporally occasioned ritual	Annual meetings
Time: Irregular or occasional occurrences	Retirement parties, roasts, problem-based audits, inductions, wakes, occasional temporally occasioned ritual	Arrival of a traveling bard, coronations, institutional problems, use of nontransparent lexical items
Place	Museums, memorial displays, place-occasioned ritual	Sites of events
Artifacts	Memorial artifacts, designed displays, photo albums, object-occasioned ritual	Artifacts accidentally preserved

and artifact. The second axis is design intention: occasions specifically designed for remembering and occasions with some other primary purpose that have affordances that allow for remembering. Table 26.1 shows typical examples, although no cell gives an exhaustive list of possible occasions.

4.1   Time: regular occurrences

These are occasions with a regular time course: they occur every year, every Sunday, on the anniversary of an event to be commemorated, etc. Some are specifically designed for remembering. For example, the 50th anniversary of D day was marked by ceremonies that were created and designed to allow for narrative remembering. Religious liturgies and ceremonies tied to particular dates are another example of this type.

Other temporally regular events can be used for remembering, although that is not their primary purpose. For example, MidWest holds annual sales conventions in each region and for national top-selling agents, which form a regular occasion for narration. These conventions have formal talks by executives of the company, which regularly invoke the past to explain the present and future, as well as informal meetings of smaller groups of friends.

For American corporations, regular audits are legally mandated occasions for remembering by accounting. They have a conventional pattern, requiring personnel within an institution to present specific records in a specific form to outside auditors. But they are also an occasion for new members of the institution, particularly those involved with record-keeping, to ask questions and share stories about why the records are as they are, and the history which they record.

4.2   Time: irregular or occasional occurrences

Occasional occurences are events whose exact timing cannot be predicted, but which recur within an institution, and which require certain types of narration. Cases designed for remembering are boundary markers, like retirements or inductions. Inductions are a particular class of occasions on which a new person, or new group of persons, is admitted into the organization, or a new level of it. These occasions include orientation meetings, presentations, etc. For example, at MidWest, part of the training of new agents includes an account of the founding and subsequent history of the company.

There are also irregularly occurring occasions that can be used for remembering. For example, in committee meetings, someone may propose changing a policy. This is often, though not necessarily, the occasion for someone to object by recounting the story of previous problems that the policy was designed to prevent.

One small-scale but important type of temporally irregular occasion is the use of nontransparent lexical items. Unusual words or acronyms may provide the opportunity for the narration of parts of the institutional memory. For example, MidWest Insurance uses the pair of terms "MOC" and "SOC," pronounced "mock" and "sock," which stand for "Moveable Object Collision" and "Stationary Object Collision." Although all auto insurance now protects against both, initially MidWest only provided protection against MOCs, since the founder felt that someone who hit a stationary object was an incompetent driver who should not be driving. Stationary object coverage was added later. These terms provide occasions for stories about how many changes the company has undergone, and about the determined and moral character of the founder.

4.3   Place

Certain places give occasions for narrative remembering. Sites like historical museums or memorial statues or displays are designed to represent or elicit certain stories, such as the memorized stories told by museum guides or available in invariant form in taped tours. Even here, though, some freer and more personal stories may be occasioned. White (1997) describes tour guides at the Pearl Harbor museum, as part of the official tour, describing their own war experiences in relation to the bombing of Pearl Harbor.

Sites of notable events may allow for the retelling of those events, while not being specifically designed for memory: Basso (1996) has described the extensive use which the Western Apache make of places and place names as occasions for stories that function as moral instruction in how to behave. A corporate example comes in passing "the first building, where we started," or "the old fire company." This can occasion a story about the founding or the early days. Such occasioning is also used for personally significant spaces: "That's the office I used to have." "Oh, you have Cindy's space."

4.4   Artifacts

Artifacts frequently serve as occasions for remembering. Some artifacts are specifically designed for remembering, like photo albums, or the memorial artifacts described above. There are also less formal memorial artifacts: T-shirts, mugs, and baseball caps that mark local milestones or events. While there have been few studies of how such artifacts are used, we have observed cases in which they serve to establish commonality. For example, a person seeing a commemorative mug on someone's desk may say, "Oh, I was at that meeting too." Further, a collection of such artifacts can serve to establish a person's history within the organization. At MidWest, over the course of a career, an agent may collect an array of memorial artifacts including plaques, model automobiles, pins and other memorabilia, all of which mark various levels of sales achievements. Such a collection is readable by insiders, and narratable to outsiders.

   Some institutions, including MidWest, make a very deliberate use of space as an occasion for the display of memorial artifacts. For example, the main lobby of the main corporate headquarters contains a small museum. This includes a Model A Ford built in the year the company was founded, the first rate chart handwritten by the founder on a piece of brown paper, posters of radio and television programs sponsored by the company, gifts given as sales performance recognitions, including top hat and white gloves, leather purses containing gold pieces, and old and new plaques, pins, and statuettes used as rewards for agents. The main headquarters building also contains low-relief bronze busts of the first five presidents in the main atrium, which are used by tour guides and training sessions as occasions for narratives about these men. (See Samuel 1994 for a discussion of English banks which maintain "mini-museums" in their lobbies, containing photographs or wax models and memorial objects of famous clients, such as Florence Nightingale or Lord Nelson, or a letter from Lord Byron asking for an extension of credit.)

   Another important form of maintenance of memory is the use of publicly displayed photographs and plaques, which serve to occasion stories. For example, as we walked through MidWest's headquarters to our next meeting, we passed a photo of a now-retired vice-president, and were told that he was the father of someone we had met. This occasioned stories about the careers of both men.

5   Silences: Stories That Are *Not* Told

Having discussed how narratives are maintained and occasioned within institutions, it is now important to turn to the question of silences: what stories are *not* told. This raises the methodological question of how it is possible to give an account of what is not said. Obviously, there are an infinite number of things that are not said. However, what is relevant is what is saliently unsaid, what could be said but is not. Different circumstances allow different forms of access to what is saliently unsaid. For example, for institutions with opposed interests, such as an employer and a labor union, each institution will have some pieces of the past which it remembers, and some which it does not. Investigating the union's representation of the past is likely to provide stories upon which the employer's memory is silent, and vice versa. (See Pilcher 1972.) In the case of MidWest, since we conducted an extensive field study, we had access not only to official representations, but also to a broad range of unofficial conversations, meetings, interviews, etc. This allowed us a considerable amount of information about material that is *not* represented in the official account of the past.

There are several different types of oppositional stories. For example, the support staff of a company may pass along tales of their manager's incompetence. These may have a radically critical nature: the guy is incompetent, and should be fired. Or they may be stories of carnival reversal, which do not permanently subvert the established order. For instance, a receptionist's story about how the boss tried to make a pot of coffee for a meeting and blew up the coffee machine, drenching his pants, is humorously critical, but does not propose a radical reordering of relations between bosses and support staff.

There are also countermemories and counterhistories, which are explicitly critical of existing power relations and of the official institutional memory. For example, Tulviste and Wetsch (1995) describes the relation between official and unofficial history in Estonia. While the official history of the Soviet domination of Estonia was coherent and well organized, the unofficial history was carried by "isolated observations, reference to public individuals and events, stories about specific public episodes, and relatives' personal stories about their own or others' experiences (e.g. in Siberian camps)" (1995: 321). This unofficial history was relatively unstructured, lacking a systematic, all-encompassing narrative. Its structure was a counterstructure, a rebuttal of the official history, given its shape by the form of the official history.

In addition to countermemories, we must also consider erasures. There can be silences with and without erasure. An institution may be silent about a given event, that is, have no official account of the event. Erasure is stronger. It is an attempt by an institution to eliminate all accounts of an event in the past that differ saliently from the official one. A clear example of erasure is the former USSR's attempt to erase all accounts of the existence of the gulags.

There are a number of silences in MidWest's official narratives. The major one is the absence of an account of a suit brought against the company in the late 1970s, charging it with discriminating against women in the hiring of agents. In the mid-1980s, the company settled the suit, and began a program of recruiting women and minorities. These facts are public, available in the public press, and of course known to agents and employees of the company who lived through these years. Yet they are rarely if ever mentioned in the company's official statements.

How might we discover this silence? The official history of the company was published in 1955, so it could have no account of this event. However, in 1992, MidWest's official magazine printed a series of 12 articles on company history, including highlights of each decade. The highlights for the 1970s and 1980s included items about changes in the leadership of the company, growth of number of policies, record sales, record losses, unveiling of a portrait of the president, and the induction of the founder into the Business Hall of Fame. The lawsuit and its consequences are not mentioned, although it caused perhaps the largest change in corporate policy of those decades.

This is a silence in the official institutional memory, but it is not an erasure. That is, while the lawsuit and its consequences are not directly discussed, they are unofficially discussable, and there have been no efforts to erase any indication of the changes. For example, as part of regional sales conventions, a yearbook of agents in the region is distributed. This yearbook is set up with pictures of the agents, their names, and the length of their tenure with the company, arranged first by half-decade. The book begins with agents of 45+ years of service, then 40+, etc. At 10+ and particularly 5+, the number of faces of women and minorities begin to approach their representation in the general population. Anyone flipping through this book, knowing nothing of the company's history, could guess that a major change in recruiting happened in the early 1990s. Yet if MidWest had wished to erase this obvious shift in policy, it could have organized the book not temporally but alphabetically, thus blurring the representation of this major change.

Why did it not do so? Why was there no erasure? One reason is the obvious fact that the change in policy cannot be erased, since it forms a part of so many people's memories. Another reason is that tenure within the company is very important to people's identities, a key way in which people characterize themselves. An alphabetical arrangement would wipe out this very salient characterization, and probably make the yearbook less appealing to and usable by the agents.

If we examine the unofficial narratives, we find neither silence nor erasure here. All agents who have been appointed within the last ten years have some relation to the lawsuit and its aftermath. While we heard no agent specifically discuss the lawsuit, many agents told stories which assume that we knew about it. For example, one agent's account of how he came to be an agent was that he spoke with several managers, and went with "the first one who had a slot for a white male." His intonation and story structure were matter-of-fact, with no evaluative comment. A woman agent, whose father had been an agent, told us that when she first expressed a desire to become an agent, she was told "But you're a girl!" After working at a variety of other jobs, she applied to MidWest when she heard that the policy had changed. As she told us: "The company was looking to hire women and minorities, that's the only reason I got hired."

In another example, a Hispanic agent explained why he did not accept the first offer to train as an agent:

> They were looking for an agent to be placed in an urban market in [Town] but they were looking for someone that was either, had to be at least 25 years old and uh, of certain racial makeup, and of which I qualified. They only problem was that I was new. I was about to be married and had no money, so there was no way I was going to go and do it.

While there is some absence of fluency in the specification of the desired racial makeup, there are two points to be made. First, the issue is speakable, at least to the extent that American discourse generally allows for discussion of race across racial or ethnic boundaries (the interviewer was Anglo-American). Secondly, the main topic is the explanation of why the speaker did not at this time accept an offer which he later was glad to accept when his own circumstances changed. Thus, these stories are tellable, without apparent embarrassment or anger, to relative outsiders, which suggests that the official silence apparently does not require a corresponding oppositional stance in an unofficial breaking of the silence.

In addition to the affirmative action suit, another notable silence in the official memory is the absence of mention of the existence of an organization of agents, described in an article in the outside business press as "a would be union" of discontented agents, who describe the company as "run for the benefit of its management and nobody else." We have heard the organization mentioned and even discussed by agents and managers, and have seen copies of the newsletter distributed by the organization to all agents. Agents and managers were quick to express publicly their distance from the organization, and their disgust with its lack of loyalty to the company. Given our position as ethnographers paid by MidWest, it is not surprising that only one person of the hundreds we talked to admitted to being a member.

6   Who Speaks for the Institution?

Another important part of understanding narratives in institutions is the question of storytelling rights: who may speak for the institution, whose account is taken up by others, whose account does *not* count as part of the institutional memory (Shuman 1986). Focusing on institutions necessarily means beginning with the official narratives, and with the accounts of those whose position grants the right to speak for the institution, whether it be the president speaking for the company, or an agent speaking for her or his own agency. That is, institutions have levels, and each of these levels has its history.

Critical theory has focused on hegemonic discourse: official accounts which attempt to naturalize the current state of affairs, to make current power relations appear to be inalterable facts of nature (Mumby 1988). Completely successful naturalization would make counteraccounts impossible, since a different state of affairs could not be imagined. Yet ethnographic accounts (for example, Scott 1985; Watson 1994; Wodak 1996) suggest that hegemonic discourse is rarely if ever fully successful.

But official representations of the institution and complete opposition to these representations are not the only possible stances. Speakers are able to create a wide range of maneuvers, including many combinations of critique, support, and suggested reform. For example, the organization of disaffected agents at MidWest regularly criticizes the management of the company for abandoning the heritage of the founder's policies. It thus makes a moral claim to a legitimate and official stance, since it claims to represent the true past and values of the company, which management has betrayed.

One of the few situated studies of the maintenance of a countertradition is Orr's account of the narratives of repair technicians, which contrast the ways in which the official documentation requires the technicians to fix particular problems with the unofficial ways that actually work (Orr 1996). More such studies are needed to provide a fuller understanding of whether and how such discourses have a life within the institutions they criticize. I suggest that posing the question in terms of institutional memory permits questions not only about what the counterhegemonic discourses are, but where they live, and how they succeed or fail in creating an on-going countermemory.

7 Conclusion

Within sociolinguistics, and particularly within the study of discourse, it has become increasingly clear that linguistic forms can only be understood within their context (Duranti and Goodwin 1992). This chapter has attempted to show that one important context for the analysis of narratives is the institution in which it is told, and the work the narrative performs in and for that institution. Such a study requires analysis of the forms and media for narratives maintained in particular institutions, the relations between these forms, the occasions for narratives, the events and evaluations of these narratives, and the identity of preferred and dispreferred speakers for given speakers (storytelling rights). These questions allow us to map the work that narratives do in institutions: maintaining identity and continuity, negotiating power relations, managing change, and marking membership, as well as transacting the daily business of the organization. Thus, research into narratives in institutions provides an empirical study of one of the primary processes of social reproduction.

Although this work might appear to be more properly located within anthropology, sociology, or folklore, in fact it is central to linguistics for a number of reasons. The first is that attention to the location of narratives within an institution permits analysis of morphological and syntactic phenomena, such as evidentials and point-of-view markers, which can be explained only by an account of a speaker's position within an institution, and what storytelling rights that person claims by a telling (Linde 1996).

Additionally, attention to institutional location allows us to specify an empirically grounded class of constraints on the form and evaluation of possible stories within that institution. For example, a story about founding one's own business which included extreme risk-taking and sacrificing one's family and health is standard in Silicon Valley, but would not be tellable in the conservative culture of MidWest. I do not want to extend the notion of starred sentences to the notion of starred narratives, which would create all too much mischief in the study of discourse. Tellability is not a matter for the intuition of the analyst, but rather for the social negotiation by members of what counts as an event and what is acceptable as an evaluation (Goodwin 1984, 1986; Linde 1993; Polanyi 1989).

In addition, a narrative takes part of its meaning from its location within an ecology of narratives. A given story in an institution has a very different meaning if it supports or contradicts the story of the founder, or the paradigmatic narrative available as a career guide. Thus, to understand the telling of the story of old Bob down the street, we must understand whether it is heard as an instance of the paradigmatic narrative, or whether old Bob is a sad example of what happens when you do not do it the right way.

Finally, attention to narrative in institutions may be seen as an extension of the ethnography of speaking. This began by asking what kinds of speech events and speech acts exist within a speech community (Hymes 1972). More recent developments have focused on issues of performance: not just the speech event, but its location and performance within a stream of activity. I propose that considering institutions as a unit of interest gives an orthogonal account of community, and provides an important unit of study for modern, industrial societies, in which the speech community cannot be defined as identical to language, dialect, or political boundaries. This chapter thus offers a paradigm for research in a wide range of sites, which are understudied and near to hand. Additional research within this paradigm could greatly add to our understanding of the work of narrative within social groups of all types and sizes.

NOTE

I would like to thank Christopher Darrouzet, who has been my invaluable colleague from the beginning of this project, as well as my other collaborators on the fieldwork of the insurance project: Libby Bishop, Renee Chin, David Fearon, Maurene Flory, Joe Harding, Nancy Lawrence, Charline Poirier, and Cheryl Lynn Sullivan. I also value greatly discussion and comments from my colleagues Susan Anderson, Michael Bamberg, Geoffrey Bowker, Bill Clancey, Penny Eckert, Meg Graham, James Greeno, Jo-anne Kleifgen, Robin Kornman, Norma Mendoza-Denton, Sigrid Mueller, Ida Obermann, Leigh Star, Etienne Wenger, and Ruth Wodak. Finally, I am extremely grateful to all the members of MidWest Insurance whose generosity with their time, and enthusiasm about their company, have made this work a delight and an excitement.

REFERENCES

Agar, Michael. 1985. Institutional discourse. *Text* 5(3): 147–68.

Bargiela–Chiappini, Francesca and Harris, Sandra J. 1997. *Managing Language: The Discourse of Corporate Meetings*. Amsterdam and Philadelphia: John Benjamins.

Basso, Keith H. 1996. *Wisdom Sits in Places: Landscape and Language Among the Western Apache*. New Mexico: University of New Mexico Press.

Conley, John and O'Barr, William. 1990. Rules versus relationships in small claims disputes. In *Conflict Talk: Sociolinguistic Investigation of Arguments in Conversations*, ed. A. D. Grimshaw (pp. 178–96). Cambridge: Cambridge University Press.

Duranti, Alessandro and Goodwin, Charles. 1992. *Rethinking Context: Language as an Interactive Phenomenon: Studies in the Social and Cultural Foundations of Language 11*. Cambridge: Cambridge University Press.

Frankel, Richard. 1983. The laying on of hands: aspects of the organization of gaze, touch, and talk in a medical encounter. In *The Social Organization of Doctor–Patient Communication*, eds S. Fisher and A. Todd (pp. 19–49). Washington, DC: Center for Applied Linguistics.

Goffman, Erving. 1981. "Footing." In *Forms of Talk*, ed. E. Goffman (pp. 124–59). Philadelphia: University of Pennsylvania Press.

Goodwin, Charles. 1984. Notes on story structure and the organization of participation. In *Structures of Social Action*, ed. J. M. Atkinson and J. Heritage (pp. 225–46). Cambridge: Cambridge University Press.

Goodwin, Charles. 1986. Audience diversity, participation and interpretation. *Text* 63: 283–316.

Hymes, Dell. 1972. Models of the interaction of language and social life. In *Directions in Sociolinguistics: The Ethnography of Communication*, eds J. Gumperz and D. Hymes (pp. 35–71). New York: Holt, Rhinehart, and Winston.

Kunda, Gideon. 1992. *Engineering Culture: Control and Commitment in a High–tech Corporation*. Philadelphia: Temple University Press.

Linde, Charlotte. 1993. *Life Stories: The Creation of Coherence*. Oxford: Oxford University Press.

Linde, Charlotte. 1996. Whose story is this? Point of view, variation and group identity in oral narrative: sociolinguistic variation – data, theory and analysis. In *Selected Papers from NWAV23 at Stanford*, eds J. Arnold, R. Blake, B. Davidson, S. Schwenter, and J. Solomon (pp. 333–46). Stanford: CSLI Publications.

Linde, Charlotte. 2000. The acquisition of a speaker by a story: How history becomes memory and identity *Ethos* 28(4): 608–32.

Michaels, Sarah. 1981. Sharing time: children's narrative styles and differential access to literacy. *Language in Society* 10: 423–42.

Mumby, Dennis. 1988. *Communication and Power in Organizations: Discourse, Ideology and Domination*. Norwood NJ: Ablex.

O'Barr, William M., and Conley, John. 1996. Ideological dissonance in the American legal system. In *Disorderly Talk: Narrative, Conflict and Inequality*, ed. C. L. Briggs. Oxford and New York: Oxford University Press.

Orr, Julian. 1990. Sharing knowledge, celebrating identity: community memory in a service culture. In *Collective Remembering*, eds

D. Middleton and D. Edwards (pp. 169–89). London and Thousand Oaks, CA: Sage.

Orr, Julian. 1996. *Talking about Machines*. Ithaca, NY: ILR Press.

Pilcher, William W. 1972. The Portland longshoremen: a dispersed urban community. In *Case Studies in Cultural Anthropology*, ed. G. A. L. Spindler. New York: Holt, Rhinehart, and Winston.

Polanyi, Livia. 1989. *The American Story*. Cambridge, MA: MIT Press.

Samuel, Raphael. 1994. *Theatres of Memory Volume 1: Past and Present in Contemporary Culture*. London and New York: Verso.

Scollon, Ron and Scollon, Suzanne B. K. 1981. The literate two-year-old: the fictionalization of self. In *Narrative, Literacy, and Face in Interethnic Communications*, eds R. Scollon and S. Scollon (pp. 169–89). Norwood, NJ: Ablex.

Scott, James. 1985. *Weapons of the Weak: Everyday Forms of Peasant Resistance*. New Haven, CT: Yale University Press.

Shuman, Amy. 1986. *Storytelling Rights: The Uses of Oral and Written Texts by Urban Adolescents, (Cambridge Studies in Oral and Literature Culture, No. 11)*. Cambridge: Cambridge University Press.

Smith, Wilfred C. 1993. *What is Scripture?* Minneapolis: Fortress Press.

Todd, Alexandra. 1981. A diagnosis of doctor–patient discourse in the prescription of contraception. In *The Social Organization of Doctor–Patient Communication*, eds S. Fisher and A. Todd (pp. 159–88). Washington, DC: Center for Applied Linguistics.

Tulviste, Peeter, and Wetsch, James V. 1995. Official and unofficial history: the case of Estonia. *Journal of Narrative and Life History* 4(4): 311–31.

Wasson, Christina. 1996. Covert Caution: Linguistic Traces of Covert Control.

Doctoral dissertation, Yale University, Department of Anthropology.

Watson, Rubie. 1994. *Memory, History and Opposition Under State Socialism*. Santa Fe, NM: School of American Research Press.

Whelan, Jack. 1995. A technology of order production: computer-aided dispatch in public safety communications. In *Situated Order: Studies in the Social Organization of Talk and Embodied Activities*, eds P. ten Have and

G. Psathas. Lanham, MD: International Institute for Ethnomethodology and Conversation Analysis and University Press of America.

White, Geoffrey M. 1997. Museum/memorial/shrine: national narrative in national spaces. *Museum Anthropology* 21(1): 8–26.

Wodak, Ruth. 1996. *Disorders of Discourse, Real Language Series*. London and New York: Longman.

B   Culture, Community, and Genre

27 Discourse and Intercultural Communication

RON SCOLLON AND
SUZANNE WONG SCOLLON

0 Introduction: Preliminary Definitions

In current usage, the term "discourse analysis" is polysemic. On the one hand, it refers to the close linguistic study, from different perspectives, of texts in use. On the other hand, discourse refers to socially shared habits of thought, perception, and behavior reflected in numerous texts belonging to different genres. In the first sense, discourse analysis grows out of a heterogeneous group of disciplines including linguistic analysis, French structuralism, the ethnography of communication, Hallidayan functional linguistics, linguistic philosophy, pragmatics, and variation analysis (McCarthy 1991; Schiffrin 1994), all of which focus on the analysis and interpretation of texts in use. In the second sense, discourse analysis grows out of critical, sociocultural, sociological, or historical analysis. To distinguish this sense from the narrower use of "discourse," writers speak of Discourses, orders of discourse, or discursive formations (Foucault 1973a, 1973b, 1976, 1977a, 1977b; Fairclough 1989, 1992, 1995a, 1995b; Gee 1986, 1989, 1996, 1999; Wodak 1996). For example, Gee defines Discourses as "ways of being in the world, or forms of life which integrate words, acts, values, beliefs, attitudes, and social identities, as well as gestures, glances, body positions, and clothes" (Gee 1996: 127). Foucault (1976) uses "discursive formation" to refer to the statements characteristic of clinical medicine, grammar, or economics of a particular time and place. In this line of development the primary focus is on society and social practice, with an attenuated or even absent interest in texts or discourse in the narrower linguistic sense.

This historical polysemy merged in the decade of the 1990s. In most analysis of discourse as text, the analysis seeks to position itself as well as the discourse being studied within a broader sociocultural or historical context. At the same time, those broader studies of social practice are coming to ground themselves in the close analysis of concrete texts. Perhaps the central tenet of this line of thought is that social practice and discourse are mutually constitutive phenomena (Chouliaraki and Fairclough 1999). That is, social practices are understood as being constituted in and through discursive social interaction while at the same time those social interactions are taken as instantiations of pre-existing social practices. It is maintained that we become who we are through discourse and social interaction, at the same time providing evidence of previous patterns of formative discursive social interaction.

"Intercultural communication" and "cross-cultural communication" are problematical in relationship to discourse analysis in that they have developed out of a conceptually wider range of disciplines including anthropology, sociology, social psychology, speech communication, management or business communication, and even international political science. Adding to this problematicity has been the largely practical or applied nature of intercultural and cross-cultural communication studies. Researchers have often had much greater involvement with nonacademic colleagues in workplaces and with professionals than has been the case with most discourse analysts until relatively recently.

Further, there is sometimes an ambiguity in the use of the terms "intercultural" and "cross-cultural" communication. Although there is no widespread agreement on this, we take "intercultural communication" to signal the study of distinct cultural or other groups *in interaction with each other*. That is to say, the comparative analysis of the groups or synthesis between them arises in this framework as part of the interaction of members of different groups with each other, and the analyst's role is to stand outside of the interaction and to provide an analysis of how the participants negotiate their cultural or other differences. As with cross-cultural analysis, the groups under study are often presupposed.

While not all researchers would agree, we take "cross-cultural communication" to signal the independent study of the communicative characteristics of distinct cultural or other groups (e.g. Bond 1986, 1988, in psychology and Hofstede 1993 in business communication). In the cross-cultural framework comparative analysis or synthesis is made by the analyst or researcher. That is to say, in research designed within the cross-cultural paradigm, the members of the distinct groups do not interact with each other within the study but are studied as separate and separable entities. In actual instances the distinctiveness of the groups under analysis is often presupposed. For example, Chinese are often contrasted with westerners, the considerable variability within each group being glossed over.

Our purpose in this chapter is first to give a brief historical account of several of the main lines of development of these different perspectives. Then we will look more closely at the presuppositions about the nature of discursive and communicative research which underlie these different approaches. Finally we will discuss some of the problematical areas which remain in the intersection of discourse analysis and intercultural communication.

1   The Coming Together of Discourse Analysis and Intercultural Communication

Dating the start of a field is, of course, impossible, but we would support McCarthy's (1991) argument that discourse analysis as a term was fixed by Harris in 1952 in a paper of that title (cited in McCarthy). Other chapters in this *Handbook* will provide elaboration of the specific developments of discourse analysis as the analysis of texts as well as of critical discourse analysis.

By comparison with these two lines of discourse analysis we would date the field of intercultural communication as beginning with Bateson's "Culture contact and schismogenesis" (1935, reprinted in 1972). In that article he set out two of the principal problems of the field which he continued to elaborate in later work (1936, 1972). The first was the problem of reifying cultures as entities. That is, he argued that cultures must not be thought of as discrete, separable objects contacting each other, but as mere abstractions. Therefore it would be a mistake of false concreteness to use a metaphor of contact, influence of one upon another, and the rest of the Newtonian language of structures in the analysis of culture.

The second problem he set out was that of developing an analytical language by which differences between cultures or groups – he clearly identified men and women, older generations and younger generations, different classes, clans, and young children and caretakers as relevant analytical groups – would be analyzed as mutually co-constructive, to use more contemporary terminology. Men and women position each other as members of different gender in their ordinary everyday interaction. By extending the study of contact to these groups which coexist in dynamic equilibrium, he hoped to understand the processes by which groups in conflict could become more harmoniously engaged.

Very closely related to this perspective, but more difficult to place historically because of the early lack of communication with the West, is the group now most frequently referenced through citations of Bakhtin (e.g. 1981) including Vygotsky (1978) and Vološinov (1986). British scholars began to reference this literature through Kristeva (1986; see also Fairclough 1992), though Goffman's (1974) citation of Uspensky (1973), who, in turn, cites Bakhtin, may show the entrance of this line of thought, first developed in the Soviet Union in the 1920s, into discourse analysis in North America in the 1970s. In any event, by the late 1970s or early 1980s it was coming to be taken as central that intertextuality and interdiscursivity were the fundamental nature of all texts. That is, all texts represent different voices engaged in implied if not actual dialog with each other. Uspensky (1973) analyzes Tolstoy's use of different naming practices and different languages to represent different points of view. As texts have become understood as embedded in sociocultural contexts, all communication or discourse in this view is "intercultural."

Paralleling this work was that of Gumperz (e.g. 1982) and a number of his students (notably Tannen 1984, 1986) and others[1] who brought discourse analysis to the service of solving problems of interracial, interethnic, and intercultural communication. Despite recent critiques of this work (Meeuwis 1994; Meeuwis and Sarangi 1994; Sarangi 1994; Shea 1994) as having ignored sociohistorical practice, power, and institutional racism as factors in intergroup communication, we would argue that this line of research was the first, at least in North America, to seek to bridge the gap between discourse analysis and intercultural communication. Under the influence of Bateson, Gumperz and others in this group were seeking to analyze the production of social, economic, and racial discrimination in and through discourse as situated social practice.

Key elements of intercultural communication within this perspective were the focus on the production of complementary schismogenesis, contextualization cues, and the problematizing of reified cultures and other groups. Bateson (1972) defined complementary schismogenesis as the processes in social interactions by which small initial differences become amplified in response to each other through a sequence of

interactional moves and ultimately result in a rupture in the social interaction. Contextualization cues are the metacommunicative cues (especially paralinguistic and
prosodic features such as tone of voice and intonation) by which primary communication is interpreted. It was the insight of Gumperz that much of the complementary
schismogenesis which results in racial, class, and other group stereotyping arises
from differing uses and interpretation of contextualization cues. Because these
contextualization cues are normally less explicitly referenced in communication, they
are much more difficult to address by participants, and therefore their intention to
"repair" the schismogenic interaction remains out of the conscious reach of people
engaged in social interaction. This line of research acknowledges that socially given
stereotypes which are brought to the process of communication are major factors
in the interpretation of contextualization cues and therefore, as practical applied
research, this work directed itself toward the explication of the processes by which
stereotypes are formed.

2   Nondiscursive Cross-cultural and Intercultural Communication

Research such as that of Hofstede (1993) clearly exemplifies the field of cross-cultural
research within a business or organizational context. Workers in this area tend to date
their beginnings much more recently[2] and seem relatively little aware of the much
earlier research we have cited just above.

Another group, cross-cultural psychologists (e.g. Bond 1986, 1988, 1993, 1996), date
their origins largely from Cole et al. (1971), though some scholars in this area do not
recognize the very important connections of Cole and his colleagues with the much
earlier work of Vygotsky and Bakhtin. Perhaps most distinctive about this research is
that it is largely experimental-quantitative in research design, that the cultural entities
being researched are largely presupposed – often national or "world" cultures – and
that there is rarely any specific focus upon or analysis of concrete texts or discourses.
Most of the scholars working in this line of research would use the term "cross-
cultural" rather than "intercultural," and application to concrete situations is achieved
through experimentally derived inferences made by the researcher, not normally
through the analysis of concrete, mutually co-constructed discourses.

As we have just suggested, there is a bifurcation between cross-cultural studies
of the Hofstede type, in which the characteristics of groups are analyzed through
experimental or quantitative survey analysis, and the cross-cultural studies of the
sociocultural school. This latter group, which would include Cole, Wertsch, and Gee,
has sought to resolve what Wertsch calls the individual–society antinomy through a
focus on mediated actions – that is, concrete situations in which action is being taken
through the use of cultural tools appropriated for that purpose. With the mediated
action as the unit of analysis, a typical situation calls for the use of what Wertsch
(1991) terms a privileged cultural tool such as the vocabulary of scientific explanation
mastered by some but by no means all students in science classes. Thus in this view,
the role of texts is as tools for social action. This sociocultural school of psychologists
references the same historical literature as the critical discourse analysts, such as

Fairclough, Wodak, and van Dijk, though they rarely make reference to each other. Also, as we have pointed out above, the interactional sociolinguistic group has at least indirectly inherited this same perspective through Goffman via Uspensky. Thus we would argue that there has been a convergence among linguistic, discursive, or interactional sociolinguistic study of text on the one hand and a separation of this line of thinking from scholars who take a more apriorist view of languages and cultures on the other.

While it is outside the scope of this chapter to consider it here, it has been argued elsewhere (R. Scollon 1997) that much of the research in cross-cultural communication (as we have defined it here) follows in a direct line from the military or governmental studies of national character (Bateson 1972; Benedict 1946) beginning during World War II,[3] and extended after that by Hall and others at the Foreign Service Institute in Washington DC (Hall 1992). Thus this national focus, perhaps legitimate within wartime conditions, has been carried along without further problematization into contemporary analyses of "cultures" on behalf of business, governmental, and military organizations.[4]

3   Foucaultian Discourse

In a series of highly influential books Foucault (1973a, 1973b, 1976, 1977a, 1977b) deconstructed the contemporary social sciences as reflecting what he called "epistemes" in some works and "orders of discourse" in others. Central to Foucault's writing is the concept that within sociocultural and historical periods are particular ways of seeing, analyzing, and acting in the world which distribute power such that participants in these periods take on the discipline of living out their periods' discourses. While Thomas Kuhn's analysis of scientific paradigms was focused more narrowly on the paradigm shifts which take place from time to time in science, many researchers across fields not normally thought of as discourse analysis found in the concept of Discourses (Gee 1989, 1996, 1999) or "orders of discourse" a conceptual framework that supported the deconstruction of reified cultural or social entities on the one hand and of apriorist views of the person on the other. Thus a number of researchers with an interest in literacy as a sociocultural phenomenon took up the question of whether literacy itself was an order of discourse.

This line of thinking, like the intercultural studies and discourse analysis studies mentioned earlier, also bifurcated in time between what Gee (1986) called "Great Divide" theorists – those who saw literacy as a broad sociocultural and reified entity that equipped persons and societies endowed with this special gift of abstraction with the machinery by which civilized society as we know it can flourish – and the social practice theorists, who viewed literacy in terms of specific habits and skills inculcated in distinctive social settings. These latter, including Scribner and Cole (1981), analyzed literacy from the point of view of activity theory, thus problematizing the broad orders of discourse of the great divide theorists. Analyzing the development of literate practices as continuous with habits of speaking and interacting that identify readers and writers as members of particular classes of families takes the mystery out of literacy. There is a tension between determinism imposed by orders of discourse and individual human agency associated with the appropriation of cultural practices in mediated action toward one's own ends.

4 The Viability of the Concept of "Culture" in Intercultural Communication

These several lines of research have never been pursued entirely independently of each other, with the exception of the "Soviet" group, whose work was largely unreferenced in the West until the late 1970s and early 1980s. Since the early 1970s, it is fair to say that the concept of culture has been progressively restructured into other units or discourses which are seen as instantiations of social practices. The question is whether or not there is a useful notion of culture in a postcritical discourse world. Within discourse analysis and intercultural communication, cultural units have been dissolved into boundaryless forms of intertextuality and interdiscursivity. Culture has largely been demoted to the status of a minor discursive formation at best. That is, culture in the sense of "Chinese culture" or "European culture" might be used as one of a very wide range of discourses at play in any particular instance of discourse. At most, culture might be considered a kind of array or complex of other discursive formations.

In Orwellian fashion other historical forces are at play as well. For example, researchers working within sociocultural discourse analysis acknowledge their historical line of descent from the Soviet school of sociocultural analysis. In other places, however, this line of descent has taken rather particularistic turns. In China, for example, what is called "sociocultural historical psychology" arrived there from the Soviet Union in the form of Pavlovian conditioning in the strictest of experimental laboratory studies. During the Cultural Revolution this line of study was critiqued as having little to do with the practical lives of the people, and research in this tradition was suspended (Zhu 1989; Pan and Jing 1991). Even now, over two decades after the end of the Cultural Revolution, sociocultural research in China is attenuated at best. Thus we have the situation where many scholars in the West are taking up the sociocultural theme at just the time when scholars in China and the former Soviet Union are embracing the interculturalist or cross-culturalist research paradigms for the distance it gives them from earlier Marxist utopian paradigms (Kamberelis and Scott 1992), as research itself becomes globalized.

5 Discourse as Constitutive of Cultural Categories

While researchers have arrived at the position from rather different directions, perhaps we can say that a strongly unifying theme of discourse analysis and intercultural communication in the present decade is that all communication is constitutive of cultural categories. From this point of view the focus has shifted away from comparison between cultures or between individuals to a focus on the co-constructive aspects of communication.

With this change of focus has come a change in assumptions about the purposes of research and of the entities upon which analysis should be focused. Rather than seeking an explanation of how given identities and meanings are communicated or fail to be communicated, what is sought is an understanding of how identities and meanings are constituted in and through the interaction itself. The role of culture and other a priori categories in this model is as historical and cultural archives of tools through which social actions are taken by participants.

We have called our own approach to intercultural communication a "discourse approach" (Scollon and Scollon 1995) and we have preferred to call what we do "interdiscourse communication." We take the position that in any instance of actual communication we are multiply positioned within an indefinite number of Discourses (in the Gee sense) or within what we have called discourse systems. These discourse systems would include those of gender, generation, profession, corporate or institutional placement, regional, ethnic, and other possible identities. As each of these discourse systems is manifested in a complex network of forms of discourse, face relationships, socialization patterns and ideologies, this multiple membership and identity produces simultaneous internal (to the person) and external contradictions. Thus, we argue, it is as important a research problem to come to understand how a particular person in a particular action comes to claim, say, a generational identity over against the other multiple identities also contradictorily present in his or her own habitus (Bourdieu 1977, 1990) as it is to try to come to understand any two individuals as positioned as culturally or ethnically different from each other. An interdiscursive approach to intercultural communication has led us to prefer to set aside any a priori notions of group membership and identity and to ask instead how and under what circumstances concepts such as culture are produced by participants as relevant categories for interpersonal ideological negotiation.

For us, this approach to intercultural communication as discourse analysis has led to what we would now call mediated discourse (R. Scollon 1995, 1997, 1999; Scollon and Scollon 1997, 1998; S. Scollon 1998). A mediated discourse perspective shifts from a focus on the individuals involved in communication, and from their interpersonal or intercultural or even interdiscursive relationship, to a focus on mediated action as a kind of social action. The central concern is now not persons but social change.

In conclusion, we might sketch out quite roughly how these different approaches would handle a characteristic research problem. The approach implied by the title of this chapter would assume first that individuals are members of different cultural groups and that their communication can be studied as a problem in communication through a discursive analysis of the characteristic communication of members of those groups. Thus a cross-cultural approach would begin with the problem that a German was to communicate with a Chinese. This might be derived from business or diplomatic concerns on the practical side or from an anthropological or social psychological perspective on the theoretical side. In either case, one might expect that experimentally designed studies or quantitative survey studies would be set up to test differences in values, perceptions, the typical structure of genres, rates of speaking and of turning over turns, gestural and other nonverbal communication systems, or of world view and ideology.

An intercultural or interactional sociolinguistic approach would identify people from these different groups who are in social interaction with each other. Through a close analysis of the discourse actually produced, the analyst would first identify breakdowns in communication, then try to find the sources of the breakdowns in the language used as well as in the misinterpretation of contextualization cues. Differences between the participants would most likely be understood as arising from a history of socialization to different groups and therefore a misunderstanding of contextualization cues in the actual situation of communicating with each other.

A mediated discourse approach would begin by asking why the problem was posed in the first place as a problem in communication between members of different cultural or other discourse-based groups. The primary question would be: what is the social action in which you are interested and how does this analysis promise to focus on some aspect of social life that is worth understanding? This concern with social action would treat the group identities of the participants as problematical only to the extent that such membership can be shown to be productive of ideological contradiction, on the one hand, or that the participants themselves call upon social group membership in making strategic claims within the actions under study, on the other. Thus the analysis would not presuppose cultural membership but rather ask how does the concept of culture arise in these social actions. Who has introduced culture as a relevant category, for what purposes, and with what consequences?

In this sense a mediated discourse analysis is a way of erasing the field of intercultural communication by dissolving the foundational questions and reconstituting the research agenda around social action, not categorial memberships or cultural genres. Conversation or narrative or talk itself is not given pride of place. Discourse is just one of the ways in which social action may be mediated, albeit commonly a very significant one. Thus culture is possibly relevant when it is empirically an outcome (or means) of actions taken by social actors, but to start from culture or intercultural (or interdiscourse) memberships is to start with a theoretical commitment to groups which is not a primary conceptual entity in mediated discourse theory; groups such as cultures are taken to be the outcomes of social actions and of histories but to have no direct causal status in themselves.

NOTES

1   Though not students of Gumperz, we would consider ourselves in the 1970s and 1980s to be part of this community of practice (Scollon and Scollon 1979, 1981). S. Scollon's influence from Gregory Bateson was more direct, as she participated in his graduate seminar at the University of Hawaii in the late 1960s.

2   A search on the worldwide web under "intercultural communication" yields some 4622 entries. One of the first is the following:

Kern On-line – Intercultural Communication conference
Intercultural Communication conference. Twenty-five years have passed since the intercultural communication field began! The Intercultural Communication 1996 conference celebrates this with . . . (Internet, March 13, 1997)

3   The pre-war concern of Bateson to avoid the conceptual reification of

groups was held in abeyance by him, Mead, and others during their "national character" period of study (Bateson 1972).

4   Befu (1993) makes the parallel argument that to a considerable extent the characteristics of Japanese interactional and cultural style so often put forward derived in part from Japanese militarism and the attempt to forge a distinctive Japanese character.

REFERENCES

Bakhtin, M. M. 1981 (Originally published 1934–5). *The Dialogic Imagination.* Austin: University of Texas Press.

Bateson, Gregory. 1936. *Naven: A Survey of the Problems Suggested by a Composite Picture of the Culture of a New Guinea Tribe Drawn from Three Points of View.* Cambridge: Cambridge University Press.

Bateson, Gregory. 1972. *Steps to an Ecology of Mind.* New York: Ballantine.

Befu, Harumi. 1993. *Cultural Nationalism in East Asia.* Berkeley, CA: University of California, Institute of East Asian Studies.

Benedict, Ruth. 1946. *Chrysanthemum and the Sword.* Boston: Houghton Mifflin.

Bond, Michael Harris. 1986. *The Psychology of the Chinese People.* New York: Oxford University Press.

Bond, Michael Harris. 1988. *The Cross–cultural Challenge to Social Psychology.* Newbury Park, CA: Sage.

Bond, Michael Harris. 1993. Between the yin and the yang: the identity of the Hong Kong Chinese. Professorial inaugural lecture series 19. *Chinese University Bulletin*, Supplement 31. Hong Kong: Chinese University of Hong Kong.

Bond, Michael Harris, ed. 1996. *The Handbook of Chinese Psychology.* Hong Kong: Oxford University Press.

Chouliaraki, Lilie and Norman Fairclough. 1999. *Discourse in Late Modernity: Rethinking Critical Discourse Analysis.* Edinburgh: Edinburgh University Press.

Cole, Michael, J. Gay, J. Glick, and D. Sharp. 1971. *The Cultural Context of Learning and Thinking.* New York: Basic Books.

Fairclough, Norman. 1989. Language and ideology. *English Language Research Journal* 3: 9–27.

Fairclough, Norman. 1992. *Discourse and Social Change.* Cambridge: Polity.

Fairclough, Norman. 1995a. *Critical Discourse Analysis: The Critical Study of Language.* London and New York: Longman.

Fairclough, Norman. 1995b. *Media Discourse.* London: Edward Arnold.

Foucault, Michel. 1973a. *The Birth of the Clinic.* London: Tavistock.

Foucault, Michel. 1973b. *The Order of Things.* New York: Random House.

Foucault, Michel. 1976. *The Archaeology of Knowledge.* New York: Harper and Row.

Foucault, Michel. 1977a. *Language, Counter-memory, Practice.* Ithaca, NY: Cornell.

Foucault, Michel. 1977b. *Discipline and Punish.* New York: Pantheon Books.

Gee, James Paul. 1986. Orality and literacy: from "The Savage Mind" to "Ways with Words." *TESOL Quarterly* 20: 719–46.

Gee, James Paul. 1989. Literacy, discourse, and linguistics: essays by James Paul Gee. *Journal of Education* 171(1): entire issue, 1–176.

Gee, James Paul. 1996. *Social Linguistics and Literacies: Ideology in Discourses.* Second edn. Bristol, PA: Taylor and Francis.

Gee, James Paul. 1999. *An Introduction to Discourse Analysis: Theory and Method.* London: Routledge.

Goffman, Erving. 1974. *Frame Analysis.* New York: Harper and Row.

Gumperz, John. 1982. *Discourse Strategies.* New York: Cambridge University Press.

Hall, Edward T. 1992. *An Anthropology of Everyday Life: An Autobiography.* New York: Anchor Books.

Hofstede, Geert. 1993. Cultural constraints in management theories. *Academy of Management Executive* 7(1): 81–93.

Kamberelis, George and Karla Danette Scott. 1992. Other people's voices: the coarticulation of texts and subjectivities. *Linguistics and Education* 4: 359–403.

Kristeva, J. 1986. Word, dialogue and novel. In T. Moi (ed.), *The Kristeva Reader.* Oxford: Blackwell. 34–61.

McCarthy, Michael. 1991. *Discourse Analysis for Language Teachers.* Cambridge: Cambridge University Press.

Meeuwis, Michael. 1994. Leniency and testiness in intercultural communication: remarks on ideology and context in interactional sociolinguistics. *Pragmatics* 4(3): 391–408.

Meeuwis, Michael and Srikant Sarangi. 1994. Perspectives on intercultural communication: a critical reading. *Pragmatics* 4(3): 309–13.

Pan Shu and Jing Qicheng. 1991. *Zhongguo da baike quanshu: Xinlixue (The Great Chinese Encyclopedia: Psychology).* Beijing and Shanghai: Zhongguo Da Baike Quanshu Chubanshe.

Sarangi, Srikant. 1994. Intercultural or not? Beyond celebration of cultural differences in miscommunication analysis. *Pragmatics* 4(3): 409–27.

Schiffrin, Deborah. 1994. *Approaches to Discourse.* Cambridge: Blackwell.

Scollon, Ron. 1997. Current trends in intercultural communication studies. Lecture presented to the School of English Language Communication, Beijing Foreign Studies University, April.

Scollon, Ron and Suzanne B. K. Scollon. 1979. *Linguistic Convergence: An Ethnography of Speaking at Fort Chipewyan, Alberta.* New York: Academic Press.

Scollon, Ron and Suzanne B. K. Scollon. 1981. *Narrative, Literacy and Face in Interethnic Communication.* Norwood, NJ: Ablex.

Scribner, Sylvia and Michael Cole. 1981. *The Psychology of Literacy.* Cambridge, MA: Harvard University Press.

Shea, David P. 1994. Perspective and production: structuring conversational participation across cultural borders. *Pragmatics* 4(3): 357–89.

Tannen, Deborah. 1984. *Conversational Style: Analyzing Talk Among Friends.* Norwood, NJ: Ablex.

Tannen, Deborah. 1986. *That's Not What I Meant!* New York: Ballantine Books.

Uspensky, Boris. 1973. *A Poetics of Composition.* Berkeley, CA: University of California Press.

Vološinov, Valentin N. 1986. *Marxism and the Philosophy of Language.* Cambridge, MA: Harvard University Press.

Vygotsky, L. S. 1978. *Mind in Society: The Development of Higher Psychological Processes.* Cambridge, MA: Harvard University Press.

Wertsch, James V. 1991. *Voices of the Mind: A Sociocultural Approach to Mediated Action.* Cambridge, MA: Harvard University Press.

Wodak, Ruth. 1996. *Disorders of Discourse.* New York: Addison Wesley Longman.

Zhu Zhixian. 1989. *Xinlixue dacidian (The Great Dictionary of Psychology).* Beijing: Bejing Shifan Daxue Chubanshe.

28 Discourse and Gender

SHARI KENDALL AND DEBORAH TANNEN

0 Introduction

The study of discourse and gender is an interdisciplinary endeavor shared by scholars in linguistics, anthropology, speech communication, social psychology, education, literature, and other disciplines. Many researchers have been concerned primarily with documenting gender-related patterns of language use, but the field has also included many for whom the study of language is a lens through which to view social and political aspects of gender relations. Tensions between these two perspectives arose in early research and continue today, as witness, for example, the interchange between Preisler (1998) and Cameron (1999). Regardless of the vantage point from which research emanates, the study of gender and discourse not only provides a descriptive account of male/female discourse but also reveals how language functions as a symbolic resource to create and manage personal, social, and cultural meanings and identities.

1 The Field Emerges

The year 1975 was key in launching the field of language and gender. That year saw the publication of three books that proved pivotal: Robin Lakoff's *Language and Woman's Place* (the first part appeared in *Language and Society* in 1973), Mary Ritchie Key's *Male/Female Language*, and Barrie Thorne and Nancy Henley's edited volume *Language and Sex: Difference and Dominance*. These pioneering works emerged during the feminist movement of the 1970s, as scholars began to question both the identification of male norms as human norms, and the biological determination of women's and men's behavior. A conceptual split was posited between biological "sex" and sociocultural constructs of "gender."[1] Early language and gender research tended to focus on (1) documenting empirical differences between women's and men's speech, especially in cross-sex interaction; (2) describing women's speech in particular; and, for many,

(3) identifying the role of language in creating and maintaining social inequality between women and men.

1.1   *Lakoff's* Language and Woman's Place

The third goal is evident in the field's foundational text, *Language and Woman's Place*. Lakoff describes her book as "an attempt to provide diagnostic evidence from language use for one type of inequity that has been claimed to exist in our society: that between the roles of men and women" (1975: 4). She posits a cycle that begins with the unequal role of women and men in society, resulting in differential gender socialization by which girls learn to use a "nonforceful style" because unassertiveness is a social norm of womanhood, given men's role in establishing norms. The use of "women's language," in turn, denies women access to power, and reinforces social inequality.

Lakoff identified the linguistic forms by which "women's language" weakens or mitigates the force of an utterance: "weaker" expletives (*oh, dear* versus *damn*); "trivializing" adjectives (*divine* versus *great*); tag questions used to express speakers' opinions (*The way prices are rising is horrendous, isn't it?*); rising intonation in declaratives (as seen in the second part of the sequence, *"What's for dinner?" "Roast beef?"*); and mitigated requests (*Would you please close the door?* versus *Close the door*) (1975: 10–18).

Lakoff's observations provided a starting point from which to explore the complexity of the relationship between gender and discourse. In one frequently cited followup study, O'Barr and Atkins (1980) examined features of "women's language" in courtroom discourse and found that the features Lakoff identified were related to the status (social class, occupation, and experience as a witness) rather than the sex of the speaker. They suggested that women use this style more than men in everyday interaction because they are more likely to be in lower-status positions. Later studies, however, showed that this is not necessarily the case. Cameron et al. (1989), finding that speakers who took up the role of conversational facilitator tended to use more tag questions, posited that women were more likely to do so because they were more likely to assume this role. Similarly, Preisler (1986) examined problem-solving situations in an industrial community, and found that managers who contributed most actively to the accomplishment of a task also used more linguistic "tentativeness features," and these managers were usually women. Tannen (1994a) also found women managers using strategies, including indirectness, to save face for subordinates when making requests and delivering criticism. Neither conversational facilitator nor manager is a low-status position.

1.2   *The personal as political*

In another influential early study, Zimmerman and West (1975) found that men interrupted women more than the reverse in thirty-one dyadic conversations tape-recorded in private residences as well as in "coffee shops, drug stores and other public places in a university community." The authors concluded that "just as male dominance is exhibited through male control of macro-institutions in society, it is also exhibited through control of at least a part of one micro-institution" (1975: 125). Their conclusion confirms the 1970s feminist slogan, "the personal is political," by positing that asymmetries in everyday conversational practices reflect and reproduce asymmetries found in the wider social environment.

Though their methods were questioned by Murray (1985), Murray and Covelli (1988), and others, West and Zimmerman instigated numerous studies of interruption in language and gender research, continuing through the present (e.g. Ahrens 1997; Beattie 1981; Esposito 1979; Greenwood 1996; West 1984). Moreover, their framework of looking to language for reflections of unequal gender relations also influenced subsequent research. For example, Fishman (1983) examined naturally occurring conversations tape-recorded by three heterosexual couples in their homes, and found that the women performed more of the conversational "support work" required to sustain conversational interaction with their partners: they produced more listening cues (*mhm, uhuh*), asked more questions, used *you know* and attention-getting beginnings (*This is interesting*) more frequently (presumably to encourage a response), and actively pursued topics raised by the men. On the other hand, men were more likely to not respond to turns and topics initiated by the women, and to make more declarative statements. Fishman argues that women's supportive role in private conversations reflects and reproduces sex-based hierarchies of power within the public sphere. (Tannen 1990 suggests a concomitant explanation for the linguistic imbalance: the central role of conversation in establishing intimacy among women, in contrast with the primacy of copresence and shared activity in creating intimacy among men.)

1.3   Lakoff in current research

Innumerable studies inspired by Lakoff either confirmed her observations or found exceptions in particular contexts. Nonetheless, as Bucholtz and Hall (1995: 6) note, Lakoff's description of gender-related language "continues to be accepted by diverse groups of speakers as a valid representation of their own discursive experiences." Although her account of "women's language" does not represent the way each individual woman speaks, it nonetheless represents the norms by which women are expected to speak, or what Bucholtz and Hall call "the precise hegemonic notions of gender-appropriate language use," which represents "the idealized language of middle-class European American women." Thus Lakoff remains an invaluable tool for current studies of gender and discourse, as seen, for example, in Barrett (1999) and Hall (1995).

2   Cultural Influences on Gender, Language, and Society

The early focus on women's speech, sex discrimination through language, and asymmetrical power relations was maintained in two influential edited volumes: McConnell-Ginet et al.'s *Women and Language in Literature and Society* (1980) and Thorne et al.'s *Language, Gender and Society* (1983). However, several chapters in these volumes represent another major strand of research in discourse and gender, one that emphasizes the complexity of the relationship among gender, society, and language. This work is strongly influenced by the theoretical perspectives of Erving Goffman and John Gumperz.

2.1 Gender differences as communicative strategies

Ethnographic work influenced by Goffman explores gender and discourse as an organizing component of social interaction. Drawing on Goffman's (1967: 5) concept of face, Brown (1980) examined politeness phenomena in a Mayan community. She found that Tenejapan women used more speech particles to strengthen or weaken an utterance, as well as strategies that were qualitatively more polite than those used by men. For example, women tended to use irony and rhetorical questions in place of direct criticism (*Just why would you know how to sew?* implying *Of course you wouldn't*), which both de-emphasized negative messages and emphasized in-group solidarity. In addition (as Lakoff predicted), although both women and men used hedging particles in cases of genuine doubt, only women used them to hedge the expression of their own feelings (*I just really am sad then because of it, perhaps*) (Brown 1980: 126). In contrast, Brown claimed, the men's communicative style was characterized by a lack of attention to face, and the presence of such features as sex-related joking and a "preaching/declaiming style" (1980: 129).

McConnell-Ginet (1988: 85) observes that Brown's contribution was crucial because it shifted the framework "from a system one acquires . . . to a set of strategies one develops to manage social interactions." Brown explains that women's and men's linguistic choices are "communicative strategies"; that is, humans are "rational actors" who choose linguistic options to achieve certain socially motivated ends in particular circumstances (1980: 113).

Goffman's influence is also seen in the pioneering ethnographic work of Goodwin (1978, 1980a, 1990), based on fieldwork with African American children in an urban neighborhood. Goodwin found that girls and boys in same-sex play groups created different social organizations through the directive–response sequences they used while coordinating task activities: the boys created hierarchical structures, whereas the girls created more egalitarian structures. For example, the boys negotiated status by giving and resisting direct directives (*Gimme the pliers!*), whereas the girls constructed joint activities by phrasing directives as suggestions rather than commands (*Let's go around Subs and Suds*). Goodwin points out that the girls can and do use the forms found in boys' play in other contexts (for example, when taking the role of mother in playing "house"), emphasizing that gender-related variations in language use are context-sensitive.

2.2 Male–female discourse as cross-cultural communication

Maltz and Borker (1982) surveyed research on gendered patterns of language use and concluded that difficulties in cross-sex communication could be understood within the framework Gumperz (1982) developed for understanding cross-cultural communication. In this framework, miscommunication stems from differences in women's and men's habits and assumptions about how to participate in conversation. For example, in considering the finding that women tend to use more minimal responses (*mhm, uhuh, yeah*) than men, Maltz and Borker suggest that women tend to use these responses to indicate "I'm listening," whereas men tend to use them to indicate "I agree." The reason, then, that women tend to use more of these utterances is that they are listening more often than men are agreeing. Based primarily on Goodwin (1978, 1980a, 1980b) and Lever (1976, 1978), Maltz and Borker suggest that women and men acquire such different conversational habits during childhood and adolescence as they play in same-sex groups.

Tannen (1989a) also brings a cross-cultural perspective to bear on cross-gender discourse. She uses "interruption" as a paradigm case of a discourse feature whose "meaning" might seem self-evident (a display of conversational dominance and usurpation of speaking rights), but which is in fact a complex phenomenon whose very identification is subject to culturally variable meanings and interpretations. In earlier work, Tannen (1984) showed that for many speakers, "overlapping" can be a show of enthusiastic participation rather than a hostile or dominating attempt to steal the floor. However, if one participant expects cooperative overlapping, but the other expects one person to speak at a time, the latter may perceive overlapping as interruption and stop speaking. Thus dominance created in interaction does not always result from an attempt to dominate, nor does it necessarily reflect the societal domination of one social group over another. This view of interruption is supported by a review of the literature on gender and interruption by James and Clarke (1993), who found that many of the studies following West and Zimmerman concluded that conversations among women exhibited more interruptions than conversations among men, but the purpose of the "interruptions" was to show rapport rather than to gain the floor.

3   The Field Develops

Throughout the next decade, scholars refined and advanced our understanding of the relationship between gender and discourse. Research focused on talk among women (e.g. Johnson and Aries 1983; Coates 1989); narrative (Johnstone 1990); language socialization (e.g. selections in Philips et al. 1987, and Schieffelin and Ochs 1986); language among children and adolescents (Eckert 1990; Goodwin 1990; Goodwin and Goodwin 1987; Sheldon 1990); and language and gender in particular contexts such as doctor–patient interaction (Ainsworth-Vaughn 1992; West 1990). Numerous journal articles were supplemented by edited collections (Todd and Fisher 1988; Cameron 1990; Coates and Cameron 1989; Philips et al. 1987); monographs (Cameron 1985; Preisler 1986); and introductory textbooks (Frank and Anshen 1983; Coates 1986; Graddol and Swann 1989).

3.1   *Tannen's* You Just Don't Understand

The publication of *You Just Don't Understand* in 1990 can be seen as ushering in the next phase of discourse and gender research, based on the attention this book received both within and outside the field. During much of the 1990s, it served (as Lakoff had before) as the point of departure for numerous studies, both as a touchstone for developing further research and as a bête noir against which to define arguments. Written for a general rather than an academic audience, this book combined a range of scholarly work with everyday conversational examples to illustrate the hypothesis that conversations between women and men could be understood, metaphorically, as cross-cultural communication.

3.2   Gender-related patterns of talk

Combining the cross-cultural perspective of Gumperz, the interactional principles of Goffman, Lakoff's framework of gender-related communicative style, and her own work on conversational style, Tannen (1990) posited that gender-related patterns of discourse form a coherent web that is motivated by women's and men's understanding of social relationships. Building on Maltz and Borker's reinterpretation of the research on children's interaction, she concluded that patterns of interaction that had been found to characterize women's and men's speech could be understood as serving their different conversational goals: whereas all speakers must find a balance between seeking connection and negotiating relative status, conversational rituals learned by girls and maintained by women tend to focus more on the connection dimension, whereas rituals learned by boys and maintained by men tend to focus more on the status dimension. Put another way, conversational rituals common among women focus on intimacy (that is, avoiding the loss of connection which results in being "pushed away"), whereas conversational rituals common among men focus on independence (that is, avoiding the one-down position in a hierarchy, which results in being "pushed around").

Given these orientations, women tend to choose linguistic options based on symmetry. For example, Tannen describes a conversational ritual common among women, "displaying similarities and matching experiences" (1990: 77). Supporting this finding, Coates (1996: 61) notes that "reciprocal self-disclosure" characterizes talk between women friends. This mirroring is realized linguistically through the repetition of syntactic patterns and key words and phrases (1996: 79–81, 84). Furthermore, these conversations frequently involve matching troubles. Tannen notes that bonding through talk about troubles is a common activity for women throughout the world (1990: 100).

In contrast, Tannen (1990, 1994a, 1994c, 1998) finds, many conversational rituals common among men are based on ritual opposition or "agonism." This is seen, for example, in "teasing, playfully insulting each other, or playing 'devil's advocate'" to develop and strengthen ideas (through, for example, challenges, counter-challenges, and debate) (1998: 196). Just as troubles talk appears among women cross-culturally, men in disparate parts of the world engage in a "war of words," in which they "vie with one another to devise clever insults, topping each other both in the intensity of the insult and the skill of the insulter" (1998: 194). Tannen stresses that it is the use of *ritualized* opposition, or "agonism," that is associated with boys and men. Girls and women certainly fight in the *literal* sense (1998: 197). Thus, little boys frequently play-fight as a favored game. Whereas little girls rarely fight for fun, they do fight when they mean it.

3.3   The "difference" and "dominance" debates

During the 1990s, scholars routinely classified research into two categories: the "power" or "dominance" approach focused on unequal roles as the source of differences (Fishman 1979, 1983; West and Zimmerman 1983; Zimmerman and West 1975) whereas the "cultural" or "difference" approach focused on sex-separate socialization as the source (Maltz and Borker 1982; Tannen 1990). This characterization of research, as initially proposed by Henley and Kramarae (1991), is clearly disciplinary: research labeled as "dominance" stemmed from communication and sociology, whereas research labeled as "difference" stemmed from anthropological linguistics.

The distinction has been used primarily to fault the "difference" approach for, purportedly, not incorporating power into the analysis of gender and discourse. Recent descriptions attribute the distinction to scholars' theoretical explanations: hierarchical power structures in a dominance approach, and divergent paths of language socialization in a difference approach. This characterization exposes the falseness of the dichotomy, because the first is an underlying cause of gender differences, whereas the latter is a sociolinguistic means through which gender differences may be negotiated and acquired. As such, the latter does not preclude unequal power relations as an underlying cause of socially learned patterns. Quite the contrary, as Tannen (1994b) notes in calling for researchers to abandon the dichotomy, a fundamental tenet of interactional sociolinguistics (see Gumperz, this volume), the theoretical framework for the cross-cultural approach, is that social relations such as dominance and subordination are constructed in interaction. Therefore, the cultural approach provides a way to understand how inequalities are created in face-to-face interaction.

A more viable basis for distinguishing between approaches is identified by Cameron (1995), who traces Tannen's non-judgmental evaluation of women's and men's discursive styles to the linguistic tradition of cultural relativity. Although she rejects cultural relativity as inappropriate in the language and gender domain, Cameron explains (1995: 35–6):

> for the linguist, inequality is conceived as resulting not from difference itself but from intolerance of difference. Thus linguists have insisted it is wrong to label languages "primitive" or dialects "substandard"; it is wrong to force people to abandon their ways of speaking, or to judge them by the yardstick of your own linguistic habits. Throughout this century, the norm in linguistics has been linguistic and cultural relativism – "all varieties are equal". It has always been an honorable position, and sometimes an outright radical one.

Thus researchers working in a linguistic tradition do not evaluate one style as superior to the other, but emphasize the underlying logic of both styles. Nonetheless they recognize – and demonstrate – that gender-related differences in styles may produce and reproduce asymmetries.

4 The Field Explodes

After 1990, the field grew exponentially with the publication of numerous edited collections (Bergvall et al. 1996; Bucholtz et al. 1999; Coates 1997b; Etter-Lewis and Foster 1996; Hall and Bucholtz 1995; Johnson and Meinhof 1997; Kotthoff and Wodak 1997a; Leap 1996a; Livia and Hall 1997b; Mills 1995; Tannen 1993; Wodak 1997); the proceedings from the influential Berkeley Women and Language Conference (Bucholtz et al. 1994; Hall et al. 1992; Warner et al. 1996; Wertheim et al. 1998); monographs (Coates 1996; Crawford 1995; Holmes 1995; Leap 1996b; Matoesian 1993; Talbot 1998; Tannen 1994a, 1994b); and second editions (Cameron [1985]1992, [1990]1998b; Coates [1986]1993).

4.1 Heterogeneity in gender and discourse

In the 1990s, research on gender and discourse expanded in many directions from its earlier focus on "women's language" to include the language of men and of other social groups who had not been widely included in earlier studies. In addition, researchers increasingly considered the interaction between gender and other social identities and categories, such as ethnicity (Mendoza-Denton 1999; Orellana 1999), social class (Bucholtz 1999a; Eckert and McConnell-Ginet 1995; McElhinny 1997; Orellana 1999), and sexuality (Barrett 1999; Jacobs 1996; Leap 1996a, 1996b, 1999; Livia and Hall 1997a; Wood 1999). In this way, the field followed the perhaps inevitable progression from prototypical to less typical cases, including those which Bucholtz (1999b: 7) describes (positively) as "bad examples": people who assume social and sexual roles different from those their cultures legitimize.

4.2 Language and masculinity

The study of men's use of language reached a milestone in 1997 with the publication of Johnson and Meinhof's edited volume, *Language and Masculinity*. In these and other studies of men's discourse, a pattern identified by Tannen (1990) is found in a wide range of contexts: men tend to discursively take up roles of expertise or authority. Coates (1997a), for example, reports, based on an extensive corpus of women's and men's friendly talk, that men are more likely to take up the role of the expert, whereas women are more likely to avoid this role. In conversations between male friends, she finds, men take turns giving monologues – some quite extensive – about subjects in which they are expert (1997a: 120). For example, in one conversation, the men talk about "home-made beer-making; hi-fi equipment; film projectors and the logistics of switching from one to the other" (1997a: 120). Thus, each man gets a turn at being the expert.

Kotthoff (1997) finds that men are more likely to take up expert positions in the public sphere. She examines the discursive negotiation of expert status in television discussions on Austrian TV by comparing the actual expert status of the guests ("extrinsic rank") and the status they interactionally achieve ("intrinsic rank"). Crediting Tannen (1990) for identifying the centrality of lecturing in men's conversational strategies, Kotthoff finds that high-ranking men always gained a high intrinsic status through the use of lecturing, characterized by suspension of turn-taking, assertions of debatable claims in a straightforward manner, and a lack of subjectivizers (e.g. *I think*) (1997: 165). (Significantly, even lower-ranking men sometimes gained a high intrinsic status, but lower-ranking women never did.)

4.3 The language of African American and Latina women

Recent research addresses the discourse of African American women (Bucholtz 1996; Etter-Lewis 1991; Etter-Lewis and Foster 1996; Foster 1989, 1995; Morgan 1991, 1999; Stanback 1985) as well as Latina women (Mendoza-Denton 1999; Orellana 1999). Morgan (1999: 29) describes three interactional events with which, barring a few exceptions, "women who have been socialized within African American culture are familiar": the first is girls' he-said-she-said disputes in which girls go to great lengths to determine who said what behind someone's back. She contrasts this speech event with "signifying," or ritual insulting, which is a game played mostly by boys. The second is teenagers' and young adults' instigating, in which older girls focus on who intended to start a confrontation. Finally, adult women participate in "conversational signifying," focusing on the speaker's right to be present to represent her own experience. (See also Goodwin 1978, 1990.)

Based on ethnographic fieldwork in a northern California urban public high school, Mendoza-Denton (1999) examines Latina girls' use of turn-initial *"No"* to manage interactional conflict. She finds a pattern of "collaborative opposition" or "conflictive corroboration" by which the girls manage shifting alignments, or stances. Goodwin (1999), based on ethnographic fieldwork among second-generation Mexican and Central American girls in an elementary school in Los Angeles, found that the Spanish–English bilingual girls engage in complex and elaborate negotiations about the rules of the game of hopscotch.

5 Analyzing Gender and Discourse

As our understanding of the relationship between language and gender has progressed, researchers have arrived at many similar conclusions, although these similarities frequently go unrecognized or unacknowledged. This section presents some of the most widely accepted tenets – and the most widely debated issues – that have emerged. Points of agreement include (1) the social construction of gender, (2) the indirect relationship between gender and discourse, (3) gendered discourse as a resource, and (4) gendered discourse as a constraint. The most widely debated issues are gender duality and performativity.

5.1 The social construction of gender

A social constructivist paradigm has prevailed in gender and discourse research. That is, scholars agree that the "meaning" of gender is culturally mediated, and gendered identities are interactionally achieved. In this sense, the field has come full circle from Goffman's pioneering work to the currently fashionable performative approach commonly credited to feminist theorist Judith Butler (1990, 1993). Goffman (1976) demonstrated, with illustrations from print advertisements, that the gendered self is accomplished through the display of postures that both ritualize subordination and are conventionally associated with gender, such as the "bashful knee bend," receiving help and instruction, and smiling more frequently and more expansively than men. Similarly, in Butler's (1993: 227) conception of performativity, local practices bring gender into being "through the repetition or citation of a prior, authoritative set of practices."

The distinctions and usefulness of Goffman's social constructivist approach and Butler's performative approach are currently being debated. See, for example, Livia and Hall (1997b), who discuss performativity in gender and language research; Kotthof and Wodak (1997b), who compare Butler and Goffman, and argue in favor of the latter; and discussions in Preisler (1998) and Meyerhoff (1996).

5.2   *The indirect relationship between gender and discourse*

Tannen (1994c) draws on Goffman (1977) to claim that discourse and gender are "sex-class linked" rather than sex linked. That is, ways of speaking are not identified with every individual man or woman but rather are associated with the class of women or the class of men (in Russell's sense of logical types) in a given society. By talking in ways that are associated with one or the other sex class, individuals signal their alignment with that sex class. A similar theoretical perspective is provided by Ochs (1992), who posits that ways of speaking are associated with stances that are in turn associated with women or men in a given culture. Thus, ways of speaking "index gender."

Because the relationship between gender and discourse is indirect, individuals may not be aware of the influence of gender on their speaking styles. For example, in interviews with four prominent Texan women, Johnstone (1995) found that the women proudly acknowledged the influence of being Texan but denied that their behavior was related to gender. Yet, in discussing her success as a litigator, one woman said (among other things): "I try to smile, and I try to just be myself." Tannen (1994c: 216) notes that, as Goffman (1976) demonstrated, this woman's way of being herself – smiling – is sex-class linked.

Based on an ethnographic study of police officers, McElhinny (1992: 399–400) notes that the indirect relationship between gender and discourse enables women to assume typically male verbal behavior in institutional settings: "female police officers can interpret behaviors that are normatively understood as masculine (like noninvolvement or emotional distance) as simply 'the way we need to act to do our job' in a professional way." Ironically, McElhinny's article is titled, "I Don't Smile Much Anymore."

5.3   *Gendered discourse as a resource*

The constructivist approach entails a distinction between expectations or ideologies and actual discursive practices. In other words, "gendered speaking styles exist independently of the speaker" (Bucholtz and Hall 1995: 7), so gendered discourse provides a resource for women's and men's presentation of self. As Tannen (1989b: 80) explains, cultural influences do not determine the form that a speaker's discourse will take; instead, they "provide a range from which individuals choose strategies that they habitually use in expressing their individual styles."

Hall (1995) demonstrates that phone-sex workers draw on gendered discourse as a resource by using "women's language" to construct the gendered identity required for economic gain in their occupation. They use "feminine" words (*lacy*) and nonbasic color terms (*charcoal* rather than *black*) (as described in Lakoff 1975); they use "dynamic" intonation, characterized by a relatively wide pitch range and pronounced and rapid shifts in pitch (McConnell-Ginet 1978); and they actively maintain the interaction through supportive questions and comments (Fishman 1983).

5.4   Gendered discourse as a constraint

If gendered discourse strategies are a resource, they are simultaneously a constraint. Both views underlie Tannen's (1994c) framing approach by which a researcher asks, first, what alignments each speaker is establishing in relation to interlocutors and to the subject of talk or task at hand; second, how these alignments balance the needs for both status and connection; and, third, how linguistic strategies are functioning to create those alignments. Only then should one ask how these language patterns are linked to gender. Tannen analyzes workplace communication to show that language strategies used by those in positions of authority are not simply ways of exercising power but are ways of balancing the simultaneous but conflicting needs for status and connection – ways that are sex-class linked. She compares two instances of small talk between status unequals. In one interaction, two men who are discussing a computer glitch negotiate status and connection through challenges; bonding against women; and alternating displays of helping, expertise, and independence (needing no help). In the other example, four women negotiate status and connection through complimenting, a focus on clothing and shopping, the balancing of display and gaze, and expressive intonation.

In both interactions, participants' linguistic strategies, and the alignments they create, reflect both status and connection. The women's conversation occurred while the highest-status woman was telling a story to two lower-ranking colleagues. When a female mail clerk entered, the speaker stopped her story and complimented the mail clerk on her blouse, and the others joined in. The complimenting ritual served as a resource for including the clerk and attending to her as a person, thus creating connection; however, it also reflected and reproduced relative status because it was the highest-status person who controlled the framing of the interaction, and the lowest-status person who was the recipient of the compliment. But gendered discourse is also a constraint, in the sense that negotiating status and connection through challenges and mock insults was less available as a resource to the women, and doing so through the exchange of compliments on clothing and discussion of shopping and fashion was less available as a resource to the men. Finally, the relationship between gender and discourse is indirect insofar as, in each case, speakers chose linguistic options to accomplish pragmatic and interactional goals.

The notion of gendered discourse as a constraint also underlies Eckert and McConnell-Ginet's (1992: 473) influential exhortation that language and gender researchers examine women's and men's language use in "communities of practice": groups of people who "come together around mutual engagement in some common endeavor." They explain that "speakers develop linguistic patterns as they act in their various communities in which they participate." These sites of engagement are relevant to the relation between microactions and macrosocial structures, because "the relation between gender and language resides in the modes of participation available to various individuals within various communities of practice as a direct or indirect function of gender." For example, in a study of the Kuna Indians of Panama, Sherzer (1987) found that language and gender were linked through gender-differentiated speaking roles that determined who had the opportunity to take up those roles in the first place. In a similar spirit, Lakoff (1995: 30) describes the increase in women's public access to "interpretive control, their ability to determine the meaning of events in which they are involved." She discusses five events that received "undue attention" in the media because they concerned the "identities and possibilities of women and men" (1995: 32).

Again, the notion of gendered discourse as a constraint is captured by a framing approach. Kendall (1999), examining family talk at dinnertime, shows that the parents create gendered identities through framing and through the alignments that constitute those frames. The mother accomplished multiple tasks by creating and maintaining several interactional frames, whereas the father participated minimally, and maintained only one frame at a time. For example, the mother served food (Hostess), taught her daughter dinnertime etiquette (Miss Manners), assisted her daughter (Caretaker), and managed her daughter's social life (Social Secretary). The father took up only one parental frame, Playmate, through which he created more symmetrical relations with his daughter, but sometimes undercut the mother's authority as well.

5.5   Gender dualism

Perhaps the most hotly debated issue in gender and discourse research is that of gender dualism. During the past decade, scholars have questioned "the division of speech on the basis of a binary division of gender or sex" (Bing and Bergvall 1996: 3). However, as a substantial number of studies find, theoretical frameworks of gender and discourse cannot summarily dismiss sex- or gender-based binary oppositions (Cameron 1998a; Johnson 1997; Preisler 1998). In a review of Bergvall et al. (1996), Cameron (1998a: 955) concludes that, although many researchers "approach the male–female binary critically, . . . in most cases their data oblige them to acknowledge its significance for the speakers they are studying."

Conceptualizing gendered discourse as a resource and a constraint within a framing approach may help resolve continuing tensions in the field concerning the role of sex/gender binary in a theoretical model of gender and discourse. The conception of gendered discourse as a resource accounts for diversity in speaking styles: many women and men do not speak in ways associated with their sex; they use language patterns associated with the other sex; there is variation within as well as between sex groups; gender interacts with other socially constructed categories, such as race and social class; individuals create multiple – and sometimes contradictory – versions of femininity and masculinity; and women and men may transgress, subvert, and challenge, as well as reproduce, societal norms.

The conception of gendered discourse as a constraint accounts for the stubborn reality that if women and men do not speak in ways associated with their sex, they are likely to be perceived as speaking and behaving like the other sex – and to be negatively evaluated. This is demonstrated at length by Tannen (1994a) for women and men in positions of authority in the workplace. Tannen found pervasive evidence for what Lakoff had earlier identified as a double bind: women who conformed to expectations of femininity were seen as lacking in competence or confidence, but women who conformed to expectations of people in authority were seen as lacking in femininity – as too aggressive.

Bergvall (1996) similarly demonstrates that, in a number of small group discussions at a technological university, a female student displays linguistic behaviors in some ways associated with stereotypically "masculine" speech ("assertively") and in other ways considered feminine ("cooperative, affiliative, instrumental"). However, her "assertive and active engagement" was negatively assessed by her peers in the class, "both orally and through written evaluations." Bergvall concludes that, when this woman "fails to enact the traditional supportive feminine role, she is negatively sanctioned and is silenced by the gender-normative activities of the class" (1996: 186).

Recent research has focused on linguistic behavior that "transgresses" and "contests" gender-linked expectations or ideologies, but it also concludes that such transgressions are typically perceived by speakers in terms of male/female duality. For example, Wood (1997), in examining lesbian "coming out stories," finds that the women refer to beliefs and practices that transgress gender ideologies, but do so by referring to cultural expectations of gender, attraction, and sexuality. Similarly, Hall and O'Donovan (1996: 229) find that hijras in India, who are often referred to as a "third gender" in gender theory (e.g. Lorber 1994), define themselves in their narratives in relation to a male–female dichotomy, characterizing themselves as "'deficiently' masculine and 'incompletely' feminine." Hall and O'Donovan conclude that "instead of occupying a position outside the female–male dichotomy, the hijras have created an existence within it."

As a result, scholars are increasingly wary of studies that view "discourse as an omnipotent force to create reality" (Kotthof and Wodak 1997b: xi). Walters (1999: 202) notes that, "In an effort to escape biological essentialism, sociolinguists have, I fear, preferred to act as if individuals do not have bodies." A framing approach incorporates the agency of performativity, but also relates – without attributing – individuals' agentive behavior to biological sex. Likewise, Kotthof and Wodak argue for a return to Goffman's social constructivist approach because it grounds the construction of gender within the social institutions that produce and perpetuate gender. As Goffman (1977: 324) put it, institutions "do not so much allow for the expression of natural differences between the sexes as for the production of that difference itself."

6 Conclusion

Research on language and gender has increasingly become research on gender and discourse (although variationist studies such as Eckert 1989, 1998 demonstrate a promising symbiotic relationship between quantitative and qualitative methods). A movement toward the study of language within specific situated activities reflects the importance of culturally defined meanings both of linguistic strategies and of gender. It acknowledges the agency of individuals in creating gendered identities, including the options of resisting and transgressing sociocultural norms for linguistic behavior. But it also acknowledges the sociocultural constraints within which women and men make their linguistic choices, and the impact of those constraints, whether they are adhered to or departed from. In a sense, the field of gender and discourse has come full circle, returning to its roots in a Goffman-influenced constructivist framework as seen in the groundbreaking work of Brown, Goodwin, Lakoff, and Goffman himself.

NOTE

1 As Maccoby (1988) observes, this distinction is illusory since it presupposes that we know a priori which aspects of behavior are culturally learned, and which are biologically given, when in fact we can not do so. Moreover, the distinction is increasingly muddied as the term "gender" is now used as a euphemism for "sex" in many contexts, such as forms that ask people to indicate their male or female "gender."

REFERENCES

Ahrens, Ulrike. 1997. The interplay between interruptions and preference organization in conversation: new perspectives on a classic topic of gender research. In Kotthoff and Wodak 1997a, 79–106.

Ainsworth-Vaughn, Nancy. 1992. Topic transitions in physician–patient interviews: power, gender, and discourse change. *Language in Society* 21.409–26.

Barrett, Rusty. 1999. Indexing polyphonous identity in the speech of African American drag queens. In Bucholtz et al. 1999, 313–31.

Beattie, Geoffrey W. 1981. Interruption in conversational interaction and its relation to the sex and status of the interactants. *Linguistics* 19.15–35.

Bergvall, Victoria L. 1996. Constructing and enacting gender through discourse: negotiating multiple roles as female engineering students. In Bergvall et al. 1996, 173–201.

Bergvall, Victoria L., Janet M. Bing, and Alice F. Freed (eds) 1996. *Rethinking Language and Gender Research: Theory and Practice*. London and New York: Longman.

Bing, Janet M., and Victoria L. Bergvall. 1996. The question of questions:

beyond binary thinking. In Bergvall et al. 1996, 1–30.

Brown, Penelope. 1980. How and why are women more polite: some evidence from a Mayan community. In McConnell-Ginet et al. 1980, 111–36.

Bucholtz, Mary. 1996. Black feminist theory and African American women's linguistic practice. In Bergvall et al. 1996, 267–90.

Bucholtz, Mary. 1999a. Purchasing power: the gender and class imaginary on the shopping channel. In Bucholtz et al. 1999, 348–68.

Bucholtz, Mary. 1999b. Bad examples: transgression and progress in language and gender studies. In Bucholtz et al. 1999, 3–24.

Bucholtz, Mary, and Kira Hall. 1995. Introduction: 20 years after *Language and Woman's Place*. In Hall and Bucholtz 1995, 1–22.

Bucholtz, Mary, A. C. Liang, and Laurel A. Sutton (eds). 1999. *Reinventing Identities: The Gendered Self in Discourse*. New York and Oxford: Oxford University Press.

Bucholtz, Mary, A. C. Liang, Laurel A. Sutton, and Caitlin Hines (eds). 1994. *Cultural Performances: Proceedings of the Third Berkeley Women and Language Conference*. Berkeley, CA: Berkeley Women and Language Group.

Butler, Judith. 1990. *Gender Trouble: Feminism and the Subversion of Identity*. New York and London: Routledge.

Butler, Judith. 1993. *Bodies That Matter*. New York: Routledge.

Cameron, Deborah. 1985. *Feminism and Linguistic Theory*. London: Macmillan. Second edition 1992.

Cameron, Deborah (ed.). 1990. *The Feminist Critique of Language: A Reader*. London and New York: Routledge. Second edition 1998b.

Cameron, Deborah. 1995. Rethinking language and gender studies: some issues for the 1990s. In Mills 1995, 31–44.

Cameron, Deborah. 1998a. Gender, language and discourse: a review. *Signs: Journal of Women, Culture and Society* 28: 945–73.

Cameron, Deborah. 1999. Dialogue: feminist linguistics: a response to Bent Preisler's review article: deconstructing "Feminist Linguistics." *Journal of Sociolinguistics* 3.121–5.

Cameron, Deborah, Fiona McAlinden, and Kathy O'Leary. 1989. Lakoff in context: the social and linguistic functions of tag questions. In Coates and Cameron 1989, 74–93.

Coates, Jennifer. 1986. *Women, Men and Language: A Sociolinguistic Account of Sex Differences in Language*. London and New York: Longman. Second edition, 1993.

Coates, Jennifer. 1989. Gossip revisited: language in all-female groups. In Coates and Cameron 1989, 94–122.

Coates, Jennifer. 1996. *Women Talk: Conversations between Women Friends*. Oxford and Cambridge, MA: Blackwell.

Coates, Jennifer. 1997a. One-at-a-time: the organization of men's talk. In Johnson and Meinhof 1997, 107–29.

Coates, Jennifer (ed.). 1997b. *Language and Gender: A Reader*. Oxford: Blackwell.

Coates, Jennifer, and Deborah Cameron (eds). 1989. *Women in their Speech Communities: New Perspectives on Language and Sex*. London: Longman.

Crawford, Mary. 1995. *Talking Difference: On Gender and Language*. London: Sage.

Eckert, Penelope. 1989. The whole woman: sex and gender differences in variation. *Language Variation and Change* 1.245–67.

Eckert, Penelope. 1990. Cooperative competition in adolescent "girl talk." *Discourse Processes* 13.91–122. Rpt in Tannen 1993, 32–61.

Eckert, Penelope. 1998. *Variation as Social Practice*. Oxford: Blackwell.

Eckert, Penelope, and Sally McConnell-Ginet. 1992. Think practically and look locally: language and gender as community-based practice. *Annual Review of Anthropology* 21.461–90.

Eckert, Penelope, and Sally McConnell-Ginet. 1995. Constructing meaning, constructing selves: snapshots of language, gender, and class from Belten High. In Hall and Bucholtz 1995, 469–507.

Esposito, Anita. 1979. Sex differences in children's conversation. *Language and Speech* 22.213–20.

Etter-Lewis, Gwendolyn. 1991. Standing up and speaking out: African American women's narrative legacy. *Discourse and Society* 2.425–37.

Etter-Lewis, Gwendolyn, and Michèle Foster (eds). 1996. *Unrelated Kin: Race and Gender in Women's Personal Narratives*. London: Routledge.

Fishman, Pamela. 1979. What do couples talk about when they're alone? In *Women's Language and Style*, eds Douglas L. Butturff and Edmund L. Epstein, 11–22. Akron, OH: University of Akron.

Fishman, Pamela. 1983. Interaction: the work women do. In Thorne et al. 1983, 89–101.

Foster, Michèle. 1989. "It's cookin' now": a performance analysis of the speech events of a black teacher in an urban community college. *Language in Society* 18.1–29.

Foster, Michèle. 1995. Are you with me?: power and solidarity in the discourse of African American women. In Hall and Bucholtz 1995, 329–50.

Frank, Francine, and Frank Anshen. 1983. *Language and the Sexes*. Albany: State University of New York Press.

Goffman, Erving. 1967. *Interaction Ritual: Essays on Face-to-face Behavior*. New York: Pantheon Books.

Goffman, Erving. 1976. *Gender Advertisements*. New York: Harper and Row.

Goffman, Erving. 1977. The arrangement between the sexes. *Theory and Society* 4: 301–31.

Goodwin, Marjorie Harness. 1978. Conversational practices in a peer group of urban black children. Philadelphia, PA: University of Pennsylvania, dissertation.

Goodwin, Marjorie Harness. 1980a. Directive–response sequences in girls' and boys' task activities. In McConnell-Ginet et al. 1980, 157–73.

Goodwin, Marjorie Harness. 1980b. He-said-she-said: formal cultural procedures for the construction of a gossip dispute activity. *American Ethnologist* 7.674–95.

Goodwin, Marjorie Harness. 1990. *He-Said-She-Said: Talk as Social Organization among Black Children*. Bloomington, IN: Indiana University Press.

Goodwin, Marjorie Harness. 1999. Constructing opposition within girls' games. In Bucholtz et al. 1999, 388–409.

Goodwin, Marjorie Harness, and Charles Goodwin. 1987. Children's arguing. In Philips et al. 1987, 200–48.

Graddol, David, and Joan Swann. 1989. *Gender Voices*. Oxford and Cambridge, MA: Blackwell.

Greenwood, Alice. 1996. Floor management and power strategies in adolescent conversation. In Bergvall et al. 1996, 77–97.

Gumperz, John J. 1982. *Discourse Strategies*. Cambridge: Cambridge University Press.

Hall, Kira. 1995. Lip service on the fantasy lines. In Hall and Bucholtz 1995, 183–216.

Hall, Kira, and Mary Bucholtz (eds). 1995. *Gender Articulated: Language and the Socially Constructed Self*. New York and London: Routledge.

Hall, Kira, and Veronica O'Donovan. 1996. Shifting gender positions among Hindi-speaking hijras. In Bergvall et al. 1996, 228–66.

Hall, Kira, Mary Bucholtz, and Birch Moonwomon (eds). 1992. *Locating Power: Proceedings of the Second Berkeley Women and Language Conference*. Berkeley, CA: Berkeley Women and Language Group.

Henley, Nancy M., and Cheris Kramarae. 1991. Gender, power, and miscommunication. In *"Miscommunication" and Problematic Talk*, eds Nikolas Coupland, Howard Giles, and John M. Wiemann, 18–43. Newbury Park, CA: Sage.

Holmes, Janet. 1995. *Women, Men and Politeness*. London and New York: Longman.

Jacobs, Greg. 1996. Lesbian and gay male language use: a critical review of the literature. *American Speech* 71.49–71.

James, Deborah, and Sandra Clarke. 1993. Women, men, and interruptions: a critical review. In *Gender and Conversational Interaction*, ed. Deborah Tannen. 231–80. New York and Oxford: Oxford University Press.

Johnson, Sally. 1997. Theorizing language and masculinity: a feminist perspective. In Johnson and Meinhof 1997, 8–26.

Johnson, Sally, and Ulrike Hanna Meinhof (eds). 1997. *Language and Masculinity*. Oxford and Cambridge, MA: Blackwell.

Johnson, Fern, and Elizabeth Aries. 1983. The talk of women friends. *Women's Studies International Forum* 6.353–61.

Johnstone, Barbara. 1990. *Stories, Community, and Place: Narratives from Middle America*. Bloomington, IN: University of Indiana Press.

Johnstone, Barbara. 1995. Sociolinguistic resources, individual identities and public speech styles of Texas women. *Journal of Linguistic Anthropology* 5: 1–20.

Kendall, Shari. 1999. The interpenetration of (gendered) spheres: a sociolinguistic analysis of mothers and fathers at work and at home.

Washington, DC: Georgetown University dissertation.

Key, Mary Ritchie. 1975. *Male/Female Language: With a Comprehensive Bibliography*. Metuchen, NJ: Scarecrow Press.

Kotthoff, Helga. 1997. The interactional achievement of expert status: creating asymmetries by "teaching conversational lecture" in TV discussions. In Kotthoff and Wodak 1997a, 139–78.

Kotthoff, Helga, and Ruth Wodak (eds). 1997a. *Communicating Gender in Context*. Amsterdam: Benjamins.

Kotthoff, Helga, and Ruth Wodak. 1997b. Preface. In Kotthoff and Wodak 1997a, vii–xxv.

Lakoff, Robin. 1973. Language and woman's place. *Language in Society* 2.45–79.

Lakoff, Robin. 1975. *Language and Woman's Place*. New York: Harper & Row.

Lakoff, Robin. 1995. Cries and whispers: the shattering of the silence. In Hall and Bucholtz 1995, 25–50.

Leap, William L. (ed.). 1996a. *Beyond the Lavender Lexicon: Authenticity, Imagination, and Appropriation in Lesbian and Gay Languages*. Buffalo, NY: Gordon and Breach.

Leap, William L. 1996b. *Word's Out: Gay Men's English*. Minneapolis and London: University of Minnesota Press.

Leap, William L. 1999. Language, socialization, and silence in gay adolescence. In Bucholtz et al. 1999, 259–72.

Lever, Janet. 1976. Sex differences in the games children play. *Social Problems* 23.478–83.

Lever, Janet. 1978. Sex differences in the complexity of children's play and games. *American Sociological Review* 43.471–83.

Livia, Anna, and Kira Hall (eds). 1997a. *Queerly Phrased: Language, Gender, and*

Sexuality. New York and Oxford: Oxford University Press.

Livia, Anna, and Kira Hall. 1997b. "It's a girl!": bringing performativity back to linguistics. In Livia and Hall 1997a, 3–18.

Lorber, Judith. 1994. *Paradoxes of Gender*. New Haven and London: Yale University Press.

Maccoby, Eleanor. 1988. Gender as a social category. *Developmental Psychology* 24.755–65.

Maltz, Daniel N., and Ruth A. Borker. 1982. A cultural approach to male–female miscommunication. In *Language and Social Identity*, ed. John J. Gumperz, 196–216. Cambridge: Cambridge University Press.

Matoesian, Gregory M. 1993. *Reproducing Rape: Domination through Talk in the Courtroom*. Chicago: University of Chicago Press.

McConnell-Ginet, Sally. 1978. Intonation in a man's world. *Signs* 3.541–59.

McConnell-Ginet, Sally. 1988. Language and gender. In *Linguistics: The Cambridge Survey, Vol. IV: The Sociocultural Context*, ed. Frederick Newmeyer, 75–99. New York: Praeger.

McConnell-Ginet, Sally, Ruth Borker, and Nelly Furman (eds). 1980. *Women and Language in Literature and Society*. New York: Praeger.

McElhinny, Bonnie S. 1992. "I don't smile much anymore": affect, gender, and the discourse of Pittsburgh police officers. In Hall et al. 1992, 386–403.

McElhinny, Bonnie S. 1997. Ideologies of public and private language in sociolinguistics. In Wodak 1997, 106–39.

Mendoza-Denton, Norma. 1999. Turn-initial "no": collaborative opposition among Latina adolescents. In Bucholtz et al. 1999, 273–92.

Meyerhoff, Miriam. 1996. Dealing with gender identity as a sociolinguistic variable. In Bergvall et al. 1996, 202–27.

Mills, Sara (ed.). 1995. *Language and Gender: Interdisciplinary Perspectives*. London and New York: Longman.

Morgan, Marcyliena. 1991. Indirectness and interpretation in African American women's discourse. *Pragmatics* 1.421–51.

Morgan, Marcyliena. 1999. No woman no cry: claiming African American women's place. In Bucholtz et al. 1999, 27–45.

Murray, Stephen. 1985. Toward a model of members' methods for recognizing interruptions. *Language in Society* 13.31–40.

Murray, Stephen, and Lucille H. Covelli. 1988. Women and men speaking at the same time. *Journal of Pragmatics* 12.103–11.

O'Barr, William M., and Bowman K. Atkins. 1980. "Women's language" or "powerless language"? In McConnell-Ginet et al. 1980, 93–110.

Ochs, Elinor. 1992. Indexing gender. In *Rethinking Context: Language as an Interactive Phenomenon*, eds Alessandro Duranti and Charles Goodwin, 335–58. Cambridge: Cambridge University Press.

Orellana, Marjorie Faulstich. 1999. Good guys and "bad" girls: identity construction by Latina and Latino student writers. In Bucholtz et al. 1999, 64–82.

Philips, Susan U., Susan Steele, and Christine Tanz (eds). 1987. *Language, Gender, and Sex in Comparative Perspective*. Cambridge: Cambridge University Press.

Preisler, Bent. 1986. *Linguistic Sex Roles in Conversation: Social Variation in the Expression of Tentativeness in English*. Berlin: Mouton de Gruyter.

Preisler, Bent. 1998. Deconstructing feminist linguistics. *Journal of Sociolinguistics* 2.281–95.

Schieffelin, Bambi B., and Elinor Ochs (eds). 1986. *Language Acquisition and Socialization across Cultures.* Cambridge: Cambridge University Press.

Sheldon, Amy. 1990. Pickle fights: gendered talk in preschool disputes. *Discourse Processes* 13.5–31. Rpt in Tannen 1993, 83–109.

Sherzer, Joel. 1987. A diversity of voices: men's and women's speech in ethnographic perspective. In Philips et al. 1987, 95–120.

Stanback, Marsha Houston. 1985. Language and black woman's place: evidence from the black middle class. In *For Alma Mater: Theory and Practice in Feminist Scholarship*, eds Paula A. Treichler, Cheris Kramarae, and Beth Stafford, 177–93. Urbana: University of Illinois Press.

Talbot, Mary M. 1998. *Language and Gender: An Introduction.* Cambridge: Polity.

Tannen, Deborah. 1984. *Conversational Style: Analyzing Talk among Friends.* Norwood, NJ: Ablex.

Tannen, Deborah. 1989a. Interpreting interruption in conversation. *Papers from the 25th Annual Regional Meeting of the Chicago Linguistic Society. Part Two: Parasession on Language in Context*, eds Bradley Music, Randolph Graczyk, and Caroline Wiltshire, 266–87. Chicago: Chicago Linguistic Society. Rpt in Tannen 1994b, 53–83.

Tannen, Deborah. 1989b. *Talking Voices: Repetition, Dialogue, and Imagery in Conversational Discourse.* Cambridge: Cambridge University Press.

Tannen, Deborah. 1990. *You Just Don't Understand: Women and Men in Conversation.* New York: Ballantine.

Tannen, Deborah (ed.). 1993. *Gender and Conversational Interaction.* New York and Oxford: Oxford.

Tannen, Deborah. 1994a. *Talking from 9 to 5: Women and Men in the Workplace:*
Language, Sex and Power. New York: Avon.

Tannen, Deborah. 1994b. *Gender and Discourse.* New York and Oxford: Oxford University Press.

Tannen, Deborah. 1994c. The sex–class linked framing of talk at work. In Tannen 1994b, 195–221.

Tannen, Deborah. 1998. *The Argument Culture: Stopping America's War of Words.* New York: Ballantine.

Thorne, Barrie, and Nancy Henley (eds). 1975. *Language and Sex: Difference and Dominance.* Rowley, MA: Newbury House.

Thorne, Barrie, Cheris Kramarae, and Nancy Henley (eds). 1983. *Language, Gender and Society.* Rowley, MA: Newbury House.

Todd, Alexandra D., and Sue Fisher (eds). 1988. *Gender and Discourse: The Power of Talk.* Norwood, NJ: Ablex.

Walters, Keith. 1999: "Opening the door of paradise a cubit": educated Tunisian women, embodied linguistic practice, and theories of language and gender. In Bucholtz et al. 1999, 200–17.

Warner, Natasha, Jocelyn Ahlers, Leela Bilmes, Monica Oliver, Suzanne Wertheim, and Melinda Chen (eds). 1996. *Gender and Belief Systems: Proceedings of the Fourth Berkeley Women and Language Conference.* Berkeley, CA: Berkeley Women and Language Group.

Wertheim, Suzanne, Ashlee C. Bailey, and Monica Corston-Oliver (eds). 1998. *Engendering Communication: Proceedings from the Fifth Berkeley Women and Language Conference.* Berkeley, CA: Berkeley Women and Language Group.

West, Candace. 1984. When the doctor is a "lady": power, status and gender in physician–patient encounters. *Symbolic Interaction* 7.87–106.

West, Candace. 1990. Not just doctor's orders: directive–response sequences in patients' visits to women and men physicians. *Discourse and Society* 1.85–112.

West, Candace, and Don H. Zimmerman. 1983. Small insults: a study of interruptions in cross-sex conversations between unacquainted persons. In Thorne et al. 1983, 102–17.

Wodak, Ruth (ed.). 1997. *Gender and Discourse*. London: Sage.

Wood, Kathleen M. 1997. Narrative iconicity in electronic-mail lesbian coming-out stories. In Livia and Hall 1997a, 257–73.

Wood, Kathleen M. 1999. Coherent identities amid heterosexist ideologies: deaf and hearing lesbian coming-out stories. In Bucholtz et al. 1999, 46–63.

Zimmerman, Don H., and Candace West. 1975. Sex roles, interruptions and silences in conversation. In Thorne and Henley 1975, 105–29.

29 Discourse and Aging

HEIDI E. HAMILTON

0 Introduction

Consider Ruth Watkins, Gerald Miller, and Viola Green. Dr. Watkins is a single 83-year-old retired university administrator. Her considerable difficulties with hearing and walking barely slow her down; her community activism centers on environmental and child welfare issues. Mr. Miller, a 95-year-old self-educated businessman, just last month stopped going to work everyday upon discovering he has pancreatic cancer. His three children, ten grandchildren, and fourteen great-grandchildren have decided to come together next week to help celebrate "Pa's" full life before he dies. Mrs. Green is a 72-year-old retired kindergarten teacher who has recently moved into a private nursing home. Her children had struggled for a couple of years to keep her at home, but the confusion and wandering of Alzheimer's disease proved to be too powerful. Mrs. Green's current joy comes from looking through old personal papers and photographs and talking with the smiling faces of friends and family members she seems not to place.

Now consider the scholar caught up in the endless fascination of exploring the interrelationships between aging and discourse: does Dr. Watkins's hearing loss affect how she interacts in city council meetings? Will her shift to e-mail as a primary form of communication change how she keeps up with friends? Has Mr. Miller's talk at work changed over the course of 80 years as a businessman? How will he interact with his oncologist as he faces decisions regarding his cancer? What does Mrs. Green enjoy talking about? What seems to frustrate her? Would she be better off in a specialized care unit where she can talk with other individuals who have Alzheimer's disease?

As recently as the early 1980s, that researcher's bookshelves devoted to this juxtaposition of interests would have been nearly empty: *Language and Communication in the Elderly: Clinical, Therapeutic, and Experimental Aspects*, edited by Obler and Albert (1980), and *Aging, Communication Processes and Disorders*, edited by Beasley and Davis (1981), would have taken their place next to Irigaray's (1973) study of dementia in France (*Le langage des dements*), Gubrium's (1975) *Living and Dying at Murray Manor*, and doctoral dissertations by Lubinski, "Perceptions of oral-verbal communication by residents and staff of an institution for the chronically ill and aged" (1976), and Bayles, "Communication profiles in a geriatric population" (1979). File folders containing the published report of a case study on language function in dementia by Schwartz et al. (1979), a discussion of senility by Smithers (1977), and an analysis of baby talk to the institutionalized aged by Caporeal (1981) would have almost completed the literature available at the time.

In the year 2000, however, that same scholar's bookshelves and file drawers are overflowing with studies. The 1980s and 1990s were filled with scholarly activities extending and deepening the understanding based on the small amount of early groundbreaking work.[1] A quick glance displays a dizzying array of topics and approaches. Some scholars[2] describe the language and/or communicative abilities that accompany aging, looking both at healthy individuals and at those dealing with health problems that directly affect language use, such as Alzheimer's disease and aphasia. Others[3] assume that people's language choices help to construct their social identities (including an elderly identity or patient identity) and relate these choices to issues of mental and physical health. Still others[4] recognize the critical importance of communicative relationships across the life span and investigate talk among friends and family members, both at home and within health-care facilities.

In this chapter, I discuss the multiple disciplinary perspectives and approaches that underlie this diversity (section 2), tracing in some detail the different modes of inquiry (section 3) and areas of inquiry (section 4) that characterize the literature on discourse and aging today. Before moving on to those discussions, however, I turn first to consider the notion of old age (section 1).

1 Who Is Old? Conceptualizations of Old Age

Researchers who work with elderly individuals come to the nearly immediate realization that age is much more complex than a simple biological category. Chronological age tells only a small part of anyone's story – and, in fact, can be quite misleading at times. Finding that simple chronological age did not correlate well with the facts of linguistic change in her research within the Labovian paradigm, Eckert (1984) turned to differences in speakers' aspirations, roles, and orientation to society to account for their linguistic behavior. Later, Eckert (1997: 167) argued that researchers must direct their focus "away from chronological age and towards the life experiences that give age meaning."

People often feel older or younger than their chronological age (Boden and Bielby 1986; cf. discussion of "disjunctive aging" in Coupland et al. 1989). Sometimes this difference between perception and calendar years can be traced to what Counts and Counts (1985) call "functional age" – changes in a person's senses (e.g. sight or hearing), appearance, and mental and physical health, as well as activity level. Other times "social age" (Counts and Counts 1985) may be at play; e.g. people who are experiencing the same "rite of passage" in society may feel more alike in terms of age than their individual chronological ages would predict. To illustrate, 45-year-old first-time parents may feel more like 25-year-old first-time parents than like their 45-year-old neighbors who just became grandparents. Likewise, a 60-year-old member of the graduating class of the local university may feel quite different from her 60-year-old friends who all graduated from college almost 40 years ago.

Finally, there is the possible influence of what Copper (1986: 52) calls "societal aging" (another term for ageism), where a generalized other is projected onto individuals which does not correspond to their own self-image. Randall (1986: 127) elaborates: "The dislocation created out of the contradictions between how I feel and look – and *what I know* – and how society perceives me – physically, socially, economically, emotionally – is a very real element in every day." Even well-meaning researchers in gerontology may unwittingly contribute to this situation by "expect[ing] that age will have a central significance and . . . look[ing] for its effects in our research of the elderly" (Ward 1984: 230) rather than striving to understand lives of the elderly "as they are lived" and highlighting age only when it is salient (see also Rosenfeld 1999).

Feeding into some of the disparities between perceived and chronological age is the extreme heterogeneity of the older segments of the population. Nelson and Dannefer (1992) observe that this increasing diversity over the life span does not appear to be specific to any particular domain; i.e. marked heterogeneity emerges as a finding across physical, personality, social, and cognitive domains. Elderly people can be expected, therefore, to differ greatly from each other in terms of memory, cognition, attitudes toward self and others, physical health, and communicative needs. Differences may also exist in terms of what kinds of people elderly women and men actually have to talk with, as well as where and how often this talk takes place. Issues here include social networks and attitudes of those in the networks both toward the particular individual in question and toward elderly people in general. Is the individual's lifetime partner (if any) still alive? Is his or her social network getting smaller and smaller as age-related peers die or move into nursing homes? Is the individual making new friends from younger generations? Is the individual talking a great deal to people who hold ageist attitudes?

This extreme variation makes it difficult to talk about normative language use. Wiemann et al. (1990) argue that, in order to be able to understand whether people are aging successfully, standards need to be ascertained for different stages of aging. At present, language used by elderly people is usually compared to the communicative, social, and psychological standards of typical middle age. As Eckert (1997: 157–8) points out, "Taking middle-aged language as a universal norm and developmental target obscures the fact that ways of speaking at any life stage are part of the community structuring of language use, and that the linguistic resources employed at any stage in life have social meaning for and within that life stage."

2   Embracing Multiple Disciplinary Perspectives

After reading the preceding discussion, one might feel a sense of anxiety and confusion when faced with the task of addressing the relationships between discourse and aging. Both Chafe (1994) and Moerman (1996), however, offer another possibility. Chafe, in an insightful discussion of data and methodologies related to linguistics and the mind, argues that no single approach can be inherently the correct one. In his opinion, all types of data "provide important insights, and all have their limitations" (1994: 12). Each methodology makes a contribution, but "none has an exclusive claim on scientific validity" (1994: 18). Moerman (1996: 147) compares the field of conversation analysis to the swidden fields of Southeast Asia, which, in contrast to sessile farms planted with a single crop, support a great variety of mutually sustaining plants. Although they appear untidy in their early stages of growth, swidden fields are productive and supportive. Following Chafe and Moerman, then, I argue that, not only should no single disciplinary approach be understood as the dominant paradigm in issues of discourse and aging, but excluding any disciplinary approach a priori will almost certainly result in a less-than-complete understanding of such issues. The field is far too complex to be understood by looking through one set of filters.

However, simply agreeing that multidisciplinarity (possibly leading to interdisciplinarity) should be embraced does not get the job done. Any scholar who has worked seriously on issues that cross disciplines knows that such work can be a true challenge. Different dominant paradigms often point to different kinds of research questions that are thought to be both answerable and useful or important. These paradigms also influence which (and how many) participants and settings are included in research studies, what kinds of language data are collected and how, and what types of theoretical frameworks and analytical units are brought to the research, as well as what counts as research findings, and how those findings are reported.

With an eye to that goal – and in the firm belief that we can only welcome multidisciplinarity if we try to understand some of these differences – I now turn to a discussion of disciplinary influences in terms of the preferred mode of inquiry into issues of discourse and aging. Areas touched on include: theory-driven versus data-driven approaches, selection of informant(s), length and breadth of study, and contexts of talk examined. Section 4 then characterizes disciplinary influences on preferred types of research questions as evidenced by the state of the literature in this area.

3   Modes of Inquiry

3.1   Different starting points

Possibly the most obvious paradigmatic difference relates to the choice of a theory-driven (top-down) or data-driven (bottom-up) approach to questions of discourse and aging. Researchers who align themselves with the natural sciences tend to take a theory-driven approach; they start with a question and motivation that derive from a theory which they deem important and relevant. Once the motivated question has been posed, they determine which and how many subjects are necessary to carry out the study as well as the context(s) of the subjects' language use. In this approach, the analytical tools necessary to the examination of language use are usually determined ahead of the actual data collection.

In contrast to the theory-driven approach, researchers who align themselves with anthropology tend to take a data-driven approach. This often starts with an interest (which could be understood to be a motivation for the study – albeit a different kind than that emanating from theory) in particular subjects and/or contexts which leads to the collection of language used by these subjects within these contexts. The researchers usually have a general research question in mind, but this question is allowed to evolve as the investigation proceeds. Interesting patterns and unexpected language use by these subjects within these contexts lead the researchers to decide which analytical tools to employ; the analysis and the research question proceed hand in hand, each informing the other until the researchers are convinced that they have understood the discourse in an interesting and thorough way.

3.2   Who should be studied?

Despite the complexity relating to the notion of age and the hetereogeneity of the elderly population discussed in section 1 above, many researchers working on questions of discourse and aging still select subjects for their studies based on chronological age, often in conjunction with various measures of health status. Time constraints frequently do not allow for the kinds of complex evaluations necessary to take into account individuals' *perceived* age, levels of activity and independence, etc., when selecting subjects. Sometimes researchers set up categories to distinguish between the young-old and the old-old or even the oldest-old as a way of taking into account observations that 65-year-olds are often different in many significant ways from 85-year-olds or those over 100 years of age (see especially Baltes and Mayer 1999). And, of course, in some studies, the researchers are specifically interested in chronological age, not perceived age, as it relates to a variety of other factors, and, therefore, select subjects based solely on chronological age.

3.3   How many subjects?

Researchers deal with the issue of heterogeneity in different ways. Often researchers argue that the best way of compensating for wide variation within the population to be studied is to include very large numbers of subjects. The large numbers are seen as means to greater generalization of the findings of the study; i.e. in a large study, it is more likely that researchers will be working with a set of individuals who represent the larger population of elderly individuals in relevant ways. In a case study or one involving very few subjects, it is more likely that the individuals will not represent the larger population in these ways.

   On the other hand, proponents of case studies and small-scale studies argue that the extreme variation that exists within the elderly population makes it likely that large-scale studies simply average out these large differences, and that the averages found, therefore, are actually not representative of large numbers of the elderly population in any meaningful way. Case studies and small-scale studies are seen as being able to investigate in a more in-depth fashion the interrelationships among a variety of discursive and social factors, leading to well-grounded research questions and methodologies that can be used in subsequent large-scale studies.[5]

3.4   *Synchronic or diachronic?*

Some researchers separate their subjects into several age-based groups, carry out the tasks that will produce the discourse to be examined, and compare the "snapshots" of these groups. Although this cross-sectional study design is tempting in that discourse of different age groups can be elicited simultaneously, there are some potential problems with this approach. For example, differences found across groups may not reflect actual changes in individuals over the life span (therefore relating to aging), but instead may have to do with differential socialization of the groups regarding the importance of talk, gender roles and identities, etiquette, or with differing amounts of formal school education (which would not relate to aging per se). Even when similarities (not differences) across groups are identified, the researcher is faced with another type of challenge, in that he or she needs to differentiate those discourse patterns which are similar for both groups *for the same reasons* from those patterns which are similar *for different reasons* (see Hamilton 1992: 246–7 for an illustration).

The most obvious way to deal with issues evoked by the cross-sectional research design is to invoke a longitudinal design, in which each subject is followed over time, thereby acting as his or her own control. In this way it is possible to identify changes that take place over time within individuals' own discourse, rather than having to infer these changes in the cross-sectional design. Despite its advantages in this way, researchers involved in a longitudinal study must be alert to a possible skewing of data over time as some individuals stay with the study and others either opt out over time or die. Although the longitudinal approach can be employed in studies of individuals (see Hamilton 1994a) and single age groups, it is most effective in combination with the cross-sectional approach, where, for example, the discourse used by people in their 30s, 40s, 50s, 60s, 70s, etc., is tracked every five years.

3.5   *Contexts of talk*

Discourse and aging studies typically examine language used within one or more of the following contexts: (1) standardized tests, (2) interviews, (3) conversations, and (4) real-life interactions "listened in on." Since differences inherent in these interactional contexts can result in differences in the discourse produced (and comprehended), some researchers have identified these contexts as being (at least partially) responsible for contradictory findings across studies.[6] It is with an eye to these differences that I now turn to a brief characterization of these four contexts.

3.5.1   *Standardized test situation*

The discourse in this context tends to be tightly constrained. The language tasks are very clearly identified so that any deviation from what is expected can be characterized as outside the range of normal. In one such task, the speaker describes what is going on in a black-and-white line drawing of a kitchen scene, in which a child is standing on a stool and reaching for a cookie jar (Goodglass and Kaplan 1972). In another task, the speaker retells a well-known fairy tale, such as "Little Red Riding

Hood." One clear benefit of this context is that the researcher can find out a good deal about a wide range of discourse abilities and compare the results with a large number of other individuals who have previously taken the test within a limited amount of time. A disadvantage of this context is that its predetermined tasks limit the display of the test-taker's discourse abilities to just those under investigation. Another possible disadvantage is that the test-taker's performance on the test may bear little resemblance to his or her actual discourse abilities as displayed in everyday situations (ecological validity). For example, if the data elicitation relies a great deal on working memory or attention to task, older individuals may perform worse than younger ones (where the memory or attention problems have not reached the point where they are recognizable in real-life situations). Furthermore, if the task is one which is relatively abstract, older individuals might perform worse than younger individuals since they are "out of practice" performing these kinds of tasks, which are more typical of school than of everyday life.

3.5.2   Interview with the researcher

The discourse in this context tends to be somewhat topically constrained and the participant roles and communicative division of labor fairly clear cut. The interviewer is usually understood to be in charge of asking the questions, while the interviewee is expected to answer them. Although there may be no "right or wrong" answers to mark the interviewee as being within or outside the range of normal (as is the case with standardized tests), subjects still know that they are not to veer very far off the proposed topics of discussion. One benefit of this communicative context is that the researcher can find out in a fairly quick and straightforward way what the interviewee has to say about a given set of topics. The use of open-ended questions allows the interviewees to frame their answers in whatever terms they feel are meaningful (in comparison to a questionnaire with predetermined answer options, for example). This freedom not only gives the researcher greater insight into the interviewees' way of thinking but also provides rich discourse for more microlevel analyses of language choices by the interviewee. One disadvantage of the interview (as compared with standardized testing) is that the open-endedness of the questions allows for the possibility that certain linguistic or communicative behavior will not be displayed.[7] Depending on the degree to which the interviewee feels uncertain about the purposes of the interview or feels uncomfortable talking with a relative stranger, the answers *about* communicative practice given in the interview may bear little relationship to what the interviewee *actually* does in practice.

3.5.3   Conversations with the researcher

The language in this context is usually more free-wheeling than that in the interviews and testing situations discussed above. In conversations, topics come and go relatively freely, being initiated, elaborated upon, and closed by either party. This symmetry may result in the elderly individual displaying a fuller range of linguistic and communicative abilities than in a more asymmetrical context. Another benefit of undirected conversations is that the researcher can identify issues of importance to the elderly individual that might never have come up in a more topically constrained discourse. Self-selected and designed conversational contributions can be windows on emotions and reflections that would probably have gone unnoticed within a more constrained context. One disadvantage of the conversation as well as the interview context (as compared with the testing situation) is the possibility that not all linguistic abilities judged to be relevant to the researcher may be displayed. Another disadvantage (as compared with the interview situation) is that it is more difficult for the researcher to maintain any sense of "agenda" when the elderly interlocutor may introduce new topics at any time, choose not to elaborate upon topics introduced by the researcher, etc.

In all three contexts just described – in tests, conversations, and interviews with the researchers – the testers/interviewers/conversational partners need to be alert to the possibility that they may unwittingly influence the language used by those whose discourse is of interest to them. Coupland et al. (1988) point out the subconscious overaccommodation by younger-generation interlocutors to the (falsely) perceived needs of their older-generation conversational partners. This overaccommodation can effect lower performance levels on the part of the older individual. My four-and-a-half-year longitudinal case study of Elsie, an elderly woman with Alzheimer's disease (Hamilton 1994a), is replete with examples of interactional influences – both positive and negative – on Elsie's talk.

3.5.4 *Real-life situations "listened in on" by the researcher*

In these situations, the elderly individuals whose language is of interest are going about their business in a usual fashion and "just happen" to be observed; for example, on visits to the doctor and in support group conversations. One distinct advantage of this type of interaction, as contrasted with the contexts discussed above, is that there is no direct influence by the researcher on the language used by the elderly individuals. In cases where the researcher is in the immediate vicinity taping the interaction or taking notes, there may be a moderate indirect influence on the interaction due to the Observer's Paradox (see Labov 1972 for discussion of the fact that it is impossible to observe people who are *not* being observed). Another advantage in situations where the researcher is of a younger generation than his or her subjects (and, by definition, is involved in *intergenerational* encounters when talking with elderly individuals) is that it is possible to gain access to *intra*generational interactions such as conversations held among residents in a nursing home. Also the researcher can examine language used by elderly interlocutors with persons *they* have chosen to talk with in everyday life situations that are meaningful to *them*, as contrasted with interactions, such as the tests, interviews, and conversations, which usually take place outside their usual stream of life.

One possible disadvantage of "listening in on" real-life interactions has to do with the fact that the researcher is not part of the interaction. Because the talk is not constructed with the researcher in mind, it is quite likely that the researcher will not be privy to some of what is being talked about, will *think* he or she understands what is going on but actually does not, or will have a rather "flat" understanding of the discourse. These problems can be overcome to a certain extent through the use of playback interviews (see Tannen 1984), in which the original participants listen to the taped interaction along with the researcher. During or after the listening session, the researcher can ask questions for clarification, or the original participants can make comments on their own.

4   Areas of Inquiry

As I mentioned in section 2, disciplinary differences extend beyond the kinds of considerations regarding design and execution of research that we have just been discussing; they go right to the heart of what kinds of questions and research topics are thought to be answerable and useful or important. In this section I identify three areas of inquiry that have served to center clusters of research in the area of discourse and aging and that I predict will continue to be important magnets for research in the future: (1) language and communicative abilities in old age; (2) identity in old age; and (3) social norms, values, and practices in old age. Of course it is impossible to draw clear lines around these areas; for example, a particular discourse practice (type 3) or marked change in discourse ability (type 1) can serve as resources for the construction of the speaker's identity (type 2). Decisions regarding where to place individual studies in this review were based on my understanding of each author's primary focus and goals.

4.1   *Language and communicative abilities in old age*

Some scholars interested in the relationship between discourse and aging are drawn to questions relating to the relative decline, maintenance, or (occasionally) improvement of language and communicative abilities which accompany human aging. The majority of these scholars work in the disciplines of psycholinguistics, neurolinguistics, and speech-and-language pathology; their findings are typically based on the discourse produced and comprehended within standardized test batteries by large numbers of strategically selected elderly subjects. Some of these researchers look specifically at subgroups of the overall elderly population who are known to have difficulties with communication, such as individuals with Alzheimer's disease,[8] different types of aphasia,[9] and hearing loss.[10] Others attempt to characterize the decline, maintenance, or improvement of such abilities within the healthy elderly population.[11]

The long list of references in the notes to the paragraph above should not mislead the reader into thinking that these translate clearly into one set of unambiguous findings regarding discourse abilities and aging. This picture is still far from clear. Cloudiness in the form of contradictory findings across studies has several sources, including: insufficient differentiation among ages of subjects in some studies; the ceiling on age categories being set too low (for example, where 60 is used as the oldest age) in some studies; widely different discourse elicitation tasks across studies (see discussion in section 3.5); and a somewhat prescriptive predisposition within speech-language pathology which takes a negative view of what sociolinguists may see as a normal range of discourse variation (see Hamilton 1994c for discussion).

Despite the somewhat cloudy picture, many scholars point to the following changes that accompany healthy aging: (1) increasing difficulty with lexicon retrieval; e.g.

naming objects on command or coming up with words and proper nouns in conversation;[12] (2) decreasing syntactic complexity in spoken and written discourse production;[13] (3) increasing "off-target" verbosity;[14] and (4) decreasing sensitivity to audience when gauging given and new information (Ulatowska et al. 1985) as well as when using highly context-dependent linguistic features such as pronouns and deictic terms.[15]

Generally speaking, researchers whose studies are highlighted in this section are not satisfied with the mere identification of language changes that accompany aging, but frequently design their studies in such a way as to determine the cause of such changes (deterioration of the underlying linguistic system, problems of working memory, general slowing down of mental and physical processes, etc.). Such laudable efforts are often thwarted, however, by the complexity of what needs to be understood and differences in research design (as addressed in section 3) in the extant scholarly literature.

Near the end of their careful review of the state of research in this area, Melvold et al. (1994: 336) conclude: "We are only beginning to understand how and to what extent aging affects discourse." I believe that this picture will become ever clearer as researchers shift their focus from groups of elderly individuals selected by chronological age, health status, and educational background to carefully defined subcategories of elderly individuals carrying out specific discourse tasks in specific contexts (as one way to deal with the heterogeneity discussed in section 1). To this end, researchers trained in the areas of psycholinguistics and neurolinguistics are encouraged to (continue to) collaborate with linguistic discourse analysts in discussions of ecologically valid task design, possible influence of the researcher on subjects' language use, and the tying of discourse variation to features of its context.

4.2   Identity in old age

Other scholars working in the area of discourse and aging are drawn to issues of identity.[16] These researchers tend to be trained in the fields of social psychology, sociolinguistics, anthropological linguistics, and anthropology. Generally, they are not primarily interested in characterizing language abilities and disabilities of elderly individuals (or, if they do so, these are seen as interactional resources in identity construction). Instead these scholars attempt to identify patterns and strategies in discourse by and with (usually healthy) elderly interlocutors and relate these to the ongoing construction of a range of identities for the speakers as the discourse emerges. Most of the findings are based on a small number of individuals in conversations, interviews, or naturally occurring interactions "listened in on," due to the intense microlevel analysis required in this work.

Though it is not usually stated explicitly in the scholarly literature, virtually all of the researchers working in this area assume that their subjects display a range of identities as they speak or write (e.g. mother/father, wife/husband, child, competent adult, professional, friend, patient, etc.), some of which have nothing at all to do with their age. Of course the notion of turn-by-turn construction of identities in discourse – of self-positioning and positioning of others – is nothing new in the analysis of naturally occurring discourse. What *is* somewhat different about this issue with regard to aging is how this construction of identities gets played out in intergenerational interactions, where overt or subliminal ageism may be present,[17] especially within institutional settings such as nursing homes[18] or doctors' offices,[19] and exacerbated by any physical and/or mental health problems the elderly person may have.[20] It is in this way, then, that interactions between elderly adults and their personal and professional caregivers may actually be the sites where these elderly individuals (despite displaying a full range of identities in their discourse) come to see themselves primarily as patients or decrepit old people.

Ryan et al. (1986: 14) argue that mismanaged, demeaning, and deindividuating language by younger nursing staff to elderly nursing home residents, based on stereotypic notions of the communicative needs of these elderly residents (e.g. "Let's get you into bed," "shall we get our pants on?" in Ryan et al. 1995), may not only "induce momentary feelings of worthlessness in elderly people but may also lead to reduced life satisfaction and mental and physical decline in the long run."[21]

Lubinski's (1976, 1988) extensive study of the quality of the communication environment in nursing homes speaks of the gradual process of "institutionalization" of patients to an unreinforcing communicative environment. According to this view, communication attempts on the part of residents (especially those seen to be communicatively impaired or incompetent) with staff members or even with other more communicatively competent residents can be "extinguished through lack of response or curt, condescending replies" (Lubinski 1988: 295); through this process, these residents gradually come to expect little communication. Smithers (1977: 252) describes a similar type of socialization in which new nursing home residents' existing conceptions of self based on the world outside of the nursing home rapidly become "invalidated by a complex variety of discrediting and depersonalizing procedures that exist within the organizational framework" of the nursing home. Baltes and colleagues[22] have identified what they term the "dependency-support script" which is typically adhered to by caregivers of older adults within institutional settings. Baltes and her colleagues argue that behavior that is consistent with this script, such as dressing a nursing home resident or washing his or her face, is based both on negative stereotypes of aging and on a desire on the part of nursing home staff to enact an ideal "helper role."

In fact, Baltes et al. (1994: 179) report that, of all behaviors by older adults in institutions, dependent behavior is the "most likely to result in social contact and attention" from their caregivers. As Coupland et al. (1991: 70) argue, "the discourse sequences in which such self-presentations are embedded ('is my projected identity credible? credited? challenged? endorsed?') are likely to be key processes constituting the bottom line of people's self-appraisals."

It is not only the case, however, that elderly individuals who see themselves as relatively strong and independent are positioned as weak and dependent in interaction with others. It can work the other way as well, as illustrated by Taylor's (1992, 1994) studies of elderly individuals who actively construct themselves as old and frail (e.g. "I feel like a worn-out agent or man. Finished. Right near the edge of life" in Taylor 1994: 193). In these cases, younger conversational partners do not allow the elderly individual's frail identity to stand, but instead "redefine their disclosure as an issue of performance and competence (e.g. 'N'yer doin' a good job!'), shying away, perhaps, from what is threatening to those partners in an ageist culture: accepted mortality" (Taylor 1994: 193–4).

Whatever the outcome, here we see the great influence of conversational partners on the active, emergent, turn-by-turn construction of identities by/with/for elderly individuals in interaction. These provocative findings have wide-reaching implications, not only for family members, friends, and professional caregivers of elderly people, but for researchers engaged in data collection as well (see related points in section 3.5.3).

4.3   Social norms, values, and practices in old age

Another group of scholars interested in the relationship between aging and discourse focuses primarily on characterizing discourse practices by elderly individuals that display or reflect the speakers' social norms and values. These researchers come from the fields of anthropology, sociology, sociolinguistics, and communication studies; they study discourse from interviews, conversations, and interactions "listened in on."

Perhaps not surprisingly, when we step back from the individual studies, we notice that many of the identified practices can be understood as responses to change; e.g. comparing "the way it is" with "the way it was", disclosing painful information about the self even in conversations with relative strangers and in initial medical encounters, complaining, gossiping, disclosing chronological age, viewing friendship differently in older adulthood, and using service encounters to socialize.[23]

In this sense, we can see that elderly people have formed solid expectations about how life is – and their place in it – by having lived it for so many years. Now perched near the end of life, change bombards them from all sides – from within and from without. Decreased vision, hearing, mobility. Problems remembering. Loss of friends and family. New residence in a retirement community or a nursing home. New technology: computers, the Internet, CDs, DVDs. Increased sexuality on television and in the movies. Different patterns of immigration and neighborhood demographics in their hometowns.

Boden and Bielby (1986) noticed that the elderly speakers in their study frequently made direct comparisons between "the way it was" and "the way it is" as topic organizers in get-acquainted conversations with age-peers (e.g. "I've seen quite a few changes in Santa Clara," "I have too. I don't like it as well as I did when I came here.")[24] Not knowing each other's personal life experiences, these speakers referred frequently to historical events, time periods, and social experiences they assumed they must have shared due to their chronological age. In their study of get-acquainted conversations (both age-peer and intergenerational), Coupland et al. (1991: 112ff) noticed that their elderly speakers were prone to disclosing painful information about their lives, including bereavement, immobility, loneliness, and health problems (e.g. "My eyes are not so good," "I've got two false hips," "I've got emphysema"). Although Coupland et al. do not relate this practice to the "way it was" practice identified by Boden and Bielby, the same kind of contrast seems to underline these disclosures, but on a more personal level ("the way *I* was" vs. "the way *I* am"). This kind of discursive practice is much more typical of the elderly women in Coupland et al.'s study than of the younger women: elderly speakers disclosed something painful in 27 of the 30 conversations that included at least one elderly speaker (Coupland et al. 1991: 112ff), whereas younger speakers disclosed something painful in only seven of the 30 conversations in which they were involved.

These contrasts also lie at the heart of many of the complaints heard and discussed by Cattell (1999) in her ethnographic fieldwork among elderly people in rural western Kenya and in Philadelphia, Pennsylvania. These complaints often centered on perceived differences between young and old generations regarding family obligations (e.g. "The young don't want to walk with us" or "They don't want to sit and eat with us") and perceived ethnic changes in residential neighborhoods and shopping districts (e.g. "We don't speak the same language. We can't even talk to each other" and "I never see anyone I know on 5th Street any more"). Cattell (1999: 312) argues that researchers should not dismiss such complaints as "just what all old people do," but should recognize the strategic use of this practice through which the complainers "assur[e] their physical security and reassur[e] themselves as persons in settings of rapid social and cultural change."

Comparing the past to the present. Disclosing painful information. Complaining. These discursive practices can be seen as reasonable responses to change, but ones that may be subject to misinterpretation when (over)heard by those who do not share the same experiences of changing physical environments, changing bodies, and changing relationships. Eckert (1984: 229) reminds us of the danger inherent in intergenerational research (and, I would add, in intergenerational encounters of all kinds): "The elderly, being the farthest from the experience of the young and middle-aged researchers, comprise the age group that is most subject to stereotyping in linguistics as well as other research."

5   Conclusions

The goal of understanding how discourse and aging are related to each other challenges us to understand how language is used by large numbers of elderly individuals in many and varied contexts, both experimental and natural. Much progress has been made since the early 1980s or so. As on a painter's canvas that had been blank, bold strokes have been made in several areas and the background sketched out. Clusters of carefully detailed work can be found. Connections are starting to be made between these clusters. The only way to get closer to completing the picture, however, is through continued research from multiple perspectives. Ironically, perhaps, the biggest potential barrier to this goal is precisely this multidisciplinarity.

How, then, to proceed? First, it can be assumed that disciplinary training will often lead researchers to study only certain kinds of problems and to propose the most effective way of approaching only these problems (and, of course, certain problems may indeed be more easily solved with a particular approach); we should take care, however, not to allow this situation to blind us to the possibility of the creative solutions that can be found if one is brave enough to cross disciplinary boundaries.[25] To this end, we need to stay informed about developments within discourse analysis as well as within fields related to aging that may impact on discourse, such as memory, studies of social relationships, and ethnographies of nursing homes, hospitals, and hospices. Such awareness will open our eyes to areas of possible collaboration across disciplines and facilitate subsequent cross-disciplinary discussion. In this effort to understand aging and discourse, we should not forget that, in order to gain a true "insider's" perspective, we need to listen to voices of those who are old – either by incorporating them as coresearchers or at the minimum by finding out what they think in playback sessions or focus groups (see also Swallow 1986: 199; Copper 1986: 56).

Second, in order to make headway in understanding how discourse and aging are interrelated against the unceasing motion of the seemingly uncountable moving parts that represent the heterogeneity of the elderly population (see section 1), we need to continue to carry out studies of well-defined subgroups of the aging population who are engaged in specific activities in specific settings. It is only through studying particularity (Becker 1984) that we will come to illuminate more general issues. Each of these two areas – aging and discourse – is so large and multifaceted as to preclude any real understanding of their interconnections if each is not broken down into manageable parts.

Finally, despite the possible consequences of the previous paragraph, we need to take care *not* to lose sight of the human beings who are at the center of our research. Since scholarly literature typically reports findings regarding fairly narrowly defined discourse produced by *different* elderly individuals in *different* contexts, it is easy to forget that each participant in each study is a more complete human being than can be made apparent in any given context of language use. The Ruth Watkins whose ability to name objects in conversation was judged to be quite impaired by a standardized test is the same Ruth Watkins who writes the most persuasive letters-to-the-editor of all the environmental activists in her community. The Gerald Miller who hardly spoke a word in his visit to the oncologist is the same Gerald Miller who tells story after marvelous story to his squealing great-grandchildren. The Viola Green who cannot remember whether her husband is alive or not is the same Viola Green who can flawlessly recite a poem she learned in the seventh grade – 59 years ago.

In closing, then, the future of research into the interrelationships between discourse and aging looks bright if scholars continue to reach out to collaborators, both to experts in other disciplines and to members of the elderly population. Mounting evidence from multiple well-defined studies of particular groups of aging individuals will help us reach our goal: understanding how the biological, social, and psychological changes that people identify as aging influence the way these people use language and, conversely, how people's use of language can impact on the biological, social, and psychological changes that people perceive and identify as aging.

NOTES

1   More regular venues are also available now for discourse analysts who would like to present their work to other researchers interested in gerontological issues. The largest multidisciplinary conference on gerontology in the United States, the annual meeting of the Gerontological Society of America (GSA), welcomes both qualitative and quantitative analyses of discourse and has as part of its organization an informal interest group on language and communication. Additionally, the International Conference on Communication, Aging, and Health

meets regularly and sees itself
as providing a forum for sharing
state-of-the-art research as
well as contributing a coherent
interdisciplinary research agenda
on communication, aging, and
health.

2   E.g. Obler and Albert (1980); Bayles
and Kaszniak (1987); Ulatowska
(1985).

3   E.g. Coupland et al. (1991); Giles
et al. (1990); Hamilton (1996).

4   E.g. Hummert et al. (1994); Nussbaum
et al. (1989); Lubinski (1981).

5   See Caramazza (1986); McCloskey and
Caramazza (1988); Caramazza and
Badecker (1989); Moody (1989); and
Caramazza (1991); Hamilton (1994a)
for further discussion of this issue.

6   See, for example, Bower (1997: 266–9);
Hamilton (1994a: 17–19); Light (1993:
907–8); Melvold et al. (1994: 334).

7   It has often been noted, for example,
that individuals with early stages
of Alzheimer's disease can "mask"
the degree of their communicative
problems, such as naming difficulties,
by cleverly giving answers in such a
way as not to point to the problem
areas.

8   E.g. Bayles (1982); Bayles and
Kaszniak (1987); Ripich and Terrell
(1988); Hamilton (1994a, 1994b);
Blonder et al. (1994); Ramanathan
(1997); Obler et al. (1999); Emery
(1999).

9   E.g. Brownell and Joanette (1993);
Ulatowska et al. (1999).

10   E.g. Villaume et al. (1994).

11   Obler (1980); Obler et al. (1985);
Ulatowska et al. (1985, 1986); Kemper
(1987, 1990); Light (1988); Kemper
et al. (1990, 1992); Glosser and
Deser (1992); Emery (1999); Barresi
et al. (1999).

12   Bowles and Poon (1985); Nicholas
et al. (1985).

13   Walker et al. (1981, 1988); Kynette
and Kemper (1986); Kemper (1987).

14   Sandson et al. (1987); Gold et al.
(1988, 1994); Arbuckle and Gold
(1993).

15   Obler (1980); Ulatowska et al. (1985,
1986); Kemper (1990); Kemper et al.
(1990).

16   Bower (1997, 1999); Coupland and
Nussbaum (1993); Coupland and
Coupland (1995); Hamilton (1996);
Paoletti (1998); Rosenfeld (1999);
Sabat and Harré (1992); Taylor
(1992, 1994).

17   Ryan et al. (1986); Baltes and Wahl
(1992); Baltes et al. (1994).

18   Lubinski (1976, 1988); Smithers
(1977); Grainger et al. (1990);
Grainger (1993); Shadden (1995).

19   Coupland et al. (1992, 1994);
Coupland and Coupland (1998,
1999).

20   Sabat and Harré (1992); Hamilton
(1996).

21   See also Caporeal (1981); Culbertson
and Caporeal (1983); Caporeal and
Culbertson (1986); Kemper (1994);
Orange et al. (1995).

22   See, for example, Baltes and Wahl
(1992, 1987); Baltes et al. (1991).

23   Comparing: Boden and Bielby (1986).
Disclosing to strangers: Coupland et al.
(1991); Okazaki (1999). Disclosing in
initial medical encounters: Greene
et al. (1994). Complaining: Cattell
(1999). Gossiping: Saunders (1999).
Disclosing age: Coupland et al.
(1991); Giles et al. (1994). Viewing
friendship differently: Nussbaum
(1994). Socializing: Fredrickson
and Carstensen (1991). Wiemann
et al. (1990).

24   Examples from Boden and Bielby
(1986: 78). Transcription has been
simplified.

25   For example, when I began my
investigations of natural conversations
with an elderly woman who had been
diagnosed with Alzheimer's disease
in the early 1980s (as written up in
Hamilton 1991, 1994a, 1994b, 1996),

most scholars I talked with indicated to me that I should carry out my research within the paradigms recognized by psycholinguistics or neurolinguistics. The existing theoretical frameworks and methodologies in those literatures did not, however, allow me to capture what I sensed was potentially most significant about my subject's communicative abilities and how they were interrelated with my own communicative behavior in our conversations. In the face of these comments and recommendations, I had to continually ask myself what a sociolinguistic approach to this problem would look like and, indeed, whether it was possible. I found as time went on that such a crossing of the boundaries was not only possible but fruitful.

REFERENCES

Arbuckle, T. Y. and Gold, D. P. 1993. Aging, inhibition, and verbosity. *Journal of Gerontology: Psychological Sciences* 48: 225–32.

Baltes, Margret M. and Wahl, Hans-Werner. 1987. Dependency in aging. In: L. L. Carstensen and B. A. Edelstein (eds), *Handbook of Clinical Gerontology*, 204–11. New York: Pergamon Press.

Baltes, Margret M. and Wahl, Hans-Werner. 1992. The dependency–support script in institutions: generalization to community settings. *Psychology and Aging* 7: 409–18.

Baltes, Margret M., Neumann, Eva-Maria and Zank, Susanne. 1994. Maintenance and rehabilitation of independence in old age: an intervention program for staff. *Psychology and Aging* 9: 179–88.

Baltes, Margret M., Wahl, Hans-Werner, and Reichert, M. 1991. Successful aging in institutions? *Annual Review of Gerontology and Geriatrics* 11: 311–37.

Baltes, Paul B. and Mayer, Karl Ulrich (eds). 1999. *The Berlin Aging Study: Aging from 70–100*. Cambridge: Cambridge University Press.

Barresi, Barbara A., Obler, Loraine K., Au, Rhoda, and Albert, Martin L. 1999. Language-related factors influencing naming in adulthood. In: Heidi Hamilton (ed.), *Language and Communication in Old Age: Multidisciplinary Perspectives*, 77–90. New York: Garland.

Bayles, Kathryn. 1979. Communication profiles in a geriatric population. Unpublished PhD dissertation, University of Arizona.

Bayles, Kathryn. 1982. Language function in senile dementia. *Brain and Language* 16: 265–80.

Bayles, Kathryn and Kaszniak, A. 1987. *Communication and Cognition in Normal Aging and Dementia*. Boston: Little, Brown.

Beasley, D. S. and Davis, G. A. (eds). 1981. *Aging, Communication Processes and Disorders*. Orlando, FL: Grune and Stratton.

Becker, A. L. 1984. The linguistics of particularity: interpreting superordination in a Javanese text. *Proceedings of the Tenth Annual Meeting of the Berkeley Linguistics Society*, 425–36. Berkeley, CA: University of California Press.

Blonder, Lee Xenakis, Kort, Eva Deane, and Schmitt, Frederick A. 1994. Conversational discourse in patients with Alzheimer's disease. *Journal of Linguistic Anthropology* 1994: 50–71.

Boden, Deirdre and Bielby, Denise D. 1986. The way it was: topical organization in elderly conversation. *Language and Communication* 6: 73–89.

Bower, Anne. 1997. The role of narrative in the study of language and aging. *Journal of Narrative and Life History* 7: 265–74.

Bower, Anne. 1999. Evaluation in bereavement narratives of elderly Irish American widowers. In: Heidi E. Hamilton (ed.), *Language and Communication in Old Age: Multidisciplinary Perspectives*, 135–76. New York: Garland.

Bowles, N. L. and Poon, L. W. 1985. Aging and retrieval of words in semantic memory. *Journal of Gerontology* 40: 71–7.

Brownell, H. and Joanette, Y. (eds). 1993. *Narrative Discourse in Normal Aging and Neurologically Impaired Adults.* San Diego, CA: Singular.

Caporeal, Linnda. 1981. The paralanguage of caregiving: baby talk to the institutionalized aged. *Journal of Personality and Social Psychology* 40: 876–84.

Caporeal, Linnda and Culbertson, G. H. 1986. Verbal response modes of baby talk to the institutionalized aged. *Language and Communication* 6: 99–112.

Caramazza, A. 1986. On drawing inferences about the structure of normal cognitive systems from the analysis of impaired performance: the case for single-patient studies. *Brain and Cognition* 5: 41–66.

Caramazza, A. 1991. Data, statistics, and theory: a comment on Bates, McDonald, MacWhinney, and Applebaum's "A maximum likelihood procedure for the analysis of group and individual data in aphasia research." *Brain and Language* 41: 43–51.

Caramazza, A. and Badecker. 1989. Patient classification in neuropsychological

research. *Brain and Cognition* 10: 256–95.

Cattell, Maria. 1999. Elders' complaints: discourses on old age and social change in rural Kenya and urban Philadelphia. In: Heidi E. Hamilton (ed.), *Language and Communication in Old Age: Multidisciplinary Perspectives*, 295–318. New York: Garland.

Chafe, Wallace. 1994. *Discourse, Consciousness, and Time.* Chicago: University of Chicago Press.

Copper, Baba. 1986. Voices: on becoming old women. In: Jo Alexander, Debi Berrow, Lisa Domitrovich, Margarita Donnelly, and Cheryl McLean (eds), *Women and Aging: An Anthology by Women*, 47–57. Corvallis, OR: Calyx Books.

Counts, Dorothy Ayers and Counts, David R. 1985. *Aging and its Transformations: Moving toward Death in Pacific Societies.* Lanham, MD: University Press of America.

Coupland, Justine, Coupland, Nikolas, and Robinson, J. D. 1992. "How are you?": negotiating phatic communion. *Language in Society* 21: 207–30.

Coupland, Justine, Robinson, Jeffrey D., and Coupland, Nikolas. 1994. Frame negotiation in doctor–elderly patient consultations. *Discourse and Society* 5: 89–124.

Coupland, Nikolas and Coupland, Justine. 1995. Discourse, identity, and aging. In: Jon F. Nussbaum and Justine Coupland (eds), *Handbook of Communication and Aging Research*, 79–103. Mahwah, NJ: Lawrence Erlbaum.

Coupland, Nikolas and Coupland, Justine. 1998. Reshaping lives: constitutive identity work in geriatric medical consultations. *Text* 18, 159–89.

Coupland, Nikolas and Coupland, Justine. 1999. Ageing, ageism, and anti-ageism: moral stance in geriatric medical discourse. In: Heidi E. Hamilton (ed.), *Language and*

Communication in Old Age: Multidisciplinary Perspectives, 177–208. New York: Garland.

Coupland, Nikolas and Nussbaum, Jon F. (eds). 1993. *Discourse and Lifespan Identity*. Newbury Park, CA: Sage.

Coupland, Nikolas, Coupland, Justine, and Giles, Howard. 1989. Telling age in later life: identity and face implications. *Text* 9: 129–51.

Coupland, Nikolas, Coupland, Justine, and Giles, Howard. 1991. *Language, Society, and the Elderly*. Oxford: Blackwell.

Coupland, Nikolas, Coupland, Justine, Giles, Howard, and Henwood, K. 1988. Accommodating the elderly: invoking and extending a theory. *Language in Society* 17: 1–41.

Culbertson, G. H. and Caporeal, L. R. 1983. Complexity and content in baby talk and non-baby talk messages to institutionalized elderly. *Personality and Social Psychology Bulletin* 9: 305–12.

Eckert, Penelope. 1984. Age and linguistic change. In: David Kertzer and Jennie Keith (eds), *Age and Anthropological Theory*, 219–33. Ithaca, NY: Cornell.

Eckert, Penelope. 1997. Age as a sociolinguistic variable. In: Florian Coulmas (ed.), *The Handbook of Sociolinguistics*, 151–67. Oxford: Blackwell.

Emery, Olga. 1999. On the relationship between memory and language in the dementia spectrum of depression, Alzheimer Syndrome, and normal aging. In: Heidi E. Hamilton (ed.), *Language and Communication in Old Age: Multidisciplinary Perspectives*, 25–62. New York: Garland.

Fredrickson, B. L. and Carstensen, Laura L. 1991. Social selectivity in old age. Paper presented at the 44th Annual Scientific Meeting of the Gerontological Society of America, November 22–5, 1991. San Francisco, CA.

Giles, Howard, Coupland, Nikolas, and Wiemann, John M. (eds). 1990. *Communication, Health and the Elderly*. Manchester: Manchester University Press.

Giles, Howard, Fox, Susan, Harwood, Jake, and Williams, Angie. 1994. Talking age and aging talk: communicating through the lifespan. In: Mary Lee Hummert, John M. Wiemann, and Jon F. Nussbaum (eds), 130–61. *Interpersonal Communication in Older Adulthood*. Thousand Oaks, CA: Sage.

Glosser, Guila and Deser, Toni. 1992. A comparison of changes in macrolinguistic and microlinguistic aspects of discourse production in normal aging. *Journal of Gerontology* 47: 266–72.

Gold, Dolores Pushkar, Arbuckle, Tannis Y. and Andres, David. 1994. Verbosity in older adults. In: Mary Lee Hummert, John M. Wiemann, and Jon F. Nussbaum (eds), 107–29. *Interpersonal Communication in Older Adulthood*. Thousand Oaks, CA: Sage.

Gold, Dolores Pushkar, Andres, David, Arbuckle, Tannis Y., and Schwartzman, A. 1988. Measurement and correlates of verbosity in elderly people. *Journal of Gerontology* 43: 27–33.

Goodglass, H. and Kaplan, E. 1972. *Assessment of Aphasia and Related Disorders*. Philadelphia: Lea and Febiger.

Grainger, Karen. 1993. "That's a lovely bath dear": reality construction in the discourse of elderly care. *Journal of Aging Studies* 7: 247–62.

Grainger, Karen, Atkinson, Karen, and Coupland, Nikolas. 1990. Responding to the elderly: troubles-talk in the caring context. In Howard Giles, Nikolas Coupland, and John M. Wiemann (eds), *Communication, Health, and the Elderly*, 192–212.

Manchester: Manchester University Press.

Greene, Michele G., Adelman, Ronald D., Rizzo, Connie and Friedmann, Erika. 1994. The patient's presentation of self in an initial medical encounter. In: Mary Lee Hummert, John M. Wiemann, and Jon F. Nussbaum (eds), 226–50. *Interpersonal Communication in Older Adulthood.* Thousand Oaks, CA: Sage.

Gubrium, Jay. 1975. *Living and Dying at Murray Manor.* New York: St. Martin's.

Hamilton, Heidi. 1991. Accommodation and mental disability. In Howard Giles, Justine Coupland, and Nikolas Coupland (eds), *Contexts of Accommodation: Developments in Applied Sociolinguistics*, 157–86. Cambridge: Cambridge University Press.

Hamilton, Heidi. 1992. Bringing aging into the language/gender equation. In: Kira Hall, Mary Bucholtz, and Birch Moonwomon (eds), *Locating Power*, 240–9. Berkeley, CA: Berkeley Women and Language Group.

Hamilton, Heidi. 1994a. *Conversations with an Alzheimer's Patient: An Interactional Sociolinguistic Study.* Cambridge: Cambridge University Press.

Hamilton, Heidi. 1994b. Requests for clarification as evidence of pragmatic comprehension difficulty: the case of Alzheimer's disease. In: Ronald L. Bloom, Loraine K. Obler, Susan DeSanti, and Jonathan S. Ehlich (eds), *Discourse Analysis and Applications: Studies in Adult Clinical Populations*, 185–99. Hillsdale, NJ: Lawrence Erlbaum Associates.

Hamilton, Heidi. 1994c. Ethical issues for applying linguistics to clinical contexts: the case of speech–language pathology. In: Jeff Connor-Linton and Carolyn T. Adger (eds), special issue on Ethical Issues for Applying

Linguistics, *Issues in Applied Linguistics*: 207–23.

Hamilton, Heidi. 1996. Intratextuality, intertextuality, and the construction of identity as patient in Alzheimer's disease. *Text* 16: 61–90.

Hamilton, Heidi (ed.). 1999. *Language and Communication in Old Age: Multidisciplinary Perspectives.* New York: Garland.

Hummert, Mary Lee, Wiemann, John M., and Nussbaum, Jon F. (eds). 1994. *Interpersonal Communication in Older Adulthood.* Thousand Oaks, CA: Sage.

Irigaray, Luce. 1973. *Le langage des dements.* The Hague: Mouton.

Kemper, Susan. 1987. Life-span changes in syntactic complexity. *Journal of Gerontology* 42: 323–8.

Kemper, Susan. 1990. Adults' diaries: changes made to written narratives across the life span. *Discourse Processes* 13: 207–23.

Kemper, Susan. 1994. Elderspeak: speech accommodations to older adults. *Aging and Cognition* 1: 17–28.

Kemper, Susan, Kynette, D., and Norman, S. 1992. Age differences in spoken language. In: R. West and J. Sinnott (eds), *Everyday Memory and Aging: Current Research and Methodology*, 138–52. New York: Springer Verlag.

Kemper, Susan, Rash, S., Kynette, D., and Norman, S. 1990. Telling stories: the structure of adults' narratives. *European Journal of Cognitive Psychology* 2: 205–28.

Kynette, D. and Kemper, Susan. 1986. Aging and the loss of grammatical forms: a cross-sectional study of language performance. *Language and Communication* 6: 65–72.

Labov, William. 1972. *Sociolinguistic Patterns.* Philadelphia: University of Pennsylvania Press.

Light, Leah. 1988. Language and aging: competence versus performance. In: J. E. Birren and V. L. Bengtson (eds),

Emergent Theories of Aging, 177–213.
New York: Springer.

Light, Leah. 1993. *Language Change in Old Age*. In: Gerhard Blanken, Juergen Dittmann, Hannelore Grimm, John C. Marshall, and Claus W. Wallesch (eds), *Linguistic Disorders and Pathologies: An International Handbook*, 900–18. Berlin: Walter de Gruyter.

Lubinski, Rosemary. 1976. Perceptions of oral–verbal communication by residents and staff of an institution for the chronically ill and aged. Unpublished PhD dissertation, Columbia University Teachers College.

Lubinski, Rosemary. 1981. Language and aging: an environmental approach to intervention. *Topics in Language Disorders* 1: 89–97.

Lubinski, Rosemary. 1988. A model for intervention: communication skills, effectiveness, and opportunity. In Barbara Shadden (ed.), *Communication Behavior and Aging*, 294–308. Baltimore: Williams and Wilkins.

McCloskey, M. and Caramazza, A. 1988. Theory and methodology in cognitive neuropsychology: a response to our critics. *Cognitive Neuropsychology* 5: 583–623.

Melvold, Janis L., Au, Rhoda, Obler, Loraine K., and Albert, Martin L. 1994. Language during aging and dementia. In: Martin L. Albert and Janice Knoefel (eds), *Clinical Neurology of Aging* (2nd edn), 329–46. New York: Oxford University Press.

Moerman, Michael. 1996. The field of analyzing foreign language conversations. *Journal of Pragmatics* 26: 147–58.

Moody, H. 1989. Gerontology with a human face. In: L. E. Thomas (ed.), *Research on Adulthood and Aging*, 227–40. Albany: SUNY Press.

Nelson, E. Anne and Dannefer, Dale. 1992. Aged heterogeneity: fact or fiction? *Gerontologist* 32: 17–23.

Nicholas, M., Obler, L., Albert, M., and Goodglass, H. 1985. Lexical retrieval in healthy aging. *Cortex* 21: 595–606.

Nussbaum, Jon. 1994. Friendship in older adulthood. In: Mary Lee Hummert, John M. Wiemann, and Jon F. Nussbaum (eds), *Interpersonal Communication in Older Adulthood*, 209–225. Thousand Oaks, CA: Sage.

Nussbaum, Jon F., Thompson, Teresa, and Robinson, James D. 1989. *Communication and Aging*. New York: Harper and Row.

Obler, Loraine K. 1980. Narrative discourse style in the elderly. In: Loraine K. Obler and Martin L. Albert (eds), *Language and Communication in the Elderly: Clinical, Therapeutic, and Experimental Aspects*, 75–90. Lexington, MA: D. C. Heath.

Obler, Loraine K. and Albert, Martin L. (eds). 1980. *Language and Communication in the Elderly: Clinical, Therapeutic, and Experimental Aspects*. Lexington, MA: D. C. Heath.

Obler, Loraine K., Nicholas, M., Albert, Martin L., and Woodward, S. 1985. On comprehension across the adult lifespan. *Cortex* 21: 273–80.

Obler, Loraine K., Obermann, Lorraine, Samuels, Ina, and Albert, Martin L. 1999. Written input to enhance comprehension of dementia of the Alzheimer's type. In: Heidi Hamilton (ed.), *Language and Communication in Old Age: Multidisciplinary Perspectives*, 63–75. New York: Garland.

Okazaki, Shoko Yohena. 1999. "I can't drive": painful self-disclosure in intergenerational talk. In: Heidi Hamilton (ed.), *Language and Communication in Old Age: Multidisciplinary Perspectives*, 233–63. New York: Garland.

Orange, J. B., Ryan, Ellen Bouchard, Meredith, Sheree D., and MacLean, Michael. 1995. Application of the communication enhancement model for long-term care residents with

Alzheimer's disease. *Topics in Language Disorders* 15: 21–37.

Paoletti, Isabella. 1998. *Being an Older Woman: A Study in the Social Production of Identity*. Mahwah, NJ: Lawrence Erlbaum Associates.

Ramanathan, Vai. 1997. *Alzheimer Discourse: Some Sociolinguistic Dimensions*. Mahwah, NJ: Lawrence Erlbaum Associates.

Randall, Margaret. 1986. From: The Journals. In: Jo Alexander, Debi Berrow, Lisa Domitrovich, Margarita Donnelly, and Cheryl McLean (eds), *Women and Aging: An Anthology by Women*, 127–30. Corvallis, OR: Calyx Books.

Ripich, D. and Terrell, B. 1988. Patterns of discourse cohesion and coherence in Alzheimer's disease. *Journal of Speech and Hearing Disorders* 53: 8–15.

Rosenfeld, Elif. 1999. When and how old age is relevant in discourse of the elderly: a case study of Georgia O'Keeffe. In: Heidi Hamilton (ed.), *Language and Communication in Old Age: Multidisciplinary Perspectives*, 209–32. New York: Garland.

Ryan, Ellen Bouchard, Hummert, Mary Lee, and Boich, Linda H. 1995. Communication predicaments of aging: patronizing behavior toward older adults. *Journal of Language and Social Psychology* 14: 144–66.

Ryan, Ellen Bouchard, Giles, Howard, Bartolucci, Giampiero, and Henwood, Karen. 1986. Psycholinguistic and social psychological components of communication by and with the elderly. *Language and Communication* 6: 1–24.

Sabat, Steven and Harré, Rom. 1992. The construction and deconstruction of self in Alzheimer's disease. *Ageing and Society* 12: 443–61.

Sandson, J., Obler, L. K., and Albert, M. L. 1987. Language changes in healthy aging and dementia. In: S. Rosenberg (ed.), *Advances in Applied Psycholinguistics*, vol. 1, 264–92. New York: Cambridge University Press.

Saunders, Pamela. 1999. Gossip in an older women's support group: a linguistic analysis. In: Heidi Hamilton (ed.), *Language and Communication in Old Age: Multidisciplinary Perspectives*, 267–93. New York: Garland.

Schwartz, M. F., Marin, O., and Saffran, E. 1979. Dissociations of language function in dementia: a case study. *Brain and Language* 7: 277–306.

Shadden, Barbara B. (ed.). 1995. Language and communication in the nursing home environment. *Topics in Language Disorders* 15: 2.

Smithers, Janice. 1977. Dimensions of senility. *Urban Life* 6: 251–76.

Swallow, Jean. 1986. Both feet in life: interviews with Barbara Macdonald and Cynthia Rich. In: Jo Alexander, Debi Berrow, Lisa Domitrovich, Margarita Donnelly, and Cheryl McLean (eds), *Women and Aging: An Anthology by Women*, 193–203. Corvallis, OR: Calyx Books.

Tannen, Deborah. 1984. *Conversational Style: Analyzing Talk Among Friends*. Norwood, NJ: Ablex.

Taylor, Bryan C. 1992. Elderly identity in conversation: producing frailty. *Communication Research* 19: 493–515.

Taylor, Bryan C. 1994. Frailty, language, and elderly identity: interpretive and critical perspectives on the aging subject. In: Mary Lee Hummert, John M. Wiemann, and Jon F. Nussbaum (eds), *Interpersonal Communication in Older Adulthood: Interdisciplinary Theory and Research*, 185–208. Thousand Oaks, CA: Sage.

Ulatowska, Hanna (ed.). 1985. *The Aging Brain: Communication in the Elderly*. San Diego, CA: College-Hill Press.

Ulatowska, Hanna, Chapman, Sandra Bond, and Johnson, Julene. 1999. Inferences in processing of text in elderly populations. In: Heidi

Hamilton (ed.), *Language and Communication in Old Age: Multidisciplinary Perspectives*, 91–144. New York: Garland.

Ulatowska, Hanna, Cannito, M. P., Hayashi, M. M., and Fleming, S. 1985. Language abilities in the elderly. In: Hanna Ulatowska (ed.), *The Aging Brain: Communication in the Elderly*, 125–39. San Diego, CA: College-Hill Press.

Ulatowska, Hanna, Hayashi, M. M., Cannito, M. P., and Fleming, S. G. 1986. Disruption of reference in aging. *Brain and Language* 28: 24–41.

Villaume, William A., Brown, Mary Helen, and Darling, Rieko. 1994. Presbycusis, communication, and older adults. In: Mary Lee Hummert, John M. Wiemann, and Jon F. Nussbaum (eds), *Interpersonal Communication in Older Adulthood*, 83–106. Thousand Oaks, CA: Sage.

Walker, V. G., Roberts, P. M., and Hedrick, D. L. 1988. Linguistic analyses of the discourse narrative of young and aged women. *Folia Phoniatrica* 40: 58–64.

Walker, V. G., Hardiman C. J., Hedrick, D. L., and Holbrook, A. 1981. Speech and language characteristics of an aging population. In: N. J. Lass (ed.), *Advances in Basic Research and Practice*, vol. 6, 143–202. Orlando, FL: Academic Press.

Ward, Russell. 1984. The marginality and salience of being old: when is age relevant? *Gerontologist* 24: 227–32.

Wiemann, J., Gravell, R., and Wiemann, M. 1990. Communication with the elderly: implications for health care and social support. In: Howard Giles, Nikolas Coupland, and J. Wiemann (eds), *Communication, Health and Ageing*, 229–42. Manchester: Manchester University Press.

30 Child Discourse

JENNY COOK-GUMPERZ AND
AMY KYRATZIS

0 Introduction: Placing Child Discourse in a Tradition

In the years since Ervin-Tripp and Mitchell-Kernan published the first book on child discourse (Ervin-Tripp and Mitchell-Kernan 1977), the field has moved through a series of changes. By turning to a discourse-centered approach, researchers have been able to shift focus, placing the child's learning process and productive pragmatic use at the center of their concern. The early discourse approach developed as a counter to traditional language acquisition studies, which centered on discovering how children could overcome the limitations of their incomplete grammatical system. Such studies made judgments of the child's ability to approximate to the adult norm based on direct elicitation in quasi-experimental settings. The impact of *Child Discourse* (Ervin-Tripp and Mitchell-Kernan 1977) along with *Developmental Pragmatics* (Ochs and Schieffelin 1979), began a movement towards situationally embedded activities as the domain of child language studies.

Researchers' interests began to turn away from exclusively psycholinguistic concerns with factors underlying the development of formal structures to concentrate on contextually situated learning. The discourse focus looked at children in naturally occurring settings and activities, and paid attention to their speech and communicative practice in everyday situations (Cook-Gumperz and Gumperz 1976; Keller-Cohen 1978). This research went beyond linguistic competence to what became known as the child's acquisition of communicative competence, which is seen as the knowledge that underlies socially appropriate speech. This approach was influenced by ethnography of communication (which saw communicative competence as a contrastive concept to the Chomskyan notion of linguistic competence), and involved theories of sociolinguistics, speech act usage, and conversational analysis. Although little conversational analytic work was done at that time, by the late 1970s and 1980s there was a growing interest in children's conversational competence (McTear 1985; Ochs and Schieffelin 1979).

0.1   Language socialization and the acquisition of discourse

The ethnographic approach to acquisition served to refocus studies of children's acquisition to the problem of how language learners are able to be participating members of a social group by acquiring social and linguistic skills necessary for interaction. The term **language socialization** came to represent this new focus. As Ochs and Schieffelin, who provided one of the first collections to address these concerns (Ochs and Schieffelin 1986), commented: language socialization involves "both socialization through language and socialization to use language" (Ochs and Schieffelin 1986: 2). The focus on language-mediated interactions as the mechanism of production–reproduction is the unique contribution of language socialization to the core problem of how societies continue. From this perspective both the sociocultural contexts of speaking, and the ways of speaking within specifically defined speech events of a social group or society, became primary research sites (Heath 1983). In contrast to earlier studies of language acquisition, which focused on the acquisition of grammatical patterns, and later studies, which looked at children's speech acts, the new approach looked at speaking embedded in specific interactive situations and at the communicative, as distinct from linguistic, competence that these practices revealed (Hymes 1962).

By the mid-1980s the shift to language socialization was responsible for highlighting what it means for a young child to participate in meaningful language exchanges and to become an active agent in her or his own development, to which discourse competence was an essential key (Cook-Gumperz et al. 1986). Children require both broad cultural knowledge about social relationships and an understanding of the social identities that define their position in a social world. Yet they also need to be active producers of the linguistic practices that construct these identities. While language socialization studies introduced the idea of studying child-centered communicative activities, interest in the later 1980s in peer speech redirected these concerns toward the child as member of a culture that was different from that of the adult world (Corsaro 1985). As part of this rising interest in peers and peer cultures came a concern with the particular speech activities that children generate for themselves. Goodwin's collection *He-Said-She-Said* was an example. This ethnographic study looked at the role of children's disputes in organizing peer cultures (Goodwin 1990). Within this peer context, the whole notion of conversational competence was shifted, such that children became the arbiters of their own conversational practices and rules of appropriateness.

Thus the growing interest in how the child's language knowledge differs from adult linguistic knowledge, and helps children organize their social and emotional worlds, refocused child discourse inquiry. For example, the edited collection *Narratives from the Crib* (Nelson 1989) represents a new direction focusing on different genres of communicative activity. In this volume, a young girl's bedtime narratives are instrumental in her understanding of the social and emotional events taking place in her life.

To summarize, in child discourse research through the 1980s, discourse-centered studies address the following areas. First, what does it mean socially and psychologically for the child to have an ever-increasing linguistic control over her or his social environment? Secondly, these studies focus on sociolinguistic practices and on events that are meaningful from the child's point of view, such as games, teasing rituals, and pretend play routines. They explore children's developing competence in their own peer world. Thirdly, child discourse studies began to focus on children's lives in a broader sociocultural context, looking at children as learners of particular social-cultural and linguistic knowledge. The studies look at how using language and acquiring language is part of what it means to become a member of a wider society.

0.2   Present-day studies of children's discourse

The themes that most characterize the field today, and that we pick up on in this chapter, involve looking at the child within a more complicated social context, one which leaves some space for her or him to have a role in its construction. Current studies are for the most part looking at a much richer notion of context, at children making meaning in their lives, not just having transmitted to them an already-formed notion of culture from adults. They look at children's worlds as a valid part of socialization theory. The concept of children's social worlds is one in which children organize their concerns and social experiences through talk. From this perspective, researchers look at how talk is part of an interactional sequence and at how it realizes social goals. Finally, we suggest that children's discourse studies have come full circle from language acquisition, which started with diary studies of children's language in meaningful contexts (e.g. Halliday 1977; Locke 1993), to now, when concern with the implications of language for self-relevance, for sense-making, and for the construction of peer cultures and children's worlds once again focuses on detailed studies over time of a child or children's language and discourse. An example is M. Shatz's *A Toddler's Life* (1997), which looks not just at children's patterns of acquisition, but at how a space is made for children to become effective communicators and sense-makers of their world.

   With these issues in mind, we will review some of the most relevant studies in two main situational domains: adult–child discourse and child–child discourse. Under adult–child discourse, we review studies in pragmatics of family life, personhood and self-identity (where space is made for the child to begin to reflect on her or his own experience), and morality in the talk of everyday life (such as dinner-table narratives, politeness routines, and other adult–child exchanges). Under child–child discourse, we review studies in the areas of peer talk for organizing peer group ranking and morality within the peer group and the interactional accomplishment of gender.

1   Adult–Child Discourse

1.1   The pragmatics of family life

The world of the family, with its often subtle distinctions of power and authority, provides children with their earliest learning experiences of how verbal communication can effect interpersonal relationships. By participating in family life, children gain practical experience of family dynamics and how talk is used to control, to persuade, or to conceal real intentions. Family discourse, particularly at mealtimes and on other ceremonial occasions, provides the essential testing-ground where children hone their skills as communicators. It is in the family group that children listen to and learn to construct narratives, tales that reflect past and future events (Heath 1982). And it is through the pragmatic conventions of daily conversations that the relative positioning of family members is constructed as part of daily discursive practice. In family discussion, children are able to observe how talk reflects, and at times constructs, status relationships of gender, age, and power by the ways people talk to each other and about each other. It is also through family discussion that children first become aware of relationships in a world beyond the family.

1.1.1 Issues of power and control

Ervin-Tripp, focusing on the pragmatic conventions of family talk, provides important insights into the linguistic means by which interpersonal relationships are negotiated through the daily activity of family talk. Her analysis concentrates specifically on the speech acts or activities, such as requests, directives, greetings and politeness expressions, jokes, and complaints, that demonstrate control of one person over another. In a paper on "Language and power in the family" (Ervin-Tripp et al. 1984: 119), she points out the need to distinguish between effective power, "the ability in a face-to-face interaction to get compliance from an addressee," and esteem, "as the right to receive verbal deference." In other words, there is not a direct correspondence between descriptors of status and everyday verbal behavior. Rather, by looking at everyday discourse, we become aware of the variety of factors of context, interactants, social position, and/or emotional involvement, as well as activity scene, that all enter into choices of verbal strategies, and on a situation-specific basis determine pragmatic choice. Ervin-Tripp et al., for example, examine how these factors influence choice of request forms (1984). Among other things, Ervin-Tripp argues that there is a relationship between the degree of indirectness of the request, the esteem of the person to whom the request is made, and the power of the speaker making the request (Ervin-Tripp et al. 1990). It is now well known that children will issue direct commands to younger children in play, while recognizing the need to be indirect to those older and with higher status in the play situation. However, such indirect strategies are not necessarily employed with parents, with whom the child has a greater emotional involvement, for parents in their turn insist at least on politeness markers as a symbol of nominal deference to their adult status (Gleason 1988; Ervin-Tripp 1976, 1977; Wootton 1997). Thus, pragmatic choices, in something as apparently simple as request forms, reveal the real complexities of the discourse knowledge necessary for children to become competent communicators in everyday settings.

The range and complexity of children's social knowledge is further revealed by the way they act out family roles in pretend play (Andersen 1990). In a pioneering study of children's understanding of family and other adult roles, Andersen used puppets as supportive props for children to play out a freely chosen selection of roles and scenes, involving, among others, medical and family settings. Her findings go further in showing the range of children's knowledge of status relationships. In role-playing games, children reveal a range of understandings of the complexities of directives and requests. The social cost of the request becomes a part of the choice of pragmatic form. There is no absolute right and wrong form but a situationally appropriate choice (Andersen 1990; Mitchell-Kernan and Kernan 1977). For example, in a doctor-and-nurse game, while doctors may give direct orders, nurses must make indirect requests. The higher-status role will also use more discourse markers such as "OK," "now," and "so" (e.g. Andersen's example of the teacher puppet saying "OK, now, so"). In both medical settings and family play, girls and boys in nursery school compete for the high-status positions. They do not see any of these roles as being gender-specific, but rather as giving local power within the game action to exert control or give rewards (Cook-Gumperz in press).

1.1.2　Dinner-table talk

A key site for looking at children's complementary roles within the family is dinner-table conversations. Children's discourse has been explored from the point of view of the participation frameworks of family routines and in particular looking at children's speech strategies during dinner-table talk and narratives. Richard Watts (1991), in a study of power in family discourse, states that the distribution of power in families can be directly related to members' success in verbal interaction, and in particular the ability to achieve and maintain the floor to complete any interactional goal. Blum-Kulka, looking at family dinner-time narratives in Israeli and American middle-class families, shows that in families, children are less likely to master the more complex kinds of interruptions and only manage to gain the floor if it is conceded to them by adults. Moreover, there is cultural variation in how interruptions of another's turn are interpreted, whether as involvement or as inappropriately taking the floor (Blum-Kulka 1997).

Ochs and Taylor (1995) documented children's understanding of the linguistic marking of status and power relationships within families in a different way. They focused on the participation structure of dinner-time storytelling among family members. In white middle-class American families, mothers and children share reports of trouble and fathers take the role of problematizer, often negatively evaluating other members' actions. This participation structure, in which children share, helps to construct power differentials within the family.

One way in which the child becomes aware of the social order is that it is modeled for them by the adult caretakers around them. Their place in the social ordering can differ cross-culturally or with other social-cultural factors, such as social class, family size, and birth order. As we explore in the next section, the child's identity is not a social given, not merely an expression of the social world into which she or he is born; rather it is realized through the interactive use of language.

1.2　Personhood and self-identity

1.2.1　How children understand their own position in a social world

How the child gains a realization of who she or he is as a person within a social and cultural world is a critical part of child discourse inquiry. Language is used by the child actively to construct a social identity and a self-awareness that comes with the self-reflexiveness made possible through the grammatical, semantic, and pragmatic resources of language.

Shatz, in a diary study of her own grandson, Ricky's, language development through the first three years of his life, describes how, in acquiring a language, the child becomes a social person. She comments:

> I argue that the toddler acquires in language a powerful tool for learning. By coupling language with self-reflectiveness and attention to internal states that have begun to manifest themselves, the toddler can learn in new ways about new things. She can get from others information not based on immediate experience, and she can compare her own experience of feelings and thoughts with statements of others about theirs. Thus, the world becomes many-faceted, beyond immediate experience and limited perspectives. (1994: 191)

With many examples, Shatz shows how Ricky gives voice to a sense of social belonging. One example describes his growing awareness of familial group membership, of belonging to a social entity with common practices and discourse. At age three, during a family gathering, he looked around the dinner table at everyone and said, "I think you call this a group" (Shatz 1997: 191). Yet at the same time, this dawning sense of his or her place in the familial group provides the child with a reflexive awareness of himself or herself as a person who is able to recognize the group and his or her own place within it. The child's growing ability to refine his or her language to be able to discuss and consider whether events are possible and to contemplate nonimmediate phenomena requires a growing control over complex grammatical features like verb aspect and modality. The result becomes the ability to realize someone else's viewpoint as different from your own and to hold these two contradictory views in mind at once. Shatz gives an example of Ricky's situationally embedded counterfactuals. He is able to say to his grandmother when he surprises her for a second morning without his pajamas, "You thought they was wet," as they had been the previous morning. The intent is counterfactual but relies on the situation rather than the more explicit lexical means of adult usage. Although this is a fairly simple utterance, Ricky's joke depended on his ability to recognize his grandmother's perspective as different from his own, and only a detailed discourse study would be able to capture such events and so account for the child's growing competence.

In a similar vein, Budwig shows how children's uses of self-reference pronouns give rise to differences of perspective on their social world and their position as an actor and active agent within it. Looking at the development of agentive causality and the use of self-reference forms, she points out that it is only by focusing on discursive practice that the real range of children's usage can be appreciated (Budwig 1990). In a detailed study of six different children's developmentally changing uses of self-reference forms between two and three years of age, she noted that the idea of personal agency appears earlier in children's discourse than the ability to attribute intentions to others (that becomes part of a wider sense of independent agency). Budwig discovers a major difference in orientation between children who habitually use only first person reference pronouns ("I") and those who in similar situations use two different forms, "I" and "me–my." These choices did not vary with age or gender but rather reflect what could be considered a personal difference in orientation to the world, as either ego-focused or nonego-focused. Other studies have found similar differences in children's choice of self-reference forms that seem to reflect a difference in self-as-experiencer/reflector-on-world and self-as-agent/controller-of-the-world (Gerhardt 1988). Through these means children can be seen as experiencers/reflectors-on-reality as well as actors-on-reality.

The child's sense of herself or himself as a reflective person able to distinguish her or his own feelings and thoughts from others is illustrated by many of the chapters in Nelson's edited volume *Narratives from the Crib* (Nelson 1989). In this volume, researchers analyze the bedtime monologues of a two- to three-year-old child, Emily. They demonstrate how, through her night-time retellings of the day's events to herself, the little girl learns to come to terms with her feelings and her reactions to the events surrounding the arrival of her new baby brother. At the same time, she gains awareness of herself as a separate person within the nexus of her family. By examining how the narratives become linguistically and pragmatically more complex, Nelson and her collaborators provide a basis for the understanding of the relations between a growing narrative skill and the development of the sense of personhood.

1.3   Talk and the morality of everyday life

As the growing child engages others within a complex set of relationships, issues of right and wrong arise. What actions mean to others, whether hurtful or supportive, and what others mean by their words and deeds, become the subject of both adult–child and peer exchanges. It is through such everyday conversations that children gain knowledge of the fabric of everyday morality, that is, of how the social world works. Talk about emotions, caring for others' feelings, recognizing your own feelings, and how to manage your body and self in socially appropriate ways all have culturally different and conventionally expected ways of expression. Such cultural differences in ways of talking about these matters range from formulaic expressions of regret for such minor infringements as bodily noises (Clancy 1986), through sanctions against overtly expressing annoyance (Briggs 1997; Scollon and Scollon 1981), through expressions of care showing concern for others and responsibility for younger siblings and other children (as Schieffelin (1989) shows with the Kaluli), to children's use of respect forms of address which show the obligations not only of caring for others (Nakamura 2001) but of paying respect across generations (Ochs 1988; Schieffelin 1990; Watson-Gegeo and Gegeo 1986).

1.3.1   Rules and routines

However, moral talk essentially is embedded within the routines of daily life and its ordinary talk about actions, events, and the outcomes of these. For example, Wootton (1986) argues that morality is not a matter of learning to match behavior to abstract rules or principles, but rather depends on awareness of the local possibilities for actions that follow in response to sequences of talk. That is, it is through situated action that the child becomes aware of the social ordering of relationships and grows to realize the obligations these entail. In a later detailed study of a two-year-old learning to use request forms, Wootton demonstrates how sequencing in everyday talk contexts provides local occasions of social knowledge of rights and wrongs. He shows how a two-year-old protests when a parent, having forgotten what she had previously said, proposes a course of action that conflicts with the child's expectation (Wootton 1997). Children, in other words, pay close attention to adults' actions and words, early in life developing a sense of the infringement of a "moral order" that results from what they see as inconsistencies. In this way, a sense of right and wrong emerges from involvement in apparently trivial daily discourse. It is through participation in such communicative encounters that children become everyday moralists, who, by paying attention to the details of interactions and talk, hold others to the expected outcomes of what has been said.

1.3.2   *Expressing feelings and politeness*

A critical aspect of moral learning is emotional socialization. Children develop the capacity to recognize the consequences of actions for their own and others' feelings, and learn to express these feelings in an accepted form. Mothers' and other caretakers' expressions of love, joy, annoyance, displeasure, concern, and admonishment provide their children with moral insight into human relations and how these are encoded in a discourse of feeling. In enacting family relationships during peer play, children reveal and often overcommunicate mothers' or fathers' caring talk by scolding, shouting, cajoling, and other expressions of concern for the correct behavior of others. In this way, what Cook-Gumperz (1995) has called "the discourse of mothering" not only reproduces a version of the activity but enables the child to practice the situational enactment of relationships through talk. The process of acquisition here is somewhat similar to that illustrated in earlier grammar acquisition studies, namely an overgeneralization followed by a progressive refinement of patterns governing both grammar and a discourse of feeling (Ochs 1988; Duranti 1992). Schieffelin goes further in her ethnographic study of the Kaluli children by showing how children are socialized into the performance of the relationship of talk in action, by making appropriate voicing and prosody to communicate concern. That is, as both Ochs and Schieffelin (1987) argue, it is not only through the correct formulaic expressions and the appropriate lexical and syntactic forms that emotion is conveyed, but through correct performance in which children may learn to display an appropriate understanding or stance vis-à-vis their own and others' actions. In a similar vein, Heath (1983) in the Trackton study and Miller (1982) in south Baltimore have shown how many working-class mothers encourage their children to engage in challenging verbal routines, even with adults, which reveal their ability to be resilient in a difficult public world. These community-based displays of toughness can be problematic for children in the multicommunity-based context of school and preschool (Corsaro and Rosier 1992). In teasing routines, child and adult enter into a mutual verbal sparring exchange. These are part of a cultural nexus of challenge that enables children to rehearse the skills deemed necessary by adults to show resilience to life's adversities (Eisenberg 1986; Miller and Sperry 1988).

Politeness strategies constitute an alternative to verbal challenges, and may be seen as a way to avoid offense and anticipate or deflect possible difficulties (Brown and Levinson 1987). And as Brown has shown in a traditional Highland Chiapas village, women in particular engage in complex strategies such as hedging and the use of indirectness markers to manage their relations with others, and these strategies become part of young women's talk (Brown 1994). Similarly, in Nakamura's (2001) study of pretend play, for Japanese nursery children, the use of politeness becomes a part of the rehearsal of adult roles (1999).

1.3.3   Narrative accounts as everyday morality: narrative form and topic inclusion

One of the key discourse domains in which everyday morality is most apparent is personal narratives used to justify actions, to recall past events, or to express opinions about others. Blum-Kulka (1997), in comparing family dinner-table talk, found that Israeli and American middle-class families differed in the extent to which they allowed the child to be the focus of the storytelling attention, and the extent to which parents stressed that "tall tales" or exaggerations were inappropriate. In contrast, working-class families, such as the Trackton African-American working class community that Heath (1983) studied, and the white working-class families studied by Miller et al. (1986), valued exaggerations as a display of linguistic competence (smart talk). It is just such mismatches in the expectations about discourse practices between the home and mainstream school community that can be a source of difficulty for young children (Michaels 1986).

As Gee (1988) and Michaels (1988), among others, have shown, adults take up topics that children offer in conversation and use these to guide children toward telling stories that display canonical narratives. These narratives are in line with a literate standard, having a beginning, a middle of complicating actions, and a highlighted ending (Gee 1986; Michaels 1988). Other studies exploring spontaneously occurring narratives between parents and their young children that happen during daily activities at home also show how adults appraise children's stories and see their own role as encouraging them to find a coherent story line, and how children can differentiate narrative genres (Hicks 1991; Hudson and Shapiro 1991).

Discourse analysis focuses on the ways in which children give narrative sequencing to events, provide coherence to the actions in the story, and are able to attribute motives to themselves and others, as well as provide an emotional evaluation. In this way, recent study of narratives, building on Heath's original point in "What no bedtime story means" (Heath 1982), shows that narratives become not only a means of developing a literate sense of story, but also a means of knowing how to express feelings and thoughts in culturally acceptable ways. In this way, narrative experiences help to develop a moral sensibility about the consequences of actions for both the self and others.

2   Child–Child Discourse

2.1   The language of children as peers: creating discourse cohesion and coherence

As described, peer talk is important in the development of the study of child discourse, in that it shifts the focus away from how children reproduce culture as it is transmitted to them from adults to how they produce culture for themselves. One area in which this has been explored extensively is in that of gender, where children appropriate gender ideologies from the adult culture, displaying and altering them for their own purposes. This topic is explored below.

One of the earliest concerns in the study of peer talk was in the creation of coherence and cohesion (McTear 1985). This concern arose from Piaget's (1926) claim that children were incapable of nonegocentric speech until age seven. Piaget characterized children's peer conversations in the pre-operational period of development as "collective monologue," conversations where children's responses to their conversational partners were noncontingent. Only older children were capable of engaging in cooperative speech. Later researchers, including Parten (1933) and Bakeman and Gottman (1986), graded levels of the cline between noncontingent and cooperative speech.

McTear (1985) examined turn-taking in children's conversations. It had been proposed that children's turn-taking differs from the model proposed by Sacks et al. (1974) for adults in that there are fewer overlaps and longer gaps. Children have difficulty projecting possible turn completion points; Garvey and Berninger (1981) reported that gaps were only slightly longer than in adult conversation in their child data. McTear (1985) reported that in a longitudinal sample of two children's talk, overlaps increased as the children grew older. However, even younger children displayed the ability to monitor the turn in progress, not only for its projected completion, but for its projected content, as seen in self-initiated other-repair when the partner had trouble completing her turn.

McTear (1985) also studied the development of coherent dialogue. He examined children's use of various surface devices which are used to show cohesive ties between utterances, including ellipsis, pronouns, and connectives. Even at younger ages, children could use various functions. "Now" would be used to signal a switch in topic and "well" to indicate a dispreferred response. "Because" was used first as an attention-getter ("it crashed because it's broken") before it was used in the sense of strict event causality ("it crashed because I dropped it"). This mirrors other researchers' developmental findings. Kyratzis et al. (1990) and Kyratzis and Ervin-Tripp (1999), relying on terminology developed by Sweetser (1990), found that speech act-level uses of "because" developmentally preceded content-level uses. In speech act-level uses, the reason justifies why the speaker is making a specific claim or speech act (as in McTear's "it crashed because it's broken") rather than explaining why an event happened, that is, in a content- or event-based sense. This developmental progression from pragmatic to mathetic uses was explained in terms of children's discourse practices. Young children are more likely to seek to justify and get compliance for requests than to explain event contingencies in the world, a more cognitive-reflective practice (see also Sprott 1992).

In terms of coherence, the earliest type that children could construct was that between questions and answers. Responses to questions initially tended to be repetitions of the partner (Ervin-Tripp 1976). Older children could respond to statements as well as questions, but they also did this first through repetition. Older children displayed more diverse ways of creating continuity in dialog. McTear (1985) examined children's next-contributions. He found that most were relevant, but older children were more likely to add new information, such as justifications and elaborations, to which partners could, in turn, respond. Younger children's next-contributions tended to be responses without initiations, meaning that conversational topics abruptly ended and new ones had to be introduced abruptly, lending a choppier feel.

Children's coherence has been examined in play and dispute exchanges (McTear 1985; Garvey 1974). These start out as series of rounds, repeatable exchange units. In both play and disputes, young children often engage in ritual cycles of assertion/counterassertion. In play, this can take the form of sound play. In disputes, it takes the form of rounds of assertion, challenge, and counterchallenge. What develops to move children away from rounds-structure in disputes is the ability to supply justifications (Dunn and Munn 1987). Dunn and Munn's findings can be reformulated in terms used in McTear's (1985) analysis. While younger children's next-contributions were relevant (e.g. objections), older children could add new information (e.g. justifications for the challenges) which in turn could be responded to (e.g. challenged and justified). Younger children display format-tying through repetition while older children do it through more varied means, introducing new elements (Brenneis and Lein 1977).

2.2   *The language of children as peers: organizing ranking in the peer group*

The early work on peer talk dealt heavily with how children use repetition and other strategies to display format-tying and create cohesion, and how they violate norms, rules, and context-specific expectations in playful ways to create meaning in play and humor (Garvey 1977). The focus was on linguistic competence. More recent work has focused on how children use linguistic strategies to create their own norms of the peer culture.

Ervin-Tripp (1976), for example, argued that while it is possible to view the forms directives take as related to sincerity conditions underlying requests (Garvey 1975), the actual choice of directive type is socially motivated. For example, Ervin-Tripp et al. (1990) found that children use deferent forms with older, higher-status peers, who are more likely to expect deference as a condition of compliance, than with parents, especially mothers. So it is not only having linguistic knowledge, but having the ability to use it in manipulating status, that differentiate the competent speaker.

Children's sensitivity to status in using linguistic markers was studied first in play-acting contrastive status relationships such as doctor–nurse–patient, mother–father–child, and teacher–student in puppet play and role play (Andersen 1990). More recent work has gone beyond role and puppet play to examine how children index and construct status or hierarchical ranking in their peer and friendship groups (Goodwin 1990, 1993). Goodwin (1993) examined how girls accomplished hierarchical forms of social organization in their own peer relationships. Older, more powerful girls used pretend directives, (e.g. "pretend I'm the mother"), showing they had the power to shift the frame of play. They also allocated to themselves more powerful pretend roles (e.g. mother vs. child).

Goodwin (1990) examined how African-American children use discrediting stories to organize hierarchical forms of social organization within neighborhood friendship groups. She found that boys used discrediting stories about present group co-members to help win ongoing arguments, while girls used stories about nonpresent co-members to rally support against those co-members and form future alliances. Goodwin (1990a; b) emphasized that girls are not only as skilled at argumentation as boys but have types of arguments that are both more extended and more complex in their participant structure. While most studies examine how oppositional stances are created through such talk, children's strategies for displaying positive alignments are also examined. Hoyle (1998) examined two boys engaged in play-acting a sportscasting and how, by aligning to one another's pretend selves in role play, the two boys took a positive footing toward one another.

It is notable that children, even preschoolers, use language to organize hierarchical forms of social organization. Kyratzis (2000), observing a friendship group of preschool girls' drawing-table talk, found that the girls told past and future narratives about staying over at one another's houses. Some girls were consistently prevented from participating. Obstacles would be put up to their participation (e.g. one girl was told she could not come over to the leader's house because her babysitter characteristically came too late). This was a source of great anxiety to the excluded girl. Children command an impressive repertoire of linguistic strategies to organize hierarchy among themselves, including frame-shifting and role-allocation in pretend play, ways of manipulating participant structures in the telling of stayover narratives and discrediting stories, and other strategies.

2.3 Peer moral talk: how the norms of the peer group are realized through gossip, chit-chat, pretend play, and conflict

2.3.1 Chit-chat and gossip in older children

In addition to recognizing the importance of ranking within children's peer groups, researchers of peer talk began to study how children use talk to organize the social norms of the group. Many studies of older children, middle-school and beyond, have looked at gossip and chit-chat among peers. Those interested in younger children have focused on studies of pretend play. (These studies will be discussed below.)

With respect to chit-chat, Eckert's (1993) study, "Cooperative competition in Adolescent 'Girl Talk,'" a two-and-a-half-year ethnographic study, documented how, through their "girl talk", a group of adolescent girls negotiated the norms of the peer group. Eckert argued that, like adult women, girls gain "symbolic capital" and status through their relations with others and hence need to negotiate norms of behavior and balance conflicting needs for independence and popularity. Eder (1993) observed adolescent girls engaged in sexual and romantic teasing and argued that teasing provides girls with ways of reinforcing bonds, experimenting with gender roles, and managing newly experienced jealousy feelings. These are means to group belonging through working out a common ground of views and values (Eder 1993).

Jennifer Coates (1994) similarly studied the talk among a friendship group of girls, adding a developmental perspective. The girls she observed practiced the discourses of others (mothers, teachers) and subverted these discourses in a variety of ways. They accomplished femininity through positioning themselves as different kinds of feminine subjects, sometimes in conflict with one another. Developmentally, as they reached 14, a new type of talk, self-conscious in nature, emerged. Life was more serious. As they struggled with changes in their world, they looked to one another for support.

While the early years of middle childhood are the period of the morality of concern for each others' feelings, as Kyratzis (in press) detailed in her study of young girls' talk about emotions, the morality of later childhood and adolescence is most vividly revealed in moral outrage, either at personal affronts or at group norm infringements. Gossip is a key mechanism through which such outrage can be expressed without totally risking the long-term life of the friendship group. As Marjorie Goodwin has brilliantly shown in the *He-Said-She-Said* accounts of children's peer group talk (1990), members of friendship groups rely on the gossip chain to convey disapproval of others' actions. She shows how ritualized routines become a uniquely effective way for one girl's discontent with the actions of another to involve the entire group in repeating or denying their participation in the gossip chain.

Much of the peer talk work has looked at how norms (e.g. values about girls' "meanness": Hughes 1993) are negotiated through talk in girls' friendship groups. However, studies have looked at talk within boys' groups as well. Eder (1998) looked at collaborative narration in both girls' and boys' groups as a means of challenging adult perceptions and establishing adolescent peer culture: "A major theme of adolescent peer culture developed in collaborative narration is an opposition to adult views about teenagers. One way in which storytellers voice such opposition is by incorporating imagined adult dialogue into a narrative to dramatize the gulf between their own perceptions and those of salient adults in their lives" (1998: 86).

2.3.2   Pretend play in young children

Hoyle (1999) documented how peers display alignments to one another by aligning to one another's pretend selves. Kyratzis (1998, in press) documented how preschool children explore possible selves and gender issues via dramatic play narratives of pretense. Their protagonists explore possible selves organized around gendered themes of power and physical strength for boys (e.g. "Shy Wizards," "Power Rangers") and of beauty, graciousness, caring for others, and nurturance for girls ("Batman's girl-friend," "Owner with Baby Kitties," "Making Chinese Friends"). Moral socialization goes on in these narratives, as children evolve norms of gender-appropriate emotion display. Girls develop positive attitudes toward nurturance/caring and boys evolve negative attitudes toward the display of fear. Children invoke gender-associated scripts of play (house for girls, good guys and bad guys for boys) even when materials do not readily afford them (e.g. boys enact a space scenario with domestic toys) (Sheldon and Rohleder 1996).

The norms-socialization that occurs among preschool-aged girls reproduces adult gender roles such as nurturance and mothering but has another aspect, resistance. In Cook-Gumperz's (in press) study, she finds that girls enact dramatic play scripts of mothering but incorporate antinurturance themes, such as boiling babies.

Pretend play may be an easier venue for norm-negotiation among preschoolers than chit-chat, although the latter can be observed on rare occasions (among preschool girls during drawing-table talk) as well (Kyratzis 2000).

2.3.3   Arguments

Arguments have been thought to be an important venue for peer moral socialization. Dunn (1996) reports that it is in conflict with close friends that children are most likely to use reasoning that takes account of the others' point of view or feelings, more so than when they are in conflict with their siblings. Children may care more about managing to maintain continuous harmonious communication with their friends than with family members. For example, Kerry, in conflict with her friend over who should have a prized crown, says "I know – we'll both be queens because we both want to. Two queens in this palace, and you'll have the crown first, then it'll be my turn" (Dunn 1996: 192). A norm is invoked about turn-taking and equal partnership.

Kyratzis and Guo (2001) show how two girls use disputes over turns as "kitties" to negotiate their status:

> *Jenny*:   kitty, I'll rub the other kitty's back first/
> *Peg*:   why?
> *Jenny*:   Sue's back/
> *Peg*:   why?
> *Jenny*:   'cause ("because") Sue is- is nicer/
> *Peg*:   no/I'm nicer to you too/
> *Jenny*:   you're both nicer to me, so I'll rub *both of your backs/
> *Peg*:   at the same time?
> *Jenny*:   I think I have to rub one at a time and then I'll rub yours second/

In this argument, Peg, like Kerry in the Dunn example above, invokes a norm, that if you are nice, you should have your back scratched. Jenny, in turn, appears to support this norm by countering that since both kitties are nicer, both will get their backs scratched. Implicit in Jenny's message is the continuance of her status as the person who sets the rules of the game. When points of view differ, standards are invoked to ground opponents' positions, hence rendering arguments a good forum for moral socialization.

2.4   Peer socialization about gender and its interactional accomplishment

According to Coates's (1986) review of research on gender and communicative competence among children, the current thinking is that peers are largely responsible for gender-associated communication styles. Maltz and Borker (1983) framed an influential theory which has guided much of the more recent work on children's communicative competence, often referred to as the Separate Worlds Hypothesis (henceforth, SWH). This hypothesis states that as a result of gender segregation in childhood, with girls playing predominantly with other girls and boys playing predominantly with other boys, girls and boys evolve quite different goals for social interactions and distinct communicative styles.

Maltz and Borker (1982) argued that different activity practices of girls and boys, as noted by Lever (1976) and others, lead them to develop different genres of speech and different skills for doing things with words. Girls learn that talk is for: (1) creating and maintaining relationships of closeness and equality; (2) criticizing others in acceptable ways; and (3) interpreting accurately the speech of other girls. Boys learn that talk is for: (1) asserting a position of dominance; (2) attracting and maintaining an audience; and (3) asserting themselves when another speaker has the floor. Girls' talk is collaboration-oriented and boys' talk is competition-oriented. Maltz and Borker, and later Tannen (1990b), proposed that "the ways of speaking that adults learn growing up in separate social worlds of peers" are so different that male–female communication in our society constitutes "cross-cultural communication" (1990b: 131), often leading to miscommunication.

In terms of research, there have been several supportive studies (see Coates 1986 for an earlier review). Goodwin (1980), which influenced Maltz and Borker, reported that the girls in the African-American Philadelphia neighborhood where she observed friendship groups of 9–13-year-olds talked negatively about the use of direct commands to equals, seeing it only as appropriate in speech of older to younger children. While disputes were common, girls phrased their directives as proposals for future action (e.g. "let's . . ."). These mitigated the imposition of the request and helped constitute a more egalitarian form of social organization.

Tannen (1990b) analyzed the conversations of same-sex pairs of best friends aged between eight and 16 years asked to talk about something serious or intimate. Pairs of male friends seemed uncomfortable with the task, avoided eye contact, and sat parallel to one another rather than face-to-face. Pairs of female friends, in contrast, willingly discussed intimate topics, and when they did so, supported one another.

Several studies with younger children, aged five and below, show differences between girls' and boys' discourse. Miller et al. (1986) found that in arguments, 5–7-year-old boys used a more heavy-handed style, while girls used mitigated strategies (e.g. compromise, evasion, or acquiescence). Amy Sheldon (1990), observing topically similar disputes within a girls' and a boys' triadic grouping, found that the boys used a more adversarial style than the girls. Boys' conflicts were extended and disrupted fantasy play, while girls' conflicts were more quickly resolved. Girls seemed to strive to maintain interconnectedness through compromise and conflict resolution. A study by Kyratzis and Ervin-Tripp (1999) similarly found that among dyads of four- and seven-year-old best friends, girls were more likely to sustain a joint pretense narrative while boys were more likely to lapse into arguments about how to proceed, disrupting joint fantasy. Leaper (1989) observed five- and seven-year-olds and found that verbal exchanges among girls employed collaborative speech acts involving positive reciprocity while exchanges among boys employed speech acts promoting negative reciprocity. Sachs (1987/1995), observing pretend play among groups of preschool girls and boys, found that girls used more mitigated forms of directives, forms that invited agreement (e.g. "pretend . . .", "let's . . .") while boys used more direct forms of requests (e.g. direct commands and declarative directives – "you have to . . .").

Several studies, then, supported the view that girls and boys have different sociolinguistic subcultures. In same-sex groups, girls interact so as to sustain interaction and realize group goals, and boys interact so as to top or one-up conversational partners and realize self-goals. Several features of communicative style go along with these goals.

Despite these sociolinguistic strategies that children learn in the friendship groups of childhood, they also have to learn situational variation. As Ervin-Tripp (1978) argues, we may expect that some situations maximize, while others minimize, gender marking. We need to examine situational influences upon styles within individuals' repertoires.

Goodwin (1993) found that the form of social organization that evolved in girls' pretend play (playing house) differed from that which characterized their task activities, making it "imperative that studies of girls' play be grounded in detailed analyses of specific contexts of use" (1993: 161). Goodwin (1990) found that girls shifted their style toward using more direct forms of requests when playing with boys rather than with other girls. Siblings vs. peers as an interactive context also influences language style; Dehart (1996) extended research on peer talk to the sibling context and did not find differences noted previously in peer talk research (e.g. Sachs 1987). Nakamura (2001), examining masculine and feminine marking among Japanese children's speech, found strong contextual variation. Feminine marking among girls was high in a gender context of family play and masculine marking among boys was high in a gender context of superhero (good guy and bad guy) play. However, gender-linked marking was reduced among both girls and boys when play was videotaped in a neutral context (e.g. grocery store play). We need to acknowledge that both girls and boys have a repertoire of speech strategies available to them and that they manipulate speech style for given interactive goals.

Sociolinguistic strategies such as directness in requests and conflict strategies may be a reflection of power as well as gender, as has been found for adults by O'Barr and Atkins (1980). Children have to learn the contexts where power display is warranted. Goodwin (2001) conducted a longitudinal study of talk within middle-school-aged children's friendship groups during recess. Both males and females used assertive forms when they were high in status, that is, experts on a topic (i.e. hopscotch). As children's expertise shifted over time, so did dibs over who used assertive forms of requests. In a mixed-sex nursery school friendship group, Kyratzis and Guo (2001) observed that preschool children varied their use of direct conflict strategies by context. Boys seemed to be licenced to use these strategies in doctor play, while girls seemed to be licenced to use these in borderwork play. Cook-Gumperz and Szymanski (2001) found that in contexts where domestic and family scenarios are instantiated, middle-school-aged Latina girls dominated boys during cooperative groupwork. So among themselves, children seem to work out that certain contexts licence males to be powerful while others licence females to take positions of authority.

In sum, the early research suggested that girls and boys spent much of their time in segregated groups and worked out among themselves different goals and styles of speech. These were thought to evolve fortuitously but to lead to fairly set ways of speaking that were consistent across context. More recent research has suggested that young children are sensitive to the power ramifications of different forms of speech, and allocate power among themselves in contextually sensitive ways that sometimes reflect gender-based links between specific contexts and power. Children show contextual fluidity in their use of speech registers.

3   Conclusion

As stated in the introduction, current research interests can be summarized in terms of the following themes: (1) focus on the child in a much richer, more complicated social context; and (2) a view of the child as constructing her or his own identity. Children in other words organize their concerns and thoughts through talk within children's social worlds. Finally, (3) peer cultures within children's worlds can use-fully be studied through a fuller, diary-like, ethnographic, context-rich approach. As we have shown in the trajectory of themes of the chapter, increasingly, children get a sense of themselves in a wider social world as well as within the context of the family. Developmentally, children move from having to fit into the family discourse space and participant roles and identities as adults construct them in pragmatics of family life, then begin to make a space for reflecting and thinking about social worlds in personhood, and then later begin to organize others as well as themselves, in terms of social organization and morality, in peer talk.

In this chapter, it would have been possible to focus on the structural features of discourse analysis, such as cohesion, coherence, and discourse markers alone. Instead, we have chosen to focus on language socialization as more representative of current interests. In other words, our purpose has been to show how the field of child discourse studies has shifted focus onto children as active constructors of their world within the domains of adult–child and peer discourse.

REFERENCES

Andersen, E. S. (1990). *Speaking with Style: The Sociolinguistic Skills of Children*. London: Routledge.

Bakeman, R. and Gottman, J. M. (1986). *Observing Interaction*. Cambridge: Cambridge University Press.

Blum-Kulka, S. (1997). *Dinner Talk: Cultural Patterns of Sociality and Socialization in Family Discourse*. Mahwah, NJ: Lawrence Erlbaum.

Brenneis, D. and Lein, L. (1977). "You fruithead": a sociolinguistic approach to children's dispute settlement. In S. Ervin-Tripp and C. Mitchell-Kernan (eds), *Child Discourse* (pp. 9–65). New York: Academic Press.

Briggs, J. (1997). Mazes of meaning: how a child and a culture create each other. In W. Corsaro and P. J. Miller (eds), *Interpretive Approaches to*

Children's Socialization (pp. 25–50). San Francisco: Josey–Bass.

Brown, P. (1994). Gender, politeness and confrontation in Tenjapa. In D. Tannen (ed.), *Gender and Interaction* (pp. 144–55). New York: Oxford University Press.

Brown, P. and Levinson, S. (1987). *Politeness: Some Universals in Language Use*. Cambridge and New York: Cambridge University Press.

Budwig, N. (1990). The linguistic marking of agentivity and control in child language. *Journal of Child Language*, 16, 263–84.

Clancy, P. (1986). The acquisition of communicative style in Japanese. In B. Schieffelin and E. Ochs (eds), *Language Socialization across Cultures* (pp. 213–50). New York: Cambridge University Press.

Coates, J. (1986). *Women, Men, and Language.* Second edition. London: Longman.

Coates, J. (1994). Discourse, gender, and subjectivity: the talk of teenage girls. In M. Bucholtz, A. C. Liang, L. A. Sutton, and C. Hines (eds), *Cultural Performances* (pp. 316–25). Proceedings of the Third Berkeley Women and Language Conference. Berkeley: Berkeley Women and Language Group.

Cook-Gumperz, J. (1995). Reproducing the discourse of mothering: how gendered talk makes gendered lives. In K. Hall and M. Bucholtz (eds), *Gender Articulated* (pp. 401–20). London and Boston: Routledge.

Cook-Gumperz, J. (in press). The interactional accomplishment of gender and girls' oppositional stances: young children between nursery school and family life. In B. Baron and H. Kothoff (eds), *Gender in Interaction.* Amsterdam and Philadelphia: John Benjamins.

Cook-Gumperz, J. and Gumperz, J. (1976). Context in children's talk. In N. Waterson and C. Snow (eds), *The Development of Children's Language* (pp. 3–25). London and New York: John Wiley.

Cook-Gumperz, J. and Szymanski, M. (2001). Classroom "families": cooperating or competing – girls' and boys' interactional styles in a bilingual classroom. In A. Kyratzis (ed.), *Gender Construction in Children's Interactions: A Cultural Perspective,* special issue of *Research on Language and Social Interaction,* 34(1), 107–29.

Cook-Gumperz, J., Corsaro, W., and Streeck, J. (1986). *Children's Worlds, Children's Language.* Berlin: Mouton de Gruyter.

Corsaro, W. A. (1985). *Friendship and Peer Culture in the Early Years.* Norwood, NJ: Ablex.

Corsaro, W. A. and Rosier, K. B. (1992). Documenting productive–reproductive processes in children's lives: transition narratives of a black family living in poverty. In W. A. Corsaro and P. J. Miller (eds), *Interpretive Approaches to Children's Socialization: New Directions for Child Development* (pp. 67–91). San Francisco: Jossey–Bass.

De Hart, G. B. (1996). Gender and mitigation in 4-year-olds' pretend play talk with siblings. *Research on Language and Social Interaction,* 29(1), 81–96.

Duranti, A. (1992). Language in context and language as context: the Samoan respect vocabulary. In C. Goodwin and A. Duranti, *Rethinking Context* (pp. 77–100). New York: Cambridge University Press.

Dunn, J. (1996). Arguing with siblings, friends, and mothers: developments in relationships and understanding. In D. I. Slobin, J. Gerhardt, A. Kyratzis, and J. Guo (eds), *Social Interaction, Social Context, and Language: Essays in Honor of Susan Ervin-Tripp* (pp. 191–204). Mahwah, NJ: Lawrence Erlbaum.

Dunn, J. and Munn, P. (1987). The development of justification in disputes. *Developmental Psychology,* 23, 791–8.

Eckert, P. (1993). Cooperative competition in adolescent "girl talk." In D. Tannen (ed.), *Gender and Conversational Interaction* (pp. 32–61). Oxford: Oxford University Press.

Eder, D. (1993). "Go get ya a French!" Romantic and sexual teasing among adolescent girls. In D. Tannen (ed.), *Gender and Conversational Interaction* (pp. 17–30). Oxford: Oxford University Press.

Eder, D. (1998). Developing adolescent peer culture through collaborative narration. In S. Hoyle and C. T. Adger (eds), *Language Practices of Older Children* (pp. 82–93). New York: Oxford University Press.

Eisenberg, A. (1986). Teasing: verbal play in two Mexicano homes. In B. Schieffelin and E. Ochs (eds), *Language Socialization across Cultures* (pp. 182–98). New York: Cambridge University Press.

Ervin-Tripp, S. M. (1970). Discourse agreement: how children answer questions. In R. Hayes (ed.), *Cognition and Language Learning* (pp. 79–107). New York: Wiley.

Ervin-Tripp, S. M. (1976). Is Sybil there? The structure of some American English directives. *Language in Society*, 5, 25–66.

Ervin-Tripp, S. M. (1977). Wait for me roller skate! In S. Ervin-Tripp and C. Mitchell-Kernan (eds), *Child Discourse* (pp. 165–88). New York: Academic Press.

Ervin-Tripp, S. M. (1978). What do women sociolinguists want? Prospects for a research field. *International Journal of Sociology of Language*, 17, 17–28.

Ervin-Tripp, S. M. (1982). Ask and it shall be given you: children's requests. In H. Byrnes (ed.), *Georgetown Roundtable on Languages and Linguistics* (pp. 232–45). Washington, DC: Georgetown University.

Ervin-Tripp, S. and Gordon, D. P. (1980). The development of requests. In R. L. Schiefelbusch (ed.), *Language Competence: Assessment and Intervention* (pp. 61–95). Beverly Hills, CA: College Hills Press.

Ervin-Tripp, S. and Mitchell-Kernan, C. (1977). *Child Discourse*. New York: Academic Press.

Ervin-Tripp, S. M., Guo, J., and Lampert, M. (1990). Politeness and persuasion in children's control acts. *Journal of Pragmatics*, 14, 195–219, 307–32.

Ervin-Tripp, S., O'Connor, M. C., and Rosenberg, J. (1984). Language and power in the family. In M. Schulzand and C. K. Ramerae, *Language and Power* (pp. 116–35). Belmont, CA: Sage.

Ervin-Tripp, S., Guo, J., and Lampert, M. (1990) Politeness and persuasion in children's control acts. *Journal of Pragmatics*, 14.

Feldman, C. (1989). Monologue as a problem solving narrative. In K. Nelson (ed.), *Narratives from the Crib* (pp. 98–102). Cambridge, MA: Harvard University Press.

Garvey, C. (1974). Some properties of social play. *Merrill-Palmer Quarterly*, 20, 163–80.

Garvey, C. (1975). Requests and responses in children's speech. *Journal of Child Language*, 2, 41–63.

Garvey, C. (1977). Play with language and speech. In S. M. Ervin-Tripp and C. Mitchell-Kernan (eds), *Child Discourse* (pp. 27–47). New York: Academic Press.

Garvey, C. and Berninger, G. (1981). Timing and turn-taking in children's conversations. *Discourse Processes*, 4, 27–57.

Gee, J. P. (1986). The narrativization of experience in the oral style. *Journal of Education*, 167, 9–35.

Gerhardt, J. (1988). The development of morphology and forms of self-reference in the speech of a two-year old. *Journal of Child Language*, 15, 337–94.

Gleason, J. B. (1988). Language and socialization. In F. S. Kessel (ed.), *The Development of Language and Language Researchers: Essays in Honor of Roger Brown* (pp. 205–15). Mahwah, NJ: Lawrence Erlbaum.

Goodwin, M. H. (1980). Directive/response speech sequences in girls' and boys' talk activities. In S. McConnell-Ginet, R. Borker, and N. Furman (eds), *Women and Language in Literature and Society* (pp. 157–73). New York: Praeger.

Goodwin, M. H. (1990). *He-Said-She-Said: Talk as Social Organization Among Black Children*. Bloomington, IN: Indiana University Press.

Goodwin, M. J. (1993). Accomplishing social organization in girls' play: patterns of competition and cooperation in an African-American working-class girls' group. In S. T. Hollis, L. Pershing, and M. J. Young (eds), *Feminist Theory and the Study of Folklore* (pp. 149–65). Urbana, IL: University of Illinois Press.

Goodwin, M. H. (2001). Organizing participation in cross-sex jump roles: situating gender differences within longitudinal studies of activities. In A. Kyratzis (ed.), *Gender Construction in Children's Interactions: A Cultural Perspective*, special issue of *Research on Language and Social Interaction*, 34(1), 75–105.

Halliday, M. (1977). *Learning How to Mean*. London: Edward Arnold.

Heath, S. B. (1982). What no bedtime story means: narrative skills in home and school. *Language in Society*, 11, 49–76.

Heath, S. B. (1983). *Ways with Words: Language, Life and Work in Communities and Classrooms*. Cambridge: Cambridge University Press.

Hicks, D. (1991). Kinds of narrative: genre skills among first graders from two communities. In A. McCabe and C. Peterson (eds), *Developing Narrative Structure* (pp. 59–88). Hillsdale, NJ: Lawrence Erlbaum.

Hoyle, S. M. (1999). Register and footing in role play. In S. Hoyle and C. T. Adger (eds), *Language Practices of Older Children* (pp. 47–66). New York: Oxford University Press.

Hudson, J. A. and Shapiro, L. R. (1991). From knowing to telling: the development of children's scripts, stories and personal narratives. In A. McCabe and C. Peterson (eds), *Developing Narrative Structure*. Hillsdale, NJ: Lawrence Erlbaum.

Hughes, L. A. (1993). You have to do it with style: girls' games and girls' gaming. In S. T. Hollis, L. Pershing, and M. J. Young (eds), *Feminist Theory and the Study of Folklore* (pp. 130–47). Urbana, IL: University of Illinois Press.

Hymes, D. (1962). The ethnography of speaking. In T. Gladwin and W. Sturtevant (eds), *Anthropology and Human Behavior* (pp. 15–53). Washington, DC: Anthropological Society of Washington.

Keller-Cohen, D. (1978). Context in child language. *Annual Review, Anthropology*, 7, 453–82.

Kyratzis, A. (2000). Tactical uses of narratives in nursery school same-sex groups. *Discourse Processes*, 29(3), 269–99.

Kyratzis, A. (1999). Narrative identity: preschoolers' self-construction through narrative in friendship group dramatic play. *Narrative Inquiry*, 9, 427–55.

Kyratzis, A. (in press). Constituting the emotions: a longitudinal study of emotion talk in a preschool friendship group of boys. To appear in H. Kotthoff and B. Baron (eds), *Gender in Interaction*. Amsterdam: John Benjamins.

Kyratzis, A. and Ervin-Tripp, S. M. (1999). The development of discourse markers in peer interaction. In K. Meng and S. Sromqvist (eds), *Discourse Markers in Language Acquisition* (pp. 1321–38), special issue of *Journal of Pragmatics*.

Kyratzis, A. and Guo, J. (2001). Preschool girls' and boys' verbal conflict strategies in the United States and China. In A. Kyratzis (ed.), *Gender Construction in Children's Interactions: A Cultural Perspective*, special issue of *Research on Language and Social Interaction*, 34(1), 45–73.

Kyratzis, A., Guo, J., and Ervin-Tripp, S. M. (1990). Pragmatic conventions influencing children's use of causal expressions in natural discourse. In *Proceedings of the Sixteenth Annual Meeting of the Berkeley Linguistics*

Society, 16, 205–15. Berkeley, CA: Berkeley Linguistics Society.

Lakoff, R. (1973). Language and women's place. *Language in Society*, 2, 45–80.

Leaper, C. (1991). Influence and involvement in children's discourse: age, gender and partner effects. *Child Development*, 62, 797–811.

Lever, J. (1976). Sex differences in the games children play. *Social Problems*, 23, 478–87.

Locke, J. (1993). *The Child's Path to Spoken Language*. Cambridge, MA: Harvard University Press.

Maltz, D. N. and Borker, R. A. (1983). A cultural approach to male–female miscommunication. In J. A. Gumperz (ed.), *Language and Social Identity* (pp. 195–216). New York: Cambridge University Press.

McTear, M. (1985). The development of coherent dialogue. Conversational processes: turn-taking. In *Children's Conversations* (pp. 164–83). Oxford: Blackwell.

Michaels, S. (1986). Narrative presentations: an oral preparation for literacy. In J. Cook-Gumperz (ed.), *The Social Construction of Literacy* (pp. 303–52). Cambridge and New York: Cambridge University Press.

Michaels, S. (1991). Dismantling of narrative. In A. McCabe and C. Peterson (eds), *Developing Narrative Structure* (pp. 303–52). Hillsdale, NJ: Lawrence Erlbaum.

Miller, P. J. (1982). *Amy, Wendy, and Beth: Learning Language in South Baltimore*. Austin, TX: University of Texas Press.

Miller, P. J. and Sperry, L. (1988). Early talk about the past: the origins of personal stories about past experience. *Journal of Child Language*, 15, 293–316.

Miller, P. M., Danaher, D. L., and Forbes, D. (1986). Sex-related strategies for coping with interpersonal conflict in children aged five and seven. *Developmental Psychology*, 22(4), 543–8.

Mitchell-Kernan, C. and Ervin-Tripp, S. (eds) (1977). *Child Discourse*. New York: Academic Press.

Mitchell-Kernan, C. and Kernan, K. (1977). Pragmatics of directive choice among children. In S. Ervin-Tripp and C. Mitchell-Kernan (eds), *Child Discourse* (pp. 189–209). New York: Academic Press.

Nakamura, K. (2001). Gender and language in Japanese preschool children. In A. Kyratzis (ed.), *Gender Construction in Children's Interactions: A Cultural Perspective*, special issue of *Research on Language and Social Interaction*, 34(1), 15–43.

Nelson, K. (ed.) (1989). *Narratives from the Crib*. Cambridge, MA: Harvard University Press.

O'Barr, W. and Atkins, S. (1980). "Women's language" or "powerless language?" In S. McConnell-Ginet, R. Borker, and N. Furman (eds), *Women and Language in Literature and Society* (pp. 93–110). New York: Praeger.

Ochs, E. (1988). *Culture and Language Development: Language Acquisition and Language Socialization in a Samoan Village*. New York: Cambridge University Press.

Ochs, E. and Schieffelin, B. (1979). *Developmental Pragmatics*. New York: Academic Press.

Ochs, E. and Schieffelin, B. (1986). *Language Socialization across Cultures*. New York: Cambridge University Press.

Ochs, E. and Schieffelin, B. (1989). Three developmental stories. In R. Shweder and R. Levine (eds), *Culture Theory: Essays in Mind, Self, and Emotion* (pp. 276–320). New York: Cambridge University Press.

Ochs, E. and Taylor, C. (1995). The "father knows best" dynamic in dinnertime narratives. In K. Hall and M. Bucholtz (eds), *Gender Articulated: Language and the Socially Constructed Self* (pp. 97–120). London: Routledge.

Parten, M. (1933). Social play among preschool children. *Journal of Abnormal and Social Psychology*, 28, 136–47.

Piaget, J. (1926). *The Language and Thought of the Child*. New York: Meridian Books.

Sachs, J. (1987). Preschool girls' and boys' language use in pretend play. In S. U. Phillips, S. Steele, and C. Tanz (eds), *Language, Gender, and Sex in Comparative Perspective* (pp. 178–88). Cambridge: Cambridge University Press.

Sacks, H., Schegloff, E. A., and Jefferson, G. (1974). A simplest systematics for the organization of turn-taking for conversation. *Language*, 50, 696–735.

Scollon, R. and Scollon, S. W. (1981). *Narrative, Literacy and Face*. Norwood, NJ: Ablex.

Shatz, M. (1994). *A Toddler's Life*. New York: Oxford University Press.

Sheldon, A. (1990). Pickle fights: gendered talk in preschool disputes. *Discourse Processes*, 13, 5–31.

Sheldon, A. and Rohleder, L. (1996). Sharing the same world, telling different stories: gender differences in co-constructed pretend narratives. In D. I. Slobin, J. Gerhardt, A. Kyratzis, and J. Guo (eds), *Social Interaction, Social Context, and Language* (pp. 613–32). Mahwah, NJ: Lawrence Erlbaum.

Sprott, R. A. (1992). Children's use of discourse markers in disputes: form-function relations and discourse in child language. *Discourse Processes*, 15, 423–39.

Sweetser, E. (1990). *From Etymology to Pragmatics: Metaphorical and Cultural Aspects of Semantic Structure*. Cambridge: Cambridge University Press.

Tannen, D. (1990a). *You Just Don't Understand: Women and Men in Conversation*. New York: Ballantine Books.

Tannen, D. (1990b). Gender differences in topical coherence: physical alignment and topical cohesion. In B. Dorval (ed.), *Conversational Organization and its Development* (pp. 167–206). Norwood, NJ: Ablex.

Thorne, B. (1993). *Gender Play: Girls and Boys in School*. New Brunswick, NJ: Rutgers University Press.

Watson-Gegeo, K. A. and Gegeo, D. (1986). The social world of Kwara'rae children: acquisition of language and values. In J. Cook-Gumperz, W. Corsaro, and J. Streeck (eds), *Children's Worlds and Children's Language* (pp. 109–20). Berlin: Mouton de Gruyter.

Watts, R. J. (1991). *Power in Family Discourse*. Berlin: Mouton de Gruyter.

Wootton, A. (1986). Rule in action, the orderly features of actions that formulate rules. In J. Cook-Gumperz, W. Corsaro, and J. Streeck (eds), *Children's Worlds, Children's Language*. Berlin: Mouton de Gruyter.

Wootton, A. (1997). *Language and the Development of Mind: A Study of Children's Conversation* (pp. 147–68). New York: Cambridge University Press.

31 Computer-mediated Discourse

SUSAN C. HERRING

0 Introduction

0.1 Definition

Computer-mediated discourse is the communication produced when human beings interact with one another by transmitting messages via networked computers. The study of computer-mediated discourse (henceforth CMD) is a specialization within the broader interdisciplinary study of computer-mediated communication (CMC), distinguished by its focus on *language and language use* in computer networked environments, and by its use of methods of *discourse analysis* to address that focus.

Most CMC currently in use is *text-based*, that is, messages are typed on a computer keyboard and read as text on a computer screen, typically by a person or persons at a different location from the message sender. Text-based CMC takes a variety of forms (e.g. e-mail, discussion groups, real-time chat, virtual reality role-playing games) whose linguistic properties vary depending on the kind of messaging system used and the social and cultural context embedding particular instances of use. However, all such forms have in common that the activity that takes place through them is constituted primarily – in many cases, exclusively – by visually presented language. These characteristics of the medium have important consequences for understanding the nature of computer-mediated language. They also provide a unique environment, free from competing influences from other channels of communication and from physical context, in which to study verbal interaction and the relationship between discourse and social practice.[1]

0.2 A brief history of CMD research

Human-to-human communication via computer networks, or *interactive networking*, is a recent phenomenon. Originally designed in the United States in the late 1960s to facilitate the transfer of computer programs and data between remote computers in the interests of national defense (Levy 1984; Rheingold 1993), computer networks caught on almost immediately as a means of interpersonal communication, first among computer scientists in the early 1970s (Hafner and Lyon 1996), then among academic and business users in elite universities and organizations in the 1980s, and from there into popular use – facilitated by the rise of commercial Internet service providers – in the 1990s. The first wide-area network, the US defense department sponsored ARPANET, was replaced in the early 1980s by the global network Internet, which as of January 1999 comprised more than 58,000 networks supporting an estimated 150 million users (Petrazzini and Kibati 1999).

The study of computer-mediated discourse developed alongside of interactive networking itself, as scholars became exposed to and intrigued by communication in the new medium. As early as 1984, linguist Naomi Baron published an article speculating on the effects of "computer-mediated communication as a force in language change." The first detailed descriptions of computer-mediated discourse soon followed, with Denise Murray's (1985) research on a real-time messaging system at IBM, and Kerstin Severinson Eklundh's (1986) study of the Swedish COM conferencing system. However, it was not until 1991, with the publication of Kathleen Ferrara, Hans Brunner, and Greg Whittemore's "Interactive written discourse as an emergent register," that linguists and language scholars began to take serious notice of CMD. The immediately following years saw the rise of a wave of CMD researchers,[2] working independently on what has since emerged as a more or less coherent agenda: the empirical description of computer-mediated language and varieties of computer-mediated discourse.[3] Since the mid-1990s, CMD research has continued to expand at a rapid rate, staking out new areas of inquiry and resulting in an ever-growing list of published resources.

In part, the first wave of CMD scholarship was a reaction against misunderstandings about CMD that had gone before. Popular claims – some endorsed by published research – held that computer-mediated communication was "anonymous," "impersonal," "egalitarian," "fragmented," and "spoken-like," attributing these properties to the nature of the medium itself, and failing to distinguish among different types and uses of CMD. Ferrara et al. (1991), although contributing useful observations on one form of real-time experimental CMD, also overgeneralized, characterizing what they termed "interactive written discourse" as a single genre. In fact, subsequent research has revealed computer-mediated language and interaction to be sensitive to a variety of technical and situational factors, making it far more complex and variable than envisioned by early descriptions.

The remainder of this chapter is organized into four broad sections, each of them representing a currently active area of CMD research. Section 1, on the "classification of CMD," addresses the nature of CMD in relation to written and spoken language, and identifies some technologically and culturally determined CMC types. Section 2 describes the structural properties of CMD at the levels of typography, orthography, word choice, and grammar. Section 3 considers how participants in CMD negotiate turn-taking and maintain cross-turn coherence, despite constraints on interaction management imposed by CMC systems. Section 4, entitled "social practice," discusses CMD in the service of social goals ranging from self-presentation to interpersonal interaction to the dominance of some groups by others. The chapter concludes by considering the prospects for CMD research in the future.

1   Classification of CMD

1.1   *Medium and channel*

Computer networks are often considered a *medium* of communication distinct from writing and speaking. Thus CMD researchers speak of electronic "medium effects" on CMD, rather than treating CMD as a form of "writing" (typing) that happens to be distributed by electronic means (see, e.g., Murray 1988). The justification for this is that while the means of production of CMD is similar to that of other forms of typing, including allowing for the editing and formatting of text in asynchronous modes, other aspects of computer-mediated communication preclude easy classification with either writing or speaking. CMD exchanges are typically faster than written exchanges (e.g. of letters, or published essays which respond to one another), yet still significantly slower than spoken exchanges, since even in so-called "real-time" modes, typing is slower than speaking. Moreover, CMD allows multiple participants to communicate simultaneously in ways that are difficult if not impossible to achieve in other media, due to cognitive limits on participants' ability to attend to more than one exchange at a time (Herring 1999a). In addition, the dissemination of computer-mediated messages involves distribution to an unseen (and often unknown) audience, while at the same time creating an impression of direct and even "private" exchanges (King 1996). For these and other reasons, participants typically experience CMD as distinct from either writing or speaking, sometimes as a blend of the two, but in any event subject to its own constraints and potentialities.

Media may differ in the number of *channels*, or sources of communication, they comprise. Face-to-face communication is a "rich" medium, in that information is available through multiple channels: visual, auditory, gestural, etc. In contrast, CMD is a "lean" medium (Daft and Lengel 1984), in that information is available only through the visual channel, and that information is limited to typed text. This has led some to posit that the computer medium is "impoverished" and unsuitable for social interaction (Baron 1984). However, there is ample evidence that users compensate textually for missing auditory and gestural cues, and that CMD can be richly expressive. This is perhaps nowhere better illustrated than by the popularity of "virtual sex" (Deuel 1996; McRae 1996) – sex being an activity that normally requires *more* channels of communication than face-to-face speech (e.g. touch) – in which acts of physical intimacy are textually enacted.

1.2   *Medium variables*

While the case for the deterministic influence of the computer medium on language use is often overstated, properties of computer messaging systems nonetheless play a significant role in shaping CMD. One important distinction relates to *synchronicity* of participation (Kiesler et al. 1984). Asynchronous CMD systems do not require that users be logged on at the same time in order to send and receive message; rather, messages are stored at the addressee's site until they can be read. E(lectronic)-mail is

Table 31.1 Classification of some common CMD modes according to medium variables

	One-way transmission	Two-way transmission
Synchronous	Chat (IRC, webchat, etc.); MUDs and MOOs	UNIX "talk"; VAX "phone"; ICQ
Asynchronous	E-mail; e-mail-based systems (listserv discussion lists, Usenet newsgroups, etc.)	–

an example of this type. In synchronous CMD, in contrast, sender and addressee(s) must be logged on simultaneously, and messages are more ephemeral, scrolling up and off participants' computer screens as new messages replace them. "Real-time" chat – such as takes place in the chatrooms of commercial service providers and via Internet Relay Chat (IRC) – is a popular form of synchronous CMD.

A cross-cutting technological dimension has to do with whether or not simultaneous feedback is available; that is, whether the message transmission is *one-way* or *two-way* (Cherny 1999). In *one-way* transmission, a message is transmitted in its entirety as a single unit, with the result that recipients do not know that a message is being addressed to them until it arrives, thereby precluding the possibility of simultaneous feedback. Most CMD in current use makes use of one-way transmission. In contrast, oral modes of communication (such as face-to-face and telephone conversations) are *two-way*, with speaker and addressee both able to hear the message as it is produced. There are also two-way CMD systems, in which participants' screens split into two or more sections, and the words of each participant appear keystroke by keystroke in their respective sections as they are typed. An example of two-way synchronous CMD on the Internet is the currently-popular ICQ ("I seek you") protocol.[4]

Some common modes of CMD are classified according to synchronicity and transmission type in table 31.1.

Other physical properties of messaging systems that shape language use include limits on message size (what Cherny 1999 calls message "granularity"), the "persistence" of the text (whether, and for how long, previous messages remain accessible to participants; Condon and Čech forthcoming), what categories of communication commands a system makes available (Cherny 1995), the ease with which a system allows users to incorporate portions of previous messages in their responses (Severinson Eklundh and Macdonald 1994; Severinson Eklundh forthcoming), whether a system allows messages to be sent anonymously (Selfe and Meyer 1991), and whether it allows users to filter out or "ignore" messages from others selectively (Lunsford 1996; Reid 1994). Finally, the availability of channels of communication in addition to text, such as audio, video, or graphics, can have consequences for language use (Yates and Graddol 1996).

1.3   CMD modes

Another useful classification is in terms of emic (culturally recognized) categories of computer-mediated communication, or CMD mode. Popular modes such as private e-mail, listserv mailing lists, Usenet newsgroups, IRC, and MUDs are socially as well as technologically defined, each having its own unique history and culture of use.[5] For example, listserv mailing lists and Usenet newsgroups are both asynchronous, multiparticipant discussion groups to which messages are contributed ("posted") via e-mail. Yet there are recognizably distinct listserv and Usenet "cultures," the former tending to attract more academic professionals, and the latter, younger (predominantly male) users engaged in contentious exchanges of opinion.[6] The greater degree of contentiousness on Usenet (including a high incidence of "flaming," or targeting an addressee with overtly hostile message content; Kim and Raja 1991) is due in part to the fact that social accountability in the Usenet system is low – whereas listserv participants must subscribe to mailing lists, providing their name and e-mail address in the process, Usenet messages are publicly posted for anyone with access to a newsreader to read. It also reflects the history of Usenet, which was invented by young male "hackers" in the late 1970s as an alternative to the "elitist," government-funded ARPANET (Rheingold 1993), and which has continued to define itself in terms of "frontier" values (Pfaffenberger 1996).

Real-time chat modes also differ from one another culturally. Although IRC and chat in a social MUD are both types of synchronous, one-way CMD, and make use of similar commands (the ability, for example, to distinguish between an utterance and an action, and the ability to message someone privately), the nature of the conversations and the conventions associated with each are different. As Cherny (forthcoming: 12–13) notes,

> [a]lthough many abbreviations are common [to IRC and ElseMOO, the social MUD I studied], certain outsider forms are sneered at: e.g. "u" for "you", "r" for "are." When I asked ElseMOO regulars, "What part of the Internet do you think abbreviations like 'r u going 2 c the movie' are from?", two replied "the icky part" and "the part I avoid like the plague." One thought perhaps IRC users sometimes use those forms but admitted to an anti-IRC bias. When one new visitor came to ElseMOO (apparently used to IRC) and said, "this is just like IRC <g> . . . with fun things to do," Bonny, a regular, responded, "except we don't say <g> here."[7]

The fact that MUDding requires some computer programming skills to do well may account for the perception of Cherny's informants that their MUD culture is more sophisticated than that of IRC.

With these distinctions as background, we now move to consider some properties of computer-mediated discourse.

2   Linguistic Structure

It is a popular perception that computer-mediated language is less correct, complex, and coherent than standard written language. Thus a writer for *Wired* magazine describes messages posted to the Internet as "a whole new fractured language – definitely not as elegant or polished as English used to be."[8] Similarly, Baron (1984: 131) predicted that participants in computer conferences would use "fewer subordinate clauses" and "a narrower range of vocabulary" – and that as a result of computer communication over time, the expressive functions of language could be diminished.

Actually, although computer-mediated language often contains nonstandard features,[9] only a relatively small percentage of such features appears to be errors caused by inattention or lack of knowledge of the standard language forms (see, e.g. Herring 1998a). The majority are deliberate choices made by users to economize on typing effort, mimic spoken language features, or express themselves creatively (Cho forthcoming; Livia forthcoming). Economy of effort seems to be the motivating force behind Murray's (1990: 43–4) observation that computer science professionals using synchronous CMD in a workplace environment "delete subject pronouns, determiners, and auxiliaries; use abbreviations; do not correct typos; and do not used mixed case", as illustrated in the following exchange between Les and Brian:

(1) *Les1*:   as it stands now, meeting on weds?
    Les2:   instead of tues
    Brian1:   idiot Hess seemed to think you were there tues morning
    Brian2:   thot that mtg from 9 to 10 would solve
    Brian3:   if you not in ny I'm going to have mtg changed to wedne.

Another deliberate practice that results in unconventional orthography is the textual representation of auditory information such as prosody, laughter, and other non-language sounds, as illustrated in the following message posted to Usenet (from MacKinnon 1995):

(2) Al,
   hahahahahahahhahahahahahahahahahahahahahaa
   sniff waaaaaaaaaaaaaaaaaaaaaaaaaaaahhhhhh
   I laughed, i cried. . . . that post was GREAT! :-)
   Amusedly,
                  -Mirth-

Strategies such as these, rather than reflecting impoverished or simplified communication, demonstrate the ability of users to adapt the computer medium to their expressive needs. Significantly, this results in a linguistic variety that, despite being produced by written-like means, frequently contains features of orality.

One medium variable, however, does exercise a powerful influence over structural complexity: synchronicity. Just as the structure of unplanned speech reflects cognitive constraints on real-time language encoding, for example in length of information units, lexical density, and degree of syntactic integration (Chafe 1982), so too synchronous modes of CMD impose temporal constraints on users that result in a reduction of linguistic complexity relative to asynchronous modes. Thus in a study of InterChange, a type of synchronous CMD used in educational settings, Ko (1996) found fewer complements, more stranded prepositions, and shorter words than in a comparably sized corpus of formal writing. Moreover, for features involving "information focus and elaborateness" (e.g. lexical density, ratio of nouns to verbs, and use of attributive adjectives), the InterChange messages had lower average frequencies than *either* writing or speaking. Ko attributes this finding to the heavy production and processing burden placed on users by the InterChange system – not only must they type, which is slower and requires more conscious attention than talking, but they must type quickly, leaving little time for message planning.

In contrast, asynchronous CMD permits users to take their time in constructing and editing messages. Variation in structural complexity in e-mail messages, therefore, must be understood as reflecting social situational factors which determine what level of formality – and with it, standardness and structural complexity – is appropriate to the context. For example, staff in an Australian university exchange private e-mail filled with informal, spoken language features: contractions, abbreviations, use of lower case in place of upper case, omission of punctuation, and omission of grammatical function words (Cho forthcoming). Yet the same e-mail technology, when used by computer scientists interacting professionally in a public discussion group on the ARPANET, produced highly standard messages containing features of syntactic complexity such as nominalizations, subordinate and complement clauses, use of the passive voice, and heavy noun phrases (Herring 1998a). Still, the ARPANET case notwithstanding, e-mail tends not to be as formal as other edited forms of writing. This is due in part to the less formal purposes e-mail is typically used to fulfill, and in part to the relative openness of e-mail as a new communication mode that has not yet been colonized by rigid prescriptive norms.[10]

3   Interaction Management

Along with claims of structural fragmentation, text-only CMD is sometimes claimed to be interactionally incoherent, due to limitations imposed by computer messaging systems on turn-taking. In contrast with the spoken conversation ideal of "no gap, no overlap" (Sacks et al. 1974), computer-mediated exchanges involve unpredictable and sometimes lengthy gaps between messages, and exchanges regularly overlap, although strictly speaking, individual transmissions cannot (Cherny 1999; Lunsford 1996; Murray 1989).[11] Two properties of the computer medium create obstacles to interaction management: (1) disrupted turn *adjacency* caused by the fact that messages are posted in the order received by the system, without regard for what they are responding to, and (2) lack of simultaneous *feedback* caused by reduced audiovisual cues (Herring 1999a).

The first property lends to many computer-mediated exchanges an initial aura of fragmentation. Consider the phenomenon of overlapping exchanges, as illustrated by the following excerpt of interaction from the Internet Relay Chat channel #punjab (from Paolillo forthcoming). Note that the IRC system automatically appends the user's name (in this case, the pseudonymous nickname selected by the user herself or himself) at the beginning of each message. Messages preceded by asterisks (***) are also generated automatically by the system, and indicate that a user has joined or left the channel. (Numbers in square brackets were added by the author for ease of reference.)

(3)   [1]   <ashna> hi jatt
    [2]   *** Signoff: puja (EOF From client)
    [3]   <Dave-G> kally i was only joking around
    [4]   <Jatt> ashna: hello?
    [5]   <kally> dave-g it was funny
    [6]   <ashna> how are u jatt
    [7]   <LUCKMAN> ssa all[12]
    [8]   <Dave-G> kally you da woman!
    [9]   <Jatt> ashna: do we know eachother?. I'm ok how are you
    [10] *** LUCKMAN has left channel #PUNJAB
    [11] *** LUCKMAN has joined channel #punjab
    [12] <kally> dave-g good stuff:)
    [13] <Jatt> kally: so hows school life, life in geneal, love life, family life?
    [14] <ashna> jatt no we don't know each other, i fine
    [15] <Jatt> ashna: where r ya from?

Two different dyadic interactions are interleaved in this stretch of discourse, one between ashna and jatt, and the other between Dave-G and kally. To complicate matters further, in l. 13, jatt addresses kally. However, despite the fact that almost every initiation–response pair is disrupted by intervening material, it is possible to track the intended recipient of each message because in each case, the message sender explicitly names the addressee. This practice, termed *addressivity* by Werry (1996), makes it possible to separate out the two dyadic interactions as follows:

(3′) [1]   <ashna> hi jatt
    [4]   <Jatt> ashna: hello?
    [6]   <ashna> how are u jatt
    [9]   <Jatt> ashna: do we know eachother?. I'm ok how are you
    [14] <ashan> jatt no we don't know each other, i fine
    [15] <Jatt> ashna: where r ya from?

(3″) [3]   <Dave-G> kally i was only joking around
    [5]   <kally> dave-g it was funny
    [8]   <Dave-G> kally you da woman!
    [12] <kally> dave-g good stuff:)

Addressivity is one means by which users adapt to constraints on turn-taking in multiparticipant synchronous CMD.

A similar referential tracking problem, and an analogous adaptation, occur in asynchronous CMD such as takes place in discussion groups on the Internet. *Linking* is the practice of referring explicitly to the content of a previous message in one's response (Baym 1996; Herring 1996b), as for example when a message begins, "I would like to respond to Diana's comment about land mines." *Quoting*, or copying portions of a previous message in one's response (Severinson Eklundh and Macdonald 1994; Severinson Eklundh forthcoming), may also function as a type of linking, as in the following example from a soap opera fan newsgroup (example from Baym 1996: 326). In this example, the name and e-mail address of the person quoted are given in a system-generated "pointer" line that precedes the quote, and each line of quoted text is set off with an angle bracket (>). The writer's comments follow the quote:[13]

(4)   janed@ABC.bigtel.com (Jane Doe) writes:
       >I can't believe how horrible Natalie looks. Has she put on a lot of weight?

       I agree, but she has always had a somewhat round face, so if she did put on weight, I think that would be accentuated.

Quoting creates the illusion of adjacency in that it incorporates and juxtaposes (portions of) two turns – an initiation and a response – within a single message. When portions of previous text are repeatedly quoted and responded to, the resulting message can have the appearance of an extended conversational exchange (Hodsdon forthcoming; Severinson Eklundh forthcoming).

The analysis of turn-taking in asynchronous CMD is additionally complicated by the fact that a single message may contain two or more conversational moves which are physically, but not functionally, adjacent (Baym 1996; Condon and Čech forthcoming). This creates problems for equating "messages" with "turns," since some e-mail messages effectively convey what would have been communicated through multiple turns in synchronous interaction.[14] Conversely, a synchronous message may contain less than a turn, as when for example a sender has more to say than fits in a single message (which in some chat systems is limited to about 100 characters), and continues his or her turn in an immediately following message (Lunsford 1996; Murray 1989). However, as soon as a message is sent, the possibility exists for a message from another participant to follow, effectively "interrupting" the first person's turn. In order to retain the floor through an extended turn, therefore, some synchronous CMD users have innovated floor-holding conventions, for example appending a special character at what might otherwise appear to be a turn-completion point to indicate that the turn is not yet finished (Herring 1999a). Alternatively, an empowered participant may allocate turns to other participants by calling on them by name, perhaps after they have put in a bid for the next turn by "raising their hand" (e.g. typing "[Character name] raises his hand"; Cherny 1999: 181). These adaptive strategies compensate for a lack of simultaneous feedback in one-way computer communication systems by providing explicit mechanisms for speaker change.

4   Social Practice

Many early researchers believed that computer-networked communication was a "cool" medium well suited to the transfer of data and information, but poorly suited to social uses (Baron 1984; Kiesler et al. 1984). Others saw in CMC a utopian, egalitarian potential – with social status cues "filtered out," anyone could participate freely in open, democratic exchanges (Landow 1994; Poster 1990). The social life that teems on the Internet in the late 1990s bears out neither of these idealized visions, but it does provide a rich source of data for the study of discourse and social practice.

4.1 Socially conditioned variation

Language use is highly variable in computer-mediated environments, even within a single mode. This variation reflects the influence on the linguistic choices of CMD users of social factors such as participant demographics and situational context.

That participant demographics make a difference in an "anonymous" (faceless, bodiless) medium such as the Internet is interesting in and of itself. It also raises problems for traditional variationist methods which assume that reliable information about participant gender, age, social class, race, geographical location, etc., is available to the researcher (e.g. Labov 1966). The dispersed nature of Internet groups renders the *geographic location* of users difficult to determine, and less relevant than in studies of face-to-face communication, since physical proximity is not a condition for shared membership in a computer-mediated speech community. *Social class, race*, and *ethnicity* have also tended to be relatively invisible on the Internet, although this may reflect the fact that until recently, most people participating in public group CMD have been highly educated, middle- to upper-middle-class, white speakers of English (Nakamura 1995; Reid 1991).[15] Even in racially polarizing debates, the racial identity of participants may only be inferable from the content of their messages, not from their language use (Hodsdon forthcoming). The exception to this generalization is intra-group CMD – especially when race/ethnicity is the theme that defines the group, as in the soc.culture newsgroups on Usenet – which makes use of discursive markers of racial and ethnic identity, including culture-specific lexis and verbal genres, and code-switching between English and the group's ethnic language (Burkhalter 1999; Georgakopoulou forthcoming; Jacobs-Huey forthcoming; Paolillo 1996, forthcoming). Provided that participants' names or language competencies do not identify them, signaling race or ethnicity on-line appears to be an option at the participants' discretion (Burkhalter 1999).

In contrast, other features of "real-life" identity are relatively apparent, even when the participants themselves do not orient toward them consciously, and may actively seek to mask them (cf. Danet 1998). Information about participants' *educational level* is given off largely unconsciously by their sophistication of language use, including adherence to prescriptive norms (e.g. Herring 1998a); similarly, *age* is often revealed through the preoccupations and life experiences communicated in message content (Herring 1998c). Most apparent of all is participant *gender*, which is indicated by participants' names in asynchronous discussion groups, and is often a focus of conscious attention even in pseudonymous synchronous CMD. Participants in chat rooms request and provide information about their real-life genders, and many choose gender-revealing nicknames, e.g. Cover_Girl, sexychica, shy_boy, and GTBastard. On a less conscious level, participants "give off" gender information through adherence to culturally prescribed gendered interactional norms,[16] sometimes interacting in ways that exaggerate the binary opposition between femaleness and maleness, for example by engaging in stereotyped behaviors such as supportiveness and coyness for females, and ritual insults and sexual pursuit of females for males (Hall 1996; Herring 1998c; cf. Rodino 1997).

Traditional gender stereotypes can be reified even when people believe they are freely choosing their on-line gender identity in nontraditional ways, as illustrated in the comment of one social MUD participant:

(5)   Gilmore says, "And in a V[irtual]R[eality], people can become someone else. I can be a 6'5" steroid stud, or someone can be a sexy hot babe and do things they'd never hve the guts to do IRL['in real life']."

In his attempt to imagine new, liberatory gender identities, this MUDder instead evokes a traditional male gender fantasy: the "steroid stud" and the "sexy hot babe." The author further cues his gender by his choice of a male character name and use of a first person pronoun in reference to "steroid stud." Other linguistic behaviors for which (presumably unconscious) gender differences have been observed in CMD include message length, assertiveness (Herring 1993), politeness (Herring 1994, 1996a), and aggression (Cherny 1994; Collins-Jarvis 1997), including "flaming" (Herring 1994).[17]

Variation in CMD is also conditioned by situational factors that constitute the context of the communication. Different *participation structures* (Baym 1996) such as one-to-one, one-to-many, or many-to-many; the distinction between public and private exchanges; and the degree of anonymity provided by the system all have potential consequences for language use. Participants' previous *experience*, both off and on the Internet, also shapes linguistic behavior; thus users may transfer terms and practices from off-line cultures into CMD (Baym 1995), and experienced users may communicate systematically differently from new users or "newbies" (Weber forthcoming).

Over time, computer-mediated groups develop *norms* of practice regarding "how things are done" and what constitutes socially desirable behavior; these may then be codified in "Frequently Asked Question" documents (FAQs; Voth 1999) and netiquette guidelines (e.g. Shea 1994). Norms vary considerably from context to context; for example, flaming is proscribed in many academic discussion groups, but positively valued in the Usenet newsgroup alt.flame (Smith et al. 1997).

This last example points to the importance of communication *purpose* – recreational, professional, pedagogical, creative, etc. – in shaping language use. Social and pedagogical IRC, for example, may differ widely in level of formality, use of directive speech acts, and topical coherence (Herring and Nix 1997). Discourse *topic* and *activity* type (such as "greeting", "exchanging information," "flaming," etc.) also condition linguistic variation. Thus, for example, contractions are used more often in discussing "fun" topics (such as profanity) than serious topics on an academic linguistics discussion list, and more often in information exchanges than in extended debates (Herring 1999c). These findings on socially motivated variation show that CMD, despite being mediated by "impersonal" machines, reflects the social realities of its users.

4.2   Social interaction

In addition to being shaped by social circumstances, CMD constitutes social practice in and of itself. Text-only CMD is a surprisingly effective way to "do" interactional work, in that it allows users to choose their words with greater care, and reveals less of their doubts and insecurities, than does spontaneous speech (Sproull and Kiesler 1991). Thus participants negotiate, intimidate, joke, tease, and flirt (and in some cases, have sex and get married)[18] on the Internet, often without having ever met their interlocutors face to face.

Computer users have developed a number of compensatory strategies to replace social cues normally conveyed by other channels in face-to-face interaction. The best-known of these is the use of emoticons, or sideways "smiley faces" composed of ascii characters (Raymond 1993; Reid 1991), to represent facial expressions. While the prototypical emoticon, a smile :-), usually functions to indicate happiness or friendly intent, emoticons cue other interactional frames as well: for example, a winking face sticking its tongue out, ;-p (as if to say "NYA nya nya NYA nya"), can signal flirtatious teasing, and Danet et al. (1997) describe a spontaneous IRC "party" where emoticons were creatively deployed to represent the activity of smoking marijuana.[19]

In addition to facial expressions, physical actions can be represented textually. Typed actions such as <grin> and *yawn* may serve as contextualization cues (Gumperz 1982) for a playful or relaxed discourse frame. Synchronous CMD such as MUDs and IRC further provides a special communication command which can be used to describe actions or states in the third person. This command is often used to expand dialog into narrative performance, as in the following flirtatious IRC exchange (example from Herring 1998c):

(6) <Dobbs> come on, Danielle!!
     <Danielle> No.
     <Danielle> You have to SEDUCE me . . .
     *** Action: jazzman reaches out for Danielle's soft hand.
     *** Danielle has left channel #netsex
     *** Action: Dobbs whispers sweet nothings in Danielle's ear
     *** Action: Butthead moves closer to Danielle
     <jazzman> danielle's gone dumbass

In this example, the four present tense actions (preceded by asterisks) are *performative* in nature; they count as "acts" (in this case, of seduction) solely by virtue of having been typed.

Since anyone can potentially create reality in this way, it follows that participants may type different, incompatible versions of reality, resulting in what Kolko (1995) calls a "narrative gap." Gaps of this sort may require the involvement of a third participant to resolve which version of the virtual reality will stand. The following MUD example is reported in Cherny (1995):

(7) The guest hugs Karen.
     Karen is NOT hugged by Guest.
     [another character later addresses Karen, referring to "the guest who hugged you"]

In this example, Karen attempts to deny the performative nature of the guest's unwelcome action, but the third participant's comment affirms it – as Cherny notes, "[i]n some sense, the action occurred as soon as the message showed up on people's screens."

From this and other research into on-line social interaction, language emerges as a powerful strategic resource – indeed, the primary resource – for creating social reality in text-based CMC.

4.3   *Social criticism*

The socially constitutive power of computer-mediated language is not limited to the accomplishment of interactional work between individuals. We owe to Foucault (1980) the insight that societal institutions are themselves constructed and maintained through discourse. Nowhere is this more true than on the Internet, where "communities" of users come together, sharing neither geographical space nor (in the case of asynchronous CMD) time, and create social structures exclusively out of words (Jones 1995; Rheingold 1993; Smith and Kollock 1999). In some on-line communities, this process generates rules, sanctions against the violation of those rules, and systems of governance to enforce the sanctions, headed by empowered individuals or groups (Kolko and Reid 1998; Reid 1994, 1999). That is, "virtual communities" may develop internal power hierarchies, contrary to utopian claims that computer-mediated communication is inherently egalitarian.

CMD also inherits power asymmetries from the larger historical and economic context of the Internet. These include the traditional dominance of the United States as the leading source of computer network technology (Yates 1996b), the fact that the cost of the equipment required to set up and access computer networks creates "haves" and "have nots," both within the US and globally (Petrazzini and Kibati 1999), and the continuing overrepresentation of white, middle-class, English-speaking males in positions of control as Internet mode and site administrators (Shade 1998). These circumstances advantage certain groups of Internet users over others, and thus call for critical CMD analysis that is sensitive to issues of power and control.

One area that has been explored extensively for Internet groups is gender asymmetry.[20] Much of this research finds that gender differences in CMD, such as those described in section 4.1 above, disproportionately disfavor female participants. In discussion groups, for example, the contentiousness of many male messages tends to discourage women from responding, while women's concerns with considerateness and social harmony tend to be disparaged as a "waste of bandwidth" in male-authored netiquette guidelines (Herring 1996a). Even extreme acts of aggression, such as narrative enactments of sexual violence against women, find ideological justification in dominant male discourses – for example, through invoking principles of "freedom of expression" (Herring 1998b, 1999b), or denying the pragmatic force of words to constitute actions in the case of a MUD rape (Dibbell 1993). Critical discourse analysis exposes the mechanisms that are employed to create and maintain gender asymmetry in computer-mediated environments, as well as analyzing the discourse strategies that are used by women to resist such attempts (Herring 1999b; Herring et al. 1995).

Another growing concern is the dominance of the English language on the Internet, and the possible effects of this dominance on the global spread of US values and cultural practices (Mattelart 1996; Yates 1996). Discourse analysts address these issues by studying the communication – including the language choices and attitudes – of speakers of other languages on the Internet. Paolillo (1996, forthcoming) finds little use of South Asian languages in CMD among South Asians, but suggests that nondominant languages may fare better when computer networks are located entirely within the nation or region where the language is natively spoken, when fonts are readily available which include all of the characters of the language's writing system, and when there has been no colonial legacy of English within the home culture. Other researchers are less sanguine: Yoon (forthcoming) finds that young people in Korea tend to accept the dominance and importance of English on and for the Internet without question, and concludes that this is due to the symbolic power of the technology, which is fueled by commercially driven mass media. These findings point to a need for critical analysis not just of CMD, but of public discourse about computer technology which transmits ideological (including commercial) messages.

Computer networks do not guarantee democratic, equal-opportunity interaction, any more than any previous communication technology has had that effect. Pre-existing social arrangements carry over into cyberspace to create an uneven playing field, and computer-mediated communication can be a tool of either oppression or resistance. While utopian theorists might be disappointed by this outcome, for socially oriented discourse analysts, it is a boon. The discursive negotiation and expression of social relations in cyberspace, including asymmetrical relations, constitutes one of the most promising areas of future investigation for students of computer-mediated discourse.

5 Conclusions

As the above discussion shows, we have come far from the view of CMD as a single genre. It should also be clear that not all properties of CMD follow necessarily and directly from the properties of computer technology. Rather, social and cultural factors – carried over from communication in other media as well as internally generated in computer-mediated environments – contribute importantly to the constellation of properties that characterizes computer-mediated discourse.

The wide variety of discourse activities that take place in CMD and the range of human experiences they evoke invites multiple approaches to analysis, including approaches drawn from different academic disciplines as well as different subfields of discourse analysis. This richness and diversity of CMD, concentrated into a single (albeit vast) phenomenon which is the Internet, is its strength. CMD study enables us to see interconnections between micro- and macrolevels of interaction that might otherwise not emerge by observing spoken or written communication, and potentially to forge more comprehensive theories of discourse and social action as a result.

That said, further specialization in CMD research is desirable and inevitable, given that the field covers a vast array of phenomena and is still new. In this overview, I have focused on issues of categorization, linguistic structure, interaction management, and social practice in computer-mediated environments. Other important topics, such as the effects of computer mediation on language change over time (Herring 1998a, 1999c), children's learning and use of CMD (Evard 1996; Nix 1998, forthcoming), pedagogical CMD (Herring and Nix 1997; Warschauer 1999; Zyngier and de Moura 1997), and cross-cultural CMD (Ma 1996; Meagher and Castaños 1996), have not been treated here. Each potentially constitutes a subdiscipline of CMD research that can be extended in its own right.

The future prospects for the field of CMD analysis are very bright. As of this writing, new research on computer-mediated communication is appearing almost daily, and a growing proportion of that work is making language its focus. This flurry of activity is certain to turn up new areas of research, as well as problematizing existing understandings; such are the signs of a vital and growing field of inquiry. Moreover, as CMC technology continues to evolve at a rapid pace, new and up-to-the-minute research will be needed to document its use. For example, we can anticipate structural and cultural changes in on-line communication as the worldwide web increasingly integrates Internet modes such as e-mail, newsgroups, and chat rooms under a single graphical interface. We can also look forward to new understandings (and new analytical challenges) as CMD enhanced by audio and video channels comes into more popular use. CMD is not just a trend; it is here to stay. For as long as computer-mediated communication involves language in any form, there will be a need for computer-mediated discourse analysis.

NOTES

1   This chapter does not consider the discourse properties of documents on the worldwide web. Web "pages" tend to be prepared in advance and monologic rather than reciprocally interactive; as such, they constitute a separate phenomenon deserving of study on its own terms. Nor does the chapter take up the question of what leads users to choose a particular medium of communication (CMD as opposed to speaking or writing) or mode of CMD (e.g. e-mail as opposed to real-time chat) for any given communicative purpose, as this falls outside our focus on the properties of computer-mediated exchanges themselves. For an early but still instructive treatment of this issue, see Murray (1988).

2   For example, Nancy Baym, Lynn Cherny, Brenda Danet, Susan Herring, Elizabeth Reid, and Simeon Yates; see references for examples of this early work.

3   The term "computer-mediated discourse" as a label for this kind of research was first used, to the best of my knowledge, at a pre-session of the Georgetown University Round Table on Languages and Linguistics that I organized in March of 1995.

4   I know of no examples of two-way asynchronous CMD, perhaps because it would serve no useful function for messages to be transmitted one keystroke at a time to the screens of addressees who were not present to appreciate the temporal aspects of the transmission.

5   Listserv mailing lists are thematically based discussion groups to which individuals "subscribe" by sending an e-mail request to the appropriate listserver; once added to the list of subscribers, they receive all communications posted to the list in the form of e-mail messages. Usenet is a large collection of "newsgroups" or discussion groups to which messages are posted as if to an electronic bulletin board; individuals must access Usenet using a web browser or newsreader in order to read the messages. IRC is a network of servers, accessed via a piece of software called an IRC client, which permits individuals to join a chat "channel" and exchange typed messages in real time with others connected to the channel. MUDs (Multi-User Dimensions or Multi-User Dungeons, from the early association of MUDs with the role-play

adventure game Dungeons and Dragons) and MOOs (MUDs, Object Oriented) are text-based virtual reality environments which, in addition to allowing real-time chat among connected users, are programmable spaces through which individuals can navigate and create text-based descriptions and objects. Access to all four modes is free via the Internet. Useful descriptions of mode-specific cultural practices include Hert (1997) for an academic discussion list, Baym (1995) and Pfaffenberger (1996) for Usenet, Reid (1991) for IRC, and Cherny (1999) and Reid (1994) for social MUDs.

6   However, see Baym (1993, 1995, 1996) for an example of a Usenet newsgroup, rec.arts.television.soaps (r.a.t.s.), that is predominantly female and cooperative in its orientation.

7   The abbreviation <g> or <grin> represents the action of grinning.

8   Jon Katz, quoted in Hale (1996: 9).

9   See, e.g., Danet (1992); Ferrara et al. (1991); Kim (1997); Maynor (1994); Murray (1990); Reid (1991); Ulhírová (1994); Werry (1996); and Wilkins (1991).

10 Recent evidence suggests that this may already be starting to change. As e-mail use becomes more common, increasingly replacing other forms of writing for both formal and informal purposes, expectations seem to be rising that e-mail language will be standard and "error-free," even in relatively informal communication (Erickson et al. 1999). For a study that documents a trend toward increasing formality over the 1990s in messages posted to a listserv discussion group, see Herring (1999c).

11 Unless otherwise noted, remarks in this section refer to one-way CMD.

12 The abbreviated Punjabi greeting "ssa" – "sat siri akal" (lit. "God is truth" = "hello") – illustrates the tendency toward reduction in synchronous CMD.

13 Quoted portions of previous messages may also appear after or interspersed with the writer's comments, depending on where the writer chooses to position the quotes, and on the default position of the cursor in relation to the quote for any given mailer system (Severinson Eklundh forthcoming).

14 In this sense, asynchronous CMD is more efficient than synchronous modes of communication; see Condon and Čech (1996, forthcoming.)

15 For current statistics on the demographics of Internet users, updated semi-annually, see the Graphic, Visualization, and Usability Center's WWW User Survey at http://www.cc.gatech.edu/gvu/user_surveys/.

16 The notion that people "give off" information about themselves unconsciously through their self-presentation is from Goffman (1959).

17 See Herring (2000) for a recent summary of research on gender differences in computer-mediated communication.

18 Weddings have been reported in MUD environments, in which the bride and groom exchange vows in a public ceremony, with other MUD participants as witnesses and guests. In some cases, the bride and groom also have a relationship "in real life." In other cases, the relationship exists only in the virtual realm (Jacobson 1996; Turkle 1995).

19 One such sequence looks like this: :-Q :| :| :\sssss :) (Danet et al. 1997).

20 See, for example, Collins-Jarvis (1997); Ebben (1994); Hall (1996); Herring (1992, 1993, 1994, 1996a, *inter alia*); Herring et al. (1992, 1995); Hert (1997); Kendall (1996); Kramarae and Taylor (1993); Savicki et al. (1997); Selfe and Meyer (1991); Sutton (1994); We (1994).

REFERENCES

Baron, Naomi S. 1984. "Computer-mediated communication as a force in language change." *Visible Language*, XVIII 2, 118–41.

Baym, Nancy. 1993. "Interpreting soap operas and creating community: Inside a computer-mediated fan culture." *Journal of Folklore Research*, 30(2/3), 143–76.

Baym, Nancy. 1995. "The emergence of community in computer-mediated communication." In S. Jones (ed.), *Cybersociety: Computer-Mediated Communication and Community*, 138–63. Thousand Oaks, CA: Sage.

Baym, Nancy. 1996. "Agreements and disagreements in a computer-mediated discussion." *Research on Language and Social Interaction*, 29(4), 315–45.

Bechar-Israeli, Haya. 1995. "From <Bonehead> to <cLoNehEAd>: Nicknames, play and identity on Internet Relay Chat." *Journal of Computer-Mediated Communication*, 1(2). http://www.ascusc.org/jcmc/vol1/issue2/

Burkhalter, Byron. 1999. "Reading race online: Discovering racial identity in Usenet discussions." In M. Smith and P. Kollock (eds), *Communities in Cyberspace*, 60–75. London: Routledge.

Chafe, Wallace L. 1982. "Integration and involvement in speaking, writing, and oral literature." In D. Tannen (ed.), *Spoken and Written Language: Exploring Orality and Literacy*, 35–53. Norwood, NJ: Ablex.

Cherny, Lynn. 1994. "Gender differences in text-based virtual reality." Available at ftp://ftp.lambda.moo.mud.org/pub/MOO/papers/GenderMoo.ps

Cherny, Lynn. 1995. "The modal complexity of speech events in a social MUD." *Electronic Journal of Communication/La revue électronique de communication*, 5(4). http://www.cios.org/www/ejc/v5n495.htm

Cherny, Lynn. 1999. *Conversation and Community: Chat in a Virtual World*. Stanford: CSLI Publications.

Cherny, Lynn. Forthcoming. "Winning and losing: Abbreviations and routines as community register markers on a social MUD." In S. Herring (ed.), *Computer-Mediated Conversation*.

Cho, Natasha. Forthcoming. "Linguistic features of electronic mail." In S. Herring (ed.), *Computer-Mediated Conversation*.

Collins-Jarvis, Lori. 1997. "Discriminatory messages and gendered power relations in on-line discussion groups." Paper presented at the 1997 annual meeting of the National Communication Association, Chicago, IL.

Condon, Sherri L. and Claude G. Ćech. 1996. "Discourse management strategies in face-to-face and computer-mediated decision making interactions." *Electronic Journal of Communication/La revue électronique de communication*, 6(3). http://www.cios.org/www/ejc/v6n396.htm

Condon, Sherri L. and Claude G. Ćech. Forthcoming. "Discourse management in three modalities." In S. Herring (ed.), *Computer-Mediated Conversation*.

Daft, Richard L. and Robert H. Lengel. 1984. "Information richness: A new approach to managerial behavior and organization design." In B. M. Staw and L. L. Cummings (eds), *Research in Organizational Behavior*, 6, 191–233. Greenwich, CT: JAI Press.

Danet, Brenda. 1992. "Books, letters, documents: Implications of computer-mediated communication for three genres of text." Unpublished

manuscript. Noah Mozes Dept of
Communication and Journalism:
Hebrew University of Jerusalem.

Danet, Brenda. 1998. "Text as mask:
Gender and identity on the Internet."
In S. Jones (ed.), *Cybersociety 2.0:
Revisiting Computer Mediated
Communication and Community*,
129–58. Thousand Oaks, CA: Sage.

Danet, Brenda, Lucia Ruedenberg-Wright,
and Yehudit Rosenbaum-Tamari.
1997. "Smoking dope at a virtual
party: Writing, play and performance
on Internet relay chat." In S. Rafaeli,
F. Sudweeks, and M. McLaughlin
(eds), *Network and Netplay: Virtual
Groups on the Internet*. Cambridge,
MA: AAAI/MIT Press.

Deuel, Nancy R. 1996. "Our passionate
response to virtual reality." In S.
Herring (ed.), *Computer-Mediated
Communication: Linguistic, Social and
Cross-Cultural Perspectives*, 129–46.
Amsterdam: John Benjamins.

Dibbell, Julian. 1993. "A rape in
cyberspace, or how an evil clown, a
Haitian trickster spirit, two wizards,
and a cast of dozens turned a
database into a society." *Village Voice*,
Dec. 21, 36–42.

Ebben, Maureen M. 1994. "Women on the
net: An exploratory study of gender
dynamics on the soc.women
computer network." Unpublished
doctoral dissertation. University of
Illinois at Urbana Champaign.

Erickson, Thomas, David N. Smith,
Wendy A. Kellogg, Mark Laff, John T.
Richards, and Erin Bradner. 1999.
"Socially translucent systems: Social
proxies, persistent conversation, and
the design of 'Babble'." Paper
presented at CHI99. http://
www.pliant.org/personal/
Tom_Erickson/loops.chi99.paper.html

Evard, Michele. 1996. " 'So please stop,
thank you': Girls online." In
L. Cherny and E. R. Weise (eds),
Wired_Women: Gender and New

Realities in Cyberspace, 188–204.
Seattle: Seal Press.

Ferrara, Kathleen, Hans Brunner, and
Greg Whittemore. 1991. "Interactive
written discourse as an emergent
register." *Written Communication*,
8(1), 8–34.

Foucault, Michel. 1980. In C. Gordon (ed.),
*Power/Knowledge: Selected Interviews
and Other Writings*, 1972–7. Brighton:
Harvester.

Georgakopoulou, Alexandra. Forthcoming.
" 'On for drinkies?': E-mail cues of
participant alignments." In S. Herring
(ed.), *Computer-Mediated Conversation*.

Goffman, Erving. 1959. *Presentation of Self
in Everyday Life*. Garden City, NY:
Anchor.

Gumperz, John J. 1982. "Contextualization
conventions." *Discourse Strategies*,
130–52. Cambridge: Cambridge
University Press.

Hafner, Katie and Matthew Lyon. 1996.
*Where Wizards Stay Up Late: The
Origins of the Internet*. New York:
Simon and Schuster.

Hale, Constance (ed.). 1996. *Wired Style:
Principles of English Usage in the Digital
Age*. San Francisco: HardWired.

Hall, Kira. 1996. "Cyberfeminism." In
S. Herring (ed.), *Computer-Mediated
Communication: Linguistic, Social and
Cross-Cultural Perspectives*, 147–70.
Amsterdam: John Benjamins.

Herring, Susan C. 1992. "Gender and
participation in computer-mediated
linguistic discourse." Washington,
DC: ERIC Clearinghouse on
Languages and Linguistics. Document
no. ED345552.

Herring, Susan C. 1993. "Gender and
democracy in computer-mediated
communication." *Electronic Journal of
Communication*, 3(2). http://
www.cios.org/www/ejc/v3n293.htm.
Reprinted (1996) in R. Kling (ed.),
Computerization and Controversy, 2nd
edn, 476–89. New York: Academic
Press.

Herring, Susan C. 1994. "Politeness in computer culture: Why women thank and men flame." In M. Bucholtz, A. Liang, L. Sutton, and C. Hines (eds), *Cultural Performances: Proceedings of the Third Berkeley Women and Language Conference*, 278–94. Berkeley: Berkeley Women and Language Group.

Herring, Susan C. 1996a. "Posting in a different voice: Gender and ethics in computer-mediated communication." In C. Ess (ed.), *Philosophical Perspectives on Computer-Mediated Communication*, 115–45. Albany: SUNY Press. Reprinted (1999) in P. Mayer (ed.), *Computer Media and Communication: A Reader*, 241–65. New York: Oxford University Press.

Herring, Susan C. 1996b. "Two variants of an electronic message schema." In S. Herring (ed.), *Computer-Mediated Communication: Linguistic, Social and Cross-Cultural Perspectives*, 81–106. Amsterdam: John Benjamins.

Herring, Susan C. 1998a. "Le style du courrier électronique: Variabilité et changement." *Terminogramme*, 84–5, 9–16.

Herring, Susan C. 1998b. "Ideologies of language on the Internet: The case of 'free speech'." Paper presented at the 6th International Pragmatics Conference, Reims, France, July 21.

Herring, Susan C. 1998c. "Virtual gender performances." Paper presented at Texas A and M University, September 25.

Herring, Susan C. 1999a. "Interactional coherence in CMC." *Journal of Computer-Mediated Communication* 4(4). Special issue on *Persistent Conversation*, T. Erickson (ed.). http://www.ascusc.org/jcmc/vol4/issue4/

Herring, Susan C. 1999b. "The rhetorical dynamics of gender harassment on-line." *Information Society* 15(3), 151–67. Special issue on *The Rhetorics of Gender in Computer-Mediated Communication*, L. J. Gurak (ed.).

Herring, Susan C. 1999c. "Actualization of a counter-trend: Contractions in Internet English." Paper presented at the 14th International Conference on Historical Linguistics, Vancouver, Canada, August 13. Forthcoming in H. Andersen (ed.), *Actualization Patterns in Language Change*. Amsterdam/Philadelphia: John Benjamins.

Herring, Susan C. 2000. "Gender differences in CMC: Findings and implications." *Computer Professionals for Social Responsibility Newsletter*. http://www.cpsr.org/publications/newsletters/

Herring, Susan and Carole Nix. 1997. "Is 'serious chat' an oxymoron? Academic vs. social uses of Internet relay chat." Paper presented at the American Association of Applied Linguistics, Orlando, FL, March 11.

Herring, Susan, Deborah Johnson, and Tamra DiBenedetto. 1992. "Participation in electronic discourse in a 'feminist' field." In K. Hall, M. Bucholtz, and B. Moonwomon (eds), *Locating Power: The Proceedings of the Second Berkeley Women and Language Conference*, 250–62. Berkeley: Berkeley Women and Language Group. Reprinted (1998) in J. Coates (ed.), *Language and Gender: A Reader*, 197–210. Oxford: Blackwell.

Herring, Susan, Deborah Johnson, and Tamra DiBenedetto. 1995. "'This discussion is going too far!' Male resistance to female participation on the Internet." In M. Bucholtz and K. Hall (eds), *Gender Articulated: Language and the Socially Constructed Self*, 67–96. New York: Routledge.

Hert, Philippe. 1997. "Social dynamics of an on-line scholarly debate." *Information Society*, 13, 329–60.

Hodsdon, Connie Beth. Forthcoming. "Conversations within conversations: Intertextuality in racially antagonistic dialogue on Usenet." In S. Herring (ed.), *Computer-Mediated Conversation.*

Jacobs-Huey, Lanita. Forthcoming. ". . . BTW, how do YOU wear your hair? Identity, knowledge and authority in an electronic speech community." In S. Herring (ed.), *Computer-Mediated Conversation.*

Jacobson, David. 1996. "Contexts and cues in cyberspace: The pragmatics of naming in text-based virtual realities." *Journal of Anthropological Research*, 52, 461–79.

Jones, Steven G. 1995. "Understanding community in the information age." In S. Jones (ed.), *Cybersociety: Computer-Mediated Communication and Community*, 10–35. Thousand Oaks, CA: Sage. Reprinted (1999) in P. Mayer (ed.), *Computer Media and Communication: A Reader*, 219–40. New York: Oxford University Press.

Kendall, Lori. 1996. "MUDder? I hardly know 'er! Adventures of a feminist MUDder." In L. Cherny and E. R. Weise (eds), *Wired_Women: Gender and New Realities in Cyberspace*, 207–23. Seattle: Seal Press.

Kiesler, Sara, Jane Siegel, and Timothy W. McGuire. 1984. "Social psychological aspects of computer-mediated communication." *American Psychologist*, 39, 1123–34.

Kim, Esther Hyunzee. 1997. "Korean romanization on the Internet." Unpublished master's thesis, University of Texas at Arlington.

Kim, Min-Sun and Narayan S. Raja. 1991. "Verbal aggression and self-disclosure on computer bulletin boards." Washington, DC: ERIC Clearinghouse on Languages and Linguistics. Document no. ED334620.

King, Storm. 1996. "Researching Internet communities: Proposed ethical guidelines for the reporting of results." *Information Society*, 12(2), 119–27.

Ko, Kwang-Kyu. 1996. "Structural characteristics of computer-mediated language: A comparative analysis of InterChange discourse." *Electronic Journal of Communication/La revue électronique de communication*, 6(3). http://www.cios.org/www/ejc/v6n396.htm

Kolko, Beth. 1995. "Building a world with words: The narrative reality of virtual communities." *Works and Days* 25/26, 13(1, 2). http://acorn.grove.iup.edu/en/workdays/toc.html

Kolko, Beth and Elizabeth Reid. 1998. "Dissolution and fragmentation: Problems in online communities." In S. Jones (ed.), *Cybersociety 2.0: Revisiting Computer Mediated Communication and Community*, 212–29. Thousand Oaks, CA: Sage.

Kramarae, Cheris and H. Jeanie Taylor. 1993. "Women and men on electronic networks: A conversation or a monologue?" In H. J. Taylor, C. Kramarae, and M. Ebben (eds), *Women, Information Technology, and Scholarship*, 52–61. Urbana, IL: Center for Advanced Study.

Labov, William. 1966. *The Social Stratification of English in New York City*. Washington, DC: Center for Applied Linguistics.

Landow, George (ed.). 1994. *Hyper/Text/Theory*. Baltimore: Johns Hopkins University Press.

Levy, Steven. 1984. *Hackers: Heroes of the Computer Revolution*. New York: Dell.

Livia, Anna. Forthcoming. "BSR ES TU F?: Brevity and expressivity on the French Minitel." In S. Herring (ed.), *Computer-Mediated Conversation.*

Lunsford, Wayne. 1996. "Turn-taking organization in Internet relay chat." Unpublished MS, University of Texas at Arlington.

Ma, Ringo. 1996. "Computer-mediated conversations as a new dimension of intercultural communication between East Asian and North American college students." In S. Herring (ed.), *Computer-Mediated Communication: Linguistic, Social and Cross-Cultural Perspectives*, 173–85. Amsterdam: John Benjamins.

MacKinnon, Richard C. 1995. "Searching for the Leviathan in Usenet." In S. Jones (ed.), *Cybersociety: Computer-Mediated Communication and Community*, 112–37. Thousand Oaks, CA: Sage.

Mattelart, Armand. 1996. "Les enjeux de la globalisation des réseaux." *Internet: L'Extase et L'Effroi* (special issue of *Le Monde Diplomatique*), 10–14.

Maynor, Natalie. 1994. "The language of electronic mail: Written speech?" In M. Montgomery and G. Little (eds), *Centennial Usage Studies*, 48–54. Publications of the American Dialect Society Series. University of Alabama Press.

McLaughlin, Margaret L., Kelly K. Osborne, and Christine B. Smith. 1995. "Standards of conduct on Usenet." In S. Jones (ed.), *Cybersociety: Computer-Mediated Communication and Community*, 90–111. Thousand Oaks, CA: Sage.

McRae, Shannon. 1996. "Coming apart at the seams: Sex, text and the virtual body." In L. Cherny and E. Weise (eds), *Wired_Women*, 242–63. Seattle: Seal Press.

Meagher, Mary Elaine and Fernando Castaños. 1996. "Perceptions of American culture: The impact of an electronically-mediated cultural exchange program on Mexican high school students." In S. Herring (ed.), *Computer-Mediated Communication: Linguistic, Social and Cross-Cultural Perspectives*, 187–202. Amsterdam: John Benjamins.

Murray, Denise E. 1985. "Composition as conversation: The computer terminal as medium of communication." In

L. Odell and D. Goswami (eds), *Writing in Nonacademic Settings*, 203–27. New York: Guilford.

Murray, Denise E. 1988. "The context of oral and written language: A framework for mode and medium switching." *Language in Society*, 17, 351–73.

Murray, Denise E. 1989. "When the medium determines turns: Turn-taking in computer conversation." In H. Coleman (ed.), *Working With Language*, 251–66. New York: Mouton de Gruyter.

Murray, Denise E. 1990. "CmC." *English Today*, 23, 42–6.

Nakamura, Lisa. 1995. "Race in/for cyberspace: Identity tourism and racial passing on the Internet." *Works and Days*, 25/26, 13(1, 2). http://acorn.grove.iup.edu/en/workdays/toc.html

Nix, Carole G. 1998. "The effects of e-mail use on fourth graders' writing skills." Unpublished doctoral dissertation, University of Texas at Arlington.

Nix, Carole G. Forthcoming. "Talking to strangers: Children's conversational openers on the Internet." In S. Herring (ed.), *Computer-Mediated Conversation*.

Paolillo, John C. 1996. "Language choice on soc.culture.punjab." *Electronic Journal of Communication/La revue électronique de communication* 6(3). http://www.cios.org/www/ejc/v6n396.htm

Paolillo, John C. Forthcoming. "Conversational codeswitching on Usenet and Internet relay chat." In S. Herring (ed.), *Computer-Mediated Conversation*.

Petrazzini, Ben and Mugo Kibati. 1999. "The Internet in developing countries." *Communications of the ACM*, 42(6), 31–36.

Poster, Mark. 1990. *The Mode of Information: Poststructuralism and Social Context*. Cambridge: Polity.

Raymond, Eric (ed.). 1993. *The New Hacker's Dictionary* 2nd edn. Cambridge, MA: MIT Press.

Reid, Elizabeth M. 1991. "Electropolis: Communication and community on Internet relay chat." Senior honours thesis, University of Melbourne, Australia. http://www.ee.mu.oz.au/papers/emr/index.html

Reid, Elizabeth M. 1994. "Cultural formations in text-based virtual realities." Master's thesis, University of Melbourne, Australia. http://www.ee.mu.oz.au/papers/emr/index.html

Reid, Elizabeth M. 1999. "Hierarchy and power: Social control in cyberspace." In M. Smith and P. Kollock (eds), *Communities in Cyberspace*, 107–33. London: Routledge.

Rheingold, Howard. 1993. *The Virtual Community: Homesteading on the Electronic Frontier*. Reading, MA: Addison-Wesley.

Rodino, Michelle. 1997. "Breaking out of binaries: Reconceptualizing gender and its relationship to language in computer-mediated communication." *Journal of Computer-Mediated Communication*, 3(3). http://www.ascusc.org/jcmc/vol3/issue3/

Sacks, Harvey, Emanuel Schegloff, and Gail Jefferson. 1974. "A simplest systematics for the organization of turn–taking for conversation." *Language*, 50, 696–735.

Savicki, Victor, Dawn Lingenfelter and Merle Kelley. 1997. "Gender language style and group composition in Internet discussion groups." *Journal of Computer-Mediated Communication*, 2(3). http://www.ascusc.org/jcmc/vol2/issue3/

Selfe, Cynthia L. and Paul R. Meyer. 1991. "Testing claims for on-line conferences." *Written Communication*, 8(2), 163–92.

Severinson Eklundh, Kerstin. 1986. *Dialogue Processes in Computer-Mediated Communication: A Study of Letters in the COM System*. Linköping Studies in Arts and Sciences 6. University of Linköping.

Severinson Eklundh, Kerstin. 1994. "Electronic mail as a medium for dialogue." In L. van Waes, E. Woudstra, and P. van den Hoven (eds), *Functional Communication Quality*, 162–73. Amsterdam/Atlanta: Rodopi.

Severinson Eklundh, Kerstin. Forthcoming. "To quote or not to quote: Setting the context for computer-mediated dialogues." In S. Herring (ed.), *Computer-Mediated Conversation*.

Severinson Eklundh, Kerstin and Clare Macdonald. 1994. "The use of quoting to preserve context in electronic mail dialogues." *IEEE Transactions on Professional Communication*, 37(4), 197–202.

Shade, Leslie Regan. 1998. "A gendered perspective on access to the information infrastructure." *Information Society*, 14(1), 33–44.

Shea, Virginia. 1994. *Netiquette*. San Francisco: Albion.

Smith, Christine B., Margaret L. McLaughlin, and Kerry K. Osborne. 1997. "Conduct controls on Usenet." *Journal of Computer-Mediated Communication*, 2(4). http://www.ascusc.org/jcmc/vol2/issue4/

Smith, Marc A. and Peter Kollock (eds). 1999. *Communities in Cyberspace*. London: Routledge.

Sproull, Lee and Sara Kiesler. 1991. *Connections: New Ways of Working in the Networked Organization*. Cambridge, MA: MIT Press.

Sutton, Laurel. 1994. "Using Usenet: Gender, power, and silence in electronic discourse." *Proceedings of the 20th Annual Meeting of the Berkeley Linguistics Society*, 506–20. Berkeley: Berkeley Linguistics Society.

Turkle, Sherry. 1995. *Life on the Screen: Identity in the Age of the Internet.* New York: Simon and Schuster.

Uhlírová, Ludmila. 1994. "E-mail as a new subvariety of medium and its effects upon the message." In Svétla Ćmejrková and František Štícha (eds), *The Syntax of Sentence and Text: A Festschrift for Frantísek Danes*, 273–82. Amsterdam: John Benjamins.

Voth, Christine. 1999. "The facts on FAQs: Frequently asked questions documents on the Internet and Usenet." Unpublished master's thesis, University of Texas at Arlington.

Warschauer, Mark. 1999. *Electronic Literacies: Language, Culture, and Power in Online Education.* Mahwah, NJ: Lawrence Erlbaum.

We, Gladys. 1994. "Cross-gender communication in cyberspace." *Electronic Journal of Virtual Culture*, 2(3). ftp byrd.mu.wvnet.edu/pub/ejvc

Weber, H. L. Forthcoming. "Missed cues: How disputes can socialize virtual newcomers." In S. Herring (ed.), *Computer-Mediated Conversation.*

Werry, Christopher C. 1996. "Linguistic and interactional features of Internet relay chat." In S. Herring (ed.), *Computer-Mediated Communication: Linguistic, Social and Cross-Cultural Perspectives*, 47–63. Amsterdam: John Benjamins.

Wilkins, Harriet. 1991. "Computer talk: Long-distance conversations by computer." *Written Communication*, 8(1), 56–78.

Yates, Simeon J. 1996. "English in cyberspace." In S. Goodman and D. Graddol (eds), *Redesigning English: New Texts, New Identities*, 106–40. London: Routledge.

Yates, Simeon and David Graddol. 1996. "'I read this chat is heavy': The discursive construction of identity in CMC." Paper presented at the 5th International Pragmatics Conference, Mexico City, July 8.

Yoon, Sunny. Forthcoming. "Internet discourse and the habitus of Korea's new generation." In C. Ess and F. Sudweeks (eds), *Culture, Technology, Communication: Towards an Intercultural Global Village.* Albany: SUNY Press.

Zyngier, Sonia and Maria Lucia Seidl de Moura. 1997. "Pragmatic aspects of spontaneous electronic communication in a school setting." *Text*, 17(1), 127–56.

32 Discourse Analysis and Narrative

BARBARA JOHNSTONE

0 Introduction

Narrative has been one of the major themes in humanistic and social scientific thought since the mid-twentieth century. The essence of humanness, long characterized as the tendency to make sense of the world through rationality, has come increasingly to be described as the tendency to tell stories, to make sense of the world through narrative. In linguistics, narrative was one of the first discourse genres to be analyzed, and it has continued to be among the most intensively studied of the things people do with talk.

I begin with a brief description of structuralist narratology, the most immediate context for discourse analysts' work on narrative. I then turn to some of the earliest and most influential American work on narrative in linguistics, that of Labov and Waletzky (1967; Labov 1972: 354–96). Subsequent sections cover other important work on the linguistic structure of narrative and on its cognitive, cultural, social, and psychological functions, on the development of narrative skills and styles in children, and on variation in narrative. I then touch on some work on narrative in other disciplines which bears on and often draws on linguistic discourse analysts' work: work on "narrative knowing" and narrative rhetoric, on history as story, on the "narrative study of lives" as a research method in education, psychology, and sociology, and on poststructuralist literary narratology. The final section discusses the current state of narrative study in discourse analysis and sketches some directions in which new work is going.

1 Structuralist Narratology

Two related but somewhat different approaches to the structure of narrative became known in the West beginning in the mid-1950s. One was that of the Russian Vladimir Propp, whose *Morphology of the Folktale* (1968) was published in Russian in 1928 but first translated into English in 1958. Although Propp borrowed the term "morphology" from biology rather than linguistics, his technique for showing what all folktales have in common and how they can differ is essentially that of linguistic analysis. Propp's work might more accurately be called the *syntax* of the folktale, since its fundamental claim is that all folktales have the same syntagmatic deep structure, the same sequence of "functions" or meaningful actions by characters. Once characters and their initial situation are introduced ("A little girl and her little brother lived with their elderly parents"), an interdiction is addressed to the hero or heroine and some family member leaves home ("One day the parents said to the girl, 'We are going into town. Take care of your brother and don't go out of the yard.' Then they left"). Next the interdiction is violated (the little girl leaves the yard) and a villain appears on the scene (geese swoop down and snatch the little brother). And the tale continues, one more or less predictable function after another.

While Propp's approach to characterizing the universal features of folklore is like that of formal syntax, Claude Lévi-Strauss's (1955, 1964, 1966) is more similar to formal semantics. Lévi-Strauss's interest was in describing the abstract elements of meaning that are expressed in myth, semantic contrasts such as male/female and raw/cooked. His claim is that traditional narrative around the world, though superficially varied, all deals with a limited number of basic themes. A number of French philosophers and literary theorists, writing in the late 1960s, adapted Propp's and Lévi-Strauss's ideas or similar ones to the analysis of literary narrative. The best known of these is probably Roland Barthes, whose "Introduction to the Structural Analysis of Narratives" was published (in French) in 1966. Others are A. J. Greimas (1966), Tzvetan Todorov (1967), and Gérard Genette (1966). (See Culler 1975: ch. 9 for an overview of structuralist theory about literary narrative.)

These structuralist approaches to myth and literature were not all the same, but they all shared two assumptions. One was that there are abstract levels on which structures and meanings that seem different superficially are really the same. The other was that narrative can be separated from the events it is about. This assumption is discussed most explicitly in the work of French linguist Émile Benveniste (1966), who distinguished between *histoire* and *discours*, or "story" – the events – and "discourse" – the presentation of the events in a narrative. Both these ideas were current in the American linguistics and literary theory of the 1960s (the former most obviously in Transformational/Generative Grammar), and, as Hopper (1997) points out, both were taken into the first American work on narrative discourse.

2   "Oral Versions of Personal Experience": Labov and Waletzky

William Labov's influential work on personal experience narrative (PEN) began in the context of his research about the social correlates of linguistic variation on Martha's Vineyard, in New York City, and elsewhere. In order to elicit unselfconscious, "vernacular" speech, Labov had people tell stories about themselves, often (though not always) stories about dangerous or embarrassing experiences. Fourteen of these stories formed the basis for "Narrative analysis: oral versions of personal experience" (Labov and Waletzky 1967), published in the proceedings volume of the 1966 meeting of the American Ethnological Society. (The paper has since been reprinted as Labov and Waletzky 1997.) In this paper, Labov and Waletzky propose a "formal" approach to PEN. The goal was to describe the invariable semantic deep structure of PEN, with an eye to correlating surface differences with the "social characteristics" of narrators. Labov's project was similar to Vladimir Propp's in its attempt to lay out the underlying syntagmatic structure of plot elements in narrative, except that Labov's focus was on the functions of individual clauses rather than larger chunks.

According to Labov and Waletzky, a clause in PEN can serve one of two functions, referential or evaluative. Referential clauses have to do with what the story is about: events, characters, setting. Evaluative clauses (and evaluative aspects of referential clauses) have to do with why the narrator is telling the story and why the audience should listen to it: evaluative material states or highlights the point of the story. Labov and Waletzky (1967) concentrates on reference in narrative, especially reference to events. A later, more easily accessible book chapter about narratives by young gang members from Harlem (Labov 1972: 354–96) concentrates on evaluation. I will summarize both versions together here, focusing mainly on the parts of each that have been most influential.

Any narrative, by definition, includes at least two "narrative clauses." A narrative clause is one that cannot be moved without changing the order in which events must be taken to have occurred. If two narrative clauses are reversed, they represent a different chronology: "I punched this boy / and he punched me" implies a different sequence of events than "This boy punched me / and I punched him." For Labov, "narrative" is not any talk about the past, or any talk about events; it is specifically talk in which a sequence of clauses is matched to a sequence of "events which (it is inferred) actually occurred" (Labov 1972: 360).

Although "minimal narratives" like the two about punching in the previous paragraph consist of just two narrative clauses, most PEN is more complex, including more narrative clauses as well as "free" clauses that serve other functions. A "fully developed" narrative may include clauses or sets of clauses with the following functions, often roughly in this order:

1 abstract
2 orientation
3 complicating action
4 evaluation
5 result or resolution
6 coda.

Each of these elements of PEN serves a double purpose, making reference to events, characters, feelings, and so on that are understood to have happened or existed outside of the ongoing interaction, and at the same time structuring the interaction in which the story is being told by guiding the teller and the audience through the related events and insuring that they are comprehensible and worth recounting.

The **abstract** consists of a clause or two at the beginning of a narrative summarizing the story to come. In response to Labov's "danger of death" question, for example, a person might begin, "I talked a man out of – Old Doc Simon I talked him out of pulling the trigger," then going on to elaborate with a narrative. (Examples are

Labov's.) The abstract announces that the narrator has a story to tell and makes a claim to the right to tell it, a claim supported by the suggestion that it will be a good story, worth the audience's time and the speaking rights the audience will temporarily relinquish.

Orientation in a narrative introduces characters, temporal and physical setting, and situation: "It was on a Sunday, and we didn't have nothin' to do after I – after we came from church"; "I had a dog – he was a wonderful retriever, but as I say he could do everything but talk." Orientation often occurs near the beginning, but may be interjected at other points, when needed. The characteristic orientation tense in English is the past progressive: "I was sittin' on the corner an' shit, smokin' my cigarette, you know;" "We was doing the 50-yard dash."

Complicating action clauses are narrative clauses that recapitulate a sequence of events leading up to their climax, the point of maximum suspense. These clauses refer to events in the world of the story and, in the world of the telling, they create tension that keeps auditors listening. The **result or resolution** releases the tension and tells what finally happened. Often just before the result or resolution, but also throughout the narrative, are elements that serve as **evaluation**, stating or under-scoring what is interesting or unusual about the story, why the audience should keep listening and allow the teller to keep talking. Evaluation may occur in free clauses that comment on the story from outside: "And it was the strangest feeling"; "But it was really quite terrific"; or in clauses that attribute evaluative commentary to characters in the story: "I just closed my eyes / I said, 'O my God, here it is!' " Or evaluation can be embedded in the narrative, in the form of extra detail about characters ("I was shakin' like a leaf"), suspension of the action via paraphrase or repetition; "intensifiers" such as gesture or quantifiers ("I knocked him *all* out in the street"); elements that compare what did happen with what did not or could have happened or might happen; "correlatives" that tell what was occurring simultaneously; and "explicatives" that are appended to narrative or evaluative clauses. (Strategies for evaluation are treated in detail in Labov 1972: 354–96.)

At the end of the story, the teller may announce via a **coda** that the story is over ("And that was that"), sometimes providing a short summary of it or connecting the world of the story with the present ("That was one of the most important;" "He's a detective in Union City / And I see him every now and again").

Labov's characterization of narrative reflected contemporary concerns and anticip-ated and influenced later work in discourse analysis in several ways. Labov was one of a number of linguists who, beginning in the 1960s, started to show that connected talk is orderly and describable in terms of its structure and function. This observation makes linguistic discourse analysis possible. Labov's work with Americans' narratives, along with work by Grimes (1975), Longacre (1976, 1983), and others comparing dis-course syntax and semantics across languages, began to illustrate the functional reasons for grammatical choices, anticipating subsequent work in functional grammar and grammaticalization (see the chapters in part I of this volume). The suggestion that discourse, like syntax, can be modeled in terms of variable surface structure and invariable deep structure has been taken up by scholars interested in formal models of discourse (see Polanyi, this volume). Labov's illustration that reference is not the only function of talk, that a great deal of what speakers and audiences do serves to create rapport and show how their talk is to be understood, was part of the move during the

1960s away from the Bloomfieldians' completely referential view of language, a move which is reflected in almost every other chapter in this volume as well.

Two aspects of Labov's work have, however, caused recurrent confusion. One of these has to do with the meaning of the term "narrative." For Labov, a "narrative" was a sequence of clauses with at least one temporal juncture, but a "complete" or "fully formed" narrative included such things as orientation and evaluation as well. "Personal experience narrative" included both "minimal" and more elaborate types. Many subsequent researchers continued to use the same term – "narrative" – both for any talk representing a sequence of past events and for talk specifically meant to get and keep someone interested in listening to a recounting of events. This has resulted in confusion both in the design and in the reporting of narrative research, since the two uses of "narrative" refer to two levels of analysis, "narrative" in the first sense being a necessary part of "narrative" in the second sense. Some scholars have accordingly found it helpful to substitute another term, such as "story," for the second sense. Following Polanyi (1985), I adopt this distinction in what follows, using "narrative" to mean talk that represents events in the past and "story" to mean roughly what it does in everyday parlance: narrative with a point.

A second source of confusion has been the inadvertently normative sound of some of Labov's terminology, and, partly in consequence, the normative way in which his analysis has sometimes been read. Labov's claim to be describing "the normal structure of narrative" or characterizing "fully developed" or "complete" narratives have led some to suppose that he was making more universal and/or more judgmental claims than were probably intended. It has been observed over and over that not all stories have abstracts or codas and that PEN is often less monologic than were the stories Labov analyzed. It has been easy for researchers to forget that the PEN Labov characterized was mainly collected in research interviews with relative strangers, and that the fact that stories arising in different contexts turn out to be different actually does more to support Labov's claims about the connection between narrative form and contextual function than to debunk them.

3   Other Work on the Structure of Narrative

Although Labov's work on narrative has been particularly influential (at least in the English-speaking world; see Gülich and Quasthoff 1985 for an overview of narrative analysis in the northern European context), Labov was by no means alone in his interest in generalizing about the underlying formal and semantic structure of narratives and stories. Some research has aimed to produce completely explicit models for how people (and other potential information processors, such as computers) produce and comprehend stories. This includes, for example, work by van Dijk and Kintsch (van Dijk, 1977, 1980; Kintsch and van Dijk 1978) describing semantic "macrostructures" and the "macrorules" that model how stories are understood, as well as work on "story grammar" by Fillmore (1982), Rumelhart (1980), de Beaugrande (1982), and others. In a similar vein but with a more ethnographic purpose, Polanyi (1981, 1985) shows how "adequate paraphrases" of conversational stories by Americans can be a way of arriving at the most basic statements of their beliefs about the world.

One particularly influential approach to the organization of oral narrative is that of Dell Hymes (1981), who showed that Native American myth was performed in poetic lines and stanzas marked by grammatical parallelism, recurring words or particles such as *see, I say,* or *lo,* and repeated numerical patterns of phrases. Other analyses of the line-by-line structure of narrative are those of Chafe (1980a), Sherzer (1982), Tedlock (1983), and Woodbury (1987); line-based transcription systems arising from these scholars' observation that oral discourse is not produced in paragraphs have been widely adopted in narrative research.

A second approach to the structure of narrative examines how storytelling is embedded in its interactional context. Research in this framework examines how the structure of stories reflects the fact that stories perform social actions (Schiffrin 1984, 1996) and how audiences are involved, directly or indirectly, in their construction (Ochs et al. 1989; Norrick 1997). Polanyi (1985: 63–74) shows, for example, how in one case the responses of a story's audience made the teller completely change the point of her story. Goodwin (1982) examines "instigating" in the discourse of urban African American girls, showing how the framing of a story in the larger social context of gossip-dispute affects how the story has to be told, understood, and reacted to. Watson (1973) articulates Labov's work with Burkean (Burke 1945, 1950) rhetorical theory to suggest a way of describing how the structure of stories is affected by the social contexts in which they are performed.

A third set of questions that have been asked about the structure of stories has had to do with linguistic features that are characteristic of this discourse genre. The use of the English simple present tense in narrative in place of the past, traditionally referred to as the Historical Present, is the focus of analysis by Wolfson (1982), Schiffrin (1981), Johnstone (1987), and others, who have connected this usage with the marking of evaluative high points and the characterization of social relations. Tannen (1986, 1989) examines how and why storytellers "construct" dialogue for characters in their stories, sometimes giving them words they could not possibly have said or words the narrator could not possibly have heard. Romaine and Lange (1991) and Ferrara and Bell (1995) discuss the history of quotatives, the verbs such as *say, go, ask,* and so on with which narrators introduce constructed dialogue, focusing particularly on the emergence of the new quotative *be like.* Other narrative framing devices, strategies by which narrators and audiences negotiate transitions between the "storyworld" of the ongoing interaction and "talerealm" in which the narrated events are located, are discussed by Young (1987) and others.

4   Why People Tell Stories

In addition to asking questions about the form of narrative talk, discourse analysts have also asked questions about its function. Talking about the past is apparently something all humans do. Rosen (1988) suggests that the "autobiographical impulse," the urge to make our lives coherent by telling about them, must be universal; personal narrative is how we make sense of ourselves as individuals and as members of groups. As Linde (1993: 3) puts it, "In order to exist in the social world with a comfortable sense of being a good, socially proper, and stable person, an individual needs to have a coherent, acceptable, and constantly revised life story." Schiffrin (1996) shows how two storytellers create individual identities, situating themselves in their families and in society through choices they make as they narrate; Johnstone (1996) discusses self-expressive reasons for individuals' storytelling styles.

Shared stories, as well as shared ways of telling stories and shared uses for stories, also make groups coherent. Among the earliest work by ethnographers of communication were studies of the functions of narrative and speech events in which narrative was central (Kirschenblatt-Gimblett 1974; Darnell 1974), and ethnographers have continued to explore the uses of narrative in various parts of the world (see, for example, Scollon and Scollon 1981; Basso 1986; Patrick and Payne-Jackson 1996). Smaller-scale social groupings are also constituted and maintained partly through shared uses of narrative. Bauman (1986), for example, discusses stories and storytelling events as they serve to negotiate social relations in Texas; Johnstone (1990) talks about how storytelling creates community and a shared sense of place in the American Midwest; Shuman (1986) examines the uses of stories by urban adolescents; Coates (1996) shows how "telling our stories" defines the interrelationships of a group of female friends.

5   The Development of Narrative Skill and Style

Even very young children appear to want to talk about the past (Miller and Sperry 1988). As they learn to take other people's perspectives, children gradually learn to provide orientational and evaluative detail that can keep audiences informed and involved. Kernan (1977) shows how evaluative devices develop with age, younger children implying their feelings and rarely recreating speech while older children rely more on explicit strategies such as telling how they felt and constructing dialog for themselves and other story characters. Romaine (1984: 146–58) uses Labov's characterization of story structure to analyze narratives by Scottish pre-adolescents, suggesting that while evaluative strategies vary, the syntax tends to be simple and relatively iconic, avoiding such strategies as passivization and subordination. McCabe and Peterson (1991a) studied pre-adolescents' uses of connectives such as *then*, *and*, and *because* in elicited stories. Hudson and Shapiro (1991) examine how developing expertise in remembering and representing events, constructing narrative macrostructures, using tense, aspect, pronouns, and anaphora, and interpreting the context all come together as children mature. Other studies of the development of storytelling ability are Botvin and Sutton-Smith (1977), Umiker-Sebeok (1979), Bennett-Kastor (1983, 1986), Preece (1987), Cook-Gumperz and Green (1984), Berman (1988), and many of the chapters in McCabe and Peterson (1991b).

As they acquire cognitive and linguistic abilities, children are also socialized into the functions of narrative in their communities. Among the best-known studies of this process is Heath's (1982, 1983) work with families in two working-class communities in the southern United States. Working-class white children in "Roadville" were taught to tell "factual" stories that ended with morals about what they had learned; working-class African American children in "Trackton" were encouraged to entertain others with fantastic tales. This and other differences in pre-school socialization have implications for children's success in school, where, for example, white children may already know to tell "sharing time" stories the way teachers expect but African American children may not (Michaels and Collins 1984). Among other work on narrative socialization is McCabe and Peterson (1991a).

6   Variation in Narrative

Much of the research discussed so far is aimed at discovering and describing what is generally or even universally true about the structure and function of narrative. But discourse analysts have also devoted considerable attention to how and why stories and their uses differ. For one thing, the basic plot structure described by Propp, Labov, and others is characteristically western. In his work (1979) on "textbuilding" in Southeast Asia, Becker shows, for example, that Javanese shadow puppet plays have a structure very different from that of the Aristotelian tragedy or the American PEN. Shadow theater plots are made coherent through spatial coincidence, as characters in different substories set in different eras come together in the same place, rather than chronologically, via rising tension leading to a cathartic climax. While European-American plots often revolve around sets of three (daughters, tasks, lead-ups to the punch line), Hymes (1981) shows that a significant set of recurrences in Native American myth may number two, four, or five. In a set of studies that involved showing a short, wordless film, Chafe and his coworkers (1980b) examined how people from various places, speaking various languages, put what they had seen into words. Clancy (1980), for example, found differences between Japanese speakers and English speakers in how nominals were used in the introduction of characters. Tannen (1980) found that Greeks tended to narrate the film in a more dramatic, story-like way than Americans, who tended to aim for referential completeness and accuracy in their retellings.

There are also cross-cultural differences in the functions of narrative. Scollon and Scollon (1981) claim, for example, that for Athabaskans experiences and stories about them are the primary source of knowledge, as reality is socially constructed through narrative. This claim has been made more generally about "oral" cultures by scholars such as Goody and Watt (1968) and Ong (1982). Blum-Kulka (1993) compared dinner-table storytelling in American and Israeli families, finding that middle-class American families tended to ritualize the telling of stories about the day, particularly by the children, while in the Israeli families storytelling was more collaborative and more evenly distributed among family members. Etter-Lewis (1991) describes personal storytelling by African American women, and Riessman (1988) compares narratives by an Anglo-American woman and a Puerto Rican, pointing out that social class as well as ethnicity is a factor in the women's different experiences and different recountings.

On the whole, though, there has been relatively little work correlating variation in narrative structure and style with social class, except to the extent that class is inevitably intertwined with other ways people position themselves socially and are positioned by others. Exceptions are Dines (1980) and Ferrara (1997), who correlate differences in the use of the narrative discourse markers *and stuff like that* and *anyway* with social class differences.

More attention has been paid to the ways narrative enters into the construction and expression of gender. Talbot (1999: ch. 4) provides an overview of some of this work. Johnstone (1993) shows how Midwestern women and men construct different worlds in their stories via different plot types and different uses of detail and constructed dialog, the women's stories focused more often on community and the men's on contests. Porter (1988) compares PEN by mothers and their daughters, showing how women's life histories "situate and construct both their past and present experience" (1988: 545) as women, mothers, and daughters, and Silberstein (1988) uses courtship stories by several generations of women in one family to examine how narrative "creates and maintains gender" (1988: 126). Ochs and Taylor (1992) discuss how dinner-table storytelling in the American families they studied helps maintain the patriarchal role of the father.

There are also studies of variation in narrative connected with situation and purpose and with medium. Comparing literary narrative with spontaneous conversational storytelling, Pratt (1977) suggests that one difference between the two has to do with how audiences interpret violations of their expectations: in the literary speech situation, says Pratt, violations must be interpreted as intentional floutings of the conventions, done for a purpose, rather than as mistakes. Walker (1982) shows that witnesses in court proceedings, bringing with them their knowledge about the necessity of evaluation in everyday storytelling, find themselves repeatedly cut off and corrected for interpreting as they narrate. Stahl (1979) and Tannen (1982) compare oral and written versions of personal experience stories, cataloging differences in what gets told and how.

7   Narrative Research Across Disciplines

Narrative has come to seem important to people throughout the humanities and social sciences. Beginning in the late 1970s, new, narrative ways of understanding history and humanity and doing research have become more and more prominent. The narrative aspects of the human mind – the ways in which the making of stories enters into how we understand the world and ourselves – are now seen to be as crucial as our rational side (Bruner 1986; Schafer 1981; Polkinghorne 1988). The observation made by White (1981) and others that history can only be selective storytelling about the past helped give rise to a way of imagining the historical enterprise which is sometimes called the "New Historicism" (Cox and Reynolds 1993). As Miller (1990) points out, each contemporary theoretical framework for literary and cultural studies – deconstruction, feminism, Marxism, psychoanalysis, reception theory, Bakhtinian dialogism, and so on – makes significant claims about narrative. In anthropology, Turner (1981) and others showed how societies make the world coherent by constructing dramatic plots to model human actions, and narrative rhetoric is now taken seriously alongside traditionally more highly valued strategies such as argumentation (Fisher 1987). Qualitative social-scientific research based on life histories, sometimes referred to as "narrative analysis" (Manning and Cullum-Swan 1994) or "the narrative study of lives" (Josselson 1996), is challenging the methodological hegemony of quantitative research paradigms in education, sociology, and psychology; and anthropologists have experimented with narrative as a way of representing other worlds of belief and experience (see Clifford and Marcus 1986; van Maanen 1995).

8   Current State of the Field

As scholars across disciplines have gotten more and more interested in narrative, the study of narrative has become more and more often interdisciplinary. The Fifth International Conference on Narrative, held in 1996, included panelists from departments of English, rhetoric, communication, education, foreign languages and comparative literature, psychology, nursing, political science, sociology and social work, history, art, philosophy, marketing, and organizational behavior, as well as linguistics. A 1997 collection of short papers marking the thirtieth anniversary of the publication of Labov and Waletzky's key article (Bamberg 1997) includes contributions by linguists, psychologists, sociologists, anthropologists, literary scholars, educational researchers, and rhetoricians. Whether the questions we try to answer are primarily about language – how narrative is structured, how grammatical resources for framing, narrating, orienting, and so on are developed and deployed – or primarily about speakers and social interaction – how people use stories to display sociolinguistic identities, how narrative circulates social power and creates and perpetuates social relations – linguistic discourse analysts have much to learn from theories about systems and society developed by others, as well as much to offer in showing others the value of close, systematic reading and listening.

Current research suggests several ways in which work on narrative may continue to develop. For one thing, discourse analysts continue to refine and fill in details in our understanding of the structure of narrative and its functions, examining new framing devices, asking new questions about the discursive representation and construction of time and space, and looking at how narrative functions in new contexts. Following the lead of sociolinguists, discourse analysts interested in narrative are beginning to consider new and different ways of accounting for variation in addition to the by now traditional explanatory variables (place of origin, social class, gender, ethnicity, and so on). We are thinking more, for example, about how language ideology affects linguistic choices (Schieffelin et al. 1998) in narrative and elsewhere, and about the role played by situated, changeable social identities that can be expressed through fleeting or long-term mixings and borrowings (LePage and Tabouret-Keller 1985). Work on formal modeling of narrative for computational purposes continues and grows in sophistication, drawing on new ways of explaining dynamic systems, such as chaos theory (Wildgen 1994).

As we continue to think about the uses of narrative in human life, we are paying increasing attention to the political effects of narrative, seeing storytelling not only as a way of creating community but as a resource for dominating others, for expressing solidarity, for resistance and conflict; a resource, that is, in the continuing negotiation through which humans create language and society and self as they talk and act. We see narrative more and more as a way of constructing "events" and giving them meaning, as we pick out bits of the stream of experience and give them boundaries and significance by labeling them. Like all talk and all action, narrative is socially and epistemologically constructive: through telling, we make ourselves and our experiential worlds.

REFERENCES

Bamberg, M. (ed.) (1997). Oral versions of personal experience: Three decades of narrative analysis. Special issue of *Journal of Narrative and Life History* 7, 1–415.

Barthes, R. (1966). Introduction à l'analyse structurale des récits. *Communications* 8, 1–27.

Basso, E. (1986). Quoted dialogues in Kalapalo narrative discourse. In J. Sherzer and G. Urban (eds), *Native South American Discourse* (pp. 119–68). Berlin: Mouton de Gruyter.

Bauman, R. (1986). *Story, Performance, and Event: Contextual Studies of Oral Narrative*. Cambridge: Cambridge University Press.

Becker, A. L. (1979). Text-building, epistemology, and aesthetics in Javanese shadow theater. In A. L. Becker and A. Yengoyan (eds), *The Imagination of Reality: Essays in Southeast Asian Coherence Systems* (pp. 211–44). Norwood, NJ: Ablex.

Bennett-Kastor, T. (1983). Noun phrases and coherence in child narratives. *Journal of Child Language* 10, 135–49.

Bennett-Kastor, T. (1986). Cohesion and predication in child narrative. *Journal of Child Language* 13, 353–70.

Benveniste, É. (1966). *Problèmes de linguistique générale*. Paris: Gallimard.

Berman, R. (1988). On the ability to relate events in narrative. *Discourse Processes* 11, 469–97.

Blum-Kulka, S. (1993). "You gotta know how to tell a story": Telling, tales, and tellers in American and Israeli narrative events at dinner. *Language in Society* 22, 361–402.

Botvin, G. J. and B. Sutton-Smith. (1977). The development of structural complexity in children's fantasy narratives. *Developmental Psychology* 13, 377–88.

Bruner, J. (1986). *Actual Minds, Possible Worlds*. Cambridge, MA: Harvard University Press.

Burke, K. (1945). *A Grammar of Motives*. Berkeley: University of California Press.

Burke, K. (1950). *A Rhetoric of Motives*. Berkeley: University of California Press.

Chafe, W. (1980a). The deployment of consciousness in the production of a narrative. In W. Chafe (ed.), *The Pear Stories: Cognitive, Cultural, and Linguistic Aspects of Narrative Production* (pp. 1–50). Norwood, NJ: Ablex.

Chafe, W. (ed.) (1980b). *The Pear Stories: Cognitive, Cultural, and Linguistic Aspects of Narrative Production*. Norwood, NJ: Ablex.

Clancy, P. M. (1980). Referential choice in English and Japanese narrative discourse. In W. Chafe (ed.), *The Pear Stories: Cognitive, Cultural, and Linguistic Aspects of Narrative Production* (pp. 127–202). Norwood, NJ: Ablex.

Clifford, J. and G. E. Marcus, G. E. (eds) (1986). *Writing Culture: the Poetics and Politics of Ethnography*. Berkeley: University of California Press.

Coates, J. (1996). *Women Talk: Conversation Between Women Friends*. Oxford: Blackwell.

Cook-Gumperz, J. and Green, J. L. (1984). A sense of story: Influences on children's storytelling ability. In D. Tannen (ed.), *Coherence in Spoken and Written Discourse* (pp. 201–18). Norwood, NJ: Ablex.

Cox, J. N. and Reynolds, L. J. (1993). The historicist enterprise. In J. N. Cox and L. J. Reynolds (eds), *New Historical Literary Study: Essays on Reproducing Texts, Representing History* (pp. 3–38). Princeton, NJ: Princeton University Press.

Culler, J. (1975). *Structuralist Poetics: Structuralism, Linguistics, and the Study of Literature*. Ithaca, NY: Cornell University Press.

Darnell, R. (1974). Correlates of Cree narrative performance. In R. Bauman and J. Sherzer (eds), *Explorations in the Ethnography of Speaking* (pp. 315–36). New York: Cambridge University Press.

de Beaugrande, R. A. (1982). The story of grammars and the grammar of stories. *Journal of Pragmatics* 6, 383–422.

Dines, E. (1980). Variation in discourse – "and stuff like that." *Language in Society* 9, 13–31.

Etter-Lewis, G. (1991). Standing up and speaking out: African American women's narrative legacy. *Discourse and Society* 2, 425–37.

Ferrara, K. (1997). Form and function of the discourse marker *anyway*: Implications for discourse analysis. *Linguistics* 35, 343–78.

Ferrara, K. and Bell, B. (1995). Sociolinguistic variation and discourse function of constructed dialogue introducers: The case of *be + like*. *American Speech* 70, 265–90.

Fillmore, C. (1982). Story grammars and sentence grammars. *Pragmatics* 6, 451–54.

Fisher, W. R. (1987). *Human Communication as Narration: Toward a Philosophy of Reason, Value, and Action*. Columbia, SC: University of South Carolina Press.

Genette, G. (1966). *Figures*. Paris: Seuil.

Goodwin, M. H. (1982). "Instigating": Storytelling as social process. *American Ethnologist* 9, 799–819.

Goody, J. and Watt, I. (1968). The consequences of literacy. In J. Goody (ed.), *Literacy in Traditional Societies* (pp. 27–84). Cambridge: Cambridge University Press.

Greimas, A. J. (1966). *Sémantique structurale*. Paris: Larousse.

Grimes, J. E. (1975). *The Thread of Discourse*. Berlin, New York, Amsterdam: Mouton.

Gülich, E. and Quasthoff, U. M. (1985). Narrative analysis. In T. van Dijk (ed.), *Handbook of Discourse Analysis, Vol. 2* (pp. 169–97). New York: Academic Press.

Heath, S. B. (1982). What no bedtime story means: Narrative skills at home and school. *Language in Society* 11, 49–76.

Heath, S. B. (1983). *Ways with Words: Language, Life, and Work in Communities and Classrooms*. Cambridge: Cambridge University Press.

Hopper, P. J. (1997). Dualisms in the study of narrative: A note on Labov and Waletzky (1967). *Journal of Narrative and Life History* 7, 75–82.

Hudson, J. and Shapiro, L. R. (1991). From knowing to telling: The development of children's scripts, stories, and personal narrative. In A. McCabe and C. Peterson (eds), *Developing Narrative Structure* (pp. 89–136). Hillsdale, NJ: Lawrence Erlbaum.

Hymes, D. (1981). *In Vain I Tried to Tell You: Essays in Native American Ethnopoetics*. Philadelphia: University of Pennsylvania Press.

Johnstone, B. (1987). "He says . . . so I said": Verb tense alternation and narrative depictions of authority in American English. *Linguistics* 25, 33–52.

Johnstone, B. (1990). *Stories, Community, and Place: Narratives from Middle America*. Bloomington: Indiana University Press.

Johnstone, B. (1993). Community and contest: Midwestern men and women creating their worlds in conversational storytelling. In D. Tannen (ed.), *Gender and Conversational Interaction* (pp. 62–80). Oxford: Oxford University Press.

Johnstone. (1996). *The Linguistic Individual: Self-Expression in Language and Linguistics*. New York: Oxford University Press.

Josselson, R. (ed.) (1996). *Ethics and Process in the Narrative Study of Lives*. Thousand Oaks, CA: Sage.

Kernan, K. T. (1977). Semantic and expressive elaboration in children's narratives. In S. Ervin-Tripp and C. Mitchell-Kernan (eds), *Child Discourse* (pp. 91–102). New York: Academic Press.

Kintsch, W. and van Dijk, T. (1978). Toward a model of text comprehension and production. *Psychological Review* 85, 363–94.

Kirschenblatt-Gimblett, B. (1974). The concept and varieties of narrative performance in east European Jewish culture. In R. Bauman and J. Sherzer (eds), *Explorations in the Ethnography of Speaking* (pp. 283–308). Cambridge: Cambridge University Press.

Labov, W. (1972). *Language in the Inner City*. Philadelphia: University of Pennsylvania Press.

Labov, W. and Waletzky, J. (1967). Narrative analysis: Oral versions of personal experience. In J. Helm (ed.), *Essays on the Verbal and Visual Arts* (pp. 12–44). Seattle: University of Washington Press.

Labov, W. and Waletzky, J. (1997). Narrative analysis: Oral versions of personal experience. *Journal of Narrative and Life History* 7, 3–38.

LePage, R. B. and Tabouret-Keller, A. (1985). *Acts of Identity: Creole-Based Approaches to Language and Ethnicity*. Cambridge: Cambridge University Press.

Lévi-Strauss, C. (1955). The structural study of myth. *Journal of American Folklore* 68, 428–44.

Lévi-Strauss, C. (1964). *Mythologiques: Le Cru et le Cuit*. Paris: Plon.

Lévi-Strauss, C. (1966). *Mythologiques: Du Miel aux Cendres*. Paris: Plon.

Linde, C. (1993). *Life Stories: The Creation of Coherence*. Oxford: Oxford University Press.

Longacre, R. E. (1976). *An Anatomy of Speech Notions*. Lisse: Peter de Ridder Press.

Longacre, R. E. (1983). *The Grammar of Discourse*. New York: Plenum Press.

Manning, P. K. and Cullum-Swan, B. (1994). Narrative, content, and semiotic analysis. In N. K. Denzin and Y. Lincoln (eds), *Handbook of Qualitative Research* (pp. 463–77). Thousand Oaks, CA: Sage.

McCabe, A. and Peterson, C. (1991a). Getting the story: A longitudinal study of parental styles in eliciting narratives and developing narrative skill. In A. McCabe and C. Peterson (eds), *Developing Narrative Structure* (pp. 217–53). Hillsdale, NJ: Lawrence Erlbaum.

McCabe, A. and Peterson, C. (1991b). *Developing Narrative Structure*. Hillsdale, NJ: Lawrence Erlbaum.

Michaels, S. and Collins, J. (1984). Oral discourse styles: Classroom interaction and the acquisition of literacy. In D. Tannen (ed.), *Coherence in Spoken and Written Discourse* (pp. 219–44). Norwood, NJ: Ablex.

Miller, J. H. (1990). Narrative. In F. Lentricchia and T. McLaughlin (eds), *Critical Terms for Literary Study* (pp. 66–79). Chicago: University of Chicago Press.

Miller, P. J. and Sperry, L. L. (1988). Early talk about the past: The origins of conversational stories of personal experience. *Journal of Child Language* 15, 293–315.

Norrick, N. (1997). Collaborative narration of familiar stories. *Language in Society* 26, 199–220.

Ochs, E., Smith, R., and Taylor, C. (1989). Detective stories at dinner-time: Problem solving through co-narration. *Cultural Dynamics* 2, 238–57. Also in C. Briggs (ed.) (1996), *Conflict Talk* (pp. 95–113). New York: Oxford University Press.

Ochs, E. and Taylor, C. (1992). Family narrative as political activity. *Discourse and Society* 3, 301–40.

Ong, W. (1982). *Orality and Literacy.* London and New York: Methuen.

Patrick, P. and Payne-Jackson, A. (1996). Functions of Rasta talk in a Jamaican Creole healing narrative: "A bigfoot dem gi' mi." *Journal of Linguistic Anthropology* 6, 47–84.

Polanyi, L. (1981). What stories can tell us about their tellers' world. *Poetics Today* 2, 97–112.

Polanyi, L. (1985). *Telling the American Story: A Structural and Cultural Analysis of Conversational Storytelling.* Norwood, NJ: Ablex.

Polkinghorne, D. E. (1988). *Narrative Knowing and the Human Sciences.* Albany: State University of New York Press.

Porter, M. (1988). Mothers and daughters: Linking women's life histories in Grand Bank, Newfoundland, Canada. *Women's Studies International Forum* 11, 545–58.

Pratt, M. L. (1977). *Toward a Speech Act Theory of Literary Discourse.* Bloomington: Indiana University Press.

Preece, A. (1987). The range of narrative forms conversationally produced by young children. *Journal of Child Language* 14, 353–73.

Propp, V. (1968). *Morphology of the Folktale* (trans. L. Scott). Austin: University of Texas Press.

Riessman, C. K. (1988). Worlds of difference: Contrasting experience in marriage and narrative style. In A. Dundas Todd and S. Fisher (eds), *Gender and Discourse: The Power of Talk* (pp. 151–73). Norwood, NJ: Ablex.

Romaine, S. (1984). *The Language of Children and Adolescents.* Oxford: Blackwell.

Romaine, S. and Lange, D. (1991). The use of *like* as a marker of reported speech and thought: A case of grammaticalization in progress. *American Speech* 66, 227–79.

Rosen, H. (1988). The autobiographical impulse. In D. Tannen (ed), *Linguistics in Context: Connecting Observation and Understanding* (pp. 69–88). Norwood, NJ: Ablex.

Rumelhart, D. E. (1980). On evaluating story grammars. *Cognitive Science* 4, 313–16.

Schafer, R. (1981). Narration in the psychoanalytic dialogue. In W. J. T. Mitchell (ed.), *On Narrative* (pp. 25–49). Chicago: University of Chicago Press.

Schieffelin, B. B., Woolard, K. A., and Kroskrity, P. V. (eds) (1998). *Language Ideologies: Practice and Theory.* New York: Oxford University Press.

Schiffrin, D. (1981). Tense variation in narrative. *Language* 57, 45–62.

Schiffrin, D. (1984). How a story says what it means and does. *Text* 4, 313–46.

Schiffrin, D. (1996). Narrative as self-portrait: Sociolinguistic constructions of identity. *Language in Society* 25, 167–203.

Scollon, R. and Scollon, S. B. K. (1981). *Narrative, Literacy, and Face in Interethnic Communication.* Norwood, NJ: Ablex.

Sherzer, J. (1982). Poetic structuring of Kuna discourse: the line. *Language in Society* 11, 371–90.

Shuman, A. (1986). *Storytelling Rights: Uses of Oral and Written Texts by Urban Adolescents*. New York: Cambridge University Press.

Silberstein, S. (1988). Ideology as process: Gender ideology in courtship narratives. In A. D. Todd and S. Fisher (eds), *Gender and Discourse: the Power of Talk* (pp. 125–49). Norwood, NJ: Ablex.

Stahl, S. K. D. (1979). Style in oral and written narratives. *Southern Folklore Quarterly* 43, 39–62.

Talbot, M. (1999). *An Introduction to Language and Gender*. Malden, MA: Blackwell.

Tannen, D. (1980). A comparative analysis of oral narrative strategies: Athenian Greek and American English. In W. Chafe (ed.), *The Pear Stories: Cognitive, Cultural, and Linguistic Aspects of Narrative Production* (pp. 51–87). Norwood, NJ: Ablex.

Tannen, D. (1982). Oral and literate strategies in spoken and written narratives. *Language* 58, 1–21.

Tannen, D. (1986). Introducing constructed dialogue in Greek and American conversational and literary narrative. In F. Coulmas (ed), *Direct and Indirect Speech* (pp. 311–32). Berlin, New York, Amsterdam: Mouton de Gruyter.

Tannen, D. (1989). *Talking Voices: Repetition, Dialogue, and Imagery in Conversational Discourse*. Cambridge: Cambridge University Press.

Tedlock, D. (1983). *The Spoken Word and the Work of Interpretation*. Philadelphia: University of Pennsylvania Press.

Todorov, T. (1967). *Littérature et signification*. Paris: Larousse.

Turner, V. (1981). Social dramas and stories about them. In W. J. T. Mitchell (ed.), *On Narrative* (pp. 137–64). Chicago: University of Chicago Press.

Umiker-Sebeok, J. (1979). Preschool children's intraconversational narratives. *Journal of Child Language* 6, 91–109.

van Dijk, T. (1977). *Text and Context: Explorations in the Semantics and Pragmatics of Discourse*. London: Longman.

van Dijk, T. (1980). *Macrostructures: An Interdisciplinary Study of Global Structures in Discourse, Interaction and Cognition*. Hillsdale, NJ: Erlbaum.

van Maanen, J. (ed.) (1995). *Representation in Ethnography*. Thousand Oaks, CA: Sage.

Walker, A. G. (1982). Discourse rights of witnesses: Their circumscription in trial. *Sociolinguistic Working Paper Number 95*. Austin, TX: Southwest Educational Development Laboratory.

Watson, K. A. (1973). A rhetorical and sociolinguistic model for the analysis of narrative. *American Anthropologist* 75, 243–64.

White, H. (1981). The value of narrativity in the representation of reality. In W. J. T. Mitchell (ed.), *On Narrative* (pp. 1–23). Chicago: University of Chicago Press.

Wildgen, W. (1994). *Process, Image, and Meaning: A Realistic Model of the Meanings of Sentences and Narrative Texts*. Amsterdam/Philadelphia: John Benjamins.

Wolfson, N. (1982). *CHP: The Conversational Historical Present in American English Narrative*. Dordrecht: Foris.

Woodbury, A. C. (1987). Rhetorical structure in a Central Alaskan Yupik Eskimo traditional narrative. In J. Sherzer and A. C. Woodbury (eds), *Native American Discourse: Poetics and Rhetoric* (pp. 176–239). New York: Cambridge University Press.

Young, K. G. (1987). *Taleworlds and Storyrealms*. Boston: Martinus Nijhoff.

33 Discourse and Conflict

CHRISTINA KAKAVÁ

0 Introduction

In the past, the linguistic means of conducting conflict among adults did not receive much attention in either linguistic or anthropological linguistic research, in part because, as Briggs (1996) puts it, conflict constitutes a type of "disorderly discourse." As a result, either researchers did not venture into this form of "backstage language behavior" (Goffman 1959) or this kind of data was not easily gathered. Consequently, several studies exist that talk *about* conflict (e.g. Watson-Gegeo and White 1990), but few focusing on a turn-by-turn analysis of how conflict is conducted among adults, except among adults in interaction with children. Only recently has conflict generated much-needed interest which has provided us with some new insights and directions.[1]

Initially, researchers focused on the structural properties of arguments or disputes, but gradually the focus shifted to more contextual strategies, and more recently, scholars are investigating how the self or selves is or are constituted through conflict and how ideology is constructed and reflected through conflict talk.

This chapter will discuss research that has been conducted on language and conflict, broadly defined as any type of verbal or nonverbal opposition ranging from disagreement to disputes, mostly in social interaction. The discussion will not include cases of "language conflict" – in other words, conflict over language choice, e.g. Nelde (1997). The chapter will cover representative research that has been done on: (1) the structural properties of conflict; (2) the communicative strategies of conducting conflict; (3) conflict negotiation and resolution; and (4) the meanings of conflict. In the conclusion, some recent trends and future directions in the area of conflict talk will be outlined.

1 Structural Properties of Conflict

The structural elements of different types of conflict are the focus of this section. Whereas some studies center on the structure of disputes or arguments and their components, others investigate the sequential organization of disagreement, and its status in social interaction. Almost no study limits itself to examining just the structural properties of conflict, but what these studies share is their interest in unearthing how conflict or disagreement is initiated and how it develops.

One of the earlier studies on children's conflict is Brenneis and Lein's (1977) investigation of role-played disputes among white middle-class children in the first, third, and fourth grades from an elementary school in Massachusetts. They found that the children's argumentative sequences fell into three structural patterns: repetition, escalation, and inversion. They also identified "stylistic tactics" (suprasegmental elements) that characterized the tone of the children's exchanges. A reciprocal redundancy was noted between content and style. The shorter and more repetitive the content exchange, the more stylistically elaborate it was. Conversely, the more semantically complex exchanges were not stylistically elaborate.

In a subsequent study, Lein and Brenneis (1978) investigated whether the features of arguments observed in their study from New England would be used cross-culturally, so they examined arguments in three speech communities: white American middle-class children from a small town in New England (the same as in their 1977 study), black American children whose parents were migrant harvesters, and Hindi-speaking Fiji Indian children from a rural community. As in their previous study, they used role-played arguments as data. No significant differences were found in terms of content and style of disputes among the three different communities, even though there was some variation regarding the use of stress.

The three communities, however, differed in their organization of arguments, particularly in the turn-taking system. The Indian children showed a much higher tolerance for overlapping talk than did the black children, who had no instances of it. White children showed organization patterns similar to those of the black students. The occasional cases of overlap that were recorded among the white children occurred when a speaker was perceived to have finished his or her utterance.

Higher tolerance for overlaps and interruptions in the course of arguments have been reported in adult studies as well for some cultures and specific contexts, for example among Greeks (Kakavá 1993a), Tzotzil speakers (Haviland 1997), British broadcast news (Greatbatch 1992), and talk-radio shows (Hutchby 1992).

The development of verbal disputing in part-Hawaiian children from their childhood to their adolescence was examined by Boggs (1978). Boggs used tape-recorded data which came from three sources: naturally occurring conversations among 5-year-olds recorded by their mothers, recordings of children's interactions at a kindergarten, and conversations among older boys and girls at their school and during camping trips. Boggs found that a pattern of disputing – direct contradiction prefaced by "not" – was very pervasive not only among the 12-year-olds but even among the 5-year-olds; he called it a "contradicting routine." However, for the 12-year-olds, the pattern seemed to be turning into what he called "situational joking," where disputants would end up laughing with each other.

The structural patterns of a dispute, Boggs reports, were similar to the ones described by Lein and Brenneis (1978). Contradicting routines started with assertions, challenges, and threats followed by contradiction, and then by another round of assertions or challenges or insults. If an insult was followed by a counterinsult, the dispute was likely to end.[2]

Maynard (1985a) focused on what constitutes an oppositional move besides a verbal action. He investigated the initial stage of an adversative episode, the so-called "antecedent event," basing his analysis on the videotaped recordings of first-grade reading groups of white middle-class native speakers of English. Maynard shows that bodily and presuppositional claims are integral parts of an oppositional move. However, Maynard claims an oppositional move does not always prompt a dispute, so he calls such a move "argumentative" to indicate that it has a potential to provoke a dispute but may not end up doing so.

Marjorie Harness Goodwin (1983, 1990a, 1990b, and in collaboration with Charles Goodwin, in Goodwin and Goodwin 1987, 1990) has produced some of the most detailed ethnographic analysis of disputes among African American children and young teenagers (from the ages 4 to 14). Goodwin (1983) and Goodwin and Goodwin (1987) examine forms of opposition that were expressed as either correction or disagreement. Contrary to studies which argued that disagreement is usually prefaced or mitigated (see the discussion of Pomerantz 1975, 1984, below), children were found to use several lexical, syntactic, and phonological properties, such as substitutions and format tying (partial or total repetitions at the phonological, syntactic, and semantic level) to initiate and sustain an opposition. Goodwin (1983) termed this form of disagreement which enhances polarity "aggravated." This type of opposition was also found in studies among adults in Taiwanese (Kuo 1991), Greek (Kakavá 1993a), and Korean (Song 1993).

In her influential studies with data from adults, Pomerantz (1975, 1984) introduced the term "dispreferred-action turn shape" to refer to second assessments that display features such as silence or delays after an assessment has been introduced. Building on the notion of preference, as introduced by Sacks (1973), she defines an action as dispreferred if it is not "oriented to" the talk as it was "invited" to be. These dispreferred actions are structurally marked, displaying what she calls "dispreference" features such as "delays, requests for clarification, partial repeats, and other repair initiators, and turn prefaces" (Pomerantz 1984: 70). She argues that when conversants feel that they are expected to agree with an assessment, yet disagree, they usually express their disagreement with some form of delay. Some of the forms of delay that she lists are initial silence in response to forthcoming talk and repair initiators.[3]

Subsequent studies have examined specific contexts and have reported findings contrary to Pomerantz's. Atkinson and Drew (1979), in their study of judicial discourse, found that after accusations, the preferred response is an unmitigated disagreement. This is consonant with Bayraktaroğlu's (1992) finding in Turkish troubles talk. Bayraktaroğlu reports that during troubles talk, the weakness displayed by the disclosing party is met with disagreement to repair the interactional equilibrium. Similarly, in psychotherapy groups, Krainer (1988) posits that the expression of discord is expected, since disagreement, complaints, and dissatisfactions should be discussed "in the open." She found both strong and mitigated challenges in her data. The strong challenges were intensified by prosodic emphasis and other intonational features and included overt features of negation, negative evaluative lexical items, etc. Pauses, requests for clarifications, and "discord particles" such as *well* marked mitigated challenges.

Kakavá (1993a, 1993b) and Kotthoff (1993) also provide counterevidence to the structural markedness of disagreement. Kakavá finds that in casual conversations among Greeks, disagreements do not often display dispreference markers, a finding that is echoed in Kotthoff's study on conversations among Chinese and German speakers. Moreover, Kotthoff found that within the context of an argument, concessions displayed the dispreference markers that Pomerantz had identified, once a dissent-turn sequence was established. Thus, these two empirical studies confirmed a claim that Bilmes (1988) had earlier made about the preferred status of disagreement within the context of an argument.

Furthermore, Greatbatch (1992) argues that in the context of British television news interviews, the notion of preference is suspended due to the positioning and design of the turn allocation. Since the moderator controls the turn-taking, interviewees never address each other directly, which, Greatbatch posits, allows unmitigated disagreement to occur. Myers (1998), however, found that participants in focus groups issued unprefaced disagreement when disagreeing with the moderator, but not when they disagreed directly with another participant, in part because the moderator encouraged disagreement.

Finally, another study addresses the concept of preference and the shape that oppositional turns take, but in a different medium: computer-mediated communication. Baym (1996) investigates agreement and disagreement patterns in a mostly female newsgroup. The disagreement patterns she discovered matched those suggested by Pomerantz, but some major differences emerged due to the medium, gender, context, and interactive goals: disagreements included quoting, were linked to previous discourse, and had pervasive elaboration. Interestingly, accounts and justifications emerged with agreements, and not just disagreements, as the notion of preference predicts.

This section has provided an overview of some representative studies from children's and adults' oppositional discourse which had as one of their main foci the structural properties of a conflict episode. Whereas some studies focused on the structure of a larger unit such as a dispute or argument, others investigated the types of features that one could expect once a disagreement has been issued. Furthermore, we have seen that in recent studies (Greatbatch, Kakavá, Kotthoff, Baym), researchers have pointed out how contextual constraints (e.g. situation or speech event) can affect the structural form disagreement turns take. These constraints and others are further explored in the following section.

2 Communicative Strategies of Conducting Conflict

The studies reviewed in this section indicate the researchers' interest in exploring not just textual features of conflict or argument but discourse-level phenomena as well, including irony, joking, stories, reported speech, etc. Another aspect that distinguishes these studies is that they examine macro- and microcontextual factors to determine the effect they have on the oppositional strategies chosen; for instance, cultural interactional rules, style, and gender, as well as speakers' interactional goals.

Schiffrin (1985) focuses on the organization of an argument, and she identifies two types of arguments: rhetorical and oppositional. By rhetorical she refers to a "discourse through which a speaker presents an intact monologue supporting a disputable position." Oppositional is defined as "discourse through which one or more speakers support openly disputed positions" (1985: 37). She finds that both types of arguments share the same discourse properties in that a speaker, in order to support his or her position, will try to undermine another speaker's. This is accomplished, Schiffrin claims, through the constant "negotiation of referential, social, and expressive meanings" (1985: 45).

Johnstone (1989; see also Johnstone 1986) claims that certain styles correlate with certain persuasive strategies, which speakers choose depending on the context. She proposes three types of persuasive strategies: quasilogic, presentation, and analogy. Quasilogic is based on the assumption that persuasion can be achieved by using a type of informal reasoning. Presentation involves the processes of moving and involving the listener in order to persuade. Finally, analogical persuasion is based on the assumption that "by calling to mind, explicitly or implicitly, traditional wisdom, often in the form of parable- or fablelike stories", people will be persuaded by undertaking "abductive leaps between past events and current issues" (1989: 149). These three strategies are then mapped onto three corresponding styles based on "conceptual correlates." The quasilogic style seems to be dominant in western culture but not exclusively. Presentational and analogical styles correspond to eastern cultures, and especially, to the older and more religious tradition.

Even though Johnstone creates these broad correspondences between strategies, style, and culture, she does not claim that culture will determine linguistic choices made in rhetorical situations. Instead, she suggests, culture may predispose people toward a particular strategy. Therefore, she believes that cross-cultural misunderstandings have their root not merely in different styles but instead in people's failure to adapt to and understand different persuasive strategies.

Silence has been found to be a strategy used in conflict talk either to disengage from or to intensify a conflict. Examining the role of silence in an Italian village, Saunders (1985) suggests that silence is comparable to extreme noise in some cases. People may opt for silence rather than confront someone when the potential for conflict is high. In contrast, they prefer direct confrontation for trivial forms of conflict. Tannen (1990a) supports Saunders's conclusion about the functional equivalency of noise and silence by investigating the role silence played in the British play *Betrayal*, by Harold Pinter, and in the American short story "Great Wits," by Alice Mattison. Both genres displayed a similar view about the destructive nature of direct confrontation. In *Betrayal*, the playwright used pauses to indicate escalations of conflict, but used silence where characters actually confronted "potentially explosive information" (1990a: 260). By way of comparison, in the short story "Great Wits," breaching silence at highly confrontational moments resulted in irreparable damage to the protagonists. Tannen suggests that some cultural underpinnings are present in the two genres; British playwrights tend to mask negative emotion by the use of pauses and silence, whereas American writers have their characters "express strong negative emotion loudly and explicitly" (1990a: 273).

The following three studies (Kuo 1991; Kakavá 1993a; Song 1993) have two common features: (1) they investigate a broad range of argumentative strategies in three different cultures, and (2) they classify strategies as aggravated or mitigated (see Goodwin 1983) and account for the variation by examining interpersonal, situational, and cultural constraints.

Kuo (1991) studied means of negotiating conflict in Taiwanese casual friends' conversations and parliamentary interpellations. Regarding overall argumentative strategies, she found that participants in the sociable arguments among friends employed several forms of aggravating disagreement. Formulaic expressions, initiations of disagreement latching to each other's talk with the Chinese equivalent of the contrastive marker *but*, uncooperative interruption, and wh-questions with partial repetitions and substitutions marked forthcoming disagreement. In the parliamentary interpellations, sarcasm and accusatory questions were added to the list of forms and types of disagreement.

Kakavá (1993a) and Song (1993) provide a qualitative analysis of the linguistic strategies of engaging in conflict in two different cultures: Greek and Korean, respectively. Some of the strategies found in the Greek data were direct disagreements sometimes accompanied by figurative kinship terms, contrastive repetition, sarcasm, personalization of an argument, accounts, and stories.[4] In Korean, Song lists formulaic expressive adverbials, repetition, code-switching, silence, and personal experience stories among others.

Whereas the studies just reviewed dealt with the culture-specific strategies of conducting conflict mostly from a qualitative perspective, Muntigl and Turnbull (1998) examine quantitatively the conversational structure of disagreement sequences and how it relates to the negotiation of face. They claim that facework is a major determinant of the type of turn sequence a speaker will use. They initially identify four major types of disagreement, ranked from most to least aggravated: irrelevancy claims, challenges, contradictions, and counterclaims. They then found that the more a second turn threatens the face of the speaker who made a claim as a first turn, the more likely it is that the third turn will contain further support of that first speaker's claim.

Centering on popular public discourse, McIlvenny (1996) explores the different strategies used by hecklers of Hyde Park speakers, and the driving forces behind these evoked participation frameworks. He demonstrates that through an arsenal of linguistic strategies, participants in this public oratory become active interpreters of meaning, at times supporting a speaker's or a participant's talk, while at other times contesting it with heckling and disaffiliative responses. McIlvenny also claims that one-upmanship and loss of face are the driving interactional forces behind these types of public debates, which additionally illustrate how different types of collective responses can emerge as a result of the constant shifting of alignments.

Gender as a factor contributing to the emergence of specific patterns of oppositional discourse is the main focus of the following studies. Goodwin (1990a, 1990b; Goodwin and Goodwin 1987) reports that African American boys' and girls' argumentative strategies tend to be rather similar in many ways, but she also observes some qualitative differences. Girls have argumentative skills equal to the boys' but the girls also use some more extended types of arguments than the boys. One of them is what she terms "he-said-she-said," a type of accusation behind someone's back that may lead to the ostracism of the offending girl. In terms of the stories boys and girls tell in disputes, Goodwin (1990a, 1990b) finds two patterns: boys use stories to sustain a dispute, and they alter their participation framework according to a social hierarchy. In contrast, Goodwin notes, girls employ stories to transform the alignments of the participants. The "instigating" stories jeopardize the participation framework of a girl, since she is often shunned for days or months.

Sheldon (1996) refers to a discourse strategy that she has termed "double-voice discourse," a type in which the speakers orient themselves toward the addressees' interests and goals.[5] Sheldon (1996) maintains that girls engage in this type of discourse, which manifests itself as both mitigation and concern for self-interest. In contrast, boys employ "single-voice" discourse, which is characterized by direct and aggravated forms of talk. Nevertheless, she also suggests that each type of discourse can be used by either boys or girls as long as they share the social goals associated with each style.

In a series of studies, Tannen (1990b, 1994, 1998) has provided numerous examples of the different strategies boys and girls (and later, men and women) use to engage in conflict in casual and professional settings. Although, as she constantly reminds the readers, not all females and males behave similarly, she maintains that patterns of gender-specific preferences exist and that these need to be identified, since people experience normative pressures to act according to their gender. Tannen claims that boys and men tend to engage in direct confrontations or use opposition as a way of negotiating status, whereas girls and women tend to seek at least overt expression of agreement and avoid direct confrontations. Often boys' and men's use of conflict is ritual (in her terms, "agonism"), such as playful roughhousing among boys, and men's use of verbal challenges as a way of exploring ideas ("playing devil's advocate"). However, Tannen also notes that other contextual parameters, such as conversational style, emergent context, and interactive goals, can affect the engagement or disengagement from confrontation irrespective of gender.

A rather similar empirical finding from another culture is reported in Makri-Tsilipakou's (1991) study of spontaneous, tape-recorded conversations among Greek couples and friends. She reports that in her study women expressed disagreement indirectly, off-record, using intraturn delays, hedges, and pre-disagreement tokens, which were followed by weak disagreements. Women tended to use more upgraders, and they accompanied their disagreement with qualifications and accounts. Men, however, usually used interturn delays, in the form of either silence or insertion sequences, and they postponed their disagreement over several turns. When they expressed disagreement, it was usually strong, bald-on-record, and unaccounted for.[6] Makri-Tsilipakou (1994b) also shows, though, how through scorn, ridicule, or disapproval Greek women engage in the public destruction of the face of their male spouses, partners, friends, or relatives to "protest" their discontent with them.

The women of Tenejapa, Mexico, are also found to use conventionally indirect means to be impolite when engaging in disputes in court cases in Brown's (1990) study. The Tenejapa women use rhetorical questions issued with irony "sarcastically to be impolite," to indicate "lack of cooperation, disagreement, hostility," Brown reports (1990: 123). However, in a qualitative study, Kakavá (1994b) finds that irony was used similarly by both Greek men and women to attain the goal reported in Brown's study: to express disagreement.

In another medium, computer-mediated communication, Herring (1994, 1996a, 1996b, Herring et al. 1995) finds that women posting messages on e-mail lists tend to disagree by cushioning their disagreements with affiliative comments, posing questions rather than making assertions. In contrast, men posters tend to use an adversarial style (putting down a participant while promoting their own claims). She also finds that both men and women are more interested in exchanging views than information.

Interestingly, though, her evidence suggests that listserve members of the minority gender shift their style in the direction of majority gender norms to fit in with the rest (Herring et al. 1995: 82).

Although the studies reviewed take into account different aspects of gendered patterns in opposition, Hasund (1996) claims that research on gender and conflict cannot be complete unless it takes into account class and social network, as well as other factors.[7] Based on a qualitative analysis of a section of the COLT (Corpus of London Teenage Language) data, Hasund argues that there is a correlation between class, gender, and forms of opposition. She reports that working-class teenage girls issued more oppositional turns than middle-class ones, and also tended to use more aggravating strategies. Additionally, the strategies that were used differed by type. Working-class girls' oppositions dealt with sexual promiscuity and obscenity, taking the shape of ritual insults. In contrast, middle-class girls exchanged oppositions over trivial or serious issues, and subsequently cushioned these oppositions by mitigated turns. However, Hasund also reports that there was a lot of intraspeaker variation in the data, which was accounted for by factors such as communicative style and degrees of intimacy present in the participants' relationship.

This section explored some representative features and strategies of engaging in conflict and the combination of contextual factors affecting the form they take. The next section will examine how interactants negotiate conflict and what the main patterns of conflict resolution in social interaction have been.

3   Conflict Negotiation and Resolution

How children negotiate conflict or resolve it has been the focus of several studies. A seminal paper is that of Eisenberg and Garvey (1981), who examined videotaped play sessions of 48 dyads of already acquainted preschoolers and 40 dyads of unacquainted preschoolers who met at a laboratory and were observed through a one-way mirror. Children rarely used "nonadaptive" strategies, that is, insistence, repetition, or paraphrase of their utterance. Instead they employed "adaptive" strategies, such as supporting their moves with reasoning, justifications, and requests for clarification to resolve their conflicts.

Building on his earlier research, Maynard (1986) focuses on the dynamics involved in multiparty disputes among children, using as data videotaped sessions of reading groups. He points out that some disputes may start as two-sided, yet end up being multiparty. Different "parties" may, invited or uninvited, align with a displayed position, stance, claim, or counterposition, and may challenge a particular position "for different reasons and by different means" (1986: 281). He also found fluid patterns of collaboration in this type of dispute that depended upon the children's emergent alignments.

Qualitative cultural differences of negotiating disputes were reported in Corsaro and Rizzo's (1990) study of American and Italian nursery school children between the ages of 2 and 4. Italian children had many more disputes involving claims than the American children had, and these disputes were often unresolved and rather lengthy. Corsaro and Rizzo argue that the claim disputes in the Italian data displayed the element of *discussione*, that is, the "enjoyment of argumentation," which they compare to the aggravated disagreement found in Goodwin (1983, 1990a) and Goodwin and Goodwin (1987). This element also manifested itself in the "dispute routines" found only in the Italian data. During these routines, Italian children engaged in a "skillful performance" to tease, enacting "complex, stylistic, and aesthetically impressive routines" (Corsaro and Rizzo 1990: 40). This "emphasis on style" characterized all Italian children's disputes in contrast to the American ones.

Looking at conflict termination turns from a sequential approach, yet drawing inferences from the notion of face, Vuchinich (1990) found that "stand-off," the case where participants drop the issue at stake and change the speech activity, was the most common type of conflict termination in his data. He examined terminal exchanges from 64 video- and audiorecordings of black and white American family dinners and he proposed five termination formats: "submission," when a participant "gives in" and accepts the participant's position; "dominant third-party intervention"; "compromise"; "stand-off"; and "withdrawal." Differences by generation were also observed due to power differences (parents versus children), but Vuchinich acknowledges that in some of the arguments that ended with parent–child stand-offs, power was not a prominent factor, since they were sociable arguments (Schiffrin 1984). Vuchinich also accounts for the higher frequency of stand-offs, the lack of compromise, or the inability to reach consensus by attributing a desire to the participants to keep their positions, yet not lose face.

Vuchinich's finding in terms of the most common type of conflict termination (i.e. stand-off) is consonant with what Genishi and di Paolo (1982) observed in their study of upper-middle-class children's disputes in a classroom setting. It was found that resolutions were not usually attained but arguments tended to be diffused.

The negotiation of conflict through different activities is the focus of Schiffrin's (1990) study. She investigates the role of two speech activities – expressing an opinion and telling a story – within the context of an argument, in which participants can be competitive yet cooperative, negotiating the values of "truth" and "sincerity" by adjusting the participation framework of talk. Opinions were found to have the paradoxical nature of both starting and finishing an argument. By way of contrast, stories provided support to a speaker's claim and invited the audience to share responsibility with the "principal" (Goffman 1981).

Maintaining one's belief or opinion by denying or contesting contradictory evidence in conflict resolution is the strategy that Mehan (1990) examines in her study of a psychiatric exam – what she refers to as "oracular reasoning." She demonstrates that this type of strategy is used by both doctors and patients, but it is the doctors' reasoning that prevails because of their institutional authority.

The role a third party plays in conflict resolution is explored in Maley's (1995) work. He investigates Australian courts and divorce mediation sessions and finds that these two different contexts affect the nature and the purpose of the activity and even shape the discursive practices involved. Whereas the adjudication context of the court case lends itself to direct and powerful intervention by a judge, the mediation context is characterized by indirect types of intervention by the mediator, who lacks both power and authority to control the outcome of the mediation. Maley also notes that the judge may act as a mediator but the mediator cannot act as a judge. This echoes in part Philips's (1990) argument about a judge's role in American court cases.

She presents evidence that the judges' interactional moves vary from merely mediative to adjudicative, depending on the context.

Conflict resolution strategies and the way that gender affects the strategies chosen are the research area of the following studies. Sheldon (1990, 1996) analyzed the conflict talk of 3-year-old friends in same-sex triads, and found that the strategies used by the two groups confirmed proposals made by Maltz and Borker's (1982) anthropological linguistic model of gender-marked language use and Gilligan's (1987) psychological framework. In Sheldon's study, the children were videotaped while playing with toys. The two disputes (one representative triad for each gender) that she analyzed displayed different discourse strategies. The girls used patterns of opposition–insistence–opposition sequences. However, they also used a variety of means to reach a negotiation (e.g. reasons). The boys' dispute was much more extended and with more opposition–insistence–opposition sequences than the girls'. In contrast to the girls' strategies, the boys did not "*jointly negotiate* a resolution" (1987: 27), even though they did offer some compromises.

This finding echoes comparable observations from a study that focused on six female teenagers. In an ethnographic study of six adolescent females, Eckert (1990) found that even when their ideas differed, the girls tried through negotiation to achieve consensus so that their cooperation would remain intact.

Different types of confrontation and negotiation of conflict were observed in Eder's (1990) study. She conducted ethnographic work with white adolescent females from working-class and lower-working-class families in a middle-school setting and obtained audio- and videotapes of 59 students from sixth to eighth grade. Focusing on the direct exchanges of conflict, she found that teenagers would use several strategies to resolve normative conflict, but the most successful one was the strategy that addressed "the real issues behind the conflict" (1990: 81). Eighth graders were found to be the most skillful in handling conflict resolution and insulting exchanges. Those students belonged to more stable social groups. She suggests that that could be the reason why they felt more comfortable engaging in direct confrontation with their familiar peers. Furthermore, social class seemed to play a role, Eder observes, since ritual insulting was more common among students from working and lower classes, where being "tough" was more highly regarded than being "polite."

As shown from the studies reviewed, although participants may choose different strategies to negotiate conflict based on their gender, yet more often than not, and irrespective of gender, conflict tends not be resolved. In some cases, it seems that engagement in conflict is pursued for its own sake for reasons that are more thoroughly examined in the next section.

4 The Meanings of Conflict

The studies reviewed in this section offer suggestions about the situated, cultural, and social meanings of conflict, a step that brings us closer to how conflict is viewed in different societies and by different groups.

Status negotiation has been one of the most commonly cited meanings of conflict talk among children and adults. Maynard (1985b), using the same data as in his previous study (Maynard 1985a), claims that conflict among children latently functions to "develop their sense of social structure and helps reproduce authority, friendship, and other interactional patterns that transcend single episodes of dispute" (1985b: 220).

A clearer association between conflict and status is found in Emihovich's (1986) study. Using an ethnographic perspective, she examined the role of disputes among white and black boys of two integrated kindergartens in a medium-sized urban city. Following Mitchell-Kernan and Kernan's (1977) argument, she claimed that the reason arguments occur during children's play is because children view argumentative talk as "status assertion." The use of directives in their play challenges their status and their opposition to these challenges is a means of defending it. An important aspect of the boys' disputes was to establish a dominance hierarchy which helped them frame their role in a relationship (who the leader was) and the outcome of disputes (usually the "tough" one would use physical means and end a dispute).

Katriel (1985) finds the ritual *brogez* ("being in anger") to function as a form of "status competition" among Israeli children who belong in the same "social sphere." *Brogez*, she reports, is a type of ritual insult and threat similar to *sounding* in African American discourse (Abrahams 1962; Labov 1972; Kochman 1983), which allows both girls and boys in same-sex groups to vent their anger and hostility through "ritually constrained interactional channels" (Katriel 1985: 487). It is also used as a means to discover social hierarchies (e.g. who has leadership qualities).

Venting one's anger in a nonconfrontational manner or just being antagonistic in ritual insults or verbal duelings has also been reported in other cultures, for example Turkish (Dundes et al. 1972), Chamula Indian (Gossen 1976), Cretan (Herzfeld 1985), Balinese (Sherzer 1993), Yoruba (Omoniyi 1995), and Cypriot (Doukanari 1997).[8]

Some of the cultural and social constraints of ritual insult are reported in Heath's (1983) ethnographic study. She reports that whereas working-class black school age boys and girls engaged in exchanges of insults and play songs, white children of the same class did not. First- or second-grade females did not engage in one-liners, couplets, or verses, (forms of insults and play songs) the way the boys did, until they were in upper primary grades. Girls preferred physical confrontation in challenges of peer relations with groups of girls from other communities, but they used verbal challenges with friends or girls with whom there was no confrontation in status relations.

Moving from ritual insults to ritualistic oppositional stances in casual conversations, the following studies demonstrate that opposition is positively valued by certain cultures and subcultures. Israelis have been found to engage in direct confrontation, which may strike a foreigner as rude, yet for Israelis, *dugri* "straight" talk has a positive norm, Katriel (1986) maintains (see also Blum-Kulka and Olshtain 1984). Goffman's (1967) rule of considerateness, Katriel claims, is not commensurate with *dugri* speech. Her explanation is that Sabra Israelis place more emphasis on "true respect – rather than consideration" (Katriel 1986: 17). The speaker's assumption is that a listener "has the strength and integrity required to take the speaker's direct talk as sincere and natural" (1986: 117).

Schiffrin (1984) provides linguistic and cultural evidence to show that disagreement among East European Jews is not an action that threatens social interaction, but instead is a form of sociability. This claim is reached after the examination of arguments among adults of a lower-middle-class East European Jewish community in Philadelphia, where Schiffrin conducted sociolinguistic interviews. Building on Simmel's (1961) notion of sociability, she defines sociable argument as a "speech activity in which a polarizing form has a ratificatory meaning" (Schiffrin 1984: 331). Schiffrin found that the participants were constantly nonaligned with each other, yet managed to maintain their intimate relationships.[9]

A similar positive evaluation of conflict has been reported for some other cultures and subcultures, for example Byrnes (1986), Kotthoff (1993), and Straehle (1997) for Germans, Kakavá (1993a, 1993b, 1993c) for Greeks, Kochman (1981) for African Americans, and Tannen (1990b, 1994, 1998) for men. In addition, some studies report a positive evaluation of conflict in some contexts, for example, in friendly conversations in Taiwanese (Kuo 1991) and in Korean (Song 1993).

Investigating ritualistic forms of opposition, Tannen (1998) examines practices from domains as diverse as the press, law, politics, and education. She demonstrates that all of these domains are permeated by forms of agonism, or ritualized opposition. She offers examples from other cultures that have not valorized the direct expression of conflict, among them the Chinese and Japanese, who traditionally view the open expression of conflict more negatively.

Jones (1990), however, finds in her study of Japanese conversations that the norm of harmony seems to be a myth, since the participants in her study used agonistic stances such as explicit expressions of conflict and sustained disagreement, and they rarely compromised. However, the norm of harmony did impose a constraint on the emotional expression of conflict in conversations. Only when the interaction became too "hot" did the participants reframe the interaction or change topics.

In summary, conflict has been viewed as a means to negotiate status, in particular among males, and it has been evaluated as either positive or negative, depending on one or more of the following factors: culture, gender, class, or situational context.

5 Conclusion: Recent Trends and Directions in Conflict Research

Recent studies of conflict build on the properties already reviewed. For example, they discover either structural features or interactional strategies, but they also seek to describe the social roles participants take in the course of an argument or they seek to delineate what other resources participants will use to construct an oppositional format. Furthermore, some studies observe a fluidity of opinions or attitudes, and alignments. Thus these studies seek to discover how opinions, roles, identities, and consequently ideologies are constructed, supported, or contested through conflict talk.

Billig (1989) presents qualitative evidence from a family's discourse that people who hold strong opinions display a variability of attitudes which, he claims, presupposes "that the speaker has access to culturally produced variability of views" (1989: 219). A similar type of variability is reported in Kakavá (1994b), who found that the participants in a casual Greek conversation constructed gendered ideologies which at times subscribed to cultural ideology but at other times contested it.

Competing voices also emerge in Kulick's (1993) study of women in Gapun.[10] He investigates how these women use *kros*, a form of conflict talk aired in public, to construct their identities. He argues that the women who engage in this type of talk confirm stereotypes about women as disruptive or in need of control, but they also undermine these stereotypes by constructing identities of powerful personae who can "publicly speak and demand hearing" (1993: 534).

Brody (1996) demonstrates another type of balancing act among Tojolab'al women. During barter, Tojolab'al women skillfully straddle the line between competition and cooperation to balance their competing needs: to achieve the highest economic bene-fit of the transaction, yet retain their communal identification by invoking shared values. Sidnell (1998) reports on a similar yet different type of collaboration and competition among women of an Indo-Guyanese village. He examines how the spa-tial description and place formulation enter the arena of conflict as both its locus and its resource in the production of oppositional formats and participant structures. The women in his study seem to use the social and interactional construction of space to exercise and contest social power. Significantly, the women had to jointly collaborate, despite their differences, on creating an interactional space to voice concerns over space, morality, and gender.

What one can conclude from all the studies reviewed is that some of the features and strategies used to engage in conflict are shared among diverse languages (see for example structural repetition in English, Taiwanese, Greek, and Korean; overlaps in Chiapas, Greek, etc.; and silence in English and Korean), whereas others may not be shared, or at least there is not sufficient evidence that they are shared (e.g. personal analogy in Greek; Kakavá 1994a). What also emerged is that certain strategies are indexical to contextual constraints such as speech event (family talk versus parliament-ary interpellations, for example), face, or gender. Since linguists have always searched for universals or implicational universals, it could be viable, if other microstudies of conflict are conducted, to create a matrix of commonly shared structural and interactional features and produce a typology of them across different contexts. Muntigl and Turnbull's (1998) work, for example is a first step toward correlating the force of a subsequent claim and face considerations. Will their claims hold in other cultural settings and contexts?

Furthermore, no study has focused on the nonverbal means of conducting conflict (i.e. gestures and facial expressions), although Maynard (1985a), Goodwin (1994), Taylor (1995), and Ochs and Taylor (1995) refer to some nonverbal oppositional stances in their papers. Consequently, there is a lacuna as to how nonverbal means of ex-pressing conflict can index the linguistic means of expressing conflict and vice versa. Could some gestures or postures constitute argumentative icons, and how do these vary by culture? Kendon (1992, 1993), for example, demonstrates how the closed fist accompanies argumentation in Italian, while Goodwin (1994) shows a postural oppositional stance among Hispanic girls. Future research can attempt to provide these missing links, which could grant a much more integrated typology of the means of engaging in conflict.

Another area that needs further investigation is how conflict is evaluated in a particular society and/or context. This line of research will shed more light on theor-etical frameworks that view disagreement either as a threatening act that needs to be avoided at any cost (Pomerantz 1984; Heritage 1984; Brown and Levinson 1987; Leech 1983) or as a positive action that enhances sociability (Simmel 1961). While we do have evidence from some cultures for either the positive or negative evaluation of conflict (e.g. Schiffrin 1984; Keenan 1974), researchers have started to question whether conflict can have either a positive or a negative value in a particular culture. Tannen (1993b), for example, has argued and shown that conflict can be potentially polysemous, in that it can create solidarity or power. As we also saw, gender (e.g. Tannen 1990b, 1994) and interactional context have emerged as important factors affecting the value conflict has. It seems that we still need to furnish more qualitative, within- and across-contexts research to study not just how conflict works but also how it is evaluated.

Just as recent work in sociolinguistics has shifted its attention to individual speaker variation (Rickford and McNair-Knox 1994; Johnstone 1996), we need to have more studies on both intra- and interspeaker variation to explore the mechanisms that lead a speaker to use one strategy over another in the course of the same or different conflict episode.[11]

An area that further needs exploration is women's conflicts, as Kulick (1993) also points out. It has often been assumed that conflict, argument, and opposition are a male domain. However, as Kulick (1993) and Sidnell (1998) show, a microanalysis of women's types of oppositional discourse, coupled with ethnographic research, is capable of discovering the multiplicity of women's voices as they emerge through discourse. It is through these types of analyses that we can learn more about not just what conflict is and how it is managed but also whether it is an act of subversion or compliance to cultural norms and expectations.

Due to the emergence and flourishing of computer-mediated discourse, researchers have begun to investigate forms, patterns, and meanings of conflict in this medium as well. As in the studies of noncomputer-mediated discourse, gender differences have been reported for listserves (see Herring 1994, 1996a, 1996b; Herring et al. 1995, for example, reviewed above). The area that has not yet been investigated is that of synchronous computer-mediated conversations (SCMCs). These real-time interactions, where users simultaneously log on to remote servers to engage in conversation, provide researchers with a new frontier of investigation: how conflict is managed through these texts that in some ways mirror conversations of verbal interaction, yet are distinctive due to their specific nature. Some preliminary findings indicate that conflict management, if present at all, is handled differently in these chat rooms (Edwards 1999). If indeed that is the case, it is important to explore what makes these types of SCMCs different and what the contributing factors are.

Finally, over a decade ago, Grimshaw (1990) urged researchers of conflict to explore the full range of texts available and not limit themselves to local or familiar loci of conflict but discover the processes that govern international disputes as well. It seems to me that his call is as pertinent now as it was then. Although as discourse analysts we have shed light on conflict management at home and in the workplace, we have not shifted our attention to international types of dispute, where the ramifications and consequences are even more dire, as we have recently experienced. Tannen (1986: 30) once wrote, referring to cross-cultural communication: "Nations must reach agreements, and agreements are made by individual representatives of nations sitting down and talking to each other – public analogs of private conversations. The processes are the same, and so are the pitfalls. Only the possible consequences are more extreme." We need to refocus our energies on these public conversations, which turn out to be more problematic than the ones we have already investigated, if we want to increase our contributions to humankind.

NOTES

This chapter was written with the support of a Mary Washington Faculty Development Grant. The author also acknowledges the editorial assistance of Paul D. Fallon.

1 See for example papers cited in Brenneis (1988) and Grimshaw (1990), and recent PhD dissertations such as Meyer (1996); Dorrill (1997); Scott (1998); among others discussed below.

2 See also similar types of observations for adults in Millar et al. (1984); Coulter (1990); Antaki (1994).

3 See also Levinson (1983) for a more detailed list of dispreference markers.

4 See also Tannen and Kakavá (1992); Kakavá (1993b, 1993c, 1994a, 1995).

5 See also Sheldon (1990) for a thorough overview of research on children's conflicts.

6 See also Makri-Tsilipakou (1994a) for a discussion of similar interruption patterns and disagreement.

7 See also Eder's (1990) study discussed in section 3.

8 See also discussions of verbal dueling in McDowell (1985) and Tannen (1998).

9 See also Modan (1994).

10 See also Kulick (1992).

11 See some preliminary findings in Kakavá (1995); Hasund (1996).

REFERENCES

Abrahams, Roger D. 1962. Playing the dozens. *Journal of American Folklore*, 75, 209–20.

Antaki, Charles. 1994. *Explaining and Arguing: The Social Organization of Accounts*. London: Sage.

Atkinson, J. Maxwell, and Paul Drew. 1979. *Order in Court*. Atlantic Highlands, NJ: Humanities Press.

Bauman, Richard, and Joel Sherzer (eds). 1974. *Explorations in the Ethnography of Speaking*. Cambridge: Cambridge University Press.

Baym, Nancy. 1996. Agreements and disagreements in a computer-mediated discussion. *Research on Language and Social Interaction*, 29, 315–45.

Bayraktaroğlu, Arin. 1992. Disagreement in Turkish troubles-talk. *Text*, 12, 317–42.

Billig, Michael. 1989. The argumentative nature of holding strong views: A case study. *European Journal of Social Psychology*, 19, 203–23.

Bilmes, Jack. 1988. The concept of preference in conversation analysis. *Language in Society*, 17, 161–81.

Blum-Kulka, Shoshana, and Elite Olshtain. 1984. Requests and apologies: A cross-cultural study of speech-act realization patterns (CCARP). *Applied Linguistics*, 5, 196–213.

Boggs, Steven T. 1978. The development of verbal disputing in part-Hawaiian children. *Language in Society*, 7, 325–44.

Brenneis, Donald. 1988. Language and disputing. *Annual Review of Anthropology*, 17, 221–37.

Brenneis, Donald, and Laura Lein. 1977. "You fruithead": A sociolinguistic approach to children's dispute settlement. In Ervin-Tripp and Mitchell-Kernan 1977: 49–65.

Briggs, Charles (ed.) 1996. *Disorderly Discourse: Narrative, Conflict, and Inequality*. Oxford: New York.

Brody, Jody. 1996. Competition as cooperation: Tojolab'al women's barter. In *Gender and Belief Systems. Proceedings of the Fourth Berkeley Women and Language Conference*, Natasha Warner, Jocelyn Ahlers, Leela Bilmes, Monica Oliver, Susanne Wertheim, and Melinda Chen (eds), 99–108. Berkeley, CA: Berkeley Women and Language Group.

Brown, Penelope. 1990. Gender, politeness, and confrontation in Tenejapa. *Discourse Processes*, 13, 123–41. Also in Tannen 1993a: 144–62.

Brown, Penelope, and Stephen C. Levinson. 1987. *Politeness: Some Universals in Language Usage*. Cambridge: Cambridge University Press.

Bucholtz, Mary, A. C. Liang, Laurel A. Sutton, and Caitlin Hines (eds). 1994. *Cultural Performances. Proceedings of the Third Berkeley Women and Language Conference*. Berkeley, CA: Berkeley Women and Language Group.

Byrnes, Heidi. 1986. Interactional style in German and American conversation. *Text*, 6, 186–206.

Corsaro, William A., and Thomas A. Rizzo. 1990. Disputes in the peer culture of American and Italian nursery-school children. In Grimshaw 1990: 21–66.

Coulter, Jeff. 1990. Elementary properties of argument sequences. In *Studies in Ethnomethodology and Conversation Analysis, No. 1: Interaction Competence*, George Psathas (ed.), pp. 181–203. Washington, DC: University Press of America.

Dorrill, Masako A. 1997. Disagreement in Japanese: Three case studies. Unpublished PhD thesis, University of South Carolina.

Doukanari, Elli. 1997. The Presentation of gendered self in Cyprus rhyming improvisations: A sociolinguistic investigation of Kipriaka Chattista in performance. Unpublished PhD dissertation, Georgetown University, Washington, DC.

Dundes, Alan, Jerry W. Leach, and Bora Özkök. 1972. The strategy of Turkish boys' verbal dueling rhymes. In Gumperz and Hymes 1972: 130–60.

Eckert, Penelope. 1990. Cooperative competition in adolescent "girl talk." *Discourse Processes*, 13, 91–122. Also in Tannen 1993a: 32–61.

Eder, Donna. 1990. Serious and playful disputes: Variation in conflict talk among female adolescents. In Grimshaw 1990: 67–84.

Edwards, Crystal. 1999. Sugar and spice and everything nice: Gender and disagreement in computer-mediated conversation. Unpublished MS, Mary Washington College, Fredericksburg, VA.

Eisenberg, Ann R., and Catherine Garvey. 1981. Children's use of verbal strategies in resolving conflicts. *Discourse Processes*, 4, 149–70.

Emihovich, Catherine. 1986. Argument as status assertion: Contextual variations in children's disputes. *Language in Society*, 15, 485–500.

Ervin-Tripp, Susan, and Claudia Mitchell-Kernan (eds). 1977. *Child Discourse*. New York: Academic Press.

Genishi, Celia, and Marianna di Paolo. 1982. Learning through argument in a preschool. In *Communicating in the Classroom*, L. C. Wilkinson (ed.), pp. 49–68. New York: Academic Press.

Gilligan, Carol. 1987. Moral orientation and moral development. In *Women and Moral Theory*, Eva Feder Kittay and Diana T. Meyers (eds), pp. 19–33. Totowa, NJ: Rowman and Littlefield.

Goffman, Erving. 1959. *The Presentation of Self in Everyday Life*. Garden City, NY: Doubleday Anchor Books.

Goffman, Erving. 1967. *Interaction Ritual: Essays on Face to Face Behavior.* Garden City, NY: Anchor Books.

Goffman, Erving. 1981. *Forms of Talk.* Philadelphia: University of Pennsylvania Press.

Goodwin, Charles, and Marjorie H. Goodwin. 1990. Interstitial argument. In Grimshaw 1990: 85–117.

Goodwin, Marjorie Harness. 1983. Aggravated correction and disagreement in children's conversations. *Journal of Pragmatics,* 7, 657–77.

Goodwin, Marjorie Harness. 1990a. *He-Said-She-Said: Talk as Social Organization among Black Children.* Bloomington: Indiana University Press.

Goodwin, Marjorie Harness. 1990b. Tactical use of stories: Participation frameworks within girls' and boys' disputes. *Discourse Processes*, 13, 33–71. Also in Tannen 1993a: 110–43.

Goodwin, Marjorie Harness. 1994. "¡Ay Chillona!": Stance-taking in girls' hopscotch. In Bucholtz et al. 1994: 232–41.

Goodwin, Marjorie Harness, and Charles Goodwin. 1987. Children's arguing. In *Language, Gender and Sex in Comparative Perspective,* Susan U. Philips, Susan Steele, and Christine Tanz (eds), pp. 200–48. Cambridge: Cambridge University Press.

Gossen, Garry H. 1976. Verbal dueling in Chamula. In *Speech Play: Research and Resources for the Study of Linguistic Creativity*, Barbara Kirshenblatt-Gimblett (ed.), pp. 121–48. Philadelphia: University of Pennsylvania Press.

Greatbatch, David. 1992. On the management of disagreement between news interviewees. In *Talk at Work: Interaction in Institutional Settings,* Paul Drew and John Heritage (eds.), pp. 268–301. Cambridge: Cambridge University Press.

Grimshaw, Allen D. (ed.), 1990. *Conflict Talk: Sociolinguistic Investigations of Arguments in Conversations.* Cambridge: Cambridge University Press.

Gumperz, John J. (ed.). 1982. *Language and Social Identity.* Cambridge: Cambridge University Press.

Gumperz, John J., and Dell Hymes (eds). 1972. *Directions in Sociolinguistics: The Ethnography of Communication.* New York: Holt, Rhinehart and Winston.

Hasund, Ingrid Kristine. 1996. Colt conflicts: Reflections of gender and class in the oppositional turn-sequences of London teenage girls. Hovedfag thesis, University of Bergen, Bergen, Norway.

Haviland, John. 1997. Shouts, shrieks, and shots: Unruly political conversations in indigenous Chiapas. *Journal of Pragmatics*, 7, 547–73.

Heath, Shirley Brice. 1983. *Ways with Words: Language, Life, and Work in Communities and Classrooms.* Cambridge: Cambridge University Press.

Heritage, John. 1984. *Garfinkel and Ethnomethodology.* Cambridge: Polity.

Herring, Susan. 1994. Politeness in computer culture: Why women thank and men flame. In Bucholtz et al. 1994: 278–94.

Herring, Susan. 1996a. Posting in a different voice: Gender and ethics in computer-mediated communication. In *Philosophical Perspectives in Computer-Mediated Communication*, Charles Ess (ed.), pp. 115–45. Albany: SUNY Press.

Herring, Susan. 1996b. Bringing familiar baggage to the new frontier: Gender differences in computer-mediated communication. In *CyberReader*, Victor Vitanza (ed.), pp. 144–54. Boston: Allyn and Bacon.

Herring, Susan, Deborah A. Johnson, and Tamra DiBenedetto. 1995. "This discussion is going too far!": Male resistance to female participation on the Internet. In *Gender Articulated: Language and the Socially Constructed Self*, Kira Hall and Mary Bucholtz (eds), pp. 67–96. New York: Routledge.

Herzfeld, Michael. 1985. *The Poetics of Manhood: Contest and Identity in a Cretan Mountain Village*. Princeton: Princeton University Press.

Hutchby, Ian. 1992. Confrontation talk: Aspects of "interruption" in argument sequences on talk radio. *Text*, 12, 343–71.

Johnstone, Barbara. 1986. Arguments with Khomeini: Rhetorical situation and persuasive style in cross-cultural perspective. *Text*, 6, 171–87.

Johnstone, Barbara. 1989. Linguistic strategies and cultural styles for persuasive discourse. In *Language, Communication, and Culture: Current Directions*, Stella Ting-Toomey and Felipe Korzenny (eds), pp. 139–56. Newbury Park, CA: Sage.

Johnstone, Barbara. 1996. *The Linguistic Individual: Self-expression in Language and Linguistics*. New York: Oxford University Press.

Jones, Kimberly Ann. 1990. Conflict in Japanese conversation. Unpublished PhD thesis, University of Michigan, Ann Arbor, MI.

Kakavá, Christina. 1993a. Negotiation of disagreement by Greeks in conversations and classroom discourse. Unpublished PhD thesis, Georgetown University, Washington, DC.

Kakavá, Christina. 1993b. Aggravated corrections as disagreement in casual Greek conversations. Proceedings of the First Annual Symposium about Language and Society – Austin (SALSA). *Texas Linguistic Forum*, 33, 187–95.

Kakavá, Christina. 1993c. Conflicting argumentative strategies in the classroom. In *Georgetown University Round Table 1993*, James Alatis (ed.), pp. 395–414. Washington, DC: Georgetown University Press.

Kakavá, Christina. 1994a. "If it was your sister . . .": Personalization in arguments. In *Themes in Greek Linguistics: Papers from the First International Conference on Greek Linguistics, Reading, September 1993*, Irene Philipp.aki-Warburton, Katerina Nicolaides, and Maria Sifianou (eds), pp. 261–8. Amsterdam: John Benjamins.

Kakavá, Christina. 1994b. "Do you want to get engaged, baby?": The cultural construction of gender through talk. In Bucholtz et al. 1994: 344–54.

Kakavá, Christina. 1995. Directness and indirectness in professor–student interactions: The intersection of contextual and cultural constraints. In *Georgetown University Round Table 1995*. James E. Alatis and Carolyn A. Straehle (eds), pp. 229–46. Washington, DC: Georgetown University Press.

Katriel, Tamar. 1985. *Brogez*: Ritual and strategy in Israeli children's conflicts. *Language in Society*, 14, 467–90.

Katriel, Tamar. 1986. *Talking Straight*: Dugri *Speech in Israeli Sabra Culture*. Cambridge: Cambridge University Press.

Keenan, Elinor. 1974. Norm-makers, norm-breakers: Uses of speech by men and women in a Malagasy community. In Bauman and Sherzer 1974: 125–43.

Kendon, Adam. 1992. Some recent work from Italy on *quotable gestures (emblems)*. *Journal of Linguistic Anthropology*, 2, 92–108.

Kendon, Adam. 1993. Gestures as illocutionary and discourse structure markers in Southern Italian conversation. Paper presented in the symposium "Recent contributions to the study of gesture in the context of talk" at the 67th Annual Meeting of the Linguistic Society of America, Los Angeles, CA.

Kochman, Thomas. 1981. *Black and White Styles in Conflict*. Chicago: University of Chicago Press.

Kochman, Thomas. 1983. The boundary between play and nonplay in black verbal dueling. *Language in Society*, 12, 329–37.

Kotthoff, Helga. 1993. Disagreement and concession in disputes: On the context sensitivity of preference structures. *Language in Society*, 22, 193–216.

Krainer, Elizabeth. 1988. Challenges in a psychotherapy group. In *Proceedings of the Fourteenth Annual Meeting of the Berkeley Linguistics Society*, Shelley Axmaker, Annie Jaisser, and Helen Singmaster (eds), pp. 100–13. Berkeley, CA: Berkeley Linguistics Society.

Kulick, Don. 1992. Anger, gender, language shift and the politics of revelation in a Papua New Guinean village. *Pragmatics*, 2, 281–96.

Kulick, Don. 1993. Speaking as a woman: Structure and gender in domestic arguments in a New Guinea village. *Cultural Anthropology*, 8, 510–41.

Kuo, Sai-hua. 1991. Conflict and its management in Chinese verbal interactions: Casual conversations and parliamentary interpellations. Unpublished PhD thesis, Georgetown University, Washington, DC.

Labov, William. 1972. *Language in the Inner City: Studies in the Black English Vernacular*. Philadelphia: University of Pennsylvania Press.

Leech, Geoffrey. N. 1983. *Principles of Pragmatics*. London: Longman.

Lein, Laura, and Donald Brenneis. 1978. Children's disputes in three speech communities. *Language in Society*, 7, 299–309.

Levinson, Steven. C. 1983. *Pragmatics*. Cambridge: Cambridge University Press.

Makri-Tsilipakou, Marianthi. 1991. Agreement/disagreement: Affiliative vs. disaffiliative display in cross-sex conversations. Unpublished PhD dissertation, Aristotle University of Thessaloníki, Thessaloníki, Greece.

Makri-Tsilipakou, Marianthi. 1994a. Interruption revisited: Affiliative vs. disaffiliative intervention. *Journal of Pragmatics*, 21, 401–26.

Makri-Tsilipakou, Marianthi. 1994b. Greek women and the public destruction of face. In Bucholtz et al. 1994: 462–77.

Maley, Yon. 1995. From adjudication to mediation: Third party discourse in conflict resolution. *Journal of Pragmatics*, 23, 93–110.

Maltz, Daniel. N. and Ruth A. Borker. 1982. A cultural approach to male–female miscommunication. In Gumperz 1982: 196–216.

Maynard, Douglas W. 1985a. How children start arguments. *Language in Society*, 14, 1–30.

Maynard, Douglas W. 1985b. On the functions of social conflict among children. *American Sociological Review*, 50, 207–23.

Maynard, Douglas W. 1986. Offering and soliciting collaboration in multi-party disputes among children (and other humans). *Human Studies*, 9, 261–85.

McDowell, John H. 1985. Verbal dueling. In *Handbook of Discourse Analysis, vol. 3: Discourse and Dialogue*, Teun A. van Dijk (ed.), pp. 203–11. London: Academic Press.

McIlvenny, Paul. 1996. Heckling in Hyde Park: Verbal audience participation in popular public discourse. *Language in Society*, 25, 27–60.

Mehan, H. 1990. Oracular reasoning in a psychiatric exam. In Grimshaw 1990: 160–77.

Meyer, Thomas W. 1996. Language and power in disagreements: Analyzing the discourse of male, female, and male/female couples. Unpublished

PhD thesis, University of Pennsylvania.

Millar, Frank E., L. Edna Rogers, and Janet Beavin Bavelas, 1984. Identifying patterns of verbal conflict in interpersonal dynamics. *Western Journal of Speech Communication*, 48, 231–46.

Mitchell-Kernan, Claudia, and Keith T. Kernan, 1977. Pragmatics of directive choice among children. In Ervin-Tripp and Mitchell-Kernan 1977: 189–208.

Modan, Gabriel. 1994. Pulling apart is coming together: The use and meaning of opposition in the discourse of Jewish American women. In Bucholtz et al. 1994: 501–8.

Muntigl, Peter, and William Turnbull. 1998. Conversational structure and facework in arguing. *Journal of Pragmatics*, 29, 225–56.

Myers, Greg. 1998. Displaying opinions: Topics and disagreement in focus groups. *Language in Society*, 27, 85–111.

Nelde, Peter Hans. 1997. Language conflict. In *The Handbook of Sociolinguistics*, Florian Coulmas (ed.), pp. 285–300. Oxford: Blackwell.

Ochs, Elinor, and Carolyn Taylor. 1995. The "Father Knows Best" dynamic in dinnertime narratives. In *Gender Articulated*, Kira Hall and Mary Bucholtz (eds), pp. 97–120. New York: Routledge.

Omoniyi, Tope. 1995. Song-lashing as a communicative strategy in Yoruba interpersonal conflicts. *Text*, 15, 299–315.

Philips, Susan. 1990. The judge as third party in American trial-court conflict talk. In Grimshaw 1990: 197–209.

Pomerantz, Anita. 1975. Second assessments: A study of some features of agreements/disagreements. Unpublished PhD dissertation, University of California, Irvine.

Pomerantz, Anita. 1984. Agreeing and disagreeing with assessments: Some

features of preferred/dispreferred turn shapes. In *Structures of Social Action: Studies in Conversation Analysis*, J. Maxwell Atkinson and John Heritage (eds), pp. 57–101. Cambridge: Cambridge University Press.

Rickford, John R., and Faye McNair-Knox. 1994. Addressee- and topic-influenced style shift: A quantitative sociolinguistic study. In *Sociolinguistic Perspectives on Register*, Douglas Biber and Edward Finegan (eds), pp. 235–76. New York: Oxford University Press.

Sacks, Harvey. 1973. On the preferences for agreement and contiguity in sequences in conversation. Public lecture at the Linguistic Institute, University of Michigan. Pub. 1987 in *Talk and Social Organization*, Graham Button and John R. E. Lee (eds), pp. 54–69. Clevedon: Multilingual Matters.

Saunders, George. 1985. Silence and noise as emotion management styles: An Italian case. In Tannen and Saville-Troike 1985: 165–83.

Schiffrin, Deborah. 1984. Jewish argument as sociability. *Language in Society*, 13, 311–35.

Schiffrin, Deborah. 1985. Everyday argument: The organization of diversity in talk. In *Handbook of Discourse Analysis, vol. 3: Discourse and Dialogue*, Teun van Dijk (ed.), pp. 35–46. London: Academic Press.

Schiffrin, Deborah. 1990. The management of a co-operative self during argument: The role of opinions and stories. In Grimshaw 1990: 241–59.

Scott, Suzanne. 1998. Patterns of language use in adult face-to-face disagreements. Unpublished PhD thesis. Northern Arizona University.

Sheldon, Amy. 1990. Pickle fights: Gendered talk in preschool disputes. *Discourse Processes*, 13, 5–31. Also in Tannen 1993a: 83–109.

Sheldon, Amy. 1996. You can be the baby brother, but you aren't born yet: Preschool girls' negotiation for power and access in pretend play. *Research on Language and Social Interaction*, 29, 57–80.

Sherzer, Joel. 1993. On puns, comebacks, verbal dueling, and play languages: Speech play in Balinese verbal life. *Language in Society*, 22, 217–33.

Sidnell, Jack. 1998. Collaboration and contestation in a dispute about space in an Indo-Guyanese village. *Pragmatics*, 8, 315–38.

Simmel, George. 1961. The sociology of sociability. Reprinted in *Theories of Society*, T. Parsons, E. Shils, K. D. Naegele, and J. R. Pitts (eds), pp. 157–63. New York: Free Press.

Song, Kyong-Sook. 1993. An interactional sociolinguistic analysis of argument strategies in Korean conversational discourse: Negotiating disagreement and conflict. Unpublished PhD thesis, Georgetown University, Washington DC.

Straehle, Carolyn. A. 1997. German and American conversational styles: A focus on narrative and agonistic discussion as sources of stereotypes. Unpublished PhD dissertation, Georgetown University, Washington DC.

Tannen, Deborah. 1986. *That's Not What I Meant!: How Conversational Style Makes or Breaks your Relations with Others*. New York: William Morrow.

Tannen, Deborah. 1990a. Silence as conflict management in fiction and drama: Pinter's *Betrayal* and a short story, "Great Wits." In Grimshaw 1990: 260–79.

Tannen, Deborah. 1990b. *You Just Don't Understand: Women and Men in Conversation*. New York: William Morrow.

Tannen, Deborah (ed.). 1993a. *Gender and Conversational Interaction*. New York: Oxford University Press.

Tannen, Deborah. 1993b. The relativity of linguistic strategies: Rethinking power and solidarity in gender and dominance. In Tannen 1993a: 165–88.

Tannen, Deborah. 1994. *Talking from 9 to 5: How Women's and Men's Conversational Styles Affect Who Gets Heard, Who Gets Credit, and What Gets Done at Work*. New York: Morrow.

Tannen, Deborah. 1998. *The Argument Culture: Moving from Debate to Dialogue*. New York: Random House.

Tannen, Deborah, and Christina Kakavá. 1992. Power and solidarity in modern Greek conversation: Disagreeing to agree. *Journal of Modern Greek Studies*, 10, 11–34.

Tannen, Deborah, and Muriel Saville-Troike (eds). 1985. *Perspectives on Silence*. Norwood, NJ: Ablex.

Taylor, Carolyn. 1995. "You think it was a fight?": Co-constructing (the struggle for) meaning, face, and family in everyday narrative activity. *Research on Language and Social Interaction*, 28, 283–317.

Vuchinich, Samuel. 1990. The sequential organization of closing in verbal family conflict. In Grimshaw 1990: 118–38.

Watson-Gegeo, Karen Ann, and Geoffrey M. White (eds). 1990. *Disentangling: Conflict Discourse in Pacific Societies*. Stanford, CA: Stanford University Press.

IV Discourse across Disciplines

34 The Analysis of Discourse Flow

WALLACE CHAFE

0 Introduction

Language is a dynamic process. It is easy to forget that fact when one is working with language that has been frozen on paper or a computer screen, where it has been turned into something that can be examined as if it were a fixed object. So much of linguistic analysis has dealt with language in written form that there is a temptation to think of language itself as having the same static quality (cf. Linell 1982). But language in action is better captured with the metaphor of a flowing stream.

There are, in fact, two streams, one a stream of thoughts, the other of sounds. The two have very different qualities. It is instructive to compare the experience of listening to a familiar language with listening to a language one does not know. In the former case it is the thoughts, not the sounds, of which one is conscious, but in the latter case only the sounds. Sounds are easier for an analyst to deal with, simply because they are publicly observable. Thoughts are experienced within the mind, and for that reason are less tractable to objective research. On the other hand thoughts enjoy a priority over sounds in the sense that the organization and communication of thoughts is what language is all about. The sounds exist in the service of the thoughts, and follow wherever the thoughts may take them. It is the thoughts that drive language forward. A basic challenge for discourse analysis is to identify the forces that give direction to the flow of thoughts.

1 Topics

Important among these forces are what I will be calling *topics*. This word has been used in different ways, and I should make it clear that I am not using it to apply to a constituent of a sentence, as when one speaks of a sentence having a "topic and comment" (e.g. Hockett 1958: 201), or of "topic-prominent" languages (Li and Thompson 1976), or of "topicalization" or "topic continuity" (e.g. Givón 1983). Rather,

I am using it to refer to what is sometimes called a "discourse topic" (Brown and Yule 1983: 71), as in "the topic of this paragraph." A topic in this sense is a coherent aggregate of thoughts introduced by some participant in a conversation, developed either by that participant or another or by several participants jointly, and then either explicitly closed or allowed to peter out. Topics typically have clear beginnings, although that is not always the case (cf. Tannen 1984: 41–3), and their endings are sometimes well defined, sometimes not. As long as a topic remains open, participants in a conversation experience a drive to develop it. I began chapter 10 of Chafe (1994) with a quote from William James that nicely captures this drive:

> In all our voluntary thinking there is some topic or subject about which all the members of the thought revolve. Half the time this topic is a problem, a gap we cannot yet fill with a definite picture, word, or phrase, but which . . . influences us in an intensely active and determinate psychic way. Whatever may be the images and phrases that pass before us, we feel their relation to this aching gap. To fill it up is our thought's destiny. Some bring us nearer to that consummation. Some the gap negates as quite irrelevant. Each swims in a felt fringe of relations of which the aforesaid gap is the term. (James 1890, vol. 1: 259)

Sensitivity to the topic structure of talk may be a trait that varies with individuals. Casual observation suggests that people are constrained to varying degrees by the need to develop a topic fully before the conversation moves on to another, and that there is variable recognition of the social right to topic development. One wonders if such differences in conversational style can be traced to differences in the degree to which a person experiences James's aching gap and the need to fill it.

A first step in discourse analysis can be to listen to a recording of a conversation with the goal of identifying topics, segments of discourse during which one or more of the speakers talk about "the same thing." Topics are identifiable above all from their content, but there are likely to be phonetic cues as well: sometimes, though certainly not always, a longer-than-normal pause before a new topic is introduced; sometimes heightened pitch, loudness, acceleration, or a new voice quality at the outset; sometimes a tapering off in these same prosodic features at the end. One may find topics varying greatly in length. There may be occasional stretches of discourse during which there appears to be no topic at all. But most parts of most conversations lend themselves well to analysis into units of this kind.

There appears to be a basic level of topic-hood, with topics at that level typically included within more inclusive *supertopics*. The latter also have identifiable beginnings and endings, but they lack the internal structure that characterizes basic-level topics and do not generate the same drive for closure, James's aching gap. Each time a basic-level topic is concluded, any participant in a conversation has the option of abandoning the current supertopic and, by introducing a new basic-level topic, introducing a new supertopic at the same time. With no internal structure of their own, supertopics can be abandoned whenever any included basic-level topic has been completed.

After a particular basic-level topic, or some sequence of them, has been chosen for further study, the next step can be to reduce the flow of language to some written form. The word *reduce* is appropriate. There is no way in which the richness of natural speech, with all its prosodic complexity, its accompanying gestures and shifts of gaze, and ultimately the entire physical, social, and cognitive context in which it took place – no way in which all these factors can be captured in any presently conceivable written form. Thus, any attempt to transcribe spoken language on paper inevitably leaves much out. The transcriber needs a system that is more or less adequate for the questions addressed, but needs always to keep in mind that any system only selects from the totality of observations that might be relevant (Du Bois et al. 1993; Chafe 1993, 1995).

It is useful in this process to identify a unit of transcription that reflects another level of organization. In addition to basic-level topics, language gives evidence of the organization of thoughts from moment to moment into a focus and a periphery: a limited area of fully active consciousness surrounded by a penumbra of ideas in a semiactive state. Each focus is expressed in sound with a brief prosodic phrase, typically one to two seconds long, whose properties include one or more of the following: a distinctive terminal intonation contour, an initial resetting of the pitch baseline, the presence of silence before and after, a change of tempo at the beginning or end, and boundary changes in voice quality such as whispering or creaky voice. Intonation units are a pervasive feature of natural speech. Not only do they provide a useful way of segmenting speech, they are profitably viewed as expressing constantly changing foci of consciousness, and hence their relevance to understanding the flow of thought (Chafe 1994: 53–81).

2   Topic Navigation

In this perspective a topic can be seen as a conceptual unit that is too large to be accommodated within the limited capacity of fully active consciousness. A topic as a whole can thus be present only in a semiactive state. Once a topic has been introduced, the more limited focus of active consciousness navigates through it, activating first one included idea and then another until the topic is judged to have been adequately covered and closure is judged appropriate. This navigation process is often guided by a *schema*, some familiar pattern that provides a path for a speaker to follow (e.g. Bartlett 1932; Chafe 1986). It may also be driven, alternatively or simultaneously, by the less predictable interaction between conversational participants (Chafe 1994: 120–36).

I will illustrate this process with an excerpt from a long conversation in the course of which three women, whose names will be given here as Kathy, Sally, and Chris, were discussing teaching practices in an elementary school classroom. Kathy was an experienced teacher, Sally was a less experienced teacher, and Chris was a less involved onlooker. We can take up this conversation at a point where its forward movement was momentarily at a standstill. The previous topic had just been closed, and if the conversation was to continue someone had to choose and introduce a new topic. The preceding topics had fallen within the domain of a supertopic I will label Classroom Experiences.

The default option during such a lull in a conversation is for any of the participants to open a new basic-level topic that remains within the current supertopic, in this case to talk about another classroom experience. That choice would leave the supertopic Classroom Experiences open, a situation that can be represented with an open parenthesis. The introduction of a new basic-level topic would then create its own open parenthesis, included within the other. This situation can be represented as follows, where the supertopic is shown in italics:

> (*Classroom Experiences* (Classroom Experience 1) (Classroom Experience 2) (Classroom Experience 3

There are two open parentheses that demand eventually to be closed.

An alternative would be for any of the participants in the conversation to introduce a basic-level topic that would close the current supertopic with Classroom Experience 2 and establish a new and different one. Imagine, for example, that someone began talking now about a movie she had just seen, introducing a new basic-level topic that would simultaneously open a new supertopic that could be labeled Current Movies. The effect would be:

> (*Classroom Experiences* (Classroom Experience 1) (Classroom Experience 2))
> (*Current Movies* (A movie just seen by X

As it happened, Sally chose the default option, opening another topic that remained within the Classroom Experiences supertopic. What she said was:[1]

(1)   Sally   (0.5) Whát I was gonna téll you about that rèally frústrates me is that,

No one but Sally knew where this topic would lead, and for the moment we can give it the label Something Frustrating. Later we will see how the flow of the conversation would make a different label appropriate.

The words *what I was gonna tell you about* suggest that Sally had planned to introduce this topic earlier. Examination of the larger context reveals that she had tried earlier to do just that. She was unsuccessful in that first attempt because Chris interrupted her with a different topic. What she said earlier was (numbered (0) because it lay outside the excerpt with which we will be principally concerned):

(0)   Sally   . . Méanwhile in the príncipal's òffice they're tèlling me,

Two other topics intervened before Sally returned to what she had tried to start in (0), a topic that must have remained alive in her semiactive consciousness while the other topics were being developed. It was thus easily available to be reintroduced in (1), which was followed by a second intonation unit whose wording closely resembled that of (0), as we will see.

3   Navigation by Schema

We can now follow this conversation as it unfolded for those engaged in it. At the end we can view a transcript of the conversation as a whole, at the same time considering what, exactly, such a transcript represents. The Something Frustrating topic was at first developed by Sally as a monologue. There is a ubiquitous schema for narrative topic development whose maximum components can be listed as follows (cf. Chafe 1994: 120–36):

- summary
- initial state
- complication
- climax
- denouement
- final state
- coda.

Labov and Waletzky (1967) suggested a similar schema, but inexplicably omitted the climax. An opening summary may or may not be present. Closer to being obligatory is the presentation of an initial state that gives the topic a spatiotemporal and/or epistemic orientation. The complication section disturbs the initial state with events that lead to a climax, an unexpected event that constitutes the point of the topic, the reason for its telling. The denouement then provides a relaxation toward a final state in which new knowledge provided by the climax has been incorporated. There may or may not be a coda, a metacomment on the topic as a whole.

Sally's statement in (1) summarized the content of what would follow by saying that it would entail something frustrating. Not only did she open a new topic and assume the floor, but at the same time by using the word *frustrates* she foreshadowed its organization, creating an expectation that it would involve something desirable followed by an explanation of why that desirable outcome could not be realized. Deciding just how to proceed required additional mental processing time on Sally's part, an interval during which she uttered a prolonged hesitation sound, followed by 1.3 seconds of silence and then an audible breath before she continued:

(2) Sally   (0.2) ùh=,

(3)   (1.3) (breath) the (0.1) the péop . . the príncipal and stuff they sày to me,

In (3) she repeated, with only partially different words, her earlier attempt to introduce this topic, shown above as intonation unit (0). Early in (3) she decided to mention the people who had given her advice. Her truncated *the peop* was an attempt at categorizing that idea, but she quickly found a better categorization and produced the interestingly hedged phrase *the principal and stuff*, followed by the quote-introducer *they say to me*.

Looking back at (1), we can see that Sally's consciousness was then operating in what I have called the *immediate mode* (Chafe 1994: 195–223). That is, Sally was talking about what was still frustrating her at the very time she was talking. With (3), however, she moved into the *displaced mode* by shifting to things that had been said to her at one or more times in the past, displaced from the here and now of this conversation. Furthermore, the choice of the *generic mode* (*they say to me*, without reference to any particular event) anticipated that the quote to follow would be generic as well.

She was not talking about a particular act of advice-giving, but of events less locally specified. (The context makes it clear that she was not using the historical present here.)

Sally then began the quote, shifting her voice iconically to a higher pitch that lay noticeably above her normal range. The first element in the quote established an affective stance on the part of the principal and the others toward what they were telling her:

(4)   Sally   (0.9) (tsk) (breath) (begin higher pitch) óh wèll,

The alveolar click (*tsk*) as well as the prosody and wording *oh well* conveyed something of the lack of concern Sally had perceived in the advice: the principal and stuff felt that coping with the third-graders was no big deal.

The next focus established a frame for the recommended action: the idea that Sally should do something specific:

(5)   Sally   . . whàt you dò with those thírd-gràders,

With this utterance Sally created a second level of displacement. Having begun in the immediate mode in (1) (experiencing her current frustration), she used (3) to shift into the displaced world in which she was given advice, and now with (5) she moved into the further displaced world of the recommended action, a more hypothetical world that might be realized at some future time. Thus the sequence of (1), (3), and (5) established a setting that was increasingly displaced from the immediacy of the present conversation:

what frustrates me	(immediate)
the principal and stuff say to me	(past and generic)
what you do with those third-graders	(future and generic)

With this orientation in place, Sally arrived at a point where she could begin expressing the advice that had been given her. Putting it all together and deciding how to express it took a little more time, some of which she filled with two intonation units that shed light on still other aspects of discourse flow:

(6)   Sally   you knòw,

(7)   is you jùst like,

There are two problems that confront anyone engaged in talk. They are created by two kinds of *unconformity*, to borrow a term from geology, where it refers to a discontinuity in rock strata. I use it here to refer to disparate aspects of human experience that must somehow be brought into approximate (but only approximate) conformity if one is to interact with one's fellow humans. First, there is the inevitable unconformity between an individual's experiences – perceptions, actions, and evaluations that are either immediate, remembered, or imagined – and the limited resources a language provides for verbalizing them. Second, there is the unconformity that inevitably exists between one mind and another. There is, in short, both a *verbalization* problem and an *interaction* problem. The language people produce often gives indications that a speaker recognizes both, and (6) and (7) are examples.

So far as the verbalization problem is concerned, language cannot fully or adequately express an inner experience. The verbalization process allows a speaker to get a useful handle on the experience and share it to some degree with others, but the linguistic organization of ideas is not the same as the experience itself. The ubiquitous *like*, found here in (7), is one way a speaker can show recognition of the unconformity between ideas and their verbal expression – a small and passing way in which Sally showed her recognition that what she was about to say would be only a roughly satisfactory representation of what she was thinking.

So far as the interaction problem is concerned, one mind can never fully know what another mind is experiencing, and language can only imperfectly bridge the gap. Someone engaged in a conversation needs both to clothe an inner experience in language that will more or less adequately express it, and at the same time find language that will more or less satisfactorily take account of what is believed to be present in other minds, to the extent that that is possible. The equally ubiquitous *you know*, the sole content of (6), is one way a speaker can show recognition of the unconformity between his or her own mind and the mind of another, in this case signaling that what she was about to say was, to some degree at least, what her listeners might have expected and not something that would be totally surprising to them. (It can be noted that (6) and (7) were attributed to the people characterized as *the principal and stuff*, not to Sally herself, but of course there is no way to know whether they were anything the principal or anyone else had actually said.)

It was time now to move on to the complication section of the narrative schema, in this case the actions recommended by the principal and stuff:

(8)   Sally   (0.8) táke them=,

(9)   and pút them=,

(10)   you knòw with= òne of the smárter fóurth-gràders who's vèry [vér]bal and,

(11) Chris [Uh huh,]

(12) Sally   (0.1) and wèll-beháved.

(13)   (0.5) And you . . hàve them wòrk as a téam you know;

(14)   so that the (0.4) (breath) fóurth-gràder can help the thírd-gràder.

At the end of (14) the prosody conveyed a definitive closure of this section. The climax then came with a bang, its impact heightened by the nearly two seconds of silence that preceded it as well as by the forceful wording:

(15) Sally   (1.7) (loud) But . . that's búllshit.

The immediately following denouement served to justify this evaluation:

(16)   Sally   (0.1) Because,

(17)   (0.5) thát just tèaches the thírd-gràder=,

(18)   with the lèsser intélligence that,

(19)   (0.9) that he's wórthless;

(20)   . . you know that he càn't léarn [sùmpm on his ów=n.]

4   Navigation by Interaction

With (20), Sally completed her own development of the topic she had opened in (1). Can we say that the conversation had now returned to a state where it would have been appropriate for any of the participants to introduce a different topic, either staying within the Classroom Experiences supertopic or introducing a new supertopic? The question is whether (20) qualifies as a topic ending. We can only speculate on Sally's goal in opening her topic in the first place, but we might suppose that she was using (1)–(20) as a way of eliciting some reaction, perhaps sympathy and advice, from her interlocutors. In any case Kathy reacted in a way that may not have been what Sally was hoping for. What she said overlapped the end of (20):

(21)   Kathy   [Nó it's nót;

(22)   nó it's] nót,

(23)   you cán put them in tèams like thàt;

   With these three intonation units Kathy succeeded in reorganizing the structure of the ongoing topic. Until now Sally's topic had been organized around the idea that teams do not work, the idea I labeled Something Frustrating. Kathy now introduced the idea that teams *do* work, thereby organizing the topic into a bipartite structure of thesis and antithesis: into the subtopics Teams Do Not Work and Teams Do Work. Thus, the topic we are studying could now be relabeled as Using Teams. But what followed took a path that no one could have anticipated.
   Kathy began by justifying her statement in (23) by trying to modify Sally's conception of the make-up of the teams:

(24)   Kathy but you dón't put óne with óne;

(25)   you pút like twó fóurth-gràders with–

Before she finished (25), however, she decided that her intent would come across more clearly if she could establish the relative numbers of third- and fourth-graders in Sally's class. After nearly a second of silence she briefly thought in (26) of asking for raw numbers, but truncated that attempt also and quickly replaced it with a request for a ratio instead:

(26) Kathy   (0.8) Hów many thírd-gràders d–

(27)   What's the . . [1 rátio of thìrd- 1] [2 graders to fòurth-graders. 2]

In the middle of (27) there occurred one of those conversational moments when people talk at cross-purposes, a turbulence in the stream of interactive thought. Sally did not immediately hear Kathy's question about the ratio of third-graders to fourth-graders, and not only Sally but also Chris began to pursue directions of their own, overlapping most of (27):

(28) Sally   [1 But they're nót 1]

(29) Chris   [2 You mean so they dòn't feel sìngled 2] [3 óut or whát. 3]

But Sally quickly abandoned whatever she had begun in (28) and responded to Kathy's question in (27) with some precise information:

(30) Sally   [3 Nów I have 3] like fíve thírd-gràders.

(31)   I have like (0.3) twénty-two kíds.

These two statements elicited the first of the misunderstandings that drove the remainder of this topic. Sally's answer invited some hasty arithmetic that should have yielded the correct number of fourth-graders, but Kathy made an error:

(32) Kathy   (0.2) Ókay,

(33)   só you have fífteen fóurth-gràders and fíve thírd-gràders?

We can only speculate on why Kathy said *fifteen*, but the subsequent conversation suggests that she had been hoping for a whole number ratio like fifteen to five, so that each team could have contained three fourth-graders and one third-grader.

The question in (33) was a confirmative one, anticipating a positive answer, but of course Sally responded with a correction:

(34) Sally   (0.6) Nó;

(35)   (0.9) uh= nó.

(36)   (0.1) I have like (0.2) séven (noise) fòurth-graders.

(37)   (0.1) (sotto voce) And fíve thìrd-graders.

During (36) there was an extraneous background noise that masked the last syllable, *teen*, of the word *seventeen*, so that Kathy heard only *seven*. On the basis of ordinary expectations regarding class size she responded with surprise, communicated especially by her prosody:

(38)   Kathy   You have twélve kíds?

Now it was Sally's turn to be surprised. Thinking she had just explained that the correct numbers were 17 fourth-graders and five third-graders, Kathy's question made no sense:

(39)   Sally   (0.5) Whát?

But Kathy could only repeat it:

(40)   Kathy   (0.1) You ónly have twélve kíds?

Sally repeated her previous answer, this time free of the noise:

(41)   Sally   (0.4) Nó.

(42)   (0.3) Séventéen;

Kathy stood corrected:

(43)   Kathy   (0.2) Óh ókay,

Sally wanted to make certain that Kathy knew that 17 was not the total number in the class, but only the size of the subset on which she had focused:

(44)   Sally   fóurth-grà[ders,]

   Amid all this confusion Kathy abandoned her plan to be precise about the numerical composition of the teams. If she had hoped to specify that each team would be composed of three fourth-graders and one third-grader, she now found it pointless to insist on such exactitude and fell back on a less precise recommendation:

(45)   Kathy   [so] thén what you dó is you sprínkle the fífth-gràders out évenly.

(46)   (0.6) And you máke . . [the fóurth-gràders] (0.1) táke the responsibílity
            for téaching them.

In (45) she made another error, saying *fifth-graders* instead of *third-graders*, probably because Kathy herself had taught a fifth–sixth-grade combination in which it was the fifth-graders who were the less advanced. Sally corrected her with a questioning intonation while Kathy was uttering *fourth-graders* in (46):

(47)   Sally   [Thírd-gràders?]

Kathy then went on to supplement what she had said in (46):

(48)   Kathy   And yóu engráin in them,

(49)   that it's théir responsibìlity to hèlp those lìttle kíds.

She added a coda that would drive home the success of the recommended procedure. Sandwiched between her final two intonation units was a protest by Sally, evidently to the effect that she herself had done the same:

(50)   Kathy   Thát's what Í did,

(51)   Sally   I háve been.

(52)   Kathy   [and it wórks.]

Even before Kathy finished (52), Chris overlapped with a question whose effect was to open a new, though closely related topic:

(53)   Chris   [But thén you]

(54)   can you sáy it's a [pàrt of your] gráde?

There followed a lengthy discussion of whether and how one should grade the fourth-graders for their mentoring activities. The situation created by (54) was thus as follows:

> (*Classroom Experiences* (Classroom Experience 1) (Classroom Experience 2) (Using Teams) (Assigning Grades

  My intention with this extended example has been to illustrate how the stream of language is propelled forward by the opening of a topic and the creation of a drive for the topic's development until closure is judged appropriate. I have discussed a basic-level topic, ultimately called Using Teams, as an example of the highest level of topic-hood at which there is a coherent trajectory of development. Once open, a topic may be kept moving along a path provided by a schema, or by the interaction of separate minds engaged in the conversation, or by some combination of both. Interactive topic development may be driven by an interlocutor's desire to agree with or contradict something said by another, or to request needed information the other may possess. This example shows especially well how forward movement may be driven by momentary misunderstandings.

5   The Text

By stringing together all the intonation units that were introduced piecemeal above, one can produce a transcript of this entire segment of the conversation. This kind of object is often called a *text*, and it is the traditional object of discourse study:

1	Sally	(0.5) Whát I was gonna téll you about that rèally frústrates me is that,
2		(0.2) ùh=,
3		(1.3) (breath) the (0.1) the péop . . the príncipal and stuff they sày to me,
4		(0.9) (tsk) (breath) (begin higher pitch) óh wèll,
5		. . whàt you dò with those thírd-gràders,
6		you knòw,
7		is you jùst like,
8		(0.8) táke them=,
9		and pút them=,
10		you knòw with= òne of the smárter fóurth-gràders who's vèry [vér]bal and,
11	Chris	[Uh huh,]
12	Sally	(0.1) and wèll-beháved.
13		(0.5) And you . . hàve them wòrk as a téam you know;
14		so that the (0.4) (breath) fóurth-gràder can help the thírd-gràder.
15		(1.7) But . . that's búllshit.
16		(0.1) Because,
17		(0.5) thát just tèaches the thírd-gràder=,
18		with the lèsser intélligence that,
19		(0.9) that he's wórthless;
20		. . you know that he càn't léarn [sùmpm on his ów=n.]
21	Kathy	[Nó it's nót;
22		nó it's] nót,
23		you cán put them in tèams like thàt;
24		but you dón't put óne with óne;
25		you pút like twó fóurth-gràders with–
26		(0.8) Hów many thírd-gràders d–
27		What's the . . [1 rátio of thìrd- 1] [2 graders to fòurth-graders. 2]
28	Sally	[1 But they're nót 1]
29	Chris	[2 You mean so they dòn't feel sìngled 2] [3 óut or whát. 3]
30	Sally	[3 Nów I have 3] like fíve thírd-gràders.
31		I have like (0.3) twénty-two kíds.
32	Kathy	(0.2) Ókay,
33		só you have fifteen fóurth-gràders and fíve thírd-gràders?
34	Sally	(0.6) Nó;
35		(0.9) uh= nó.
36		(0.1) I have like (0.2) séven (noise) fòurth-graders.
37		(0.1) (sotto voce) And fíve thìrd-graders.
38	Kathy	You have twélve kíds?
39	Sally	(0.5) Whát?
40	Kathy	(0.1) You ónly have twélve kíds?
41	Sally	(0.4) Nó.
42		(0.3) Séventéen;
43	Kathy	(0.2) Óh ókay,
44	Sally	fóurth-grà[ders,]
45	Kathy	[so] thén what you dó is you sprínkle the fífth-gràders out évenly.

46		(0.6) And you máke . . [the fóurth-gràders] (0.1) táke the responsibílity for téaching them.
47	Sally	[Thírd-gràders?]
48	Kathy	And yóu engráin in them,
49		that it's théir responsibìlity to hèlp those lìttle kíds.
50		Thát's what Í did,
51	Sally	I háve been.
52	Kathy	[and it wórks.]
53	Chris	[But thén you]
54		can you sáy it's a [pàrt of your] gráde?

What kind of thing is this? Does it have any validity beyond being a visual representation of a concatenation of utterances that were produced in sequence as the conversation unfolded through time? One possibility, easily discardable, is that it represents something in the minds of one or more of the participants before these things were said. But of course no one could have planned the above, or have predicted that the conversation would proceed in this way. Is it, then, something that remained in the minds of the participants afterwards? Again the answer must be no, though perhaps this time not quite so unqualified a no. Although some of the ideas expressed here were probably retained in some form, varying from one participant to another, for at least a while, the details of how these thoughts were activated and verbalized during the conversation were surely quickly lost. The participants may have remembered for a time that they talked about using teams in the classroom, that Sally did not like the idea, that Kathy did like it, and so on. But the particular sequence of ideas and exactly how they were expressed was surely ephemeral.

It is worth noting that spontaneous conversations differ from "oral literature" in this respect. A person may remember a ritual or story or joke and repeat it later in another setting, though with language and content seldom if ever identical. But people do not repeat casual conversations in the same way. Someone might say, "That was a good conversation," but no one would be likely to exclaim, "Let's say the whole thing again tomorrow." If people do remark occasionally, "I think we've had this conversation before," they are hardly thinking of a verbatim repetition. It is worth reflecting on the fact that the collection and study of texts has in the past been slanted toward narratives and rituals whose value lies in something closer to (though seldom identical with) verbatim repetition. Discourse of that kind is more persistent in memory, and in that respect is a little more like written language. In other words, earlier discourse studies have tended to favor material that has been closer in nature to written text (Chafe 1981).

I do not mean to suggest that a text like the above has no use. What it gives us is a lasting record of evanescent happenings that we can examine visually at our leisure. As a kind of time machine, it is a resource that allows us as analysts to view all at once the dynamic processes by which a sequence of linguistic events was produced. It is a useful tool that can further our understanding of how minds and language proceed through time. By freezing temporal events it helps us identify the forces responsible for creating them. My point is that we should not be misled into interpreting this artificial aid to understanding as something that possesses a transcendent reality.

One may sometimes hear the view that participants in a conversation are engaged in the joint construction of a text. I suggest that it is better to think of a conversation as a uniquely human and extraordinarily important way by which separate minds are able to influence and be influenced by each other, managing to some extent, and always imperfectly, to bridge the gap between them, not by constructing any kind of lasting object but through a constant interplay of constantly changing ideas. The example that has been discussed here suggests a few of the ways in which that can happen.

NOTES

1   Conventions followed in this and the following transcriptions of speech include the following. The numbers in parentheses are measurements (to tenths of a second) of periods of silence. The acute and grave accents mark the nuclei of syllables with primary and secondary accents respectively. Periods show a decisively falling pitch contour, often accompanied by creaky voice, whereas semicolons show a less decisive fall. Commas show any other terminal contour, except that the high rising pitch associated with a yes-no question is shown by a question mark. The equals sign shows a prolongation of the preceding sound. Square brackets show overlapping speech, sometimes indexed with numbers when there might be ambiguity. That is, a segment enclosed in [1 . . . 1] overlaps with another segment indexed in the same way, etc.

REFERENCES

Bartlett, Frederic C. 1932. *Remembering: A Study in Experimental and Social Psychology.* Cambridge: Cambridge University Press.

Brown, Gillian, and George Yule. 1983. *Discourse Analysis.* Cambridge: Cambridge University Press.

Chafe, Wallace. 1981. Differences between colloquial and ritual in Seneca, or how oral literature is literary. In Wallace Chafe, Alice Schlichter, and Leanne Hinton (eds), *Reports from Survey of California and Other Indian Languages,* No. 1, pp. 131–45. Berkeley: University of California, Department of Linguistics.

Chafe, Wallace. 1986. Beyond Bartlett: Narratives and remembering. In Elisabeth Gülich and Uta M. Quasthoff (eds), *Narrative Analysis: An Interdisciplinary Dialogue.* Special issue of *Poetics,* 15, 139–51.

Chafe, Wallace. 1993. Prosodic and functional units of language. In Jane A. Edwards and Martin D. Lampert (eds), *Talking Data: Transcription and Coding in Discourse Research,* pp. 33–43. Hillsdale, NJ: Lawrence Erlbaum.

Chafe, Wallace. 1994. *Discourse, Consciousness, and Time: The Flow and Displacement of Conscious Experience in Speaking and Writing.* Chicago: University of Chicago Press.

Chafe, Wallace. 1995. Adequacy, user-friendliness, and practicality in transcribing. In Geoffrey Leech, Greg

Myers, and Jenny Thomas (eds), *Spoken English on Computer: Transcription, Mark-up, and Application*, pp. 54–61. New York: Longman.

Du Bois, John W., Stephan Schuetze-Coburn, Susanna Cumming, and Danae Paolino. 1993. Outline of discourse transcription. In Jane A. Edwards and Martin D. Lampert (eds), *Talking Data: Transcription and Coding in Discourse Research*, pp. 45–89. Hillsdale, NJ: Lawrence Erlbaum.

Givón, T. 1983. *Topic Continuity in Discourse: A Quantitative Cross-Language Study*. Amsterdam and Philadelphia: John Benjamins.

Hockett, Charles F. 1958. *A Course in Modern Linguistics*. New York: Macmillan.

James, William. 1890. *The Principles of Psychology*. 2 vols. New York: Henry Holt. Reprinted 1950, Dover: New York.

Labov, William, and Joshua Waletzky. 1967. Narrative analysis: Oral versions of personal experience. In June Helm (ed.), *Essays on the Verbal and Visual Arts: Proceedings of the 1966 Annual Spring Meeting of the American Ethnological Society*, pp. 12–44. Seattle: University of Washington Press.

Li, Charles N., and Sandra Thompson. 1976. Subject and topic: A new typology of language. In Charles N. Li (ed.), *Subject and Topic*, pp. 457–89. New York: Academic Press.

Linell, Per. 1982. *The Written Language Bias in Linguistics*. Linköping, Sweden: University of Linköping Press.

Tannen, Deborah. 1984. *Conversational Style: Analyzing Talk Among Friends*. Norwood, NJ: Ablex.

35 The Discursive Turn in Social Psychology

ROM HARRÉ

0 Introduction

Fully to grasp the depth of the change that attention to discourse[1] has brought about in social psychology it is necessary to understand something of the early history of this branch of the human sciences. The general topic of social psychology is simply defined: the study of certain kinds of interaction between people, such as friendship, leadership, aggression, the influence of other people's opinions on an individual's beliefs, and so on. The fundamental presupposition of what is now called the "old paradigm" privileged the cognitive and emotional states of individuals as the source of the properties of the patterns of social interactions they engaged in.

The methodology that grew out of this root metaphysical principle was exclusively experimental. People were defined as subjects. The treatments to which they were subjected in laboratories were partitioned into independent variables, and the reactions of the subjects to these treatments were analysed into dependent variables. The upshot was a catalogue of correlations between independent and dependent variables. In one famous study the result purported to display a correlation between the frequency with which people met and the degree of their liking for one another. For the most part the experimental program paid no attention to the meanings which subjects might have given to what was happening, nor were the conversations that ordinarily surround and partly constitute social interactions included within the methodological scope of mainstream research. The "frequency/liking study" (Zajonc 1984) abstracted from all real situations to a laboratory stimulus consisting of meaningless symbols. It was widely assumed that the real cultural and historical contexts of social action could be ignored, since the laboratory was deemed to be a culturally neutral place. What people did in the laboratory was taken to be indicative of general psychological laws, of comparable scope to the laws of physics. They were taken to cover all instances of a type of being and to underlie their patterns of behavior – in this case all human beings and their social interactions. Both these paradigm-defining assumptions were flawed. This way of doing social psychology was well entrenched by the 1950s, and particularly strongly so in the United States. The reactions of undergraduate psychology majors became the main database for far-reaching generalizations about human behavior.

The research program that initiated the study of social psychology that became the "old paradigm" was concerned with the phenomenon of social facilitation. How does the presence of other people affect an individual's performance? This question is germane to athletics as much as it is to factory work. With his studies in both these areas, Triplett (1897) established a certain way of thinking about and studying social interactions. The metaphysics was causal, in that he thought of the reactions of a target person as the effects of the stimuli provided by the onlookers, coworkers, pacemakers, etc. The methodology was experimental, in that the effect was to be understood by treating the phenomenon as if it could be analyzed into a relation between the enhanced or declining performance of the subject, treated as the dependent variable, and the character of the surrounding situation, taken to be the independent variable.

It is a remarkable tribute to the persistence of a "convenient" paradigm in the face of mountains of conflicting evidence that the majority of social psychologists, in academic psychology, still work within the old paradigm, descended from Triplett's framework. The effect of this has been to make most of the academic research in social psychology little more than a study of local customs and practices, in fact a kind of local anthropology. For example, studies of the conditions under which people would help one another presumed a base-line "Christian" ethics in place among the people studied.

Two sets of influences led to the development of new-paradigm social psychology. It was realized that the old paradigm focused attention on the supposed states of individuals and their cognitive processes figuring as causal mechanisms, so largely ignoring the dynamics of the episodes in which these people were engaged. Indeed much of the work was quite static, or involved changes in the tendencies of individuals when subject to experimental treatments. The shift from contrived experiments to a study of real-life social episodes changed the underlying assumptions of social psychology quite radically. Context became important (Marsh et al. 1977) and the role of language took centre stage (Giles and Robinson 1990). What were people doing in extended social interactions, and what was the main medium by which social interaction was sustained? What did people have to know to be able to engage in such episodes? Patently the old-fashioned "experimental" method of the old paradigm would be useless in these conditions.

Perhaps these shortcomings could be overcome by staging realistic experiments, real-life episodes in laboratories. The failure of this compromise led to a second set of influences coming to bear. A series of experiments on obedience and authority, staged by Zimbardo (1969), had to be called off since dangerous situations developed among the people involved. Those playing the role of the warders in a simulated prison were just too tough on those playing inmates. The attempt to simulate the conditions which supposedly made the Holocaust psychologically possible resulted in the morally equivocal treatment of experimental subjects (Milgram 1974). In Milgram's study, subjects were deceived into thinking that they were giving dangerous, even lethal electric shocks to people, under the orders of a psychologist. Some became greatly distressed by the situation.

It was also realized that the methods of inquiry in most experimental projects were shot through with radical ambiguities. The interpretations that people were giving to the experimental "treatments" often bore little relation to the interpretation with which the psychologist conducting the experiment was working. For example, Milgram thought he was investigating obedience while all along the people involved were interpreting the episode in terms of trust. The many who continued to deliver shocks to the presumed victim explained their actions in terms of the trust they had in the integrity of the scientific community, rather than in terms of Milgram's interpretation of their actions as obedience to constituted authority.

The moral problems of the old paradigm were tackled by moving from reality to fantasy, by asking people to reply to questionnaires about what they would do, feel, and so on in imagined situations. This method was assimilated to the old paradigm by lexical legislation. Questionnaires were called "instruments" and the business of answering them was called an "experiment." Unfortunately the same method, statistical analysis of correlations, reappeared in the new, discursive frame, a story or vignette being labeled "stimulus object" and the answers correspondingly being called "responses." The effect of this was to maintain the metaphysics of causation in the new situation, in which it no longer made any sense at all. Semantic relations between meanings are not causal relations between stimuli and responses.

The problem of divergent interpretations has never been tackled by adherents to the old paradigm. An honest, open-minded appraisal of academic social psychology could only lead to the abandonment of the metaphysics and the methodology that had led to these impasses. What would a clear-eyed view disclose? First of all that social episodes are more often than not carried through by the use of language, and secondly that answering questionnaires is not an experiment but a formalized conversation *about* this or that type of episode, in short nothing but a stripped-down account.

Here we have fertile soil for the development of a more sophisticated psychology, sensitive to unexamined metaphysical assumptions and ready to undertake the time-consuming and painstaking analysis of the complex phenomena of real social interactions, mediated by meanings and made orderly by the following of rules.

In this chapter we will be following the growth of a new paradigm, which is much indebted to the rather simple insight that people do a lot of their social interacting by talking, displaying symbolic objects, and so on.

1   From State to Process: The Moral/Political Dimension

The shift from a social psychology of individual mental states, or even of individual biological reactions, to one of collective social processes is not just a shift of focus. It is also a profound reconstructing of the moral and political conceptual framework within which psychological research is carried on. Anthropologists and historians are very familiar with the polarization of cultures along an axis from the highly individualistic to the strongly collectivist. American society has taken the Enlightenment ideal of the morally and socially autonomous individual, amplified by various influences, toward the individualistic pole. At the same time, individuals are assumed to be the focus of moral assessment, so there is strong motivation to find ways of easing the burden of individual moral responsibility. This feature, found to a lesser extent in other societies tending toward individualism, accounts for the paradox that strikes thoughtful foreigners: the seeming incompatibility in American social arrangements between democracy in the large and autocracy in the small.[2] From the point of view of the metaphysics and methodology of psychology the same contrast appears in the attempts to give causal accounts of social behavior, typical of much American work. This orientation is opposed to the agentive metaphysics of work elsewhere, for example the "activity" psychology approach of von Cranach (von Cranach 1981). If what one does is the effect of some causal mechanism, one can hardly be held responsible for one's actions. Extravagant and reckless shopping used to be looked on as a moral failing to be censured. People who got into debt were expected to take better control of their lives. Lately we have had "shopping" classified as an addiction, with the implication that the shopper is the victim of a causal mechanism for which a display of goods is a stimulus and purchasing some a response. One is no more responsible for one's escalating credit card debts than is the influenza victim for an escalating temperature. Experts must be called in to effect a cure.

There are two caveats to be entered vis-à-vis the new paradigm change from causal to normative or rule-referring explanations. The shift to "the rules," as extrapersonal constraints, *can* be made to serve in a causal explanatory framework. Rules have been interpreted not as discursive devices for making one's action intelligible and warrantable, but as causal influences. But what would motivate such a strained interpretation?

One could look on a social psychology based on a cause/effect metaphysics and a neobehaviorist experimental methodology as a socially potent device for making alibis available.[3] In many respects social psychology, and indeed other branches of both clinical and academic psychology, are not sciences, but part of the everyday apparatus by which people escape the consequences of their own actions. Paradoxically again, attention to episodes of collective and joint action forces one to pay attention to the individuals who enter into life episodes as responsible beings.

The shift from an interest in the cognitive mechanisms or biological reactions that are the focus of individualist research paradigms, to an interest in the way that people actively engage, with others, in projects of various kinds and levels, involves a new view of the relevant phenomena. There is not only a moral/political contrast between repudiating and claiming responsibility for one's action, but a shift from states of individuals to structures of multiperson episodes as defining the basic level of "what there is."

From the new theoretical point of view, what is new-paradigm research going to be engaged on? And what exemplars can we rely on to help bring a true *science* of human thought, feelings, and conduct to fruition?

2 First Steps in Methodology: How To Do Science

We are presented with a world of enormous complexity and indeterminacy. This is true of our world in both its physical and its cultural aspects. The greatest innovation in technique, an innovation that made physics possible, was the development of the technique of building, imagining, and using models. The first steps in this radical shift in methodology were taken between 1400 and 1600. A model is an analogue of its subject.

Let me illustrate two important roles of model making, both of which have an important part to play in psychology, with examples from early modern physics. The technique of model making is fairly simple in elementary physical sciences, though the same general plan is preserved into the very much more complex procedures required when the subjects of our models are human actions themselves and the cognitive processes and states produced by them. There are two main families of models in use in all the sciences.

2.1   Heuristic abstractions

It often happens that the real-world object or process that seems to be at the heart of some phenomenon of interest is too difficult to study in itself. In the case of physical systems it may be too large or happening too rapidly or too slowly. In 1600 William Gilbert published his great work, the *De Magnete*, the definitive work on the properties of simple magnets. Gilbert was interested in the problems of navigation and particularly in the use of the magnetic compass as a navigational instrument. To experiment on the whole earth was then impossible, so to shrink the world to manageable size Gilbert constructed a "terrella," a little earth, a sphere of lodestone with the magnetic and geographical poles coinciding. The oceans were carved out as depressions on the surface, and he attempted to chart the magnetic variation from true north as he moved a miniature compass across the micro-oceans. Such models have been variously named. I shall call models in this family "heuristic abstractions." The physical sciences and engineering are full of these models. Some are created out of material stuff and manipulated in the laboratory. For example, wind-tunnel models of airliners are analogs of the real thing, "flying" in an analog of the atmosphere. Some are imagined and their behavior studied by developing mathematical models of the basic physical entities of the model, or run on computers, for example models of the solar system from Exodus to Einstein. Heuristic abstractions do no more and no less than represent the nature of the things we can observe, in a manageable form. But there is another family of models, serving a different purpose.

2.2   Explanatory models

Francis Bacon was puzzled by the anomalous effect of heat on different solids. For instance, wax was liquefied by heating but clay was solidified. How could this be? He tried to explain the difference in the effects by imagining what solids might be like: assemblages of small, hard particles, or corpuscles. His model for heat itself was a motion of the constituent parts of bodies. By assigning wax atoms and clay atoms different degrees of adhesion he was able to invent an explanation. In the hands of Boyle, Newton, J. J. Thomson, Rutherford, Feynman, and many others, this primitive model of matter has been amazingly refined and elaborated. Explanatory models are invented and applied to the reality they model, whereas heuristic abstractions are abstracted from it.

So we have families of models distinguished by their subjects, that of which they are models. But neither heuristic abstractions nor explanatory models are freely constructed. They are constrained by sources. There is a limit to what we are permitted to imagine as explanatory models. They must, if plausible, be possible realities. The way to ensure that is to set up a double analogy. The model is an analog of the unobservable state, object, or processes we are assuming really explain the phenomena of interest. But in most cases the model is itself an analog of something we can already observe. The corpuscular model of an atom is modeled on a small material particle, say a grain of sand. Democritus is said to have thought of the atomic model of matter by observing the dancing motes in the sunbeam. So that Bacon's corpuscles are not unlike the grains of sand that can be made to stick together into a sandcastle or more drastically into glass. Heuristic models too are constrained by reference to sources. How do we know what to look for in abstracting an analog from a complex phenomenon? How do we ensure that we abstract the same way in all aspects of our construction? The technique of the physical scientists has been to double the analogy here too. Darwin's famous "natural selection" model directs our attention to certain features of the biosphere, but his abstractions were controlled by thinking of the living world as if it were a huge farm. He knew a great deal about creating varieties by domestic selection of favored breeding pairs. He looked for something similar in nature, and found it in the greater breeding potential of plants and animals that were most "at home" in their environments.

Both kinds of models deal with problems of observation. In the one case the reality is too difficult to observe and study conveniently, while in the other it cannot be observed at all. An experiment is not primarily a test of a hypothesis, but the running of a working model of some process in the world under study that cannot conveniently be examined in its natural form. Studying genetics by experimenting with garden peas and drosophilas in a jar is an example of the making of models of aspects of the natural world and seeing how they run. Experiments in the human sciences too must have this character to be scientifically acceptable.

3   Models in the Human Sciences

There are plenty of examples of both types of model in human studies, and indeed in the patterns of thinking of everyday life. Every time one consults a map one is using a heuristic abstraction from the countryside. Maps are simplified and reduced abstractions from the reality of a region. Every time one declares oneself to be fighting off a virus one is thinking in terms of an explanatory model. Viruses, until recently as unobservable as quarks, were invented to explain the onset and course of diseases for which no bacterial cause could be found. But what about models for psychological phenomena themselves?

The dramaturgical model in social psychology that has been used to good effect in several contexts is an abstraction from the messy goings-on it is used to represent, for example the behavior of the staff of a restaurant. To the student of social psychology, the shift of style and other indicators of cognitive slant as a waiter moves from kitchen to dining room presents a puzzle to be solved. How are these performances to be accounted for? By trying to abstract a pattern from the events, controlled by the idea of likening the work of a restaurant to the performance of a play, the decor to the stage sets, and so on, Goffman (1957) was able to present the work of the restaurant in a simplified but illuminating way. Similarly the fine structure of football hooliganism was revealed by Marsh et al.'s (1977) use of the idea of a status-creating and status-confirming ritual to abstract a pattern from what seemed at first sight to be chaotic acts of violence.

Cognitive psychology is rich in explanatory models. For instance, the use of cost-benefit analysis to analyze the thinking of lovers may seem somewhat unromantic, but it has offered a possible explanatory account of the ups and downs of love affairs. More technically impressive has been the use of the famous analogy through which artificial intelligence has spawned some interesting explanations in cognitive science. The model-creating analogy looks like this:

> Computer : Running a program :: Brain : Thinking

The slogan that the brain is a kind of computer is a rather extravagant way of stating the thesis that computation is a model of some, perhaps all, kinds of cognition. Here we have a very powerful, though ultimately flawed, explanatory model. It is flawed because the number and weight of ways in which brains and their functioning are unlike computers vastly outweighs the number and weight of ways they are alike.

It is not too much to say that a great deal of thinking, perhaps all, is a matter of model making, sometimes richly imagined but sometimes taking the form of highly schematized formal representations. The model-engendering relation is analogy. To what is social interaction analogous? Is there a kind of social interaction that could serve as a heuristic (and perhaps even an explanatory) model for social interaction of many or most kinds?

3.1   Conversation: the leading model for discursive psychology

I have been arguing that cognitive psychology ought to be focused on the public uses of words and other symbolic devices that active people use to carry out all sorts of projects. The means adopted in most cases involve a great deal of public and private talk. "Conversation" can be given an extended role as the leading metaphor for making sense of those aspects of episodes that seem to be mediated by other symbolic devices, though these are not conveyed by speech. Some of the concepts appropriate for analyzing linguistic interactions, such as syntax and semantics, may have a metaphorical use in nonlinguistic contexts. For example, what people do is effective insofar as it has a more or less shared meaning in the group involved. To be fully comprehensible and socially efficacious, say as an apology, the meaningful gesture, etc., must take place within a tacit system of norms that would, if stated explicitly, express the loosely bounded set of possible courses of thought and action that these people would regard as justified, sensible, and proper. Since conversation is literally a subtle symbolic public activity, often but not always directed to some overt or covert end, and occurring within the bounds of certain conceptions of what is a possible conversation, it ought to serve as a model for all types of meaningful inter-personal interaction, whatever be the medium (including, as I shall show, tennis).

It further follows that in so far as *all* human encounters are meaningful and norm-bound, the conversation or discursive model should straddle the boundaries between social orders and their cultural realizations. In the examples to follow, I will try to illustrate the literal use of the concept of "conversation" as a guide to building work-ing models of psychological phenomena. This is the basis of the conversational or discursive analogy.

4   What is the Field of Interest for Social Psychology?

4.1   Task and tool: a fruitful metaphor

Suppose we adopt the new-paradigm stance, and define our task as the discovery of the aims and norms of small-scale collective joint action, revealing the nature of interaction episodes. What about the people who engage in them? Where is the psychology? If we see episodes as people doing things, then the most natural organ-izing principle within which to frame our studies is the task/tool distinction. What are the socially relevant tasks that people are engaged in and what are the tools they are using to accomplish them? Tools for executing social tasks fall into two classes. There are symbolic devices such as words, gestures, flags, music, and so on. Then there are tools that individual people use to manage these symbolic tools, namely their own bodily organs such as brains and tongues. These too are tools.

Now the work of the social psychologist becomes complicated, because the concept that links a person to the task that he or she is jointly performing with others is their skill. To have a skill is to have a certain kind of procedural knowledge, know-how; and also some propositional knowledge, some know-that. Matters become still more complicated, since there has been a good deal of work that shows that in a group of people engaged in some activity, deficits in the skills of some members are made up for by the others. This familiar aspect of joint action has been called psychological symbiosis. We have then a three-fold structure:

1   There is the task/tool distinction to be applied to any given type of episode, say the building of friendship.
2   There is the tool/skill distinction by which individual actors are seen as working on the production of the psychological phenomenon in question.
3   There is the mutual pattern of interactions between team members, in which various relations, such as psychological symbiosis, completing the inadequate social performance of someone else can be observed.

One of the more difficult ideas for traditionalists, practitioners of old-paradigm social psychology, to accept is the central thesis that most cognitive phenomena have their primary location in the flow of interpersonal, joint action. I will describe this key concept more concretely in the case of remembering below, but there are plenty of models for the genesis of something cognitive in interpersonal interaction.

Let us take tennis as an illustration, and apply it as the source of our heuristic model of some cognitive phenomenon in the unfolding of collective action, for example remembering. How are we to understand an *act* of remembering as a social performance? According to the discursive point of view it is like the score "40/30" in a tennis match, say between Agassi and Sampras. This score is a cognitive phenomenon that was jointly produced by the players, acting in accordance with the norms of tennis matches, which neither could have produced singly, and for which both are responsible. Conformity is ensured publicly, and thus the joint construction of that score is rendered possible, by social norms personified in the umpire. In subsequent play the competitors must take account of that score, though in the plays that follow the fateful role may change. Let us say the game evolves through "Deuce" to "Advantage Agassi" to "Game." Remembering, I shall try to show, is rather like that. We notice also that to create that score and the subsequent "match" both players must be skilled at tennis, both as a material practice and as a discourse. Had I been playing Sampras the score would have been 6–0, 6–0, 6–0.

4.2   *Speech as social action: performative utterances as speech acts*

The notion of discourse has its home in linguistic exchanges, storytelling, and the like. Before I go on to show how the scope of the concept must be enlarged to include nonlinguistic interchanges of certain sorts, we need to ground the whole enterprise in a suitable account of language as a discursive medium. Why do we say things to one another? For almost two millennia it was assumed that it was to exchange information. The job of language was primarily descriptive. "How many eggs this morning?" "Six." But think about some more of this conversation. "Come to breakfast." "How do you like them done?" "Sunny side up." "The yolks are too hard." "You're always complaining! Cook them yourself." "Aw! Mum!" We all know that even "You're always complaining" is not a simple description of someone's habitual behavior. It is at just this point that social psychology and linguistic analysis intersect. The last six utterances are performances of certain social acts: inviting, questioning, answering, complaining, expressing resentment, and apologizing. Seen thus the conversation is a complex social episode, with its own rules and conventions.[4] Here we have a social episode and the medium is literally discursive. Utterances like those above have been called "performative" by Austin (1964), and the work they do "speech acts."

It is very important to resist the temptation to fall back into psychological individualism at this point.[5] Austin realized that what someone said was effective only if it was said by the right person in the right circumstances, and if it was so understood by the other people involved. He was insistent that the intentions and states of mind of speakers played a secondary role. To keep the distinction between what an individual speaker intended and what was jointly produced, I shall adopt the well-known distinction between actions (individual intended behavior) and acts (the jointly constructed social meanings of actions) in distinguishing between speech actions – what someone intends by an utterance – and speech acts – what is jointly accomplished by that utterance in context. Thus I may intend to praise you when I say "Not a bad show, old pal," while you and everyone else around take me to be belittling your achievement.

Now if we put the question: "Why do we say things to one another?" the answer will be: "To accomplish all sorts of practical and social tasks." We are back at the point of transition from old- to new-paradigm social psychology. Instead of a cause/effect metaphysics we adopt the agentic framework, in which active and skilled beings set about jointly accomplishing projects. Of course this leaves room for odd-balls, mavericks, weirdos, nerds, squares, and so on. We shall see later how we must acknowledge a multiplicity of overlapping customs and constraints on what we do and say to one another in creating and managing the next episode in our joint lives.

5   Positioning: The Microstructure of Social Order

Not everyone present in some scene is authorized to do or say everything that might be said on the occasion. The notion of "role" was introduced to express the way certain kinds of actions belonged to certain persons as role holders. It was not the individual but the role that authorized this or that kind of action. "In the role of . . ." certain things were possible, but out of that role the very same person could not perform the act without censure or futility. Only as a licensed medical practitioner can anyone prescribe certain pharmaceutical drugs. Only as a father do I have a right to decide the schooling of my child, and so on. But the notion was used in such a catholic fashion that it soon was both too rigid, emphasizing formal and closed roles like judge and priest, and also too loose, emphasizing informal and open roles like "the role of women." Furthermore, the shift from a static to a dynamic conception of social interaction led to dissatisfaction with the relatively fixed character of what was picked out by the concept of role. In the attempt to understand the fluid exchanges of everyday episodes, something more dynamic was needed. This was provided from several sources. Goffman (1975, 1981) contributed the concept of "footing"; from Torode came a social psychological appropriation of the literary concept of "voice" (Torode 1977) and from the unlikely partnership of business studies and feminism (Hollway 1984) came "position." A major contribution to the development of the concept of "position" came from Davies (1989). For reasons not germane to this exposition I have come to prefer "position" as the most satisfactory term for this concept.

A position in an episode is a momentary assumption or ascription of a certain cluster of rights, duties, and obligations with respect to what sorts of things a certain person, in that position, can say and do. It is important to emphasize the ephemeral character of positions. They can be challenged, transformed, repudiated, exploited, expanded, and so on, and in those transformations the act-force of the joint actions of an episode ebb and flow. Furthermore, each speaker/hearer in an episode may construe what is said and done by reference to a different positioning, and so act in relation to different acts, even though all hear, in one sense, the same speech action. He may think he has commiserated with her, while she may think what he said patronizing. He uttered "Too bad the job turned out not so good."

In order to follow the unfolding of those fateful episodes in which friendships are sealed, love affairs disintegrate, bargains are struck, deadly insults are exchanged, jokes are made, decisions are arrived at, and so on and so on, close attention must be paid to the dynamics of positioning, as the episode develops.

What explains the sequential structures of speech acts, understood in the light of our intuitions as to the positions of the interactors? This question could not be posed within the framework of the old paradigm, with its essentially static conception of social interaction. Here we return to the important notion of model.

The most powerful and the most ancient heuristic abstraction used to throw the relevant structure of an episode into high relief is the dramaturgical model. Shakespeare famously used it, drawing on the social psychology of the Elizabethan era in authors such as Erasmus. It was revived as a deliberate counterforce to behaviorism by Kenneth Burke (1945), and subsequently inspired some of Goffman's most illuminating studies (Goffman 1967). The idea is very simple: we juxtapose the staging of a play to the living out of an episode of everyday life, using the concepts from the stage to analyze the otherwise opaque happenings of the lived episode. Burke recommended a five-fold basic scheme: act, scene, agent, agency, and purpose. One would approach a scene from *Hamlet* with these in mind, and Burke recommended that we approach the scenes of everyday life with the same scheme. Taken in pairs he called them "ratios." He thought that the model could be enriched by looking for the act/scene relationship, the agency/purpose relationship and so on. So to force the guilty pair to confess (act) Hamlet stages the play within the play (scene). The agency is the playlet while the purpose is to secure a confession. In like manner one might study the stages of the formation of a friendship as the unfolding of a drama.

6   Narrative: The Microstructure of Social Episodes

Burke's dramaturgical model is not the only fruitful borrowing discursive social psychology can make from literary studies. How are we to discern the sequential structure of social episodes?[6] Two heuristic abstractions have been much in vogue.

6.1   Life as ceremony

It is sometimes fruitful to look on social episodes as if they were literally ceremonials. This model has the advantage that some social episodes are indeed so. Ceremonials consist of hierarchically organized patterns of social acts, performed by the authorized role-holders, in the right settings. In the course of the performance some larger act is accomplished, often one in which the social relations that existed at the beginning of the episode are ritually changed or revised. Marriages are created, people are deprived of civil rights, presidents are created by swearing in, and so on. The social psychology of these episodes is on the surface, since the rules for the performance of the ceremony and the conditions that individuals have to meet to be acknowledged as role-holders are clearly and formally laid down. No one is condemned to death inadvertently or sworn in as President of the United States accidentally. Things do go wrong with trials and elections, but these are not matters of inadvertence or accident.

In discussing the social psychology of friendship, I shall illustrate the use of ceremonial as a heuristic model for revealing the structure and meaning of the episodes in which friendships are brought into being. For now it is enough to say that it requires hierarchical patterns of social acts of a kind taken as proper in a particular society, with the active cooperation of certain people having well-understood roles. Unlike in true ceremonials, there are no formal rules, no written protocols, and no formal criteria for acceptance as a role-holder. We shall see how the ceremonial model contrasts with the cause/effect metaphysics, in which friendship is treated as an effect and the investigator tries to find some condition that is its cause.

6.2 Life as narrative

Jerome Bruner (1986, 1991) and others have developed a second heuristic model to do similar work to the ceremonial analog. He noticed how much of life is recounted through stories. When people get together they tell each other anecdotes, bits of their lives. They present episodes to one another in the form of stories. Folk social psychology consists very largely of the skills and resources needed for storytelling. Stories are not just catalogues of events, but narratives, with customary forms and often with plots. Some of the plots are traditional, collected and analyzed by such students of everyday narratives as Opie and Opie (1972) and Propp (1924). The role of narrative in accounts has been nicely summarized by Bernstein (1990: 55):

> One of the ways human beings assess and interpret the events of their life is through the construction of plausible narratives. Narratives represent events not as instances of general laws but rather as elements of a history where a continuing individual or collective subject suffers or brings about dramatic, i.e. meaningful, change.

Bernstein goes on to remark that narratives have plots in which there is a narrative conclusion, which is related to what has gone before not by logic but by its appropriateness to the story line. The psychological point of this approach is that whatever happened in the past, it is the construal of the past in terms of the presently told narrative that provides the stepping-off point for how the narrator's life will be carried on. Since the process of narrative reappraisal is never ending, the form of a life is a kind of continual but subtly transformative reappropriation of the past, through which it is effectively recreated for the purpose in hand.

In introducing the idea of positioning I pointed out that the speech act-force of this or that speech action is dependent on the positions that the actors acknowledge each other to be speaking and acting from. There is a third component in this pattern of mutual influences: the story line that those engaged in the episode are working out. Story lines are potential narratives, the raw material for reworkings of episodes along lines that disclose themselves as possibilities as the episode and others connected to it unfold.

7 Accounts

A remarkable feature of human social interaction, in contrast to that of other primates, is the overlaying of the first-order action, be it in a conversational medium or some other, with an interpretative gloss, a second-order discourse, an account. Human social life is potentially, and often actually, multilayered. The collection and analysis of accounts has been part of the methodology of new-paradigm social psychology from its inception in the late 1960s. Ethnomethodologists were the first to notice that intentional actions were not only oriented to audiences, but that insofar as they were so oriented they were potentially accountable. Scott and Lyman (1968) were the first to suggest that the elicitation of accounts was a powerful method for the understanding of social episodes.

An account is an interpretive and justificatory discourse, the topic of which is a social interaction. In exculpatory talk we find both claims about the meanings of social actions as acts, and assertions of the relevant norms, in light of which what has been done can be seen as reasonable and proper. Accounts address the question of the intelligibility and warrantability of actions, insofar as they are seen as the performance of acts.

However, accounting is itself a form of social action, and as such is potentially accountable at a third level, and so on. Accounting is hierarchical. Philosophers have addressed the question of the closure of accounting hierarchies. Taylor (1989) has suggested that they terminate in "existential" declarations: "That's the sort of person I am!" Wittgenstein has argued (1953: §§217–44) that in the case of hierarchies of rules, closure can be achieved only by citing either a practice, into which one has been trained, and to which one has, therefore, no further reason for conforming, or a natural regularity, explicable biologically. From the point of view of the discursively oriented social psychologist, the collection of accounts need proceed only so far as is necessary to establish a working interpretation of the actions that constitute a social episode. All interpretations are capable of further refinement.

Worked example 1: Friendship as an accomplishment

The nearest old-paradigm psychologists got to studying friendship was to try to find out the conditions under which people came to like one another. The flaws in this work are very instructive. The best-known piece of research was carried out by R. B. Zajonc (1984). Fully immersed in the causal metaphysics of psychological individualism, he tried to show that the more frequently people met the more they would like one another. But instead of studying people meeting people, he experimented with people meeting meaningless signs, pseudo-Turkish words. Lo and behold, the subjects in his experiments declared that they most liked the words which had been presented the most. This experiment has two major flaws. The first is its lack of applicability to human relations, in that in that case it is the meaning of frequent meetings that plays a role. Liking is not an effect produced by a cause. This is so obvious it is hardly worth reiterating. But the second flaw is more deep seated. It has been shown that whatever is the attribute asked for in the experiment, the more frequently an object is shown to a person the more she or he is likely to declare it has the salient attribute. The question "Which is the brightest?" also gets the most frequently seen as the object of choice. It would be interesting to test this explanation in the realm of audition. Is the most frequently presented sound picked as the most pleasant, or the loudest? I am fairly confident we will get the same sort of result.

A good deal of research in the general area of interpersonal attraction does actually use discursive methods, but presents them as if they were experiments. For instance, Byrne (1971) asks people to form an impression of another person by consultation of a written profile. Of course this is a task in discursive psychology, part of the psychology of literary interpretation; for instance: "Do you like Ophelia more than you like Rosalind?"

Turning away from the simplicities of old-paradigm research to the more sophisticated work of anthropologists and microsociologists, we find a quite different research focus. Instead of the static cause/effect metaphysics of the old paradigm we find a dynamic metaphysics for modeling the processes of making friends, including the way we mark stages in the development of a relationship in different cultures, the differing levels of commitment at each stage, and so on. Still the most interesting work published on the topic is by Douglas (1972), in which she tracks the development of a relationship through successive rituals, particularly ritual meals. In our extended notion of discourse these are socially significant as acts, having their own "semantics" and their proper order and sequence, their own "syntax." She shows how people pass from unstructured mutual entertainment ("drinks") to highly structured ("dinners") through to informal ("pot luck"). The sequence defines and records the stages from acquaintance to intimacy. What is the psychology of this process? Once again it is a matter of local knowledge, knowing the meaning of this or that stage in the process and how it relates to those that have gone before and might subsequently occur.

In their classic study of the social psychology of childhood, Opie and Opie (1972) identified and described a number of friendship rituals by which a relationship is sealed. For example, there are mixing of blood, dividing a coin, exchanges of ritual gifts, and so on.

But, it might be said, what is characteristic of the people who are willing to take part in the discursive construction of friendship (or its opposite)? Are there not personal characteristics that draw people to one another? This might have been true were there any such thing as context-independent personal attributes. Despite the attempts at the revival of the discredited trait theory, flawed in the same way as original trait theories by statistical fallacies, it seems that people have psychological and characterological attributes only in those moments when they are interacting as pairs, triads etc. It turns out that personal and characterological attributes change with imagined respondent in much the same way as they do when we each interact with different respondents in real-life episodes. So it cannot be that the relationship develops out of a pre-existing similarity of taste, or agreement in opinions, if those similarities and agreements are themselves the product of the coming to be of the relationship. Once one is committed to a person, one adjusts oneself to the other and the other adjusts himself or herself to one. People who stick to the opinions and so on that they bring into a relationship doom it to an unpleasant end. Trait theorists seem to see stable traits because it is they who are interacting with the subjects of their studies, or if they are using a questionnaire method, the local discursive conventions constrain answers within a certain framework.

According to the discursive point of view, friendship and the liking that goes with it are an accomplishment, a relatively permanent aspect of interpersonal interactions in a variety of episodes that are framed within the local system of norms of ritual interaction. The discursive study of friendship and other interpersonal relations is still undeveloped, despite the large number of data available concerning destructive and constructive ways of conversing, for example within families.

Worked example 2: Remembering as a social act

There has been a great deal of confusion of thought in the old-paradigm attempts to develop a psychology of remembering. The source of the confusion lies in the failure to realize the role of the experimenter in the process that is being studied. Remembering is not just personal recollecting and reporting what one recollects, though these are often the very same act. It is also recollecting correctly. In laboratory experiments, a genre of episodes deriving more or less directly from the work of Ebbinghaus, the experimenter fixes the past, and determines, a priori, what it is. This is usually done by creating "stimulus materials" that are reckoned to be durable, and to persist unchanged throughout the experiment. This ensures that the past is available in the present in a way that is almost never found in everyday life. In our terms, traditional remembering experiments are poor models of people engaged in the activity of remembering in memorial episodes. Experimenters, following the tradition of Ebbinghaus, though not experimenting only on themselves, smuggle in this way of guaranteeing that they know what the past situations to be remembered were. So the normative aspect of remembering is concealed. To remember is to recollect the past correctly.

If we turn to real life and ask how remembering is done, the phenomenon turns out to be dynamic, social, and complex. The one device that is almost never available is that used by the laboratory experimenter, namely a guaranteed material relic of the past. Very little material evidence for past situations and happenings survives even for 24 hours. This fact is obvious enough in courtrooms, but has been overlooked by psychologists. How then is correctness assessed, if it is not by some sort of quotidian archaeology? Individual people entertain themselves with their recollections, scarcely ever bothering to check them out. When an old diary does surface in the back of the drawer it makes startling reading. Very little was as it is now remembered. What matters, it turns out, and as might have been expected, is that the "facts of the past" are settled by social negotiation (Middleton and Edwards 1990). People propose various possible recollections and these are discussed, assessed, and negotiated amongst those involved in a memorial episode. Furthermore, Marga Kreckel showed (Kreckel 1981) that in most memorial episodes there is a fairly clear distribution of memorial power. Some people have greater standing as determiners of the past than others. While the psychology of memory continues to be a laboratory-based study, with developments into psychoneurology (the biochemical basis of recollection), the topic of remembering as a psychological phenomenon, as a feature of discursive practices, is neglected. Note the grammar. Memory, the noun, is used by those psychologists who think that the topic of research is finally states of the brain. Remembering, the gerund, is used by those psychologists who think that the topic of research is how people recall the past. The asymmetry is itself interesting, in that while people interested in remembering would regard the work on individual neurological processes of recollection to be one leg of a dualistic research project, those who are interested in memory tend to be naive reductionists and to pay no attention at all to the real-life processes by which putative rememberings are sorted and certified. Remembering is in important respects a conversational phenomenon, existing as a feature of discourse. In these respects it is not an attribute or state of individuals, which comes to be expressed publicly. It is a public phenomenon.

8 What Do the Results of New-paradigm Research Look Like?

Episode-focused studies should come up with dynamic models of joint action that would simulate the episodes we find in real life. To achieve this we need to know what acts are to be performed to accomplish the overall project of the episode, or nested set of episodes. We also need to know the rules and conventions that are realized in the way acts are sequenced in episodes, and the positions and roles of the actors who are their proper performers. In short, we need to bring out the "semantics" of actions and the "syntax" of their building up into intelligible episodes. In laying out the task of social psychology this way, we have extended the notions of semantics from words to utterances, and of syntax from sentences to discourses. At the same time we have extended the notion of discourse from conversations to episodes of many other kinds. But, as I have argued, that is the essence of scientific method: drawing on well-understood sources to create working models of that which we do not yet understand.

8.1 The semantics of social acts

To recruit the notion of meaning to discuss the act/action distinction seems entirely natural. What better way of describing the relation between farewelling and purposively waving than to take the former as the meaning of the latter? Acts are the meanings of actions. Well and good. But "meaning" is not an uncontroversial term itself. Disillusioned with referential or denotative accounts of meaning that purported to be quite general, Wittgenstein (1953) famously proposed that meaning should be understood in terms of practice, that is in terms of use. This suggestion fits well with the act/action distinction. What is waving for? To farewell someone. What is saying "Look out!" for? To warn someone. And so on. Meaning seems to be well treated as social function. And this fits in nicely with the Austinian insight that most utterances are speech acts rather than descriptions.[7] To give the semantics of a repertoire of actions just is to carry out an analysis of their social roles, facilitated by the analysis of the second-order discourses or accounts with which ambiguities are cleared up, unfortunate actions remedied, and so on.

8.2   *The syntax of social episodes*

The conversational model serves as both a first- and a second-order account of the orderliness of social episodes. In accordance with the tool/task metaphysics and the substitution of "skill" for "cause," we need to find an expression to catch what it is skilled actors must know to produce a sequence of acts that do accomplish the social task which they intend. The commonsense notion "they know the rules" can be recruited to a more strictly defined role. To act correctly a person must have explicit or implicit knowledge of the relevant norms, and this knowledge can be expressed as a set of rules.[8] However, the psychology of rule conformity is complex. This is because there are two ways that the concept of "rule" has been used. In Wittgenstein's terminology there is the case of following a rule, a way of acting in which the actor attends to a discursive presentation of the rule, and treats it like an instruction or order, doing what it says. But there is also the case of acting in accordance with a rule. Here we are using the word "rule" metaphorically, to express an insight about the norm that seems to be immanent in the practice. Failure to keep the distinction between literal and metaphorical uses of the word "rule" has led to some serious mistakes, particularly prominent in cognitive psychology. It has been assumed by Fodor (1975), for example, that acting in accordance with a rule is just like following a rule, only the following takes place unconsciously. There seems to be no good ground for this claim, and it has been roundly criticized by Searle (1995) and others.

We can write down rule systems to express *our* hypotheses about the norms relevant to the kinds of episodes we are studying, but we must bear the above distinctions in mind when we interpret them psychologically, in the task/tool/skill framework. The following of an explicit rule is a different kind of skilled action from acting in accordance with rule, which should properly be assimilated to habit.

9   Conclusion

Social episodes are not unconnected sequences of stimulus/response pairs. They are structured and accountable action/act sequences given meaning and warrantability by complex normative constraints, some immanent in the action and others explicitly formulated as rules of procedure. Following the general principles that govern good scientific work in the physical sciences, we must set about constructing working models of social interactions, analogous to them and, at the same time, analogous to some phenomenon we do have some understanding of. The fact that social interaction is accomplished symbolically immediately suggests adopting a generally discursive approach to the understanding of social life. The most natural model to choose is the conversation, refined in relation to various sources, such as ceremonies and dramas. There are other possibilities too, for example the court of law, and certain games, of which, for me, that of tennis is the most powerful model, since it is itself both a material practice and a discursive episode. By shifting to the episode as the unit of analysis, we open up social interaction to a more sophisticated research methodology than the simplistic "experimental" method of the old paradigm, which enshrined so many errors, not least the commitment to a certain unexamined political ideology.

NOTES

1 For a textbook treatment of discursive psychology in general see Harré and Gillett (1994).

2 To someone coming from a 900-year-old tradition of democratic management of universities the extraordinary degree of authoritarian rule in US universities comes as a great surprise. But the clash between macro- and microideals of governance is visible everywhere in the United States.

3 The same can be seen in the recent trend of blaming tobacco companies for illnesses that are the result of one's own self-indulgence and weakness of will.

4 Marga Kreckel (1981) noticed that there were two codes of conduct in play in family life. The family she studied shared a homodynamic code with other families of the local culture, but

also made use of a heterodynamic code all their own.

5 Despite taking his start from Austin, Searle (1979) has only recently taken full account of the fact that speech acts are joint actions (Searle 1995).

6 Working from Goffman's way of expressing these distinctions, Tannen has developed the concept of discourse framing (cf. Tannen 1993).

7 Austin came to change his mind on the depth of this distinction, since he realized that even in describing something to someone one is engaged at one level in a social act, roughly: "Trust me!"

8 The one respect in which I would go along with transformational linguistics is the emphasis on syntactic knowledge ("competence") as knowledge of rules.

REFERENCES

Austin, J. L. (1964) *How To Do Things with Words*. Oxford: Oxford University Press.

Bernstein, J. M. (1990) Self-knowledge as praxis: Narrative and narration in psychoanalysis. In C. Nash (ed.), *Narrative in Culture*. London: Routledge, pp. 51–77.

Bruner, J. S. (1986) *Actual Lives, Possible Worlds*. Cambridge, Mass.: Harvard University Press.

Bruner, J. S. (1991) The narrative construction of reality. *Critical Inquiry* 17, 1–21.

Burke, K. (1945) *A Grammar of Motives*. Englewood Cliffs, N.J.: Prentice-Hall.

Byrne, D. (1971) *The Attraction Paradigm*. New York and London: Academic Press.

Davies, B. (1989) *Frogs and Snails and Feminist Tales*. Sydney: Allen and Unwin.

Douglas, M. (1972) Deciphering a meal. *Daedelus* (Winter).

Fodor, J. A. (1975) *The Language of Thought*. New York: Crowell.

Giles, H. and Robinson, W. P. (1990) *Handbook of Language and Social Psychology*. Chichester: Wiley.

Goffman, E. (1957) *The Presentation of Self in Everyday Life*. New York: Doubleday.

Goffman, E. (1967) *Interaction Ritual*. Chicago: Aldine.

Goffman, E. (1975) *Frame Analysis*. Harmondsworth: Penguin.

Goffman, E. (1981) *Forms of Talk*. Oxford: Blackwell.

Harré, R. and Gillett, G. (1994) *The Discursive Mind*. London and Los Angeles: Sage.

Hollway, W. (1984) Gender difference and the production of subjectivity. In J. Henriques et al., *Changing the Subject*, ch. 20. London: Methuen.

Kreckel, M. (1981) *Communicative Acts and Shared Knowledge*. London: Academic Press.

Marsh, P., Rosser, E., and Harré, R. (1977) *The Rules of Disorder*. London: Routledge and Kegan Paul.

Middleton, M. and Edwards, D. (1990) *Collective Remembering*. London: Sage.

Milgram, S. (1974) *Obedience to Authority*. London: Tavistock.

Opie, P. and Opie, I. (1972) *The Lore and Language of Schoolchildren*. Oxford: Oxford University Press.

Propp, V. (1924) *The Morphology of the Folk Tale*. Austin: Texas University Press.

Scott, M. B. and Lyman, S. M. (1968) Accounts. *American Sociological Review* 33, 46–62.

Searle, J. R. (1979) *Expression and Meaning*. Cambridge: Cambridge University Press.

Searle, J. R. (1995) *The Construction of Social Reality*. London: Allen Lane.

Tannen, D. (1993) *Framing in Discourse*. New York: Oxford University Press.

Taylor, C. (1989) *Sources of the Self*. Cambridge, Mass.: Harvard University Press.

Torode, B. (1977) The revelation of a theory of the social world as grammar. In R. Harré (ed.), *Life Sentences*, ch. 11. Chichester: Wiley.

Triplett, N. (1897) The dynamogenic factors in pacemaking and competition. *American Journal of Psychology* 9, 507–33.

von Cranach, M. (1981) The psychological study of goal-directed action: basic issues. In M. von Cranach and R. Harré (eds), *The Analysis of Action*, pp. 35–73. Cambridge: Cambridge University Press.

Wittgenstein, L. (1953) *Philosophical Investigations*. Trans. G. E. M. Anscombe. Oxford: Blackwell.

Zajonc, R. B. (1984) On the primacy of affect. *American Psychologist* 39, 117–23.

Zimbardo, P. G. (1969) *Influencing Attitudes and Changing Behavior*. Reading, Mass.: Addison-Wesley.

36 Discourse Analysis and Language Teaching

ELITE OLSHTAIN AND MARIANNE CELCE-MURCIA

0 Introduction: The Interface of Discourse Analysis and Language Teaching

The **communicative approach** to language teaching, which began in the early 1970s and gradually took over most of language teaching in the world, at least in "ideology" if not in practice, has made people aware of the need to focus on communicative features of language use as an integral part of the teaching program. It is widely accepted in the field that we teach both "language *for* communication" and "language *as* communication." In other words, the objective of language teaching is for the learners to be able to communicate by using the target language, even if at times this is limited communication, and the most effective way to teach language is by *using* it for communication. So, given this premise, the *goal* of language teaching is to enable the learner to communicate and the *method* for teaching is for the learner to experience and practice relevant instances of communication.

It would be ill-advised to teach language via the communicative approach without relying heavily on **discourse analysis**. In fact discourse analysis should provide the main frame of reference for decision-making in language teaching and learning. Creating suitable contexts for interaction, illustrating speaker/hearer and reader/writer exchanges, and providing learners with opportunities to process language within a variety of situations are all necessary for developing learning environments where language acquisition and language development can take place within a communicative perspective.

Discourse analysis and pragmatics are relevant to language teaching and language learning since they represent two related discourse worlds that characterize human communication. The first represents **intended meaning** transmitted within context, and is, therefore, concerned with sequential relationships in production; and the other explains the **interpreted meaning** resulting from linguistic processing and social interaction, all the while taking into account a variety of contextual factors, at the receptive end. Language teaching needs to focus on both (1) strategies of message construction to facilitate learner production of the communicative intent and (2) strategies of interpretation, in order to ensure some ability on the learner's part to process inferentially (even if only approximately) the speaker/writer's intent.

For many years during the first half of the twentieth century and well into the second half, language teaching, like linguistics, used the **sentence** as its basic unit of analysis. In language teaching this meant that rules, examples, exercises, and activities focused on individual sentences. Consequently, this was an approach which legitimized decontextualized language practice. Individual sentences can be interesting, unusual, or mysterious, but when separated from context, they lack real meaning. Generations of learners practiced sentences in the target language and remained quite incapable of linking these sentences into meaningful stretches of discourse. In the more recent approaches to language learning and teaching, **discourse** or **text** has become the basic unit of analysis. More recent language textbooks present texts, short or long, as a basis for both understanding and practicing language use within larger meaningful contexts. This approach has greatly altered the type of activities undertaken in language classrooms. Learners need to focus, therefore, on various discourse features within any specified language activity.

Another perspective that was added to language materials and classroom activities, once discourse became the unit of analysis, is the set of sociolinguistic features that accompany any natural interaction. The real or imaginary participants involved in a communicative activity in the classroom become important. If the classroom activity is to represent real-life interaction, then age, social status, and other personal characteristics of the interactants cannot be ignored, and learners are expected to develop awareness of the linguistic choices which are related to such features. They need to gain experience in decision-making related to choices of linguistic representations that are compatible with the characteristics of the participants and with the pragmatic features of the given situation. Simulated speech events become an important feature of the language classroom, and although such a simulated speech event is a classroom artifact, it must represent as closely as possible a real speech event that could occur in natural interaction.

Prior to adoption of the communicative approach to language teaching, the main goal of the language classroom was to supply students with the ability to produce and recognize linguistically acceptable sentences. The communicative approach added a very important new dimension: communication strategies. The underlying notion of the approach recognizes the fact that learners may never achieve full linguistic competence and yet they will need to use the target language for various types of communication. One needs to develop, therefore, communication strategies that overcome and compensate for the lack of linguistic knowledge. Such communication strategies are partly "universal" in nature from the learner's point of view, since some can successfully be transferred from the first language. Thus, learners who are "good communicators" in their first language have a good chance of also becoming effective communicators in their second, although they may not know the second language nearly as well as the first. We are referring here to the ability to paraphrase, use circumlocution and gestures, among other things, during spoken communication. These abilities seem to be quite transferable if the language classroom provides sufficient opportunities for using such strategies in the second language.

As a result of the general acceptance of the communicative approach, language learning and language teaching have had to fully incorporate communicative interaction into the curriculum. The fact that language users exhibit linguistic, cultural, and social identities in a real-life interaction affects the teacher's choice of simulated or specially designed classroom interactions which attempt to recreate the main features of the real-world event within the language classroom. The competent language teacher can no longer limit herself or himself to being an educator and a grammarian. To a certain extent, she or he also has to be a sociolinguist, aware of and interested in various aspects of discourse analysis.

Fortunately, there are several books now available to address this educational need. Cook (1989) introduces the theory of discourse analysis and demonstrates its practical relevance to language learning and teaching for those with little background. In the first part, which deals with theory, the author provides accessible definitions for basic concepts in discourse analysis. In the second half, he demonstrates the incorporation of discourse analysis into language teaching. Nunan (1993) also directs his work at beginning students in discourse analysis, and, like Cook, he addresses language teachers who want to incorporate discourse analysis into their teaching. The main purpose of the book, as stated in the introduction, is to give the reader "some of the key concepts in the field and to provide [the reader] with an opportunity of exploring these concepts in use" (1993: ix). Nunan's choice of texts helps clarify and deepen the reader's understanding of discourse analysis.

The three other texts described below present more extensive theoretical grounding for applying discourse analysis to language teaching. McCarthy (1991) goes into the details of how discourse analysis relates to the different language areas (grammar, vocabulary, phonology) and to spoken and written language. The main objective of the book is to help language teachers become knowledgeable about discourse analysis. The book encourages teachers and material developers to use natural spoken and written discourse in their textbooks, teaching materials, and classroom activities. Hatch (1992) aims to give teachers and other practitioners in the field of language teaching a better understanding of how the general theory of communication, and discourse analysis in particular, can and should relate to language teaching. She includes discussion of scripts, speech acts, and rhetorical analysis, among other areas. Perhaps the most comprehensive text available is McCarthy and Carter (1994), which presents the relevance of a basic description of the properties of discourse analysis to language teaching. The book describes research and findings in the area of discourse analysis and shows how these findings can be applied to classroom teaching. It is rich in authentic texts, which provide data for analysis and exemplification.

From this brief review, it seems obvious that a number of key texts have come out recently in an attempt to initiate and guide teachers into the era of discourse analysis and language teaching. Even if the implementation of this view is not being carried out everywhere, teachers and practitioners today are aware of the importance of pedagogical discourse analysis.

1   Shared Knowledge: The Basis for Planning the Teaching/Learning Continuum

The discourse perspective in language teaching places particular importance on the notion of **shared knowledge**. This notion relates to one's general knowledge of the world – knowledge to which participants in an interaction can appeal before, during, and after a communicative event. This appeal to or reliance on knowledge of the world is not always conscious, but it always affects the communicative interaction by either easing it along or interfering and even blocking it. The extent to which the participants share such knowledge will, therefore, affect the degree to which the communicative interaction will be effective.

Speakers assume shared knowledge when they address others and plan their utterances accordingly; listeners appeal to prior knowledge while interpreting the flow of speech; writers plan their texts according to what they presume their intended audience knows about the world, and readers appeal to their prior knowledge while processing written texts. Furthermore, interactants select or prefer language which accommodates and strengthens some of the shared and mutually perceived situational features. When we misjudge shared knowledge or the perceptions of the other participants in the interaction, we potentially run the risk of creating instances of minor or serious miscommunication. This can happen among speakers of the same language and within the same sociocultural setting, but it occurs much more frequently across linguistic and cultural barriers. Shared knowledge must therefore include both general knowledge of the world and sociocultural knowledge related to the target speech community whose language the learner is trying to acquire.

In the literature about reading and writing the term **prior knowledge** plays a very central role. It is the conceptual knowledge that enables interactants to communicate with one another via the written or spoken text. Marr and Gormley (1982: 90) define prior knowledge as "knowledge about events, persons, and the like which provides a conceptual framework for interacting with the world." Schallert (1982) further expands the notion to refer to *everything* a person knows, including tacit and explicit knowledge of procedures and typical ways of expressing information. Alexander et al. (1991) develop a conceptual framework of knowledge including domain and discipline knowledge as part of general **content knowledge**, and knowledge of text structure, syntax and rhetoric as part of one's **discourse knowledge**.

Effective communicative interaction among language users is achieved, therefore, when there is a basic sharing of prior content and discourse knowledge between the producers and the interpreters of the text. There needs to be a matching of three types of background knowledge: prior factual or cultural knowledge; prior work or life experience; and prior familiarity with the relevant discourse community. For spoken language the interlocutors need to be familiar with sociocultural conventions and interaction management. Considerations of politeness norms, of turn-taking conventions, and of forms of address are important for maintaining social harmony and for personal negotiation. For written language, writers and readers need to share writing conventions, familiarity with genre types, and rhetorical traditions.

In formal language teaching we need to distinguish between adult learners and adolescents or children in school. Adult language learners come not only from a different language background but also from a different cultural background, and as was mentioned before, this cultural background is very much part of their knowledge of the world. For such adult learners, the modern language classroom needs to take into account cross-cultural differences that might interfere with successful communication in the target language (Tannen 1985). It is therefore important to plan the language curriculum so as to accommodate communicative interaction that will enable learners to both experience and reflect on cross-cultural differences.

When we are concerned with students in school as language learners, we have to take into account another perspective: the students' maturational development and their acquisition of world knowledge. A text in the target language brought to class might present content difficulties because of the subject matter, which might not yet be known to the students, or it might be difficult because of cultural information with which they are not familiar. Planning the language curriculum and planning the language lesson have to take into account the need to accommodate the learner's prior knowledge in order to build up the shared knowledge necessary for the learners to interact successfully within the planned communicative event.

A discourse perspective on language teaching places significant emphasis on the notion of **shared knowledge**, since this factor is at the heart of successful interpersonal communication. Classroom pedagogy can no longer limit itself to the linguistic corpus of the target language; it has to expand its activities and planning to include sociocultural and pragmatic considerations. In order to use a language effectively, the language user needs to have knowledge of the various factors that impact human communication. A discourse-based model for language pedagogy perceives shared knowledge as consisting of layers of mutually understood subcategories: content knowledge, context knowledge, linguistic knowledge, discourse knowledge, etc. (Johns 1997). Therefore, shared knowledge is of primary importance in modern language pedagogy.

2 Discourse in the Language Classroom: The Basis for Creating the Context for Language Learning

If we think of a discourse community as a group of people who share many things – a considerable body of knowledge, a specific group culture, an acceptable code of behavior, a common language, a common physical environment, and perhaps a common goal or interest – we can easily see how the language classroom is a unique discourse community. The students and their teacher make up a group that shares almost all of the factors mentioned above. But beyond these factors they also have an unwritten "contract" with respect to the obligations and commitments they have to the group. Thus it is quite common in a foreign language class for the students and the teacher to share the understanding that communication will take place in the target language even though the teacher and the students could communicate more effectively in their first language. Similarly, in any language class that uses the communicative approach, it is known that many of the classroom events and activities are not "real" in terms of the classroom situation, but are used as representations of real situations in the world outside the classroom.

Swales (1990: 24) has developed six defining characteristics that are necessary and sufficient for identifying a group of people as a **discourse community**, and we adapt these to the language classroom:

1 "A discourse community has a broadly agreed set of common public goals." The public goal of a language classroom is quite obvious: to promote the students' acquisition of the target language, as a group and as individuals, in as effective a

manner as possible. Sometimes, certain classes will have other specific goals for particular periods of time, but those specific objectives will usually fall within the more global goal of acquiring the language.

2   "A discourse community has mechanisms of intercommunication among its members." Any classroom, the language classroom included, has well-recognized mechanisms for intercommunication. The teacher communicates instructions, knowledge, and guidance to the students in various ways and the students communicate with the teacher via homework assignments, group activities, and other educational projects. The students also communicate with one another within the classroom context – sometimes this is real communication pertinent to the situation and at other times this is part of the "make-believe" world that is part of classroom activities.

3   "A discourse community uses its participatory mechanisms primarily to provide information and feedback." The language classroom has unique participatory mechanisms that provide feedback on students' participation in learning activities, feedback on the degree of approximation of their language performance to the target, information to prepare them for subsequent work, etc. Typically, however, within the classroom context the teacher is in complete control of the initiation of the information and feedback flow, while the students are at the receiving end. In more modern educational contexts the students can also become initiators of the information and feedback flow.

4   "A discourse community utilizes and hence possesses one or more genres in the communicative furtherance of its aims." According to Bhatia (1993: 16), "each genre is an instance of a successful achievement of a specific communicative purpose using conventionalized knowledge of linguistic and discourse resources." The language classroom has definitely developed, and continues to develop, expectations for discourse that are compatible with its goals and with the type of activities that go on in the classroom. The instruction and guidance that teachers direct at their students take on a genre that the students recognize. As part of the interaction, students also learn which genre is appropriate for *their* linguistic production within various classroom activities. Many features of these genres may be common to all classrooms, and certainly to all language classrooms, since they share common goals and conventions, yet any particular classroom may also develop its own unique genre, which fits the common goals and preferences of that particular teacher and that particular group of students. In any case, it is obvious that anyone joining a classroom after the start of the school year, for instance, will have to learn specific features of the genre of that class.

5   "In addition to owning genres, a discourse community has acquired some specific lexis." Again this requirement fits the classroom context quite well: school language has its specific lexis, language learning has its specific lexis, and a particular classroom may have some of its own lexis. Any teacher, but particularly a language teacher, may have his or her own preferred stock of words and phrases, which then become the lexis of the classroom. Sometimes students who act as leaders in the classroom also add their own word and phrase preferences to the common lexis.

6   "A discourse community has a threshold level of members with a suitable degree of relevant content and discoursal expertise." With respect to this particular

requirement, classrooms have some universal features which are part of any school system. At the beginning of every school year, only the teacher is normally considered an "expert"; however, each particular group of students is "initiated" into the discourse code of their class. In terms of their participation in their discourse community, one could consider each year's "new" students as novices, who will become experts in certain skills and areas by the end of the year.

When the language classroom functions as a discourse community, it thereby creates its own context within which the students and the teacher can develop linguistic and cross-cultural discourse practices that further their efforts toward the common goal of improving the students' target language competence and performance. Language teachers and curriculum developers can and should capitalize on the language classroom as a discourse community – or, as Breen (1985) has said, they should exploit the social context of the language classroom more fully, since it reflects what happens in society more generally. One can, for instance, make the distinction between truly authentic interaction that deals with the actual affairs of the class and its members, and the "representative" material which becomes real only as part of the group's "make-believe" contract. In the teaching–learning situation the truly authentic elements will carry considerable weight, since there is no doubt that these are instances where the students will focus more on the meaning than on the message. In other words, during actual classroom interactions the students will not always think of the language in which they interact but focus on the goals of their interaction. This creates authentic communication in the target language and allows students to accumulate significant experience in using that language. During the simulated, representative interactions, on the other hand, they will need to suspend immediate reality and create represented reality on a make-believe basis. Authentic interactions will further enrich their experience in the target language, leading to more effective acquisition.

Furthermore, the fact that a language classroom is part of a school system, and that students need to show "results" or outcomes based on their learning experiences, will usually motivate students to engage in reflection and metacognition, which will then facilitate the conscious learning process. A special type of discourse will develop for each of these three different types of interaction: the real interaction between students and teacher and among the students themselves when dealing with real matters relating to their immediate environment, instances of practice that are part of the learning curriculum, and instances of reflection which relate to what has been learned and are an attempt to mentally encode the learning experiences for future encounters. Somewhat different discourse rules will develop for each of these subdiscourses.

3 Discourse Analysis and the Teaching of the Language Areas

Within the teaching context, discourse analysis has significant applications in the language areas of phonology, grammar and vocabulary. The teaching of phonology interacts with the teaching of oral discourse. **Phonology**, in particular the prosodic or suprasegmental elements, provides the range of possible rhythm and intonation combinations. Yet the context is what determines the most appropriate choice of prosody in any given situated utterance. The general pragmatic strategy used by English speakers, for example, is to de-emphasize given information (what is already known) and emphasize new information, thereby utilizing prosody for information management and interaction management. In other words, in any language class where oral skills are taught, the interaction of discourse and prosody must be highlighted and taught, since contextually appropriate control of rhythm and intonation are an essential part of oral communicative competence.

In the area of interaction between phonology and discourse it is important to emphasize information management. In oral interactions the difference between new and old information is signaled via prosody, and contrast and contradiction are also marked by a shift of focus in the ongoing discourse. Students need to be alerted to these prosodic features in the target language, but they also need to be alerted to similarities and differences in rhythm and intonation between their native language and the target language. Much more difficult to describe and teach, however, are the social functions of intonation, which may reveal things such as the speaker's degree of interest or involvement, the speaker's expression of sarcasm, etc. Without a doubt, the discourse analysis of oral interaction is highly relevant to the teaching of pronunciation in a communicative classroom.

A discourse-oriented approach to **grammar** places importance both on the texts within which grammatical points are presented and on the connecting roles fulfilled by the various grammatical forms. As McCarthy (1991: 62) claims: "grammar is seen to have a direct role in welding clauses, turns and sentences into discourse." Knowing grammar can no longer mean knowing only how a form functions within a given sentence, but must also include discourse features of grammatical forms. Thus knowing the tense–aspect system in English cannot mean only knowing which forms constitute each tense–aspect combination, but must also mean knowing how each tense–aspect combination can be used to create temporal continuity as well as signaling other relationships within the larger text.

Students learning a new language need to become aware of the repertoire of grammatical choices in that language, but more importantly they need to become aware of the conditioning role of discourse and context, which guides the language user in making appropriate choices. It is the context-dependent, pragmatic rules of grammar that play an important role in a discourse approach to grammar. In English, such grammatical choices as passive versus active voice, sentential position of adverbs, tense–aspect–modality sequences, and article use, among others, are context-dependent. Similar lists of context-sensitive "rules" can be generated for any language. In all such cases, the speaker/writer's ability to produce the form or construction accurately is but part of a much larger process in which the semantic, pragmatic, and discourse appropriateness of the form itself is also judged with respect to the context in which it is used. Similarly, the interpretation process can be facilitated or hindered depending on the learner's understanding of what functions a given grammatical form plays within the given context.

Some of the most obvious structural features of connected discourse are the type of cohesive ties identified and discussed by Halliday and Hasan (1976, 1989): reference, substitution, ellipsis, and conjunction. Textual cohesion is achieved by choosing among and using these cohesive devices appropriately – speakers and writers incorporate them as they produce texts, and listeners and readers attend to them as they interpret texts.

In the teaching and learning of **vocabulary** the discourse perspective stands out very clearly. Vocabulary cannot be taught or learned out of context. It is only within larger pieces of discourse that the intended meaning of words becomes clear. Granted, one could claim that most content words have one or more basic "dictionary" definition which could be learned as such. But the intended and complete meaning of a word can only be derived from the combination of a given dictionary meaning and the contextual frame within which the word appears. Furthermore, when talking about learners of another language we must remember that so-called equivalent words in two different languages might function quite differently in terms of collocations, range of specific meanings, and typical discourse functions.

Vocabulary can be literal or figurative (with figurative language including idiomatic use and metaphorical use (Lakoff and Johnson 1980)). For example, a sentence such as "He got the ax" may mean literally that some male person fetched a tool for chopping wood or figuratively that he was fired from his job, i.e. terminated. The interpretation one arrives at may well depend on the cotext. If the discourse continues, "and he chopped down the tree," the literal interpretation takes hold. If the subsequent discourse is "so now he's looking for another job," the figurative interpretation is the coherent one. The language learner needs both to acquire a word's potential range of meaning and to be able to recognize the particular meaning which is compatible with the context and the discourse within which the word appears. Although this is true for any vocabulary item, in a general sense, this is especially true of a large number of vocabulary items which have specialized meanings when used within a particular context.

A specialized field such as biology or physics may well have three types of vocabulary: (1) a core vocabulary it shares with all sciences and technologies; (2) a specific vocabulary for its own branch of science; and (3) an even more specific vocabulary known primarily to those in a specific subarea (e.g. microbiology or plasma physics). Discourse analysis and concordance analysis (i.e. having access to tokens of word forms in context for an appropriate corpus) can identify the most frequent vocabulary items of each type, which, in turn, is useful information for the language teacher working with second language learners who study these disciplines.

Words that serve a discourse function rather than expressing semantic content are much more dependent on context for their meaning and use. For example, the English function word *else* is a useful and relatively frequent lexical item, yet it is not well treated in ESL/EFL textbooks, where sentence-level grammar and vocabulary exercises are the norm. Like other reference words (e.g. personal pronouns, demonstratives, etc.), *else* generally requires some prior discourse for its interpretation. Sentence-level exercises cannot possibly convey to nonnative speakers the importance of the word *else* and the ways in which it is used in English. What is needed are many fully contextualized examples (taken or adapted from authentic materials) to provide learners with the necessary exposure to and practice with *else*, a function word that is semantically, grammatically, and textually complex.

4   Discourse Analysis and the Teaching of the Language Skills

When using language for communication, we are faced with two major types of processes: transmitting our ideas and intentions to an addressee or interpreting and understanding the text or message produced by an interlocutor. The first places the initiator of the discourse at the production end of the continuum while the second places the interpreter at the reception end. When **producing** discourse, we combine discourse knowledge with strategies of speaking or writing, while utilizing audience-relevant contextual support. When **interpreting** discourse, we combine discourse knowledge with strategies of listening or reading, while relying on prior knowledge as well as on assessment of the context at hand. The language skills can be grouped in two different ways: we can talk about productive versus receptive skills or we can talk about the skills which refer to spoken language versus those that refer to written language.

For productive skills, learners need to develop effective communication strategies based on either oral or written production. For receptive skills, learners need to develop interpretation skills related to either listening to or reading a text. Yet for each skill the language user requires unique strategies. For interactive listening, for instance, language learners need to develop strategies and routines that elicit clarifications, repetitions, and elaborations from the speaker, in order to facilitate the comprehension process when she or he is having interpretation difficulties. It seems, therefore, that when using the spoken language, in a face-to-face exchange, it is necessary to resort to a variety of compensatory skills to overcome lack of language resources, since the nature of oral exchange is such that immediate remedies have to be found in order to maintain the flow of speech. This can be true for both the speaker and the listener; the speaker lacking linguistic knowledge may resort to situational and other contextual features to make himself or herself understood, while the listener makes use of similar features in order to understand.

Prior and shared knowledge for receptive skills, at the macroprocessing stage, involves activation of schematic and contextual knowledge. **Schematic knowledge** is generally thought of as two types of prior knowledge (Carrell and Eisterhold 1983): content schemata, which are the background information on the topic and relevant sociocultural knowledge, and formal schemata, which are knowledge of how discourse is organized with respect to different genres, topics, or purposes. **Contextual knowledge** is the overall perception of the specific listening or reading situation (i.e. listeners observe who the participants are, what the setting is, what the topic and purpose are; readers consider the place where the text appeared, who wrote it, and for what purpose). Listeners and readers also make use of their understanding of the ongoing discourse or cotext (i.e. listeners remember what has already been said and anticipate what is likely to be said next, while readers consider the title of the text and subtexts, the larger framework within which the text appeared, etc.). In teaching language, the teacher should exploit the processing features that listening and reading skills share.

Language teachers can provide learners with a variety of listening activities which will engage them in listening practice at the discourse level. During such activities it is important that learners have the opportunity to combine the following: recognition of **phonological** signals, such as stress, pause, and intonation; recognition of **lexicogrammatical** signals, such as discourse markers, lexical phrases, and word order; knowledge of **content organization**; and incorporation of **contextual** features. A successful and effective listener will combine all of the above in an attempt to understand the spoken message.

Geddes and Sturtridge (1979) suggest the use of "jigsaw" listening activities for a useful integration of all the above signals and features. During the jigsaw activity, each of several small groups of learners listens to a different part of a larger piece of discourse (e.g. a story, a recipe, a mini-lecture, a news broadcast) and writes down the important points. Later each group shares its information with another group, and then another, so that gradually each group is able to piece together the larger discourse. The different listening subskills are used in this activity, while the students also get an opportunity to share their experiences and thoughts and thus become more metacognitively aware of the listening process. Various strategies and tactics that rely on discourse features can be discussed and are thereby improved for future use.

A variety of other activities can be developed to accommodate the changing environment within which listening becomes crucial. Voice-mail systems and telephone answering machines are important instances of authentic listening to which students should be exposed. Recordings of interactive telephone conversations, during which students are asked to listen first and then interpret and sum up what they have heard, can be helpful practical listening activities. It can also be useful for second language learners to listen to recorded segments of radio or TV news broadcasts as well as to short lectures on a variety of topics. Material developers and curriculum planners need to incorporate such listening experiences into the language classroom (Celce-Murcia 1995a).

In addition, one must not forget that even advanced-level foreign language learners may experience microlevel problems in decoding the normal stream of speech while listening. In some cases the overall context compensates for such problems; in other cases it does not. For example, the university student listening to a lecture who hears "communist" instead of "commonest" may misunderstand an entire lecture segment. Therefore, attention should be given to issues of segmentation and phonemic decoding, as well as to the global features described above, when teaching listening skills to learners.

In order to process a written text, rather than a spoken one, the reader has to perform a number of simultaneous tasks: **decode** the message by recognizing the written signs, **interpret** the message by assigning meaning to the string of written words, and finally **figure out** the author's intention. In this process there are at least three participants: the **writer**, the **text**, and the **reader**. Researchers in this field have been studying and describing the interactive nature of the reading process since the late 1970s (Rumelhart 1977, 1980, 1984; Rumelhart and McClelland 1982; Stanovich 1980, 1981, 1986). The reading task requires readers to choose, select, and apply some of what they know to each new text. It seems that "good" readers do this very effectively while poorer readers encounter many difficulties.

A well-written text exhibits two important features which facilitate its interpretation during the reading process: coherence and cohesion. **Coherence** is the quality that makes a text conform to a consistent world view based on one's experience, culture, or convention. It can also be viewed as a feature of the text which incorporates the ways and means by which ideas, concepts, and propositions are presented. Coherence is the result of a reader's appropriate response to the writer's plan and relates to the discourse world of written texts, to pragmatic features, and to a content area; it usually fits a conventionally and culturally acceptable rhetorical tradition in terms of sequence and structure. In the process of interpreting a written text, the reader assesses his or her specific purpose for reading and then recruits his or her knowledge of the world, previous experience in reading, and familiarity with writing conventions and different types of genres to arrive at that degree of interpretation deemed necessary.

Cohesion refers to those overt features of a text which provide surface evidence for its unity and connectedness. Cohesion is realized linguistically by devices and ties which are elements or units of language used to form the larger text. Since cohesion relies heavily on grammatical and lexical devices, deficiencies in the reader's linguistic competence may cause the reader to miss important cohesive links and, as a result, to have difficulties in the interpretation process. The language learner needs to develop good strategies of combining linguistic knowledge with the other types of knowledge mentioned above in order to apply them all simultaneously in the interpretation process.

Reading courses should provide learners with activities that help them develop strategies employing all the types of knowledge related to the interpretation process. Personal involvement in such reading activities would most likely result in the development of effective, individual reading strategies. A discourse-oriented reading course will allow learners to negotiate their interaction with texts by constantly involving them in making choices and decisions with respect to a text. Learners need to engage in the processing of a large stock of multipurpose reading matter in order to become independent and strategic readers. The combination of intensive work on the knowledge component and ample exposure to processing activities makes for a successful reading course. However, in order to ensure the development of strategic readers the teacher must also devote attention to reader awareness and metacognition. These encourage learners to become independent readers and to regulate their interpretation strategies during the reading process.

Psycholinguistic models of reading have placed special emphasis on the reader's ability to combine personal knowledge with textual information in order to get at the meaning of written texts. Accordingly, textbook writers and reading specialists often recommend that readers guess the meaning of unfamiliar words by using clues from the text, thus minimizing the use of dictionaries. This practice is useful, is generally very effective, and provides readers with important shortcuts to increase decoding speed. However, there are some serious pitfalls that readers need to watch out for. Haynes (1993), in her studies of the "perils of guessing," finds that English as a Second Language readers can be good guessers only when the context provides them with immediate clues for guessing. Insufficient context or a low proficiency level on the part of the learner, on the other hand, may lead to mismatches in word analysis and recognition, which can then cause confusion and misinterpretation of the target text. Haynes recommends that teachers make students aware of these difficulties and encourage them occasionally to double-check their guesses by using the dictionary.

Dubin and Olshtain (1993) further emphasize the need for teachers to consider the extent to which a given text provides useful contextual clues. The authors arrived at a set of parameters of the contextual support in the text necessary for proper interpretation of unfamiliar lexical items, which includes thematic clues derived from the main idea of the text as well as semantic information at the paragraph and sentence level. Only when readers can combine their general knowledge with information drawn from the text is there a good chance that guessing word meaning from context will be successful.

Writing, when viewed as a language skill for communication, has much in common with both reading and speaking: it shares the features of written text with reading, and it shares the production process with speaking. The writer communicates his or her ideas in the form of a written text from which known or unknown readers will eventually extract their ideas and meanings. The writer is responsible, therefore, for creating a "well-written" text that has cohesion and coherence and takes the potential reader's background knowledge into account. Learners need to gain practice in writing within the language classroom so as to develop experience and effective strategies for a "reader-based" approach, which continually considers and accommodates an absent "reader–audience" (Chafe 1982; Flower 1979; Olson 1977, 1994; Ong 1982). A writer cannot rely on the context to provide support for interpretation. In fact, writing competence develops as a gradual liberation from the dependence on context for meaning. This "liberation" is achieved through skillful mastery of the potential linguistic repertoire, matched with effective use of conventional rhetoric through a revision process leading to the written text. Furthermore, successful adult academic writing is the result of the writer's autonomous and decontextualized production process, which, in turn, results in texts that are self-contained and potentially communicative to readers who are removed in place and time from the writing process itself.

Another school of thought takes a more social view of writing and therefore perceives it as being similar to speech. Such an approach often compares writing to speech events (Myers 1987) that need to adhere to specific writing conventions. The social interactionist view (Nystrand 1982) perceives conversational dialog to be as important for the development of writing competence as it is for the development of spoken discourse. Perhaps the strongest relation between speech and writing was expressed by Vygotsky (1962, 1978), who viewed writing as monologic speech based on socialized dialogic speech.

Classroom activities leading to writing competence, such as those described above, place emphasis on "writing for a reader and matching the writer's and reader's potential schemata while doing so." A child often reaches school with some basic knowledge of the letters of the alphabet, and perhaps with a very limited number of reading experiences and even fewer experiences in interactive writing. The school environment is usually the first and also the principal situation in which young people are expected to partake in writing tasks, and students often perceive the teacher as their only reader–audience. Developing a more expanded notion of reader–audience is part of becoming a "good communicator" in the written mode.

While cohesion, as mentioned above, relies heavily on grammatical knowledge, coherence is grounded in the thinking process. An important consideration in the creation of coherence in a text is the choice of genre and rhetorical format, which in turn is closely related to one's purpose for writing. At the most general level we distinguish between the narrative genre and factual or expository writing. McCarthy and Carter (1994) refer to these as the two prototype genres. The narrative is structured around a chronological development of events and is centered on a protagonist. Consequently, a narrative is usually personalized or individualized and tells about the events related to the person or persons involved. An expository text, on the other hand, has no chronological organization but rather a logical one, and is usually objective and factual in nature. Both types of writing may be important in the language classroom, but it is the expository text which requires the type of training and experience that only the classroom can provide.

One of the important features of a well-formed text is the unity and connectedness which make the individual sentences in the text hang together and relate to each other. This unity is partially a result of the coherent organization of the propositions and ideas in the passage, but it also depends considerably on the painstaking process carried out by the writer in order to create formal and grammatical cohesion among the paragraphs and among the sentences in each paragraph. Thus, by employing various linguistic devices the writer can strengthen a text's coherence, create global unity, and render the passage in a manner which conforms to the expectations of experienced readers. A significant amount of writing activities should be carried out in language classrooms in order to enable learners to develop the skills and strategies which lead to improved personal writing.

The speaking skill, although sharing the production process with the writing skill, is very different from the act of writing, since spoken language happens in the here and now and must be produced and processed "on line" (Cook 1989). In such oral communication there is always room for mismatches and misunderstandings, which could derive from any of the following:

- The speaker does not have full command of the target language and produces an unacceptable form.
- The necessary background knowledge is not shared by the speaker and the hearer and they bring different expectations to the spoken interaction.
- The speaker and the hearer do not share sociocultural rules of appropriateness, and therefore the speaker may have violated such a rule from the hearer's point of view due to pragmatic transfer from the first language.

The basic assumption in any oral interaction is that the speaker wants to communicate ideas, feelings, attitudes, and information to the hearers or wants to employ speech that relates to the situation. The objective of the speaker is to be understood and for the message to be properly interpreted by the hearer(s). It is the speaker's intention that needs to be communicated to her or his audience. However, a "faulty" production in any one of the above three areas could create a piece of spoken discourse that is misunderstood.

In an attempt to ensure proper interpretation by the hearer, the speaker has to be concerned with the factors of medium, which are linguistically controlled, as well as the factors of appropriateness, which are pragmatically controlled by the speech situation and by the prevailing cultural and social norms. Factors of medium relate to the speaker's linguistic competence as well as to the possibility of faulty delivery of the spoken utterance. The language learner needs to constantly improve his or her mastery of linguistic and sociocultural knowledge, while gaining ample experience in spoken communicative interactions, in order to develop useful speech production strategies. These strategies are most important in overcoming linguistic and other types of deficiencies that often are typical of nonnative speakers.

5   Conclusion

The biggest obstacle with regard to moving beyond ad hoc approaches to communicative language teaching, and arriving at a communicative approach that is fully informed by discourse analysis at both the theoretical and practical levels, is to provide language teachers and other teaching professionals (curriculum developers, textbook writers, language testers) with proper grounding in discourse analysis. Many language teaching professionals receive training in grammar, phonetics, and the teaching of the language skills such as reading, writing, and speaking. A few programs also include a theoretical course in discourse analysis, but such a course generally does not make practical connections with the language classroom. Courses in "pedagogical discourse analysis" are still the exception in teacher training programs, despite the fact that a body of appropriate pedagogical material exists (see the review of texts in section 0). The need for professional training in pedagogical discourse analysis is clear not only for second and foreign language teachers but also for first language educators and literacy specialists. Until training catches up with need, appropriate reading materials, in-service training, and professional conferences are some of the ways to fill the gap.

Language teachers also require training in cross-cultural communication, since many modern classrooms are multicultural in nature. A multicultural class may be composed of new immigrants of different ethnic groups. Each of these groups comes from a specific cultural background, which may contain discourse and interactional features that are different from the target language promoted by the school system, and which may even be unfamiliar to the teacher and the other faculty at school. In such multicultural contexts, it is important for all personnel to become aware of cultural differences and to learn to respect them, so that they do not unwittingly penalize learners for being different from the target culture while adhering perfectly to the norms of their own culture. Here the notion of shared knowledge relates to the students' background; it is something that teachers must be aware of and that should guide teachers in selecting materials and teaching procedures for their classes.

In addition to having good grounding in discourse analysis and an awareness of cross-cultural differences, language teachers should also be trained in how to impart awareness of discourse and cultural features to their learners at both the macro-organizational and microstructural levels. By "the macro-organizational level" we are referring here to course-planning and content organization, which should lead to successful learning and development. By "the microstructural level" we mean more specific linguistic and pragmatic information that is relevant to particular communicative exchanges. Both teachers and learners need to take responsibility for the reflective teaching–learning process, but teachers must assume the task of enabling such sharing of responsibility.

The discourse-oriented curriculum, which should be the basis for language courses with a discourse orientation, places special emphasis on three areas: **context, text-types**, and **communicative goals**. Consequently, the delineation of goals, tasks, and procedures for language learning will always take contextual features into account: expectations related to student achievement will center on the students' linguistic and cultural background; texts and other teaching materials will be selected or designed to be compatible with the student audience; and classroom activities will simulate real needs outside the classroom. In this respect such a curriculum is different from a linguistically oriented curriculum, where contextual features might be viewed as external to the curriculum (Celce-Murcia 1995b).

A discourse-oriented curriculum encompasses the various relationships existing between discourse analysis, the language areas, and the language skills, in a manner that guides teaching practitioners in all areas to incorporate a discourse-based approach into their work. Discourse analysts, sociolinguists, and other researchers can consider the classroom environment as one rich and varied context (among many) for discourse investigation. What needs to be examined more closely is both the discourse occurring in the classroom itself (i.e. the spoken and written communication between the teacher and students and among students) and the discourse of teaching materials and assessment instruments (i.e. the discourse structure of these materials as well as the discourse they elicit when used in the classroom). The results of such classroom-centered research in turn will enhance our understanding of discourse-based approaches to education in general and to language teaching in particular.

REFERENCES

Bhatia, V. K. (1993). *Analyzing Genre: Language Use in Professional Settings.* London: Longman.

Breen, M. (1985). The social context for language learning: A neglected situation? *Studies in Second Language Acquisition*, 7: 1, 135–58.

Carrell, P. L. and Eisterhold, J. C. (1983). Schema theory and ESL reading pedagogy. *TESOL Quarterly*, 17: 4, 553–74.

Celce-Murcia, M. (1995a). Discourse analysis and the teaching of listening. In G. Cook, and B. Seidlhofer (eds), *Principles and Practice in Applied Linguistics: Studies in Honour of H. G. Widdowson*, pp. 363–77. Oxford: Oxford University Press.

Celce-Murcia, M. (1995b). On the need for discourse analysis in curriculum development. In P. Hashemipour, R. Maldonado, and M. van Naerssen (eds), *Studies in Language Learning and Spanish Linguistics: In Honor of Tracy D Terrell*, pp. 200–13. San Francisco: McGraw Hill.

Chafe, W. (1982). Integration and involvement in speaking, writing, and oral literature. In D. Tannen (ed.), *Spoken and Written Language*, pp. 35–53. Norwood, NJ: Ablex.

Cook, G. (1989). *Discourse*. Oxford: Oxford University Press.

Dubin, F. and Olshtain, E. (1993). Predicting word meanings from contextual clues: Evidence from L1 readers. In T. Huckin, M. Haynes, and J. Coady (eds), *Second Language Reading and Vocabulary Learning*, pp. 181–202. Norwood, NJ: Ablex.

Flower, L. S. (1979). Reader-based prose: A cognitive basis for problems in writing. *College English*, 41: 1, 19–37.

Geddes, M. and Sturtrige, G. (1979). *Listening Links*. 3 cassettes, teacher's book, student's book. London: Heinemann.

Halliday, M. A. K. and Hasan, R. (1976). *Cohesion in English*. London: Longman.

Halliday, M. A. K. and Hasan, R. (1989). *Language, Context, and Text: Aspects of Language in a Socio-semiotic Perspective*. Oxford: Oxford University Press.

Hatch, E. (1992). *Discourse and Language Education*. Cambridge: Cambridge University Press.

Haynes, M. (1993). Patterns and perils of guessing in second language reading. In T. Huckin, M. Haynes, and J. Coady (eds), *Second Language Reading and Vocabulary Learning*, pp. 46–64. Norwood, NJ: Ablex.

Johns, A. (1997). *Text, Role and Context*. Cambridge: Cambridge University Press.

Lakoff, G. and Johnson, M. (1980). *Metaphors We Live By*. Chicago: University of Chicago Press.

McCarthy, M. (1991). *Discourse Analysis for Language Teachers*. Cambridge: Cambridge University Press.

McCarthy, M. and Carter, R. (1994). *Language as Discourse: Perspectives for Language Teaching*. London: Longman.

Myers, M. (1987). The shared structure of oral and written language and the implications for teaching writing, reading, and literature. In J. R. Squire (ed.), *The Dynamics of Language Learning*, pp. 121–46. Urbana, IL: NCTE.

Nunan, D. (1993). *Introducing Discourse Analysis*. London: Penguin.

Nystrand, M. (1982). Rhetoric's "audience" and linguistics' "speech community": Implications for understanding writing, reading, and text. In M. Nystrand (ed.), *What Writers Know*, pp. 1–28. New York: Academic Press.

Olson, D. R. (1977). From utterance to text. *Harvard Educational Review*, 47, 257–81.

Olson, D. R. (1994). *The World on Paper: The Conceptual and Cognitive Implications of Writing and Reading*. Cambridge: Cambridge University Press.

Ong, W. (1982). *Orality and Literacy*. London: Methuen.

Rumelhart, D. E. (1977). Toward an interactive model of reading. In S. Dornic (ed.), *Attention and Performance* 6, pp. 573–603. New York: Academic Press.

Rumelhart, D. E. (1980). Schemata: The building blocks of cognition. In R. J. Spiro, B. C. Bruce, and W. R. Brewer (eds), *Theoretical Issues in Reading Comprehension*, pp. 33–58. Hillsdale, NJ: Lawrence Erlbaum.

Rumelhart, D. E. (1994). Understanding understanding. In J. Flood (ed.), *Understanding Reading Comprehension* (pp. 1–20). Newark, DE: International Reading Association.

Rumelhart, D. E. and McClelland, J. L. (1982). An interactive activation model of the effect of context in perception. *Psychological Review*, 89, 60–94.

Stanovich, K. E. (1980). Toward an interactive-compensatory model of individual differences in the development of reading fluency. *Reading Research Quarterly*, 16, 32–71.

Stanovich, K. E. (1981). Attentional and automatic context effects in reading. In A. Lesgod and C. Perfetti (eds), *Interactive Processes in Reading*, pp. 241–67. Hillsdale, NJ: Lawrence Erlbaum.

Stanovich, K. E. (1986). Matthew effects in reading: Some consequences of individual differences in the acquisition of literacy. *Reading Research Quarterly*, 21: 4, 360–407.

Swales, J. M. (1990). *Genre Analysis: English in Academic and Research Settings*. Cambridge: Cambridge University Press.

Tannen, D. (1985). Cross-cultural communication. In T. A. van Dijk (ed.) *Handbook of Discourse Analysis*, Vol. 4, pp. 203–15. New York: Academic Press.

Vygotsky, L. S. (1962). *Thought and Language*. Cambridge, MA: MIT Press.

Vygotsky, L. S. (1978). *Mind in Society*. Cambridge, MA: Harvard University Press.

37 Discourse Analysis in Communication

KAREN TRACY

0 Introduction

Communication refers to many things: it is the process through which individuals as well as institutions exchange information; it is the name for the everyday activity in which people build, but sometimes blast apart, their intimate, work, and public relationships; it is a routinely offered solution to the problems engendered in societies in which people need to live and work with others who differ from themselves; it is a compelling intellectual issue of interest to scholars from diverse academic disciplines; and it is the name of the particular academic discipline I call home. In this chapter I offer my take on the field of Communication's take on discourse analysis. I draw attention to this chapter being my view, not to undermine what I have to say, but because I am an individual speaking for "the group," where the group is a diverse, squabbling family that does not see things the same way.

The chapter begins with background about the field of Communication[1] and how it connects with discourse analytic studies. Then, I focus on five exemplars of discourse research, book-length analyses that make apparent differences among traditions within Communication. In discussing each example, additional studies that are topically and/or methodologically similar are identified. I conclude by identifying the intellectual features that give discourse studies conducted by communication scholars a family resemblance.

1 Background on Communication

Although the importance of communication in everyday life is relatively transparent, what exactly Communication is as a discipline is not so. The field of Communication is a particularly American phenomenon, tracing its institutional origins to around 1900, when it initially existed as a pedagogical area within English departments (Cohen 1994). College speech teachers, as communication professionals then thought of themselves, broke away to form their own departments to give oral practices such as public speaking and debate the attention that, in English departments, were given only to written literary texts. In the ensuing decades the communication field underwent multiple transformations: becoming research-oriented, rather than primarily teaching, changing the name of its professional associations from "speech" to communication, expanding the oral practices it studied from public speaking and debate to group discussion, communication in developing relationships and among intimates, interaction in work and institutional settings, and mediated communications of all forms (e.g. radio, TV, computers).

Interestingly, scholars (Rogers 1994) who study mass communication often frame the birth of the field[2] in the post-World War II era, with communication's turn to social science and the start of research institutes at several major universities. This version of history, however, does not fit well for discourse researchers, who typically developed their scholarly identities in the (then) speech departments, where social science inquiry coexisted, sometimes happily and at other times acrimoniously, with its humanistic counterpart, rhetorical studies.

Fields divide their intellectual terrain into areas. These decisions, or perhaps more accurately "historical happenings," influence the shape of issues in ways that scholars involved in them often themselves do not fully understand. In linguistics, for instance, scholars are typically divided into areas by which aspect of the code they study (phonology, syntax, semantic, pragmatics). Communication's central way of dividing scholars is by contexts of focal interest (face-to-face, commonly called interpersonal communication, organizational communication, mass communications, and rhetorical studies (study of public, civic life)). Any simple categorization system creates problems, and communication scholars (e.g. Chaffee and Berger 1987) have been critical of dividing by context. While the criticism has been influential – many communication researchers regard dividing the field by context as a poor way to organize information and intellectual issues – nonetheless, because no better macrosystem has emerged, it continues to shape intellectual activities in a myriad of ways. Most relevant to this review is the fact that discourse analytic work began among interpersonal communication researchers.

Until relatively recently, research in interpersonal communication predominantly used experimental methods and sophisticated statistical testing procedures to study interaction among people. Against this set of taken-for-granted practices, scholars doing discourse analysis were taking a radical methodological turn. An upshot of the disciplinary context within which discourse studies emerged is that "discourse analysis"[3] in communication is conceived as a method of inquiry. This contrasts with linguistics (Schiffrin 1994), for instance, in which discourse is typically treated as a level of linguistic analysis: from a linguistic viewpoint, discourse analysts are scholars who study a particular unit of language (above the sentence) or how language is used socially. Since virtually all communication research focuses on language units larger than individual sentences and considers what people do with language, as well as other symbolic forms, linguistics' definition was not especially useful in Communication. Instead, what separated discourse analysts in Communication from their nondiscourse colleagues was the study of these topics in everyday situations[4] rather than in the laboratory or through questionnaires. Within Communication, then, discourse analysis is the *study of talk (or text) in context, where research reports use excerpts and their analysis as the central means to make a scholarly argument.* Moreover, since choosing discourse analysis was choosing a method that was not standard, this methodological choice required explicit justification, and, at least some of the time, showing how the choice tied to a researcher's commitments about the purpose of inquiry.

Within the area of interpersonal communication, for instance, social (or interpretive) approaches to inquiry are typically contrasted with quantitative behavioral ones. Quantitative approaches study communication actions out of their social context with a goal of generating broad-based explanations; often, although by no means exclusively, the explanations are cognitive. Interpretive theorists (e.g. Lannamann 1991; Leeds-Hurwitz 1995; Sigman 1987, 1995), in contrast, have argued for the importance of studying communication as a socially situated activity. In comparison to discourse scholars from other disciplines, then, communication research includes more metatheoretical commentary and methodological elaboration – explication about how talk materials are selected, transcribed, and interpreted. Whatever the topical focus of a discourse analytic study in communication, it is flavored by the backgrounded controversy of whether study of face-to-face interaction is better done through close study of small amounts of naturally occurring talk or through examining theoretically prespecified variables for larger numbers of people in controlled settings.

In the first handbook of discourse analysis van Dijk (1985) identified classical rhetorical writers (e.g. Aristotle, Quintilian, and Cicero) as the first discourse analysts. Within Communication this claim has two sides. At one level, rooting contemporary discourse studies in classical rhetoric is unproblematic: classical rhetoric is the intellectual starting point for much of what goes on in the communication field today. At another level, however, it generates confusion. Within the field the study of public life (rhetorical criticism and theory) is an ongoing area of scholarly work and is, itself, a distinct academic specialization. Scholars who label themselves rhetorical theorists and critics are rarely the same individuals as ones who consider themselves discourse analysts. Rhetorical criticism and discourse analysis share the commitment to close study of texts in context. Yet the commitment gets understood and pursued against markedly different intellectual backdrops. Rhetorical criticism is pursued within a humanistic frame where analyses of texts are related to literary criticism, political and continental philosophy, history, film studies, and so on. Discourse analysis, in contrast, is typically grounded in social science and considers its cognate disciplines to be psychology, sociology, linguistics, education, and so on. Moreover, where rhetorical critics tend to study speeches and unique political actions,[5] discourse analysts tend to study those aspects of social life that are ordinary and unremarkable. Although the division between social science and humanistic work is considerably more blurred than it was in the late 1980s (e.g. Mumby and Clair 1997; Taylor 1993), it continues to demarcate intellectual communities.

One distinctive feature of Communication is its recognition, even embracing, of the value of multiple perspectives on issues. Communication has an openness to other fields' ideas and models of inquiry rarely found in other academic disciplines. On the negative side, this openness can make it difficult to figure out how a piece of communication research is distinct from one in a neighboring discipline. For instance, depending on one's place in the field, communication researchers might be asked how their research is different from social psychology, business and industrial relations, anthropology, political science, sociology, pragmatic studies within linguistics, and so on. Yet as I will argue at this review's end, the discourse analytic work carried out by communication scholars reflects a shared disciplinary perspective. Although the distinctiveness of the perspective has not always been well understood, even by its practitioners, the perspective embodies a set of intellectual commitments that can enliven and enrich the multidisciplinary conversation about discourse.

2   Five Examples

2.1   *Telephone talk (Hopper)*

Telephone Conversation (Hopper 1992a) extends and synthesizes studies by Robert Hopper and his colleagues about the interactional structure in telephone talk (e.g. Hopper 1989, 1990/1; Hopper and Doany 1988). At the book's start Hopper provides evidence that talking on the telephone is a significant part of everyday life, noting, for instance, that "U.S. citizens spent 3.75 trillion minutes on the phone during 1987" (1992a: 3). Hopper traces the historical evolution of the telephone and the ways that face-to-face talk differ from telephone talk, and then introduces conversation analysis and argues why it is a particularly helpful approach for understanding communication on the phone.

The heart of the book is an explication of telephone talk in terms of its interactional processes. Drawing upon his own work, as well as related conversation analytic work, Hopper describes the canonical form for telephone openings, considers summons and answers, and how identification and recognition work, examines how switchboards and call answering shape telephone exchanges, and investigates the influences of relationships between callers and national culture. In addition, he looks at turn-taking, overlaps, and interruptions in telephone conversation, and considers how speakers project transition relevance places. Toward the book's end, Hopper analyzes play episodes on the phone, considers how telephone technology is transforming people's relationships, and identifies implications of the study for people's everyday telephone conduct.

The central news of Hopper's study is its explication and extension of key conversation analytic ideas in the context of telephone conversations. Conversation analysis (e.g. Atkinson and Heritage 1984; Boden and Zimmerman 1991; Schegloff and Sacks 1973), more than any other discourse approach, has been adopted (and adapted) by communications scholars. In turn, communication researchers[6] have contributed to the growing body of knowledge about the interactional structures of conversation, and members' sense-making practices. For instance, communication research has offered analyses of: (1) features of turn-taking (Drummond and Hopper 1993; Thomason and Hopper 1992); (2) conversational repair (Zahn 1984), (3) specific adjacency pairs (Beach and Dunning 1982; Pomerantz 1988); (4) laughter's interactional work (Glenn 1989, 1991/2); (5) discourse makers such as "okay" (Beach 1993, 1995) and "I don't know" (Beach and Metzger 1997); (6) how marital couples' storytelling practices enact them as an intimate unit (Mandelbaum 1987, 1989); and (7) how stigmatized individuals do "being ordinary" (Lawrence 1996).

In addition, there is a growing interest in extending the typical focus on vocal and language features of talk to considerations of the way interaction is physically embodied, performed, and materially situated (e.g. Goodwin and Goodwin 1986; Goodwin 1995; Hopper 1992b; LeBaron and Streeck 1997, in press; Streeck 1993), and in extending study of conversation processes in informal conversation to medical and therapy settings (e.g. Morris and Chenail 1995; Pomerantz et al. 1997; Ragan 1990; Robinson 1998). Too, studies of institutional talk in Communication display a greater concern about the consequences of action, thereby giving them a somewhat different flavor from other conversation analytic work (e.g. Bresnahan 1991, 1992).

As noted earlier, discourse analytic work within communication has been occurring within an intellectual milieu where methodological practices are contested. As a result, discourse scholars have worked to explicate the method and substance of conversation analysis (Hopper et al. 1986; Nofsinger 1991; Pomerantz and Fehr 1997) and argue for its value in comparison with other methods. Hopper and Drummond (1990), for instance, showed how close studies of talk reveal a rather different picture of relationships than what scholars get when they have people give accounts of what caused a relationship break-up, and Beach (1996) shows how knowledge about grandparent care-giving and health problems like bulimia can be enhanced by incorporating conversation analytic methods within surveys and interviews. Too, colloquia in journals have explored methodological controversies surrounding the value of conversation analysis (CA) versus quantitative coding (Cappella 1990; Jacobs 1990; Pomerantz 1990), whether CA can be combined with quantitative coding (Wieder 1993), the most persuasive ways to make discourse claims (Jackson 1986; Jacobs 1986), the combining of ethnographic methods with conversation analysis (Hopper 1990/1), and the legitimacy and meaning of different kinds of "context" in analysis (Tracy 1998).

2.2 Accounting (Buttny)

Richard Buttny (1993) introduces his study of social accountability in communication by highlighting how calls for accounts and the offering of them are transformative discursive practices. Because communicators are moral beings who hold themselves and others accountable for actions, the study of accounting offers a window on a culture's "folk logic of right action" (1993: 2). The study of accounts has been an area of lively intellectual activity in communication. To a large degree, however, it had been conducted within an empiricist metatheoretical frame (Bostrom and Donohew 1992) that used quantitative coding and statistical analysis to reveal relationships among kinds of people, features of situations, and types of accounts (e.g. Cody and McLaughlin 1990). Buttny highlights the problematic nature of studying accounts in this way, and argues for an alternative methodological approach, what he labels "conversation analytic constructionism." His book provides a philosophical exploration of what this approach means and guidance about how to do it. Conversation analytic constructionism shares many similarities with conversation analysis. It studies naturally occurring talk and grounds claims in recipient responses. But in response to the rather straightforward readings of recipients' interactional meanings that CA offers, constructionism presumes meaning is socially constructed (and hence always carries potential to be otherwise).

The heart of Buttny's book is its analysis of accounting episodes in couples therapy, a Zen class, and welfare and news interviews (see also Buttny 1996; Buttny and Cohen 1991). Also explored are the relationships among accounting and emotion talk. A key way that Buttny's work differs from most conversation analytic research is that it explicitly situates itself in an interpretive social constructionist frame (for reviews see Pearce 1995; Shotter 1993). This metatheoretical exploration gives a self-consciously reflective flavor to the research absent in CA studies.

Other discourse studies about accounting explore: (1) functions of accounts (Morris et al. 1994), (2) the structure of episodes (Hall 1991), (3) how a person's calling for an account can itself become a disputed issue (Morris 1988), (4) how accounts change over time (Manusov 1996), (5) their occurrence in particular institutions such as service encounters (Iacobucci 1990), and (6) issues that arise when speakers are accounting for success (Benoit 1997). Accounts are but one kind of problematic, morally implicative event, but many others have also been studied. Talk about emotion and feelings in close relationships (Staske 1998) and in emergency service calls (Tracy and Tracy 1998b), relational and identity issues involved in computer-mediated conversations (Baym 1996; Rintel and Pittam 1997), the interactional sensitivities in giving criticism (Tracy and Eisenberg 1990/1) or advice (Goldsmith and Fitch 1997), teasing (Alberts 1992; Yeddes 1996), how parents seek to regulate children's behavior (Wilson et al. 1997), positioning self in relation to God (Bruder 1998a, 1998b), and how college students use reported speech to talk about sensitive topics such as race on campus (Buttny 1997) have also been explored.

2.3   Straight talk (Katriel)

Dugri is a culturally specific form of speech in Israeli society that Tamar Katriel (1986) explores in her book *Talking Straight: Dugri Speech in Israeli Sabra Culture*. Rooted in the ethnography of communication tradition (Hymes 1974), Katriel traces the socially rich roots of *dugri* that led to its becoming an especially valued way of talk among Israelis of European descent. *Dugri*, a term originally from Arabic that is now part of colloquial Hebrew, is used both to describe the act of speaking straight to the point, and as a label for an honest person who speaks in this way. Katriel illuminates how *dugri* takes its meaning from its being embedded in Zionist socialism, a system committed to making Zionist Jews everything that the Diaspora Jew was not. *Dugri* as a speech action is an assertion of character within a cultural group committed to fostering an egalitarian, socially responsible community. Katriel explores the meanings and functions of *dugri* within Israeli culture by focusing on its typical expressive forms, as well as its occurrence in several historically significant events. Throughout, Katriel shows how *dugri* relates to speech forms valued in other cultures and how it challenges politeness theory's (Brown and Levinson 1987) assumption that most talk is grounded in rules of considerateness.

The ethnography of communication tradition was brought into the communication field initially by Philipsen (1975, 1992, 1997) in his studies of the communicative code of Teamsterville, a working-class, urban, white community. This tradition has been extended in significant ways through Philipsen's students' studies of the enactment of personal relationships, address, directives, and leave-taking practices among

Colombians (Fitch 1991a, 1991b, 1994, 1998; Fitch and Sanders 1994), understanding of address forms and the activity of speaking in tongues in an American Christian community (Sequeira 1993, 1994), through studies of *griping* and *behibudin* (a ritualized sharing practice among children) in Israeli culture (Katriel 1991), and rules of self-expression in American life in work, play, and public arenas (Carbaugh 1988, 1996; Coutu in press; Hall and Valde 1995; Philipsen in press) and their differences with Soviet society (Carbaugh 1993).

In an overview of approaches to discourse analysis, Schiffrin (1994) treats ethnography of communication as one tradition of discourse analysis. Within communication, ethnography's identity is not so straightforward. While there is little dispute about the contribution that ethnography of communication studies makes to language and social interaction research, studies in this tradition are not usually regarded as discourse analysis. To the degree that an ethnography is evidenced through observation and informant interviews collected through field notes, a study will typically not be seen as discourse analysis. To the degree that an ethnography of communication study is evidenced through analysis of recorded and transcribed talk, it will be. Hybrid discourse analytic/ethnographic studies are increasingly common. From a disciplinary perspective, then, some of the studies noted above would more readily be judged ethnographies than discourse analysis. However, because discourse analysis in its larger interdisciplinary context (e.g. van Dijk 1997a, 1997b) is defined as much, if not more so, by topic (studies of language and social interaction) rather than method, it would be a serious oversight not to mention this work.

2.4 Controlling others' conversational understandings (Sanders)

Most people, at least some of the time, experience communication as problematic. The reason for this, Sanders (1987) argues, is that people have other purposes when they communicate than just expressing what they are thinking or feeling: "On at least some occasions, people communicate to affect others – to exercise control over the understandings others form of the communicator, the situation, their interpersonal relationships, the task at hand, etc., thereby to make different actions and reactions more or less likely" (1987: vii). How people do this is Robert Sanders's focus in *Cognitive Foundations of Calculated Speech*, a book that proposes a theory of strategic communication grounded in people's interpretive practices. Beginning with Grice's (1975) notion of conversational implicature and the work of speech act scholars (e.g. Austin 1962; Searle 1969), Sanders distinguishes three types of meaning that utterances can have. Simply put, an utterance's propositional content can be distinguished from the illocutionary act that it performs, and from the conversational implicatures that may be triggered. Typically, Sanders argues, while all of these meanings are available, only one is focal. How the particular level (and content) of meaning becomes focal depends on specific choices a speaker makes about wording construction and delivery. Wording an utterance one way will constrain a fellow conversationalist from offering responses that a speaker does not want to get, and channels him or her toward desired other responses. This constraining (channeling) process is never more than partial, but it is the communicative resource that every communicator seeks to use as an exchange unfolds to accomplish his or her preferred goals. Thus while every utterance constrains what may reasonably follow, subsequent actions may cause prior utterances to be reinterpreted.

The key challenge in a theory of meaning-making, as Sanders sees it, is to identify how relatively stable aspects of meaning are acted upon by the shaping and changing power of context (especially prior utterances). A set of forecasting principles which communicators use to make decisions about what to say next is identified. Sanders draws upon a range of procedures to assess his theory. In addition to using hypothetical examples and experiments that assess interpretive preferences for utterance sequences, the principles are applied to a range of interpersonal and public conversations and written texts. Through analysis of multiple instances of very different kinds of discourse, the broad applicability of the theory is displayed. In this regard, like studies in the ethnography of communication tradition, Sanders's work would be regarded as a methodological hybrid that is part discourse analytic (see also Sanders 1984, 1985). Studies that combine discourse analysis and quantitative coding are in fact a common methodological hybrid (e.g. Tracy and Eisenberg 1990/1; Villaume et al. 1997).

Another line of communication research centrally informed by speech act theorizing comprises studies of argumentative discourse. Van Eemeren et al. define argumentation as the use of "language to justify or refute a standpoint, with the aim of securing agreement in views" (1993: 208). Making of an argument, then, is conceived as performing a complex speech act in which the propositional content of the act can be specified, as well as its sincerity and preparatory conditions. Texts whose arguments have been analyzed include advertisements (Jacobs 1995), divorce mediation proceedings (Aakhus 1995), interviews with police officials (Agne and Tracy 1998), school board elections (Tracy in press), college classes in critical thinking (Craig 1998; Craig and Sanusi in press), and group decision-making occasions that are mediated by computers (Aakhus 1998; Brashers et al. 1995). More explicitly than in other discourse traditions, studies of argumentative discourse meld empirical description with normative theorizing. As linguist Cameron (1995) has argued, language use not only is, but should be conceptualized as, a normative practice. A normative stance undergirds studies of argumentative discourse, and within this tradition the focus is on assessing the practical usefulness and moral reasonableness of different normative proposals (Jacobs and Jackson 1983; van Eemeren et al. 1993).

Understanding how discourse links to speakers' interactional goals, a primary focus in Sanders's work, also has received considerable attention, both in general theoretical conceptions (e.g. Bavelas 1991; Craig 1986; Mandelbaum and Pomerantz 1991; Sanders 1991; Tracy 1991; Tracy and Coupland 1990) and in particular contexts; for example, intergenerational conversations (Coupland et al. 1991a, 1991b).

Sanders's work reflects an interest in philosophy of language issues that have been the focus of attention within pragmatics research in linguistics. Other links with pragmatics by communication researchers include studies of conversational cohesion and coherence (Craig and Tracy 1983; Ellis 1992; Ellis and Donohue 1986; Penman 1987), and analyses of speech acts of different types such as requests (Bresnahan 1993; Craig et al. 1986) or complaints (Alberts 1988a, 1988b). Studies that tap into Brown and Levinson's (1987) politeness theory and more broadly Goffman's (1967) notion of facework are especially numerous (see Ting-Toomey 1994; Tracy 1990 for reviews). Linnell and Bredmar (1996) examine facework in the talk between midwives and expectant mothers, Penman (1990, 1991) in courtroom interrogation, Beck (1996) in debates, and Tracy and Tracy (1998a) in 911 emergency calls. At the broadest level Haslett (1987) has argued that adopting a functional pragmatic perspective would enrich the field's studies of children's communication development, classroom interaction, and issues in intimate relationships.

2.5   *Academic colloquium (Tracy)*

A last example of discourse work within communication is to be seen in a study of my own about the dilemmas of academic scholarly talk (Tracy 1997a).[7] Discussing ideas and debating issues is a common activity and a taken-for-granted good in academic life. In typical characterizations of this speech activity, though, people are invisible – ideas "have it out with each other." *Colloquium* views the problems of academic talk from the vantage of its participants: "What worries do faculty and graduate students bring to this occasion? What problems do participants face as they talk with each other? How are problems made visible in talk and given attention through talk?" (1997: 3). Using tape-recorded presentations and discussions from weekly colloquia in a PhD program, and interviews with graduate students and faculty participants, *Colloquium* explores the host of dilemmas that confront participants in their institutional and interactional roles. As presenters, for instance, faculty members and graduate students needed to make decisions about how closely to position themselves in relation to the ideas about which they talked. Close positioning – done through mention of tangible by-products of intellectual work such as articles or grants, or time references that made apparent lengthy project involvement – acted as a claim to high intellectual ability and therein licensed difficult questions and challenges. More distant positioning made a presenter's making of errors and inability to handle certain intellectual issues more reasonable, but became increasingly problematic the higher one's institutional rank (beginning versus advanced graduate student, assistant versus full professor).

In their role as discussants, participants struggled with how to challenge supportively: how could participants pursue important intellectual issues yet avoid contributing to others' humiliation? The conversational dilemma faculty and graduate students faced was that conversational moves that displayed a person to be taking an idea seriously were the same ones that might be used as evidence that a discussant was being self-aggrandizing or disrespectful. Dilemmas at the group level included managing emotion in intellectual talk, and fostering discussion equality among a group in which members varied considerably in experience and expertise.

In sum, *Colloquium*: (1) analyzed the problems that confronted a group of academics in their roles as graduate students and faculty, presenters and discussants, and group members; (2) described the conversational practices that made problems visible and the strategies used to manage them; and (3) identified the normative beliefs this group of academics held about how intellectual discussion ought to be conducted. At the book's end are proposals about improving colloquia that seek to recognize the dilemmatic quality of the difficulties that confront participants.

In investigating academic colloquia I developed a hybrid type of discourse analysis that I named action-implicative discourse analysis (Tracy 1995). Like much communication work, action-implicative discourse analysis has roots in ideas from diverse traditions (in particular, politeness theory, conversation analysis, critical discourse approaches, and interactional sociolinguistics). In action-implicative discourse analysis, however, these ideas are blended for the purpose of addressing questions about people and talk that are prototypically "communicative."[8] What makes discourse research especially "communicative" is addressed in the next section.

A discourse-grounded dilemmatic approach to communicative problems is seen in studies of other institutional contexts as well. Naughton (1996), for instance, describes the strategies hospice team members use to manage the dilemma of displaying patient acceptance and making medically and professionally informed evaluations; Pomerantz et al. (1997) consider the interactional tensions faced by medical residents and their supervisors as they coordinate action in front of patients; te Molder (1995) analyzes dilemmas of government communicators who create and plan "information" campaigns; and Tracy and Anderson (1999) examine the delicate conversational dance citizens do when they call the police to report a problem with a person with whom they have a connection. Studies informed by a dilemmatic or dialectical frame are commonplace in nondiscourse traditions as well (see Baxter and Montgomery 1996; Rawlins 1992 for reviews).

3   Key Features of a Communication Take on Discourse Analysis

For communication researchers, then, discourse analysis is the close study of talk (or text) in context, a method that is to be distinguished from ethnographic field approaches (informant interviewing and participant observation) on the one hand, and laboratory and field-based coding studies on the other. Discourse analysis is situated within an interpretive social science metatheory that conceives of meanings as socially constructed, and needing to be studied in ways that take that belief seriously. It is: (1) empirical work, to be distinguished from philosophical essays about discourse; and (2) social scientific in world view and hence distinguishable from humanistic approaches to textual analysis (e.g. rhetorical criticism studies that analyze language and argument strategies in political speeches).

Discourse analysis provides communication researchers with a compelling way to study how people present themselves, manage their relationships, assign responsibility and blame, create organizations, enact culture, persuade others, make sense of social members' ongoing interactional practices, and so on. Stated a bit differently, taking talk seriously has enabled communication researchers to reframe and address long-standing disciplinary concerns in powerful, persuasive new ways. By now, it should be obvious how ideas from intellectual traditions outside Communication have shaped discourse work within Communication. What may be less obvious is what Communication offers the interdisciplinary discourse community.

In the final section are described intellectual commitments, habits of mind if you will, common among communication researchers.[9] None of the commitments is unique to communication scholarship. Yet taken as a set, these intellectual practices and preferences create a perspective on discourse that is identifiably "communicative." A communication perspective, I argue, brings issues into focus that are invisible or backgrounded in other disciplinary viewpoints. As such, a communicative perspective does not just apply ideas from other traditions, as occasionally has been asserted (e.g. Schiffrin 1994), but offers a valuable and distinct voice to the multidisciplinary conversation about discourse.

3.1   A preference for talk over written texts

That discourse analysts within communication privilege oral over written texts is not surprising given the history of the field. This does not mean there is no interest in written texts (e.g. Coutu in press; Tracy 1988), but it does mean that analyses of written discourse are the exception rather than the rule. The field's strong preference for the study of oral texts foregrounds certain features of discourse that can more easily be backgrounded in studies of writing. Most notable is the way studying talk increases the visibility of people as part of what is being studied – there is no way to study talk apart from persons speaking and being spoken to. Discourse analysis in Communication is the study of people talking with each other.

Typically, fields define themselves more broadly than they actually practice. In Communication, for instance, although there are no good intellectual reasons, discourse analysts typically focus on adults rather than children (cf. Barnes and Vangelisti 1995), English speakers rather than other language speakers (cf. Hopper and Chen 1996), and persons with normal communicative capacities rather than those with disorders (cf. Goodwin 1995). Moreover, because discourse analytic studies began in interpersonal communication – an area of the field that distinguishes itself from organizational and mass communication – there has been relatively little attention to talk in business settings (cf. Taylor 1993), the focal site for organizational communication study, or in mass media contexts (cf. Nofsinger 1995).

3.2   Audience design and strategy as key notions

That talk is produced in particular situations for specific aims addressed to particular others is taken for granted as important to consider in Communication studies. Put a bit differently, taking account of audience – whether the audience be a single conversational partner, a small working group, or an ambiguously bounded public – is regarded as crucial for understanding people's discourse practices. Moreover, many of Communication's questions concern how an audience shapes what gets said. That texts of all types are designed for audiences is not a claim that anyone is likely to contest, but it is a fact often ignored in research practice. The influence of conversation analysis in Communication, over other discourse approaches, and in contrast to its more limited influence in its home discipline of sociology, can be understood as arising from its taking this disciplinary commonplace seriously. With its conception of talk as recipient-designed, and the commitment to grounding claims about meaning in a recipient's response, conversation analysis has offered communications scholars a compelling way to study what they "knew" was important.

In addition to the notion that talk is directed to an audience, there is a related assumption that people are crafting their talk to accomplish their aims given the other and the character of the situation. Although structure and strategy are deeply connected (Craig and Tracy 1983; Schiffrin 1994), it is the strategic aspect of talk that is most interesting to communication researchers. Thus, communication researchers tend to think of talk occasions as situations that could have been played out in other ways. Communicators are choice-making, planning actors confronting uncertain situations and seeking to shape what happens in ways that advance their concerns. Questions to which communication researchers repeatedly return include: (1) "What identity, task, or relationship functions are served for a speaker by talking in this way rather than that?" and (2) "What are the advantages and disadvantages of selecting one strategy versus another?"

A rhetorical approach to discourse is not unique to communication. The sociologist Silverman (1994), for instance, implicitly adopts this stance in his study of patients telling counselors why they have come in for HIV testing. A group of British social psychologists (Billig 1987; Edwards and Potter 1992; Potter 1996) have argued explicitly for such an approach. But while taking a rhetorical stance is radical for psychologists, it is mainstream in communication. Admittedly, not all communication researchers see the value of looking closely at talk (preoccupation with minutiae), but few question the value of conceptualizing communication as a strategic activity.

3.3   *"Problematic" situations as most interesting*

Certain kinds of communicative tasks elicit relatively uniform responses, (e.g. describing an apartment); others reveal considerable individual differences (O'Keefe 1991). It is situations that social actors experience as problematic, where individuals respond differently – for example, accounting for a problem, reacting to someone else's, giving advice – that are most interesting for communication researchers. Communication scholars' interest in the problematic is displayed in the attention given to conflict and persuasion situations, as well as their visible concern about multiple-goal and dilemmatic occasions. Moreover, it is in situations where most people, or more accurately most members of a culture, do not respond in identical ways that evaluation of action is likely to become focal. When responses are not uniform, it becomes possible (and typical) to consider whether one kind of response, rather than another, does a better job of promoting relational satisfaction, minimizing group conflict, getting compliance, fostering involvement in a group decision, and so on. In such situations, a person or group's conversational choices (i.e. strategies) will be consequential.

Communication scholars study problematic situations both from the perspective of the situated actor and from that of detached observers. It is the actor perspective, however, that is less common in other intellectual traditions (Pearce 1995). An actor perspective takes seriously looking at talk though participants' eyes. The "participants' eyes" that are of interest, though, are not just immediate participants in their here-and-now particularity. That is, it is not only an interest in how people are locally making sense and acting but how they *could be* that is a particularly Communication impulse. It is in the space between what is typically done, and what might rarely be done but nonetheless is possible, that novel, interesting, and effective strategies are to be created or discovered.

3.4 An explicitly argumentative writing style

All scholarly writing is about making arguments, but not all academic writing is explicitly argumentative. An explicitly argumentative style, to identify just a few features, is one that uses a greater frequency of first person voice (I argue) rather than third person (the author found) or impersonal voice (the data show), uses verbs that locate agency in the author rather than the data, and treats a large range of methodological and theoretical matters as "decisions" requiring justification, rather than as procedures to be described. The counterpoint to an explicitly argumentative style is one that seeks to be descriptive, framing what a researcher is doing as reporting rather than persuading. A descriptive style is expected when members of a community understand the significance of an action, issue, or person similarly. There is no surer way to mark oneself as a novice or outsider to a community than to argue for what is regarded as obvious. Similarly, to provide no evidence for assertions a community regards as contentious is a sign of ignorance of some type. An argumentative stance is expected when one is dealing with issues that members of a targeted group regard as debatable. Stated a bit differently, an argumentative style legitimates other views of the world – it frames an issue as something others may see differently. Effective scholarly writing requires weaving descriptive and argumentative moves together. But the characteristic way this is done – the relative frequency of descriptive and argumentative devices – tends to differ according to scholarly disciplines (Bazerman 1988). In a study I did (Tracy 1988) comparing journal articles from four intellectual traditions (discourse processing, conversation analysis, interactional sociolinguistics, and communication), the communication report used the most explicitly argumentative style. The use of a relatively explicit argumentative style is a marker of Communication work.

At a practical level, the argumentative style can be attributed to the intellectual diversity within Communication. There are few things that everyone in the discipline would give assent to. Because of this diversity it is necessary to use a more explicitly argumentative style than is displayed in other disciplines. However, the argumentative writing style is not merely a practical necessity, it is the embodiment of a disciplinary attitude toward people. A writing style that is relatively argumentative does two things. First, it treats a larger range of others as audience. Since "givens" begin to disappear as one moves across intellectual traditions, explicit arguing is a way of informing others they are included among the addressed. Additionally, to the degree the argumentative style extends to the people and practices about whom an author writes, research participants are treated as reflective agents who weigh alternatives and make choices rather than as "subjects" whose discursive behavior is being explained. In sum, while an explicitly argumentative style has disadvantages – most notably, slowing intellectual progress to deliberate about issues that on particular occasions might better be ignored – it is consistent with a valuing of different perspectives, and it is an impulse that is strong in Communication work.

3.5   *Viewing talk as practical and moral action*

Talk is not just a phenomenon to be scientifically described and explained, it is moral and practical action taken by one person toward others. Talk not only can be evaluated, but should be. Just as people in their everyday lives are inescapably evaluating their own and others' actions, so, too, do scholars have a responsibility to take the moral and practical dimensions of talk seriously. It would be inaccurate to say that viewing talk as practical and moral action is a dominant view among communication researchers. Many, like their linguistic counterparts, define themselves as scientists whose job it is to describe and explain their phenomena, and, as best as possible, to keep values out of their work and avoid "prescribing."

Yet while the scientific view may still be dominant in Communication, there are changes afoot. Intellectual streams are fast becoming rivers. Normative theorizing – theories that consider what ought to be, as well as what is – have long been part of the field. Rhetorical humanistic work, by definition, takes a critical stance toward discursive objects and involves a normative component, as do critical studies of organizational life (Deetz 1992). In studies of argumentative practices and small group decision-making, there has been considerable theorizing considering how practices ought to be conducted.

Robert Craig (Craig 1989, 1992, 1995, 1999; Craig and Tracy 1995) has argued that the discipline of Communication should think of itself as a "practical" rather than a scientific one. Craig's notion of "practical" has some features in common with the area in linguistics labeled "applied." Gunnarsson defines applied linguistics as having the goal "to analyze, understand, or solve problems relating to practical action in real-life contexts" (1997: 285). Craig's view of Communication as a practical discipline also regards problems as the starting point for research. But what distinguishes Craig's model from Gunnarsson's description of applied linguistic work is practical theory's assumption that problems are not self-evident things. To the contrary, the most difficult and important part of the research process is defining the problems of a practice. Whose view of the difficulties should be taken? How should people's notions about "the problem" be put together? Since definitions of problems invariably imply blame and responsibility for change, defining "the problem" is highly consequential. Moreover, defining problems well is more than a matter of empirical observation. Good problem definitions require careful thought about the likely moral and practical consequences of defining problems one way rather than another. As Craig notes in the preface to an edited volume about social approaches to the study of communication:

> [S]ocial approaches imply that communication research has an active role to play in cultivating better communicative practices in society. The responsibility of such roles follows from the *reflexivity* inherent in our research practices. . . . Communication is not a set of objective facts just simply "out there" to be described and explained. Ideas about communication disseminated by researchers, teachers, and other intellectuals circulate through society and participate in social processes that continually influence and reshape communication practices. Our choice, as interpersonal scholars, is not ultimately *whether* to participate in those processes but *how* to participate. We should be asking not just what communication *is*, but also what it *should* be. If we're going to help make it, let's at least try to make it better. (Craig 1995: ix)[10]

4 Conclusion

In this chapter I have spoken for my diverse, squabbling family. I have "described" what discourse analytic research looks like in Communication. This describing has, of course, involved selection. In essence I have taken a single photograph from the family album, enlarged it, framed it, and talked about it as "discourse analysis in communication." I have worked to select a picture most family members would regard as reasonable, but given the family is large, I have had to make decisions about whose faces (arms, feet) could be occluded or left fuzzy, and whose should be big and clear. To push this photography analogy just a bit further, let me conclude by giving my reasons for choosing this particular snapshot. From my perspective, this image of "discourse analysis in Communication" is a nice one because it shows the importance of neighbors and friends in Communication's definition of itself, because it highlights features that are distinctively "Communication," therein making it easy to spot a Communication person in a crowd, and because it should make evident why Communication is a lively and interesting family that others would benefit from getting to know better.

NOTES

My thanks to the faculty members and graduate students in the discourse data group at the University of Colorado, and Kristine Fitch and the graduate students in the discourse analysis seminar (summer 1997) at the University of Iowa, for helpful comments.

1 To make the chapter more readable, the word "communication" is capitalized when it refers to the academic field of study (Communication), and is in lower case when it refers to the everyday activity or communication as a topic.

2 Within the field there is an important distinction between "communication," without the "s," and "communications," with the "s". Communications with an "s" is used to refer to mass communications (media-related areas). Communication in the singular is the preferred term for other areas of the field. A person's command (or lack thereof) of this distinction is a marker of discipline knowledge.

3 Some years ago Levinson (1983) made a distinction between conversation analysis and discourse analysis. At that point in time the distinction was a reasonable one, although even then not completely accurate (e.g. Gumperz 1982a, 1982b). Analyses of talk were limited, and without major distortion could be divided into those that began with more formal structures (speech acts) and those that began with "unmotivated looking" and a concern about interactional structure. In the ensuing years there has been an enormous growth in discourse studies where this simple dichotomy no longer very well captures the intellectual terrain. Many of these new approaches have been strongly influenced by conversation analysis (CA), but are not addressing the kinds of questions that have been

focal in CA. Thus, although this distinction is still used by some scholars, and particularly by conversation analysts, I do not make the distinction. Instead, like Schiffrin (1994) I treat discourse analysis as an umbrella term, and conversation analysis as one particular kind of discourse analysis, characterized both by a specific set of questions about social life and by a distinct method of analysis.

4   "Naturally occurring talk" is not a transparent category but has been an issue of debate. Are interviews naturally occurring talk? Do conversations generated in laboratory simulations count? These are ongoing concerns among communication researchers, with people taking different positions.

5   There is increasing convergence between texts that rhetoricians and discourse analysts take as objects of study. Some rhetoricians study everyday exchange forms (e.g. Hauser 1998) and discourse analytic studies of campaign or political oratory can be found (Tracy in press). However, in each case what is taken for granted differs. Rhetoricians tend to justify the reasonableness of focusing on the ordinary, "vernacular rhetoric" instead of rhetoric in its unmarked forms (i.e. speeches, debates), whereas discourse analysts would be likely to explicitly argue for the value of studying a public monologic text in contrast to the more typical interactive ones.

6   To decide whether a scholar is a communication researcher I considered (1) if the person received his or her PhD in a communication program, (2) if the person is/was a faculty member in a communication program, and (3) if the person publishes articles in the field and participates in its professional

conferences. For the vast majority of authors cited in this review, all three criteria apply; for some, however, only two apply. For instance, Chuck Goodwin and Anita Pomerantz are included as communication scholars. Goodwin received his PhD in a communication program but since graduate school has been in anthropology and linguistics departments; Pomerantz received her degree in sociology but for more than a decade and a half has been a faculty member in communication departments. Persons who attend national or international communication conferences or publish occasional papers in the field's journals without one, or both, of the other two criteria are not considered communication scholars. My classification means that there will be a small set of people that more than one discipline will claim as its own. In addition, co-authored work between scholars in different disciplines is treated as communication if at least one of the authors is a communication researcher.

7   Parts of the analysis in the book initially appeared as journal articles (Tracy and Baratz 1993, 1994; Tracy and Carjuzaa 1993; Tracy and Muller 1994; Tracy and Naughton 1994).

8   To say that my own work is prototypically communicative may seem self-aggrandizing. In making this claim I have no intention of implying a quality judgment. Quality is a different judgment than tradition typicality, which may or may not be a desirable feature. More than most communication scholars, however, I have been interested in articulating how discourse analysis by communication scholars is distinctively "communicative." That is, I have sought to articulate and

foster in my own work the intellectual moves that are valued and commonplace in Communication while shaping these moves in ways that take advantage of the interesting work in other disciplines.

9 In describing what are central disciplinary impulses, I am offering a construction of "the field." This construction is crafted so that knowledgeable others would regard it as a reasonable description of what is actually there. At the same time, "the description" is my attempt to regularize and strengthen impulses in the field that I find attractive while decreasing the influence of others.

10 The volume was addressed to interpersonal communication researchers and in the quote several references to communication actually said "interpersonal communication."

REFERENCES

Aakhus, M. (1995). The rational consequences of argument management. In F. van Eemeren, R. Grootendorst, J. A. Blair, and C. A. Willard (eds), *Special Fields and Cases: Proceedings of the Third ISSA Conference on Argumentation* pp. 593–605. Amsterdam: Sic Sat.

Aakhus, M. (1998). Settlement on the electronic frontier: The management of argumentation with group decision support systems. In J. F. Klumpp (ed.), *Argument in a Time of Change* pp. 132–7. Annandale, VA: National Communication Association.

Agne, R., and Tracy, K. (1998). Not answering questions: A police chief's strategies in a sensationalized murder. In J. F. Klumpp (ed.), *Argument in a Time of Change* pp. 238–42. Annandale, VA: National Communication Association.

Alberts, J. K. (1988a). A descriptive taxonomy of couples' complaints. *Southern Communication Journal 54*, 125–43.

Alberts, J. K. (1988b). An analysis of couples' conversational complaint interactions. *Communication Monographs 55*, 184–97.

Alberts, J. K. (1992). An inferential strategic explanation for the social organization of teases. *Journal of Language and Social Psychology 11*, 153–77.

Atkinson, J. M., and Heritage, J. (eds) (1984). *Structure of Social Action: Studies in Conversation Analysis.* Cambridge: Cambridge University Press.

Austin, J. L. (1962). *How To Do Things with Words.* Oxford: Oxford University Press.

Barnes, M. K., and Vangelisti, A. (1995). Speaking in a double-voice: Role-making as influence in preschoolers' fantasy play situations. *Research on Language and Social Interaction 28*, 351–90.

Bavelas, J. B. (1991). Some problems with linking goals to discourse. In K. Tracy (ed.), *Understanding Face-to-Face Interaction: Issues Linking Goals and Discourse* pp. 119–30. Hillsdale, NJ: Lawrence Erlbaum.

Baxter, L. A., and Montgomery, B. M. (1996). *Relating: Dialogues and Dialectics.* New York: Guilford.

Baym, N. (1996). Agreements and disagreements in a computer-mediated discussion. *Research on Language and Social Interaction 29*, 315–45.

Bazerman, C. (1988). *Shaping Written Knowledge: The Genre and Activity of the Experimental Article in Science.*

Madison: University of Wisconsin Press.

Beach, W. A. (1993). Transitional regularities for "casual" "okay" usages. *Journal of Pragmatics 19*, 325–52.

Beach, W. A. (1995). Preserving and constraining options: "Okays" and "official" priorities in medical interviews. In G. H. Morris and R. Chenail (eds), *Talk of the Clinic* pp. 259–89. Hillsdale, NJ: Lawrence Erlbaum.

Beach, W. A. (1996). *Conversations about Illness: Family Preoccupations with Bulimia*. Mahwah, NJ: Lawrence Erlbaum.

Beach, W. A., and Dunning, D. G. (1982). Pre-indexing and conversational organization. *Quarterly Journal of Speech 68*, 170–85.

Beach, W. A., and Metzger, T. R. (1997). Claiming insufficient knowledge. *Human Communication Research, 23*, 562–88.

Beck, C. S. (1996). "I've got some points I'd like to make here": The achievement of social face through turn management during the 1992 vice presidential debate. *Political Communication 13*, 165–80.

Benoit, P. J. (1997). *Telling the Success Story: Acclaiming and Disclaiming Discourse*. Albany: SUNY Press.

Billig, M. (1987). *Arguing and Thinking: A Rhetorical Approach to Social Psychology*. Cambridge: Cambridge University Press.

Boden, D., and Zimmerman, D. H. (ed.) (1991). *Talk and Social Structure*. Cambridge: Polity Press.

Bostrom, R., and Donohew, L. (1992). The case for empiricism: Clarifying fundamental issues in communication research. *Communication Monographs, 59*, 109–29.

Brashers, D. E., Adkins, M., Meyers R. A., and Nittleman, D. (1995). The facilitation of argument in computer-mediated group decision-making interactions. In F. van Eemeren, R. Grootendorst, J. A. Blair, and C. A. Willard (eds), *Special Fields and Cases: Proceedings of the Third ISSA Conference on Argumentation* pp. 606–21. Amsterdam: Sic Sat.

Bresnahan, M. I. (1991). When a response is not an answer: Understanding conflict in nonnative testimony. *Multilingua 10*, 275–93.

Bresnahan, M. I. (1992). The effects of advisor style on overcoming client resistance in the advising interview. *Discourse Processes 15*, 229–47.

Bresnahan, M. I. (1993). Gender differences in initiating requests for help. *Text 13*, 7–23.

Brown, P., and Levinson, S. C. (1987). *Universals in Language Usage: Politeness Phenomena*. Cambridge: Cambridge University Press.

Bruder, K. A. (1998a). A pragmatics for human relationships with the divine: An examination of the monastic blessing sequence. *Journal of Pragmatics 29*, 463–91.

Bruder, K. A. (1998b). Monastic blessings: Deconstructing and reconstructing the self. *Symbolic Interaction 21*, 87–116.

Buttny, R. (1993). *Social Accountability in Communication*. London: Sage.

Buttny, R. (1996). Clients' and therapists' joint construction of the clients' problems. *Research on Language and Social Interaction 29*, 125–53.

Buttny, R. (1997). Reported speech in talking race on campus. *Human Communication Research 23*, 477–506.

Buttny, R., and Cohen, J. R. (1991). The uses of goals in therapy. In K. Tracy (ed.), *Understanding Face-to-Face Interaction: Issues Linking Goals and Discourse* pp. 63–77. Hillsdale, NJ: Lawrence Erlbaum.

Cameron, D. (1995). *Verbal Hygiene*. London: Routledge.

Cappella, J. N. (1990). The method of proof by example in interaction analysis. *Communication Monographs* 57, 236–42.

Carbaugh, D. (1988). *Talking American: Cultural Discourse on Donohue.* Norwood, NJ: Ablex.

Carbaugh, D. (1993). "Soul" and "self": Soviet and American cultures in conversation. *Quarterly Journal of Speech 79*, 182–200.

Carbaugh, D. (1996). *Situating Selves: The Communication of Social Identities in American Scenes.* Albany: SUNY Press.

Chaffee, S. H., and Berger, C. R. (1987). What communication scientists do. In C. R. Berger and S. H. Chaffee (eds), *Handbook of Communication Science* pp. 99–122. Newbury Park, CA: Sage.

Cody, M., and McLaughlin, M. (eds) (1990). *The Psychology of Tactical Communication.* London: Multilingual Matters.

Cohen, H. (1994). *The History of Speech Communication: The Emergence of a Discipline, 1914–45.* Annandale, VA: Speech Communication Association.

Coupland, J., Coupland, N., Giles, H., and Henwood, K. (1991a). Formulating age: Dimensions of age identity in elderly talk. *Discourse Processes 14*, 87–106.

Coupland, N., Coupland, J., Giles, H., and Henwood, K. (1991b). Intergenerational talk: Goal consonance and intergroup dissonance. In K. Tracy (ed.), *Understanding Face-to-Face Interaction: Issues Linking Goals and Discourse* pp. 79–100. Hillsdale, NJ: Lawrence Erlbaum.

Coutu, L. (in press). Communication codes of rationality and spirituality in the discourse of and about Robert S. McNamara's *In Retrospect. Research on Language and Social Interaction.*

Craig, R. T. (1986). Goals in discourse. In D. G. Ellis and W. A. Donohue (eds), *Contemporary Issues in Language and Discourse Processes* pp. 257–74. Hillsdale, NJ: Lawrence Erlbaum.

Craig, R. T. (1989). Communication as a practical discipline. In B. Dervin, L. Grossberg, B. J. O'Keefe, and E. Wartella (eds), *Rethinking Communication: Vol. 1 Paradigm Issues* pp. 97–122. Newbury Park, CA: Sage.

Craig, R. T. (1992). Practical communication theory and the pragma-dialectical approach in conversation. In F. H. van Eemeren, R. Grootendorst, J. A. Blair, and C. A. Willard (eds), *Argumentation Illuminated* pp. 51–61. Amsterdam: Sic Sat.

Craig, R. T. (1995). Foreword. In W. Leeds-Hurwitz (ed.), *Social Approaches to Communication* pp. v–ix. New York: Guilford.

Craig, R. T. (1998). Reflective discourse in a critical thinking classroom. In J. F. Klumpp (ed.), *Argument in a Time of Change* pp. 356–61. Annandale, VA: National Communication Association.

Craig, R. T. (1999). Communication theory as a field. *Communication Theory 9* 119–61.

Craig, R. T., and Sanusi, E. (in press). "I'm just saying": Discourse markers of standpoint continuity. Proceedings of the 4th ISSA Conference on Argumentation. Amsterdam: Sic Sat.

Craig, R. T., and Tracy, K. (eds) (1983). *Conversational Coherence: Form, Structure and Strategy.* Beverly Hills: Sage.

Craig, R. T., and Tracy, K. (1995). Grounded practical theory: The case of intellectual discussion. *Communication Theory 5*, 248–72.

Craig, R. T., Tracy, K., and Spisak, F. (1986). The discourse of requests: Assessments of a politeness approach. *Human Communication Research 12*, 437–68.

Deetz, S. A. (1992). *Democracy in an Age of Corporate Colonization: Developments in Communication and the Politics of Everyday Life.* Albany: SUNY Press.

Drummond, K., and Hopper, R. (1993). Acknowledgement tokens in a series. *Communication Reports 6*, 47–53.

Edwards, D., and Potter, J. (1992). *Discursive Psychology*. London: Sage.

Ellis, D. G. (1992). *From Language to Communication*. Hillsdale, NJ: Erlbaum.

Ellis, D. G., and Donohue, W. A. (1986). *Contemporary Issues in Language and Discourse Processes*. Hillsdale, NJ: Lawrence Erlbaum.

Fitch, K. (1991a) The interplay of linguistic universals and cultural knowledge in personal address: Colombian madre terms. *Communication Monographs 58*, 254–72.

Fitch, K. (1991b). Salispuedes: Attempting leave-taking in Colombia. *Research on Language and Social Interaction 24*, 209–24.

Fitch, K. (1994). A cross-cultural study of directive sequences and some implications for compliance-gaining research. *Communication Monographs 61*, 185–209.

Fitch, K. L. (1998). *Speaking Relationally: Culture, Communication, and Interpersonal Connection*. NY: Guilford.

Fitch, K. L., and Sanders, R. E. (1994). Culture, communication, and preferences for directness in expression of directives. *Communication Theory 4*, 219–45.

Glenn, P. J. (1989). Initiating shared laughter in multi-party conversations. *Western Journal of Speech Communication 53*, 127–49.

Glenn, P. J. (1991/2). Current speaker initiation of two-party shared laughter. *Research on Language and Social Interaction 25*, 139–62.

Goffman, E. (1967). *Interaction Ritual*. Garden City, NY: Anchor.

Goldsmith, D. J., and Fitch, K. (1997). The normative context of advice as social support. *Human Communication Research 23*, 454–76.

Goodwin, C. (1995). Co-constructing meaning in conversations with an aphasic man. *Research on Language and Social Interaction 28*, 233–60.

Goodwin, M. H., and Goodwin, C. (1986). Gesture and coparticipation in the activity of searching for a word. *Semiotica 62*, 51–75.

Grice, H. P. (1975). Logic in conversation. In P. Cole and J. Morgan (eds), *Syntax and Semantics, Vol. 3: Speech Acts* pp. 41–58. New York: Academic Press.

Gumperz, J. J. (1982a). *Discourse Strategies*. Cambridge: Cambridge University Press.

Gumperz, J. J. (ed.) (1982b). *Language and Social Identity*. Cambridge: Cambridge University Press.

Gunnarsson, B-L. (1997). Applied discourse analysis. In T. A. van Dijk (ed.), *Discourse as Social Interaction* pp. 285–31. London: Sage.

Hall, B. J. (1991). An elaboration of the structural possibilities for engaging in alignment episodes. *Communication Monographs 58*, 79–100.

Hall, B. J., and Valde, K. (1995). "Brown-nosing" as a cultural category in American organizational life. *Research on Language and Social Interaction 28*, 391–419.

Haslett, B. (1987). *Communication: Strategic Action in Context*. Hillsdale, NJ: Lawrence Erlbaum.

Hauser, G. A. (1998). Vernacular dialogue and the rhetoricality of public opinion. *Communication Monographs, 65*, 83–107.

Hopper, R. (1989). Sequential ambiguity in telephone openings: "What are you doin?" *Communication Monographs 56*, 240–52.

Hopper, R. (ed.) (1990/1). Ethnography and conversation analysis after *Talking Culture* (special section). *Research on Language and Social Interaction 24*, 161–387.

Hopper, R. (1992a). *Telephone Conversation*. Bloomington, IN: Indiana University Press.

Hopper, R. (1992b). Speech errors and the poetics of conversation. *Text and Performance Quarterly 12*, 113–24.

Hopper, R., and Chen, C-H. (1996). Language, cultures, relationships: Telephone openings in Taiwan. *Research on Language and Social Interaction 29*, 291–313.

Hopper, R., and Doany, N. (1988). Telephone openings and conversational universals: A study in three languages. In S. Ting-Toomey and F. Korzenny (eds), *Language, Communication and Culture* pp. 157–79. Newbury Park, CA: Sage.

Hopper, R., and Drummond, K. (1990). Emergent goals at a relational turning point: The case of Gordon and Denise. In K. Tracy and N. Coupland (eds), *Multiple Goals in Discourse* pp. 39–66. Clevedon Multilingual Matters.

Hopper, R., Koch, S., and Mandelbaum, J. (1986). Conversation analysis methods. In D. G. Ellis and W. A. Donohue, *Contemporary Issues in Language and Discourse Processes* pp. 169–86. Hillsdale, NJ: Lawrence Erlbaum.

Hymes, D. (1974). *Foundations in Sociolinguistics: An Ethnographic Approach*. Philadelphia: University of Pennsylvania Press.

Iacobucci, C. (1990). Accounts, formulations and goal attainment. In K. Tracy and N. Coupland (eds), *Multiple Goals in Discourse* pp. 85–99. Clevedon: Multilingual Matters.

Jackson, S. (1986). Building a case for claims about discourse structure. In D. G. Ellis and W. A. Donohue (eds), *Contemporary Issues in Language and Discourse Processes* pp. 129–48. Hillsdale, NJ: Lawrence Erlbaum.

Jacobs, S. (1986). How to make an argument from example in discourse analysis. In D. G. Ellis and W. A. Donohue (eds), *Contemporary Issues in Language and Discourse Processes*

pp. 149–68. Hillsdale, NJ: Lawrence Erlbaum.

Jacobs, S. (1990). On the especially nice fit between qualitative analysis and the known properties of conversation. *Communication Monographs 57*, 243–49.

Jacobs, S. (1995). Implicatures and deception in the arguments of commercial advertising. In F. van Eemeren, R. Grootendorst, J. A. Blair, and C. A. Willard (eds), *Special Fields and Cases: Proceedings of the Third ISSA Conference on Argumentation* pp. 579–92. Amsterdam: Sic Sat.

Jacobs, S. and Jackson, S. (1983). Strategy and structure in conversational influence attempts. *Communication Monographs 50*, 286–304.

Katriel, T. (1986). *Talking Straight: Dugri Speech in Israeli Sabra Culture*. Cambridge: Cambridge University Press.

Katriel, T. (1991). *Communal Webs: Communication and Culture in Contemporary Israel*. Albany: SUNY Press.

Lannamann, J. W. (1991). Interpersonal communication research as ideological practice. *Communication Theory 1*, 179–203.

Lawrence, S. G. (1996). Normalizing stigmatized practices: Achieving co-membership by "doing being ordinary." *Research on Language and Social Interaction 29*, 181–218.

LeBaron, C., and Streeck, J. (1997). Space, surveillance, and the interactional framing of experience during a murder interrogation. *Human Studies 20*, 1–25.

LeBaron, C. D., and Streeck, J. (in press). Gesture, knowledge, and the world. In D. McNeil (ed.), *Review of Language and Gesture: Window into Thought and Action*. Cambridge: Cambridge University Press.

Leeds-Hurwitz, W. (ed.) (1995). *Social Approaches to Communication*. New York: Guilford.

Levinson, S. C. (1983). *Pragmatics*. Cambridge: Cambridge University Press.

Linnel, P., and Bredmar, M. (1996). Reconstructing topical sensitivity: Aspects of face-work in talks between midwives and expectant mothers. *Research on Language and Social Interaction 29*, 347–79.

Mandelbaum, J. (1987). Couples sharing stories. *Communication Quarterly 35* 144–70.

Mandelbaum, J. (1989). Interpersonal activities in conversational storytelling. *Western Journal of Speech Communication, 53*, 114–26.

Mandelbaum, J., and Pomerantz, A. (1991). What drives social action? In K. Tracy (ed.), *Understanding Face-to-Face Interaction: Issue Linking Goals and Discourse* pp. 151–66. Hillsdale, NJ: Lawrence Erlbaum.

Manusov, V. (1996). Changing explanations: The process of account-making over time. *Research on Language and Social Interaction 29*, 155–79.

Morris, G. H. (1988). Finding fault. *Journal of Language and Social Psychology 7*, 1–26.

Morris, G. H., and Chenail, R. J. (eds) (1995). *The Talk of the Clinic: Explorations in the Analysis of Medical and Therapeutic Discourse*. Hillsdale, NJ: Lawrence Erlbaum.

Morris, G. H., White, C. H., and Iltis, R. (1994). "Well, ordinarily I would, but": Reexamining the nature of accounts for problematic events. *Research on Language and Social Interaction 27*, 123–44.

Mumby, D. K., and Clair, R. P. (1997). Organizational discourse. In T. A. van Dijk (ed.), *Discourse as Social Interaction* pp. 181–205. London: Sage.

Naughton, J. M. (1996). Discursively managing evaluation and acceptance in a hospice team meeting: A dilemma. Ann Arbor: UMI Dissertation Services.

Nofsinger, R. E. (1991). *Everyday Conversation*. Newbury Park, CA: Sage.

Nofsinger, R. E. (1995). Micromanaging expert talk: Hosts' contributions to televised computer product demonstrations. In B. R. Burleson (ed.), *Communication Yearbook 18* pp. 345–70. Thousand Oaks, CA: Sage.

O'Keefe, B. J. (1991). Message design logic and the management of multiple goals. In K. Tracy (ed.), *Understanding Face-to-Face Interaction: Issues Linking Goals and Discourse* pp. 131–50. Hillsdale, NJ: Lawrence Erlbaum.

Pearce, W. B. (1995). A sailing guide for social constructionists. In W. Leeds-Hurwitz (ed.), *Social Approaches to Communication* pp. 88–113. New York: Guilford.

Penman, R. (1987). Discourse in courts: Cooperation, coercion, and coherence. *Discourse Processes 10*, 210–18.

Penman, R. (1990). Facework and politeness: Multiple goals in courtroom discourse. *Journal of Language and Social Psychology 9*, 15–38.

Penman, R. (1991). Goals, games and moral orders: A paradoxical case in court? In K. Tracy (ed.), *Understanding Face-to-Face Interaction: Issues Linking Goals and Discourse* pp. 21–42. Hillsdale, NJ: Lawrence Erlbaum.

Philipsen, G. (1975). Speaking "like a man" in Teamsterville: Cultural patterns of role enactment in an urban neighborhood. *Quarterly Journal of Speech 61*, 13–22.

Philipsen, G. (1992). *Speaking Culturally: Exploration in Social Communication*. Albany: SUNY Press.

Philipsen, G. (1997). Toward a theory of speech codes. In G. Philipsen and T. Albrecht (eds), *Developing Communication Theories* pp. 119–56. Albany: SUNY Press.

Philipsen, G. (in press). Permission to speak the discourse of difference. *Research on Language and Social Interaction*.

Pomerantz, A. (1988). Offering a candidate answer: An information seeking strategy. *Communication Monographs, 55*, 360–73.

Pomerantz, A. (1989/90). Constructing skepticism: Four devices used to engender the audience's skepticism. *Research on Language and Social Interaction, 22*, 293–313.

Pomerantz, A., and Fehr, B. J. (1997). Conversation analysis: An approach to the study of social action as sense making practices. In T. A. van Dijk (ed.), *Discourse as Social Interaction* pp. 64–91. London: Sage.

Pomerantz, A., Fehr, B. J., and Ende, J. (1997). When supervising physicians see patients: Strategies used in difficult situations. *Human Communication Research 23*, 589–615.

Potter, J. (1996). *Representing Reality: Discourse, Rhetoric and Social Construction*. London: Sage.

Ragan, S. L. (1990). Verbal play and multiple goals in the gynaecological exam interaction. *Journal of Language and Social Psychology 9*, 61–78.

Rawlins, W. K. (1992). *Friendship Matters: Communication, Dialectics and the Life Course*. New York: Aldine de Gruyter.

Rintel, E. S., and Pittam, J. (1997). Strangers in a strange land: Interaction management on Internet relay chat. *Human Communication Research 23*, 507–34.

Robinson, J. D. (1998). Getting down to business: Talk, gaze, and body orientation during openings of doctor–patient consultations. *Human Communication Research 25*, 97–123.

Rogers, E. M. (1994). *A History of Communication Study*. New York: Free Press.

Sacks, H., Schegloff, E. A., and Jefferson, G. (1974). A simplest systematics for the organization of turn taking for conversation. *Language 50*, 696–735.

Sanders, R. E. (1984). Style, meaning, and message effects. *Communication Monographs 51*, 154–67.

Sanders, R. E. (1985). The interpretation of nonverbals. *Semiotica 55*, 195–216.

Sanders, R. E. (1987). *Cognitive Foundations of Calculated Speech: Controlling Understandings in Conversation and Persuasion*. Albany: SUNY Press.

Sanders, R. (1991). The two-way relationship between talk in social interaction and actors' goals and plans. In K. Tracy (ed.), *Understanding Face-to-Face Interaction: Issues linking Goals and Discourse* pp. 167–88.

Schegloff, E. A., and Sacks, H. (1973). Opening up closings. *Semiotica 8*, 289–327.

Schiffrin, D. (1994). *Approaches to Discourse*. Oxford: Blackwell.

Searle, J. R. (1969). *Speech Acts*. Cambridge: Cambridge University Press.

Sequiera, D. L. (1993). Personal address as negotiated meaning in an American church community. *Research on Language and Social Interaction 26*, 259–85.

Sequeira, D. L. (1994). Gifts of tongues and healing: The performance of charismatic renewal. *Text and Performance Quarterly 14*, 126–43.

Shotter, J. (1993). *Conversational Realities: Constructing Life through Language*. Thousand Oaks, CA: Sage.

Sigman, S. J. (1987). *A Perspective on Social Communication*. Lexington, MA: Lexington Books.

Sigman, S. J. (ed.) (1995). *The Consequentiality of Communication*. Albany: SUNY Press.

Silverman, D. (1994). Describing sexual activity in HIV counselling: The cooperative management of the moral order. *Text 14*, 427–57.

Staske, S. A. (1998). The normalization of problematic emotion in conversations between close relational partners: Interpersonal emotion. *Symbolic Interaction 21*, 59–86.

Streeck, J. (1993). Gesture as communication I: Its coordination with gaze and speech. *Communication Monographs 60*, 275–99.

Taylor, J. R. (1993). *Rethinking the Theory of Organizational Communication: How to Read an Organization*. Norwood, NJ: Ablex.

te Molder, H. (1995). Discourse of dilemmas: An analysis of government communicators' talk. PhD dissertation. Netherlands: Copyprint 2000, Enschede.

Thomason, W. R., and Hopper, R. (1992). Pauses, transition relevance, and speaker change. *Human Communication Research 18*, 429–44.

Ting-Toomey, S. (ed.) (1994). *The Challenge of Facework: Cross-Cultural and Interpersonal Issues*. Albany: SUNY Press.

Tracy, K. (1988). A discourse analysis of four discourse studies. *Discourse Processes 11*, 243–59.

Tracy, K. (ed.) (1991). *Understanding Face-to-Face Interaction: Issues Linking Goals and Discourse*. Hillsdale, NJ: Lawrence Erlbaum.

Tracy, K. (1990). The many faces of facework. In H. Giles and P. Robinson (eds), *The Handbook of Language and Social Psychology* pp. 209–26. Chichester: John Wiley and Sons.

Tracy, K. (1995). Action-implicative discourse analysis. *Journal of Language and Social Psychology 14*, 195–215.

Tracy, K. (1997a). *Colloquium: Dilemmas of Academic Discourse*. Norwood, NJ: Ablex.

Tracy, K. (1997b). Interactional trouble in emergency service requests: A problem of frames. *Research on Language and Social Interaction 30*, 315–43.

Tracy, K. (ed.) (1998). Using context in analysis. Special issue of *Research on Language and Social Interaction 31*.

Tracy, K. (1999). The usefulness of platitudes in arguments about conduct. In F. H. van Eemeren, R, Grootendorst, J. A. Blair, and C. A. Willard (eds), *Proceedings of the 4th International Conference of the International Society for the Study of Argumentation* (pp. 799–803). Amsterdam: Sic Sat.

Tracy, K., and Anderson, D. L. (1999). Relational positioning strategies in calls to the police: A dilemma. *Discourse Studies 1*, 201–26.

Tracy, K., and Baratz, S. (1993). Intellectual discussion in the academy as situated discourse. *Communication Monographs 60*, 300–20.

Tracy, K., and Baratz, S. (1994). The case for case studies of facework. In S. Ting-Toomey (ed.), *The Challenge of Facework* pp. 287–305. Albany: SUNY Press.

Tracy, K., and Carjuzaa, J. (1993). Identity enactment in intellectual discussion. *Journal of Language and Social Psychology 12*, 171–94.

Tracy, K., and Coupland, N. (eds) (1990). *Multiple Goals in Discourse*. Clevedon: Multilingual Matters.

Tracy, K., and Eisenberg, E. M. (1990/1). Giving criticism: A multiple goals case study. *Research on Language and Social Interaction 24*, 37–70.

Tracy, K., and Muller, N. (1994). Talking about ideas: Academics' beliefs about appropriate communicative practices. *Research on Language and Social Interaction 27*, 319–49.

Tracy, K., and Naughton, J. (1994). The identity work of questioning in intellectual discussion. *Communication Monographs 61*, 281–302.

Tracy, K., and Tracy, S. J. (1998a). Rudeness at 911: Reconceptualizing face and face-attack. *Human Communication Research 25*, 225–51.

Tracy, S. J., and Tracy, K. (1998b). Emotion labor at 911: A case study and theoretical critique. *Journal of Applied Communication 26*, 390–411.

van Dijk, T. A. (ed.) (1985). *Handbook of Discourse Analysis, Vols 1–4*. London: Academic Press.

van Dijk, T. A. (1997a). Discourse as interaction in society. In T. A. van Dijk (ed.), *Discourse as Social Interaction* pp. 1–37. London: Sage.

van Dijk, T. A. (1997b). The study of discourse. In T. A. van Dijk (ed.), *Discourse as Structure and Process* pp. 1–34. London: Sage.

van Eemeren, F. H., Grootendorst, R., Jackson, S., and Jacobs, S. (1993). *Reconstructing Argumentative Discourse*. Tuscaloosa, AL: University of Alabama Press.

Villaume, W., Brown, M. H., Darling, R., Richardson, D., Hawk, R., Henry, D. M., and Reid, T. (1997). Presbycusis and conversation: Elderly interactants adjusting to multiple hearing losses. *Research on Language and Social Interaction 30*, 235–62.

Wieder, D. L. (ed.) (1993). Colloquy: On issues of quantification in conversation analysis. *Research on Language and Social Interaction 26*, 151–226.

Wilson, S. R., Cameron, K. A., Whipple, E. E. (1997). Regulative communication strategies within mother–child interactions: Implications for the study of reflection-enhancing parental communication. *Research on Language and Social Interaction 30*, 73–92.

Yeddes, J. (1996). Playful teasing: Kiddin' on the square. *Discourse and Society 7*, 417–38.

Zahn, C. (1984). A re-examination of conversational repair. *Communication Monographs 51*, 56–66.

38 Discourse and Sociology: Sociology and Discourse

ALLEN GRIMSHAW

0 Introduction

In 1946 I took an introductory chemistry course in a highly regarded engineering school. During the following 13 years I took degrees in anthropology and sociology. I have had little to do with chemistry in the half century since I took the course; I have spent the past four decades deeply involved in teaching and research on society with a particular focus, for more than 30 years, on language in use in social contexts.

In the spring of 1998 I went to hear a chemist colleague deliver a distinguished research lecture on laser analyses of molecular structure. It was fascinating, as is the work of other chemist colleagues in a range of specialties in their discipline. Some social research is also fascinating and "relevant." The difference between chemistry (and *some* of the other physical sciences) and social science disciplines is that most of the topics of interest, questions asked, and methods of contemporary chemistries were seldom even vaguely adumbrated in the text and lectures of my introductory course while *most* concerns, questions, and methods of the social sciences were well limned half a century ago.

0.1 Language in sociology

One possible exception to this observation is that of language (discourse, written and spoken discourse, talk, conversation, and so on) and social life (micro and macro, social structure, social organization, social interaction, and so on); this has been a recent development. While a diverse set of scholars, ranging from the Russian psychologist Vygotsky, studying language acquisition, to a heterogeneous swarm of philosophers of language from Austin to Voloshinov and Wittgenstein, commented on issues of language in society, older readers of this chapter know that attention to language *by sociologists* was modest indeed as recently as the late 1940s. Among disciplinary founders, Durkheim and Weber had little to say about language. Pareto was interested in a range of issues from ambiguity and argument to a Whorfian-like social semantics to language and ideology; his work never attracted much of a following among sociologists. Simmel addressed issues relating to the management of interaction in everyday life, including matters having to do with written and spoken text as interactional resources. Sociologists as early as the 1920s were reading his work; none followed up what would now be seen as sociolinguistic implications. After World War II sociology graduate students in the United States were told about, and in some departments read, Cooley, Dewey, and Mead. The focus was on social psychological issues of self, role, individual, and interaction, but *not* on the part played by language. Most American sociological theorists in the years following World War II were little more interested. Merton, Parsons, Sorokin, and their contemporaries seldom attended to language matters at either the micro- or macrolevels (Parsons did say in 1951 that language is a societal prerequisite). Among sociologists read by most Americans, only Erving Goffman foregrounded language and talk in the early post-war decades. Few sociologists heard of Alfred Schutz, fewer read his work. As recently as the early 1970s there were only two journals specializing on topics considered in this *Handbook*, and anthologies, monographs, and texts numbered in the low hundreds.[1]

There has been a sea change in sociological attention to language since the 1940s. Proportionately far more sociologists are attending to language than were in the 1940s, 1950s, and 1960s.[2] Almost any sociologist's list of influential living theorists would include at least a few from a longer roll including Bourdieu, Collins, Garfinkel, Giddens, Habermas, and Latour – all of whom accord central importance to considerations of language in use in social contexts.[3] Dozens of journals publish hundreds of articles exploring the interrelationships of language and social structures and behaviors. Dozens of handbooks and encyclopedias provide summaries of these articles and additional hundreds of monographs. This great richness notwithstanding, Russell's (1979) characterization remains apposite:

> Psychologists, sociologists, anthropologists, philosophers, and linguists have advanced the study of discourse without the common descriptive terminology, without the shared theoretical or methodological predilections, and without the set of paradigmatic studies around which a unified and cumulative body of knowledge can be constructed. Proliferation of contrasting paradigms in each of the above mentioned disciplines renders the possibility of a comprehensive (and unifying) theory of language extremely remote. (1979)

I do not claim that a unified theory of language in society is imminent; I *will* note below what I consider to be some encouraging/promising developments.

Changes in chemistry and other natural sciences have resulted in part from the discovery of tiny particles and DNA strings and of such astronomical phenomena or possibilities as black holes, quasars, and false vacuums, through a combination of ever-improving instrumentation and imaginative theorizing.[4] In the case of language and society the phenomena of interest have always been accessible; they were, until recently, overlooked.[5] While foundational pieces on humans and language in society began to appear in English in the mid-1960s (e.g. Berger and Luckmann, Cicourel, Garfinkel, and Schutz, with Chomsky's *Aspects* appearing in 1965) and Foucault and Habermas translations early in the following decade, it is my belief that the emergence of the reciprocal interests of my title have resulted as much from demonstration to sociologists of the value of linguistic knowledge and language data (discourse) for sociology, and of sociological knowledge and data for students of language in use, as from direct exposure to these rich but often difficult theorists and philosophers of language.

I have room for no more than a personal sampling of work bearing on discourse–sociology relationships which I have found to be thoughtful and provocative.[6] I begin with an illustration drawn from Urban's work (1991, 1996), employing a "discourse-centered approach to culture" (DCAC), of how ways of talking in a society simultaneously reflect, constitute, and reproduce social organization (including kin relationships), cultural beliefs (including mythology), and norms about everyday living (including those regarding gender relations). I next illustrate how discourse illumines social processes, focusing particularly on the talk of social conflict. I continue with sketches of a sampling of studies of discourse in institutional settings (medical, public, and business) that illumine issues of long-standing sociological concern.[7] I conclude with very brief mention of some unattended questions and demonstrations.

1   Discourse-centered Approach to Culture: An Illustration

Perhaps the most important reason that sociologists and other students of society historically did not attend to language phenomena has been that these phenomena are so central to our lives that we notice them only when they become in some way problematic; for example, through failing hearing, or for American English monolinguals through situations which require coping with other languages. Actually, of course, far more is involved in cross-cultural "coping" than differences in language itself; *Weltanschauung* and perceptual frames may so vary that even with "accurate" translations another culture may be baffling indeed. The following illustrations from Urban's own work and from a range of other apparently quite different researches hopefully provide partial demonstration and some illumination of these complexities.

Urban begins his 1991 book about a small Indian group in Brazil by declaring, "The DCAC is founded on a single proposition: that culture is localized in concrete, publicly accessible signs, the most important of which are actually occurring instances of discourse" (1991: 1); he has published two books dedicated to elucidation/demonstration of this perspective.

Depending upon context, interlocutors, and audiences, English speakers may have a wide variety of collectivities in mind when employing first person plural pronouns (nonexhaustively: age cohort, ethnic group, gender, nationality, political party, religion: I have shown elsewhere (1994) how the ambiguity of pronominal reference in English can be used to manipulate group boundaries). Urban (1996) asserts that "his" people[8] typically use few first person plural pronouns, but that when they do, they use them to make a distinction between "we the living" and "they the dead," and not for the sorts of collections named above. Nor, Urban claims, do these people reference kin in terms of some standardized set of kin terms which reference biological relationships. Rather they draw on a collection of kin terms whose meaning in specific talk is revealed by the ways in which contexting discourse is employed in talking about *relationships*. Urban argues that perceptions are shaped by discourse and, specifically, by discourse that maximally circulates publicly. Nothing terribly controversial in such an observation. But Urban goes on to claim that "to keep discourse circulating at P.I. Ibirama, you must avoid disputable referential content" and "make sure that it cannot be contradicted by immediate experience" (1996: 87). Such a world of discourse is one quite different from that with which we are familiar; and quite different too in behavioral consequences. Urban is not propounding some naive Sapir–Whorfianism. He is demonstrating that differences in discursive practices generate truly different world views and perceptual and interpretive frames. Table 38.1

Table 38.1 Some possible/imagined relationships between discourse/talk and perceptions of the world: Shokleng (P.I. Ibirama) and mother-tongue English-speaking North Americans

Shokleng		*USA English*	
Features of discourse/talk	*World view*	*Features of discourse/talk*	*World view*
Personal pronoun avoidance	Collective as contrasted to individual identity	Widespread use of personal pronouns/ referential ambiguity	Individuation of self
We–they used for alive–dead distinction	Continuity/ sharing rather than difference/ differentiation	We–they for multiple memberships	Recognition of social heterogeneity
Careful formulation of talk to avoid exposure to contradiction from hearers	Blurring of biological kin relations – foregrounding of ceremonial (fictive) and socially recognized relationships	Frequent challenge of facts, opinions	Emphasis on empirical accuracy – believability *or* obfuscation *or* recognition of speaker challengeability
Eschewing of personal narrative(s)	The world is stable	Personal narrative salient	Foregrounding of cause–effect relations/ recognition of continuity with change
Mode of learning origin myths	Truncation of temporal axis/ history repeats itself	Constant decentering of text	Nothing is as it appears

suggests some contrasts between Shokleng and English-speaking North Americans in perceptions of the world – and the rootedness of those perceptions in discourse practices.

1.1   Different theories for differing discourse

Consider an example closer to home. People attentive to talk would not argue nowadays that there are no differences between the ways men and women talk in contemporary American society. It is indisputable, moreover, that women in American society are relatively disadvantaged compared to men. What *is* in dispute is whether gender differences in discourse are best explained as resulting from differences in male and female *culture* (as Tannen 1992 uses the term) or from differences in male and female *power* (Troemel-Ploetz 1991; see also Thorne and Henley 1975; Thorne et al. 1983). Troemel-Ploetz appears to believe that men (specifically middle-class white American males) act and talk with the end of domination (or accommodating to the greater power of other males) and are not interested in more successful cross-gender communication – females can just accommodate. Tannen agrees that power and domination are important considerations in all talk but argues that problems in cross-gender communication occur because of differences in the very understanding of what talk is all about, such that, for example, even males wanting to be supportive when females express discomfort simply do not know how (i.e. males give suggestions about what to do while women want to be told that what has happened or is happening is really a bad thing).

Urban's view is more complex. According to the DCAC perspective, if people are exposed to the same discourses, they ought to have the possibility of abstracting from those discourses/signs a shared framework. His explanation for continuing difficulties in cross-gender communication stems from the conclusion – based on the circulation notion – that there must *not* be wholly shared access to public signs, that there must be some measure of differential circulation among men and women, out of which the social organizational difference is precipitated. In short, differential circulation of discourse within a larger community of more or less shared public signs leads to crystallization of the social categories of "men" and "women." Urban suggests that the "power" solution only displaces the problem from the level of circulation (its empirical locus) and gives the false image that the asymmetry exists outside of circulatory processes, and, moreover, is probably immutable. He finds such a view wrong and cites major shifts in the US since the 1960s as evidence of changes in social organization and concomitant circulatory patterns – with the former perhaps being a consequence of the latter.

Tannen's view of cross-gender discourse differences is consonant with Urban's DCAC and differences of Brazilian Indian culture and discourse from that of the North American English of both men and women. Urban foregrounds the importance of public circulation of discourse. Troemel-Ploetz issues a call to the gender barricades. The implications for differently understanding relations between discourse and social organization are immense.

1.2 *Different modes, codes, ways of talking, and so on, within languages/cultures*

Many sociologists and linguists now share quite sophisticated awareness of class and regional dialectal differences in speech; there is increasing attention to differences in opportunities which often accompany those in speech production. More importantly for present purposes, scholars in several disciplines have identified distinctions in discourse fairly directly related to immediate interactional outcomes and, perhaps, to cultural reproduction as well. Space permits only brief mention of some categorizations which help in understanding discourse in society.

In the late 1950s Bernstein[9] began to publish papers on differences in educational and familial discourse as shaped by social class in England. Over the next 30 years or so he addressed more and more encompassing themes beginning with a public–formal language distinction which evolved into his well-known (but less understood) elaborated and restricted codes (less and more context-dependent utterances, respectively), to classification and frame as modes of organizing knowledge, to, ultimately, issues of the very reproduction of society and culture. Bernstein came to argue that realizations of elaborated and restricted code manifested in specific texts (speech utterances) are simultaneously: (1) the *result* of the location of specific social actors with reference to class (and therefore to different "control modes") and practices of agencies of transmission, and (2) a *basis* for maintenance of class (and privilege) through symbolic differentiation in thought ways and *Weltanschauung* (Bernstein uses the term "mental structures"). It could be argued that such a perspective is not incompatible with DCAC.[10]

In the mid-1970s Lakoff (1975) identified differences between men's and women's talk, which came to be labeled "powerful" and "powerless" speech and initiated disputes over interpretation and implied tactics, which continue (see above). Then O'Barr (1982) and his associates discovered that many of the differences identified were isomorphic to those between the courtroom speech of witnesses of different social class and education, which generated differences in credibility such that, for example, hesitancy or hedging or other manifestations of uncertainty are seen as indicators that witness evidence is less trustworthy. O'Barr's findings are again compatible with Urban's DCAC – they further underline the critical importance of context in influencing both the production and interpretation of speech.

1.3 Intra*textual difference, multivocality, entextualization, decentering*

I have been talking about how differences in discourse in use across different societies/cultures and in different subcultures within societies/cultures result in differences in societal features as wide-ranging as collective identity (who *is* "we"), gender-related self-esteem, and maintenance of class privilege. Another group of scholars has been looking not at different texts in different contexts but at differences (in several senses) of *"same"* texts.

Silverman and Torode (1980) organize their approach to text analysis around three polarities: (1) "appearance–reality" as manifested in actual texts;[11] (2) what theorists of language say and actually do *in their own texts*, and; (3) "interpretation versus interruption" as modes of textual analysis. Interruption denies the "conventional assertion" of the neutrality of language in use; it attempts by "political intervention" to make explicit the "political choices" which are made in using language. Most discourse – whether in everyday interaction, fiction, or scholarship – takes for granted such epistemological assumptions as subject–object relations and linear causality. Interruption of discourse can provide access to the "reality" referenced by "appearances." Identification of multiple "voices" is one result of interruption; attention to multivocality has implications for highly productive theoretical developments in linguistics (inter alia, problems of reference, coreference, referential ambiguity, and textual cohesion), sociology (inter alia, role, reference groups, self, and identity), and sociolinguistics, especially pragmatics and issues of multifunctionality in utterances. Silverman and Torode focus especially on theorists of language,[12] but they also comment on the work of students of talk, including Labov and Sacks – and Kafka. Any social actor (or analyst) who asks "what is meant by what is being said" (Cicourel 1974; Grimshaw 1989; Labov and Fanshel 1977) or who is interested in how text is related to social organization or ideology may well end up "interrupting."

A second variety of difference in sameness is that examined by Silverstein and Urban and their colleagues (1996) in their practice of what has come to be labeled "decentering of text." Some of what "decenterers" do is very much like the "interruption" of Silverman and Torode. A deeply interesting dimension is added, however, by scrutiny of a "same" text in different manifestations; for example, an original oral rendition, electronic recording, phonetic transcription, transcription in original language and in translation. Consider, further, these different renditions incorporated in one or both languages into oral scholarly presentations, scholarly and popular papers, presentation to the original informant or performer, or whatever. The meaning of such a text, as perceived by both emitters and audiences, will be influenced by a host of variables including contexts of text and of situation (as conceptualized by, e.g., Cicourel 1994; Duranti and Goodwin 1992; Halliday and Hasan 1989; Hymes' SPEAKING heuristic 1974) and others, from Collins's (1981) "irreducible macrofactors" (for present purposes (1) the dispersion of individuals in physical *space*, (2) the amount of *time* that social processes take, and (3) the *numbers* of individuals involved *and* Collins's argument that people are all participants in chains of interaction in which, in every situation, interactional resources are gained, maintained, or lost) to Goffman's participation statuses (1974). Contemplate how different history would have been and how different our world, absent certain discourses, *or* with different readings/interpretations of discourses which have occurred. Consider how carefully lawyers study contracts looking for possible variant interpretations – or diplomats and the military study treaties, or critics prose and poetry. Consider further again the complexities added when contracts or treaties are intended to regulate behaviors of parties of different languages/cultures[13] or critics to assess productions in translation, or, still further, when notes employed in generating the several varieties of texts are available for use in the search for meaning(s). The value of discourse for understanding society and vice versa is evident.

2 Discourse and Social Processes – Discourse in Social Process

Most non-language-oriented sociologists asked about possible usefulness of language data would probably suggest not revelation of cultural differences through discourse (see above) or substantive illumination of institutions/organizations (see below) but investigation of face-to-face interaction.[14] Such research *is* important and increasingly visible, in the now generally recognized specialty of conversation analysis (CA), in interdisciplinary study of discourse associated with specific social processes such as social conflict or negotiation, and in research directed to specification of "interactional moves" in ongoing interaction. CA is discussed elsewhere (see Schegloff, this volume); I here briefly mention propositional studies of conflict talk.[15]

2.1 Immersion, {multiple/serial} cases, verstehen: exploratory, summary, and testable propositions

Persuasive and compelling dramatic and other fictional renderings of the discourse of conflict have been around for millennia. While there are long traditions of research on social conflict (and other social processes), until fairly recently scholarly attention to what is *said* in conflictful interaction has been modest (there *were* studies of written diplomatic exchanges in periods leading up to war). As recently as 1983 Goldman critically remarked the absence of "even *one* complete dispute transcript";[16] in the years since, hundreds of audio-, film, and videorecordings and transcriptions of these records (at least some of them "complete" – whatever that may mean)[17] have been published and/or archived in equal numbers of articles, chapters in collections, and individual monographs (see, illustratively, references in Brenneis, 1988; Grimshaw, 1990a).

There are hundreds of propositional statements about social conflict; they vary very considerably in scope, specificity, elegance, and rigor of formulation, are drawn from both contemporary and historical case studies, experiments, and statistical analyses, and are informed by perspectives from all the social and clinical sciences as well as the humanities (again illustratively, see Coser 1956; Dahrendorf 1957; Mack and Snyder 1957; Williams 1947). Similar distillation has not been attempted with studies of conflict talk; I believe formulation of summary and, ultimately, testable propositions is a feasible and potentially highly productive enterprise.

I can here illustrate only instances of discourse rules, propositions, and testable propositions or hypotheses (the following discussion draws heavily on chapter 13 of my 1990).

2.1.1 Discourse/(conversational, interactional) rules

Labov and Fanshel (1977, henceforward LF) formulate their discourse rules as "if . . . then" propositions. Many disputes include assignment of blame or responsibility (see especially Fillmore 1971). A discourse rule for this behavior might look like the following:

01. *Rule for assigning blame (responsibility).*[18] If A asserts B should and could have performed a behavior X_1, but wilfully did not, or that he should and could have avoided performing a behavior X_2, but nonetheless wilfully performed it, then A is heard as blaming B for the non-occurrence or occurrence of X_1 or X_2 respectively.

2.1.2   Observational propositions or postulates

In 1989 I formulated a set of summary propositions or postulates about how the sociological variables of (1) relations of power and (2) of affect and (3) outcome characteristics influence (determine would be too strong; there are, for example, important contextual constraints) choice of ways of talking to get things socially accomplished. Analogous rules about conflict talk might look like the following (adapted from Grimshaw 1990b):

02. Probability of an initial move varies directly with a potential initiator's perception of his or her stake in a possible outcome and with the initiator's power relative to that of a potential opponent;
03. The "taking up" of an oppositional move (i.e. occurrence of conflict talk) varies directly with an offended party's perception of her or his stake in a possible outcome and with the party's power relative to that of the offending party;
. . .
06. Within the range of conflict-talk modes available because of power considerations, specific selection is constrained by the interaction of relations of affect, perceived stakes, likely third party (audience) reactions, and so on.

2.1.3   Testable propositions/(hypotheses?)

Such (and further) specification of observations[19] allows formulation of testable propositions like the following:

07. A will not attempt to avoid a dispute (or need to) if A has the power to overcome B *and* is willing to risk generation of negative affect (in self, in B, in self–B relations, or possibly in other interactants or bystanders).

Successful verification or falsification of propositions about conflict (or other varieties of) talk and establishment of links among validated propositions are steps toward theory construction and an ultimate goal of what Hymes (1974) has called a "unified/ [integrated] theory of sociolinguistic description."[20]

3   What about Paradigms? Now? Soon? Ever?

As I observed earlier, I do not believe it can be said that the massive increase in attention to language matters by sociologists and other social scientists in recent years either constitutes or reflects a new paradigm in the social sciences. Indeed, I am not at all certain that there *are* either dominant or competing paradigms in the social sciences (it might be argued that social psychological and social structural perspectives are such competing paradigms). To a very substantial extent, what seems to go on in social behavioral studies and specifically in work on language in use in social contexts seems closer to what Kuhn could have characterized as "pre normal science" (*not* his term):

> In the absence of a paradigm or some candidate for paradigm, all of the facts that could possibly pertain to the development of a given science are likely to seem equally relevant. As a result, early fact-gathering is a far more nearly random activity than the one subsequent scientific development makes familiar. Furthermore, in the absence of a reason for seeking some particular form of more recondite information, early fact-gathering is usually restricted to the wealth of data that lie close to hand. (1970: 15)[21]

There is no dearth of theoretical perspectives on language in use in social contexts. Heuristics (e.g. Hymes's 1974 SPEAKING acronym), proto theories (e.g. Garfinkel's 1967 original ethnomethodology), theories of the middle range (e.g. the Bourdieu–Bernstein conceptualization of cultural reproduction, Brown and Levinson's 1978 on politeness phenomena, or Cicourel's 1974 cognitive sociology), and sensitizing perspectives (e.g. Gumperz's 1982 interpretive sociolinguistics, sometimes also called interactional sociolinguistics or referred to as the theory of conversational inference – see Gumperz, this volume; Gumperz and Hymes's 1972 ethnography of speaking) abound.[22] However, while many articles and monographs informed by one or another or several of these orientations are published, many (perhaps most) publications on discourse and society consist not of the testing and extension of theories or of paradigms but rather of observation, description, and documentation of constituent elements of talk as employed in social interaction. I believe much study of discourse has not progressed beyond collection and classification of interesting specimens (I hasten to acknowledge that such collection and classification lie at the foundation of all theoretical work).

I devote my remaining space to three promising exceptions,[23] namely, (1) employ of comprehensive discourse analysis (CDA) in study of interactional accomplishment in ongoing conversational discourse, (2) study of narrative and employ of text analysis more generally to study stability, conflict, and change in cultural, economic, political, and social institutions, and (3) demonstration of the value of Collins's formulation of "micro foundations of macro sociology" through intensive examination of discourse within business organizations.

3.1   Comprehensive discourse analysis

Immediately after the pessimistic portrayal of prospects for a comprehensive and unifying theory of language in society cited above (section 0.1), Russell continues with the following characterization of Labov and Fanshel's (LF) *Therapeutic Discourse*:

> Amidst such diversity, points of theoretical convergence are sufficiently rare, or abstract, or short-lived to seriously deter sustained empirical applications. One would not expect a meticulous empirical investigation of fifteen minutes of discourse to provocatively engage, not only the specific theoretical propositions with which it is motivated, but approaches to discourse analysis and interpretation that have little

more in common than their avowed concern with linguistic performance. . . . LF is just such a work. (1979: 176)

While both predecessors and followers of LF have looked at conversation in its social context(s), LF differ in the explicitness with which they foreground their concern to extend the scope of linguistic analysis to conversation as a whole (i.e. being "account-able to an entire body of conversation, attempting to account for interpretations of all utterances and the coherent sequencing between them" (Labov and Fanshel 1977: 354)). Their ambitious agenda includes apprehending the relation between what is said and what is meant *and* how things get socially accomplished with talk. In the course of this project LF found themselves involved in ever-evolving editing of their target text as they attended to fields of discourse, paralinguistic cues (including "key"), knowledge shared by interactants, sequencing, and so on, in order to identify expansions of text (what is "actually" being said/meant), propositions (recurrent communications), rules of discourse, and interactional moves. LF generated an array of innovative and well-honed methodological conceptualizations, clear specification of risks of their approach, and a clearer understanding of what gets done in the therapeutic interview *and* demonstration of how that done is socially accomplished than had been previously available.

LF recognized that similar studies of other types of conversations would neces-sarily antecede efforts at constructing a unified theory of conversational description. Such studies consume prodigious amounts of time and energy – my four studies[24] of a 12-minute sound–image record of three to five participants involved in a disserta-tion defense engaged me for more than ten years;[25] few (if any) other investigators have taken up LF's challenge. My CDA studies of the dissertation defense allowed me to both (1) promulgate *sociological* propositions about processes of social evalu-ation, conflict talk, and social boundary work and about communicative nonsuccess, and (2) identify sociological *constraints* on language in use in social contexts. CDA remains an unexploited richness.

3.2   *Narrative and textual analysis*[26]

Since its original publication in 1967 Labov and Waletsky's (1997, hereafter LW) specification of the structure of narrative has been both inspiration and guide for investigators from across a range of disciplines; the more than 50 authors who contributed to Bamberg's (1997) volume on the impact of LW across the intervening years represent linguistics and language and literature programs as well as those in psychology, the social sciences, and special programs ranging from child develop-ment to ethnic studies (see Johnstone, this volume). This broad appeal and influence notwithstanding, Labov wrote (in his contribution to the anniversary volume):

> The discussion of narrative and other speech events at the discourse level rarely allows us to prove anything. It is essentially a hermeneutic study, in which con-tinued engagement with the discourse as it was delivered gains entrance to the perspective of the speaker and the audience, tracing the transfer of information and experience in a way that deepens our own understanding of what language and social life are all about. (1997: 396)

I believe that the following examples demonstrate that Labov has been too modest.

Two principal motivations driving the development of CDA were Fanshel's concern to better understand and thereby to improve what goes on in therapeutic interviews, and Labov's to better understand conversation. Lyotard's (1984; see also Jameson 1984) motivation to develop a theory (philosophy?) of narrative sprang in part from his dissatisfaction with contemporary views on "legitimation," "paradigm," "postmodernism," "science," "truth and falsity," and a bundle of more and less closely related emergent and redefined concepts. His aim is to investigate the nature of postmodern knowledge, the bases of assertion of priority in claims of legitimacy of science, logic, and narrative, and the somewhat antinomian employ of narrative in popularizing science, and to raise a variety of interesting questions relating to different varieties of training (with unmentioned implications for Bernstein's (*passim*) elaborated and restricted codes and classification and framing of knowledge) and the nature of universities.

Lyotard invokes real-world cases only anecdotally.[27] Barbara Czarniawska and Bruno Latour, in contrast, have quite different conceptualizations of narrative and of its usefulness in social analysis, but are alike in that they focus heavily on empirical cases.

Czarniawska (1997)[28] bases her analyses on discourse materials produced in and about Swedish public organizations, including inter alia: (1) autobiographies and biographies, (2) speeches of varying levels of formality, (3) conversations, (4) interviews, (5) bureaucratic memos, (6) annual reports, (7) budgets, and (8) media coverage. She seeks to demonstrate a central descriptive and analytic role, *for the study of organizations*, of stories/narratives and a dramaturgical perspective. She does this via depoliticization of Lyotard and employ of resources of anthropology, literary theory, and the institutional school within sociology. Change is a major focus for Czarniawska and she demonstrates nicely how *stories*, *themes*, and *serials* can be employed to elucidate the role of "good" and "bad" friction in social change, how new and old ways of acting have been integrated, and how new processes of "companyization" and "computerization" change the workplaces of individuals as well as the larger bureaucratic landscape. In her 1999 study Czarniawska pursues her interest in organization by investigating organizational theory as a literary genre.

Latour focuses not on narratives produced by organizational members and others who have stakes in an organization's performance, which themselves constitute data for the study of those organizations, but, rather, on narratives about events and "actants" (see Linde, this volume).[29] His Actant Network Theory posits outcomes which result from interaction of a sweeping range of "things," including human actors, machines, and fiscal structures (see n. 29). In his study/story about a failed technological project called Aramis (Latour 1996b; see also Laurier and Philo 1999), intended to provide a massively innovative and efficient modern mass transport system for Paris, Latour collects data similar to that employed by Czarniawska but uses it to demonstrate how, among other things, Aramis itself became a player with goals and aspirations, subject to disappointment, and even deliberately resisting behaviors of other participants (including human ones). In an earlier study of Pasteur's work on lactic acid (1992), Latour demonstrated how a literary perspective on scientific texts can illuminate in new ways issues which are at the heart of sociological concern in *that* variety of interaction between human and nonhuman "actants." While I am sufficiently traditional to be skeptical indeed about the notion of nonhuman actants being volitional and able to experience emotions (note again Latour's denial that such ascription is metaphorical), it is hard to deny that behavior involving the sort of actants he identified (note 29) can be compellingly engrossing.[30]

Studies focused on other varieties of narratives have pursued different analytic and theoretical ends. Agar (e.g. 1980; Agar and Hobbs 1982) looked at an extensive life history of a heroin addict, with, amongst others, ends of identifying themes and stories, cultural and subcultural knowledge required to understand life histories, and life histories as careers. More recently (1997), Ries collected conversational narratives about economic catastrophes and food and commodity shortages and strategies in Perestroika-era Moscow, with an end to portraying a Russian (Moscow) culture of complaint, disappointment, and resignation.[31] With only occasional exceptions (e.g. Czarniawska 1997: 145ff); these authors' analyses of discourse material are very different from the CDA of LF or the CA-influenced project of Boden described immediately below; all demonstrate persuasively the value of discourse (and specifically of narrative) in investigation of sociological questions – and of sociological theory in elucidating meanings of discourse.

3.3   *Microfoundations and institutional stability and change*

In the late 1960s I had a continuing argument with Harvey Sacks and his conversation analysis (CA) associates. I told them I found their work highly original, exciting, and of great potential value to sociology, and urged them to integrate CA methods and concepts into more traditional sociology – simultaneously showing how traditional sociological concepts and perspectives could help in interpreting CA findings. Sacks's response was that he *was* doing sociology, that what I wanted him to do was not relevant to *his* sociology, and that sooner or later all but the most stubborn of the rest of us would come to accept his vision.

Increasing numbers of researchers across the social sciences (and the humanities) have come to value CA as an approach to everyday talk; only recently has a CA-trained sociologist undertaken to *demonstrate* the value of talk as data for studying fundamental sociological questions such as how social organization is constituted, reproduced, and modified – and how members contribute to that constitution, reproduction and modification through talk – in what may appear to be singularly mundane and unremarkable interaction. Boden (1994),[32] like Czarniawska, studies organizations; her interest similarly is to demonstrate the centrality of spoken and written discourse in organizational life. Some of her data are the same; not her analyses.[33]

Boden's demonstration is persuasive. Using audiorecorded talk from telephone calls and meetings of varying levels of formality, collected in organizations ranging from a travel agency and a local television station through hospitals and a university administrative department to the Oval Office, Boden shares with her readers her understanding of the (sometimes) extraordinarily delicate but analytically identifiable ways in which talk is employed to "inform, amuse, update, gossip, review, reassess, reason, instruct, revise, argue, debate, contest, and actually *constitute* the moments, myths and, through time, the very *structuring* of [the] organization" (1994: 8; cf. LF on interactional terms). The dawning awareness of an accountant that physicians in different departments might differently view policy change that could improve a hospital's overall revenue position but reduce "their" money (1994: 58ff) is a nice case in point.[34]

Boden shows how members of organizations can at the same time account for their behaviors in terms of a "rational actor" model and be unaware of how actual decision-making is accomplished incrementally, in fragments of unremembered and individually unremarkable chat, rather than by focused weighing of "rational" considerations. Boden simultaneously shows how concurrent and articulated employ of the previously segregated conceptual apparatuses of general sociology and of CA (e.g. adjacency organization, agenda, bracketing, placement, sequence (*centrally and critically*), turn, and so on) is mutually enhancing. Boden argues that stages of (1) collection of actual talk, (2) identification of sequentiality in that talk, and (3) discovery in the talk and its sequentiality of the fundamental stuff and fundamentals of organization (4) allow/contribute to sociological theory at levels of considerable abstractness (1994: 206ff). While it may please neither Boden nor Collins, I find in Boden's study a nice *demonstration* of Collins's (1981) "microfoundations of macrosociology" perspective. Valuable complementarity is again evident.

4 More Questions

I hope that this eclectic sampling of new developments linking discourse and sociology will whet readers' appetites.[35] Many critical questions about sociology–discourse relations have not even been dimly adumbrated. Consider only two questions central to sociological concerns, answers to which either require, or are at least more easily understood with, discourse (or text, or utterance, and so on) data. What, for example, is the relationship between the talk (or written communication) of interacting individuals or small groups (a concern of microsociology) and matters of language spread, maintenance, decline, loyalty, standardization, conflict, and so on (concerns of macrosociology)? Relatedly, how do cultures and societies (and for that matter, languages) reproduce themselves – or change?

NOTES

Thanks are due to colleagues Tom Gieryn, Kate O'Donnel, Ron Scollon, Greg Urban and, especially, Michael Silverstein, and are gratefully given. None of them (or others I may have consulted and then forgotten) is responsible for my skimpy attention to non-USA and other specific literatures. Several complained about it.

1 Curiously, an innovative text published right after the war (LaPiere 1946) treated not only language topics but matters of war (another topic generally neglected by sociologists) as well. It apparently disappeared without a trace.

2 I find hyperbolic Lemert's (1979: 184) characterization of the situation of the early 1970s as one in which "language has become the prominent topic in sociology"; he elsewhere in the same treatment states more soberly, "it is not a surprise that a sociology living

and working in the twilight of man has begun cautiously to turn to language" (1979: 229). I agree with Lemert that a sea change does not constitute a paradigm shift.

3   My own list would include theorists such as Basil Bernstein, Aaron Cicourel, and Thomas Luckmann, who have been more closely identified with issues of discourse and sociology.

4   It is interesting that when *U.S. News and World Report* initiated a section on science in June 1998, the first topic explored was baby talk. It is also interesting that the focus was on nonsocial dimensions of the phenomenon. In seeking scientific status and public interest at the same time, the authors emphasized a "nature" versus "nurture" dichotomy which could not currently be characterized as central to language studies.

5   One reader labels this characterization as "nonsense," stating that the situations and changes in situations are/have been "exactly the same" in the two disciplines – or in sociology at different points in time. Perhaps.

6   I have written in other places on criteria for handbook articles. One criterion is completeness of coverage. Such coverage is not possible in a chapter of the length assigned me. Moreover, I was told by the editors that a piece touching on unresolved issues and new directions of research would be more appropriate than a literature review. I *have* covered a wider range of issues in other places.

7   I have discussed several of these and other defining issues elsewhere. See, e.g. my 1974, 1992 (causal perspectives), 1973a, 1973b, 1981 (rules and other regularities), 1987a (sociology of language versus sociolinguistics), and 1987b (micro and macro dimensions). Many of

these issues are treated at some length in the introductory and concluding chapters of the Multiple Analysis Project volumes (Grimshaw 1989; Grimshaw et al. 1994).

8   Called Shokleng in Urban (1991) and referenced as "people of P.I. (Posta Indígena) Ibirama" in Urban (1996). What these people are to be called itself constitutes a problem of labeling – and perception.

9   Collected in Bernstein's 1971 and 1975 volumes. On the characterization on the place of text in Bernstein's maturing theory which appears at the end of this paragraph, see my 1976.

10 Nor, Michael Silverstein has observed (personal communication), with Bakhtinian "voice" effects in heteroglossia.

11 In their perspective there *is* a world of "reality" constituted by material relations and an infinitely large number of symbolic characterizations or "appearances" of that world. The folk view that the relation between "reality" and "appearance" is isomorphic is wrong.

12 Althusser, Austin, Barthes, Bernstein, Culler, Derrida, Foucault, Habermas, Heidegger, Hussell, Schutz, Vološinov, and Wittgenstein, among others.

13 On diplomatic negotiation, see, e.g., Smith's (1989) intriguing examination of USA–USSR negotiations; on negotiation by high-ranking military officers see Grimshaw (1992a).

14 Sociologists are increasingly aware of literatures on variation in speech production, especially those associated with class and gender (Scherer and Giles 1979 is a useful early collection; Peter Trudgill continues to write on socially based differentiation in speech production) and even with institution-based researches such as those of

Czarniawska and Boden, to be discussed shortly. However, most sociologists tend to perceive research on language in terms of conversation analysis or of studies of social interaction as manifest in talk in small groups.

15 Reference to interactional moves is made below. On constraining sociological variables, see my 1989.

16 Minimally a hyperbolic claim (one perhaps less charitable reader characterized the term complete as "nonsensical"). Scheflen (1973) included not only a full "lexical" transcript of a four-party therapeutic session but also a transcription of a film record. More detailed transcriptions were made available even earlier as part of the Natural History of an Interview project. See, more recently, Merlan and Rumsey (1991).

17 On the chimera of completeness, see inter alia Grimshaw et al. (1994: *passim*) (including the discussion there of the Natural History of the Interview project and its attempt to generate a "complete" transcript), Cicourel (1994), Lucy (1993), and Silverstein and Urban (1996). Articles in the Lucy and in the Silverstein and Urban volumes are abundantly suggestive of new questions on the topic of this article and rich in identification of directions in which research directed to answering those questions could profitably be pursued. A useful discussion of these materials would require far more space than is available in this handbook chapter.

18 Michael Silverstein (personal communication), who like other readers is uncomfortable with the use of "propositional" in talking about ways of talking, suggests, "this utterance form *counts as* 'assigning blame' or 'blaming.'" He observes

that a "rule" for identifying praise might look quite similar. That is, in part, the point.

19 For example, specification of considerations of intensity, hostility, and violence. Grimshaw (1990a) includes an attempt to formulate propositions about relations among external threat, internal cohesion, and invocation of external threat in attempts to recruit allies in the course of conflict talk.

20 There is no space in this brief chapter on some new (or recast) ways of looking at relationships among linguistics, sociolinguistics, and sociology and their common resource of discourse to address hoary issues of similarities and differences in treatment of regularities of behavior. Terms such as explanation, law, norm, principle, proposition, regularity, rule, universal, and their variants, with modifiers such as absolute, variable, statistical, substantive, and so on, have not traveled well across disciplinary boundaries. Nor is there agreement on discovery procedures.

21 Kuhn continues by observing that technological improvements have often been vital in the development of new sciences. Studies of language in use in social contexts in any of their currently familiar forms would not be possible without modern electronic equipment.

22 Halliday's systemic-functional theory (various; see also de Joia and Stenton 1980) is perhaps the most comprehensive in terms of coverage of looking at what utterances *do* and how; the perspective does not appear to have generated a wide following in the United States. In Halliday's own hands the theory is highly illuminating; see, especially his 1994. In any case, however productive the theory, it has not been articulated in a

manner which makes it possible to consider it paradigmatic.

23   Space constraints make it impossible for me to more than mention a number of other profoundly thoughtful, exciting, and promising projects. Among omissions particularly disappointing to me and to early readers: (1) the language and identity industry generated by Anderson (1991), (2) the rich emerging literature on language and ideology, and (3) so-called "critical discourse analysis" and related topics of language and social control. All these topics are, as a favorite teacher used to say, "inextricably interrelated and intertwined." See also research in the volumes cited in n. 17.

24   Of (1) negotiation of an evaluation, (2) communicative nonsuccess, (3) conflict, and (4) employ of referential ambiguity in pronominal usage in social boundary work (see Grimshaw 1989; Grimshaw et al. 1994).

25   A more complete (comprehensiveness is an unattainable goal) analysis of a contextually situated conversation than is usually possible can be essayed through having multiple analysts investigate the same sound–image data record. My studies were part of the Multiple Analysis Project (Grimshaw et al. 1994) in which nine independent scholars did eight studies of the dissertation defense materials. See McQuown (1971), Zabor (1978), or chapter 1 in Grimshaw et al. (1994) for a pioneering collaborative project, The Natural History of an Interview.

26   See, again, section 1.3.

27   For this reason Silverstein (personal communication) prefers Latour as empirically foundational.

28   For a marginally more detailed characterization of Czarniawska's excellent book, see my 1998.

29   An "actant" is any entity, human or otherwise, and including not just other sentient beings such as animals, but also corporate entities (the IRS, workplaces, countries) events (Christmas, weddings, deadlines), things in nature (Mount Everest, Hurricane Andrew, the Black Death, environmental pollution), ideas, ideologies, and obsessions (salvation, independence, justice, mathematical proofs), and everything else in the world. Latour wants to assign greater autonomy to nonhumans and less to humans in all events; he says he uses the notion "actant" nonmetaphorically.

30   While less specifically oriented to literary perspectives and matters of discourse, Latour's (1996a) examination of interaction in a baboon troop is also fascinating, provocative, and highly sociological in its implications.

31   Ries reports that her conversational partners were not interested in suggestions (or questions) about ameliorative actions, and greeted "What can be done?" queries with silence – followed by more "horror stories." Examination of responses of action or resignation in other shortage situations such as wartime sieges or protracted drought should be useful.

32   I again draw on my review. See my 1995.

33   CA methods are increasingly employed by sociologists. Atkinson and Drew (1979) on court proceedings, Maynard (1984) on plea bargaining, and Goodwin (1990) on black children's play groups are impressive examples. These studies do not as directly as Boden foreground the epistemological issues implied by Sacks's posture as limned above (see, for example, Boden 1994: 214–15).

34 Michael Silverstein (personal communication) suggests that the physicians themselves may not be conscious of why they take one or another position.

35 Nn. 17 and 23 refer to a number of exciting and as yet undone researches. Anyone doubting that there are exciting things to study at the intersection of discourse and sociology should carefully read Steiner (1992). The book is putatively about issues of translation but filled with observations and notions about language in use in social contexts.

REFERENCES

Agar, Michael (1980). Stories, background knowledge and themes: problems in the analysis of life history narratives. *American Ethnologist*, 7, 223–39.

Agar, Michael and Jerry R. Hobbs (1982). Interpreting discourse: coherence and the analysis of ethnographic interviews. *Discourse Processes*, 5, 1–32.

Anderson, Benedict R. O. (1991, 1983). *Imagined Communities: Reflections on the Origin and Spread of Nationalism*. London: Verso.

Atkinson, J. Maxwell and Paul Drew (1979). *Order in Court: The Organisation of Verbal Interaction in Judicial Settings*. Atlantic Highlands: Humanities Press.

Bamberg, Michael G. W. (ed.) (1997). Oral versions of personal experience: three decades of narrative analysis. Special issue, *Journal of Narrative and Life History*, 7 (Numbers 1–4).

Berger, Peter L. and Thomas Luckman (1962). *The Social Construction of Reality: A Treatise in the Sociology of Knowledge*. New York: Doubleday.

Bernstein, Basil (1971). *Class, Codes and Control 1: Theoretical Studies Toward a Sociology of Language*. London: Routledge and Kegan Paul.

Bernstein, Basil (1975). *Class, Codes and Control 3: Towards a Theory of Educational Transmissions*. London: Routledge and Kegan Paul.

Boden, Deirdre (1994). *The Business of Talk: Organizations in Action*. Cambridge: Polity.

Brenneis, Donald (1988). Language and disputing. *Annual Review of Anthropology*, 17, 221–37.

Brown, Penelope and Stephen Levinson. (1978). Universals in language usage: politeness phenomena. In Esther N. Goody (ed.), *Questions and Politeness: Strategies in Social Interaction* (pp. 56–289, 295–310). Cambridge: Cambridge University Press.

Chomsky, Noam (1965) *Aspects of the Theory of Syntax*. Cambridge: MIT Press.

Cicourel, Aaron V. (1964). *Method and Measurement in Sociology*. New York: Free Press.

Cicourel, Aaron V. (1974). *Cognitive Sociology: Language and Meaning in Social Interaction*. New York: Free Press.

Cicourel, Aaron V. (1994). Theoretical and methodological suggestions for using discourse to recreate aspects of social structure. In Allen D. Grimshaw, Peter J. Burke, Aaron V. Cicourel, Steven Feld, Jenny Cook-Gumperz, Charles J. Fillmore, John J. Gumperz, Ruqaiya Hasan, Michael A. K. Halliday, David Jenness, and Lily Wong Fillmore, *What's Going on Here? Complementary Studies of Professional Talk*, Vol. 2 of the Multiple Analysis

Project (pp. 61–94). Norwood, NJ: Ablex.

Collins, Randall (1981). On the microfoundations of macrosociology. *American Journal of Sociology*, 86, 984–1014.

Coser, Lewis A. (1956). *The Functions of Social Conflict*. Glencoe: Free Press.

Czarniawska, Barbara (1997). *Narrating the Organization: Dramas of Institutional Identity*. Chicago: University of Chicago Press.

Czarniawska, Barbara (1999). *Writing Management: Organization Theory as a Literary Genre*. Oxford: Oxford University Press.

Dahrendorf, Ralf (1957). *Class and Class Conflict in Industrial Society*. Stanford: Stanford University Press.

De Joia, Alex and Adrian Stenton (1980). *Terms in Systemic Linguistics: A Guide to Halliday*. New York: St. Martin's Press.

Duranti, Alessandro and Charles Goodwin (eds) (1992) *Rethinking Context: Language as an Interactive Phenomenon*. Cambridge: Cambridge University Press.

Fillmore, Charles J. (1971). Verbs of judging: an exercise in semantic description. In Charles J. Fillmore and D. Terence Langendoen (eds), *Studies in Linguistic Semantics*. New York: Holt, Rhinehart and Winston.

Garfinkel, Harold (1967). *Studies in Ethnomethodology*. Englewood Cliffs: Prentice-Hall.

Goffman, Erving (1974). *Frame Analysis*. New York: Harper and Row.

Goldman, Laurence (1983). *Talk Never Dies: The Language of Huli Disputes*. London: Tavistock Publications.

Goodwin, Marjorie Harness (1990). *He-Said She-Said: Talk as Social Organization among Black Children*. Bloomington: Indiana University Press.

Grimshaw, Allen D. (1973a). Rules in linguistic, social and sociolinguistic systems and possibilities for a unified

theory. In Roger W. Shuy (ed.), *Twenty-third Annual Roundtable, Monograph Series on Language and Linguistics (1972)* (pp. 289–312). Washington, DC: Georgetown University Press.

Grimshaw, Allen D. (1973b). Social interactional and sociolinguistic rules. *Social Forces*, 58, 789–810.

Grimshaw, Allen D. (1974). Sociolinguistics. In Wilbur Schramm, Ithiel Pool, Nathan Maccoby, Edwin Parker, Frederick Frey, and Leonard Fein (eds), *Handbook of Communication* (pp. 49–92). Chicago: Rand McNally.

Grimshaw, Allen D. (1976). Polity, class, school, and talk: the sociology of Basil Bernstein. Review article of Basil Bernstein, *Class, Codes, and Control, 3: Towards a Theory of Educational Transmissions, Theory and Society*, 3, 553–72.

Grimshaw, Allen D. (1981). Talk and social control. In Morris Rosenberg and Ralph H. Turner (eds), *Sociological Perspectives on Social Psychology* (pp. 200–32). New York: Basic Books.

Grimshaw, Allen D. (1987a). Sociolinguistics versus sociology of language: tempest in a teapot or profound academic conundrum? In Ulrich Ammon, Norbert Dittmar, and Klaus Mattheier (eds), *Sociolinguistics: An International Handbook of the Science of Language and Society*, Vol. 1 (pp. 9–15). Berlin: de Gruyter.

Grimshaw, Allen D. (1987b). Micro–macrolevels. In Ulrich Ammon, Norbert Dittmar, and Klaus Mattheier (eds), *Sociolinguistics: An International Handbook of the Science of Language and Society*, Vol. 1 (pp. 66–77). Berlin: de Gruyter.

Grimshaw, Allen D. (1989). *Collegial Discourse: Professional Conversation among Peers*. Vol. 1 of the Multiple Analysis Project. Norwood, NJ: Ablex.

Grimshaw, Allen D. (ed.) (1990a). *Conflict Talk: Sociolinguistic Investigations of*

Arguments in Conversations. Cambridge: Cambridge University Press.

Grimshaw, Allen D. (1990b). Research on conflict talk: antecedents, resources, findings, directions. In Allen D. Grimshaw (ed.), *Conflict Talk: Sociolinguistic Investigations of Arguments in Conversations* (pp. 280–324). Cambridge: Cambridge University Press.

Grimshaw, Allen D. (1992a). Research on the discourse of international negotiations: a path to understanding international conflict processes? *Sociological Forum*, 7, 87–119.

Grimshaw, Allen D. (1992b). Sociolinguistics. In Edgar Borgatta and Marie Borgatta (eds), *Encyclopedia of Sociology* (pp. 2000–11). New York: Macmillan.

Grimshaw, Allen D. (1994). Referential ambiguity in pronominal inclusion: social and linguistic boundary marking. In Allen D. Grimshaw, Peter J. Burke, Aaron V. Cicourel, Steven Feld, Jenny Cook-Gumperz, Charles J. Fillmore, John J. Gumperz, Ruqaiya Hasan, Michael A. K. Halliday, David Jenness and Lily Wong Fillmore *What's Going on Here? Complementary Studies of Professional Talk*. Vol. 2 of the Multiple Analysis Project (311–71). Norwood, NJ: Ablex.

Grimshaw, Allen D., Peter J. Burke, Aaron V. Cicourel, Steven Feld, Jenny Cook-Gumperz, Charles J. Fillmore, John J. Gumperz, Ruqaiya Hasan, Michael A. K. Halliday, David Jenness, and Lily Wong Fillmore (1994). *What's Going on Here? Complementary Studies of Professional Talk*. Vol. 2 of the Multiple Analysis Project. Norwood, NJ: Ablex.

Grimshaw, Allen D. (1995). Review of Deirdre Boden, *The Business of Talk: Organizations in Action*, *Contemporary Sociology*, 24, 585–7.

Grimshaw, Allen D. (1998). Review of Barbara Czarniawska, *Narrating the*

Organization: Dramas of Institutional Identity, *Contemporary Sociology*, 27, 262–3.

Gumperz, John J. (1982). *Discourse Strategies*. Cambridge: Cambridge University Press.

Gumperz, John J. and Dell Hymes (eds) (1972). *Directions in Sociolinguistics: the Ethnography of Communication*. New York: Holt, Rhinehart and Winston.

Halliday, Michael A. K. (1994). So you say pass . . . thank you three muchly. In Allen D. Grimshaw, Peter J. Burke, Aaron V. Cicourel, Steven Feld, Jenny Cook-Gumperz, Charles J. Fillmore, John J. Gumperz, Ruqaiya Hasan, Michael A. K. Halliday, David Jenness, and Lily Wong Fillmore, *What's Going on Here? Complementary Studies of Professional Talk*. Vol. 2 of the Multiple Analysis Project (pp. 175–229). Norwood, NJ: Ablex.

Halliday, Michael A. K. and Ruqaiya Hasan (1976). *Cohesion in English*. London: Longman.

Hymes, Dell (1974). *Foundations in Sociolinguistics: An Ethnographic Approach*. Philadelphia: University of Pennsylvania Press.

Jameson, Frederic (1984). Foreword. In Jean-François Lyotard, *The Post-Modern Condition: A Report on Knowledge* (trans. Geoff Bennington and Brian Massumi) (pp. vii–xxi). Minneapolis: University of Minnesota Press.

Kuhn, Thomas S. (1970, 1962). *The Structure of Scientific Revolutions*. Chicago: University of Chicago Press.

Labov, William (1997). Some further steps in narrative analysis. In Michael G. W. Bamberg (ed.), *Oral versions of personal experience: three decades of narrative analysis. Special issue, Journal of Narrative and Life History*, 7 (Numbers 1–4), 395–415.

Labov, William and David Fanshel (1977). *Therapeutic Discourse: Psychotherapy as*

Conversation. New York: Academic Press.

Labov, William and Joshua Waletsky (1997 [1967]). Narrative analysis: oral versions of personal experience. In Michael G. W. Bamberg (ed.), *Oral versions of personal experience: three decades of narrative analysis.* Special issue, *Journal of Narrative and Life History,* 7 (Numbers 1–4), 3–38.

Lakoff, Robin (1975). *Language and Woman's Place.* New York: Harper Colophon.

LaPiere, Richard T. (1946). *Sociology.* New York: McGraw-Hill.

Latour, Bruno (1992). Pasteur on lactic acid yeast: a partial semiotic analysis. *Configurations,* 1, 129–146.

Latour, Bruno (1996a). On interobjectivity. *Mind, Culture, and Activity,* 3, 228–45.

Latour, Bruno (1996b). *Aramis, or the Love of Technology* (trans. Catherine Porter). Cambridge, MA: Harvard University Press.

Laurier, Eric and Chris Philo (1999). X-morphising: review essay of Bruno Latour's *Aramis, or the Love of Technology, Environment and Planning A,* 31, 1047–71.

Lemert, Charles (1979). *Sociology and the Twilight of Man: Homocentrism and Discourse in Sociological Theory.* Carbondale: Southern Illinois University Press.

Lucy, John A. (ed.) (1993). *Reflexive Language: Reported Speech and Metapragmatics.* Cambridge: Cambridge University Press.

Lyotard, Jean-François (1984). *The Post-Modern Condition: A Report on Knowledge* (trans. Geoff Bennington and Brian Massumi). Minneapolis: University of Minnesota Press. (Original work published 1979.)

Mack, Ray and Richard Snyder (1957). The analysis of social conflict – toward an overview and synthesis. *Journal of Conflict Resolution,* 1, 212–48.

Maynard, Douglas W. (1984). *Inside Plea Bargaining: The Language of Negotiation.* New York: Plenum.

McQuown, Norman (1971). The natural history method – a frontier method. In Alvin R. Mahrer and Leonard Pearson (eds), *Creative Developments in Psychotherapy* (pp. 431–8). Cleveland: Case Western Reserve University.

Merlan, Francesca and Alan Rumsey (1991). *Ku Waru: Language and Segmentary Politics in the Western Nebilyer Valley, Papua, New Guinea.* Cambridge: Cambridge University Press.

O,Barr, William (1982). *Linguistic Evidence.* New York: Academic Press.

Ries, Nancy (1997). *Russian Talk: Culture and Conversation during Perestroika.* Ithaca, NY: Cornell University Press.

Russell, R. L. (1979). Speech acts, conversational sequencing, and rules. *Contemporary Sociology,* 8, 176–9.

Scheflen, Albert E. (1973). *Communicational Structure: Analysis of a Psychotherapy Transaction.* Bloomington: Indiana University Press.

Scherer, Klaus R. and Howard Giles (eds) (1979). *Social Markers in Speech.* Cambridge and Paris: Cambridge University Press and Editions de la Maison des Sciences de l'homme.

Silverman, David and Brian Torode (1980). *The Material Word: some Theories of Language and its Limits.* London: Routledge and Kegan Paul.

Silverstein, Michael and Greg Urban (eds) (1996). *Natural Histories of Discourse.* Chicago: University of Chicago Press.

Smith, Raymond F. (1989). *Negotiating with the Soviets.* Bloomington: Indiana University Press.

Steiner, George (1992). *After Babel: Aspects of Language and Translation* (second edition). Oxford: Oxford University Press.

Tannen, Deborah (1992). Response to Senta Troemel-Ploetz's "Selling the apolitical", *Discourse and Society*, 3, 249–54.

Thorne, Barrie and Nancy Henley (eds) (1975). *Language and Sex: Difference and Dominance*. Rowley, MA: Newbury House.

Thorne, Barrie, Cheris Kramarae, and Nancy Henley (eds) (1983). *Language, Gender and Society*. Rowley, MA: Newbury House.

Troemel-Ploetz, Senta (1991). Selling the apolitical: review of Deborah Tannen's *You Just Don't Understand*, *Discourse and Society*, 2, 489–502.

Urban, Greg (1991). *A Discourse-Centered Approach to Culture: Native South American Myths and Rituals*. Austin: University of Texas Press.

Urban, Greg (1996). *Metaphysical Community: The Interplay of the Senses and the Intellect*. Austin: University of Texas Press.

Williams, Robin M., Jr. (1947). *The Reduction of Intergroup Tensions*. New York: Social Science Research Council.

Zabor, Margaret (1978). Essaying Metacommunication: a Survey and Contextualization of Communication Research. Unpublished PhD dissertation, Indiana University.

39 Imagination in Discourse

HERBERT H. CLARK AND
MIJA M. VAN DER WEGE

0 Introduction

Taking part in discourse often demands a vivid imagination. In the depths of World War I, Franz Kafka traveled from Prague to Munich to give a public reading of his yet to be published short story "The Penal Colony." Max Pulver (1953: 52) described hearing Kafka speak (our translation):

> With his first words, an indistinct smell of blood seemed to spread out, and an extraordinarily faint taste settled on my lips. His voice might have sounded apologetic, but it forced its pictures into me with razor sharpness, like icy needles of acute torment. It wasn't just that the torture and instruments of torture were described in the executioners' words of suppressed ecstasy. It was that the listener himself was dragged into this hellish torture. He lay as a victim on the gently rocking rack, and each new word, like a new thorn, tore slowly into his back.

Pulver was not alone in his experience. Soon one woman fainted and had to be carried out, and then so did two more. Many in the audience fled before they were overwhelmed by Kafka's words. By the end, there was almost no one left in the hall.

At the heart of Kafka's story is what he intended us to *experience* from it. But how is it possible for words – mere words – to get people to smell blood, feel pain, faint, and flee? Kafka's audience may seem old-fashioned in their reactions, but most of us have had similar experiences. At the cinema, we have felt fear, anger, elation, and tension, and found ourselves crying, hiding our eyes, or leaving the theater. With novels, we have seen the images sketched for us and felt fear, anger, excitement, suspense, and sexual arousal. How is it possible for us to experience such things about fictional objects?

A crucial part of the answer is imagination. But what is imagination, and how does it work? In this chapter, we will describe the challenges that imagination poses for accounts of discourse and then evaluate several answers to these challenges. One of the greatest challenges is to explain what happened to Kafka's audience.

1   Imagination in Narratives

When people tell stories, and when they listen to them, they think about what is going on in the worlds being described. We will consider six types of evidence that they do that.

1.1   *Visual and spatial representations*

People appear to create visual or spatial representations as they understand many utterances. In one classic demonstration (Bransford et al. 1972: 195), people read either (1) or (2), among other sentences, and were asked to remember it:

(1)   Three turtles rested on a floating log and a fish swam beneath it.

(2)   Three turtles rested beside a floating log and a fish swam beneath it.

If we change the word *it* to *them* in 1 and 2, we get 1' and 2':

(1')   Three turtles rested on a floating log and a fish swam beneath them.

(2')   Three turtles rested beside a floating log and a fish swam beneath them.

Note that the scenes described in (1) and (1') are consistent with each other, for if a fish swam beneath the log it also swam beneath the turtles. The scenes described in (2) and (2'), however, are not consistent. In a test of memory for (1) or (2), people were given all four sentences (in a random order) and asked to say which one they had seen. People who had seen (1) often chose (1') by mistake. But those who had seen (2) rarely chose (2') by mistake. Conclusion: they must have represented not the sentence *per se*, but the scene described – possibly in the form of a visual or spatial image.

   People need to create imaginal representations simply to interpret single words. Take *approach* in these three descriptions:

(3)   I am standing on the porch of a farm house looking across the yard at a picket fence. A tractor [or: mouse] is just approaching it.

(4)   I am standing across the street from a post office with a mailbox in front of it. A man crossing the street is just approaching the post office [or: mailbox].

(5)   I am standing at the entrance to an exhibition hall looking at a slab of marble. A man is just approaching it with a camera [or: chisel].

In one experiment (Morrow and Clark 1988: 282–5), people were given one of the two alternatives of these and other descriptions and asked to estimate the distance of, say, the tractor, or mouse, from the picket fence. The average estimates were as follows:

(3')   tractor to fence, 39 feet; mouse to fence, 2 feet

(4')   man to post office, 28 feet; man to mailbox, 13 feet

(5')   man with camera to marble slab, 18 feet; man with chisel to marble slab, 5 feet

People arrived at a denotation for *approach* apparently by considering how near one object must be to a landmark in order to be in "interaction with it" for its assumed purpose. Tractors come into interaction with a fence at 39 feet, whereas mice do so only at 2 feet. These judgments depended on the size of the referent object (3), the size of the landmark (4), and the approachers' purpose (5).

   These findings should not be surprising – and they are just a sample of a large literature on such effects. But they remind us that imagination is needed for even the simplest descriptions. We need to imagine the appearance or arrangement of turtles, logs, tractors, and fences to come to the right interpretations.

1.2   Deixis and point of view

Narratives are ordinarily told from particular points of view. Melville's *Moby-Dick* is a first person account of a sailor, Ishmael, who describes his experiences aboard a whaler. When Ishmael moves from one place to the next, his point of view changes too. We are to imagine the world as he sees it in passing through it. We need first a visual, spatial, and conceptual representation of that world. We must then track not only where he is in that world, but which way he is moving, what he is looking at, and what he is hearing. We must track his moment-by-moment perceptual experiences.

   Tracking the narrator, or the protagonist, requires following a *deictic center* – the *I*, *here*, and *now* of the narrator's point of view. This is especially important for interpreting deictic expressions like *come* and *go*, *this* and *that*, and *here* and *there* (see Bühler 1982; Duchan et al. 1995; Fillmore 1975). In Hemingway's *The Killers*, the narrator opens his story this way:

(6)   The door to Henry's lunchroom opened and two men came in.

As Fillmore (1981) noted, the narrator must be inside the lunchroom, because he describes the door as opening by unseen forces and the men as "coming" in, not "going" in. The deictic center is inside the room. Point of view is essential to many of the narrator's choices, and imagining the scene from the narrator's or protagonist's vantage point is crucial to getting that point of view right.

   Abrupt changes in point of view require abrupt changes in the imagined representation, and these are sometimes difficult to perform. In a demonstration by Black et al. (1979: 190–1), people were asked to read simple descriptions such as these two:

(7)   Bill was sitting in the living room reading the paper, when John came [or: went] into the living room.

(8)   Alan hated to lose at tennis. Alan played a game of tennis with Liz. After winning, she came [or went] up and shook his hand.

As Black et al. suggested, we can think of point of view in (7) and (8) by setting up a camera to view the scenes. For the first clause in (7), we would set it up in the living room and leave it there when John "comes" in. Not so when John "goes" in, for the camera would need to be moved out of the living room. In (8), the camera would be near Alan for the first two sentences, so it would not need to be moved when Liz "comes" up to him. It *would* need to be moved when she "goes" up to him. Changing point of view (as with "went" in (7) and (8)) should be disruptive to understanding, and it was. People took reliably longer to read the passages with the changed points of view, and they were also more likely to misrecall them (see also Bruder 1995).

People are expected to follow the protagonists even when there are no deictic expressions. In a study by Glenberg et al. (1987: 78), people were given paragraphs to read, one sentence at a time. Some read one of the two versions of 9:

(9)   Warren spent the afternoon shopping at the store.
      He picked up [or: set down] his bag and went over to look at some scarves.
      He had been shopping all day.
      He thought it was getting too heavy to carry.

The pronoun *it* in the last sentence refers to the bag mentioned in the second sentence. When the verb in the second sentence is *picked up*, Warren keeps the bag with him when he looks at the scarves, but when the verb is *set down*, he leaves it behind. The bag's location was important to the interpretation of the pronoun. People read the final sentence a full 0.6 seconds faster when the verb was *picked up* than when it was *set down*. The assumption is that they could readily locate the referent for *it* when the bag was still with Warren, but not when it was not. They must therefore be consulting such a spatial model in determining the referent (see also Bower and Morrow 1990).

But how do people figure out where the protagonist is? In an experiment by Morrow (1985: 393), people were shown a small model house and asked to memorize its layout. They then read brief narratives that ended like this and answered the question at the end:

(10)   She walked from the study into the bedroom.
       She didn't find the glasses in the room.
       Which room is referred to?

For different people, the first sentence had different prepositions (*from* vs. *through* vs. *past the study* and *into* vs. *to the bedroom*) and different verb modalities (*walked* vs. *was walking*). All these differences affected which room people took to be the referent of *the room* in the second sentence. Here are the results of just two of the variants (in percent of choices by the participants):

(11)   She walked *from* the study *into* the bedroom
       The room referred to: the bedroom, 77 percent; the study, 21 percent; other rooms, 2 percent

(12)   She walked *past* the study *to* the bedroom
       The room referred to: the bedroom 21 percent; the study 73 percent; other
       rooms, 6 percent

In (11), most people took the protagonist to be in the bedroom, but in (12), most of
them took her to be near the study. Again, people were remarkably consistent in their
judgments.

It is difficult to overstate Glenberg's and Morrow's challenge for how people deploy imagination in discourse. To make these judgments, people must create a spatial
representation of the protagonist's environment and keep track of where he or she is.
And to create these representations, they must rely not just on the descriptions given,
but on their practical knowledge of houses, department stores, acts of walking, and
other common items and events. They must combine information from many sources
in the descriptions themselves – e.g. the verb (*walked*), the prepositional phrases (*from
the study* and *into the bedroom*), and other items (*the bag*).

1.3   Gestures

Narrators often produce gestures that refer to the world they are talking about
(Goodwin 1981; Kendon 1980; McNeill 1992; Schegloff 1984). Some of the gestures are
iconic and depict things, and others are *deictic* and locate things. Many do both. But
all of these gestures require imagination and, in turn, aid imagination of the story
world.

Iconic gestures are common in spontaneous narratives. In an example analyzed by
Kendon (1980: 219), Fran is telling a joke based on the film *Some Like it Hot*. Her
speech is on the left, divided into four so-called intonation units, and her gestures are
on the right:

(13) | | **Speech** | **Gestures** |
       | --- | --- | --- |
       | 1. | they wheel a big *table* in | Fran sweeps her left arm inward in a horizontal motion. |
       | 2. | with a big with a big [1.08 sec] *cake* on it | During pause Fran makes series of circular motions with forearm pointing downward and index finger extended. |
       | 3. | and the *girl* | Fran raises her arm until it is fully extended vertically above her. |
       | 4. | jumps *up* | |

While describing the scene in words, Fran uses her hands and arms to portray selective pieces of it.

Iconic gestures make heavy demands on imagination, as Fran's story illustrates. In
intonation unit 2, she depicts a large birthday cake by drawing its circular outline in
the air. She intends her audience to put the gesture together with what she is saying
("with a big with a big cake on it") and *visualize* a cake that is the size and shape of
her outline. Fran moves immediately from that gesture into a depiction of the "girl"
jumping up out of the cake. In unit 2, the vantage point of Fran's gesture is outside

the cake, and in unit 3, it is inside the cake on the table. Fran changes her point of view in a trice, and she expects her audience to follow.

Deictic gestures are equally demanding. Consider an example from a Tzetal narrative recorded by Haviland (1996: 305–6), presented here in translation:

(14)   There were indeed people living there [pointing to a fence in the imaginary space of the narrative]. Beside the path [vertical hand moving up and down, representing an imaginary gate]. (That house) was the same size at this house here [pointing at *actual* house nearby].

The narrator first points at an *imaginary* fence in the space in which he has situated the story around him, and with an iconic gesture, he adds an *imaginary* gate. But then he points at an actual house nearby, saying, in effect, "That house [whose gate I can point to in the imaginary narrative space] is the same size as this house [which I can point to here]." As Haviland noted, narrators and their audience must keep track of the imaginary and the actual spaces separately and in relation to each other.

Narrators must represent the appearances and locations of objects and events to produce iconic and deictic gestures. With each gesture, they make reference to locations, shapes, and events in imaginary or actual spaces around them. Although they may use some of these gestures to help themselves keep track, they use at least some of them as part of what they are telling their addressees, who could not interpret the gestures without creating the corresponding imaginary locations, shapes, and events.

1.4   Voices

Most narratives require us to imagine more than one voice. Take the first lines of a joke told by Sam to Reynard (Svartvik and Quirk 1980: 42–3):

(15)   let me tell you a story, - - -
        a girl went into a chemist's shop, and asked for, . contraceptive tablets, - -
        so he said "well I've got . all kinds, and . all prices, what do you want,"
        she said "well what have you got,"

Here we find four voices. The first is Sam's announcing the story to Reynard. The second belongs to the fictional narrator as he describes the girl and chemist's conversation. With the quotation in 1. 3, we move to the chemist's voice, and in l. 4, to the "girl's" voice. Some of these voices are introduced by "he said" or "she said," but others later in the joke are not. As David Lodge (1990: 144) noted, "[The] alternation of authorial description and characters' verbal interaction remains the woof and warp of literary narration to this day."

Quotations, like gestures, are clear aids to imagination. Narrators use them to help us imagine specific individuals, what they say, how they speak. Narrators often dramatize the voices for gender, emotion, dialect, and much more (Clark and Gerrig 1990; Tannen 1989; Wade and Clark 1993). For one recorded story, Tannen (1989: 121) observed, "There are at least five different voices animated in this narrative, and each of these voices is realized in a paralinguistically distinct acoustic representation: literally, a different voice." She described the various voices as sobbing, innocent, upset, hysterically pleading, and bored. Still other quotations are accompanied by the quoted person's gestures, as in this example about a woman in a hospital (Polanyi 1989: 89):

(16)   I went out of my mind and I just screamed I said "Take that out! that's not for me!" . . . And I shook this I-V and I said "I'm on an I-V, I can't eat. Take it out of here!"

As part of her two quotations, the woman "shakes her arm as if shaking the I-V and shouts in the conversational setting as she shouts in the story" (1989: 92), and this helps us imagine her physical actions together with her voice.

Narrators may also use what is called free indirect speech – a curious mixture of quotation and description. Here are examples from spontaneous and literary narratives in which the direct quotations are with quotation marks and the free indirect quotations with cross-hatches:

(17)   and I said. #did she mean for lunch or dinner,# - - and she said "oh either" (Svartvik and Quirk 1980: 98)

(18)   #The picture! How eager he had been about the picture! And the charade! And a hundred other circumstances; how clearly they had seemed to point at Harriet! . . . # (Jane Austen, *Emma*)

In (17) Nancy quotes herself, but instead of saying "Do you mean for lunch or dinner?" she puts the quotation in the third person and past tense, "Did she mean for lunch or dinner?" Likewise, in (18) the narrator in Jane Austen's *Emma* depicts Emma's first person thoughts, but only halfway, leaving them in the third person and past tense. Free indirect quotation is also an aid to imagination, and as in (18), it can be used to vivify the protagonist's private thoughts (Cohn 1978).

Quotation is for showing, or what Plato called *mimesis*, whereas authorial description is for telling, or Plato's *diegesis*. As Lodge (1990: 144) put it, "Roughly speaking, mimesis gives us the sense of reality in fiction, the illusion of access to the reality of personal experience, and diegesis conveys the contextualising information and framework of values which provide thematic unity and coherence." Both telling and showing require imagination, but showing is the more direct aid as it helps us see and hear the characters in pictures and sounds.

1.5   *Mimetic props*

Narratives are often equated with conversational or written stories, but they take other forms as well: theatrical plays, radio plays, operas, operettas, puppet shows, films, television comedies, soap operas, film cartoons, comic books, songs, and pantomimes.

Table 39.1

Medium	Mimetic props
Printed novels	Direct speech, free indirect speech
Audiotaped novels	Expressive direct speech, free indirect speech
Spontaneous stories	Expressive direct speech, free indirect speech, iconic and deictic gestures
Operas	Actors, sung speech, sound effects, limited visible enactments, limited scenery, expressive music
Stage plays	Actors, "stage" speaking, sound effects, limited visible enactments, limited scenery
Films	Actors, naturalistic speaking, sound effects, visible enactments close up, rich scenery, expressive music

These forms range widely in how much they show and tell, and in how effectively they engage our imagination.

Many narratives have appeared in several media. Take Shakespeare's *Hamlet*. We can read it in the original, read it in a comic book version, hear it performed as a radio play, see it performed on stage, or see it as a film. Or there's *Emma*. We can read it, hear it read on audiorecording, or see the film. Shaw's *Pygmalion* is better yet. We can read the play, hear it read, or see it performed on stage, or we can take in a performance of the musical *My Fair Lady* as an audiorecording, stage version, or film. The several forms of these narratives are not equivalent. They induce different thoughts, experiences, and emotions. But how?

Every medium relies on *mimetic props* – devices that aid directly in imagining the story world. Table 39.1 shows six media with some of their props.

Suppose we want to imagine people talking. With indirect quotation in a novel, we have to imagine what the participants might have said and how they might have sounded. With direct quotation, we get the words uttered, but we have to imagine the voice, its accent, its emotional tone. If we hear the novel read, we get help from the reader's dramatization of each quotation, which may include voice, accent, and emotional tone. In spontaneous stories, we may get the accompanying gestures. In operas, we get highly stylized versions of speech in a musical idiom that we are to interpret as happy, sad, angry, or surprised. In stage plays, we get help from actors delivering their lines in expressive, though conventionalized dramatizations of their lines. In films, we get more naturalistic speech, along with close-ups of the actors' faces and gestures. As we go down the list, the mimetic props take on greater variety and verisimilitude.

Mimetic props are engineered to aid imagination. In reading *Emma*, we work hard to imagine what Emma looks like – her hair, clothing, and mannerisms. Without a background in nineteenth-century English style, we may get many of these features wrong. In seeing the film *Emma*, we are *shown* what she looks like – her hair, clothing, mannerisms – so all we must imagine is that this particular actress (say, Gwyneth Paltrow) is in fact Emma. It may seem that the greater the verisimilitude of the mimetic props, the better the aid to imagination, but that is not always true. Background music in films is hardly realistic, and yet it too is an effective prop.

1.6   Emotion

Imagining a story usually includes experiencing emotions. Take what Walton (1978) called **quasi-fear**. When we see a horror film, we are afraid of what the monster will do to the heroine. Our hearts beat faster, our muscles tighten, and our knuckles turn white as the monster approaches her. But do we warn her as we would if all this were happening in front of us? Or take what Gerrig (1989a, 1989b, 1993) called **anomalous suspense**. Ordinarily, suspense is a state in which we "lack knowledge about some sufficiently important target outcome" (Gerrig 1993: 79). Yet, as Gerrig documented, when we read suspense stories, we often feel suspense even when we know how they turn out. As with Walton's quasi-fear, we compartmentalize our emotional experience as part of the story world and not the actual world.

Most narratives are designed to elicit emotion. Novels are classified into genres largely by the emotions they evoke. Mysteries lead to suspense and fear; adventures to excitement, fear, and elation; horror stories to horror, loathing, and fear; light romances to sexual excitement; heavier romances to erotic arousal; satires to amusement; and so on. Films evoke many of the same emotions. Here we come full circle to Kafka's "The Penal Colony" and the reactions it evoked. We imagine story worlds as if we were now experiencing them before our very eyes. At the same time, we recognize that we are still in the actual world.

2   Participating in Narratives

Over the years cognitive scientists have proposed many models of discourse. Some were intended to be comprehensive, but most were aimed at limited aspects of discourse. The arguments we have reviewed suggest that these theories must account for at least four phenomena:

1 *Experience:* People experience selective features of the narrative world as if they were actual, current experiences. These include visual appearances, spatial relations, points of view, movement and processes, voices, and emotions.
2 *Mimetic props:* People's imaginings appear to be aided by well-engineered mimetic props – direct quotation, gestures, stage sets, sound effects, background music.
3 *Participation:* Speakers and writers design what they say to encourage certain forms of imagination, but listeners and readers must willingly cooperate with them to succeed.
4 *Compartmentalization:* In participating in narratives, people distinguish their experiences in the story world from their experiences in the real world.

The models of discourse proposed can be classified roughly into four categories: schema theories; mental models; mental simulations; and joint pretense. We will evaluate these theories against the four phenomena.

2.1 Schema theories

In the early 1990s, psychologists developed the notion of **schema** to account for how people understand and remember stories. A schema is a set of cultural preconceptions about causal or other types of relationships. In the classic experiments by Bartlett (1932), people were told a Native American folk story, "The War of the Ghosts," which included many elements unfamiliar to western norms. In retelling that story, people often distorted it to fit their cultural expectations. For example, many changed "hunting seals" into "fishing," a more likely pastime in their schema.

Schemas of a different type were proposed for the structure of stories themselves. According to one account (Rumelhart 1975), stories consist of setting followed by an episode; an episode consists of an event plus a reaction to it; a reaction consists of an internal response plus an external response; and so on. Listeners are assumed to parse stories into these functional sections in much the way they parse sentences into constituents. In a rather different account (Labov 1972), narratives of personal experience consist of six parts: (1) an abstract, briefly summarizing the story; (2) an orientation, a stage setting about the who, when, what, and where of the story; (3) a complicating action; (4) an evaluation of these actions; (5) the result or resolution of the complicating action; and (6) a coda, a signal of completion. Narrators and their audience presumably refer to such schemas in producing and understanding stories.

A third class of schemas, called **scripts**, was proposed as representations for events (Schank and Abelson 1977). The argument was that scripts guide our expectations about the presence and order of everyday events. When we go to a restaurant, our "restaurant script" informs us that we need to order from a menu, wait for our food, and pay at the end. When we hear a description about going to a restaurant, we appeal to the same script. Even if not explicitly told, we assume that the protagonist ordered food and paid the bill in the proper order (Bower et al. 1979). If we are told that the events occurred in an unusual order, e.g. the protagonist paid before ordering food, we may recall the events in their usual order because that fits our "restaurant script."

Schemas have also been proposed for categories and concepts. When a narrator uses the word *house*, so it is argued, listeners interpret it according to a "house" schema. They may infer that it is a building, that people live in it, that it is made of wood, bricks, or stone (Anderson 1990). Unfortunately, what might count as valid inference in one situation may not be valid in another. In a study by Labov (1973), people were inconsistent in using "cup" to describe drawings of various cup-like objects. They were more likely to call the same object a "bowl" than a "cup" when they imagined it filled with mashed potatoes than when they imagined it empty.

Schemas were designed, then, to explain how people can have a mental representation of a narrative that is more detailed than the original narrative. People can take the limited input and, by applying schemas, elaborate on it in various ways. By themselves, however, schemas are of little help in accounting for our four criteria. They do not account for the *experience* of imagining a story world, the use of mimetic props, the willing participation in narratives, or the compartmentalization of experience.

2.2   Mental models

Whereas schemas are cultural preconceptions that people bring to a narrative, mental models are mental constructions in which people represent specific objects, events, and relationships in utterances or narratives (Johnson-Laird 1983). They are mental instantiations of the world being described. People create mental models based upon the discourse, the situation, and the purposes they have to serve. So, people trying to understand (1) and (2) create mental models of ponds, logs, fish, and turtles so that they can estimate where they are in relation to each other. People trying to interpret *approach* in (3), (4), and (5) create mental models of the scenes described in order to judge where the various objects must be. According to one proposal (Just and Carpenter 1980, 1987), readers create mental models for each utterance they read in order to help them parse and understand it. They can change the model if the next word is not what was expected in the model so far. Mental models begin, in effect, with the generic information represented in schemas, and add visual and spatial relationships to represent instantiations of a scene or event.

Mental models can also represent dynamic events. If you are asked how many windows there are in your house, you are likely to imagine yourself walking around the house counting the windows – a dynamic process (Shepard and Cooper 1982). According to Hegarty (1992; Hegarty et al. 1988), people understand diagrams of pulleys in much the same way – through dynamic mental models (see also Gentner and Stevens 1983). These seem eminently suited for representing the dynamic course of events people consult in telling and understanding narratives.

Despite their advantages, mental models fail to account for several features of imagination in discourse. They do not really say what it is to imagine the events in a story – to see things from particular vantage points or to experience fear or suspense. They do not say how mimetic props such as gestures, films, and voices aid in these experiences. They do not account for the different roles speakers and listeners play in creating these experiences. Nor do they deal with the compartmentalization of our experiences of the real and narrative worlds.

2.3   Mental simulations

Mental simulations, as proposed by Kahneman and Tversky (1982), are a type of dynamic mental model in which people can modify the initial settings of the model and compare the outcomes. People might simulate a process for many purposes: (1) to predict its outcome; (2) to assess its probability; (3) to assess counterfactual alternatives ("if only . . ."); and (4) to project the effects of causality. When people simulate alternative endings to a story, for example, they tend to make "downhill" changes to scenarios – they remove unusual or unexpected aspects of the situation. They rarely make "uphill" changes, which introduce unusual aspects, and never make "horizontal" changes, which alter arbitrary aspects (Kahneman and Tversky 1982). Mental simulations, therefore, represent the process of *pretending* to work through an event.

Mental simulations are well suited for imaginary experiences (see Davies and Stone 1995). These include emotional experiences. When people go back over fatal accidents of loved ones, they often experience guilt, anger, or regret as they mentally simulate alternatives for those accidents – as they think "if only she hadn't driven down that street" or "what if he had left two minutes earlier" (Kahneman and Tversky 1982). Mental simulations require the active participation of the participants, and they introduce a boundary between reality and the simulation (taking the system "off-line" and feeding it pretend inputs). Still, there is no account for how they are aided by mimetic props, and many of their specifics have yet to be tested experimentally.

2.4 Joint pretense

A joint pretense is an activity in which two or more people jointly act as if they were doing something that they are not actually, really, or seriously doing at that moment (Clark 1996; Goffman 1974; Walton 1978, 1983, 1990). The prototype is the game of make-believe. Suppose Sam and Rogers, both aged five, are jointly pretending to be lion and lion-tamer. To succeed, they must coordinate their imaginings. They must simulate the way a lion and lion-tamer would behave toward each other. They must also imagine the back yard as a circus ring, the back porch as a lion cage, and much, much more. The crucial point is that Sam and Rogers are simultaneously engaged in two layers of joint action. At layer 1, they are Sam and Rogers playing a game of make-believe. At layer 2, they are a lion and lion-tamer performing in a circus (Clark 1996).

Participating in narratives can be viewed as a type of joint pretense (Bruce 1981; Clark 1996; Currie 1990; Walton 1979, 1983, 1990). Take (15), in which Sam is telling Reynard a joke. When Sam says "A girl went into a chemist's shop and asked for contraceptive tablets," he is asking Reynard to join with him in pretending that he is a reporter, that Reynard is a reportee, and that he is telling Reynard about an actual girl going into an actual chemist's shop. Or take *Moby-Dick*, which begins "Call me Ishmael." Melville is asking his readers to join him in the pretense that these are the words of an actual sailor telling his contemporaries about his actual adventures in pursuing a great white whale. Or take Clark Gable in *Gone with the Wind*. When he says to Vivien Leigh, "Frankly, my dear, I don't give a damn," we viewers are invited to pretend with him, producer David Selznick, and MGM that he is actually Rhett Butler, and that he is telling Scarlett O'Hara that he doesn't give a damn.

Joint pretense addresses all four phenomena that are characteristic of imagining in narratives – at least in principle. When people engage in a pretense, they simulate selective aspects of the narrative world as if it were the actual world. These require mental simulations, as in reading *Moby-Dick* or seeing *Gone with the Wind*, but may also require physical simulations, as in playing lion and lion-tamer in the back yard. People are aided in these simulations by mimetic props, which help them step into the characters' shoes and do what the characters do. Joint pretense brings out the roles of narrator and listener: the two must coordinate their imaginings in just the right way. And, finally, the layering of joint pretense enables the participants to compartmentalize their as-if experiences from their actual experiences, as they should (Clark 1996; Gerrig 1993).

3   Conclusion

Narratives would be dull if they did not transport us into exciting new worlds. People do not tell stories just to get us to understand what they mean. They do it to get us to experience those worlds. As the novelist John Gardner put it, "The writer's intent is that the reader fall through the printed page into the scene represented" (1983: 132). That, in turn, takes imagination – not unfettered imagination, but imagination coordinated by the narrator and audience, or what Gardner called "controlled dreaming." Only then will we experience the penal colony the way Kafka meant us to – seeing the dreadful visions, feeling sick to our stomachs, wanting to escape.

In imagining story worlds, people represent at least these features: visual and spatial relations, point of view, pointing and iconic gestures, voices, mimetic props, and emotion. For a theory of narratives to be complete, it must account for the experience of imagining, the role of mimetic props, the coordination of imagining between narrators and their audience, and the compartmentalization of imagination from reality. Most theories fail on these criteria, but theories of joint pretense show promise. On this view, narrators and their audience join in the pretense that what the narrators are telling and showing the audience is true then and there, and that allows the audience to simulate the narrative world – to fall through the printed page into the scene represented.

REFERENCES

Anderson, J. R. (1990). *Cognitive Psychology and its Implications*. New York: W. H. Freeman.

Bartlett, F. C. (1932). *Remembering: A Study in Experimental and Social Psychology*. Cambridge: Cambridge University Press.

Black, J. B., Turner, T. J., and Bower, G. H. (1979). Point of view in narrative comprehension. *Journal of Verbal Learning and Verbal Behavior, 18*, 187–98.

Bower, G. H., and Morrow, D. G. (1990). Mental models in narrative comprehension. *Science, 247* (4938), 44–8.

Bower, G. H., Black, J. B., and Turner, T. J. (1979). Scripts in memory for text. *Cognitive Psychology, 11*, 177–220.

Bransford, J. D., Barclay, J. R., and Franks, J. J. (1972). Sentence memory: A constructive vs. interpretive approach. *Cognitive Psychology, 3*, 193–209.

Bruce, B. (1981). A social interaction model of reading. *Discourse Processes, 4*, 273–311.

Bruder, G. A. (1995). Psychological evidence that linguistic devices are used by readers to understand spatial deixis in narrative text. In J. F. Duchan, G. A. Bruder, and L. E. Hewitt (eds), *Deixis in Narrative: A Cognitive Science Perspective* (pp. 243–60). Hillsdale, NJ: Lawrence Erlbaum Associates.

Bühler, K. (1982). The deictic field of language and deictic words. In R. J. Jarvella and W. Klein (eds), *Speech, Place, and Action* (pp. 9–30). Chichester: John Wiley.

Clark, H. H. (1996). *Using Language*. Cambridge: Cambridge University Press.

Clark, H. H., and Gerrig, R. J. (1990). Quotations as demonstrations. *Language, 66,* 764–805.

Cohn, D. (1978). *Transparent Minds: Narrative Modes for Presenting Consciousness in Fiction.* Princeton: Princeton University Press.

Currie, G. (1990). *The Nature of Fiction.* Cambridge: Cambridge University Press.

Davies, M., and Stone, T. (eds). (1995). *Mental Simulation.* Oxford: Blackwell.

Duchan, J. F., Bruder, G. A., and Hewitt, L. E. (eds). (1995). *Deixis in Narrative: A Cognitive Science Perspective.* Hillsdale, NJ: Lawrence Erlbaum Associates.

Fillmore, C. (1975). *Santa Cruz Lectures on Deixis.* Bloomington, IN: Indiana University Linguistics Club.

Fillmore, C. (1981). Pragmatics and the description of discourse. In P. Cole (ed.), *Radical Pragmatics* (pp. 143–66). New York: Academic Press.

Gardner, J. (1983). *The Art of Fiction: Notes on Craft for Young Writers.* New York: Alfred Knopf.

Gentner, D., and Stevens, A. (eds). (1983). *Mental Models.* Hillsdale, NJ: Erlbaum.

Gerrig, R. J. (1989a). Reexperiencing fiction and non–fiction. *Journal of Aesthetics and Art Criticism, 47,* 277–80.

Gerrig, R. J. (1989b). Suspense in the absence of uncertainty. *Journal of Memory and Language, 28,* 633–48.

Gerrig, R. J. (1993). *Experiencing Narrative Worlds: On the Psychological Activities of Reading.* New Haven, CT: Yale University Press.

Glenberg, A. M., Meyer, M., and Lindem, K. (1987). Mental models contribute to foregrounding during text comprehension. *Journal of Memory and Language, 26* (1), 69–83.

Goffman, E. (1974). *Frame Analysis.* New York: Harper and Row.

Goodwin, C. (1981). *Conversational Organization: Interaction Between Speakers and Hearers.* New York: Academic Press.

Haviland, J. B. (1996). Projections, transpositions, and relativity. In J. J. Gumperz and S. C. Levinson (eds), *Rethinking Linguistic Relativity* (pp. 271–323). Cambridge: Cambridge University Press.

Hegarty, M. (1992). Mental animation: Inferring motion from static displays of mechanical systems. *Journal of Experimental Psychology: Learning, Memory, and Cognition, 18* (5), 1084–102.

Hegarty, M., Just, M. A., and Morrison, I. R. (1988). Mental models of mechanical systems: Individual differences in qualitative and quantitative reasoning. *Cognitive Psychology, 20* (2), 191–236.

Johnson-Laird, P. N. (1983). *Mental Models.* Cambridge: Cambridge University Press.

Just, M. A., and Carpenter, P. A. (1980). A theory of reading: From eye fixations to comprehension. *Psychological Review, 87,* 329–54.

Just, M. A., and Carpenter, P. A. (1987). *The Psychology of Reading and Language Comprehension.* Boston, MA: Allyn and Bacon.

Kahneman, D., and Tversky, A. (1982). The simulation heuristic. In P. Slovic, D. Kahneman, and A. Tversky (eds), *Judgment Under Uncertainty: Heuristics and Biases,* (pp. 201–8). Cambridge: Cambridge University Press.

Kendon, A. (1980). Gesticulation and speech: Two aspects of the process of utterance. In M. R. Key (ed.), *Relationship of Verbal and Nonverbal Communication* (pp. 207–27). Amsterdam: Mouton de Gruyter.

Labov, W. (1972). The transformation of experience in narrative syntax. In W. Labov (ed.), *Language in the Inner City: Studies in the Black English Vernacular* (pp. 354–96). Philadelphia, PA: University of Pennsylvania Press.

Labov, W. (1973). The boundaries of words and their meanings. In

C.-J. N. Bailey and R. W. Shuy (eds), *New Ways of Analyzing Variations in English* (pp. 340–73). Washington, DC: Georgetown University Press.

Lodge, D. (1990). Narration with words. In H. Barlow, C. Blakemore, and M. Weston–Smith (eds), *Images and Understanding* (pp. 141–53). Cambridge: Cambridge University Press.

McNeill, D. (1992). *Hand and Mind.* Chicago: University of Chicago Press.

Morrow, D. G. (1985). Prepositions and verb aspect in narrative understanding. *Journal of Memory and Language, 24,* 390–404.

Morrow, D. G., and Clark, H. H. (1988). Interpreting words in spatial descriptions. *Language and Cognitive Processes, 3,* 275–91.

Polanyi, L. (1989). *Telling the American Story.* Cambridge, MA: MIT Press.

Pulver, M. (1953). *Erinnerungen an eine Europäische Zeit.* Zurich: Orell Füssli Verlag.

Rumelhart, D. E. (1975). Notes on schemas for stories. In D. G. Bobrow and A. M. Collins (eds), *Representation and Understanding: Studies in Cognitive Science* (pp. 211–36). New York: Academic Press.

Schank, R. C., and Abelson, R. P. (1977). *Scripts, Plans, Goals, and Understanding.* Hillsdale, NJ: Erlbaum.

Schegloff, E. A. (1984). On some gestures' relation to talk. In J. M. Atkinson and J. Heritage (eds), *Structures of Social Action: Studies in Conversation Analysis* (pp. 262–96). Cambridge: Cambridge University Press.

Shepard, R. N., and Cooper, L. A. (eds) (1982). *Mental Images and their Transformations.* Cambridge, MA: MIT Press.

Svartvik, J., and Quirk, R. (eds) (1980). *A Corpus of English Conversation.* Lund: Gleerup.

Tannen, D. (1989). *Talking Voices: Repetition, Dialogue and Imagery in Conversational Discourse.* Cambridge: Cambridge University Press.

Wade, E., and Clark, H. H. (1993). Reproduction and demonstration in quotations. *Journal of Memory and Language, 32* (6), 805–19.

Walton, K. L. (1978). Fearing fictions. *Journal of Philosophy, 75,* 5–27.

Walton, K. L. (1983). Fiction, fiction–making, and styles of fictionality. *Philosophy and Literature, 8,* 78–88.

Walton, K. L. (1990). *Mimesis as Make-believe: On the Foundations of the Representational Arts.* Cambridge, MA: Harvard University Press.

40 Literary Pragmatics

JACOB L. MEY

0 Introduction: Author and Reader

Human language activity unfolds mainly along the two dimensions of the spoken and the written word. The former is commonly known as "conversation"; the latter comprises (but not exclusively) what is often referred to as "literature." Together, they constitute the principal ways in which humans produce **text**. In addition to the spoken, **oral** text, with its corresponding competence (often called "orality" or "oracy"), there are the written productions (mainly **literary** texts) that are the subject of the present chapter.

Along with human oral competence, we thus encounter the phenomenon of "literacy," interpreted either as the simple ability to read and write, or as the actual production and consumption of written texts. As long as the emphasis is on language as it is *spoken* (especially in conversation), the role of pragmatics does not seem to be in doubt (witness the inclusion of topics such as "conversation analysis" in most current handbooks); the question up for discussion in the present chapter is whether pragmatic findings can be assigned any validity or explanatory significance for literary production as well.

Recently, an increasing interest in the pragmatics of literary texts has been making itself felt across the disciplines of both literary science and linguistics. The magisterial synthesis provided by Fludernik in her 1993 book was followed by another milestone work by the same author in 1996. Earlier, the work by Banfield (with all its "sound and fury," as McHale characterized the reception of this work in 1983) had been followed by incisive studies such as the one by Ehrlich (1990). Lesser-known studies, as well as older ones, did not fail to make their impact, either; suffice it to name works by Iser (1978), Cohn (1978), or the original narratological-theoretical works by people like Genette (1980), Stanzel (1982), and Bal (1985), and of course the gigantic earlier efforts by literary critics such as Horkheimer, Benjamin, Kermode, Hillis Miller, Fish, and others. Add to this the ongoing discussions on literary-pragmatic subjects (such as is carried on in the pages of *Poetics Today*, *Poetics*, *Text*, and other journals), and efforts toward comprehensive theory such as that undertaken recently by Tsur (1992), and one cannot escape the conclusion that the debates are not just about peripheral questions such as to how to interpret this poem or that piece of prose, but that something more is afoot: the question of literature as such, and what it is doing in our lives. After all, books are there to be read; literature is for users to peruse. Saying that, we have also planted ourselves *in mediis rebus pragmaticis*: if literature is for the users, and the use of language is what determines pragmatics, then literary pragmatics is the expression not just of a trendy tendency, but of some deeper need for clarification of the relationships between humans, their words, and their worlds.

In keeping with the general definition of pragmatics that I have formulated elsewhere (cf. Mey 2000: section 1.2), the question "What is the significance of pragmatics for the study of written text?" or more broadly "How do literature and pragmatics relate?" has to be seen from the angle of the **language user**. But who is this user, when it comes to literature?

At first glance, we seem to recognize the **reader** as the user *par excellence*: it is he or she who acquires the products of someone else's literary activity, and by consuming ("reading") them, satisfies a personal need (and indirectly provides the author, the producer of the text, with a living). As I have argued elsewhere (Mey 1994, 1995), this relationship is not just one of buying and selling a regular commodity; authors and readers, while being distinguished by their different positions on the supply and demand sides of the literary market, have more in common than your regular sellers and buyers. It is this commonality, and the resulting *cooperation* between authors and readers, which makes the world of literary producing and consuming different from a regular marketplace.

Reading is a collaborative activity, taking place between author and reader. The work that the author has done in producing the text has to be supplemented and completed by you, the reader. You do not just buy a book: you buy an author to take home with you. Reading is a cooperative process of **active re-creation**, not just the passive, preset and predetermined use of some "recreational facility." As a contemporary novelist has expressed it succinctly: "[A novel] is made in the head, and has to be remade in the head by whoever reads it, who will always remake it differently" (Byatt 1996: 214). The reader, as an active collaborator, is a major player in the literary game. His or her contribution consists in entering the universe that the author has created, and by doing so, becoming an actor, rather than a mere spectator. As a result, we do not only have cooperation, but also *innovation*. By acting the reader changes the play: what the reader reads is, in the final analysis, his or her own coproduction along with the author. I call this interaction a **dialectic** process (see Mey 1994, 1999: sections 11.2, 12.3), inasmuch as the author depends on the reader as a presupposition for his or her activity, and the reader is dependent on the author for guidance in the world of fiction, for the "script" that he or she has to internalize in order to successfully take part in the play, have his or her "ways with words," to borrow a felicitous expression due to Shirley Brice Heath (1988).

The pragmatic study of literary activity focuses on the features that characterize this dialectic aspect of literary production: the text as an author-originated and -guided, but at the same time reader-oriented and -activated, process of wording. The reader is constrained by the limitations of the text; but also, the text provides the necessary degrees of freedom in which the reader can collaborate with the author to construct the proper textual universe, one that is consonant with the broader contextual conditions that mark the world and times in which the reader lives.

In the following, I will take a closer look at the mechanisms that language makes available to realize this joint textual production.

1 Author and Narrator

In her novel *A república dos sonhos* (*The Republic of Dreams*), the Brazilian author Nélida Piñon (1984) tells the story of an old woman, Eulália's, last days. Telling this story implies giving an account of Eulália's long life, an account which is provided through "flashbacks" and retrospective narrative, attributed, among others, to a young woman, Eulália's granddaughter Breta.

In telling her story, Breta assumes a double narrative perspective: for one, she lets the life story unfold through the voice of her grandmother (as "heard" by Breta herself); in addition, she tells us how she experienced her grandmother's final hours. Neither of these narrative levels is directly linked to the *author* of the book: Piñon speaks, as it were, through the voice of her characters, among which Breta is the central figure. Breta is given a crucial part in the telling of the story, the process of narrating; Breta is a major narrative "voice," distinct from the author's own. But there is more.

Toward the end of the book, Breta remarks to herself that, when all the funeral fuss is over, she will sit down and tell the story of what happened in grandma's bedroom – that is, the story she just has been telling us! Breta the narrator suddenly becomes another person: Breta the author. This new author has, so to speak, caught us unawares in a flying start, organized by the "real" author, Nélida Piñon. Before we have had time to realize it, we have already met the author Breta, who enters the fictional world of *The Republic of Dreams* to become the new, so to say "prospective," narrator in the literary universe created by the "real" author. Thus, Breta is at the same time an author *and* a narrator; however, she can only be this by the grace of the real author and, as we will see, by the reader's active acceptance of this division of roles. (I will have more to say on this in section 3.)

What this case makes clear is the important difference that exists in a literary production between author and narrator. The author creates the narrator, whether or not the latter explicitly manifests himself or herself on the narrative scene. Either way, the narrator is a "character" in the story, a character, furthermore, who cannot be held responsible for the actions and opinions of the other characters.

The pragmatic relevance of the distinction between author and narrator is in the different approach that the readers have toward the production and consumption of a piece of text. It is important for the readers to realize that the narrator's persona does not identify with that of any of the other characters. Neither (and I would say a fortiori) can the author be identified with the actions and opinions of the characters; which explains the occurrence of the familiar disclaimers on the inside of the front cover of novels, to the effect that "all the characters occurring in this book are fictitious, and any resemblance to any living persons is purely coincidental."

Such statements need not be "true," in the sense that the author may indeed have drawn on actually existing persons, sometimes even letting this fact be known, by subtle or not-so-subtle hints, as in the roman à clef. The point is that while a writer, as a narrator, may be permitted to actually portray her or his persons as real characters, as an author (crudely defined as the person who gets the royalties), she or he is not allowed to reproduce actual experiences when depicting living persons unfavorably; doing so would inevitably result in a costly lawsuit for libel. Modifying D. H. Lawrence's famous quip (quoted by Toolan 1994: 88), "Never trust the teller, trust the tale," we could say, "Never trust the narrator (or author); trust the text, and your own abilities as a reader to make sense of it."

As we see, the pragmatics of authorship vs. "narratorship" are of the utmost importance for the successful cooperation between the users involved in the production and consumption of the literary work. Narrativity, however defined, is always a pragmatic quality of both readers and texts, and of the interplay between the two. The next section will go into some detail as to the textual mechanics of these pragmatic presuppositions. (Cf. Mey 2000: section 7.2.3.)

2   Textual Mechanisms

How do readers use the textual mechanisms mentioned above in their efforts to understand a text, as it has been situated in place, time, and discourse by the author? I will start out by discussing the phenomena of place and person reference (mainly deixis); next, I will have something to say on time/tense and discourse.

2.1   *Reference*

Consider the following extract: ". . . he returned home only to find her the wife of his hated cousin and mother of many little ones with his features but not his" (Byatt 1992: 176). This is said about a sailor who has been to sea for many years, and whose return was not expected – least of all by his wife, who had remarried a cousin of her husband's (referred to as "hated" in the extract). The marriage had been successful, one could say, at least in the way of fertility (hence the "many little ones"); but to the original husband, the sight of all these children bearing the features of the despised cousin rather than (being) his own[1] must have been pretty appalling.

All this information we glean without special difficulty just by quickly perusing the above text. Yet, the phrase "many little ones with his features but not his," taken by itself, sounds a little odd, not to say contradictory; out of its context, it is not easy to understand. In particular, the double occurrence of the personal pronoun *his* cannot be determined using linguistic rules of deixis; the correct assignment of reference depends entirely on the context.

The question is now: what precisely is this context, and how do we go about interpreting it?

Our understanding of the fictional world is contingent upon our acceptance of the author as an "authority," as an *auctor* in the classical sense: a creator, one who speaks the word by which the creatures become alive, or at least one who, having been "present at the Creation" (cf. Proverbs 8), is allowed to act as a major mouthpiece for the creative force. By entering the world of the text, by becoming participants in the drama enacted in the narrative, we become at the same time understanders of the ways in which the personae interact, and how they are textually referred to. In this particular case, many of us have read about, maybe even known, people who were assumed to have died and still came back "from the dead," as the expression goes; post-Holocaust Europe was full of happenings like these. Such an understanding is prior to, and conditions, any further or deeper understanding of the text; the establishment of the correct references (such as the two occurrences of "his" in the above passage from Byatt) is a consequence of such an understanding, not its effective cause.

Having seen how the textual world is both pragmatically dependent upon, and preconditional to, the establishment of linguistic reference, let us now spend a few moments considering the problem of **tense** in a literary text.

2.2 *Tense*

When it comes to the use of tense in literary works, the situation is no different from that surrounding deixis. Again, the question is how to use the resources that the language puts at our disposal in order to understand the text, in this case to determine who is saying what at which point of time in the narrative. The so-called **indexical** function of tense may be considered as a means of situating an utterance in time relative to a user. (See Mey 1999: ch. 3.)

A simple schema is that proposed by Ehrlich (1990), following the classical distinction introduced by the logician Hans Reichenbach in the 1940s (Reichenbach 1947). Ehrlich establishes the following distinctions: First, we have the time at which the utterance is spoken: this is "speech time" (ST). Then, there is the time at which the event that is spoken about took place: this is called "event time" (ET). And finally, we have the time that is indicated by the temporal indicators of the utterance (that is to say, both verbal tense morphemes and adverbs of time). This "temporal perspective" is called "reference time" (RT).

To show the contrast between the different "times," as expressed by these temporal indicators, Ehrlich provides the following example (1990: 61):

> John had already completed his paper last week.

Here, "the RT is last week, the ET is an unspecified time prior to last week, and the ST occurs after both RT and ET" (*ibid.*).

What this example does not show is the influence that a possible *context* may have on the use of tense. In a context of use, the various relations between RT, ST, and ET may well be disrupted, such that we only can understand what is going on by appealing to our understanding of the *pragmatic* world in which the interplay between the tenses is taking place. It is a bit like what happens when we are confronted with so-called "flashbacks" in a novel or on the screen. A story unfolds in (event) time, but suddenly the time perspective is broken, and events anterior to those related are "intercalated," inserted into the stream of events, thus establishing a different time reference (sometimes, but not necessarily, accompanied by a change in time of "speaking"). In such cases, the morphemes of tense are not always sufficient by themselves to shore up a tottering, broken, or "unvoiced" narrative (Mey 1999: section 7.3).

Moreover, while most languages cannot do without some morphological indication of time (such as is embodied in the category of tense and its indexical function), its use may vary enormously from language to language. Naturally, this can cause complications for our understanding of a text, especially in those cases where the translator is not aware of the intricate differences between the grammars of different languages. Here's an example in which a translated tense misfires: in the beginning of Mikhail Bulgakov's classical satirical novel *Master i Margarita* (*The Master and Margarita*), two gentlemen (one of them called Ivan) appear on the scene, walking and talking with each other in a Moscow park. Their discussion is interrupted by the purchase of some soft drinks at a nearby stand, and by a momentary fit of dizziness, accompanied by a hallucinatory experience, on the part of Ivan. When things are back to normal, we are told that:

> . . . – povel rec, prervannuju pit'em abrikosovoj.
>   Rec èta, kak vposledstvie uznali, sla ob Isuse Xriste.

> (. . . – [he (sc. Ivan)] continued the discussion interrupted by the drinking of the apricot soda.
>   This conversation, as we learned subsequently, was about Jesus Christ.)
> (Bulgakov 1969: 8; Engl. transl. 1967: 5).

On reading this fragment in its English translation, the baffled reader asks himself or herself how to reconcile the two conflicting time indications expressed here. The time adverb "subsequently" refers to a point of time in the future. This reference time (RT) is posterior to "event time" (ET), that is, it must occur some time after the events depicted in the preceding passage; more specifically, after the two interruptions in the gentlemen's conversation, caused by soda drinking and hallucinating. In contrast, speech time (ST) and event time (ET) are simultaneous, the conversation occurring more or less at ET.

By any account, the RT established by "learned" (a past tense) has to be *prior* to ET, according to the rules for the use of the past tense in English (and in most languages), and hence would exclude the use of an adverb such as "subsequently," denoting *posterior* time. This conundrum can only be solved by appealing to the understanding that we have of the situation: the conversation (about whose content we have not been informed so far) will, at a future point of time (RT), be disclosed as having had to do (at ET/ST) with the person of Jesus Christ. This is what our common "readerly" sense tells us has to be the meaning of this obscure passage.

The example analyzed here shows two things:

1   The occurrence of a linguistic anomaly (such as a verbal past tense combined with a future time adverbial) can only be explained by reference to a larger frame of narration in which such a combination makes sense. This is the "readerly," *pragmatic* interpretation of the difficulty.
2   While the occurrence of a particular linguistic form is not sufficient, by itself, to make the correct inferences, linguistic forms are certainly a much-needed help in the analysis of a text's pragmatic content.[2]

Let us now have a look at how textual understanding is made possible in the totality of contextual conditions that are often subsumed under the general appellation of **discourse**.

2.3   *Discourse*

Discourse has been defined as "the ensemble of phenomena in and through which social production of meaning takes place" (Mumby and Stohl 1991: 315). Since a text, in my understanding, is a typically *social* product, created by users in an environment of socially determined conditions, discourse (in the sense defined above) looms large in all textual interpretation. The "ensemble of phenomena" referred to by Mumby and Stohl is what I call the **universe of discourse**; it comprises, but not exclusively, the phenomena usually dealt with in logic or linguistics, the latter comprising such phenomena as the earlier discussed deixis and tense.

However, the discourse aspect of a text is not just a passive one, a reader being (more or less successfully) entertained by an author; on the contrary, the success of the text depends on the reader's active collaboration in creating the textual universe (cf. Mey 1995). The reader is party to the textual discourse as much as is the author: only in the "meeting of their heads" (varying Byatt's expression quoted above) will the real story be successfully delivered and see the light of day.

In this readerly process of (self-)activation, the key word is *credibility*: the author has to establish a universe of discourse that the reader is willing to accept on the writer's "author-ity"; that authority in its turn is dependent on how skillfully the author manages to arrange the events and persons she or he is depicting, and how cleverly she or he manages to assign the characters their proper "voices," as we will see in the next section. Just as the time of the narrative event need not coincide either with "real" time, or with time as it proceeds, in orderly fashion, through our lives, so the levels of narration need not coincide with those of reality. Our knowledge about what can happen in narrative is conditioned by our cultural and social presuppositions, as well as by the particular "contract" that we enter into upon opening a novel; in other words, by the totality of discourse, in the sense defined above.

But how are readers able to "find their feet," to know where they are in the narration? How can they hold on to the thread of a narrative despite many hitches and breaks? In this connection, the all-important question that readers must ask themselves at any given point of the narrative is whose "voice" they are hearing. The next section will deal with this question in detail.

3   Voice and "Point of View"

As we have seen, readerly control of the narration's vagaries is sustained though a variety of devices, some of which are linguistic, while others belong to the domain of "reader pragmatics." Among the latter, there is one that stands out by its importance and frequent use: the phenomenon recognized as "focalization," "voice," or "point of view." Despite its importance for the analysis and understanding of text, this contextual device has found no accepted place in the deliberations of those pragmatically oriented researchers who hail from various linguistic backgrounds: in most cases, their span of attention is limited by the purely grammatical, cotextual phenomena.

In the traditional view, authors create a text by inventing some characters, who then proceed to act out some series of events, called "stories." The characters are the author's "creatures": we attribute the creational origin of a particular character (e.g. Huckleberry Finn) to its creator, a particular author (here Samuel Clemens, a.k.a. Mark Twain). It is essential for the author (as it is for any decent creator) that his or her creatures stay in line and do not transgress the boundaries of the story universe, or of the parts they have been assigned in the play; in particular, the characters should preferably stick to their authorized roles.

However, characters do not always "behave." Authors frequently complain that their personae assume independent lives and voices, and that the plot starts to develop by an inner logic of its own, with the author as a bemused spectator on the sidelines, following the antics of his or her creatures and chronicling them as best he or she can. In extreme cases, the characters may confront the author with their demands and enter onto the stage by themselves, as real, live persons, as has been immortalized in the famous play by Luigi Pirandello, *Six Characters in Search of an Author* (1921).

My use of the "stage image" above is more than a facile illustration: it serves to highlight some of the points that I have been trying to make with regard to the process of narration. A stage play basically consists of characters speaking in the *voices* that have been assigned them by the playwright. These voices are used in the context of an actual setting, that is, a context created by the physical stage, by the director's interpretation of the text, but most of all by the wider ambiance of the literary playhouse and its temporary inhabitants, the audience, the latter representing the broader context of society.

The process by which (theatrical or literary) voices are created is called **voicing**. The voices appearing on the scene are embodied in the *dramatis personae*, originally "personified" (as the word indicates: *persona* is Latin for "mask") by the masks worn in the classical theatrical performance. Voices are made possible within the *universe of discourse*, that is, they neither represent independently created roles, to be played at will as exponents of the actor's self-expression, nor are they strictly grammatically produced and semantically defined units, to be interpreted by linguists and text analysts according to the rules of grammar or narration. Rather, voices have to be understood in an interactive process of ongoing collaboration between all the parties involved. It is this **contextual cooperation** that the process of "voicing," in the final analysis, presupposes and represents.

Successful voicing depends on the interplay of the agents in the narrative process, narrator and "narratee" in concert making up the successful narration. In the following, I will illustrate the crucial role of "voice" (understood as the verbal expression of a particular character's role) in a pragmatic approach to text. I will do this by sketching out the interplay of the various voices in Nélida Piñon's *The Republic of Dreams*; in particular, I will show how Breta, the granddaughter, is given a different voice, depending on her position in the narrative.[3]

First of all, we have the *author*, Nélida Piñon, who is responsible for the literary work as such. She speaks to us indirectly, as it were, as a *narrator*, through the device of storytelling. As the "narrative instance" in charge, she has all the attributes that we ordinarily associate with a storyteller: omnipotence, omniscience (specifically, knowledge of what goes on in the heads and "inner sancta" of the persons described), omnipresence, and so on. In this narrative, as is usual, the narrator remains *implicit* (see Mey 1999: section 8.4.2): we are told that "Eulália had started to die on Tuesday" (the opening sentence of the book; Piñon 1984: 3), but no official, *explicit* "sender" of this message is provided. The *voice* we are hearing is the voice of the narrator, not that of the author: the latter only speaks to us *through* the former.

Similarly, we are introduced to Breta as Eulália's granddaughter by the same implicit narrative voice:

> Eulália watched them [the grandchildren coming into her room to say goodbye]. . . . Eulália noted Breta's presence. . . . She had always handed over this granddaughter to her husband. (1984: 14)

Later on in the book, some of the *characters* tend to become narrators in their own rights. This starts already a couple of pages down from the previous quote, where the grandfather introduces himself as a narrator by saying:

> The story of Breta, and of this family, began at my birth. (1984: 16)

As to Breta herself, she assumes her role as an homodiegetic ("I") narrator with the words:

> When I was a little girl, Grandfather surprised me with presents and unexpected proposals. (1984: 66)

These continuous shifts between third person and first person narration are characteristic of this particular novel; but in order to pin down the "I-voice" of a particular piece of first person narrative, we have not only to invoke the grammatical or linguistic resources at our command, but in addition, we have to enter the "fictional world" (Mey 1994), the world of narration, by identifying with the particular voice that is speaking. For instance, in the case of Madruga, the grandfather, introducing himself as an "I" on p. 16, we are at first uncertain whom the narrative voice belongs to: Eulália (who also has been present throughout the preceding section), or Madruga, her husband. As we read on, it turns out that the voice is that of a boy: his passion for fishing, his burgeoning attraction to women, all bespeak the gender of the young Madruga.

When, towards the end of the book, after many allusions to her future role as a family chronicler (e.g. on p. 17, where her grandfather muses: "What if she were to be the first writer in the family?"), Breta "comes out" as an author ("I will write the book nonetheless," p. 662), it is the voice of Breta, as a *character turned narrator*, telling us this. And when we close the book, on the last sentence:

> I only know that tomorrow I will start to write the story of Madruga. (1984: 663)

we are in the presence of a narrative voice that tells us that what the Breta character is going to do as an *author* is to write the story, parts of which she has just told us in her own, *character-become-narrator*'s voice. By this narratorial trick, Breta the *presumptive* author hands back the narrative relay to the *actual* author who has created her, Nélida Piñon, thus closing the narrative score on a final, impressive flourish.

4   Conclusion

It is only through an active cooperative effort, shared between reader and author, that the interplay of voices can be successfully created and recreated. Reading is a *cooperative* act; the pragmatics of literary texts spell out the conditions for this collaborative effort, without which the text would not properly exist as text. Only through a *pragmatic act* of reading can the text be realized; without such an act, and its corresponding actor, the *reader*, the "letters of literature" will forever be dead.[4]

NOTES

1   Both readings, "his own" and "being his own", are possible. Thanks to Deborah Tannen for pointing this out.
2   The Russian text contains more clues in this respect than does the English translation I have quoted (despite the fact that the translator is a native-born Russian). A recent English translation of Bulgakov's work fares slightly better: "as was learned subsequently" is how Burgin and O'Connor render the discussed passage (1995: 6). Even so, the tense problem remains.
3   In the following, the translations are my own; the page references are to the original, Brazilian edition of the novel.
4   On "pragmatic acts", see Mey (2000: ch. 8).

REFERENCES

Bal, Mieke. 1985. *Narratology. Introduction to the Theory of Narrative*. Toronto: University of Toronto Press. (Original Dutch title: *De Theorie van het Vertellen en Verhalen*. Muiderberg: Coutinho, 1981.)

Banfield, Ann. 1983. *Unspeakable Sentences: Narration and Representation in the Language of Fiction*. London: Routledge and Kegan Paul.

Bulgakov, Mikhail A. 1969. *Master i Margarita (The Master and Margarita)*. Frankfurt: Posev. English trans. Mirra Ginsburg, New York: Grove Press. 1967; new trans. Diana Burgin and Katherine Tiernan O'Connor. Dana Point, Calif.: Ardis. 1995. [1940; first Russian edn 1966–7.]

Byatt, A. S. 1992. *Angels and Insects*. London: Chatto and Windus.

Byatt, A. S. 1996. *Babel Tower*. New York: Random House.

Cohn, Dorrit. 1978. *Transparent Minds: Narrative Modes for Presenting Consciousness in Fiction*. Princeton, N.J.: Princeton University Press.

Ehrlich, Susan. 1990. *Point of View: A Linguistic Analysis of Literary Style*. London and New York: Routledge and Kegan Paul.

Fludernik, Monika. 1993. *The Fictions of Language and the Languages of Fiction.: The Linguistic Representation of Speech and Consciousness*. London: Routledge and Kegan Paul.

Fludernik, Monika. 1996. *Towards a "Natural" Narratology*. London: Routledge and Kegan Paul.

Genette, Gérard. 1980. *Narrative Discourse: An Essay in Method*. Ithaca, N.Y.: Cornell University Press. (French original: *Figures III: Discours du Récit*. Paris: Seuil, 1972).

Heath, Shirley Brice. 1988. *Ways with Words*. London: Routledge and Kegan Paul.

Iser, Wolfgang. 1978. *Die Art des Lesens*. Munich: Pieper.

McHale, Brian. 1983. Review of Banfield 1983. *Poetics Today* 4.

Mey, Jacob L. 1994. Edifying Archie or: How to fool the reader. In Herman Parret, ed., *Pretending to Communicate*. Berlin: Walter de Gruyter. pp. 154–72.

Mey, Jacob L. 1995. Pragmatic problems in literary texts. In Sharon Millar and Jacob Mey, eds, *Form and Function in Language*. Odense: Odense University Press. pp. 151–70. (= *RASK* Suppl. Vol. 2).

Mey, Jacob L. 1999. *When Voices Clash: A Study in Literary Pragmatics*. Berlin and New York: Mouton de Gruyter.

Mey, Jacob L. 2000. *Pragmatics: An Introduction*. Oxford and Malden, Mass.: Blackwell. (Second, entirely revised edition). [1993.]

Miller, J. Hillis. 1985. *The Linguistic Moment: From Wordsworth to Stevens*. Princeton, N.J.: Princeton University Press.

Mumby, Dennis K. and Cynthia Stohl. 1991. Power and discourse in organization studies: absence and the dialectic of control. *Discourse and Society* 2(3): 313–32.

Piñon, Nélida. 1984. *A República dos Sonhos (The Republic of Dreams)*. Rio de Janeiro: Alves. [Engl. trans. Helen Lane. New York: Knopf. 1989.]

Pirandello, Luigi. 1921. *Sei Personaggi in Cerca d'Autore (Six Characters in Search of an Author)*. Milan: Mondadori.

Reichenbach, Hans. 1947. *Elements of Symbolic Logic*. New York: Free Press.

Stanzel, Franz Karl. 1982. *Theorie des Erzählens*. Göttingen: Vandenhoeck and Ruprecht.

Toolan, Michael. 1994. *Narrative: A Critical Linguistic Introduction*. London: Routledge and Kegan Paul. [1988.]

Tsur, Reuven. 1992. *Toward a Theory of Cognitive Poetics*. Amsterdam and New York: North-Holland/Elsevier.

41 Computational Perspectives on Discourse and Dialog

BONNIE LYNN WEBBER

0 Introduction

Computational work on discourse and dialog reflects the two general aims of natural language processing:

- that of modeling human understanding and generation of natural language in terms of a system of computational processes. Work in this area is usually called **computational linguistics**.
- that of enabling computers to analyze and generate natural language in order to provide a useful service. Work in this area has been called **applied natural language processing**, **natural language engineering**, or more recently **language technology**.

These aims go back as far as the earliest research and development in natural language processing (NLP), which began with work on machine translation in the early 1950s. Early machine translation work pointed out serious problems in trying to deal with unrestricted, extended text in weakly circumscribed domains. This led NLP researchers in the 1960s and early 1970s to focus on question-answering dialogs in restricted domains, such as baseball games in Green et al. (1961), airline schedules in Woods (1968), analyses of lunar rocks in Woods et al. (1972), and a "blocks world" in Winograd (1973). But as the development of meaning representations and reasoning needed for effective language processing became less and less language issues, the attention of NLP researchers shifted from developing natural language systems to solving individual language-related problems – e.g. developing faster, more efficient parsers; developing "weaker" and hence more realistic grammars whose complexity is only slightly more than context-free (cf. Joshi 1999); developing ways of handling referring expressions; modeling communicative goals and plans and their realization in language, etc. But now we have come full circle, and the recent explosion in information available over computer networks, and demands for less frustrating automated telephone-based service facilities made possible by advances in speech technology, have refocused interest on dealing with unrestricted extended text and dialog.

With new attention being paid to discourse and dialog, the aims of computational work in these areas can be seen to be similar to those of NLP in general:

- that of modeling particular phenomena in discourse and dialog in terms of underlying computational processes;
- that of providing useful natural language services, whose success depends in part on handling aspects of discourse and dialog.

By "phenomena" in discourse and dialog, I mean either (1) a word, phrase, and utterance whose interpretation is shaped by the discourse or dialog context, or (2) a sequence of utterances whose interpretation is more than the sum of its component parts. What computation contributes is a coherent framework for modeling these phenomena in terms of resource-limited inferential search through a space of possible candidate interpretations (in language analysis) or candidate realizations (in language generation).

Inference here refers to any form of reasoning. The reasoning may be **nondefeasible**, according to logical principles that guarantee the correctness of its conclusions, as in correctly concluding from "John went to the zoo again" that John had gone to the zoo at least once before. Or the reasoning may be **defeasible**, producing plausible conclusions that are not necessarily correct, as in concluding from "John went to the zoo. He saw an owl" that John had seen the owl at the zoo.

Search refers to how one goes about determining discourse interpretation: there are often several *possible* ways to interpret a word, phrase, utterance, or sequence of utterances in context, and one needs to find the intended, or at least the most likely, one. **Inferential search** refers to the roles that inference can play in this process: it can serve to (1) grow the search space in which the interpretation of an utterance will be found (or alternatively, the search space in which the surface realization of some underlying conceptual form will be found), or (2) provide evidence relevant to evaluating candidate interpretations or surface realizations, or both. For example, in:

(1) a. John arrived at an oasis. He saw the camels around the water hole and . . .
     b. John arrived at an oasis. He left the camels around the water hole and . . .

inference can play one or both roles in interpreting the definite noun phrase "the camels." It can be used to link the camels to the oasis or to the means by which John got there. (This use of inference is sometimes called **bridging**.) And it can also be used in choosing which interpretation is more plausible – camels already at the oasis in (1a), since they are something John might observe and whose observation might be mentioned, and camels that John brought with him to the oasis in (1b), since they are something he could then leave.

Resource-limited refers to the fact that the computational processes used in discourse and dialog do not have unlimited time or memory in which to carry out the search. Resource-limited search can manifest itself in terms of restrictions on the context from which search begins and/or as constraints on the way the search space can develop. For example, if there is a cost associated with inference, as in Hobbs et al. (1993) and Thomason and Hobbs (1997), that cost can be used to direct the growth of the search space toward low-cost solutions or to prune more expensive ones from it.

(It can also be used to choose the lowest-cost interpretation among those that can be completed, but that would not be a resource-limited process, as it would require first producing them all.)

This is not to imply that all computational work on discourse and dialog involves resource-limited inferential search. Recent language technology work on discourse (mainly coreference identification) and dialog (mainly call routing and other simple service interactions) exploits probabilistic methods based on frequencies gathered from large tagged corpora. I will say a bit more about this in section 2.

Section 1 of this chapter provides a brief discussion of computational models of discourse and dialog from the perspective of computational linguistics. Section 2 describes language technology in the area of discourse and dialog, while section 3 speculates on future directions and developments.

More extensive discussion of recent computational research and development can be found in the individual papers cited throughout this chapter, in textbooks by Allen (1995) and by Jurafsky and Martin (2000), in a survey by Cohen (1996), and in the websites of the Association for Computational Linguistics' Special Interest Group on Discourse and Dialogue (SIGDial) (http://www.sigdial.org) and the Language Engineering Telematics project, MATE (http://mate.nis.sdu.dk/).

1   Discourse, Dialog, and Computation

1.1   *Computational models of cognitive processes in discourse and dialog*

Many aspects of language have their use and interpretation shaped by the discourse context:

- forms of reference, such as pronominal anaphora and deixis, and definite and deictic noun phrase (NP) reference;
- certain forms of ellipsis such as VP ellipsis, sluicing – e.g. "I know John goes swimming on New Year's Day but I don't know why" – and background ellipsis – e.g. Q: "Will the shop open in June?" A: "No." Q: "In July?" (Other forms of ellipsis, such as gapping and conjunction reduction, are generally considered purely within the domain of syntax and do not appeal to the resources or processes associated with discourse.)
- the interpretation of clauses in terms of eventualities and their temporal, causal and rhetorical relations to one another.
- aspects of intonation and syntactic choice generally associated with **information structure** (i.e. notions of theme/rheme and background/focus).

What these phenomena share are *constraints* on their use, associated with a continually changing context that they contribute to, and reliance on *inference* to find and/or verify candidate intepretations. These features come from the resource-limited inferential search processes that underlie their generation and interpretation.

Consider, for example, pronominal reference. One of the earliest computational models of pronoun reference appears in LUNAR (cf. Woods 1978), which allowed geologists to pose English-language queries to a large database concerning the *Apollo 11* lunar samples. LUNAR's treatment of pronominal anaphora in follow-up questions such as:

(2) User: Do the breccias contain olivine?
LUNAR: . . .
User: Do they contain magnatite?

(3) User: What is the silicon content of each volcanic sample?
LUNAR: . . .
User: What is its magnesium concentration?

followed Karttunen (1976) in taking pronouns and definite NPs to refer to **entities** in a model of the discourse. In LUNAR, entities could be evoked through indefinite and definite NPs in a user's query, and referenced in the same or a subsequent query. Only the ten most recently evoked or referenced entities were considered possible referents for a subsequent pronoun or definite NP. Entities were tested for semantic fit in order of recency, with the first to fit taken to be the intended referent. This had the side effect of updating the referent's position in the **reference list**, removing it from its current position and inserting it at the start of the list, thereby delaying its dropping off the end. Recent theories of contextual reference based on an approach to contextual modeling called **centering**, developed in the mid-1980s by Grosz et al. (1995), have similar features.

Centering follows work by Sidner (1982) in imposing a finer structure on context than LUNAR, by assigning to each utterance in a discourse both a unique **backward-looking center** C_b and a rank-ordered list of **forward-looking centers** C_f. The C_f-list for one utterance comprises the possible candidate referents for pronouns in the next utterance. One question is how to structure this search, and different ordering metrics have been proposed for different languages (for Italian in Di Eugenio 1997, for Turkish in Turan 1995, and for Japanese in Iida 1997). Another question is how to use the C_b in identifying a preferred solution. For example, Brennan et al. (1987) introduced the idea of **center transition preferences** that prefer interpreting a pronoun in a way that retains the same C_b between utterances, or barring that, only changes it in particular ways. The C_b and C_f-list are then updated at the end of each utterance.

Brennan et al.'s treatment is not incremental. In contrast, Strube (1998) proposed a simpler form of centering that returns to models such as LUNAR in (1) abandoning the backward-looking center C_b and center transitions and (2) using only a finite ordered list of salient candidates. This allows updating to take place as soon as a referring expression is processed, with an entity's insertion into the list determined by how the speaker has chosen to specify it with respect to the "familiarity scale" given in Prince (1981). In this scale, Prince distinguishes between entities presented as **new** to the discourse, entities presented as already **evoked** by the discourse or the outside situation, and entities presented as **inferable** from something already introduced into the discourse. A feature of this scale is that well-known individuals, when first introduced into a discourse, are nevertheless considered new (in Prince's terms, **unused**). In Strube's incremental approach, if an entity is already on the list, its position on the list may change on subsequent reference, reflecting how it has been specified. Besides being simpler, Strube's algorithm better reflects intended interpretations than other centering algorithms, although it still does not provide a complete account of pronominal reference.

It should be noted that centering and earlier focus models have also been used to guide decisions about the use of pronouns in generating text in work by McKeown (1985) and by Dale (1992), though the decision process is not simply the reverse of that used in interpretation. More recently, McCoy and Strube (1999) have considered whether considering changes in temporal focus could explain a speaker's decision to use a name or definite NP where centering allows the use of a pronoun: it is a better model, but still incomplete.

Computational models of other discourse phenomena – including other forms of contextual reference – highlight other features of the resource-limited inferential search that can be seen to underpin their processing.

1.1.1   Definite NPs

The intended referent of a definite NP need not have been explicitly mentioned in the prior discourse, as long as it can be inferred from what has been. For example, in:

(4)   Phone "Information". *The operator* should be able to help you.

the definite NP *the operator* refers to the telephone operator you reach when phoning information. The referent of a definite NP can but need not be a member of the set of initial candidates that a reference resolution process begins with. Computational research attempts to specify not just what these additional candidates may be, but the specific search processes by which they will be found and the intended referent correctly identified, as in Bos et al. (1995); Hahn et al. (1996); Hobbs et al. (1993); Markert and Hahn (1997). From the perspective of text generation, choosing whether to use a definite NP (and, if so, choosing one sufficient to refer uniquely to the intended referent) involves both search and inference for other entities in the context that block referential uniqueness, and search for properties that distinguish the intended referent from the remaining others, as in Dale and Haddock (1991); Dale and Reiter (1995); Horacek (1997); Stone and Doran (1997); Stone and Webber (1998).

1.1.2   Demonstrative pronouns

These expressions highlight the need for an augmented candidate set for reference – not only the individuals and/or sets evoked by individual NPs (or sets of NPs) but also properties and eventualities evoked by predicates, clauses and larger units of discourse (**discourse segments**). For example:

(5)   Phone "Information". *That* should get you the information you need.

As discussed in Webber (1988, 1991) and later in Asher (1993) and Stone (1994), resolution of demonstrative pronouns appears, in part, parasitic on an update process for discourse segments to provide possible referents. Where demonstratives refer to individuals, Davies and Isard (1972) have pointed out the role of stress in preferring one candidate over another in resolving a demonstrative pronoun versus an anaphoric pronoun:

(6)   Think of a number, square it, and then multiply [*it, that*] by three.

In NL generation, I am not aware of any more recent attempt to articulate the processes involved in generating demonstrative pronouns than the work of Davey (1974), generating explanations of what happened in a game of tic-tac-toe.

1.1.3   Clausal relations

It has long been noted that a discourse composed of a sequence of clauses requires recognizing intended relations between them (often called **coherence relations**), although Scott and de Souza (1990) and others have pointed out that similar relations hold between phrases and between phrases and clauses as well. Such relations have been taken to contribute to the underlying substructures and their interpretation as explanations, descriptions, proposals, corrections, etc. For example, one must recognize the different relations between the clauses in (7a) and in (7b), in order to understand them correctly:

(7)   a. Phone "Information". The operator will have the number you want.
      b. Phone "Information". It won't cost you anything.

Rhetorical Structure Theory, as presented in Mann and Thompson (1988), posits a fixed set of relations with constraints on their applicability, but not how they would be used in any kind of process involved in understanding or generation. Identifying clausal relations appears resource-limited in two ways: in establishing what the current clause is related to – the previous clause or some larger segment in which it is embedded – and in establishing what relation(s) hold between them. With respect to the former, while a speaker may be describing more than one event or situation at a time or connecting up many strands into an explanation, the listener, nonetheless, appears limited in terms of how many things she or he can be attending to or keeping in mind simultaneously and on how she or he can use evidence in deciding how a new clause fits in. Computational work here has focused on the updating process, including the role of tense and aspect as evidence for what should be updated and how. Relevant work here includes that of Hitzeman et al. (1995); Kameyama et al. (1993); Kehler (1994); Moens and Steedman (1988); Webber (1988). Different inferential processes that could be used in recognizing the intended relations between clauses within a discourse are described in Hobbs et al. (1993); Lascarides and Asher (1993); Thomason and Hobbs (1997). Discussion of bases for relating clauses in discourse can be found in Grosz and Sidner (1986); Moore and Pollack (1992); Moser and Moore (1996); Webber et al. (1999b, 1999c).

1.1.4   Information structure

Information structure deals with: (1) what a speaker conveys as being the topic under current discussion and, consequently, his or her contribution to that topic (**theme** vs. **rheme**), and (2) what a speaker takes to be in contrast with things a hearer is or can be attending to (**focus** vs. **background**) (cf. Halliday 1967b, 1970; Steedman 2000). Information structure manifests itself in both sentential syntax and intonation.

Just as interpreting a clause as an eventuality requires identifying its temporal, causal, and/or rhetorical relations with others in the discourse, the process involved in recognizing the theme of an utterance also requires recognizing its relation to the theme of the previous utterance or, more generally, to context. This again requires an inferential search process. So too do elements marked intonationally or syntactically as being in contrast require searching through a limited set of elements that could serve as a source of contrast, and inferring the intended alternative set to which both source and contrast item belong. This again is a resource-limited inferential search process. Less work has, to date, been done on characterizing and modeling these processes, but cf. Hajicova et al. (1995); Prevost (1995); Prevost and Steedman (1994); Steedman (1996a). Interest in the area is growing due to its use in improving intonation in spoken language generation.

1.1.5   Repetition and restatement

Speakers have been observed to often restate information already introduced into a dialog. This would contradict the Maxim of Quantity in Grice (1975), unless, as suggested in Walker (1996a, 1996b), there are resource-limitations on the propositions a listener can be attending to and all propositions needed to draw an inference must be attended to simultaneously. In Walker's model, recently introduced or mentioned propositions are held in an unordered cache (rather than an ordered list), and various cache management strategies are explored to see which correspond more closely to observed human behaviors.

There are other discourse phenomena whose interpretation depends on context – from the contextual presuppositions of individual words such as "also" and "other" (cf. Bierner and Webber 1999) to the contextual presuppositions of clauses headed by "when" and "since." Eventually, all such phenomena should be brought within the purview of a computational account framed in terms of resource-limited inferential search.

1.2   Computational models of rational agency

Discourse and dialog pragmatics (including speech acts, relevance, Gricean maxims, etc.), in the procedural view taken here, emerge from considerations of speaker and hearer as rational agents. Rational agency views discourse and dialog as behavior arising from and able to express an agent's beliefs, desires, and intentions (i.e. what the agent is committed to achieving), constrained by its resource limitations, as described in Bratman (1987); Bratman et al. (1988). Both **planning** – the process that maps an agent's intentions into actions, primarily communicative in the case of speakers as agents – and **plan recognition** – the process by which a hearer recognizes what the speaker is trying to accomplish – are resource-limited inferential search processes. However, they are shaped by two factors beyond those discussed in the previous section:

- The context in which they operate *changes continually* in consequence of actions.
- The changing context will only ever be *partially known*.

The former means that any look-ahead or precomputations they do must reflect the fact that beliefs and intentions of speaker and hearer can evolve or even change precipitously during the course of a discourse or dialog. The latter means that these processes must be able to elicit essential information; to provide useful output on the basis of assumptions as well as facts; and to modify or efficiently recompute new output if and when these assumptions are found inconsistent or wrong.

The basic framework for this work comes from the "goal (intention) begets plan" approach to planning developed and used in artificial intelligence since the late 1960s, following ideas in Newell and Simon (1963). The most widely known version is called the STRIPS algorithm, described in Fikes and Nilsson (1971). The data structures used by this algorithm capture such elements of intention and action (including communicative action) as the fact that actions have preconditions that must hold for them to have their intended effects, and that they may therefore be themselves adopted as goals realizable through further communicative actions; and that actions may have several different effects on the world. Later versions incorporated additional features such as a view of actions at different levels of aggregation and abstraction, in work by Di Eugenio (1998), Di Eugenio and Webber (1996), and Moore (1995); actions that can be done to acquire information, which can then affect the further plan or trigger further planning; and the fact that changing an agent's beliefs can cause him or her to adopt particular goals, etc., in the work of Allen (1995); Appelt (1985); Cohen and Perrault (1979); Litman and Allen (1990). This is all well described in Allen (1995).

More recently, researchers have begun to develop more complex computational models of language as rational planned action, reflecting, inter alia:

- that the beliefs of the planner/speaker might differ from those of the hearer and even be incorrect. Pollack (1986) shows how, for a speaker's communicative actions and underlying plan to be understood with respect to her or his beliefs, the hearer must be able to infer or elicit what beliefs support the speaker's inferred plan as well as inferring that plan itself.
- that dialog can be used to explore and negotiate possible courses of action, not just accomplish action, shown in the work of Di Eugenio et al. (1998) and Lambert and Carberry (1992, 1999).
- that dialog involves a collaboration among all its participants. Thus, Grosz and Kraus (1996); Grosz and Sidner (1990); Lochbaum (1998); McRoy and Hirst (1995) all show that the planning process for achieving goals through dialog is more complex than when only a single planning agent is involved.
- that planning agents have preferences shaping the way they choose to realize goals as plans of action. Thus, both Chu-Carroll (1997) and Carberry et al. (1999) show that in an advisory dialog, the participant in the advisory role must be able to infer or elicit those preferences, as well as the advisee's possibly incorrect beliefs.

- that communicative actions – e.g. to justify one course of action over another, to explain how a process works, etc. – may not succeed in their goal, requiring the speaker to use the hearer's feedback to produce a new or augmented plan whose communicative actions will accomplish the goal or support the initial communication in doing so (e.g. through clarification or explanation), as in the work of Moore (1995) and Young et al. (1994).
- that a communicative action conveys information to achieve particular intentions – (cf. Grosz and Sidner 1986; Moore and Paris 1993; Moore and Pollack 1992); that there is a potentially many-to-many relation between information and intention (cf. Di Eugenio and Webber 1996; Moore and Pollack 1992; Pollack 1991; Stone and Webber 1998); and that information and intention must be combined in generating communicative actions and extracted in understanding them. How to do this harkens back to discussions of the **modularity** of syntax and semantics in Fodor (1983). That is, Moore and Pollack (1992) argue that the recognition of informational relations cannot be ordered a priori before the recognition of intentional relations, and vice versa. But whether, in human language processing, the processes operate nondeterministically in parallel on distinct data structures, as in Hobbs (1996), or are integrated into a single process operating on a single integrated database, as in Moore (1995), or something in between, as in Thomason and Hobbs (1997), is not clear. Nor is the optimal form of integration yet known from a purely computational engineering perspective.

The brief discussions in the next two sections will show an ever-increasing number of applications in the areas of discourse and dialog. As in the past, this will also likely act as a spur to increased theoretical understanding of discourse and dialog in terms of cognition and rational agency.

2   Discourse, Dialog, and Language Technology

As noted in section 0, computational work on discourse and dialog has been driven equally by the desire to understand these phenomena as manifestations of intrinsically computational processes and by the desire to satisfy existing or potential consumer needs. In the early days of NLP, those needs were taken to be machine translation (MT) and database question/answering. The latter drove much of the early research on discourse and dialog (cf. section 1.1 and work on "cooperative question answering" such as Cheikes and Webber 1988; Joshi 1982; Joshi et al. 1987; Pollack 1986; Webber 1986). But despite early attempts to provide NL "front ends" to database systems to handle user queries, and NL "back ends" to produce cooperative responses, the consumer base of casual users of database systems, for whom such "wrappers" were designed, never really materialized.

Recently however, there has been renewed interest in cooperative dialogs, made possible by improvements in automated speech recognition and spurred by corporate desires for automated (spoken) telephone and web-based service interactions (cf. Litman et al. 1998; Walker et al. 1998). Similarly, for most of its history, MT ignored discourse and dialog as a relevant factor in translation, but again, speech recognition has made a difference: now the effort to provide "translating telephones" requires making use of whatever sources of knowledge can be brought to bear. Finally, the recent explosion of freely available electronic text and services on the worldwide web (WWW) has become a potent driver of language technology, including work on discourse and dialog.

By and large, language technology methods aim toward broad coverage at low cost. They eschew understanding, tolerating what may, from a theoretical perspective, appear to be a high rate of errors, as long as they individually or together lead to significant improvements in overall task performance. In web-based information retrieval, such improvements may involve either increasing **precision** (i.e. reducing the large number of "false positives" in any search that tries to avoid missing too many "true positives") or increasing **recall** (i.e. increasing the number of "true positives" that might otherwise be missed when anaphora and ellipses replace more lexically "revealing" evidence). The former is being addressed indirectly, by trying to identify what parts of a text might potentially be relevant (subtopic identification) and by trying to identify the sentences in a (short) document that best reveal its content and outputting those sentences as a summary of the text, as in Kupiac et al. (1995) and Mani and Maybury (1998), thereby enabling people to make relevance judgments faster, based on a smaller portion of the text, as in the work of Hearst (1994) and Reynar (1998). Where those sentences themselves contain context-dependent discourse phenomena, efforts are made to include sufficient previous text that people can resolve them. The latter is being tackled by superficial methods of coreference resolution that may guess incorrectly in places or only attempt the easy cases (cf. Baldwin 1997; Kameyama 1997; Kennedy and Boguraev 1996).

Work is also being done on developing and using **dialog models** to support more effective telephone- and web-based computer services, including call-routing (cf. Chu-Carroll and Carpenter, 1999), emergency planning-support systems (cf. Allen et al. 1996; Heeman et al. 1998), and travel information (cf. Bennacef et al. 1996; Carlson and Hunnicut 1996; Flycht-Eriksson and Jonsson 1998; Seneff et al. 1998). A dialog model is an efficient description of standard patterns of action in a dialog, often encoded as a finite-state or probabilistic automaton to reflect the role of the current state in predicting (or constraining) the next one. The development of a dialog model thus requires two things:

- a classification scheme for dialog actions that (1) can be annotated reliably (cf. Carletta et al. 1997) on the basis of superficial evidence, and (2) can support effective predictions. Dialog acts are commonly classified functionally, at some abstract level connected with the type of task being performed (e.g., *greet, suggest, reject*, etc. as in Samuel et al. 1998 (meeting planning dialogs); *restate plan, elaborate plan*, etc. as in Heeman et al. 1998 (complex task-planning dialogs), also (cf. Poesio and Traum 1997; Reithinger and Klesen 1997; Traum and Hinkelman 1992). But they can also be usefully classified by the topic they address, as in Chu-Carroll and Carpenter (1999) and Jokinen et al. (1998).
- a reliable method of correlating evidence from dialog actions and their context with the classification of dialog actions, so that the dialog model can be used in speech recognition, dialog understanding, and/or response generation. The usual problem is that one does not know which combination of which surface features

– including particular vocalizations, particular words and/or phrases, particular surface-syntactic features, the class of the previous utterance(s), etc. – provides reliable evidence, including potentially different features and a different combination for each class in the scheme. So data must first be reliably annotated for features that could serve as evidence. After that, a machine-learning method such as decision-tree induction, transformation-based learning (cf. Samuel et al. 1998), or neural network learning can be used to build the classification scheme. For clarity, one may use sets of probabilistic automata, each trained to a different kind of evidence, combined using the standard calculus of probabilities, as in the dialog managers developed by Stolcke et al. (1998) and Taylor et al. (1998).

A dialog model can also be designed to make use of a **dialog strategy**, embodying decisions for how to respond to dialog actions on the part of the human user that admit a variety of system responses. Here, both machine learning and purely statistical techniques are being used to identify effective strategies and evaluate their effectiveness (cf. Litman et al. 1998; Walker et al. 1998).

3   Speculations on Future Directions and Developments

Before closing this chapter, I would like to add my speculations on where useful future developments are likely to occur in computational work on discourse and dialog.

- The development of a single integrated account of context management (updating, evolution, and retrieval) will provide better understanding of the whole range of resource-bounded, context-linked discourse phenomena, including contextual reference, information structure, and clausal relations.
- The development of an integrated account of both informational and intentional aspects of discourse and dialog will initially support more principled and effective text and speech generation systems and, eventually, understanding systems as well.
- The emergence of new tasks related to discourse and dialog will turn researchers' attention to additional communicative phenomena. For example, broadening communication channels to support "face-to-screen" or even "face-to-face" spoken interaction with computer systems will focus attention on information to be gained from a speaker's gestures and their use in enriching the speaker's message or in disambiguating it, as in the work of André et al. (1998); Cassell et al. (1994); Cassell and Stone (1999); Koons et al. (1993); McGee et al. (1998).
- Improvements in the handling of current phenomena, such as clausal reference and clausal relations, will be needed to support more difficult future tasks involving "mapping" natural language texts to formal specifications (e.g. for software, to support system construction and verification) or to terminologies (e.g. in medicine, to support knowledge discovery and refinement of practice standards).

- Just as at the sentence level, lexical semantics poses more difficult representational and reasoning problems than Montague-style formal semantics, at the discourse level, the semantics of events and actions poses as yet unsolved problems in representation and reasoning. The emergence of solutions to these problems should lead to improved performance on information retrieval and text summarization tasks, and may also support vision systems to use natural language discourse and dialog to talk about what they see as they act in the world.
- Just as sentence-level processing has sought lexically based syntactic/semantic formalisms that can facilitate both understanding and generation (cf. Tree-Adjoining Grammar, described in Joshi 1987; Combinatory Categorial Grammar, described in Steedman 1996b, 2000, etc.), similar efforts by Danlos (1997) and by Webber et al. (1999a, 1999b, 1999c) will contribute to facilitating both discourse understanding and generation.
- As in grammar modeling, where the utterances that people produce are influenced by a wide range of structural and performance factors and where probabilistic models may provide the most reliable predictions, probabilistic models used in discourse and dialog will improve as they move to incorporate more and more sophisticated models of the phenomena they aim to approximate.
- More and more on-line documents are being prepared using mark-up languages like SGML or document-type declarations specified in XML. Mark-up reflecting function (e.g. heading, citation, pie chart, etc.) rather than appearance (e.g. italics, flush right, etc.) will likely facilitate more effective information retrieval and other language technology services such as summarization and multidocument integration.

There seems no doubt that computational approaches are contributing their share to our understanding of discourse and dialog and to our ability to make use of discourse and dialog in building useful, user-oriented systems.

NOTE

I would like to thank Sandra Carberry, Barbara Di Eugenio, Claire Gardent, Aravind Joshi, Mark Steedman, and Michael Strube, who have provided me with useful direction and comments in the orientation, organization, and presentation of this chapter.

REFERENCES

Allen, James, 1995. *Natural Language Understanding*. Redwood City CA: Benjamin/Cummings, second edition.

Allen, James, Miller, Bradford, Ringger, Eric, and Sikorski, Tiresa, 1996. "A robust system for natural spoken dialogue." In *Proceedings of the 34th Annual Meeting, Association for Computational Linguistics*. University of California at Santa Cruz, 62–70.

André, Elisabeth, Rist, Thomas, and Muller, Jochen, 1998. "WebPersona: a life-like presentation agent for the world-wide web." *Knowledge-Based Systems* 11:25–36.

Appelt, Douglas, 1985. *Planning English Sentences*. Cambridge: Cambridge University Press.

Asher, Nicholas, 1993. *Reference to Abstract Objects in Discourse*. Boston, MA: Kluwer.

Baldwin, Breck, 1997. "CogNIAC: high precision coreference with limited knowledge and linguistic resources." In *Proceedings of the ACL/EACL Workshop on Operational Factors in Practical, Robust Anaphora Resolution for Unrestricted Texts*. Madrid, 38–45.

Bennacef, S., Devillers, L., Rosset, S., and Lamel, L., 1996. "Dialog in the RAILTEL telephone-based system." In *Proceedings of the Fourth International Conference on Spoken Language Processing*. Philadelphia, PA, 550–3.

Bierner, Gann and Webber, Bonnie, 1999. "Inference through alternative set semantics." In *Inference in Computational Semantics, Proceedings*. Amsterdam, 39–52. Extended version in *Journal of Language and Computation*. 1(2), Spring 2000, 259–74.

Bos, Johan, Buitelaar, Paul, and Mineur, Anne-Marie, 1995. "Bridging as coercive accommodation." In *Proceedings of the CLNLP Workshop*. Edinburgh.

Bratman, Michael, 1987. *Intentions, Plans and Practical Reason*. Cambridge, MA: Harvard University Press.

Bratman, Michael, Israel, David, and Pollack, Martha, 1988. "Plans and resource-bounded practical reasoning." *Computational Intelligence* 4(4):349–55.

Brennan, Susan E., Friedman, Walker, Marilyn, and Pollard, Carl J., 1987. "A centering approach to pronouns." In *Proceedings of the 25th Annual Meeting, Association for Computational Linguistics*. Stanford University, Stanford, CA, 155–62.

Carberry, Sandra, Chu-Carroll, Jennifer, and Elzer, Stephanie, 1999. "Constructing and utilizing a model of user preferences in collaborative consulation dialogues." *Computational Intelligence* 15(3):185–217.

Carletta, Jean, Isard, Amy, Isard, Stephen, Kowtko, Jacqueline, Doherty-Sneddon, Gwyneth, and Anderson, Anne, 1997. "The reliability of a dialogue structure coding scheme." *Computational Linguistics* 23(1):13–31.

Carlson, Rolf and Hunnicut, Sheri, 1996. "Generic and domain-specific aspects of the Waxholm NLP and dialog modules." In *Proceedings of the Fourth International Conference on Spoken Language Processing*. Philadelphia PA, 677–80.

Cassell, Justine and Stone, Matthew, 1999. "Living hand to mouth: psychological theories about speech and gesture in interactive dialogue systems." In *Proceedings of AAAI Fall Symposium on Psychological Models of Communication in Collaborative Systems*, 34–42.

Cassell, Justine, Badler, Norman, Douville, Brett, Pelachaud, Catherine, Steedman, Mark, and Stone, Matthew, 1994. "Animated conversation: rule-based generation of facial expressions, gesture and spoken intonation for multiple conversational agents." In *Proceedings of SIGRAPH'94*. Anaheim, CA, 413–20.

Cheikes, Brant and Webber, Bonnie, 1988. "The design of a cooperative respondent." In *Proceedings of the Workshop on Architectures for Intelligent Interfaces*. Monterey, CA, 3–17.

Chu-Carroll, Jennifer, 1997. "A plan-based model for response generation in collaborative negotiation dialogues." PhD thesis, Department of Computer and Information Science, University of Delaware.

Chu-Carroll, Jennifer and Carpenter, Bob, 1999. "Vector-based natural language call routing." *Computational Linguistics* 25(3):361–88.

Cohen, Philip, 1996. "Discourse and dialogue: dialogue modelling." In Ron Cole (ed.), *Survey of the State of the Art in Human Language Technology*, Oregon Graduate Institute: NSF/EC/CSLU, ch. 6.3. http://www.cse.ogi.edu/CSLU/HLTsurvey/HLTsurvey.html

Cohen, Philip and Perrault, C. Raymond, 1979. "Elements of a plan-based theory of speech acts." *Cognitive Science* 3(3):177–212.

Dale, Robert, 1992. *Generating Referring Expressions*. Cambridge, MA: MIT Press.

Dale, Robert and Haddock, Nick, 1991. "Content determination in the generation of referring expressions." *Computational Intelligence* 7(4):252–65.

Dale, Robert and Reiter, Ehud, 1995. "Computational interpretations of the Gricean maxims in the generation of referring expressions." *Cognitive Science* 18:233–63.

Danlos, Laurence, 1997. "G-TAG: a formalism for text generation inspired from tree adjoining grammar." In Anne Abeille and Owen Rambow (eds), *Tree-adjoining Grammar*, Stanford, CA: CSLI Press.

Davey, Anthony, 1974. "The formalisation of discourse production." PhD thesis, Department of Artificial Intelligence, University of Edinburgh.

Davies, D. J. M. and Isard, Stephen, 1972. "Utterances as programs." In Donald Michie (ed.), *Machine Intelligence 7*, Edinburgh: Edinburgh University Press. 325–40.

Di Eugenio, Barbara, 1997. "Centering theory and the Italian pronominal system." In Marilyn Walker, Aravind Joshi, and Ellen Prince (eds), *Centering in Discourse*, Oxford: Oxford University Press. 115–38.

Di Eugenio, Barbara, 1998. "An action representation formalism to interpret natural language instructions." *Computational Intelligence* 14(1):89–133.

Di Eugenio, Barbara and Webber, Bonnie, 1996. "Pragmatic overloading in natural language instructions." *International Journal of Expert Systems* 9(2):53–84.

Di Eugenio, Barbara, Jordan, Pamela W., Moore, Johanna D., and Thomason, Richmond H., 1998. "An empirical investigation of proposals in collaborative dialogues." In *Proceedings of COLING/ACL'98*. Montreal, Canada, 325–9.

Fikes, Richard and Nilsson, Nils, 1971. "STRIPS: a new approach to the application of theorem proving to problem solving." *AI Journal* 2:189–208.

Flycht-Eriksson, Annika and Jonsson, Arne, 1998. "A spoken dialogue system using spatial information." In *Proceedings of the International Conference on Spoken Language Processing*. Sydney, 1207–11.

Fodor, Jerry, 1983. *The Modularity of Mind*. Cambridge, MA: MIT Press.

Green, Bert, Wolf, Alice, Chomsky, Carol, and Laughery, Kenneth, 1961. "BASEBALL: an automatic question answerer." In *Proceedings of the Western Joint Computer Conference*. 219–24. Reprinted in B. Grosz et al. (eds) 1986, *Readings in Natural Language Processing*, Los Altos, CA: Morgan Kaufman. 545–50.

Grice, H. P., 1975. "Logic and conversation." In Peter Cole and Jerry Morgan (eds), *Syntax and Semantics*, New York: Academic Press, vol. 3. 41–58.

Grosz, Barbara and Kraus, Sarit, 1996. "Collaborative plans for complex group actions." *Artificial Intelligence* 86(2):269–357.

Grosz, Barbara and Sidner, Candace, 1986. "Attention, intention and the structure of discourse." *Computational Linguistics* 12(3):175–204.

Grosz, Barbara and Sidner, Candace, 1990. "Plans for discourse." In Philip Cohen, Jerry Morgan, and Martha Pollack (eds), *Intentions in Communication*, Cambridge, MA: MIT Press. 417–44.

Grosz, Barbara, Joshi, Aravind, and Weinstein, Scott, 1995. "Centering: a framework for modelling the local coherence of discourse." *Computational Linguistics* 21(2):203–25.

Hahn, Udo, Markert, Katja, and Strube, Michael, 1996. "A conceptual reasoning approach to textual ellipsis." In *Proceedings of the 12th European Conference on Artificial Intelligence*. Budapest, 572–6.

Hajicova, Eva, Skoumalova, Hana, and Sgall, Petr, 1995. "An automatic procedure for topic-focus identification." *Computational Linguistics* 21(1):81–94.

Halliday, Michael, 1967b. "Notes on transitivity and theme in English, part II." *Journal of Linguistics* 3:199–244.

Halliday, Michael, 1970. "Language structure and language function." In John Lyons (ed.), *New Horizons in Linguistics*, Harmondsworth: Penguin. 140–65.

Hearst, Marti, 1994. "Multi-paragraph segmentation of expository text." In *Proceedings of the 32nd Annual Meeting of the Association for Computational Linguistics*. Las Cruces, NM, 9–16.

Heeman, Peter, Byron, Donna, and Allen, James, 1998. "Identifying discourse markers in spoken dialogue." In *Proceedings of the AAAI Spring Symposium on Applying Machine Learning and Discourse Processing*. Stanford University, CA, 44–51.

Hitzeman, Janet, Moens, Marc, and Grover, Claire, 1995. "Algorithms for analysing the temporal structure of discourse." In *Proceedings of the Annual Meeting of the European Chapter of the Association for Computational Linguistics*. Dublin, 253–60.

Hobbs, Jerry, 1996. "On the relation between the informational and intentional perspectives on discourse." In Eduard Hovy and Donia Scott (eds), *Computational and Conversational Discourse: Papers from the NATO Advanced Research Working Group on Burning Issues in Discourse*, Berlin: Springer Verlag. 139–57.

Hobbs, Jerry, Stickel, Mark, Martin, Paul, and Edwards, Douglas, 1993. "Interpretation as abduction." *Artificial Intelligence* 63(1–2): 69–142.

Horacek, Helmut, 1997. "An algorithm for generating referential descriptions with flexible interfaces." In *Proceedings of the 35th Annual Meeting of the Association for Computational Linguistics (ACL97/EACL97)*. Madrid, Spain. Palo Alto, CA: Morgan Kaufmann, 206–13.

Iida, Masayo, 1997. "Discourse coherence and shifting centers in Japanese texts." In Marilyn Walker, Aravind Joshi, and Ellen Prince (eds), *Centering in Discourse*, Oxford: Oxford University Press. 161–80.

Jokinen, Kristina, Tanaka, Hideki, and Yokoo, Akio, 1998. "Context management with topics for dialogue systems." In *Proceedings of COLING/ACL'98*. Montreal, 631–7.

Joshi, Aravind, 1982. "Mutual beliefs in question answering systems." In N. Smith (ed.), *Mutual Belief*, New York: Academic Press. 181–97.

Joshi, Aravind, 1987. "An introduction to tree adjoining grammar." In Alexis Manaster-Ramer (ed.), *Mathematics of Language*, Amsterdam: John Benjamins. 87–114.

Joshi, Aravind, 1999. "Computational linguistics." In R. Wilson and Frank Keil (eds), *MIT Encyclopedia of Cognitive Sciences*, Cambridge, MA: MIT Press. 162–4.

Joshi, Aravind, Webber, Bonnie, and Weischedel, Ralph, 1987. "Some aspects of default reasoning in interactive discourse." In Ronan Reilly (ed.), *Communication Failure in Dialogue and Discourse*, Amsterdam: North-Holland. 213–20.

Jurafsky, Dan and Martin, James, 2000. *Speech and Language Processing*. Englewood Cliffs, NJ: Prentice-Hall.

Kameyama, Megumi, 1997. "Recognizing referential links: an information extraction perspective." In *Proceedings of the ACL Workshop on Operational Factors in Practical, Robust Anaphora Resolution for Unrestricted Texts*. Madrid, 46–53.

Kameyama, Megumi, Passonneau, Rebecca, and Poesio, Massimo, 1993. "Temporal centering." In *Proceedings of the Annual Meeting of the Association for Computational Linguistics*. Columbus, OH, 70–7.

Karttunen, Lauri, 1976. "Discourse referents." In James McCawley (ed.), *Syntax and Semantics*, New York: Academic Press, vol. 7. 363–85. Earlier circulated as a 1966 Indiana University Linguistics Club pre-print.

Kehler, Andrew, 1994. "Temporal relations: reference or discourse coherence." In *Proceedings of the 32nd Annual Meeting of the Association for Computational Linguistics (ACL), Student Session*. Las Cruces, NM, 319–21.

Kennedy, Christopher and Boguraev, Branimir, 1996. "Anaphora in a wider context: tracking discourse referents." In *Proceedings of the 12th European Conference on Artificial Intelligence*. Budapest, 582–6.

Koons, David B., Sparrell, Carlton J., and Thorisson, Kristina R., 1993. "Integrating simultaneous input from speech, gaze and hand gestures." In Mark T. Maybury (ed.), *Intelligent Multimedia Interfaces*, Cambridge, MA: MIT Press. 257–79.

Kupiac, Julian, Pedersen, Jan, and Chen, F., 1995. "A trainable document summarizer." In *Proceedings of the 18th ACM-SIGIR Conference*. Seattle, WA, 68–73.

Lambert, Lynn and Carberry, Sandra, 1992. "Using linguistic, world and contextual knowledge in a plan recognition model of dialogue." In *COLING92, Proceedings of the 14th International Conference on Computational Linguistics*. Nantes, 310–16.

Lambert, Lynn and Carberry, Sandra, 1999. "A process model for recognizing communicative acts and modeling negotiation subdialogues." *Computational Linguistics* 25:1–53.

Lascarides, Alex and Asher, Nicholas, 1993. "Temporal interpretation, discourse relations and commonsense entailment." *Linguistics and Philosophy* 16(5):437–93.

Litman, Diane and Allen, James, 1990. "Discourse processing and commonsense plans." In Philip Cohen, Jerry Morgan, and Martha Pollack (eds), *Intentions in Communication*, Cambridge, MA: MIT Press. 365–88.

Litman, Diane, Pan, Shimei, and Walker, Marilyn, 1998. "Evaluating response strategies in a web-based spoken dialogue agent." In *Proc COLING-ACL'98*. Montreal, 780–6.

Lochbaum, Karen, 1998. "A collaborative planning modal of intentional structure." *Computational Linguistics* 24(4):525–72.

Mani, Inderjeet and Maybury, Mark, 1998. *Advances in Automatic Abstracting*. Cambridge, MA: MIT Press.

Mann, William and Thompson, Sandra, 1988. "Rhetorical structure theory: toward a functional theory of text organization." *Text* 8(3):243–81.

Markert, Katya and Hahn, Udo, 1997. "On the interaction of metonymies and anaphora." In *Proceedings of International Joint Conference on Artificial Intelligence (IJCAI)*. Nagoya, 1010–15.

McCoy, Kathleen and Strube, Michael, 1999. "Taking time to structure discourse: pronoun generation beyond accessibility." In *Proceedings of the 21st Annual Conference of the Cognitive Science Society*. Vancouver, 378–83.

McGee, David, Cohen, Phil, and Oviatt, Sharon, 1998. "Confirmation in multimodal systems." In *Proceedings of COLING/ACL'98*. Montreal, 823–9.

McKeown, Kathleen, 1985. *Text Generation: Using Discourse Strategies and Focus Constraints to Generate Natural Language Texts*. Cambridge: Cambridge University Press.

McRoy, Susan and Hirst, Graeme, 1995. "The repair of speech act misunderstandings by abductive inference." *Computational Linguistics* 21(4):435–78.

Moens, Marc and Steedman, Mark, 1988. "Temporal ontology and temporal reference." *Computational Linguistics* 14:15–28.

Moore, Johanna, 1995. *Participating in Explanatory Dialogues*. Cambridge, MA: MIT Press.

Moore, Johanna and Paris, Cecile, 1993. "Planning text for advisory dialogues: capturing intentional and rhetorical information." *Computational Linguistics* 19(4):651–95.

Moore, Johanna and Pollack, Martha, 1992. "A problem for RST: the need for multi-level discourse analysis." *Computational Linguistics* 18(4):537–44.

Moser, Megan and Moore, Johanna, 1996. "Toward a synthesis of two accounts of discourse structure." *Computational Linguistics* 22(3):409–19.

Newell, Allen and Simon, Herbert, 1963. "GPS, a program that simulates human thought." In Edward Feigenbaum and Julian Feldman (eds), *Computers and Thought*, New York: McGraw-Hill. 279–93. Reprinted by AAAI Press, 1995.

Poesio, Massimo and Traum, David, 1997. "Conversational actions and discourse situations." *Computational Intelligence* 13(3):309–47.

Pollack, Martha, 1986. "Inferring domain plans in question-answering." PhD thesis, Department of Computer and Information Science, University of Pennsylvania.

Pollack, Martha, 1991. "Overloading intentions for efficient practical reasoning." *Noûs* 25:513–36.

Prevost, Scott, 1995. "A semantics of contrast and information structure for specifying intonation in spoken language generation." PhD thesis, Department of Computer and Information Science, University of Pennsylvania. IRCS TR 96-01.

Prevost, Scott and Steedman, Mark, 1994. "Specifying intonation from context for speech synthesis." *Speech Communication* 15:139–53.

Prince, Ellen, 1981. "Toward a taxonomy of given–new information." In Peter Cole (ed.), *Radical Pragmatics*, New York: Academic Press. 223–55.

Reithinger, Norbert and Klesen, Martin, 1997. "Dialogue act classification using language models." In *Proceedings of EuroSpeech'97*. 2235–8.

Reynar, Jeffrey, 1998. "Topic segmentation: algorithms and applications." PhD thesis, Department of Computer and Information Science, University of Pennsylvania.

Samuel, Ken, Carberry, Sandra, and Vijay-Shankar, K., 1998. "Dialogue act tagging with transformation-based learning." In *Proceedings of COLING/ACL'98*. Montreal, 1150–6.

Scott, Donia and de Souza, Clarisse Sieckenius, 1990. "Getting the message across in RST-based text generation." In Robert Dale, Chris Mellish, and Michael Zock (eds), *Current Research in Natural Language Generation*, London: Academic Press. 47–73.

Seneff, Stephanie, Hurley, Ed, Lau, Raymond, Pao, Christine, Schmid, Philipp, and Zue, Victor, 1998. "A reference architecture for conversational system development." In *Proceedings of the International Conference on Spoken Language Processing*. Sydney, 931–4.

Sidner, Candace, 1982. "Focusing in the comprehension of definite anaphora." In Michael Brady and Robert Berwick (eds), *Computational Models of Discourse*, Cambridge, MA: MIT Press. 267–330.

Steedman, Mark, 1996a. "Representing discourse information for spoken dialogue generation." In *Proceedings of the Second International Symposium on Spoken Dialogue*. Philadelphia, PA, 89–92.

Steedman, Mark, 1996b. *Surface Structure and Interpretation*. Cambridge, MA: MIT Press. Linguistic Inquiry Monograph 30.

Steedman, Mark, 2000. *The Syntactic Process*. Cambridge, MA: MIT Press.

Stolcke, Andreas, Shriberg, Elizabeth, Bates, Rebecca, Taylor, Paul, Ries, Klaus, Jurafsky, Dan, Coccaro, Noah, Martin, Rachel, Meteer, Marie, and Ess-Dykema, Carol Van, 1998. "Dialog act modeling for conversational speech." In *Proceedings of the AAAI Spring Symposium on Applying Machine Learning to Discourse Processing.*

Stanford, CA. Extended version pub. as: Stolcke, Andreas, Ries, Klaus, Coccaro, Noah, Shriberg, Elizabeth, Bates, Rebecca, Jurafsky, Daniel, Taylor, Paul, Martin, Rachel, Ess-Dykema, Carol Van, and Meteer, Marie, 2000. "Dialog act modeling for automatic tagging and recognition of conversational speech." *Computational Linguistics* 26(3):339–74.

Stone, Matthew, 1994. "Discourse deixis, discourse structure and the semantics of subordination." Manuscript, University of Pennsylvania.

Stone, Matthew and Doran, Christine, 1997. "Sentence planning as description using tree adjoining grammar." In *Proceedings of the 35th Annual Meeting of the Association for Computational Linguistics (ACL97/EACL97)*. Madrid, 198–205.

Stone, Matthew and Webber, Bonnie, 1998. "Textual economy through closely coupled syntax and semantics." In *Proceedings of the Ninth International Workshop on Natural Language Generation*. Niagara-on-the-Lake, 178–87.

Strube, Michael, 1998. "Never look back: an alternative to centering." In *Proceedings, COLING/ACL'98*. Montreal, 1251–7.

Taylor, Paul, King, Simon, Isard, Stephen, and Wright, Helen, 1998. "Intonation and dialogue context as constraints for speech recognition." *Language and Speech* 41:493–512.

Thomason, Richmond and Hobbs, Jerry, 1997. "Interrelating interpretation and generation in an abductive framework." In *Proceedings of the AAAI Fall Symposium on Communicative Action in Humans and Machines*. Cambridge, MA.

Traum, David and Hinkelman, Elizabeth, 1992. "Conversational acts in task-oriented spoken dialogue." *Computational Intelligence* 8(3): 575–99.

Turan, Umit, 1995. "Null vs. overt subjects in Turkish discourse: a centering analysis." PhD thesis, Department of Linguistics, University of Pennsylvania.

Walker, Marilyn, 1996a. "The effect of resource limits and task complexity on collaborative planning in dialogue." *Artificial Intelligence* 85(1–2):181–243.

Walker, Marilyn, 1996b. "Limited attention and discourse structure." *Computational Linguistics* 22:255–64.

Walker, Marilyn, Fromer, Jeanne, and Narayanan, Shrikanth, 1998. "Learning optimal dialogue strategies: a case study of a spoken dialogue agent for email." In *Proceedings of COLING-ACL'98*. Montreal, 1345–51.

Webber, Bonnie, 1986. "Questions, answers and responses: interacting with knowledge base systems." In Michael Brodie and John Mylopoulos (eds), *On Knowledge Base Systems*, New York: Springer-Verlag. 365–401.

Webber, Bonnie, 1988. "Tense as discourse anaphor." *Computational Linguistics* 14(2):61–73.

Webber, Bonnie, 1991. "Structure and ostension in the interpretation of discourse deixis." *Language and Cognitive Processes* 6(2):107–35.

Webber, Bonnie, Knott, Alistair, and Joshi, Aravind, 1999a. "Multiple discourse connectives in a lexicalized grammar for discourse." In *Third International Workshop on Computational Semantics*. Tilburg, 309–25.

Webber, Bonnie, Knott, Alistair, Stone, Matthew, and Joshi, Aravind, 1999b. "Discourse relations: a structural and presuppositional account using lexicalised TAG." In *Proceedings of the*

36th Annual Meeting of the Association for Computational Linguistics. College Park, MD, 41–8.

Webber, Bonnie, Knott, Alistair, Stone, Matthew, and Joshi, Aravind, 1999c. "What are little trees made of: a structural and presuppositional account using lexicalised TAG." In *Proceedings of International Workshop on Levels of Representation in Discourse (LORID'99)*. Edinburgh, 151–6.

Winograd, Terry, 1973. "A procedural model of language understanding." In Roger Schank and Ken Colby (eds), *Computer Models of Thought and Language*, W. H. Freeman. 152–186. Reprinted in B. Grosz et al. (eds), 1986 *Readings in Natural Language Processing*, Los Altos, CA: Morgan Kaufman.

Woods, William, 1968. "Procedural semantics for a question-answering machine." In *Proceedings of the AFIPS National Computer Conference*. Montvale. NJ: AFIPS Press. 457–71.

Woods, William, 1978. "Semantics and quantification in natural language question answering." In *Advances in Computers*, New York: Academic Press, vol. 17. 1–87.

Woods, William, Kaplan, Ron, and Nash-Webber, Bonnie, 1972. "The Lunar Sciences Natural Language Information System: final report." Technical Report 2378, Bolt Beranek and Newman, Cambridge, MA.

Young, R. Michael, Moore, Johanna D., and Pollack, Martha E., 1994. "Towards a principled representation of discourse plans." In *Proceedings of the 16th Annual Conference of the Cognitive Science Society*. Atlanta, GA, 946–51.

Index